Law Among Nations

An Introduction to Public International Law

Law Among Nations

An Introduction to Public International Law

Tenth Edition

GERHARD VON **GLAHN**

University of Minnesota-Duluth

JAMES LARRY **TAULBEE**

Emory University

Boston   Columbus   Indianapolis   New York   San Francisco   Upper Saddle River
Amsterdam   Cape Town   Dubai   London   Madrid   Milan Munich   Paris   Montreal   Toronto
Delhi   Mexico City   São Paulo   Sydney   Hong Kong   Seoul   Singapore   Taipei   Tokyo

Senior Acquisitions Editor: Vikram Mukhija
Editorial Assistant: Beverly Fong, Isabel Schwab
Marketing Manager: Wendy Gordon, Lindsey Prudhomme
Production Manager: Fran Russello
Project Coordination and Text Design: Niraj Bhatt/Aptara® Corp. Inc.
Cover Illustration/Photo: Paul Vreeker/Reuters/Corbis
Printer and Binder: Courier Companies, Inc.

Library of Congress Cataloging-in-Publication Data
Von Glahn, Gerhard
 Law among nations : an introduction to public international law / Gerhard von Glahn, James
Larry Taulbee. — 10th ed.
   p. cm.
 Includes bibliographical references and index.
 ISBN-13: 978-0-205-85577-3
 ISBN-10: 0-205-85577-6
 1. International law. I. Taulbee, James Larry, II. Title.
 KZ3185.V6 2013
 341—dc23

                                                                2011049530

10 9 8 7 6 5 4 3 2 —CRW—15 14 13

ISBN-13: 978-0-205-85577-3
ISBN-10:   0-205-85577-6

In memory of Gerhard von Glahn (1911–1997)
Viro benignitatis doctrinaeque

To
Ryan, Jake, McKinlee, Kohen, and Walker
May their world be more peaceful than our collective past.

BRIEF CONTENTS

CONTENTS

PREFACE

As an introduction to the tenth edition of *Law Among Nations*, it seems fitting to quote from the preface to the first edition with regard to the purpose of the book. Professor von Glahn noted that he intended to write "a text adapted specifically for the typical undergraduate course in international law . . . using the traditional approach to the subject but incorporating in the actual text, whenever called for as illustrative materials, abstracts of classic and modern cases." He chose the title *Law Among Nations* to emphasize the essential structure of the international legal system.

The world has changed markedly since the first edition. The end of the Cold War; the continuing revolution in communication technologies; the dense web of financial and other functional linkages between countries that involve individuals and agencies at every level of society, not just foreign offices, as well the continuing growth, both formal and informal, of international institutions have added many dimensions to the idea of "AMONG." To illustrate this in simple fashion, consider the factual elements in the following case:

> A French court will hear a criminal libel case involving a review, written in English by a German law professor, of a book published by a Dutch company, written in English by a French citizen who lives in Israel. The review appeared on a website based in the United States and moderated by an American professor of law.[1]

While a problem in private international law, it nonetheless illustrates perfectly the world of the present and its challenges. Even when Professor von Glahn prepared his last edition (seventh), this would not have been a possibility.

As the world has changed, we have questions about how quickly "law'" may change to reflect new circumstances. In updating the text, I have taken especial notice of the problems. In many areas, agreements have proliferated, but many questions remain about the depth of commitment when governments have to make hard decisions that may affect powerful domestic interests. In controversial areas such as human rights, the environments, the law of the sea, and issues associated with the use of force, I have identified the issues and the ongoing competing arguments.

NEW TO THIS EDITION

Beginning with a discussion in Chapter 2, which addresses the promises and problems of globalization and the idea of global governance, I have revised the material in each relevant chapter to reflect these ideas. Through the use of small case studies

---

[1]A. Liptak, "Book Review Brings Libel Lawsuit with Global Reach," *The International Herald Tribune* (February 22, 2011), 3.

and references to other chapters, I have also made an effort to point out and connect issues that connect across many dimensions and issue areas in an attempt to present a dynamic process rather than the "still" pictures that most books reflect. Most issues do not exist in isolation; they are embedded in broader concerns. The book continues to evolve in that it focuses upon process in terms of application as much as "the letter of the law." In addition, I have increasingly tried to tie the subject matter closer to mainstream scholarship in international politics.

In response to the reviewers, I have extended the discussion of peaceful resolution of disputes. I have also tied the procedures more closely to what I see as the central problem of "process and procedures." Would we teach a course in some aspect of domestic law without presuming that students first knew the court structure, levels of determination, and alternative methods of dispute resolution?

One of the most difficult problems faced in revising a textbook comes from the temptation to revise by accretion. Texts can rapidly become like river deltas, slowly expanding in a sprawling manner to fill available space. In updating chapters, I understand that instructors have their own preferences regarding the appropriate emphasis on historical background, topics, cases, and political science–international relations theory. As both a teacher and an author I am very much aware of the competing demands of making a very complex area of international interaction fit into a semester course. Appending the word "introduction" actually complicates rather than simplifies the problems. What in terms of prior knowledge can instructors expect students to bring with them to the course? I have kept these ideas in mind as I have updated, added, and deleted.

This means doing a revision involves some difficult choices. As always, in keeping with the original vision, I have tried to balance history, jurisprudence, controversies, and discussions of the substantive law with illustrative cases. Because of space limitations, I may have deleted some material that individual instructors have found useful. I welcome your comment here.

Chapter 1 has a much more coherent discussion of the relationship of IR theory to international law. This plays into a revised Chapter 2 that now more systematically addresses the roots and problems associated with the idea of "globalization," as well as the evolution of modern international law. Also, in Chapter 2, with the exception of Grotius, I have reduced the discussion of early writers to their essence, while somewhat expanding the discussion of the role of natural law. I return to this theme in Chapter 16 on human rights. I have totally rewritten Chapter 5 to highlight the decision process in terms of why and when these techniques might be employed to resolve issues, and the relevance of and possible roles of law in the decision.

This serves as a backdrop to the chapters on substantive areas, particularly those on human rights, international criminal law, the law of the sea, international environmental law, and international economic law. I have totally rewritten Chapters 7, 8, and 9, compressing the three rather rambling chapters into two that more clearly define the central issues of "statehood" and the problems of "failed states." All chapters have been edited to reflect current controversies and problems. But, in particular, I have updated the discussions of the continuing problem of piracy and slavery in Chapter 16, as well as the activities and decisions of international courts, including those of the ad hoc criminal courts in Chapters 18 and 22.

FEATURES

The book does reflect my personal point of view in one respect. I believe that one of the fundamental problems of teaching (and understanding) how international law works comes from a lack of attention to international legal process. A course in American constitutional law has a simple format—one court, one constitution, and one legislature. A course in the *law among nations* requires that students first understand what method, "source," or forum applies and why, before they tackle the question of what substantive law may apply and why. For this reason, I have "front-loaded" the discussion of the structure and processes of the international legal system. In response to the reviewers, I have again put the "peaceful resolution of disputes" in a separate chapter but have tried to tie it more closely to what I see as the central problem of "process and procedures."

Such chapters often present still pictures when the critical question involves understanding the dynamic process. After all, is not law about the peaceful resolution of disputes according to appropriate rules? Why do we often discuss all of the "substantive issues and rules," and then suddenly decide that we will then deal with process as a secondary issue? Does not "process" apply all through the course? Would we teach a course in some aspect of domestic law without presuming that students first knew the court structure, levels of determination, and alternative methods of dispute resolution?

SUPPLEMENTS

Pearson is pleased to offer several resources to qualified adopters of *Law Among Nations* and their students that will make teaching and learning from this book even more effective and enjoyable.

MySearchLab: For over 10 years, instructors and students have reported achieving better results and better grades when a Pearson MyLab has been integrated into the course. MySearchLab provides engaging experiences that personalize learning, and comes from a trusted partner with educational expertise and a deep commitment to helping students and instructors achieve their goals. A wide range of writing, grammar and research tools and access to a variety of academic journals, census data, Associated Press newsfeeds, and discipline-specific readings help you hone your writing and research skills. To order MySearchLab with this text, use ISBN 0-205-85594-6.

Passport: Choose the resources you want from MyPoliSciLab and put links to them into your course management system. If there is assessment associated with those resources, it also can be uploaded, allowing the results to feed directly into your course management system's gradebook. With MyPoliSciLab assets like videos, mapping exercises, Financial Times newsfeeds, current events quizzes, politics blog, and much more, Passport is available for any Pearson political science book. To order Passport with this book, use ISBN 0-205-85595-4.

Longman Atlas of World Issues (0-205-78020-2): From population and political systems to energy use and women's rights, the *Longman Atlas of World Issues* features full-color thematic maps that examine the forces shaping the world. Featuring maps from the latest edition of *The Penguin State of the World Atlas*, this excerpt includes critical thinking exercises to promote a deeper understanding of how geography affects many global issues.

Goode's World Atlas (0-321-65200-2): First published by Rand McNally in 1923, *Goode's World Atlas* has set the standard for college reference atlases. It features hundreds of physical, political, and thematic maps as well as graphs, tables, and a pronouncing index.

The Penguin Dictionary of International Relations (0-140-51397-3): This indispensable reference by Graham Evans and Jeffrey Newnham includes hundreds of cross-referenced entries on the enduring and emerging theories, concepts, and events that are shaping the academic discipline of international relations and today's world politics.

Research and Writing in International Relations (0-205-06065-X): With current and detailed coverage on how to start research in the discipline's major subfields, this brief and affordable guide offers the step-by-step guidance and the essential resources needed to compose political science papers that go beyond description and into systematic and sophisticated inquiry. This text focuses on areas where students often need help—finding a topic, developing a question, reviewing the literature, designing research, and last, writing the paper.

ACKNOWLEDGMENTS

I gratefully acknowledge the perceptive reviewer comments of Ali R. Abootalebi, University of Wisconsin, Eau Claire; Robert Bledsoe, University of Central Florida; John Ferguson, Baylor University; Robert Gorman, Texas State University; Ellen Pirro, Iowa State University; Jacques Fomerand, John Jay College; and Joel Jenswold, Oklahoma State University.

I also need to thank my editor, Vikram Mukhija, for the opportunity to undertake this new edition and for his encouragement throughout the process. Those associated with preparation of the manuscript for publication also deserve kudos for a job well done on a difficult manuscript. My students and colleagues over the years have provided perceptive commentary on many subjects covered in this text. For that I am very appreciative. They have often made me think about the issues from very different perspectives. Nonetheless, any errors of omission or commission remain mine.

J.L.T.
Atlanta, Georgia
August 2011

ABBREVIATIONS

Certain sources utilized frequently throughout this volume are cited in abbreviated form as follows:

BOOKS

Bishop	Bishop, *International Law: Cases and Materials* (2nd ed., 1962).
Brierly	Brierly, *The Law of Nations* (6th ed., by Sir Humphrey Waldock, 1963).
Claude	Claude, *Swords into Plowshares: The Problems and Progress of International Organizations* (3rd ed., rev. 1964).
Fenwick	Fenwick, *International Law* (4th ed., 1965).
Friedman	Friedman, *The Law of War: A Documentary History* (2 vols, 1972).
Hackworth	Hackworth, *Digest of International Law* (8 vols, 1940–1944).
Hudson	Hudson, *Cases and Other Materials on International Law* (1951).
Hyde	Hyde, *International Law Chiefly As Interpreted and Applied by the United States* (3 vols, 2nd ed., 1945).
Jessup	Jessup, *A Modern Law of Nations: An Introduction* (1949).
Lauterpacht's	Oppenheim, *International Law: A Treatise. Vol. 1, Peace* (8th ed., H. Lauterpacht, 1955); Vol. 2, Disputes, *War and Neutrality* (7th ed., H. Lauterpacht, 1952).
Moore	Moore, *A Digest of International Law* (8 vols, 1906).
Nussbaum	Nussbaum, *A Concise History of the Law of Nations* (rev. ed., 1954).
Sørenson	Sørenson, ed., *Manual of Public International Law* (2 vols, 1968).
Verzijl	Verzijl, *International Law in Historical Perspective* (11 vols, 1968–).
von Glahn	von Glahn, *The Occupation of Enemy Territory: A Commentary on the Law and Practice of Belligerent Occupation* (1957).
Whiteman	Whiteman, *Digest of International Law* (15 vols, 1963–1973).

PERIODICALS AND OTHER SOURCES

AJIL	*American Journal of International Law*
APSR	*American Political Science Review*
BYIL	*British Yearbook of International Law*
CYIL	*Canadian Yearbook of International Law*
Current Policy	*U.S. Department of State, Bureau of Public Affairs publication*
Gist	*U.S. Department of State, Bureau of Public Affairs publication*
EJIL	*European Journal of International Law*
ICJ Reports	*International Court of Justice, Reports of Judgments, Advisory Opinions, and Orders (1947–)*
ICLQ	*International and Comparative Law Quarterly*
ILC	*International Law Commission*
ILM	*International Legal Materials*
NYT	*The New York Times*
Proceedings	*Proceedings of the American Society of International Law*
Tijdschrift	*Nederlands, Tijdschrift voor International Recht*
TGS	*Transactions of the Grotius Society [London]*
T.I.A.S.	*Treaties and Other International Acts Series*
LNTS	*League of Nations Treaty Series*
U.S. (in case citations)	*United States Reports (Supreme Court of the United States).* Cases before 1875 are cited by the name of the reporter: Dallas (1790–1800) Cranch (1801–1815) Wheaton (1816–1827) Peters (1828–1842) Howard (1843–1860) Black (1861–1862) Wallace (1863–1874)
U.S.C.	*United States Code*
U.S.C.A.	*United States Code Annotated*
UNESCOR	*United Nations Economic and Social Council official records*
UNGAOR	*United Nations General Assembly official records*
UNSCOR	*United Nations Security Council official records*
UNTS	*United Nations Treaty Series*
Y.B.	*Yearbook*

The Law of Nations

The Nature of International Law

E vidence of international law as a vital concern in the everyday relations between states appears regularly in the headlines of the world's newspapers. Consider the following, culled from reports on events during a recent two-week period.

Pirate Sentenced

The stiff prison sentence given a Somali pirate in US federal court is meant to be a deterrent to armed attackers who would board and hold for ransom unarmed commercial ships.[1]

Book Review Has International Implications

A French court will hear a criminal libel case involving a review, written in English by a German law professor, of a book published by a Dutch company, written in English by a French citizen who lives in Israel. The review appeared on a website based in the United States and moderated by an American professor of law.[2]

Extradition for Mongolian Spy

A British judge has ruled that Mongolian spy chief Bat Khurts, who claims he was lured to the UK so that he could be arrested and jailed under a European arrest warrant, can be extradited to Germany.[3]

Cyprus Parliament Ratifies Agreement with Israel on Delimitation of EEZ

The agreement, signed in December last year, is set to consolidate Cyprus' EEZ in that it complements similar agreements Cyprus has signed with Egypt and Lebanon. The delimitation of the EEZ is based on the Law of the Sea Convention.[4]

---

[1]B. Knickerbocker, "Somali Pirate Gets Stiff Sentence in US Court. Will It Deter Piracy?" Christian Science Monitor (February 16, 2011).

[2]A. Liptak, "Book Review Brings Libel Lawsuit with Global Reach," *The International Herald Tribune* (February 22, 2011), 3.

[3]T. Moynihan, "Extradition for Mongolian Spy," *The Independent* (London) (February 19, 2011).

[4]Cyprus News Agency, BBC Monitoring Europe—Political (February 18, 2011).

Piracy, jurisdiction over an international dispute involving free speech, cooperation with respect to criminal prosecution, and delimiting maritime borders between adjacent states all constitute matters that fall squarely into the realm of international law. In an era of increasing "globalization," international law forms a critical part of the framework that promotes sustained cooperation among states. While skeptics may continue to question the scope and impact of international law as real law, simple observation should quickly provide strong evidence that states do regard international law as an important factor in their everyday relations with one another.

THE NATURE OF THE LAW

To begin, we need to establish some points of reference. Why do we need an "international" law, distinct from the laws of individual states, that seeks to establish principles and procedures to govern relations with other states? If international law does exist, what distinguishes international law from domestic law? The answer to the first question should be obvious. With nearly 200 states in the world today, consider the confusion and problems of dealing with potentially 200 different sets of procedures and standards on such simple matters as necessary travel documents, mailing a letter to a foreign county, or establishing and maintaining diplomatic relations. Many areas of contemporary international life require common practices to facilitate necessary international contacts and cooperation. International law provides that common referent. Answering the second question requires a more extended discussion focused upon the nature and function of law in society.

We need to emphasize here that this book focuses upon *public* international law—the law among nations. As we shall see, public international law also includes an emerging area of international law, international criminal law, that deals with the actions of individuals including issues of how governments (individuals in responsible positions) treat their citizens. Private international law, also characterized as conflict of laws, deals with the private (nongovernmental) transactions and disputes between parties (companies, individuals, nongovernmental organizations [NGOs]) from differing nations. Generally, courts and others use this body of law to determine which law to apply when there is a conflict between the domestic laws of the parties in a dispute. So private international law would come into play when Siemens AG (Germany) has a dispute with Sony Corporation (Japan) over a joint manufacturing agreement that involves component suppliers in China and an assembly plant in Indonesia.

Some Definitions

Traditionally, writers have defined international law as that body of principles, customs, and rules recognized as effectively binding obligations by *sovereign states* and such other entities that have been granted *international personality.* In contemporary international politics, states are not the only actors subject to international law. The United Nations (UN), the Organization of American States (OAS), and many other intergovernmental organizations (IGOs) are examples of entities other than states that have international legal personality (Chapter 7). The International Committee of the Red Cross (an NGO) also has limited international legal "personality" with respect to certain functions related to the Geneva Conventions (Chapter 19). This definition pulls together the essential elements suggested by most contemporary writers on international law. It does not represent, by any means, the only acceptable definition. Professor Philip Jessup, drawing upon an old and perhaps apocryphal Chinese proverb, has counseled, "One should always have in the background of one's mind a multiplicity of definitions covering the subject at hand in order to prevent oneself from accepting the most obvious."[5] This applies especially to international law because controversy does surround the subject matter. Therefore, in the spirit of Professor Jessup's advice, we offer the following additional definitions. Professor James Brierly, in his classic text, asserts:

> The Law of Nations, or International Law, may be defined as the body of rules and principles of action which are binding upon civilized states in their relations with one another.[6]

A more contemporary definition from the American Law Institute extends this definition somewhat:

> "International law," as used in this Restatement consists of rules and principles of general application dealing with the conduct of states and of international organizations and with their relations inter se, as well as with some of their relationships with persons, whether natural or juridical.[7]

Note one important difference between these last two definitions. Professor Brierly's definition rests upon the traditional assumption that only *states* can be the *subjects* of international law in the sense of having legal rights and obligations. Traditional definitions of international law assume a "hard-shell" definition of *sovereignty,* meaning that international law has nothing to say about how rulers treated their subjects or how governments treated their citizens. Hence, international law applies between and among states but has no power or authority to intrude into the affairs of the domestic community. The more modern definition from the *Restatement* acknowledges that, increasingly, international law in the form of evolving human rights norms also applies to the relationship between *individuals* and their states and may specify rights and duties for individuals in certain circumstances (Chapter 14).

The difference between the Brierly and the *Restatement* definition also highlights an important point for the reader. All law embodies a dynamic process. Law must change to reflect changing circumstance. States make the law in response to their interests and concerns. Circumstances and interests change. One hundred years ago, states could resort to war to settle their disputes without violating any law. Seventy years ago, the idea of genocide as an international crime against

---

[5]P. Jessup, *A Modern Law of Nations: An Introduction* (1949), 4. Professor Jessup served a short term as the American judge on the International Court of Justice.

[6]J. L. Brierly, *The Law of Nations,* 6th ed., edited by H. Waldock (1963), 1.

[7]American Law Institute, *Restatement of the Law, Third, The Foreign Relations Law of the United States* (1988), para. 101, 222.

humanity did not exist. Twenty years ago, the question of establishing controls over the Internet had little salience to governments because the Internet did not exist in its current form. Ten years ago, while cell phones were becoming ubiquitous, the possibility of texting and "tweeting" lay in the future.

Law and Politics at the International Level

"International law is to law as professional wrestling is to wrestling."[8] The skepticism of this quip reflects the belief of many that international law has no real substance. Critics believe that at best international law may provide window dressing for states to justify their actions, but, to use contemporary jargon, it does not exert any definitive *compliance pull* in the sense that a government will obey if an obligation requires that it act in a way that would result in a short-term loss vis-à-vis an important interest. Skeptics believe that governments comply with international law only if convenient to do so and feel free to ignore it otherwise. These criticisms come from eminent philosophers, statesmen, and men of letters. Montesquieu wrote:

> International Law is better known in Europe than in Asia, yet it can be said that royal passions, the submissiveness of their subjects and sycophantic writers have corrupted all its principles. In its present state, this branch of law is a science which explains to kings how far they can violate justice without damaging their own interests.[9]

Abba Eban, then the Israeli ambassador to the United States, noted, "International law is the law which the wicked do not obey and the righteous do not enforce."[10] In *Tiger at the Gates,* Jean Giradoux provides a pointed critique of both the character of international lawyers and what he saw as the infinitely flexible nature of international law, characterizing the field as "[t]he training ground for the imagination."[11] During the debate over whether NATO should take action against Serbia, when British Foreign Secretary Robin Cook told U.S. Secretary of State Madeleine Albright that he had "problems with our lawyers" over using force against Yugoslavia without UN Security Council approval, Secretary Albright reportedly responded, "Get new lawyers."[12]

The structure of the international political system encourages skepticism about law. An examination of the international political systems will find *none* of the institutions and features normally associated with "the law" as a factor in modern domestic societies. Most international relations textbooks begin by telling us

---

[8]S. Budiansky, *US News and World Report* (September 20, 1993), 8.

[9]C-L. de Secondat (Montesquieu), *The Persian Letters,* trans. J. R. Loy (1961), 176.

[10]A. Eban, interview with Edward R. Murrow on *Person to Person* (CBS television broadcast, September 20, 1957).

[11]J. Giradoux, *Tiger at the Gates (La guerre de Troie n'aura pas lieu),* trans. C. Fry (1955), 45. Giradoux has Busiris, a famous international lawyer at the court of Priam (Troy) when the Greek ships first sail into the harbor, engage in what we might call "good lawyering" twice!

[12]Reported by James Rubin, U.S. Secretary of State Madeleine Albright's press spokesman at the time of the Kosovo Conflict, *Financial Times* (September 29, 2000).

that *anarchy* best describes the international milieu. While *anarchy* simply means the absence of central political rule (not necessarily chaos or disorder), in talking about a system that does not have a legislature to enact authoritative prescriptions, a central executive authority with an effective police power, or a court system with compulsory jurisdiction over state activities, how can we speak seriously of law as a reality that affects the behavior of states? The answer to this question has provided many generations of legal scholars and political theorists with a puzzle they have yet to solve to everyone's satisfaction. Indeed, because of the close association of law with the hierarchic authority structure of government, Nicholas Onuf has described international law as the vanishing point of jurisprudence.[13]

The absence of formal institutions and especially the lack of any effective enforcement mechanisms give some credence to those who question the efficacy of international law. Skeptics, looking at the few examples given at the beginning of this chapter, still might say, "So what?" Pointing to a few instances where advocates assert that international law *presumably* has had an effective role does not really address the fundamental issues, nor does it help us understand why and how international law does work without the institutional framework normally associated with making, implementing, adjudicating, and enforcing legal rules. We suggest that criticisms come from two common misperceptions: unrealistic comparisons of international law with domestic law and visions of international politics that underestimate the incentives for cooperation.

To paraphrase Giradoux, in answering the challenges of critics, we do need to "train our imagination" because understanding how law works at the international level requires that we move beyond some simple definitions of law and even simpler conceptions of the role and impact of law in domestic societies. Critics tend to make comparisons between an idealized system of domestic law as it presumably *ought* to operate in advanced industrialized democracies and the obvious deficiencies of international law. Such comparisons will always overestimate the efficacy of the domestic legal system and underestimate the scope and impact of international law.

In large part, the comparison problem occurs because of a set of *default assumptions*—that is, "propositions and facts" that everyone believes without question (regardless of whether they are true)—about how "the law" operates in well-ordered societies. Here you should note that, *by default,* we almost always assume the legal systems of Western industrialized democracies (or, more precisely, the United States) provide the ideal model of a well-constructed, functioning legal system. These default assumptions are hard to rebut through abstract counterargument and even through explicit examples because they draw upon an emotional "mythology" surrounding the law that seems ingrained into Western culture.[14] Individuals "know what they know." To counter these default assumptions, we will offer a short tour through "the law in action" in domestic society.

Before proceeding to an examination of these default assumptions, we need to define *law.* By defining international law before offering a definition of law, we quite literally have put the cart before the horse—because the definitions of international

---

[13]N. G. Onuf, "The International Legal Order as an Idea," 73 *American Journal of International Law* (1979), 244.

[14]See J. Shklar, *Legalism: Law, Morals, and Political Trials* (1986).

law assumed that we all have a good definition of law in general, know how law differs from other codes of behavior, and have some grasp of what law does at the domestic level. Again, following Professor Jessup's sage advice, we now offer three definitions. The three definitions represent an attempt to provide the general characteristics that distinguish legal rules from other types of rules such as those found in religious or moral codes or international *comity*. We have created the first two from a composite reading of works about the law. The third comes from the *Oxford English Dictionary*:

> A set of binding rules enjoining a certain behavior on all subjects under specified and comparable conditions.
>
> A method of ensuring social order by commanding requisite behavior through the threat of physical sanctions. A rule of conduct imposed by authority.
>
> The body of rules, whether proceeding from formal enactment or from *custom*, which a particular state or community recognizes as binding on its members or subjects.[15] (Emphasis added)

Although only the second definition specifically mentions sanctions, the other two imply some type of penalty for *noncompliance* with any of the "binding obligations." Note that we deliberately use the term *noncompliance*, rather than the more graphic *breaking the law*, because the term more accurately reflects a civil/administrative perspective while capturing what happens when you "break" the criminal law.

Default Assumptions and International Law

The first default assumption that colors our assessment is that we all almost automatically associate *law* with the "cop on the corner"/"thieves ought to be punished" model of the *criminal* law—a rule backed by a sanction that says if you do the crime, you do the time.[16] "Breaking the law" conjures up the principles and procedures of the criminal law and the premise that thieves ought to be punished. However, a singular focus on the criminal law and its operations misleads because the criminal law forms only part, and *perhaps the lesser part,* of the legal code in modern states. Law as a reality and dominant force in domestic societies is much more than a coercive order aimed at punishing those who commit criminal acts. The proof of this comes from a simple fact: The practice of the greatest number of lawyers in the United States (and other advanced industrialized democracies) falls within the area of *civil* and *administrative* law—contracts, labor relations, domestic relations, wills, trusts, property, tenants' rights, and a host of other relationships. Violations of civil and administrative obligations here do not necessarily involve "punishment," but rather a course of action that will make the situation "whole" in terms of regulations or contractual understandings.

---

[15]*Oxford English Dictionary.*

[16]These two ideas come from J. H. E. Fried, "How Efficient Is International Law?" in *The Relevance of International Law,* edited by K. Deutsch and S. Hoffmann (1968), 93–132.

Moreover, the "thieves ought to be punished" model simply does not capture the function of law as an important constitutive factor, that is, as the force forming the basis for the validity of constitutions—the force giving substance to arrangements that authoritatively allocate power to legislate, enforce, or adjudicate. The rules in the Constitution of the United States define what branches of various governmental agencies have the legal obligation/authority to perform what duties with respect to governing. In disputes over the relative powers of various branches of government, that is, questions that involve the fundamental law of the country, clearly the "cop on the corner"/"thieves ought to be punished" model has no relevance.[17] Can you imagine the president of the United States trying to use the FBI to arrest members of Congress on the charge of violating the Constitution?

Responses to noncompliance in many areas of the noncriminal law in domestic societies somewhat parallel what occurs in the international legal system. Certainly, noncriminal law does have penalties attached for noncompliance, but these do not rely on the criminal law presumption of how one ensures compliance. "Contracts must be observed" forms a fundamental rule of civil law. But enforcement of the norm, if one party to the contract feels a breach has occurred, depends upon *the party alleging violation* taking the first step to deal with noncompliance. No "cop on the corner" steps in to escort the "accused" to jail. Moreover, the action to seek compliance regarding the alleged breach may not involve an immediate resort to the machinery of the courts, but rather direct negotiation, mediation, or arbitration. Circumstances of the moment may dictate the remedy and the method of redress the aggrieved party elects. Breaches of contract *may* involve penalties for noncompliance, but the criminal law comes into play only if the breach resulted from clearly criminal conduct such as a deliberate fraud or misrepresentation.

The second default assumption deals with presumptions of efficiency. Critics tend to assume that domestic law (and, in particular, the criminal law) works efficiently under all circumstances. We have noted earlier that default assumptions about law often draw from the operations of the criminal law and the associated justice system. To examine the second assumption concerning efficiency, we confine our comments to the criminal justice system because of the presumed efficiency of central enforcement. Looking at U.S. Department of Justice Statistics or merely reading the newspapers every day gives sufficient evidence to rebut the idea that central institutions necessarily mean effective enforcement. Indeed, for many crimes, "how effective" in terms of statistics may surprise you. Table 1.1, drawn from statistics compiled annually by the U.S. Department of Justice, summarizes the data on crimes and arrests from the year 2009. The reader needs to understand that the data include only those crimes that were *reported* to a law enforcement agency. Other data from the same report estimate how many crimes may go unreported each year. In examining the table, we need only point out the relatively high probability that burglars will escape apprehension or that the data support the comment by an anonymous insurance executive in Los Angeles that "to own a nice car is to have it stolen."

---

[17]See, for example, *Goldwater v. Carter,* 444 U.S. 996, 100 S.Ct. 533, 62 L.Ed.2d 428 (1979). The U.S. Supreme Court sometimes avoids questions involving disputes over issues of separation of powers not clearly defined in the Constitution, terming these "political questions," www.bulk.resource.org/courts.gov/c/US/444/444.US.996.79-856.html.

TABLE 1.1

Offenses Known to Police and Cleared by Arrest or Exceptional Means, 2009

Total Agencies (14,274)	Known Offenses	Percent Cleared by Arrest
Violent Crime	1.14+ million	47.1
Robbery	352,125	28.2
Murder/Manslaughter	13,242	66.2
Forcible Rape	76,276	41.2
Property Crime	8.3 million	18.6
Larceny/Theft	5.56 million	21.5
Burglary	1.96+ million	12.5
Vehicle Theft	714,131	12.4
Arson	53,852	18.5

Source: U.S. Department of Justice, Federal Bureau of Investigation, Crime in the United States (September 2010), www2.fbi.gov/ucr/cius2009/data/table_25.html.

Looking at the noncriminal law, pure food and drug standards hardly spare us from contaminated foodstuffs; oligopoly is a dominant feature of many contemporary industrial sectors; and the fallout from Enron, WorldCom, and Bernie Madoff indicates that abuse of security and exchange regulations seems to occur on a regular basis. Just for good measure, let us also include the general lack of observance of speed limits. Do not dismiss this as a trivial concern. Speed and alcohol or drugs are contributing factors in a majority of fatal traffic crashes. True, some people do get caught in all of the examples just given, but seemingly not enough to have a deterrent effect on others. Reports of rape, robbery, and homicide do not necessarily lead to a conclusion at the domestic level that the laws against these offenses have little effect and are meaningless. Most people obey most of the law most of the time. Some people do not comply with the law some of the time, and a few of those may actually pay a penalty some of the time. What, then, should we make of the often-repeated criticism that international law does not have the strength to deter violations?

The third default assumption emphasizes the difference between "law" and politics, implying a relative absence of political considerations at the domestic level. We will simply concede that, because of the absence of centralized institutions, many applications of law at the international level *are* likely to have a much higher political content than are those within states. Nonetheless, this does not mean the total absence of political considerations from domestic legal systems. On the contrary, most law at the domestic level results from the highly politicized process associated with legislatures. The ongoing very contentious debate over prohibiting abortion provides a very good example. While at their core all domestic legal codes seem to share some common rules such as prohibitions against murder, theft, and violent assault against persons, others depend upon the attitudes of those subject to the specific law code. To give but one quick example, the standards that separate *fraud* from just a "sharp business practice" differ not only from society to society but also even within societies with respect to specific techniques and procedures. What *is* the line between false advertising and good promotion of a product?

Rules may become the target of challenge or change because of shifts in public opinion or political ideology. We can point both to quantum shifts such as the abolition of the "separate but equal" doctrine in U.S. law as unconstitutional and to the ongoing controversies over abortion and gay rights to emphasize this observation. Similarly, issues relating to immigration (e.g., who deserves entry, and the status and rights of illegal immigrants once here) form the core of a continuing and contentious debate. Certain rules may simply be unenforceable or go unenforced. Those who enforce the law have considerable discretion in many areas. For example, many states still have laws on their books prohibiting adultery, but these go unenforced. During periods of heavy traffic, police will watch traffic flow at 15–20 mph over the speed limit if traffic is moving smoothly. After evicting tenants for nonpayment of rent, landlords seldom sue for what the tenants may owe in arrears because the time and cost of litigation plus the potential costs of collecting any judgment will normally far outweigh the gains in recovery. Keep these examples in mind when we turn the discussion to enforcement at the international level.

Additionally, within the United States, district attorneys, state attorneys general, solicitors, sheriffs, and judges are elected officials in many jurisdictions. At the local level, the decision to charge an individual with a specific crime or the recommendation of a specific sentence may depend upon the district attorney's reading of public sentiment (or available prison space).[18] Nor does the appointment of officials cancel out politics. Appointment merely shifts the venue in which politics applies. Politicians still participate in, and define the criteria for, the selection process. In a change of administrations, a newly elected U.S. president can appoint U.S. attorneys for various jurisdictions. Every judicial appointment at the federal level revolves around political issues.[19] Clearly, those involved in the appointment process have political agendas they feel can be either protected or accomplished with the appointment of like-minded individuals to the bench. The contemporary concern with "failed" states such as Somalia provides additional confirmation of this observation.

VISIONS OF INTERNATIONAL POLITICS

Focusing upon default assumptions and their implications for legal systems at all levels still leaves open the question of how we can speak of law and its impact in a political system that has no central institutions. Here we advance a simple proposition. The *fundamental assumptions* (default assumptions) that an analyst makes about "how international politics really works" will determine the evaluation of international law as an important or inconsequential factor. Several "schools of

---

[18]What will the district attorney do with the case of the teenager who, in her haste to escape from being caught by the resident of the house that she and her friends had just "rolled" with toilet paper, drove off the road and killed three of her companions in the car? Only she survived. Does the district attorney go for the indictment for vehicular homicide, or has she "been punished enough"?

[19]See S. G. Stolberg, "The High Costs of Rising Incivility on Capitol Hill," *New York Times* (November 30, 2003), sec. 4, 10.

thought"—realism, liberalism/neoliberalism, and constructivism—currently compete as paradigms that claim to provide the best insight into the essence of contemporary international politics. In the following section, we will briefly discuss how these three paradigms affect views about the role and potential effectiveness of international law.

Political Realism

Based on Thomas Hobbes's graphic description of the state of nature, political realism forms one of the dominant theories in contemporary scholarship on international politics. For those who subscribe to realism as the preferred theoretical approach to explaining international politics, international law cannot exist as "law." Realists believe the anarchical condition of the international system means that states constantly seek out their own interest and constantly seek to enhance their own power and power position to ensure their survival. For realists, the lack of any measures or institutions for third-party enforcement means that agreements or cooperative ventures have a temporary quality because states will abandon them when their interest and power dictate that they can. Hobbes argues:[20]

> And covenants, without the sword, are but words and of no strength to secure a man at all. Therefore, notwithstanding the laws of nature (which every one hath then kept, when he has the will to keep them, when he can do it safely), if there be no power erected, or not great enough for our security, *every man will and may lawfully rely on his own strength and art for caution against all other men.* (Emphasis added)

For political realists, some rough "rules of the game" may evolve from temporary balances or from situations where one state has the ability to dominate and impose its will. Because of the fundamental drive of states to acquire power and power position to assure security, long-term, binding rules are impossible.[21] Advocates of political realism argue that the current situation that promotes increased interaction and cooperation exists only because of an anomaly in power distribution.[22] Hence, a recent study asked a cogent, but as yet unanswered, question: Is globalization a phenomenon with its own independent roots, or does it depend upon American hegemony and action to promote and open world markets?[23]

The refusal to acknowledge any impact of law beyond the very narrow association with formal institutional arrangements permeates the influential work of Kenneth Waltz. Waltz argues that the system of international relations may exhibit some qualities that make it structurally similar to a market, but only up to a point. Waltz concludes, "International politics is more nearly a realm in which anything

---

[20]T. Hobbes, *The Leviathan II,* XVII, 2, www.oregonstate.edu/instruct/phl302/texts/hobbes/leviathan-c.html#CHAPTERXVII.

[21]For useful, concise discussions, see J. Donnelly, *Realism and International Relations* (2000), 6–31; M. Doyle, *Ways of War and Peace: Realism, Liberalism and Socialism* (1997); and J. Vasquez, *The Power of Power Politics: From Classical Realism to Neotraditionalism* (1998).

[22]See, for example, J. J. Mearsheimer, *The Tragedy of Great Power Politics* (2001).

[23]N. P. Ripsman and T. V. Paul, *Globalization and the National Security State* (2010).

goes."[24] Implicitly, Waltz suggests that the principal difference between the law, as he understands it to operate at the domestic level, and comparable international rules is the greater efficacy of the former due to the perceived lack of enforcement mechanisms at the international level.

From a slightly different perspective, Henry Kissinger argues that rigid legal and judicial principles may interfere with the flexibility statesmen need in order to conduct a successful foreign policy:

> The danger lies in pushing the effort to extremes that risk substituting the tyranny of judges for that of governments; historically, the dictatorship of the virtuous has often led to inquisitions and even witch-hunts. . . . The role of the statesman is to choose the best option when seeking to advance peace and justice, realizing that there is a tension between the two and that any reconciliation between the two is likely to be partial.[25]

Note in particular the reasoning of Kissinger. He is correct in that statesmen, not judges, make decisions about critical foreign policy issues. Note also, this does **not** mean that law has no relevance to a decision.

Liberalism/Neoliberalism

While attractive on its face as a concise statement of the harsh realist picture of international relations that many find intuitively appealing, liberal internationalists assert that Waltz's characterization does not capture the complexity of contemporary state relationships, nor, on reflection, does it embody the experience of the greatest part of the industrial age. Realism assumes that state interests must always be competitive and never congruent, yet liberal critics cite the increasing institutionalization of modern international life to suggest that states can and do cooperate on a sustained basis because they cannot otherwise achieve their goals. One cannot always assume that scarcity, competition, and lack of third-party regulators always result in an arena where power does reign in the sense that others must bow to the will of the dominant. In the modern world, particularly in states where democratic institutions have emerged, security also involves economic progress and stability. The enormous expansion of international institutions at every level serves as a simple validation of this observation. Given the time, effort, and resources invested in building these institutions, we cannot simply dismiss them as short-term products that flow from stalemates in competition.[26]

Liberal critics argue that many of the assumptions essential to the realist perspective overplay the efficiency of domestic orders, even in the criminal law models. But the most obvious problem with realists comes from their willful disregard of the rules, formal and otherwise, that do impinge on state action. These range from fundamental rules inhibiting the absorption of lesser states by larger ones, to extensive institutional support for international monetary and financial coordination, to laws

---

[24]K. Waltz, *Theory of International Politics* (1979), 91.

[25]H. A. Kissinger, "The Pitfalls of Universal Jurisdiction," 80 Foreign Affairs (2001), 86, 95.

[26]See J. J. Mearsheimer, "The False Promise of International Institutions," 19 *International Security* (1994–1995), 5.

protecting diplomats and state visitors, to nutritional standards sponsored by the Food and Agricultural Organization (FAO). Realists may dismiss these as "housekeeping rules," or sometimes as *low politics* in contradistinction to the *high politics* of statecraft where vital interests come into play. Nonetheless, we will point out that "housekeeping rules" form the essential fabric of everyday interaction among states. We will discuss "vital interests" and the law in some detail later in this chapter.

Liberal institutionalists argue that merely by looking at some facts of modern international life that we all tend to take for granted, we can easily see international law at work. Modern national constitutions contain references to international law. Foreign ministries in other governments and the U.S. Department of State employ many legal advisers out of concern for observance of obligations. Why bother if law has such little importance? Beyond this, the basic structure of modern international relations rests upon legal definitions and practice. Law defines who the legitimate players are (states, IGOs, etc.), their essential characteristics (i.e., the qualities any player must possess to be considered eligible to enter the game), how they qualify to come into the game (recognition, constitutive treaty), and the rules of formal interaction (diplomatic relations).

Additionally, beyond the examples cited at the beginning of this chapter, simple acts such as making a direct-dialed long-distance phone call, mailing a letter to a person in another country, or traveling to another country for business or pleasure are possible because international law provides the framework through which states cooperate in regulating these activities. International law regulates every flight by an international air carrier into a country. Every international IGO—the UN, the OAS, and the World Trade Organization (WTO), to cite a few examples—has a constitutive document based on a *multilateral agreement* among states that establishes the purposes and powers of the organization as well as the obligations of member states. The multilateral agreements that brought the International Telecommunications Union (ITU) and the International Postal Union (IPU) into existence define the powers granted to the ITU and IPU to set down the rules and regulations for handling your telephone calls or letters directed to other countries.

Constructivism

Constructivism is a relative newcomer as a widely accepted approach to understanding important features of international politics. Like political realism and liberalism, constructivism embodies a number of variant approaches that share some fundamental assumptions. At base, constructivism concerns the "making and remaking" of international politics.[27] Where realism and liberalism are substantive theories of international politics in that they offer specific hypotheses about how states respond to the anarchical structure of international politics, constructivism is a social theory that focuses on how each state (as an agent) engages and deals

---

[27]M. Barnett, "Social Constructivism," in *The Globalisation of World Politics*, edited by J. Bayliss, et al. (2008), 162; J. Brunnee and S. Toope, "International Law and Constructivism: Elements of an Interactional Theory of International Law," 39 *Columbia Journal of Transnational Law* (2000), 19–74.

with the consequence of anarchy as the essential structural element of international politics. Constructivism offers no predictions about regularities or trends in world politics; rather, it seeks to explain why the world is organized the way it is.[28]

Constructivism as a social theory centers more on how we ought to think about international politics, rather than positing answers drawn from initial premises. It deals with the development and evolution of shared ideational concepts (notions, values) that define what we accept as knowledge (facts), important symbols (why do we honor the American flag), methods of expression (language), and rules. Constructivism addresses the social processes that generate shared norms and rules. It seeks to explain how state behaviors converge to produce international norms and institutions.[29] In Wendt's cogent phrase, "anarchy is what states make of it," not what it makes states do.[30] Realism and liberalism make important assumptions about this process rather than seeking to dissect and describe it. Constructivism insists that we need to examine the process carefully.

For constructivists, law is seen as legitimate not because it flows from some perceived authority but because the actors have internalized the values as legitimate. Legitimate norms are mutually constructed as common understanding evolves. One recent commentary argues that "law is persuasive when it is viewed as legitimate, largely in terms of internal process values, and when, as a result of the existence of basic social understandings, it can call upon reasoned argument . . . to justify its processes and its broad substantive ends, thereby creating shared rhetorical knowledge."[31] Interactions over time help develop the sense of legitimacy. In this process, nonstate actors, NGOs, corporations, informal intergovernmental expert networks, and many other groups that share transnational transaction links are important elements—other than states—that are actively engaged in creating shared understandings (knowledge) and promoting learning among states. Slaughter argues that important interactions occur both horizontally and vertically. Horizontal networks embrace government officials of similar functions across states. Horizontal networks "bring together regulators, judges or legislators to exchange information and to collect and distill best practices."[32] The recent meetings of EU central bankers and others with respect to the fall 2008 financial crisis provide a good example. Vertical networks involve close ties between national officials and their supranational counterparts in various IGOs. Vertical networks can operate as enforcement mechanisms or as harmonization networks.[33] In both cases, the interactions would help build and reinforce the intersubjective consensus (agreement among participants) necessary for generating and maintaining international legal norms.

---

[28]M. Barnett, note 27, at 171.

[29]N. G. Onuf, *World of Our Making* (1988); M. Finnemore and K. Sikkink, "International Norm Dynamics and Political Change," 52 *International Organization* (1998), 887, 888.

[30]A. Wendt, "Anarchy Is What States Make of It: the Social Construction of Power Politics," 46 *International Organization* (1992), 391–425.

[31]Brunnee and Toope, note 27, at 72.

[32]A. Slaughter, *A New World Order* (2004), 19.

[33]Slaughter, note 32, at 21.

As a very young approach, constructivism has proven better at explaining "what is," and how it evolved, than at exploring the mechanisms of change. It does, however, provide an interesting approach to investigating the validity of norms apart from traditional theories that rely upon assumptions of hierarchy and external enforcement.

Vital Interests and Law: High Politics

In fairness to critics, when the vital interests of states appear to be at stake, law may play a secondary role. Few would argue with former Secretary of State Dean Acheson when, analyzing the role of law in the Cuban Missile Crisis, he said, "The survival of states is not a matter of law."[34] Acheson is technically correct. In a severe crisis, with vital interests at stake, decision makers probably will not look to international law to provide a solution. The question is, however, *how often* do states and governments face situations that threaten their survival? Moreover, in analyzing accounts of the Cuban Missile Crisis, arguably a confrontation where potentially survival was at stake, one finds that a concern for the law runs throughout the deliberations.[35] During the crisis and in its aftermath, the Kennedy administration spent a great deal of time in justifying the U.S. response as an initiative that reflected a legal right.[36] We should not take the fact that law may play a subsidiary role in acute crises as a criticism that diminishes its role otherwise. True, law may not provide an absolute guide to resolving these crises, but those who make these assertions seem to imply that every international transaction, whether crisis driven or not, involves a complex deliberation over whether to obey or disobey particular rules. This quite simply does not reflect the reality of real-world decision making. In this respect, realists make quite unrealistic assertions.

WHY DO STATES OBEY INTERNATIONAL LAW?

Though the international system lacks impartial third-party mechanisms to enforce international law, international lawyers routinely assert that states comply with most international law most of the time. We would expect international lawyers to defend their discipline, but consider as well the statement of Hans Morgenthau, a central figure in the revival of political realism after World War II:

> It is also worth mentioning, in view of a widespread misconception in this respect, that during the four hundred years of its existence international law has in most instances been scrupulously observed. . . . [T]o deny that

---

[34]D. Acheson, "Remarks by the Honorable Dean Acheson, Former Secretary of State," 57 *Proceedings of the AJIL* 13 (1963), 14.

[35]In particular, see the memoir of R. Hilsman, *The Cuban Missile Crisis: The Struggle over Policy* (1996), and his earlier discussion in *To Move a Nation: The Politics of Foreign Policy in the Administration of John F. Kennedy* (1967).

[36]J. S. Campbell, "The Cuban Crisis and the U.N. Charter: An Analysis of the United States Position," 16 *Stanford Law Review* 160 (1963); D. G. Partan, "The Cuban Quarantine: Some Implications for Self Defense," *Duke Law Journal* 696 (1963).

international law exists at all as a system of binding legal rules flies in the face of all the evidence.[37]

Still, any discussion of ensuring compliance must deal directly with the issue of power. We should note that while Professor Morgenthau believed that states generally obey international law, he also observed that the structure of the international legal system "makes it easy for the strong both to violate the law and to enforce it, and consequently puts the rights of the weak in jeopardy."[38] Indeed, although many realists may have an incomplete picture of contemporary international politics, the fear expressed by Professor Morgenthau that the structure of the legal system provides little in the way of deterrence or restraint *if* a powerful state chooses to ignore the rules always lurks in the background of discussions concerning compliance and enforcement.

From our earlier analysis and extended comments to follow, the reader should understand that acknowledging the lack of a potent central enforcement agent to curb the activities of the powerful does *not* mean, therefore, that powerful states *constantly* ignore international obligations with no expectations of adverse results. Granted, the lack of central institutions suggests the possibility that *powerful* states *could,* but the question still becomes, How often *do* they take advantage of the possibility? Critics can cite spectacular failures as evidence of noncompliance. Singular failures prove nothing. Perfect compliance suggests the triviality of a standard. Compliance and obedience rest upon a much more complex set of factors than a simple fear of punishment. As we argued earlier, clearly, the fear of punishment does not necessarily deter powerful individuals and organizations from noncompliance or outright defiance of the law within domestic societies. Public employee labor unions still go on strike. Corporate officials still engage in fraud and insider trading. Drug dealers at all levels still sell drugs and kill each other.

The question remains, if the system has no effective third-party authority to force states to utilize judicial means or to enforce decisions, and if no hierarchy of courts with compulsory jurisdiction exists under which a dispute between states can move by appeal from lower to higher levels and/or awards made by existing courts and tribunals, why *do* states obey international law? How do states enforce international law? The following sections deal with issues of compliance and enforcement at the international level.

Motivation for Obedience

Much of the discussion regarding this question has centered on the unproved assumption that the only real motivation for obedience to the law flows from the fear of physical sanction by a superior (Thomas Hobbes, John Austin).[39] Critics have a simple argument: Because no such superior exists in the international sphere, except for the use of UN forces or direct unilateral intervention by one of

---

[37]Hans J. Morgenthau, *Politics Among Nations,* 3rd ed. (1961), 277.

[38]Morgenthau, note 37, at 294, 295.

[39]See, for example, J. Austin, *The Province of Jurisprudence Determined* (1832), in which he defines law as "the command of the sovereign."

the great powers, nations have no reason to obey the law. Assuredly, fear of "punishment" may on occasion play a part in bringing about a willingness, expressed by word or deed, to abide by the rule of law, but other and more important causative factors appear to play a part. To understand this, we again need to engage our imagination.

Desire for Order and Predictability

We should be very careful about making comparisons between those factors motivating individuals and those motivating aggregate or collective entities like states. However, a fundamental factor in the development of law flows from the simple fact that, given a choice, most individuals will prefer order and predictability. Brierly summarizes the matter very well:

> The ultimate explanation of the binding force of all law is that man, whether he is a single individual or whether he is associated with other men in a state, is constrained, in so far as he is a reasonable being, to believe that order and not chaos is the governing principle of the world in which he has to live.[40]

Maintaining normal relations with other countries depends upon the predictable behavior of others. The observance of the known rules of international law thus becomes a requirement for states.

The desire to observe the law can be discerned in the *standing instructions* issued to government personnel who, because of their role or mission, may have occasion to deal with situations that could produce serious international incidents. Standing instructions try to anticipate potential problems and give specific procedures for dealing with them according to international law.[41] Coast Guard officers, embassy staff, and many times local police (particularly in Washington, DC, and New York City, which host very large diplomatic communities) need guidance. To give a real example, how should local police have handled the case of the consul general from a very important trading partner who, while on the way home from a private party where he had overindulged, wrapped his car around a power pole on the main thoroughfare in front of a dozen witnesses? (We discuss this example further in Chapter 14.) For individuals dealing with situations that could have international implications, the time, care, and effort invested to ensure they understand the elements of the relevant law in these cases are proof that governments take the obligations seriously and do try to interpolate them into everyday interactions.

Consent and Obedience

Many writers believe that because states make the law through their formal consent, they necessarily feel obligated to honor the rules in order to achieve specific common aims. States make the law, which also means that such law is more likely

---

[40]Brierly, note 6, at 56.

[41]See, for example, the U.S. Department of State, *Guidelines on Protection of Foreign Missions*, 22 C.F.R. § 2a.1 (1987).

to reflect common interests. In the well-known *Lotus* case, the Permanent Court of International Justice stated:

> International law governs relations between independent states. The rules of law binding upon states emanate from their own free will as expressed in conventions or by usages generally accepted as expressing principles of law and established in order to regulate the relations between co-existing independent communities or with a view to achievement of common aims.[42]

But the traditional reliance on consent alone does not adequately explain the way states act in relation to the law. Moreover, asserting that consent alone binds states begs the question because then we must ask these questions: Where does the rule setting consent as the binding factor derive from, and what makes it binding?[43]

EXTRALEGAL FACTORS THAT PROMOTE COMPLIANCE

Enlightened Self-Interest: The Interdependence of Policies

A number of interrelated extralegal factors help explain why states obey the law. Some of these also play a role in well-ordered domestic legal systems, but as subsidiary considerations. Much of the law embodies identical or complementary interests—meaning that *self-interest* plays a great role as a motivating force rather than as a divisive element. Fundamentally, all of these extralegal factors flow from the interdependent nature of policymaking in the contemporary world. Interdependence in the political sense arises because while problems may appear as discrete events, they must be solved within the framework of priorities that define the importance of the problem in relation to other interests. The maintenance of relatively stable patterns of rules characterized as a legal order depends upon relevant decision makers utilizing operational maxims that reflect important shared values among the members of the order. Andrew Hurrell provides a useful perspective:

> Being a political system, states will seek to interpret obligations to their own advantage. But being a legal system that is built on the consent of other parties, they will be constrained by the necessity of justifying their actions in legal terms.[44]

We should remember that the key players in most disputes between states are not judges (although lawyers may be involved), but political officials who have quite different modes of search and discovery regarding applicable rules. Because many courses of action will affect others as well as the decision makers' own state, political advisers must take into account the attitudes of allies, adversaries, and onlookers about what constitutes permissible conduct within the parameters of a specific incident. Will a particular course of action incur approval, acquiescence, or resistance

---

[42]The S. S. *Lotus,* PCIJ, Ser. A, No. 10 (1927).

[43]G. G. Fitzmaurice, "The Foundations of Authority of International Law and the Problem of Enforcement," 19 *Modern Law Review* (1956), 8.

[44]A. Hurrell, "International Society and the Study of Regimes: A Reflective Approach," in *Regime Theory and International Relations,* edited by V. Rittberger and P. Mayer (1993), 61.

from other states? And which states will utilize the foregoing judgments in what manner? How will a particular decision affect future relations with other states? Law may not determine the answers to all of these questions, but it will be a factor in evaluating responses.

Credibility and Reputation

International relations textbooks tend to ignore credibility and reputation except as factors when the use of force comes into play. Nonetheless, these are important considerations in the everyday interaction between governments. Consider credibility and reputation as the "credit rating" that states earn through their dealings with other states. Having the reputation of keeping one's word and dealing within the law can facilitate good relations and aid in achieving goals that require the cooperation of others. A reputation for principled behavior and for being dependable and reliable is an asset not to be undervalued. Conversely, having the reputation of not honoring one's bargains or playing by the rules can seriously inhibit the pursuit of goals, no matter how powerful you may be.

Law Habit

We should not dismiss or discount habit as a motivating factor in the observance of law. Routine observance of the rules promotes a "habit of law"—a simple acceptance of the law as a factor in everyday decision making. At the individual level, as we grow up, we acquire certain attitudes and beliefs as part of the socialization process. As individuals, most of us routinely obey most of the law most of the time without consciously thinking about it. The same holds true for decision makers. As we noted earlier, even in the discussion about how to deal with the Cuban Missile Crisis, when the survival of the United States might have been at stake, the participants could not stray very far from questions of law. Outside of crisis situations, the complementarities of law and interest make this habit relatively easy to sustain. Professor Harold Koh furnishes an interesting explanation of how the law habit may evolve based on the necessity of dealing with the international political environment:[45]

> In tracing the move from the external to the internal, from one-time grudging compliance with an external norm to habitual internalized obedience, the key factor is repeated participation in the international legal process. That participation helps to reconstitute national interests, to establish the identity of actors and to develop the norms that become part of the fabric of emerging international society.

Reciprocity

In his classic and influential treatise, Emmerich de Vattel stated a proposition that he described as the "Golden Rule of Sovereigns": One cannot complain when

---

[45]H. H. Koh, "Why Do Nations Obey International Law?" 106 *Yale Law Journal* 2599 (1997), 2655.

he is treated as he treats others.[46] Any government contemplating a violation of a rule of law must consider the reactions of other states. Considering again the extent to which the law reflects common and complementary interests, the converse of Vattel's proposition holds as well: A government's observance of an obligation stands as the condition that guarantees the observance of other governments, and vice versa. When Vattel wrote (in 1758), states, particularly great powers, had few relationships—beyond those connected with diplomacy—where reciprocity played a vital role. His Golden Rule stands as a piece of prudent political advice to his contemporaries, but serves as a warning of consequences, not a fundamental legal principle. Vattel counseled self-interested restraint, if not an enlightened self-interest.

In the contemporary world, increasing interdependence has broadened the areas where reciprocity has a real impact as a pragmatic calculation. In one form, reciprocity yields a practical nonlegal explanation based on self-interest as to why states observe treaties. A treaty is no more than a set of *conditional promises:* To get the benefits promised by the other party, governments must give the benefits they have promised. In this case, the presumption is that, having consented to the treaty in the first place, the state has a compelling self-interest in seeing the provisions executed.

Reciprocity has other uses as well. National legislators may attempt to create or affect international relationships by passing reciprocity legislation. Hence, the Congress of the United States might enact a statute that would permit individuals from a foreign country to exercise certain rights within the United States *only if* the foreign state extends the same rights and privileges to American citizens within its borders. For example, the right of citizens from State X to own certain mineral resources within the United States would depend upon State X, in reciprocal legislation, according that same opportunity to U.S. citizens to own resources in, or controlled by, State X.

The clearest and most common illustration of how reciprocity works comes from the law regulating diplomatic relations. Every receiving state most likely has diplomats of its own in other countries. Observing and enforcing the rules of protocol and immunity for resident diplomats are primary conditions of having other states treat your diplomats in the same manner. This presupposes, of course, that a state cares about the well-being of its diplomats abroad and about its reputation in general. Belarus, Libya, Iran, and China (during the Cultural Revolution) have all engaged in activities that fundamentally violated the rules protecting diplomats from abuse. While concern for maintaining the general principle of immunity—and for nationals traveling or resident in these countries—precluded retaliation against the diplomats or embassies of the offenders (*note* the interdependence of interests here and the importance other states placed upon maintaining the principle), these states did not escape unpunished. We return to this issue in Chapter 14.

---

[46]E. de Vattel, *The Law of Nations (Le droit des gens)*, trans. C. G. Fenwick (1995, reissue of 1916 edition), 4. See also R. O. Keohane, "Reciprocity in International Relations," 40 *International Organization* 1 (Winter 1986), 1–27, for a more general discussion of the role of reciprocity in contemporary international politics.

World Opinion

Some writers and statesmen have claimed that world opinion forms an important element in encouraging states to obey the rules of international law. This is difficult to prove. Most modern writers have discounted world public opinion as a factor because of the difficulty in defining the idea and in establishing meaningful measures of its expression. For example, what "publics" should we include in the assessment? Opinion *within* individual states may support or inhibit certain actions by governments, but to be an effective factor in supporting international law, these opinions would have to demonstrate consistency, clarity of substantive content, and salience across a wide spectrum of states.

Methods of Ensuring Compliance: How Do States Enforce International Law?

Any discussion about enforcing compliance with international law must include two rather distinct concepts: violation of the rules of law themselves and failure to carry out arbitral awards or judicial decisions. We address the issue of arbitral and judicial awards later (see Chapter 15). Here we focus primarily on enforcing compliance with the law itself. To understand the role of enforcement, we must consider what outcomes enforcement should produce. As discussed earlier, this is not a simple matter. While mentioning enforcement inevitably conjures up the "punishment" aspect of the criminal law, what a state may wish in a particular circumstance is merely assurances of future compliance and action to repair any damage caused by nonperformance rather than any type of punitive action "to teach a lesson." Of course, situations do occur where punishment does constitute the sole or primary purpose, but the question we all need to keep in mind is, How often, and in what circumstances, do states seek punishment as the primary goal in trying to repair a breach of obligation?

For the most part, enforcement at the international level depends upon *the party alleging violation* taking the first step to deal with noncompliance. *Every state must guard its own interests*. The primary mode of securing compliance in the face of a breach is *self-help*. At base, every state sits as ultimate judge in its own case, that is, as the entity that can make decisions about a settlement, unless the parties can agree to submit the dispute to some form of third-party settlement: arbitration, a relevant court, a regional organization, or the UN Security Council. Because inequalities of power and interdependence of policy interests may come into play, this process can be very difficult. Circumstances of the moment may dictate both the method sought to redress an act of noncompliance and *the nature of the remedy* the aggrieved party elects.

Politics may come into play because settlements may reflect a desire for continued good relations rather than a strict demand for reparations to "repair the breach." Moreover, many of the procedures for resolving disputes over legal questions serve as methods for resolving disputes that may have nothing to do with legal questions. Not every dispute between states involves a breach of the law, nor does the law necessarily provide a method or remedy for resolving all disputes. To reiterate an earlier point, the same holds true (but to a lesser extent) in domestic legal systems. Disputes between individuals, and between states, may raise certain issues that lie outside of the area where the law provides a solution. In the absence of restrictive homeowner covenants defining acceptable color schemes, painting your house purple with orange polka dots and chartreuse trim may cause infinite hassles with neighbors who do not share your taste, but neighbors may find the law of little use in trying to force you to repaint using a less flamboyant set of colors.

In considering the consequences of noncompliance, one should keep in mind that violation of the rules of law by a given state—even if no sanction is attempted—*does not render the rule invalid.* We make this point explicitly because critics often seem to imply that the fact that states violate any rule in any circumstance proves the invalidity of that rule as law. The same conclusion about the validity of a rule of international law holds true, of course, in the sphere of domestic (municipal) legal systems. Violations of, say, a federal law, a Minnesota or Georgia statute, or a city ordinance do not vitiate, set aside, or nullify the rule in question. Indeed, as just mentioned, perfect compliance would suggest the irrelevance or triviality of a particular rule.

The Supreme Court of Hong Kong stated this principle clearly in the arbitration concerning the S.S. *Prometheus* when it held that

> [t]he resistance of a nation to a law to which it has agreed does not derogate from the authority of the law because that resistance cannot, perhaps, be overcome. Such resistance merely makes the resisting nation a breaker of the law to which it has given its adherence, but it leaves the law, to the establishment of which the resisting nation was a party, still subsisting. Could it be successfully contended that because any given person or body of persons possessed for the time being to resist an established municipal law such law had no existence? The answer to such a contention would be that *the law still existed, though it might not for the time being be possible to enforce obedience to it.*[47] (Emphasis added)

SUGGESTED READINGS

Kunz, "Sanctions in International Law," 54 *AJIL* 324 (1960).

Kunz, "The Swing of the Pendulum: From overestimation to Underestimation of International Law," 44 *AJIL* 135 (1950).

Lauterpacht's *Oppenheim*, I, 15.

Nardin, *Law, Morality and the Relations of States* (1983).

Onuf, *World of Our Own Making* (1989).

Renwick, *Economic Sanctions* (1981).

Reus-Smit, ed., *The Politics of International Law* (2004).

Sanctions and Law

Shklar, *Legalism* (1986), Part I: *Law and Morals.*

S. Silverburg, ed., *International Law: Contemporary Issues and Future Developments* (2011)

Whiteman, I, 58.

DISPUTE SETTLEMENT

Dahlitz, *Peaceful Resolution of Major International Disputes* (1999).

Evans, ed., *Remedies in International Law: The Institutional Dilemma* (1998).

Hamilton, ed., *The Permanent Court of Arbitration: International Arbitration and Dispute Resolution—Summaries of Awards, Settlement Agreements, and Reports* (1999).

Jackson, *Sovereignty, the WTO and Changing Fundamentals of International Law* (2006).

Merrils, *International Dispute Settlement,* 5th ed. (2011).

[47] *Hong Kong L.R.* (1904), 207, 225.

INTERNET RESOURCES

The American Society of International Law
www.asil.org/resource/home.htm

The International Law Institute
www.ili.org

Lyonette Louis-Jacques, "Legal Research on International Law Issues Using the Internet"
www.lib.uchicago.edu/~llou/forintlaw.html

If your library has access to JSTOR:

American Journal of International Law
www.jstor.org/journals/00029300.html

NATURE OF THE LAW IN GENERAL

Brierly, 1, 41.

Butler, ed., *Control over Compliance with International Law* (1991).

Campbell, "International Law and Primitive Law," 8 *Oxford Journal of Legal Studies* 169 (1988).

Caney, *Justice Beyond Borders: A Global Political Theory* (2005).

Chayes and Chayes, "On Compliance," 47 *international Organization* 175 (1993).

Chayes and Chayes, *The New Sovereignty: Compliance with International Regulatory Agreements* (1998).

Conlon, *United Nations Sanctions Management: A Case Study of the Iraq Sanctions Committee, 1990–1994* (2000).

Damrosch, ed., *Enforcing Restraint: Collective Intervention in Internal Conflicts* (1993).

Dyzenhaus, "Positivism and the Pesky Sovereign," 22 *EJIL* 363 (2011).

Goldsmith and Posner, *The Limits of International Law* (2005).

Gowlland-Debbas, ed., *United Nations Sanctions and International Law* (2001).

Hall, "The Persistent Spectre: Natural Law, International Order and the Limits of Legal Positivism," 12 *EJIL* 269 (2001).

Henkin, *How Nations Behave: Law and Foreign Policy*, 2nd ed. (1979).

Higgins, *Problems and Process: International Law and How We Use It* (1994).

Keohane, *Moravcsik, and Slaughter, "Legalized Dispute Resolution: Interstate and Transnational," 54 International Organization 457* (2000).

Waldron, *"Are Sovereigns Entitled to the Benefit of the International Rule of Law?" 22 EJIL 315* (2011).

Development of Law Among Nations

EARLY DEVELOPMENT OF INTERNATIONAL LAW

Pre-Greek Civilizations

International law, as we know it today, primarily developed from the ideas and practices of Western civilization.[1] Its existence in modern form covers only the past 500 years or so, but its roots extend into the distant past. Some have attempted to link the modern law with the customs and usages of pre-Greek civilizations, but it now appears that our present law cannot claim such an impressive genealogy. We can, however, find evidence in contemporary law of rules and procedures that parallel those in the earliest documents describing relations between states. For instance, a treaty concluded in the very dawn of recorded history—about 2100 B.C.—between the rulers of two communities in Mesopotamia, Lagash and Umma, provided for the settlement of a boundary dispute through arbitration and involved the taking of solemn oaths for observance of the agreement. Any examination of Hebrew, Assyrian, Babylonian, Hindu, and early Chinese records in the fields of warfare and diplomacy reveals many customs and usages corresponding to the practice of modern states.[2] Do not assume, however, that we can trace the modern law directly to those early civilizations. The world of antiquity lacked the modern concept of a community or society of nations. The interests of each unit were local and parochial, not "international."

---

[1]See, inter alia, A. Nussbaum, *A Concise History of the Law of Nations* (1954); D. Bederman, *International Law in Antiquity* (2001); R. Cohen, *On Diplomacy in the Ancient Near East: The Amarna Letters (Israel)*, Clingendael Discussion Papers in Diplomacy, Netherlands Institute of International Relations, no. 2, February (1995).

[2]See Nussbaum, note 1, at 1–5; Lauterpacht, *Oppenheim*, I: 72; and F. M. Russell, *Theories of International Relations* (1936), chs. 1–4.

Greek Contributions

Greek civilization, great though its achievements were in many other spheres, did not *directly* contribute to the development of modern international law.[3] We have deliberately used the word *directly*. As with other civilizations, the Greeks developed practices that parallel modern international law. The Greeks shared common bonds of race, culture, language, and religion as well as a distinct feeling of enmity toward all non-Greeks (the "barbarians"). On the other hand, we find the well-known passion of the Greeks for local independence (decentralization). The central issues in the debate over Greek contributions revolve around a perception of whether the Greeks shared a common conception of mutual state relations under a common rule of law. Considerable evidence exists to support the contention that, among the Greek city-states of the pre-Alexander era (338 B.C.), a customary law governing interactions did exist based upon mutual respect and common cultural heritage.[4] The Greeks

> intuitively understood within the Hellenic community, international justice meant that there were commonly shared expectations of behavior, understood and respected even though they were not the subject of diplomatic adjustment or codification in a treaty.[5]

Post Alexander, it is difficult to speak of a state system in the eastern Mediterranean governed by any commonalities.

Roman Contributions

Ancient Rome contributed immensely to the development of Western law as well as to the subsequent evolution of modern international law. Ironically, the Greeks may have failed to establish a community based upon common practice, but Greek ideas played a central role in the development of the Roman legal system. Roman legal writers defined two kinds of law: *jus civile,* the laws that each country created for itself, and *jus gentium,* a body of law established among all men by reason, based on ideas or ideals of justice, and observed by all countries. As Rome expanded from a city-state in central Italy to a far-flung multiethnic empire, the *jus civile* that had applied to Rome proper became inadequate for the problems generated by the broader context. The *jus gentium,* originally considered as the law that governed the relationship between foreigners and Roman citizens, supplanted the old Roman *jus civile.*

The idea of *natural law (jus naturale),* generally attributed in origination to the Greek *Stoic* philosophers, that underlay the *jus gentium* was considered to

---

[3]See C. Phillipson, *The International Law and Custom of Ancient Greece and Rome* (1911); Scupin, "History of the Law of Nations: Ancient Times to 1648," in *Encyclopedia of Public International Law,* vol. 2, edited by R. Berhardt (Amsterdam: North Holland, 1984); and W. K. Pritchett, *The Greek State at War* (5 vols, 1967–1991). For a summary of the debate over Greek contributions, see Bederman, note 1, at 34–41.

[4]See R. Bauslaugh, *The Concept of Neutrality in Classical Greece* (1991), 36, 52.

[5]Bederman, note 1, at 40; Lauterpacht, note 2, I: 71.

embody the common principles on which the laws of civilized societies ought to be constructed.[6] These principles, derived from the nature of humanity and the world, stood independent from any human action, and as universally and eternally valid. Of course, the interesting questions here stem from identifying the process or methods through which one may ascertain these principles and rules with certainty. The technical philosophical differences among the schools of thought that developed to explore these problems need not concern us here. The importance comes from the emphasis on reason, rationality, and universality. These left an indelible print on how we think about international law. In the contemporary era, we find the reemergence of a form of natural law theorizing in association with the development of various human rights regimes.[7]

FROM MEDIEVAL TO EARLY MODERN EUROPE

The fall of the Roman Empire and its administrative structures resulted in a period of political fragmentation and instability. Even so, contrary to a widespread belief, the medieval period did contain some of the seeds of a future international law. Legal thinkers of the Middle Ages preserved and developed the ideas associated with *jus gentium*, increasingly emphasizing the existence of a universal law applicable to all states. On the other hand, the medieval period lacked the conditions under which a system akin to modern international law could evolve. The word *Germany* did not describe a state, but a geographic area that alone encompassed more than 300 political units with some claim to independent status. Most of these units seldom exerted influence beyond their immediate localities.[8] Relationships were based primarily upon landholding (grants) and other personal ties such as family and marriage.[9] The holdings of King Henry II of England (1133–1189) illustrate the complexity of the medieval political landscape. Through his father and mother, Henry inherited Maine, Anjou, Normandy, and other land in western France. Marriage added Aquitaine and Gascony. These landholdings made him a vassal, although a very powerful one, to the King of France.[10] This relationship would later produce the motivating justifications for the Hundred Years'

---

[6]See, for example, Cicero, *De Legibus,* I: 18; Also, B. W. Frier, *The Rise of the Roman Jurists* (1985). Natural law as a term encompasses both moral and legal theories. The nexus and overlap between the two, that is, how and to what extent does moral theory provide the rationales for legal theory, have generated an interesting literature over the ages. In the modern era, both Lon Fuller (*The Morality of Law*, 1964) and Ronald Dworkin (*Law's Empire*, 1986) have made influential contributions to the discussion.

[7]See, for example, J. Waldron, ed., *Theories of Rights* (1984) (chapters by R. Dworkin, A. Gewirth, and H. L. A. Hart).

[8]In addition to secular principalities of various descriptions (kingdoms, duchies, principalities, dominions, margravates, landgravates, free imperial cities), many ecclesiastical territories (Archbishoprics, Bishoprics, even some abbeys/monasteries) enjoyed an independent status as well. Note that Andorra at one time was a *condominium* (joint rule) between the Bishop of Urgell (Spain) and the Count of Foix (France).

[9]For a readable account of relationships and politics, see B. Tuchman, *A Distant Mirror: The Calamitous 14th Century* (1987).

[10]R. Bartlett, *England Under the Norman and Angevin Kings: 1075–1225* (2000).

War (1337–1453, House of Valois vs. the House of Plantagenet).[11] In this political milieu, the ideas associated with sovereignty and the role of the modern state that form the building blocks of modern law have no referents.

The view of Roman rule as a unified, civilizing influence played a central role in European politics until the Treaty of Westphalia. We find two competing entities striving to claim the mantle of leadership presumably conferred on the heir(s) to Roman rule. First and foremost, the Catholic Church furnished an integrating factor. The existence of a single religion with its increasingly centralized administrative structure and the evolution of a common law (canon or ecclesiastical law) applicable to members—irrespective of race, nationality, or location—provided a semblance of unity. Often church and state were intertwined, with church officials holding important government offices. Ecclesiastical law, as it developed during the medieval period, influenced many areas regarded today as lying within the sphere of international law: the conclusion of treaties and their observance, authority over territory, the right of conquest with the sanction of the Church ("just war"), papal activity in *arbitration* and the general emphasis in canon law on arbitration as a desirable method for settling disputes, and, above all, regulations concerning many facets of warfare. Few chapters in Western intellectual history are more fascinating than the repeated attempts by the Church to eliminate *private war* and to mitigate the evils of legitimate international conflict.[12] In addition, as trade developed, so did the need for rules to manage business and maritime activity.

The Holy Roman Emperor emerged as the second claimant to the heritage of Rome. Presumably established on Christmas Day in A.D. 800 with the crowning of Charlemagne as *Imperator Augustus* (emperor) by the pope ("Holy" did not become part of the title until the mid-1100s), the empire's territorial boundaries varied over its history. At its peak, it encompassed Germany, including Austria (western Francia), Switzerland, northern Italy, and holdings associated with Burgundy (eastern France). Although the title implied unity, it primarily consisted of hundreds of smaller subunits, principalities, duchies, counties, free imperial cities, as well as various other domains (see footnote 8). Despite the name, for most of its history, the Holy Roman Empire did not include Rome within its borders.[13] Strong emperors played a leading role in European politics, but the emperor did not have absolute authority over the component pieces. As a result, the empire never attained any great degree of unity. As one commentary noted, when the emperor was in Germany, his Italian subjects rebelled; when he was in Italy, his German subjects rebelled.[14] Relations between the pope and ambitious emperors were often fractious as well. At times the emperor had sufficient power to dethrone and install popes. The Reformation (sixteenth century) further weakened

---

[11]For an excellent discussion of the issues, see C. Allmand, ed., *War, Government and Power in Late Medieval France* (2000).

[12]See Nussbaum, note 1, at 17, 18, on the role of the Church; W. Ullmann, *Law and Politics in the Middle Ages* (1975); M. Keen, *The Laws of War in the Late Middle Ages* (1965); T. Meron, *Henry's Wars and Shakespeare's Laws: Perspectives on the Law of War in the Later Middle Ages* (1993); and F. H. Russell, *Just War in the Middle Ages* (1975).

[13]J. Sypeck, *Becoming Charlemagne: Europe, Baghdad and the Empires of A.D. 800* (2007); J. Coy, D. Marschke and D. Sabean, eds, *The Holy Roman Empire Reconsidered* (2010).

[14]*The Holy Roman Empire*, http://faculty.ucc.edu/egh-damerow/holy_roman_empire.htm.

the authority of the emperor within his German dominions. The issues generated by the schism(s) eventually led to the Thirty Years' War (1618–1648), which culminated with the Treaty of Westphalia.

The Treaty of Tordesillas (1493–1494)

The Treaty of Tordesillas (Spain–Portugal, 1493–1494) illustrates the role of the pope in secular affairs in this era. The late 1400s had witnessed a great expansion in European exploration. States had many motives, but perhaps the most pressing concerned trade with the East—India and China. To make trade more efficient and profitable, Portugal attempted to find a direct water route to India and China and thus bypass Arab merchants who controlled the land routes to Asia. After Columbus discovered the "New World" in 1492, a competition arose between Spain and Portugal concerning claims to territory in the newfound region. This marked a very different type of issue because heretofore acquisition of land outside of Europe had not played a great role in the competition between European states. The possibility that the New World had vast resources (particularly of gold and silver) led to a bitter competition between Spain and Portugal.

The two states had negotiated a treaty (in 1493) to divide any new discoveries. In 1493, Pope Alexander VI acted to clear up any confusion that may have arisen over territorial claims. He issued a decree that established an imaginary line running north and south through the mid-Atlantic, 100 leagues (300 nautical miles) from the Cape Verde Islands. Spain would have possession of any unclaimed territories to the west of the line, and Portugal would have possession of any unclaimed territory to the east of the line. After further exploration, the Portuguese grew dissatisfied with the agreement when they realized how much more land Spain had received. In June 1494, the two states renegotiated the dividing line, and the agreement was officially ratified during a meeting in the Spanish town of Tordesillas. The Treaty of Tordesillas reestablished the line 370 leagues (1,110 nautical miles) west of the Cape Verde Islands. This explains why Portuguese is the national language of Brazil. Note that the agreement did not include any other states.

Writers and Ideas

Before continuing with the historical narrative, we will briefly summarize a few of the more prominent writers who contributed to the early development of international law. Space limitations prevent the inclusion of many authors famous in the history of international law, such as Pierino Belli and Balthazar Ayala on the laws of war; Richard Zouche and Samuel Rachel on positive law; and Christian Wolff, the great teacher of Vattel, and Georg von Martens on the natural rights of states and on certain aspects of positive law.[15] *These writers represent the concerns of their age.* Not surprisingly, the bulk of their work focused upon war.

---

[15]Fortunately for the serious student, virtually all the classics in international law are available in the famous *Classics of International Law,* sponsored by the Carnegie Endowment for International Peace. Summaries of the most important writers are found in Nussbaum and in Lauterpacht, I: 85. Much material on selected writers, such as Vitoria and Grotius, may also be found in standard histories of Western political thought.

Until the beginning of the eighteenth century, much of the writing about law built upon *natural law* foundations. As we noted earlier in this chapter, the Catholic Church played a central part in this endeavor. Many of the more prominent contributors were clerics. Perhaps the best known and most influential arguments were produced by Thomas Aquinas. For Aquinas, natural law formed an aspect of divine providence that produced the plan that orders all creation. Natural law constituted the basic principles of practical rationality. By extension, the precepts of the natural law are universally binding by nature. All human beings possess a basic knowledge of the principles of the natural law. Aquinas argues that the fundamental principle of the natural law is that *good is to be done and evil avoided.* Unfortunately, he does not identify a set of axioms through which we might identify norms (acts) that fall within these general parameters. He does suggest that context, motives, and ends would provide guides.[16]

Francisco de Vitoria (1480–1546) He was a well-known Dominican friar and professor of theology at the University of Salamanca in Spain, Vitoria. Scholars often characterize Vitoria, along with Grotius (see later in text), as the founder of modern international law.[17] He primarily focused on the question of what made a war a just one, but also examined the bases of Spanish authority in the Americas, particularly with regard to relations between Indians and Spaniards. In his writings, one should note his remarkable concern for the rights of indigenous peoples and their fair treatment.

Francisco Suárez (1548–1617) Suárez,[18] a Jesuit priest and professor of theology at the University of Coïmbra in Spain, built on the legacy of Vitoria. In his *Treatise on Laws and God as Legislator* (1612), he held that the *jus gentium* differed in kind from natural law because it formed a body of law that applied between independent states rather than a law common to all states. As such, the argument laid the foundation for the idea of consent as the basis of a distinct set of rules voluntarily instituted by men.

An Important Note

The perspective of the next writer, Grotius, reflects a response to the impact of the Thirty Years' War (1618–1648) on Europe (discussed later in this chapter). Grotius lived through the events of the war. He died in 1645 just as negotiations began to end it. Earlier, Grotius had also written an influential work challenging assumptions about the law as it evolved to deal with issues concerning ships and the sea (*Mare Liberum*, 1609). These ideas had great influence on the development of the modern law of the sea.

---

[16]*Treatise on Law: The Complete* Text (2009).

[17]J. B. Scott, *The Spanish Origin of International Law: De Vitoria and His Law of Nations* (1934). While this is a thorough examination of Vitoria's writings, many of Scott's major premises should be treated with some skepticism.

[18]Nussbaum, note 1, at 80.

Huigh Cornets de Groot (Hugo Grotius, 1583–1645) Modern analysts accept de Groot,[19] better known as Hugo Grotius, as the *father* of international law.[20] Because we earlier referred to Vitoria as the *founder* of modern international law, we need to explain the difference. The work of Grotius stands as the first extensive treatment of international law that attempted to develop a systematic jurisprudence. In discussing the nature of the traditional *jus gentium,* Grotius went to considerable lengths to explain that it represented, in his opinion, law both human (i.e., not divine in origin) and volitional, a body of rules deliberately created by human beings to serve human needs. Perhaps the best measure of his influence over the next hundred years or so comes from Adam Smith, who noted in 1762: "Grotius seems to have been the first who attempted to give the world anything like a regular system of natural jurisprudence, and his treatise *On the Laws of War and Peace,* with all of its imperfections, is perhaps at this day the most complete work on the subject."[21]

In developing his thesis on the laws pertaining to warfare, Grotius leaned heavily on the Scholastic writers, with frequent citations from the works of Vitoria. His approach proved innovative in a number of ways. Virtually all forerunners of Grotius had limited their learned discussions of war, both just and unjust, to the beginning of a conflict. Grotius opened a vast new area for speculation and debate when he included in his work a detailed discussion of the conduct of military operations and their legal consequences and considerations. With insight, tolerance, and an eloquent use of examples borrowed from the past, he urged moderation in warfare and discussed the status and fate of hostages, the destruction of property, the problem of the defeated peoples' religious beliefs, and a host of other questions ignored or evaded by his predecessors. He did not believe that this particular portion of the *Law of War and Peace* represented a collection of legally binding principles. Rather, he saw his discussion of the conduct of hostilities as a form of personal advice to statesmen and military commanders. His early readers and even his critics regarded this section of the work as one of his most important contributions.

Another novel aspect associated with the concept of lawful or just war advanced by Grotius involves the question of war as a punitive measure. Earlier writers had maintained that only "superiors" were entitled to inflict punishment. Grotius, on the other hand, believed that equals could also inflict penalties or sanctions. He regarded war as a punitive action aimed against state crimes, analogous to the domestic punishment of crimes committed by individuals.[22] Sovereigns could thus lawfully exact punishment not only for injuries sustained by them or their subjects

---

[19]See E. Dumbauld, *The Life and Legal Writings of Hugo Grotius* (1969); E. Keene, *Beyond the Anarchical Society: Grotius, Colonialism and Order in World Politics* (2002); K. Haakonssen, ed., *Grotius, Pufendorf, and Modern Natural Law* (1999); and H. Bull et al., eds, *Hugo Grotius and International Relations* (1990).

[20]See Nussbaum, note 1, at 102, and Lauterpacht, note 2, I: 91. The two major works of Grotius are available in English: *The Law of War and Peace,* trans. F. W. Kelsey (1925) (the Kelsey edition draws from the second, vastly revised version by Grotius, written near the conclusion of the Thirty Years' War) and *The Freedom of the Seas,* trans. R. Magoffin (1916).

[21]A. Smith, *Lectures on Justice, Police, Revenue and Arms,* edited by Edwin Canaan (1896), 1.

[22]H. Grotius, *Law of War and Peace* (1625), bk. II, ch. 20.

but also against any person whatsoever if the injurious acts constituted a violation of the law of nature or international law. This right of punishment originated in the law of nature, according to Grotius. The modern reader will find in the relevant pages of Grotius strong echoes of the demands voiced during World War II for the punishment of war criminals. In fact, the following chapter (bk. II, ch. 21) contains a striking passage to the effect that subjects made themselves responsible for crimes of their sovereign if they consented to it or acted illegally under his persuasion or command. Thus, Grotius would have denied that one could escape just punishment for war crimes by pleading the defense of "superior orders."

After Grotius The distinction made by Grotius between a natural law of nations, as developed by him, and the customary or voluntary law, expounded by Richard Zouche (1590–1661), led to the rise of three separate schools of legal philosophy in the seventeenth and eighteenth centuries: the naturalists, the *positivists*, and the Grotians. The naturalists, led by Samuel Pufendorf, denied that any positive law of nations originated from custom or treaties; they maintained, with Thomas Hobbes, that international law merely formed a part of the law of nature. The positivists, in turn, opposed the followers of Pufendorf in believing that a positive law of nations had its true origin in custom and treaties, hence in the consent of states, that is, the actions of human beings. They argued that this law was far more important than any natural law of nations. Some writers of this school went so far as to deny the very existence of a law of nature. The leading positivist was the famous Dutch jurist Cornelius van Bynkershoek (discussed later in this section). The Grotians held to a middle position in the controversy, asserting that Grotius himself had drawn tenable distinctions between natural and voluntary law. But many of his disciples differed from the founder in insisting that both kinds of law were equally important. We should note in passing that, since the seventeenth century, the trend has moved away from the naturalists and strongly toward the position of the positivists.

The idea that an international society (a community of nations) exists with rules to govern its conduct, however derived, flows from Grotius. Followers of the Grotian tradition acknowledge the harsh realities sovereign states may face, while emphasizing the common interests (interdependence) they share. Grotius attempted to develop a middle way, wedding the idea of natural law to positivism-idealism and realism—what should be to what is factual practice. The Grotian tradition underlies the general analytical approach of the contemporary "English school" of analysis in international relations.[23] Because the processes associated with globalization and interdependence have had an impact, the assumptions of the English school seem to have gained some currency.[24]

Samuel Pufendorf (1632–1694) Pufendorf was the world's first professor of international law. Scholars still disagree, in a surprisingly voluminous literature, about whether he contributed much or little to the growth of the law beyond

---

[23]For example, see H. Bull, *The Anarchical Society* (1977).

[24]B. Buzan, *The English School: A Bibliography* (April 2009), www.polis.leeds.ac.uk/research/international-relations-security/english-school/resources.php.

being the founder of the so-called naturalist school of legal philosophy. Pufendorf implicitly believed in the existence of a state of nature antedating the historical state and held that in this pre-political situation, a law of nature was binding on all men. Only this law, rather than the consent of states, could establish legally binding principles and hence had to be regarded as the sole source of international law. His concept of the law of nature embraced those standards of behavior that experience and reason (the latter growing out of both experience and instruction) showed men, as they grew in knowledge, to be essential for their own good and for the good of human society, of which they formed a part in accordance with the design of nature.

Cornelius van Bynkershoek (1673–1743)   Although he never wrote a comprehensive treatise, Bynkershoek became the leading exponent of the positivist school. Most of Bynkershoek's contributions to the development of the law consisted in elaborating the rules governing neutral rights and duties, blockade (closely related to neutrality), prize law, and the subject of treaties in general.[25] As with Grotius, who earlier had advanced the doctrine of "freedom of the high seas," Bynkershoek clearly argued the legal positions that would permit the Dutch to enhance their shipping and trade with as little interference from others as possible, even in wartime. His writings on the necessity of limiting the territorial sea probably had great influence on the practice of states because of their wide circulation.

Christian Wolff (1679–1764)   Better known as a philosopher, Wolff published a work in 1749 entitled *Jus Gentium* as the ninth and last part of a major study on natural law. He promoted the concept of a world state (*civitas gentium maxima*) possessing considerable authority over its component member units. Vattel (discussed next), while clearly influenced by other ideas promoted by Wolff, specifically rejected this possibility.

Emmerich de Vattel (1714–1767)   A leading proponent of the Grotian school of legal philosophy, Vattel served in various diplomatic and policy-making roles during most of his adult life. His major work, *International Law: Or, Principles of Natural Law Applied to the Conduct and Affairs of Nations and of Sovereigns* (1758), designed as a practical manual for statesmen, became the standard European reference work in international law and is still cited on rare occasions even today.[26] Perhaps his most enduring contribution was the insistence that full sovereignty meant equality with respect to international law. Even considering the vital contributions of Grotius, until modern times no single writer has exercised as

---

[25]Many writers cite Bynkershoek as the originator of one of the more enduring myths of international legal history. In trying to justify claims to the width of the territorial sea, he utilized a security-based rationale, arguing that control of territorial waters should extend as far as a land-based cannon shot could carry. As the story goes, the typical cannon of the time had a range of approximately 3 nautical miles; therefore, the limit to claims became 3 nautical miles. While Bynkershoek was not the first to advance this rationale, his writings on limiting the territorial sea probably had great influence on the practice of states because of their wide circulation.

[26]Translated into English by C. G. Fenwick (1916).

much direct and lasting influence on those conducting international affairs in the legal sphere as did Vattel.[27]

THE IMPACT OF WESTPHALIA (1648)

During the Reformation in the sixteenth and seventeenth centuries, the Catholic Church gradually lost its direct influence in international affairs as Protestant entities emerged to contest the authority of the pope and Holy Roman Emperor. Historians and political scientists generally regard the Peace of Westphalia (actually the treaties of Münster and Osnabrück, two cities in Westphalia), ending the long and bloody Thirty Years' War, as the transition point between the old *hierarchical feudal order* based upon a network of complex personal relationships, loyalties, and obligations to the modern *horizontal* order based upon the idea of independent, self-governing *(sovereign)* states that recognize no superior political authority. Given its impact on both political and religious landscapes of the time, one can understand the reaction of Pope Innocent X when he said, "The Peace [of Westphalia] is null, void, invalid, unjust, damnable, reprobate, inane, empty of meaning and effect for all time."[28]

Textbooks and international relations literature routinely refer to the Westphalian state system, but to understand the evolution of international law, we must understand what the agreement at Westphalia did and did not do. One school of thought sees the immediate emergence of an international "society" based upon reciprocal obligations. The treaties did contain some language that established the twin ideas of sovereign independence and equality (i.e., all states regardless of size or religious persuasion had the protection of the law such as it was), some rudimentary requirements for the pacific settlement of disputes, and the possibility of collective action against any state violating the treaty. In addition, the collective grant of recognition to the Swiss Confederation and the United Provinces (the Netherlands) as independent sovereign states and the rhetoric contained in some treaty instruments do provide some idea of a nascent "club" with formal rules for admission. For many, publicists aside, Westphalia marks the political beginning point of modern international law because of the "deliberate enactment of common regulation by concerted action."[29]

This surely overplays the political reality of the prior 100 years as well that of the next 150. While we take treaties ending major conflicts as convenient historical markers, they usually merely register, in static form (i.e., as a snapshot rather than as a dynamic moving picture), trends already well under way but perhaps not

---

[27]Vattel's writings, now largely ignored except in France, have been criticized severely by modern legal historians. Most of the adverse comments center on his deliberate diminishment of the importance attributed to natural law, compared with that accorded to voluntary law. Nevertheless, despite theoretical weaknesses, Vattel's work went through edition after edition. It remained a best seller among legal commentaries for many decades. Vattel found particular favor in the United States. As late as 1887, a decision of the Supreme Court of the United States cited Vattel as an authority.

[28]Quoted in K. J. Holsti, *Peace and War: Armed Conflicts and International Order: 1648–1989* (1991), 25.

[29]L. Gross, "The Peace of Westphalia, 1648–1948," 42 *AJIL* (1948), 20–41.

yet fully developed. When the signatories signed off on Westphalia, they entered a totally uncharted realm. The treaties certainly signaled the absolute end of the old hierarchical order but did not produce a system of authoritative rules to govern the new circumstances of "freedom." It is one thing to destroy the old; it is entirely a different enterprise to put something new in place of the old that satisfies all. Westphalia did not produce a binding set of obligations to govern future relations. These evolved slowly over the next two centuries.

We should emphasize that an idea of Europe as a collective set of states with a distinctive common heritage of law and civilization had evolved—a rudimentary society existed, bound together by close common links among the great powers.[30] Over the next 150 years, while war continuously pitted European states against each other, the idea also grew that Europe formed an organic society of states bound together by common ties of family relationship, religion, and historical tradition that set Europe apart as "civilized." While fighting each other, the states also engaged in a competition for empire overseas. Wars may occur in Europe, but presumably the connections (and the resolution) were more significant than the sporadic outbreaks of violence. The questions revolve around the extent to which this really generated internal European norms that states took as serious obligations. In sum, Westphalia resolved some important questions, but the answers to other questions here do not comfort. As Holsti aptly notes, "Westphalia produced a peace and a type of order designed to guarantee *that* particular peace, but not peace in general."[31]

To understand the evolution of international law, we must understand the gap between the abstract ideas of the Enlightenment (eighteenth century)—embraced by many monarchs as the fashion of the time—and the dedicated pursuit of self-interest by those same monarchs. The gap between ideals and the pursuit of self-interest could not have been wider. As a school of thought, political realism applies with few caveats to the latter part of the seventeenth century and the whole of the eighteenth. In this era, "sharks and minnows" was a real game with real consequences. Territorial expansion formed an integral part of the state-building exercise. Sharks gobbled minnows with little fear of retribution, even though the minnows may have had technical "equality." Historians and political scientists analyze this period as the era of "classical balance of power," arguing that the great powers acknowledged some important "rules of the game." Yet these rules were rudimentary and certainly not legal. We should understand that the economic and social linkages *(transaction links)* that today often play into calculations of self-interest did not exist, or did not exist to the point of forming an important priority in interstate relations. States went to war because they had few options that would exert pressure on other states other than war or the threat of war. The most that can be said here is that the *idea* of a system of a European concert of powers floated around the salon circuit. Craig and George note:

> Writers on politics often talked of it as a desirable thing, in the sense that if it could really be brought into being, it might be able to develop the already

---

[30]See F. H. Hinsley, *Power and the Pursuit of Peace* (1963).

[31]Holsti, note 28, at 41. See also W. P. Guthrie, *The Later Thirty Years War: From the Battle of Wittstock to the Treaty of Westphalia* (2003).

recognized rules of international behavior into a more effective code of law that would restrain international violence and reduce the constant drain that war imposed upon state resources.[32]

Law did not presume to govern the relationship between war and peace—it governed relationships *in war and in peace* (see Chapter 20). International law said nothing about the transition, the decision to go from peace to war. One set of obligations applied in peace, and quite another in war.

In one sense, the foregoing may seem harsh. It measures the growth of international law in exactly the terms we rejected in Chapter 1 as the appropriate standard—the ability to restrain the resort to war. But note that the lack of important transaction links between states—trade, for example—meant states lacked means other than war (or force short of war) to influence other states. Mercantilism as the dominant economic philosophy (self-sufficiency, or autarky, as a political goal) reinforced narrow, self-interested policies of monarchs. In looking at Vattel and others, we can see the evolution of certain housekeeping arrangements necessary for transacting the business of state—the law associated with diplomatic intercourse (necessary for "high" politics), admiralty law (although many aspects associated with the rights of neutrals remained in dispute), the law merchant, and even the *jus in bello*. Here we should point out the importance and relevance of Vattel's Golden Rule of Sovereigns as a maxim counseling political prudence and restraint.

THE NINETEENTH CENTURY

Understanding the evolution of international law during the nineteenth century requires consideration of the major changes that occurred in the political, economic, and social relations both within and among states.[33] The end of the *eighteenth* century witnessed two important "revolutions"—the French, which changed the way individuals thought about the internal governance of states, and the "Industrial," which changed the material basis of all politics, domestic and international. We can summarize the international political climate during the nineteenth century in two sentences. For the first 40 years after the Congress of Vienna (1814–1815), the great powers were afraid of themselves in the sense of the potent challenges concerning internal governance produced by the French (and American) examples. For the second 40 years, they were afraid of each other because of the evolution (and costs) of military power produced by the Industrial Revolution. Both of these generated trends that would have major implications for how international law developed. The nineteenth century marks the true beginnings of law that reflects contemporary issues. Interestingly, the gap between publicists of the era and practice

---

[32]G. A. Craig and A. L. George, *Force and Statecraft,* 3rd ed. (1995), 19.

[33]By simply comparing the index of topics covered by Vattel with those covered by the first edition of Henry Wheaton's text (1836) and with the first edition of Hall's classic work (1858), then with Lassa Oppenheim's first edition in 1905, we can easily see the important developments in the nineteenth century. To complete the tour to the present, one should then look at the *ninth* edition of Oppenheim, published in 1992. While the Vattel–Wheaton–Hall–Oppenheim first edition comparison is striking, the difference between the first and ninth editions of Oppenheim is even more so. The 1992 edition runs to more than 1,330 pages dealing only with the law of "peace."

does not seem great. Positivism became the primary doctrine associated with developments in the nineteenth (and twentieth) centuries. Note that the first part of the century does not seem to produce a great writer on international law. We mention Henry Wheaton, in passing, because he emerged as the first American to write a systematic treatise.

The French Revolution gave birth to the modern idea of the *citizen* who has rights and duties, as opposed to a mere subject whose primary duty often was just paying taxes. Throughout the period immediately following the Congress of Vienna (1814–1815) that marked the end of the Napoleonic Wars, monarchs feared the rise of "republican" sentiment—that is, the idea that "the governed" should have any say in how they were governed. In many instances, the fear of republican revolution at home may have dulled the enthusiasm for war abroad. Despite their best efforts, "nationalism" in the form of demands for popular sovereignty grew apace. For entities like the multi-"national," multiethnic Austro-Hungarian Empire, the growing demands for *self-determination* by various groups foreshadowed their ultimate demise and the important role nationalism would play in the twentieth century. Yet note that the absence of nationalism permitted France, considered an essential player as a great power by other members of the society, to reenter the community of nations as a full member quickly and with only minor reparations. Contrast this with the treatment of Germany after World War I (100 years later).

One feature often emphasized as resulting from Vienna is the Concert of Europe, a series of consultations among the great powers held sporadically throughout the nineteenth century to deal with common problems. While the conferences mark some evolution in the sphere of cooperation, there was nothing systematic about them, no permanent organization associated with them, and no general abstract agreement concerning their purpose. In this sense, they flowed from the idea that having won the war through cooperation, some form of continuing cooperation would be necessary to keep the peace. This vague feeling had marked the aftermath of the treaties of both Westphalia (1648) and Utrecht (1713), both of which had ended the equivalent of world wars, yet no substantive basis for cooperation had emerged. The difference after Vienna arose because revolution and "national liberation" continued to pose a common threat to widely shared common ideas about the basis for stability and balance. Despite the lack of formal arrangements other than a provision in the Quadruple Alliance that called for periodic summit meetings, European states did hold 25 meetings between 1830 and 1884. Until the Crimean War (1854–1856), war avoidance rather than assertive pursuit of foreign policy goals formed the essence of great power practice.[34] No incidents in the interim provided clear and compelling lessons that would stimulate influential elements of political and military elites to consider fundamental changes. The concert did manage territorial change, and in general, managed to avert war or to keep wars localized.

The Industrial Revolution provided the basis for economic growth within states and the foundation for increasing contacts and trade between them. Manufacturing

---

[34]Of the 25 infantry battalions Great Britain initially sent to the Crimea, only 6 had seen service since the end of the Napoleonic Wars. Consequently, a very small minority of either officers or men had any prior combat experience. E. M. Spiers, *The Army and Society, 1815–1914* (1980), 98.

complexes linked by railroads and telegraphs changed patterns of internal growth. Slowly, the ideas of liberal trade theory (free trade is a good) replaced those of mercantilism. With expanding international contacts came the necessity for evolving rules to deal with the new circumstances and international organizations such as the International Telecommunications Union (ITU, founded in 1865) to help coordinate and deal with the international implications of the new technologies and circumstances. In many respects, the growing transaction links may explain the reluctance of states, in line with liberal trade theory, to resort to force (war destroys important links). Certainly, when Kaiser Wilhelm wrote an angry note to his prime minister demanding that Germany support his brother monarch in Spain against the United States with regard to Cuba (1897), he probably did not expect a quite reasoned reply detailing the important trade links and relationship that such a course might damage or terminate.

The Crimean War (1854–1856) marks a transition in many ways. The rapid change in the nature of armies made possible by social and political changes within states and advances in military technology would radically change beliefs about the nature of warfare and its potential as a tool of statecraft. Crimea stands as the last old-fashioned war (at least in Europe). The Prussian–German military model of professional cadre expanded by citizen-soldiers when necessary came to dominate military organizations shortly after. The relatively short wars fought by Germany against Austria (1866) and France (1870–1871) had raised expectations that war could be controlled. The International Committee of the Red Cross (founded in 1863) and the two Hague Conferences (1899 and 1907)[35] worked to develop elaborate codes to make war more humane. *The resort to war, and force short of war, remained legal, meaning the results of war (such as conquest) had legal standing.* We can see an effort to rein in and regulate the use of force short of war in the 1907 Hague (II) Convention on the Limitation of Employment of Force for Recovery of Contract Debts.[36]

INTERNATIONAL LAW AS "INTERNATIONAL" BEFORE WORLD WAR I

A great irony infuses the development of international law during the nineteenth century. On the one hand, it spread through the imperial activities of the European powers; on the other, it became more parochial because it reflected European values and applied in full only to those states admitted to the very exclusive club of "civilized" nations, determined of course by the current members of the club. Publicists often referred to international law as the *"public law of Europe."* Many important questions turned on who belonged to the club and who did not (see Table 2.1).

Consider, in this respect, the admission of Turkey into the company of "civilized" nations as part of the settlement of the Crimean War in 1856, while China and Japan remained outside the fold, subjected to unequal treaties and other indignities. Most

---

[35]We should note that the follow-on scheduled for 1915 was canceled because of war.

[36]October 18, 1907; see www.icrc.org/ihl.nsf/INTRO/150?OpenDocument.

TABLE 2.1	
Europe, 1870	
Austria–Hungary	The Netherlands
Belgium	Portugal
Denmark	Russia
France	Serbia
Germany	Spain
Great Britain	Sweden–Norway
Greece	Switzerland
Italy	Turkey
Montenegro	

Romania (1878–1879) and Bulgaria (1878–1886) were added before the end of the nineteenth century.

areas in Africa, the Middle East, and Asia became colonial possessions or dependencies that in turn had no rights under *international* law because the members of the club refused to acknowledge that these territories enjoyed any independent legal status (*juridical personality*). How, and under what circumstances, such possessions might *ever* emerge from their dependent status to become "states" would become one of the most important questions in the twentieth century.

TWENTIETH CENTURY

World War I destroyed four empires—the German, the Austro-Hungarian, the Russian, and the Turkish (Ottoman)—and accelerated trends that would eventually undermine the surviving colonial empires. It also destroyed the general belief in moral and material progress that had grown up with the advance of industrial societies during the latter part of the nineteenth century. On the other hand, the demise of empires meant a significant expansion of the state system. The world became much less Eurocentric with the emergence of the United States and Japan as important powers. The devastation flowing from World War I reinforced the idea that states should seek peaceful settlement of disputes if possible. The League of Nations, drawing on the legacy of the prewar Hague Conferences and the Concert of Europe, attempted to build on what statesmen saw as a genuine sentiment to limit war. The League *did not* outlaw the resort to war. Its procedures embodied the idea that through rational discourse and fact-finding, reasonable persons can find solutions to disputes. The League had no independent "enforcement" capability in the sense of enacting collective sanctions or sending troops. In the end, the League would fail because its members lacked the will to stand against persistent aggression. Still, the League did promote the idea that resort to force ought to be seriously limited—that war as an instrument of unilateral policy no longer had legitimacy. The Kellogg–Briand Treaty (1928) made aggressive war illegal for its signatories.

While the League may eventually have failed in its primary purpose, under its auspices, the Permanent Court of International Justice (PCIJ), the first true international court, came into existence in 1921.[37] After World War II, the PCIJ would become the International Court of Justice (ICJ) within the UN system. From its inception, the League had a concern with the rights of minorities in many of the small new states that emerged from the breakup of empires. With the mandate system for the former colonial possessions of the defeated states, there is a fledgling acknowledgment that these territories might one day emerge as states. The League seriously tackled the labyrinth of disarmament and the equally knotty problems of defining aggression. The interwar period also saw the birth of many intergovernmental organizations (IGOs), such as the International Labor Organization (ILO). This trend would accelerate in the aftermath of World War II. Legal scholarship flourished, much of it focused on describing the proceedings of the many international conferences aimed at dealing with common problems and with systematizing and codifying international law.

The United Nations

World War II proved even more devastating than World War I. The design of the new international organization, the United Nations, was evolutionary and conservative, drawing upon the structure of the League to a surprising extent.[38] It balanced Westphalian assumptions of sovereignty with the open-ended obligations of collective security. The UN Charter enshrined the state as the essential building block of postwar order by its emphasis on the norm of absolute territorial integrity and through its provision that only sovereign states qualified for membership. The principal duties and scope of authority related only to conflicts between states. Other functions of the organization were designed to enhance the qualities associated with statehood. In sum, the Charter legitimated the state as the quintessential form of political organization necessary for participation in international society.

At its heart, the design depended upon a plan to centralize the use of force in service of maintaining order *(collective security)*. Force would be used only as an authorized sanction taken after appropriate collective deliberation.[39] The model depended upon the collective authority and power invested in the UN Security Council to dampen conflicts, while limiting the rights of individual states to initiate the use of force except in the contingency of self-defense. *In theory*, with collective procedures in place, the need for states to utilize unilateral force as a measure of self-help would no longer exist. The wedding of Westphalian assumptions to Wilsonian ideals of collective security produced a profoundly conservative set of governing assumptions.[40] The Charter design sought to provide mechanisms to resist violent challenges to a status quo composed of well-defined, peace-loving

---

[37]The Permanent Court of Arbitration associated with the Hague Conventions was neither permanent in the sense of having a seat and stable membership nor, technically, a court.

[38]See L. M. Goodrich, "From League of Nations to United Nations," 1 *International Organization* (February 1947), 3–21; R. B. Russell, *A History of the United Nations Charter: The Role of the United States, 1940–1945* (1958); and Wilhelm Grewe, "The History of the United Nations," in *The Charter of the United Nations*, edited by B. Simma (1994), 1ff.

[39]Charter, Chapter VII, §39–50; www.un.org/en/documents/charter/index.shtml.

[40]On the intellectual origins, see Hinsley, note 30.

sovereign states. Such states would have internationally acknowledged governments and borders, and the governments would also be considered legitimate by constituent populations. The world visualized by the Charter divided states into two categories: peace lovers and aggressors.

The Cold War and Anticolonial Movement

The postwar world visualized in the Charter never materialized. The conflict that rapidly emerged between the United States and the Union of Soviet Socialist Republics (USSR) meant that the United Nations could not work as planned. More ironically, a second set of unexpected problems, caused by the rising tide of nationalism in colonial areas, arose. The Charter was constructed to deal with a particular kind of challenge—it (as well as the customary law) rests upon a very specific conception of military conflict and its conduct. The Charter presupposes that armed conflict will occur only between two territorial states and will be conducted by regular army forces clearly identified through distinctive uniforms and insignia.[41] Over the past 50 years, incidents that fit this characterization have formed the exception rather than the rule. The United Nations found itself in the position of having to deal with demands for self-determination and/or independence from French, Dutch, Portuguese, Belgian, and British colonies.

Regarding organizational concerns, struggles for independence from colonial regimes and postcolonial rivalries dominated the scene. While claims of self-defense and domestic jurisdiction did arise within the context of colonial wars for independence, these generally were not the basis used by third parties to urge a solution. Practice with regard to these early cases reflects, in nascent form, an aspirational corollary to Charter prohibitions geared to support the goal of self-determination: *A state may not assert a right of self-defense against people seeking to free themselves from colonial domination, alien occupation, or racist regimes.* Resistance to legitimate movements for self-determination became an illicit use of force. The dissolution of colonial empires led to an unprecedented expansion in the number of states in the state system. For the first time, politics became truly global in nature.

Impact of Communist and New States on the Development of International Law

National sovereignty formed the keystone of Soviet legal thought, with particular emphasis on nonintervention. We should note that this meant nonintervention, of course, in the affairs of the Soviet Union. This emphasis may strike observers as incongruous, in view of the Soviet Union's actual foreign policy practice that clearly evidenced a double standard, but, as a society claiming to have a revolutionary

---

[41]For the attempt to update the *jus in bello* to reflect the varieties of post–World War II conflict, see United Nations, "Protocol Additional to the Geneva Conventions of 12 August 1949, and Relating to the Protection of Victims of International Armed Conflicts (Protocol I) and Protocol Additional to the Geneva Conventions of 12 August 1949, and Relating to the Protection of Victims of Non-international Armed Conflicts (Protocol II)," 16 *International Legal Materials* (1977), 1391–1449.

agenda promoting necessary reform, presumably it and its friends had already been reformed. After World War II, Soviet writers tended to emphasize a tripartite division in international law: One body of rules applied to relations between "socialist" (Communist) states, another body of rules applied between non-Communist ("bourgeois") states, and a third group of principles and rules applied to relationships between socialist and bourgeois nations. The last of these groupings appeared to rely heavily on the twin concepts of consent and absolute sovereignty.[42]

In the late 1950s, Professor G. I. Tunkin, head of the Department of International Law at the Moscow State University and probably the foremost exponent of relevant Soviet legal opinion, differed sharply with these earlier views of Soviet legal scholars who believed in the concurrent existence of three sets of rules of international law. Tunkin furthermore anticipated that peaceful coexistence between socialist and nonsocialist states would lead to an effort to agree on certain specific rules of conduct for states (lawmaking treaties, continued development of customary law, the UN General Assembly's resolutions, decisions of international judicial agencies, and so on). In connection with the foregoing, Tunkin stressed the absolute acceptance of the existence of state sovereignty and nonintervention.[43]

Contrary to popular belief, the Soviet Union routinely observed most of the rules of customary international law as well as the nonpolitical (technical) agreements concluded with other states and public international organizations. Russian acceptance and observance of international law found their obvious basis in expediency dictated by the need for coexistence with non-Communist states as well as by the obvious fact that selected interests of Communist and non-Communist states did coincide. On the other hand, the USSR utilized international law extensively and frequently to promote the political and ideological aims of the Soviet state.

Propaganda campaigns in Third World nations as well as in Latin America centered repeatedly on slogans based on ideas culled from the principles of international law, primarily on component parts of sovereignty, such as self-determination, nonintervention, and equality. With the disintegration of the USSR and the end of the Cold War, the Russian Federation now seemingly has adopted a mainstream view of the role of international law but one that still emphasizes nonintervention and self-determination.

Chinese Concepts of Law

Western conceptions of law never played a great part in traditional Chinese society. Behavior depended more on example and individual moral behavior than on external regimes of sanctions imposed for misdeeds.[44] Moreover, during the nineteenth century, China did not gain admission to the European club and suffered many indignities with respect to unequal treatment. While not treated as a colony,

---

[42]W. W. Kulski, "The Soviet Interpretation of International Law," 49 *AJIL* 518 (1955).

[43]For an abstract of other aspects of Tunkin's teachings, see Slywotzsky's review of Tunkin's major work in 16 *Harvard Int'l Law J.* 767 (1975), or, preferably, consult the book itself: G. I. Tunkin, *Theory of International Law*, trans. R. Butler (1974); R. A. Mullerson, "Sources of International Law: New Tendencies in Soviet Thinking," 83 *AJIL* 494 (1989).

[44]R. Unger, *Law in Modern Society* (1976), 86–100.

China was forced to sign treaties giving extraterritorial rights to European states. A French or British citizen who committed a crime in China would thus be tried by a British or French court, not by a Chinese one. This experience left a bitter legacy. Largely isolated from mainstream international politics during a good part of the Cold War, the People's Republic of China (PRC) seemingly took a realpolitik view of international law, adhering to those rules and principles that served their policies and interests, and ignoring those that did not.

With its decision to play a more central global role, particularly regarding trade and development issues, the PRC's attitudes have evolved toward the mainstream, but the country retains attitudes that clearly reflect its past experience. Current statements and practice indicate an adherence to the "hard shell" sovereignty concept. The PRC has been extremely reluctant to approve any type of intervention into the internal affairs of any state, no matter how compelling rationale may be. On the flip side, perhaps because of Tibet and the ongoing Taiwan issues, it has also not jumped to recognize secessionist movements.[45] As a state that has an arsenal of nuclear weapons, the PRC has supported nonproliferation efforts.

The "New" States

Not unexpectedly, as those areas that were formerly colonial dependencies became independent in some number, they attacked many of the principles and structures of what they perceived as a law that still reflected Eurocentric interests. Some traditional doctrines they adopted without hesitation—the ideas of sovereignty and nonintervention, for example. Others, particularly those in the economic realm, they found perpetuated an inequality they found unacceptable. One of the earliest manifestations of this was the founding of the United Nations Conference on Trade and Development (UNCTAD) to represent their viewpoints as the counterpart to the General Agreement on Tariffs and Trade (GATT), to which most of the developed states belonged. A second impact came with the demands to control their own natural resources and the subsequent nationalization of mines and oil fields. Still a third impact came in the extended negotiations that produced the UNCLOS III when major rifts developed over issues, the width of the territorial sea for example, that had long histories in customary practice. Attempts by the United Nations Educational, Scientific and Cultural Organization (UNESCO) to control news reporting and information flow caused several states to suspend funding and the United States to withdraw.[46] Important questions concerned with the spread of globalization

---

[45]See L. Zhu, "Chinese Practice in Public International Law: 2007," 7 *Chinese Journal of International Law* (2008), 485–507, for a summary of recent Chinese statements and practice.

[46]B. D. Ayres Jr., "U.S. Affirms Plan to Leave UNESCO at End of Month," *New York Times* (December 20, 1984), A1, and "Still No on UNESCO," *Washington Post* (May 1, 1996), A24. See in addition R. Pear, "Baker Would Ask Cutoff of Funds if U.N. Agencies Upgrade P.L.O.," *New York Times* (May 2, 1989), A12; P. Lewis, "U.S. Cuts Funds to U.N. Food Agency over P.L.O.," *New York Times* (January 10, 1990), A5; L. H. Diuguid, "OAS Reducing Staff by 269 Workers; U.S., Others Late in Paying Share of Operating Budget," *Washington Post* (December 30, 1988), A4; D. Johnston, "O.A.S. Says Aid Programs Are Imperiled," *New York Times* (July 25, 1988), 13; D. E. Sanger, "I.M.F. Resists 'Blackmail' by Russia and U.S.," *New York Times* (September 25, 1998), A10; and J. Mathews, "Delinquency Diplomacy," *Washington Post* (March 10, 1997), A17.

have highlighted many issues, such as intellectual property rights, human rights, and access to technology, that will comprise the grist for future debates.

In part, many of the issues identified with the "North–South" split have been less than effectively advanced due to the great diversity of the "South." After the anticolonial revolution, these states found that often their everyday interests divided as much as, if not more than, promoted a basis for unity. We should not find this surprising, given that most members of the United Nations qualify as "South" based on their level of economic development. In this respect, compare the economic position and potential of Chad with that of Brazil. On the other hand, the bundle of issues associated with economic development and the South will play a continuing major role in the future development of international law.

Islam and International Law

Like its traditional Western counterpart, Islam does divide legal relationships into rules governing times of peace and rules governing relationships during war.[47] Peacetime relationships are based upon human brotherhood, protection of rights, a commitment to the rules of ethics and morality (the "pillars of civilization"), justice, international cooperation, the sanctity of covenants, and reciprocity.[48] However, the roots of the law do not flow from mutual consent or reciprocity. They are directly derived from the Qur'an and the Hadith.[49] The questions stem from asking, to whom does the law apply? Writing about the relationship of Islamic law to modern international law, Professor Majid Khadduri noted:[50]

> In contrast with the modern law of nations, which presupposes . . . states enjoying sovereign rights and equality of status, the law of Islam recognizes no other nation than its own. Similarly to the law of ancient Rome and the law of medieval Christendom, the law of Islam was based on the theory of a universal state . . . one community, bound by one law and governed ultimately by one ruler.

Reflecting this perspective, the world is divided into lands of the converted (*dar al-Islam*) and everyone else (*da al-harab*—people of the war). Some scholars have suggested a third category, *dar al-àhd* (or *dar as-sulh*)—the abode of covenant.[51] Those in the abode of covenant are non-Muslims who live in Islamic territory according to a covenant. "The abode of war comprises countries which are outside the scope of Islamic sovereignty and where the religion and political rules of Islam are not implemented; its people are belligerents."[52] In the traditional law, those in

---

[47]Sheikh W. al-Zuhili, "Islam and International Law," 87 *International Review of the Red Cross* (2005), 270; See also N. A. Shah, *Islamic Law and the Law of Armed Conflict* (2011).

[48]al-Zuhili, note 47, at 272–276.

[49]The Hadith is the oral tradition that embodies the words and deeds of the Prophet Muhammad (the Messenger of Allah).

[50]M. Khadduri, "Islam and the Modern Law of Nations," 50 *AJIL* 358 (1956), 356.

[51]al-Zuhili, note 47, at 276. The author notes that, while traditional, these categories have no textual support either in the Qur'an or in the Hadith.

[52]al-Zuhili, note 47, at 276.

the *dar al-Islam* had a legal duty to bring all others into the fold (*jihad* equals the just war, *bellum justum,* of the West). From a legal standpoint, it is a permanent state of war.[53]

In theory, war is justified only to resist aggression against Muslims, to ward off injustice, to redress injury, or in self-defense. Muslims should not utilize force for purposes of conversion. Al-Zuhili states: "Before the declaration of either war or *jihad*, the enemy should be made to choose one of three options: Islam as a token of peacefulness, reconciliation or a peace treaty with Muslims; or finally war."[54] At the time he wrote (mid-1950s), Professor Khadduri noted that the Islamic states had seemingly come to grips with the realities of dealing with, and within, the community of nations. The newly emergent question has become the extent to which this may be so, given the resurgence of fundamentalist movements in many states that view themselves as continuing victims of injustice at the hands of others.

Globalization and Global Governance

Popular commentary tends to identify globalization with the spread of an economic interdependence based upon market principles as the basis for international exchanges of goods and services. The underlying ideas here flow from the liberal tradition (John Locke, Adam Smith, Immanuel Kant, John Stuart Mill, Richard Cobden). An implicit corollary associated with that fundamental set of assumptions holds that globalization also promotes the spread of democracy as the internal basis for governing states. A second corollary postulates a gradual but progressive spread of liberal values partially from the interdependent benefits of economic exchange, but also because the shared values underpin the growth of a global civil society as law and an interlocking web of institutions reduce the scope for autonomous state action. Based upon these assumptions, some theorists have argued that the evolution of economic interdependence and democracy has dampened the tendency for states to resort to war.[55]

Simply explained, market principles rest upon an assumption of self-interested behavior based upon a mutual economic advantage gained from the exchange of goods and services free from regulation or other interference from outside the market. But the expansion in international trade forms only one dimension of the globalization phenomenon. The term reflects a broader set of trends in the contemporary international system. First, no one state has the capability by itself to deal with problems such as terrorism, the traffic in narcotics, or issues that involve environmental degradation that often reach across borders. The dramatic rise in the numbers of IGOs since World War II attests to this trend. Second, the revolution in transportation, communication, and other technologies has enabled individuals in like-minded groups to reach out and organize across borders (nongovernmental organizations, NGOs). This revolution also has encouraged state officials other

---

[53]Khadduri, note 50, at 359. Note also the word *mujahada,* translated as "militant struggle."

[54]al-Zuhili, note 47, at 281.

[55]See E. Silberner, *The Problem of War in Nineteenth Century Economic Thought* (1946); B. Russett and J. O'Neal, *Triangulating Peace: Democracy, Peace and International Organizations* (2001); R. Keohane and J. Nye, *Power and Interdependence,* 3rd ed. (2000).

than employees of foreign ministries for forge discussion links (policy networks) that focus on solutions to common problems such as immigration, housing, development, and health issues. Note that, with the exception of the Department of Interior, every cabinet department of the U.S. government has an "international" section that maintains contacts with their counterparts in other countries. Foreign policy is no longer the sole province of the Department of State or Foreign Ministries in other states. Third, consider as well that these factors have also facilitated the growth of an international commercial economy based upon market principles. Talking about state-to-state interaction abstractly masks the multitude of ways in which contemporary states interact, and the role of other important players on the contemporary international stage.[56]

In this respect, please note the term "governance" in this section heading. The term does not imply the evolution of an international government. "Governance" refers to a process that involves coordinating these "horizontal" links between states, IGOs, NGOs, companies, and various other transnational groups rather than the traditional hierarchical (vertical) structures we tend to associate with "governing." Globalization and the need for governance go hand in hand. Moreover, the interconnected nature of financial markets evidenced by the recession that began in the United States in December of 2007 and then spread across the globe over the next few months illustrates both the extent of globalization (in the sense of how interconnected many issue areas have become) and the need for "governance" in the sense of international cooperation to evolve rules to regulate activities that may have transborder connections and consequences.

One facet of globalization clearly promotes increased integration as states have found ways to forge cooperative ventures in areas of congruent or complementary interest. Globalization has meant that the scope and relevant concerns of international law have rapidly expanded.[57] As states have acted on a perceived need to cooperate, the proliferation of international organizations has meant a proliferation of important "housekeeping rules." This has resulted in states willingly giving up some traditional sovereign rights. By the same token, the proliferation of international institutions and interest groups has made the process of lawmaking much more complex. International institutions often have very narrow mandates with respect to issues within their competence. For example, when the International Maritime Organization (IMO, then IMCO) sought to prepare a treaty dealing with the very important issues of oil spills at sea, it had to coordinate with 11 different agencies and organizations in addition to the states and interest groups involved.

Expansion of issue areas covered by law has meant greater complexity as well. Apart from the sheer volume of international lawmaking efforts, contemporary international issues do not necessarily fit neatly into single categories. The treaty on Trade-Related Aspects of Intellectual Property Rights (TRIPs), for example, combines issues involving both economic and human rights fields. This dichotomy can generate considerable tension in any dispute because the

---

[56]A. Hurrell, *On Global Order: Power, Values and the Constitution of International Society* (2007), 95, 96.

[57]For an enlightening discussion of the extent of "internationalization"/"globalization" across many sectors, but particularly in terms of legal concerns, see A. Slaughter, *A New World Order* (2004).

fundamental principles associated with each issue area dictate different results.[58] The case of alleged libel cited at the beginning of Chapter 1 illustrates the complexity of contemporary relations.

The emergence of NGOs in the contemporary system has had a great impact as well. A recent commentary notes: "The exact number of NGOs is not known, but estimates range from tens of thousands to more than one hundred thousand."[59] Not all NGOs play an international role. As we shall discuss in the chapters on substantive law, NGOs play the role of advocates and monitors. Their activities can play a pivotal role in placing an issue on the international agenda, moving it forward, and then assessing compliance with any solution producing. At the international level, NGOs increasingly work as advisors to national governments, international agencies and the UN. In the past, NGOs often convened separate and autonomous meetings alongside UN conferences to critique UN agendas, mobilize local organizations and to advocate for political, social and economic changes. Today NGOs are at the table, enriching intergovernmental discussions with grass-roots knowledge and subject matter expertise.[60]

Médecins Sans Frotieres (Doctors Without Borders), the International Committee of the Red Cross, CARE, Human Rights Watch, Greenpeace, the World Wildlife Fund, and Amnesty International are examples of large-scale NGOs with extensive activities in a number of different countries.

Given the diversity of organizations that make up the contemporary international system, even with its expansion in terms of issue areas, public international law comprises only one component of the "rules" and structures associated with the idea of governance. Public international law provides the foundation for IGOs such as the United Nations, the World Trade Organization (WTO), and the World Health Organization (WHO) through their constitutive treaties (Chapter 4), and it provides for the fundamental structure for international action and contacts, but it does not presume to apply to all actors. Multinational corporations, nonprofit organizations, social movements, academics, tourists, artists, transborder ethnic and linguistic groups (i.e., the Kurds, the Basques)—to name a few—are also part of the contemporary mix. Among others, John Locke made a division between the proper realm of government activity and that of civil society where more informal rules including those of comity and morality may regulate interactions. Contemporary theorists have adopted the term *global civil society* to describe the complexity of contemporary international relations.

[58]Agreement on Trade-Related Aspects of Intellectual Property Rights, Annex 1C of the Marrakesh Agreement Establishing the World Trade Organization, signed in Marrakesh, Morocco, on April 15, 1994, www.wto.org/english/tratop_e/trips_e/t_agm0_e.htm.

[59]Harvard Law School Nongovernmental Organizations (NGOs), www.law.harvard.edu/current/careers/opia/planning/public-international-work/nongovernmental-organizations.html. See also, Duke University Libraries—NGO Research Guide, http://library.duke.edu/research/subject/guides/ngo_guide/; University of California at Berkeley Library, www.lib.berkeley.edu/doemoff/govinfo/intl/gov_ngos.html; Duke University Libraries International Governmental Organizations, http://library.duke.edu/research/subject/guides/igo_guide/.

[60]Harvard Law School Nongovernmental Organizations, note 59.

Globalization and Its Discontents

As we noted earlier, one impact of globalization has been to promote integration. We see this in Europe. Still, for many, the market system creates winners and losers. From a macroeconomic perspective, over the past 50 years, the gap in terms of GNP between the industrialized and the lesser developed has widened, not narrowed.[61] While there have been some spectacular gains by states like India and China, many others have faced stagnant growth or recession.[62] In some places, the global market may actually undermine state building attempts. We see the problems in complaints about how little certain workers are paid as companies seek to minimize labor costs. We also see the disintegrative effects in the UN initiative to outlaw "blood diamonds." In certain parts of Africa, rebel groups and warlords do not wish to control the government; they wish to gain and maintain control over a resource coveted by international traders because they can support themselves by selling the resource on the open market.

The point here is that the effects of globalization have been very uneven. Certainly, many states have benefitted and have been drawn into an expanding web of interdependent relationships. Many others, identified as part of the global South, exist on the periphery. Challenges to the ideas that drive globalization come from many different sources, the most obvious being "backlash movements" many times driven by a perception that biases in the system have denied them a rightful share of benefits.[63] This captures only part of the problem. The processes associated with globalization have run up against some very "deep-rooted sets of domestic social, political and economic structures and very distinctive national traditions."[64] These often run counter to some of the important ideas, norms, and practices associated with globalization. We see this in the mantra of radical Islamic groups who reject what they perceive as hostile Western ideas that controvert their fundamental beliefs about the appropriate structure of society, individual rights, and justice.

Advocates of globalization often underplay the role of asymmetry and power in the system. The questions here relate to the nature of progress and the extent to which states, and particularly powerful states, may commit to reform in existing institutions that might move them forward in terms of purpose. How deep does the idea of shared values and purposes run? In many areas, we find an impressive number of agreements. Upon inspection, numbers mean little because the agreements

---

[61]"Income Gap Between Rich and Poor Is Huge and Growing, Warns UN Report," UN News Service (October 16, 2008).

[62]The most prominent critique is J. Stiglitz, *Globalization and Its Discontents* (2002). Stiglitz, a Nobel Prize winner, focuses upon what happens when people lack important information needed for the decisions they have to make, or when markets for important kinds of transactions are inadequate or do not exist at all. The implication of each of these flaws is that free markets, left to their own devices, do not necessarily deliver the positive outcomes claimed for them by textbook economic reasoning. Economic theory presumes that people have full information, can trade in complete and efficient markets, and can depend upon satisfactory legal and other institutions.

[63]See, for example, E. Bircham and J. Charlton, eds, *Anti-Capitalism: A Guide to the Movement* (2001).

[64]Hurrell, note 56, at 213

contain suggested guidelines rather than hard requirements and firm goals, or they may contain weak or nonexistent sanctions for noncompliance, or they may contain multiple loopholes and escape clauses. These observations do not mean that little progress has occurred. It does reflect a perspective that suggests further meaningful progress may be very difficult in certain areas.

In this respect, we should not overlook the demands on the global South for liberalization by states and powerful private actors who in turn resist doing the same.[65] Along these same lines, we should note the voices within developed states that warn against policies that erode the ability to act autonomously. Finally, building on this last point, questions arise about the long-term sustainability of cooperative regimes as competition increases over scarce resources such as food, fuel, and water.

A Balance Sheet

As we approach each issue area, we need to assess progress, but the critical questions may revolve around future progress. Globalization may have eroded sovereign prerogatives to some extent in some areas, but states and particularly powerful states remain the primary actors in the system. An imperative of cooperation has not totally replaced short-term calculations of narrow self-interest. Given the complexity of the system, interdependence could actually impede progress in that linkages between issue areas (e.g., trade and the environment, national security and the environment) may require trade-offs between interests that will prove unacceptable for many states. Questions remain as well about the ability of current institutions to make adequate responses to future problems.

SUGGESTED READINGS

The study of international law involves many intellectually challenging issues. The "history" of international law, as with any "history" worth studying, has generated many very technical academic arguments. This section does not attempt to outline or define all of the controversies; it offers a guide to further reading.

DEVELOPMENT OF THE LAW: GENERAL

Anand, *Studies in International Law and History: An Asian Perspective* (2004).

Benton, *Law and Colonial Cultures: Legal Regimes in World History, 1400–1900* (2001).

Jacobini, *A Study of the Philosophy of International Law as Seen in Works of Latin American Writers* (1954).

Janis, *The American Tradition of International Law: Great Expectations 1789–1914* (2004).

Janis, *The Influence of Religion on the Development of International Law* (1991).

Neff, *War and the Law of Nations: A General History* (2005).

Nussbaum, *A Concise History of the Law of Nations* (1954).

Slaughter, *A New World Order* (2004).

Verzijl, *International Law in Historical Perspective* (11 vols, 1968–1976).

---

[65]Hurrell, note 56, at 209.

THE ANCIENT WORLD

Bederman, *International Law in Antiquity* (2001).

Gagarin, *Early Greek Law* (1986).

Numelin, *The Beginnings of Diplomacy* (1950).

Phillipson, *The International Law and Custom of Ancient Greece and Rome* (1911).

MIDDLE AGES TO EARLY MODERN

Guthrie, *The Later Thirty Years War: From the Battle of Wittstock to the Treaty of Westphalia* (2003).

Keen, *The Laws of War in the Late Middle Ages* (1965).

Meron, *Henry's Wars and Shakespeare's Laws: Perspectives on the Law of War in the Later Middle Ages* (1993).

Russell, *Just War in the Middle Ages* (1975).

Ullman, *Law and Politics in the Middle Ages* (1975).

SELECTED CLASSICAL WRITERS

Ayala, Balthazar, *Three Books on the Law of War and on the Duties Connected with War and on Military Discipline (De Jure et Officiis Bellicis et Disciplina Militari Libri III)*, trans. John Pawley Bate (reprint, 1964).

van Bynkershoek, Cornelius, *Quaestionum Juris Publici Libri Duo*, 1930 Carnegie ed., trans. T. Frank (1930; reprint, New York: Oceana, 1964).

Gentili, Alberico, *De Iure Belli Libri Tres*, 1612 ed., trans. J. C. Rolfe (1612; reprint, New York: Oceana, 1964).

da Legnano, Giovanni, *Tractatus De Bello, De Represaliis et De Duello*, edited by T. E. Holland, trans. J. L. Brierly (New York: Oceana, 1964).

Suárez, Francisco, *Selections from Three Works of Francisco Suarez, S.J.*, Classics of International Law series, vol. 2, edited by J. B. Scott (Oxford: Clarendon Press, 1944).

de Vattel, Emer, *Le Droit de Gens, ou Principes de la Loi Naturelle*, trans. C. G. Fenwick (Buffalo, NY: Hein, 1995).

Wolff, Christian, *Jus Gentium Methodo Scientifica Pertractatum*, trans. Joseph H. Drake (reprint, New York: Oceana, 1964).

GROTIUS AND HIS TIMES

Bull, Kingsbury, and Roberts, eds, *Hugo Grotius and International Relations* (1990).

Dumbauld, *The Life and Legal Writings of Hugo Grotius* (1969).

Haakonssen, ed., *Grotius, Pufendorf, and Modern Natural Law* (1999).

Keene, *Beyond the Anarchical Society: Grotius, Colonialism and Order in World Politics* (2002).

Murphy, "The Grotian Vision of World Order," 76 *AJIL* 477 (1982).

Sources of the Law

The determination or location of the specific rule of international law that would apply to a given dispute between two countries forms a common difficulty experienced by students, lawyers and other practitioners, and judges. At the international level, the lack of a unified legal code, constitution, central legislative authority, and judicial structures with compulsory jurisdiction makes this a far more daunting excursion for international seekers of the relevant law than for their domestic counterparts. In an ideal world, we would have an international law code that would specify all existing rules (and exceptions) and various national interpretations. The mode of search and discovery would then move closely parallel to that of domestic lawyers and judges. Unfortunately, no such code exists as yet, despite numerous private attempts, often of great value, to compile codes for various subfields or on specific subjects and despite the commendable efforts of the International Law Commission of the United Nations.

How, then, can we determine with any certainty the rules of international law germane to a given case? More to the point at this stage of our exploration of the subject, if no unified legal code exists, where then should we go to look? Moreover, if we find a rule, how will we know if it constitutes a *legal* rule rather than one of morality, good manners *(comity)*, or just a convenient usage? Is there an authoritative guide that we might use to locate international rules and principles? To give a short answer to all of the questions, some general agreement on relevant sources appears to have been reached in drafting Article 38 of the Statute of the International Court of Justice (ICJ).[1] Article 38(1) identifies three major sources of international law and two subsidiary possibilities for determining relevant rules of that law when the major sources offer little or incomplete guidance. The Article directs the Court to apply the following:

- *International conventions* (treaties), whether general or particular, establishing rules expressly recognized by the contesting states

---

[1]International Court of Justice, *Statute of the International Court of Justice* (June 26, 1945); 1055 T.S. No. 993, 3 Bevans 1179. All members of the United Nations are automatically parties to the statute.

- *International custom,* as evidence of a general practice accepted as law
- The general principles of law recognized by civilized nations
- Judicial decisions
- *The teachings of the most highly qualified publicists* (writers; subject to the provisions of Article 59)

Article 38(2) also states, "This provision shall not prejudice the power of the Court to decide a case *ex aequo et bono* if the parties agree thereto." Literally, *ex aequo et bono* means what is right (just) and good. Legally it means in fairness and good conscience. The requirement of prior state consent significantly limits the potential use of Article 38(2) by the Court. The Court has never decided a case solely on this principle although judges have occasionally used the idea of "equity" in their reasoning when straightforward application of existing principles would result in an obvious injustice (e.g., the *North Sea Continental Shelf Case*).[2]

Some controversy does surround the provisions of Article 38 because critics argue that it does not capture the dynamic evolution of international law and that it reflects a European bias regarding sources.[3] For the moment, we will simply note the critics and their position. Largely, the controversy has to do with the importance of "general principles of law" as a source supplementing the two traditional "sources," custom and treaties. In the following discussion, we first examine the nature and characteristics of the sources included in Article 38 and then briefly look at and evaluate other possibilities suggested by the critics of Article 38.

INTERNATIONAL TREATIES (CONVENTIONS)

International agreements go by many names. We shall discuss the rules relating to agreements in Chapter 4. For this section, we will use *treaty* and *convention* as interchangeable terms. In contrast with the commentaries of 100 years ago, treaties and conventions now generally constitute the major source of international law.[4] One must be wary, however, of taking such a statement too literally. Obviously, the thousands of bilateral treaties concluded among nations may create specific obligations or laws for the two states that consent to them, but these may not create one single general rule of international law, although *they may be based on* more general rules. A commercial treaty between Guatemala and France or an extradition or consular treaty between the United States and

---

[2]North Sea Continental Shelf (Federal Republic of Germany/Denmark) (Federal Republic of Germany/Netherlands), International Court of Justice, Judgment of February 20, 1969, www.icj-cij.org/docket/files/51/5535.pdf. See also Chapter 17, "Adjudication."

[3]See, for example, B. Cheng, *General Principles of Law: As Applied by International Courts and Tribunals* (1953, 1987).

[4]Without getting too far into the technical and semantic questions here, we should note that Sir Robert Jennings (who served as a judge on the International Court of Justice) noted that treaties are not a "source" of law but a source of "obligation." The "source" of the relevant law is the antecedent *pacta sunt servanda* ("treaties must be observed"), which flows from the customary law. R. Y. Jennings, "Recent Developments in the International Law Commission: Its Relation to the Sources of International Law," 13 *American Journal of International Law* 385 (1964).

Sri Lanka cannot create a general rule of conduct for the community of nations. At best such instruments are declaratory, based upon existing rules derived from other sources.

With that understanding, treaties (or other types of international agreements) as explicit and deliberate agreements between or among states constitute the closest parallel to a legislative function at the international level. The complexity of modern life has increased the need for agreements at many levels. Just consider the range of issues involved in facilitating international travel: standardizing travel documents (passports, visas, and stateless documents), establishing procedures to permit routine commercial airline access, and establishing rules for telephone, fax, and mail communication to permit individuals to find a place to stay and/or to arrange a series of business meetings. All of these are potentially contentious areas covered by international agreements. Just consider the implications if the U.S. government had to negotiate bilateral agreements to cover these everyday transactions with every state where Americans might travel, make a telephone call, or send a letter. Now think about how many other everyday international transactions might require such agreements among all states in the community of nations (or at least a significant number).

Bilateral treaties (two states) or a treaty involving only a few states may create limited obligations. In contrast, states have engaged in a form of international legislation by drafting, signing, and ratifying *multilateral conventions* (treaties)—that is, treaties concluded among a number of countries acting in their joint interest explicitly intended to codify (make consistent) customary practice, create new rules, or perhaps create a new international agency (e.g., the International Criminal Court). Unlike other treaties, the lawmaking treaty has as its purpose the creation of rules that have *universal or general* relevance. The Vienna Convention on Diplomatic Relations (1961) and the Vienna Convention on the Law of Treaties (1969) exemplify efforts to establish uniform rules based upon long-standing (but somewhat inconsistent) customary practice. The importance of this effort will become more evident after the discussion of the problems of determining rules of customary law in the following section. The International Covenant on Civil and Political Rights (1966); the Convention Against Torture and Other Cruel, Inhuman or Degrading Treatment or Punishment (1975); and the Convention on the Elimination of All Forms of Discrimination Against Women (1979) represent initiatives to establish new international rules.

To understand the limits of lawmaking treaties, note first that the provisions will apply only to those states that have *signed* and *ratified,* or deposited an *instrument of accession to,* a particular convention (see Chapter 4 for additional discussion). We have emphasized the element of *consent* throughout this introduction. Signature and ratification (or accession) indicate a state's consent, with ratification (or accession) forming the most important element because it certifies final acceptance. Note that if the initial number of ratifying states is small (or does not include the powerful), the treaty will not create a new rule of general international law but only a rule of particular or regional application among the consenting states. The rule may become more general by the acquiescence of nonparty states in practice that supports the new rule (see following discussion on custom), or by formal ratification or accession to the instrument embodying the new rule. On the other hand, as we discuss later, states that specifically refuse to acquiesce in the new rule by refusing to ratify the treaty or to adhere to it are, of course, not *normally* bound by the rule, principle, or interpretation in question.

Even though a lawmaking treaty may not achieve close to universal acceptance through signature and ratification, it may nevertheless represent a source of international law for the broader community. It may be considered as a codification of preexisting customary law. If adopted by a majority of states *having a very vital interest* in the subject area, or who represent the major powers in a geographic area, it may still have some influence on cases between states that have not formally accepted the treaty. The convention may serve as a source that applies to particular issues or to the geographic region. To give one example, on most issues related to the law of the sea, the consent or dissent of landlocked states (e.g., Bolivia, Uganda, Nepal, and Afghanistan) will have far less impact than that of states with extensive coastlines, large navies, or sizeable merchant marines. The Declaration of Paris of 1856 abolished privateering and redefined the rights of neutrals in naval warfare. The treaty technically bound only those states that signed the final act,[5] but in fact, many other states accepted the rules as part of an evolving *customary law* because the major sea powers had ratified it. We will explore the issues associated with treaties and other international instruments in more detail in Chapter 4.

INTERNATIONAL CUSTOM

Custom represents a second source of international law. In contrast with the normal meaning of the term—the description of a habit—a legal custom represents a usage with a definite obligation attached to it. Customary law says that a state should follow the normal habits useful in facilitating international contacts considered essential to peaceful relations, even though no formal written agreement exists to define the obligations in detail. Although no formal legal code specifies the obligations, failing to follow a rule established through legal custom raises the possibility of punishment, sanctions, or retaliation because it entails a binding duty toward other nations. Until shortly after the end of the nineteenth century, customary rules comprised the bulk of accepted general international law. Many of the rules that originally governed such diverse areas as jurisdiction over territory, freedom of the high seas, the privileges and immunities of states and diplomats, the law of land warfare (*jus in bello*),[6] and the rights of aliens have stemmed from customary practice.

Some contemporary writers have downplayed the role of custom as not responsive to the rapidly changing international milieu. This runs counter to what many have argued forms the essential strength of custom—the ability to adapt to rapidly changing circumstances.[7] To understand the nature of this

---

[5]The states that signed were Austria, France, Prussia, Russia, Sardinia, Turkey, and Great Britain.

[6]The law governing the conduct of individual soldiers in warfare (*jus in bello*), as opposed to the law governing the resort to force by a state (*jus ad bellum*—right to war).

[7]See M. Byers, *Custom, Power and the Power of Rules* (1999) for a thorough evaluation of the literature and issues connected with international customary law; A. Roberts, "Traditional and Modern Approaches to Customary International Law: A Reconciliation," 95 *AJIL* 757 (2001); and A. D'Amato, *The Concept of Custom in International Law* (1971).

argument, we need to note two major factors that complicate the determination of a customary rule in the contemporary international system—the number of states and the weight exerted by the opinion of each state. Determining a customary rule was much easier when the relevant opinions and practices involved those of less than 40 states instead of more than 190. This statement somewhat exaggerates the difficulty because establishing a rule of customary law does not involve simple counting.

As we noted earlier, power, interest, and sometimes technical capability may play a considerable role in developing and defining a customary rule. The practice of states with the greatest interest and most influence will have greater weight. While landlocked states such as Uganda and Bolivia might have a view on the management and control of fisheries, most states will look to the activities of states with large fishing industries—like Japan, Norway, Peru, the United Kingdom, and Russia—for evidence relating to practice. Treaties do not yet cover all areas of the law; many states have refused to sign and ratify major lawmaking treaties. If a lawmaking treaty presumably embodies a codification of customary law in an issue area, a non-signatory state may still be considered bound by the preexisting customary practices. Customary law still has relevance.

Determining a customary rule of law can be a difficult and contentious process. Some customary law, particularly before World War I (1914–1918), originated through the practices of a very few states. Consider that as late as 1880, the European state system had only 17 (see Chapter 2) identifiable members, and at least 4 of those did not enjoy full sovereign rights.[8] This point deserves some emphasis because contemporary international law has largely evolved from the body of practice often described as the *public law of Europe,* which was accepted as the international law of its time. In the nineteenth century, a state had to be a member of the club (a very exclusive club) to have its practice and viewpoint counted. This excluded China and Japan (and the rest of Asia), Africa, Central America, and the Middle East (except for Turkey). The United States and a few independent South American states existed on the periphery but hardly had a major impact on *European practice.* Indeed, as we shall see, they drew on European practice.

Origin and Proof of Rules: What Can We Know and When Can We Know It?   To advance a simple proposition about how customary law comes into existence and evolves, consider that *need* defined by functionality lies at the heart of the matter. This does not argue that pure need for an appropriate rule always generates an appropriate rule, but observing the areas in which customary practice first evolved widely recognized rules considered as law, the combination of need and functionality supplies a good explanation even within the parameters of political realism. By definition, a customary rule must have two distinct elements: (1) a material element defined by *systematic practice* over time and (2) a psychological element, the *opinio juris* or evidence that states regard the practice

---

[8]See S. D. Krasner, *Sovereignty: Organized Hypocrisy* (1999) for a provocative and challenging discussion of many of the ideas we will discuss as fundamental parts of an international legal order.

as a legal obligation. Observed repeated practice by itself offers insufficient evidence that a rule of customary law exists. States must have indicated in some manner that the practice involved a legally required duty. In sum, just because a state or government consistently follows a certain course of conduct regarding a particular set of issues does not establish that it has necessarily accepted those actions as a *legal* obligation.

Some obvious questions should spring to mind regarding practice. In terms of time, how often (repetition) and how long must a particular practice be observed? In terms of subjects, the questions are how many states (extent of observance) and, many times equally important, the identity of the states that seemingly have accepted the rule? In terms of justifications, how should we weigh what states do against what states say they do? How should we weigh what states do against what they *do not do?* Do the objections of some states count (weigh) more heavily than that of others?

Here, one other complicating factor enters the mix: Have any states actively protested against a particular practice as a rule? If they have not (and if they have not regularly done so), does silence have probative value? Does silence mean acquiescence, indifference, or ignorance? Does it matter which state or states protest? Obviously, given the multiple parameters for determination, judges and lawyers may have many differences about the exact point at which a habitual act (usage) by certain states becomes transformed into a rule of customary law. How often (or how long), and by how many different states, does a habitual act have to be performed or be accepted without protest to achieve the status of a principle or rule of law entailing a legal obligation? How long, by how many states, and how often does dissent have to occur to call into question claims that a customary rule exists? There are no straightforward answers to these questions. The answers depend largely upon the states involved in the case and the specific circumstances (context) of the case. The rule derived may be a *general rule* keyed into particular needs and circumstances rather than a universal rule binding on all.

The following case raised a great deal of controversy. At the time of the decision, almost every international lawyer of note denounced the conclusion and reasoning as incorrect. Nonetheless, it addresses many of the issues alluded to in the preceding discussion.

THE LOTUS

Permanent Court of International Justice (PCIJ), 1927

Facts

A French merchant vessel, the *Lotus,* rammed and sunk a Turkish vessel on high seas. Despite all possible rescue efforts by the French vessel, several Turkish nationals aboard the Turkish vessel lost their lives.

(continued)

The French vessel proceeded to a Turkish port. A French officer came ashore to testify at the request of Turkish officials. The officials placed him under arrest, then tried and sentenced him under provisions of Turkish law. France protested the trial and conviction. Both countries agreed to submit the case to the PCIJ. There was a treaty between France and Turkey that was relevant, but the treaty only stated that questions of jurisdiction shall be decided in accordance with the principles of international law.

Issue

Has Turkey violated international law in asserting jurisdiction by arresting and trying the French officer?

Decision

Turkey has not violated any provisions of international law (divided court).

Reasoning

The central question became "What were the relevant principles of international law?" In maritime cases, jurisdiction normally follows the flag on the high seas. The French would have had the duty to punish the officer at fault. The Turkish claim was made under a law extending jurisdiction through the passive personality principle (i.e., Turkish citizens were the objects/victims). The Court held that in these circumstances, there existed a permissive rule (see following) that justified the Turkish claim. France claimed that Turkey must show a positive basis under international law for assuming jurisdiction. Turkey claimed that it need only to point out the absence of any restrictions upon the exercise of its jurisdiction (whatever is not explicitly forbidden is permitted). The Court supported the Turkish view: "Restrictions upon the independence of states cannot be presumed."

The French government (properly) relied upon treaties, decisions of municipal and international courts, and the opinions of publicists in supporting its contentions. These are the relevant sources and evidence of international law. If there were a point of international law to support the French view, this is the appropriate way to find it. However, in the opinion of the court, France did not find enough evidence to support its contention. In this case, while France clearly demonstrated that states in the position of Turkey had abstained from prosecution, France did not present persuasive evidence that these states had done so out of a belief that they were legally barred from doing so. A state in the position of Turkey might see fit *not* to exercise its (concurrent) jurisdiction, but this would be as a matter of policy, not necessarily out of a sense of legal obligation. In sum, in the opinion of the Court, France had established a practice, but failed to establish the *opinio juris* that would establish it as a legal obligation.

Note

At the time, the decision was widely criticized. A diplomatic conference meeting in Brussels in 1952 disagreed with the conclusions of the PCIJ in the *Lotus* decision. In consequence, the participants drafted the International Convention for the Unification of Certain Rules Relating to Penal Jurisdiction in Matters of Collision and Other Incidents of Navigation (signed May 10, 1952, at Brussels). The provisions of this instrument concerning trials of alleged offenders in connection with collisions on the high seas have been reiterated in the 1958 Geneva Convention on the High Seas and the 1981 UNCLOS III Treaty: On the high seas, jurisdiction follows the flag.

In general, silence equals acquiescence to a rule of customary law only *if* a rule exists *and* the state knows that it exists. Equally, with protests, there must be a rule and the protest must have some reasonable substantive content. Again, no one cares much about the position of landlocked states on maritime issues (other than access to the sea).

Keep in mind that determining a customary rule is not a science and that *one can never determine a customary rule in an absolute sense.* Although from time to time states have sought to establish rules for finding customary law, they have yet to decide upon an authoritative method. At best, one can say that a preponderance of evidence supports a particular rule in question. To illustrate these points, consider the opinion of the ICJ in the *Nicaragua v. United States* case:

> It is not to be expected that in the practice of States the application of the rules in question should have been perfect. . . . The Court does not consider that, for a rule to be established as customary, the corresponding practice must be in absolutely rigorous conformity with the rule. . . . [T]he Court deems it sufficient that the conduct of States should, *in general* be consistent with such rules, and that instances of state conduct inconsistent with a given rule should generally have been *treated as breaches of that rule,* not as indications of the recognition of a new rule.[9] (Emphasis added)

The decision in the case of the *Scotia* supplies a good illustration of the evolution of a set of concepts from rudimentary and habitual beginnings to the status of a legal principle.

▶ THE SCOTIA

United States Supreme Court, 1872, 14 Wall. (81 U.S.) 170

Facts

Appeal from U.S. Circuit Court, Southern District of New York, in a case of collision between the American sailing vessel *Berkshire* and the British steamer *Scotia,* by which the *Berkshire* was lost. The owners of the *Berkshire* sued in the district court to recover their losses, claiming that the collision occurred through the fault of the *Scotia*. The court ruled against the plaintiffs, holding that courts of admiralty were required to take judicial notice of the existence of British orders-in-council promulgating regulations for preventing collisions at sea and of the fact that because so many maritime states had accepted those regulations, there existed a general rule and usage. By the regulations in question and in accordance with an Act of Congress in 1864, the *Berkshire* was bound to show only colored

(continued)

---

[9]*Nicaragua v. United States* (Merits), *ICJ Reports of Judgments* (1986), 98, para. 186.

lights. Because it had failed to do so, no remedy could be obtained for the loss of the vessel. When the case was appealed to the circuit court, the decree of the district court was affirmed.

It appears that the *Berkshire* did not display any colored lights at all but only a white light, at the bow, fastened about 4 feet above deck level. The *Scotia,* acting in accordance with the regulations mentioned, mistook the white light for the masthead light of a steamer, assuming in consequence that the presumed steamer was some distance away. Subsequently the two vessels collided, the *Scotia* obeying at all times the steering and sailing regulations required under the rules of the sea.

Issue

What was the law prevailing at the place and time of the collision?[10]

Decision

The prevailing law was the law of the sea, which the *Berkshire* violated by not displaying appropriate lights. Decision of lower court affirmed.

Reasoning

1. In 1863, the British government issued orders-in-council prescribing rules and regulations for the display of lights and for movements of both sailing vessels and steamers. Before the end of 1864, nearly all maritime nations had adopted the same regulations respecting lights.

2. No single nation can change the law of the sea, which rests on the common consent of civilized communities. It has force because it has been generally accepted as a rule of conduct. But when navigation rules originally laid down by two countries (Great Britain and later the United States) are accepted as obligatory rules by more than 30 of the principal maritime nations, those rules have become a part of the law of the sea, a usage has been changed into a legal custom, and the rules in question were the law at the place and at the time the collision occurred.

Notice the evidence the court used to establish the rule(s) in this case. While Great Britain was the leading maritime power at the time, more than 30 other principal maritime states including the United States had adopted the British standards. To reiterate an important point, *national legislation by itself* cannot establish an international rule, **but** *a consistent pattern of national legislation by the principal states* engaged in a particular area or activity may do so.

Evidence for Existence of a Rule   Unlike lawmaking treaties, which are easily available for study and reference, the evidence for the existence of customary law is scattered and at times extremely difficult to locate. The evidence the judges examined in the *Lotus* and the *Scotia* cases indicates some of the materials that courts will evaluate in trying to establish a rule. The most obvious of these would encompass sources produced by the various organs and officials of the state: legislation, judicial decisions, statements by responsible public officials, official manuals, standing instructions, published diplomatic correspondence, and other similar documents.

---

[10]Note that we have excluded a number of other issues, important at the time, to focus on the role of custom in the decision.

Some states have published *digests of practice*.[11] Patterns of claims against other states, historical accounts, newspapers, and the writing of eminent publicists from a state may provide additional clues to the existence of legal custom.

Replacement of Rules   Reading the ICJ opinion in the *Nicaragua* case raises an interesting question: What marks the difference between behavior that simply violates a rule of customary law and behavior aimed at establishing a new rule of customary law? Two important factors come into play here. The first would be the strength of the rule, gauged in terms of clarity and breadth of acceptance. The stronger the rule, the stronger the evidence in terms of competing or contrary practice needed to offset or overturn it. Second, any challenge (or opposition) must be principled, that is, not just challenge for the sake of challenge. Curiously, the duration of a rule may have little weight if convincing evidence for a clear new rule emerges in favor of supplanting a very old, ambiguous one. The weight of proof or an alternative rule *rests with the challenger.* Until the alleged new rule gains sufficient recognition through other states adhering to it, the challenger may simply be deemed a lawbreaker. In understanding the nature of claims made here, two terms apply. States adhering to the status quo will claim *de lege lata* (or *lex lata*), the law as presently found. Challengers will argue *de lege ferenda* (or *lex ferenda*), the law as it ought to be.

A somewhat different status attaches to a state that has protested the application of a rule from the start. The ICJ in the *Anglo-Norwegian Fisheries*[12] case found that a customary rule determining how territorial waters ought to be delimited on jagged coastlines such as Norway's did not apply, because Norway had always resisted any attempt to apply it to its coast. Presumably, a state that opposed a rule of customary law from its inception would not be bound by it. This would not affect obligations considered *jus cogens*.

The strength of customary law is that new customary rules may emerge rapidly, particularly in the wake of technological change that produces situations inadequately covered by the old law. Initially the rules relating to airspace and outer space evolved quite quickly as aircraft and rockets became part of international life. So, too, did the law with respect to the continental shelf as its economic potential became apparent (Chapter 12). The relevant rules in all three areas still depended upon the reactions *(consent)* of states to the changes. The rules that emerged look "instantaneous" only in retrospect because they did not require long periods to coalesce around agreed behaviors. While an interesting argument for technical specialists, simply put, customary law *by definition* rests upon practice.

Jus Cogens (Peremptory Norms)   One category of *customary* rules deserves special attention: *Jus cogens,* or *peremptory norms,* describe rules of customary

---

[11]Since 1973, the United States has published an annual *Digest of United States Practice in International Law*. Before 1973, M. M. Whiteman (1963–1973), G. H. Hackworth (1940–1944), and J. B. Moore (1906) published *Digests*. These include diplomatic notes, policy statements, judicial decisions, briefs and memoranda, and other documents that might be of use in deducing customary international law. For a listing of European and other digests, see the suggested readings at the end of this chapter.
[12]*ICJ Reports* (1951), 116.

law considered so fundamental and significant to the structure and functioning of the international community that they bind states even if the state has not given formal consent. Needless to say, the corollary is that states have no right to opt out of, or protest, the application of these rules. Prohibitions against genocide, the waging of aggressive war, and war crimes clearly form norms of *jus cogens*. Many have argued that many other human rights norms have entered into that status as well (Chapters 15 and 16). As one might expect, considerable controversy surrounds the question of what norms do and do not have peremptory status.

The International Law Commission, in drafting the Vienna Convention on the Law of Treaties, held that the law of the Charter prohibiting the use of force presupposed the existence in international law of peremptory rules. The commission concluded that a treaty would be void if it conflicted with a peremptory norm of general international law "from which no derogation was permitted and which could be modified only by a subsequent norm of general international law having the same character" (Vienna Convention, Article 53). The Convention itself defines a *peremptory norm of general international law* as a "norm accepted and recognized by the international community of states as a whole as a norm from which no derogation is permitted and which can be modified only by a subsequent norm of general international law having the same character."[13]

The concept of *jus cogens,* or peremptory norms, subsequently has appeared in a number of other agreements, most notably the 1986 Convention on Treaties Between States and International Organizations or Between International Organizations. The current widely accepted view asserts that peremptory norms do exist. Writers assert that to be considered *jus cogens,* rules must satisfy at least four criteria: (1) they must be norms of *general* international law; (2) they must be accepted by the community of states *as a whole*; (3) they must not be capable of derogation; and (4) there must not exist any possibility that such norms could be modified in any way except by the appearance of new peremptory norms of the same character.

It is, of course, difficult to identify the peremptory norms in existence today. While no authoritative list exists, many commentators on the law believe that all main principles laid down in the UN Charter qualify as peremptory norms, citing Article 103 of the Charter in support of their views. That Article specifies that obligations of states under that instrument enjoy precedence over all other national commitments. That provision alone appears sufficient to place those principles above any other principles or norms.

In addition, the traditional rule of the inviolability of diplomatic agents appears to qualify as a peremptory norm. Hannikainen listed at least five other categories of such norms possessing peremptory character: (1) the prohibition on the use of aggressive force between states; (2) respect for the self-determination of peoples; (3) respect for basic human rights; (4) respect for the rules guaranteeing the international status of sea, air, and space beyond the limits of national jurisdiction; and (5) respect for the basic international rules governing armed conflicts.

---

[13]See L. Hannikainen, *Peremptory Norms (Jus Cogens) in International Law: Historical Development, Criteria, Present Status* (1988), 21.

One should also note that the Vienna Conference was cognizant of the strong criticisms voiced against the concept of *jus cogens*. The conferees added Article 66(a) of the Vienna Convention, which provides that "any one of the parties to a dispute concerning the application or the interpretation of Article 53 or 64 may, by a written application, submit it to the International Court of Justice for a decision or the parties, by common consent, could agree to submit the dispute to arbitration." This provision means that the convention included a procedure through which, at least in theory, rules of *jus cogens* could emerge from judicial or arbitration decisions as well as from the practice of states.

Treaties and Custom

The movement to treaties represented by the conscious efforts to codify relevant practice in the twentieth century illustrates the widespread dissatisfaction with custom as the basis for development and growth of international law. Nonetheless, the relationship between treaty law and customary law represents a complex jigsaw puzzle. A rule may develop over the same time in *both* treaty and customary law. A new lawmaking treaty overrides an earlier conflicting rule of customary law unless the latter represents a rule of *jus cogens*. When a lawmaking treaty modifies or replaces a rule of customary international law, the changes in question affect, of course, *only* the states that have signed and ratified the agreement. In their relations with nonparty states, the old rules of customary law would still apply. Hence, a given rule of international law may be part of conventional law for some states (parties to a treaty) and part of customary international law for all other states. If a party to the treaty in question should withdraw, it would still be bound by the relevant rule of customary international law found in the lawmaking treaty.[14]

This principle proved of great importance in *Nicaragua v. United States* (Merits). The ICJ first found that a U.S. reservation prevented the Court from seizing jurisdiction over Nicaragua's claim based on violations of the UN Charter and Charter of the Organization of American States (OAS). But the Court decided that it could apply customary international law rather than the conventional restraints found in the multilateral and bilateral treaties cited as at issue. The Court held that merely because principles of customary and general international law had been codified or embodied in multilateral lawmaking conventions, this did not mean that those principles had ceased to exist. The principles still applied as rules of customary law even for countries that were states parties to such conventions. Principles such as the nonuse of force, nonintervention, and respect for the independence and territorial integrity of states continued to be binding as part of customary international law, despite their incorporation into conventional law in documents such as the UN Charter or the Charter of the OAS.[15]

---

[14]E. W. Vierdag, "The Law Governing Treaty Relations Between Parties to the Vienna Convention on the Law of Treaties and States Not Party to the Convention," 76 *AJIL* 779, 786 (1982); see R. Y. Jennings, "Recent Developments in the International Law Commission: In Relation to the Sources of International Law," 13 *Int'l. Comp & Law Q* 385 (1964).

[15]*Nicaragua v. United States* (Merits), para. 174, 184.

General Principles of Law

General principles of law recognized by civilized nations form the third source of international law.[16] Today the expression *civilized nations,* a relic from an earlier era, means only *states.* The meaning and scope of *general principles of law* have generated extensive discussion. Two prominent opinions have emerged. One view holds that the phrase refers to the general principles underlying domestic jurisprudence that can also be applied to international legal questions. Such principles might include the concepts that both sides in a dispute should have a fair hearing or that agreements require "good faith" in negotiation and execution. The other view asserts that the phrase refers to general principles of law drawn from natural law as interpreted during recent centuries in the Western world—that is, the transformation of broad universal principles of a law applicable to all of humankind into specific rules of international law.[17] Of the two opinions, the first best describes the majority view in contemporary thought (and court use). From a legal standpoint, the law of nature represents at best a vague and ill-defined source of international law.[18]

Most modern writers appear to regard general principles of law as a secondary source of international law, infrequently used in practice but possibly helpful on occasion. When the Committee of Jurists put this source into the Statute of the PCIJ in 1920, they offered several interpretations of its meaning. Generally, the purpose of including this source would seem to avoid the chance that the Court might fail to hand down a decision because no "positive applicable rule" existed. Lacking a clear rule, the phrase "general principles" presumably would enable the Court to go outside the generally accepted sources of international law and draw on relevant principles common to various domestic legal systems.[19] The exact scope of what this might include has formed the substance of continued scholarly debate, but the bulk of the opinion tends toward a very conservative interpretation—general principles encompass only those applied by a great many states. The questions here, as with customary practice, focus upon which states and how many.

---

[16]Some trace the idea that one may draw relevant international legal rules from other than custom and treaty to the Martens Clause in the preambles of the 1899 and 1907 Hague Conventions:

> Until a more complete code of the laws of war has been issued, the High Contracting parties deem it expedient to declare that, in cases not included in the Regulations adopted by them, the inhabitants and belligerents remain under the principles and protection of the law of nations as they result from the usages established among civilized peoples, *from the laws of humanity, and the dictates of the public conscience.* They declare that it is in this sense especially that Articles 1 and 2 of the Regulations must be understood. (Emphasis added)

For a discussion of this and its impact on international humanitarian law, see A. Cassese, "The Martens Clause: Half a Loaf or Simply Pie in the Sky," 11 *European Journal of International Law* (2000), 187–216; T. Meron, "The Martens Clause, Principles of Humanity, and Dictates of Public Conscience," 94 *AJIL* (2000), 78–89.

[17]See W. Friedmann, "The Uses of 'General Principles' in the Development of International Law," 57 *AJIL* 279 (1963); consult Whiteman, I: 5, 21, esp. 90–94.

[18]See discussion in J. L. Kunz, "Natural-Law Thinking in the Modern Science of International Law," 55 *AJIL* 951 (1961).

[19]See M. O. Hudson, "On Article 38," in his *The Permanent Court of International Justice, 1920–1942* (1943), 606–620; R. B. Schlesinger, "Research on the General Principles of Law Recognized by Civilized Nations," 51 *AJIL* 734 (1957).

We should point out that the provision in 38(1)(c) is a *permissive* rule. The Court does not have to use general principles to fill gaps (*lacunae*) in the law. In the *Right of Passage over Indian Territory (Portugal v. India)* case,[20] the Court did not draw on well-established domestic principles dealing with easements or servitudes,[21] even though it might have reasonably done so. For obvious political reasons, it chose instead to deal with the issues in the narrowest possible way that might resolve the dispute. Still, a number of court decisions have utilized the general principles concept. The PCIJ in the *Chorzów Factory Case* noted that "it is a general conception of law that every violation of an engagement involves an obligation to make reparation."[22] In the very first case heard by the ICJ, the *Corfu Channel* dispute, the court alluded to the use of circumstantial evidence as being admissible "in all systems of law."[23] To come to a meaningful decision in the *Barcelona Traction Case*,[24] which concerned the status of a privately held power company forced into bankruptcy by the Spanish government, the ICJ had to rely heavily on the domestic legal definition of a corporation as a limited liability company because nothing equivalent or parallel in the way of institutions or law existed at the international level.

Judicial Decisions

We have already mentioned two ways in which judicial decisions may play a part as a source of international law—as part of the evidence to establish a customary rule in specific disputes and as evidence of general principles of law in application. In either instance, judges and courts do not *make* law; they interpret it. Sir Robert Jennings noted:

> I should explain that I have not forgotten that Article 38 of the Hague Court's Statute speaks of judicial decisions as a "subsidiary means for the determination of rules of law." This provision I understand as a necessary recognition that judges, whether national or international, are not empowered to make new laws. Of course we all know that interpretation does, and indeed should, have a creative element in adapting rules to new situations and needs. . . . Nevertheless, the principle that judges are not empowered to make new law is a basic principle of the process of adjudication.[25]

Moreover, as a reminder, the opinions of one court in one country, no matter how powerful, cannot directly modify existing rules or spawn new ones. The

[20]*Right of Passage over Indian Territory (Portugal v. India)*, *ICJ Reports* (1960), 6. Because of its position, the ICJ pays close attention to the political climate. This case, involving the status of a number of colonial enclaves within India, occurred just as the sentiment for decolonization reached a boiling point. The Court chose to deal with the incident in the narrowest possible framework rather than to examine the possibility of a general custom establishing some inherent right of transit or passage over territory.

[21]Easements and servitudes give rights to nonowners to enjoy some benefit or rights regarding a property.

[22]*The Chorzów Factory Case* (Claim to Indemnity—Jurisdiction), *PCIJ*, Ser. A, No. 9 (1928), 31, and the same case (Claim to Immunity—Merits), *PCIJ*, Ser. A, No. 17 (1928), 29.

[23]*The Corfu Channel Case (Great Britain v. Albania)*, *ICJ Reports* (1949), 22.

[24]*Barcelona Traction, Light, and Power Co.* (Belgium v. Spain), *ICJ Reports* (1970), 3, 37.

[25]R. Y. Jennings, "The Judiciary, International, and National and the Development of International Law," 45 *International and Comparative Law Quarterly* (1996), 3.

questions here primarily relate to the relative weight given to decisions by national courts and arbitral tribunals in contrast with those of international courts.

Consistent decisions by national courts over a period of time will have some impact on the interpretation of particular rules. Court decisions not only reflect the interpretation of other courts as to the existence or content of a rule of international law, but also indicate the specific meaning and application of that rule for the country in question at the time of the decision. U.S. Supreme Court Chief Justice John Marshall eloquently expressed this view in the case of *Thirty Hogsheads of Sugar v. Boyle:*

> The law of nations is the great source from which we derive those rules, which are recognized by all civilized and commercial states throughout Europe and America. This law is in part *unwritten,* and in part conventional. To ascertain that which is unwritten, we resort to the great principles of reason and justice; but, as these principles will be differently understood by different nations under different circumstances, we consider them as being, in some degree, fixed and rendered stable by a series of judicial decisions. The decisions of the Courts of every country, so far as they are founded upon a law common to every country, will be received not as authority, but with respect. *The decisions of the Courts of every country show how the law of nations, in the given case, is understood in that country, and will be considered in adopting the rule which is to prevail in this.*[26] (Emphasis added)

As precedents and recorded decisions have multiplied over the years, a vast and instructive body of opinion has evolved for inspection and study. We should also note that as interdependence increases through the processes of globalization, increasingly national courts are called upon to deal with issues involving international law. The change in the nature of issues may not be readily apparent because in response to change, legislatures have converted international practice into domestic legislation.

To repeat an earlier point, the number of international courts applying international law has multiplied enormously since World War II. The decisions of international tribunals, including arbitral tribunals, are playing an increasingly important part in determining the existence and meaning of rules of international law. This holds especially true of the ICJ, even though Article 59 of the ICJ *Statute* states, "The decision of the Court has no binding force except between the parties and in respect of that particular case." From our earlier brief discussion, the logic of this provision should be obvious. Court decisions can bind only those states that consent to them. Notwithstanding the disclaimer in Article 59, the very nature of an international tribunal such as the ICJ—a group of carefully chosen and able legal authorities representing many different legal backgrounds and systems, with its presumed advantage over a national court conceivably influenced by nationalistic or political considerations—tends to elevate the decisions and advisory opinions of such a body above domestic court decisions. Strictly speaking, the ICJ does not consider prior decisions as precedents in the manner of the common law but does strive to maintain consistency regarding basic principles and approaches.[27]

---

[26]13 U.S. (9 Cranch) 191; 3 L.Ed. 701, 703 (1815).

[27]See M. Shahabuddeen, *Precedent in the World Court* (1996), and D. W. Bowett et al., *The International Court of Justice: Process, Practice and Procedure* (1997).

Commentators, text writers, and judges often cite many parts of PCIJ and ICJ reasoning and decisions as authoritative renderings of various aspects of the law. Even decisions that many thought disastrous may have an impact. Many disagreed with the PCIJ decision in the *Lotus* case (presented earlier), and subsequent treaty provisions nullified it, but because of the panel's careful and thorough examination of the factors involved in proving a rule of customary law, many writers and jurists still utilize the case to illuminate the process and pitfalls.

Writings of Publicists

The writings of publicists—the works of text writers and other private commentators—represent a subsidiary source of international law. Today they serve primarily as a means for determining varying interpretations of the law. In reading various commentators, one often runs across the phrase "the law in action versus the law in books," meant to suggest that scholars of the law may have a rather idealized version of what the law requires. True, no contemporary judge turns to a text to find the relevant rules, and no text writer or commentator creates international law, regardless of his or her professional eminence. At most, outstanding writers may state what the law is in their own time, may provide information on its historical development, and may speculate on future developments.[28] To the extent that their government may adopt their suggestions and utilize them in developing a usage, or incorporate them in a lawmaking treaty concluded with several other states, the writer may be regarded as an indirect source of international law. In past centuries (see Chapter 2), the publicist's work had great importance. The writings of Grotius, Gentili, Vattel, and other notables in the history of the law played a vital part in the growth of international law.

Comity

Reports on international events occasionally refer to *rules of comity* (French, *courtoisie internationale*). An example is the practice of a sending state not publishing the text of a diplomatic note before its receipt by the receiving state. Comity represents regular modes of state behavior that do not involve a binding legal obligation. If such an obligation existed, of course, the rule in question would be one not of comity but of either customary or conventional law. Comity is the international equivalent of good manners.

A rule may, of course, shift from one sphere to another. For example, the salute expressed through the dipping of the flag by one warship to another representing a friendly foreign nation on the high seas formerly represented a rule

---

[28]The most striking modern example of a publicist's influence on the development of new rules of law has been the work of Rafael Lemkin, who, through his work, contributed materially to the framing of the Convention on Genocide by the United Nations. Lemkin coined the term *genocide*. See, generally, "Les actes constituant un danger general (interétatique) consideres comme delites des droit des gens," *Expilications additionelles au Rapport spécial présentè à la V-me Conférence pour l'Unification du Droit Penal à Madrid* (14-2O.X.1933). (Translation: "Acts Constituting a General (Transnational) Danger Considered as Crimes under International Law"), trans. J. T. Fussell, www.preventgenocide.org/lemkin/; *Axis Rule in Occupied Europe: Laws of Occupation—Analysis of Government—Proposals for Redress* (1944), ch. 9; and "Genocide as a Crime under International Law," 41 *AJIL* (1947), 145–151.

of customary international law; today, the practice is viewed merely as part of international comity. On the other hand, a rule of comity could become a part of conventional law by treaty or may evolve into a component of customary law. In the *Paquette Habana*[29] (see Chapter 6) case, which dealt with the seizure of fishing vessels during the Spanish–American War, the United States contended, based upon a prior British case (1798), that exemption of such boats rested only upon grace, comity, or courtesy. The counsel for the boat owners persuaded the Court that in the interim 100 years, the practice had evolved into an obligatory rule of customary law. The essential determinant in all cases, however, is the existence or absence of a legally binding obligation. A violation of a rule of comity can be viewed at most as an unfriendly act, with no claims to reparation attached.

Equity

Few would dispute that equity and fairness represent fundamental goals of the law.[30] As a guide to legal decision, equity and fairness do not necessarily involve *abstract* ideas of "justice" or "equality." They refer to such concepts as proportionality, balance, and impartiality in the endeavor of a court to take into account the particular circumstances of a situation to avoid inequities that would result from a straightforward judicial application of a general rule of law. In the case of *The Diversion of Water from the Meuse (Netherlands v. Belgium)*, Judge Manley Hudson noted one application of the claims and counterclaims in the case:

> It would seem to be an important principle of equity that where two parties have assumed an identical or a reciprocal obligation, one party which is engaged in a continuing non-performance of that obligation should not be permitted to take advantage of a similar non-performance of that obligation by the other party.[31]

In the *North Sea Continental Shelf Cases,* the ICJ asserted, "Whatever the legal reasoning of a court of justice, its decision must by definition be just, and therefore in that sense equitable" and that "equity does not necessarily imply equality."[32] To emphasize these points, consider in addition the ICJ decision in the *Libya–Tunisia Continental Shelf* case. Tunisia had argued that because it was poor and Libya comparatively rich from its oil wealth, Tunisia should be given an extraordinarily favorable portion of the continental shelf shared by these adjacent countries (some reasonable expectation existed that substantial oil and gas deposits lay under the continental shelf). The Court rejected the argument, instead relying upon

> a reasonable degree of *proportionality,* which a delimitation carried out through equitable principles ought to bring about between the extent of the continental shelf areas appertaining to the coastal state and the coastline of the state and the length of the relevant parts of its coast.[33] (Emphasis added)

---

[29]175 U.S. 677 (1900).

[30]See M. Akehurst, "Equity and General Principles of Law," 25 *ICLQ,* 801 (1976).

[31]*Diversion of Water from the Meuse (Netherlands v. Belgium)*, PCIJ, Ser. A/B, No. 70 (1937), 77.

[32]*Federal Republic of Germany v. Denmark, Federal Republic of Germany v. Netherlands, ICJ Reports* (1969).

[33]*Libya–Tunisia Continental Shelf, ICJ Reports* (1982), para. 133 (A)(5).

The Court then strongly suggested to the parties a practical method to determine proportionality.

While drafting their opinion in the Libyan–Tunisian case, the justices of the ICJ were well aware of Article 83 in the United Nations Convention on the Law of the Sea (UNCLOS) III Treaty,[34] then in draft stage, that mandated all disputes concerning the delimitation of the continental shelf between states with opposite or adjacent coastlines should be on the basis of "international law . . . in order to achieve an equitable solution." We find the same language in Article 74 concerning the division of exclusive economic zones (EEZs), while Article 59 provides that EEZ disputes between coastal states and others should be resolved "on the basis of equity in light of all the relevant circumstances."

BEYOND ARTICLE 38 OF THE STATUTE

Resolutions and Declarations of International Organizations

Inevitably, questions arise about the role and legal significance of declarations and resolutions produced by universal and regional intergovernmental organizations (IGOs). Understandably, most of the debate concerns the United Nations and its role in the development of international law. This question actually has five constituent parts. Four of these are straightforward. First, most IGOs, the UN included, have the authority to legislate for themselves in terms of *internal* rules and operating procedures not specified in the constitutive document. Second, the UN Security Council (under Chapter VI of the UN Charter) has the power to make decisions that bind all members regarding the circumstances surrounding the grant of authority in Article 39 to deal any threat to the peace, breach of the peace, or act of aggression. Third, the UN General Assembly has promoted the development of lawmaking treaties, particularly regarding human rights. Fourth, the practice of the institutions in carrying out their missions will create rules in terms of precedents as they find it necessary to fill in gaps in treaties, or deal with new problems. The fifth part, the status of UN General Assembly recommendations and resolutions, serves as the focus of some debate.[35]

Can the General Assembly through its actions "legislate" international law in some instances? The short, traditional answer—in looking at the Charter and 60 years of practice—is no. The Charter assigns no formal lawmaking authority to the General Assembly. Its resolutions do not enact, formulate, or alter international law. By definition, because General Assembly resolutions are only *recommendations,* they lack the critical element of *opinio juris.* Erik Suy, then legal counsel of the United Nations, wrote:

> The General Assembly's authority is limited to the adoption of resolutions. These are mere recommendations having no legally binding force for member states. Solemn declarations adopted either unanimously or by consensus have no different status, although their moral and political impact will be an important factor in guiding national policies. Declarations frequently

---

[34]*Convention on the Law of the Sea,* UN A/CONF, 62/122, 21 I.L.M. 1261 (1982).

[35]R. A. Falk, "O n the Quasi-Legislative Competence of the General Assembly," *AJIL* 60 (1966), 782–791.

contain references to existing rules of international law. They do not create, but merely restate and endorse them. Other principles contained in such declarations may appear to be new statements of legal rules. But the mere fact that they are adopted does not confer on them any specific and automatic authority.[36]

Chamber Three of the Iran–United States Claims Tribunal, in its award in *SEDCO, Inc. v. National Iranian Oil Co.*, refused to accept references to General Assembly resolutions as having any legal effect.[37] The Chamber, when discussing standards of compensation, declared that the General Assembly resolutions cited lacked any legal substance and could not even be considered evidence of customary law. The Chamber held that only one relevant General Assembly resolution, no. 1803,[38] had received approval by a sufficiently broad majority of states to reflect international legal standards of compensation. Similarly, in the Texaco Overseas Petroleum Company (TOPCO) arbitration, the sole arbitrator rejected the Libyan claim that several General Assembly resolutions it put forth as customary law supported its refusal to submit to compulsory arbitration to resolve the dispute.[39] The arbitrator noted that support for the resolutions did not represent a valid cross section of the international community, because all of the economically developed states had voted no or abstained.

Yet this does not quite tell the whole story. Some have theorized that resolutions passed almost unanimously year after year with virtually the same wording might have some evidentiary value in establishing customary law. The answer is possibly—consensus as expressed in the General Assembly may represent nothing more than a hopeful exhortation or may address relatively short-lived concerns. In the exceptional cases in which a General Assembly resolution may contribute to the development of international law, it does so *only if* the resolution meets three criteria: (1) if it gains virtually universal support, (2) if the members of the General Assembly share a lawmaking or law-declaring intent, and (3) if the content of that resolution is then reflected in general state practices.[40]

Soft Law

Soft law,[41] an apparent contradiction in terms, has two different meanings in international law literature. Some analysts use the term to refer to treaty provisions that

---

[36]E. Suy, *Innovations in International Law-Making Processes* (1978); quote reprinted in S. M. Schwebel, "The Effect of Resolutions of the UN General Assembly on Customary International Law," *American Society of International Law Proceedings* (1979), 304, 305.

[37]ITL 59-129-3, The Hague, March 27, 1986, and 80 *AJIL*, 969 (1986).

[38]GA Res. 1803, 17 UN GAOR Supp. (no. 17) at 15, UN Doc. A/5217 (1962); 57 *AJIL*, 710 (1963).

[39]*Texaco Overseas Petroleum et al. v. Libyan Arab Republic* (January 19, 1977), in 17 *International Legal Materials* (1978), 1.

[40]See J. E. Alvarez, *International Organizations as Lawmakers* (2005), for a comprehensive discussion; and S. Bleicher, "The Legal Significance of Re-citation of General Assembly Resolutions," 63 *AJIL* (1969), 444–478.

[41]For a concise but perceptive discussion, see H. Hilgenberg, "A Fresh Look at Soft Law," 10 *EJIL* (1999), 499–515; see also D. Shelton, "Soft Law," in *Routledge Handbook of International Law*, edited by D. Armstrong (2009), 68–80.

cannot be implemented because they lack specificity.[42] More recently, the term has come to describe the fluctuating borderline between the politics of policymaking and customary law. Not all international agreements come in treaty form. Declarations, joint statements of policy or intention, signify agreements and establish commitments but not binding legal obligations. Statesmen may prefer nontreaty arrangements for many reasons. The following list is meant to be suggestive, not exhaustive. Many of the reasons may overlap or complement one another: confidence building, impetus for coordinated national legislation, avoidance of cumbersome domestic approval procedures, or the creation of a preliminary regime with hope for development. As with comity, Professor David Bederman argues that this last reason, the possibility of evolution (or devolution), should be highlighted:

> When international actors develop a standard of conduct, and even when it is expressly couched in the idiom of aspiration or informality, the inevitable trend is that soft law hardens into legal obligation. I believe that in any rules, standards, or typology for norms, there is an asymmetric dynamic at work. Rules rarely dissolve into standards, but standards (my surrogate for soft law in an international context) will usually solidify into legal rules.[43]

Thus, in many cases we might regard soft law as *de lege ferenda*—that is, as law in development or as an aspirational goal. In particular, this seems to hold true for economic and environmental agreements.

Advocates often cite the Helsinki Final Act of the 1975 Conference on Security and Cooperation in Europe (CSCE) as a prime example of soft law. Article X of the Final Act[44] declared that the parties had agreed to "pay due regard to, and implement the provisions in the Final Act" and expressed "their determination fully to respect and apply these principles . . . in all aspect to their mutual relations." A follow-up memorandum of understanding instructed the government of Finland to transmit the document to the secretary-general of the United Nations, but also declared that the document did not qualify as a treaty and thus did not have to be registered (see Article 102 of the Charter). While not regarded as a treaty, the document still had enormous impact because of its publication and dissemination within Eastern Europe and the very public commitments made by the governments that signed the agreement.

Pragmatically, the *political* difference between the binding power of treaty and nontreaty arrangements may be minimal. There is little evidence to suggest that states regard soft law agreements less seriously than formal treaty obligations. Both treaties and nonlegal agreements depend upon continuing cooperation between or among the parties to secure the benefits. If that willingness to cooperate erodes or disappears, then neither treaty nor "soft law" agreement will remain viable. As we discussed earlier, in theory the aggrieved state may seek redress for the nonperformance of a treaty obligation; in practice the possible political and material costs may outweigh the desire for redress or punishment.

---

[42]For example, see P. Weil, "Towards Relative Normativity in International Law?" 77 *AJIL* (1983), 414.

[43]D. J. Bederman, "Constructivism, Positivism, and Empiricism in International Law," 89 *Georgetown Law Journal* (2001), 490.

[44]August 1, 1975; 14 *ILM* 1292 (1975).

The International Law Commission

The General Assembly of the United Nations created the International Law Commission (ILC) in 1947 to promote the development and codification of international law.[45] Article 15 of the Statute establishing the Commission defines the difference between the two purposes. *Progressive development* entails "the preparation of draft conventions on subjects which have not yet been regulated by international law or in regard to which the law has not yet been sufficiently developed in the practice of States." *Codification* means "the more precise formulation and systematization of rules of international law in fields where there already has been extensive State practice precedent and doctrine." The early work—defining and developing rules relating to the continental shelf, the Convention on Reduction of Statelessness (1961), and the work leading to the Draft Code of Crimes against the Peace and Security of Mankind—represents examples of progressive development. The Vienna Convention on Diplomatic Relations (1961), the Vienna Convention on Consular Relations (1963), and the Vienna Convention on the Law of Treaties (1969) illustrate efforts at codification.

We need to emphasize that neither the General Assembly nor certainly the Commission as a body created by the Assembly has the power to formulate binding rules of international law for states. Clearly the founders of the United Nations did not intend the Assembly to serve as a legislature. On the other hand, as a forum where all states participate, it does provide a venue for study, discussion, and recommendation. Typically, the work of the ILC results in a draft convention that gives states the option of signature and ratification. The recent work of the Commission in developing the Rome Statute of the International Criminal Court (ICC) serves as a good example of the process. Since 1949, the ILC has published a yearbook detailing its work in each session.[46] Topics currently under discussion and development include diplomatic protection, reservations to treaties, international liability for injurious consequences arising out of acts not prohibited by international law, and responsibility of international organizations.

SOME PRINCIPLES AND CONVENTIONS DEVELOPED BY THE ILC

- Vienna Convention on the Law of Treaties, 1969
- Vienna Convention on the Law of Treaties Between States and International Organizations or Between International Organizations, 1986
- Draft Declaration on Rights and Duties of States with commentaries, 1949

(Continued)

---

[45]See United Nations, *International Law Commission,* www.un.org/law/ilc/, for detailed information about current projects. The Commission, composed of 34 members (elected for five-year terms), meets annually. Unlike other UN bodies, in theory, members serve in their individual capacities, not as official representatives of their governments.

[46]See http://untreaty.un.org/ilc/publications/yearbooks/yearbooks.htm.

- Vienna Convention on Succession of States in respect of State Property, Archives and Debts, 1983
- Vienna Convention on the Representation of States in Their Relations with International Organizations of a Universal Character, 1975
- Convention on the Reduction of Statelessness, 1961
- Principles of International Law Recognized in the Charter of the Nürnberg Tribunal and in the Judgment of the Tribunal with commentaries, 1950

SUGGESTED READINGS

SOURCES OF THE LAW

Akehurst, "The Hierarchy of the Sources of International Law," 47 *British Yrbk of Int. L.* (1974–1975), 273.

Alvarez, *International Organizations as Lawmakers* (2005).

Boyle and Chinkin, *The Making of International Law* (2007).

Byers, *Custom, Power and the Power of Rules* (1999).

Danilenko, *Law-Making in the International Community* (1993).

Dekker and Post, eds, *On the Foundations and Sources of International Law* (2003).

Koskenniemi, ed., *Sources of International Law* (2000).

Roberts, "Traditional and Modern Approaches to Customary International Law: A Reconciliation," 95 *AJIL* (2001), 757.

Rossi, *Equity and International Law* (1993).

Talmon, "The Security Council as World Legislature," 99 *AJIL* (2005), 175.

Van Hoof, "Rethinking the Sources of International Law," 23 *Columbia J. of Transnational L.* 705 (1985).

Wolfke, *Custom in Present International Law*, 2nd ed. (1993).

International Agreements

TYPES OF AGREEMENTS

Treaties and other forms of international agreements have been in evidence throughout recorded history. We noted earlier an agreement between Umma and Lagash, defining the boundary between them, at the very dawn of recorded history. On display in Ankara, one of the most noted treaties involves a negotiated peace between Egypt and the Hittite Empire (modern Turkey) after the Battle of Kadesh (c. 1294 B.C.).[1] In modern times, beginning with the writings of Grotius, writers and diplomats have depended mostly on rules of law governing contractual relations between private individuals in developing the principles regulating contractual arrangements between states. Only in the past few decades have states made serious attempts to develop systematic international rules governing treaties and other interstate agreements. Even so, the general principles applied by states in actual practice have achieved a high degree of uniformity.

International agreements underpin much of the everyday business of international politics. No other mechanism really exists that reflects the explicit agreed preferences of states.[2] The United States has over **10,000** treaties in force.[3] All writers, from Hugo Grotius onward, have pointed out that the *names* or *titles* of international agreements included under the general term *treaty* have little or no legal significance in and of themselves. Simply put, what those drafting the instrument choose to call it—whether a treaty, convention, or protocol—has no intrinsic legal meaning. Indeed, the variety of names given over the years to various international agreements is astounding. Besides the common varieties, such as *convention, agreement, protocol, treaty,* and *covenant,* and the less common *final act, general*

---

[1]Dates for this battle vary. Indeed, dele one edition, the *Encyclopedia Britannica*, in three different articles mentioning the battle, gives three different dates.

[2]On the general subject of treaties, consult Hackworth, IV, 1; Moore, V, 155; and McNair, *The Law of Treaties* (reiss. 1986).

[3]U.S. Department of State, "Treaty Affairs," www.state.gov/s/l/treaty/index.htm. The State Department also publishes *Treaties in Force* (TIF) each January, as well as the *Treaties and Other International Agreements* (TIAS) series.

act, and *declaration,* a bewildering array of relatively rare terms confronts the student. Among them, to list but a few, are *arrangement, accord, code, compact, contract, regulation, concordat,* and *statute.*[4] Certain terms are more common, but they furnish little more than general designations of category.

A treaty in the accepted sense of the term may be characterized in the words of Sir Gerald G. Fitzmaurice:[5]

> A *treaty* is an international agreement embodied in a single formal instrument (whatever its name, title or designation) made between entities both or all of which are subjects of international law possessed of an international personality and treaty-making capacity, and intended to create rights and obligations, or to establish relationships, governed by international law.

The *Restatement of [American] Foreign Relations Law* notes that a "treaty is one of many terms used to describe an international agreement." An *international agreement* has been defined as "an agreement among two or more states or international organizations that is intended to be legally binding and is governed by international law."[6] In fact, both of these definitions emphasize the legal rather than the practical aspect. In practical form, a treaty represents a set of *mutually conditional promises* that both states consider legal obligations. Translated into personal terms, this means that I promise in good faith to keep my promises if you keep your promises, and you promise in good faith to keep your promises if I keep my promises. Simply keep in mind that *intent* constitutes the most important element here. The parties must *intend* to create a binding set of mutual legal obligation by their actions. Not all international instruments create binding legal obligations. Some may merely state commonly held political beliefs or principles (see the discussion of "soft law" in Chapter 3).

Bilateral Treaties

Bilateral agreements are between only two states or parties and are closely related, at least by analogy, to contracts between individuals. A bilateral treaty is concluded between two states desiring to promote or regulate interests or matters of particular interest to them alone. Hence, bilateral treaties create limited obligations. For example, extradition treaties are normally bilateral instruments.

Multilateral Treaties

States also conclude multilateral (multiparty) treaties—agreements negotiated by and involving more than two parties. Some of these agreements do not create new principles or rules of international law but merely serve as expanded versions of bilateral treaties. Multiparty alliances such as the North Atlantic Treaty Organization

---

[4]D. P. Myers, "The Names and Scope of Treaties," 51 *American Journal of International Law* 574 (1957), 575.

[5]Later a judge on the International Court of Justice. G. G. Fitzmaurice, *Third Report on the Law of Treaties: Yearbook of the International Law Commission* (1958), II, 24.

[6]*Restatement (Third) of Foreign Relations Law,* § 301 (1987).

(NATO) or its Eastern Bloc adversary, the Warsaw Pact, form two good examples. Multilateral treaties created the United Nations, the Organization of American States (OAS), and other international agencies such as the World Health Organization and the World Trade Organization (WTO). Multilateral treaties that have as their principal purpose the codification of existing law or the elaboration of new principles of law governing a particular issue area are often characterized as *lawmaking treaties*. The International Covenant on Civil and Political Rights and other human rights instruments provide good illustrations of lawmaking treaties.

A Note on Lawmaking Treaties   Many multilateral treaties do have as their principal purpose the codification of existing customary law (Chapter 3) or the establishment of a new international governmental organization (IGO). The Vienna Convention on Diplomatic Relations (1961) and the Vienna Convention on the Law of Treaties (1969) exemplify efforts to establish uniform rules based upon long-standing (but somewhat inconsistent) customary practice. The International Criminal Court (ICC), as the most recent high-profile addition to the IGO ranks, exemplifies the constitutive function.

Others intend to put in place new general principles of law governing a particular issue area. These are often characterized as lawmaking treaties. The International Covenant on Civil and Political Rights (ICCPR; 1966), the Convention Against Torture and Other Cruel, Inhuman or Degrading Treatment or Punishment (1975), and the Convention on the Elimination of All Forms of Discrimination Against Women (1979) represent initiatives to establish new general rules of international law.

To understand the limits of lawmaking treaties, note first that the provisions will apply only to those states that have **signed and ratified, or deposited an instrument of accession with the United Nations** for, a particular convention. We have emphasized the element of consent throughout this introduction. Signature and ratification or accession indicate a state's consent, with ratification or accession forming the most important element because it certifies final acceptance. *Accession* to a treaty has exactly the same effect as signature and ratification. Often treaties will specify a time frame in which the treaty will be open for signature. While states may sign a treaty during this time, the act of signing does not mean that they have any time frame in which to ratify it. If a state does not sign the treaty during the time frame when it is open for signature (perhaps the state did not exist when the treaty was first open for signature, for example), it bypasses the signature phase by simply depositing an instrument of accession with the secretary-general of the United Nations. This action formally signals state consent, just as an instrument of ratification would.

Thus, the impact of the treaty in the sense of establishing a general rule *still depends upon **which** states and how many*. If the initial number of ratifying states is small, the treaty does not create a new rule of general international law but only a rule of particular or regional application among the consenting states. The International Convention Against the Recruitment, Use, Financing and Training of Mercenaries opened for signature in 1989. It needed only 22 ratifications to enter into force, but did not receive those until December 2001. Currently, it has only 32 states parties. No major state has ratified the treaty or submitted an instrument of accession. As a result, the impact of the treaty in terms of establishing the prohibitions in the treaty as general rules of international law remains marginal.

Obviously, rules may become more general as acquiescence in practice that supports the new rule by nonparty states (review the discussion on custom, Chapter 3), formal ratification or accession to the instrument embodying the new rule, or adherence to it by additional states increases. On the other hand, as we shall discuss later in text, states that specifically refuse to acquiesce in the new rule by refusing to ratify the treaty or to otherwise acknowledge its provisions are, of course, not *normally* bound by the rule, principle, or interpretation in question. The active opposition of the United States to the Rome Statute creating the ICC serves as a paradigm case.

Even though a lawmaking treaty may not achieve close to universal acceptance in terms of signature and ratification, it may nevertheless represent a source of international law for the broader community. The provisions, if adopted by a majority of states that have a very vital interest in the subject area, or who represent the major powers in a geographic area, may still have some influence on the resolution of issues between states that have not formally accepted the treaty. The convention may serve as a source that applies to particular issues or to the geographic region. To give one example, the consent or dissent of landlocked states on most issues related to the law of the sea (e.g., Bolivia, Uganda, Nepal, and Afghanistan) will have far less impact than that of those states that have extensive coastlines, large navies, or sizeable merchant marines. The Declaration of Paris of 1856 abolished privateering and redefined the rights of neutrals in naval warfare. The treaty technically bound only those states that signed the final Act,[7] but in fact, many other states accepted the rules as part of an evolving customary law (Chapter 3).

Declarations

Declarations are a peculiar type of agreement resulting from inter-American conferences and meetings of foreign ministers. They produce statements of legal principles applying, on a regional basis, in the Western Hemisphere. Thus, the Preamble of the Act of Chapultepec (Conference on Problems of War and Peace, Mexico City, 1945) states, "the American States have been incorporating in their international law, since 1890, by means of conventions, resolutions and *declarations,* the following principles." The governments of states in Latin America do not differentiate, in regard to legal status or binding force, between rules laid down in formal treaties and those found in resolutions or declarations; they regard all such rules as having equal standing.

Executive Agreements

Executive agreements represent a unique American practice in conducting relations with other states. Unlike a treaty concluded by the president (or his agents, such as the secretary of state), which requires submission to the U.S. Senate for its "advice and consent" before ratification, an executive agreement does not require

---

[7]Austria, France, Prussia, Russia, Sardinia, Turkey, and Great Britain.

the Senate's final approval. It is a binding international obligation made *solely* by the executive branch. At times the authority may come from prior congressional authorization (presidential grants of most favored nation status), a prior treaty (individual agreements with NATO partners), or without prior authority from the powers generally recognized as vested by the Constitution solely in the presidential office (e.g., power granted as commander in chief and chief executive). Recent examples include a new United States–Brazilian Defense Cooperation Agreement (April 2010)[8] and U.S. accession to the ASEAN Treaty of Amity and Cooperation (July 2009).[9]

▶ DAMES & MOORE V. REAGAN

United States Supreme Court, 1981 453 U.S. 654, 101 S.Ct. 2972, 69 L.Ed. 2d 918

Facts

On November 4, 1979, a group of Iranian militants seized the U.S. embassy in Teheran and detained the diplomatic personnel as hostages. In response, President Carter issued an executive order to block the Iranian government from the use of any of its assets (money, property, etc.) subject to the jurisdiction of the United States. In response, the Treasury Department issued a regulation providing that unless "licensed or authorized . . . any attachment, judgment, decree, lien, execution, garnishment or other judicial process is null and void with respect to any property in which on or since November 14, 1979 there existed an interest of Iran."

Dames & Moore filed suit in the U.S. District Court for Central California against the Atomic Energy Organization of Iran and a number of Iranian banks, claiming that the Atomic Energy Organization of Iran owed the company more than $3.4? million for

performance of services under a contract. In January 1981, through the mediation efforts of Algeria, the United States and Iran reached an agreement on terms for the release of the hostages. The agreement stipulated that all litigation between "the Government of each party and the nationals of the other" would immediately terminate. Instead, claims for damages would be submitted to binding arbitration. On that same day, President Carter issued a series of executive orders implementing the terms of the agreement. On February 24, 1981, President Reagan issued an executive order "ratifying" the earlier action of President Carter. He also "suspended" all claims in any U.S. court that might be presented to the arbitration tribunal.

Dames & Moore received a summary judgment against the government of Iran. They attempted to execute the judgment by obtaining writs of garnishment and execution in state courts in Washington

(*continued*)

---

[8]U.S. Department of State, www.state.gov/r/pa/prs/ps/2010/04/140059.htm.

[9]U.S. Department of State, "United States Accedes to the Treaty of Amity and Cooperation in Southeast Asia," Press Release, July 22, 2009, www.state.gov/r/pa/prs/ps/2009/july/126294.htm.

state. The district court stayed these attempts, and in light of the executive orders, vacated all attachments and prohibited further action against the defendants. Dames & Moore then filed for declaratory and injunctive relief against the United States and the secretary of the Treasury, seeking to prevent enforcement of the executive orders and Treasury Department regulations on the grounds they exceeded the statutory and constitutional powers of any agency.

Issues

1. Can the president of the United States unilaterally override the interests of private citizens in obtaining redress through the courts by invoking broader concerns of national interest?

2. Can he do so through executive agreement?

Decision

The executive orders and Treasury regulations fall within the powers and authority granted by the Constitution.

Reasoning

"When the President acts pursuant to an express or implied authorization from Congress, he exercises not only his powers but also those delegated by Congress."

Much of the controversy surrounding executive agreements has concerned questions relating to unilateral presidential commitments that seem to compel congressional approval because of funding or other need for legislation to implement the commitment successfully (i.e., separation of powers issues).[10] In August 1972, President Richard Nixon signed the Case Act (Pub. L. 92–404), which requires that international agreements, other than treaties, thereafter entered into by the United States should be transmitted to Congress within 60 days after the agreements have been executed (i.e., concluded).[11] The Act came in response to congressional irritation over secret agreements that generated commitments that might potentially require action by the legislature. The law did not question the right of the president to make executive agreements. It sought to restore a proper balance between the branches.

---

[10]See, for example, *Dames & Moore v. Reagan,* 453 U.S. 654, 101 S.Ct. 2972 (1981); *United States v. Guy W. Capps, Inc.,* U.S. Court of Appeals, 4th Cir., 1953, 204 F.2d 655, digested in 48 *AJIL* 153 (1954); for the problem of a conflict between an executive agreement and a state law, see *United States v. Pink,* U.S. Supreme Court, 1942, 315 U.S. 203.

[11]Text of the law in 11 *International Legal Materials* 1117 (1972); see also the statement by the legal adviser, Department of State (May 18, 1972), excerpted in 66 *AJIL* 845 (1972), and letters from the acting secretary of state (January 26, 1973), 67 *AJIL* 544 (1973); and (September 6, 1973), 68 *AJIL* 117 (1974). The Act was amended by Pub. L. 95–426 (Foreign Relations Authorization Act, Fiscal Year 1979, of October 7, 1978) to include all agencies. The law states that the secretary of state shall transmit to the Congress the text of any international agreement, other than a treaty to which the United States is a party, as soon as practicable after such agreement has entered into force regarding the United States but in no event later than 60 days thereafter. However, any such agreement the immediate disclosure of which would, in the president's opinion, be prejudicial to the national security of the United States shall not be so transmitted to the Congress but shall be transmitted to the Committee on Foreign Relations of the Senate and the Committee on Foreign Affairs of the House of Representatives under an appropriate injunction of secrecy to be removed only upon due notice from the president. This ensures that Congress is aware of commitments made by the executive branch on behalf of the U.S. government. See further L. Henkin, *Constitutionalism, Democracy, and Foreign Affairs* (1990), 58.

Perhaps the Far Eastern Agreement (signed at Yalta on February 11, 1945) stands as the most famous and controversial modern executive agreement post World War II. President Roosevelt clearly regarded the document as an executive agreement, yet did not admit this in his actual verbal report to Congress on March 1, 1945.[12] The circumstances surrounding the Yalta Agreement illustrate the circumstances the Case Act sought to correct. President Roosevelt requested Congress to "concur in the general conclusions" reached at Yalta, yet Congress could take no such action because the text of the agreement was not released by the Department of State until February 1946. In the meantime, however, the U.S. government, through the executive branch, undertook to carry out the measures called for in the agreement.

WHAT MAKES A TREATY VALID?

First, the validity of treaties rests upon a principle of customary law, *pacta sunt servanda, or treaties must be observed*.[13] We should add here the corollary that states must act in *good faith* in performing treaty obligations. Without this principle, we cannot speak of international agreements as instruments that create binding legal obligations. Skeptics may question this precept. We ask the reader to review the material in Chapter 1 on "why do states obey international law" as an answer to the skepticism. Keep in mind that states make agreements because the agreements reflect mutual interests.[14] All states have a vital interest in protecting the general principle of *pacta sunt servanda*.

Second, to reiterate a fundamental principle, whether bilateral or multilateral, as evidence of state consent, international agreements are *normally* binding *only* upon those states that have signed *and* ratified them or otherwise indicated consent through accession. As with every general rule, some exceptions exist. We will discuss the exceptions at the appropriate places in this chapter. Some treaties, the Charter of the United Nations for one, do contain rules of *jus cogens* (peremptory norms) considered binding on all regardless of formal consent.

Third, treaties are made between or among *states* (or, in certain cases, between or among international organizations and states), not governments. A change in government, even a radical change in the form of government, does not release the

---

[12]See C. Y. Pan, "Legal Aspects of the Yalta Agreement," 46 *AJIL* 40 (1952); the essentially opposing views of H. W. Briggs, "The Leaders' Agreement of Yalta," 40 *AJIL* 376 (1946) (text of the agreement is reprinted in full in both sources); and O. Schachter, "The Twilight Existence of Nonbinding International Agreements," 71 *AJIL* 296 (1977).

[13]See Vienna Convention on the Law of Treaties of May 23, 1969. Text and elaborate commentary in 61 *AJIL* 263 (1967 Supp.); text of convention and related documents in 63 *AJIL* 875 (1969), and in 8 *ILM* 679 (1969); text also at www.untreaty.un.org/ilc/texts/instruments/english/conventions/1_2_1986.pdf; entered into force January 27, 1980. The United States has not ratified the convention.

[14]One of the crazier comments voiced during the Cold War was "We should not approve this agreement because it is in the interest of the Soviet Union." Well, why would the Soviet Union sign *any* agreement that was *not* in its interest? Why would the United States sign any agreement that was not in its interest?

state from the treaty obligation. A quick review of the relevant cases on recognition in Chapter 7 will illustrate this principle.

Fourth, to be valid, a treaty must be *registered* with the United Nations. This has become a principle since World War I, when the League of Nations pioneered the idea. Many attributed the events leading to World War I to treaties negotiated in secret (and kept secret) that states felt bound to honor. Registration became the practical means to ensure President Woodrow Wilson's insistence that all treaties should be "open covenants, openly arrived at."

FORMATION OF TREATIES

Because constitutions differ, nothing useful can be said in general about *who* may have the authority within a particular state to engage in treaty making. International law leaves the question of internal arrangements strictly to the state.[15] On the other hand, the process at the international level generally has four identifiable stages, several of which may occur concurrently:

1. Negotiation (including the drawing up and authentication of the text)
2. Provisional acceptance of the text, normally through the affixing of the signatures of the negotiators
3. Final acceptance of the treaty by states, normally through ratification
4. The treaty's official entry into force of the treaty (and registration with the United Nations)

Negotiation

No prescribed format exists regarding the generation and acceptance of the text of a treaty. Negotiations may occur in many different settings. The crucial consideration for the negotiation stage is that individuals engaged in the process must have the official authority to do so. Representatives negotiating a treaty must be duly authorized to carry out their tasks and normally are required to have credentials to that effect. Complex and controversial multilateral treaties such as that establishing the ICC may go through many different stages of development during which delegates and others debate and amend the text. Organizations such as the International Law Commission (ILC) or the International Maritime Organization (IMO) may work to produce a draft text that will be considered by delegates to a subsequent conference convened specifically to produce a final document. In some instances, the UN General Assembly has served as the principal forum for debate and approval (e.g., the International Convention Against the Recruitment, Use, Financing and Training of Mercenaries).[16]

---

[15]See the *Memorandum* (October 15, 1973) of the acting legal adviser, U.S. Department of State, on the functions of the secretary of state regarding treaties, excerpted in 68 *AJIL* 322 (1974).

[16]G.A. Res. 44/34, U.N. GAOR, 6th Comm., 44th Sess., Supp. No. 49, at 306, U.N. Doc. A/44/766 (1989).

The United Nations sponsored the developmental stages of the Rome Statute of the ICC, but approval of the final text involved a separate conference where states and others had an opportunity to suggestion additions, amendments, or alternative wording.[17]

A Note on NGOs and Conference Diplomacy   We should note that the Rome conference marks one of the first where NGOs played an important role.[18] In fact, by their activities, they had an important role in the dynamic development of the text. To understand their role, one needs to understand how international conferences work. As with legislatures, the important work happens in committees. Large states can afford to have enough people in their delegation to have someone attend all sessions of committees. This gives larger delegations an edge in terms of information and input. At the Rome conference, representatives from various NGOs attended committee session with laptop computers. They took notes on the committee proceedings and then distributed the information to interested delegations, thus leveling the playing field in terms of access to information. This permitted smaller states to play a much greater part in constructing the language of the final text that emerged from the deliberations. We can note this as one of the unanticipated consequences of the revolution in communications that underlies many of the changes we attribute to globalization (Chapter 2).

Adoption/Authentication/Consent

Once the text of a treaty has been drafted in formal form by negotiation, the parties must indicate their consent. For bilateral agreements, this is by mutual consent of the two parties. For treaties negotiated between a limited number of states, this is usually by unanimous consent. For multilateral instruments negotiated by an international conference, this is by the voting rules adopted by that conference. For treaties drawn up in an international organization or at a conference convened by such an organization, this is according to the voting rules provided either by the constitution of the organization or by the decision of an organ or agency competent to issue such rules. *Treaties will also normally include a stipulation about what official/authentic versions of the text will be accepted in terms of* **language**. Because translation is not an exact art, this is an important condition.[19]

Adoption of a final text by the negotiators is followed by authentication. This step may take place in a number of ways: The negotiators may simply initial the text on behalf of their states; the text may be incorporated in the final act of the conference at which it was drawn up; the text may be incorporated in a resolution

[17]See W. A. Schabas, *An Introduction to the International Criminal Court* (2011); B. N. Schiff, *Building the International Criminal Court* (2011).

[18]See M. J. Struett, *The Politics of Constructing the International Criminal Court: NGOs, Constituency and* Agency (2008).

[19]See R. Cohen, *Negotiating Across Cultures: Communication Obstacles in International Diplomacy* (rev. ed. 1997).

adopted by an organ of an international organization; or, most commonly, the negotiators may append their signatures to the text of the agreement. Any of these procedures confirm that the text of the treaty is in its final form (Vienna Convention, Article 10).

Signature

Who may sign a treaty? Obviously, only persons with the capacity (authority) to do so—those with the *plenipotentiary power* (the authority to bind their state). Heads of states or governments and ministers of foreign affairs usually have the authority to sign. In other cases, representatives of states to whom full (plenary) powers to negotiate and sign have been issued may sign. Article 18 of the Vienna Convention contains the logical assertion that once a state has signed a treaty, it is obliged to refrain from all acts that would defeat the treaty's object and purpose, at least until that state has ratified the agreement or has indicated it does not intend to become a party to the agreement.

Ratification

Most modern international treaties become effective only upon ratification. International law does not specify how a state carries out the ratification process. Virtually every state has developed detailed domestic regulations spelling out the process of treaty ratification. Constitutional provisions vary greatly from country to country. Until such acceptance is forthcoming, a treaty does not create binding obligations for the state in question except in the extremely rare instance of an agreement that becomes effective and binding on signature alone.[20]

In the United States, the president transmits the authenticated and signed text of a treaty to the Senate. To accept a treaty, the Senate must approve it by a two-thirds majority. Upon Senate approval, the final step requires that the president *proclaim* the treaty by issuing a formal statement indicating the United States now considers the treaty in effect. Many descriptions of the U.S. treaty-making process leave out the last, but vital, step of *proclamation*.[21]

Understandings

An *understanding* is an attempt by a state to specify in advance its own interpretation of certain parts of an agreement. These statements will accompany the notification of ratification or accession when it is transmitted to the secretary-general. These statements have no binding force. Understandings simply reflect the views of one state. However, in a dispute, they may prove useful as a quick way to determine the views of other states regarding the meaning of certain provisions.

---

[20]For an interesting discussion concerning ratification, see R. D. Putnam, "Diplomacy and Domestic Politics: The Logic of Two Level Games," 42 *International Organization* 427 (1988).

[21]See M. J. Glennon, "The Senate Role in Treaty Ratification," 77 *AJIL* 257 (1983).

Reservations

Obviously during the negotiation phase, states will try to shape an agreement in a manner that best reflects their own interests.[22] Sometimes these efforts will not produce an acceptable outcome. In other cases, states may have chosen not to participate in the original negotiations, or, in the case of new states, they may not have been eligible to participate. In other cases, state organs involved in the process of ratification may not find certain provisions acceptable. In these cases, a state may wish to become a party to a treaty because of the overall benefits, but it may have objections to certain requirements as stated.

A *reservation* is a statement by which a state indicates its nonacceptance or interpretation of an article in a multilateral treaty. Unlike an understanding, a *reservation* is a statement of *amendment* inserted into a treaty by one party as a specified condition of ratification (Vienna Convention, Articles 19–23). It is an attempt either to opt out (exempt itself) or to modify certain "unacceptable" conditions. Like an understanding, a reservation constitutes a *unilateral* statement of position. Other states may or may not accept such reservations.

If the treaty is a *bilateral agreement,* few problems arise over a reservation. The other party either ratifies the original agreement as altered by the reservation or refuses to ratify it and thus kills the agreement. Reservations to multilateral treaties obviously pose a different problem. Before World War II, two approaches existed. The secretary-general of the League of Nations adopted the position that a state proposing a reservation to a multilateral treaty could not become a party unless *all* other states parties accepted the reservation. In sum, without unanimous consent to the proposed alteration by those states that had accepted the provisions "as is," the party seeking to join the regime on its own terms would be precluded from doing so. On the other hand, the Governing Board of the Pan-American Union (the precursor to the Organization of American States) expressed a much more flexible view:[23]

1. The treaty shall be in force, in the form in which it was signed, as between more countries that ratify it without reservations, in the terms in which it was originally drafted and signed.
2. It shall be in force as between the governments that ratify it with reservations and the signatory states that accept the reservations in the form in which the treaty may be modified by said reservations.
3. It shall not be in force between a government that may have ratified with reservations and another that may have already ratified, and which does not accept such reservations.

With the proliferation of multilateral treaties post World War II—many of which addressed controversial subjects like human rights—the question of reservations

---

[22]See G. G. Fitzmaurice, "Reservations to Multilateral Conventions," *2 Int'l. and Comp, L. Q.* (1953); and Hackworth, V, 130 (one of the clearest statements on this point). See also the unusual approach adopted in J. K. Gamble, "Reservations to Multilateral Treaties: A Macroscopic View of State Practice," 74 *AJIL* 372 (1980). The new standard work on the subject is F. Horn, *Reservations and Interpretive Declarations to Multilateral Treaties* (1988).

[23]See 45 *AJIL* 3 (1951 Supp.); refer also to C. G. Fenwick, "Reservations to Multilateral Treaties," 45 *AJIL* 145 (1951).

became an ongoing subject of debate. At base, the question involves the tension between the desire for certain treaty regimes to be as inclusive (as broadly accepted) as possible and the hard question of how accepting states that pose reservations may affect the integrity and effectiveness of the established regime. Post World War II, the debate over reservations focused upon the Genocide Convention (1948), the first of the major human rights treaties. In an advisory opinion, the International Court of Justice (ICJ) expressed the opinion that a state that had proposed a reservation that raised objections from one or more parties to the convention, but not by others, could still be accepted as a party *if* the reservation "is compatible with the object and purpose of the Convention."[24] After much further debate, the ILC adopted the ICJ position in constructing its draft of the Vienna Convention on the Law of Treaties. In addition, the ILC promoted the idea that each future multilateral treaty should contain specific stipulations concerning how reservations should be treated.

Articles 20 and 21 of the Vienna Convention give the best evidence of current law. To summarize the important points:

1. A reservation expressly authorized by a treaty does not require subsequent acceptance by the other contracting states unless the treaty so provides.
2. When the object and purpose of a treaty that the application of the treaty in its entirety between all the parties is an essential condition of the consent of each one to be bound by the treaty, a reservation requires acceptance by all the parties.
3. When a treaty is a constitutive instrument of an international organization (i.e., its constitution) and unless otherwise specified, a reservation requires the acceptance of the competent organ of that organization.
4. An objection by another contracting state to a reservation does not preclude the entry into force of the treaty as between the objecting and reserving states unless a contrary intention is definitely expressed by the objecting state.
5. An act expressing a state's consent to be bound by the treaty and containing a reservation is effective as soon as at least one other contracting state has accepted the reservation.
6. A reservation established with regard to another party in accordance with Articles 20 and 23 modifies for the reserving state in its relations with that other party the provisions of the treaty to which the reservation relates to the extent of the reservation, and modifies those provisions to the same extent for that other party in its relations with the reserving state (Article 21). The reservation does *not* modify the provisions of the treaty for the other parties to the treaty inter se.

As the Vienna Convention illustrates, the post–World War II environment promoted a more flexible stance with respect to reservations in an attempt to build the broadest base for many emerging regimes. On the other hand, recent practice has again tended toward more restrictive views, especially for complicated, comprehensive treaties involving multi-subject issue areas—such as the United

---

[24]*Reservations to the Genocide Treaty, ICJ Reports* (1951), 24; *ICJ Reports, 1951* (Pleadings, Oral Arguments), May 28, 1951, in 45 *AJIL* 579 (1951); see also Y.-L. Liang, "The Third Session of the International Law Commission: Review of Its Work by the General Assembly—I," 46 *AJIL* 483 (1952), for a detailed analysis of the opinion.

Nations Convention on the Law of the Sea (UNCLOS III—see Chapter 12) and the Rome Statute establishing the ICC. We discuss the role of reservations in dispute resolution later, when the questions have relevance in resolving a dispute.

Accession

Related to both signature and ratification is the subject of accession—the formal act of acceptance by a state that had not originally signed or ratified a treaty. In some circumstances, the permission of the original parties to the treaty may be required before non-signatories may join in the agreement (e.g., admission to an alliance group or organization set up by treaty). Accession commonly applies only to general multilateral agreements such as the Law of the Sea Treaty, the Vienna Convention on Treaties, or the Genocide Convention. We should note that, *if permitted,* states may make reservations upon accession.

Succession

On occasion, a newly independent state, formerly part of another entity (such as a former British colony), joins a multipartite agreement to which its former governing authority (i.e., the United Kingdom) had been a party. For example, on April 2, 1982, Kiribati deposited with the UN Secretariat its *notification of succession* to the Vienna Convention on Diplomatic Relations (see Chapter 7 on state succession).

The Vienna Convention on the Law of Treaties

To illustrate one possible sequence of how treaties evolve, we shall briefly examine the genesis of the Vienna Convention on the Law of Treaties (May 23, 1969). The ILC developed draft articles on the Law of Treaties in several of its sessions, culminating in January 1966 in a draft convention, complete with an elaborate commentary. That draft was discussed at the first session of the United Nations Diplomatic Conference on the Law of Treaties, held in Vienna from March 26 to May 24, 1968. Delegates adopted 65 of the original 75 articles in question (many with relatively minor changes) by the Committee of the Whole, deferred action on 9 articles, added 4 new ones, and totally deleted 1.

At the second sessions of the conference (April 9 to May 22, 1969, in Vienna), delegates again discussed the revised draft in its entirety and then voted on the text, article by article. This resulting text was then produced for submission to governments for a final vote on the whole. States adopted the text of the Vienna Convention on the Law of Treaties (hereafter referred to as the Vienna Convention) on May 22, 1969, by a vote of 79 in favor and 1 against (France), with 19 abstentions (including all members of the Soviet Bloc). Article 85 stated, "Chinese, English, French, Russian and Spanish texts are equally authentic." Adoption or approval of the text then meant the treaty was open for formal signature.

Article 81 declared the convention open for signature until April 30, 1970. After that date, states could become a party by *accession,* a formal notice of acceptance deposited with the secretary-general of the United Nations. Article 84 provided that *the treaty would enter into force* on the 30th day after the 35th deposit of a notice of ratification or accession with the secretary-general. The convention entered into force on January 27, 1980. The United States has signed the original, but has not, as of this writing, ratified the convention. Most provisions of the Vienna Convention, including Articles 31 and 32 on matters of treaty interpretation, are considered declaratory of customary international law.[25] On the other hand, the Preamble states, "rules of customary international law will continue to govern questions not regulated by the provisions of the present Convention."

Self-Executing and Non-Self-Executing Treaties

In the United States, treaties may be either *self-executing* or *non-self-executing* in nature.[26] A self-executing treaty becomes domestic law as soon as the Senate acts and the president signs and proclaims it (instrument enters into force internationally). Judges will then deal with the treaty as if the provisions had been enacted by the Congress and signed by the president into statutory law. Non-self-executing agreements require *implementing legislation* before they come into effect domestically. In the United Kingdom (and most other states), this distinction does not have the importance it does for U.S. courts, because treaties cannot become the "law of the land" until the Parliament acts formally to so incorporate them. In the United Kingdom, for example, the Parliament has no formal role in treaty making including ratification. That prerogative lies solely with the Crown/executive. Yet the treaty cannot go into force in the United Kingdom in the sense of having domestic courts apply provisions unless the Parliament takes formal action to adopt the treaty as domestic law. So, even though Parliament has no formal role, the need for its ultimate consent gives the legislature some informal power. Presumably because the prime minister also heads a parliamentary majority (or coalition majority), problems seldom occur.

In the United States, the decision about the category into which a given treaty falls has usually been made by the judicial branch, based on the intentions of the parties as shown in the wording of the treaty or other evidence such as statements by the chief executive or legislative body. In *Asakura v. City of Seattle* (Chapter 6), after a very long examination of the issue, the court regarded the relevant treaty as self-executing. Note that the United States has regarded *all **human rights treaties** as **non-self-executing*** (see Chapter 15). For example, even though the United States signed the Genocide Treaty in 1948, ratification took place in 1988 only after the Congress wrote very detailed implementing legislation. In the United States and elsewhere, the courts look at such implementing legislation in arriving at a decision in relevant cases. Legal scholars are virtually unanimous in believing that whether a treaty falls into one or the other of the two categories is immaterial as far as the legal obligations of a party to that treaty are concerned. Naturally, if a country fails to adopt implementing legislation in the case of a non-self-executing treaty, it cannot carry out its obligations under that agreement, but from the standpoint of international law, it will still be obligated by that instrument (see Chapter 6).

---

[25]At this writing (August 2011), the convention had received 45 signatures and had 111 states parties. The International Law Commission also promoted the development of the Convention on Treaties Concluded Between States and International Organizations or Between International Organizations done at Vienna on March 21, 1986. This convention has not yet entered into force. See www.state.gov/s/l/treaty/faqs/70139.htm for the U.S. position.

[26]See S. I. Vladeck, "Non-self-executing Treaties and the Suspension Clause After St. Cyr," 113 *Yale L.J.* 2007 (2004).

RAFFINGTON v. CANGEMI

U.S. Court of Appeals for the Eighth Circuit (2004) 399 F.3d 900; 2005 U.S. App. LEXIS 1809

Facts

Sherneth Raffington,[27] an alien in custody awaiting removal to Jamaica, appealed the district court's denial of her petition for a writ of habeas corpus. Raffington argued that the government cannot remove her because of its frivolous appeal of the immigration judge's (IJ) grant of suspension of deportation and, further, that the district court erred in failing to consider the merits of her belated claim for relief under the Convention Against Torture (CAT).

Raffington had reentered the United States illegally in April 1988. The Immigration and Naturalization Service (INS) initiated deportation proceedings (now called removal proceedings) in October 1994. The IJ granted suspension of deportation in December 1996, and the INS appealed. In September 2001, the Board of Immigration Appeals sustained the appeal and denied Raffington's application for suspension of deportation.

After Raffington was taken into custody pursuant to a warrant of removal, she petitioned for habeas corpus relief. The district court denied relief, concluding that the INS had a good faith basis to appeal the IJ's grant of suspension of deportation. The IJ noted that Raffington's attempt to assert a claim under the CAT in her reply brief was untimely. Raffington moved to reopen the case to present her CAT claim. The district court denied leave to file a motion for reconsideration because they found "no evidence to suggest that Raffington could obtain relief under the Convention." She appealed both orders. The district court granted a stay pending appeal because removal may cause irreparable injury and Raffington "raises a substantial question as to whether her Convention Against Torture claim has been adequately adjudicated."

Issue

Does Raffington have grounds to stay the deportation order under the Convention Against Torture?

Decision

No. She may have requested a stay, but the law does not require she receive one.

Reasoning

Raffington argued that the district court erred in refusing to consider her request for relief under the CAT because that claim has never been adjudicated on the merits. The court stated, "At the outset, we seriously doubt whether this claim is even cognizable in habeas. As ratified by the United States, the CAT is a *non-self-executing treaty,* which means *there is no direct right of action for violation of the treaty,* only for violation of any domestic law implementing the treaty. The relevant statute provides that implementation of CAT shall be in accordance with nonreviewable agency regulations, and that judicial review of the denial of CAT relief must be 'as part of the review of a final order of removal.'" (Emphasis added)

---

[27]See also *Wang v. Ashcroft*, U.S. Court of Appeals Second Circuit (2003), 320 F.3d 130; 2003 U.S. App. LEXIS 2086.

Rejection of Treaties

Technically, even though its representatives have signed a treaty, a state is not bound by the treaty's obligations until ratification has taken place. Instances abound where states have signed but not ratified a treaty. In the United States, the Senate is free to deny its consent to a treaty negotiated by the executive branch even though the action might generate ill-feeling among the other parties to the agreement. Under such circumstances, the president has no independent authority to proclaim the treaty as the "law of the land." Among the more noted instances of Senate refusal stand the Treaty of Versailles (ending World War I), which included the Covenant of the League of Nations. More to the point, a state may not ratify an agreement because politics within the state may make acceptance difficult or impossible. Negotiation of terms acceptable at the international level may not be so at the domestic level.[28] It took the United States 40 years to ratify the Genocide Convention. In many instances, the president has not submitted a treaty to the Senate for ratification or has withdrawn it before a vote because of a calculation that the Senate would reject it. President Carter submitted the Strategic Arms Limitation Treaty II (SALT II) with the Soviet Union to the Senate, but chose to withdraw it before a formal vote because he knew it had no chance of ratification. He then, in a statement designed to reassure the Soviet Union, emphasized that the United States would adhere to the provisions of the treaty as official "policy" even though the Senate had not ratified the treaty. The United States signed the Rome Statute creating the ICC, but neither President Clinton nor President Bush has submitted the treaty to the Senate because of perceived opposition.

The United States did not originally sign the Rome Statute that established the ICC. It had opposed many features of the Rome Statute before and during the conference (1997) that produced the final text (see Chapters 15 and 22).[29] When finally signing the treaty in December 2000, President Clinton reiterated American objections and said he would not submit the treaty to the Senate for ratification unless other states would consent to revise the treaty to take into account American objections.[30] In May 2002, President George W. Bush "unsigned" the ICC treaty. The decision to "unsign" was unprecedented and raised many questions about the legal significance of the withdrawal as well as the importance of the precedent.[31]

Simply stated, the U.S. action raised the question of the legal significance of signature alone. As noted earlier, Article 18 of the Vienna Convention arguably

---

[28]See Putnam, note 20.

[29]Letter from John R. Bolton, undersecretary of state for arms control and international security, to UN Secretary-General Kofi Annan (May 6, 2002), www.state.gov/r/pa/prs/2002/9968.htm, in keeping with the role of the United Nation as treaty depository.

[30]W. J. Clinton, president of the United States, "Statement on Signature of the International Criminal Court Treaty, Washington, DC," at 1 (December 31, 2000), 37 *Weekly Comp. Press Doc.* 4 (January 8, 2001). Note that President Clinton's signature occurred in the very last days of his administration and on the last possible day for a "signature without ratification," as specified in the Statute.

[31]D. C. Scott, "Presidential Power to 'Unsign' Treaties," 69 *U. Chi. L. Rev.* 1447 (2002), discusses the circumstances surrounding the possibility that the United States might also unsign the Comprehensive Test Ban Treaty. See also E. T. Swaine, "Unsigning," 55 *Stan. L. Rev.* 2061 (2003), for a concise discussion of issues and positions.

obligates states that have signed a particular instrument to refrain from any acts that might hinder or disrupt the operation of the treaty regime.[32] This presumably obligates states not to act in bad faith or in a way that might affect the legitimate expectations of benefits other states hoped to achieve in agreeing to the treaty. The first unanswered question then becomes the permissibility of unsigning. The second then depends upon the answer to the first: If permissible, does unsigning release the United States from the obligation not to disrupt the purpose and operations of the treaty?

Registration of Treaties

The registration of international treaties[33] is not a new idea. Before World War I, the practice of states was governed largely by secret diplomacy. The search for the causes of World War I led to strong criticism of secret diplomacy. President Woodrow Wilson emerged as the leader of a segment of international public opinion favoring not only open diplomacy but also the registration of treaties as a means of ensuring publicity for their contents. Although the expectation that open diplomacy and full public knowledge concerning the making and contents of all kinds of agreements among nations would eliminate a major cause of war has proven illusory, the idea of registering treaties has survived largely as the result of Wilson's crusade. Article 18 of the League Covenant provided that "every treaty or international engagement entered into hereafter by any Member of the League shall be forthwith registered with the Secretariat and shall as soon as possible be published by it. No such treaty or international engagement shall be binding until so registered."

The Charter of the United Nations in Article 102 requires the compulsory registration of international treaties and agreements:

1. Every treaty and every international agreement entered into by any member of the United Nations after the present Charter comes into force shall as soon as possible be registered with the Secretariat and published by it.
2. No party to any such treaty or international agreement that has not been registered in accordance with the provisions of paragraph 1 of this Article may invoke that treaty or agreement before any organ of the United Nations.

The significant change in the Charter from the provisions of Article 18 of the Covenant is the avoidance of the principle that unregistered treaties would lack binding force for the parties in question. The Charter simply says that presumed obligations under unregistered treaties may not be used in any dispute taken up by any organ of the United Nations. Post World War II, we have no cases where states have attempted to invoke an unregistered instrument in this way.

---

[32]As noted earlier, many states—including the United States—have not ratified the Vienna Convention but have nonetheless accepted it as declaratory of customary law.

[33]The interested reader will find suggestive materials in P. C. Jessup, "Modernization of the Law of International Contractual Agreements," 41 *AJIL* 378, 381 (1947); see also Vienna Convention, Articles 76–80.

Interpretation of Treaties

Once an international agreement comes into force, the interpretation[34] of its meaning and purposes will often continue to be a problem. Negotiators are not psychics, and new problems not part of the negotiations will emerge. Disarmament and arms control agreements are particularly fragile because technologies change, and competitive states will seek loopholes. Consider in this respect the attempt of President Reagan's administration to "reinterpret" the antiballistic missile ban (ABM) Treaty that formed an integral part of the first Strategic Arms Limitation Treaty talks and agreement (SALT I) to permit continued research, testing, and development of the technologies associated with the Strategic Defense Initiative (colloquially known as "Star Wars"). While some "schools" of thought have proposed *canons*[35] for interpretation, a thorough discussion of these lies far beyond the tasks of an introductory text. An examination of these is not necessary to grasp the fundamental principles. Most modern writers agree that three basic principles govern the interpretation of treaties: (1) ordinary meaning in context, that is, determination of the real meaning of the parties' accepting the instrument; (2) good faith; and (3) intent and purpose. Unless there is substantial evidence to the contrary, interpretations must assume that the parties intended a treaty to have effect and must not produce an absurd result (see Vienna Convention, Articles 31–33).

Wording   A fundamental objective of interpretation is, therefore, to discover just what the parties to a treaty understood the agreement to mean when they entered into it. The process parallels that of a lawyer in seeking to give effect to contracts, wills, trusts, and other arrangement within the domestic context. If the instrument's terms are clear and specific, no contrary intent can be asserted by either party to the agreement. A commonly cited example illustrates this principle. Article III, Section 1, of the Hay–Pauncefote Treaty of 1901 provided that the Panama Canal should be "free and open to the vessels of commerce and war of all nations observing these Rules, on terms of entire equality." The United States asserted, however, that the term *all nations* did not include the United States—because the United States had built the canal, continued as its owner, and thus had the right to grant preferential treatment to its own ships, namely, exemption from payment of tolls under the Panama Tolls Act. Elihu Root, one of the most prominent international lawyers in the United States, sided with the British government in its protest that the clear terms and intentions of the treaty had been violated by the exemptions in question. After much discussion in Congress, the exemptions were eventually repealed in 1914.

The words used in the agreement are to be interpreted in their usual, ordinary meaning unless, by some chance, such an interpretation would produce absurd, contradictory, or impossible consequences. Because a treaty is expected to reflect the intentions of the parties involved, it may be necessary in interpretation to depart

---

[34]The literature on the subject is extensive and diversified in its approach. Consult, inter alia, Lauterpacht, *Oppenheim*, I: 950 (which, incidentally, lists an unusually large total of 16 rules to be applied to the interpretation of treaties), and the illuminating opinions of the legal adviser of the Department of State concerning the 1963 Nuclear Test Ban Treaty, reprinted in 58 *AJIL* 175 (1964).

[35]A *canon* is a rule or, more particularly, a body of rules established as fundamental and valid for a particular area of study.

from the literal meaning of certain words in order to avoid conclusions quite obviously contrary to the treaty's intent. Moreover, difficulties in translation may produce anomalies because many words and terms do not translate literally from one language to another. Treaties can also be interpreted, on occasion, in the light of other conventions covering the same subject matter. This was done, for example, by the Permanent Court of International Justice in the *River Oder Commission* case.[36]

Rules for Interpreting Multilingual Treaties When a treaty is concluded in two or more languages, all texts being authentic, there may be considerable difficulties in interpretation. For instance, a given term may have a broad, liberal meaning in one of the languages, and its equivalent in another language may have a restrictive, narrow meaning. Under such conditions, the tendency has been to use the **narrower meaning** in interpreting the treaty. As in the case of virtually all other rules applicable to the subject, limitations exist, the most commonly cited being the decision of the Permanent Court of International Justice in the *Mavrommatis Palestine Concessions* case. A question about the narrower meaning of *contrôle public* and the more extensive meaning of *public control* was decided in favor of the meaning of the English term.[37]

On occasion, a term in a treaty may have a different meaning in the countries that are parties to the agreement. In this case, one commonly employed solution is to apply the meaning prevalent in the country where the action contemplated by the treaty is to take place. If, of course, such action is scheduled for, say, both parties to such agreement, then the application of this rule might result in the rather odd—and perhaps unacceptable—spectacle of different procedures or actions being taken in two countries under the terms of the same instrument.

The following two examples may serve to illustrate the linguistic problems encountered on occasion in the interpretation of treaties. Article 5(3) of the Fourth Geneva Convention Relative to the Protection of Civilian Persons in Time of War (1949) provides that spies and saboteurs, "in case of a trial, shall not be deprived of the rights of fair and regular trial." The governing French text reads, "in case of pursuit" rather than the English "in case of trial." Second, in the Hague regulations of 1907, now regarded not only as treaty law but also as customary international law, Article 43 refers, in the French version, to *l'ordre et la vie publics* (public order and safety of occupying forces, or public life, or social functions of everyday life), whereas the common English translation refers to "public order and safety."

Logical Interpretation If grammatical analysis should prove insufficient to interpret a treaty, logical interpretation may be called into play. In other words, a given term or provision in an international instrument may be given a meaning that is logical and in harmony with the other parts of the agreement.[38] Such an interpretation

---

[36]*River Oder Commission* case (*Six Gov'ts v. Poland*), PCIJ, Ser. A, No. 23 (1929), at 26 of the *Judgment* of September 10, 1929.

[37]PCIJ, Ser. A, No. 2 (1924).

[38]See such pertinent opinions of the Permanent Court of International Justice as the one on the *Interpretation of the Statute of Memel, PCIJ*, Ser. A/B, No. 49 (1932), on the *Minority Schools in Upper Silesia,* Ser. A., No. 15 (1928); the *Mosul* case, Ser. B, No. 12 (1925); and the opinion on the *Postal Service in Danzig,* Ser. B, No. 11 (1925).

seeks to construe dubious passages or terms in their context—a principle one can find little to quarrel with.

Historical Interpretation Courts have occasionally applied a historical interpretation to certain treaties, although this method requires considerable caution in its application. As long as a court restricts itself in this sphere to an examination of records concerned with negotiation of the agreement and related documents (*travaux préparatoires,* or preparatory work and discussions), the historical approach to interpretation appears quite reasonable. But once a court accepts previous history (historical relations among the parties, for example), it begins to tread on highly questionable ground. In this same vein, a court may examine *common practice* regarding the treaty that might establish a common understanding of the meaning of the terms.[39]

Purpose and Function Still another approach to treaty interpretation—all others having failed—is to relate one's inquiry to the function intended to be served by the treaty.[40] A court may attempt to interpret the instrument based on its purposes.

SPECIAL PROBLEMS

Effects on Third Parties

At this point, we need to address certain special problems with the interpretation of international agreements. One of these is the effect of such instruments on third parties. Many agreements, by their positive terminology, have been clearly intended to benefit third parties. This is particularly true when a treaty contains an adhesion or accession clause, enabling third states to become parties to the instrument and to acquire by such a step a variety of legal privileges that otherwise might—or might not—have been conceded to them. On the other hand, *no treaty can create legally binding obligations or rights for a third party without the latter's consent.* If that consent is stated expressly, then the third party accepts the obligation established intentionally by the treaty. A legal right is created if the parties to the treaty intend to grant that right to a third party, to a group of states that party belongs to, or to all states, but in every instance, the third party must assent to the right. That assent, however, need not be expressed specifically (as in the case of a

---

[39]See E. Lauterpacht, "Some Observations on the Preparatory Work in the Interpretation of Treaties," 48 *Harvard L. J.* 549 (1935); also the Advisory Opinion of the Permanent Court of International Justice in *Jurisdiction of the European Advisory Commission of the Danube Between Galatz and Braila, PCIJ,* Ser. B, No. 14 (1927), 18.

[40]See Permanent Court of International Justice advisory opinions on the *Acquisition of Polish Nationality,* Ser. B, No. 7 (1923); on the *Competence of the International Labour Organization to Regulate, Incidentally, the Personal Work of Employers,* Ser. B, No. 13 (1923); on *Interpretation of the 1919 Convention Concerning Employment of Women During the Night,* Ser. A/B, No. 50 (1932); in the judgment on *Certain German Interests in Polish Upper Silesia,* Ser. A, No. 7 (1926); and in the *Chorzów Factory* case, Ser. A, No. 17 (1928).

treaty-created obligation); as long as the third party does not voice an objection to the right granted, assent is assumed by the parties to the treaty.[41]

Charters and Constitutions of International Organizations

Special problems of interpretation may arise in connection with the charters or constitutions of international organizations. A majority of such instruments, certainly in the case of most contemporary specialized agencies of the United Nations, contain provisions specifying how any disputes concerning interpretation are to be settled. But the Charter of the United Nations lacks such a precise formulation, even though it does contain a number of hints about possible methods of interpretation. The absence of specific provisions might indicate that unilateral interpretation is permissible, but designation in Article 92 of the ICJ as "the principal judicial organ of the United Nations" could lead to the logical conclusion that the court should serve as the agency of interpretation. Finally, the provision of Article 10, which grants competence to the General Assembly to "discuss any questions or any matters relating to the powers and function of any organs provided for in the present Charter," could be viewed as authority for the General Assembly to interpret at least certain aspects of the Charter. The factual development of Charter interpretation in the United Nations appears to have emphasized interpretation by the political organs of the United Nations, but on occasion not only the ICJ but also the secretary-general has handed down rulings as to the applicable meaning of Charter provisions.

VALIDITY OF TREATIES

One of the oldest principles in international law is usually rendered as *pacta sunt servanda*: "treaties must be observed."[42] However, as in the case of domestic contracts as well as domestic legislation, circumstances or conditions may occur that will invalidate either. Hence, we must examine not only the validity of the principle itself but also the conditions under which treaties will be considered valid or invalid. A state may not render an agreement invalid by just verbally condemning it, as Pope Innocent X did in the instance of the Treaty of Westphalia, calling it "null, void, invalid, iniquitous, unjust, damnable, reprobate, inane, empty of meaning and effect for all times." Rather, specific conditions or situations affect the validity of an agreement; that is, validity is determined by the existence, or lack thereof, of binding force on the parties involved. Many considerations play a part in this matter, any or many of which may nullify an international agreement.[43]

---

[41]Based on Vienna Convention, Articles 34–38, on the effect of treaties on third parties. See also Permanent Court of International Justice, *Free Zones of Upper Savoy and Gex, PCIJ*, Ser. A/B, No. 46 (1932), in W. Friedman, 367.

[42]See the historical analysis of the maxim in H. Wehberg, "Pacta Sunt Servanda," *53 AJIL 775* (1959), as well as the heavily documented study of J. L. Kunz, "The Meaning and the Range of the Norm *Pacta Sunt Servanda*," *39 AJIL* 180 (1945); and Vienna Convention, Article 26.

[43]Validity, invalidity, and termination of treaties are dealt with in the Vienna Convention, Articles 26–75.

1. *Capacity to contract.* A treaty is invalid if one of the parties to a bilateral agreement lacks the capacity to contract (i.e., international personality; see Chapter 7).

   Certain international organizations have the right to conclude valid international agreements with states and/or among themselves. This ability adds a new aspect to the problems of capacity to contract: In the case of such organizations, the governing statutes, charters, or constitutions may have to be checked carefully to determine whether a given organization has the capacity to conclude a certain agreement or commit itself to specific obligations.

2. *Authority granted to agents.* The validity of an international agreement depends on the authority granted by the respective government to the agents entrusted with its negotiation. If an agent exceeds the powers conferred on him/her, the resulting agreement will lack validity if the other parties have been notified beforehand of the restrictions on his/her authority to conclude an agreement.

3. *Personal duress or intimidation.* A treaty is invalid when personal duress has been brought to bear against the negotiators of one party (Vienna Convention, Article 51).

   Note one exception to this general rule. Every peace treaty imposed at the end of a war by the victors on the vanquished lacks the element of voluntary consent. However, the same writers who stress the need of free assent also maintain that the particular duress involved in a peace treaty does not negate its validity, and thus they place peace treaties in an essentially separate category. The traditional view—that the consent of the defeated state is required to make a peace treaty legally valid—has been replaced in some modern instances by a new attitude. The consent of Italy was not required for giving effect to the peace treaty after World War II. Although Italy, Bulgaria, and Finland did sign their respective peace treaties, Hungary and Romania did not. No one has claimed that the latter peace treaties lacked validity.

4. *Use of fraud in negotiation.* A treaty whose negotiation involved fraud would be considered invalid. Modern history can show very few instances in which outright fraud formed a part of treaty negotiation, but this does not preclude the possibility of such instances occurring in the future. However, mere failure to disclose some facts during negotiation when such disclosure would weaken the case or argument of one of the negotiating parties should not be taken as a case of fraud. Only **deliberate** fraudulent misrepresentation during the course of negotiation, such as the use of falsified maps or documents or false statements as to facts, would have the effect of invalidating the resulting agreement (Vienna Convention, Article 49).

5. *Corruption of a state agent.* At the insistence of several Third World delegations at the 1969 Vienna Conference, Article 50 was added to the Vienna Convention. It provides that if the expression of a state's consent to be bound by a treaty has been procured through the corruption of its representative directly or indirectly by another negotiating state, the first state may invoke this corruption as invalidating its consent to be bound by the treaty (Vienna Convention, Article 50).

6. *Substantial error.* A treaty is void *ab initio* (from the beginning) if it can be shown that the agreement was based upon a substantial error concerning the

facts. In other words, if in the course of negotiation and ratification, an incorrect assumption is made by one or both of the parties, then the treaty may lack validity, or the party in question may consider it "voidable" and refuse to be bound by the agreement. An illustrative instance might be the use of an incorrect map. Note that in this case (to distinguish this point from the one in item 3), this would be an *erroneous* map, not one deliberately falsified to defraud the other party (see Vienna Convention, Article 48).

7. *Conformity to other agreements.* A treaty is not necessarily invalid if its provisions do not conform to earlier agreements concluded among the same parties. In the event of inconsistency between a new treaty and earlier agreements between the same parties, the latest agreement prevails (as the latest evidence of intent and purpose).

8. *Inconsistency with provisions of UN Charter.* A treaty inconsistent with the provisions of the Charter of the United Nations has to yield to the Charter, provided that all parties to the agreement are members of the United Nations.

9. *Conflict with international law.* Is a treaty invalid if its provisions contradict principles of general customary or conventional international law? Most writers believe this is the case. Their attitude reflects a conviction that a combination of the rules of customary law and the rules laid down in lawmaking treaties constitutes a body of principles to which treaties between states must conform, even if one of the parties to the agreement has not ratified or acceded to a specific lawmaking treaty touching on the subject matter of the agreement in question.

10. *Immoral object.* Is a treaty void or voidable because it has an immoral object as its substance? Lauterpacht has given a most persuasive affirmative answer. But dissent must be registered, because the position taken by Lauterpacht implies both that whatever is immoral is ipso facto illegal and that states may generally agree on actions considered immoral. Certainly there are grave doubts about both assumptions. As yet, morality and legality have not been united in marriage. Moreover, definitions of immorality may—and indeed do—differ greatly, not only among different civilizations in the world but also among the member states of the "Western" group.

11. *Oral agreement.* An agreement is not invalid simply because it is an oral agreement rather than a written instrument. An agreement reached verbally between agents of states who are capable of binding their respective governments is quite sufficient, provided the evidence confirms that the individuals in question intend at the time to conclude a binding agreement. Nevertheless, a written instrument is preferable to a verbal agreement, if only to prevent subsequent disputes about the nature of the understanding that has been reached.

   In conclusion, we must call attention to Article 42(1) of the Vienna Convention: "the validity of a treaty or of the consent of a state to be bound by a treaty may be questioned only through application of the relevant procedures contained in the provisions of the Convention." In other words, no state bound by the convention may make allegations about the invalidity of a given agreement without reference to the provisions of the Convention.

Textual Elements

While most treaties follow an established pattern in regard to their format, no general rules specify a particular formula. Many agreements have a preamble stating the reasons for the agreement and the results expected to arise from it. Others incorporate such a statement of purpose in the opening paragraphs of the actual text of the agreement. Following the statement of purpose, however made, will come the substantive part of the agreement, containing the detailed provisions of the treaty—the mutual obligations to which each state has consented. The following sections will then deal normally with the issues of implementation, such as the details of the ratification process, the effective date of the treaty, the duration of the treaty, the time the instrument will remain open for signature, dispute resolution procedures, registration, method(s) of termination (if applicable), and other details the negotiators feel are important. In some cases, implementation issues will be included in an ancillary protocol rather than in the primary document.

Treaties vary regarding the detail the parties feel necessary to include. For example, as noted earlier, the SALT I Interim Agreement and the ABM Treaty were very concise (remarkably so). On the other hand, the agreement between President Reagan and General Secretary Mikhail Gorbachev of the Soviet Union that dealt with the removal of intermediate-range ballistic missiles (INF Treaty) ran to 166 pages. The ABM Treaty (May 26, 1972)[44] consisted of two parts. Part I contained the preamble and text. Part II consisted of agreed statements, common understandings, and unilateral statements regarding the treaty. As discussed earlier, Part II involves the efforts of the parties to specify more precisely their views of certain provisions of the agreement. In this case, questions always arose concerning the *legal* standing of Part II because President Nixon and General Secretary Leonid Brezhnev technically signed only Part I. To handle disputes concerning implementation and compliance, Article XIII set up a Standing Consultative Committee (SCC). Article XIV authorized the SCC to undertake a review of the treaty every five years with an eye toward amendment or modernization as technologies and political circumstances change.

Termination of Treaties

States may terminate treaties in six basic ways: (1) according to the terms of the treaty itself; (2) by explicit or tacit agreement of the parties concerned; (3) through violation of the provisions of the agreement by one party, the second party then asserting, if it so desires, that it considers violation as terminating the treaty; (4) by one party on the grounds that fundamental conditions on which the treaty rests have changed; (5) through the emergence of a new peremptory norm of general international law conflicting with the treaty; and (6) through the outbreak of hostilities between parties to the agreement (Vienna Convention, Articles 54–64). A seventh, and obvious, cause of termination—particularly true in the case of bilateral agreements—is the disappearance (extinction) of one of the parties. Unless specified in the text, theoretically treaties are in effect forever. The fact that we have listed so many

---

[44]Text at www.fas.org/nuke/control/abmt/ (accessed August 1, 2005).

ways of termination indicates that few treaties will last forever, but we should note that this observation applies more to bilateral treaties than multilateral treaties.

Many treaties contain specific provisions about termination. In general, such provisions envisage three basic causes for the end of the agreement: lack of performance, arrival of a fixed termination date, and denunciation of the agreement as outlined therein. Some treaties end when the acts called for by the agreement have been performed by the parties involved. An example would be the voluntary cession of territory by sale. When the purchasing state has transmitted the appropriate sums to the selling state, the title to the affected area is transferred and the treaty is terminated. The actual documents remain, of course, as evidences of the transaction and may help settle any disputes about the performance of the acts involved.

Many treaties contain a specific expiration date. On that date, the treaty becomes null and void unless the parties have made appropriate arrangements for extending the life of the agreements, and the parties concerned have acted in accordance with that provision to extend their agreement's duration. Many treaties contain provisions permitting denunciation (sometimes termed *renunciation*) of the agreement. Usually such provisions set a minimum duration of the agreement. After the date on which this minimum life comes to an end, the treaty continues in force but may terminate when renounced by either party. Commonly termination, in regard to the renouncing party, does not occur immediately but after a time interval (six months or a year is a period frequently utilized) between the time the notice of denunciation was filed and the effective termination of the agreement for the denouncing party. For example, the ABM Treaty states that it shall be of "unlimited duration" but contains the following stipulation in Article XIV.2:

> Each Party shall, in exercising its national sovereignty, have the right to withdraw from this Treaty if it decides that extraordinary events related to the subject matter of this Treaty have jeopardized its supreme interests. It shall give notice of its decision to the other Party six months prior to withdrawal from the Treaty. Such notice shall include a statement of the extraordinary events the notifying Party regards as having jeopardized its supreme interests.

Obviously, any agreement between states may end by **mutual consent** of the parties to the instrument. Such agreement would normally take the form of a written declaration by which the parties state their intention to terminate. Similarly, states may terminate a treaty by implication—that is, through the conclusion of another treaty that obviously supersedes prior agreements among the same parties without mentioning such agreements in the text of the new instrument. And, on occasion, it appears that a treaty has been terminated by a tacit agreement among the parties involved to let the treaty lapse through nonobservance. In other words, each in turn fails to comply with the terms of the treaty, and no one protests such nonobservance, because all are in tacit agreement that they no longer wish to be bound by the provisions of the instrument.

Violations as a Cause for Termination   For obvious reasons, the questions here relate mainly to bilateral treaties. In the event that one of the states involved in a treaty violates any of its provisions, the treaty does not by that fact automatically become invalid or void. States may *not* unilaterally cancel a *mutual* obligation.

Many treaties, such as the ABM Treaty discussed earlier, contain provisions dealing with alleged violations (i.e., the SCC). Where treaties do not specify rules for resolving conflicts, this question has no good answer in the abstract because the answer or outcome really depends upon the nature and intent of the violation. Moreover, while in some ways the principles that apply to contracts in municipal law yield a parallel, those at the international level seem more imprecise and less evident in terms of consistent practice. At the very least, the other part may suspend its performance. *If* the violation is of such a nature that it has eliminated the basis for the agreement, and the state committing the violation has deliberately undertaken the action, clearly the requirement of good faith no longer applies. Under these circumstances, abrogation would seem permissible (see Article 60 of the Vienna Treaty concerning "material breach").[45] In some circumstances, a state may undertake an act of *retorsion* or *reprisal* as a measure of punishment in an effort to have the violator redress the grievance. We find few instances of punishment (see Chapter 1) because enforcement or "teaching a lesson" may affect other relationships and values (in particular, relationships and values involving third states).

Many multilateral treaties such as those setting up the WTO and the UNCLOS III contain explicit and compulsory dispute resolution mechanisms. The Charter of the United Nations contains a harsh-sounding approach to the question of unilateral violation. Article 6 states:

> a Member of the United Nations which has persistently violated the Principles contained in the present Charter may be expelled from the Organization of the General Assembly upon the recommendation of the Security Council.

This has never occurred.

Changed Circumstances Is a treaty void or voidable because circumstances have altered in fundamental ways since the agreement's inception? This question represents one of the most irritating problems in the realm of international agreements. Unilateral denunciation of a treaty on the grounds of changed circumstances has been accepted as a doctrine, though often regretfully, by almost all modern writers on international law. Since Vattel's time, the correctness of the concept of *rebus sic stantibus* has been recognized not only by writers but also by the secretary-general of the United Nations, in commenting on the termination of European treaties protecting minorities (between 1939 and 1947) through basic changes in conditions. Numerous modern court decisions have also referred to the doctrine, so that it may now be invoked by states. The ICJ itself affirmed the doctrine of *rebus sic stantibus* in the *Fisheries Jurisdiction* case [46] when it held that

> this principle and the conditions and exceptions to which it is subjected, have been embodied in Art. 62 of the Vienna Convention which may in many respects be considered as a codification of existing customary international law.

---

[45]Article 60(3) of the Vienna Convention says, "A material breach of a treaty, for the purpose of this article, consists in; (a) a repudiation of the treaty not sanctioned by the present Convention; or (b) the violation of a provision essential to the accomplishment of the object or purpose of the treaty."

[46]*United Kingdom v. Iceland, Jurisdiction*, ICJ Reports (1973), 18.

Article 62 of the Vienna Convention contains two conditions for the application of the doctrine: (1) the existence of the circumstances subsequently changed "must have constituted an essential basis of the consent of the parties to be bound by the treaty" (i.e., a fundamental change) and (2) the effect of the changes must have been such as "radically to transform the extent of obligations still to be performed under the treaty."

The real problem in the doctrine of *rebus sic stantibus* arises when one looks for its invocation in actual practice. Few writers and fewer diplomats appear to be able to agree on the circumstances under which the doctrine could be justifiably invoked. The most recent use of the doctrine involved the enormous Gabcíkovo–Nagymaros Project on the Danube River, originally based on a Hungarian–Czechoslovak treaty of 1977 (see Chapter 18). Hungary unilaterally terminated the treaty in 1992. A Special Agreement of July 2, 1993, between Hungary and the Slovak Republic submitted existing differences to the ICJ. In examining the circumstances in light of Article 62, the ICJ concluded:[47]

> The changed circumstances advanced by Hungary are, in the Court's view, not of such a nature, either individually or collectively, that their effect would radically transform the extent of the obligation still to be performed in order to accomplish the Project. A fundamental change of circumstance must have been unforeseen; the existence of the circumstances at the time of the Treaty's conclusion must have constituted an essential basis of the consent of the parties to be bound by the Treaty . . . [T]he stability of treaty relations requires that the plea of fundamental change of circumstances be applied only in exceptional cases.

An Interesting Question: Termination in the United States   President Jimmy Carter chose to terminate the Mutual Defense Treaty with the Republic of China in accordance with the terms of the instrument. He invoked Article X of the 1954 treaty, which stated that termination would occur after one year's notice by either party. This was fully in accord with Article 67(2) of the Vienna Convention:

> Any act declaring invalid, terminating, withdrawing from or suspending the operation of a treaty pursuant to the provisions of the treaty or of paragraphs 2 or 3 of Article 65 shall be carried out through an instrument communicated to the other parties. If the instrument is not signed by the Head of State, Head of Government or Minister for Foreign Affairs, the representatives of the state communicating it may be called upon to produce full powers.

The arguments concerning the legal aspects of President Carter's termination of the Mutual Defense Treaty with the Republic of China did not address the *international law* aspects of the matter. Rather, they related to internal questions of constitutional authority (separation of powers). The U.S. Constitution gives the president the power to make treaties with the advice and consent of the Senate. The Constitution is silent concerning who may "unmake" (i.e., terminate) a treaty. President Carter's critics argued that logic dictated that, if the president

---

[47]*Case Concerning the Gabcíkovo–Nagymaros Project (Hungary v. Slovakia)*, International Court of Justice, Judgment of September 25, 1997, General List No. 92, www.icj-cij.org/docket/files/92/7375.pdf.

could make a treaty only with the advice and consent of the Senate, then the president also needed the advice and consent of the Senate to "unmake" (terminate) a treaty.[48] He had no authority to do it unilaterally. The Supreme Court determined this to be a nonjusticiable "political question"—something that had to be decided between the executive and the Congress. By leaving controversy moot, the Court in essence approved the president's action.

One further note here: No rule of international law requires that all treaties with a "derecognized" government terminate automatically with the end of recognition, provided the agreements in question relate to the area (territory) actually under the control of the derecognized government. Hence the U.S. government announced, some time after the denunciation of the Mutual Defense Treaty, that the slightly fewer than 60 other agreements concluded earlier with the Republic of China (Taiwan) would be regarded as continuing in force.[49]

SUGGESTED READINGS

EXECUTIVE AGREEMENTS

CASES

Dames & Moore v. Reagan, 453 U.S. 654, 101 S.Ct. 2972 (1981).

United States v. Guy W. Capps, Inc., U.S. Court of Appeals, 204 Fed. Reporter, 2nd Series 665, in 48 AJIL 154 (1954).

TREATY INTERPRETATION

Gardner, *Treaty Interpretation* (2008).

McDougal, Lasswell, Miller, *The Interpretation of Agreements and World Public Order Principles of Content and Procedure* (1994).

TREATIES: GENERAL

Aust, *Modern Treaty Law* (2007).

Cannizzaro, *The Law of Treaties Beyond the Vienna Convention* (2011).

Chiu, *The People's Republic of China and the Law of Treaties* (1999).

Cohen, *Negotiating Across Cultures: Communication Obstacles in International Diplomacy* (rev. ed. 1997).

Lauterpacht, *Oppenheim*, I: 877.

Piris, *The Lisbon Treaty: A Legal and Political Analysis* (2010).

Reisenfield, "The Doctrine of Self-Executing Treaties and *U.S. v. Postal*: Win at Any Price?" 74 *AJIL* 892 (1980).

---

[48]*Goldwater et al. v. Carter et al.,* U.S. Court of Appeals, DC, November 30, 1979, 617 F.2d 697, in 18 *ILM* 1488 (1979). See especially 1501–1502 on the presidential power to recognize governments and to void a treaty without congressional action. On appeal, the Supreme Court vacated the judgment of the court of appeals and remanded the case to the district court with directions to dismiss the complaint: U.S. Supreme Court, No. 79–856, December 13, 1979, in 19 *ILM* 239 (1980), and in 74 *AJIL* 441 (1980). On the other hand, see the *Memorandum, Termination of Treaties: International Rules and Internal United States Procedure,* by the deputy assistant legal adviser for Foreign Affairs, Department of State, in Whiteman, XIV, 461, in which the author asserted that "matters of policy or special circumstances may make it appear to be advisable or necessary to obtain the concurrence or support of Congress or the Senate."

[49]*New York Times* (December 18, 1978), A1, A10; see also U.S. Pub. L. 96–8, the "Taiwan Relations Act" of April 10, 1979, in 18 *ILM* 873 (1979). See also United States Senate Foreign Relations Committee, *Termination of Treaties: The Constitutional Allocation of Power* (2005).

POWER TO CONCLUDE TREATIES

Asakura v. City of Seattle, U.S. Supreme Court, 1924, 265 U.S. 332.

Raffington v. Cangemi, 399 F.3d 900; 2005 (8th Cir. 2004), U.S. App. LEXIS 1809.

WHO and Dole v. Carter, U.S. Court of Appeals, 10th Cir., 1977, 569 F.2d 1109, in 72 *AJIL* 665 (1978).

Interpretation of the 1919 Convention Concerning Employment of Women During the Night, Advisory Opinion, *PCIJ,* Ser. A/B, Nso. 50 (1932).

VALIDITY, INVALIDITY, AND TERMINATION OF TREATIES

David, *The Strategy of Treaty Termination: Lawful Breaches and Retaliations* (1975).

Henkin, "Litigating the President's Power to Terminate Treaties," 73 *AJIL* 647 (1979).

Kontou, *The Termination and Revision of Treaties in Light of New Customary International Law* (1995).

Scheffer, "The Law of Treaty Termination as Applied to the United States De-recognition of the Republic of China," 19 *Harvard Int'l. L.J.* 931 (1978).

United States Senate Foreign Relations Committee, *Termination of Treaties: The Constitutional Allocation of Power* (2005).

International Legal Process

O ne prominent analyst has defined a dispute as "a specific disagreement concerning a matter of fact, law or policy in which a claim or assertion of one party is met with refusal, counter-claim, or denial by another."[1] Because politics involves questions about the control, use, and distribution of scarce tangible and intangible resources, conflict is built into the system. As we have discussed in Chapters 1 and 2, the organization of the system into sovereign states of varying size and economic capacity means that disputes over allocation of coveted or needed resources occur as a matter of course. Scarcity means that often states may want the same thing or have issues over how certain resources are apportioned.[2] Prevailing ideas about appropriate policy means and ends may also promote conflict. As we noted in Chapter 2, globalization has provided many incentives that encourage cooperation, but it also has produced situations that fuel great discontent as well. Many in lesser developed countries see globalization as promoting policies that permit states (and individuals) who already have great advantage, to attain greater advantage. Nonetheless, the techniques and procedures we shall discuss in this chapter do not focus on why or how conflicts occur, but rather on the means and methods available to parties to help them resolve conflicts in a dispute when they do occur. More narrowly, we will focus on techniques relevant to resolving disputes over legal issues.

Several observations seem appropriate here. First, disputes obviously vary in terms of intensity and thus importance to states. Not every issue entails a matter of vital interests, although the anarchic nature of the international system permits the governing authorities of each state to attach whatever level of importance they choose to any dispute no matter how trivial it may seem to third-party observers. Ethiopia and Eritrea fought a bloody war (more than 100,000 casualties) ostensibly over a border dispute that involved a few square miles of desert.[3] Second,

---

[1] J. G. Merrills, *International Dispute Settlement,* 5th ed. (Cambridge University Press, 2011), 1.

[2] See, D. Easton, *The Political System. An Inquiry into the State of Political* Science (1953); H. Lasswell, *Politics: Who Gets What, When, How* (1935).

[3] Global Issues (December 20, 2000), www.globalissues.org/article/89/conflict-between-ethiopia-and-eritrea.

although the methods discussed in this chapter may be used to resolve legal disputes, *not every dispute between states involves a breach of a legal obligation.* Third, even when legal principles do have relevance, or when a breach of legal obligation has occurred, the resolution of the dispute may not involve strict adherence to legal principles and procedures. As we noted in Chapter 1, although lawyers may be involved, dispute resolution at the international level often involves political officials whose goals, methods of operation, fact collection, reasoning, and standards of evaluation may be far different from those utilized by lawyers and judges. As we shall discuss later in this chapter, at the international level, a bias against formal judicial methods exists because legal methods do seek to insulate the decision process from the vagaries of political decision. Remember that lawyers and judges seek comparable and reliable answers to similar situations. Politicians-statesmen seek acceptable solutions. These two ends may often be incompatible. Moreover, this points out an important point: The role of law in dispute resolution and the role of adjudication in dispute resolution form two different sets of considerations. By definition, adjudication requires law, but legal principles may play a role absent a framework for adjudication. As we shall see later, the use of law without adjudication defines the normal circumstance in international politics.[4]

Note that the process of resolving disputes at the domestic level may often involve procedures other than litigation in court (alternative dispute resolution or ADR). For certain types of domestic civil or administrative law cases—divorce or other contractual problems, for example—the parties may prefer mediation or arbitration to litigation. A district attorney may prefer a plea bargain (negotiation) to trial for many reasons. In comparison to most domestic legal systems, the international legal process involves a myriad of methods, with formal methods of adjudication ranking near the bottom in preference. We will discuss the role of courts in some detail in a separate chapter (Chapter 17).

This chapter will focus on peaceful means of resolving disputes. We will examine the legitimate use of force as a sanction or response to disputes and the law that regulates the conduct of the use of force in Chapters 20 and 21. For reasons we discussed in earlier chapters, the use of force has played a central role in the evolution of the Westphalian state system. Nonetheless, beginning with the treaties of Westphalia, every treaty that ended a major conflict has had within it an obligation to use peaceful means to settle disputes.[5] The reasons states continued to resort to war flowed from the simple fact that, despite the increasing costs of war, no viable alternatives were available. The treaties may have included aspirational obligations, but did not spell out specific arrangements by which these goals might be accomplished. Even if the treaties had contained language that set up mechanisms for resolution, the material elements, both tangible and intangible, necessary to support their application in practice

---

[4]See J. L. Taulbee, "The Politics of International Law," in *International Law Contemporary Issues and Future Developments,* edited by S. Silverburg (2011).

[5]See K. J. Holsti, *Peace and War: Armed Conflicts and International Order 1648–1989* (1991); F. H. Hinsley, *Power and the Pursuit of Peace* (1963).

were absent. Not until the latter part of the nineteenth century, as the Industrial Revolution and its accompanying ideas took widespread hold in Western Europe and the United States, did the idea of "peaceful settlement" as a normal course of action gain currency.

In the contemporary system, Article 2(3) of the UN Charter obligates states to "settle their international disputes by peaceful means in such a manner that international peace and security, and justice, are not endangered." Article 33(1) further requires that "The parties to any dispute, the continuance of which is likely to endanger the maintenance of international peace and security, shall, first of all, seek a solution by negotiation, enquiry, mediation, conciliation, arbitration, judicial settlement, resort to regional agencies or arrangements, or other peaceful means of their own choice." Some of these—conciliation and inquiry, for example—are seldom used. As international law has evolved, many multilateral treaties such as the United Nations Convention on the Law of the Sea (UNCLOS III) and the World Trade Organization (WTO) now include procedures to resolve disagreements among the parties. Failure to achieve compliance through the normal methods for peacefully settling disputes can lead to the imposition of sanctions.

These techniques should not be taken as self-contained, independent methods in that the use of one might preclude another. In many cases they may form complementary or even additive procedures. For example, negotiation will form part of an agreement to set up mediation, conciliation, or arbitration, or to submit the dispute to the International Court of Justice.[6] Consider as well that the goals of the states involved will determine the selection of a particular technique. One should *not* presume that finding an immediate solution is the most immediate concern of the parties in a dispute. Building external support for your position, "taking the high road" as a matter of prestige and reputation, or merely as a way of seeking to delay any effort to resolve in hope that unfavorable circumstances might change in your favor, may be interim goals.

DIPLOMATIC CORRESPONDENCE: GOVERNMENT-TO-GOVERNMENT CLAIM OR NEGOTIATION

Lodging protests through normal diplomatic channels forms the oldest and most used method for addressing violations of international law or resolving other disputes. Diplomatic correspondence utilizes the normal adversarial briefs designed to give the most advantageous construction to the facts and the applicable law. Anyone examining the exchange must understand the partisan and contentious nature of the process and seek to evaluate the totality of the correspondence. States prefer this method for many claims because it gives them a measure of control over the outcome. Negotiation uses normal diplomatic channels.

---

[6]See, for example, the website of the American Arbitration Association, www.adr.org/sp.asp?id=33994; see also U.S. Government, "Primer on International Alternative Dispute Resolutions" (March 2005), www.osec.doc.gov/ogc/occic/adr.html.

MORTENSEN V. PETERS

Great Britain, High Court of Justiciary of Scotland, 1906 (1906) 8 S.C., 5th Series, 99, 14 Scot. L.T227

Facts

Appeal from decision of a sheriff who had imposed a fine of £50, with the alternative of 15 days in prison.

Mortensen, a Danish citizen resident in England and master of a trawler registered in Norway, had been charged with violating the Sea Fisheries Act and Herring Fisheries (Scotland) Act by "otter trawling" in the Moray Firth at a distance of more than 3 marine, or nautical, miles (approximately 1.15 statute, or land, miles) from the nearest land. The statutes in question, and a bylaw enacted by the Fishery Board in 1892, forbade the fishing method in question in the Moray Firth, that body of water having a mouth of approximately 75 miles across from point to point.[*] Mortensen appealed, arguing that the statutes and bylaw applied only to British subjects or to persons within British territory and that the place in question—that is, the location where the alleged violation of law had taken place—was outside British territory under international law and hence not subject to the statutes and bylaw.

Peters, the procurator-fiscal of the Court, argued in reply that the terms of the statutes and bylaw were universal and that even if international law were applied, the offense had been committed in British waters, and that even if the Moray Firth were not part of British territory for all purposes, the British government was fully entitled to undertake protective measures as regards fishing in those waters.[†]

Issues

1. Whether a British statute applied not only to British subjects but also to all other persons within British territory
2. Whether the waters of the Moray Firth outside the 3-mile limit were British territorial waters and hence subject to British jurisdiction
3. Whether domestic courts were bound by a statute contravening a rule of international law

Decision

The court ruled unanimously in the affirmative on all three issues and upheld Mortensen's conviction.

Reasoning

See discussion in Chapter 6.

Resolution

Following the decision in *Mortensen v. Peters,* several foreign masters of trawlers registered in Norway were arrested and

(*continued*)

---

[*]Normally the territorial sea of Great Britain, at that time, extended *3 marine miles* from the low-tide mark; hence, a body of water fronting on the ocean and having a width at the mouth of 75 miles included a goodly portion of waters termed *high seas,* not subject to the jurisdiction of the coastal state. See Chapter 12 for a detailed discussion of the subject of territorial waters.

[†]The Norwegian registration of Mortensen's vessel by its British owners represented a common subterfuge adopted at that time by British operators of fishing vessels, apparently to avoid compliance with the protective legislation that, they believed, did not apply to ships flying a foreign flag and plying their trade beyond the 3-mile limit.

convicted in Scotland for the same offense in the same place. They were released, however, following *a series of protests by the Norwegian government.* Norway then issued a warning to all trawlers registered under its flag that no further diplomatic protection would be extended if charges of illegal fishing in the Moray Firth were lodged against them. It also amended its own regulations to make it more difficult to register foreign vessels in Norway.

The British Foreign Office in turn admitted through Mr. Walter Runciman in the House of Commons in 1907 that the Fisheries Acts as interpreted in the Mortensen case were "in conflict with international law." Subsequently, Parliament enacted a statute prohibiting the landing and selling in Great Britain of any fish caught by prohibited methods in the prohibited areas in question.

Needless to say, the process has a high political content. The resulting negotiations may produce a settlement that achieves a satisfactory result for the parties but leaves the legal issues unresolved. The exchange may not successfully resolve the issues. Success in the end depends upon the willingness of the parties to seek a negotiated solution, which in turn relies upon mutual flexibility and goodwill. Hence, diplomatic exchange may not resolve the issues. We will examine the claims process in some detail later in Chapter 11 ("State Responsibility: Responsibility for Injuries to Aliens"). The *Mortensen* case furnishes an interesting example of how diplomatic correspondence/protest may work in practice.

Note that, in the aftermath of this controversy, *both* states altered their policies. Norway tightened up its regulations regarding ship registration, thereby acknowledging a problem and the desire to avoid future conflicts. Great Britain changed its legislation from a questionable extension of legislative authority to a law prohibiting actions that it clearly had the authority and absolute right to control. The new law prohibited activity falling clearly within Great Britain's own *territorial jurisdiction.* You should make note of the legal issues in this case because we shall return to this case and the other issues in Chapter 6 when discussing the relationship between international law and domestic law.

The *Case Concerning the Conservation and Sustainable Exploitation of Swordfish Stocks in the South-Eastern Pacific Ocean* (Chile v. The European Union) illustrates the interrelationship between negotiation and other means of settlement.[7] In December 2000 the two parties submitted the dispute to the International Tribunal for the Law of the Sea (ITLOS). After a series of postponements, the two parties began bilateral negotiations that resulted in an agreement in November 2009. The two parties then notified the ITLOS that they had reached mutual agreement on a settlement and requested withdrawal of the case.

Although states may prefer negotiation as a method, the technique has some important limitations. Effectiveness depends upon normal diplomatic relations and a strong common interest in finding a solution. The absence of formal diplomatic ties does not preclude all contacts, but it does seriously inhibit communication. In addition, the ability to negotiate an acceptable solution directly depends

---

[7]Order, *Case Concerning the Conservation and Sustainable Exploitation of Swordfish Stocks in the South-Eastern Pacific Ocean* (Chile v. The European Union), ITLOS (Case No. 7) (December 16, 2009).

upon the level of consensus (compatibility) between the disputants. A lack of formal relations often reflects a serious rift between the states. If so, then the material conditions necessary for a settlement in terms of common interests will not be present. Simply stated, resolution through negotiation depends upon how much value states place upon what is at stake. The level of consensus between them will play a major role in determining value in both tangible and intangible factors. In many cases, a combination of low level of consensus and the high value of the stakes at issue will preclude a negotiated settlement. The questions surrounding creation of an independent state of Palestine, or those surrounding the dispute over Kashmir between India and Pakistan, provide good examples here.

Inquiry and Fact-Finding

In any dispute, domestic or international, establishing the facts relating to the incident to the satisfaction of both parties forms one of the most challenging tasks. Remember that diplomatic exchanges constitute the equivalent of adversarial briefs. In some cases, states may resort to third parties—that is, states or organizations not involved in the dispute—to undertake an investigation to establish the facts. Early in the twentieth century, commissions of inquiry enjoyed some prominence in the international law community. Article 9 of the 1907 Hague Convention (drawn from the 1899 Hague Convention) defined the task of a commission of inquiry as follows: "to facilitate a solution by means of an impartial and conscientious investigation."[8] Commissions of inquiry have proven useful although seldom used. In his comprehensive study, Merrills lists only six cases in the period 1900 to date (Table 5.1).

Beginning in the administration of President Woodrow Wilson and lasting until the outbreak of World War II, the United States negotiated 48 bilateral treaties that included commissions of inquiry as the preferred method of resolving disputes.[9] The Letelier and Moffitt Case listed in Table 5.1 is the sole instance in

TABLE 5.1	
Cases Involving Inquiry (1900–Date)	
The Dogger Bank	Russia and Great Britain (1904)
The *Tavignani*	France and Italy (1912)
The *Tiger*	Norway and Germany (1917)
The *Tribantia*	Netherlands and Germany (1916/1922)
The *Red Crusader*	Denmark and United Kingdom (1961)
Letelier and Moffitt Case	Chile and United States (1976/1988–1990)

---

[8]*Hague Convention (I) for the Pacific Settlement of International Disputes,* October 18, 1907, 54. LNTS 435; 2 *American Journal of International Law* Supp 43: full text available from the Avalon Project, www.yale.edu/lawweb/avalon/lawofwar/pacific.htm.

[9]N. Bar-Yaacov, *The Handling of International Disputes by Inquiry* (London: Oxford University Press 1974), ch. 5.

which any of these treaties played a part. In theory, impartial fact-finding would seem a good way to resolve disputes, but in contemporary practice, states rarely resort to formal commissions of inquiry, investigative commissions, or other formal mechanisms types of third-party fact-finding.

While states have seldom utilized formal commissions of inquiry, the League of Nations, the United Nations, and various regional international organizations have found it a useful method. Nongovernmental organizations (NGOs) such as Amnesty International, the International Committee of the Red Cross, and Human Rights Watch; various UN agencies; and other interested parties regularly monitor the compliance of states with various treaties and prepare reports on their findings independent of specific requests.[10] For example, the United Nations Commission on Human Rights (UNCHR) monitors problems related to its more than 40 thematic mandates (e.g., torture, extrajudicial execution, rights of the child, and violence against women; see Chapter 15). In the strictest sense, these activities do not comprise fact-finding or inquiry. Still, the information gathered may furnish states with an outside view of the facts in a particular situation.

Good Offices, Facilitation, and Mediation

The techniques of good offices, facilitation, and mediation all center on encouraging states to resolve their disputes themselves through negotiations. A third state, an intergovernmental organization (IGO), an individual such as the secretary-general of the United Nations or the pope, or a group of states may seek to move states toward direct negotiation. None of these methods alone produces legally binding obligations as an outcome. Resolution still depends upon the will of the parties to accept and act on the end result.

A third party may extend *good offices,* an offer to act as a go-between, to persuade states to enter into negotiations to end a dispute. In this capacity, the state or states proffering the service may shuttle messages and suggestions back and forth but will have no other role. If negotiations result, the role of the third party comes to an end.

Facilitation may be defined as "extended" good offices. As a technique, it occupies an intermediate position between good offices and mediation. Because facilitation often seems only a stage in moving disputing parties to mediation or to other forms of settlement, analysts often ignore it altogether as a separate process. The facilitator's role goes beyond setting up the negotiations to undertaking tasks associated with the negotiations themselves and devising strategies to keep the talks going once started. Unlike mediators, who take an active part in the substantive exchange between parties, facilitators make no proposals but focus on ways to keep communication flowing between the principals.[11] This may entail secret "back-channel" talks, funding, or simply providing a neutral place to meet and supplying appropriate support services. In contemporary practice, facilitation

---

[10]See, for example, Report of the High Commissioner for Human Rights, "Situation of Human Rights in the Darfur Region of the Sudan," U.N. Doc. E/CN.4/2005/3, May 7, 2004.

[11]H. van der Merwe, "Facilitation and Mediation in South Africa: Three Case Studies," www.gmu.edu/academic/pcs/vander~1.htm.

often plays an important part in moving parties in internal conflicts to engage in face-to-face negotiations.[12]

In contrast to facilitators, *mediators* take an active role in the negotiations between parties. An obvious prerequisite for a mediator is the perception by *both* parties of impartiality. Mediators may shuttle proposals back and forth, clarify points, evaluate consequences, or even make their own proposals for settlement. The role is difficult because active engagement may produce perceptions of bias by one side or the other. The product of mediation does not legally bind either party. The Camp David Accords (Egypt and Israel) and the Beagle Channel dispute (Chile and Argentina) represent prominent and often-cited examples of successful mediation. Because of the political interplay and consequent difficulties over the course of the dispute, we have chosen to highlight the Beagle Channel dispute.

▶ THE BEAGLE CHANNEL DISPUTE[13]

Argentina v. Chile

Facts

The Beagle Channel conflict involved a dispute over the exact location of the border between Argentina and Chile. The dispute centered on three islands south of Tierra del Fuego—Picton, Nueva, and Lennox.[14] The islands are barren and virtually uninhabited, but because of their geostrategic position, their ownership has great importance for navigation rights, claims to other islands in the area, the delimitation of the Strait of Magellan, and questions relating to the maritime boundaries south of Cape Horn. These questions included possible competing claims to portions of Antarctica.

Demarcation of the border had been in contention from the earliest days of Argentina and Chile as independent countries. The Boundary Treaty of 1881 attempted a definitive solution, but omitted an important consideration. It failed to specify the eastern terminus of the Beagle Channel. Because the treaty granted Chile possession of all islands south of the channel, the longitudinal range (and exact course) of the channel became a key ongoing question.[15] Between

(continued)

---

[12]Van der Merwe, note 11; see also A. Kelleher and J. L. Taulbee, "Building Peace Norwegian Style: Studies in Track I 1/2 Diplomacy," in *Subcontracting Peace: The Challenges of NGO Peacebuilding*, edited by O. P. Richmond and H. F.. Carey (2005); and J. Bercovitch, *Studies in International Mediation* (2003).

[13]See M. Laudy, "The Vatican Mediation of the Beagle Channel Dispute: Crisis Intervention and Forum Building," www.mendeley.com/research/vatican-mediation-beagle-channel-dispute-crisis-intervention-forum-building-1/.

[14]Tierra del Fuego (literally "land of fire") is an archipelago at the southernmost tip of South America. An 1881 treaty divided the area between Argentina and Chile. The archipelago consists of a main island (Isla Grande de Tierra del Fuego, often called Tierra del Fuego as well) and a group of smaller islands. The Strait of Magellan separates the archipelago from the continent. The southern point of the archipelago, in Chile, forms Cape Horn. See "Tierra del Fuego," Wikipedia, http://en.wikipedia.org/wiki/Tierra_del_Fuego.

[15]Laudy, note 13, at 295.

1915 and 1964, there were at least five unsuccessful attempts to submit the issues to arbitration.[16]

The issues became more salient with changes in the law of the sea during the mid-twentieth century. When Chile and Argentina signed the Boundary Treaty, international customary law limited claims to territorial waters to 3 nautical miles. The negotiations for UNCLOS III (opened for ratification in 1982) had clearly indicated a widespread consensus for 12 nautical miles of territorial seas and for an additional claim to a 200-mile exclusive economic zone (EEZ). In addition, a Chilean law establishing a controversial method of drawing baselines to delimit its territorial seas raised issues concerning navigation, military security, and fishing rights in areas Argentina considered crucially important.[17]

In 1971, the two countries signed an agreement to submit the dispute to binding arbitration under the auspices of Great Britain. The arbitral court consisted of five judges from the International Court of Justice. In May 1977, the panel awarded the three islands to Chile and established a boundary running roughly through the center of the channel. Subsequent negotiations between the two states over implementation proved unfruitful. Argentina repudiated the British award in January 1978. Tension between the two states over the issues heightened to the point of imminent war. Further negotiations failed to produce a settlement. Argentina accepted a Chilean proposal for mediation in November, but the two governments could not agree upon an acceptable mediator. At this point, Pope John Paul II informed the two governments that he would send a personal envoy to meet with the two governments in an effort to resolve the dispute.

The negotiations proceeded slowly until a change in government in Argentina (a return to democratic rule) in December 1983. The two parties then rapidly negotiated a settlement. The Treaty of Peace and Friendship was signed in Rome in November 1984.

Issue

What longitudinal point formed the eastern terminus of the Beagle Channel?

Outcome

Argentina renounced title to the islands. Chile dropped its demand for joint use of the Argentine maritime zone and accepted a relatively narrow territorial sea.

Note

Mediation clearly has high political content. Settlements rely on the willingness of the parties to accept the terms. The domestic political situation in Argentina during most of the dispute clearly inhibited progress toward settlement. The military leadership feared that making concessions to Chile would be a "face-losing" proposition that might result in domestic problems. While the change in government played the pivotal role, in this case the moral authority of the pope may have prevented a war, and the pressure of other potential political and economic trends softened the impact of the cession.[18]

---

[16]Laudy, note 13, at 299.

[17]Laudy, note 13, at 296.

[18]Laudy, note 13, at 315, 316.

Conciliation

As a method, conciliation involves a Commission, set up by the parties, that has the task of finding "terms of settlement susceptible of being accepted by them," or providing other aid upon request.[19] Conciliation differs from inquiry in that the commissioners make explicit proposals for settlement. It differs from mediation in that the commissioners do not participate in an ongoing exchange of proposals between the parties, although the process may involve ongoing input from the disputants. The primary duties of a conciliation commission are to investigate the situation surrounding the dispute and suggest grounds for a possible settlement. In practice the commission may do much more depending upon the nature of the instructions and presentations of the parties. As with arbitration, much depends upon the protocol (treaty, understanding) that sets up the process. The instructions in the protocol setting up the process may narrowly define the issues, or otherwise constrict the duties, functions, and mission of the commission, or they may permit a considerable amount of independent initiative and inquiry.

The process of conciliation may utilize a commission of inquiry, but does not necessarily have to do so. If it chooses to do so, the parties do not have to accept the results of the inquiry, nor do they have to accept the proposals for settlement developed by the Commission. Indeed, acceptance of the proposed settlement presumably has no impact beyond the fact that the parties have come to an agreement. Agreements have no value in terms of precedent. According to a widely cited report of the *Institut de Droit International*, "the acceptance by one party of a proposal of settlement in no way implies any admission by it of the considerations of law or of fact that may have inspired the proposal of settlement"[20]

For our purposes, we will focus upon the role of conciliation in resolving disputes over treaty obligations. In the early 1920's several treaties specified conciliation as a method to resolve differences. These early treaties, however, did not contain any language that provided guidance with respect to the specific procedures that states might utilize when deciding upon "conciliation" as a method of resolving differences. A 1925 treaty between France and Switzerland defined the process in terms that became a model for later treaties.[21] Post World War II, the use of conciliation in resolving disputes relating to bilateral treaties declined. Interestingly, during the same period, many significant multilateral treaties incorporated conciliation as a method of resolving disputes between and among states parties. In particular, treaties involving commercial interests, human rights, and environmental protection specify conciliation as a method of reconciling differences. Table 5.2 indicates a few of the more important treaties that include this method.

Conciliation works best when the issues are primarily legal, the interests involved are of secondary importance, and the parties wish an equitable solution.[22] In terms of negatives, conciliation is expensive and nonbinding. As we have

---

[19]Institute of International Law, *Regulations on the Procedure of International Conciliation* (30th Commission: Salzburg 1961), Article 1, www.idi-iil.org/idiE/resolutionsE/1961_salz_02_en.pdf.

[20]Institute of International Law, note 19, Preamble.

[21]Merrills, note 1, at 59.

[22]Merrills, note 1, at 81.

> ### TABLE 5.2
>
> **Selected Multilateral Treaties Incorporating Conciliation (1945–2011)**
>
> Pact of Bogota (1948)
> European Convention on Human Rights (1950)
> European Convention for the Peaceful Settlement of Disputes (1957)
> Vienna Convention on the Law of Treaties (1969)
> Vienna Convention on the Succession of States with Respect to Treaties (1978)
> Convention on the Representation of States in Their Relations with International
>   Organizations of a Universal Character (1975)
> Vienna Convention for the Protection of the Ozone Layer (1985)
> Convention on Biological Diversity (1992)
> Energy Charter Treaty (1994)

pointed out earlier with respect to other nonbinding methods, many other forums and techniques are available including the United Nations as well as various intergovernmental organizations that deal with specific functional issue areas.

Arbitration and Judicial Settlement

To this point, we have focused on the techniques that involve or encourage direct state-to-state engagement as the preferred method of dispute resolution. Alternatively, states may elect to use an arbitration tribunal or an international court. These methods embody the idea of an impartial "third-party" participation that produces a *binding* settlement on the parties. This idea springs from the role of adjudication in domestic legal systems. Still, the use of these options depends upon the willingness of governments to commit to procedures where they do not have a measure of control over the result. Political consideration becomes very important because arbitration and judicial proceedings yield legally binding decisions in a process where the participants can exert only indirect influence after the process begins. When a state moves to adjudication, it loses much control over the factors that might influence the final proposal for settlement. At the international level, judicial means will work only if the states involved have agreed to accept the outcome of the process.

Arbitration may involve either a single prominent individual chosen by both sides or, more usually, a commission consisting of one member from each state and a neutral member chosen by mutual agreement. States may choose more members if they wish to do so. While we will explore the use of arbitration in settling claims more thoroughly in Chapters 11 and 17, the following case represents a classic example of arbitration in practice. Note that the panel comprised five commissioners instead of the more normal three.

Courts

The International Court of Justice (ICJ), the newly formed International Criminal Court (ICC), the International Criminal Tribunal for Yugoslavia (ICTY), the

International Criminal Tribunal for Rwanda (ICTR), the Special Court for Sierra Leone (SCSL), the Special Tribunal for Cambodia (STC), the European Court of Justice, and the European Court of Human Rights represent the judicial ideal in contemporary international relations. Some treaties further specify that alleged violations should be referred to the ICJ. Other treaty regimes, the WTO, and UNCLOS III have their own dispute resolution procedures as part of the treaty provisions. While falling far short of the ideals associated with its founding, the ICJ still has greatly influenced the development of contemporary international law. States do not regularly refer contentious cases to the ICJ, but as with its predecessor, the Permanent Court of International Justice (PCIJ), opinions issued by 15 prominent international jurists carry a great deal of weight. Because it represents a new institution, the ICC does not yet have a history to evaluate. However, an examination of the politics surrounding its creation and the ongoing political saga over its possible jurisdiction (U.S. opposition) can help us understand the possibilities and limits of judicial means.

THE ALABAMA CLAIMS COMMISSION

United States v. Great Britain (1872)

The Alabama claims arose out of the U.S. Civil War. The Treaty of Washington in 1871 set up the Alabama Claims Commission to adjudicate claims based upon the U.S. contention that Great Britain had failed to enforce its neutrality laws diligently during the Civil War. The United States contended that commerce raiders built in British shipyards caused great material loss during the war. The panel consisted of five members: one each from the United States and Great Britain, one named by the king of Italy, one by the president of the Swiss Confederation, and one by the Emperor of Brazil. The panel began its deliberations in Geneva in December 1871.

Facts

Confederate agents had contracted for warships from British boatyards; but to circumvent British neutrality laws, they had disguised their intent by characterizing the construction as merchant vessels. The Confederate States of America (CSA)

had always intended to use the ships as commerce raiders. The most successful of these cruisers was the *Alabama,* launched on July 29, 1862. The *Alabama* captured 58 Northern merchant ships before a U.S. warship engaged and sank it in June 1864 off the coast of France. Besides the *Alabama,* other British-built ships in the Confederate Navy included the *Florida, Georgia, Rappahannock,* and *Shenandoah.* Together, they sank more than 150 Northern ships and impelled much of the U.S. merchant marine to adopt foreign registry.

The United States demanded compensation from Britain for the damage wrought by the British-built, Southern-operated commerce raiders, based on the argument that the British government, by aiding the creation of a Confederate Navy, had failed to enforce its neutrality laws diligently.

Issue

Could Britain be held *internationally responsible* (at fault) for failing to interdict the escape of the five ships?

(continued)

Decision

The panel voted 4–1 for the United States (the British commissioner dissenting, of course). In the case of the *Alabama* and the *Florida,* the panel found Great Britain had failed to fulfill its neutrality obligations: it had permitted the vessels to be constructed within British jurisdiction, had failed to detain them, and later had extended the convenience of its colonial ports. With the *Shenandoah,* there was no fault in permitting departure; but later, the British had permitted the ship to recruit crews and augment its armament in Australia.

No responsibility attached for the other two vessels. The British paid the sum of $15,500,000 in gold to settle all claims.

Reasoning

The decision turned upon the definitions of the standards of alertness defined by *due diligence.*[†] The United States maintained that the standard must be a diligence keyed to the power of the state and the magnitude of the results of any potential negligence. The British countered that due diligence meant that a state was not bound to exercise more care than it would for its own safety.

SANCTIONS AND CENTRALIZED ENFORCEMENT

Inevitably, because of our experience with—and the resulting default assumptions about—the domestic law model, we all immediately focus on centralized measures of enforcement. The extensive discussion of *decentralized techniques* should help place the role of *centralized enforcement* in perspective. Not every alleged violation of an international obligation reaches the point of threatening international peace and security—that is, when it becomes a concern of more than just the states involved in the dispute. As we noted earlier, failure of a state to perform an obligation that may have limited or localized effect on states affected by the action will not automatically generate a response from any central authority in an effort to compel compliance. In the greatest majority of cases, action to repair the breach will involve a bilateral or limited multilateral context. Hence, we need to understand when central enforcement may apply and when it may not.

The methods of enforcement discussed thus far seldom involve issues of international peace and security. States use these methods to resolve the problems arising from everyday interaction. **In this respect, you should consider how few issues do actually raise real problems of international peace and security.** Of course, states may always refer a dispute to a universal international organization such as the General Assembly or Security Council of the United Nations or to a regional agency such as the OAS. States seldom do so willingly, for the same reasons, they seldom utilize judicial means of settlement.

To this point, we have tried to emphasize how complex the question of enforcement and compliance may be. Seldom does an allegation or an act of non-compliance raise the "thieves ought to be punished" model. In noting this, we did *not* mean to imply "thieves are seldom punished" as the appropriate standard when considering the effectiveness of international law. *The important point is that "punishment" may not reflect what a state or government may want in many*

[†]Make note of this term. It plays a part in some cases discussed later in the book.

situations. Moreover, at the international level, thieves can and do get punished—perhaps as often as burglars or car thieves do in the U.S. criminal justice system.

Sanctions

States do not have the right to resort unilaterally to forcible means of seeking compliance for most alleged breaches of obligations. The UN Charter, which most have ratified or otherwise acknowledged, forbids *the use of force* by individual states except in self-defense. This does not mean that individual states cannot impose a sanction when another state fails to honor a legal obligation.

Older textbooks often mention two techniques available to states as possible enforcement tools: *retorsion* and *reprisal. Retorsion* refers to perfectly legal, but unfriendly actions a state may take in response to a violation. For example, a state could cut off economic or military aid or pass legislation eliminating certain privileges (see the section "Reciprocity," Chapter 1) granted on a reciprocal basis to nationals of the offending state. A *reprisal* is an ***illegal*** act justified by the prior violation. A state might cancel a treaty unilaterally or raise tariffs only on goods imported from the violator. The *prior illegal* act by the target state makes reprisal a *legal* response. These two techniques actually play a minor role in contemporary practice.

Self-help remains the norm, but states will often seek collective sanctions **because the effects of interdependence and globalization means that very few states possess the power and position to impose effective sanctions by themselves.** States seeking to impose sanctions individually could potentially damage themselves as much as the target. As much as a state may wish to press for the advancement of human rights and highlight abuses, it may still hesitate to push for economic sanctions if the errant state happens to be a major trading partner. In this respect, consider the ongoing debate within the United States over these issues. In a world of complex interdependence, few relationships involve straightforward bilateral linkages.[23] Small states may have little or no effective unilateral recourse against violations because they either lack the means or cannot bear the costs.

The Theory and Politics of Centralized Enforcement

In exploring the idea of central enforcement, we focus primarily on the United Nations because it plays a primary role in contemporary international enforcement. Even though other IGOs have sought occasionally to circumvent its procedures (NATO in Kosovo, for example) and states have bitterly complained about both its actions and its failures to act, the UN Charter still stands at the center of discussions of enforcement. Currently the United Nations has close to universal membership, meaning that almost every state in the contemporary world has *consented* to accept the obligations in the Charter. That alone gives the organization a status no other IGO can match.

The Charter sets up a *collective security* regime. The theory of collective security also underlies the domestic criminal law system. In a collective security regime, central enforcement agents represent the community. The community, as established

---

[23]See R. O. Keohane and J. S. Nye, *Power and Interdependence,* 3rd ed. (2001), chs. 1, 2, for an extended treatment of this point.

in the state, has a monopoly on the use of violence. This means that individual members give up their right to use violence to "enforce" their rights by taking individual action with the understanding that the central authority will do so effectively. In domestic law we see this model illustrated by the way criminal cases are often presented—the *People v. John Doe/Jane Doe,* where "the people" represent the community interest (represented by the district attorney, solicitor, or prosecutor) in prosecuting the case against "John Doe/Jane Doe" after the police as representatives of the central authority have arrested him or her. We expect the central authority to protect us, but as individuals we have a *circumscribed* right to use violence in self-defense when agents of the central authority are not readily available to protect our lives and property.

Hence, as the fundamental obligation in the collective security regime established by the Charter, states party to the treaty accept the obligation to "refrain in their international relations from the threat or use of force against the territorial integrity or political independence of any state or in any other manner inconsistent with the purposes of the United Nations" (Article 2.4). Because almost every recognized state in the world today has signed and ratified the treaty, the *prohibition on the unilateral use of force* by states stands as a fundamental principle of contemporary international law. Chapter VII (Article 39) of the Charter empowers the Security Council to act as the central enforcement agent in situations involving aggression, a threat to the peace, or a breach of the peace. Individual states do not have the right to resort to force as a method of enforcing a breach of international law or, further, as a means of resolving other disputes. According to the Charter (Articles 51 and 52), the only legitimate use of force by an individual state or a group of states would be an action in self-defense or collective self-defense (see Chapter 20).

While the Security Council authorized military action to counter Iraq's invasion of Kuwait in 1991, measures recommended by the Security Council may not necessarily entail the use of force. In fact, the threat of sanctions, as punishment for violating the rules of the law, has shifted from the use of outright force to nonmilitary techniques. Among these are the rupture of diplomatic and consular relations; economic sanctions, ranging from selective reductions to total stoppage of trade; travel limitations; financial restrictions on the flow of currencies; and the elimination of transportation (land, sea, and air) and mail service and other means of communication to and from the state being sanctioned. Further, the offending state may be suspended or even expelled from membership in an international agency and thus be deprived of the benefits accruing from such membership as well as the ability to vote on policies and decisions. Several UN agencies may constitutionally revoke aid or membership as an enforcement measure. A member of the UN organization itself, once enforcement action has been begun by the Security Council under Article 5 of the Charter, may be suspended from membership, and a member that has persistently violated the principles of the Charter may be expelled by the General Assembly on recommendation of the Security Council (Article 6 of the Charter). We might note that this has never happened.

For many reasons, the Charter regime has never worked as its framers intended, yet the organization still plays a central role. For example, the United States requested UN Security Council action to impose economic sanctions against

Iran after Iranian militants seized its embassy in Teheran in November 1979. Even though the Soviet Union vetoed the proposal in the Security Council, the proposal still received extensive publicity for the alleged failure to comply with the rules of the law and a great outpouring of public condemnation of the delinquent state from other states, but, more important, it built support and legitimacy for collective sanctions apart from UN action.

Sanctions aside, common consent still appears to be the primary reason for obeying the law. The states of the world have agreed to be bound by generally accepted rules for conducting their international relations, particularly in view of the reciprocal need for predictable state behavior in the activities covered by the accepted rules. However—and this has caused much distress to overly optimistic defenders of the law—the principles of international law do not, as yet, make very stringent demands on states and do not generally impinge much on what the states consider "vital national interests." Thus, the record indicates that the primary reasons for obedience to the law seem to coincide with Jessup's view that "international law reflects and records those accommodations which over centuries states have found it to their interest to make."[24] Self-interest, enlightened or not, still appears to be the basic reason for compliance. All other factors mentioned must be assigned a secondary or lesser role. Consent to the law, and self-limitation in abiding by that consent, are essential underpinnings of the rules of international law. Because of this, Vattel's Golden Rule still stands as a valid guide for modern statesmen.

SUGGESTED READINGS

Dahlitz, *Peaceful Resolution of Major International Disputes* (1999).

Evans, ed., *Remedies in International Law: The Institutional Dilemma* (1998).

Hamilton, ed., *The Permanent Court of Arbitration: International Arbitration and Dispute Resolution: Summaries of Awards, Settlement Agreements, and Reports* (1999).

Merrils, *International Dispute Settlement,* 5th ed. (2011).

---

[24]Philip Jessup, "International Law in 1953 A.D.," *Proceedings* (1953), 8, 10.

The Relationship Between International and Municipal Law

In Chapter 1, we discussed the complexity of the international legal process. International law as a system of law applies to states and the relationship between states. Because of the structure of the international political system, the lack of central institutions and authority, the rules normally have effect only when and if put into effect by the legislatures, courts, and executive agencies of individual, sovereign states that form the membership of the international community. Accordingly, the decisions of national courts as well as the responses and application of state political authorities are an important component of international legal process (see the discussion of customary law in Chapter 3). International law contains no specifications—that is, no rules concerning the procedures through which states must apply its rules. The guiding assumption is simply that states will carry out their obligations in good faith and that failure to do so will engage the "responsibility" of the state with the possibility of appropriate redress or penalties (see Chapters 8 and 11).

We need to remember that each state possesses its own constitution (or the equivalent) and its own distinct system of allocating competence to decide important questions among the traditional executive, legislative, and judicial branches we associate with the modern state. The questions here revolve around *how* the executive, legislative, and judicial institutions of individual states deal with international law. To understand some of the problems, we shall first briefly explore a classic debate over the relationship between international and national law. We then examine the premises that determine how *domestic courts* in different states apply international law. Please note that this discussion *does not* apply to *international* courts such as the International Court of Justice (ICJ) or the International Criminal Court (ICC). We consider the procedures and practice of international courts later in this text.

MONISM AND DUALISM: WHAT IS THE RELATIONSHIP BETWEEN INTERNATIONAL AND DOMESTIC LAW?

Before analyzing procedures, we should take note of a debate among international law academics and practitioners that has run through the law literature over the past century or so. We cover the debate briefly here because it is relevant from the perspective of states. Note, however, *it has no meaning for international courts* that deal only with international law. Consider that much of international law can be applied and enforced only by states. *Monists* believe that international and domestic law form one legal system and that international law is *hierarchically superior*. Provisions of international law would thus override conflicting provisions of domestic law. *Dualists* believe that the two legal systems *are totally separate,* operating in two entirely different realms, and that international law can be applied in domestic legal systems only *if, and to the extent that,* the relevant rules have been transformed or incorporated into the domestic legal system. In practice, the greatest majority of contemporary states, the United States among them, adhere to a *dualist* position. In contemporary politics, the monist position is often advanced by human rights advocates who wish to build the strongest case possible for limiting the claims of states that abuse their own citizens (see Chapters 15 and 16).

APPLYING INTERNATIONAL LAW

Judges routinely note, "International law is part of our law." In probing deeper, we find that this simple statement masks a somewhat more complex reality, particularly when applying customary international law. To understand the problems of translating international law into "part of our law," we must examine the judicial process in applying international law and consider how it differs from normal judicial process. In applying international law, and especially in applying customary international law, judges must find and interpret law that has *developed largely through the actions of other states* or sometimes through the decisions of international courts. Customary law may be the "common law of nations," but the practice that defines the relevant rules does not issue solely from the actions of any one state. Consequently, applying international customary law may present a court with a set of interesting issues related to the expectations associated with its own judicial tradition.[1] The processes connected with determining a rule of customary international law come very close to judicial "legislation" or lawmaking, especially when the law is undergoing change or evolution. This may prove less of a problem in the contemporary world. Because of the push toward codification of international law through lawmaking treaties, the opportunities where customary law may come into play continue to diminish.

Some constitutions give guidance; some do not. For example, the French, Indian, and Irish constitutions explicitly refer to customary law, but the U.S. Constitution does not. While the U.S. Constitution does give Congress the power "to define offenses against the law of nations" (Article I), the Congress has seldom availed itself of this option. Even though no explicit statement about international customary law

---

[1]P. R. Trimble, "A Revisionist View of Customary International Law," 33 *UCLA Law Review* (1986), 665.

being "the law of the land" exists, in practice, Congress has traditionally ceded to presidents the authority to assert the U.S. position on matters of customary law and practice as part of the foreign affairs power. But, as with any political matter involving choice, the Congress still has considerable power to influence the direction—if not the decision—if it so chooses. The U.S. Supreme Court has declared customary international law as judicially applicable,[2] but because they hesitate to engage in judicial lawmaking, American judges may prefer not to use customary law in the absence of executive branch guidance. On the other hand, Article VI of the U.S. Constitution declares *ratified* treaties to be the "law of the land." Courts may apply them just as they apply statutes enacted by Congress. *Hence, when American judges speak of "international law" in their discourses, they refer exclusively to* customary *international law,* not treaties to which the Congress has given its advice and consent or other written international agreements. The same observation holds true (for slightly different reasons) for British (United Kingdom) judges as well. Keep this in mind when evaluating the cases presented in this chapter.

The practical concerns of applying international law raise a set of issues based on the question of how national judges proceed when dealing with the following situations:

1. A rule of customary international law when no domestic legislation exists
2. A rule of customary law when conflicting domestic legislation exists
3. Treaties and other international agreements when no domestic legislation exists
4. Treaties and other international agreements when conflicting domestic legislation exists
5. A rule of customary or treaty law when a conflict with constitutional provisions exists

In the United States, we must additionally consider the role of *executive agreements* and other *soft law* agreements (see Chapter 3). To begin our discussion, we offer the following summary/decision tree. We will elaborate it as needed to illustrate important points.

HOW DOMESTIC COURTS PROCEED IN ANALYZING A CASE

First consideration: what kind of law is involved—is it customary or derived from a treaty or international agreement?

   I. *If a rule of customary* law: Despite the common assertion that international law is part of our law, courts in *all* states (customary law tradition or civil law tradition) will look for
       a. a rule of relevant domestic law;
       b. domestic legislation/constitutional provisions/other relevant considerations that authorize the court to apply customary law;
       c. some evidence that the state has *consented* to a particular rule; and/or

                                                 (continued)

---

[2]*The Paquette Habana,* 175 U.S. 677, 700 (1900).

> d. conflicts between domestic law and customary international law.
>   1. If a domestic statute exists, courts in *common law states* will tend to give effect to the domestic statute (will of the legislature). If a *conflict* exists between a domestic statute and a rule of customary law, judges may attempt to mitigate the conflict by assuming that the legislature did not intend to violate international law.
>   2. Courts in *civil (code) law states* vary in their response. Some state practice assumes that international law is hierarchically superior to domestic law; *however,* in dealing with customary international law, that assumes that the relevant rule of customary international law can be derived with some assurance. A domestic statute will be given precedence over an inconsistent or vague customary rule. Seldom will a clear customary rule be invoked over a later, inconsistent, vague rule of domestic law.
> II. *If a rule derives from a treaty or other international agreement:* Has the state signed/ratified the relevant treaty (i.e., has it approved the treaty according to its own constitutional procedures)?
>   a. *Courts of common law states* will treat the treaty as equal to domestic legislation (anterior/posterior). Again, individual judges will often assume that the legislature did not intend for a particular piece of legislation to conflict with the treaty.
>   b. *Courts of civil (code) law states,* depending upon their constitution and legal heritage, will treat international law as hierarchically superior to domestic legislation; that is, a treaty (no matter how old, if still in force) will supersede any later domestic legislation.

Customary International Law: No Domestic Statute

The classic case cited by most casebooks used in the United States to illustrate the application of international law when no domestic statute applies is the *Paquette Habana.* The case has some ambiguity despite the decision, because the court applied admiralty law.[3] Admiralty law forms a distinctive body of law that presumably applies equally to all maritime nations and has clearly formed part of U.S. practice from colonial times. The U.S. Constitution (Article III.2, 3) explicitly establishes federal power over admiralty and maritime issues. The *Paquette Habana* involved questions relating to "prize law," that is, the practice of capturing enemy shipping (vessels and cargo) during wartime for sale at auction in the home state.[4] Because of the long-established acceptance of admiralty and maritime law as an essential part

---

[3]See F. L. Maraist and T. C. Galligan, *Maraist and Galligan's Admiralty in a Nutshell,* 5th ed. (2005).

[4]Actually, the statutes governing prizes still remain on the books (10 U.S.C.A. § 7651 et seq.). The nature of contemporary naval warfare makes prize law less relevant. World War I marks a great shift here. Consider the German strategy linked to the U-boat fleet of simply *sinking* enemy shipping rather than taking it as prizes. The capture of prizes was the principal purpose of privateering (outlawed in 1856). If readers have seen the film *Master and Commander* (or read the Patrick O'Brien books from which the screenplay was drawn) or have followed the Horatio Hornblower series on A&E (or read the C. S. Forrester novels), they should understand that the taking of prizes (the richer the better) played a big part in warfare prior to World War I. The captains and crews of warships shared the monies received from selling the captured vessels (and their cargoes) at auction under the supervision of a prize court. Every sailor in the British Navy dreamed of earning enough prize money to retire comfortably.

of U.S. practice—it formed a major concern of the newly formed United States—the questions relate to the representative nature of the case. In what respects does this case reflect reasoning transferable as precedent to cases that involve less well settled areas of customary law?

▶ THE *PAQUETTE HABANA*; THE *LOLA*

U.S. Supreme Court 175 U.S. 677 (1900)

Facts

Two appeals from decrees at the U.S. District Court, Southern District of Florida, which had authorized the sale of two fishing vessels and their cargoes seized as prizes of war during the Spanish–American War. Each vessel, operating out of Havana, regularly engaged in fishing in Cuban coastal waters, sailed under the Spanish flag, and was owned by a Spanish subject of Cuban birth, living in Havana. The cargo, when the vessels were seized, consisted of fresh fish. Apparently neither captain had any knowledge, until the capture of the vessels, that a state of war existed between Spain and the United States and that the United States had proclaimed a blockade of Spanish ports. Both vessels were brought to Key West and condemned in the U.S. District Court, with a decree of sale of both vessels and cargoes.

Issue

Whether unarmed coastal fishing vessels of one belligerent are subject to capture as prizes by vessels of another belligerent.

Decision

1. Unarmed coastal fishing vessels are exempt from seizure by a belligerent.
2. Decree of district court reversed; proceeds of the sale of vessels and cargoes to be restored to the claimants, with damages and costs.

Reasoning

1. By an ancient usage among civilized nations, beginning centuries ago and "gradually ripening into a rule of international law," coastal fishing vessels pursuing their vocation have been recognized as exempt, with their cargoes and crews, from capture. This usage can be traced by means of documents back as far as A.D. 1403 in England. Subsequent evidence indicates that France and other countries followed the same usage. Eminent writers on international law have indicated through the past few centuries that the usage became general in scope.
2. The United States had recognized the immunity of coastal fishing vessels as far back as the Mexican War of 1846.
3. In most recent times, many states had issued specific orders to naval commanders concerning fishing vessels, recognizing their exemption from seizure unless military operations should make it necessary.
4. "International law is part of our law, and must be ascertained and administered by courts of justice of appropriate jurisdiction, as often as questions of right depending upon it are duly presented for their determination. *For this purpose, where there is no treaty and no controlling executive or legislative act or judicial decision,*

(continued)

resort must be had to the customs and usages of civilized nations, and, as evidence of these, to the works of jurists and commentators, who by years of labor, research, and experience, have made themselves peculiarly well acquainted with the subjects of which they treat. Such works are resorted to by judicial tribunals, not for the speculations of their authors concerning what the law ought to be, but for trustworthy evidence of what the law really is" (*Hilton v. Guyot,* 159 U.S. 131; emphasis added).

5. "[A]t the present day, by the general consent of the civilized nations of the world, and independently of any express treaty or other public act, it is an established rule of international law, founded on considerations of humanity to a poor and industrious order of men, and of the mutual convenience of belligerent States, that coast fishing vessels, with their implements and supplies, cargoes and crews, unarmed and honestly pursuing their peaceful calling of catching and bringing in fresh fish, are exempt from capture as prize of war."

6. *The President had issued a proclamation that declared, "It being desirable that such war should be conducted upon principles in harmony with the present views of nations and sanctioned by their recent practice."* The Court continued, "[T]he proclamation clearly manifests the general policy of the Government to conduct the war in accordance with the principles of international law." (Emphasis added)

7. "This rule of international law is one which prize courts, administering the law of nations, are bound to take judicial notice of, and to give effect to, in the absence of any treaty or other public act of their own government in relation to the matter."

Despite the importance and salience of admiralty law, in the reasoning leading to the decision, the court took particular pains to point out that **both** the president and the secretary of the Navy had indicated the intention of the United States to adhere to international law in conducting the war. Recalling that *no explicit constitutional provisions authorize courts to apply customary international law*, and considering that most admiralty law at this time was the product of *custom*, the question lurking in the background is whether, in the absence of a presidential proclamation (*clear evidence of consent*), the court would have felt comfortable in issuing this decision. The issues here have never been fully explored in the United States because American courts have seldom had to deal with the situation. Trimble notes that there are "almost as many cases in which the courts rejected the application of customary international law as there are examples in which courts actually applied it."[5] Of more than 2,000 cases involving international law since 1789, only 50 or so have had to cope with customary law in situations where no guidance from the political branches existed.[6] Many of these cases involved conflicts with domestic statutes. We shall deal with those issues shortly.

Two British cases illustrate the issues and problems associated with the tension between consent and the presumed processes and strengths of customary law

[5]Trimble, note 1, at 687.
[6]Trimble, note 1, at 685.

(*lex ferenda* versus *lex lata*). In the first, *West Rand Central Gold Mining,* the court took a simple position—it found a relevant rule, but no consistent evidence of formal consent by any organ of the British government. Like the American court in the *Paquette Habana,* the position adopted by the British court represents the doctrine of **transformation**—courts need evidence of prior consent by political authorities in order to apply any rule of customary international law, or evidence of a rule *so fundamental and universal (jus cogens)* that no "civilized state" could opt out.

The following case (1977) took a very different view of the role of British courts in applying customary international law. Lord Denning argued that the doctrine of **incorporation**, the idea that judges had the authority to use customary law as they found it at the time regardless of any indication of political consent, was the correct approach.

Still, this discussion does not tell the whole story. The court in *Trendtex* also came to the radical conclusion that *stare decisis* (precedent) did not necessarily apply in cases involving customary international law. Up to this decision, British courts had routinely accepted that precedent applied regardless of possible changes. As we discuss later, this stance could have a major impact in several areas of contemporary international law, most notably with respect to human rights.

▶ **TRENDTEX TRADING CORPORATION V. CENTRAL BANK OF NIGERIA**

England, Queen's Bench, 1977 (1977) Q.B. 529, 553–554

Issue

Was the bank entitled to sovereign immunity as an organ of the Nigerian government; that is, was the bank immune from being sued in the courts of England?

Background

At the time of the case, the applicable rules of customary international law did not require the court to grant sovereign immunity to the bank. Considering the doctrine of *transformation* (and, nominally, the role of precedent) enunciated in *West Rand Central,* could the Court, in the absence of any action by Parliament, apply the current rule?

Decision

As a commercial entity, the bank could not claim sovereign immunity (see Chapter 7 for more discussion concerning the evolution of this rule).

Reasoning

1. The doctrine of *incorporation* predates that of transformation. The judge, Lord Denning, traced it back to 1737.

2. If the law of nations formed part of the law of England, then the law of England must change as international law changes, and international law does change.

3. Prior courts have given effect to changes without prior parliamentary approval.

4. Because international law changes and evolves, *stare decisis* does not always hold: "It follows . . . that a decision of this court—as to what was the ruling of international law 50 or 60 years ago—is not binding on this court today."

Finally, to add a piece needed to understand the next section, we should note another important consideration. British courts are not entirely free to utilize incorporation. We find an important limitation in the opinion of Lord Atkin in *Chung Chi Cheung v. The King:*[7]

> The courts acknowledge the existence of a body of rules which nations accept among themselves. On any judicial issue they seek to ascertain what the relevant rule is, and having found it they will treat it as incorporated into the domestic law, *so far as it is not inconsistent with rules enacted by statutes.* (Emphasis added)

Statutes, or acts of Parliament, will take precedence over customary law. In the United States, laws enacted by Congress will also take precedence over customary law. To digress slightly in support of this point, we should note the anomalous decision in *United States v. Postal,*[8] where the court held that a consistent exercise of customary rights (law) by the United States took precedence over a more recently ratified treaty that more narrowly circumscribed those rights. Remember—there are rules and exceptions. Memorize the rule, but also memorize the exceptions and be sure that you understand **why** they form exceptions.

Customary International Law in Conflict with Domestic Statute

Interestingly, conflicts with domestic statutes do not occur often. When they do, judges often try to reconcile the difference. However, for the most part, the first general rule for domestic courts is *that they must give effect to the will of the legislature* (unless there is a constitutional problem). To explore this, we shall revisit a case first discussed in Chapter 5: *Mortensen v. Peters.*

MORTENSEN V. PETERS

Great Britain, High Court of Justiciary of Scotland, 1906 (1906) 8 S.C., 5th Series, 99, 14 Scot. L.T227

Background

The case involved the enforcement of an Act of Parliament with regard to prohibiting fishing by foreign vessels in areas of Moray Firth (see Chapter 5).

Issues

1. Whether a British statute applied not only to British subjects but also to all other persons within British territory;

(continued)

---

[7](1939): AC 160; 9 ILR, 264.

[8]U.S. Court of Appeals 589F.2d 862, 5th Cir. (1979). The court ruled the treaty in question was non-self-executing.

2. Whether the waters of the Moray Firth outside the 3-mile limit were British territorial waters and hence subject to British jurisdiction; and
3. Whether domestic courts were bound by a statute contravening a rule of international law.

Decision

The court ruled unanimously in the affirmative on all three issues and upheld Mortensen's conviction.

Reasoning

1. The wording of the legislation in question—that is, the use of such expressions as "it shall not be lawful," "every person who," and so on—clearly indicated that the legislature intended, for this purpose, to have the statutes apply against all persons, regardless of nationality. The purpose of the legislation would have been defeated if only British fishermen had been controlled and all others would have been free to use any method of fishing in the area.
2. Many instances were on record in which a given nation legislated for waters beyond a 3-mile limit and land embraced by that nation and in which the validity of such legislation had been upheld by the courts.
3. "There is no such thing as a standard of international law extraneous to the domestic law of a kingdom, to which appeal may be made. International law, so far as this Court is concerned, is the body of doctrine regarding the international rights and duties of States *which has been adopted and made part of the law of Scotland.* It may probably be conceded that there is always a certain presumption against the Legislature of a country asserting or assuming the existence of a territorial jurisdiction going clearly beyond limits established by the common consent of nations—that is to say, by international law. Such assertion or assumption is of course not impossible. *A Legislature may quite conceivably, by oversight or even design, exceed what an international tribunal (if such existed) might hold to be its international rights. Still, there is always a presumption against its intending to do so.* In this Court we have nothing to do with the question of whether the Legislature has or has not done what foreign powers may consider a usurpation in a question with them. Neither are we a tribunal sitting to decide whether an Act of the Legislature is *ultra vires* [in excess of authority conferred by law and hence invalid] as in contravention of generally acknowledged principles of international law. *For us an Act of Parliament duly passed by Lords and Commons and assented to by the King, is supreme, and we are bound to give effect to its terms.*" (Emphasis added)

Considering the date of the case, 1906 (see *West Rand Central*), the court here clearly adheres to the idea of *dualism* regarding customary international law and follows the doctrine of *transformation*. The court does not, in this case, try to determine if the statute contravenes international law, though it notes the possibility. The court does put forth another important doctrine—courts should presume that, *as a rule, legislatures do not deliberately intend to violate international law.* In U.S. practice, this is known as the *Charming Betsy* rule.

THE CHARMING BETSY (MURRAY V. SCHOONER CHARMING BETSY)

U.S. Supreme Court 6 U.S. (2 Cranch) 64 (1804)

Facts

In February 1800, during the undeclared war with France, Congress passed the Non-intercourse Act suspending all commercial intercourse between the United States and France. Implementation of the Act included instructions issued by the president. In July 1800, Captain Alexander Murray, commanding the U.S. *Constellation,* captured the vessel *Charming Betsy* and confiscated its cargo as it sailed toward Guadeloupe, a French possession. At the time Jared Shattuck, a Danish trader born in the United States, owned the vessel.

Issue

Can an act of Congress adopted to suspend trade between the United States and France authorize the seizure of neutral vessels if such seizure would violate customary international law?

Decision

"*[A]n act of Congress ought never to be construed to violate the law of nations, if* any other possible construction remains" (Emphasis added). Ship and cargo returned to their owner.

Reasoning

1. If Congress intended that any American vessel sold to a neutral should, in the possession of that neutral, be liable to the commercial disabilities imposed on her while she belonged to citizens of the United States, it should have *plainly expressed "such extraordinary intent."* (Emphasis added).

2. If the legislation was designed to prohibit the sale of American vessels to neutrals, it should have done so straightforwardly.

3. Determining that the *Charming Betsy* was the bona fide property of a Danish burgher, Chief Justice Marshall concluded that the ship was not subject to forfeit even though it was employed in carrying on trade and commerce with a French island.

Similarly in a later case, the *Over the Top (Schroeder v. Bissell, Collector),*[9] the plaintiffs argued that the seizure of the ship owned by a British citizen—flying the British flag, and ostensibly in international waters (19 nautical miles from the coast)—when an illegal sale of whiskey took place *violated a rule of customary international law* that limited such jurisdiction to 3 nautical miles. In his decision the judge noted:

If we assume for the present that the national legislation has, by its terms, made the acts complained of a crime against the United States even when committed on the high seas by foreign national upon a ship of foreign registry, *there is no discretion vested in the federal court,* once it obtains jurisdiction,

---

[9]Admiralty No. 2796; No. 2797; No. 2798; Equity No. 1746, U.S. District Court, District of Connecticut, 1925, 5 F.2d 838. For similar statements, see *The Nereide,* U.S. Supreme Court 1815 (9 Cranch) 388; *Tag v. Rogers,* 267 F.2d 664, D.C. Cir. (1959); and *Garcia-Mir v. Meese,* 788 F.2d 1446, 11th Cir. (1986).

to decline enforcement. *International practice is law only in so far as we adopt it,* and like all common or statute law it bends to the will of the Congress. *It is not the function of court to annul legislation; it is their duty to interpret and by their judicial decrees to enforce it.* . . . There is one ground only upon which a federal court may refuse to enforce an act of Congress and that is when the act is held to be unconstitutional. (Emphasis added)

After making this declaration, the judge continued, arguing that while the court cannot simply annul a statute, it may assume "that the congressional act did not deliberately intend to infringe" principles of international law (*Charming Betsy* rule). The statute in question had explicitly extended the customs jurisdiction of the United States to 12 nautical miles (4 marine leagues). The judge observed that Congress could do so if it wished and could extend jurisdiction 4 leagues more if it decided to do so. *In this instance, the court would have enforced the extension because it had no choice.* The judge then pointed out that, as the statute was currently written, Congress had extended jurisdiction to only 12 nautical miles. At 19 miles off the coast, the sale and consequent arrest took place beyond the legal reach of the U.S. Treasury and Coast Guard. The court voided the seizure of the ship and cargo.

In discussing the role of *customary law,* some advocates have suggested that a clear rule of international customary law may override a later vague, inconsistent rule of domestic law. The simple answer to this hypothesis for the United States and the United Kingdom is *no.* The District of Columbia Court of Appeals has stated, "[T]he law in this Court remains clear: no enactment of Congress can be challenged on the ground that it violates customary international law."[10] While this position is theoretically possible in some civil code states (the Netherlands and Germany, perhaps, considering their constitutional provisions), *its advocates have not* produced cases to substantiate their claims. Treaties have a very different status due to the explicit process of adoption that clearly involves consent.

An important question here arises when the conflict with the domestic statute cannot be resolved in a way consistent with the international rule. If the statute and the rule of customary law cannot be reconciled, then here we can most easily see the impact of dualism. In the United States, the Constitution does not prohibit the president or the Congress from violating international law. As we have seen, American courts will uphold acts of the political branches in violation of customary law as long as such acts are within the constitutional authority of the branch in question.[11] Keep in mind, however, that if a given government does violate a rule of that law by an executive or legislative act, while the statute will take precedence *domestically,* internationally the state in question has committed a violation *(delict)* and remains *responsible* for any violations of the obligations in its international relations (see Chapter 11). Simply stated, no state can opt out of a binding international obligation merely by citing its own laws or constitution.[12]

---

[10]*Committee of United States Citizens Living in Nicaragua v. Reagan,* U.S. Ct. of Appeals, 859 F.2d 929, Dist. C. (1988).

[11]See L. Henkin, *Foreign Affairs and the Constitution,* 2nd ed. (1996), 221. See also the interesting papers on "May the President Violate Customary International Law?" 80 *American Journal of International Law* 913 (1986); J. J. Paust's dissenting "The President *Is* Bound by International Law," 81

[12]*Polish Nationals in Danzig,* PCIJ, Ser. A/B, No. 44 (1933), 24.

Treaties When No Domestic Legislation Exists

How states go about incorporating treaties and other international agreements into instruments usable by their domestic institutions varies widely because constitutional provisions differ. Because treaties do make national law in some form, most national legislatures have a role in ratification or accession (see Chapter 4).[13] The U.S. Constitution does not define the term *treaty,* but has two relevant provisions dealing with treaty practice. Under Article II, § 2.2, the president has the power "with the advice and consent" of *two-thirds* of the Senate to make treaties. Article VI, § 2, declares that "all Treaties made, under the Authority of the United States, shall be the supreme Law of the Land; and the Judges in every State shall be bound thereby." In addition to "treaties," the president has the power to make other *international agreements:* (1) on the basis of congressional authorization, (2) on the basis of his own foreign relations power, or (3) on the basis of authority contained in an earlier treaty made pursuant to Article II. These agreements are also considered to be federal law. U.S. courts will apply them in the same way that they apply acts of Congress or treaties.

Oddly, in the United Kingdom, Parliament has no formal constitutional role in treaty making. The treaty-making power is vested solely in the executive (the Cabinet), acting on behalf of the Crown. Practically, the difference may have little consequence. Parliament must be involved when treaties (1) have direct financial implications requiring the assent of Parliament because they affect revenue or (2) are so politically controversial that one or both of the governments involved may wish to safeguard positions by writing an express requirement for parliamentary approval into the text. In any case, all treaties requiring formal ratification or accession are subject to the Ponsonby procedure whereby a treaty is laid before Parliament for comment (and possible debate) for 21 days before the executive can take formal action to ratify.[14] Shaw argues that the ostensible omission of Parliament from the process has little meaning, because any treaty purporting to create rights and duties enforceable in the United Kingdom cannot directly do so without enabling legislation from Parliament (note the presumption of *dualism*).[15] All such treaties, by definition, are not *self-executing* (see Chapter 4). In a recent decision, Lord Oliver stated:[16]

> [T]he royal prerogative, whilst it embraces the making of treaties, does not extend to altering the law or conferring rights on individuals or depriving individuals of rights which they enjoy in domestic law without the intervention of Parliament. . . . Quite simply a treaty is not part of English law unless and until it has been incorporated into the law by legislation.

From time to time, the scope of the treaty power in the United States has fueled impassioned debate. Earlier concerns over the possibility that treaties might yield sufficient grounds for challenges to policies relating to racial discrimination, labor

---

[13]Accession arises when a government adopts a treaty although it was not an original signatory when the treaty was open for signature.

[14]House of Commons Information Office, "Treaties," Factsheet P14, Procedure Series (Rev. June 2003), www.parliament.uk/directories/hcio.cfm.

[15]M. N. Shaw, *International Law,* 5th ed. (2003), 138, 139.

[16]*Maclaine Watson v. Department of Trade and Industry,* 3 All ER 523, 531; 81 *International Law Review* (1989), 671, 684.

standards, or the usurpation or erosion of the rights reserved to the individual states in the Constitution have led to some interesting exchanges. In the late 1940s and early 1950s, many individuals pushed for adoption of the Bricker Amendment to the Constitution, which would have made any law enacted by Congress superior to any treaty provision.[17] Today, while specific treaties—such as the Rome Statute establishing the ICC—may generate passionate criticism and defense, the treaty power itself is not at the center of the controversy. Our concern here relates simply to the issues that, once adopted through "advice and consent" (and proclamation), what status do treaties have in relationship to other rules of domestic law?

For the United States, treaties as "law of the land" stand as enforceable elements of domestic law *and* as instruments that create international obligations. The Supreme Court in *Missouri v. Holland*[18] stated:

> [B]y Article II, § 2, the power to make treaties is delegated expressly, and by Article VI treaties made under the authority of the United States, along with the Constitution and laws of the United States made in pursuance thereof, are declared the supreme law of the land. If the treaty is valid there can be no dispute about the validity of the statute under Article I, § 8 as a necessary and proper means to execute the powers of the Government.

This case stemmed from a challenge by the State of Missouri that the subject matter of the treaty, regulating migratory birds, violated the Constitution because it arrogated to the federal government rights reserved to the states in the Tenth Amendment. The court in this instance rejected the claim while noting that valid international agreements as *federal law* override the laws of the various individual states of the union and the laws and ordinances of their political subdivisions such as cities and counties. Moreover, a determination of *international law* (customary) by the Supreme Court will also be considered binding in the same way.

The principal controversy for treaty application in the United States centers on the procedures necessary to put treaties into an appropriate form for implementation. Courts and the Congress regard some treaties as *self-executing,* meaning they require no additional legislation or action beyond ratification by Congress and proclamation by the president for the courts to utilize them directly. Other agreements fall into the *non-self-executing* category and thus require legislation or appropriate administrative action in promulgating regulations (Chapter 4). The importance here stems from the fact that non-self-executing treaties, despite being the "supreme law of the land," **do not by themselves** create *a rule of decision* for U.S. courts. Without enabling legislation to provide guidelines for application (decision rules), non-self-executing treaties are unenforceable through action in a U.S. court.[19]

Unless a specific agreement carries with it a stipulation as to its status, the United States may determine how it wishes to deal with the agreement—the only expectation regarding international law being "good faith" in implementation. At the time

---

[17]See J. L. Taulbee, "A Call to Arms Declined: The United States and the International Criminal Court," 14 *Emory Int'l L. R.* 105 (2000), 115.

[18]U.S. Supreme Court, 252 U.S. 416 (1920).

[19]A non-self-executing treaty "does not by itself give rise to domestically enforceable federal law." *Medellin v. Texas*, 128 S. Ct. (2008) at 1356.

of ratification, either the president or the Congress has the option of deciding if current law will suffice, or if implementation will require new legislation. Occasionally, at the time of treaty ratification and proclamation, neither the Congress nor the president will specify the treaty status. This position often gives rise to interesting discourse over the status of the treaty when the courts later have to decide its relevance to a particular case. Consider the list of factors that judges may examine:[20]

> The extent to which an international agreement establishes affirmative and judicially enforceable obligations without implementing legislation must be determined in each case by references to many contextual factors: the purposes of the treaty and the objectives of its creators, the existence of domestic procedures and institutions appropriate for direct implementation, the availability and feasibility of alternative enforcement methods and the immediate and long-range social consequences of self- or non-self-execution.

The following case, *Asakura v. City of Seattle*, illustrates two of the principles just discussed: the supremacy of federal law in the form of international agreements *and* the importance of the status of a treaty as self-executing or non-self-executing.

▶ ASAKURA V. CITY OF SEATTLE

U.S. Supreme Court 205 U.S. 332 (1924)

Facts

Mr. Asakura, a citizen of Japan, had resided in the United States since 1904. In 1915, he invested $5,000 in a pawnbroking business in Seattle. In July 1921, the City of Seattle passed an ordinance, repealing an earlier one, that required all pawnbrokers to obtain a license and to be citizens of the United States. Asakura brought suit against the city, claiming that the ordinance violated the treaty between the United States and Japan, ratified and proclaimed in April 1911.[21] The Superior Court of King County found for Asakura; the Supreme Court of the State of Washington held the ordinance valid and reversed the finding of the Superior Court.

Issue

Does the city ordinance violate the treaty?

Decision

For Mr. Asakura, the treaty provisions apply, and the ordinance violates the treaty.

(continued)

---

[20]*People of Saipan v. United States Department of Interior*, U.S. Court of Appeals, 502F.2d 90, 9th Cir. (1974). For a recent discussion dealing with the Supreme Court's decision in *Medellin v. Texas*, 128 S. Ct. (2008), see C. A. Bradley, "Intent, Presumptions, and Non-Self-Executing Treaties," 102 *AJIL (2008), 540–551.*

[21]The case has one other important feature. The treaty involved *reciprocal* rights and privileges (Chapter 1) to enter, travel in, and reside in the territories of the others; to carry on trade, wholesale and retail; to own or lease and occupy houses, manufactories, warehouses, and shops; to employ agents of their choice; to lease land for residential and commercial purposes; and generally to do anything incident to, or necessary for, trade upon the same terms as native citizens or subjects.

Reasoning

1. A treaty made under the authority of the United States is the "supreme law of the land," and judges in every state shall be bound thereby.
2. Regarding the treaty, "The rule of equality established by it cannot be rendered nugatory in any part of the United States by municipal ordinances or state laws. It stands on the same footing of supremacy as do the provisions of the Constitution and laws of the United States. *It operates of itself without the aid of any legislation, state or national; and it will be applied a given authoritative effect by the courts."* (Emphasis added)

Acts of Congress in Conflict with Treaties

Treaties (and other international agreements) enjoy parity as federal law with statutes enacted by Congress. Thus, if a conflict between the two arises, courts will ordinarily use the rule to deal with conflicts in statute law to resolve the inconsistency. A treaty or statute adopted later overrides an earlier inconsistent statute. The problem, of course, comes when a later treaty conflicts with an earlier one, or when an act of Congress conflicts with an earlier treaty. As with customary law, the *Charming Betsy* rule forms a relevant consideration for the court. Hence, judges first try to reconcile the conflict through a reasonable construction of purpose and intent. If the court cannot find a way to resolve the differences, then the treaty, to the extent of the conflict, no longer has effect. Again, while the statute will be in effect as domestic law, the legislation will not relieve the United States of its *international obligations* and the possibility of being held *internationally responsible* for any breach of duty (Chapter 11). Note the reasoning of the District of Columbia Court of Appeals in *Diggs v. Schultz* (1972).

▌ DIGGS V. SCHULTZ

U.S. Court of Appeals, District of Columbia, 1972 470 F.2d 461 cert. denied, 411 U.S. 931, 93 S.Ct. 1897 (1973)

Facts

In 1966 the Security Council (SC) of the United Nations, *with the affirmative vote* of the United States, adopted a resolution directing all member states to impose an embargo on trade with Southern Rhodesia. The SC reaffirmed and enlarged the action in 1968. In 1971, Congress adopted the so-called Byrd Amendment to the Strategic and Critical Materials Stock Piling Act. The amendment prohibited the president from placing an embargo on any "strategic" materials produced by a non-Communist country if the United States currently imported those materials from a Communist country. Because Southern

(continued)

Rhodesia was considered a non-Communist country and produced "strategic" raw materials currently imported by the United States from Communist countries, the amendment prevented the president from continuing to enforce the embargo.

Issue

Does Congress have the authority to nullify, in part or in whole, a treaty commitment?

Decision

Under the Constitution, Congress has the authority to abrogate a treaty commitment.

Reasoning

After some consideration of nonjusticiability, the court found the following:

1. "We think that there can be no blinking the purpose and effect of the Byrd Amendment. It was to detach this country from the U.N. boycott of Southern Rhodesia in blatant disregard of our treaty undertakings."

2. "Under our constitutional scheme, *Congress can denounce treaties if it sees fit to do so, and there is nothing the other branches of government can do about it.* We consider that this is precisely what Congress has done in this case." (Emphasis added)

Notes

1. The passage of the Byrd Amendment caused great comment within the United Nations. The Security Council again reaffirmed the sanctions in February 1972, noting that failure to support the embargo "would be contrary to the obligations of states."

2. At the behest of President Jimmy Carter, in 1977 Congress repealed the Byrd Amendment. When Southern Rhodesia became the independent state of Zimbabwe in 1979, the United Nations removed all sanctions.

3. Article 27 of the Vienna Convention on the Law of Treaties holds that "a party may not invoke the provisions of its internal law as justification for its failure to perform a treaty."[22] Though technically not applicable here because the treaty had not entered into force, the question involves the status of this principle as a rule of *customary law*. The United States had not ratified this treaty (and still has not), but insofar as Article 27 reflects a codification of customary law, the United States could not escape the onus of violation.

In *Missouri v. Holland,* the court carefully noted that it must honor "treaties made under the authority of the United States, along with the Constitution and laws of the United States." The State of Missouri had challenged the treaty on the grounds that it violated constitutional guarantees to the various states of the federal union. Remember that courts may decline to apply a federal law only if they find some (or all) of the statute unconstitutional. For the purposes of domestic law, the U.S. Constitution stands *hierarchically superior* to *all* federal law. Indeed, most litigation involving challenges to executive agreements (and the scope of presidential authority) entails questions of *internal constitutional law* beyond the scope of this discussion (see Chapter 4). This fact should suggest that if an international agreement conflicts with constitutional guarantees, then—just like any act of Congress—it would be void to the extent of the inconsistency.

---

[22]Of May 23, 1969, U.N. Doc. A/CONF. 39/27; entered into force January 27, 1980.

The Supreme Court in *Reid v. Covert* (1957)[23] addressed the issues relating to such conflicts. In this case, a principal question became whether an executive agreement and subsequent implementing legislation by Congress could, under certain circumstances, override an individual's rights to a fair trial as defined by the relevant sections of the U.S. Constitution.[24] Mrs. Covert had killed her husband while living on a U.S. Air Force Base in England. Under an executive agreement between the United States and Great Britain, implemented through congressional legislation, the United States had authority to prosecute in its *military courts* all crimes committed by U.S. service personnel or their civilian dependents. In considering Mrs. Covert's trial and conviction, the court noted:

> The prohibitions of the Constitution were designed to apply to all branches of the National Government and they cannot be nullified by the Executive or by the Executive and the Senate combined. There is nothing new or unique about what we say here. . . . [W]e conclude that the Constitution in its entirety applied to the trials of Mrs. Smith and Mrs. Covert. [24,25]

In passing, we should note that the question of international responsibility and/or obligation did not arise here. First, the decision voided only *part* of the agreement. Note the phrase "to the extent of the conflict." Second, the decision did not say that the United States could not try (and punish if found guilty) civilian dependents who committed crimes in England (or Japan). The court declared that any trial of a civilian dependent could not take place in military courts-martial, because such trials must meet the standards contained in the Constitution.

One question still remains—the compatibility of the U.S. Constitution (or of any national constitution) with international law. Be assured that this is not a silly or irrelevant question. The United States has refused to ratify a number of human rights treaties because of a perception that international standards for certain rights do not correspond with those as guaranteed in the Constitution and elaborated over the years through decisions of the Supreme Court. The opposition does not come exclusively from the political "left" or the political "right." The usual simplistic political rhetoric, based upon "liberal" and "conservative," which informs so much of contemporary political exchange in the United States fails to account for the complexity of the issues. We will explore this issue further in Chapter 15.

CIVIL CODE STATES AND THE EUROPEAN UNION

Thus far, with occasional references to countries that utilize traditional civil code as the basis for national law, we have concentrated on the practice of the Anglo-American tradition. For states that have adopted the tradition, practice does not

---

[23]U.S. Supreme Court, 354 U.S. 1 (1957).

[24]The prior and underlying issue was the extent to which the Constitution should apply to crimes committed by citizens while overseas.

[25]Mrs. Smith had killed her husband under similar circumstance in Japan.

vary a great deal. As we have noted, in many instances, practice in civil code states does not vary all that much concerning the role of customary law. Detailing the points of variance on a country-by-country tour, while perhaps useful to a practicing lawyer, would add little to our understanding of how states regard and use custom.

On the other hand, the status of treaties in civil code countries varies. Some states regard almost all international agreements as non-self-executing (e.g., Belgium). Others proceed on a treaty-by-treaty basis. Some constitutions, the Russian Federation for example, have taken international treaty law to be hierarchically superior to national law; some have not. Some, such as France (Article 55 of the French Constitution), will consider treaties hierarchically superior on the basis of *reciprocity*—that is, if the other party or parties to the agreement hold the same views. This matters, of course, because while all states tend to accept as a matter of course that a treaty will supersede inconsistent prior legislation, taking treaties as superior means that treaties will override inconsistent future legislation. To help understand why this matters, we must consider two important rules of international treaty law (see Chapter 4):

1. Treaties are made by the state, the continuing political entity; when a specific government negotiates, signs, and ratifies a treaty, it binds its successors as well. Changes in government (however effected, whether by election or revolution) do not necessarily void treaty rights.
2. Unless states have specifically decided to limit the treaty obligations in time by including appropriate language, treaties presumably remain in effect in perpetuity.

Consider the implications of these two rules for states with a long history. If the rules are taken literally, courts at times may have to apply nineteenth-century treaties to twenty-first-century cases despite more recent and relevant legislation.

The treaty creating the European Union (EU) has the status of a constitution for the state parties (those who have signed and ratified or deposited instruments of accession). No domestic legislation may contravene the obligations created by ratification of, or accession to, the treaty. An even more interesting result here stems from the fact that the institutions of the EU produce regulations, directives, and decisions that bind member states. In effect, members have surrendered some of their sovereign prerogatives as the price of the benefits produced by the EU. The amount of litigation in the European Court suggests that, as with any "constitution" or legal code, states look for "wiggle room" to maximize their own interests.

SUGGESTED READINGS

Bradley, "Intent, Presumption, and Non-Self-Executing Treaties," 102 *AJIL 540 (2008).*

Leigh, "Is the President Above Customary International Law?" 86 *AJIL* 757 (1992).

Nanda, *Litigation of International Disputes in U.S. Courts* (2005).

Whiteman, I: 103.

CASES

The Scotia, 1871, 14 Wallace 170.

Certain German Interests in Polish Upper Silesia, PCIJ, Ser. A., No. 7 (1926).

Medellin v. Texas, 128 S. Ct (2008)

THE INTERNATIONAL/MUNICIPAL RELATIONSHIP IN GENERAL

Bishop, 71.

Charney, "The Power of the Executive Branch of the United States Government to Violate Customary International Law," 80 *AJIL* 913 (1986).

Ferdinandusse, *Direct Application of International Law in National Courts* (2006).

Franck and Gregory, *International Law Decisions in National Courts* (1995).

Glennon, "Raising *The Paquete Habana*: Is Violation of Customary International Law by the Executive Unconstitutional?" 80 *NW U. L. Rev.* 322 (1985).

Kirgis, "Federal Statutes, Executive Orders and 'Self-executing Custom,'" 81 *AJIL* 371 (1987).

Koh, "Is International Law Really State Law?" 111 *Harvard Law Rev.* 1824 (1998).

Reinisch, *International Organizations Before National* Courts (2008).

Shany, *Regulating Jurisdictional Relations Between National and International Courts* (2009).

Subjects of International Law

Subjects of International Law: Recognition

THE COMMUNITY OF NATIONS

The existence and application of a system of law relating to all civilized states presuppose a system of common values and attitudes—or, in other words, that vague concept sometimes called the *community,* or *family,* of nations.[1] As we noted in Chapter 2, the idea had a firm place in the European tradition by the time international law assumed its modern form, even though no formal machinery existed through which the community could operate in the legal or political sphere.

Reality of the Community Concept

The concept of a community of humankind has one of the oldest lineages in Western civilization and thought. We can trace it back to the Stoic philosophers of antiquity and see it as part of such conceptions as the brotherhood of all humanity, the social nature of humanity, and the idea that all individuals share membership in a worldwide community ruled by right reason (natural law). Such beliefs, transmitted through the centuries by philosophers such as Cicero and Seneca, by Roman jurists, and by the Christian Church received new vigor during the Renaissance, when legal theorists faced the problem of a politically divided Europe. Renaissance thought, well expressed by Francisco Suárez and other scholars, held that man's nature, need, and desire for mutual help could not be fulfilled in individual states but involved humanity as a whole in one great society. Moreover, that society, just like its component political parts, needed a body of law to regulate and order the relations between those parts.

Thus, a long tradition holds that a worldwide community has developed, composed of states and other units, and that these units possess rights, responsibilities, and moral obligations. Indeed, such a community does exist, for the simple reason

---

[1]Note that, even though a considerable debate exists over the precise definitions of *community* and *society* and how they may apply at the international level, we shall use these terms interchangeably. For our purposes here, the extent or depth of "community" in its narrowest sense does not matter.

that many people talk, write, and, within limits, behave as if there were such a community. We should not assume that this essentially hypothetical community has the coherence and unity of societies organized on more limited scope and basis, such as the state and smaller associations of people. As writers have pointed out, on numerous occasions the community of states has failed to achieve even minimum standards of coherence on many dimensions. Yet in the contemporary world, no state has sufficient resources to stand completely on its own. For the greatest majority of states, nonparticipation in the international system does not constitute a viable choice.

Beginnings of the Community of Nations

As we noted in Chapter 2, historians and political scientists usually take the Peace of Westphalia, marking the end of the Thirty Years' War (1648), as the true beginning of the modern community of nations. The European states participating in the peace settlements at Münster and Osnabrück constituted the charter members of a community that remained very limited in the number of its official members until World War I. Until 1856, only Christian nations could join the group of states subject to the rules of international law. From a geographic viewpoint, legal writers were concerned with, until the beginning of the nineteenth century, about the *droit des gens de l'Europe* (the law of the nations of Europe), and referred to all other states as *pays hors chrétienté* (countries outside Christianity). By the terms of Article 7 of the Treaty of Paris (1856), the Ottoman Empire received the protection and right "to participate in the public law and system of Europe." Italy and some Balkan states subsequently were admitted into the community. The twentieth century witnessed a great expansion in the membership of the community. Today international society has more than 190 states as well as 2,000 IGOs and more than 7,300 NGOs that may also have membership in more than one country.

INTERNATIONAL JURIDICAL PERSONALITY

Under the law, an entity must meet certain minimum qualifications in order to enjoy the benefits of legal rights or must have an obligation to perform certain legal duties. In international law, entities meeting those minimum qualifications have international *juridical personality*. In this chapter, we discuss the fundamental requirements for obtaining juridical personality and describe entities that now have, had in the past, or do not have juridical personality. Not surprisingly, given the complex contemporary international scene, one cannot expect to find simple answers and procedures. Even the word *state* involves a surprising number of permutations that satisfy the fundamental requirements. The formal process by which a state is acknowledged as a member is termed *recognition*.

The most important thing to understand here is the corporate or *collective* nature of international juridical personality. In future chapters, we use the phrase "collective responsibility" to describe circumstances that will make a *state* legally liable for certain acts or omissions. This means that from the perspective of international law, *individuals* will seldom have any *personal responsibility* (see Chapters 11, 15, and 16). The claim or action will be filed against the *state* as the appropriate subject of the law, not against a specific individual as an officer of the state (see Chapter 10). Officers of the state, as agents responsible for carrying out certain duties, may bear personal liability with respect to domestic laws or constitutions, but remember that international law does not specify forms of government or make any demands about how states or other entities meet their obligations, so long as they meet them.

In fact, a limited analogy with corporations (incorporated companies) in domestic law might clarify what we mean by *collective* (corporate) *responsibility and liability*. For example, debts or assets accrued by operating a business belong to the corporation as a legal entity, not to the individuals who make up the corporation as officers and employees. If a corporation fails and files for bankruptcy, the individual officers and employees do not have a *personal* (i.e., individual) responsibility for repayment of the debts (unless they have engaged in some form of illegal activity such as appropriating corporate assets for personal use). The obligations fall upon the corporation as a legal (i.e., juridical) person, and the corporation as a legal person has the responsibility, as best it can, to satisfy the claims against it. In similar fashion, the president of the United States has the constitutional responsibility to see that U.S. obligations are fulfilled. But if the United States, for some reason, does not honor a legal obligation, the president's personal property and assets *are **not** at risk* even though he may have failed in his duty.

Members of the Community of Nations

Who are the principal members of the community of nations, in the sense of having international juridical personality? *Territorial states* alone, by definition, are eligible for such membership. Although certain international agencies and organizations—such as the European Union (EU), the International Committee of the Red Cross (ICRC), and the United Nations—may possess limited juridical personality through the treaties creating them, they are not full "persons" in the context of being primary subjects of international law. States constitute the essential core and building blocks of the political and legal system. As we discussed in Chapter 1, state practice and actions form the essence of the international legal system. For the most part, states are the primary *subjects* of international law. Later in this text, we discuss the circumstances and issue areas (see Chapters and) where international law may directly place obligations (duties) on individuals. For the next several chapters, we shall concentrate on the rights and duties of states. However, not all subjects of international law are "states" in the narrow sense of the definition.

Fully Sovereign and Independent States

To have full legal (juridical) personality, a state must have certain characteristics. A set of minimum facts defines the *legal idea* of a state. According to the *Restatement (Third) of Foreign Relations Law of the United States*, § 201 (1987),

> International law generally defines a "state" as "an entity that has defined territory and a permanent population, under the control of its own government, and that engages in, or has the capacity to engage in, formal relations with other such entities."

Table 7.1

Contemporary States

Country	Size (sq. mi.)	Population
Vatican City	0.17 (109 acres)	850
Monaco	0.73	30,500
Nauru	8	9,600
Tuvalu	9	10,300
San Marino	24	25,650
Liechtenstein	62	33,406
Washington, DC	69	570,898
Rhode Island	1,212	988,500
Republic of Georgia	26,911	4,693,892
State of Georgia, *United States*	58,910	7,644,000
Russia	6,592,900	148,190,450
Canada	3,849,700	29,857,400
United States	3,787,500	265,089,800
China	3,689,700	1,210,005,000
Brazil	3,286,500	162,661,300
Australia	2,996,200	18,260,863
India	1,237,100	952,107,700
Argentina	1,073,400	34,673,000
Kazakhstan	1,049,200	16,916,500

A state, first of all, must occupy a fixed *territory* over which a stable *government* exercises exclusive jurisdiction. *Population* represents an obvious third characteristic of a state. Without population, no government would be possible. *Recognition* by other existing states implies an acknowledgment that the entity has the capacity to fulfill its international duties and obligations as a state and that other states will deal with it as a sovereign equal. In the contemporary world, states come in many different sizes. As Table 7.1 illustrates, *recognition* does not depend upon minimum territorial size, nor does it have a minimum population requirement. To understand what this may mean, think about the implications for Nauru or Tuvalu, which are theoretically equal to all other states as independent sovereign entities in their relations with China, Russia, or the United States.

The presence of territory, government, and population does not, however, necessarily guarantee the existence of an international state in the legal sense. For instance, Puerto Rico (3,435 square miles, 3.9 million population) has territory, a government, and a population, yet it does not have an independent legal status as a state in the "international law" meaning of the term. It lacks the final and decisive requirement to qualify as a member state—*recognition of its independence by those states already in existence.* As another example, even though it is more than twice the size of, and has one-third more population than, the *international* state of Georgia, the U.S. state of Georgia cannot make a treaty with a foreign government or state, cannot bring a case before the International Court of Justice (ICJ), cannot join the United Nations, cannot accept and accredit ambassadors or other diplomatic personnel, and cannot issue its own travel documents because it lacks the legal capacity, the international juridical personality, that would permit it to do so. All of those rights belong to the central federal government of the United States.

While international law specifies the requisite facts that define a state, *each existing state has the right to determine for itself if the set of facts as reflected in each individual situation* merits the *judgment* that a new state exists. Let us emphasize again the fundamental nature of the legal process: One must first determine the facts before making a legal judgment. Because each state has the right to determine the facts for itself, the process of recognition can produce very uneven results. Many Arab states do not recognize Israel as a state. During the Cold War, Eastern Bloc states recognized East Germany, whereas Western Bloc states recognized West Germany and refused the idea that East Germany had any attributes of a state. During the Vietnam War, many Western states recognized South Vietnam (capital Saigon) as a state; many other states recognized North Vietnam (capital Hanoi) as the rightful government of all of Vietnam. These anomalies often show up when states, in response to demands for self-determination, break up into smaller parts.

Another contemporary difficulty comes from the phenomenon of "failed states." While still retaining formal recognition as states, failed states lack an effective central government. Because of coups, interventions, or the fortunes of civil war, these states often have had a succession of temporary governments. Liberia, Sierra Leone, Somalia, and the Democratic Republic of the Congo (formerly Zaire), among others, currently fall into this category. The Soviet Union and Yugoslavia both have broken up into several constituent states. Many of these new states still struggle to maintain coherence and order.

Recognition in General

The term *recognition* means "a formal acknowledgment or declaration by the government of an existing state that it intends to attach certain customary legal consequences to an existing set of facts." In most cases, recognition has a more specialized meaning in international law, relating to the acknowledgment of the existence of a new state, or of a new government in an existing foreign state (after a *nonconstitutional* change such as a revolution or coup d'état), coupled with an expression of willingness by the recognizing state to enter into relations with the recognized entity or government. Recognition in international law also applies to a broader range of relationships as well: to belligerent communities or insurgents, in connection with the validity of title to territory (e.g., recognition of conquest or other means of acquisition), and with reference to the commission of other acts by governments that have international consequences.

In theory, the basic function of recognition is a formal acknowledgment as *fact* of something that has had uncertain status up to the point of formal acknowledgment. Granting recognition indicates the willingness of the recognizing state to accept the legal consequences of its act. In practice, many factors intervene. Despite much reasoned argument to the effect that recognition of new states (and new governments) constitutes a legal matter, most writers as well as state practice support the conclusion that recognition is *a political act with legal consequences.* We can demonstrate this convincingly by simply pointing to the deference of national courts to decisions by political organs of governments concerning new states and governments.

If recognition were a simple matter of *pure legal fact,* national courts would have the latitude to determine the existence of a state or of a new government (after a nonconstitutional change) through their own means of search and discovery apart from the actions of political authorities. In the United States and the United Kingdom, the authority to grant recognition to new states and governments rests in the executive—the president (through the State Department) and the prime minister (through the Foreign Office), respectively. A quick review of the discussion of members of the community of nations and the requirements of "statehood" above should clearly illustrate that recognition may often involve important political questions beyond the simple acknowledgment of legal fact. The case of Palestine provides a graphic example. Sixty years of bloody history have brought the issues to resolution.

Palestine   The reaction to the Palestine National Council's (the "legislature" of the Palestine Liberation Organization [PLO]) declaration of independence of the "State of Palestine" on November 15, 1988, gives a prime example of the political character of the act of recognition. The new entity

- lacked a defined territorial jurisdiction,
- lacked an identifiable and functioning government, and
- lacked a coherent population—great numbers of those claimed as potential "people" lived in surrounding Arab states (many in refugee camps) or in areas under Israeli occupation.

Nevertheless, 23 states granted recognition to the "State of Palestine" within two days, and 70 governments had done so by mid-January 1989. In some instances, recognition fell short of the traditional format: On November 18, 1988, the Soviet Union announced that it recognized the *proclamation* of the Palestinian State, a formula also utilized by Czechoslovakia. On the other hand, the PLO opened (January 1, 1989) the "Embassy of Palestine" in Riyadh in a building donated by the king of Saudi Arabia, and a number of states had upgraded PLO missions to embassy status (Jordan, Iraq, Algeria, Bahrain, and the United Arab Emirates).

The decentralization in this process can produce a situation where an international legal process might render a very different decision from a domestic court bound by the policy of its executive authority and constitution (see the *Tinoco Arbitration,* later in this chapter). Without going too far afield here, just consider that having the United Nations accept a state as a member on the one hand now certifies that a critical number of states have accepted that entity as a state. In the calculus of world politics, admission to the United Nations does not mean that *every* current member has granted formal recognition to the new member; conversely, UN membership does not imply that every other member state has a duty to recognize a new member. In this respect, consider as well the anomalous position of Taiwan (Republic of China) discussed later in this chapter.

De Facto, De Jure, and "Provisional": The Politics of Recognition

The terms *de facto* and *de jure* have caused much confusion because of inconsistency of application in practice and because of continuing disputes among publicists over exactly what the two terms convey regarding the status of the state or government so recognized.[2] The confusion further emphasizes the *ad hoc* political element that seems to be part of many decisions, despite attempts by writers to emphasize legal principles.

Some consensus does exist concerning the intent of states and governments when they employ the terms. If an existing state has characterized the transaction as *de facto*, this means the recognizing government has doubts about the long-term survival of the putative state or government or has political or moral qualms about its origin, but has found it necessary to deal with its representatives on a formal and ongoing basis. The toughest decisions here have always come about when existing governments must deal with *civil wars for the control of the existing state, or with secessionist movements* (for example, Chechnya) seeking to form their own state. In these cases, government authorities must make some pragmatic and difficult decisions.

The terms *de facto* (in fact) and *de jure* (by law) run throughout both state practice and discussions of recognition policies. Some publicists have characterized the question as *de facto recognition* versus *de jure recognition*. This totally misses the point by focusing upon the type of recognition rather than the parameters of the situations. These terms do not describe the nature or type of recognition, but rather a judgment about the status of the state or government receiving recognition. Hence, correctly the emphasis should be on recognition of a *de facto* state or government or recognition of a *de jure* state or government.

Do the semantics here make a very great difference? Clearly, the use of *de facto* in any statement concerning recognition indicates that the state (government) extending recognition has some misgivings about either the long-term stability or the nature (political acceptability) of the new government. In surveying the record, the debate has had little impact on state practice—or perhaps more accurately, state practice has simply provided further grist for debate. In some frustration, the British government stopped using the term *de facto* in the late 1940s (though British scholars still debate the issue). The current *Restatement* notes that, because of confusion (and possible political consequences), the United States does not currently use these terms.[3] When the United States recognizes a state or government, it presumably implies *de jure* status. In sum, recognition is recognition. *It has the same effect whether granted de facto or de jure*—no difference exists between *de facto* and *de jure* with respect to international *legal* rights and duties.

The origin of attempts to construct provisional or partial forms of recognition clearly flows from the simple fact that statesmen have sought flexibility in dealing with situations, such as civil wars, that may produce indeterminate outcomes. They often have to balance many different considerations, ranging from concern for the well-being and lives of citizens who may be caught in the conflict

---

[2]For a concise summary of the issues here, see M. J. Peterson, *Recognition of Governments: Legal Doctrine and State Practice 1815–1995* (1997), 92–98.

[3]Sec. 202.

to questions of preserving property and other rights (contracts, mineral concession rights, etc.) during and after the conflict. Forms of provisional recognition were attempts to deal with entities on the basis of, and to the extent that they exercised, control over a specific territory. While of historic interest, the terms have little significance today because most states have largely abandoned their use.

The Consequences of Recognition

In theory, the recognition of a new government means that the recognizing government acknowledges the stability of the new government as well as its willingness to honor its obligations. The recognizing government acknowledges its willingness to enter into normal international interactions with the new state (government). An important point to remember here is that the actual date on which a state grants recognition may not be the *effective date* of recognition. A state may make recognition of either a state or a government retroactive to some past date, representing a judgment concerning effective control. As we shall see later, a retroactive effective date could have considerable impact on litigation, state responsibility, and other legal matters. This principle was expressed extremely well in the case of *Underhill v. Hernandez* (168 U.S. 250 [1897]). The court held that if the party seeking to dislodge the existing government succeeds, and if the independence of the government it has set up is recognized, then the acts of such government, from the commencement of its existence, can be regarded as legitimately binding.

Recognition means the government of the new state now has the right to establish formal diplomatic relations under the rules of international law with other states that have granted recognition and enjoy the benefits of formal channels of diplomatic intercourse. Recognition does *not* mean that a state *must* set up a diplomatic mission in the recognizing state. Indeed, the presence or absence of formal diplomatic relations forms a choice based on the level of interaction and level of mutual interests, not a legal requirement. No state, including the United States, has an ambassador (or consular official) in every country it has recognized. Recognition cannot impose such a burden in terms of money and people, because few could afford the costs. In this respect, think about Nauru—half the population of the island would be in the diplomatic service posted some place overseas—that is, if they could find the money to support the missions. Finally, just as recognition does not imply a necessary establishment of formal diplomatic relations, *breaking diplomatic ties as a form of protest does not mean withdrawal of recognition* (see Chapter 13).

Recognition of Governments

Recognition of a government as a political act differs from the recognition of a state **only** in the nature of the entity being recognized. As we noted earlier, logically the recognition of a new state automatically entails the recognition of the government in control at the time. A government constitutes the operative agency of a state—that is, the group of individuals responsible for exercising the rights or carrying out the obligations imposed by the principles and rules of international law. So long as changes in governments occur through constitutional or other legitimate means, foreign governments and states do not have to acknowledge the change by a formal act of recognition. The real problems in the recognition of governments occur when a government's form changes through an *unconstitutional* or otherwise irregular transfer of authority from one group to another group (coup d'état, revolution, etc.) within the state in question. The issue then becomes the willingness of foreign states to accept the new government as the official representatives, *the official international agents*, of that state and deal with them accordingly.

A most interesting contemporary case is that of Afghanistan under the Taliban government (1996–2001). Backed by Pakistan and funded by Saudi Arabia, Afghanistan promised to put an end to the factional warfare that had claimed thousands of lives in the years following the defeat of the country's Soviet puppet government in 1991. Although they controlled the capital, Kabul, and much of the country for five years, the Taliban regime (the Islamic Emirate of Afghanistan) gained diplomatic recognition from only three states: Pakistan, Saudi Arabia, and the United Arab Emirates.[4] Most notably, the regime welcomed Osama Bin Laden. On September 22, 2001, the United Arab Emirates and Saudi Arabia withdrew recognition of the Taliban as the legal government of Afghanistan. A United States–led invasion in October of 2001 resulted in the seating of a new government in late December 2001. Recent reports indicate the Taliban have regrouped and again are sponsoring an insurgency in the areas around Kandahar.

We should note that changes in the form of a *government* or in its personnel do not affect the continuing existence of the *state* involved. The classic example commonly cited is that of France between 1791 and 1875. During that period, a succession of constitutional changes produced a transition from monarchy to a republic, then from a republic to an empire, followed by a return to monarchy, development of another empire, and finally evolution into the Third Republic. During all of these changes in government form, France remained the "State of France," the identical international legal person, with the same rights and immunities and with the same unchanged international obligations. In emphasizing points made in Chapters 4 and 6, international law binds the *state*. The government is only the *agent* of the state. If you understand the earlier discussion about the nature of international legal personality, then you should note that the *identity* of the agent does not matter so long as the agent has received recognition. The case of the *Sapphire* illustrates this principle.

▶ THE *SAPPHIRE*

United States, Supreme Court, 1871, 11 Wallace 164

Facts

The private American ship *Sapphire* and the French naval transport *Euryale* collided in the harbor of San Francisco on December 22, 1867. The *Euryale* suffered heavy damage. Two days later, a suit was filed in the district

(continued)

---

[4]Tony Karon, "TIME.com Primer: The Taliban and Afghanistan" (September 18, 2001), www.time.com/time/nation/article/0,8599,175372,00.html (accessed April 20, 2009).

court, in the name of Napoleon III, Emperor of the French, as owner of the *Euryale,* against the *Sapphire.* The owners of the American ship filed an answer, alleging that the damage had been caused through the fault of the French vessel. The district court decided in favor of the libelant (Napoleon III) and awarded him $15,000, representing the total amount claimed. The owners of the *Sapphire* appealed to the circuit court, which, however, upheld the verdict of the lower court. The owners then appealed to the Supreme Court of the United States in July 1869. In the summer of 1870, Napoleon III was deposed as emperor. The case was argued before the Supreme Court on February 16, 1871.

Questions

1. Did the emperor have a right to bring a suit in U.S. courts?
2. If such a suit had been brought rightly, had it not become abated by the deposition of Emperor Napoleon, or, in other words, did the French state, because of the change in its form of government, lose the identity that had permitted it to sue in a foreign court?

Decision

The Supreme Court held that the officers of the *Euryale* had also been at fault and that, both parties being at fault, the damages should be equally divided between them. It therefore reversed the decree of the circuit court and remitted the cause to that court with directions to enter a decree in conformity with the opinion of the Supreme Court. The suit brought originally in the name of Napoleon III had not become abated by the emperor's removal from power. The right to sue and receive compensation belonged to the French state as a legal entity.

Reasoning

1. Question (1): There was no doubt in the minds of the court as to the right of a recognized friendly foreign sovereign to sue in U.S. courts. "A foreign sovereign as well as any other foreign person, who has a demand of a civil nature against any person here, may prosecute it in our courts. To deny him this privilege would manifest a want of comity and friendly feeling."

2. Question (2): "The reigning sovereign represents the national sovereignty, and that sovereignty is continuous and perpetual, residing in the proper successors of the sovereign for the time being. Napoleon was the owner of the *Euryale,* not as an individual, but as sovereign of France. . . . On his deposition the sovereignty does not change, but merely the person or persons in whom it resides. The foreign state is the true and real owner of its public vessels of war. The reigning emperor, or National Assembly, or other actual person or party in power, is but the agent and representative of the national sovereignty. A change in such representative works no change in the national sovereignty of its rights. The next successor recognized by our government is competent to carry on a suit already commenced and receive the fruits of it. The vessel has always belonged and still belongs to the French nation."

Contemporary Controversies

In theory, a government's judgment as to the existence of another new state or the existence of a successor government after a revolution or a coup should be based upon answers to certain objective tests: (1) Does the government of the new entity exercise effective control over its country's administrative machinery, (2) is there any resistance to the government's authority, and (3) does the government appear to have the backing of a substantial segment of the people in its country? Indeed, many other factors may play a role in the decision to recognize. As we discuss later, governments have occasionally sought to hedge their bets by applying various other criteria or attempting to extend provisional recognition.

Thus, the decentralization of the recognition process gives rise to many interesting situations. The debate here illustrates an important point that arises throughout our examination of how law works in the contemporary world. Law presumably provides consistent, reliable answers under comparable circumstances. By itself, the declaration that "I know one when I see one" is the antithesis of legal process and judgment: Without definition and guidelines for applications, each person could freely make a determination according to whatever criteria he or she felt appropriate at the moment. Legal judgments depend upon sets of definitions, rules, and guidelines (operational criteria) of sufficient specificity that, when utilized, would lead each person observing the event to approximately the same conclusion. In this respect, vague or open-ended standards that produce erratic decisions erode claims that law governs or guides the process.

Operational tests (guidelines or standards) provide the essential bridge between abstract, ideal definitions and the reality of application to the diverse circumstances of the real world. The problem here stems from the lack of common objective operational criteria for the elements of the definition. We have examined intuitively the question, "What makes a state?" But even though we have suggested some objective tests, we still have no explicit common guidelines to answer the question, "When should recognition be granted?" While we find many discussions warning against "premature" recognition, these fail to address the question of reliable operational tests to guide us in knowing when a state or government merits recognition—that is, in knowing when recognition might be "premature." The authors of these discussions tend to debate the effects of premature recognition without addressing the issue of how we might distinguish between the deserving and the undeserving.

Governments may use subjective tests. Between roughly 1913 and 1929, the U.S. government insisted that to be recognized by the United States, a new government had to come into office by legal and constitutional means. The United States applied the so-called Wilson Doctrine (named after U.S. President Woodrow Wilson) to new governments in Mexico, El Salvador, Costa Rica, and Nicaragua. The doctrine denied to the peoples of those states the right to select their own governments by whatever means they chose. It meant that the U.S. government claimed the right to determine the legal basis of a foreign government. More interestingly, many contemporary writers have suggested an entirely new set of objective criteria based upon human rights considerations. According to the "democratic entitlement" theorists, "We are witnessing a sea change in international law, as a result of which the legitimacy of each government someday will be measured definitively by international rules and processes."[5] These analysts claim that modern human

---

[5]T. M. Franck, "The Emerging Right to Democratic Governance," 86 *AJIL* (1992), 50. See also G. H. Fox, "The Right to Political Participation in International Law," 17 *Yale Journal of International Law* 539 (1992); G. H. Fox and B. R. Roth, eds, *Democratic Governance and International Law* (2000).

rights law has extended the ideas of legitimacy based upon popular sovereignty to the international level. The idea has played a role in "nation-building" efforts by international organizations such as that in East Timor.[6] The following two cases, both from the breakup of the former Yugoslavia, as well as the discussion of China later in this chapter illustrate the problems.

Kosovo and FYROM

The debate over Kosovo illustrates contemporary problems. In February 2008, Kosovo declared its independence from Serbia. Despite denials that their intervention a decade ago was not aimed at separating Kosovo from Serbia, the United States, Britain, France, and Germany quickly granted recognition.[7] Other EU members did not follow suit. Spain, Greece, Romania, and Cyprus severely criticized the effort to make Kosovo independent. The Russian Federation (Serbia's key ally) and China remained adamantly opposed to Kosovo's independence, warning of the danger of inspiring separatist movements around the world. Those opposed to the secession noted a Security Council Resolution that had explicitly recognized Kosovo as part of Serbia during the earlier debate.[8] Members of Kosovo's Serb minority indicated they will never recognize the declaration of independence and have pledged allegiance to authorities in Belgrade. They have begun to form separate governing and law enforcement bodies in Serb enclaves, particularly in northern Kosovo, which borders Serbia. Some fear that this activity could lead to demands to partition Kosovo.

In early October 2008, the UN General Assembly approved a Serbian motion to submit the issue to the ICJ.[9] The court will be asked to give an advisory opinion on whether the unilateral declaration of independence by the temporary self-rule institutions in Kosovo is in line with international law. The resolution received was opposed by the United States and Albania, but was supported by Brazil, China, India, Mexico, Russia, and South Africa. Of the 27 members of the European Union, 22 abstained. Cyprus, Greece, Romania, Slovakia, and Spain voted in support. Each of these states worries that Kosovo's independence will reinforce separatist or autonomist tendencies in their own countries. Immediately after the General Assembly vote, the Former Yugoslav Republic of Macedonia (FYROM) and recently separated Montenegro granted recognition to Kosovo.[10] In July 2010,

---

[6]See S. D. Murphy, "Contemporary Practice of the United States Relating to International Law," 94 *AJIL* 102 (2000), 106ff.

[7]P. Finn and P. Baker, "Kosovo Gains Recognition by U.S., Some in Europe," *Washington Post* Foreign Service (February 19, 2008), A09.

[8]UNSCOR, S/RES1244 of June 10, 1999.

[9]Request for an advisory opinion of the International Court of Justice on whether the unilateral declaration of independence of Kosovo is in accordance with international law, UNGAOR, A/RES/63/3 of October 8, 2008. Only Albania, the Marshall Islands, the Federated States of Micronesia, Nauru, and Palau voted with the United States.

[10]T. Barber, "Serbia Scores a Partial Victory," *Financial Times* (October 22, 2008).

the ICJ issued its Advisory Opinion.[11] By a 10–4 vote, it found that the unilateral declaration had not violated international law. By March of 2011, Kosovo had received recognition from 76 states, including the United States and most members of the European Union (but not even from half of the current membership of the United Nations). The situation in Kosovo has political implications for other states in the Balkans with large Serbian minorities as well.

The crisis caused by the breakup of Yugoslavia included a prolonged crisis over recognition of the FYROM. This case illustrates the problems nonrecognition may cause in the contemporary world. Curiously, in contrast with the violent struggles in Croatia and Bosnia-Herzegovina, the FYROM gained independence quite easily and with little bloodshed. The quest for recognition, however, proved much more difficult even though the great majority of European states favored immediate recognition of the FYROM upon its effective severance of membership in the old Socialist Federal Republic of Yugoslavia (SFRY) in 1991. Clearly, the FYROM met the objective criteria for statehood. In seceding, it had not violated any provision of international law, but Greece had major objections to the use of certain national symbols and to the use of the name *Macedonia* (also the name of a province in northern Greece).

The controversy had a significant impact on the effectiveness of the sanctions the European Union (EU) had adopted to punish Serbia and Montenegro for their actions in Bosnia and Croatia. Without recognition, the FYROM refused to cooperate with the EU in enforcing the sanctions, thus allowing its territory to serve as a conduit for prohibited items in transit to the war zones. Greece further exacerbated the crisis by adopting a unilateral trade embargo against the FYROM in direct defiance of a collective EU decision to open economic ties with the new state.[12] Six EU member states recognized the FYROM in December 1993, but Greece continued to resist until 1995. Though the two states normalized relations, the dispute over the name still simmers under the surface. In October 2008, a UN mediator proposed the name Republic of Northern Macedonia to replace the awkward FYROM.[13] The dispute has very real consequences because Greece has actively blocked Macedonia's NATO aspirations and its attempts to join the EU.

Other Special Cases

Neutralized States   A *neutralized* state differs from a neutral state in that the status of permanent neutrality (except for the obvious right of self-defense in the case of direct attack) is imposed on the neutralized state by a group of outside powers.

---

[11] *Accordance with International Law of the Unilateral Declaration of Independence in Respect of Kosovo*, International Court of Justice (July 22, 2010). Judges Tomka (Slovakia), Bennouna (Morocco), Koroma (Sierra Leone), and Skolnikov (Russian Federation) voted against the majority. Note that Judge Hanqin (China) voted with the majority.

[12] T. D. Grant, *The Recognition of States* (1999), 185; the embargo caused the European Commission to file suit against Greece in the European Court of Justice. See *Commission of the European Communities v. Hellenic Republic* [1994] ECR I-3037; 100 *ILR* 222.

[13] "UN Proposes Name 'Northern Macedonia'," Reuters (October 8, 2008). FYROM has suggested a double-name solution—one for internal use, one for international use. Greece has resisted this solution.

A self-declared neutral state, for example Sweden, has itself chosen to adopt a *policy* of neutrality. A neutralized state cannot enter into an alliance requiring its participation in any future conflict. The powers requiring its neutrality in turn obligate themselves to respect that status. The number of neutralized states has never been very large: Switzerland (since 1815), Austria (1955), and Laos (1962). In 1920, the League of Nations "recognized" the permanent neutrality of Switzerland. On the demise of the League, Switzerland initially decided not to become a member of the United Nations but "participated" in the operation of the ICJ and various other agencies affiliated through the Economic and Social Council. It finally formally joined the United Nations in 2002.

Divided States   A peculiar phenomenon in the post-1945 world, reflecting the bipolar orientation of world politics during the Cold War, was the emergence of several states divided into two entities, each having an operative government: Germany (Federal Republic and Democratic Republic), Korea (Democratic People's Republic and the Republic of Korea), China (Republic of China and People's Republic), Vietnam (North and South), and Cyprus. The division of Korea, China, and Cyprus continues today.

China   After the flight of the Nationalist government, led by Chiang Kai-shek, to Taiwan (1949) and the takeover of power on the mainland by Communist forces led by Mao Tse-tung, the United States continued to recognize the *government* in Taipei (capital of Taiwan, the Republic of China [ROC]) as the lawful and only government of all of China. Even though Taiwan did not officially claim itself as a separate state, its claim to be the government of all of China challenged the legitimacy of the mainland government in its own claim to be the government of all of China. The United States continued to recognize the Nationalist government of Chiang and refused to recognize the government of the People's Republic of China (PRC) led by Mao in Beijing (see Chapter 5).

This dispute technically involves issues related to the recognition of a *government* rather than recognition of a new state, although currently Taiwan (Republic of China) functions as an independent state for those who have recognized it. However, because of the peculiar circumstances associated with the Cold War, the rapid economic development of Taiwan, the increasing participation and influence of Beijing in international political affairs, and Beijing's territorial claim to Taiwan as Chinese territory, the issues have changed somewhat over time, yet remain unresolved. Beijing (the capital of mainland China), because of the obvious challenge to its *legitimacy*, has refused to accept a "two Chinas policy" from any state. It has demanded that any state that recognized Beijing could not at the same time recognize (or continue to recognize) Taipei. If a state had previously recognized Taipei, Beijing demanded as a condition that state's withdrawal of recognition from Taiwan. Consider how unusual this situation is for international politics—Beijing, not the community, has set its own conditions for recognition. On the other side, because the Chinese government in Beijing has remained under Communist Party control, the United States and its allies have steadfastly insisted that Taiwan has a right of self-determination. This means that any union would require the consent of the people of Taiwan.

The PRC replaced the ROC as the representative of "China" in the United Nations on October 25, 1971, by action of the General Assembly. The General Assembly refused to permit Taiwan to continue as a member under any circumstances. This meant that the Beijing government now occupied the Chinese seat on the Security Council. While the United States had supported the admission of the People's Republic, it had opposed the expulsion of the Republic of China, but both Chinese governments had emphatically rejected the "two Chinas" concept of membership before the General Assembly action took place. Fifteen attempts by Taiwan to join the United Nations have failed—most recently in 2007.[14]

President Richard Nixon took the first move toward U.S. recognition of Beijing in 1972 by making an unprecedented visit to the mainland, but official recognition and establishment of official relations did not occur until President Carter made the formal declaration in January 1979. The United States, for its part, recognized the government of the People's Republic as the sole legal government of China. The United States agreed that on the same date, it would notify the government on Taiwan that it was withdrawing U.S recognition and that the Mutual Defense Treaty of 1954 between the Republic of China and the United States would be terminated in accordance with the provisions of that treaty (at the end of 1979—see Chapter 4). The United States also withdrew all military personnel from Taiwan.

From a factual standpoint, the Republic of China continues to exist as an independent entity, recognized by about two dozen members of the family of nations.[15] The U.S. government has assured the authorities on Taiwan that nongovernmental relations between them and the United States would continue, through a corporation created in the United States for that purpose, and that the United States would continue its shipment of "defensive" military supplies to Taiwan.

Korea Following World War II, Korea was split. The northern half came under Communist rule and the southern portion became Western oriented. We should note that the Korean War (1950–1953) ended without a peace treaty and that the two states are technically still at war.[16] The government of the Republic of Korea (South) was long accepted by most UN members as the only lawful government of all of Korea; the People's Republic of Korea (North), on the other hand, was recognized only by members of the Socialist Bloc. In 1972, the two governments engaged in negotiations at Panmunjom with the object of improving their mutual relations and reunifying their country. The series of meetings soon lapsed without substantive agreement. In May 1973, the People's Republic (North) was admitted to membership in the World Health Organization (WHO); within weeks, it received observer status at the Geneva headquarters of the United Nations, and in June 1973, it obtained observer status (already enjoyed for a long time by South Korea) at the UN New York headquarters.

---

[14]See www.whydemocracy.net/house/news/node/42 (accessed April 20, 2009).

[15]For current information, see "Political Status of Taiwan," www.answers.com/topic/political-status-of-taiwan. Interestingly, the Holy See recognizes the ROK, mainly out of protest of the PRC's suppression of the Catholic faith on the mainland.

[16]See Whiteman, I: 320; and *US News and World Report* (August 20, 1990), 41.

Both governments at first vigorously denounced and opposed a "German solution" to their problems—each preferring to adhere to the concept of an eventual unification solution. In mid-June 2000, the leaders of the two Koreas held their first summit meeting in Pyongyang. The summit led to a joint statement by the two leaders that supported, in general terms, the goals of eventually reunifying the two Korean states, reuniting families divided since the Korean War, and securing economic cooperation. However, in December 2002, North Korea repudiated a 1994 agreement on nuclear weapons and facilities, and expelled UN monitors, raising fears it would produce nuclear weapons. Developments in inter-Korean relations since 2002 have been mixed. The North shelled Yeonpyeong Island in November 2010, killing two South Korean soldiers and causing a great deal of property damage. The question of nuclear weapons and missile production by the North continues as an issue.[17]

Cyprus Cyprus gained independence from the United Kingdom in 1960, with constitutional guarantees by the Greek Cypriot majority to the Turkish Cypriot minority. In 1974, a Greek-sponsored attempt to seize the government was met by military intervention from Turkey, which soon controlled almost 40 percent of the island. In 1983, the Turkish-held area declared itself the Turkish Republic of Northern Cyprus (TRNC) but was recognized only by Turkey. Beginning in January 2002, the United Nations sponsored direct talks between the two sides to reach a comprehensive settlement for division of the island. The talks culminated with a referendum of all Cypriots on April 21, 2004, in which the citizens of the TRNC voted to accept the plan for reunification put forth by Kofi Annan. Cyprus (minus the TRNC) was admitted to the EU on May 1, 2004. The EU approved the TRNC as a "tertiary" state (a customs union), pending completion of the reunification process.

Special Subjects

The City of the Vatican (The Holy See) For historical reasons, if not for its contemporary status, the City of the Vatican must be included as a member of the community of nations. The governing authority of the Roman Catholic Church (RCC) is generally known as the Vatican, with the pope as its head. The Holy See is the RCC's secular diplomatic agent, and Vatican City is its independent territory. Most of the questions that had plagued relations between the Holy See and Italy since the extinction of the Papal States in 1870 were resolved by the Lateran Treaty of 1929.[18] That agreement recognized the State of the City of the Vatican as a sovereign and independent state occupying 108.7 acres in Rome. In 1984, a *concordat* (agreement—see Chapter 4) between the Holy See and Italy modified certain of the earlier treaty provisions, including the primacy of Roman Catholicism as the

---

[17]"North Korea's Conflict with the South: Timeline," *The Telegraph* (November 23, 2010), www.telegraph.co.uk/news/worldnews/asia/southkorea/8153048/North-Koreas-conflict-with-the-South-timeline.html.
[18]U.S. Department of State, "Background Note: Holy See," www.state.gov/r/pa/ei/bgn/3819.htm.

Italian state religion. Present concerns of the Holy See include religious freedom, international development, the Middle East, terrorism, interreligious dialogue and reconciliation, and the application of church doctrine in an era of rapid change and globalization. The Vatican is a member of, or has official observer status with, several international organizations and maintains a small accredited observer mission at the United Nations in New York. After a long hiatus (117 years), the United States reestablished formal diplomatic relations with the Vatican in 1984.

The independence and sovereignty of the Vatican were upheld in July 1987 when the Italian Court of Cassation voided arrest warrants against Archbishop Paul Marcinkus, head of the Vatican Bank, and two other senior Vatican Bank officials, all charged with being accessories to fraudulent bankruptcy in the Italian Banco Ambrosiano scandal. The court ruled that the 1929 Lateran Treaty protected "central bodies" of the church from "every interference" by the Italian government.

Sovereign Military Order of the Knights of Malta   A second special subject of international law, yet not really a member of the community of nations, is the Sovereign Military Order of the Knights of Malta. Founded in the days of the Crusades as the Order of St. John, it was engaged in the care of the wounded and the sick. Originally based in the Crusader town of Acre (now located in Israel), it moved in 1291 to Cyprus and then, in 1310, to the island of Rhodes. In 1522 the Turks drove the Order from Rhodes, and they relocated in Malta in 1530. Successively, French occupation in 1798, followed by conquest and annexation in 1800 by Great Britain, left the order with no state authority of its own. It moved to Rome, where today its headquarters occupy about one large city block.[19] The Knights of Malta, with a membership of about 8,000, operate hospitals, hospices, and other medical facilities in many parts of the world. The Order maintains diplomatic relations with the City of the Vatican and with some 40 countries, mostly located in Latin America. It also has concluded postal agreements with 10 countries and has been recognized as a (landless) sovereign nation by some 40 countries. Because of its special status, the Order can be classified as a ***non-state*** subject of international law, although of a somewhat peculiar nature.

Associated States   Before leaving the "state" discussion on the subjects of international law, we should mention a new category in that group: ***associated states***. This contemporary term refers to an entity that has delegated certain governmental functions (primarily foreign affairs and/or defense) to a "principal state" while retaining its own international status. Other states in the family of nations still regard the entity as a member state with full rights, privileges, and obligations. In the Pacific area, the Federated States of Micronesia, the Commonwealth of the Northern Marianas, the Republic of the Marshall Islands, and the Republic of Palau fall into the category of associated states. All were former trust territories of the United States. Individuals in these states have U.S. *nationality* for the purposes of travel and other activities, but *they do not have the rights of citizenship*. So they cannot vote in any U.S. election, even that for president. As we shall discuss

---

[19]Order of Malta, www.orderofmalta.org/?lang=en.

in Chapter 8, nationality does not necessarily entail the full rights of *citizenship*. Nationality and citizenship **are not** coextensive principles.

The Principality of Sealand   The motivations concerning the establishment of Sealand[20] reflect the romantic desire of many to find an uninhabited island (or buy one) and set up an independent domain free of taxes and regulations. It also illustrates the difficulties of doing so. Among these ventures, Sealand has the most extensive history.[21]

During World War II, the United Kingdom decided to establish a number of offshore military bases to defend England against German air raids. These human-made "islands," built just outside of territorial waters along the east coast of England, housed 150–300 troops who manned and maintained artillery designed to shoot down German aircraft and missiles. One of these, Roughs Tower (area, approximately 14,000 square feet—for comparison, a Nimitz-class aircraft carrier has a flight deck of 275,184 square feet), was situated slightly north of the Thames River estuary about 7 nautical miles from the coast. Because at that time the United Kingdom claimed a territorial sea of only 3 nautical miles, Roughs Tower stood in international waters in the North Sea. At the end of World War II, the government withdrew all troops from these bases. Subsequently, all of these forts except Roughs Tower were dismantled.

In September 1967, Paddy Roy Bates, a British citizen, occupied Roughs Tower and claimed it as his own with the original idea of setting up a commercial "pirate" radio operation. Bates argued that as a deserted and abandoned piece of "territory" outside the jurisdiction of any state, Roughs Tower constituted *terra nullius* ("no one's land") open for the taking. Bates then declared the old fort an independent state, with him and his wife (Joan) as its sovereign rulers. In 1968, the British Navy allegedly attempted to evict the new inhabitants of Roughs Tower. Bates responded by firing several shots at the vessels. When he subsequently came onshore for supplies, authorities arrested him. In November 1968, the court held that it had no jurisdiction because the episode had occurred outside of the United Kingdom's legitimate territorial jurisdiction. The government, while upset, did not appeal for fear that another court might give some substance to the claims of independence.

Although *no state has granted formal recognition to Sealand*, its website boasts that it has all the necessary features of a state, including a constitution, a flag, a national anthem, a national motto, postage stamps, currency (1 Sealand dollar equaling 1 U.S. dollar), and passports (although no state has ever accepted them as official travel documents).[22] It also has had a coup attempt by a group of potential

---

[20]For a short history, see www.sealandgov.org; see also T. Dennis, "The Principality of Sealand: Nation Building by Individuals," 10 *Tulsa J. Comp. & Int'l L.* 261 (2002); S. P. Menefee, "Republics of the Reefs: Nation-Building on the Continental Shelf and in the World's Oceans," 25 *Cal. W. Int'l L.J.* 81 (1984); S. Baker, "Seized Gun Platform Puzzles Britain," UPI, December 23, 1982.

[21]Principality of Sealand, www.sealandgov.org/.

[22]While Bates denied that Sealand sold "citizenship," those associated with the venture certainly did sell passports. After a scandal of major proportions that involved criminal activity, approximately 150,000 Sealand passports were revoked in 1997. E. Owen, "Rogue Ruler of 'Fantasy Land' Held in Passport Con Probe," *The Express* (April 6, 2000).

investors and developers who intended to set up a luxury hotel and casino in the structure.[23] With the Internet revolution, Sealand attracted attention because it housed a firm that offered the equivalent of offshore banking to companies seeking to provide maximum privacy for their data and e-commerce transactions.[24] The success of this now seems in doubt because the website for HavenCo shut down in November 2008. As of July 2011, the "sovereign family" of Sealand was looking for a buyer.

National Liberation Movements　After World War II, as the anticolonial movement gained momentum, attempts to give various groups engaged in struggles to expel colonial occupiers' visibility and leverage figured prominently in the politics to seat representatives of these groups at international meetings normally restricted to members of the community of nations. A typical instance took place at the 1974 conference to revise the 1949 Geneva Conventions on the Rules of War, convened by Switzerland in Geneva. On the insistence of the Organization of African Unity (OAU) and their allies, 14 national liberation movements participated in the diplomatic conference as members without vote. The OAU member states were determined that "recognized" national liberation movements be awarded an international character. At the same time, these states tried to limit the potential reach of "national liberation" doctrine because they had little desire to be the object of local national liberation movements within their own borders.[25] Except for continuing questions surrounding the Palestinian Liberation Organization (PLO), the issues here have little salience in contemporary politics, though secessionist movements continue in many areas of the world.

International Organizations　Public international organizations (IGOs)—agencies established for state purposes by states—in some cases do have a limited international personality. Some have the power to conclude binding international agreements (within the scope of competence granted), of appearing as plaintiffs or defendants before international tribunals, and of being able to claim immunity from legal process for defined categories of their officials in the same manner as for accredited representatives of members of the community of nations.

From its inception, the United Nations has clearly possessed a limited international personality. The framers of the UN Charter, to avoid real or fancied defects in the League Covenant, included numerous articles in the Charter (Articles 24, 26, 41, 42, and 104) specifically outlining the legal powers and the responsibilities of the United Nations and spelling out its status as an international legal person. The EU united three earlier entities: the European Economic Community (or Common Market), the European Coal and Steel Community, and the European Atomic Energy Commission. The EU is authorized to conclude binding agreements with nonmember

---

[23]See M. Lucas, "Seven Miles off the Suffolk Coast, the Principality of Sealand Is Europe's Smallest Self-Proclaimed Independent State," *The Independent* (November 27, 2004).

[24]See J. Libbenga, "Offshore Hosting Firm HavenCo Lost at Sea," The Register (November 25, 2008), www.theregister.co.uk/2008/11/25/havenco/ (accessed April 16, 2011).

[25]K. Suter, *An International Law of Guerilla Warfare: The Global Politics of Law Making* (1984), 147ff.

countries and IGOs, and it can make regulations binding its member states as well as industrial concerns operating within its functional sphere. The EU has the status of an international legal person with limited rights granted to it by treaty.

Nongovernmental Organizations For our purposes here, the exact definition of a nongovernmental organization (NGO) does not matter. Whether solely confined to one state or transnational in membership (i.e., having members from many states), NGOs do not have international juridical personality. NGOs cannot make treaties, bring cases to the ICJ, or have a formal membership in an IGO.[26] One should not conclude that the absence of legal personality necessarily translates into a lack of political influence in many important areas of contemporary international life. As we discuss later (see Chapters 14, 15, and 18), NGOs such as Amnesty International, Human Rights Watch, and the International Committee of the Red Cross (ICRC) have played important roles in developing contemporary law and practice in the areas of human rights, the environment, and international humanitarian law.

Status of Tribes A few writers once held that tribes in North America and elsewhere were equivalent to international persons. States, on the other hand, have usually denied such status to tribes; agreements made with them were subsequently often (and quite unfairly) denied the character of binding treaties, regardless of the nomenclature applied to the original agreement when it was made. While domestic law may give tribes a certain amount of autonomy with a state, tribes do not constitute independent members of the community of nations.[27]

A Note on Leased Territory

Leases of territory, regardless of the length of time specified in the relevant agreements, do not confer title or create changes in sovereignty. China leased Port Arthur and Dalny to Russia; Kiao-chao to Germany; Wei-hai-wei, Tientsin, and the so-called New Territories on the mainland opposite the island of Hong Kong to Great Britain; Macao to Portugal; and Kwang-chau-wan to France. None of these agreements transferred legal title to the areas involved from the lessor to the lessee.[28] The same doctrine applies to the former lease of the Canal Zone granted by Panama to the United States and the current ongoing U.S. lease of Guantánamo Bay from

---

[26]See R. Wedgwood, "Legal Personality and the Role of Non-governmental Organizations and Non-state Political Entities in the United Nations System," in *Non-state Actors as New Subjects of International Law*, edited by R. Hofmann (Berlin: Dunker and Humblot, 1999), 21; D. Shelton, "The Participation of Non-governmental Organizations in International Judicial Proceedings," 88 *AJIL* 611 (1994).

[27]In an effort to promote the interests and welfare of tribes and certain indigenous peoples, the International Labor Organization adopted Convention No. 169 in June 1989, the Convention Concerning Indigenous and Tribal Peoples in Independent Countries. The text of the instrument is reproduced, with a background/content summary, in 28 *ILM* 1382 (1989), www.ilo.org/indigenous/Conventions/no169/lang--en/index.htm. It entered into force on September 5, 1991. See also the detailed footnote 5 in 89 *AJIL* 351 (1995).

[28]See *In re Ning Yi-Ching and Others*, Great Britain, Vacation Court, August 23, 1939, 56 *Times L. R.* 1, 3, reprinted in 34 *AJIL* 347 (1940). On leased territories in general, consult Whiteman, II: 1216.

Cuba. Authorities and diplomats have agreed that a lease treaty only transfers jurisdictional rights and does not at all bring about an alienation of territory. In other words, sovereign *rights* are exercised by the leasing state, but *title* to the territory remains indisputably with the state granting the lease. This is true even when the lease entails use of the territory as a naval or military base by the leasing state (e.g., Guantánamo Bay in Cuba, leased by but not ceded to the United States).[29] All of these leases, except the U.S. lease of Guantánamo, have been canceled.[30]

Constitutive and Declaratory Theories

Debate continues within the international legal community over whether recognition is the only means through which an entity may gain statehood as well as over the criteria that a de facto (in fact) authority must meet to be considered a state or government for the purposes of international law.[31] Let us assume a community that has all the necessary elements to qualify as a state—people, territory, and effective government—but for some reason has not gained recognition from any existing state. Does such an entity have any status in international law? Older textbooks discuss two theories: recognition as *constitutive* of international personality and recognition as merely *declaratory* of international personality. The constitutive theory holds that the putative "state" has no legal existence until recognized. Declaratory theory states that the existence of a state is a matter of pure objective fact. The act of recognition simply marks official notice that the entity meets the basic conditions of fact associated with statehood and registers the intention to treat the entity as a state. *Recognition presupposes a state's existence; it does not create it.* The current Restatement leans heavily toward this position but also notes that a state must act as if an unrecognized entity were a state if it meets the minimum standards of statehood.[32] Again, this observation seems more pragmatic advice than legal requirement. The declaratory position still begs the question of who initially determines that an entity meets the criteria of statehood. Does recognition by Nauru, Tuvalu, Kiribati, and the Vatican necessarily have any meaning at all for other states?

Neither of these theories quite covers the complexity of issues involved with recognition in the contemporary world, but they are worth exploring briefly.[33] Prior to World War I, the constitutive theory clearly reflected practice. We need

---

[29] *Treaty Between the United States of America and Cuba*, May 29, 1934, www.yale.edu/lawweb/avalon/diplomacy/cuba/cuba001.htm (accessed April 26, 2009). A nominal rent of $3,386.25 was paid annually by the United States until 1960, when the Cuban government refused to accept further payments on the grounds that the base should not be allowed to remain in U.S. hands; *New York Times* (February 4, 1964), 14; and *New York Times* (August 30, 1977), 4.

[30] See P. W.-Smith, *Unequal Treaty, 1898–1997: China, Great Britain and Hong Kong's New Territories* (1980); the text of the 1984 treaty is found in 23 *ILM* 1366 (1984).

[31] For good, concise summaries of the debate, see, for example, James R. Crawford, *The Creation of States in International Law* (1970), 16–25; Lauterpacht, *Recognition in International Law* (1948), ch. IV; Grant, note 12, at chs. 1, 2.

[32] Sec. 202; see also "Reporter's Notes to Restatement," Sec. 202.

[33] R. Y. Jennings and A. Watts, eds, *Oppenheim's International Law*, 9th ed. (1992), 128ff.

only to look at the diplomatic record to see how areas considered to be non-members of the club governed by the "public law of Europe" were treated. With the evolution of the public law of Europe as the framework to a true *international* law, and with the dissolution of colonial empires, the declaratory theory more closely paralleled state practice. As former colonial holdings shed their status as colonial possessions and claimed independence, most states acknowledged most of the transitions to "statehood" without closely examining the minimum facts. Some have suggested that this practice undermined the idea of statehood because many of these entities lacked a government with sufficient capacity to carry out the duties imposed by international law.

Questions relating to recognition once more became salient with the breakup of the former Yugoslavia and the former Soviet Union into a number of constituent states in the 1990–1994 period. The evidence from the more recent cases strongly suggests that the editorial opinion favoring declaratory doctrine in the Restatement does not reflect either recent American practice or that of any major state.[34] The question of the viability of a secessionist movement, particularly like that of Biafra from Nigeria, illustrates the difficulty of ascertaining "pure fact" apart from political interest. The struggles of the Former Yugoslav Republic of Macedonia to overcome Greek objections illustrate the fundamental problems of the declaratory position. Actually, Croatia and Bosnia–Herzegovina both serve as interesting cases because the states of the European Union (EU) granted recognition when rebel forces still occupied significant portions of their claimed territories. The governments of these states clearly did not exercise "effective control" over all of their claimed territory at the time.

While we have asserted that law should provide reliable answers, in contemporary state practice we can find no definitive answer as to which theory may provide the best explanation. Clearly, recognition forms a prerequisite to formal, official bilateral relations with the recognizing state, but as we noted earlier, the decentralized nature of the process may produce many anomalies. To reemphasize an important point, the extent to which a state "belongs" to the community of nations depends upon the extent of its bilateral relationships with other states as determined by their *unilateral* acts of acknowledgment. Clear examples come from the isolation of the Turkish Republic of Northern Cyprus (TRNC), the diplomatic record associated with the divided states during the Cold War, the claims of the founders of Sealand, the status of the Ukrainian Soviet Socialist Republic and the Byelorussian Soviet Socialist Republic as members of the United Nations from its founding, and the current status of the Republic of China (Taiwan).

The questions revolve around the status of an unrecognized entity that may ostensibly meet all the requirements for statehood except formal recognition. If recognition is "constitutive" of legal personality, then what "rights" and "duties" does an unrecognized entity have? Clearly an unrecognized entity does not have the right of formal diplomatic contact, but can it then simply ignore all international obligations because it does not have juridical personality and hence technically cannot either exercise rights or be subject to duties? To complicate the problem, even though an "entity" may not have *formal* rights, many insist that it must

---

[34]Grant, note 12, at 22–24.

observe the duties and obligations (the rules) of international law and could, after formal recognition, be held legally responsible for any delicts[35] before recognition that might engage international responsibility. Other than the obvious pragmatic political observation that if you wish to join the club, you must not openly flout the rules of the club, what is the *legal* basis for making this assertion? As circumstances have changed, some writers espousing this position have claimed that existing states have a duty to recognize an entity if it meets the minimum standards. Nothing in state practice indicates any such obligation.[36]

Continuing Questions: Self-Determination Is What States Make of It   As with the breakup of Yugoslavia, the breakup of the former Soviet Union continues to pose contemporary problems in terms of generating secessionist movements.[37] Pridnestrovie (Moldova), Chechnya (Russia), Abkhazia and South Ossetia (Georgia), and Nagorno-Karabakh (Azerbaijan) have made claims to independence. While Russia has actively sought to suppress the Chechen bid for independence, it has lent support to the others.[38] It officially recognized the independence of Georgia's two breakaway provinces, South Ossetia and Abkhazia. On August 25, 2008, Russia threatened to extend recognition to Pridnestrovie and Nagorno-Karabakh if Western states recognize Kosovo. Presently, only Armenia has recognized Nagorno-Karabakh. In an interesting twist, the "unrecognized" states in waiting have recognized each other. At the moment (June 2011), even though all four have managed to resist control from their former states and have the trappings of sovereignty, none of these entities has garnered support for independence from the broader international community. Contrast their struggles with the latest member of the international community, South Sudan, which gained independence from Sudan after a long and bloody war.[39]

Implied (Tacit) Recognition   In 1944,[40] President Franklin Roosevelt received a message that General Charles de Gaulle, leader of the French resistance in North Africa, had sent a rare white gorilla as a gift. The gift posed a problem: To accept it might send the message that the United States had implicitly or tacitly acknowledged that General de Gaulle, as the de facto (in fact) political leader of the Free French movement, had some formal political status. Not to accept the gift would have angered the general, whose touchiness over status was well known, at a crucial point in the coordination of plans and consultation. Fortunately, the gorilla must have been a born diplomat. He died on the voyage over, thus solving the problem.

---

[35]A *delict* is a violation of international law.

[36]On this point, see Peterson, note 2, at 31–35.

[37]S. Pegg, "*De Facto* States in the International System" (Institute of International Relations, The University of British Columbia, Working Paper #21, 1998). "Regions and Territories: South Ossetia," BBC NEWS (April 23, 2009), http://news.bbc.co.uk/2/hi/europe/country_profiles/3797729.stm.

[38]Russia confirms support of Abkhazia's and Ossetia's independence, mosnews.com (March 20, 2009), www.mosnews.com/politics/2009/03/20/ossetabkhaz/.

[39]"South Sudan Becomes World's Newest Nation," AP Wire (July 9, 2011).

[40]For an extended discussion of possible conditions and terms, see B. R. Roth, *Governmental Illegitimacy in International Law* (2001).

Similarly, in preparing for reciprocal visits between the heads of state of East and West Germany during their rapprochement in 1972–1973, the East German government had planned the full red carpet treatment with salutes, flags, and high-profile official receptions. The West German head of state, Willy Brandt, demurred and asked that the visit remain low-key with no official ceremonies. The refusal had a simple root—reciprocity. If East Germany honored Brandt as head of state with the red carpet treatment, his East German counterpart would have expected the same on his visit to West Germany. Remember that neither West Ger-many nor any of its allies had yet recognized East Germany as a state. The West German salute, use of flag, and VIP treatment might be construed as an implied recognition of East Germany as an equal and a state. At that point, West Germany did not wish to do anything that might imply recognition of the East German regime before reaching an agreement defining the relationship between the two.

Presumably, implicit (tacit) recognition occurs when a government engages in an act, or establishes a contact or interaction, inconsistent with nonrecognition. The literature on tacit recognition uniformly asserts this position. Yet during the American Civil War, Great Britain sent a number of official agents to the Confederate states, but never formally recognized the latter as an independent entity. Many other governments have acted similarly in modern history. The problem stems from lack of agreement on what types of interactions might be considered as reliable indicators of recognition. Cold War disagreements raised an interesting question germane to other areas of international law: Should we consider the inherent nature of the act or consider its intention? What kinds of contacts between states imply recognition?

In contemporary relations, while diplomats may fear taking some action that might inadvertently be read as recognition, the facts of most cases indicate that even sustained contact—if done through low-ranking officials or "back channels"—does not constitute implicit or tacit recognition. Modern life with its tour-ism, business contacts, and the range of other interactions flowing from "globalization" may generate the need for ad hoc contacts with unrecognized regimes to deal with issues that arise without raising the presumption of formal recognition. Protection of citizens or property may necessitate dealings with an unrecognized state or government. For example, after an unconstitutional change in government, diplomats often may stay at their posts because of the need to remain in contact with the new government.[41] Continuing contact in this instance would signal continued recognition of the state without necessarily implying formal recognition of the new government.

During the Cold War, necessary contacts with divided states or Communist/non-Communist contenders for power often led to informal contacts with disclaimers. For example, consider the saga of U.S. relations with the People's Re-public of China. In this case, even a visit from President of the United States Richard Nixon to Beijing was not taken as a sign of official recognition. The United States, although it had not recognized the government of the People's Republic of China, dealt directly with that government from 1955 through the arrangement of over

---

[41]Peterson, note 2, at 103.

100 "ambassadorial talks" originally held in Geneva from 1958 to 1968, in 1970 in Warsaw, and in 1972 in Paris. Participants were the Chinese and American ambassadors accredited to Poland, and later those accredited to France. The U.S. government had indicated repeatedly that these talks did not mean recognition of the Beijing government. On February 22, 1973, the United States and China announced the forthcoming establishment of official government liaison offices in Washington and Beijing to hasten normalization of relations between the two countries. In late May 1973, those offices came into being. Official recognition did not happen until January 1, 1979.

Other examples of *relations officieuses* in the absence of formal recognition abound in modern international relations. The United States successfully mediated the settlement of the Angola–South Africa conflict even though the United States had not recognized the Angolan government since Angola's independence. Again, the Holy See (the Vatican) occasionally dealt with the State of Israel despite failing to "recognize" the latter. Such dealings took place through a mission headed by an Apostolic Delegate lacking diplomatic (ambassadorial) status. The Vatican did not formally recognize Israel until December 1993.

On the other side of the coin, as we have noted, the Vatican played important diplomatic roles even though it lacked explicit recognition from many states, including the United States. From 1797 to 1867, the United States had stationed a consul, a chargé d'affaires, or a "minister resident," at the Papal States, but then the United States closed its legation. The Kingdom of Italy formally annexed the Papal States in 1870, leaving the status of the Vatican in limbo because the Church no longer had a secular territorial base. Not until 1929, with the signing of the Lateran Pact and Concordat, did the Vatican reemerge as a totally independent entity. President Franklin Roosevelt appointed a personal representative—a position devoid of any diplomatic status—in 1939. After President Harry Truman failed to gain Senate approval for his ambassadorial nominee, the United States had no regular contact with the Vatican until President Richard Nixon recreated the post of personal representative. Following Senate approval of President Ronald Reagan's nominee, William A. Wilson (March 7, 1984), the United States became the 108th state to grant formal recognition to the Vatican. In 1982, Great Britain, Denmark, Norway, and Sweden (Protestant states) all granted recognition and restored full diplomatic relations with the Vatican after a 400-year hiatus.

Nonrecognition

Nonrecognition clearly limits the extent of bilateral contacts, but questions concerning the extent of the limitation persist. To emphasize a point made earlier in the chapter, many cases of extensive and prolonged "informal" contact with unrecognized regimes have occurred. The difficulties found in sorting through effects stem from the lack of systematic analysis of different factual situations by international legal scholars. All cases of nonrecognition tend to be lumped into one category without considering motive, length, or context. In particular, scholars have failed to distinguish between lengthy periods of nonrecognition based on political hostility or legal obligation (e.g., the United States regarding the incorporation of the Baltic Republics by the Soviet Union) and those based on doubt about the stability of the new regime.[42]

Nonetheless, most writers do agree that nonrecognition of an existing state or government represents a rather ineffective political measure unless it embodies a broad consensus among major states. Nonrecognition has a number of disadvantages, including that the legitimate interests of one's citizens cannot adequately be protected in the unrecognized entity. If nonrecognition lasts for any period of time, administrative agencies and courts will have to face the problem of maintaining necessary contacts and protecting private rights. Potentially, nonrecognition could raise such questions as the validity of marriages, divorces, travel documents, and contracts executed under the laws of the unrecognized regime. We examine some of these issues when we examine the case law later in this chapter.

The crisis caused by the breakup of Yugoslavia and the prolonged crisis over recognition of the Former Yugoslavian Republic of Macedonia (FYROM) illustrates the problems nonrecognition may cause in the contemporary world. The controversy had a significant impact on the effectiveness of the sanctions the European Union (EU) had adopted to punish Serbia and Montenegro for their actions in Bosnia and Croatia. Without recognition, the FYROM refused to cooperate with the EU in enforcing the sanctions, thus allowing its territory to serve as a conduit for prohibited items in transit to the war zones. Greece further exacerbated the crisis by adopting a unilateral trade embargo against the FYROM in direct defiance of a collective EU decision to open economic ties with the new state.[43] Though the two states normalized relations, the dispute over the name still simmers under the surface. The dispute has very real consequences because Greece has actively blocked FYROM's NATO aspirations and its attempts to join the EU.

Belligerent Communities and Insurgents

The post–World War II era has witnessed many violent internal struggles. Communities have sought to achieve independence from a parent country, or groups have sought to secure control of an entire state for their own purposes. These groups lack statehood, but after the initiation of hostilities, may effectively occupy territory extensive enough to move the conflict beyond a purely local uprising. When this point is reached in the development of a rebellion, other states may grant to the community a limited measure of international personality by recognizing a status of belligerency and terming the group a *belligerent community*.

Recognition of belligerency is *not* synonymous with recognition as a state or as a government. The belligerent community is still considered legally an integral part of the state against whose government it is conducting hostilities. The issues here involve judgments about effective control. The community will acquire statehood in the legal sense only if it succeeds in its enterprise, by either achieving independence as a new entity or replacing the lawful government of its state by its own chosen representatives. Until it has such success, the belligerent community possesses only very limited, temporary aspects of international personality.

---

[42]Peterson, note 2, at 121.

[43]Grant, note 12, at 185; the embargo caused the European Commission to file suit against Greece in the European Court of Justice. See *Commission of the European Communities v. Hellenic Republic* [1994] ECR I-3037; 100 *ILR* 222.

Legally, this places on the belligerents, as well as on the government opposing them, responsibility for all violations of the laws of war and for the treatment of foreign property and citizens. Rights acquired by the belligerents then include the rights of blockade, visitation, search, and seizure of contraband articles on the high seas, and abandonment of claims for reparation on account of "damages suffered" through the conflict by foreign citizens. On the other hand, a belligerent community lacks the right to send or receive diplomatic agents, to join international organizations, or to benefit from multilateral conventions concerned with peacetime international relations and activities of states.

Recognition of belligerent communities has posed many of the more perplexing problems connected with recognition. Traditionally, insurgents had to satisfy two criteria: (1) they had to have established at least a rudimentary government and military organization reasonably in operative control of a substantial area of the parent state (or overseas territory, if a colonial revolt) and (2) the scope of the rebellion had to have reached a stage beyond a mere local uprising, that is, a status equivalent to conflicts between states. If other states have satisfied themselves that rebel groups satisfy the criteria, recognition of the rebels as a belligerent community frees the parent state from all international responsibility for the acts of the rebels from the inception of the revolt (see Chapter 10). This last statement holds true, however, *only* if the parent government has made some attempt, implied in the second criterion, to assert its authority over the rebels.

One of the more recent instances of the recognition of a belligerent community occurred in June 1979, during the then 19-month-old civil war in Nicaragua. The so-called Andean Group (Bolivia, Colombia, Ecuador, Peru, and Venezuela) declared that "a state of belligerency" existed in Nicaragua and that the forces of the Sandinista National Liberation Front (FSLN) represented a "legitimate army." That declaration then permitted the members of the Andean Group to aid the rebels with weapons and other supplies.[44]

As with all acts of recognition, the right lies with each individual foreign state. The acts of the parent state cannot control the policies of others. Hence, even if the lawful government has recognized the rebels as a belligerent community, each foreign state remains free to grant or withhold the same recognition. If the foreign state withholds recognition, then it has a duty to refrain from assisting the rebel group but is free to grant or withhold aid to the lawful government. Likewise, even if the lawful government does not recognize the rebels as a belligerent community, a foreign state retains the right to grant or withhold such recognition.

In contrast, a rebellion that has not yet achieved the standing of a belligerent community is said to be in a state of *insurgency*—a condition described as intermediate between internal tranquility and civil war. Recognition of insurgency normally entails issuing a proclamation calling public attention to the existence of an insurgent group in a foreign country and cautioning the public to exercise due caution regarding travel, business relations, and other dealings with and in the area in question. Such a proclamation of a state of insurgency does not correspond to the recognition of a belligerent community.

---

[44]D. R. Gordon and M. R. Munro, "The External Dimension of Civil Insurrection," 25 Journal of *Inter-American Studies and World Affairs* (1983), 59–81.

Recognition and Access to Courts

Indeed, regardless of theories, recognition does have a constitutive element in one vital area. Unrecognized states or governments do not have access to domestic courts. Unrecognized states and governments can neither sue nor be sued with respect to areas outside of those where sovereign immunity applies (see Chapter 8). We do need to make one important qualification here. The constitutive theory does **not** necessarily apply to *cases in private international law* unless an issue of public policy arises (i.e., an embargo, a boycott, a sanction regime). Regarding private international law, and what courts have seen as nonpolitical issues, the question of recognition as controlling becomes much more complex.

Recognition permits a new government (or the government of a new state) access to the courts of the recognizing state. Courts in both civil law and common law states begin with the proposition that recognition is a decision within the province of the executive authority. Courts in both systems have developed methods of consultation to determine the position of the executive branch on particular questions. In civil law states, the foreign ministry will produce a document known as an *avis*. In United Kingdom and Commonwealth common law, the Foreign Office provides a *certificate*. In the United States, guidance may come from a statement from the State Department or with the appearance of the executive branch as an intervenor.[45] While courts in all states consider themselves bound *not* to contradict the foreign policy preferences of the executive, this procedure does not necessarily produce clear guidance. The documents, particularly in situations of civil conflict, often leave considerable room for judicial search and interpretation. We explore some of these issues next, through case law and discussion.

In contemporary practice, the explanation for some leeway stems from the increased willingness of governments to make determinations that separate international relations and foreign policy issues (high politics) from the question of who actually exercises effective control for purposes of domestic law and conflict of laws (private law) issues. The expansion of private contacts (the impact of globalization) has caused many governments to find ways to mitigate the potential effects of nonrecognition on private interests by separating the imperatives of "high" politics, presumably underpinning the decision to withhold recognition, from the demands of "low" politics, stemming from the increasing density of transactional contacts at the individual level. These issues may involve the validity of marriages, divorces, property rights, and contracts executed under the auspices of an unrecognized regime:[46]

> The change also puts decisions about each in the hands of different decision-makers. Though courts still work to avoid direct conflict with executive policy, the change increases the likelihood that an unrecognized regime will be accepted as an effective administrator for *private law* questions even when the executive branch refuses it recognition. (Emphasis added)

---

[45]Peterson, note 2, at 143.

[46]Peterson, note 2, at 144.

Next we will consider the following problems posed by litigation in national courts involving unrecognized regimes:

1. Those initiated by a party against an unrecognized regime
2. Those initiated by an unrecognized regime
3. Those involving the claims of an unrecognized regime to property located within the court's jurisdiction
4. Private international law disputes that cannot be resolved without reference to the laws or administrative actions of an unrecognized regime
5. The consequences of the withdrawal or loss of recognition

Note the role of recognition in the following cases.

> **LEHIGH VALLEY RAILROAD COMPANY V. STATE OF RUSSIA**
>
> # Supreme Court of the United States 275 U.S. 571; 48 S. Ct. 159; 72 L. Ed. 432; 1927 U.S. LEXIS 590
>
> ### Facts
>
> The State of Russia sued the Lehigh Valley Railroad Company in U.S. District Court for breach of contract of carriage, arising out of the Black Tom explosion and fire on July 30, 1916. The incident caused the loss of a large shipment of explosives and ammunition being sent to Russia for use in World War I. At the time of loss, the goods in question had been the property of the State of Russia. In February 1917, following widespread unrest, the Duma approved the establishment of a provisional government in an attempt to restore order in the capital. On March 2, 1917, Tsar Nicholas abdicated the throne in favor of his brother Michael, who renounced his claim the next day. For 9 months, the provisional government, first under Prince Lvov and then under Alexander Kerensky, unsuccessfully attempted to establish its authority. On October 25, 1917, the Bolsheviks led by Vladimir Lenin successfully deposed the Kerensky government. The U.S. government did not recognize the Bolshevik government; hence, the provisional government remained as the government of Russia officially recognized by the United States.
>
> Boris Bakhemeteff had received accreditation on July 5, 1917, by the U.S. Department of State as the official representative of the provisional Russian (Lvov/Kerensky) government. He continued to act as its representative until July 30, 1922, when he retired. Thereafter, the Department of State recognized Mr. Ughet, the financial attaché of the Russian embassy, as Bakhemeteff's successor.
>
> Bakhemeteff initiated the suit against the Lehigh Valley Railroad Company on July 23, 1918, even though by this time the government he represented had already ceased to exercise any authority in Russia. The railroad moved for dismissal of the suit, arguing that, because his government no longer exercised power, Mr. Bakhemeteff (and his successor) had no standing to initiate suit on behalf of Russia.
>
> (*continued*)

Issue

Did Bakhemeteff (and his successor) have standing to initiate and continue the suit against the railroad on behalf of the State of Russia even though the government they represented no longer governed Russia?

Decision

Bakhemeteff had the requisite standing because the U.S. government recognized him as the representative of the State of Russia and as the custodian of all property and interests of that state in the United States.

Reasoning

The court held that the State of Russia survived and that Bakhemeteff and Ughet, recognized as its official agents by the Department of State, could lawfully continue suits on behalf of the State of Russia. "The suit did not abate by the change in the form of government in Russia; the state is perpetual, and survives the form of its government. . . . The recognized government may carry on the suit, at least until the new government becomes accredited here by recognition."

In 1970, the Republic of Vietnam (South Vietnam) filed a complaint alleging that various American drug companies had acted in violation of the antitrust laws of the United States in selling broad-spectrum antibiotics.[47] At that point, South Vietnam could accurately describe itself as "a sovereign foreign state with whom the United States of America maintains diplomatic relations." However, in April 1975, the status of the Republic of Vietnam changed dramatically. South Vietnam surrendered unconditionally to the military forces of North Vietnam. In July 1976, the former territory of the Republic of Vietnam was formally attached to that of North Vietnam. The resulting state took the name of the Socialist Republic of Vietnam. The Republic of Vietnam (South Vietnam) became extinct. The United States did not grant recognition to the Socialist Republic of Vietnam.

In September 1975, Pfizer filed a motion to dismiss the action "on the ground that the plaintiff as named and described in the amended complaint no longer exists in any form recognizable by this Court and has not been succeeded by any government, entity or person that has capacity to sue in this Court." In early December 1976, the District Court dismissed South Vietnam's suit with prejudice.[48] Agents acting on behalf of the Socialist Republic of Vietnam contended that the District Court erred in dismissing this action with prejudice rather than suspending it in anticipation of recognition by the United States of a new government representative of the national sovereignty of Vietnam. The Court noted:

> The law is well settled that a foreign government that is not recognized by the United States may not maintain suit in state or federal court. . . . The recognition of foreign governments is a function of the executive branch and is wholly outside the competence of the judiciary. . . . While executive action

---

[47] *Republic of Vietnam v. Pfizer, Inc.*, 556 F.2d 892 (8th Cir. 1977).

[48] If a court enters a judgment with prejudice, this signifies that the court has made a decision on the merits of the case and a final disposition, thus barring the plaintiff from bringing a new lawsuit based on the same subject.

pertaining to the recognition or nonrecognition of a foreign government is binding on the courts, the courts are nevertheless free to determine the legal consequences of that executive action upon pending litigation. . . . On occasion, suit has been brought by a foreign government recognized by the United States and, during the pendency of the action, diplomatic recognition of the party plaintiff has been withdrawn. Under these circumstances, courts have traditionally responded by either dismissing the action or suspending it *sine die* pending recognition of a new government by the United States. . . . The official position of the executive branch is set forth in a letter of June 9, 1975, from the Department of State to the Department of Justice: "The Government of South Vietnam has ceased to exist and therefore the United States no longer recognizes it as the sovereign authority in the territory of South Vietnam. The United States has not recognized any other government as constituting such authority. . . . The Department of State would not advise any requests to the Court to suspend, rather than dismiss, the proceedings" . . . Plaintiff has failed to demonstrate any basis for holding that the dismissal of the present suit constituted an abuse of discretion.

We might note one policy that states have pursued in the event of nonrecognition of a new foreign government—the freezing, by the state, of all assets of the new foreign government found in the territory of the state denying recognition. Examples abound in recent history, such as the actions of the United States in freezing the governmental assets of Cambodia and South Vietnam (1975), North Vietnam, North Korea, Cuba, Rhodesia (now Zimbabwe), and the People's Republic of China (1950–1979).

In light of the court's holding in the Pfizer case, note the following case.

REPUBLIC OF CHINA v. MERCHANTS' FIRE ASSURANCE CORPORATION OF NEW YORK

United States, Court of Appeals, Ninth Cir., 1929, 30 F. [2d] 278

Facts

The Republic of China had insured certain of its public buildings with the defendant company, among them the building of the Chinese Government Telephone Administration in Wuchang. Fire damaged this particular structure. After the loss occurred, Wuchang was captured by the troops of the "National Government" from the lawful government of the Republic of China. Soon afterward, the National

Government, by then controlling 15 of the 18 provinces of China, demanded payment for the loss from the insurance company. When the latter refused payment, the National Government filed suit against the company in the [then] U.S. Court for China.

The insurance company claimed that the plaintiff was not the Republic of China but merely a revolutionary organization not recognized as the government of the Republic of China, hence without any legal

(continued)

capacity to sue in U.S. courts. The company was sustained, and the case was dismissed. The National Government appealed this dismissal.

Issue

Under what conditions, and when, may an unrecognized government originating through unconstitutional or revolutionary acts sue in the courts of a foreign state?

Decision

The National Government won its appeal. In view of events that had taken place *since* the dismissal of the suit in the lower court, that is, the recognition of the National Government by the United States, the circuit court reversed the original decision.

Reasoning

1. The courts of a state cannot acknowledge the existence of a government that originated in revolution until it has first been recognized by the *political* department of the government under which such courts function. By this standard, the National Government, unrecognized at the time it sought access to the U.S. Court for China, had no legal capacity to sue in that court.

2. However, on July 25, 1928, a commercial treaty was concluded between the American minister to China and the minister of finance of the National Government of the Republic of China.

This treaty, although not yet given consent for ratification by the Senate of the United States, constituted recognition by the Executive Department of the United States of both the National Government and its accredited representatives. In addition, a telegram from the U.S. secretary of state to the circuit court stated that the minister of the National Government had been officially received by the president of the United States.

These actions, the court held, conclusively settled the question of the United States's recognition of the National Government: Implicit recognition had taken place through entering into negotiations, sending a diplomatic agent, and receiving a diplomatic agent in formal audience. The changes that had taken place had to be acknowledged by the court, and the recognition extended to the National Government validated the suit already begun by it in the U.S. courts.

Note

Following recognition, the new government will acquire title to its predecessor's assets located in the territory of the recognizing state, including bank deposits, investments, embassy or legation buildings, the contents of consular offices, and so on. The new government also falls heir to all claims previously asserted by its predecessor government.

CONTEMPORARY PRACTICE

As we noted earlier, in principle, a nonrecognized government does not have a right of access to the courts of states that have withheld recognition. Because it lacks international legal personality, an unrecognized government cannot initiate a suit in the courts of a country that has denied recognition. In surveying the contemporary international political landscape, <u>we have noted that national courts</u> have found ways to make exceptions to the access rule *when gross inequities* _would have resulted_. While we normally think of international law as "high politics," state policy also influences the legitimate everyday business of citizens. In a landmark case dealing with these issues, U.S. Supreme Court Judge Benjamin Cardozo said:[49]

> Juridically, a government that is unrecognized may be viewed as no government at all, if the power withholding recognition chooses thus to view it. In practice, however, since juridical conceptions are seldom, if ever, carried to the limit of their logic, the equivalence is not absolute, but is subject to _self-imposed limitations of common sense and fairness_. (Emphasis added)

Both British and American courts have permitted suits from unrecognized regimes if the executive authority has indicated a willingness to permit the plaintiff entity to litigate its claims. Consider the following situation:

> An American company makes a contract for delivery of merchandise from a state trading company owned by a government unrecognized by the United States. U.S. law does not prohibit the transaction. The company delivers the merchandise as stipulated in the contract. The party receiving the merchandise then defaults on the contract by refusing to pay. The state trading company seeks to enforce the contract through filing suit in an appropriate U.S. court. In litigation the American company raises the defense that, as an organ of government of an unrecognized regime, the company does not have access to U.S. courts.[50]

In this case, the court applying Judge Cardozo's tests of common sense and fairness noted:[51]

> [N]onrecognition, while a material fact, is only a preliminary one. A foreign government, although not recognized by the political arm of the United States Government, may, nevertheless, have _de facto_ existence which is juridically cognizable. To exculpate itself from payment for the merchandise which it received, defendant would have to allege and prove that the sale upon which the trade acceptance was based, or the negotiation of the trade acceptance itself, violated public or national policy. Such a defense would constitute one in the nature of illegality and could render all that ensued from the transaction void and unenforcible, but to sustain such a defense it must be shown that the transaction or the assignment violated our laws or some definite policy.

In another more recent case, _Transportes Aereos de Angola v. Ronair, Inc.,_ the executive branch permitted a company wholly owned by the unrecognized state of Angola to pursue its claims on the basis that the company constituted a separate

---

[49] _Sokoloff v. National City Bank_, 239 N. Y. 158 [1924] at 165.

[50] Hypothetical case based upon _Walter Upright, Appellant, v. Mercury Business Machines Co., Inc., Respondent,_ Supreme Court of New York, Appellate Division, First Department 13 A.D.2d 36; 213 N.Y.S.2d 417; 1961 N.Y. App. Div. LEXIS 11469.

[51] _Walter Upright_, note 50, at 2.

juridical entity—that is, the company was not merely an alter ego of the government, but a "discrete and independent entity."[52] The court noted:

> In those cases in which an instrumentality of an unrecognized government or the government itself has been precluded from adjudicating a legal claim in the United States, the executive branch ordinarily steadfastly opposed the foreign party's standing to sue, thus leaving the court with no recourse but to give effect to the critical issue of non-recognition. In this case, however, not only did the Department of Commerce, in consultation with the Department of State, place its imprimatur on TAAG's (the Angolan corporation) commercial dealings with Ronair by issuing a license to export the Boeing aircraft to Angola, but the State Department itself has unequivocally stated that allowing TAAG access to this Court would be consistent with the foreign policy interests of the United States.

International Versus National (Bilateral) Effects of Recognition   Advocates of the declaratory theory often rely heavily upon the *Tinoco Arbitration* (1923) in making their case. The difficulty of this position flows from the provisions of the treaty setting up the arbitration (Chapter 3). Because he was not bound by any prior determination of a political authority, the sole arbitrator, Chief Justice of the U.S. Supreme Court William Howard Taft, had the authority under the treaty to make an independent determination of the status of the Tinoco government. In doing so, he found two facts compelling. First, although Great Britain had not recognized the Tinoco government, 20 other states had done so. Second, clearly, by asserting the rights of British citizens, Great Britain obviously had concluded that the regime had met the minimum standard for legal capacity to conclude the agreements (effective control) regardless of its unrecognized status.[53]

Immunity of a Nonrecognized Government   Nonrecognized governments present somewhat of a catch-22 situation. On the one hand, if indeed they have no legal personality, they cannot be the focus of a suit because litigation cannot be brought against something that does not exist. On the other hand, if we presume that the government exists and effectively controls the territory in question, others must concede jurisdiction. In the classic case, *Wulfsohn v. Russian Socialist Federated Soviet Republic*,[54] the court noted that even the plaintiff conceded that the RSF Soviet Republic was the existing *de facto* government of Russia regardless of whether the United States had extended recognition. Therefore, its acts *within its own territory* (contrast with the *Lehigh Valley Railroad* case) could not be the subject of challenge in a U.S. court. We will return to this point in the discussion of the Act of State doctrine in Chapter 8.

---

[52] *Transportes Aereos de Angola v. Ronair, Inc.*, 544 F.Supp. 858, 862 (D.Del.1982). See also *Amtorg Trading Corporation v. United States*, 71 F.2d 524 [CCPA 1934]; *Banco Para el Comercio v. First National City Bank*, 658 F.2d 913 [C.A. 2, 1981].

[53] Taft also noted that because the incidents occurred during and in the immediate aftermath of World War I, many U.S. allies might have deferred to the American policy of nonrecognition in refusing to recognize the Tinoco government.

[54] U.S. Court of Appeals of New York, 1923 234 N.Y. 372.

STATE SUCCESSION

International law uses the rather vague term *state succession* to describe the legal consequences resulting from a change in sovereignty over territory.[55] Technically, according to the International Law Commission, state succession "means the replacement of one state by another in terms of the *responsibility* for the international relations of territory." State succession has occurred throughout history but has happened most frequently in the decades following World War II. Decolonization and, more recently, the fragmentation of the former Soviet Union (FSU) and of the Socialist Federal Republic of Yugoslavia have raised interesting issues about the extent to which new states remain liable for the duties and obligations incurred by the previous state.[56]

Curiously, despite the number of recent cases, no coherent, generally accepted body of legal norms has emerged to provide guidelines for the varieties of change that have occurred in sovereignty. After more than a decade of preparatory work by the International Law Commission, two UN-sponsored conventions have emerged: the Convention on Succession of States in Respect of Treaties (Vienna, 1978) and the Convention on Succession of States in Respect of State Property, Archives and Debts (Vienna, 1983).[57] The titles of these conventions tell you why the issues here have great importance. In the case of secession, partition, or combination (Syria and Egypt to form the United Arab Republic, for example), the members of the international community have a great interest in knowing who, if anyone, will assume the treaty obligations, who will have a claim to state property (and bank accounts) in other states, and who will have the duty to repay government loans.

Issues relating to state succession arise in a number of ways. We will focus on three main categories:

1. Achievement of independence by a territory previously under sovereignty protection, mandate, trusteeship, or other form of control by another state. (This includes secession from a state; e.g., Croatia, Slovenia, Macedonia (FYROM), Bosnia, 1991–1994.)
2. Loss of the status of a state through annexation, merger, or imposition of a protectorate by another state (e.g., union of the two German states).
3. Change in sovereignty over a territory from one state to another through cession.

In cases of the first category, treaties called *devolution agreements* have normally decided the division of rights and obligations between the predecessor state and the

---

[55]For a comprehensive treatment of this topic, see J. R. Crawford, *The Creation of States in International Law*, 2nd ed. (2006), 374–448.

[56]The standard work on the subject is still D. P. O'Connell, *State Succession in Municipal Law and International Law* (2 vols, 1967). See also Y. Z. Blum, "UN Membership of the 'New' Yugoslavia: Continuity or Break?" 86 *AJIL* 4 (1992), 830, 833.

[57]The Convention on Succession of States in Respect of Treaties entered into force on November 6, 1996, but still has only 18 parties. As of June 1, 2005, the Convention on Succession of States in Respect of State Property, Archives and Debts had not entered into force and had been ratified by only six states. Text of 1978 convention in 72 *AJIL* 971 (1978), and of the 1983 instrument in 22 *ILM* 308 (1983).

newly independent entity. These will determine the extent to which the latter would assume rights and duties originally created by treaties for the predecessor state. In cases of the second category, domestic legislation of the successor state or premerger agreements between the prospective parties have determined the status of both rights and obligations of each entity. In cases of the third category, the successor state alone decides the fate of both rights and obligations of the extinct predecessor entity.

In all three categories, rules of international law enter into the picture, regulating the rights and obligations of predecessor and successor in relation to outside states or other third parties. Before entering into detail, we must emphasize that the *international personality* of a state normally remains unaffected by increases or losses in territory (with corresponding gains or reductions in population) unless the changes in question create a change so profound that the new situation alters the central organization (basic structure) of the state or involves a loss to the state of the "core area" in which the government center had been located.

Today, questions usually revolve around shrinkage in the territory of a given state through secession. The dissolution of the Soviet Union and the former Yugoslavia may yet be followed by the disintegration of other political entities. Ethnic, religious, and historic enmities alone provide reasons for groups desiring their own state. In the wake of the Cold War, the revival of nationalism has created many new claims for groups seeking their own state. The standard examples usually cited show that despite often drastic losses of territory, the legal personality of the states remained unaffected: Poland (partitions of 1772 and 1793) was unchanged from a legal standpoint until 1795, when it disappeared after a third partition. Turkey—despite territorial losses in 1856, 1878, and 1911–1913, and as a result of World War I—remained legally unaffected. As a result of the treaties ending World War I, Hungary was reduced to one-third of its prewar size. If the Confederate States of America had succeeded in its secession plans, the legal identity of the United States would have remained unchanged, even though a new entity would have become a player. On the other side, what happened to the obligations of Latvia, Lithuania, and Estonia after their absorption into the Soviet Union, or those of Austria after its incorporation into Germany in 1938? Upon its reconstitution after World War II, did the "new" Austria have to assume the obligations of the "old," pre-1938 Austria?

Extinction by Voluntary Act

How may a state become extinct? The international personality of a state can be ended by a voluntary act. One instance is the breakup of a federation into separate states, as in the case of the Republic of Colombia when it separated in 1828–1830 into three separate states (Ecuador, Venezuela, and New Granada). One of these states, New Granada, later reverted to the name of Colombia and possibly retained the legal personality of Colombia even after 1830. Extinction also may come about through merger with another state: The cases of Texas (union with the United States) and Syria (temporary merger with Egypt in the United Arab Republic) come to mind. In the contemporary world, these issues came into play with the reunification of Germany. They would also apply if Taiwan and the People's Republic of China negotiated a merger, or if North and South Korea were reunited.

Extinction by Forcible Means

Forcible annexation by conquest has been a common method for the extinction of hitherto independent states. World history is filled with examples; the Transvaal in 1901 and Korea in 1910 are favorite illustrations. Currently, the Charter of the United Nations prohibits conquest as an acceptable method of acquiring good title.

Rights and Obligations of a Totally Extinct State

When one state is absorbed by another, the question arises as to the extent to which the successor state acquires both the rights and the obligations of the defunct state.[58] These issues will normally be dealt with as part of the merger agreement. If third states have any claims against the state that loses its international identity, the settlement of such obligations is up to the successor state. Unless provided for in the merger agreement, the citizens of the defunct state have no right of appeal under international law against any actions taken by the annexing state because their former country has lost its international personality. Thus, it is no longer a subject of international law. Any claims by or against citizens of the defunct state involving their former government become domestic questions of the annexing state.

Extinction of the personality of a state traditionally results in an abrogation of all political and military treaties previously concluded between the now extinct entity and other states. This holds true, of course, only in the case of total extinction. If succession involves only a portion of the original sovereign territory, the latter will still be bound by treaties with other countries because, as such, its legal personality continues intact. Only those provisions of treaties relating to lost parts of the territory would no longer bind the former sovereign. Despite the absence of applicable rules of law, successor states have generally been willing to assume contractual obligations of the extinct state with respect to third states or the citizens of such states. This has been true in the case of contracts involving concessions such as mining rights and transportation facilities.

On the other hand, no common practice can be discovered regarding the debts contracted by the predecessor state. Debts owed to the citizens of the former state become domestic questions of the annexing state. In the case of partial succession of the sort described in the next section, the instrument transferring the areas in question may regulate such issues. Debts owed to third states or their citizens may or may not be honored by the successor state. The government of the United States took over the debts of its member states in 1790, but it refused in 1845 to assume the obligations of the Republic of Texas, although arrangements were made to pay the contested sum by using proceeds from the sale of public land in Texas. Croatia and Slovenia appear to have taken over a portion of the Yugoslav national debt (1991–1992).[59] On January 13, 1992, the Ministry of Foreign Affairs of the

---

[58]K. J. Keith, "Succession to Bilateral Treaties by Seceding States," 61 *AJIL* 521 (1967); E. Dumbauld, "Independence Under International Law," 70 *AJIL* 425 (1976); R. Mushkat, "Hong Kong and Succession of Treaties," 46 *International and Comparative Law Quarterly* 181 (1997).

[59]Bosnia and Herzegovina-Croatia, "Preliminary Agreement Concerning the Establishment of a Confederation," 33 *International Legal Materials* 605 (1994); C. Stahn, "The Agreement on Succession Issues of the Former Socialist Federal Republic of Yugoslavia," 96 AJIL 379 (2002).

Russian Federation informed all foreign missions in Moscow that the Federation should be considered as a party to all international agreements in force in place of the USSR. The Federation thereby assumed all treaties that had been binding on the Soviet Union at the time of its demise.

Partial Succession

Partial succession occurs when a state assumes sovereignty over portions of territory formerly belonging to another state, when a new international personality is created by the secession of a territory from an existing state or when a member state of a federation or a confederation obtains independence. Partial succession poses many complicated problems centering on the distribution or division of the rights and obligations somehow attached to the territory involved in the succession.

Effects Upon Public and Private Property Rights

Normally, only two parties are involved in questions of property rights. Fortunately, experience has taught most states to specify how issues will be settled between them. Such matters are usually incorporated in the instrument transferring title to the territory. On occasion, however, third parties may be involved in partial succession, usually through claims of their citizens that relate in some way to the transferred territory. Unless otherwise agreed on by the states concerned or by some appropriate international organization, the passing of state property of the predecessor to the successor state or states takes place without compensation. This principle applies to both partial and total extinction of the predecessor state. The property of third states, or the rights and interests of third states, recognized as such under the laws of the predecessor state, is not affected by state succession.

Under partial succession, the public property of the predecessor state located in the successor state normally passes to the latter. When Czechoslovakia partitioned itself into the Czech Republic and the Republic of Slovakia, all immovable state property (buildings and so on) was allocated to the republic in which it was located. Movable state property, down to office furniture, was split on a 2:1 ratio, corresponding to the relative size of the two state populations involved. The two new entities used the same ratio to allocate state property located abroad. For example, if the Czech state received an embassy, Slovakia received title to a cultural center. Some 20 embassies (in Asia, Africa, and South America) were slated to be sold, and the proceeds were to be divided. On the other hand, the Russian Federation claimed title to all foreign property of the former Soviet Union instead of dividing it with the other 14 successor republics. This claim was justified by Russia's assumption of the Soviet Union's debt. Private property rights in territory ceded by one state to another or annexed by another are not formally affected by the change. Titles to land—provided they are complete and perfect at the time of change—are usually protected by the successor state unless the new government subscribes to some form of socialism that demands the nationalization of all land.

In another instance involving a division of assets, the International Monetary Fund (IMF) determined in December 1992 that the Socialist Federal Republic of Yugoslavia had ceased to exist and therefore had ceased to be a member. The IMF then decided that the successor states of Bosnia and Herzegovina, Croatia, Macedonia, Slovenia, and the Federal Republic of Yugoslavia (Serbia and Montenegro) were the successors to the assets and liabilities of the former Yugoslavia in the IMF.

When part of a state is transferred to another state, the passing of the state debt (internal) from predecessor to successor normally is settled by negotiation and agreement between the parties. Article 37(2) of the 1983 Vienna Convention provides that in the absence of such an agreement, the predecessor's state debt is to pass to the successor state "in an equitable proportion." On the other hand, when the successor is a newly independent state (say, an ex-protectorate or an ex-colony), no state debt of the predecessor state normally passes to the new entity unless an agreement between the parties provides otherwise in view of the link between the predecessor's state debt and its activities in the newly independent area. When two or more states unite to form one successor state, the state debt of the predecessors passes on to the new entity. When part or parts of a state's territory separate from that legal person and form a new state, the state debt of the predecessor state passes to the successor state on a proportional basis unless the parties agree otherwise. And finally, when a state dissolves and ceases to exist and the parts of the predecessor state's territory form two or more successor states, the state debt of the dissolved unit passes, normally, in equitable proportions to the successor states. Unless otherwise decided between the parties (states) involved, debts owed to the predecessor state because of its activities in the territory to which title is being passed become debts owed to the successor state.

Effects of Treaties   One other aspect of state succession merits brief examination, due to the number of controversies it has caused in international relations. In the case of universal succession, political treaties, such as alliance, are abrogated at once—as are treaties of commerce, navigation, and extradition. In the case of partial succession, political treaties are abrogated. Other agreements may be terminated after consultation between a successor state and the other party or parties to any given agreement. If one party to an international agreement changes its form of government or expands or contracts its geographic boundaries, the provisions of any treaties in question are usually not affected by such changes, even if the expansion of territory involves the inclusion of other former states in the one that is a party to the agreement. Unless the changes suggested the desirability of new treaties, the prior agreements have generally been regarded as remaining in full force and effect.

The Vienna Convention on State Succession of States in Respect of Treaties answers almost all questions imaginable, yet by its very breadth (and technical detail), it exceeds the limits of discussion possible in a general text. But one aspect of the subject should be kept in mind—the new instrument covers in detail the absence of applicability of past treaties concluded by the original sovereign in relation to former colonial territories as well as seceding territories (unless, of course, the newly independent colony or newly seceded territory agrees specifically to be bound by the treaties in question). The fate of the treaties concluded by the former Soviet Union illustrates what may happen in the instance of total extinction. In the so-called Minsk Declaration of December 8, 1991, the Commonwealth of Independent States (CIS) asserted that the "States members undertake to discharge the international obligations incumbent on them under treaties and engagements entered into by the former Union of Soviet Socialist Republics." Since then, individual ex-Soviet successor states have acceded to a variety of the multipartite treaties to which the Soviet Union had been a party. In the case of the defunct Yugoslavia, successor states have deposited with the UN Secretariat statements of succession to a large number of multipartite agreements such as the genocide convention, the human rights covenants, and the antislavery convention.

SUGGESTED READINGS

Crawford, The *Creation of States in International Law,* 2nd ed. (2007).

Tocci, "The 'Cyprus Question': Reshaping Community Identities and Elite Interests Within a Wider European Framework," Center for European Policy Studies, Working Paper 14 (September 2000).

CASES

The Helena, Great Britain, High Court of Admiralty, 1801, 4 Ch.Rob.3.

The Indonesia Case, Security Council of the UN, July 31–August 1, 1947, in 3 *United Nations Bulletin* 215 (1947).

Nationality Decrees Issued in Tunis and Morocco, Advisory Opinion, *PCIJ,* Ser. B, No. 4 (1923).

Principality of Monaco v. Mississippi, U.S. Supreme Court, 1933, 291 U.S. 643 and 292 U.S. 313.

MISCELLANEOUS ISSUES

Clark, "China's Unlawful Control over Tibet: The Tibetan People's Entitlement to Self-Determination," 12 *Ind. Int'l & Comp. L. Rev.* 293 (2002).

Hofmann, ed., *Non-state Actors As New Subjects of International Law* (1999).

Levie, *The Status of Gibraltar* (1983).

Necatigil, *The Cyprus Question and the Turkish Position in International Law,* 2nd ed. (1993).

Shelton, "The Participation of Non-governmental Organizations in International Judicial Proceedings," 88 *AJIL* 611 (1994).

Sloane, "The Changing Face of Recognition in International Law: A Case Study of Tibet," 16 *Emory Int'l L. Rev.* 107 (2002).

Rights and Duties of International Legal Persons

TRADITIONAL VIEWS

Up to the end of the nineteenth century, almost all in the international legal community agreed that the states belonging to the community of nations possessed a package of fundamental rights. These rights—equality, existence, external independence, self-defense, and territorial supremacy (*sovereignty*)—presumably belonged to any community recognized as a state. In part, the justification for such rights came from natural law. The underlying theory maintained that the rights represented legal principles on which all *positive* international law rested. This contention ignored the obvious fact that legal principles can only be created by a legal order and could not be presupposed by it. This controversy over jurisprudence forms one of the continuing controversies concerning the nature of international law as true law.

RIGHTS OF STATES

Curiously, we find a gap in subject matter. Until recently, only the regional inter-American community made any effort to develop a general and definitive declaration of the rights of states. Starting with the Declaration of the Rights and Duties of Nations of the American Institute of International Law in 1916, the inter-American community considered the issues at a succession of conferences: Rio de Janeiro (1927), Havana (1928), Montevideo (1933), Buenos Aires (1936), and Lima (1938). At the Montevideo Conference, the states adopted a convention.[1] The subsequent conferences witnessed a reaffirmation of the basic rights.

---

[1] *Montevideo Convention on the Rights and Duties of States*, signed at Montevideo on December 26, 1933, and entered into force on December 26, 1934. Article 8 reaffirmed by protocol, December 23, 1936. Bolivia alone among the states represented at the Seventh International Conference of American States did not sign the Convention. The United States of America, Peru, and Brazil ratified the Convention with reservations. Text available at www.taiwandocuments.org/montevideo01.htm (accessed April 21, 2009).

The most ambitious modern attempt to define the rights and duties of states began with Resolution 178 (II) of the General Assembly of the United Nations (November 21, 1947), which asked the International Law Commission to prepare a draft declaration of such rights and duties. This draft, delineating four rights (independence, territorial jurisdiction, equality in law, and self-defense) and ten duties, was criticized on many counts, both during its formulation and afterward. To date, no further progress on the project has been reported. In December 1974, the General Assembly did pass a rather controversial resolution (3281-XXIX), the Charter of Economic Rights and Duties of States (120 in favor, 6 against, and 10 abstentions).[2] As a resolution and with certain key countries opposing its adoption, the resolution has had no binding effect, yet it has been referred to frequently by Third World countries in the United Nations. The same holds true for the Declaration on Principles of International Law Concerning Friendly Relations and Co-operation Among States in accordance with the Charter of the United Nations.[3]

THE RIGHTS OF EXISTENCE AND INDEPENDENCE

The so-called right of existence has been asserted as the fundamental condition for all other rights claimed by a state. However, *existence* in the narrow meaning of the term represents an essential inherent characteristic of a state, not a right. Simple logic tells us that the inability to continue existence would lead to the extinction of the legal personality of any member of the community of nations. Governments have frequently insisted on this right but have styled it variously as the "right of self-defense" and the "right of self-preservation." From a practical standpoint, then, the "right" is one to a *continued* existence—the preservation of a state's corporate integrity through self-defense or some other mechanism. This "right" generates many questions in the contemporary era. For example, what happens when the presumed right of integrity conflicts with the asserted new right of self-determination?

Oppenheim argued that, as with existence, the independence of a state and its territorial and personal supremacy (supreme authority in its territory and over its citizens) did not constitute rights but rather other recognized and protected qualities or characteristics of states as international persons.[4] *Independence,* or *domestic independence,* means that a state has freedom to manage its affairs without interference from other states.[5] A state may organize its government as it sees fit, adopt a constitution to suit its own needs, lay down rules and regulations for the property and personal rights of its citizens and subjects, determine under what

---

[2]Text in 14 *International Legal Materials* 251 (1975).

[3]*Declaration on Principles of International Law Concerning Friendly Relations and Co-operation Among States in Accordance with the Charter of the United Nations*, G.A. res. 2625, Annex, 25 UN GAOR, Supp. (No. 28), U.N. Doc. A/5217 (1970), 121, www1.umn.edu/humanrts/instree/principles1970.html (accessed April 21, 2009).

[4]Lauterpacht, *Oppenheim*, I: 286; for further details on the subject in general, consult Whiteman, V: 88.

[5]See *Attorney-General of New Zealand v. Ortiz* [1982] 3 W.L.R. 570, United Kingdom, Court of Appeal, May 21, 1982, reported in 77 *American Journal of International Law* 631 (1983).

specific conditions foreigners will enter its territory, and so on. In other words, an independent state is "absolute master" in its own house, subject only to the limitations imposed on it either by the rules of general international law or by treaty arrangements it has made with other states.

A second aspect of independence relates to the right of a state to conduct its foreign relations to the best of its ability in such manner as it desires without supervisory control by other states *(external independence)*. By definition, a country must have the authority to act as a free agent in contracting and fulfilling international obligations it chooses to assume with other states. External independence is regarded as a basic test for the admission of new members into the community of nations.

Asserting a "right" of independence underlies the frequently voiced claim to a right of *self-determination*. This term appears to imply a right of any group of people to choose its own political institutions (including, of course, its own government). Many legal writers and political leaders have supported the idea that "national" or "ethnic" groups possessed a right to "self-determination." The concept itself made its appearance shortly before the settlements at the Versailles Peace Conference after World War I. President Woodrow Wilson supported the idea but with some ambivalence, because he did not favor self-determination within the borders of what was then Russia proper. After World War II, the principle of self-determination emerged even more clearly and soon took the form of an assertion that a *legal right* of self-determination existed. The Charter of the United Nations [Articles 1(2); 73; 76(b)] and resolutions passed by the General Assembly have affirmed the existence of such a right. The push for the right was an influential factor in the wave of decolonization in the ensuing decades. On the other hand, not all legal writers became enamored of the new right. Some have expressed strong doubts about its existence.[6] Some have argued that promoting a right of self-determination for some foreign group may violate the prohibition on intervention found in the Charter of the United Nations (Article 2[4]).[7] We should note that the International Court of Justice (ICJ) endorsed the right in its 1975 Advisory Opinion on the Western Sahara.[8]

---

[6]See T. M. Franck, "Legitimacy in the International System," 82 *AJIL* 705, 746 (1988); and F. L. Kirgis, "The Degrees of Self-Determination in the United Nations Era," 88 *AJIL* 304 (1994), particularly 306–307 for the "right" as applied in actual listed disputes.

[7]See the 1960 Declaration on the Granting of Independence to Colonial Countries and Peoples, in which the General Assembly endorsed the idea that "any attempt aimed at the partial or total disruption of the national unity and the territorial integrity of a country is incompatible with the purposes and principles of the Charter of the United Nations." General Assembly Res. 1564, U.N. Doc. A/4684 (1960), 66; see also V. Nanda, "Self-Determination in International Law," 66 *AJIL* 321 (1972).

[8]*Advisory Opinion on the Western Sahara*, 1975 *International Court of Justice* Rep. 12, 33 (Advisory Opinion of October 16); text in 14 *ILM* 1355 (1975). Note that while African states pushed the idea of self-determination as a right, they did so with the proviso that self-determination did not then apply to postcolonial issues of "self-determination" that might arise because of the crazy-quilt borders the new states inherited as a result of colonial division.

THE RIGHT OF EQUALITY

One of the oldest rights claimed for states has been the right of equality. Publicists have asserted this principle since the days of Hugo Grotius. An impressive array of jurists and countless governmental proclamations have affirmed this right, particularly among the American republics. Obviously, in most aspects, the states of the world are not at all equal. They differ in area, population, resources, access to oceans, armament, and generally all the factors entailed by the concepts of national power and power politics. The "right" to equality simply means an equality in law, or an equality before the law, of all members of the community of nations.

The Permanent Court of International Justice (PCIJ), in 1935, distinguished between equality in fact and equality in law in its opinion on the *Minority Schools in Albania*:

> It is perhaps not easy to define the distinction between the notions of equality in fact and equality in law; nevertheless, it may be said that the former notion excludes the idea of merely formal equality. . . . Equality in law precludes discrimination of any kind; whereas equality in fact may involve the necessity of different treatment in order to attain a result which establishes an equilibrium between different situations.[9]

Ironically enough, Article 2 of the Charter of the United Nations contains, among other principles, the notion of the "sovereign equality of its Members." Yet the structure of the Security Council, which grants special status to the five permanent members, clearly violates this principle. Article 23 grants permanent seats on the Security Council to the United States, Russian Federation (originally the USSR), China, Great Britain, and France. The other ten members of the body are elected for two-year terms. The ten nonpermanent members of the Security Council suffer a diminution of their "sovereign equality" through the provisions of Article 27, which spells out the voting procedure in the Security Council, including the veto power of the permanent members. On the other hand, Article 23 may be taken to represent a realistic appraisal of the role traditionally played in international relations by the great powers.

Equality in law means that a state has one vote (unless it has agreed to the contrary) whenever a question has to be settled by consent among states. It means that *legally* the vote of the smallest state carries as much weight as does the vote of the largest and most powerful member of the community of nations. Hence, the deposit of a ratification or accession of a new multilateral treaty by Vanuatu will count as much toward the number necessary for the treaty to enter into force as one deposited by China or the Russian Federation (Chapter 4). *Practically*, as we discussed earlier, it does **not** mean that, in terms of the operational impact of the treaty, Vanuatu and China are equally important.

---

[9]*Minority Schools in Albania*, Advisory Opinion, *Permanent Court of International Justice*, Ser. A/B, No. 64 (1935).

THE RIGHT OF IMMUNITY

Equality and independence mean that no state may exercise legal jurisdiction over another (Chapter 7). Practically, this means that one independent sovereign state cannot, *without its consent,* be made a defendant in the courts of another independent sovereign state. This right permits "sovereigns" to act in what they perceive as their nation's own best interest without concern that others might attempt to use the courts in another country to disrupt their policies. Domestically, the doctrine also ensures that the public property of the state and that of other states cannot be attached or encumbered in any way. In the era before the twentieth century, the "hard shell" idea of immunity served well because of the clear distinction between the idea of *public actions* (*acta jure imperii*), directly imputable to the government, and *private actions* (*acta jure gestionis*), clearly not the province of government. In the early twentieth century, states became involved in trade and other activities normally considered the province of the private sector. State-controlled trading companies and state-owned airlines, telecommunications, and media became common.

When states began to engage in everyday commercial transactions that had nothing to do with the activities normally associated with security or other "public" purposes, the question of the *scope* of immunity became an important topic of debate. As we will see later, the problem became the operational tests or standards used to distinguish between *acts of state* (*acta jure imperii*), protected by immunity, and other acts (*acta jure gestionis*) for which the state should bear responsibility as if they were ordinary juristic persons (e.g., a corporation). For example, contracts for ordinary services made in good faith should have remedies for nonperformance. If a state-owned airline company contracts for aircraft from a private manufacturer, it should not be able to invoke sovereign immunity as a defense against failure to honor the contract by not paying for planes delivered. We will return to this issue later.

Personal Sovereign Immunity

According to customary international law, a foreign head of state and his or her family enjoy personal sovereign immunity. They have complete immunity from suit or judicial process in the territory of another state. Foreign sovereigns or heads of state enjoy personal immunity from suit, and they cannot be named as a party defendant to a suit brought against them in their official capacity as the representative of their state. During President George W. Bush's official state visit in 2004, Canadian courts refused to act upon several attempts by a Canadian peace group, Lawyers Against the War, to have him either arrested or declared *persona non grata*.[10]

In June 2001, the *Cour de Cassation*[11] (e.g., Supreme Court) in Paris issued its decision concerning a case brought against Muammar al-Gaddafi, the leader of the Socialist Libyan People's Jamahiriya, for conspiracy to commit murder and terrorism. The case concerned the destruction by a bomb of a UTA (*Union des Transports Aériens*) airlines DC-10 over the Ténére desert (Niger) on September

[10]"Canada Blocks Torture Charges Against Bush," Lawyers Against the War, www.lawyersagainstthewar.org/press.html#December%206,%202004; www.lawyersagainstthewar.org/press.html (accessed April 30, 2009).
[11]*Arrêt of the Cour de Cassation*, March 13, 2001, No. 1414, at 1.

19, 1989. The crash resulted in the death of 171 individuals. At the time, UTA was the largest privately owned, independent airline in France. The dead also included several people who had French nationality (see Chapter 9).

The *Cour d'Assises* tried and convicted *in absentia* six members of the Libyan secret service—including the chief (the brother-in-law of Gaddafi)—for murder, destruction of an aircraft, and terrorism.[12] Based on these convictions, a French *nongovernmental organization* (NGO), SOS Attentats,[13] and the families of several victims subsequently filed a petition of complaint alleging the complicity of the Libyan government in the bombing with French authorities. Acting on the complaint, a *juge d'instruction* (magistrate)[14] brought charges against Gaddafi for complicity in acts leading to terrorism and murder. The *chambre d'accusation*[15] confirmed the indictment. The prosecutor filed a motion to quash the indictment with the *Cour de Cassation,* arguing that Gaddafi, as head of state, had immunity. The court agreed and voided the indictment.[16] Similarly, in the Ndombasi case (*Democratic Republic of the Congo v. Belgium*), the ICJ found that as minister of foreign affairs, Abdoulaye Ndombasi had immunity from prosecution.[17]

In the United States, passage of the Foreign Sovereign Immunities Act of 1976 (FSIA; see following discussion) had the interesting consequence of separating questions concerning the immunity of the state from those involving the actions of the head of state. Before passage of this act, practice assumed that the immunity of the state presumably attached directly to the head of state. Unlike British legislation of the same vintage, U.S. legislation does not explicitly deal with the question of immunity for foreign heads of state.[18] Thus, immediately after the 1976 legislation, U.S. courts experienced an increase in suits filed against foreign heads of state.[19] The State Department here again assumed an ad hoc role that has resulted in inconsistent outcomes. The ruling in *Lafontant v. Aristide* (1994)[20] suggested that foreign heads of state are protected by absolute immunity, thus clearly separating any personal liability due to their position from any liability incurred by the *state*.

---

[12]Felonies related to terrorism or illegal drug trade are judged by a special *Cour d'Assises*. The court consists of seven professional judges on first instance and nine professional judges on appeal.

[13]SOS Attentats describes its mission as defending the rights of victims of terrorism and the fight (struggle) against terrorism.

[14]A *juge d'instruction* conducts criminal investigations. He or she does not hear cases.

[15]This chamber of the Court of Appeal hears appeals of indictments.

[16]For an interesting critique of this judgment, see S. Zappala, "Do Heads of State in Office Enjoy Immunity from International Crimes," 12 *European Journal of International Law* (2001), 595–612.

[17]Arrest Warrant of April 11, 2000; Judgment of February 14, 2002. See further Chapters 13 and 18. Note also that this ruling applies only to national courts that attempt to utilize universal jurisdiction. The Statutes of the International Criminal Court and the UN ad hoc tribunals explicitly state that formal position in any government does not preclude prosecution because of an assertion of immunity.

[18]See K. Highet, G. Kahale III, and J. W. Dellapenna, "*Lafontant v. Aristide.* 844 F.Supp.128," 88 *AJIL* 528 (1994). The authors point out that the Tate letter did not address the issue. The British State Immunity Act "defines a foreign state as including the sovereign or other head of the state, as well as the government of the state and related institutions and entities." *Ibid.,* at 531.

[19]Many of these suits were filed under the Alien Tort Statute, 28 U.S.C. §1350 (2004). For a discussion of the litigation here, see Chapter 16, "International Criminal Law."

[20]*Lafontant v. Aristide*, 844 F. Supp. 128, U.S. Dist. Ct., E.D.N.Y. (1994).

The courts took a different route when individuals sought redress against Robert Mugabe (president of Zimbabwe) and Stan Mudenge (foreign minister of Zimbabwe) as representatives of the Zimbabwe African National Union—Patriotic Front (ZANU-PF) for subjecting the plaintiffs and/or members of their family to torture, assault, execution, and other acts of violence. President Mugabe and Foreign Minister Mudenge had come to New York for the United National Millennium Conference.[21] The State Department filed a "suggestion of immunity" with the district court, stating that Mugabe and Mudenge had "head of state immunity." Moreover, the State Department asserted that passage of the FSIA "was not intended to affect the power of the State Department, on behalf of the President as Chief Executive, to assert immunity for heads of state or for diplomatic and consular personnel."[22] In this case, the Court of Appeals for the Second Circuit dismissed the suit on the basis that the two men enjoyed *full sovereign and diplomatic immunity*.[23]

Former Heads of State in Exile

Questions here often arise from the status of *former heads of state in exile*, particularly if a successor government of his or her state seeks extradition and has agreed to waive immunity. Such questions may involve the nature of the acts at issue. Were they acts of state or merely common acts?[24] In considering the case of Ferdinand and Imelda Marcos, the Court of Appeals for the Second Circuit held:

> Appellants concede that comity is the animating principle upon which head-of-state immunity rests. They argue nonetheless that the doctrine must also serve a "protective function" of "shield[ing] human decision-makers from the chilling effects of future liability. . . ." They suggest that this protective function be promoted at the expense of comity. Because an incumbent leader may change policies in order to avoid being forced out of office, adopting the protective function argument would serve only to reduce political accountability. Hence, we decline to impose this internal policy choice on a foreign government. Given that the Philippine government may waive the Marcoses' head-of-state immunity, the question remains whether it has done so. The district court found that there was such a waiver. The language of that waiver . . . could scarcely be stronger.[25]

The Marcos case also raises interesting issues of extradition, which we will discuss later in Chapter 10. We shall also discuss the landmark case of Augusto Pinochet, as former president of Chile, in Chapter 15.

---

[21]"Mugabe Sued Over Election Killings," *BBC News*, http://news.bbc.co.uk/1/low/world/africa/918781.stm (accessed November 12, 2005).

[22]"Immunity As Head of State for Zimbabwe's President Mugabe," 95 *AJIL* 874 (2001), 876.

[23]*Tachiona v. Mugabe*, 169 F. Supp. 2d 259, S.D.N.Y. (2001); *Tachiona v. Mugabe* [00 Civ. 6666 (VM) (JCF)], U.S. Dist. Ct. S.D.N.Y., 216 F. Supp. 2d 262; 2002 U.S. Dist. LEXIS 11979.

[24]See *Republic of the Philippines v. Marcos*, 806 F.2d 344, U.S. Court of Appeals, 2d Cir., November 26, 1986, reported in 81 *AJIL* 417 (1987).

[25]*In re Doe*, 860 F.2d 40. U.S. Court of Appeals, 2d Cir. (1988) [also *re* Ferdinand—and Imelda—Marcos], reported in 83 *AJIL* 371 (1989).

STATE IMMUNITY

In dealing with state immunity, we encounter two problems. The first involves the scope of immunity a state may enjoy in contemporary jurisprudence. The second pertains to issues connected with *executing a legitimate decision* from a municipal court against a foreign government. An individual might prevail in a lawsuit, but then may find that the assets of the defendant state cannot be attached because they support activities connected to the jus imperii. As we noted earlier, until the beginning of the twentieth century, all states adhered to the doctrine of absolute sovereign immunity.[26] In American jurisprudence, the classic case of *The Schooner Exchange v. McFaddon* states the classical view.[27]

▶ THE SCHOONER EXCHANGE V. McFADDON

United States Supreme Court, 1812 7 Cranch 116 (1812)

Facts

The defendants, McFaddon and Greetham, alleged that they were the sole owners of the *Exchange* when it sailed from Baltimore for San Sebastian, Spain, on October 27, 1809; that the schooner was seized on December 30, 1810, by persons acting under the decrees and orders of Napoleon, emperor of France, in violation of international law; that the vessel, renamed the *Balaou*, was in Philadelphia in possession of a certain Dennis Begon, although no sentence of decree of condemnation had been pronounced against the ship by any court of competent jurisdiction; and that they asked that the courts restore the vessel to their ownership. The U.S. district attorney had appeared in the district court and argued that because peace existed between France and the United States, public vessels of France could freely enter and leave the ports of the United States, and that the former *Exchange* was now a public vessel

of France, hence immune from American jurisdiction. The district court dismissed the suit of McFaddon and Greetham, a decision that was reversed by the circuit court, and so the case came, by appeal, before the Supreme Court of the United States.

Issue

Could an American citizen assert in an American court title to an armed public vessel of a foreign country, found within the waters of the United States?

Decision

Sentence of circuit court reversed, and decision of district court affirmed: The suit was dismissed for want of jurisdiction.

Reasoning

The jurisdiction of a state within its own territory is necessarily exclusive and absolute. It is not subject to any limitation not imposed by the state on itself. All exceptions to this complete and absolute jurisdiction must be

(*continued*)

---

[26]Some limitations on immunity always have existed—for example, on ownership of immovable interests not held or administered for public purposes.

[27]For Great Britain, see *The Parlement Belge*, 1880, L.R.S.P.D. 197.

traced to the consent of the nation itself. But the perfect equality and absolute independence of sovereigns have given rise to a class of cases in which every sovereign is understood to waive the exercise of parts of that complete exclusive territorial jurisdiction, and one of these applies to warships entering the ports of a friendly power. If a sovereign permits his or her ports to remain open to the public ships of friendly foreign states, the conclusion is that such ships enter by his or her assent. And ''it seems, then, to the court, to be a principle of public law, that national ships of war, entering the port of a friendly power open for their reception, are to be considered as exempted by the consent of that power from its jurisdiction.'' The courts are not competent to enforce their decisions in cases of this description.

The *Exchange* (captured by the French Navy in pursuit of its blockade of England) had been transformed in the port of Bayonne by the order of the French government into a public armed vessel of France. The vessel must be presumed to have entered American waters and the port of Philadelphia under the implied promise that while behaving in a friendly manner, it would be exempted from the jurisdiction of the United States.

At the turn of the twentieth century, civil code states began to examine the nature of transactions. By that time, many states had become involved in a variety of activities having little to do with traditional sovereign activities. The following decision by a Belgian court develops the idea of *acta jure imperii* as opposed to *acta jure gestionis*:

> Sovereignty is involved only when political acts are accomplished. . . . However, the state is not bound to confine itself to a political role, and can for the needs of the collectivity, buy, own contract, become creditor or debtor and engage in commerce. . . . In the discharge of these functions, the state is not acting as public power, but does what private persons do, and as such is acting in a civil and private capacity. When . . . the litigation concerns a civil right, within the sole jurisdiction of the courts . . . the foreign state as civil person is like any other foreign person amenable to the Belgian courts.[28] (Emphasis added)

The tension between the two concepts of immunity continued through the first half of the twentieth century. Great Britain, the United States, and Communist countries continued to adhere to the broader concept of absolute immunity, while most civil code countries continued to develop the "restrictive" concept. Before World War II, cases occasionally arose in the United States and Great Britain that challenged the idea of absolute immunity,[29] but courts in both states were reluctant to move toward the restrictive doctrine.[30]

---

[28]*Société Anonyme des Chemins de Fer Liègeois Luxembourgeois v. the Netherlands* (1903), 294, 301.

[29]See the well-known American cases of *Berizzi Brothers Co. v. SS Pesaro*, U.S. Supreme Court, 1926, 271 U.S. 562; *The Maipo* (D.C.) 252 F. 627, and 259 F. 367, as well as the British cases of *The Gagara*, L.R. [1919] P.D. 95, *The Porto Alexandre*, L.R. [1920] P.D. 30, and *The Jupiter*, L.R. [1924] P.D. 236.

[30]The Court of Appeals has now opened up the court system in the United Kingdom to suits against foreign officials for human rights abuses committed overseas. In *Jones v. the Kingdom of Saudi Arabia and Mitchell v. Al-Dali* (Ct. of App., Civil Division, Claim HQ 02X01805 (2004), www.hmcourts-service.gov.uk/judgmentsfiles/j2871/jonesandmitchell-v-saudi_arabia.htm, the claimants brought suit against Saudi Arabia [Ministry of Interior] and several individual officials in their personal capacity. In an interesting decision, the court held that the ministry could claim sovereign immunity, but the individual officials could not. We examine these issues further in Chapter 14.

The Tate Letter

A significant change in American policy regarding state immunity occurred in 1952, when the then acting legal adviser to the Department of State, Jack B. Tate, wrote a letter to the acting attorney general. In the letter, Tate indicated acceptance of the restrictive theory of immunity by the U.S. government.[31] He pointed out that the adoption of the restrictive theory by more and more countries justified the restrictions involved. He noted that henceforth from the view of the Department of State, "private activities of foreign sovereigns" should be denied immunity in American courts. The Tate letter outlined the department's policy but failed to offer any guidelines or operational standards for distinguishing between a sovereign's private and public acts. Without such standards, courts would still have to seek guidance from the State Department and defer to its judgment. This procedure resulted in great inconsistency because the State Department often made decisions based on current foreign policy considerations rather than with an eye toward developing a consistent policy. Courts remained bound by the decision in *Republic of Mexico v. Hoffman*[32] that "once the State Department has ruled in a matter of this nature, the judiciary will not interfere." Only if the Department of State did not find it expedient to respond to a request for immunity could the court then decide for itself, through the process of judicial search and decision, if sovereign immunity should apply. The following case illustrates one instance where the department left the decision to the court.

In *Victory Transport Inc. v. Comisaria General de Abastecimientos y Transportes* (1964),[33] the State Department refused to issue a certificate of immunity because the Fascist government (under Francisco Franco) of Spain was the appellant/defendant. Lacking a State Department determination of sovereign immunity, the court developed a set of operational tests by which *acta jure imperii* might be determined:

[S]ince the State Department's failure or refusal to suggest immunity is significant, we are disposed to deny a claim of sovereign immunity that has not been "recognized and allowed" by the State Department unless it is plain that the activity in question falls within one of the categories of strictly political or public acts about which sovereigns have traditionally been quite sensitive. Such acts are generally limited to the following categories:

1. internal administrative acts, such as expulsion of an alien.
2. legislative acts, such as nationalization.
3. acts concerning the armed forces.
4. acts concerning diplomatic activity.
5. public loans.

---

[31]Text in 26 *Department of State Bulletin* (June 23, 1952), 984; also in Whiteman, VI: 569. For a detailed analysis of the letter, consult W. W. Bishop Jr., "New United States Policy Limiting Sovereign Immunity," 47 *AJIL* 93 (1953).

[32]324 U.S. 30 (1945). See also *National City Bank of New York v. Republic of China*, 348 U.S. 356, 360–361, 75 S. Ct. 423, 99 L.Ed. 389 (1955).

[33]U.S. Court of Appeals, 2d Cir., 1964, 336 F.2d 354, 358–360, 362, *cert. denied*, 381 U.S. 394 (1965); key portions of the decision may be found in Whiteman, VI: 578.

We do not think that the restrictive theory adopted by the State Department requires sacrificing the interests of private litigants to international comity in other than these limited categories.

Unfortunately, courts seldom had the opportunity to explore the relevance of these standards. In other cases relating to "friendly governments," despite the intention of the Tate letter, the State Department rarely found instances that permitted judicial discretion. As we will see later when discussing *diplomatic immunity,* the courts bowed to what they perceived as the prerogative of the executive branch and accepted State Department certificates at face value.[34]

Isbrandtsen Tankers, Inc. v. Republic of India[35] highlighted the inconsistencies in applying the Tate letter procedures. The court looked at the criteria developed in *Victory Transport* and noted, "Were we required to apply this distinction, as defined, to the facts of the present case, we might well find that the actions of the Indian government were, as appellant contends, purely private commercial decisions." The court, however, chose a different path. Citing the decision in the earlier *Republic of Mexico v. Hoffman* case,[36] it noted:

> In situations where the State Department has given a formal recommendation, however, the courts need not reach questions of this type. The State Department is to make this determination, in light of the potential consequences to our own international position. Hence, once the State Department has ruled in a matter of this nature, the judiciary will not interfere.

The Foreign Sovereign Immunities Act: Beyond the Tate Letter

The inconsistency in practice led the Departments of State and Justice to work with the Congress to develop legislation to deal with the issues. After four years of work, the Congress passed the Foreign Sovereign Immunities Act of 1976.[37] The act had four objectives: (1) it vested decisions concerning sovereign immunity exclusively in the court, (2) it codified the restrictive theory of sovereign immunity

---

[34]See *Alfred Dunhill of London, Inc. v. Republic of Cuba*, U.S. Supreme Court, 96 S. Ct. 1854, May 24, 1976, reported in 70 *AJIL* 828 (1976), and in full in 15 *ILM* 35 (1976); *Petrol Shipping Corporation*, U.S. Court of Appeals, 2d Cir., April 21, 1966, 360 F.2d 103, reported in 60 *AJIL* 859 (1966); *Aerotrade v. Republic of Haiti*, U.S. Dist. Court, S.D.N.Y., May 24, 1974, reported in 16 *Harvard Int'l Law J.* 168 (1975), and in full in 13 *ILM* 969 (1974). See also *The Philippine Admiral v. Wallem Shipping* (Hong Kong), United Kingdom, Judicial Committee of the Privy Council, November 5, 1975, reported in 70 *AJIL* 364 (1976), and in 15 *ILM* 133 (1976). This last case has been cited, with approval, in several subsequent decisions dealing with the restriction of sovereign immunity. See also the instructive as well as entertaining account by Charles N. Brower, "Litigation of Sovereign Immunity Before a State Administrative Body and the Department of State: The Japanese Uranium Tax Case," 71 *AJIL* 438 (1977).

[35]U.S. Court of Appeals, 446 F.2d 1198, 2d Cir. (1971).

[36]324 U.S. 30 (1945). See also *National City Bank of New York v. Republic of China*, 348 U.S. 356, 360–361, 75 S. Ct. 423, 99 L.Ed. 389 (1955).

[37]28 U.S.C. §§ 1330, 1602–1611 (1994). Text of act in 71 *AJIL* 595 (1977). A section-by-section analysis and explanation of the act is found in 15 *ILM* 88 (1976). See also J. N. Martin, "Sovereign Immunity—Limits of Judicial Control," 18 *Harvard Int'l L. J.* 429 (1977). The act was amended twice in November 1988; see texts in 28 *ILM* 396 (1989).

with respect to U.S. law, (3) it specified the methods for beginning a lawsuit against a foreign state, and (4) it stipulated the nature of the assets U.S. citizens might attach in execution to satisfy a final judgment against a foreign state.[38] Under the act, foreign sovereigns have immunity from jurisdictions except for stated exceptions: waiver, cases arising out of commercial activity, rights to property taken in violation of international law, and personal injury and death claims. In 1988, Congress added actions to enforce arbitration agreements and resulting arbitration awards to the exceptions.

The Anti-Terrorism and Death Penalty Act of 1996 provides that immunity shall not be available when "money damages are sought against a foreign state for personal injury or death that was caused by an act of torture, extrajudicial killing, aircraft sabotage, hostage taking, or the provision of material support or resources . . . for such an act."[39] On its face, this provision seemingly opened up the possibilities for extensive litigation. The legislation, however, limited such suits to those states officially designated as supporters of terrorism.

Distinguishing Between Public and Private Acts   We noted earlier that making clear distinctions between purely public acts (*acta jure imperii*) and ordinary acts (*acta jure gestionis*), while seemingly simple, can become very complex. We also dealt with the question of *operational standards* (rules of application) that form the bridge between "theory" and "practice." In this case, we must deal with two different ways of evaluating transactions. We can characterize an act either by its nature or by its purpose. The "nature of the act" test focuses on whether or not a given sovereign act is commercial in nature. If the act is commercial, then under modern usage, the state in question lacks immunity for it in foreign courts. The "purpose" test reflects the fact that sovereign acts may indeed be commercial but reflect state purposes. In that case, the acts in question would enjoy the protection of *jus imperii* and the state would enjoy immunity abroad. To illustrate, if a state imported quantities of woolen materials for sale in its territory, that act would lack protection under the *jus imperii,* because it would be an ordinary private commercial act under *jure gestionis.* If the state imported the textiles in question for conversion into army uniforms, this would then qualify as a sovereign public act and fall under the protection of the *jus imperii.* The state would enjoy immunity from possible suit in foreign courts for any issues arising out of the transaction.

The Tate letter followed the public/private purpose of the act distinction in outlining its theory of restrictive state immunity. The Congress, in drafting the FSIA, took a different path. The FSIA, in listing exemptions to immunity, listed "commercial activity," *hence adopting the nature of the transaction approach:*[40]

> A "commercial activity" means either a regular course of commercial conduct of a particular commercial transaction or act. The commercial character of an

---

[38]Consult also the following concerning the 1976 act: "Jurisdiction of United States Courts on Suits Against Foreign States," in *Report of Committee of the Whole House on the State of the Union,* September 9, 1976, reproduced in 15 *ILM* 1398 (1976); G. R. Delaume, "Public Debt and Sovereign Immunity: The Foreign Sovereign Immunity Act of 1976," 71 *AJIL* 399 (1977).

[39]Pub. L. No. 104–32 § 221, 110 Stat. 1214. Amended section of FSIA, n. 28, is 28 U.S.C. § 1605.

[40]Definition of commercial activity in 28 U.S.C. § 1603(d); listed exemption in § 1605(a).

activity shall be determined by reference to the nature of the course of conduct or particular transaction or act, rather than by reference to its purpose.

A contract by a foreign government to buy arms, equipment, and provisions for its armed forces would thus constitute a commercial activity. The exemption then applies regardless of the public function involved.[41]

The following case marks an important transition in the journey from the old practices to the new in U.S. law. Even after passage of the FSIA, courts struggled with the sovereign immunity issue. Part of the difficulty stemmed from a lack of experience and familiarity with the issues. Because of constant State Department intervention, the judiciary had not developed a confident expertise in these issues. In this case, the court sought to establish some guidelines.

> ### CALLEJO V. BANCOMER, S.A.
>
> # U.S. Court of Appeals 764 F.2d 1101 (5th Cir., 1985)
>
> ## Facts
>
> Callejo and his wife were citizens of the United States. In 1979–1980 they purchased certificates of deposit (CDs) issued by Bancomer, S.A., a then privately owned Mexican bank. Bancomer regularly engaged in commercial activity in the United States. The Callejos had four CDs with a value of approximately $300,000. In August and September 1982, the government of Mexico promulgated exchange control regulations. The regulations required that banks pay both prinicipal and interest in pesos even if the CDs were dollar-denominated and that payments be made in Mexico. In September, the government of Mexico then nationalized all privately owned Mexican banks, including Bancomer.
>
> Pursuant to the new exchange control regulations, Bancomer notified the Callejos that it would pay the principal and interest on the four CDs in pesos at a rate of exchange substantially below the market rate. To forestall this, the Callejos renewed two CDs and filed suit alleging breach of contract and securities violations. Bancomer filed a motion to dismiss. The district court held that the Callejos' suit was not based
>
> *(continued)*

---

[41]See *Carey and New England Petroleum Corporation v. National Oil Corporation and Libyan Arab Republic*, U.S. Dist. Court, S.D.N.Y., June 16, 1978, in 17 *ILM* 1180 (1978); *Reading and Bates v. National Iranian Oil Company*, U.S. Dist. Court, S.D.N.Y., September 27, 1979, *ILM* 18, 1398 (1979); *Verlinden B.V. v. Central Bank of Nigeria*, U.S. Supreme Court, 461 U.S. 480 (1983); *Texas Trading & Milling Corp. v. Federal Republic of Nigeria*, U.S. Dist. Ct., S.D.N.Y. 500 F. Supp. 320; 1980 U.S. Dist. LEXIS 9307; *America West Airlines, Inc. v. GPA Group Ltd.*, 877 F.2d 793, U.S. Court of Appeals, 9th Cir., June 12, 1989, and *Rush–Presbyterian–St. Luke's Medical Center v. Hellenic Republic*, 877 F.2d 574, U.S. Court of Appeals, 7th Cir., June 14, 1989. Both cases reported in 84 *AJIL* 262 (1990). See also *Trans-America Steamship Corp. v. Somali Democratic Republic*, 767 F.2d 998, U.S. Court of Appeals, D.C. Cir., July 12, 1985, in 80 *AJIL* 357 (1985); *Martin v. Republic of South Africa*, 836 F.2d 91, U.S. Court of Appeals, 2d Cir., December 29, 1987, in 28 *ILM* 583 (1988); *Biton et al. v. Palestinian Interim Self-Government Authority, et al.*, Civil Action No. 01-0382 (RMC), U.S. Dist. Ct. D.C., 310 F. Supp. 2d 172; 2004 U.S. Dist. LEXIS 4238; 195 A.L.R. Fed. 623.

on Bancomer's commercial activities and therefore the bank as an instrumentality of the Mexican government was entitled to sovereign immunity. The Callejos appealed.

Issues

1. Is the Callejos' suit based upon a "commercial activity" by Bancomer?
2. Does Bancomer have immunity because of its relationship with the Mexican government?

Decision

Bancomer's activities were neither themselves sovereign nor entitled to

derivative immunity by virtue of being compelled by Mexican law.

Reasoning

Bancomer did not act as an agent of the Mexican government merely by implementing the exchange restriction. It acted as any private party would in complying with the law. It was not the central bank and had no role in effecting the monetary controls. In the sovereign immunity arena, "we start from a premise of jurisdiction. *Where jurisdiction would otherwise exist, sovereign immunity must be pleaded as an affirmative defense; it is not presumed."*

In an era of multinational holding companies, the question of the tests used to determine an instrumentality or agency of a "foreign state" continued to plague the courts. The definition in the FSIA[42] lent itself to a number of different operational tests. In *Dole Food C. v. Patrickson,*[43] the U.S. Supreme Court addressed this question:

> May a corporate subsidiary claim instrumentality status where the foreign state does not own a majority of its shares but does own a majority of the shares of a corporate parent one or more levels above the subsidiary?

The court held that a state must directly own a majority of the shares in a foreign corporation in order for the corporation to qualify as an "instrumentality" (and hence a foreign state) under FSIA. This ruling considerably narrowed the range of entities that would qualify as "foreign states" under the legislation.[44]

An interesting situation arose in *BP Chemicals v. Jiangsu Sopo Corp. Ltd.*[45] A wholly owned corporation of the Chinese government engaged another government-owned corporation to obtain high-technology products and engineering help from American firms to assist in the construction of a Chinese chemical plant based upon trade secrets and designs owned by BP. While engaged in the effort to procure the products, the agent divulged information relating to the trade secrets and designs (illegitimately obtained) to the American companies it solicited. BP sued both the principal and the agent for violation of the Missouri Uniform Trade

---

[42]Note 34, § 1603(b).

[43]538 U.S. 468 (2003).

[44]See also *USX Corp. v. Adriatic Ins. Co.,* 345 F.3d 190, 209 (3rd Cir. 2003); *Filler v. Hanvit Bank,* 378 F.3d 213 (2d Cir.), *cert. denied,* 125 S. Ct. 677 (2004); *Abrams v. Société Nationale des Chemins de Fer François,* 389 F.3d 61; 2004 U.S. App. LEXIS 23691; 125 S. Ct. 1841; 161 L. Ed. 2d 726; 2005 U.S. LEXIS 3353; 73 U.S.L.W. 3619 (*cert. denied*).

[45]*BP Chemicals v. Jiangsu Sopo Corp. Ltd.,* 285 F.3d 677, 688, 8th Cir. (2002), *cert. denied,* 123 S. Ct. 343 (2002).

Secrets Act. The court found that by employing an agent to buy the equipment, China had engaged in commercial activity and that a foreign state may lose its immunity by "virtue of activities of its agent."[46]

Problems of Executing Judgments

An ongoing issue concerns the execution of a judgment in a successful suit. Winning in court represents only half of the problem. If a state chooses not to honor the judgment voluntarily, the winning plaintiff faces the task of finding assets not protected by immunity within the jurisdiction of the forum state. Simply, a finding that a state lacks immunity from suit under a particular set of circumstances does not presume a total waiver of immunity. Sections 1609–1611 of the FSIA attempt to deal with the complexities here. Property and assets used for commercial activities lack immunity; those used for public purposes have immunity. Thus, funds used to run embassies would have immunity. Finding assets that qualify, as with judgments in domestic cases, may prove a daunting task. The following case helped to clarify several issues.[47]

▶ FIRST CITY, TEXAS–HOUSTON, N.A. V. RAFIDAIN BANK

U.S. Ct. of Appeals Second Circuit 281 F.3d 48 (2d Cir.), cert. denied, 123 S. Ct. 75 (2002)

Facts

In 1990, First City filed suit against Rafidain, Iraq's state-owned commercial bank, and Central Bank, as Rafidain's alter ego, to recover more than $50 million in unpaid principal and interest on defaulted letters of credit issued by Rafidain. The district court entered default judgment for $53.2 million against both defendants on April 26, 1991. A year later, both defendants moved to vacate the defaults; Central Bank's motion was granted on the basis that service had been insufficient, but Rafidain's motion was denied.

Following this judgment, the plaintiff served notice of discovery on both banks regarding disclosure of sources and nature of assets. After 10 years of claims and counterclaims, the court finally affirmed the original decision of the district court.

Issue

Did postjudgment jurisdiction (waiver of immunity) extend to allow discovery activities with regard to assets available to satisfy the judgment?

Decision

Yes. Given Rafidain's waiver, the district court had subject matter jurisdiction under 28 U.S.C. §§ 1330(a) and 1605(a)(2) to decide the controversy that arose from Rafidain's commercial activities carried on in the United States.

(continued)

---

[46]Note 45, at 688.

[47]See also *Hill v. Republic of Iraq and Saddam Hussein*, 328 F.3d 240, 680, D.C. Cir. (2003).

Reasoning

"We think that where subject matter jurisdiction under the FSIA exists to decide a case, jurisdiction continues long enough to allow proceedings in aid of any money judgment that is rendered in the case. In this case, that includes discovery regarding a possible alter ego of Rafidain that may have assets sufficient to satisfy First City's judgment. Discovery of a judgment debtor's assets is conducted routinely under the Federal Rules of Civil Procedure. *See* Fed. R. Civ. P. 69(a) ('In aid of the judgment or execution, the judgment creditor or a successor in interest when that interest appears of record, may obtain discovery from any person, including the judgment debtor, in the manner provided in these rules or in the manner provided by the practice of the state in which the district court is held.')."

In *Kelly v. Syrian Shell Petroleum Development B.V.*,[48] the court noted that judgment means that foreign states will be in the same position as any American debtor. On the other hand, judgment does not give the plaintiff a license to engage in a fishing expedition under the guise of discovery.

Waiver of Immunity

Waiver of immunity may be explicit or implicit. The FSIA does not define *implicit waiver,* and U.S. courts have construed the precedents very narrowly.[49] In the contemporary world, many financial and trade negotiations center on whether a foreign state or sovereign will waive its immunity for suit. In several of the cases discussed earlier, the contracts and agreements contained waiver provisions (e.g., *Rafidain*), and many specify what body of substantive law would apply to any dispute.[50]

Immunity After Severance of Diplomatic Relations

The political nature of recognition implies continued enjoyment of immunity after a severance of diplomatic relations between two states. Thus, the U.S. courts have sustained, at least since 1962, Cuban sovereign immunity despite the severance of diplomatic relations.[51] The simple point here is that formal diplomatic relations normally depend upon recognition, but that does not mean that severance of diplomatic relations implies withdrawal of recognition.

---

[48]213 F.3d 48, 2d Cir., *cert. denied,* 123 S. Ct. 75 (2002).

[49]See the discussion in *Creighton Limited v. Government of the State of Qatar,* 161 F.3d 118, D.C. Cir. (1999).

[50]For a fascinating case, see *Princz v. Federal Republic of Germany,* 26 F.3d 1166, D.C. Cir. (1994); and the discussion "International Law. Foreign Sovereign Immunities Act. D.C. Circuit Holds That Violation of Peremptory Norms of International Law Does Not Constitute an Implied Waiver of Sovereign Immunity Under the Foreign Sovereign Immunities Act," 108 *Harvard Law Review* 513 (1994).

[51]See *Rich v. Naviera Vacuba, S.A. and Republic of Cuba; Mayan Lines v. Republic of Cuba and the M/V Bahia de Nipe; United Fruit Sugar Co. v. 5,000 Tons of Sugar;* and *Navarro and Others v. the M/V Bahia de Nipe,* U.S. Ct. Appeals, 4th Cir., September 7, 1961, 295 F.2d 24, in 56 *AJIL* 526, 550 (1962).

Status of Nonrecognized Foreign Governments

Nonrecognition of a foreign government (see Chapter 7) normally results in its inability to assert immunity for its vessels in foreign ports or waters. The Soviet Union's seizure, in 1940, of the three Baltic republics of Estonia, Latvia, and Lithuania, followed by the absorption of the three states into the Soviet Union, was not recognized as lawful by a considerable number of foreign states, including notably the United States, Great Britain, and Ireland. These and other governments refused to recognize the transfers of sovereignty involved in the absorption of the three Baltic republics.

At the time of the Soviet takeover, a number of vessels belonging to private owners, particularly in Estonia and Latvia, happened to be on the high seas. Several of the ships in question came into ports of the Republic of Eire and at once became the objects of suits. The Soviet Union asserted that the vessels were state property and that as such they had immunity from the jurisdiction of Irish courts without the consent of their sovereign owner. The Soviets, who espoused a doctrine of absolute state immunity, argued that this immunity existed whether the ships were used for public purposes or for commerce and whether or not they were in the possession of the sovereign.

The plaintiffs in the cases—that is, the accredited representatives of the "defunct" Baltic governments in exile—sought to act as trustees to prevent acquisition of control over the vessels by agencies of the Soviet Union. These so-called Baltic ship cases, reinforced by corresponding decisions in a number of other countries—including the United States[52]—helped establish the doctrine that nonrecognition of an alleged successor state or government results in a failure to create immunity claimed for vessels of that state or government.

Retroactivity of the FSIA

Litigation by heirs to recover assets of Holocaust victims seized by Nazi regimes before and during World War II raised the issue of the possible retroactivity (temporal reach) of the FSIA. Constitutional lawyers may immediately protest that the FSIA, as ex post facto legislation, could not possibly apply to early cases, *but* the issue as framed by the courts in the civil law context relied upon a two-step test derived from the U.S. Supreme Court's ruling in *Landgraf v. USI Film Products*.[53] The Supreme Court in *Landgraf* noted that it must focus on the tension between two apparent contradictory canons for interpreting statutes that do not specify their temporal reach: (1) The rule that a court must apply the law in effect at the time it renders its decision[54] and (2) the axiom that statutory retroactivity is not favored.[55] The court noted that the presumption against statutory retroactiv-

---

[52]See *Zarine v. Owners, etc., SS Ramava: McEvoy & Ors. v. Owners, etc., SS Otto*; and *McEvoy and Veldi v. Owners, etc., SS Piret and SS Mall,* Eire High Court, April 29 and 30 and May 1 and 16, 1941, 75 *Irish Law Times Reports* 153, in 36 *AJIL* 490 (1942); and the American case of *Latvian State Cargo & Passenger SS Line v. McGrath,* U.S. Ct. Appeals, D.C. Cir., 1951, 188 F.2d 1000.

[53]511 U.S. 244 (1994).

[54]See *Bradley v. Richmond,* 416 U.S. 696, 711 (1974).

[55]See *Bowen v. Georgetown Univ. Hospital,* 488 U.S. 204, 208 (1988).

ity stems from elementary considerations of fairness. Individuals should have an opportunity to know what the law is and to conform their conduct accordingly. Otherwise, they would face an open-ended liability. In the criminal context, the *ex post facto* clause in the Constitution clearly expresses this idea. In the context of civil law, the question becomes one of congressional intent. Hence, the court first asked "whether Congress has expressly prescribed the statute's proper reach."[56] If the court is satisfied that Congress has done so, then the court will not proceed. If Congress has not clearly stated the reach, then a court must decide whether applying the statute to events before its enactment "would impair rights a party possessed when he acted, increase a party's liability for past conduct, or impose new duties with respect to transactions already completed."[57]

In 1998 an Austrian journalist, granted access to the Austrian Gallery's archives, discovered evidence that certain valuable works in the gallery's collection had not been donated by their rightful owners but had been seized by the Nazis or expropriated by the Austrian Republic after World War II. The journalist provided some of that evidence to Maria Altmann, who in turn filed suit to recover possession of six Gustav Klimt paintings.[58] Before the Nazi invasion of Austria, the paintings had hung in the home of Altmann's uncle, Ferdinand Bloch-Bauer, a Czechoslovakian Jew. Altmann claimed ownership of the paintings under a will executed by her uncle after he fled Austria in 1938. She alleged that the gallery obtained possession of the paintings through wrongful conduct in the years during and after World War II.

The Court of Appeals engaged in a detailed historical search before concluding that the FSIA would not attach new legal significance to the events. Applying the act retroactively, the court held that Austria could neither expect to nor would it have been entitled to immunity for its actions at the time they occurred.[59] The Supreme Court in *affirming* the decision of the circuit court rejected both the historical search and the two-pronged test in *Landgraf,* finding instead that congressional intent in terms of application was clear.[60]

We must contrast the decision in *Altmann* with that in *Abrams v. Société Nationale des Chemins de Fer Français.*[61] The plaintiffs brought suit, individually and on behalf of other Holocaust victims and their heirs and beneficiaries, against the French national railroad company, Société Nationale des Chemins de Fer Français (SNCF). The plaintiffs alleged that SNCF had committed war crimes and crimes against humanity under customary international law by knowingly transporting tens of thousands of French civilians to Nazi death and slave labor camps. During the time when these atrocities were committed, SNCF remained under

---

[56]Recall the issues in the *Over the Top* (see Chapter 6).

[57]*Landgraf,* note 53, at 280.

[58]*Altmann v. Republic of Austria,* 317 F.3d 954, 9th Cir. (2003).

[59]*Altmann,* note 58, at 964–965.

[60]*Republic of Austria, et al. v. Altmann,* 541 U.S. 677; 124 S. Ct. 2240; 159 L. Ed. 2d 1; 2004 U.S. LEXIS 4030.

[61]389 F.3d 61; 2004 U.S. App. LEXIS 23691, *cert. denied, Abrams v. Société Nationale des Chemins de Fer Français,* 2005 U.S. LEXIS 3353, U.S. (April 18, 2005).

independent civilian control. It had since been wholly acquired by the French government. The court noted:[62]

> In their supplemental briefing, appellants argue that a distinction can be drawn between SNCF and the Altmann defendants in that the former, unlike the latter, was a non-governmental entity at the time of the alleged misconduct. This fact is *immaterial* after Altmann. In determining immunity of a foreign sovereign, Altmann deems irrelevant the way an entity would have been treated at the time of the alleged wrongdoing. Thus, the distinction between a corporate entity and a government entity now only speaks to whether the tortfeasor is a sovereign, or alternatively an "agent" or "instrumentality" of the sovereign, and hence to whether FSIA is applicable at all. While SNCF was predominantly owned by civilians during World War II, it is now wholly owned by the French government and, as we have previously ruled, is an "agent" or "instrumentality" of France under the FSIA. (Abrams, 332 F.3d at 180; see also Dole Food Co. v. Patrickson, 538 U.S. 468, 480, 155 L. Ed. 2d 643, 123 S. Ct. 1655 (2003), holding unequivocally that an entity's status as an instrumentality of a foreign state should be "determined *at the time of the filing of the complaint.*") Once the railroad is encompassed by the FSIA, its prior incarnation as a private entity does not bar the statute's retroactive application. (Emphasis added)

ACT OF STATE DOCTRINE

As we have argued, international law requires each state to respect the validity of the public acts of other states, in the sense that its courts will not pass judgment on the legality or the constitutionality of a foreign sovereign's acts under its own laws within its own territory. A classic statement of this so-called act of state doctrine is found in the dictum of U.S. Supreme Court Chief Justice Melville Fuller in *Underhill v. Hernandez*:[63]

> Every sovereign state is bound to respect the independence of every other sovereign state, and the courts of one country will not sit in judgment on the acts of the government of another done within its own territory.

To this point, we have considered the question of immunity when a state's actions extend outside of its own territory. The act of state doctrine reflects the simple idea that each state must respect the validity of foreign state acts, in the sense of refusing to permit its courts to sit in judgment on the legality or constitutionality of the foreign act under foreign law.[64]

A number of decisions of the U.S. Supreme Court appeared to accept the act of state doctrine as a principle of international law. In fact, however, the practice of many states indicated they did not regard such an interpretation as correct. The

---

[62]*Abrams v. Société Nationale des Chemins de Fer Français*, 7–8 n. 61.

[63]U.S. Supreme Court, 1897, 168 U.S. 250. See also the monographic treatment in M. Zander, "The Act of State Doctrine," 53 *AJIL* 826 (1959).

[64]Briggs, 404.

U.S. Supreme Court joined this point of view in 1964, when in *Banco Nacional de Cuba v. Sabbatino* (376 U.S. 398, 421) it held that the act of state doctrine was not a rule of international law and that its application was not necessarily required by international law. In the *Sabbatino* case, the court stated that instead of laying down or reaffirming an inflexible and all-inclusive rule, the judicial branch would not examine the validity of an act of expropriation within its own territory by a foreign sovereign government (existing and recognized by the United States at the time of suit) in the absence of a treaty or other controlling legal principles, even if the allegation was made that the *expropriation* violated customary international law.[65]

As a direct consequence of the *Sabbatino* case, in 1964 Congress incorporated a new paragraph into the Foreign Assistance Act of 1961. Amended in 1965, the paragraph (620[a]2) provided that no courts in the United States were to decline on the ground of the federal act of state doctrine to determine the merits implementing the principles of international law in a case in which a claim to property was asserted, based on confiscation after January 1, 1959, by an act in violation of the principles of international law. The Department of State strongly objected to this so-called Sabbatino or second Hickenlooper Amendment.[66] The Hickenlooper Amendment, however, did not affect the determination of a foreign government's immunity from suit in U.S. courts.[67] To date, Congress has not affirmatively endorsed the doctrine in any form, nor has it created a statutory referent as a guide for application.

The last U.S. Supreme Court review of an act-of-state case of importance came in 1990, in the case of *W. S. Kirkpatrick & Co. et al. v. Environmental Tectonic Corp., International*.[68] The court held that the act-of-state doctrine precluded examination only of the validity or legality of foreign governmental acts performed in that government's territory. Justice Scalia wrote for a unanimous court in very clear language that the act of state doctrine is a "rule of decision" and that "[a] ct of state issues only arise when a court must decide—that is, when the outcome

---

[65]U.S. District Court, S.D.N.Y., 1961, 193 F. Supp. 375, digested in *55 AJIL* 741 (1961); affirmed on appeal, Court of Appeals, 2d Cir., 1962, 307 F.2d 834, reprinted in *56 AJIL* 1085 (1962); reversed and remanded, Supreme Court, 1964, 376 U.S. 398, abstracted at length in *59 AJIL* 799 (1964) (including Justice White's lengthy dissent); U.S. Dist. Court, S.D.N.Y., 1965, on remand, 243 F. Supp. 957, and Memorandum Opinion, November 15, 1965, 272 F. Supp. 836, reproduced at length in 60 *AJIL* 107 (1966); decision affirmed on appeal, Court of Appeals, 2d Cir., 1967, 383 F.2d 166; *cert. denied*, 1968, 390 U.S. 956; rehearing denied, 1968, 390 U.S. 1037. The complicated series of decisions is analyzed carefully, with supporting documents, in Whiteman, VI: 20–36.

[66]See Whiteman, II: 27–31, for details. The formal reference to the "Hickenlooper" Amendment is Section 620(e)(2) of the Foreign Assistance Act of 1961, as Amended [22 U.S.C. 2370(e)(2)]; the section in question is reprinted in *57 AJIL* 749 (1967). Consult also Lowenfeld, "The Sabbatino Amendment—International Law Meets Civil Procedure," *59 AJIL* 899 (1965).

[67]*American Hawaiian Ventures v. M V J. Latubarbary*, U.S. District Court, N.J., 1966, 257 F. Supp. 622, reported by Matthews in 8 *Harvard Int'l L. J.* 357 (1967). But see U.S.C. 9 § 15, which notes, "Enforcement of arbitral agreements, confirmation of arbitral awards, and execution upon judgments based on orders confirming such awards shall not be refused on the basis of the Act of State doctrine."

[68]*W. S. Kirkpatrick & Co. v. Envtl. Tectonics Corp.*, 493 U.S. 400 (1990); see Patrick W. Pearsall, "Means/Ends Reciprocity in the Act of State Doctrine," 43 *Columbia Journal of Transnational Law* 999 (2005).

of the case turns upon—the effect of official action by a foreign sovereign."[69] A recent commentary concludes:

> The Supreme Court's act of state opinions do not provide any singular ends that lower courts should privilege in applying the doctrine. While the Supreme Court provides lower courts with broad discretion to determine whether the act of state doctrine applies in a given case, it has simultaneously left uncertain the principle that the doctrine intends to effectuate, rendering those same judges pastured in an indeterminate jurisprudential landscape.[70]

Privilege to Bring Suit

No discussion of state immunity can be concluded without mentioning the privilege of foreign sovereigns to bring suit in the courts of a friendly state (see Chapter 7 for examples). General agreement prevails concerning the duty of such a sovereign (state) to adhere to the procedures established for and in the courts of the state in which the suit is being brought. By implication, the privilege to sue is accompanied by the consent to submit to the jurisdiction of the court in question, that is, waive its immunity, regarding any counterclaims arising out of the same suit.[71] This right does have limits: The right of access to foreign courts, however, does not permit a state to bring suit for the enforcement of its own revenue or penal laws by the foreign court, at least not in the absence of some form of reciprocal agreement to enforce such laws of another jurisdiction.

In the United States, while federal courts will not examine the validity of foreign expropriations of property located in the countries concerned, these same courts will not permit a foreign government to take property located in the United States without payment of compensation. "American courts will not give 'extraterritorial effect' to a confiscatory decree of a foreign state, even when directed against its own nationals."[72]

RIGHTS OF INTERNATIONAL ORGANIZATIONS

As we noted in Chapter 7, the subjects of international law include not only independent states but also certain other international legal persons. Of these, international organizations form the most important. Whatever the legal status of such agencies before World War II, there can be no question that since 1945 a number of organizations, created by states through international conventions, have enjoyed the position of subjects of the law. The attributes of their

---

[69]Kirkpatrick, note 68, at 406.

[70]Pearsall, note 68, at 1013.

[71]See Robert B. Looper, "Counterclaims Against a Foreign Sovereign Plaintiff," 50 *AJIL* (1956), 647–653; *Republic of China v. Pang-Tsu Mow,* U.S. Court of Appeals, Dist. of Col., 1952, 201 F.2d 195; *Banco Nacional de Cuba v. Chemical Bank New York Trust Co.,* U.S. Dist. Ct., S.D.N.Y., October 16, 1984, in 79 *AJIL* 459 (1985).

[72]*Maltina Corp.* v. *Cawy Bottling Co.,* U.S. Court of Appeals, 5th Cir., 462 F.2d 1021, *cert. denied,* 409 U.S. 1060 (1972).

international personality, however, are limited by the constitutive treaty creating each of these international agencies. The constitutive treaty alone shapes their constitution and specifies the authority delegated to them. International organizations, therefore, are not original subjects of international law but *derivative* subjects of that law.

The Advisory Opinion of the International Court of Justice on Reparations for Injuries Suffered in the Service of the United Nations serves as a fundamental statement concerning the position of international organizations in contemporary practice.[73] The court stated: "Fifty States, representing the vast majority of the members of the international community, had the power, in conformity with international law, to bring into being an entity possessing objective international personality, and not personality recognized by them alone, together with capacity to bring international claims."[74] Because states, both in their corporate capacity and in the person of the chief of state, have certain privileges, the question arises as to the possession of similar privileges by international organizations that have achieved international legal personality. Since 1945, the granting of privileges and immunities, as phrased typically in Article 105 of the UN Charter, has covered everything "necessary for the fulfillment of its purposes."[75] What matters here, however, is the status of the organizations themselves, with reference to immunity from suit and execution of judgments. Public international agencies possessing international legal personality enjoy immunity from suit for all noncommercial activity of such agencies.[76]

Immunities Act

The General Convention on the Privileges and Immunities of the United Nations (February 13, 1946, 1 U.N.T.S. 15) provided immunity from suit as well as from every other form of legal process without an explicit waiver. In contrast with the initial drafting of the UN Charter, the Convention specifically draws on the analogy with the corresponding immunity enjoyed by states. Significantly, with the International Organizations Immunities Act (59 Stat. 669, which, together with the UN Charter, *governed* UN immunities in the United States before the

---

[73]International Court of Justice, 1949, *L.C.J. Reports* (1949), 174.

[74]Ibid., reprinted in 43 *AJIL* 590 (1949); see also Q. Wright, "Responsibility for Injuries to United Nations Officials," 43 *AJIL* 95 (1949); and his "The Jural Personality of the United Nations," 509. The most comprehensive analysis available of the legal status of the United Nations is G. Weinberg, *The International Status of the United Nations* (1961).

[75]The full text of the convention, as approved by the General Assembly on February 13, 1946, is found in 43 *AJIL* (Supp. 1, 1949). Concerning immunity, see Article 4, § 11(f)(g); Article 5, § 18(e)(f); and § 19 of the convention. Consult also the "Headquarters" *Agreement Between the United States and the United Nations* of June 26, 1947, and the *Interim Agreement* of December 18, 1947, between the same parties; both documents reprinted in 43 *AJIL* 8 (January 1949 Supp.).

[76]See *Broadbent et al. v. Organization of American States et al.,* U.S. Ct. Appeals, D.C. Cir., January 8, 1980, no. 78–146, in 19 *ILM* 208 (1980), for a careful exposition of the matter; and *Standard Chartered Bank v. International Tin Council,* UK, High Court of Justice (Queen's Bench Division), April 17, 1986, in 25 *ILM* 650 (1986), a case involving jurisdictional immunity and contracts with international organizations.

latter acceded to the General Convention effective on April 29, 1970), UN immunity could be waived only expressly by contract or in relation to the purpose of any proceeding.

UN immunity under the provisions of the United Nations General Convention includes immunity for UN assets, wherever located, from any legal process; immunity of all UN premises from search, requisition, expropriation, confiscation, and any other sort of interference; immunity of archives; complete freedom from all financial controls, moratoriums, or other monetary regulations; freedom to hold funds in any desired currency or metal; freedom to transfer funds; an absolute exemption of all assets and revenue from all direct taxes; exemption from all customs duties as well as from any foreign trade prohibitions on goods needed for the official use of the organization; a guarantee of most favored diplomatic treatment in regard to rates, priorities, and so on, connected with all media of communications; exemption from all forms of censorship; the right to use codes; and the privilege of transporting correspondence by courier or otherwise under the full complement of customary diplomatic immunities.

The status of the UN headquarters in the United States, on the other hand—depending on the "housekeeping" agreement of June 26, 1947, between the United Nations and its host—presents some rather interesting deviations from the virtually absolute immunity provided for in the General Convention.[77] U.S. civil and criminal laws (federal, state, and local) apply in the zone, which is merely granted "inviolability." *Inviolability* means that although the zone is U.S. territory, U.S. officials (federal, state, or local) may enter the zone only with the consent of the secretary-general; the secretary-general must also grant specific approval if any service of legal process is contemplated by American authorities.[78] Within the area in question, the United Nations may operate its own radio station, airport, and postal service. An arbitration tribunal of three members is to settle all disputes between the host sovereign and the United Nations concerning interpretation of the agreement.

DUTIES OF STATES

We pointed out earlier that many of the alleged rights of states either reflect defining characteristics or, in other instances, represent duties or obligations. Whether or not one admits the existence of a moral code prevailing in the relations among nations, the fact remains that practicing diplomats, Machiavellian or otherwise, have agreed that some sort of code does exist (see Chapter 1). Thus, states concluding treaties among themselves expect that the agreements will be observed; whoever breaches the treaty will either deny that fact or defend it by elaborate arguments designed to show that the act was morally or legally just. It therefore becomes necessary now to investigate what may be properly included among the duties of states in their mutual relations.

---

[77]See text of agreement and related documents in 43 *AJIL* 8 (1949 Supp.); and Whiteman, XIII: 32.

[78]See *People v. Weiner*, 85 Misc. 2d 161, 378 N.Y.S. 2d 966 (Crim. Ct. of City of N.Y., 1978), reported in 18 *Harvard Int'l L. J.* 198 (1977).

The older duties of states (prohibition of intervention, etc.) developed into rules of customary international law.[79] Somewhat later, a limited number of new duties were added through the adoption of the UN Charter. In recent decades, many of the duties of states have originated through the adoption of multipartite treaties. While the applying only to states parties to them (see Chapter 4), these treaties have nonetheless affected virtually all countries involved in a given problem.

The most modern, though incomplete, listing of the asserted duties of states may be found in the Draft Convention on the Rights and Duties of States, prepared in 1949 by the International Law Commission in conformity with a resolution of the UN General Assembly. The following discussion deals with the duties mentioned by the commission, as well as with several additional obligations generally recognized as binding by the members of the community of nations.

Traditional Duties

Nonintervention   On the one hand, the Charter of the United Nations contains a duty to abstain from subversive intervention and to respect the territorial integrity and political independence of all other states. This duty includes refraining from engaging in propaganda, official statements, or legislative action of any kind with the intention of promoting rebellion, sedition, or treason against the government of another state. At the same time, there exists an equally legal obligation, enshrined in the same Charter, for the members to respect human rights and the self-determination of peoples. The problem stems from how to define *subversive intervention*. Did Libya's leader, Colonel Muammar al-Gaddafi, violate the rule when, during a 14-year period of squabbling with Morocco, he organized a radio campaign inciting the Moroccan people to overthrow their king?

Both great and small powers have practiced subversive intervention. Although the jurisdiction of any state is territorial and limited to its own domain, many states have interests abroad or follow a foreign policy that involves a cooperative response from other states. When such a foreign policy or such interests appear to demand that a friendlier, a more amenable, a more radical, or a more conservative government is needed in another state to better serve the interests of the first one, then there is a great temptation to attempt to intervene in the "domestic politics" of the other state so that the desired results are achieved. The problem of coping with such subversive intervention is complicated by considerations of freedom of opinions that may prevail in a given country and by the technical problems of stopping propaganda across national frontiers. As President Gerald Ford of the United States phrased it in his press conference of September 16, 1974, "Our Government, like other governments, does take certain actions in the intelligence field to help implement foreign policy and protect national security. I am informed reliably that Communist nations spend vastly more money than we do for the same kind of purposes." The actions Ford referred to were the activities, costing around $8 million, of the U.S. government between 1970 and 1973 in an effort to undermine,

---

[79]See also *Nicaragua v. United States* (Merits) in Chapter 3.

economically and politically, the government of President Salvador Allende Gossens of Chile.[80]

Should *private* broadcasts and telecasts attacking or libeling foreign governments be regarded as creating state responsibility in the absence of some evidence of state sponsorship? In the case of statements made through a station operated as part of the Voice of America network, government responsibility may have been created. Private intervention may also take the form of aid to rebels in another country. This action may involve funding foreign rebel movements or the actual shipment of weapons, ammunition, and other forms of military assistance. A prime example was the extensive aid of both kinds by private American sources to the illegal Irish Republican Army (IRA) in Northern Ireland.[81]

Counterfeiting   Another obligation or duty of states is that of preventing the counterfeiting, within their jurisdiction, of the coins, currencies, postage stamps, and securities of another state.[82] Even when given states have not adhered to international conventions prohibiting such practices, they tend to regard it as their obligation to prevent counterfeiting by passing appropriate domestic legislation. However, just as in the case of practically all other state duties, the advent of a state of war cancels the duty in question insofar as it applies to enemy states. In World War II, Germany counterfeited British £5 notes; for its part, Great Britain counterfeited German postage stamps to expedite the mailing of propaganda postcards addressed to random samples of German citizens in cities bombed by the Royal Air Force. Excellent imitations of German official mailbags filled with such stamped and addressed cards were dropped from planes in the hope that German citizens, believing the bags to have been lost from mail trucks during the confusion of a bombing attack, would turn them in to the nearest post office for dispatch to the addresses.

Nontraditional Duties

A duty of states, one generally accepted in theory but all too often violated in practice, is the obligation to refrain from fomenting civil strife in the territory of another state and to prevent the organization within its own territory of activities calculated to produce such civil strife. Another duty of every state is to make certain that the conditions prevailing in its territory do not menace international

---

[80]*New York Times* (September 8, 1974), 1, 26; (September 15, 1974), 1, 19, E-23; (December 5, 1975), 1, 10. See also *Covert Action in Chile* (Staff Report of the Select Committee to Study Governmental Operations with Respect to Intelligence Activities, U.S. Senate, 94th Congress, 1st Session) (Washington, DC, 1975), as well as the summary of a *Memorandum* dated October 25, 1974, by the acting legal adviser of the Department of State, in 69 *AJIL* 382 (1975); see also A. M. Scott, *Revolution in Statecraft: Intervention in an Age of Interdependence* (Durham, NC: Duke University Press, 1982), for a classic treatment of this aspect of the Cold War.

[81]See J. B. Bell, *The IRA, 1978–2000: Analysis of a Secret Army* (London: Frank Cass, 2000).

[82]See Whiteman, VI: 268; Hackworth, II: 350; and *United States v. Arjona*, U.S. Supreme Court, 1887, 120 U.S. 479. There has been in force since 1931 the International Convention and Protocol for the Suppression of Counterfeiting Currency (Geneva, 1929); the United States is not a party.

peace. This duty, developed by the International Law Commission from a portion of the Panamanian draft of the convention just mentioned, needs little comment. It appears to be a corollary to the concept of national sovereignty, with each state presumably having exclusive authority in its territory, that such authority should be wielded effectively to prevent any danger to neighboring states. If a state fails to maintain a degree of control sufficient to prevent such danger to its neighbors, then it is obligated to assume responsibility for the consequences of its failure as a sovereign government (see Chapter 10).

A duty, technically applicable only to the members of the United Nations under Article 2(3) of the UN Charter, is an obligation to settle international disputes by peaceful means. Because the Charter as a treaty is not binding on nonmembers of the organization, countries that do not belong to the United Nations appear to be entitled in law to adopt forcible measures to settle disputes among themselves, either *ab initio* (from the beginning) or after a failure of peaceful methods. Given that the United Nations now encompasses almost all members of the community of nations, this might be considered a universal norm. On the other hand, the record since 1945 shows that members of the United Nations, too, have resorted to force outside the permissible condition of self-defense.

A corollary to that duty is the duty to abstain from the resort to war as an instrument of national policy and to refrain from the threat or use of force against another state. This alleged duty depends obviously on the interpretation adopted of the status of war under current international law. Support of this duty negates one of the traditional characteristics or rights of a sovereign state—the right to go to war when other methods of obtaining justice, satisfying claims on another state, or achieving presumably essential or vital national goals have failed. In view of the debatable nature of this duty of states, its validity will be considered later in this text (Chapter 19). A member of the United Nations must also refrain from giving assistance to any state against which the United Nations is taking preventive or enforcement action. This duty is merely a restatement of Article 2(5) of the UN Charter.

Another duty, derived from Article 2(4) of the UN Charter, is to abstain from recognizing any territorial acquisitions made by a state acting in violation of the Charter's provisions. Unfortunately, this duty has not always been observed by the members of the organization. Instances such as Indian aggression against Hyderabad and in 1961 against Portuguese enclaves in India, Chinese acquisitions of Burmese and Indian territories and Tibet, and India's seizure of portions of Kashmir come to mind.[83]

Again, there is a duty for all states to carry out in good faith the obligations arising out of treaties and other sources of international law, and no state may

---

[83]See Q. Wright, "The Goa Incident," 56 *AJIL* (1962), 617; as well as Whiteman, II: 1140; C. Eagleton, "The Case of Hyderabad Before the Security Council," 44 *AJIL* (1950), 277; the pre-UN analysis by J. W. Garner, "Non-recognition of Illegal Territorial Annexation and Claims to Sovereignty," 30 *AJIL* (1936), 679; and Briggs, "Non-recognition of Title by Conquest and Limitations of the Doctrine," *Proceedings* (1940), 72.

invoke provisions in its constitution or laws as an excuse for failure to carry out this duty. As we have discussed (Chapter 4), one of the oldest principles of international law is the doctrine of *pacta sunt servanda* (treaties must be observed), even though there are differences of opinion as to the absolute nature of the rule and the possible conditions under which it can be set aside lawfully. The duty of honoring obligations in good faith is an essential and basic condition for a legal order, and there can be no doubt as to its existence. The final duty of every state, frequently asserted, is that of conducting its relations with other countries in accordance with international law. This, like the preceding duty, is a basic condition for the existence of a legal order. Although compliance in every case cannot be expected, the duty is undeniable and is a binding obligation or duty of states.

SUGGESTED READINGS

BP Chemicals v. Jiangsu Sopo Corp. Ltd., 285 F.3d 677, 688, 8th. Cir. (2002).

Hill v. Republic of Iraq and Saddam Hussein, 328 F.3d 240, 680, D.C. Cir. (2003).

Landgraf v. USI Film Products, 511 U.S. 244 (1994).

Société Iranienne du Gaz v. Société Pipeline Service, France, Cour de Cassation, May 2, 1990, reported in 85 *AJIL* 696 (1991).

ACT OF STATE DOCTRINE

Pearsall, "Means/Ends Reciprocity in the Act of State Doctrine," 43 *Columbia Journal of Transnational Law* 999 (2005).

THE SABBATINO CASE

This famous case was heard three times in the Second Circuit Court of Appeals and twice in the Supreme Court; see *Banco Nacional de Cuba v. First National City Bank,* U.S. Ct. Appeals, 2d Cir., May 11, 1973, reported in 12 *ILM* 636 (1973). The earlier history of the litigation is *First National City Bank v. Banco Nacional de Cuba,* 40 U.S. L.W. 4652 (U.S., June 7, 1972), rev'g. 442 F.2d 530 (2d Cir. 1972); 400 U.S. 1019 (1971), vacating 431 F.2d 394 (2d Cir. 1970), rev'g. 270 F. Supp. 1004, S.D.N.Y. (1967). The relevant decisions, rulings, briefs, and other related materials may be found in 6 *ILM* 898 (1967); 9 *ILM* 1125 (1970); 10 *ILM* 56, 509, 1191 (1971); 11 *ILM* 27, 348, 811 (1972). The key decisions were also reported in 65 *AJIL* 195, 391, 812 (1971) and 65 *AJIL* 856 (1972).

Falk, "The Complexity of Sabbatino," 58 *AJIL* 935 (1964).

RIGHTS: GENERAL

Carl Marks & Co. v. Union of Soviet Socialist Republics, 665 F. Supp. 323, U.S. Dist. Ct., S.D.N.Y., 1987, in 83 *AJIL* 129 (1989).

Franck, "The Emerging Right to Democratic Governance," 86 *AJIL* 46 (1992).

Franck, "Legitimacy in the International System," 82 *AJIL* 705, 746 (1988).

Kirgis, "The Degrees of Self-Determination in the United Nations Era," 88 *AJIL* 304 (1994).

Tomuschat, ed., *The Modern Law of Self-Determination* (1993).

IMMUNITIES OF STATES CASES

Lafontant v. Aristide, 844 F.Supp128, U.S. Dist. Ct., E.D.N.Y. (1994).

Tachiona v. Mugabe, 169 F. Supp. 2d 259, S.D.N.Y. (2001).

IMMUNITY TO SUIT

Delaume, "Economic Development and Sovereign Immunity," 79 *AJIL* 319 (1985).

Gordon, *State Immunity in Commercial Transactions* (1991).

Higgins, "The Death Throes of Absolute Immunity: The Government of Uganda Before the English Courts," 73 *AJIL* 465 (1979).

CASES

Abrams v. Société Nationale des Chemins de Fer Français, 389 F.3d 61; 2004 U.S. App. LEXIS 23691, *cert. denied, Abrams v. Société Nationale des Chemins de Fer Français,* 2005 U.S. LEXIS 3353 (U.S., Apr. 18, 2005).

Altmann v. Republic of Austria, 317 F.3d 954, 9th Cir. (2003); *Republic of Austria, et al. v. Altmann,* 541 U.S. 677; 124 S. Ct. 2240.

The Allocation of Competence
in International Law

Nationality

MEANING OF NATIONALITY

To this point, we have talked almost exclusively about states and governments. Many questions of international law involve the necessity of delineating responsibility for specific actions or delineating the areas where a state or government can legitimately exercise its authority and rights. In the contemporary world, *nationality,* as the essential connection between an individual and a particular state in the contemporary world, stands at the center of many issues from questions of diplomatic protection to those involving human rights. Aircraft and ships have nationality, as do companies. The ability to travel rests upon documents based primarily on nationality. In the contemporary world, *stateless* individuals—those without an identifiable nationality—may often find themselves treated as if they have no rights, because the primary concern of each state is with those individuals defined as its citizens or nationals, its true members. Nationality is the bond that unites individuals with a given state that identifies them as members of that entity, enables them to claim its protection, and also subjects them to the performance of such duties as their state may impose on them. Constitutions and laws may reserve to nationals specific rights and privileges, such as owning property or entering into particular professions within the state. For example, in the United States, radio and television licenses are reserved for American individuals or corporations; land and mineral rights possessed by the federal government may be leased only to citizens or domestic corporations; and foreign airlines may carry passengers from point to point within the United States only under explicit regulations worked out with foreign governments, often on the basis of reciprocity.

Legal writers as well as legislators in many countries employ two terms in this connection—*nationals* and *citizens*. These two terms are not synonymous. *National* has a broader meaning than *citizen* does. While a citizen is automatically a national, a national may not necessarily be a citizen. For example, before the Philippines became independent, the inhabitants of the archipelago were nationals, but not citizens, of the United States. So they traveled on U.S. passports but could not vote in U.S. elections. When the Philippines became independent, all Filipinos not naturalized in other countries (hence including all born in the islands but residing as nationals in the United States) became citizens of the Republic of the Philippines and lost their status as nationals of the United States. Today most of the 47,000 Samoans in American Samoa are U.S. "nationals," but not U.S. citizens.[1]

Because the domestic laws of states relating to citizenship vary greatly, the following discussion uses the terms *national* and *nationality* to refer more adequately to an international law approach. The relationship between state and nationality represents a link through which an individual normally can and does enjoy the protection and benefits of international law. If individuals lack a nationality tie to a state, they lack protection if injured by the action of a government. International law explicitly ties petitions for redress to nationality. Absent nationality, no state can espouse a claim for redress.

RIGHT OF THE STATE TO CONFER NATIONALITY

International law permits each state to decide who shall be its nationals; under what conditions nationality shall be conferred; and who shall be deprived of such status, and in what manner. The court in *Tomasicchio v. Acheson* clearly stated the prevailing principle:[2]

> Citizenship depends, however, entirely on municipal law and is not regulated by international law. Acquisition of citizenship of the United States is governed solely by the Constitution and by Acts of Congress.

Curiously, only a few rules of customary law, of multilateral treaties, and of "general principles" exist that deal with the subject of nationality. Despite attempts to draft comprehensive global lawmaking treaties on the subject, none has as yet met with success. Despite the acknowledgment that national law governs most of the details of nationality, a limited number of rules of international law (some general, some particular in scope) apply in this sphere. Most of these rules embody provisions that *limit the discretion* of the state to bestow nationality, particularly upon individuals who may not seek that state's nationality. In this respect, we may speak of a requirement for an *effective link* between citizen and state.

---

[1]Within British law, the term *subject* will appear, signifying an individual who owed allegiance to the British Crown, having been born within the United Kingdom or its colonies. Legislation in 1948 created "subject" as a second class of citizenship that an individual in countries like Australia and Canada (and certain other Commonwealth countries) could have alongside their primary citizenship. Until 1962, the status of subject carried with it the right of immigration to the United Kingdom. See L. Fransman, *British Nationality Laws* (1989).

[2]U.S. Dist. Court, D.C., 1951, 98 F. Supp. 166.

NOTTEBOHM CASE

Liechtenstein v. Guatemala International Court of Justice 1955 [1955] I.C.J. Rep. 4

Facts

Nottebohm was born a German national in 1881.[3] In 1905, he immigrated to Guatemala and established residence and a headquarters for his business activities in commerce and plantation management. In 1937, he became head of the Nottebohm firm in Guatemala. After 1905, he made occasional business and holiday visits to Germany and other countries and had a number of business connections in Germany. He occasionally visited a brother who had lived in the Principality of Liechtenstein since 1931. His place of domicile (fixed abode) was in Guatemala until 1943.

In 1939, Nottebohm traveled to Germany and Liechtenstein. In October 1939 he applied for naturalization as a citizen of Liechtenstein. The law in force in Liechtenstein required (1) acceptance into the "Home Corporation" of a Liechtenstein commune, (2) proof that the old nationality would be lost upon naturalization, (3) a residence of at least three years (subject to waiver), (4) proof of an agreement with Liechtenstein's tax authorities, and (5) payment of a substantial naturalization fee. The government had the duty to examine and approve the documents and then submit the application to the Diet. If approved by the Diet, the application would be forwarded to the prince, who alone could confer nationality. German law provided that Nottebohm would automatically lose his German nationality upon obtaining another through naturalization.

Nottebohm acquired all approvals, but sought and gained a waiver of the residence requirement. After taking his oath of allegiance, he obtained a Liechtenstein passport, sought and received a visa from the Guatemalan consul in Zurich, and returned to Guatemala to resume his business activities in early 1940.

When Guatemala entered World War II against Germany, the government interned Nottebohm as an enemy alien and confiscated his property. Subsequent actions transferred most of the property to the government. In 1951, Liechtenstein filed suit against Guatemala in the International Court of Justice (ICJ).

Issues

1. Did Guatemala, by arresting Nottebohm as an enemy alien and confiscating his property, violate international law?
2. Did Liechtenstein have the right to bring the claim on Nottebohm's behalf because no "durable link" existed between Liechtenstein and Guatemala?

Decision

On an 11–3 vote, the Court decided that Liechtenstein did not have standing to

(*continued*)

---

[3]*The Nottebohm Case (Liechtenstein v. Guatemala)*, International Court of Justice 1953, *Preliminary Objection* (November 18, 1953), *International Court of Justice Rep.* 111 (1953), in 48 *American Journal of International Law* 327 (1954); *Judgment* (Merits) (April 6, 1955), *ICJ Rep.* (1955), 4, in 49 *AJIL* 396 (1955); see also J. L. Kunz, "The Nottebohm Judgment (Second Phase)," 54 *AJIL* 536 (1960).

extend diplomatic protection to Nottebohm by bringing a claim on his behalf. Hence, Guatemala was within its rights.

Reasoning

The facts "clearly establish . . . the absence of any bond of attachment between Nottebohm and Liechtenstein, as it was to enable him to substitute for his status as a national of a belligerent state that of a national of a neutral State, with the sole aim of thus coming within the protections of Liechtenstein, but not of becoming wedded to its traditions, its interests, its way of life or of assuming the obligations—other than fiscal obligations. . . . Guatemala is under no obligation to recognize a nationality granted in such circumstances."

In passing, we should note an important fact: *states have the right to change their own laws defining nationality at any time they choose so long as those changes do not violate the minimal standards accepted by the international community.* In the case of Liechtenstein, the Court noted that while Liechtenstein had the absolute authority to legislate as it pleased, *the act did not have any international effect* with respect to Nottebohm because it did violate these minimum standards. Indeed, as a method of limiting liability, some states have sought to cast the web of nationality in broad terms. We explore this question further later in the chapter.

The secession of the three Baltic states from the former Soviet Union illustrates the impact that nationalism may have on nationality laws. In the case of Estonia, when that country regained its independent status in 1991 after 50 years of Soviet occupation, the government wished to create a distinctly Estonian state. Before World War II, ethnic Russians comprised about 9 percent of the population. After Soviet annexation, thousands of ethnic Russians migrated to Estonia. By 1991, approximately 475,000 individuals out of a population of 1.6 million were ethnic Russians. Estonia quickly enacted a "law on foreigners," a new citizenship law, which defined a citizen as a resident of pre–World War II Estonia and their descendants. Most post-annexation immigrants could vote in local elections but not in national elections. They could not serve in the police or hold other government jobs. To become citizens, they had to have lived in Estonia for a minimum of two years and demonstrate knowledge of 1,500 basic Estonian words.[4] Latvia enacted similar legislation where, at most, ethnic Latvians comprised only 52 percent of the residents.[5]

Modes of Acquiring Nationality

An individual may acquire nationality through five modes: by birth, by marriage, by naturalization, by adoption or legitimation, or through transfer of territory. Most of the population of almost all states acquires nationality through birth, but tens of thousands of persons each year choose to change their nationality by voluntarily seeking another through the process of naturalization. Millions

---

[4]See *Christian Science Monitor* (November 7, 1991), 5. Note that the 1968 revision of British law included the provision that a UK passport holder could enter the United Kingdom free of immigration control only if he or she, or at least one of his or her parents or grandparents, was born, naturalized, adopted, or registered as a UK citizen within the territorial boundaries of the United Kingdom itself.

[5]www.germany-info.org/relaunch/info/archives/background/citizenship.html (accessed April 22, 2009).

acquired new nationalities when the former Yugoslavia and Soviet Union broke up. When the entities that had formerly been subsidiary divisions of the larger state gained independent status and recognition as full members of international society, former nationals of the Soviet Union and Yugoslavia suddenly became Lithuanians, Latvians, Georgians, Ukrainians, Uzbekistanis, or Bosnians. German nationality law provides for a "right of return" for ethnic Germans from Eastern Europe and the Soviet successor states.[6] Before World War II, many states had laws that forced women who married a man of another nationality to take his nationality. Most state laws today permit women (and men) to make a choice by electing naturalization under a modified set of requirements.

Law of the Soil (*Jus Soli*)

By general agreement (customary international law), any individual born on the soil of a given state of parents who have the nationality of that state receives the nationality of the state in question. The United States and most Latin American states have embraced the idea that a birth that occurs within the territorial jurisdiction *(jus soli)* of a state is sufficient to create the bond of nationality, irrespective of the allegiance of the parents. For example, Brazilian law states, "those born in the Federative Republic of Brazil, even if of foreign parents, provided that they are not at the service of their country" have a claim to Brazilian nationality.[7] The same holds true for the United States. Within the United States, the policy has generated great controversy because many perceive the liberality of American policy as providing the impetus for large numbers of pregnant women to come to America illegally in order for their child to have American nationality.[8] This issue has caused other states to impose a residency requirement. In the most recent revision of German law, children born in Germany to foreign parents acquire German citizenship at birth if at least one parent has lived legally in Germany for a minimum of eight years.[9]

UNITED STATES V. WONG KIM ARK

United States Supreme Court, 1898, 169 U.S. 649

Facts

Wong Kim Ark was born in San Francisco in 1873 of Chinese parents who were subjects of the emperor of China but permanently domiciled in the United States. Because they were Chinese, the parents

(continued)

---

[6]www.germany-info.org/relaunch/info/archives/background/citizenship.html (accessed April 22, 2009).

[7]www.georgetown.edu/pdba/Constitutions/Brazil/brtitle2.html (accessed April 22, 2009).

[8]L. Alvarez and J. M. Broder, "More and More Women Risk All to Enter U.S.," *New York Times* (January 10, 2006), 1.

[9]German Nationality Law, note 6.

then could not apply for U.S. citizenship by naturalization. Wong Kim Ark went to China in 1894. On his return to the United States in 1895, authorities refused Wong admission to the United States on the grounds that he was a Chinese laborer, not a citizen, and that he did not otherwise qualify within any of the privileged classes named in the Chinese Exclusion Act then in force.

Wong Kim Ark sued for a writ of habeas corpus, claiming American nationality on the ground of birth. The case eventually came by appeal before the U.S. Supreme Court.

Issue

Would a child born in the United States of alien parents ineligible for citizenship become at birth a national (citizen) of the United States by virtue of the first clause of the Fourteenth Amendment of the Constitution: "All persons born or naturalized in the United States, and subject to the jurisdiction thereof, are citizens of the United States and of the State wherein they reside"?

Decision

The court decided in favor of Wong Kim Ark, under the Fourteenth Amendment. His birth on U.S. soil conferred citizenship on him at birth.

Reasoning

1. "It is the inherent right of every independent nation to determine for itself, and according to its own Constitution and laws, what classes of persons shall be entitled to its citizenship."

2. "The Fourteenth Amendment affirms the rule of citizenship by birth within the territory, in allegiance and under the protection of the country, including all children here born of resident aliens, with the exceptions or qualifications (as old as the rule itself) of children of foreign sovereigns or their ministers, or born on foreign public ships, or of enemies within and during a hostile occupation of our territory, and with the single additional exception of children of members of the Indian tribes owing direct allegiance to their several tribes. The amendment, in clear words and in manifest intent, includes the children born within the territory of the United States of all other persons, of whatever race or color, domiciled within the United States."

As with any general rule, exceptions exist based on comity or courtesy rather than on international law. For example, children of foreign heads of state, foreign diplomats,[10] and, in a few cases, foreign consular officials have an exemption. You should note the phrase "not at the service of their country" in the Brazilian law, quoted earlier. The reasoning here stems from a simple proposition: These individuals reside or travel here as part of their official duties. To impose nationality

---

[10]See *In re Thenault,* U.S. District Court, DC, 1942, 47 F. Supp. 952. In the United States, children born on U.S. territory to foreign diplomats *not* accredited to the American government would normally be regarded as U.S. citizens. See Department of State MS. File 130 (December 14, 1937) concerning M. de Hedry, reprinted in U. G. Whitaker, *Politics and Power* 376 (1964).

arbitrarily on their children born here would constitute an act of arrogance by the receiving state.

One other potential condition serves to void the usual application of *jus soli* in the United States. In case of war on American soil, a child born in a portion of the United States then under the occupation of enemy military forces does not acquire American nationality under *jus soli* because during such occupation the authority of the legitimate sovereign is suspended, and the enemy occupation forces exercise temporary control over the territory in question.[11] A child born there would, therefore, not be a person "born in the United States and subject to the jurisdiction thereof."

Law of the Blood *(Jus Sanguinis)*

Historically, "blood relationship," *jus sanguinis,* or "ethnicity," where nationality of a child follows that of the parents, determined the entity of primary allegiance. This meant that the status of the territory where birth occurred had no significance. Ancient Egypt used *jus sanguinis* exclusively. Hence, historians usually describe the first pharaoh of the 22nd Dynasty (Sheshonk I, 945 B.C.) as a Libyan mercenary—that is, as a non-"national" soldier who overthrew an incompetent and politically inept employer. Yet Sheshonk's father, as well as he, had been born on Egyptian soil. In more recent times, prior to the year 2000, when new legislation came into effect, Germany had one of the strictest nationality laws in Europe. Originally enacted in 1913, it used "Teutonic ancestry" as its operative test. As a result, the law effectively barred the greatest majority of some 7 million Turkish workers and their offspring from gaining German nationality.[12] The change in the law added *jus soli,* with some qualifications for length of residence, to the older *jus sanguinis* provisions.

States have the prerogative to place *conditions* on the application of *jus sanguinis.* In an indirect acknowledgment of *jus soli,* often the requirements specify that an individual born outside the territorial jurisdiction of the state, even though to parent nationals, will have to make an affirmative declaration of his or her allegiance at some point. Normally, the law will require that the individual needs to do so in some period after reaching the age of majority in terms of citizenship. Brazilian law specifies that *jus sanguinis* applies to[13]

> those born abroad, of a Brazilian father or a Brazilian mother, provided that either of them is at the service of the Federative Republic of Brazil; [or] those born abroad, of a Brazilian father or a Brazilian mother, provided that they come to reside in the Federative Republic of Brazil and opt for the Brazilian nationality at any time.

---

[11]See *Inglis v. Sailor's Snug Harbour,* U.S. Supreme Court, 1830, 3 Peters 99.

[12]See www.germany-info.org/relaunch/info/archives/background/citizenship.html (accessed April 22, 2009).

[13]Brazilian Constitution, note 7.

U.S. LAW SPECIFIES A NUMBER OF OTHER REQUIREMENTS: UNITED STATES 8 USCS § 1401 (2005)

Children Born After November 14, 1986

If both parents are U.S. citizens, one of the parents must have resided in the United States or possessions at any time prior to the child's birth.[14]

If one parent is a U.S. citizen and one a U.S. national, the U.S. citizen parent must have been physically present in the United States for at least one year continuously at any time prior to the child's birth.

If one parent is a U.S. citizen and one an alien:

1. If the child was born abroad, the U.S. citizen parent must have been physically present in the United States or possessions for at least five years prior to the child's birth, at least two of which were after the parent turned 14.

2. If the child was born in a U.S. possession, the U.S. citizen parent must have been physically present in the United States or possessions for a continuous period of one year at any time prior to the child's birth.

If the child is the *illegitimate* child of a U.S. citizen mother, the mother must have been physically present in the United States or possessions for a continuous period of one year at any time prior to the child's birth.

If the child is the *illegitimate* child of a U.S. citizen father, the father must have been physically present in the United States or possessions for five years prior to the child's birth, at least two of which were after the father turned 14; and

a. before the child turns 18, (1) the child is made legitimate, (2) the father acknowledges paternity in writing under oath, or (3) paternity is established by a court; and

b. the father must agree in writing to support the child financially until age 18.

In the examples we have given, nationality passes through both male and female sides. Still, modern state laws vary in the way in which nationality passes from parents to child. The United States, along with many other countries, with limiting conditions, permits the link to pass through both mother and father. Some states still specify that nationality passes primarily through the father.

Complications

Because many states use both *jus soli* and *jus sanguinis,* many individuals may find themselves eligible for *dual nationality*. Thus, a child born to French parents in the United States would be a French national through *jus sanguinis* as well as an

---

[14]See also the Technical Correction Act of 1994 (March 1, 1995) (8 U.S.C.S. § 1409); and the Child Citizenship Act (February 27, 2001) (14 U.S.C.S. § 1433). The Child Citizenship Act redefined the conditions under which a foreign-born child adopted by American parents could automatically acquire citizenship.

American national through *jus soli*. In the United States, that individual would be an American citizen; in France, a French citizen; and in Ghana, a citizen of both France and the United States (dual nationality). Note the provisions of Denmark's 1950 law.[15] It seeks to avoid both *dual nationality* and statelessness. Note specifically in the following the conditions that define when nationality would pass through the mother's side:

Section L (1) Danish citizenship shall be acquired at birth by:

1. A legitimate child whose father is Danish;
2. A legitimate child born of a Danish mother in Denmark if the father is not a national of any country *or* the child *does not acquire the father's nationality by birth;*
3. An illegitimate child whose mother is Danish.[16] (Emphasis added)

Generally, when two states have a claim on a person's allegiance on the basis of birth, the state exercising principal *and* actual control over the person of the individual is acknowledged by the other claimant as the state of master nationality. We discuss the question of master nationality further in the chapter on diplomatic protection and state responsibility (Chapter 11).

Naturalization

Naturalization forms the second most common mode of acquiring nationality. Naturalization is generally a voluntary act by which the national of one state becomes the citizen of another. For example, Nottebohm deliberately sought to acquire a nationality other than the German one he received at birth. In the world of today, immigrants may seek to acquire the nationality of their new state for many reasons—access to professions and jobs that require citizenship, ease of travel (e.g., a European Union passport), or simply pride. Although normally involving an individual, naturalization may also apply to whole groups through an executive or legislative act. In such collective naturalization, the voluntary aspect of individual naturalization may be absent.

Dual Nationality

As we noted earlier, persons may acquire two nationalities (dual nationality) through the automatic operation of the nationality laws of two different states. Individuals may also become dual nationals through marriage. For example, neither British nor French law stipulates the loss of citizenship if a national undergoes naturalization after marriage *unless* the person specifically renounces the previous nationality.[17]

---

[15]Denmark enacted a "consolidated" nationality law in 2003 that somewhat loosens the *jus sanguinis* requirements. Nonetheless, it still seeks to limit dual nationality. See, "New to Denmark, dk," www.nyidanmark.dk/en-us/faq/danish_nationality/danish_nationality.htm (accessed May 1, 2009).

[16]Citizenship Act No. 252 of May 27, 1950, translation by the secretariat of the United Nations.

[17]For an interesting and concise discussion of dual nationality and its practical implications, see Citizenship and Immigration Canada, "Dual Citizenship," www.cic.gc.ca/english/citizen/dualci_e.html (accessed April 22, 2009).

Current U.S. law does not mention dual nationality, nor does the law require dual nationals to make a definite choice.[18] While being a dual national may have some benefits, a dual national also owes allegiance to both countries and, depending upon the particular legal code (e.g., France), may be subject to the laws of both states even when traveling overseas. A U.S. citizen with dual nationality must use a U.S. passport to enter and leave the United States.[19] Use of valid passport from the country of second nationality while traveling outside of the United States does not endanger U.S. citizenship. Britain and France have similar requirements. Japan forces a choice:[20]

> A Japanese national who also holds foreign nationality (a person of dual nationality) shall choose one of the nationalities before s/he reaches age 22. If the person received the second nationality after s/he reached age 20, s/he should choose one nationality within 2 years after the day s/he acquired the second nationality. If s/he fails to choose one nationality, s/he may lose Japanese nationality.

Another, and formerly common, reason for dual nationality is the unwillingness of a state to grant to its nationals the right to expatriate themselves through naturalization in another state. Such an attitude illustrates the *doctrine of indelible allegiance,* originally formulated in Great Britain but later abandoned by that state. Under this theory, an individual cannot lose his or her nationality without the prior consent of his or her sovereign. A few states have insisted, down to recent years, that recognition of naturalization should hinge on explicit approval by the recognizing state of each individual's naturalization abroad. Such a recalcitrant attitude by states has, understandably, led to countless disputes because of strict adherence to the doctrine of indelible allegiance. For example, until 1965, Czechoslovakia did not recognize American-born children of Czech parents as U.S. citizens.

Irksome as it is to both states and individuals, the problem of dual nationality persists because states have not yet found the will to settle the important questions by means of a general international convention.[21] We find a modest beginning in the Convention on Certain Questions Relating to Conflict of Nationality Laws, signed at The Hague in 1930. This instrument, to which the United States did not become a party, stated that individuals having two or more nationalities could be regarded as nationals by each of the states whose nationality they possessed (Article 3); that a state could not afford diplomatic protection to one of its nationals against a state whose nationality such a person also possessed (Article 4); that in a third state, persons having dual nationality should be treated

---

[18]See U.S. Department of State, http://travel.state.gov/travel/cis_pa_tw/cis/cis_1753.html (accessed May 1, 2009).

[19]See U.S. Department of State, http://travel.state.gov/travel/cis_pa_tw/cis/cis_1753.html.

[20]See http://info.pref.fukui.jp/kokusai/tagengo/html_e/konnatoki/5kekkon/b_sentaku/sentaku.html (accessed April 22, 2009).

[21]See *Esphahanian v. Bank Tejarat,* The Hague, Iranian–United States Claims Tribunal, AWD 31-157-2, March 29, 1983, in 77 *AJIL* 646 (1983).

as if they had only one (Article 5); and that persons possessing two nationalities acquired involuntarily could renounce one of them but only with the permission of the state whose nationality they desired to surrender (Article 6). In general, states today follow in practice almost all of those provisions, despite the absence of general conventional rules.[22]

Marriage

Article 1 of the Convention on the Nationality of Married Women of January 29, 1957,[23] should immediately send a signal to the attentive reader:

> Contracting State agrees that neither the celebration nor the dissolution of a marriage between one of its nationals and an alien, nor the change of nationality by the husband during marriage, shall automatically affect the nationality of the wife.

Before World War II, many nationality laws simply "imposed" the husband's nationality on an alien spouse.[24] Until 1990, Swiss women who married a nonnational automatically lost their Swiss citizenship.[25] Today, many states (e.g., France, Japan, and Ireland) offer an expedited naturalization process for those spouses of either sex who elect to do so.[26]

The simple fact that international law permits each state to determine the methods and means of acquiring nationality means that we still see interesting variants in the treatment of women with regard to marriage. In Indonesia, a nonnational wife may easily acquire Indonesian nationality. A nonnational husband qualifies only if he has "proved meritorious and have served the interest of Indonesia. Such nationality shall be granted with the approval of the House of Representatives."[27] The current law of Iran states that non-Iranian-national women who marry Iranian citizens obtain Iranian nationality upon marriage and must convert to Islam.[28]

---

[22]See *Tomasicchio v. Acheson,* U.S. District Court, DC, June 18, 1951, 98 F. Supp. 166, reported in 46 *AJIL* 155 (1952); Rode, "Dual Nationals and the Doctrine of Dominant Nationality," 53 *AJIL* 139 (1959), as well as the report on the British case of *Oppenheimer v. Cattermole,* 1971, et seq., before the Appellate Committee of the House of Lords (1975), in 16 *Harvard Int'l L. J.* 749 (1975).

[23]See C. L. Bredbenner, *A Nationality of Her Own: Women, Marriage, and the Law of Citizenship* (1998), for an extended treatment.

[24]Entered into force August 11, 1958; text at www.unhchr.ch/html/menu3/b/78.htm. The convention currently has 70 states party. The United States did not sign the treaty and has not ratified it.

[25]Under current law (since 1992), women who lost their citizenship under the provision of the old statute qualify for "expedited" naturalization.

[26]For example, see http://oasis.gov.ie/moving_country/migration_and_citizenship/becoming_an_irish_citizen_through_marriage.html (accessed April 22, 2009).

[27]www.expat.or.id/info/nationalityact.html (accessed April 22, 2009).

[28]http://travel.state.gov/travel/cis_pa_tw/cis/cis_1142.html (accessed April 22, 2009).

Status of Children

Complicated questions have arisen with respect to the nationality of children, particularly illegitimate offspring and foundlings.[29] A number of international conventions have been developed to deal with such questions, but limited ratification has caused the problems to continue. The primary issue of interest in this connection is the status of children removed from the country of their birth by their parents when those parents subsequently became citizens of another state. Most countries hold that minor children follow the nationality of their parents. When the nationality of the parents changes through naturalization, the nationality of the minor child changes accordingly. States have declined, on occasion, to permit minor children—nationals under *jus soli*—to accompany departing parents abroad when such departure appeared likely to jeopardize the children's retention of nationality.[30]

In 1994, the U.S. Congress acted to provide relief for individuals caught in this circumstance. Under previous U.S. legislation enacted in 1952, native-born U.S. citizens taken abroad by their parents while under the age of 21 years would lose their American nationality if the parents acquired another nationality through naturalization, unless the children in question returned to the United States to establish a permanent residence before their 25th birthday.[31] The Technical Corrections Act of 1994[32] permits a child under 18 who has a citizen grandparent who meets the physical presence requirements to gain expeditious naturalization. Although the child does not have to meet the physical presence requirement, he or she would have to travel to the United States to complete the process. The Child Citizenship Act of 2000[33] eased the requirements for acquiring citizenship for both biological and adopted children born abroad. Biological and adopted children of U.S. citizens who are born overseas can automatically acquire citizenship, provided that one parent is a U.S. citizen (by birth or naturalization) and that the child is under 18 and legally residing within the United States.

---

[29]For recent U.S. practice, see *Miller v. Albright,* 523 U.S. 420 (1998); *Ngueyen v. Immigration & Naturalization Service,* 533 U.S. 53 (2001); *Jama v. Immigration & Customs Enforcement,* 543 U.S. 335 (2005).

[30]See G. Van Bueren, *The International Law of the Child* (1994). For a discussion that involves some interesting hypothetical possibilities, see D. Isaacson, "Correcting Anomalies in the United States Law of Citizenship by Descent," 47 *Ariz. L. Rev.* 313 (2005).

[31]Immigration and Nationality Act of 1952, § 349(a), para. 1. See also the famous decision in *Marie Elizabeth Elg v. Frances Perkins, Secretary of Labor et al.,* U.S. Supreme Court, 1939, 307 U.S. 325, in 33 *AJIL* 773 (1939).

[32]8 USCS § 1409 (2005). The act defines *physical presence* as the time when the grandparent was physically within the borders of the United States. This excludes any travel outside the United States, including vacation. Maintaining a residence in the United States does not constitute physical presence for the purposes of the act. See www.usembassy.org.uk/cons_web/acs/passports/robirth.htm.

[33]8 USCS § 1433 (2005); see http://travel.state.gov/family/adoption/info/info_457.html. For an analysis of an interesting set of hypotheticals based upon current law, see Isaacson, note 30.

Loss of Nationality

The acts that may result in *expatriation,* the stripping of nationality from a native-born individual, or denaturalization, rescinding the grant given to a former citizen of another country, vary from country to country. The laws of various states have included voting in foreign elections; service in the armed forces of another country (especially when an oath of allegiance forms a prerequisite for such service); acceptance of an office abroad reserved under the relevant laws for citizens of the foreign state in question; desertion in time of war; "disloyalty" (treason) and formal renunciation of nationality either through naturalization abroad or through an official declaration filed with an embassy, legation, or consul of a person's country.[34] In the United States, expatriation, a formal and explicit renunciation of citizenship, raises no further legal questions. The individual in question has voluntarily lost his or her former citizenship. In the interesting case of *Davis v. District Director of Immigration, etc.* (481 F. Supp. 1178, D.D.C. 1979), Garry Davis, a former citizen of the United States, formally renounced his nationality without obtaining naturalization from another country in order to become a "world citizen."[35] He was subsequently denied entrance as an immigrant without a visa.

Questions involving expatriation have always centered on intent. U.S. law once specified a number of actions that, if performed, would automatically deprive both native-born and naturalized citizens of American nationality. In *Marks v. Esperdy,*[36] a badly divided Supreme Court held that Herman Frederick Marks had lost his U.S. citizenship by serving in the Cuban Army. Marks, a native-born U.S. citizen from Milwaukee, Wisconsin, went to Cuba in 1958. He joined Fidel Castro's revolutionary forces fighting to overthrow the government of Fulgencio Batista. After the Castro insurgency toppled the government, Marks continued to serve as a captain in the Cuban Army. He returned to the United States after a disagreement with the Castro government. In January 1961, Marks was arrested by officers of the Immigration and Naturalization Service. The attorney general commenced deportation proceedings against him, charging that, pursuant to 8 U.S.C. § 1481(a)(3), n. 1, he had lost his American citizenship by serving in the armed forces of a foreign country without the authorization of the secretary of state and the secretary of defense. The court noted that *Marks became an alien in 1959 at the time the expatriating acts were committed,* not at the time of the judicial determination of his status. Because he

---

[34]See L. Boudin, "Involuntary Loss of American Nationality," 73 *Harvard L. R.* 1510 (1960); compare the landmark decision in *Schneider v. Rusk,* 377 U.S. 163 (1964), concerning congressional power and naturalized citizens. See also other cases listed under "Suggested Readings" at the end of this chapter.

[35]Garry Davis is still an active campaigner for world government and world citizenship. See www.garrydavis.org/.

[36]*Marks v. Esperdy,* 377 U.S. 214 (1964); 84 S. Ct. 1224; *on cert. United States ex rel. Marks v. Esperdy,* 315 F.2d 673, 676 (2nd Cir. 1963). See 8 U.S.C.S. § 1481 (3). This is the only case prosecuted under this statute. A form of this requirement has been part of U.S. neutrality law since 1917, yet the United States did not prosecute U.S. citizens who fought with the Lafayette Escadrille in World War I, those who fought in the Spanish Civil War, those who joined Canadian or British armed forces before American entry into World War II, or the "Crippled Eagles" who fought with the Rhodesian Army in the late 1970s.

had committed a crime involving moral turpitude (1951) and had entered the United States without the appropriate documents, he qualified as a deportable alien.

Over the years, the Supreme Court has held a number of the provisions in this legislation unconstitutional. The key case in a series (including that of Marks) concerning nationality was *Afroyim v. Rusk,* where the Supreme Court struck down the statute that provided for loss of nationality if a person voted in a foreign election. In this decision, the Court argued that such laws violated due process.[37] The court stated that each citizen has "a constitutional right to remain a citizen in a free country unless he *voluntarily* relinquishes that citizenship" (Emphasis added).[38] Subsequent cases involved the question of proving intent—that is, of what it means to relinquish. The case involving the controversial Rabbi Meir Kahane proves instructive in this regard. Kahane sought an injunction against officials of the U.S. Department of State to bar them from enforcing a Certificate of Loss of Nationality approved on October 7, 1988. He also sought a declaration from the court that his Oath of Renunciation of his U.S. citizenship, executed on August 16, 1988, and again on September 16, 1988, was null and void. Kahane had renounced his American citizenship because a recently enacted Israeli law mandated that only Israeli citizens could be members of the Knesset. A subsequent decision by the Israeli Supreme Court ruled Kahane ineligible to run for the Knesset because of his radical political beliefs. With his Israeli citizenship no longer politically useful, he sought to revoke his renunciation of American citizenship. The State Department refused to accept his revocation. In denying the plaintiff's request to reinstate his American citizenship, the district court noted three criteria that needed to be met to satisfy due process:[39]

> All persons born or naturalized in the United States, and subject to the jurisdiction thereof, are citizens of the United States. . . . U.S. Const. amend. XIV, § 1. In this case, the court must decide whether the plaintiff, Rabbi Meir Kahane, has lost the precious right of American citizenship. The government must prove three things if Kahane is to be deprived of his citizenship:
>
> 1. that he committed an expatriating act, as defined by statute;
> 2. that he did so voluntarily; and
> 3. that he intended to relinquish his citizenship.
>
> The court felt the government had established all three beyond question.

---

[37]As speculation, consider the possible decision of the Supreme Court if *Marks v. Esperdy* had come after *Afroyim.* The reasoning in the Marks case raises the same issues of due process.

[38]7 U.S. 253, 67 S. Ct. 1660 (1967). See "Survey of the Law of Expatriation, Memorandum Opinion of the Solicitor General" (June 12, 2002), www.usdoj.gov/olc/expatriation.htm.

[39]*Kahane v. Schultz,* 653 F. Supp. 1486; 1987 U.S. Dist. LEXIS 1275. In the summary of facts, the Court noted: "The parties agree that Kahane has committed an expatriating act, because he accepted a seat in the parliament of a foreign state, the Israeli Knesset." See 8 U.S.C. § 1481(a)(4)(A). The parties also agree that Kahane performed the expatriating act voluntarily, as required by *Nishikawa v. Dulles,* 356 [**2] U.S. 129, 133, 2 L. Ed. 2d 659, 78 S. Ct. 612 (1958). The only dispute between the parties is whether Kahane "intended to relinquish his citizenship," as required by *Vance v. Terrazas,* 444 U.S. 252, 261, 62 L. Ed. 2d 461, 100 S. Ct. 540 (1980). The State Department's Board of Appellate Review found that Kahane intended to relinquish his citizenship when he joined the Knesset; the Board therefore held that Kahane had "expatriated himself." *Kahane v. Secretary of State,* 770 F. Supp. 1162 (D.D.C., 1988).

Bobby Fischer

One of the more interesting recent nationality cases involves the odyssey of chess Grand Master Bobby Fischer. Considered one of the greatest chess minds ever, Fischer defeated Boris Spassky in a match held at Reykjavík, Iceland, in 1972 to become the first (and so far the only) American to win the official world championship. After his triumph he became a recluse, turning down endorsements and opportunities to participate in tournaments that offered prizes of as much as a million dollars. For reasons he never divulged, in 1992 Fischer defied a U.S. ban on travel to the former Yugoslavia in order to play a series of matches against Spassky in Montenegro. After the match, he lived in Belgrade for a time. A grand jury in Washington, DC, indicted him in December of 1992 for violating the International Emergency Economic Powers Act, which imposed restrictions on travel and other dealings with states that composed the former Yugoslavia. The United States pursued Fischer for the next 12 years.[40]

During that time, he lived in Germany, Hungary, the Philippines, Switzerland, and finally Japan (2001–2005). Some mystery attaches to his travels because during this time he evidently was able to use and renew his U.S. passport even after the indictment. Finally, inJuly 2004, Japanese authorities detained him for traveling on an invalid passport. Because his father had German citizenship, Fischer attempted, unsuccessfully, to gain political asylum and citizenship there. In mid-August 2004, Fischer renounced his American citizenship in a letter to the U.S. embassy in Tokyo. Japanese authorities denied his request for political asylum and issued a deportation order. He spent nine months in jail. Seeking ways to evade deportation to the United States, Fischer wrote a letter to the government of Iceland in early January 2005 and asked for Icelandic citizenship. Sympathetic to Fischer's plight, Icelandic authorities granted him an alien's passport. When this proved insufficient for the Japanese authorities, the Althing (national parliament of Iceland) agreed unanimously to grant Fischer full citizenship in late March 2005.[41] Because traveling on an invalid passport did not provide grounds for extradition, in an attempt to prevent Fischer from moving to Iceland, the U.S. government filed charges of tax evasion against him. Fischer died in Reykjavik in January 2008.

Naturalized Citizens

Naturalized citizens can lose their nationality in ways that do not apply to native-born citizens. Moving back to the country of original nationality and failing to maintain an essential link with the United States, or committing fraud or misrepresentation at the time of application, would provide grounds for deprivation.

---

[40]B. Weber, "Bobby Fischer, Chess Master, Dies at 64," *New York Times* (January 18, 2008), www.nytimes.com/2008/01/18/obituaries/18cnd-fischer.html; S. Moss, "Death of a Madman Driven Sane by Chess," *The Guardian* (January 19, 2008), www.guardian.co.uk/world/2008/jan/19/chess.sport.

[41]Bobby Fischer: "Ich bin ein Icelander!" *Chessbase News* (March 21, 2005), http://chessbase.com/newsdetail.asp?newsid=2275.

We should note that many of the defendants in recent denaturalization cases were accused of war crimes committed during World War II.[42]

In one of the most contentious cases heard over the past 25 years, a U.S. judge upheld the revocation of the citizenship of John Demjanjuk after prosecutors successfully argued that he had fraudulently become an American national after World War II by concealing his past as a guard at several Nazi concentration camps. Demjanjuk, then aged 81, lost his citizenship in 1981, when prosecutors believed he was the Nazi guard "Ivan the Terrible" from Treblinka.[43] The United States extradited Demjanjuk to Israel in 1986 to stand trial for crimes against humanity. He was convicted and sentenced to death in 1988. After Demjanjuk had spent five years on death row, the Israeli Supreme Court ruled there was reasonable doubt that he was Ivan and ordered his release. Demjanjuk returned to the United States, where prosecutors had found additional evidence to prove that although he was not Ivan, he had been a guard at other camps.

He returned to his suburban Cleveland home in 1993. His U.S. citizenship, revoked in 1981, was reinstated in 1998. However, the Justice Department renewed its case, arguing that Demjanjuk had served as a guard at death camps other than Treblinka. The government no longer tried to link him to Ivan the Terrible. Now prosecutors argued that documents kept by the Germans, and archived by the Soviet Union, showed that Demjanjuk had served in several Nazi death or forced labor camps after he was trained at Trawniki in Poland. His citizenship was again revoked in February 2002. On December 28, 2005, a U.S. immigration judge ordered his deportation to the Ukraine. Demjanjuk's lawyer again had indicated they would appeal the verdict. On April 25, 2008, his lawyers filed the final appeal in the case.[44] On May 4, 2009, the U.S. Court of Appeals in Cincinnati (6th Circuit) rejected the petition and ordered his deportation to Germany to stand trial as an accessory to the murder of 29,000 Jews.[45] At this writing, a verdict has not been handed down in the case. However, even though the trial in Germany has

---

[42]See also *United States v. Fedorenko,* U.S. Court of Appeals, 5th Cir., 1979, 597 F. 2d 946, reported in 74 *AJIL* 186 (1980); affirmed in *Fedorenko v. United States,* U.S. Supreme Court, 101 S. Ct. 737, January 21, 1981, reported in 75 *AJIL* 669 (1981). Fedorenko was deported to the Soviet Union on December 19, 1984. He had been charged with lying to immigration officials upon entering the United States in 1949 about his job as a Nazi death camp guard. Most prominent in this category of cases was the Romanian Orthodox Archbishop Valerian Trifa, also accused of war crimes. He voluntarily gave up his American citizenship before it was taken from him (in August 1980) but remained in the United States until he was deported to Portugal in October 1984. Trifa had requested deportation to Switzerland, but that government refused to take him. The United States then asked West Germany to admit him, on the grounds that he had left Romania under German SS protection during World War II, but the Federal Republic refused because Trifa was not a German citizen.

[43]See www.jewishvirtuallibrary.org/jsource/Holocaust/Demjanuk4.html (accessed April 22, 2009).

[44]*United States v. John Demjanjuk,* 367 F.3d 623; 2004 U.S. App. LEXIS 8528; 2004 FED App. 0125P (6th Cir.); 64 Fed. R. Evid. Serv. (Callaghan) 166; *Demjanjuk, v. United States,* 125 S. Ct. 429; 160 L. Ed. 2d 341; 2004 U.S. LEXIS 7307; 73 U.S.L.W. 3273, (*cert. denied*). J. Caniglia, "Demjanjuk Supporter Sues Family to Be Paid," *Cleveland Plain Dealer* (January 23, 2006), A1. In yet another bizarre twist, Jerome Brenter, a supporter who claimed he has spent $2 million of his own money on the case, has filed suit against the family for repayment.

[45]DPA, "Demjanjuk Loses Appeal to Prevent Deportation to Germany," Haaretz.com (May 4, 2009), www.haaretz.com/hasen/spages/1082544.html.

not concluded, in January 2011, a Spanish magistrate requested the issuance of an European arrest warrant as well.

In *U.S. v. Latchin*,[46] the defendant served in the Iraqi Intelligence Service (IIS). He moved to the United States with IIS approval and continued to receive an annual salary. He successfully applied for naturalization, but on his application, failed to reveal his affiliation with the IIS. After his status as a "sleeper" spy came to light, he was convicted of failing to register as a foreign agent and had his citizenship revoked.

Statelessness

Before World War II, *statelessness*, the lack of nationality, was a rare occurrence. The relatively few recorded instances usually pertained to the accidental loss of nationality without the corresponding acquisition of a new one or the deliberate expatriation of groups by a government such as occurred in postrevolutionary Russia or in Nazi Germany. Frequently, the issues involved illegitimate children. We cannot discuss the problem, however, before clarifying some terms. In the contemporary world, we find individuals who truly have no effective nationality because of circumstances and those who have a *de facto* stateless position in that they may have a nationality that does not give them protection outside their own country. The latter category includes many of the individuals commonly referred to as *refugees*. The scale of the problem of *de facto* statelessness—that is, of refugees—has been, and still is, staggering both in numbers and in terms of human misery. Ethnic conflicts, civil wars, and discriminatory policies have created large communities of individuals who no longer enjoy the protection of a functioning state. Hence, the day-to-day difficulties encountered by a stateless person are difficulties that most individuals who enjoy the benefits of nationality may not understand or appreciate. For example, stateless persons, whatever the cause, lack the fundamental link by which they might derive benefits from the protection of international law. They lack the benefits of "diplomatic protection" (Chapter 11), and they may not have access to identity documents, travel permits, work cards, marriage licenses, and other kinds of papers normally issued to citizens in the twenty-first century. Attempts to alleviate some of these problems have sometimes been successful, but, more often than not, they have failed.

RE IMMIGRATION ACTION AND HANNA

Canada, Supreme Court of British Columbia, 1957, 21 Western Weekly Rep. 400

Facts

Hanna was born at sea with no known record of his birth. Hanna knew the name of his father, but not his nationality. His mother was born in Ethiopia. Shortly after the marriage in then French Somaliland (modern Djibouti), his father left to find employment in Liberia. His mother, while

(continued)

---

[46] *U.S. v. Latchin*, U.S. Ct. Of App., 7Cir., 554 F.3d 709 (2009.)

pregnant, booked passage from Djibouti to Liberia, but one day at sea, she became ill and gave birth to Hanna. Because of the illness and birth, the ship returned Hanna's mother to French Somaliland, where she entered a hospital/home for women. She died when Hanna was six. He subsequently "raised himself" with the help of various individuals in Djibouti and Ethiopia. As he grew older, he began to have difficulty with the immigration officials of various countries because he had no documents to establish his nationality and place of residence. Lacking a birth certificate, he found that he was at the mercy of the whims of immigration officials.

In the hope of gaining asylum in another country, Hanna stowed away on an Italian tramp steamer. Unfortunately, upon each attempt to enter a country when the ship reached port, he was immediately arrested and deported back to the ship. After a year of such treatment, while in Beirut he escaped from the Italian ship to a Norwegian vessel. He fared no better. He was held prisoner on the Norwegian ship for more than 16 months (while it made three or more trips to Canada). Upon escape, he challenged the legality of his detention by the master of the Norwegian ship. The court of first instance held that the master

had the authority to hold Hanna under the regulations concerning stowaways.

Hanna then made application to enter Canada but lacked documents to prove his birth, nationality, or place of origin. A deportation order followed. He appealed the order.

Issue

Does an individual who cannot prove his or her nationality—that is, a stateless person—have any right of asylum or entry under international law?

Decision

International law permits each state to define its criteria for immigration and asylum. Under Canadian law, Hanna did not qualify, *but* strict enforcement of Canadian law in this instance would perpetuate an injustice.

Reasoning

In the opinion of the judge, of the four options for deportation, three were meaningless. The fourth, return to the ship, meant continued imprisonment aboard. The decision only releases Hanna so that immigration authorities may search for a solution. It does not mean that Hanna has established any legal right to enter Canada.

The *Hanna* case illustrates the extreme difficulties that stateless individuals may have to endure. In this regard, consider the more recent case of Marham Karimi Nasseri, whose story made it to the big screen in *The Terminal* (2004). Nasseri arrived at Charles de Gaulle Airport in Paris in November 1988 with a one-way ticket to London and no passport. He told airport authorities that his papers had been stolen at a Paris train station. Waiving the usual rules, the authorities let him fly to Heathrow. But British immigration officials refused to let him enter the country, and he was returned to Charles de Gaulle. He survived there in the passenger lounge for 11 years, relying on the kindness of strangers. While French authorities insisted that Mr. Nasseri was on French soil illegally, they could not deport him because they could find no country that would accept him. In 1999, French authorities finally relented and permitted him to enter France.[47]

---

[47] S. Daley, "11 Years Caged in an Airport; Now He Fears to Fly," *New York Times* (September 27, 1999), A4.

Multilateral Treaties and Statelessness   The entry into force of the 1951 Geneva Convention on the Status of Refugees slightly improved the condition of some stateless persons. The United States is a party to the instrument. This convention contains, among other matters, a core of basic rights accorded to stateless persons. In addition, the 1954 UN Conference on the Status of Stateless Persons drafted the Convention Relating to the Status of Stateless Persons, entered into force on June 6, 1960.[48] Originally signed by 22 states, the convention at this writing has only 57 states party. While many European countries have acceded, the United States has not chosen to sign the instrument. Similarly, the Convention on the Reduction of Statelessness, adopted in August 1961 by the UN Conference on the Elimination or Reduction of Future Statelessness, entered into force on December 13, 1975,[49] but now has only 37 states party. This multilateral treaty attempts to introduce some order into the mass of conflicting nationality laws. Finally, the Organization of African Unity (OAU) Convention on Refugee Problems in Africa of September 10, 1969, entered into force on November 27. The convention expanded the definition of *refugee* and contains specific regulations concerning nondiscrimination, voluntary repatriation, and the issue of travel documents. Although currently 41 of the 53 current OAU members have ratified the convention, it has had minimal impact on the current refugee problems generated by contemporary ethnic conflicts and civil wars. In this instance, the jealous protection of a state prerogative by members of the community of nations has impeded multilateral solutions to the problems of statelessness because an effective solution would require far-reaching intervention into, and regulation of, what virtually every state still normally regards as representing matters of exclusive national jurisdiction and determination.

Consider the following case where statelessness may have worked, in the short term, in favor of an individual.

U.S. Ex Rel. Steinvorth v. Watkins

United States Court of Appeals, 2nd Circuit, 1947, 159 F. (2d) 50

Facts

Steinvorth was born in Costa Rica of German parents who took him to Germany in 1901. During World War I, he served in the German Army; he then returned to Costa Rica as a permanent resident in 1920. In 1941, he chose Costa Rican citizenship after the German consul there

(*continued*)

---

[48]Text in 63 *AJIL* 389 (1969 Supp.); text of the protocol, 63 *AJIL* 385; see also letter from Secretary of State Dean Rusk to the president, 123–128. Two relevant cases are *Ming v. Marks*, U.S. District Court, S.D.N.Y., 367 F. Supp. 673, reported in 68 *AJIL* 534 (1974); and *Cheng v. Immigration and Naturalization Service*, U.S. Court of Appeals, 3rd Cir., 1975, 521 F.2d 1351, in 70 *AJIL* 578 (1976).

[49]Text in 8 *International Legal Materials* 1288 (1969) and at www1.umn.edu/humanrts/instree/z2arcon.htm (accessed April 22, 2009).

had informed him that this act would cancel his German citizenship. On September 23, 1944, the president of Costa Rica published an edict stating that Steinvorth had lost his Costa Rican citizenship. The next day, Costa Rican authorities arrested Steinvorth and then handed him over to American authorities, who transported him to the United States and interned him as an enemy alien. He petitioned for habeas corpus, but the District Court, Southern District of New York, denied the petition. He then appealed to the circuit court.

Issue

Was Steinvorth an enemy alien, a status that would have made his internment lawful?

Decision

The circuit court reversed the finding. Steinvorth was discharged from custody and internment because he was not an enemy alien but a stateless person.

Reasoning

Under German law, Steinvorth terminated his German citizenship by opting for Costa Rican citizenship in 1941. The 1944 cancellation of his Costa Rican nationality could not be judged by an American court, because it constituted an act of state done in a foreign jurisdiction. The American court had to accept the legislation as effectively canceling Steinvorth's citizenship in Costa Rica.

But the termination of his Costa Rican citizenship did not restore his German nationality. That could have been done only by Germany itself, and no evidence submitted indicated that anything like that had happened since September 23, 1944, to make him a German citizen again. After that date, Steinvorth was a stateless person. The government of the United States could hold Steinvorth only if he were a citizen, or a subject of a hostile country. Because he was neither of these, he had to be released.

Nationality of Business Enterprises

Corporations   Corporations as juristic persons (see Chapter 8) have nationality just as individuals do. Over the years, some controversy existed concerning the method of determining the nationality of corporations. States have used three methods: place of incorporation, location of home office, and place of principal business activity. Traditionally, Anglo-American jurisprudence relied upon the place of incorporation. In the case of unincorporated associations, nationality was determined based on the state in which they were constituted or in which their governing body normally met or was located. Among most European states, on the other hand, for a long time the concept was preferred that a corporation's nationality was determined either by the location of its home office *(siège social)* or, in a minority view, by the place in which the principal business operations occurred. A fourth test, rarely used, applies to entities that serve as mere corporate shells. In this case, nationality may be determined by the principal nationality of its shareholders.

In a classic case, *Barcelona Traction Light and Power Co., Ltd. (Belgium v. Spain)*,[50] the International Court of Justice opted to use state of incorporation as the test of nationality. Belgium had sued Spain on behalf of Belgian stockholders. The court ruled that Belgium had no standing to sue, because the corporation was chartered (incorporated) in Canada and hence Belgium did not have an effective link.

---

[50]*ICJ Reports.* (1970), 168.

Given the complexity of modern corporate organization, a full discussion of the possible permutations in this area ranges far beyond the scope of an introductory text.[51] For example, the U.S.–Iranian Claims Commission used a slightly different standard to address the question of what companies met the nationality criteria in the instrument that defined who could file for consideration for compensation.[52] In sum, the most important factor, as with individuals, is that a genuine link must exist between the state asserting nationality (protection) and the company subject to the claim.

Partnerships and Other Organizations   In the case of business enterprises without legal personality, such as partnerships, no nationality as such can be assigned to the firm. The interests involved are those of the partners, and the nationality of the partners determines which state is entitled to represent the firm's interests. It does not matter, for purposes of determining the "nationality" in question, where the operating establishment of the partnership is located: The nationality of the partners is the decisive factor.

Jurisdiction Over Nationals Abroad

Assertion of the continuing bond between a state and each of its nationals occurs most frequently in connection with the commission of crimes or other offenses by those nationals beyond the territorial jurisdiction of their state. Some countries, such as France, assert a right to punish their nationals for offenses committed regardless of the location of the offense. Other states, notably Great Britain and the United States, have traditionally restricted their criminal jurisdiction to acts committed within their territory or areas defined by "special jurisdictions" such as aircraft and ships at sea that bear their nationality. One might consider in this respect that the pragmatic limitations imposed by the necessity of constitutional requirements for fair trials are at the root of Anglo-American practice. We will examine this question of jurisdiction more fully in Chapter 10.[53]

Current U.S. statutes provide that U.S. nationals abroad can be prosecuted in this country for contempt of court (such as failure to attend a trial in a criminal action when officially summoned),[54] treason committed in the United States or

---

[51]For American cases, consult *Clark v. Uebersee Finanz-Korporation, A.G.*, U.S. Supreme Court, 1947, 332 U.S. 480; as well as *Uebersee Finanz-Korporation, A.G. v. McGrath*, U.S. Supreme Court, 1952, 343 U.S. 205. The famous and controversial *Interhandel* case, involving a Swiss company allegedly controlled by German interests and in turn controlling the General Aniline and Film Corporation complex in the United States, is so complicated that its discussion is beyond the scope of a general text.

[52]See *International Schools Services, Inc.*, 5 Iran-U.S. Cl. Trib. Rep. 338 (1984); *Flexi-Van Leasing*, 1 Iran-U.S. Cl. Trib. Rep. 455 (1982); *General Motors Corp.*, 3 Iran-U.S. Cl. Trib. Rep. 1; (1983); *Housing & Urban Services International*, 9 Iran-U.S. Cl. Trib. Rep. 313 (1985) (re: partnerships); C. Staker, "Diplomatic Protection of Private Business Companies: Determining Corporate Personality for International Law Purposes," 61 *British Yearbook of International Law* 155 (1990).

[53]See *Small v. United States*, U.S. Supreme Court 125 S. Ct. 1752; 161 L. Ed. 2d 651; 2005 U.S. LEXIS 3700; remanded by *United States v. Small*, 2005 U.S. App. LEXIS 13961 (3d Cir., June 17, 2005); *United States of America v. Yakou*, United States Court of Appeals (D.C. Cir.), 393 F.3d 231 (2005) U.S. App. LEXIS 37; *United States of America v. Delgado-Garcia*, United States Court of Appeals (D.C. Cir.) 362 U.S. App. D.C. 512; 374 F.3d 1337 (2004).

[54]*Blackmer v. United States*, U.S. Supreme Court, 1932, 284 U.S. 421, 52 S. Ct. 252.

elsewhere, and unauthorized attempts by any citizen, "wherever he may be," to influence a foreign government in its relations with the United States (Logan Act). The U.S. government also imposes its income tax on citizens wherever resident and, in time of a military draft, obligates all male citizens of the proper age to register. British laws provide for punishment for treason as well as bigamy, perjury, homicide, and other crimes committed abroad by a British subject. India's criminal laws apply to Indian nationals everywhere, regardless of the magnitude of the offense. In France, a citizen can be prosecuted for any crime and many misdemeanors committed abroad. In Germany, criminal laws apply to citizens wherever offenses have taken place, even to persons who became German citizens after committing a criminal act.

Jurisdiction Over Alien Persons

The exercise of territorial jurisdiction over aliens stands as a logical consequence of the possession of sovereignty or independence by states. Each country is free to exclude or to admit aliens as it pleases. The determination of the principles applied in this connection is one of purely domestic concern. Concurrent with the right of exclusion goes an equally unfettered right of each state to expel any alien who has illegally gained entry into its territory as well as any alien whose conduct, after legal entry, is deemed prejudicial to public order and security. Consider the following case.

NORWEGIAN STATE V. CARLILE

Norway Supreme Court (Appeals Division), 1964, Journal du Droit 96 International 438 (1969)

Facts

Carlile, a British subject, was arrested and indicted for swindling. On several occasions, he had gone to hotels in Norway and simulated stumbling, falling, and suffering injuries for which he then collected damages. He had used the same deceit several times in Denmark and Sweden. The governments of Denmark and Sweden requested the Norwegian authorities also to indict Carlile for his acts in Denmark and Sweden. They did. Thereupon Carlile objected on the ground that Norway had no jurisdiction under international law to indict him for acts done in Denmark and Sweden. On appeal, the Supreme Court held that even if international law prohibited the application of Norwegian penal law to acts committed in Denmark and Sweden, the prohibition did not apply at the stage of indictment for infractions punishable under the law of all three countries. Hence, it said, the objection was premature and would have to be ruled upon at trial.

Issue

Did Norway have a right to indict Carlile for criminal acts committed in Sweden and Denmark?

(continued)

Process

Upon learning of the decision, the British embassy in Oslo took up the matter with the Norwegian Ministry of Foreign Affairs, questioning the basis of Norway's jurisdiction over the acts committed by Carlile in Denmark and Sweden.

Outcome

At the request of the public prosecutor, the Ministry of Foreign Affairs requested an opinion from its legal adviser. He took the position that the grounds relied upon by the Supreme Court *were highly questionable,* despite the requests for prosecution made by Denmark and Sweden, so long as the United Kingdom did not consent to the exercise of jurisdiction over its national.

By decision of the Cabinet, a royal decree of April 17, 1964, voided the indictment to the extent it covered acts done in Denmark and Sweden.

Diplomatic Protection

From time to time, we have alluded to the right of a state to exercise diplomatic protection on behalf of its nationals. We need to be more precise concerning what this right permits states to do on behalf of its nationals. *Diplomatic protection* describes the efforts of states to ensure their nationals are not abused through the actions of other states. To understand the scope of this "protection," we need to examine two propositions. First, states have a duty *not* to mistreat the nationals of other states. Second, individuals who travel outside of their own country are subject to the laws of the country where they may be at the time. When in Rome, persons should behave as the laws of Italy require them to behave. If nonnationals violate a law in Italy, they are subject to the police and judicial authorities of Italy. The state of nationality may give advice on procedure, help procure attorneys, and observe the proceedings for irregularities, but it has no right to intervene directly.

If abuse does occur, the state has a right to raise a claim against Italy (usually through diplomatic correspondence and negotiation) on behalf of its national to seek redress or damages, whichever seems appropriate. We will examine the procedures and rules of claims in Chapter 10 when discussing state responsibility and denial of justice in more detail. The Carlile case illustrates a simple example of diplomatic protection.

Note that while Carlile clearly seemed guilty, British authorities still had an interest in fair treatment and the maintenance of an important principle of jurisdiction. The question was not the content of Carlile's character, but the principle involved.

SUGGESTED READINGS

NATIONALITY

Bredbenner, *A Nationality of Her Own: Women, Marriage, and the Law of Citizenship* (1998).

Conant, *Justice Contained: Law and Politics in the European Union* (2002).

Donner, *The Regulation of Nationality in International Law* (1994).

Forcese, "Shelter from the Storm: Rethinking Diplomatic Protection of Dual Nationals in Modern International Law," 37 *Geo. Wash. Int'l L. Rev.* 469 (2005).

Plender, ed., *International Migratory Law* (1988).

Huntington, *Who Are We? The Challenges to America's National Identity* (2004).

(For a lengthy critique and discussion of Huntington, see Johnson and Hing, "2005 Survey of Books Related to the Law: National Identity in a Multicultural Nation: The Challenge of Immigration Law and Immigrants: Who Are We? The Challenges to America's National Identity. By Samuel P. Huntington," 103 *Mich. L. Rev.* 1347 [2005].)

Hannum, *The Right to Leave and Return in International Law and Practice* (1987).

Seidl-Hohenfeldern, *Corporations in and Under International Law* (1987).

Smith, *Civic Ideals: Conflicting Visions of Citizenship in U.S. History* (1997).

Staker, "Diplomatic Protection of Private Business Companies: Determining Corporate Personality for International Law Purposes," 61 *BYIL* 155 (1990).

Whiteman, VIII: 1, 64, 105, 119.

CASES
GENERAL

Jama v. Immigration & Customs Enforcement, 543 U.S. 335 (2005), 125 S. Ct. 694; 160 L. Ed. 2d 708; 2005 U.S. LEXIS 626.

Kaplan v. Tod, U.S. Supreme Court, 1925, 267, U.S. 228.

Miller v. Albright, 523 U.S. 420 (1998), 118 S. Ct. 1428; 140 L. Ed. 2d 575; 1998 U.S. LEXIS 2789.

Ngueyen v. Immigration & Naturalization Service, 533 U.S. 53 (2001), 533 U.S. 53; 121 S. Ct. 2053.

Ramos-Hernandez v. Immigration & Naturalization Service, U.S. Court of Appeals, 9th Cir., 1977, 566 F.2d 638, in 72 *AJIL* 673–674 (1978).

Schmidt v. United States, U.S. Court of Appeals, 2d Cir., 1949, 177 F.2d 450, in 44 *AJIL* 414 (1950).

United States v. Best, U.S. Dist. Court Mass., 1948, 76 F. Supp. 138 and 857; and also *Best v. United States,* U.S. Court of Appeals, 1st Cir., 1950, 184 F.2d 131.

DUAL NATIONALITY

Brook v. Girois, United States District Court (E. Dist. PA) 2003 U.S. Dist. LEXIS 14051.

Falken Industries, Ltd., and Roy Janis v. Johansen, and Sautin, United States District Court (Dist. Mass) 360 F. Supp. 2d 208 (2005).

Nehme v. Immigration and Naturalization Service, U.S. Court of Appeals (5th Cir.) 252 F.3d 415; 2001.

LOSS OF CITIZENSHIP

Afroyim v. Rusk, U.S. Supreme Court, 1967, 387 U.S. 253, in 62 *AJIL* 189 (1968).

Bensky v. Powell, United States Court of Appeals (7th Cir.) 391 F.3d 894; 2004 U.S. App. LEXIS 25600.

Marks v. Esperdy, 377 U.S. 214 (1964); *United States ex rel. Marks v. Esperdy,* 315 F.2d 673, 676 (2nd Cir. 1963).

United States of America v. Wasylyk, United States District Court (N. Dist. N.Y.) 162 F. Supp. 2d 86; 2001 U.S. Dist. LEXIS 9983.

United States v. Rebelo, United States District Court (Dist. N.J.) 358 F. Supp. 2d 400; 2005 U.S. Dist. LEXIS 4233.

THE NOTTEBOHM CASE

The commentary on the *Nottebohm* case is extensive: see the literature cited in Kunz, "The Nottebohm Judgment (Second Phase)," 54 *AJIL* 536 (1960). Consult also the digests of the decision of November 18, 1953, by the Court on the Preliminary Objection, *ICJ Reports, 1953,* 48 *AJIL* 327 (1954): 111; and of the 1955 judgment in *The Nottebohm Case (Liechtenstein v. Guatemala),* International Court of Justice, April 6, 1955, *ICJ Reports, 1955,* 4, in 49 *AJIL* 396 (1955).

JURISDICTION OVER NATIONALS ABROAD

Lange and Born, eds, *The Extraterritorial Application of National Laws* (1987).

Lowe, *Extraterritorial Jurisdiction* (1985).

CASES

In considering the following cases, one should review Chapter 6 on the application of law in domestic courts. Several of these cases depend upon a judicial reading of the legislative intent of the statute.

Rex v. Neumann, Union of South Africa, Special Criminal Court, Transvaal, 1946, in 44 *AJIL* 423 (1950).

Reid v. Covert; Kinsella v. Krueger (On Rehearing), U.S. Supreme Court, 1957, 354 U.S. 1, excerpted at length in 51 *AJIL* 783 (1957).

Small v. United States, U.S. Supreme Court 125 S. Ct. 1752; 161 L. Ed. 2d 651; 2005 U.S. LEXIS 3700; remanded by *United States v. Small,* 2005 U.S. App. LEXIS 13961 (3d Cir., June 17, 2005).

United States of America v. Yakou, United States Court of Appeals (D.C. Cir.), 393 F.3d 231 (2005) U.S. App. LEXIS 37.

United States of America v. Delgado-Garcia, United States Court of Appeals (D.C. Cir.) 362 U.S. App. D.C. 512; 374 F.3d 1337 (2004).

United States v. Laub, U.S. Supreme Court, 1967, 385 U.S. 475, in 61 *AJIL* 808 (1967).

STATELESS PERSONS AND REFUGEES

Amnesty International, *Nationality, Expulsion, Statelessness, and the Right to Return* (2000).

Feller et al., eds, *Refugee Protection in International Law: UNCHRs Global Consultations on International Protection* (2003).

Goodwin-Gill, *The Refugee in International Law* (1985).

Gorman, *Coping with Africa's Refugee Burden: A Time for Solution* (1987).

Hathaway, *The Law of Refugee Status* (1991).

Lee, "The London Declaration of International Law Principles on Internally Displaced Persons," 95 *AJIL* 454 (2001).

Martin, *The New Asylum Seekers: Refugee Law in the 1980s* (1988).

Miller, "Immigration Law and Human Rights: Legal Line Drawing Post–September 11: Blurring the Boundaries Between Immigration and Crime Control After September 11th," 25 B.C. Third World L.J. 81 (2005).

Phuong, *The International Protection of Internally Displaced Persons* (2004).

Takkenberg, *The Status of Palestinian Refugees in International Law* (1998).

Von Sternberg, *The Grounds of Refugee Protection in the Context of International Human Rights and Humanitarian Law: Canadian and United States Case Law Compared* (2002).

CASES

The greatest majority of cases here involve questions of asylum. We will cover this topic further in Chapter 10 (on jurisdiction) and Chapter 15 (on human rights).

Coriolan v. Immigration and Naturalization Service, U.S. Court of Appeals, 5th Cir., 1977, 559 F.2d 993, in 72 *AJIL* 924 (1978).

Haitian Refugee Center; Inc. v. Gracey, U.S. Dist. Court, D.D.C., 600 F. Supp. 1396, January 10, 1985, in 79 *AJIL* 744 (1985).

Principles of Jurisdiction

As we have discussed, the division of the world into states gives rise to questions of how far states may go in asserting rights to perform certain actions. One primary function of international law is to set limits to state claims to exert authority in certain areas. We characterize this general function by the term "allocation of competence." In the last chapter, we focused on the rights of states to define their own nationals and the limits international law places on them in doing so. In this chapter, we look at how international law allocates the right to legislate, and delimits the right to adjudicate and enforce, norms of behavior. We emphasize the difference between prescription, adjudication, and enforcement because the right to prescribe does not always automatically carry with it the right to enforce directly. For example, states do have the right to prescribe statutes for their nationals that apply to actions outside the country. They do not have the right to enforce such laws by entering the territory of another state to arrest a national who has committed a crime so defined.

In passing, we must look at the concept of jurisdiction in some detail. Jurisdiction, or an equivalent concept, forms a fundamental structural element common to all legal systems. As with many concepts, it has many different facets. In a narrow sense, and one most often used, *jurisdiction* refers to the difference of specific function or scope of competence among courts and law enforcement agencies. We can distinguish between civil, criminal, and administrative jurisdictions, for example, or within criminal law, between those courts that try felony cases and those that try cases involving misdemeanors, or between courts that have original or first jurisdiction and those that hear appeals from courts of original jurisdiction.

In a broader sense the term *jurisdiction* refers to the allocation of legal competence to regulate certain categories of persons, events, and things within a state and among various levels and institutions of government. To illustrate the broader meaning of jurisdiction, we need look no further than the Constitution of the United States. The constitution provides for a division between persons, events, and places that may be subjected to federal law and regulation and those that are reserved to the 50 states. Hence, federal jurisdiction empowers relevant federal officials and agencies to make statutes and regulations, enforce compliance with those statutes and regulations, and adjudicate violations with respect to particular persons, events, and places. The federal government has exclusive jurisdiction over criminal offenses such as counterfeiting, espionage, treason, and crimes committed on board American aircraft and ships outside of U.S. territory. State and municipal agencies have exclusive jurisdiction, with some exceptions such as kidnapping, over common crimes like homicide, burglary, and rape.

Jurisdiction often has a territorial component as well as a functional component. Indeed, territory probably serves as the most obvious parameter of jurisdiction in *criminal law*. State legislatures, courts, and police may exercise their functions only within specific territorial limits. By focusing on the idea that each state within the United States has a criminal jurisdiction explicitly limited by territory and substantive subject matter, we can see the need for procedures that bridge the potential problems caused by such limitations of authority.

The legislature, courts, and police of Georgia or Ohio have authority only within Georgia or Ohio. With some exceptions, the force of legislation enacted by the Georgia General Assembly and the power of Georgia police authorities to enforce Georgia law cease at the state line and have no effect on the citizens of Florida or South Carolina or Alabama unless they happen to be inside the territorial boundaries of Georgia. Similarly, the same holds true for international boundaries; American authorities may not physically cross over into Canada or Mexico to retrieve a person accused of violating American law even if the violation occurred on American territory. As we discuss later in this chapter, the difference between the power to legislate and the power to enforce and adjudicate forms the most obvious instances where extradition (between U.S. states, this is technically *interstate rendition*) comes into play.

In international law, as in national (municipal) law, we must distinguish between civil and criminal law. When civil litigation between private parties involves a transnational problem, courts may have a choice of law and venue in deciding the merits of the case. The same does not hold true for cases relating to a violation of criminal law. A primary principle of customary international law holds that a court may apply only the criminal law of the state from which it derives its competence (see Chapter 4). The *Carlile* case discussed at the end of Chapter 9 illustrates this principle. Few writers have ventured opinions as to why states have insisted on maintaining exclusive control of criminal jurisdiction, but we might speculate that fear of the unfamiliar has much to do with the attitudes involved. Being subjected to foreign legal procedures, the terrors of a foreign prison, language barriers, the possibility of receiving severe penalties for crimes considered less serious in one's own country, the suspicion of an implicit bias against foreigners, and the fear of corrupt or incompetent authorities all probably play a role, most particularly so when many countries are perceived to be "less developed," undemocratic, or hostile. Historically, even within the United States, some of these perceptions concerning law enforcement and judicial authorities have operated to frustrate cooperation between authorities in different states. If these perceptions have a discernible impact on processes within the American legal system, how much more they must affect attitudes toward the even more unfamiliar operations of foreign legal systems.

Examples of these attitudes are easy to find. Despite the explicit inclusion of a "defendant's bill of rights" within the North Atlantic Treaty Organization (NATO) Status of Forces Agreement (SOFA) (Article VII.9), the U.S. Senate expressed serious doubts about the wisdom of permitting foreign courts to try American servicemen for crimes committed while off base and off duty. Through a resolution accompanying the ratification of the agreement, the Senate set up oversight procedures to ensure that American defendants in the courts of our new allies would not be denied the constitutional rights they would have enjoyed in the United States. Among other provisions, the resolution directed the commanding officer of the base to request a waiver if he had any concern that the accused would be denied all of the constitutional rights he or she would enjoy in the United States. The resolution also required that a representative of the United States attend every trial of an American conducted under the agreement by the receiving state.[1]

The treaties that European states forced China to sign in the nineteenth century—giving these states *extraterritorial* jurisdiction over the activities of their own nationals in China even when the offenses were committed against Chinese subjects—also illustrate the attitudes of states in criminal law matters. The adverse public reaction in the United States to what many perceived as moderate sentences meted out by an Italian court to the individuals convicted in the *Achille Lauro* incident, and the severe criticism of Nicaraguan procedure in the Eugene Hasenfus case, provide additional confirmation of a general public distrust of foreign criminal proceedings.

PRINCIPLES OF INTERNATIONAL JURISDICTION

As we begin this discussion of jurisdiction, we should note the *one fundamental rule* that underlies all of the principles—an essential connection (*an effective link*) must exist between the state asserting jurisdiction and the event, whether through the person, place, or nature of the action. Contemporary international practice recognizes five fundamental principles of jurisdiction: (1) territory, (2) nationality (sometimes termed *active personality*), (3) protective personality, (4) passive personality, and (5) universality. These are not separate and exclusive rules for establishing and validating claims. Because these principles may overlap in practice, in most instances, they have a hierarchical relationship in terms of priorities for sorting out issues of *concurrent jurisdiction*. Concurrent jurisdiction occurs when two states may assert a claim to prosecute based upon two valid assertions of jurisdiction that draw upon two different principles. For example, if a French citizen commits homicide within the territorial jurisdiction of the United States, France could assert a claim to jurisdiction based upon *nationality*. The United States would have a stronger claim based upon *territoriality*. This could become an interesting question if the individual flees either to a third state with both France and the United States requesting extradition or back to France.

---

[1] 4 U.S.T.A. 1828, T.I.A.S. No. 2486 at 361. Text in 48 *AJIL* 83 (1954 Supp.). Consult also Rouse and Baldwin, "The Exercise of Criminal Jurisdiction Under the NATO Status of Forces Agreements," 51 *American Journal of International Law* 29 (1957), which examines many of the difficulties encountered with such concurrent jurisdiction; as well as R. Baxter, "Jurisdiction Over Visiting Forces and the Development of International Law," *Proceedings* (1958), 174–180.

Territorial Principle

Every country has the right to prescribe and enforce rules of behavior within its own physical boundaries. As we noted earlier, the territorial principle ranks at the top of the hierarchy because it derives directly from the twin ideas of sovereign control and equality (reciprocal recognition of sovereign prerogatives) of sovereigns. For certain purposes, aircraft and ships that have nationality (see Chapters 12 and 13) may qualify as "territory" (e.g., in regard to marriage, birth, or crimes committed aboard when outside territorial waters). As we noted in the last chapter, everyone, aliens and citizens alike, must obey the laws of a state while within its legitimately defined territorial jurisdiction.

Conversely, authority over territory also carries with it the obligation to respect and protect the legitimate rights and interests of other states within its territory. Still, travelers should keep in mind a variant of an old adage: *when in Rome, do as the Romans* ought *to do* (not as the Romans do!). The 1985 arrest, trial, and conviction of an American model from South Carolina for killing her neighbor in Rome brought headlines, but no objections from the government of the United States. Of course, the arrest of an American citizen visiting or living in another country may occasionally evoke protest and outrage by U.S. authorities (or the press), but apart from working with and through the foreign government involved ("diplomatic protection"; see Chapter 9), the United States has no legal standing to interfere with foreign legal processes.

The fact that crimes may not occur solely within the territorial boundaries of one state complicates the practical application of the territorial principle. To understand the complications that may arise in the contemporary era, we offer the following hypotheticals:

> Alex, a Mexican national, and Alice, an American national, live together in San Diego. They have a fight and break up. Alice travels to Mexico, where she buys a box of chocolates, injects them with poison, and mails the box to Alex as a peace offering. He eats several pieces of the candy and dies from the poison. She then flies to Vancouver, Canada. Upon learning that Alice is in Canada, both U.S. and Mexican authorities request her extradition. Canada, instead of honoring the extradition requests, arrests Alice and places her on trial for murder. The United States enters a formal protest against Canada's action.
>
> Marvin Minuteman, upset at the flow of illegal immigrants coming across the U.S. border with Mexico, recruits a private paramilitary force to patrol the border. One night, upon seeing movement on the other side of the Rio Grande, Marvin fires across the river, killing Pancho Patrole, an officer of the Mexican Federal Police. Mexican authorities demand that the U.S. extradite Marvin to stand trial in Mexico.

In both cases, the question is simply, which of the states may claim jurisdiction and on what basis—which of the states in these cases have an essential connection to the crimes?

For the moment, we will consider only the issues connected with the principle of territoriality. *Where* did the crimes occur—in Mexico or in the United States?

The answer is that essential elements of the crimes occurred in *both* states, thus providing *concurrent jurisdiction* based upon territoriality. The actions of Alice provide Mexico with a claim to jurisdiction based upon the *subjective* territorial principle. The death of Alex from the act gives the United States a claim based upon the *objective* territorial principle. The *subjective territorial principle* gives states the authority *to prescribe* laws for actions that begin within national territory but have harmful effects outside. The *objective territorial principle* permits states to legislate for acts that occur outside of territory but have effects within it; that is, states have a right to enact legislation that has *extraterritorial* reach. Both Mexico and the United States have valid claims to jurisdiction. Canada does not. In the hypothetical example, the United States has exercised its right of diplomatic protection (Chapter 9) by protesting the Canadian actions. Canada, at the request of Mexican or American authorities, may arrest and hold Alice pending an extradition hearing but has no basis for trial because it has no essential connection to the crime.

The following case, while turning on a question of legislative intent, still illustrates the validity of the objective territorial principle in that Canada willingly complied with the American request for the extradition of one of its citizens to stand trial.

▶ U.S. V. MACALLISTER

United States Court of Appeals, 11th Circuit 160 F.3d 1304; 1998 U.S. App. LEXIS 28611

Facts

William MacAllister, a resident of Montreal, Canada, was a member of a conspiracy to export cocaine to the United States.[2] Between June 1992 and March 1993, MacAllister and Paul LaRue discussed buying cocaine from John Burns, a special agent of the Drug Enforcement Agency (DEA) based in Jacksonville, Florida. During this time, negotiations took place both within the United States and in Canada. In March 1993, several other conspirators—Ashley Castenada, Salvatore Cazzetta, and Nelson Hernandez—traveled to Jacksonville to meet with Agent Burns. During this visit, Burns accepted a down payment of 600,000 Canadian dollars in anticipation of the shipment. On March 21, 1993, Agent Burns met with LaRue in Canada to discuss final plans for the delivery of, and final payment for, the cocaine. LaRue accompanied Burns back across the border to Burlington, Vermont. Agents then arrested LaRue and Castenada. Pursuant to treaty request, Canadian authorities extradited MacAllister (a Canadian citizen) to the United States for trial.

(continued)

---

[2]*MacAllister v. United States*, Supreme Court of the United States, 528 U.S. 853; 120 S. Ct. 318; 145 L. Ed. 2d 114; 1999 U.S. LEXIS 5539; 68 U.S.L.W. 3226 (*cert. denied*).

Issue

Did the law under which MacAllister was prosecuted have extraterritorial reach?

Decision

Yes. Courts will give extraterritorial effect to penal statutes where congressional intent is clear.

Reasoning

The Court noted, "Prior to giving extraterritorial effect to a penal statute, we consider whether doing so would violate general principles of international law. . . . In this case, it would not. . . . It is sufficient to state that the objective territorial principle justifies extraterritorial application of these statutes. The objective territorial principle applies where the defendant's actions either produced some effect in the United States or where he was part of a conspiracy in which any conspirator's overt act were committed with the United States' territory."

On the other side of the problem, countries have an interest in proscribing conduct that occurs within their territory but may have extraterritorial effects. For example, sections of Title 18 of the U.S. Code Annotated (U.S.C.A.) prohibit any action with U.S. territory connected with the counterfeiting of foreign currencies (§§ 481, 488), any conspiracy to destroy foreign property located abroad (§ 956), and any activity connected with organizing a military expedition for use against a foreign government with whom the United States is at peace (§ 960).

States may use the territorial principle to extend their jurisdiction beyond their physical borders. The sea, up to 12 nautical miles from shore, and aircraft and ships registered in a country may have the same status as territory (jurisdiction follows the flag). Crimes committed aboard ships and aircraft while on or over the high seas—that is, outside the territorial waters of any state—fall exclusively under the jurisdiction of the state of registration. For the United States, crimes aboard ships and aircraft (and spacecraft) of American registry fall within the Special Maritime and Territorial Jurisdiction (18 U.S.C.A. § 7). Within the areas specified in the Special Maritime Jurisdiction, federal law covers actions detrimental not only to federal interests but also to the general maintenance of law and order, that is, criminal activity that would normally fall within the jurisdictional ambit of the 50 states. We cover this subject in more detail in Chapter 12.

The case *United States v. Flores*[3] exemplifies the potential reach of the U.S. Special Maritime and Territorial Jurisdiction. Flores was indicted for a homicide that occurred on board an American ship anchored approximately 250 miles from the mouth of the Congo River, a position clearly within the territorial jurisdiction of Belgium, which controlled the area at that time. Belgium chose not to exercise its jurisdiction. The question then became one of whether the special maritime jurisdiction of the United States extended to a ship clearly within the sovereign territory of another state. The Supreme Court held that a merchant vessel, "for purposes of the jurisdiction of the courts of the sovereignty whose flag it flies to punish crimes committed upon it, is deemed to be a part of the territory of that

---

[3] 289 U.S. 137 (1933).

sovereignty, and not to lose that character when in navigable waters within the territorial limits of another sovereignty."[4]

Other special circumstances may give rise to conflicting claims to exercise territorial jurisdiction. Perhaps the most common case arises from the operation and maintenance of military bases in foreign countries.[5] In these cases, the parties normally provide orderly settlements of possible conflicting claims by treaties that specify the circumstances under which each state may exercise jurisdiction over the citizens and soldiers of the other. The United States has Status of Forces Agreements (SOFAs) with every country where U.S. military personnel are stationed outside of American territory. Most of these treaties contain a common formula: receiving states retain the right to try ordinary violations of the law when personnel are *off duty and off base*, and the sending state has primary jurisdiction over violations of military law, situations arising out of an act or omission connected with an official duty, and offenses involving only the property, security, or nationals of the sending state. Either country has the right to waive its primary jurisdiction. The treaties also specify the circumstances under which a state party to the agreement may request extradition of an accused person.[6]

Exceptional Extraterritorial Claims to Jurisdiction The subject of extraterritorial jurisdiction became a contentious issue early in 1981. Following the establishment of martial law by the Polish government on December 13, 1981, the president of the United States announced on December 29 a series of economic sanctions against both Poland and the Soviet Union. Those steps included the suspension of export or reexport licenses to the Soviet Union of equipment and technology for the transmission and refining of petroleum and gas, regardless of preexisting contractual obligations. This included goods of U.S. origin already in foreign hands. On June 22, 1982 (effective date), the U.S. government expanded the sanctions by amendment of sections of the Export Administration Regulations.[7] The new sanctions meant that persons in a third country could not reexport U.S.-made machinery (or its components) for the exploration, production, transmission, or refinement of oil and natural gas without the permission of the U.S. government.

---

[4]Flores, note 3, at 155.

[5]For the defining case, see *Wilson v. Girard,* U.S. Supreme Court, 35 U.S. 324 (1957).

[6]See NATO SOFA, note 1. Consult the note "Criminal Jurisdiction Over American Armed Forces Abroad," 70 *Harvard L. R.* 1043 (1957); and see *United States v. Ekenstam et al.,* U.S. Court of Military Appeals, June 22, 1956, 7 U.S.M.C.A. 168, 21 C.M.R., digested in 50 *AJIL* 961 (1956). The American–Japanese Security Treaty of 1951 was replaced by a new Treaty of Mutual Cooperation and Security, signed on January 19, 1960, which also regulated the status of American armed forces in Japan: text in 38 *Current History* 293 (1960). See also *United States ex rel. Stone v. Robinson,* U.S. Dist. Court, W.D. Penna., January 23, 1970, as amended January 30, 1970, 309 F. Supp. 1261, in 64 *AJIL* 955 (1970); J. Glanz, "2nd Army Officer Charged in Iraq Rebuilding Scandal," *New York Times* (December 16, 2005).

[7]See "Economic and Political Aspects of Extraterritoriality," *Current Policy,* No. 697 (May 1985); Gist, "Controlling Transfer of Technology" (February 1984) and "Controlling Transfer of Strategic Technology" (April 1985); 18 *International Legal Materials* 1508 (1979); 21 *ILM* 164 (1982); and *id.,* 855, 864.

The European Community (now the European Union) as a group and other countries individually (such as the United Kingdom) protested immediately against the U.S. amendments of June 22, 1982. They asserted that the measures violated international law because of their extraterritorial aspects. The regulations sought to govern the conduct of companies not of U.S. nationality as to their conduct outside the United States. The U.S. amendments also sought to impose the restrictions of U.S. law by threatening discriminatory sanctions in trade inconsistent with normal commercial practice established between the United States and other countries. The U.S. amendments violated two generally accepted bases of jurisdiction in international law: territoriality and nationality.

The International Court of Justice (ICJ), in the *Barcelona Traction* case,[8] had examined the issue of corporate nationality and found two generally accepted criteria for corporate nationality: the place of incorporation and the location of the registered office of the company in question. The U.S. regulations appeared to imply that technological links to U.S. companies or the possession of U.S.-origin goods should generate a right of American jurisdiction even if the patents had been registered also in other countries. As the European Community pointed out, in its *Comments on the U.S. Regulations Concerning Trade with the U.S.S.R.*,[9] goods and technology did not have any nationality, and there were no known rules of international law for using goods or technology situated abroad as a basis for establishing jurisdiction over the persons controlling them. The American sanctions on oil and gas equipment were finally lifted on November 13, 1982.

Typical of foreign reluctance to accept U.S. insistence on extraterritorial jurisdiction was the decision of the United Kingdom's High Court of Justice (Queen's Bench Division, Commercial Court) in *Libyan Arab Foreign Bank v. Bankers Trust Co.*, of September 2, 1987.[10] The case centered on control of Libyan bank deposits in the London branch of the Bankers Trust Co. after the U.S. president had "frozen" all Libyan assets "in the United States." The Court affirmed the general rule that the law of the place where an account was kept governed jurisdiction. In this case, English law, not American regulations, applied to the London bank account. Note the application of this principle in a more recent case. While some states (Uganda, for example) refused to follow the examples of the United States and the European Union during the civil insurrection in Libya in early 2011, no state protested their right to freeze Libyan assets held by banks and other financial institutions that fell clearly within their jurisdiction.[11]

---

[8]*Case Concerning the Barcelona Traction, Light and Power Company, Ltd. (Belgium v. Spain)*, 3 *ICJ Rep.* (1970), 43.

[9]21 *ILM* 891 (1982). See also the address of the legal adviser of the Department of State (June 30, 1982) in 76 *AJIL* 839 (1982).

[10]26 *ILM* 1600 (1987). See also Canada, "Foreign Extraterritorial Measures Act" (entered into force on February 14, 1985), in 24 *ILM* 794 (1985).

[11]H. Cooper, "U.S. Freezes a Record $30 Billion in Libyan Assets," *New York Times* (February 28, 2011); A. Torello, "EU Freezes Assets of Five Libyan Entities," *Wall Street Journal* (March 11, 2011).

Nationality Principle (Active Personality)

Nationality forms the second important basis for international jurisdiction. As we discussed in Chapter 9, municipal law establishes the rights and duties of nationals with respect to their own government. A sovereign state may legislate for the activities of its own nationals in any way it chooses so long as it does not conflict with the sovereign prerogatives of another state (or perhaps, increasingly, human rights law—see Chapter 15). States may enforce their own penal code against their own nationals even when the offenses are committed abroad. Consequently, national laws may have extraterritorial effect if the state desires to enforce them in that manner. The United States and the United Kingdom recognized the validity of the principle but make little use of it. The United States does prescribe for the punishment of treason, where committed (18 U.S.C.A. § 2381); for income tax evasion (1 R.C. § 1); for avoidance of registration for military service (50 U.S.C.A. App. § 453); and for unauthorized attempts to influence a foreign government in its relations with the United States (18 U.S.C.A. § 953). Governments may also impose restrictions on foreign travel. For many years, U.S. citizens could not travel to Cuba or Mainland China because of a government ban.

For the United States, practical considerations limit the scope of the principle in actual use. The difficulties of collecting evidence according to constitutional rules because of resistance to the idea of foreign agents performing a task normally done by municipal authorities under less stringent constraints upon search, seizure, and interrogation, and the cost and inconvenience of transporting witnesses, tend to militate against extensive and consistent use of the nationality principle.

A Note on Treason

Beginning with World War II, a new and fascinating sphere of jurisdiction over nationals received much publicity: the right of a state to punish "treasonable" acts committed outside its territorial jurisdiction, either by its own nationals or by such aliens as can be held to owe allegiance to the state in question. The best-known U.S. case in this special category is *Chandler v. United States*.[12] Chandler, indicted for treason to the United States committed while residing in Germany, asserted that the constitutional definition of *treason* did not cover adherence to an enemy by one residing in enemy territory. The District Court denied this interpretation. It said:

> Treasonable acts endanger the sovereignty of the United States. It has never been doubted that Congress has the authority to punish an act committed beyond the territorial jurisdiction of the United States which is directly injurious to the Government of the United States. An alien domiciled in a foreign country as the defendant Chandler admittedly was during the period alleged in the indictment was bound to obey all the laws of the German Reich as

---

[12]*United States v. Chandler*, U.S. District Ct. Mass., 1947, 72 F. Supp. 230, reported in 42 *AJIL* 223 (1948); *Chandler v. United States*, U.S. Court of Appeals, 1st Cir., 1948, 171 F.2d 921, digested in 43 *AJIL* 804 (1949); certiorari denied by Supreme Court in 1949: 336 U.S. 918. See also www.constitution.org/cmt/jwh/jwh_treason_6.htm (accessed April 22, 2009).

long as he remained in it, not immediately relating to citizenship, during his sojourn in it. All strangers are under the protection of a sovereign state while they are within its territory, and owe a local temporary allegiance in return for that protection.

At the same time a citizen of the United States owes to his government full, complete, and true allegiance. He may renounce and abandon it at any time. This is a natural and inherent right. When he goes abroad on a visit or for travel, he must, while abroad, obey the laws of the foreign country, where he is temporarily. In this sense and to this extent only he owes a sort of allegiance to such government, but to no extent and in no sense does this impair or qualify his allegiance or obligation to his own country or to his own government.

This statement, particularly the portions dealing with a limited allegiance owed to a foreign host government, represents the generally accepted view. A citizen of state X, traveling in state Y, must obey the traffic and sanitation regulations imposed by local law; to that extent, as an example, he owes a limited and temporary allegiance to state Y. But in all other respects that person is, and remains, until renouncing it, a citizen and subject of state X.

Considering this perspective, questions of nationality and allegiance become life or death issues in treason cases. The following case illustrates one of the problems. William Joyce, as "Lord Haw-Haw," broadcast propaganda for the Nazi regime during World War II with the clear intent of trying to demoralize Allied troops. When Joyce was captured at the end of World War II, the question for the prosecution centered upon determination of his nationality.

JOYCE V. DIRECTOR OF PUBLIC PROSECUTIONS

Great Britain, House of Lords, 1946, 62 Times Law Reports 208

Facts

Joyce was born in the United States in 1906. When he was three years old, his parents took him to Ireland, where he stayed until 1921. He then went to England, where he remained until 1939. As a child, he was "brought up, educated, and settled within the King's dominions." On July 4, 1933, he applied for a British passport, describing himself as a British subject by birth, claiming to have been born in Galway. He requested the passport for the purpose of holiday touring on the Continent. Joyce received the passport, which was valid for a period of five years. On September 26, 1938, he applied for a renewal of the passport for one year, *declaring himself to be a British subject by birth.* (Emphasis added)

On August 24, 1939, he applied once more for a one-year renewal of the passport, again describing himself as

(continued)

a British subject by birth. He then left for Germany. When he was arrested, he possessed a document showing that he had been hired as an announcer of English news by the German Radio Corporation of Berlin-Charlottenburg, as of September 18, 1939. In this document, his "work book," Joyce's nationality was given as "Great Britain." Up to August 24, 1939, at least, Joyce owed allegiance as an alien resident, living in England under the protection of the British Crown, to the British government. Between the beginning of his employment in Germany and until at least July 2, 1940, Joyce broadcast propaganda on behalf of the enemies of Great Britain under the name of "Lord Haw-Haw."

At the end of World War II, he was arrested and brought to trial in London on charges of treason. The court at first instance found him guilty. He appealed. In due course, the case came to the House of Lords.

Issues

1. Could a British court assume jurisdiction to try an alien for an offense against British law committed in a foreign country?
2. Did Joyce owe any allegiance to Great Britain between September 18, 1939, and July 2, 1940? (Note specific time frame here.)
3. Because the renewal of Joyce's passport gave him no British protection, and he had no intention of availing himself of such, did he still owe any allegiance to Great Britain during the period spent in Germany?

Decision

All three (major) issues answered in the affirmative.

Reasoning

1. Joyce owed allegiance to the Crown. All who were brought within the king's protection are *ad fidem regis* and owe him allegiance from the day they came into his realm. Now, treason was the betrayal of a trust. Joyce, having long resided in British jurisdiction and because of this allegiance to the Crown, applied for and received a passport and then proceeded to adhere to the king's enemies.
2. A passport served as a means of identification. The possession of a British passport by one who was not a British subject gave him rights and imposed on the sovereign obligations that would otherwise not have been given or imposed. *Joyce maintained by his own act of obtaining the passport the bond that bound him to Great Britain* when he resided there. As one owing allegiance to the king, he sought and obtained the protection of the king for himself while abroad. In other words, he extended the duty of allegiance beyond the moment he left English territory. As long as Joyce held the passport, he was a person who, if he adhered to the king's enemies in the realm or elsewhere, committed an act of treason.
3. Because of the foregoing conclusion, a British court possessed jurisdiction to try Joyce.
4. Because the appellant had admittedly adhered to the king's enemies outside the realm, he had been rightly convicted.

Note

William Joyce was subsequently executed by hanging. Shortly thereafter, Britain abolished the death penalty.

In another celebrated case, *Gillars v. United States,*[13] the Court of Appeals, in affirming the conviction of a U.S. national for treason ("Axis Sally," who voluntarily broadcast from Germany on behalf of the German government during World War II), emphatically insisted that obedience to the law of the country of domicile or residence—local allegiance—is permissible, but this kind of allegiance does not call for adherence to the enemy and the giving of aid and comfort to it with disloyal intent. The court rejected the defendant's argument that her duties to the United States had ceased before the start of her broadcasts in Germany because an American consular officer had revoked her U.S. passport. Said the court, "The revocation of a passport does not cause a loss of citizenship or dissolve the obligation of allegiance arising from citizenship."[14] We discuss the actions that may result in a loss of nationality/citizenship later in this chapter.

Protective Principle

At first glance, this principle appears to coincide with the objective territorial principle. Under the protective principle, states seek to control activities that could have a "potentially adverse effect upon security or government functions by *nonnationals* beyond the normal reach of territorial jurisdiction."[15] The protective principle differs from the objective territorial principle in that *all elements of the crime occur outside the territorial jurisdiction of the state.* Counterfeiting of currency and other government, documents, conspiracies to overthrow the government, and drug smuggling and related activities comprise good examples of conduct normally proscribed through the protective principle. The Controlled Substance Import and Export Act of 1970 makes it a crime to manufacture a "controlled substance" with the intent of having it "unlawfully imported into the United States" (21 U.S.C.A. § 956). The act explicitly states that the legislation is "intended to reach acts of manufacture or distribution outside the territorial jurisdiction of the United States." In *Rivard v. United States,*[16] four Canadian nationals were extradited and convicted of conspiracy to smuggle heroin into the United States *even though none of the four had visited the United States prior to their extradition.* In a more recent case, *United States v. Suerta,* the court utilized the protective principle to justify the seizure of a shipment of illegal drugs on the high seas.[17]

Though most states use this principle in some form, the potential for abuse by states that define their "security" or "state interest" in very broad fashion seems clear. Suppose a Frenchman standing in French territory shouts an obscenity about

---

[13]U.S. Court of Appeals, 1950, 182 F.2d 962; 45 *AJIL* 372 (1951).

[14]See also the story of Iva Ikuko Toguri D'Aquino (Orphan Ann, or "Tokyo Rose"), who found herself stranded in Japan at the outbreak of the war. She claimed Japanese authorities forced her to broadcast propaganda and maintained her innocence, noting that she had kept her American citizenship despite pressure from authorities. After the war, she stood trial for treason and was convicted. In the early 1970s, new evidence came to light that supported her claims. President Gerald Ford pardoned her in 1977. See http://womenshistory.about.com/library/bio/blbio_toguri_iva.htm.

[15]*United States v. Pizzarusso,* 388 F.2d (2d Cir. 1968).

[16]375 F.2d 882 (5th Cir. 1967). See also *Rocha v. United States of America,* 182 F.Supp. 479 (1960); 288 F.2d 545 (1961) for a case involving sham marriages as a tactic to avoid provisions of U.S. immigration laws.

[17]291 F.3d 366 at 370 (2002).

the German chancellor across the Franco-German border. Should Germany have the right to seize jurisdiction to try the Frenchman for sedition? Texts often cite the *Cutting* case[18] as the example of such abuse. Cutting, an American national and newspaper editor in Texas, visited Mexico, where he was arrested for publication in Texas of an alleged libel against a Mexican citizen. The U.S. government protested on the basis that the Mexican government had no authority to prescribe legislation for American citizens acting within U.S. territory. The protest noted that to concede that right to states would be to open every foreign traveler in every state to an undefined and potentially unlimited criminal liability. While the Mexican government eventually released Cutting, the incident clearly illustrates the potential for misuse and abuse.

Section 403 of the *Restatement* attempts to set reasonable limits to jurisdictional claims by specifying criteria for courts to consider in their deliberations. Of particular relevance to this discussion is the requirement that the proscribed conduct must be "generally recognized as a crime under the law of states that have reasonably developed legal systems." In actuality, only the active protests of other states concerning excessive intrusion into their own spheres of competence would seem to limit the use of the principle. This principle becomes especially important in extradition cases, where broad definitions of security or other vital interests by a requesting state may put the requested state in the position of having to make a difficult value judgment concerning the validity of the petition.

Passive Personality Principle

Where the nationality (active personality principle) seeks jurisdiction over nationals who commit crimes abroad, adherents of the passive personality principle seek jurisdiction over nonnationals who commit crimes against their nationals regardless of the location of the act. The theoretical justification for asserting such a right comes from the duty states have to protect the welfare of their own nationals. Historically, both the United States and the United Kingdom have resisted recognizing claims based upon the principle. The U.S. attitude changed in the mid-1980s due to a number of terrorist incidents such as the Rome airport massacre and the *Achille Lauro* hijacking, in which American citizens were killed or injured. In this respect, the United States adopted the principle in *limited* form for exactly the same reasons Israel did after the massacre of Israeli athletes at Munich in 1972.[19] In this case, clearly the United States intent seems not to include mundane, everyday crimes such as an American victim of a barroom brawl in Rota or a mugging in Moscow.

The case of Fawaz Yunis shows the U.S. application of the principle after the legislation. In 1985, Yunis and his colleagues hijacked a Royal Jordanian airliner that had several Americans on board. Eventually all hostages were released unharmed, but the United States devised an elaborate plan ("Operation Goldenrod") to capture Yunis. They lured him aboard a yacht, chartered by the FBI, that was anchored just outside the territorial sea of Cyprus. While defense attorneys raised numerous constitutional objections to his capture and trial, Yunis eventually was found guilty of the hijacking.[20]

---

[18]*Foreign Relations of the United States* 751 (1888).

[19]Omnibus Diplomatic Security and Anti-terrorism Act, 18 U.S.C. § 2331 (1986).

[20]*Fawaz Yunis*, 924 F.2d 1086, 1091 (D.C. 1991).

France (since 1975), Israel (since 1972), and Japan also utilize the principle. Our earlier observations concerning the practical difficulties of actually seizing and trying a case under the active personality (nationality) principle apply equally as well to passive personality. At present, states that do recognize passive personality may employ it to decide claims to jurisdiction among themselves if they choose to do so. Lacking universal acceptance, this principle carries no weight in claims against those states that do not recognize it as valid.

Universality Principle

Unlike other bases of jurisdiction, which depend upon some link between the state and the crime (location, nationality, or effect), the universality principle relies on the idea that some crimes constitute a fundamental offense against the interests of *all* nations. Yet, from the point of jurisprudence, we must ask a tough question: Are "universal" crimes universal in the sense that advocates would have us believe, or do they simply constitute crimes that most nations have found it expedient to proscribe?[21] In practice, does the distinction make a difference? We raise the question in passing because it does go to the heart of many contemporary controversies over prescription and enforcement, particularly in the area of human rights law. From a traditional perspective, to protect the values affected by these "crimes of universal interest," all states have the right to apprehend and punish violators. In this respect, we must distinguish here between crimes of universal interest as defined by multilateral treaties and customary usage (*jus cogens*) and those defined in the municipal laws of states.[22] Apart from piracy and certain war crimes, treaties dealing with genocide, the slave trade, and aircraft hijacking contain provisions that permit a claim to universal jurisdiction under specified circumstances (see Chapters 13 and 16). The problem with these treaties is that a claim to such jurisdiction can issue only from a state party to the convention. Because so few states have signed and ratified many of these conventions, the relevance to actual practice is severely diminished. Some have suggested terrorism as a universal crime. As a practical observation, the controversies surrounding how to define *terrorism*, an essential prerequisite to developing standards for prosecution, undermine this argument. We will examine these issues in Chapter 16.

EXTRADITION

A staple plot in B movies of the 1940s and 1950s features an embezzler or thief fleeing to Rio de Janeiro to live happily ever after, enjoying the sun and sand on the ill-gotten gains because Brazil did not have an extradition treaty with the United

---

[21]See, for example, A. P. Rubin, *Piracy* (1997), which eloquently disputes the "universality" theory with respect to pirates.

[22]A few states have found all crime abhorrent and, through their legal codes or constitutions, have claimed universal jurisdiction regardless of any substantive connection or effect. Considering our previous discussion, needless to say, claims of jurisdiction based solely upon these municipal statutes have no validity and are seldom, if ever, advanced as serious claims.

States. While one cannot always trust the legal information gleaned from old movies, Rio in the past has been a haven for successful criminals. To cite but one prominent example, Ronnie Biggs, the mastermind of the £2.3 million Great Train Robbery in Great Britain (1963), lived in Brazil until he decided to return to England in 2002.[23] Rwanda has sought Richard McGuire from the United States, charging that he murdered his colleague, Dian Fossey, the internationally famous "gorilla lady" celebrated in the film *Gorillas in the Mist*.[24]

Post World War II, several South American countries gained a reputation as havens for Nazi war criminals. In the following discussion, toleration of local authorities plays an important role because, *in the absence of a treaty,* extradition presents states with a permissive rule. No rule of *international law* prevents a state from surrendering an alleged fugitive if it chooses to do so. Conversely, in the absence of a treaty, no state has a duty to surrender an alleged fugitive if it chooses not to do so. In U.S. practice, a request for extradition of an individual from the United States will not be granted in the absence of a "treaty or convention for extradition."[25] In extradition proceedings, U.S. courts will *not* consider any argument for extradition that relies on *customary international law* or comity.[26] This policy has the merit of avoiding situations where other countries may expect the United States to reciprocate in kind, but also puts the United States in the position of having to rely upon irregular means of rendition in many cases.[27]

---

[23]For the complete story, see http://ronnie-biggs.biography.ms (accessed April 22, 2009).

[24]"Man Convicted of Killing Dian Fossey Loses Job Offer." Fossey was hacked to death in Rwanda in 1985. McGuire was her American research assistant. The court convicted him in absentia, but he remained in the United States, *which does not have an extradition treaty with Rwanda,* www.cbc.ca/story/world/national/2005/03/14/fossey-050314.html. One should note that U.S. authorities never accepted the "evidence" submitted as sufficient to establish "probable cause."

[25]18 U.S.C.A. § 3184 (2004). In *Factor v. Laubenheimer* (290 U.S. 276, 287, 1933), the U.S. Supreme Court stated the general rule:

The principles of international law recognize no right to extradition apart from treaty. While a government may, if agreeable to its own constitution and laws, voluntarily exercise the power to surrender a fugitive from justice to the country from which he has fled, and it has been said that it is under a moral duty to do so, the legal right to demand his extradition and the correlative duty to surrender him to the demanding country exist only when created by treaty.

[26]The United States has, in the past, requested on the basis of *comity* that other states hand over fugitives in the absence of a treaty. Perhaps the most notable case of this type in American history involved the Egyptian surrender of Jon Surratt, charged in the plot to assassinate President Lincoln; 2 *Moore,* 35 (1906). Whiteman's discussion of U.S. practice (6 *Digest,* 727–1122) does not reference the Surratt case, other similar nineteenth-century cases discussed by Moore, or the later and more familiar Insull case: 2 *Foreign Relations* 552 (1933).

[27]The United States and Iran did not have a treaty of extradition. Thus, although the deposed Shah of Iran lived briefly in the United States (1979–1980), Iran made no attempt to present a formal demand for his extradition. But after the Shah had moved to Panama, Iranian authorities prepared a formal request for his detention and subsequent extradition. The 450-page document was to be presented by a French attorney representing Iran to the Panamanian government on March 24, 1980. The Shah, however, elected to leave Panama, with his family, on March 23, 1980, and moved to Egypt, at the invitation of President Anwar Sadat. Panamanian laws would have required the Shah's arrest as soon as the extradition request had been filed with the host country's foreign ministry.

Informal or Irregular Rendition

In theory, sovereignty provides a "legal hard shield" against intervention by foreign agents. Yet theory belies practice. Municipal courts seldom make a concerted inquiry into how the accused arrived before them. Israeli courts had few qualms about trying Adolf Eichmann after his kidnapping from Argentina. Italian courts seized jurisdiction over the *Achille Lauro* hijackers despite protests that the forcible diversion of the Egyptian airliner to Italian territory by American military planes violated international law. Unlike other areas of the law, in this area, courts have permitted extralegal and perhaps even patently illegal actions to create legally valid results. Only occasionally, as we will discuss later, have American courts been willing to listen to pleas based upon the illegality of arrest and transport from overseas.

Abduction and kidnapping occur when states have refused to surrender individuals. We do not suggest this occurs as an ordinary matter of course in the everyday transactions among states. In many instances where states share a common border where large numbers of persons pass during any given day, officials on both sides have developed an informal, cooperative bond regarding enforcement of low-level, everyday criminal activity that may involve border crossing. It is the high-profile cases—Eichmann, Biggs, Argoud, and Alvarez-Machain—that cause concern. Israeli agents took Adolph Eichmann, wanted for his participation in the Holocaust, from Argentina. Colonel Antoine Argoud, a leader of the Algerian revolt against the policies of Charles de Gaulle, was kidnapped from Munich and left bound and gagged in a car on a Paris street for police to find after a tip from an anonymous telephone call.[28] Biggs was kidnapped while having dinner in Rio and was found adrift in a yacht off the coast of Bermuda. Dr. Humberto Alvarez-Machain, accused of participating in the torture and death of American DEA Agent Enrique Camarena-Salazar in Mexico, was abducted by Mexican bounty hunters at the behest of the DEA and transported to the United States for trial. French agents took Ilich Ramírez Sánchez (Carlos the Jackal, one of the world's most wanted terrorists) from the Sudan.[29] Of these five cases, only Biggs escaped prosecution.

Within the United States, the classic precedent that defines U.S. practice is *Ker v. Illinois*.[30] In this case, the United States had executed extradition papers in accordance with an existing extradition treaty with Peru. U.S. agents could not deliver the papers to Peruvian authorities because, at the time, Chilean forces occupied Lima, the capital city. Chilean troops aided in the capture and placing of Ker aboard an American ship. Peru lodged no protest over the incident. The Supreme Court held that the method of arrest gave Ker no grounds to object to the trial.

The most serious challenge to the *Ker* doctrine came in *U.S. v. Toscanino*.[31] The Court ruled that violence, torture, and other inhumane treatment of the defendant in the presence of U.S. agents in Uruguay substantially rendered the

---

[28]http://news.bbc.co.uk/onthisday/hi/dates/stories/february/27/newsid_2515000/2515735.stm (accessed May 5, 2009).

[29]A. Riding, "Carlos the Terrorist Arrested and Taken to France," *New York Times* (August 16, 1994), A1.

[30]U.S. 436 7 S. Ct. 225 (1888).

[31]500 F.2d 267 (2d Cir. 1974).

arrest invalid. Despite the elation of critics, subsequent rulings have somewhat mitigated the more radical implications of *Toscanino*. The courts have tended to treat *Toscanino* as the ultimate negative standard against which the conduct of U.S. agents overseas may be gauged. Where agents have participated less directly[32] or their actions have been less violative of individual rights,[33] the courts have still followed *Ker*. An individual must do more than charge illegal capture and abduction to evade trial, provided the court otherwise can assert a valid jurisdiction. The Supreme Court in the Alvarez-Machain hearing said, "The fact of respondent's forcible abduction does not prohibit his trial in a U.S. court for violations of this country's criminal laws."[34]

Critics argue that using these methods, particularly abduction, as a means of avoiding formal legal requirements often deprives individuals of rights they might have under domestic law or treaties in force. More generally, informal rendition does generally violate the integrity of the international legal process. Some states have fought back by requesting the extradition of those involved in the abductions. Mexico filed a request for extradition of two DEA agents, only to be told that the actual kidnappers were Mexican. Canada has successfully requested and received extradition for a number of individuals involved in such abductions from Canadian territory.[35] Nonetheless, states will continue to utilize these techniques so long as courts accept the results as producing valid *in personam* jurisdiction.

COMMON ELEMENTS OF EXTRADITION TREATIES

Contemporary discussions of extradition treaties and municipal laws regulating extradition tend to emphasize the variety and complexity of provisions. Modern practice, however, has tended to converge; most new treaties contain the following common elements: (1) a definition of extraditable offenses, (2) the "specialty principle," (3) a definition of extraditable persons, (4) standards of proof required to establish the validity of the request, and (5) an exclusion for political offenses.

Extraditable Offenses

Considering the time and expense of extradition procedures, practicality normally confines extraditable offenses to only the most serious crimes and to those committed within the territorial jurisdiction of the requesting party. Treaties may permit extradition on the basis of the nationality and protective principle as well. Not surprisingly, problems of definition lie at the core of this discussion. The first

---

[32]*U.S. v. Cordero*, 688 F.2d 32 (1st Cir. 1981).

[33]*United States ex rel. Lujan v. Genglar*, 510 F.2d 62 (2d Cir. 1975).

[34]*United States of America v. Best*, 304 F.3d 308 (2007); *United States v. Alvarez-Machain*, 504 U.S. 655 (1992). We should note that at trial, Dr. Alvarez-Machain was found innocent. See further Chapter 15.

[35]B. Brown, "Pursuit Beyond the Borders of Justice: Bounty Hunters Flout International Law," *Atlanta Constitution* (April 1, 1987), A17. According to Brown, Canada had charged 10 individuals and successfully prosecuted 4.

problem is the requirement of *double criminality*. Double criminality holds that offenses must constitute crimes under the laws of both countries. The second problem involves a question of *method*—on what basis do you specify what constitutes a serious crime?

While historically some debate has occurred over the principle of *double criminality*,[36] the principle seems well established in current practice. Occasionally this requirement has produced some interesting results. After his conviction on a charge of statutory rape in California, film director Roman Polanski fled to France during the appeal.[37] France refused the extradition request because the French legal code specifies a different age of consent; thus Polanski would not have been tried in France under similar circumstances. In another famous case, the British government refused to surrender Gerhart Eisler on charges of perjury and contempt of Congress. The British defined *perjury* in an extremely narrow sense and concluded that Eisler's statements, though false, did not meet the test of perjury under British law.[38] The British panel effectively ruled that lying to the *American* Congress did not constitute perjury under *British* law. Note also the Bobby Fischer incident in Chapter 9. Japan was willing to deport Fischer, but had refused the extradition request because the requested offense did not constitute a crime under Japanese law. Julian Assange, the founder of WikiLeaks, contested his extradition to Sweden on the basis that the charge in the request did not constitute "rape" as defined in British (and more generally, in European law).[39]

The Griffiths case illustrates both the double criminality provision and how it may apply to *extraterritorial* crimes. In February 2007, Hew Raymond Griffiths became the first ever Australian extradited to the United States for "piracy" of intellectual property (computer software). Griffiths, known online by the nickname "Bandido," ran the online piracy group named DrinkOrDie. He also held leadership roles in several other well-known warez[40] groups, including Razor1911 and RiSC. In an interview published in December 1999 by an online news source, he boasted that he ran all of DrinkOrDie's day-to-day operations and controlled access to more than 20 of the top warez servers worldwide.[41] Over the years, the U.S. Department of Justice estimated that the group had been responsible for $70 million dollars in losses to the software industry.

The group suffered a debilitating blow when the Justice Department and U.S. Immigration and Customs Enforcement, as part of Operation Buccaneer in December 2001, conducted more than 70 raids in the United States and five foreign countries, including the United Kingdom, Finland, Norway, Sweden, and Australia. Sixty people were arrested worldwide, 45 of them in the United States.

Before arriving in the United States, Griffiths had spent nearly three years in a detention center in Australia while fighting his extradition in Australian courts.

---

[36]See *Factor v. Laubenheimer*, 290 U.S. 276 (S. Ct. 1933).

[37]See www.vachss.com/mission/roman_polanski.htm (accessed April 22, 2009).

[38]Whiteman, VI: 797–798.

[39]CBS News, "Assange Lawyer: Risk of 'Denial of Justice,'" (February 7, 2011), www.cbs.com/stories/2011/02/07/ap/world/main7325608.shtml.

[40]"Pirates" use this term to denote the products produced by their efforts.

[41]Department of Justice, Press Release (April 20, 2007).

The extradition treaty and supplemental protocol between the United States and Australia contains an explicit *double criminality* provision.[42] Software "piracy" is a crime in the United States and, presumably, in Australia. The challenge to the U.S. request was based on the terms in Article 1, paragraph 4 of the protocol, which stipulates that if an offense occurs outside the territory of the requesting state (the United States), extradition will be granted if the laws of the requested state (Australia) provide for the punishment of an offense committed outside its own territory in similar ways. Griffiths pled guilty to two copyright-related charges and received a 51-month sentence.[43]

The *second* set of difficulties derives from the method of definition used to specify serious offense. Treaties utilize two main methods: *stipulative* and *enumerative*. Stipulative definitions use length of sentence. The treaty would apply to all crimes punishable in both states by so many months or years of imprisonment. If the treaty uses *enumeration*, the treaty will apply only to the offenses listed within the treaty. The United States uses the *enumerative* method almost exclusively.

The enumerative method tends to be extremely clumsy. For precision, it requires great attention to detail. This, in turn, necessarily makes treaties long and complex. If, by chance or circumstance, the list omits certain categories of offenses or the treaty becomes dated as new types of crimes such as aircraft hijacking emerge as major problems, subsequent inclusion by supplementary treaty or protocol entails considerable time and effort in negotiation and ratification. The United States has maintained this method for two reason: consistency in procedural application and because the nature of sentencing provisions in the federal code (as well as those in most state codes) does not easily lend itself to the stipulative method. American statutes do not uniformly stipulate *minimum* sentences but often tend to rely on the rather indeterminate formula "not more than."

Stipulative definitions have the advantages of reducing complexity and of being easily updated as the parties update their municipal codes to control new problems. Reliance upon the stipulative method also eliminates the problem of minor differences in definitions of offenses in the laws of the parties. Conversely, the stipulative method does not work well where the two codes have notably disparate penalties for similar offenses. Modern treaties among civil code states, including the European Treaty on Extradition, tend to use the *stipulative* method exclusively.

A third requirement often found in definitions of extraditable offenses is that the crime must have been committed on the territory or within the territorial jurisdiction of the requesting state. This provision presents difficulties in that serious crimes covered by the reach of the protective or nationality principle could go unpunished because the perpetrators cannot be extradited. More recent American treaties cover this possibility by permitting extradition on the basis of either "double criminality" or reciprocity. Consider here the case of Gary McKinnon, a

---

[42]Extradition Treaty, May 14, 1974, U.S.-Austl., 27 U.S.T. 957; Protocol Amending the 1974 Treaty, September 4. 1990. U.S.-Austl., S. Treaty Doc. No. 102-23 (1992).

[43]Gross, "Extradited Copyright Infringer Sentenced," InfoWorld (June 22, 2007), www.infoworld.com/article/07/06/22/Copyright-infringer-sentenced_1.html (accessed April 23, 2009).

national of the United Kingdom. McKinnon has been described in the United States as the biggest military hacker of all time. Allegedly, he hacked into 53 U.S. Army, 26 U.S. Navy, and 16 NASA computer systems, causing more than $700,000 in damage.[44] Yet he, like Hew Griffiths, had never set foot within U.S. territory (review the *Rivard* case). After unsuccessful appeals to the House of Lords and the European Court of Human Rights (ECHR), McKinnon was extradited in early September 2008.[45]

Territoriality has one other important effect on extradition. In transporting a fugitive, passage through the territory of third states (including airspace) requires the express permission of that state. Where extradition involves common crimes, few problems result. On the other hand, when the charge entails fraud or other violations of economic relations, states may balk. Widely divergent standards and approaches among states give rise to divergent definitions of the dividing line between sharp business practice and an illegal deal. In these cases, transport of fugitives sometimes necessitates mapping circuitous routes to avoid states that might object because the behavior would not have been considered a crime if done within their jurisdiction. Once an individual comes inside their jurisdiction, objecting states would have the authority and right to demand the prisoner's release because the captors would have no right of extraterritorial enforcement.

The Specialty Principle

The speciality principle holds that an individual may stand trial only for the charges in the extradition petition. The specialty principle is merely a formal expression of an obligation to deal with equals in good faith. While its exercise may protect the rights of the individual, it primarily serves to protect the requested state from abuse of its judicial process. If a state violates the specialty principle, we must distinguish between domestic effects and international effects. In *Fioconni and Kella v. Attorney General of the United States*,[46] the court noted that a conviction of an individual for an offense not charged in the extradition warrant could not void the conviction, because *individuals* had no rights under the treaty. In this case, a separable question concerned the possible violation of U.S. foreign relations law and the reaction of the Italian government. While violation of the specialty principle may not constitute grounds to negate a subse-

---

[44]D. Campbell, "British Computer Hacker Faces Extradition to US after Court Appeal Fails," *The Guardian* (August 29, 2008). Consider here the arguments of his legal team. "The offences for which our client's extradition is sought were committed on British soil and we maintain that any prosecution of our client ought therefore to be carried out by the appropriate British authorities. . . . Our client faces the prospect of prosecution and imprisonment thousands of miles away from his family in a country in which he has never set foot."

[45]Note that McKinnon's petition to the ECHR drew on the *Soering* case. He argued that he would be subjected to inhumane conditions in a U.S. prison. "European Court of Human Rights Refuses Request for Interim Measures by Gary McKinnon," Press Release, European Court of Human Rights (August 28, 2008).

[46]464 F.2d 475 (2d Cir. 1972).

quent conviction in U.S. courts, it will complicate future relations including the processing of future extradition petitions with the requested state if it perceives a breach of good faith.

One instance of the specialty principle played a role in the case of Adnan Khashoggi. The Saudi financier, at one time held to be the world's wealthiest man, was arrested in April 1989 in Bern, Switzerland, at the request of the United States. Khashoggi had been indicted in U.S. District Court in New York for helping Ferdinand Marcos and his wife in real estate transactions involving funds stolen from the Philippine treasury as well as for a variety of racketeering charges. He was extradited to the United States in July 1989 and faced charges for mail fraud and obstruction of justice (contained also in the request for extradition). He was not tried on the racketeering charges; they were punishable in the United States but were not punishable under Swiss law.[47]

In recent years, the specialty principle has come into play concerning crimes where the death penalty may be imposed. Many countries have abolished the death penalty. Municipal laws (such as in Italy, the United Kingdom, and Canada) or, many times, constitutional provisions (such as in Germany and Spain) preclude extradition to states where the charged offenses may subject them to the death penalty. Even if the United States could have advanced a valid claim to the *Achille Lauro* hijackers, Italy would not have complied unless the United States would have agreed that the death penalty would not be a sentencing option.

One of the more interesting and high-profile cases involving death penalty issues concerns Ira Einhorn, the so-called unicorn killer.[48] In 1979, Einhorn was accused of murdering his girlfriend, Holly Maddux, in Philadelphia. He fled the country. A Pennsylvania court proceeded to try Einhorn *in absentia* in 1993. He was convicted and given the death penalty. When authorities finally located Einhorn in France, the extradition request faced two hurdles—the trial *in absentia* and the death penalty sentence. The Pennsylvania General Assembly passed a special law permitting Einhorn to petition for a new trial, and U.S. authorities pledged Einhorn would not face execution. He was finally returned to the United States in July 2001. In October 2002, Einhorn was convicted of murder and received a sentence of life in prison without parole.

Questions relating to the death penalty and the specialty principle surfaced in an unusual way in the *Soering* case.[49]

---

[47]C. Wolf, "The Marcos Verdict: Marcos Is Cleared of All Charges in Racketeering and Fraud Case," *New York Times* (July 3, 1990), A1; W. Rempel, "Imelda Marcos Acquitted on U.S. Fraud Charges," *Toronto Star* (July 3, 1990), A10.

[48]For the complete story, see www.crimelibrary.com/notorious_murders/famous/einhorn/index_1. html?sect=13 (accessed April 22, 2009). Note also that Einhorn had an additional level of appeal to the European Court of Human Rights. Another high-profile case involved the extradition from Canada of the serial killer Charles Ng charged with 11 murders in California. See www.trutv.com/library/crime/serial_killers/predators/ng/call_1.html (accessed April 23, 2009).

[49]Text of the *Soering* decision, including content summary, in 28 *ILM* 1063 (1989); Lillich's analysis of this case, 85 *AJIL* 128 (1991); Schabas, *The Abolition of the Dealth Penalty in International Law* (1993); *Kindler v. Canada* (Minister of Justice), 1991, 2 S.C.R. 779, Supreme Court of Canada (September 26, 1991), in 87 *AJIL* 128 (1993).

THE *SOERING* CASE

European Court of Human Rights, July 7, 1989

Facts

Jens Soering, 22, a German national, son of a German diplomat, was accused of murdering his girlfriend's parents in Virginia. He and the girl were arrested in the United Kingdom on a charge of check fraud, and Soering confessed to the murders, claiming to have been under the influence of the girl. The latter currently was serving multiple life sentences in Virginia as an accessory to the murders.

The United States requested extradition of Soering under the UK–U.S. Extradition Treaty of 1972. The United Kingdom attempted to obtain American assurances that the death penalty, if imposed, would not be executed. The United States replied that the UK position would be communicated to the sentencing judge. Soering thereupon lodged a complaint with the European Human Rights Commission, which brought the case before the European Court of Rights.

The complaint charged that the United Kingdom, in extraditing Soering to the United States, would be in violation of Article 3 of the European Convention for the Protection of Human Rights and Fundamental Freedoms. ["No one shall be subjected to torture or to inhuman or degrading treatment or punishment."]

Soering claimed that if he were returned to Virginia and sentenced to death, he would face years in death row under extreme conditions while appealing his sentence. His contention therefore centered not on the merits of capital punishment (allowed under certain conditions laid down in the Human Rights Convention) *but on the conditions experienced by prisoners awaiting execution and the outcome of appeals.*

Issue

Could the United Kingdom deny extradition of Soering to the United States despite the UK–U.S. Treaty, whose provisions did cover the crime of murder?

Decision

The Court ruled unanimously against Soering's extradition to the United States.

Reasoning

"Having regard to the very long period of time spent on death row in such extreme conditions, with the ever present and mounting anguish of awaiting execution of the death penalty, and to the personal circumstances of the applicant, especially his age and mental state at the time of the offense, the applicant's extradition to the United States would expose him to a real risk of treatment going beyond the threshold set by Article 3." (Several minor issues have been omitted in this abstract.)

Notes

The European Human Rights Convention, to which the United Kingdom was a party, represented a lawmaking treaty and as such took precedence over the bilateral UK–U.S. Extradition Treaty. A unanimous verdict by the full court, representing all 23 members of the Council of Europe, is rare.

After this verdict, British officials agreed to extradite Soering to the United States on the condition that the capital murder charge would not be pressed. He was subsequently extradited, tried, and sentenced by a Virginia court to two terms of life imprisonment.

The specialty principle applies in one other area. A state may not re-extradite a fugitive to a third state without the express permission of the state from which the fugitive was originally obtained. Again, the principle expresses the continuing interest of the state originally requested in seeing that its judgment and process are not abused. To illustrate, the specialty principle would prevent the United States from circumventing Italy's ban on extradition to countries with death penalties for the alleged offense by having the fugitives first extradited to an appropriate but willing accomplice state that has no such ban. That state in turn would re-extradite the fugitives to the United States.[50]

Extraditable Persons

The important considerations here relate to exclusions rather than inclusions. A requested state does not necessarily have to surrender all individuals accused or convicted of an extraditable offense. We have noted that many states will not surrender persons if they would be subject to the death penalty. Beyond these cases, the two most commonly excluded groups are nationals of the requested state and political offenders. We will treat the political offense exclusion in a separate section later. Many treaties provide that states need not extradite their own nationals—a clear illustration of our earlier observations concerning fears of foreign courts.[51] Some states, like Germany, have written the exclusion into their constitutions. Unfortunately, the record shows that unless the offense directly impinges on a state's own vital interests, the refusal to extradite often permits criminals to avoid prosecution altogether because of the costs, time, and problems of collecting evidence and witnesses. As a general principle, the practice of requiring a state that refuses extradition of a national to initiate prosecution in good faith has much to recommend it. Some multilateral treaties such as The (Hague) Convention for the Suppression of Unlawful Seizure of Aircraft (1971)[52] contain "extradite or prosecute" provisions. Of course, the obligation contained in these treaties applies only among signatories. Note the following case as an example of the complexities often involved in dealing with these issues.

---

[50]See *United States ex rel. Donnelly v. Mulligan*, 74 F.2d 220 (2d Cir. 1934).

[51]See *New York Times* (January 31, 1952), and 47 *AJIL* 150 (1953), for details of the fascinating case of *In re Lo Dolce* (United States, Dist. Court W.D.N.Y. 1952, 106 F. Supp. 455), which involved an Italian demand for surrender by the United States of two U.S. nationals for the murder of another American (Major William V. Holohan) by poisoned soup and shooting, while all three were behind enemy lines, and the embezzlement of $100,000 in gold and currency. The murder had taken place in Italy in 1944, behind the German lines, while the three men were engaged in carrying the valuables in question to Italian partisans; see Fink and Schwartz, "International Extradition: The Holohan Murder Case," 39 *American Bar Association Journal* 297 (1953), 346.

[52]10 *ILM* (1971), 133–136. See Chapter 16.

Samuel Sheinbein Case

Samuel Sheinbein[53] committed a murder in Maryland. By birth, he was a national of both Israel and the United States. His father had left Israel as a child, and Samuel had never even visited the country until he fled there to escape prosecution. While Israeli law explicitly forbade the extradition of nationals, the treaty in force explicitly prohibited refusal to extradite on the basis of nationality.

The treaty also provided that requests would be governed by the law of the requested state at the time. A district court in Israel ruled in favor of extradition, but this was reversed by the Israeli Supreme Court. While reversing the decision, the Court also noted that the law needed to be changed. Israeli authorities then tried and convicted Sheinbein. He received a 24-year sentence.

Israel then amended its law to permit extradition of nationals provided they would be permitted to serve their sentences in Israel.

Great Britain, in theory, will surrender nationals; in practice, it seldom does so. Provisions in U.S. treaties vary with no distinguishable pattern. Except in cases of skyjacking, the United States has been remarkably flexible on the issue. Consider these three instances of relatively recent treaty practice: the United States agreed to the exemption (Brazil), specifically denied the exemption (Israel), and left the decision to the discretion of the respective executive authorities (Sweden). A signatory of the 1971 Hague Convention in an effort to suppress skyjacking, the United States has entered into bilateral extradite or prosecute agreements with Cuba as well as other states through the 1978 Bonn Declaration.[54] Note that offenses under the Suppression of Unlawful Acts series of treaties sponsored by the United Nations (see Chapter 16) all contain *an extradite or try provision.*

Political Offenses: Asylum

The political offense exception to extradition is now well rooted in contemporary practice. The exemption is found in both multilateral and bilateral treaties. Many states have recognized it by enacting domestic legislation or by including it as part of their constitutions (e.g., Brazil and Spain). On the other hand, a few states such as Japan have a policy of not granting asylum on the basis of alleged political persecution or political crimes. The United States has no statutory or constitutional provisions that cover political offenses or asylum. It has, however, included an exception for political offenses in all of its bilateral extradition treaties. As international terrorism has become of greater concern, the immunity conferred by a refusal to extradite has generated considerable debate over questions of definition, judgment, and practice.

---

[53]Abramovsky and Edelstein, "The Sheinbein Case and the Israeli-American Extradition Experience," 32 *Vanderbilt Journal of Transnational Law* 305 (1999).

[54]*New York Times* (July 18, 1978), A1.

That states recognize an exclusion for political offenses today stands as an interesting commentary on how standards change over time. Until the nineteenth century, *only* political offenders were sought for extradition. The modern practice linking extradition to criminal offenses has evolved primarily over the past 150 years and coincides with the development of transportation systems that permitted the speedy escape of felons from one country to another. At the same time, the idea that *some* had committed crimes based upon *political* motives coincides with the development and spread of liberal sentiment concerning the right (obligation) of individuals to resist tyrannical rule.

In the fragmented political world of the post–Cold War era, the often mouthed sentiment that "one person's freedom fighter is another person's terrorist" has more than face validity. The divisions in contemporary politics make it difficult to develop a common definition of a "political crime" and standard tests to identify one in practice. As with other areas, states may agree in principle that individuals sought for political or religious offenses (e.g., Salman Rushdie) ought to be exempt from return, but they have not agreed upon common operational tests that easily distinguish common criminals from political or religious fugitives. Because of the potential political repercussions, these decisions often lie outside the reach of the courts unless the executive authority offers the case for resolution. In the context of domestic Italian politics, a courageous stance most often overlooked was the Italian government's decision *not* to grant political asylum to the hijackers. This judgment would have precluded domestic prosecution as well as requests for extradition. Still, at the same time the Italian government made the decision to prosecute *some* of the hijackers, it also released Abu Nidal, who was accused of masterminding the attack, and permitted him to cross the border into Yugoslavia. Moreover, given the nature of the defense mounted by the attorneys representing the hijackers who went to trial, the Italian court could have found them innocent by reason of "political motivation."

National policies vary—particularly in the contemporary, politically charged atmosphere after the 9/11 attacks. France, until the summer of 1986, proudly valued its reputation as a haven for dissidents. A policy of benign neglect, generous grants of asylum, and strict constructionist court rulings reflected a wide definition of relative political offenses. Until the fall of 1984, French governments had sheltered from extradition Basque members of Euzkadi Ta Askatasuna (ETA) wanted by Spanish authorities for various violent terrorist acts in Spain.

The decision, executive or judicial, to exempt individuals from extradition because the crimes stemmed from "political," "religious," or "military" offenses guarantees immunity from prosecution so long as the individual does not enter the jurisdiction of another state less tolerant. Writers have advanced two primary justifications for extending protection to political refugees: (1) the desire to remain neutral in the domestic conflicts of another state and (2) the humanitarian desire to prevent individuals from receiving unfair treatment at the hands of another government. Without exploring the degree to which either of these two motivations corresponds to practice, we should note that American courts have rejected the first as an acceptable defense while embracing the second.[55]

---

[55] *Abu Eain v. Wilkes,* 641 F2d (7th Cir. 1981).

Traditionally, political offenses have been divided into two categories: *pure political acts* and *relative political acts*. Some confusion exists because the term *political offense* does embrace both meanings but is often used without the qualifying adjective. *Pure* political offenses consist of acts such as sedition, espionage, and treason that are directed at the government of a state but *do not involve a common crime.* Most controversy comes from the problem of weighing the elements in *relative* political offenses where a common crime such as murder is so intertwined with a broader action directed at the government of a state that the two cannot be separated and therefore must be considered as one offense. *The court must determine if the political component outweighs the ordinary criminal component, giving the crime a predominantly political (or public) character.* This decision is a difficult one for most judges. For a judge to permit any serious crime to go unpunished, especially when an individual has not denied guilt, the proof must involve extraordinary extenuating circumstances.

Political Offenses: Standards of Determination

In American practice, U.S. courts still adhere to a substantive test[56] culled from British case law just before the turn of the twentieth century.[57]

IN RE CASTIONI

1 Q.B. 149 (1891)

Facts

During a political uprising aimed at organizing a provisional government with the idea of seceding from the Swiss confederation, Castioni shot and killed a government official who blocked access to a government building. The act took place in full view of a crowd that intended to capture the building as part of installing the new government. When Swiss federal troops crushed the rebellion, Castioni fled to England. Against the Swiss request for extradition, Castioni argued that his motives were political, not private. He had

(continued)

---

[56]See Evans, "Reflections upon the Political Offense in International Practice," 57 *AJIL* 1 (1963); Thompson, "The Evolution of the Political Offense Exception in an Age of Modern Political Violence," 9 *Yale J. World Pub. Ord.* 315 (1983); Rubin, "Extradition and 'Terrorist' Offenses," 10 *Terrorism* 83 (1987); Banoff and Pyle, "To Surrender Political Offenders: The Political Offense Exception to Extradition in United States Law," 16 *NYU J. Int'l L. & Pol.* 169 (1986); Carbonneau, "The Political Offense Exception as Applied in French Cases Dealing with the Extradition of Terrorists," 1983 *Mich Y.B. Int 'l Legal Stud.* 209 (1983); Bassiouni, "The Political Offense Exception Revisited," 15 *Den. J. Int'l L. & Pol'y* 255 (1987); Taulbee, "Political Crimes, Human Rights and Contemporary International Practice," 4 *Emory Int'l L. J.* 43 (1990).

[57]For a discussion of tests used by other states, see Taulbee, "Political Crimes, Human Rights and Contemporary International Practice," n. 49 at 50 et seq.

not known the victim before the incident and had no personal feelings against him.

Issue

Do the actions of Castioni qualify as a political offense that would exempt him from extradition?

Decision

Britain should refuse extradition to Switzerland.

Reasoning

The Court used what it termed an "objective test" to separate the private from the "public" motive. The test had three elements:

1. an *overt* act
2. done in support of a political uprising and
3. aimed at securing control of, or protecting the security of, a government.

We should compare the decision in *Castioni* with that in the following case.

IN RE MEUNIER

Great Britain, High Court of Justice, Queen's Bench Division, 1894 L.R. [1894], 2 Q.B. 415

Facts

Meunier, a French citizen and by political belief an anarchist, took it upon himself in March 1892 to cause two explosions. One, at the Café Véry in Paris, caused the death of two persons. The other occurred at the Lobau military barracks in the same city. Both incidents represented part of an anarchist effort to avenge the execution of the anarchist Ravachol.

After committing the two attacks, Meunier fled to Great Britain. A French court tried him in absentia and, on convictions on charges of murder, sentenced him to death. The French government made formal application for his arrest and extradition. Meunier was arrested on April 4, 1894, in the Victoria Station in London. He protested his arrest and pending deportation to France, and his counsel, citing the *Castioni* case, claimed that although the bombing of the barracks had been a reprehensible act, it possessed political character. His counsel also

asserted that insufficient evidence had been produced in the case of the attack on the Café Véry to lay the blame for the two deaths on Meunier.

Issue

Did Meunier's acts in Paris correspond to the accepted definition of a political offense?

Decision

The court rejected Meunier's contention that his acts constituted political offenses and ordered his continued detention until he could be surrendered to agents of the French government.

Reasoning

The Court used the *Castioni* tests. The attacks on the Café Véry and on the military barracks did not constitute political offenses. No struggle between two parties in the French state, each seeking to impose the government of its choice on the state, existed. The group with which Meunier

(continued)

identified was the enemy of all governments and desired to abolish rather than control them. The terrorist acts of anarchists, furthermore, were not directed primarily at governments (which might have given them a semblance of political character) but were usually aimed at private citizens (the attack on the Café Véry was cited as an example by the court).

"The party of anarchy is the enemy of all Governments. Their efforts are directed primarily against the general body of citizens. They may secondarily

and incidentally commit offences against some particular Government; but anarchist offences are mainly directed against private citizens."

Under the circumstances, Meunier's acts did not represent political offenses within the meaning of the British Extradition Acts of 1870 and 1873.

Note

After Meunier was taken back to France, the death sentence imposed on him in his absence was carried out.

On its face, the objective test in *Castioni* would seem reasonable. The problem arises because American courts (but not British) have until recently refused to look beyond context to content.[58] Until the mid-1980s, American courts adhered to the dicta of *In re Ezeta*.[59] This case involved a request from El Salvador for the extradition of its former president (Carlos Ezeta) and four military leaders for various offenses that included murder and robbery. These offenses allegedly occurred during an attempt to quell an armed rebellion. The court applied the criteria from *Castioni* but refused to look into the severity of the offenses in question:[60]

> Crimes may have been committed by the contending forces of the most atrocious and inhuman character, and still the perpetrators of such crimes escape punishment as fugitives beyond the reach of extradition. I have no authority, in this examination, to determine what acts are within the rules of civilized warfare, and what are not. War, at best, is barbarous, and hence it is said that the "law is silent during war."

Because the court refused to engage in an analysis of motives or means, subsequent opinion often referred to the test as "objective."[61] American courts tended to apply the *Castioni* principles mechanically, examining neither the character of the government presumably under attack nor the scope and severity of the offenses in relationship to the goal sought (proportionality).[62]

---

[58]A Cold War bias informed many decisions. The United States finally deported Andrija Artukovic in February 1986 after American courts had systematically refused Yugoslavian requests for extradition because the offenses had occurred during the German invasion of Yugoslavia. The court concluded that war in its most elemental form was a struggle for political power.

[59]62 F. 972 (N.D. Cal, 1894).

[60]*Ezeta*, n. 52 at 997.

[61]See, e.g., *Quinn v. Robinson*, 107 S. Ct. 372 (1986), *cert. denied*, 783 F.2d 776 (9th Cir. 1986).

[62]For the evolution in British approach, see *Regina v. Governor of Brixton, ex Parte Kolcynski* (Polish Seaman's case), 1 Q.B. 540 (1955); *Regina v. Governor of Brixton Prison, ex Parte Schtraks*, 1 Q.B. (1963); and *Cheng v. Governor of Pentonville Prison*, A.C. 931 (H.L., 1973). The Polish Seaman's case introduced a balancing element into British practice.

The potential problems surfaced first in the request in 1956 to the United States from Yugoslavia for the extradition of Andrija Artukovic (the "Butcher of the Balkans"), who had served during World War II as the minister of the interior (and minister of justice) in the pro-Nazi government. According to allegations in the petition, Artukovic was responsible for a campaign of systematic repression that included the execution of 200,000 Serbs.[63] Two arguments proved decisive in finding that Artukovic's actions as interior minister fell under the political offense exception. First, the court noted that the Croatian government had been subject to a number of challenges and to a wartime environment. Although Artukovic had ordered the executions in the course of his official duty, he had not personally committed murder. Thus, the court found that his offenses fell within the context of a political struggle to maintain a government. Second, the court dismissed the Yugoslavian contention that the offenses in question constituted war crimes, noting that the evidence of an existing duty to surrender war criminals was not compelling enough to overturn an interpretation of "long-standing" regard to similar treaty provisions.[64]

The court's failure to examine the mass nature of the killings, the civilian status of the victims, and the relationship of the killings to the maintenance of the regime raised serious questions about the application of the political incidence test. The reasoning of the court seemingly transformed the political incidence test into a license for gratuitous murder on a grand scale. The problem with the *Castioni* criteria used as "objective" tests is that, carried to the extreme, they would protect terrorists no matter how heinous their actions. Events of the 1970s and early 1980s caused a major rethinking of prior practice as well as a spirited debated within the American legal community.

Twenty-five years after the decision to refuse Yugoslavia's request to extradite Artukovic, the courts again seized the issue. This time, utilizing criteria developed in *Eain v. Wilkes*[65] (discussed shortly), the court found:[66]

> Those murders as to which it is hereinafter found there is probable cause to believe respondent committed *do not* come within the "political character" defense. Respondent's statement of his motives would be irrelevant. *Eain,* 641 F.2d at 520. ("For purposes of extradition, motivation is not itself determinative of the political character of any given act.") The facts and circumstances in evidence show that the murders were not of a "political character" within the meaning of the Treaty; they were for personal gain, racial or religious hatred, and/or impermissible vengeance upon disarmed enemy soldiers. Ridding a country of some of its population for such reprehensible reasons, as part of some larger political scheme, is not a crime of a "political character" and is thus not covered by the political offense exception to extradition. (Emphasis added)

---

[63]See *Karadzole v. Artukovic,* 140 F. Supp. 245 (S.D. Cal. 1956), affirmed *sub nom. Karadzole v. Artukovic,* 247 F.2d 198 (9th Cir. 1957), vacated *per curiam* 355 U.S. 393 (1958).

[64]247 F.2d at 204.

[65]*Eain v. Wilkes,* 641 F.2d 504, 520 (7th Cir.), *cert. denied,* 454 U.S. 894 (1981).

[66]*Artukovic v. Rison,* 628 F. Supp. 1370; 1985 (C.D. Cal. 1985), U.S. Dist. LEXIS 17012.

In February 1986, the United States returned Artukovic to Yugoslavia. He stood trial, was convicted, and was sentenced to death by firing squad. He died in prison (at the age of 88) in 1988.

A Turning Point in U.S. Practice

In the modern context, the parameters of many political conflicts have become less clear. Although political differences between two or more parties may exist, the situation frequently does not rise to the level of strife found in the earlier cases. Courts confronted with new forms and methods of political struggle have disagreed about the type of conflict that triggers application of the political offense exception to extradition. As the Seventh Circuit observed in *Eain v. Wilkes,* terrorist activity in particular "does not conveniently fit the categories of conflict with which the courts and the international community have dealt in the past."[67]

The court in *Eain* struggled with the traditional criteria. In applying the traditional definition of "war, revolution or rebellion," the court refused to acknowledge the contention that conduct in the ongoing struggle between the Arab States, Palestine, and Israel qualified as a political offense. Eain claimed membership in El Fatah (the military wing of the Palestinian Liberation Organization—PLO). The Israelis sought his extradition on a warrant charging Eain with indiscriminately setting off explosives that killed civilians. Eain resisted on the basis that Israel sought to try him for his political beliefs; hence the crime in the warrant fell under the political offense exception. The court decided that the dispersed nature of the PLO significantly differentiated its status from that of other groups engaged in rebellion.[68]

Critics contrasted this decision with those in several high-profile cases involving members of the Provisional Irish Republican Army (PIRA), the violent paramilitary offshoot of the Irish Republican Army (IRA).[69] In the first *Mackin* case, the court concluded that the conflict in Northern Ireland was part of "an on-going,

---

[67]641 F.2d, n. 58 at 504.

[68]Ibid., 518. The court also stretched to find support from *In re Meunier,* stating that the attack seemingly was directed at the *social,* not the *political,* structure of Israel. *Id.* at 520–521.

[69]See *In re Doherty (Doherty I),* 599 F. Supp. 270 (S.D.N.Y. 1984) (denying extradition to United Kingdom of a PIRA member convicted of murder); *United States v. Doherty (Doherty II),* 615 F. Supp. 755 (S.D.N.Y. 1985) (dismissing action for collateral review of order denying extradition), *aff'd, (Doherty III),* 786 F.2d 491 (2nd Cir. 1986); *Doherty v. U.S. Department of Justice, I.N.S. (Doherty IV)* 908 F.2d 1108 (2nd Cir. 1990); *In re Quinn (Quinn I),* No. Cr-81-Misc. (N.D. Cal 1982) (certifying extradition); *Quinn v. Robinson (Quinn II),* No. C-82-6688 RPA (N.D. Cal 1983) (granting habeas corpus), and (*Quinn III),* rev'd 783 F.2d 776 (9th Cir. 1986), *cert. denied,* 107 S. Ct. 271 (1986); *In re Mackin (Mackin I),* 80 Cr. Misc. 1, p. 54 (S.D.N.Y. 1981) (denied extradition to United Kingdom of PIRA member charged with attempted murder—appeal dismissed) (*Mackin II),* 668 F.2d 122 (2d Cir. 1981); *In re McMullen,* No. 3-78-1899 MG (N.D. Cal. May 11, 1979) (denying extradition to United Kingdom of PIRA member sought for bombing military barracks); later proceeding (*McMullen II),* 17 I. & N. Dec. 542 (Bd. of Immigration Appeals [BIA] 1980) (reversing immigration judge's finding that McMullen was not deportable), *rev'd,* 658 F.2d 1312 (9th Cir. 1981) (*McMullen III)* (finding BIA's rejection of extensive evidence that McMullen was likely to be persecuted by PIRA if deported to Ireland was not supported by substantial evidence), on remand (*McMullen IV)* I. & N. Interim Dec. No. 2967 (BIA 1984) (finding McMullen deportable because claimed persecution was not based on political opinion and ineligible for asylum because there were reasons to believe he had committed *serious nonpolitical crimes), aff'd,* 788 F.2d 591 (9th Cir. 1986) (Emphasis added). See also the discussion of the *Doherty* case in Speer, "International Decisions," 85 *AJIL* 345 (1991).

continuous uprising by the . . . [Provisional Irish Republican Army] against British domination with the goal of establishing a unified Irish nation."[70]

The ongoing difficulty led to an exceptional measure. In 1986 the United States and Great Britain negotiated a protocol that severely limited the circumstances under which acts of violence may qualify for exemption. The push for the change came from the Reagan administration in response to the inability of the United States to effect extradition of gunmen associated with the PIRA. Ratification of the protocol stalled in the U.S. Senate, but became a moot question because of changes in U.S. practice and changes that occurred in the political situation in Northern Ireland.

Policy and Law

To proceed further requires some important distinctions. Thus far we have discussed the political offense exception in terms of *asylum* for those who qualify. While the political offense exception forms one justification for granting asylum, we must distinguish between asylum based on the political offense exception, territorial asylum granted on the basis of human rights concerns (persecution, etc.), and "withholding" or deferral based upon an expectation of unfair treatment if the subject is returned. In practice, the three categories overlap in important ways because the United States has also attempted deportation in lieu of extradition (i.e., *Doherty* and *McMullen*). *Asylum* means the person may stay in the United States permanently; *withholding* means the individual has a temporary reprieve.[71] As part of the emerging concern for human rights in the late 1970s, Congress amended the Immigration and Nationality Act in 1980.[72] The Refugee Act of 1980[73] stated:

> The Attorney General shall not deport or return any alien to a country if the Attorney General determines that such alien's life or freedom would be threatened in such country on account of race, religion, nationality, membership in a particular social group, or political opinion.[74]

In the Illegal Immigration Reform and Immigrant Responsibility Act (IIRIRA) of 1996,[75] Congress revised the withholding and asylum provisions. Under current law, the attorney general may not grant asylum if he or she determines "there are serious reasons for believing that the alien has committed a serious nonpolitical crime outside the United States prior to the arrival of the alien in the United States."[76] The following case illustrates the Supreme Court's guidance in defining "serious nonpolitical crimes."[77]

---

[70]Mackin I, note 69, at 54. For similar reasoning, see Doherty I, McMullen II, note 69.

[71]See *INS v. Cardoza-Fonseca*, 480 U.S. 421 (1987), at 428–429.

[72]66 Stat. 166, 8 U.S.C. § 1101 et seq. (2005).

[73]Refugee Act, Pub. L. 96–212, 94 Stat. 102. See *INS v. Stevic*, 467 U.S. 407 (1984), at 414–416, 421–422 (1984).

[74]8 U.S.C. § 1253(h)(1) (2005).

[75]IIRIRA, Pub. L. 104–208, 110 Stat. 3009–546. The withholding provisions are now codified at 8 U.S.C. § 1231(b)(3), and the asylum provisions at § 1158.

[76]Section 1158(b)(2)(A)(iii).

[77]See also *In the Matter of the Indian Government's Request for Extradition of Kulvir Singh, Aka Kulbir Singh Barapind,* 170 F. Supp. 2d 982; (E.D. Cal 2001) U.S. Dist. LEXIS 22291.

I.N.S. v. Aguirre-Aguirre

United States Supreme Court 526 U.S. 415 (1999), 121 F.3d 521 (reversed and remanded)

Facts

The Board of Immigration Appeals (BIA) had ruled that Aguirre-Aguirre, a citizen of Guatemala, did not qualify for withholding. He had entered the United States illegally in 1994 and conceded his eligibility for deportation, but he had argued that he feared persecution for earlier political activities in Guatemala. The Court explicitly noted that the issue in the case was not whether persecution would likely occur, but whether Aguirre-Aguirre was ineligible for withholding because he committed a "serious nonpolitical crime" before his entry into the United States. Aguirre-Aguirre had admitted that, to protest government policies in Guatemala, he had burned buses, assaulted passengers, and vandalized and destroyed property in private shops. The BIA found these to be serious nonpolitical crimes. In doing so, it relied upon its previous interpretation of a serious nonpolitical crime applied in the *Matter of McMullen*.[78]

The Court of Appeals (9th Circuit) reversed the finding of the BIA. In doing so the Court of Appeals used a "balancing test" (analytical framework) that considered "the political necessity and success of Aguirre's methods," whether his acts "were grossly out of proportion to their objective or were atrocious," and the "persecution respondent might suffer upon return to Guatemala." According to the majority of the Court, the BIA's analysis of the serious nonpolitical

crime exception was legally deficient in three respects: (1) the BIA should have "consider[ed] the persecution that Aguirre might suffer if returned to Guatemala" and "balance[d] his admitted offenses against the danger to him of death," (2) it should have "considered whether the acts committed were grossly out of proportion to the[ir] alleged objective" and were "of an atrocious nature, and (3) the BIA "should have considered the political necessity and success of Aguirre's methods."

Issue

What criteria should U.S. courts use in determining if actions were serious nonpolitical offenses; that is, what criteria should courts use in determining if the criminal element of specific actions outweighed their political nature?

Decision

The court of appeals erred. The primary error was the insistence that the BIA was required to balance Aguirre-Aguirre's criminal acts against the risk of persecution he would face if returned to Guatemala.

Reasoning

The question involves which reading of the statute [§ 1253(h)(2)(C)] better represents its intent. The nature of the crime(s), not the extent of persecution, forms the most important element. Considering the risk of persecution stands as a separable factor. In

(continued)

---

[78]*McMullen IV*, note 69.

the instant case, the BIA determined that "the criminal nature of the respondent's acts outweigh their political nature" because his group's political dissatisfaction "manifested itself disproportionately in the destruction of property and assaults on civilians," and its political goals "were outweighed by [the group's] criminal strategy of strikes."

Note

An important consideration in all cases is the simple fact that in the United States, the executive has the final say in asylum cases. Throughout this opinion, the court cites numerous opinions and statements by the attorney general to support its reasoning. On territorial asylum, see Chapter 15.

We should compare the verdict in Aguirre-Aguirre with the finding in the following Canadian case.

GIL V. CANADA (MINISTER OF EMPLOYMENT AND IMMIGRATION)

Court of Appeal, Hugessen, Desjardins and Décary J.J.A. Montréal, September 12, 14; Ottawa (October 21, 1994)

Facts

Gil is an Iranian citizen. In the years 1980 and 1981, he became involved with a group of anti-Khomeini activists in incidents of bombing and arson directed against wealthy supporters of the regime. Those attacks consisted in placing bombs or Molotov cocktails in the supporters' business premises. Since the premises were usually crowded at the time of the attacks, the attacks frequently resulted in injury and even death to innocent bystanders. The Immigration and Refugee Board (Canada) concluded that Gil had a well-founded fear of persecution in the event of his return to Iran, but because he had committed "serious nonpolitical crimes," he was not eligible for refugee status under the United Nations Convention Relating to the Status of Refugees to which Canada is a state party.

Issue

Do Gil's actions qualify as political offenses?

Decision

No. While rejecting the "incidence" test, the court used a proportionality test.

Reasoning

The court noted that the "political offense" exception is thus applicable "only when a certain level of violence exists and when those resorting to violence are seeking to accomplish a particular objective such as to bring about political change or to combat violent political opposition." The court found that Iran during this era met the first test because "in the years in question, Iran was a turbulent society in which a number of armed groups were in conflict with the Khomeini regime."

In examining the second part, the court noted that the test focuses "on the need for a nexus between the crime and the alleged political objective. The nature and purpose of the offense require examination, including whether it was committed out of genuine political motives or merely

(continued)

for personal reasons or gain, whether it was directed toward a modification of the political organization or the very structure of the state, and whether there is a close and direct causal link between the crime committed and its alleged political purpose and object. The political element should in principle outweigh the common law character of the offence, which may not be the case if the acts committed are grossly disproportionate to the objective, or are of an atrocious or barbarous nature."

In this instance, the court noted, "There was no objective rational connection between injuring the commercial interests of certain wealthy supporters of the regime and any realistic goal of forcing the regime itself to fall or to change its ways or its policies. Even if some of the businesses targeted were owned by highly placed members of local revolutionary committees, the nexus between such businesses and the general structure of the Government of Iran at the time appeared far too tenuous to support or justify the kind of indiscriminate violence which the appellant admitted to. . . . The crucial point was not merely that some of the victims were innocent bystanders but, much more importantly, that the attacks themselves were not carried out against armed adversaries and were bound to injure the innocent. Violence of this sort was wholly disproportionate to any legitimate political objective."

Political events of the past 60 years, made more contentious by the rise of powerful competing ideologies, have raised some extremely difficult issues and complicated the task of responsible legal response. Political events since 9/11 have really sharpened the debate. Rather than generalize, we ask readers to consider the following questions about possible tests and parameters for weighing political offenses: Should the question of targets, whether official (public) or private, and types of casualties, intended or incidental, be a consideration? Should it matter if the action occurs within the territory of the targeted government, or should actions outside the disputed territory qualify? How should a state treat those who flee from oppressive regimes when they commit serious crimes in their effort? Should some offenses, murder for example, never qualify for an exemption? These questions pose salient issues for both municipal and international law with few firm and reliable guidelines that will reconcile legal responsibility with political acceptability. The current situation seems to breed situations where one seemingly must be sacrificed to the other.

Standards of Proof

A difference of practice between civil law and customary law countries has great importance here. In civil law states, the extradition request tends to be viewed as a tool of judicial cooperation. The assumption is that the requesting state has sufficient reason. Hence a properly executed request, barring other complications such as a claim by the requested individual for an exemption, simply sets in motion the appropriate procedures. This approach contrasts rather sharply with common law practice, where the requesting state must show "probable cause" by presenting prima facie evidence of guilt. Even among common law countries, the probable cause requirement has presented difficulty. Canadian courts have ruled against extradition because the judge felt the United States had not shown the alleged offense to be a crime under either American state or federal statutes.

Occasionally, civil law states have mistaken the prima facie requirement for a standard of *punishability* rather than one of *prosecutability*. This seems to have happened in the *Insull* case, where Greek courts refused two requests for Samuel Insull, who was wanted in the United States for embezzlement and larceny.[79] The courts in both instances proceeded to try the case and rule that the evidence furnished by the United States was insufficient to establish that Insull had deliberately intended to evade American law, and they refused the American petition. The perceived lack of cooperation caused the United States to declare a newly negotiated extradition treaty with Greece null and void.

The *Insull* case proves instructive in another way. Insull subsequently left Greece for Turkey, which had no extradition treaty with the United States. American authorities immediately made application to the Turkish government, which arrested Insull and handed him over without judicial or administrative process. As a final irony, after his return, Insull was tried and found innocent.

Acts of State

Several other interesting questions derive from our discussion of political crimes. The Iranians sought the extradition of the deposed Shah from Panama and threatened to file a request with the United States just before the occupation of the American embassy in Teheran in 1979. The year 1986 saw Jean-Claude "Baby Doc" Duvalier leave Haiti and Ferdinand Marcos leave the Philippines. Because of their official positions, can these individuals raise the issue that their official position gave them immunity for any actions taken while in office? (See Chapters 8 and 14 for further discussion of these issues.)

The United States has cooperated with requesting states in the past. The most notable case involved Marcos Perez Jiménez, a former president of Venezuela, who had taken up residence in Miami after his exile. Venezuela filed a complaint charging Jiminez with two groups of crimes: murder and participation in murder, and financial crimes for his own gain.[80] In his defense, Jiminez relied upon the political exception clause in the treaty of extradition and the "act of state" doctrine, arguing that he had immunity from prosecution for any of the acts charged because of his official position. The court denied the relevance of the defense, noting that the crimes charged—fraud, criminal malversation, and embezzlement—were quite ordinary crimes, not acts of Venezuelan sovereignty.

The cases of the Shah and Ferdinand Marcos turn on much simpler considerations. Neither the Philippines nor Iran had a valid extradition treaty with the United States. Of course, the United States could have deported Marcos and did not. It could have refused entry to the Shah and did not. Given our earlier discussion of French policy, it is doubtful that the French government would return Duvalier to Haiti, although they have publicly expressed dismay at their inability

---

[79]www.encyclopedia.com/html/I/Insull-S1.asp.

[80]*Jimenez v. Aristeguieta*, 311 F.2d 547, 5th Cir. (1962).

to find another state to take him as a political refugee. The United States put great pressure on Panama to accept the Shah. In passing, we might note that Idi Amin, the expelled Ugandan dictator, enjoyed a somewhat secluded exile in Saudi Arabia until his death in 2003.

The Extradition Process in the United States

While the locus of the final decision may vary, normally the extradition procedure begins with an application through diplomatic channels addressed to the appropriate executive authority in the requested state. Once the authorities in the requested state receive the petition, the decision may lie solely with the executive or with the judiciary, or entail some interaction between the two. The permutations and combinations here do not easily lend themselves to generalization, but the critical consideration pertains to the independence of the judiciary from executive influence. As we have seen, in France the judiciary has responsibility for the decision, but is highly responsive to the policy preferences of the executive departments.

Federal statute controls American extradition procedures (18 U.S.C. §§ 3181–3185). An authorized representative of a foreign government may file a complaint with any federal or state court in whose jurisdiction the fugitive is found. The complaint must state the charge and affirm that the offense occurred within the jurisdiction of the requesting state. The law does not require the requesting states to file a formal notification with the State Department, although most do so. In recent practice, extradition cases have been referred to magistrates, the lowest-ranking officers in the federal court system. The court will determine if a valid treaty is in effect, if the accused is the same individual charged in the complaint, if the offense charged meets the double-criminality test, and, finally, if the requesting state has presented sufficient evidence to establish a prima facie case against the accused.

Because the hearing serves the function of establishing *probable cause* rather than a trial on the merits (guilt or innocence), the Federal Rules of Evidence do not apply. Hearsay is admissible, and defendants may present only evidence that explains the circumstances (looking toward a political exception) or evidence that they are not the person sought. Defendant may not present evidence that merely contradicts or challenges the prosecution's case, since such evidence has no bearing on probable cause.[81]

The defendant may not appeal the verdict, but may apply for a writ of *habeas corpus*, the denial of which *can be* appealed to a higher court. The reasoning behind limiting the right of appeal presumably depends upon the courts' view of the nature of the extradition hearing as a preliminary hearing. When courts rule that extradition is permissible, the secretary of state may still refuse to surrender the fugitive (18 U.S.C. § 3186). The secretary of state has the authority to undertake his or her own investigation and examination of the issues and court proceedings after the completion of the hearing, but is not bound by the court record. If the court denies the petition, the requesting country does not have a right of appeal, but may refile its complaint before a different court. The following case illustrates the process.

---

[81]*Collins v. Loisel,* 259 U.S. 309 (1922).

> ## ▶ SAINEZ V. VENABLES
>
> # U.S. Court of Appeals, 9th Circuit 588 F.3d 713; 2009 U.S. App. LEXIS 26163 (2010)
>
> **Facts**
>
> Appellant arrestee sought review of a decision of the U.S. District Court for the Southern District of California, which denied his petition for a writ of *habeas corpus* challenging his arrest pending extradition on a Mexican arrest warrant for murder.
>
> **Issues**
>
> Did the appellant have sufficient justification to warrant a writ of habeas corpus?
>
> **Decision and Reasoning**
>
> The court found no cause to challenge either the original decision to extradite or the rejection of the petition for the writ. The probable cause finding of the magistrate judge was properly affirmed by the district court. The sworn statements of several witnesses to the shooting supported a reasonable inference that the arrestee had killed a man as charged. The charge and procedures clearly met treaty definitions and requirements.

SUGGESTED READINGS

JURISDICTION: GENERAL

Fischer et al., eds, *International and National Prosecution of Crimes Under International Law: Current Developments* (2001).

Inazumi, *Universal Jurisdiction in Modern International Law: Expansion of National Jurisdiction for Prosecuting Serious Crimes Under International Law* (2005).

Reisman, ed., *Jurisdiction in International Law* (1999).

Ryngaert, *Jurisdiction in International Law* (2008).

Spang-Hanssen, *Cyberspace and International Law on Jurisdiction* (2004).

Slot and Bulterman, eds, *Globalisation and Jurisdiction* (2004).

AUTHORITY OVER ARMED FORCES ABROAD

Fleck, *The Handbook of the Law on Visiting Forces* (2001).

Whiteman, VI: 379–427.

Woodlife, *The Peacetime Use of Foreign Military Installations Under Modern International Law* (1992).

CASES

Christopher Collins et al. v. Caspar Weinberger, Secretary of Defense, et al., U.S. Court of Appeals, D.C., No. 82-1857, May 17, 1983, in 22 *ILM* 799 (1983).

Holmes v. Laird, U.S. Court of Appeals, D.C., 1972, 459 F.2d 1211, in 67 *AJIL* 153 (1973); decision in full in 11 *ILM* 584 (1972).

Moore v. The United Kingdom, U.S. Court of Appeals, 9th Cir., 384 F.3d 1079, 2004.

The Netherlands v. Short, Netherlands, Supreme Court (January 26, March 30, 1990), in 29 *ILM* 1375 (1990).

Public Prosecutor v. Starks and Eaton, Republic of China, Taiwan High Court, Taichung Branch, 1971, in 70 *AJIL* 145 (1976).

United States v. Keaton, U.S. Court of Military Appeals, 1969, in 64 *AJIL* 431 (1970).

CORPORATIONS

Acquaah, *International Regulation of Transnational Corporations: The New Reality* (1986).

Seidl-Hohenveldern, *Corporations in and Under International Law* (1987).

EXTRADITION IN GENERAL

Bassiouni, *International Extradition: United States Law and Practice,* 5th ed. (2007).

Nichols, Montgomery, and Knowles, *The Law of Extradition and Mutual Assistance* (2007).

Zanotti and Rotman, *Extradition in Multilateral Treaties and Conventions* (2006).

CASES

Atkinson v. United States of America Government, United Kingdom, House of Lords, 1969, [1969] 3 W.L.R. 1074, in 64 *AJIL* 711 (1970).

Factor v. Laubenheimer, 290 U.S. 276, 287 (1933).

In re Kam-shu, U.S. Court of Appeals, 5th Cir., 1973, 477 F.2d 333, in 68 *AJIL* 125 (1974).

Royal Government of Greece v. Governor of Brixton Prison ex Parte Kotronis, United Kingdom, House of Lords, 1969 [1969] 3 W.L.R. 1107, in 64 *AJIL* 714 (1970).

United States v. Cordero, U.S. Court of Appeals, 1st Cir., 1981, 668 F.2d 32, in 76 *AJIL* 618 (1981).

POLITICAL OFFENSES

Epps, "The Validity of the Political Offender Exception in Extradition Treaties in Anglo-American Jurisprudence," 20 *Harvard Int'l Law J.* 61 (1979).

"Sorting the Revolutionary from the Terrorist: The Delicate Application of the 'Political Offense' Exception in U.S. Extradition Cases," 59 *Stanford Law Review* 181 (2006).

Molner, "Extradition: Limitation of the Political Offense Exception," 27 *Harvard Int'l L. J.* 266 (1986).

CASES

Cheng v. Governor of Pentonville Prison, A.C. 931 (H.L., 1973).

In re Ezeta, U.S. Dist. Court, N.D. Cal., 1894, 62 Fed. 972.

I.N.S. v. Aguirre-Aguirre, 526 U.S. 415 (1999), 121 F.3d 521.

In the Matter of Ktir, Switzerland, Supreme Federal Court, 1961, digested in 56 *AJIL* 224 (1962).

Ornelas v. Ruiz, U.S. Supreme Court, 1896, 161 U.S. 502.

Regina v. Governor of Brixton, ex Parte Kolcynski (Polish Seaman's case), 1 Q.B. 540 (1955).

Regina v. Governor of Brixton Prison, ex Parte Schtraks, 1 Q.B. (1963).

EICHMANN CASE

Attorney-General of the Government of Israel v. Eichmann, District Court of Jerusalem, December 11, 1961, excerpted at length in 56 *AJIL* 805 (1962); see *Israel Digest,* June 5, 1962, 1, for the summary of the dismissal (May 29, 1962) of Eichmann's appeal to the Supreme Court of Israel; see also *New York Times* (November 26, 1972), 14. Eichmann was executed by hanging on May 31, 1972.

Hausner, *Justice in Jerusalem* (1966).

Robinson, *And the Crooked Shall Be Made Straight* (1966).

Rogat, *The Eichmann Trial and the Rule of Law* (1961).

Whiteman, VI: 105.

INFORMAL EXTRADITION

Lowenfeld, "U.S. Law Enforcement Abroad: The Constitutional and International Law, Continued," 84 *AJIL* 444 (1990).

United States–Canada Agreement: Protocol of Amendment, 1988, in 82 *AJIL* 337 (1988), 399.

CASES

State v. Ebrahim, [1991] Supreme Court, South Africa (App. Div.) February 16, 1991, 2 *South African L.R.* 553(a), in 31 *ILM* 888 (1992) and 87 *AJIL* 133 (1993).

United States v. Alvarez-Machain, 504 U.S. 655 (1992).

State Responsibility: Responsibility for Injuries to Aliens

In 1985, French agents boarded the Greenpeace ship *Rainbow Warrior* while it stood moored in the harbor at Auckland, New Zealand.[1] They set explosive devices that sank the ship and killed one person on board. The *Rainbow Warrior* had come to New Zealand to take part in a planned protest against the open-air testing of nuclear weapons at Mururoa Atoll by the French government. Greenpeace had orchestrated a plan whereby the *Rainbow Warrior* would lead a large group of ships into the test area. By this action, they hoped to stop the test or to embarrass the French government if it carried out the test regardless of the potential damage. The resolution of this case, which we will discuss soon, illustrates many of the principles and problems we discussed in Chapter 3 concerning "enforcement." It also illustrates in broad form one set of issues connected with state responsibility.

Thus far we have tended to focus upon rights that states have as a matter of their statehood, but as Judge Huber concisely pointed out in the *Spanish Zone of Morocco* case,[2]

> [R]esponsibility is the necessary corollary of a right. All rights of an international character involve international responsibility. Responsibility results in the duty to make reparation if the obligation in question is not met. (Emphasis added)

This simple statement has extraordinarily complex implications. The International Law Commission (ILC) labored for over 50 years to produce a draft convention dealing with the issues related to state responsibility. To understand the political difficulties here, one only has to briefly review the history of the international system post 1945 and think about the problems of constructing a viable convention that would prove acceptable to the ideological rivals of the East–West conflict

---

[1]For a concise summary of the incident, see "New Zealand Disasters," http://library.christchurch.org.nz/Childrens/NZDisasters/RainbowWarrior.asp (accessed April 22, 2009).

[2]R.I.A.A. (1923), 641.

as well as to the emerging new states concerned about their rights as a defense against any possible challenge to their newfound independence (the "North–South" conflict).[3] The end of the Cold War resolved many controversies in this area, but others remain. We shall note them in this chapter as we address specific cases illustrating practice. Even though the ILC Draft Convention has not entered into force (see Chapter 4), it still gives us a good starting place for examining the *customary law* associated with state responsibility.

To understand the legal difficulties associated with producing the document, we need only examine the first three articles of the ILC Draft Convention on the Responsibility of States for Internationally Wrongful Acts:[4]

ARTICLE 1

Every internationally wrongful act of a State entails the international responsibility of that State.

ARTICLE 2

There is an internationally wrongful act of a State when conduct consisting of an *action or omission*:

a. Is attributable to the State under international law; and
b. Constitutes a breach of an international obligation of the State.

ARTICLE 3

The characterization of an act of a State as internationally wrongful is governed by *international law*. Such characterization is not affected by the characterization of the same act as lawful by internal law (Article 3). (Emphasis added)

A close reading of these passages points up three important considerations that everyone needs to grasp to understand the principles of state responsibility. First, *municipal law does not have a direct counterpart* because "responsibility" in the international context embraces *all* breaches of legal obligation, whether contained in treaties (bilateral or multilateral) or more generally in customary international law.[5] So we find grouped into this discussion incidents such as the *Rainbow Warrior* that involve violation of fundamental sovereign rights, other cases that involve violations of the rules governing international peace and security, still others that deal with alleged illegal expropriation of property held by foreign nationals, as well as other "denial of justice" claims based upon the modern idea of *diplomatic protection* (Chapter 8). One needs merely to review the myriad and diverse cases

---

[3]See S. N. G. Roy, "Is the Law of Responsibility of States a Part of Universal International Law?" 55 *American Journal of International Law* 866 (1961), for a discussion of this controversy.

[4]*Responsibility of States for Internationally Wrongful Acts*, adopted by the International Law Commission at its 53rd session (2001); see *Official Records of the General Assembly*, 56th session, Supplement No. 10 (A/56/10), chp.IV.E.1, www.un.org/law/ilc/texts/State_responsibility/responsibilityfra.htm (accessed April 22, 2009).

[5]Note, for example, that the ILC has also tackled the question of "liability" for injuries stemming from acts not prohibited by international law as a project separate from the state responsibility project.

discussed in the first few chapters of this book to see the breadth and complexity of the issues covered here.

Some writers have used the terms *responsibility* and *liability* interchangeably. We have resisted this because "state responsibility" as a breach of obligation on the one hand is much narrower than the idea of liability, which implies compensation for damage. For example, in municipal law, a liability may arise from the consequences of a perfectly legal but harmful act or from an accident.

On the other hand, state responsibility has aspects that are broader than strict definitions of "liability" in that redress (making the situation "whole" again) may not involve compensation at all in the ordinary sense of the word. Although we began with a case that illustrates a very high profile breach of fundamental principles, in most of this chapter we will deal with the everyday issues associated with *diplomatic protection*—primarily denial of justice—of citizens when engaged in business, travel, or other activities abroad. While these cases are not as exciting as a covert operation or outright attack, their resolutions furnish good examples of the "law in action."

The second important point, contained in Article 2, is that responsibility can stem not only from overt actions by a state but also from a *failure* of a state to act or exert control over events or persons (an *omission*) when it should have reasonably been expected to do so. Finally, Article 3 clearly states a principle we have alluded to several times in past chapters: *International law,* not municipal law, forms the basis of determination for an international wrong. A state may not evade responsibility for its conduct by pointing to a provision in its domestic legal code that validates its action.

CIRCUMSTANCES *PRECLUDING* WRONGFULNESS

Before discussing the questions associated with breaches, we need to note the circumstances that might preclude one state from invoking a claim involving responsibility against another. Chapter V of the ILC draft (Articles 20–25) lists and defines situations that exempt states from claims concerning responsibility: prior consent to the act, lawful acts of self-defense (see Chapter 19), countermeasures against a wrongful act by another state, force majeure (events clearly beyond the control of the state), and distress. The convention permits a plea of necessity only if the action in question is the *only* way of safeguarding a vital interest (Article 25(a)) and does not "seriously impair an essential interest of the State or States towards which the obligation exists, or of the international community as a whole" (Article 25(b)). States may still be required to pay compensation for any damage caused by the act (Article 27(b)).

THE *RAINBOW WARRIOR*

Acting on the basis of an anonymous tip in the wake of the explosion that destroyed the *Rainbow Warrior,*[6] New Zealand authorities detained a couple traveling on Swiss passports on the charge of violating immigration laws. New Zealand authorities

---

[6]For a narrative and chronology, see www.greenpeace.org/international/rainbow-warrior-bombing/spy-story/spy-story-2/spy-story-3/spy-story-4 and www.kauricoast.co.nz/Feature.cfm?WPID=70 (both accessed April 22, 2009).

also traced the explosives used in a chartered yacht, the *Ouvea,* which had a crew of French nationals. Before authorities could arrest the crew, the *Ouvea* sailed and was never seen again. Soon, the French media began to suggest a link between the French secret service (DGSE) and the bombing—an allegation that French President François Mitterand openly and categorically denied. President Mitterand promised full cooperation and punishment of those involved if the allegations proved to be true.

The "Swiss" couple proved to be two high-ranking agents of DGSE, as did members of the *Ouvea*'s crew. Two months after the bombing, the French government admitted complicity. Direct talks between the two governments failed to produce a satisfactory agreement. The secretary-general of the United Nations (Javier Pérez de Cuéllar) then agreed to mediate the dispute. Eventually, the French agreed to pay New Zealand NZ$ 13 million and Greenpeace, USA,$ 8 million, and issued a public apology.

The story does not end here. The two French agents in custody pled guilty to manslaughter and arson charges. They received sentences of 10 years for manslaughter and 7 years for arson, with the sentences to run concurrently. Responding to pressure from the French public, the French government demanded the return of the two agents to France. When New Zealand refused, the French instituted an embargo against a wide range of New Zealand products. As part of the mediated agreement, the two convicted agents were tranferred to the island of Hao (under French control) with the understanding that they would serve a minimum of three years. Within a year, one agent returned to France, ostensibly for medical treatment; the other returned to France less than a year later, presumably because her father was terminally ill. France ignored all protests from New Zealand. When New Zealand attempted to extradite another French agent involved in the plot from Switzerland (1991), France again applied economic pressure until New Zealand dropped the effort.

Reparations and Redress

What does this case say about reparation or redress of the breach that occurred? Several points need elaboration to illustrate the complexity of the problem. First, perception based upon the assumptions we make about appropriate punishment plays a great role here in assessing the outcome. Instinctively, due to the nature of the act, the assumptions and processes associated with municipal criminal law spring to mind. Yet we need to keep one important point in mind here. This case, because of its high profile and connection to vital interests, was not resolved through an independent court using legal methods of search, discovery, and application (see Chapters 1 and 5). As with most disputes between states that involve fundamental principles, the key players here were not judges (although lawyers probably were involved as advisers) but political officials who have quite different modes of search, discovery, and application regarding applicable rules and acceptable outcomes. Many courses of action will affect others as well as the decision makers' own state. Political advisers must take into account the attitudes of allies, adversaries, internal constituencies, and onlookers about what constitutes permissible conduct within the parameters of a specific incident. Will a particular course of action incur approval, acquiescence, or resistance from other states, and which states will utilize the foregoing judgments and in what manner? State officials seldom have the luxury of considering a high-profile incident in strictly legal terms because it does not occur in isolation from other events. Any action will have other repercussions and consequences depending upon the choice of response.

Second, because we do tend to focus on the domestic criminal law paradigm in cases such as the *Rainbow Warrior,* and because the incident certainly involved criminal acts, we often overlook the fact that in many cases involving breach of contract in municipal law, the solution relies upon what the parties negotiate and are willing to accept in terms of satisfaction. Abstract ideas of *retributive* justice give way to pragmatic concerns of what is possible and what is desirable given the circumstances. Third, even if we do rely upon domestic criminal law as our model, consider the mediation effort as the equivalent of an international plea bargain: *France publicly acknowledged guilt,* allocuted to the circumstances, and paid compensation. Even so, from a criminal law perspective and from a subjective point of view, the seeming lack of punishment for the individuals involved raises questions. France did not honor the bargain in full and used the power of the state to pressure New Zealand to return the agents to France.

Claims and Adjudication

States make demands for redress in the form of a *claim,* or formal demand for action to address the breach of obligation. As the discussion of the methods of dispute resolution in Chapter 5 illustrates, states may resolve claims in many different ways, from direct negotiation to submission to an international tribunal. Many of the cases we discuss later come from arbitration or diplomatic correspondence (direct negotiation). If an incident results in a large number of mutual claims, the states may set up a Claims Commission. The United States and Iran established such a commission in 1981 to deal with claims arising out of the events surrounding the 1979 seizure of the American embassy in Teheran. The Commission had the charge of dealing with both claims between the states parties as well as claims by nationals of one state party against the other state party. To date, it has settled over 3,900 claims.[7]

A second example is the Eritrea–Ethiopia Claims Commission for incidents arising from the armed conflict between the two states (1998–2000). Set up under the auspices of the Permanent Court of Arbitration, the statement of purpose (compromis) for the commission serves as a good summary of what such commissions seek to accomplish. The compromis instructs the commission to

> [d]ecide through binding arbitration all claims for loss, damage or injury by one Government against the other, and by nationals (including both natural and juridical persons) of one party against the Government of the other party

---

[7]Iran–United States Claims Tribunal, www.iusct.org/english/.

or entities owned or controlled by the other party that are (a) related to the conflict that was the subject of the Framework Agreement, the Modalities for its Implementation and the Cessation of Hostilities Agreement, and (b) result from violations of international humanitarian law, including the 1949 Geneva Conventions, or other violations of international law.[8]

The commission has dealt with cases that involved[9]

- Damage and injury to respective diplomatic missions
- Economic loss
- Violation of the jus ad bellum (Chapter 20)
- Loss, injury, and other damage for serial bombardment and displacement of civilians
- Prisoners of war

The commission has made a number of findings of significance with respect to the use of force and the rules of warfare. On substantive law, these have included "an elaboration of what provisions of existing agreements on international humanitarian law have become part of customary law; guidance on the application of various norms to wartime circumstances, such as target selection, treatment of prisoners, and actions against civilian property and economic activity; findings on the applicability in wartime of peacetime treaties and human rights norms; and the lawfulness of the use of force in connection with boundary disputes."[10] The commission has also made substantial contributions to procedural matters. These include the adoption of a standard of proof for serious allegations, a balanced approach toward the use of various forms of evidence, guidance on handling of allegations of rape, and proactive attitude toward resolving factual disputes.[11] We will deal with the cases from a Mexican–American Mixed Claims Commission at the end of this chapter.

Standards and Procedures for Claims   Whether states resort to negotiation, arbitration, or other forms of adjudication, a claim must still conform to certain requirements in order to go forward as a viable demand. Many texts refer to these requirements as *preliminary objections;* but that term simply describes the *validation process* through which a claim must pass in order for it to be addressed on its substantive merits. The requirements for a valid claim include (1) nationality, (2) exhaustion of local remedies, (3) nonwaiver, and (4) no unreasonable delay in presenting the case. Some texts may mention a *fifth* requirement: States may not press a claim if the injury results from improper behavior on behalf of the injured national. This "requirement" has an interesting and controversial element we will

---

[8]Agreement Between the Government of the Federal Democratic Republic of Ethiopia and the Government of the State of Eritrea, Algiers (December 12, 2000), www.pca-cpa.org/upload/files/Algiers%20Agreement.pdf.

[9]Eritrea–Ethiopia Claims Commission, www.pca-cpa.org/showpage.asp?pag_id=1151.

[10]M. J. Matheson, "Eritrea-Ethiopia Claims Commission: Damage Awards," ASIL Insights (September 4, 2009), www.asil.org/insights090904.cfm.

[11]Idem.

address later. While it seems obvious on its face, as with many "obvious" (commonsense) propositions, the devil does often lurk in the details of application.

The most fundamental principle is that the injured party must have the *nationality* of the claimant state (see Chapter 9).[12] This includes companies as well as individuals. The *Rainbow Warrior* incident had one casualty—Fernando Pereira, a naturalized citizen of the Netherlands (originally born in Portugal). New Zealand had an absolute right to arrest and prosecute those associated with the bomb plot because it took place within its territorial jurisdiction. New Zealand had an absolute right to file a claim against France for reparation of the breach and demand compensation for any damage suffered to itself due to the nature of the act. Yet New Zealand did not have standing to file a claim for compensation from France on behalf of Mr. Pereira and his heirs, even though it happened within the jurisdiction of New Zealand. This principle has such a firm basis that we can find *no* instances of exception in published practice.[13]

Second, injured aliens must first seek redress through local courts or other appropriate institutions before appealing to their government to espouse a claim (Article 44). The origin of this rule is unclear, but it seems born of pragmatism.[14] This procedural rule has two consequences. It requires the accused state to address the allegation of breach through its own institutions and keeps low-level or trivial disputes from cluttering up otherwise friendly relations between states. The exceptions to this rule come when "there is no justice to exhaust"[15] or when, as in the *Rainbow Warrior,* the requirement would provide no meaningful procedural outlet other than state-to-state negotiation or an agreed alternative. In the first

---

[12]See Hackworth, V: 802; Moore, VI: 628. Concerning the requirement of the nationality of the claimant state at the time the injury occurred, see the valuable collection of facts and documents by Myers, "Nationality of Claims," 908, in his "Contemporary Practice of the United States Relating to International Law," 53 *AJIL* 896 (1959); "United States-Israel Claims Settlement" (1980), reported in 75 *AJIL* 368 (1981). For cases illustrating the nationality aspect of the claimant, see *United States (Agency of Canadian Car & Foundry Co.) v. Germany,* United States–Germany, Mixed Claims Commission, 1939, digested in Hackworth, V: 833; and *United States (Romano-American Claim) v. Great Britain* in Hackworth, V: 702–705, 840–844.

[13]But we should call attention to Article 8c of the 1992 Treaty on European Union, which states that every person holding the nationality of a member state (hence, a citizen of the EU) may receive diplomatic protection by the diplomatic or consular authority of any member state in the territory of any third state where his or her country of nationality has not established diplomatic or consular representation. As you might have concluded from Chapter 9, individuals with dual nationality may pose special problems.

[14]See "Articles," n. 2, no. 22; See *The Panevevezys-Saldutiskis Railway Case (Estonia v. Lithuania),* Permanent Court of International Justice (*PCIJ*), Ser. A/B, No. 76 (1939), and its coverage by Hudson, 34 *AJIL* 1 (1940); Court of Justice, *Elettronica Sicula S.p.A. (ELSI) (United States v. Italy),* 1989 *ICJ Rep.* 15, in 28 *International Legal Materials* 1109 (1989); F. A. Mann, "Foreign Investment in the International Court of Justice: The *ELSI* Case," 86 *AJIL* 92 (1992); Expropriation Claims, "Exhaustion of Local Remedies and External Measures," 84 *AJIL* 887 (1990).

[15]See A. A. C. Trindade, *The Application of the Rule of Exhaustion of Local Remedies in International Law* 127 (1983). But see the *Case of Elettronica Sicula S.p.A. (ELSI) (United States v. Italy),* International Court of Justice, July 20, 1989, [1989] *ICJ Rep.* 15, in 28 *ILM* 1109 (1989); digested in 84 *AJIL* 249 (1990), in which the Court's panel held that the plaintiff had sufficiently exhausted all local remedies for the claim to be admissible. Also see M. W. Ennis, "Exhaustion of Local Remedies and External Measures," 84 *AJIL* 887 (1990).

instance, if the legislature had enacted a law (or the government had practiced a policy) that barred all foreigners from access to domestic courts with respect to any alleged injury, there would be no point in resorting to local remedies. In the second instance, the rights associated with statehood (states as equals) imply a principle of equality—often expressed as "dignity and respect"—that with regard to incidents such as the *Rainbow Warrior,* states do not have to exhaust "local" remedies. As a hypothetical exercise, can you imagine New Zealand initiating a suit in any French court where New Zealand alleges that a French covert operation violated its sovereign rights?

Third, a state may not explicitly or implicitly (by reason of its conduct) waive the right to file a claim and then later decide to pursue the claim (Article 45). One important fact needs emphasizing here. The right to file a claim, even when the claim is made on behalf of an individual or a company, belongs to the state, not to the individual or the company. An individual or a company has no right to waive the right of their state of nationality to claim for an injury. Conversely, the duty of the state alleged to have violated a right is owed to the claiming state, not to the individual or company. In this respect, the alien's national state has total discretion. It may refrain from filing at all, or it may settle the claim in any manner it considers satisfactory to its own interests. Note the following statement by the Federal Department of Foreign Affairs of Switzerland:

The state is entirely free to extend diplomatic protection or refuse it. International law places the state under no obligation to extend diplomatic protection to its nationals, and nor does any provision on Swiss law confer any such right on the individual. The sole restriction on the Federation's discretionary powers is the prohibition of the arbitrary use of power.[16]

This last point becomes important because during the nineteenth and early twentieth centuries, many Latin American states included a *Calvo clause*[17] in agreements (particularly concession agreements) with foreign companies and individuals. The Calvo clause provided that domestic courts would always be the final arbiter in all disputes concerning the contractual arrangements. Use of the Calvo clause was an obvious attempt to preclude diplomatic intervention. The argument turned on a simple assertion that foreigners should not have more rights than nationals. If nationals had to accept the results of the local court system, then certainly so should aliens. The use of the Calvo clause had little effect *because individuals cannot sign away rights they do not possess.*[18] The right of protection belongs to the state, *not* to the individual. This may be one instance where a lack of rights actually works to the advantage of an individual.

Fourth, the requirement of expeditious attention in terms of submitting a claim needs little elaboration, even though no precise standard exists that clearly defines *unreasonable delay.* As with many other standards, "reasonableness in context"

---

[16]Confédération suisse, Federal Department of Foreign Affairs, www.eda.admin.ch/eda/en/home/topics/intla/cintla/dicopr/dipr.html.

[17]This clause is named for Carlos Calvo (1824–1906), an Argentinian diplomat who originated the idea.

[18]See R. Dolzer, "New Foundations of the Law of Expropriation of Alien Property," 75 *AJIL* 553 (1981), 560.

seems to furnish the relevant parameters. Nonetheless, one should understand that the requirements refer to *submission* of a claim. As we shall see later in this chapter, resolving a claim may take many years.

Reasonableness in context still leaves open the question of injury as the result of improper behavior. On its face, excluding instances where someone suffers injury while engaged in wrongdoing seems an obvious requirement. Yet standards of punishment for various kinds of offenses vary widely among states. The widely publicized cases of a severe caning (Singapore) of an American teenager for a graffiti and vandalism incident, the imposition of the death penalty on another teenager (a citizen of the United Kingdom) in Malaysia for drug trafficking, or very lengthy prison terms (up to 50 years) for firearms and other drug-related offenses (Thailand)[19] do raise issues of proportionality. We will explore some of these issues later in this chapter and others in Chapter 15 on human rights.

Injury to Aliens

Few areas in the international law of peace have evoked more numerous and more controversial questions than have the relations between a state and nonnationals who are residing in or visiting its territory. As globalization has proceeded apace, so have immigration and travel. In its broader aspects, this sphere of the law applies to the safety and security of foreign citizens living or visiting in a given state, to contractual agreements concluded between a state and the citizens of foreign countries, and to the status and security of any property legally possessed by aliens located in a given country. *Sovereignty* means that each state has the sole authority to determine on what basis it will admit aliens and the extent to which aliens thus admitted will enjoy certain *civil* rights within its jurisdiction. Clearly, foreign nationals should not expect the right to vote in elections, hold elective office, have the opportunity to compete for certain types of jobs (particularly those in government service), or even enter and engage in certain occupations. On the other hand, beyond those *permissive* grants, states have a duty to respect that each alien, as a foreign national (and as a human being), has certain fundamental rights both as to person and to property. It is primarily in connection with those basic rights that a responsibility by the host state arises. In this sphere, claims originate and, under certain conditions, may be advanced against the host state by the government to which the alien owes allegiance.

Jurisdiction Over Alien Persons

Right of Exclusion and Deportation   The exercise of territorial jurisdiction over aliens represents a logical consequence of the possession of sovereignty or independence by states. Each country is free to exclude or to admit aliens. The determination

---

[19]For example, possession of 20 grams or more of any Class A drug at a Thai exit point is classed as trafficking. If defendant is found guilty, the death sentence may be given. In Thailand, amphetamines and ecstasy are both considered Class A drugs. M. Aquino, "Harsh Punishments for Drug Use in Southeast Asia," About.com, http://goseasia.about.com/od/travelplanning/a/seasia_drugs.htm (accessed May 5, 2009).

of the principles to be applied in this connection is of purely domestic concern. Concurrent with the right of exclusion goes an equally unfettered right of each state to expel not only any alien who has illegally gained entry into its territory but also any alien whose conduct, after legal entry, is deemed prejudicial to public order and security. Deportation of such unwanted aliens normally is made to their home state. The latter may refuse admission to such deportees. The usual reasons for such rejection center on the stateless character of some of the individuals in question or, even more commonly, on their criminal record.[20] Because deportation of aliens is not a criminal proceeding—at least not in the United States—the ex post facto doctrine is not applicable. Congress has an unquestioned right to legislate retroactively in order to provide legal standing for the expulsion of aliens for the commission of offenses that did not render them subject to deportation when the offenses were committed.[21]

Status of Aliens   Under normal conditions, aliens traveling through or residing in a given state enjoy no special privileges because of their alien status. They cannot claim any substantive rights greater than those of the citizens of their host state and, indeed, lack any special political or civil rights reserved for the latter by their own state. Likewise, aliens normally must use the same courts and the same legal procedures utilized by the local citizens in seeking redress for injuries or wrongs suffered by them. The laws of the host state protect aliens to the same degree that they protect the local citizens, subject to any existing legal limitations on the aliens' property and contract rights. Thus, if a given state should prohibit the ownership by aliens of uranium mines, a citizen of a foreign country, residing in the state in question, could not find judicial relief in the courts of the host state if he or she tried to acquire ownership of such a mine and was blocked in such endeavors.

Aliens legally admitted to the territorial jurisdiction of a state may, of course, be punished for any offenses they commit on the territory of the host state or on ships or aircraft registered in that state. As we discussed in Chapter 9, diplomatic protection extends only so far. One should take specific note of the following statement taken from the website of the U.S. Mission to Turkey: "While the Embassy is permitted to provide basic diplomatic and consular protections to incarcerated Americans, Consular Officers cannot interfere with the Turkish legal system."[22] They may be tried and punished for having, anywhere, counterfeited its currency, postage stamps, or official documents. Any state may try and then punish an alien in its territory for a crime, wherever it may have been committed, constituting piracy under the law of nations. A state may prosecute and punish aliens within its territory for a crime, regardless of its location, against its independence or security (see Chapter 10).

---

[20]*Caranica v. Nagle,* U.S. Ct. of Appeals, 9th Cir., 1928, 28 F. (2d) 955; but see *Narenji v. Civiletti,* U.S. Ct. of Appeals, D.C. Cir. (1979), 617 F.2d 745, analyzed by Kraiem in *Note* (Iranian Students in U.S.), 21 *Harvard Int'l L.J.* 467 (1980).

[21]See *Lehmann v. United States ex rel. Carson,* U.S. Supreme Court, 1957, 353 U.S. 685; and *Mulcahey v. Catalanotte,* U.S. Supreme Court, 1957, 353 U.S. 692.

[22]http://ankara.usembassy.gov/CONSULAR/ACSDRUG.HTM.

Similarly, aliens do not enjoy privileged status regarding taxes. If, however, a state does impose some form of discriminatory tax against aliens, an international claim may be lodged against it by the state whose citizens suffered the discrimination. In the past, such discrimination often was prohibited through specific provisions found in commercial and other treaties. General practice now would support a conclusion that a rule of customary international law protects aliens against discriminatory taxation—even though they are not protected against possible double taxation—by their host state and their own government, in the absence of contrary agreements.[23]

The question then arises, what does the right of diplomatic protection entail if it does not permit "direct interference"? To answer this question, we must introduce and discuss three additional topics—the definitions of *imputability* and *denial of justice,* and the idea that international law supports an *international minimum standard of justice.*

Imputability   In ordinary circumstances, actions by private individuals do not engage the responsibility of a state. However, trite as the proposition may sound, a state is responsible only for *its own actions or omissions.* Sometimes overlooked, omissions comprise situations where the state (government) failed to act when it had a duty to do so. The question becomes the process through which an act or an omission may be attributable to the state. Conduct of any organ or agency of a state, or of any official, employee, or other agent of a state, that causes injury to an alien clearly is attributable to the state if it is within the real or apparent authority or functions of such state agency or an individual agent of the state. The current ILC Draft Convention (Article 7) also includes harmful acts by state agents that may exceed their formal authority (acts *ultra vires*). The question involves the process through which an action may formally be attributed to the state. The technical name for this process is *imputability.* Imputability means the *legal* assignment of a particular act by a person or group of persons to a state or some other entity that has international legal personality for the purpose of determining responsibility. This concept and its procedural components provide the means for determining which acts may be attributable to the state.

Denial of Justice   You have had your pocket picked on the Via Veneto in Rome, or during Carnival in Rio, and have had to join the other frustrated tourists and locals standing in a long line on a very hot day to file a complaint with the local police, who seem thoroughly indifferent (and with a "prickly" attitude). When nothing further happens from your complaint, do you have a case of "denial of justice" that would engage the responsibility of Italy or Brazil? In the first instance, please consider that for your pocket-picking incident to become the subject of an international claim, you will first have to satisfy the exhaustion of local remedies criterion. What would it take for you to hang around long enough to determine that authorities have made no progress on your complaint or simply for you to take the time and effort to monitor their progress once you return home? Even then, would your state file a claim if you failed to gain satisfaction? The answer is probably not. A simple cost–benefit

---

[23]See Travers, "The Constitutional Status of State and Federal Governmental Discrimination Against Resident Aliens," 16 *Harvard Int'l L.J.* 113 (1975); *In re Griffiths,* U.S. Supreme Court 1973, 93 S. Ct. 2851; and *Sugarman v. Dougall,* 413 U.S. 634 (1973).

calculation should quickly convince you that states will undertake action only when serious breaches occur or when broader principles are at stake (review *Norwegian State v. Carlile* in Chapter 9). Petty crime happens almost everywhere as a matter of course. Can you imagine the amount of time and effort a state might have to invest if it chose to press these claims? Would states jeopardize otherwise friendly relations and expend the monies to file numerous claims that involve only a few hundred dollars each? Consider, in this respect, the discussion in Chapter 1 of the landlord who evicts a delinquent tenant. Context, that is circumstances, is important. Reasonably no state can provide an absolute guarantee of safety in all situations.

In different circumstances, what if as an alien you are exposed to an openly oppressive or discriminatory law or encounter a clearly unfair administration of a law? What if you as a foreign national were seeking redress for an injury in the courts of the host state, were denied access, or were clearly discriminated against because you are an alien? Or what if you as an alien were being prosecuted for a violation of local law and singled out for disproportionate punishment? What if state officials openly condone attacks on foreign nationals, particularly nationals from a specific country? In these instances, a denial of justice has occurred. Such incidents may justify a claim by the alien's state of nationality on his or her behalf, to secure appropriate redress. To return to a point made earlier, while the original injurious actions of private individuals may have resulted in injury, these are not directly imputable to the state. It is the failure (an omission) of the state to take action to redress the situation, punish individuals responsible, or provide reasonable means to do so that engage a state's responsibility.

Denial of justice—or, more correctly, *denial of procedural justice*—is a much disputed term, often used imprecisely. In the sense that we will use it in this discussion, the term refers to any failure by the authorities of the host state to provide adequate means of redress to the alien when his or her substantive rights have suffered injury. If the alien has violated the laws of the host state, the state has a duty to observe due process of law in the prosecution and punishment of the alien offender. A broad interpretation of the term would expand its meaning to include such matters as denial of access to the local courts, inefficiency in the performance of police and judicial processes, or an obviously unfair treatment or judicial decision. But a word of caution is necessary: The real question in a "denial of justice" has usually been whether a state was responsible internationally for some particular act or some specific omission of an act, which under international law (1) was wrongful, (2) was imputable, and (3) caused an injury to an alien.

Minimum International Standard of Justice   Clearly, standards of justice and the treatment of citizens by their governments vary considerably from country to country. Many governments, proceeding from the assumption that aliens have entered their jurisdiction voluntarily, have asserted that the aliens should receive no special favors. They must take things as they find them. This attitude raises the question, Is there a minimum standard below which no civilized state would or should go?

Until just after World War II, Latin American states tended to resist the idea of any minimum standard—a stance also adopted by the newly emergent states in the 1960s and 1970s. The United States, Great Britain, and other Western countries have insisted for many decades that such a minimum standard exists. This view is shared by a number of international arbitration tribunals.[24] As Elihu Root, the distinguished American jurist, once stated:

> If any country's system of law and administration does not conform to that standard, although the people of the country may be content and compelled to live under it, no other country can be compelled to accept it as furnishing a satisfactory measure of treatment to its citizens.[25]

Without a governing multilateral treaty, the rights of aliens may be found in the customary law, as was pointed out in *Hines v. Davidowitz et al.* (U.S. Supreme Court, 1941, 312 U.S. 52):

> Apart from treaty obligations, there has grown up in the field of international relations a body of customs defining with more or less certainty the duties owing by all nations to alien residents—duties which our State Department has often successfully insisted foreign nations must recognize as to our nationals abroad. In general, both treaties and international practices have been aimed at preventing injurious discrimination against aliens.

Questions about its existence notwithstanding, from our perspective the more important questions concern the exact requirements of the international minimum standard. This forms a matter of considerable dispute. As we noted in the chapter on jurisdiction (Chapter 10), states tend to be very protective and sensitive in matters of domestic legal procedure. The case of Michael Fay, an American teenager convicted of vandalism of cars in Singapore, illustrates this attitude. When the U.S. government voiced concerns about the harshness of Fay's sentence (six lashes of a rattan cane, four months in prison, and a fine), Singapore's minister of home affairs publicly said that, as a crime-ridden society, the United States should not seek to impose its standards on others. He noted, "It is absurd that societies so stricken with crime should attempt to apply their standards on us and teach us what to do."[26]

Still, consider that some minimum standards must exist. If not, states could justify almost any abuse of aliens on the basis that their own citizens receive the same treatment; thus, aliens should have no complaint. We believe that the closest approach to definition of a minimum standard of justice comes from the Uni-

---

[24]See Foreign Claims Settlement Commission (U.S.), Decision No. W-16119, *In the Matter of the Claim of Hugo Schlessinger and Eugene Schlessinger* (December 7, 1966), excerpted in 61 *AJIL* 823 (1967). See also the *Harry Roberts Claim (United States v. Mexico),* General Claims Commission, 1926 [1927], 4 *U.N. Rep. Int'l Arb. Awards* 77.

[25]Presidential Address, *Proceedings, American Society of International Law* (1910), 20.

[26]Associated Press Wire, April 23, 1994. Consider the following as well from "Europeans Seek to Halt Execution of Scot":

> European religious leaders and politicians, outraged by the execution sentence imposed on 29-year-old Kenneth Richey, a native of Scotland, denounced the U.S. state of Ohio's death penalty law as barbaric. While U.S. President Bill Clinton recently appealed to the government of Singapore to reconsider the flogging sentence of an Ohio teenager convicted of vandalism there, the European Parliament, which governs the European Union, passed a resolution urging U.S. authorities to stop Richey's execution. After 20 years on death row, a federal appeals court overturned the conviction in August 2007. Richey then accepted a plea bargain that essentially reduced his sentence to time served. "Kenneth Richey to Be Released after 20 Years on Death Row," TimeOnline (December 19, 2007), www.timesonline.co.uk/tol/news/uk/article3075159.ece (accessed May 4, 2009).

versal Declaration of Human Rights, adopted by the General Assembly of the United Nations on December 10, 1948. Significantly, the states of Latin America—traditionally opposed to the concept of a minimum standard—approved the American Declaration of the Rights and Duties of Man at the Ninth International Conference of American States at Bogotá in 1948. This declaration closely parallels the UN instrument. Still, one should consider the operational standard used by the commissioners in the *Neer*[27] claim (see further discussion following):

> The treatment of an alien, in order to constitute an international delinquency should amount to an outrage, to bad faith, to wilful neglect of duty or to an insufficiency of action so far short of international standards that every reasonable and impartial man would readily recognize its insufficiency.

Diplomatic Protection

To return to our earlier question about how one might define and delimit the concept of *diplomatic protection,* note that while the U.S. Embassy in Ankara may not intervene directly in Turkish legal proceedings involving an American citizen, it can and will assist in finding appropriate legal counsel and observe the process to ensure that no violation of rights under Turkish (or international) law occurs. The Permanent Court of International Justice (PCIJ) noted:[28]

> [B]y taking up the case of one of its subjects and by resorting to diplomatic action or international judicial proceedings on his behalf, a state is in reality asserting its own rights, its right to ensure, in the person of its subjects, respect for the rules of international law.

In light of this observation, consider the *Carlile* case (Chapter 9). It may appear at first glance somewhat trivial, but the claim upholds an important and fundamental principle of jurisdiction and furnishes a basic example of what "protection" may entail. While Carlile would not seem a person whom any state would wish to "protect," to reiterate the point made earlier, the issue is not Carlile's character, but the potential jeopardy that might attach to other British citizens (or other aliens) if Norway proceeded with the prosecution.

MIXED CLAIMS COMMISSIONS

Any discussion of the treatment of aliens must involve an explanation of one of the major means to settle claims for injuries to those aliens—the Mixed Claims Commission. The United States originated the practice of establishing mixed claims commissions through the Jay Treaty with Great Britain. Since then many other such commissions have been created, such as the one between the United States and Germany about World War I claims and the one between the United States and Italy after World War II. One of the most important, mentioned earlier, in terms of the amount of money and the number of claims involved, was the Iran–

---

[27]*United States (L.F. Neer) v. United Mexican States* (1926), 4 R.I.A.A., 61–62 (Mexico-U.S. General Claims Commission).

[28]*Mavrommatis Palestine Concessions Case,* PCIJ, Ser. A, No. 2 (1924), 12.

United States Claims Tribunal established to deal with claims stemming from the situation that occurred after the seizure of the U.S. Embassy in Tehran in 1979. We have also discussed the Eritrea–Ethiopia Claims Commission.

For our purposes, however, we will draw mainly from decisions of the Mexico–U.S. General Claims Commission because of the range of issues covered with respect to denial of justice. In 1923, the United States and Mexico agreed to set up a General Claims Commission in an effort to improve relations between the two countries. The commission had the form of an arbitral panel that would issue binding decisions in settlement of claims for losses or damages "originating from acts of officials or others acting for either government and resulting in injustice" allegedly suffered by nationals of either country after July 4, 1868.[29] The commission had three members: an American national (Edwin Parker, then replaced by Fred Kenelm Nielsen), a neutral (Cornelius van Vollenhoven, the Netherlands), and a Mexican national (Genaro Fernandez MacGregor). The commission met from 1924 to 1931 in both Washington, DC, and Mexico City.

Due Diligence

In the *Alabama Claims* case discussed in Chapter 5, the commissioners used the standard of *due diligence*. The United States claimed injury because Great Britain had not exercised sufficient care in observing its duties as a neutral. While this idea may seem a vague standard in the abstract, like many "operational criteria" that form the connection between the abstract standard and the actual incident, it becomes much clearer within the context of the event. In the following two cases, *imputability* depends upon an assessment of the "due diligence" displayed by authorities in dealing with the events in question. Local remedies had been exhausted because no further action by any agency could have altered the situation.

▶ **JANES CLAIM**

United States (Laura M. B. Janes Claim) v. United Mexican States United States–Mexico, General Claims Commission, 1926 (Opinions of Commissioners, 1927, 108)

Facts

Byron E. Janes, American superintendent of the El Tigre Mine at El Tigre, Sonora, Mexico, was shot to death at that location on July 10, 1918, by Pedro Carbajal, a discharged employee of the El Tigre Mining Co. The killing occurred in view of many persons living near the company office. The local police chief was informed of Janes's death within five minutes and came at once.

(*continued*)

---

[29]This agreement excluded from the jurisdiction of the General Claims Commission cases stemming from events related to revolutions or disturbed conditions in Mexico. Mexico and the United States constituted a separate Special Claims Commission to address claims arising from incidents that occurred between November 20, 1910, and May 31, 1920.

However, he delayed the assembling of his men, and then a further delay occurred because of his insistence on a mounted posse. An hour after the shooting, the posse left in pursuit of the murderer, who had hurried away on foot.

The posse found no trace of Carbajal. He remained at large even though he stayed at a ranch some 6 miles from El Tigre for a week and, so it was rumored, visited the village twice during that period. A later report had the fugitive at a mescal plant 75 miles south of El Tigre. When the Mexican civilian and military authorities were informed of this news, they took no steps to capture Carbajal until the mining company offered a reward. Then they sent a small military detachment to the mescal plant, but Carbajal had left before the soldiers arrived. Mexican authorities took no further steps beyond circulation among the judges of first instance in the State of Sonora of a request for the arrest of the fugitive killer.

Issues

Were the authorities of Sonora guilty of a lack of due diligence in the pursuit and apprehension of the killer of Byron Janes? If so, did that lack constitute a denial of justice that would engage the international responsibility of Mexico?

Decision

The General Claims Commission decided that there had been a proven case of lack of due diligence and awarded the United States, on behalf of Mrs. Janes and her children, a sum of $12,000.

Reasoning

The Mexican government was liable for not having measured up to its duty of diligently pursuing and properly punishing the offender (in both cases, through its official agents in the State of Sonora). The commissioners found the actions of local authorities displayed "a remarkable lack" of intelligent investigation.

In contrast with the Janes claim, in which the commissioners found that an appalling lack of due diligence resulted in an attribution of responsibility to the Mexican state, the following case shows what happens when reasonable diligence is exercised *given the context* of the events.

UNITED STATES (L. F. H. NEER CLAIM) V. UNITED MEXICAN STATES

United States–Mexico, General Claims Commission, 1926 Opinions of Commissioners, 1927, 71

Facts

Paul Neer, an American citizen, was superintendent of a mine near Guanacevi, State of Durango, Mexico. On November 16, 1924, about 8 P.M., when he and his wife were riding from the village to their

nearby home, they were stopped by a group of armed men. After exchanging a few words with Neer, they engaged in a gunfight in which the American was killed.

Mrs. Neer summoned help, and the village authorities went to the scene of the killing

(continued)

on the night it took place. On the following morning the local judge examined some witnesses, including Mrs. Neer. Several days passed during which a number of suspects were arrested but released subsequently due to lack of evidence. The investigation lagged because Mrs. Neer was unable to supply a detailed description of the members of the group that had been involved in the affair.

Issues

Did the actions of Mexican authorities meet any standard of due diligence? If not, was the violation of sufficient magnitude to engage the international responsibility of Mexico?

Decision

The commission rejected the American claim.

Reasoning

The commission agreed that local authorities might have acted more

vigorously in seeking to apprehend the culprits in the slaying of Neer. However, the commission also recognized that the local authorities were handicapped because Mrs. Neer, the only prosecution eyewitness to the murder, had not overheard the exchange of words between Neer and his killers, nor could she supply the authorities with any other helpful information, such as a description of the individuals involved.

In view of the steps taken by the authorities, the commission held that whatever lack of vigor had been displayed did not constitute a lack of diligence serious enough to charge the Mexican government with an international delinquency.

Note

Review the statement of the commissioners cited in this case, and then consider that statement with respect to the Chattin claim, discussed later.

A third classic case, the Youmans claim,[30] presents a slightly different set of circumstances. The Youmans claim also illustrates the complexity of many cases. The Janes and Neer claims present a relatively narrowly bounded set of considerations. In the *Youmans* case, Mexican troops that were sent to resolve a mob attack against three Americans actually joined the mob, resulting in the death and mutilation of all three. Local authorities did begin court action against 29 members of the mob. Eighteen of them were arrested. Several were then released on nominal bail with no further proceedings taken against them. Trials in absentia did occur for five persons, who were sentenced to death. Subsequently, the sentences were commuted. This had no real effect—one person had died in the meantime, and the other four had left town before they were even arrested. In other actual trials, seven were acquitted; the cases against six others discontinued. Charges against some others remained open as late as 1887, seven years after the riot had taken place, but this seemed only a formality considering previous action in the case.

First, the question centered on the action of the Mexican troops sent to disperse the mob and protect the Americans. These were official agents of the Mexican government, dispatched under specific instructions. Their actions clearly violated any expectation of "due diligence" in protection. Second, in the aftermath, did Mexican authorities proceed in a manner that indicated a positive resolve to punish those involved (including the soldiers)? The General Claims Commission

---

[30]*United States (T. H. Youmans Claim) v. United Mexican States,* United States–Mexico General Claims Commission, 1926 (Opinions of Commissioners, 1927), 150.

decided that the Mexican government had to assume responsibility for the failure to protect Youmans, and then for not taking proper steps to apprehend and punish the guilty parties (including the troops) for failing in their duty and instructions.

The next case considered raises a number of issues. Frequently, a charge of denial of justice forms the basis of a claim against a state when an alien is brought to court and later claims irregularity in proceedings, cruel treatment, or a clearly unjust sentence. The following case, despite its bizarre elements, may illustrate some of the meanings of denial of justice, but you should also review the discussion concerning preliminary objections and improper conduct, and closely consider the dissent of the Mexican commissioner. There is a high probability that Chattin was guilty as charged.

UNITED STATES (B. E. CHATTIN CLAIM) V. UNITED MEXICAN STATES

United States–Mexico, General Claims Commission, 1927 Opinions of Commissioners, 1927, 422

Facts

Chattin, an American citizen, had worked since 1908 as a conductor for the Ferrocarril Sud-Pácifico de México (Southern Pacific Railroad of Mexico). He was arrested on July 9, 1910, at Mazatlán, State of Sinaloa, on a charge of embezzlement. It appeared that Chattin and a Mexican brakeman employed by the railroad had been engaged in the fraudulent sale of railroad tickets and had kept the proceeds of their enterprise for themselves. Chattin was kept in prison until January 1911, pending trial. He was tried in that month; convicted on February 6, 1911; and sentenced to two years' imprisonment. He was released from the jail in Mazatlán in May or June 1911, when the revolutionary forces of General Francisco Madero entered the town and liberated all prisoners.

Chattin returned to the United States and filed a claim with the Department of State, alleging that the arrest, trial, and sentence had been illegal; that he had suffered inhuman treatment in jail; and that all this merited damages to the amount of $50,000.

Issues

Had a denial of justice taken place in the judicial proceedings and imprisonment involving Chattin? If such denial had occurred, did responsibility devolve on the government of Mexico?

Decision

The General Claims Commission decided in favor of the United States and ordered Mexico to pay the sum of $5,000 as damages for denial of justice sufficiently grave to create state responsibility for Mexico.

Reasoning

Note here that none of the commissioners questioned the fact that Chattin was indeed guilty of embezzlement. The commission found that Chattin had been legally arrested, although the procedure used differed from that normally employed in the United States. The commission focused on four main concerns. First, Chattin was not informed of the charges and not permitted to confront accusers. Report concluded that this was "proved by the record and to a painful extent." Second, the trial was unreasonably delayed and then lasted only five minutes. Report noted that the trial was "a pure formality," in which confirmations were made only of written documents and in which not even the lawyer of the accused conductors took the trouble to say

(continued)

more than a few words. "The whole of the proceedings discloses a most astonishing lack of seriousness on the part of the Court." Charges that the arrest was illegal and that Chattin was mistreated in prison were not proven.

DISSENT

The Mexican commissioner (Fernando McGregor) registered a vigorous dissent here. First, he noted that Chattin was tried together with several Mexican nationals who received the same treatment. Why should he benefit from a more rigorous set of procedural safeguards than the nationals of the county in which he had chosen to live?

Second, he argued about the nature of the presumed defects. He distinguished between those that do not cause damage if the final decision is just and those that make it impossible for a decision to be just. He finally noted that he felt the criticisms made of the proceedings came from a lack of substantive knowledge of the judicial system and practice of Mexico. He noted that the same goal could be reached by many different roads.

NOTE

Chattin and his fellow embezzler had appealed the decision of the Mazatlán court up to the Supreme Court of Mexico but had lost the appeals. They had exhausted local remedies.

The last case for this section deals with a slightly different situation. In light of the announcement by several paramilitary groups that they would hold training exercises along the Rio Grande in an effort to help stem the flow of illegal aliens, the following case has some salience.

UNITED MEXICAN STATES (GARCIA AND GARZA) v. UNITED STATES

U.S.–Mexico General Claims Commission, 1926 Opinions of the Commissioners (1926)

Facts

Mexico presented the claim on behalf of the parents of a girl who was killed in 1919 by a shot from a U.S. cavalry patrol while she was crossing on a raft from the American to the Mexican side of the Rio Grande. Her father was waiting on the Mexican side. The laws of both countries forbade crossing at that point, as the girl's father knew. The officer commanding the patrol was sentenced by a court-martial to dismissal from the service, but the findings and sentence were set aside by the president.

Issue

Was the patrol justified in using deadly force in this circumstance?

Decision

The use of force was unwarranted.

Reasoning

The commissioners asked if any international standard existed with respect to the taking of human life. They drew the following from the 4th Hague Convention of 1907:

1. The act of firing should not be indulged in unless the delinquency is sufficiently well stated.

2. It should not be indulged in unless the importance of preventing or repressing the delinquency by firing is in reasonable proportion to the danger arising from it to the lives of the culprits and other persons in the neighborhood.

(continued)

3. It should not be indulged in whenever other practicable ways of preventing or repressing the delinquency might be available.
4. It should be done with sufficient precaution not to create unnecessary danger, unless it be the official's intention to hit, wound, or kill.

The commission decided that these requirements had not been met.

Dissent

The American commissioner, Fred Nielsen, registered a strong dissent. He felt that the commander's actions were justified under the circumstances. One should take seriously the decision of the Board of Review and of the president. While a domestic decision cannot bind an international tribunal, he insisted on a different standard of determining responsibility—unless one can show that a domestic system of law enforcement runs counter to that adopted by other civilized nations, responsibility should not attach. No evidence of fraud or abuse of power or acts ultra vires (beyond granted authority) occurred here.

As a general note, these requirements in various forms generally underlie the use of deadly force policy for most law enforcement agencies in the United States, Japan, and Western Europe.

Expropriation

Lay opinion to the contrary, every government has the right of expropriation— that is, of eminent domain. The law of nations demands respect for private property, but it does recognize the right of a state to derogate from this principle when its superior interests so require. Thus, the law allows expropriation for reasons of public utility in time of peace and requisition in wartime.[31] For example, in 1982 the French government nationalized five major groups of industrial corporations as well as 37 banks. Compensation was paid to both foreign and domestic investors as required by the French Constitution.[32] Expropriated property may be foreign or domestic: No distinction need be drawn by the seizing government, except in the case of foreign-owned public (state-owned) property. This principle has been affirmed again and again by international tribunals.[33] As long as the following conditions outlined hold true, the action of the state does not create an international responsibility. Much as some may decry the taking away of private property by any state, there can be no question that every independent political entity has an undoubted and lawful right to exercise the power of eminent domain.

[31]Portuguese-German Arbitration (1919), *Award II* (1930), in United Nations, *Reports of International Awards, II*, 1039. See also the explanation offered by the U.S. Supreme Court in *Banco Nacional de Cuba v. Sabbatino* (376 U.S. 398, 1964, at 428) that "the Judicial Branch will not examine the validity of a taking of property within its own territory by a foreign sovereign government even if the complaint alleges that the taking violates customary international law."

[32]See www.conseil-constitutionnel.fr/tableau/tab82.htm for cases.

[33]See *Norwegian Claims Against the United States of America*, Permanent Court of Arbitration, 1922, in J. B. Scott, ed., *Hague Court Reports, II*, 40–44, 70; as well as *German Interests in Polish Upper Silesia* (Germany v. Poland), Merits, *PCIJ*, Ser. A, No. 7 (1926), esp. 22.

Expropriation of foreign private property must, generally, satisfy all of the following conditions if the question of basic state responsibility is to be avoided:

1. The taking must be by a foreign sovereign government.
2. The property must be within the territorial jurisdiction of that government.
3. The government in question must exist and must be recognized by the state of which the affected owners are citizens.
4. The taking must not violate any treaty obligations.
5. Prompt, effective, and adequate compensation must be paid, and the capacity to pay and to effect transfer of funds has a legitimate place in determining the promptness and effectiveness of compensation.
6. No discrimination must exist in the taking.
7. The taking in question must be based on reasons of public utility, security, or national interest of a nature sufficiently great to override purely individual or private interests.

Resolution 1803 (XVII) of the UN General Assembly (1962) on Permanent Sovereignty over Natural Resources summarized the customary law at the time. Article 4 noted that resolution of disputes should be made through arbitration or international adjudication.[34] As with other questions of state responsibility, the newly emergent states of the global South resisted a number of these precepts. In December 1974, by a vote of 120 to 6 (with 10 abstentions), the General Assembly of the United Nations adopted a controversial instrument entitled Charter of Economic Rights and Duties of States.[35] Under the assumption that the Charter represented merely a resolution and not newly created principles of international law, the document, reflecting the views of almost all Third World countries on a variety of topics, has led to substantial disagreement since its adoption. The cause of most of the irritation voiced by the industrialized countries of the world came from provisions in Article 2 of the charter:

1. Every State has and shall freely exercise full permanent sovereignty, including possession, use and disposal, over all its wealth, natural resources, and economic activities.
2. Each State has the right:
   a. To regulate and exercise authority over foreign investment within its national jurisdiction in accordance with its laws and regulations and in conformity with its national objectives and priorities. No State shall be compelled to grant preferential treatment to foreign investment;
   b. To regulate and supervise the activities of transnational corporations within its national jurisdiction and take measures to ensure that such activities comply with its laws, rules and regulations and conform with its economic and social policies. *Transnational corporations shall not*

---

[34]UN GAOR, 17th Sess., Supp. No. 17 (A/5217), 15, www.un.org/documents/ga/res/17/ares17.htm.
[35]GA Res. 3281 (XXIX), 29 UN GAOR, Supp. (No. 31) 50, UN Doc. 9631 (1974). Text in full in 69 *AJIL* 484 (1975). Voting against the Charter were Belgium, Denmark, the Federal Republic of Germany, Luxembourg, the United Kingdom, and the United States; www.un.org/documents/ga/res/29/ares29.htm.

intervene in the internal affairs of a host State. Every State should, with full regard for its sovereign rights, co-operate with other States in the exercise of the right set forth in this subparagraph;

   c. To nationalize, expropriate or transfer ownership of foreign property in which case appropriate compensation should be paid by the State adopting such measures, taking into account its relevant laws and regulations and all circumstances that the State considers pertinent. In any case *where the question of compensation gives rise to a controversy, it shall be settled under the domestic law of the nationalizing State and by its tribunals,* unless it is freely and mutually agreed by all States concerned that other peaceful means be sought on the basis of the sovereign equality of States and in accordance with the principle of free choice of means. (Emphasis added)

Article 2 (by design, it must be assumed) omits all reference to public utility or public purpose as the basis for expropriation—see condition 7, listed earlier. It also contains no mention of the "doctrine of alien nondiscrimination"—that is, the assertion that resident aliens are entitled at least to the same protection of persons and property as local law grants to nationals. Finally, in Section 2c, it attempts to limit the ability of states to exercise their rights of diplomatic protection by stipulating that national law and courts will become the standard and principal recourse in disputes over compensation.

The ramifications of this debate extend far beyond the bounds of an introductory text because they involve, on the one hand, broad questions of international trade and investment policy and, on the other, technical questions such as the valuation of properties as functioning enterprises that require some sophisticated accounting knowledge.[36] The states of the global South, sensitive to their prerogatives and in many cases the past victims of corporations that exhibited a heavy-handed or dismissive attitude in their dealings with governments, still need to attract foreign investment for development purposes. Yet the fear of being exploited coupled with the need for an infusion of capital from the outside have produced an ambivalence that manifests itself in many different ways, not the least of which is a suspicion that acceptance of "globalization" with its liberal economic underpinnings (emphasizing unregulated market forces) will render them a permanent underclass.[37] Looking at the 1974 Charter, one might understand its thrust better by examining the nature of the nationalizations and expropriations that have occurred.

Nationalization of Alien Properties

Confiscation without payment of compensation has frequently reached enormous proportions in terms of the monetary value of the seized alien properties. Many of

---

[36]For example, one could use book value (assets–liabilities balance), share value (capitalization), or market (sale) value. See R. Lillich, ed., *The Valuation of Nationalized Property in International Law* (1987).

[37]This is a long-standing fear. It underlies the formation of the United Nations Conference on Trade and Development (UNCTAD) in 1966 as the lesser developed states' counterpart to the then General Agreement on Tariffs and Trade (GATT), now evolved to the World Trade Organization (WTO), to level the playing field. See Roy, note 4, at 882–883.

the more contemporary questions concerning expropriation centered on various extractive industries—oil (Libya), metals and minerals (Chile), fertile agricultural lands (Zimbabwe), various utilities (i.e., electric power generation and telephones), and modes of transportation, particularly railroads. Consider in this respect the titles of the two resolutions we discussed earlier. Among the more spectacular seizures, Gamal Abdel Nasser nationalized the Suez Canal in 1956. Britain and France sent troops to force its return, but failed. The United Nations sent its first peacekeeping force (UNEF) to monitor the settlement. Several other controversial incidents of nationalization took place in the early 1970s. Between them, the Kennecott and Anaconda mining companies controlled a major part of the Chilean economy. The Chilean government under Salvador Allende nationalized these as well as the property of ITT, a multinational communications company. During the Yom Kippur War (1973) and its aftermath, Arab states, acting in concert through the cartel Organization of Petroleum Exporting Companies (OPEC), were able to restrict the flow of oil to the West. This in turn led to a series of cancellations of concessions to Western oil companies, outright expropriation, and forced renegotiation of contracts. Libya stood at the forefront of the effort to use the resource as a tool to gain leverage. In the wake of the coup that deposed the Shah, the successor government in Iran nationalized American assets in Iran. This resulted in one of the largest and most complex settlements administered by the United States.

Nationalization can take effect immediately within the territory of the taking state. The interesting legal questions come from the disposition of property and other assets located beyond the jurisdiction of the nationalizing state. While the governments of other states have no authority to question the validity of another state's actions within its own territory, they have no obligation to respect that action when it has effects within their own jurisdiction unless it conforms to accepted public policy. Hence, the "taking" state may or may not gain possession of the bank accounts or other assets and properties of the nationalized enterprise located within a third state.[38] This will depend upon the view of the third state as to the legitimacy of the act.

Global Settlements

To reiterate and emphasize some earlier points, no rule of international law *requires* a state to espouse a claim on behalf of an injured citizen or company. This is a *permissive* rule in that a state has the right to pursue such claims, if it chooses to do so. While preliminary objections apply as a method of validating a claim, no

---

[38]Nonrecognition of nationalization of assets located outside the territory of the taking state is illustrated in *Carl Zeiss Stiftung v. V.E.B. Carl Zeiss Jena,* U.S. Ct. of Appeals, 2d Cir., 1970, 433 F.2d 686, in 65 *AJIL* 611 (1971); in *United Bank Limited v. Cosmic International, Inc.,* U.S. Ct. of Appeals, 2d Cir., 1976, 542 F.2d 868, in 71 *AJIL* 351 (1977); and in *Republic of Iraq v. First National City Bank,* U.S. Dist. Ct., S.D.N.Y, 1965, 241 F. Supp. 567, *dismissal affirmed,* U.S. Ct. of Appeals, 2d Cir., 1965, 353 F.2d 47, *certiorari denied,* Supreme Court, 1966, 86 S. Ct. 556. The latter case is discussed in a *Note* by Horlings in 7 *Harvard Int'l Law Club Journal* (1966), 316. See also the Netherlands case of *Svit, N.P. v. Bata-Best B.V.,* Netherlands, District Court, 's-Hertogenbosch (First Chamber), 1975; an *Explanatory Note* by MacCrate and the decision are in 15 *ILM* 669 (1976).

rules of law govern the pursuit of an espoused claim or the manner in which the claimant state disposes of any financial settlement reached. Normally any judgment would take into consideration the nature of the injury. While the United States will usually pay all of the sums in question to the claimant citizen (with some deductions for administrative and collection costs), no rule of international law requires it to do so. Because the claim belongs to the state, it *could* retain all funds received from the delinquent state.

The settlement of the large majority of many recent cases involving expropriation has involved extended negotiations that produced an agreement for a lump-sum payment, or *global* agreement. States may negotiate lump-sum or *global* settlements to avoid the problems associated with sorting through individual claims arising from a particular incident or just to "clear the books." For example, Secretary of State Madeleine Albright announced in early March 2000 that the Clinton administration would propose a global settlement to Iran to clear up all of the remaining claims and issues in an effort to normalize commercial relations.[39] In a global settlement, the state with claims against it agrees to pay a single lump sum in satisfaction of all claims against it. The claimant state then, if it chooses, may create its own *national* claims commission to determine the distribution of the funds to those citizens with outstanding claims. The national commissioners will set the rules and decide upon the distribution of the monies.[40]

Although not produced through a direct state-to-state claim by the United States, the result of the Holocaust Victims Assets Litigation serves as a good recent example of a global settlement. As the result of several class action litigations against certain Swiss banks—alleging that they had collaborated with and aided the Nazi regime in Germany by retaining and concealing the assets of Holocaust victims, and had accepted and "laundered" illegally obtained loot and profits from slave labor—the parties reached a negotiated settlement in 1998. The Swiss banks agreed to pay a lump sum of $1.25 billion in return for an agreement that this would release and "forever discharge" the Swiss banks *and the Swiss government* from "any and all claims" relating to the Holocaust, World War II, its prelude, and its aftermath.[41] Adjudication of the claims by individuals would be through procedures drawn up and administered under the auspices of the U.S. District Court for the Eastern District of New York.

Other examples include the Soviet Union's agreement to repay some $300 million in 1933 to American owners of properties confiscated in the Soviet Union.[42] The United States also negotiated agreements with other Eastern European countries: Yugoslavia (1948), Poland (1958), Romania (1960), Bulgaria (1963),

---

[39]"Global Settlement with Iran Imminent," www.wnd.com/news/article.asp?ARTICLE_ID=20219 (accessed April 22, 2009).

[40]Consult R. B. Lillich and B. H. Weston, *International Claims: Their Settlement by Lump Sum Agreements* (1975), the most comprehensive treatment of the subject available.

[41]See "Introduction to the Claims Resolution Process," www.crt-ii.org/introduction.phtm.

[42]This formed part of the Litvinov Agreement, in which the United States recognized the Soviet government. The Litvinov Agreement was supposed to be the first step toward a more general settlement. The second step never occurred.

Hungary (1973), and Czechoslovakia (1982).[43] The Mexican government eventually agreed to a minimal payment to the owners of American oil companies expropriated by Mexico. In May 1976, the government of Sri Lanka agreed to pay $13.7 million to British owners of tea, rubber, and coconut plantations expropriated only a year earlier. In May 1979, a lump-sum settlement agreement was reached between the United States and the People's Republic of China concerning expropriations of American properties. According to the agreement, China would pay the United States a total of $80.5 million over the following six years. That sum represented a settlement at a rate of about 41 cents on the dollar of the $197 million in claims against China. In return, the United States promised the People's Republic government assistance in recovering some $80 million in assets frozen in the United States.

Compensation issues tend to be difficult where corporations and property are involved. Vague language such as *full, fair, adequate,* and *just* does not make the process easier. Moreover, the settlements often come long after the original act. Claimants may get just pennies on the dollar in settlement. Rough estimates of the proportional value of the settlements with the various Eastern European countries range from approximately 90 percent (Yugoslavia) to 20 percent (Romania).

Ex Gratia Payments

We should briefly mention one other form of compensation: payments made by a state to aliens for injuries suffered. Such payments are made not because of a judicial or arbitral award, but because of humanitarian reasons including the perception that a wrong has been done. Such compensation, termed an *ex gratia payment,* has been made on occasion. The most recent and well-publicized example was caused by the downing of Iran Air Flight 655 by the U.S.S. *Vincennes* (July 3, 1988), with a loss of all 290 persons aboard the civilian aircraft (including 66 children and 38 non-Iranians). After long negotiations, on February 22, 1996, the United States—while denying any responsibility—agreed to pay Iran $61.8 million in compensation ($300,000 per wage-earning victim, $150,000 per non-wage-earner) for the 252 Iranians killed.[44]

Iran had filed a claim against the United States (May 19, 1989) in the International Court of Justice. Iran asked the court to assert U.S. responsibility for compensation in an amount to be determined by the court. With the settlement of February 22, the two agreed that it was

> a full and final settlement of all disputes, differences, claims, counterclaims and matters directly or indirectly raised by or directly arising out of, or directly or indirectly related to, or connected to this case.[45]

---

[43]See, for example, R. Lillich, "The United States–Hungarian Claims Agreement of 1973," 69 *AJIL* 534 (1975); V. Pechota, "The 1981 U.S.-Czechoslovak Claims Settlement Agreement," 76 *AJIL* 639 (1982), as well as the extensive documentation in 21 *ILM* 371, 414 (1982).

[44]For a good brief discussion of the incident, see www.answers.com/topic/iran-air-flight-655.

[45]*Case Concerning the Aerial Incident of 3 July 1988 (Islamic Republic of Iran v. United States of America)*, International Court of Justice (1996), www.icj-cij.org/icjwww/icases/iirus/iirus_iorders/irus_iorder_19960222.pdf.

Other Means of Depriving Aliens of Property

Thus far, only the actual expropriation—that is, the assumption of title—of alien property has been considered. But there are other ways of depriving an alien of property. Governments have attempted, for instance, to limit an alien's control or use of property.[46] Entrances to a factory have been barred on grounds of preserving public order; wage legislation and labor courts have lifted the wages of the employees of an alien enterprise to prohibitively high levels; entrance visas have been denied to vitally needed foreign technical personnel; allocations of required foreign exchange have been curtailed or stopped entirely; importations of replacement parts for machinery have been prevented; portions of buildings have been prohibited for use by the alien enterprise; conservators, managers, or inspectors have been introduced by government order into an enterprise and then prevented free use and direction by the nominal foreign owners; or, by a simple prohibition on the sale of the property, the value of the assets has been sharply reduced.[47] Such interference in the utilization of an alien's property could easily bring about a decision to sell the property to the government in question—or, in extreme cases, to the closing or even the abandonment of the property.

RESPONSIBILITY OF STATES FOR THE ACTIONS OF REBELS AND INSURGENT GOVERNMENTS

The discussion of international claims arising out of the treatment of aliens has centered thus far only on acts undertaken, directly or indirectly, by the lawful, recognized government of a state. Frequently, however, aliens suffer injuries in their persons or property at the hands of rebels or insurgent movements. The rules governing such injuries are fairly simple, yet there have been numerous controversies between states because of incidents connected with civil wars and uprisings. In the event of a rebellion, the assumption of state responsibility centers on the concept of the exercise of "due diligence." Almost by definition, every government is concerned with using all available means to prevent an outbreak of rebellion. If rebellion occurs, a government must act to suppress it as effectively and as quickly as possible and then punish the rebels. If it can be demonstrated that reasonable precautions were taken to prevent a rebellion and that after an uprising began, prompt measures were taken to subdue the rebels and punish them, then the lawful government has no international responsibility for the acts committed by rebels against aliens.[48]

---

[46]For a good discussion of this issue, see L. Shore, "Expropriation," Chapter 8 in C. McLachlan, L. Shore, and M. Weiniger, *International Investment Arbitration: Substantive Principles* (2007).

[47]The list has been adapted from L. B. Sohn and R. R. Baxter, "Responsibilities of States for Injuries to the Economic Interests of Aliens," *55 AJIL 545*, 559 (1961).

[48]Home Missionary Society Case (United States v. Great Britain), United States–Great Britain, Claims Arbitration, 1920 (Claims Arbitration Under a Special Agreement of August 8, 1910—Nielsen's Report, 421).

What if the insurgents win control over the territory of the entire state and replace the lawful government? In that case, the new government may be held responsible by other states for whatever injuries were caused to aliens from the very beginning of the existence of the then insurgent group. Likewise, the new government would not assume responsibility for whatever injuries were suffered by aliens at the hands of the overthrown previous administration of the state during the course of the civil war. In other words, a lawful government is usually not responsible internationally for the acts of unsuccessful rebels—provided that due diligence in preventing or suppressing the revolt can be demonstrated. A successful insurgent group may be held responsible internationally for all acts undertaken under its authority from its inception. No responsibility can be imputed to the group for the acts of the vanished government as long as those acts were of a political or military nature, incidental to the civil war, and undertaken for public ends.

SUGGESTED READINGS

RESPONSIBILITY OF STATES: GENERAL

Cancado, *The Application of Exhaustion of Local Remedies in International Law: Its Rationale in the International Protection of Individual Rights* (1983).

Caron and Crook, eds, *The Iran–United States Claims Tribunal and the Process of International Claims Resolution: A Study by the Panel on State Responsibility of the American Society of International Law* (2000).

Lauterpacht, *Oppenheim,* I: 338.

Lillich, ed., *The International Law of State Responsibility for Injury to Aliens* (1983).

Rosenne, *The International Law Commission's Draft Articles on State Responsibility* (1991).

Weston, Lillich, and Bederman, *International Claims: Their Settlement by Lump Sum Agreements, 1975–1995* (1999).

Zegveld, *Accountability of Armed Opposition Groups in International Law* (2002).

CASES

Claims of Finnish Shipowners (Finland v. Great Britain), 1934, 3 U.N. Rep. Int'l Arb. Awards 1479.

Libyan American Oil Co. v. Libya, Sweden, Court of Appeals, 1980, in 20 *ILM* 891 (1981).

Libya v. Libyan American Oil Co., Switzerland, Federal Supreme Ct., 1980, in 75 *AJIL* 153 (1981) and 20 *ILM* 151 (1981).

United States (Noyes) v. Panama, General Claims Arbitration, 1933, *Hunt's Rep.* 155, 190.

EXPROPRIATION OF ALIEN PROPERTY

Aldrich, "What Constitutes a Compensable Taking of Property? The Decisions of the Iran–United States Claims Tribunal," 88 *AJIL* 585 (1994).

Heiskanen and O'Brien, "UN Compensation Commission Panel Sets Precedents on Government Claims," 92 *AJIL* 339 (1998).

Lillich, ed., *The United Nations Compensation Commission* (1995).

Mooney, *Foreign Seizures: Sabbatino and the Act of State Doctrine* (1967).

Mouri, *The International Law of Expropriation as Reflected in the Work of the Iran-U.S. Claims Tribunal* (1994).

Shore, "Expropriation," Chapter 8 in McLachlan, Shore, and Weiniger, *International Investment Arbitration: Substantive Principles* (2007).

von Mehren and Kourides, "International Arbitration Between States and Foreign Private Parties: The Libyan Nationalization Cases," 75 *AJIL* 476 (1981).

Weeramantry, "International Decisions: Partial and Final Arbitration Awards (Eritrea/Ethiopia): Eritrea Ethiopia Claims Commission Awards for Claims Relating to the Laws of War, Diplomatic Relations, Expropriation, and Other Matters, Arising Out of the Eritrea-Ethiopia Armed Conflict," 101 *AJIL* 616 (2007).

CASES

Alberti v. Empresa Nicaraguense de la Carne, U.S. Court of Appeals, 7th Cir., April 18, 1983, 705.

AMOCO International Finance Corp. v. Islamic Republic of Iran, AWD 310-56-3.
Iran–United States Arbitration Tribunal, *Case Concerning the American International Group, Inc./American Life Insurance Company and the Islamic Republic of Iran/Central Insurance of Iran,* December 19, 1983, *INA Corp. v. The Islamic Republic of Iran,* AWD 184-161-1, August 13, 1985, in 80 *AJIL* 181 (1986).

The Law of the Sea

E lementary geography texts point out that oceans and seas cover over 70 percent of Earth's surface. Historically, the seas as well as other waterways have served as vital conduits for travel and commerce. In Chapter 9 we noted that under certain conditions, a state may lawfully extend its jurisdiction beyond territorial limits. In this, the law of the sea provides us with a particularly fascinating study due to the convergence of changes in technology with fundamental changes in the international environment during the 1940s–1990s. Rapid advances in technology, combined with a rapid expansion of the state system flowing from the breakup of colonial empires, produced a volatile political environment. These new states were determined to have their views heard and their interests taken as important. These changes in turn resulted in the emergence of a new regime for the oceans that, while drawing substantially upon time-honored principles, has many innovative features.

Over the past 60 years or so, many controversies relating to the law of the sea have involved the *right to control and exploit resources*, whether in the form of oil, fish, or other potentially valuable commodities. Claims *to control* or *have access to* the resources of the sea resulted in unilateral claims to extensive territorial seas, exclusive economic zones, patrimonial seas, the continental shelf, or portions of the deep seabed. In response, states made an effort to codify the existing customary law. Under the sponsorship of the United Nations, states assembled in Geneva in 1958 (United Nations Conference on the Law of the Sea, or UNCLOS I). The conference produced four conventions: the Convention on the Territorial Sea and the Contiguous Zone, the Convention on the High Seas, the Convention on the Continental Shelf (ConShelf Convention), and the Convention on Fishing and Conservation of the Living Resources of the High Seas.[1] Because a number of issues, particularly the width of the territorial sea, remained unresolved despite the

---

[1]Texts: "Territorial Sea," http://untreaty.un.org/ilc/texts/instruments/english/conventions/8_1_1958_territorial_sea.pdf; l "High Seas," http://untreaty.un.org/ilc/texts/instruments/english/conventions/8_1_1958_high_seas.pdf; "Continental Shelf," http://untreaty.un.org/ilc/texts/instruments/english/conventions/8_1_1958_continental_shelf.pdf; "Fishing and Conservation," http://untreaty.un.org/ilc/texts/instruments/english/conventions/8_1_1958_fishing.pdf.

draft convention, the United Nations sponsored a second conference (UNCLOS II) in 1960. This second meeting not only failed to resolve the outstanding issues, but also gave states a forum to vent their dissatisfaction with certain other features of the four conventions (particularly the limits in the ConShelf Convention) that already seemed dated because of technological advances. The year 1960 was particularly interesting, because 17 new states emerged and were accepted into the United Nations. Over the next decade, the membership of the organization would grow from 82 in 1959 to 127 in 1970. By 1979, membership had almost doubled the 1959 total, standing at 152.[2] Needless to say, adding this number of states—most with limited experience in international affairs and jealously protective of their newfound independence—to the already fragmented negotiating environment enormously complicated the process of developing a new regime.

A third UN conference on the issues began in 1973, producing a convention (UNCLOS III) that opened for signature in 1982.[3] The United States and a number of other leading sea powers refused to sign the convention because of objections to the proposed creation of an International Seabed Authority that would control "mining" or other activities connected with the deep seabed. Other states, such as France, Italy, and Japan, while signing initially, indicated that unless modified, their governments would not submit the treaty for ratification (see Chapter 4). The treaty entered into force in 1994 with the 60th ratification, but only after an initiative by the secretary-general of the United Nations that resulted in intensive talks (1990–1994) that led to the Agreement Relating to the Implementation of Part XI of the United Nations Convention on the Law of the Sea of 10 December 1982.[4] The UN General Assembly adopted the agreement (121–0, with seven abstentions) on July 29, 1994. The United States voted for the resolution and indicated provisional acceptance through written notification as provided for in the agreement (November 16, 1994). While the United Kingdom, Japan, the Russian Federation, and the states of the European Community have now ratified UNCLOS III, the United States did not sign the original convention, and remains as the only major maritime nation that has not ratified *(accessed to)* the treaty. We discuss UNCLOS III in more detail later in this chapter.

SOME NOTES ON "LAWMAKING" AT THE INTERNATIONAL LEVEL

The genesis of UNCLOS III furnishes us with a fascinating look at the difficulties of multilateral lawmaking in the contemporary era. Consider first the following political divisions among states at the time negotiations began. The East–West conflict (Cold War) between the United States and its allies/clients and the Soviet Union (USSR) and its allies/clients formed the primary foundations for political interaction. While the emergence of large numbers of new states gave the nonaligned

---

[2]Currently, membership stands at 191 after the second expansion in the wake of the breakup of Yugoslavia and the Soviet Union, www.un.org/Overview/growth.htm (accessed April 22, 2009).

[3]Text at www.un.org/depts/los/convention_agreements/texts/unclos/unclos_e.pdf.

[4]Text at www.un.org/depts/los/convention_agreements/texts/unclos/closindx.htm.

(and neutral) movement visibility, Cold War issues still dictated important contacts and linkages between the primary players in the East–West conflict and individual states outside the formal alliance structures (NATO, Warsaw Pact/China). Second, the emergence of the so-called North–South conflict (somewhat misnamed as most of the "North" was "West" and most of the "East" was "South" in terms of relevant economic measures) that had at its heart economic issues of "fairness" and "reparations." Consider that, from the perspective of many of these newly independent nations, their former colonial metropoles had fostered a situation of exploitation where outsiders had "ripped them off." This attitude carried over into the negotiations for UNCLOS III.[5]

To complicate matters further, the states in the East–West conflict had to balance demands from four powerful interests (constituencies): drillers/miners, fishermen, the military, and scientists. Note that, for obvious reasons, drillers/miners and fishermen share interests in expanding state control over resource bases. Yet, no matter the convergence of interests, these groups did not act in concert because of a perception (primarily by the fishermen) that the two activities were not compatible. On the other hand, the military (we should say *states with navies*) and scientists share an interest in having a narrow extension of state authority to regulate the seas. They wished to preserve maximum access, either for free movement (navies) or for scientific research. Unfortunately, with respect to the overlap of interest between these two groups, the scientists wanted to dissociate themselves from the military because of fears (often justified) that association with the military would cause states to restrict access because of suspicions about the nature of their projects. Indeed, the information gathered by the physical oceanographer often is what navies want to know. Problems could also occur because states feared that such studies conducted by those outside could once again open them to exploitation. States without navies (the majority) had an interest in securing a relatively broad band of territorial control in the interest of security as well as control over resources.

GENERAL PRINCIPLES

To begin, we should note that the same basic principles of jurisdiction discussed in Chapter 10 apply to the seas as well. A separate discussion about the sea is necessary to understand how international law provides guidelines to separate competing claims to jurisdiction, because most cases involve *concurrent jurisdiction*. Moreover, as we noted earlier, the seas present an additional set of issues because of competing claims to resources. As with any question of jurisdiction, with ships, the first question asked is *where did the incident happen*. We emphasize this question because the contemporary sea has many different zones—ports (internal waters), territorial seas, contiguous zones, exclusive economic zones (EEZs), continental shelf, deep seabed, and the high seas (see Figure 12.1). Location matters because current law specifies distinct sets of rights and duties for each of these areas.

---

[5]For a short introduction, see A. Hollick, *New Era of Ocean Politics* (1974).

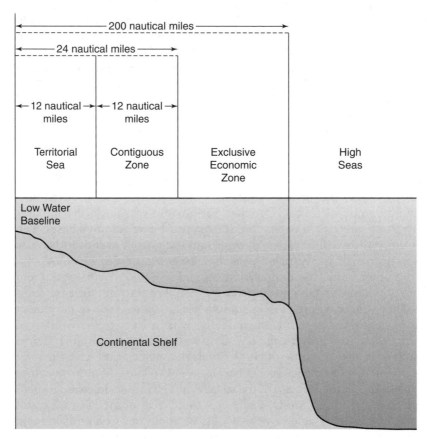

FIGURE 12.1
Maritime Zones.

BASIC PRINCIPLES

Nationality: Jurisdiction Follows the Flag

As we discussed in Chapter 9, ships have nationality. Every ship outside of its own territorial jurisdiction must fly a flag indicating the state of registry. For now remember the old formula: *Jurisdiction follows the flag.*[6] It marks the beginning of any analysis of jurisdiction involving ships or aircraft. Each state determines for itself the conditions for granting its nationality to vessels. In terms of jurisdiction, where normally territoriality stands at the top of the hierarchy of jurisdictional principles, in cases involving the law of the sea, "nationality" in terms of registry may confer "territoriality" with respect to the exercise of jurisdiction over persons and events on board. But, as we shall see, the "territoriality" derived from nationality accorded to ships is not absolute *(unless they are warships)*. It does mean that state laws and regulations apply to most acts undertaken aboard the vessel, but the ascription of "territoriality" from the standpoint of *national law* and established practice does not necessarily stand at

---

[6]Article 91, UNCLOS III. An interesting aside is that once registered, a ship attains juristic personality—it may sue and be sued. Keep this in mind while considering the issues of flags of convenience.

the top of the hierarchy of principles in determining resolution of problems associated with *concurrent jurisdiction* from the standpoint of *international law*.

Ships may also fly the flag of certain international organizations. Article 93 of UNCLOS III permits the United Nations, its specialized agencies, and the International Atomic Energy Agency to sail ships under their own flags. An interesting use of the UN flag occurred in December 1983, when, with the unanimous support of the Security Council, UN Secretary-General Javier Pérez de Cuéllar announced that for "strictly humanitarian reason," the ships that evacuated Yasser Arafat and some 4,000 soldiers of the Palestinian Liberation Organization (PLO) would be allowed to fly the UN flag alongside the flag of the country of registration (France, Greece, or Italy). The ships, chartered by Saudi Arabia, were escorted by French warships to deter any Israeli or Syrian attacks.

The law of the flag state governs matters relating to internal affairs aboard a vessel, including discipline. Within ports (internal waters) or territorial seas and contiguous zones, a ship must obey the host country's navigation and similar regulations. As we discuss later, informal pragmatic "rules of thumb" often settle matters

REGINA V. LESLIE

Great Britain, Court of Criminal Appeal, 1860 8 Cox's Criminal Cases 269

Facts

Leslie was captain of the British private merchant vessel *Louisa Braginton*. When the ship came to the Chilean port of Valparaiso, the Chilean government contacted Leslie and persuaded him to sign a contract whereby he undertook to transport several Chilean citizens to Liverpool. The individuals in question had been banished from Chile for political reasons. Under military guard, they were placed on board the ship.

Whenever the vessel touched port on the voyage back to England, the exiled Chileans demanded their release ashore, but Leslie insisted on fulfilling the contract and brought the entire group to Liverpool. There the Chileans sued Leslie on charges of false imprisonment. The lower court ruled in favor of the plaintiffs. Leslie appealed.

Issue

Was Leslie liable to an indictment in Great Britain for fulfilling his contract concluded in Chile with the government of that country?

Decision

The Court of Appeal affirmed the conviction.

Reasoning

English, not Chilean, law applied the moment Leslie left Chilean territorial waters. The conviction could not be sustained for what Leslie had done in Chile. The attitude of the Chilean government toward its citizens had to be assumed lawful.

However, as soon as Leslie left Chilean territorial waters, he and his ship came solely under the laws of England. This applied to all persons on board. His activities subsequent to the departure from Chilean jurisdiction amounted to false imprisonment because he took the Chileans, without their consent, to England when they clearly desired to leave his ship in other states. *A Chilean captain and vessel would have acted correctly under the circumstances,* but Leslie had not.

of concurrent jurisdiction over incidents that occur in these areas. On the high seas, the law of the flag state prevails.

Flags of Convenience

In the *Nottebohm* case (see Chapter 9), we found an individual attempting to adopt a "nationality of convenience." Under the law of the sea, *flags of convenience*—in essence nationalities of convenience—have been a long-standing problem.[7] For example, Aristotle Onassis was not an owner of Greek ships—he was a Greek who owned ships, most of which were registered in Liberia or Panama. Each state has the right to register vessels as it chooses under its own rules and regulations.[8] Yet the right of registry presumably entails in turn obligations and ability to police the vessels so registered. Lack of effective inspection, administration, and enforcement has raised concerns about the qualifications for masters, officers, and other classes of skilled seamen, as well as about the seaworthiness of the ships. Competition and low wages can mean quite minimal requirements. Most of the vessels so registered may never visit any port in their "home" state. Indeed, consider the surprise of one of the authors of this text, when he spotted a ship flying the flag of Luxemburg (a small landlocked state) entering the port of Savannah.

UNCLOS III attempted to address the issue by requiring a "genuine link" (Article 91.1) between states and ships. One might interpret the wording here to mean that another state could feel free to deny recognition to the asserted nationality of a vessel flying a flag of convenience, effectively making the vessel "stateless." Stateless vessels have no guaranteed right of entry to ports (internal waters) and are subject to boarding, search, and arrest by the authorities of any member of the family of nations.[9] To date, this remains a moot issue because no state has ever gone so far as to challenge the use of a flag of convenience in this manner. The United States has maintained a convenient benign blindness toward the use of flags of convenience by U.S. shipowners—but with the understanding that in time of war, American-*owned* ships, no matter where registered, can be requisitioned to support the war effort.

The reasons for adopting flags of convenience are numerous: low or no taxes (including such items as social security and unemployment levies), lower wage rates

---

[7]The following 27 countries, along with the German International Ship Register, have been declared flags of convenience (FOCs) by the Fair Practices Committee of the International Transport Workers' Federation (ITF), which runs the ITF campaign against FOCs: Antigua and Barbuda, Aruba (Netherlands), Bahamas, Barbados, Belize, Bermuda (United Kingdom), Burma, Cambodia, Canary Islands (Spain), Cayman Islands (United Kingdom), Cook Islands (New Zealand), Cyprus, German International Ship Register (GIS), Gibraltar (United Kingdom), Honduras, Lebanon, Liberia, Luxemburg, Malta, Marshall Islands (United States), Mauritius, Netherlands Antilles, Panama, St. Vincent, Sri Lanka, Tuvalu, and Vanuatu; www.lloydslist.com/ll/sector/tankers/article358721.ece.

[8]UNCLOS III, Article 91.1.

[9]See UNCLOS III, Article 92(2). Jurisdiction over stateless vessels on the high seas was involved in two interesting American cases: *United States v. Cortes*, U.S. Ct. of Appeals, 5th Cir., 588 F.2d 106, 1979, reported in detail in 20 *Harvard Int'l L. J.* 397 (1979); and *United States v. Marino-Garcia* (two consolidated cases), U.S. Ct. of Appeals, 11th Cir., 679 F.2d 1373, 1982, reported in 77 *American Journal of International Law* 630 (1983). These cases brought out the fact that all nations have the right to assert jurisdiction over stateless vessels on the high seas, even if no direct connection exists between the vessel and the state asserting jurisdiction.

than would be necessary if registered in state of ownership, and lenient health and safety regulations. Shipowners often argue that the realities of international competition mean that many regulations in economically developed countries make profitable operation impossible. Consider this statement by a Canadian shipowner:[10]

> Vanuatu is known as a "flag of convenience" country. That means if you register your ships here and fly the Vanuatu flag, you get all kinds of perks you wouldn't get in Canada. Corporate taxes are non-existent and you don't have to hire Canadians if you don't want to.

On the other side of the coin, the question of effective administration, inspection, and enforcement has become a topic of great concern in Europe because of a series of recent shipping disasters.[11] The oil tanker *Erika,* sailing under the flag of Malta, sank in the Bay of Biscay in December 1999. The *Prestige,* a Liberia-owned vessel with a Greek captain, was crewed by Filipinos, registered in the Bahamas, and chartered for the voyage by the Swiss-headquartered Russian Alfa Group oil conglomerate. The ship sank some 150 miles off the Spanish coast of Galicia on November 19, 2002. The wreck produced the third major oil slick in the region in less than 20 years.[12] These two incidents involved ships of questionable seaworthiness, thus raising a heated debate within the European Union (EU) over the issue of flag state liability for inspection and certification. The debate has not produced stricter standards—not surprising, because a number of EU member states, if not offering a flag of convenience themselves, condone their use.

Prompted by the problems created by the concept of "genuine link" and the rapid expansion in numbers of flags of convenience, the United Nations sponsored a conference to draft a new *Convention on Conditions for Registration of Ships* (1986). The convention aimed at defining the minimum elements of a genuine link that should exist between a ship and its flag state. Those minimum elements included the following: (1) the state should have a competent and adequate national maritime administration subject to its jurisdiction and control, (2) the administration actively engaged in activities to ensure that ships flying the flag of that state complied with its law and regulations, and (3) a "satisfactory part" of the complement (officers and crew) should consist of nationals of the flag state. As of August 1, 2011, the convention had only 14 states parties. Entry into force requires 40 states representing 25 percent of the relevant gross registered tonnage at the time. Of the major states, only the Russian Federation has signed (but not ratified). Of the states identified as a flag of convenience, Liberia submitted an instrument of accession in 2005.

In passing, we should note one innovative use of flags of convenience. In 1987, in an attempt to protect Kuwaiti tankers against attack during the Persian Gulf hostilities, the United States agreed to put 11 of these ships under the U.S. flag. The United States then assigned U.S. Navy vessels to escort them during their

---

[10]"The Vanuatu Connection," www.cbc.ca/disclosure/archives/030401_csl/vanuatu.html (accessed April 22, 2009).

[11]http://news.bbc.co.uk/1/hi/programmes/correspondent/883110.stm (*Erika*).

[12]P. Mitchell, "Two Years After the *Prestige* Disaster, New Sea Pollution Measures Blocked" (December 1, 2004), www.wsws.org/articles/2004/dec2004/poll-d01.shtml (accessed April 22, 2009).

sojourns in the Gulf.[13] The tankers even received new American names. One might legitimately question if an "effective link" beyond obvious American self-interest existed in this situation.

MARITIME BOUNDARIES AND JURISDICTIONAL PRINCIPLES

While the idea that ships have "nationality" goes back to the most ancient of times, the principle that the seas should be open to all—that states could not make extensive claims to significant areas of the ocean as territory—has a relatively recent origin. Carthage (from the fifth to the second century B.C.), whose lifeblood came from trade, had a large navy that ruthlessly destroyed any ships regarded as competitors found within its area of interest.[14] Consider that in 1493–1494, the pope divided the known oceans and newly found overseas territories between Spain and Portugal, then the two leading seagoing powers in Europe. While the work of Grotius in the early seventeenth century (c. 1609) set the stage, the doctrine that *the seas were open to all on an equal basis* did not take hold until the early nineteenth century. In this respect, we might note the self-interested nature of the arguments made by Grotius. As a citizen of a small power (Holland) trying to build its economy on the basis of overseas trade, his position arguing for the freedom of the high seas ran very much against the interest of the dominant sea powers—Spain, France, and Portugal—as well as that of the rising challenger, England, all of whom had a "closed sea" rationale driving their policies. Perhaps the impact of Grotius illustrates a case of making the right argument at the right time. With the fragmentation of the international system after the Treaty of Westphalia in 1648, the idea that all states had a right to use the sea as they wished found strong support among those now free to chart their own course in foreign affairs. Over the next hundred years, the expansion of trade among states witnessed the slow replacement of mercantilist mindsets by free trade rationales.

From the late seventeenth century until the mid-twentieth century, the sea had only three divisions: ports (internal waters), the territorial sea (and contiguous zone), and the high seas. Matters became more complicated in 1945, when the United States unilaterally claimed a right to exploit the seabed and subsoil of the continental shelf and then the right to manage certain fisheries for purposes of conservation. Viewing this as a claim to resources, other states, lacking continental shelves, asserted rights to very broad territorial seas. Between 1946 and 1959, Argentina, Chile, Peru, and Ecuador all enacted legislation that laid claim to a 200-nautical-mile band of territorial sea in an effort to exclude other states from the very rich fisheries off their coasts. Others responded with innovative

---

[13]M. H. Armacost (U.S. undersecretary for political affairs), "The U.S. Plan to Protect Kuwaiti Ships in the Gulf by Putting Them Under U.S. Flags" (June 16, 1987), and related documents, in 26 *International Legal Materials* 1429 (1987), and J. V. Lamar, "Rough Seas and New Names," *Time* (June 29, 1987), 13.

[14]J. L. Taulbee, "The Mercenary Option: An Apologia for Carthage," *Journal of Military and Naval History* 10 (1999).

claims to EEZs or patrimonial seas. The law of the sea, once considered one of the most stable issue areas in international law, became an active minefield of competing claims.

Internal Waters

A state has an exclusive right to exploit and control those areas designated as internal waters. These include ports, harbors, and all navigable waterways (rivers, lakes, and canals). In theory, a coastal state has the right to refuse entry to its harbors and ports (internal waters) to any ship except one in distress. Because most states actively promote trade, the really important questions normally involve the status of ships once in port, not their right to enter. For merchant ships, a right of entry is presumed unless a state has expressly indicated otherwise. Inasmuch as a port or harbor is considered internal waters, a state has the right to assert territorial jurisdiction over all *private* ships docked or moored there, meaning that it may enforce its laws in full if it chooses to do so. States may choose, for pragmatic reasons, not to exercise their rights. Note here that we have emphasized private ships. Warships constitute another category, discussed later. In practice, pragmatic concerns tend to limit the willingness of the port state to assert its authority in only the most serious crimes (peace of the port doctrine).

MALI V. KEEPER OF THE COMMON JAIL (WILDENHUS' CASE)

United States Supreme Court, 1887 120 U.S. 1

Facts

The Belgian steamer *Noordland* was docked in the port of Jersey City, New Jersey. On October 6, 1886, in a fight on board the ship, a Belgian member of the crew, Joseph Wildenhus, killed another Belgian crew member. The Jersey City Police boarded the vessel and arrested Wildenhus, who then was committed by a police magistrate to the common jail of Hudson County, New Jersey, pending trial for murder. The Belgian consul (M. Charles Mali) for New York and New Jersey then petitioned for a writ of habeas corpus, claiming that under international law *and* the provisions of the Belgian–United States Consular Convention of 1880, the offense should

be handled under the laws of Belgium. In sum, the State of New Jersey lacked jurisdiction. Article 11 of the convention invoked stated:

> The local authorities shall not interfere [with the internal order of merchant vessels] except when the disorder that has arisen is of such a nature as to disturb tranquility and public order on shore or in the port, or when a person of the country, or not belonging to the crew, shall be concerned therein.

The Belgian case rested in the assertion that no outside persons had been involved. Slayer and victim were both Belgian citizens and members of the crew. The commission of the crime aboard ship and

(continued)

below deck had not disturbed the tranquility of the port and public order.

Issue

Does murder aboard a foreign vessel in port, affecting only members of the foreign crew, constitute a disturbance of the tranquility of the port, thereby justifying assertion of jurisdiction by local law enforcement agencies?

Decision

Decision in favor of New Jersey's right to arrest and try Wildenhus.

Reasoning

The crime of murder, by its commission, disturbs tranquility and public order on shore or in a port, so it has to be regarded as falling within the exceptions in which the local authorities have a right to interfere.

While the *Wildenhus* case involved a question of interpretation of a treaty, the relevant provisions of the treaty reflect standard and long-established practice with respect to merchant vessels in port. In *Cunard v. Mellon*,[15] the United States chose to enforce the provisions of the National Prohibition Act by seizing stocks of liquor and other intoxicating beverages on board foreign vessels in port even though the prohibited items were sealed under lock and key. The Court noted:

> The merchant ship of one country voluntarily entering the territorial limits of another subjects herself to the jurisdiction of the latter. The Jurisdiction attaches in virtue of her presence, just as with other objects within those limits. During her stay she is entitled to the protection of the laws of that place and correlatively is bound to yield obedience to them. *Of course, the local sovereign may out of considerations of public policy choose to forego the exertion of its jurisdiction or to exert the same in only a limited way, but this is a matter resting solely in its discretion.* (Emphasis added)

In summary, for many reasons, including expedience, a port state may choose *not* to exercise its full jurisdictional rights over ships within internal waters. But that decision still remains within the discretion of the port state. Note that Great Britain, a major maritime power, did not protest the *Cunard* decision.

Pragmatism and practice limit the actual exercise of jurisdiction in several ways. First, as in *Wildenhus*, treaties may apply, particularly among or between states,

HYPOTHETICAL CASE: CONCURRENT JURISDICTION

The following hypothetical case illustrates the principles of jurisdiction with respect to ports. A Frenchman kills an Israeli on board a Liberian ship while docked in a Brazilian port. Who may claim jurisdiction, and why?

Brazil	territoriality (internal waters)
Liberia	flag (nationality/"territoriality")
France	nationality (active personality)
Israel	passive personality (nationality of the victim)

[15]U.S. Supreme Court, 262 U.S. 100 (1923).

with strong commercial ties that generate large volumes of maritime contact. Just as states will negotiate a Status of Forces Agreement (SOFA) to clarify jurisdictional problems to regulate common problems, states will often do the same with regard to commercial relations. Second, as a matter of *customary law*, except under extraordinary circumstances, a port state does not have the right to interfere in the internal operation of the ship. The captain's authority to discipline the crew and other matters related to internal ship operations lie outside the normal exercise of jurisdiction. Third, a state does not have to permit a warship entry (unless in distress), but once docked, a warship has absolute immunity from civil and criminal jurisdiction in that port. Members of the crew in uniform on official duty on shore enjoy immunity as well. Warship and crew are expected to obey the rules and regulations of the port state while visiting. If asked to leave by state authorities, a warship *must* do so.

REGINA V. ANDERSON

Great Britain, Court of Criminal Appeal (1868) 11 Cox Criminal Cases, 198

Facts

James Anderson, an American citizen, was indicted for murder on board a vessel registered in Great Britain. At the time of the crime, the ship was moving up the River Garonne on its way to the French city of Bordeaux, some 90 miles from the coast. The vessel was clearly in the internal waters of France. The accused was detained on the ship until it returned to England, where he was charged with murder in the Central Criminal Court in London. He was convicted of manslaughter despite his plea that the court lacked jurisdiction to try him because the offense had been committed within French territory by an American citizen.

Issue

Which country had jurisdiction to try the accused under the conditions described?

Decision

Conviction upheld. British courts had jurisdiction to try offenses committed aboard British ships.

Reasoning

The court found Anderson was subject to American law as a citizen, to French law for having committed the offense within the territorial boundaries of France, and also to British law because jurisdiction (flag) extends to the protection of British vessels no matter where those ships might be at a given time. France could have exercised its right to try but had not done so.

Ships in Distress   Curiously, neither the 1958 Convention on the Territorial Sea and the Contiguous Zone nor UNCLOS III mentions the right of a ship in distress to enter internal waters. The rules that limit state jurisdiction here form part of the *customary law* of the sea. Ships in genuine distress—that is, forced, through weather or other emergency, to enter a port or harbor for safety—are exempt from duties, fees, and customs regulations that otherwise may have applied.[16] The reasoning here is straightforward—the ship did not enter of its own choice, and therefore the state should not profit from its presence. Contemporary issues of refuge have centered on the issue of the right of a state to refuse entry if by granting entry to the ship, the state might suffer damage. In the case of the *Castor,* Morocco, Gibralter, and Spain denied refuge to a tanker "in distress." The *Castor,* carrying 30,000 tons of unleaded gasoline, had sustained severe damage in heavy weather. Because of the damage, the ship was deemed to present a serious risk of explosion and rupture of the hull. The ship existed in limbo for 35 days (late December 2000 to January 2001) until being towed to a relatively sheltered spot off the coast of Tunisia, where its cargo was safely offloaded.[17] In November 2002, Spanish authorities also demanded that the severely damaged tanker, the *Prestige,* steer a course away from the coast rather than permitting it refuge.[18] The ship sank off the coast of Galicia, causing the worst environmental disaster in Spanish history.

Spurred by these recent cases of refusal to grant entry, the International Maritime Organization (IMO) has developed some *guidelines* based upon contemporary realities.[19] The guidelines make granting access to a place of refuge a political decision that can be taken only on a case-by-case basis. In so doing, presumably states would have the right to balance the interests of the affected ship with those of the environment or public safety. Hence, as with other areas, the content of the law relating to refuge is in a state of evolution or, some might say, devolution.

Gulfs and Bays   As large indentations in the coastline, gulfs and bays have always merited separate consideration. Indeed, our previous discussion of the status of Moray Firth (*Mortenson v. Peters,* Chapters 4 and 6) applies here in regard to what states can claim as internal waters or territorial sea. Many gulfs and bays run deep into the territory of the coastal state. If the distance between the headlands of a bay or gulf is less than 24 miles, a state may claim the area as internal waters (Article 10.4, UNCLOS III). If the distance between the headlands exceeds 24 miles, states may draw a straight baseline of 24 miles within the bay to enclose the maximum amount of water possible with a line of that length.

---

[16]For a statement of traditional practice, see *Cashin v. the King* (1935), Canada, Exchequer Court, 4 D.L.R. 547, 551–552; and *The Rebecca, Hoff, Administratrix* (United States v. United Mexican States), General Claims Commission (1929), 4 U.N. R.I.A.A. 444. For an evaluation of current state practice, see C. F. Murray, "Any Port in a Storm?

The Right of Entry for Reasons of Force Majeure or Distress in the Wake of the Erika and the Castor," 63 *Ohio State Law Journal* 1465 (2002).

[17]www.oceansatlas.com/unatlas/issues/emergencies/transportation_and_telecomm/places_of_refuge. htm#Background%20on%20the%20Castor%20incident; see also R. Martin, "The New Supertanker Plague," www.oilcrash.com/articles/super.htm.

[18]B. Bahree, C. Vitzthum, and E. Portanger, "Oil Trouble the Making of a Disaster: The *Prestige*'s Last Hours Lessons of the Past Sealed Oil Tanker's Fate as Spain, Portugal, Fearing Spills, Sent It Away," *Wall Street Journal* (November 25, 2002).

[19]Resolution A.949(23) of March 5, 2004, www.imo.org/includes/blastDataOnly.asp/data_ id%3D9042/949.pdf. See also A. Chircop, "Living with Ships in Distress: A New IMO Decision-Making Framework for the Requesting and Granting of Refuge," 3 *WMU Journal of Maritime Affairs* 1 (April 2004), 31–49.

Controversies arise here over claims based upon historic status to bays and gulfs that fall outside of these rules of delimitation.[20] Canada claims Hudson Bay (600 miles wide, 1,000 miles long), but the United States disputes the claim. Similarly, the status of the Gulf of Aqaba remains in controversy, although the United States regards the gulf as international waters.

The plots of B movies in the 1930s–1960s often involved the casino on a ship docked just outside then 3-mile limit, thus being a legal gambling operation. In contemporary times, gambling cruises leave from many U.S. ports, but they now have to travel 12 nautical miles to get outside U.S. territorial waters.[21] In relation to a number of issues, consider the following case.

▶ THE PEOPLE V. STRALLA AND ADAMS

Supreme Court of California (1939) 98 California Decisions 440; 34 AJIL 143 (1940)

Facts

Stralla and Adams operated the *Rex,* a gambling ship anchored in Santa Monica Bay, 4 miles from the City of Santa Monica and 6 miles landward from a line drawn between the headlands of Santa Monica Bay. The headlands of the bay are separated by a distance of 25 nautical miles (29 statute miles). The bay has a depth from the headlands of approximately 10 miles.

The authorities of Los Angeles County raided the ship and arrested its owner-operators. The owner-operators were convicted of operating a gambling ship in violation of the laws of California. They appealed the conviction.

Issue

Was Santa Monica Bay part of the territory of California, or was the vessel anchored in the high seas and thus immune from seizure by California authorities?

Decision

The California Supreme Court affirmed the conviction.

Reasoning

All of Santa Monica Bay falls within the jurisdiction of the State of California. It is a "historic bay" claimed by California from its inception. The state constitution claims all bays and harbors along the coast as an integral part of California. The territorial sea of the United States extends 3 miles (now *12 miles*) from the baseline drawn across the headlands of the bay. Within the bay, the State of California may exercise its jurisdiction for all lawful purposes.

---

[20]For suggested criteria for determining historic status, see "Juridical Regime of Historic Waters, Including Historic Bays," 2 *Yearbook of the International Law Commission* 1 (1962).

[21]We should note a great irony here. Entrepreneurs in Savannah, Georgia used to run two types of "cruises." You could book passage on a boat that would travel a short way up the Savannah River into South Carolina, where video poker and other video gaming were legal, or you could book passage on a ship that would make its way down the river into international waters, where you could choose your game. As an aside, these cruises fell victim to (1) legislation in South Carolina that outlawed video poker and (2) competition from other land-based legal casinos.

The Gulf of Sidra   In early 1986, the United States and Libya clashed over Libyan claims to the Gulf of Sidra[22] as a historic body of water belonging exclusively to Libya. The gulf covers an area of 22,000 square miles, bordered on three sides by Libyan territory. Libya had extended its territorial sea to 12 nautical miles in 1959. In 1973, the Libyan government unilaterally announced that the entire gulf constituted an integral part of the internal waters of the country. Foreign vessels could enter only with express permission, and overflight could occur only through agreement. The seaward limit of the gulf comprised a straight baseline of approximately 300 miles from headland to headland. The United States and other countries (specifically Italy) rejected the claim because (1) the baseline exceeded current standards by more than 12 times the permissible length (24 nautical miles); (2) Libya had not claimed jurisdiction beyond territorial waters prior to 1973, thus putting the "historic" claim into doubt; (3) Libya had failed to exercise effective jurisdiction over the gulf; and (4) the international community had not recognized, or acquiesced to, the Libyan claim of historic possession. U.S. and Libyan fighters engaged in aerial battle over the Gulf in 1981. Another violent confrontation ensued when the United States directly challenged the Libyan claim by sending a naval task force across the Libyan baseline (March 23, 1986).[23] Libya responded by firing surface-to-air missiles at U.S. planes. The United States responded with attacks on Libyan patrol craft outside "territorial waters" and on missile bases on the mainland. Again in 1989, U.S. planes engaged Libyan fighters over the gulf. While the damage was minimal on both sides, the U.S. action (and the lack of criticism for it by other states) had the effect of emphasizing the lack of international recognition for the claim.

Territorial Sea and Continuous Zones

As seventeenth- and eighteenth-century writers began to treat the question of outward boundaries with respect to the extension of sovereignty, three principal considerations emerged: security/defense, control of resources such as fisheries, and freedom of movement for ships engaged in trade. The debate over the years has centered on how much of the sea states may claim where they exercise sovereign rights (territorial sea); how much of the sea they may claim where they may assert *protective* or *preventive* rights with respect to items such as customs, health regulations, or immigration; and, since 1945, who, if anyone, has the right to claim portions of the continental shelf and deep seabed for purposes of exploitation.[24]

The debate over the width of the territorial sea and how to justify claims has some interesting history. Early in the eighteenth century, a Dutch lawyer, Cornelius van Bynkershoek, proposed a security-based rationale: "the power [control] over the lands ends where the power of weapons ends."[25] At the time, sources

---

[22]See "Objection of the United States to the Assertion of Sovereignty Over the Gulf of Sirte (Sidra) by Libya," 68 *AJIL* 510 (1974).

[23]Y. Z. Blum, "The Gulf of Sidra Incident," 80 *AJIL* 668 (1986); *Gist,* December 1986; and the AP and UPI Dispatches of March 23, 1986, to March 27, 1986.

[24]See H. S. K. Kent, "The Historical Origins of the Three-Mile Limit," 48 *AJIL* (1954), 537–553.

[25]*De Domino Maris* (1702), 44.

set the approximate range of coastal cannon at 3 nautical miles. As attractive as this rationale might be from a security perspective (and that of political realism), it did not take hold as a broadly accepted principle even though writers tended to discuss variants of it throughout the eighteenth century.[26] One difficulty with any such rule stems from the variability of technology—as technology improved the range of weapons, would the range of sovereign control increase as well? States sought other rationales that would standardize usage. Pragmatism prevailed over narrowly self-interested principle. Consider the scope of the problem if the width of the territorial sea changed with every advance in weaponry. Late in the eighteenth century, an Italian jurist proposed a simple formula—states could claim 1 marine league (3 nautical miles).[27] By the end of the century, most major maritime states including Great Britain and the United States had accepted the 3-nautical-mile standard. We should note that these states also recognized (based on reciprocity) the historical claims of certain states to broader zones (Scandinavia, 4 nautical miles) so long as the claim did not materially affect the overall regime.

Problems emerged in the twentieth century as states sought unilaterally to establish fishing and conservation zones. Concern flowed from the simple fact that historically, claims to exert "jurisdiction" over areas for certain purposes tended to evolve into claims of sovereign rights.[28] The first major and unsuccessful attempt to arrive at a generally acceptable and uniform breadth of the territorial sea was made at The Hague in 1930. The divisions among the participants proved so great that not a single proposal for a limit ever came to a vote. After World War II, the International Law Commission (ILC) tackled the issue, declaring that *12* nautical miles constituted the maximum claim that could be sustained, justifying its stand by the opinion that any greater breadth jeopardized the principle of the freedom of the high seas. On the other hand, the ILC did not succeed in fixing the limit between 3 and 12 miles. The negotiations at the two UN conferences (1958 and 1960) soon bogged down in a welter of competing claims to territorial waters and fishing zones. Without a general agreement, coastal states began to announce new limits for territorial seas.

One of the best illustrations of the problems comes from a series of confrontations, known as "the Cod Wars," between Great Britain and Iceland.[29] In 1958, Iceland announced a change in its territorial sea from 3 nautical miles to 12 nautical miles. It then instituted a ban on foreign fishing vessels within the new 12-mile limit, citing declining fish stocks as the reason. The British protested and sent naval frigates to protect British trawlers fishing in the area. After several incidents over the next three years, Britain finally accepted the new limits. Peace ensued until 1972, when Iceland declared a 50-nautical-mile territorial sea.[30] The two states negotiated another agreement in 1973 in which Britain accepted restrictions on areas, numbers of trawlers, and size of catch. The agreement expired in November 1975, whereupon Iceland again expanded its claim to a territorial sea of 200 nautical miles.

---

[26]See W. L. Walker, 22 *British Yearbook of International Law* (1945), 210–231; Kent, note 24, at 538.

[27]Kent, note 24, at 537.

[28]See J. H. W. Verzijl, 3 *International Law in Historical Perspective* (1970), 60–65.

[29]For a summary, see www.american.edu/TED/icefish.htm.

[30]*Fisheries Jurisdiction (United Kingdom v. Iceland)*, International Court of Justice (1974).

In 1970, the United States shifted its position by announcing that it would support the 12-mile limit in return for guarantees of free transit privileges through all straits used for international navigation. One difficulty caused by expansive claims to territorial seas is that many straits—that is, main passages from one sea to another—would fall within a territorial boundary. Ultimately, in December 1988, the United States officially expanded its territorial sea limits from the traditional 3 nautical miles (adopted in the George Washington administration, 1793) to 12 nautical miles. Article 4 of UNCLOS III permits states to claim up to 12 nautical miles.[31]

Defining the Territorial Sea   Specifying the width of the territorial sea marks only the beginning. The most interesting questions flow from questions of appropriate standards for measurement. While states may agree on the landward point of demarcation—the low-tide mark along the coastline—problems flow from irregular coastlines. The easiest way to illustrate this problem is to point to the western coast of Norway (or Canada's Arctic coast). Practically, it would be close to impossible to delineate the territorial sea in a reasonable way by following the coastline. We chose Norway as an example because it was involved in a landmark case over the use of straight baselines to define its territorial sea.

In the *Anglo-Norwegian Fisheries* case (1951) before the International Court of Justice (ICJ), Great Britain disputed Norway's use of straight baselines to delimit its territorial sea. Britain contended that Norway had seized many British fishing ships on the high seas outside the *4-nautical-mile* limit claimed by Norway. While recognizing the right of Norway to a 4-mile band of territorial sea (based on historical grounds), Britain challenged the method of defining the territorial band. The Court found the Norwegian method reasonable and acceptable. Both the 1958 Convention on the Territorial Sea and the Contiguous Zone and UNCLOS III (Article 7) contain virtually identical specifications for drawing straight baselines.

Varying Widths of the Territorial Sea   Neither customary law nor treaties prohibit a variation in the breadth of a country's territorial sea. Article 3 of UNCLOS III simply states, "Every State has the right to establish the breadth of its territorial sea up to a limit not exceeding 12 nautical miles." Turkey has adopted the 12-mile limit in the Black Sea and the Mediterranean but a 6-mile limit in the Aegean. Japan and South Korea have adopted a 12-mile limit in the Strait of Korea except in its western channel, where a 3-mile limit prevails.

Archipelago Theory   Island groups present an interesting challenge. Both Indonesia and the Philippines claimed the right to draw a perimeter around their outermost islands and to then claim all waters within that perimeter as *historic internal waters*. Indonesia then proposed a 12-mile limit for its territorial sea, while the Philippines claimed limits that varied between 3 and 12 miles depending upon location. These claims met an overwhelming protest from others. A

---

[31]See D. D. Newsom, "Why the Three-Mile Limit Sank," *Christian Science Monitor* (January 26, 1989).

simple look at the map indicates why. Indonesia's proposed perimeter would have stretched over 3,000 miles east to west and 1,200 miles north to south; that of the Philippines would have extended 600 miles east to west and over 1,300 miles north to south. If accepted by other states, the proclaimed internal waters status of the seas enclosed would have abolished rights of free passage, the right of submarines to enter and travel submerged, and the rights of foreign aircraft to fly over the waters involved unless states had negotiated treaty rights.[32] UNCLOS III (Articles 46–51) limits the length of archipelagic baselines to a normal maximum of 100 nautical miles. In the case of very large archipelagos, up to 3 percent of the total number of baselines may exceed the limit to a maximum of 125 nautical miles. The United States has always opposed the archipelago theory. In *Civil Aeronautic Board v. Island Airline, Inc.* (1964),[33] the U.S. Circuit Court held that the channels separating the Hawaiian Islands beyond the 3-mile limit then claimed by the United States were international waters. The boundaries of Hawaii, therefore, were defined by a belt of territorial waters around each island (now 12 nautical miles).

Adjacent States   If states have adjacent or opposite coastlines, the issue of an equitable border between the two becomes an important question. Often, the contentious issues involve the right to resources of the seabed/subsoil/continental shelf, although fisheries have played some role.[34] UNCLOS III (Article 15) provides a formula for equitable division. The rule would not apply if historic title or some other special circumstance dictates a different outcome.

Sovereignty and Its Limits   A state has complete sovereign control over all areas including the airspace, waters, seabed, and subsoil within the delimited area. Custom and treaty do establish a right of innocent passage for foreign vessels, defined as "traversing the sea without entering internal waters" (Article 18). No right of innocent passage exists for aircraft. Transit must be continuous and expeditious, although a ship may stop and anchor insofar as the same are incidental to ordinary navigation or rendered necessary by weather conditions or distress. The ship in innocent passage has a duty to obey all safety and navigation rules established by the coastal state and must not engage in any activity that would be prejudicial to the "peace, good order or security of the coastal state" (Article 19). The coastal state may not exercise its criminal or civil jurisdiction on board a ship in innocent passage unless an activity does disturb the peace, good order, or security of the coastal state or the captain of the vessel requests assistance.

For example, passage of a foreign fishing vessel is not considered innocent if it fails to observe the laws and regulations prohibiting fishing by such vessels in the

---

[32]See "Indonesia: Archipelagic Waters," 83 *AJIL* 559 (1989); D. Andrew, "Archipelagos and the Law of the Sea: Island Straits States or Island-Studded Sea Space?" 2 *Marine Policy* 46 (1978).

[33]*Civil Aeronautics Bd. v. Island Airlines*, 235 F. Supp. 990 (D. Haw. 1964), *aff'd*, 352 F.2d 735 (9th Cir. 1965).

[34]For example, Germany, Denmark, and the Netherlands (North Sea); Libya and Tunisia; Libya and Malta; Nigeria and Cameroon; Romania and the Ukraine (Black Sea). For details, see www.icj-cij.org/homepage/index.php. .

territorial sea.[35] Violation of such a ban led to a violent confrontation between the Bahamas and Cuba. In May 1980, the *Flamingo,* a Bahamian patrol boat, chased and arrested two Cuban fishing boats caught fishing in the Bahamian territorial sea. Responding to a radio call from one of the fishing ships, two Cuban military planes strafed and sank the *Flamingo.* Four Bahamian marines died in the attack. After some intense negotiations, Cuba agreed to pay $10 million in reparations for the sinking of the *Flamingo* and the murder of the four marines. The eight Cuban fishermen who started it all were convicted of poaching in July 1980.[36]

Presumably, the right of innocent passage applies to warships as well as merchant ships. The United States has always insisted upon this right, but during the Cold War, the Soviet Union and its allies recorded reservations to the 1958 Geneva Convention on the Territorial Sea that made such passage dependent upon prior authorization. A survey of contemporary opinion finds a considerable split. Brownlie argues that a significant number of states, indeed perhaps a majority, make such passage subject to prior consent.[37] The draft convention of the International Law Commission included an article that gave the coastal state the right to require prior authorization, but the 1958 Convention omitted it.[38] Some, the United States included, have argued that the heading "Rules Applicable to All Ships" in UNCLOS III (Articles 17–32) applies to warships by direct inference. Brownlie disputes this as not supported by the *travaux préparatoires.*[39]

International Straits The question of free passage through straits is a major concern of maritime states. An *international strait* is any passage connecting two portions of the high seas (or EEZs). The Bosporus and Dardanelles, the Strait of Gibraltar, the Strait of Magellan, the Gulf of Aden, the Strait of Hormuz, the Straits of Tiran, and the Strait of Dover may be familiar names. Writers have identified at

---

[35]See C. B. Selak Jr., "Fishing Vessels and the Principle of Innocent Passage," 48 *AJIL* 627 (1954). Ecuador had claimed inability to control foreign shipping and had prohibited innocent passage of fishing vessels. On the other hand, UNCLOS III includes in Article 19(2) a long list of practices deemed to be in violation of innocent passage and lists, among other items, "any fishing activities," any act "aimed at collecting information to the prejudice of the defence or security of the coastal state," acts of willful or serious pollution, and so on; the list concludes with item 2–1: "Any other activity not having a direct bearing on passage." In 1979, Ecuador enacted a law banning all fishing by foreign tuna boats within 100 miles of the Ecuadorian coast, extending thereby the old limit of 60 miles.

[36]"The Flamingo Affair: A Regrettable Confusion," www.nassauinstitute.org/wmprint. php?ArtID=518.

[37]I. Brownlie, *Principles of Public International Law,* 6th ed. (2003), 188.

[38]II *Yearbook of International Law Commission* (1956), 276–277.

[39]Brownlie, note 37, at 188. A 1988 incident in the Black Sea demonstrates the potential problems and questions. Two U.S. warships entered Soviet territorial waters near a major naval base (Sevastopol) on the Crimean Peninsula. Both ships had on board sophisticated electronic gear. They proceeded on a course lateral to the coast and approximately 10 miles from shore. Two Soviet frigates were waiting. They asked the U.S. ships to leave, but received no reply. The two Soviet ships then deliberately "bumped" the two American ships, causing some minor damage but no injuries. The U.S. ships then departed the Soviet territorial sea. Questions arose concerning the nature of the passage. Was it "innocent," or a prohibited test? Ironically, in justifying their actions, both the United States and the USSR relied heavily on the UNCLOS III treaty even though neither had ratified it at the time (the United States had not even signed it).

least 120 international straits in the world that have a width of 24 miles or less.[40] As we noted earlier, the contemporary trend to expansive claims to territorial seas means that many of these passages now fall entirely within territorial seas. UNCLOS III (Article 38) grants "transit passage," defined as continuous and expeditious passage, through (and over) international straits. On its face, transit passage would seem to give the coastal state less authority over the activities of ships because no requirement of "innocence" attaches even though there is an obligation to refrain from any activities not directly connected with their normal modes of "continuous and expeditious" progress through the strait.

Zones of Special Jurisdiction

Contiguous Zones   In the introduction to this chapter, we noted that coastal states may exercise protective and preventive control over a strip or belt of the high seas contiguous (or adjacent) to their territorial waters. Since 1790, the United States has claimed jurisdiction for customs purposes up to a distance of 12 miles from the shore. Under a number of special "liquor treaties" with Great Britain and other states during the Prohibition Era, the United States had the right to stop, board, search, and seize vessels of the contracting states within one hour's sailing distance from the shore. In 1935, Congress passed the Anti-Smuggling Act, which authorized the president to establish at need so-called customs enforcement areas up to 50 nautical miles beyond the 12-mile limit.

The 1958 Convention on the Territorial Sea and the Contiguous Zone formally recognized the idea of a zone of the high seas beyond territorial waters in which states could prevent infringement of their customs, fiscal, immigration, or sanitary regulations. It firmly established under international law that states had the right to punish violations of such regulations committed in the contiguous zone.[41] UNCLOS III (Article 33) incorporated the definitions of the 1958 Convention but provided for a 24-nautical-mile limit (from shore) rather than the 12-mile limit in the original. Note that jurisdiction to prescribe and enforce extends *only* to those issue areas specifically identified in the treaty.[42] Beyond territorial waters, jurisdiction over other matters, criminal and civil, depends upon what states have chosen to do within the *permissive* grant in the convention. Some have chosen to extend their rights under the convention to the maximum possible limits (the United States); others have chosen to claim more modest limits.[43]

---

[40]On straits in general, see Whiteman, IV: 417–80; K. Kheng-Lian, *Straits in International Navigation: Contemporary Issues* (1982); J. N. Moore, "The Regime of Straits and the Third United Nations Conference on the Law of the Sea," 74 *AJIL* 77 (1980); W. M. Reisman, "The Regime of Straits and National Security: An Appraisal of International Lawmaking," 74 *AJIL* 47; and Articles 34–44 of the 1982 UN Convention on the Law of the Sea, in 21 *ILM* 1276 (1982).

[41]See *U.S. v. Baker*, U.S. Ct. of Appeals, 5th Cir., January 2, 1980, 609 F.2d 134, in 74 *AJIL* 678 (1980).

[42]Note that the treaty does *not* recognize "security" or "military zones" as a legitimate extension of jurisdiction. See H. K. Park, "The 50-Mile Military Boundary Zone of North Korea," 72 *AJIL* 866 (1978).

[43]For a summary of claims, see R. R. Churchill and A. V. Lowe, *The Law of the Sea*, 3rd ed. (1999), 471–472.

The Continental Shelf Until 1945, exploitation of the deep seabed and subsoil *outside* of the territorial sea was open to all on an equal basis. In September 1945, President Harry Truman issued a proclamation that reserved exclusive rights to the United States over an area of the ocean floor outside of the territorial sea termed the *continental shelf*.[44] In most areas of the world (the west coast of South America excluded), the seabed slopes gently away from the coast until it falls abruptly to *abyssal depths* (several thousand feet deep). The width of the continental shelf varies enormously from less than a mile to more than 100 miles. Control of the area became important to states when they discovered substantial exploitable oil and natural gas deposits under the shelf. The possibility of tapping into other resources, such as sedentary fish stocks (oysters, etc.), added to the incentive to claim exclusive rights. The Truman Proclamation attempted to balance the interest in controlling access to resources with freedom of navigation and fishing by explicitly noting that the claim involved only the seabed and subsoil, not the superjacent waters or airspace. In sum, the waters and airspace above the shelf outside of the territorial sea would retain their character as high seas.

Because of variations in width, the ILC, building on the formula in the Truman Proclamation (continuous and contiguous), proposed a limit based upon depth. In its preparatory work for the 1958 Convention on the Continental Shelf (ConShelf Convention), the ILC included a 200-meter (approximately 100 fathoms) outer limit plus a loophole based upon technology. States could make claims beyond the 200-meter *isobath*[45] "to where the superjacent waters admit of the exploitation of the natural resources of the said areas."[46] The 1958 Convention on the Continental Shelf included this language without change. The difficulty stemmed from very rapid technological change. The delimitation of the area in the ConShelf Convention was obsolete even before the treaty entered into force in July 1964. For example, at present the Norwegian oil industry has experience in drilling at depths of 1,200–1,300 meters (4,300 feet) in the Norwegian Sea and has reached a depth of 5,900 meters (more than 19,300 feet).[47] UNCLOS III (Article 76.1) permits states to claim up to 200 nautical miles from shore if the claim meets the twin tests of continuity and contiguousness. The questions here relate to the impact of the new standard as a potential rule of *customary law*.

The continental shelf gives us an interesting study in the development of an international norm. Events illustrate a strength of customary practice—the ability to respond to new phenomena expeditiously. While normally we think of customary law as evolving over a long period of time, a single, clear precedent can quickly

---

[44]Presidential Proclamation No. 2667 (September 28, 1945), 40 *AJIL* 45 (1946 Supp.), www.icj-cij. org/homepage/index.php. This did not mark the first initiative. In 1944, Argentina claimed a zone encompassing mineral resources in the "epicontinental" sea. The United States followed up its claim with the Outer Continental Shelf Lands Act of 1953, which reserved for the United States all "political" and "civil" jurisdiction both in the subsoil and in the seabed of the shelf (43 U.S.C. §§ 1331–1356, P.L. 212, ch. 345, August 7, 1953, 67 Stat. 462).

[45]A line of map passing through all points of equal depth below water.

[46]52 *AJIL* 858 (1959 Supp.). For text of the treaty, see www.un.org/law/ilc/texts/contsh.htm.

[47]http://odin.dep.no/odin/english/norway/economy/032005-990443/dok-bn.html (accessed April 22, 2009).

shape a new rule—particularly in an issue area either where no clear identifiable previous practice exists or where practice has been inconsistent or sporadic. On the other side of the coin, claims to the continental shelf also led to other states asserting claims to other resources that challenged portions of the law thought long settled. We will examine this point later.

The 1958 Convention recognized exclusive rights to the seabed and subsoil resources of the shelf (Article 2). If a state chooses not to exploit such resources, its sovereign rights preclude any other state from doing so without express consent of the littoral (coastal) state. Of particular interest here is Article 2.4 (Article 77, UNCLOS II), which gives the coastal states exclusive control over "living organisms belonging to sedentary species." This would include oysters (pearl cultivation) or other species that can move only in constant contact with the seabed.[48] With minor variations, the definition for example, the 1982 UNCLOS III incorporates most of the provisions of the 1958 instrument.[49] The only limitation to sovereign rights on the shelf relate to submarine pipelines and cables. States may not impede the laying or maintenance of submarine cables and pipelines subject to their right to take reasonable measures for the exploration of the shelf and the exploitation of its resources (Article 7). As a note in passing, the question of "cables" now has considerably less relevance because satellites have replaced cable as an essential communications link.

Subject to these restrictions, the coastal state is entitled to construct and operate installations on the shelf necessary for its exploration or the exploitation of its natural resources. For obvious reasons, no installation constructed on the shelf has the status of an island. These installations cannot generate territorial seas of their own, although states may establish reasonable safety zones around them. The convention forbids any construction that would interfere with the use of recognized sea lanes (Article 60.7). An interesting and open question concerns the right to construct defense installations on the shelf. The treaty does not address the subject. So far, no state has advanced a claim to do so.

► U.S. v. RAY

U.S. Court of Appeals (5th Cir., 1970)
423 F.2d 16

Facts

The United States brought an action to enjoin two private companies from constructing artificial islands around, and erecting buildings upon, two reefs (Triumph Reef and Long Reef) located 4.5 miles east of Elliot Key off the southeast coast of Florida. In 1963, a Bahamian corporation (Atlantis Development) whose charter authorized it to develop property in

(continued)

---

[48]See 69 *AJIL* 149 (175).

[49]Unless specifically noted, all future in-text cites are to UNCLOS III.

international waters sought to establish a new "country" on the reefs—Atlantis, Isle of Gold. The corporation built four buildings, three of them destroyed by a hurricane that struck in September of that year. The U.S. Army Corps of Engineers notified Atlantis that the reefs formed part of the Outer Continental Shelf of the United States.

In November 1964, an American corporation, Acme General Contractors, applied for a permit for dredging and construction at Triumph Reef. The company intended to establish the Grand Capri Republic on this reef, Long Reef, and two others. The Corps of Engineers denied this permit. Atlantis Development filed a complaint alleging a claim to prior ownership. Acme, in partnership with Ray (a U.S. national), began to dredge and fill at Triumph and Long Reefs without authorization. The United States filed an action to compel Acme and Ray to cease their activities. Atlantis filed a cross complaint against Acme and Ray alleging trespass and asserting its superior claim to the property.

Issues

1. Are the areas in question under the jurisdiction of the United States?
2. Can Atlantis advance a valid proprietary claim to the areas in question?

Decision

The areas are unquestionably under U.S. jurisdiction. Neither company has any basis for asserting a valid title.

Reasoning

Both by national legislation (the Outer Continental Shelf Lands Acts of 1953) and by international convention (ConShelf), the United States has an exclusive right to explore and exploit the reefs.

Additionally, the court noted, "Obviously the United States has an important interest to protect in preventing the establishment of a new sovereign nation within four and one-half miles of the Florida Coast, whether it be Grand Capri Republic or Atlantis, Isle of Gold. The rights of the United States in and to the reefs and the vital interest that the Government has in preserving the area require full and permanent injunctive relief against any interference with those rights by defendants and intervenor."[50]

Note

A delightful aspect of this case involves the thorough presentation of arguments and evidence by the attorneys for Acme and Atlantis concerning the requirements for establishing a new island nation.

Oil and fish are at the root of any number of disputes that involve the continental shelf and the exclusive economic zone (EEZ). The United States has a number of outstanding disputes with Canada over the extent of both regimes. Consider here also the dispute between Argentina and Chile over the status of the Beagle Islands (Chapter 5) as well as the incidents between Iceland and other states discussed earlier in this chapter. As *The Economist* recently noted, globally there are dozens of disputes over islands, "many of them specks that no one would care about—were it not for the oil and the fish."[51] Some problems have become more intense because of perceptions that certain fisheries may be on the

---

[50]423 F.2d 16 at 22–23.

[51]"The Lobster Wars," *The Economist* (October 13, 2007), 33–34.

verge of collapse if more effective management practices are not put into place. Before dealing with the EEZ, we will examine some of the disputes over the division of the continental shelf.

Dividing the Continental Shelf Considering the economic stakes involved (Norway went from a relatively poor northern state to a very rich one based solely on the oil resources under its continental shelf), the variation in natural and political boundaries around the world, and the relative newness of the idea of a continental shelf, the question of equitable division of resources among adjacent or opposite states can generate spirited (and sometimes expansive) claims. *The North Sea Continental Shelf Case*[52] (Denmark, the Netherlands, and the Federal Republic of Germany, February 20, 1969)[53] is among the first litigation over apportioning the shelf among adjacent and opposing states. The case had two interesting issues, one involving a plea for equity and one involving customary law. The problem of equity flowed from a geographic quirk. Due to the peculiar shape of part of the German coastline in the North Sea (deeply indented at one point), drawing the boundaries according to the equidistant principle in Article 6 of the ConShelf treaty would give Germany considerably less of the shelf than perhaps merited by the length of its coastline. Indeed, Germany advanced the novel argument, rejected by the court, that the shelf should be divided in proportion to the length of each state's coastline. The second issue involved the status of the "equidistant principle" in Article 6. Denmark and the Netherlands advanced the proposition that it formed a rule of customary law, binding on Germany even though it had not *ratified* the agreement.

The court discussed the question of equity at length. While the court has the authority to decide a case *ex aequo et bono* with the consent of the parties (see Chapter 3), it has never done so. The court struggled with the question of applicable principles. While it clearly declined to accept the idea of pure distributive justice embodied in the *ex aequo et bono* concept, the judges in their decision revising the method of drawing baselines clearly did accept the principle of *equity* in the Aristotelian sense—a tempering of injustice.[54] On the second issue, they found that while many parts of the 1958 treaty might be considered as declaratory of customary law, they could find no evidence that the method of drawing baselines in Article 6 had any substantial support in prior practice. Hence, it could not be considered a rule of customary law binding Germany.

One last note on this case seems appropriate concerning the attitude of the ICJ toward all of the cases in this issue area. In every case, the Court has expressed a strong preference that the disputing parties should negotiate the differences rather than litigate them. As we shall see, the contentious nature of

---

[52]For a map of the disputed area, see http://iilj.org/courses/documents/SketchMap.pdf.

[53]See A. E. Evans, "North Sea Continental Shelf Cases (Federal Republic of Germany/Denmark; Federal Republic of Germany/Netherlands," 63 *AJIL* 591 (1969).

[54]For an elaboration of this argument, see W. Friedmann, "The North Sea Continental Shelf Cases: A Critique," 64 *AJIL* 229 (1970); see also R. Y. Jennings, "Equity and Equitable Principles," *Annuaire Suisse du Droit International* (1986), 42, 46. See also *Case Concerning the Continental Shelf* (*Libyan Arab Jamahiriya v. Malta*), 24 *ILM* 1189 (1985).

the overall relationship between the parties has often precluded direct settlement through diplomatic means. Nonetheless, the interplay here forms a fascinating study of the "politics of international law" (legal dispute settlement).

United States, USSR, and Japan   The USSR, Japan, and the United States did successfully negotiate a series of agreements relating to the status of the king crab. Between the United States and the USSR, the issue turned on whether the area in question could be considered a traditional fishery (see following discussion of the EEZ). Both states agreed that king crab comprised a continental shelf resource subject to the exclusive control of the state where found.[55] After recognizing that abrupt cessation of king crab harvesting would work an economic hardship on the USSR, the two agreed to a gradual reduction.

On the other hand, the legal issue between the United States and Japan was "Do king crabs swim or walk?" If they swim, then they fall into the classification of fish, which then could be freely taken in the superjacent waters over the shelf outside of territorial waters. If the crabs primarily move by walking in constant contact with the shelf, then they become part of the property of the state claiming the shelf. When the negotiation began, Japan had not signed the 1958 ConShelf Convention and reserved its legal position while also, somewhat unhappily, agreeing to a reduction in its fishing activities. The United States also agreed to extend its *good offices* to help the Soviet Union and Japan resolve their conflict over their competition for king crab in the areas concerned.[56]

Greece and Turkey: The Politics of International Law   The dispute between Greece and Turkey[57] involves a fascinating pragmatic problem complicated by 2,500 years of history and less than friendly relations between the two (a mini cold war). Despite being formal allies in NATO, the bilateral relationship of these states has occasionally generated open hostilities (e.g., as in the case of Cyprus) and often simmered in an agitated state just short of war. In this case, history and geography combine to exacerbate the issues. Greece controls more than approximately 3,000 islands in the Aegean Sea. Many of these islands lie very close to the Anatolian (western) coastline of Turkey. The discovery of oil on the continental shelf near one of these islands set the stage for a classic confrontation over division of the continental shelf. The long-standing political hostilities over other issues notwithstanding, the unique features of the geographic situation combined with the ambiguities in customary and conventional law to generate innumerable contentious legal questions. Apart from the formidable problem of actual delineation, the interesting questions here stem from Greek efforts to use various international forums to exert pressure on Turkey as opposed to the Turkish insistence on bilateral negotiations in good faith.

---

[55]D. W. Windley, "International Practice Regarding Traditional Fishing Privileges of Foreign Fisherman in Zones of Extended Maritime Jurisdiction," 63 *AJIL* 490 (1969), 492–493.

[56]*Ibid.*, 493–494. The *New York Times* reported that the outcome of the negotiations left the Japanese a little "crabby."

[57]For the background of the dispute, consult C. Rozakis, *The Greek-Turkish Dispute Over the Aegean Continental Shelf* (1975); L. Gross, "The Dispute Between Greece and Turkey Concerning the Continental Shelf in the Aegean," 71 *AJIL* 31 (1977).

Greece acceded to the ConShelf treaty in 1972 and signed UNCLOS III, but did not ratify it until 1995. Turkey has not signed or otherwise indicated acceptance of either convention. In August 1976, Greece brought the dispute before the Security Council of the United Nations and unilaterally submitted an application to the ICJ asking for interim measures of protection. The Security Council almost immediately adopted a resolution asking both countries to resume direct negotiations. In September 1976, the ICJ issued a statement to the effect that the circumstances did not require interim measures of protection, reserving the question of jurisdiction for future determination. The two states then negotiated the Berne Agreement on the Continental Shelf (November 1976), in which they agreed to resume direct negotiations and refrain from any acts that might prejudice the success of negotiation. Finally, in December 1978, the ICJ held that it lacked jurisdiction in the dispute.[58] As of this writing, the issues remain unresolved.

Exclusive Economic Zones (EEZs)

Analysts of UNCLOS III tend to agree that the construction of EEZs represents a major legal as well as political achievement. EEZs are not an entirely new idea. Their early uses mainly involved claims to exclusive fisheries zones. For example, in 1945 the United States had proclaimed a *conservation zone* in the high seas contiguous to the coasts of the United States. The zone applied to areas where only American nationals had been fishing.[59] In areas where nationals of other states shared the fishery, the proclamation called for agreements with other governments to regulate activity. Proclamations of other countries attempted to exclude foreign fishermen altogether. In 1976, President Ford signed the Fishery Conservation Management Act that expanded what had been a zone of 12 miles to a breadth of 200 nautical miles.[60] The law did not prohibit all foreign fishing in the zone, but it did limit the catch of foreign vessels only to excess stock that could not be harvested by American fishermen. Conservation of fishing stocks formed the central concern of the legislation. The United States proclaimed a 200-nautical-mile EEZ in 1983. Note that the zone applies to Hawaii and Puerto Rico as well as the continental United States.

A broad consensus emerged from the conference negotiations. It attempted to balance "sovereign rights" of the coastal state over certain activities within the EEZ with the right of all states to use the area. The territorial sea ends at 12 nautical miles; the contiguous zone ends at 24 nautical miles. The EEZ may extend 200 nautical miles from the baseline used to determine the territorial sea (or 188 nautical miles from the boundary of the territorial sea—Article 56). Within

---

[58]Text of the order in *Aegean Sea Continental Shelf Case* (*Greece v. Turkey*), 15 ILM 985 (1976); Berne Agreement text in *ILM* 16 *id.,* 13 (1977); ICJ ruling in *Jurisdiction (1978) ICJ Rep.* 1, December 19, 1978, digested with copious excerpts by Evans in 73 *AJIL* 493 (1979).

[59]The text of the proclamation may be found in 40 *AJIL* 46 (1946 Supp.) and 22 *ILM* 461 (1983), including map. See also Whiteman, I: 932.

[60]Text in 70 *AJIL* 624 (1976) and in 15 *ILM* 635 (1976). Many critics of the law, including U.S. government officials, held that its provisions violated the clear wording of the 1958 Convention on Fishing and the 1958 Convention on the Conservation of the Living Resources of the Sea: see *New York Times* (July 20, 1976), 4; and Windley, note 55.

the 188-nautical-mile area, states have *limited* sovereign rights (exclusive rights) *defined by the treaty*. For example, the coastal state may not enforce customs or other regulations in the EEZ. UNCLOS III strikes a balance—the area of the EEZ does not qualify as "high seas," because the coastal state has certain limited "sovereign rights" (and certain duties).

Controversies over delimiting boundaries abound because of the potential to exert control over very large areas of the ocean that might contain important resources or that might give an important strategic advantage. The Beagle Island/Channel dispute between Argentina and Chile (Chapter 5) became so contentious because of the island's location, not because of any inherent value the land may have had. Similarly, China and Japan have had ongoing talks over Japanese claims that Okinotorishima, an atoll in the Philippine Sea, though clearly belonging to Japan forms a point from which Japan may claim a 200 mile EEZ. At issue is the definition of an "island" in UNCLOS III (Article 121).[61]

In the EEZ, the coastal state has the right to exploit and take measures to conserve and manage the natural resources, living or nonliving, of the waters above the seabed, of the seabed, and of the subsoil (Article 56). Within the zone, the coastal state has the exclusive right to determine the allowable catch of the living resources in its EEZ. It may build artificial islands and other installations and structures. Other states may enjoy rights of navigation, overflight, and the laying of submarine cables and pipelines. In general, delimiting the EEZs of opposite or adjacent states will follow the same principles as those applicable to continental shelf questions when natural gas, oil, or other natural resources are involved. In the case of fisheries, other equitable principles may come into play. In this respect, consider the dispute between the United States and Canada over the Gulf of Maine.[62] The questions concerned control over Georges Bank, one of the world's most productive fisheries. Even after the delimitation, the United States and Canada engaged in extended negotiations to work out the details of management and conservation.

An ongoing problem of fishery management stems from the simple fact that fish move. Some stocks may "straddle" the line between the coastal state's EEZ and the high seas. Others are highly migratory. UNCLOS III did not directly address the problems caused by these stocks, necessitating the development of a follow-on treaty, the *Agreement for the Implementation of the Provisions of the United Nations Convention on the Law of the Sea of 10 December 1982 Relating to the Conservation and Management of Straddling Fish Stocks and Highly Migratory Fish Stocks* (New York, August 4, 1995). This instrument entered into force on December 11, 2001.[63] The United States, Canada, Brazil, Japan, the Russian Federation, and the European Community have ratified the treaty. Significantly, Chile, Ecuador, and Peru have not signed.

---

[61]Centre for International Law, "Okinotorishima and the Rock/Island Controversy and Other Maritime Disputes in the East and South China Seas," National University of Singapore (June 3, 2009), http://cil.nus.edu.sg/programmes-and-activities/past-events/cil-seminar-series-by-prof-ted-mcdorman/.

[62]*Delimitation of the Maritime Boundary in the Gulf of Maine Area* (Canada v. United States), *ICJ Rep.* 246 (October 12, 1984); 21 *ILM* 225 (1984).

[63]As of December 1, 2008, 71 states parties.

Straddle stocks have generated great controversies.[64] During a 1997 dispute over the equitable division of catch off the Alaskan coast, Canadian salmon fishermen blockaded an American ferry in port to protest what they saw as the inaction of their government in safeguarding their interests.[65] In May 2008, the two states signed yet another bilateral treaty in an effort to resolve the issues generated by management of the fisheries.[66]

A similar dispute occurred between Australia, New Zealand, and Japan over conservation and management of the southern bluefin tuna (SBT) stock.[67] In this dispute, Australia and New Zealand requested the International Tribunal for the Law of the Sea (ITLOS) to adjudicate. The court did not issue a definitive solution but ordered interim (provisional) measures to conserve the stocks and mandated an arbitral tribunal to resolve the issues. In a totally unexpected turn of events, the arbitral tribunal found that it lacked jurisdiction and revoked the provisional conservation measures.[68] The failure of the arbitral panel forced the parties back into direct negotiation over their respective claims.

HIGH SEAS

Traditionally, the term *high seas* referred to all areas of the world's oceans located outside the limits of the territorial seas claimed by states. As we discussed previously, states have increasingly laid claim to exercise rights over resources in certain areas of the high seas (contiguous zones, EEZs, and continental shelf) and the status of the deep seabed under the high seas still remains an area of some controversy. Although UNCLOS III (Article 86) in theory excludes EEZs and archipelagic waters as belonging to the modern high seas, we have discussed the rules applying to these areas as exceptions applicable to specific circumstances and events because much of the high seas regime still applies to most ships operating in these areas.

We have briefly noted some of the political maneuvering in the fifteenth through eighteenth centuries over claims to control large parts of the ocean. Again,

---

[64]To understand the underlying causes of these disputes, we can focus on the life cycle of the Pacific salmon and its migratory patterns. The Pacific salmon is an anadromous species, which simply means that it reproduces in fresh water but journeys to the ocean before returning to its place of birth to spawn. Pacific salmon will spend several years migrating through the ocean, thus making them vulnerable to harvest by countries other than their host country. Generally speaking, salmon stocks from both Canada and the United States head north from their rivers of origin, reaching the end of their northward migration in Alaskan and adjacent waters, and then return by a southerly route to their rivers of origin to spawn. Because of the potential exposure of salmon to overharvesting, both neighboring countries and high seas fishing fleets can easily overfish the stocks. B. M. Caldwell, "The Pacific Salmon Treaty: A Brief Truce in the Canada/U.S.A. Pacific Salmon War," 57 *Advocate* (1999), www.admiraltylaw.com/fisheries/Papers/Pacific%20Salmon%20Treaty.pdf.

[65]PBS, "North American Fish Fight," ONLINE News Hour (August 1, 1997).

[66]Press Release, Pacific Salmon Commission, May 22, 2008, www.psc.org/pubs/AnnexIV/AnnexIVPressRelease22May08.pdf.

[67]Because all SBT breed in one area, they are managed as one breeding stock; unified management thus requires the cooperation of all states that harvest them. One significant management problem is that, while SBT do not breed until they are 8 years old, they are fished commercially from the age of 2 or 3.

[68]*SBT Case*, 39 *ILM* (2000), 1359, 1393.

we should make a distinction here that is important to the development of the law. Practical questions relating to the ownership and operation of specific ships, marine insurance, and other issues related to commerce and navigation stand somewhat apart from the political issues of access and free use of the oceans. So we will not address the everyday issues of *admiralty law*, much of which falls within private international law, even though many cases will depend upon the rules of *public* international law (e.g., location of the ship) in effect at the time. As the power of states favoring a "closed sea" concept waned, and the utility of that claim gave way to modern commercial and naval concerns, the rule that all states may have equal access to and use of the high seas emerged. Although the roots of the doctrine reach back to at least the early seventeenth century, widespread acceptance of the idea came only with the nineteenth century and the interest of major maritime powers in maintaining and enforcing the principle.

Prescription and enforcement on the high seas depend upon a complementary blend of custom, treaty, and national law. In some cases, UNCLOS III specifies direct obligations; in others (flag regulations), it directs states to enact appropriate measures enforceable through national means and courts. Portions of UNCLOS III are generally regarded as codification of customary law and may be considered binding and enforceable against non-signatories. UNCLOS III (Articles 88 and 89) states that the high seas shall be "reserved for peaceful purposes" and that no state "may validly purport to subject any part of the high seas to its sovereignty." Rights of states, among others, include freedom of navigation, overflight, fishing, and scientific research. Landlocked states—those having no seacoast—have a right of free access to the sea (Articles 124–132). To this end, states interposed between the sea and a landlocked state should by treaty grant freedom of transit through their territory and accord to vessels flying the flag of the landlocked state treatment equal to that accorded to their own ships.

BOLIVIA

After years of protest against being a landlocked state, in 1978, Bolivia negotiated access to a free port zone at Rosario, Argentina. You should consider the timing of this agreement in the context of the ongoing Argentine–Chilean dispute over the Beagle Channel at the time. In January 1992, after long negotiation, Peru concluded a treaty of friendship that included free Bolivian use of Peru's port facilities and the free zone at Ilo.[69] Other landlocked states have not found the same cooperative attitude from their neighbors.

Policing the High Seas   Under normal circumstances, only the crew of a warship of the same flag (nationality) can board a merchant vessel on the high seas. A warship encountering a foreign merchant vessel may board for purposes of investigation if the captain has reasonable suspicion that the vessel is engaged in improper activities such as piracy, the slave trade, unauthorized broadcasting (a pirate radio or TV station), or refusal to show its flag, or if, upon request, the flag state gives permission.[70] In the interest of suppressing certain activities such as drug smug-

---

[69]Text in 32 *ILM* 279 (1993).

[70]Note: Permission has to come from authorities of the flag state. The master (or captain) of the vessel cannot waive the requirement. The right belongs to the state, not to the ship.

gling and the slave trade, states have made cooperative agreements (based upon reciprocity and common interest) to permit a right of mutual enforcement against their merchant vessels. An example is the agreement between the United States and the United Kingdom with respect to narcotics trafficking. Still, the rules of jurisdiction may lead to some interesting problems. Consider the following two incidents that illustrate potential problems of enforcement.

THE EVERGREEN

In May 1982, the *Evergreen*, a freighter sailing *on the high seas* under the Panamanian flag, had a minor mutiny on board. Two Filipino crew members killed the first officer, a citizen of India. The Israeli master brought the ship into U.S. territorial waters and radioed for help. Before FBI agents and Coast Guard personnel boarded the ship, the crew had subdued the mutineers. Upon reaching Houston, the master surrendered the two mutinous sailors to private security guards hired by the Panamanian consul general in Houston. The sailors were then flown to Panama for trial (in the flag state). The United States, while cooperating with Panama, had no claim to try them. The sailors had committed no criminal act within any *jurisdiction* the United States could reasonably claim.

THE MAERSK *DUBAI*

In Canada, six Taiwanese officers (including the master) of the container ship *Maersk Dubai*,[71] registered in Taiwan, were accused of throwing three stowaways (of Romanian nationality) overboard on the high seas. The case presented Canadian authorities with an interesting problem. Because the crimes occurred on the high seas, Canada has no basis for jurisdiction. Romanian law permits prosecution on the basis of passive personality, but the extradition treaty with Canada specified only territoriality or its equivalent. Canada does not recognize Taiwan as an independent state and has no extradition treaty with it. After the court received assurances from Taipei that the six would be vigorously prosecuted, the judge ordered their transfer to Taiwan to stand trial.

The *Maersk Dubai* illustrates a growing problem—the smuggling of migrants. In an effort to stem the flow, Canada and many other states have enacted stiff penalties against ships and owners if caught with illegal immigrants on board. Smugglers of human cargo prey on the poor and the desperate. Horror stories abound. To maximize profits and because they care little about the lives of others, "sponsors" will cram as many individuals as they can into containers. The BBC has stated that human trafficking has replaced the drug trade as the world's largest illegal enterprise because the risks are less and the profits just as large.[72] Experts have noted that women and children are particularly at risk. They often end up as prostitutes or cheap labor in sweat shops. We will explore this issue further in Chapter 17 in the section on the contemporary slavery and slave trade.

---

[71]G. Hamilton, "Death on the High Seas," *Ottawa Citizen* (March 7, 1997), A1; "Taiwan to Hear Case of Romanian Stowaways," *Toronto Star* (March 19, 1997), A13. Compare this incident with the case of the *M. C. Ruby*, "Life Terms for Stowaway Massacre," *The Independent* (December 11, 1995), www.independent.co.uk/news/world/life-terms-for-stowaway-massacre-1525209.html.

[72]http://news.bbc.co.uk/1/hi/world/2056662.stm; see also D. Kyle and Z. Liang, "Migration Merchants: Human Smuggling from Ecuador and China," Center for Comparative Migration Studies Working Paper 43, University of California, San Diego (October 2001), www.ccis-ucsd.org/PUBLICATIONS/wrkg43.PDF.

Stateless Ships Because the flag essentially operates as a passport to the high seas, stateless vessels sail at their own risk. Every state has the right to arrest a stateless vessel, but still must observe whatever principles of national and international law that might apply. In short, a stateless vessel may not have a nationality, but it (and its passengers and crew) do not stand outside the law. States are not free to treat such individuals as pirates or as they otherwise please.

Piracy Contemporary international law mandates that each state pass appropriate national legislation to control piracy (see an extended discussion in Chapter 16). In that all states have a duty to suppress piracy (Article 100), we can speak of "universal jurisdiction" in this instance (for an extended discussion, see Chapter 17). Maritime piracy still flourishes off the coasts of Southeast Asia and Africa. It threatens the security of some of the world's most important sea lanes as well as the safe and orderly flow of international maritime commerce. Data from the U.S. Coast Guard estimate direct financial losses incurred as a result of high seas piracy at about $450 million per year. Moreover, according to data from the International Maritime Bureau (IMB) Piracy Reporting Center based in Malaysia, incidents of maritime piracy have more than doubled since 1994, averaging between 200 and 300 per year over the past five years. These figures, however, may understate the extent of the problem because many attacks (e.g., incidents involving coastal fishermen and recreational boaters) go unreported.[73]

Generally, contemporary publicists have treated Article 15 of the 1958 Convention on the High Seas (incorporated as Article 101 in UNCLOS III) as a codification of existing customary law.[74] Piracy, in simple form, consists of the following:

> Any illegal acts of violence or detention, or any act of depredation, committed for *private ends* by the crew or the passengers of a *private ship* or a private aircraft, and directed.
> On the high seas against another ship or aircraft or against persons or property on board such ship or aircraft. (Emphasis added)

Article 15 represents an attempt at innovation because it includes aircraft as well as surface vessels. Only military ships or aircraft or other official vessels and aircraft so authorized may seize ships and aircraft suspected of piracy.

Hot Pursuit If a ship commits an offense within the internal waters, territorial waters, or contiguous zone of a coastal state and then attempts to leave, the appropriate authorities of the coastal state may pursue the vessel into the high seas to effect arrest. *Hot pursuit* (Article 111) must commence within the appropriate zone, be continuous, and end if or when the fleeing ship enters the territorial sea of another state. Questions here often relate not so much to the right to pursue, but to the *methods* pursuing ships may use to bring the alleged violator into custody. Specifically, under what circumstances may a pursuing vessel resort to overt force

---

[73]See "Pirates Hijack Tsunami Aid Ship," http://news.bbc.co.uk/2/hi/africa/4636695.stm.

[74]The definition marks a significant departure from the traditional definition. See Chapter 17 for an extended discussion.

THE *I'M ALONE*

Canada v. United States 3 U.N.R.I.A.A. 1609 (1935)

Facts

An American Coast Guard patrol boat (the *Wolcott*) spotted the *I'm Alone,* flying the Canadian flag (a British ship of Canadian registry), within the contiguous zone of the United States off the Louisiana coast (12 miles at the time). Suspecting that the vessel might be engaged in smuggling alcohol, the Coast Guard vessel signaled the *I'm Alone* to heave to for boarding and examination. The master of the *I'm Alone* refused, whereupon the Coast Guard ship fired a warning shot across its bow and one through its rigging. The ship fled. A two-day chase ensued, with a second U.S. Coast Guard ship, the *Dexter,* joining the pursuit. The *Dexter* overhauled the *I'm Alone* and again requested surrender. After firing some warning shots, the *Dexter* then fired a number of shots into the hull, sinking the *I'm Alone.* One crewman drowned.

Issues

1. Did the U.S. vessel have the right to request boarding for examination?
2. Did the United States have a right of hot pursuit when the vessel refused?
3. Did the United States have the right to use force to apprehend the vessel?
4. Was the action of the *Dexter* in deliberately sinking the *I'm Alone* a reasonable and proper use of force?

Decision

The United States had good reason to board to determine "beneficial ownership and cargo." It had the right to use *reasonable* force to carry out the investigation. The chase conformed to the accepted rules of hot pursuit. The intentional sinking of the ship was not justified by any principle of international law nor by any agreement between the United States and Great Britain.

Reasoning

Given that the vessel had knowingly been employed as a "rum runner," the "United States might . . . use necessary and reasonable force for the purpose of effecting the objects of boarding, searching, seizing and bringing into port the suspected vessel; and if sinking should occur incidentally as a result of the exercise of necessary and reasonable force for such purpose, the pursuing vessel might be entirely blameless. But the Commissioners think that, in the circumstances . . . the sinking of the suspected vessel was not justified."

The United States "ought formally to acknowledge its illegality, and to apologize to His Majesty's Canadian Government therefore; and further that as a material amend in respect of the wrong the United States should pay the sum of $25,000 to His Majesty's Canadian Government."

Note that the commission denied any compensation to the owners for the loss of the ship. The monies awarded all went to the captain and the crew, "none of whom was a party to the illegal conspiracy to smuggle liquor into the United States."

in attempting to arrest a ship "on the run" that has allegedly violated a statute? In evaluating the question of reasonable uses of force in this context, consider the following two cases: the *I'm Alone*[75] and the *M/V* "Saiga" (No. 2).[76] The standard applied in both cases is "reasonable measures in context (principle of proportionality)." While this standard may sound vague in the abstract, we should note that the principle underlies the policies used by most law enforcement agencies in the United States to define when a law officer may use deadly force to apprehend a suspect. It also presumably governs many other instances where states resort to the use of force (see Chapter 20).

THE *M/V* "*SAIGA*" (NO. 2) CASE

Saint Vincent and the Grenadines v. Guinea International Tribunal for the Law of the Sea (ITLOS) 39 International Legal Materials 1323 (1999)

Facts

The *Saiga*, an unarmed tanker flying the flag of St. Vincent and the Grenadines, was pursued and arrested by Guinean authorities on suspicion that the ship had committed, or was about to commit, violations of customs and contraband laws. Guinea admitted that the arrest had occurred outside the EEZ of Guinea, but maintained that its pursuit had conformed to Article 111 of UNCLOS III.

Issues

1. Did the arrest of the *Saiga* conform to the requirements of hot pursuit as defined in Article 111 of UNCLOS III?
2. Did Guinea use unreasonable and excessive force in stopping and arresting the *Saiga*?

Decision

The tribunal found that the circumstances surrounding the incident did not justify the exercise of hot pursuit. Moreover, the actions of the arresting ships did not meet the necessary tests to sustain a claim to hot pursuit. Finally, Guinea used excessive force in apprehending the *Saiga*.

Reasoning

1. The tribunal found no evidence that the *Saiga* had violated any law or regulation.
2. The conditions for the exercise of hot pursuit are cumulative—each must be satisfied for the pursuit to be legitimate. The tribunal found that pursuit was not continuous and that, in the circumstances, the patrol boats could not have given a visual or auditory signal to stop the tanker.
3. Guinea had no reasonable basis for opening fire upon a fully laden tanker. Guinean officers also had no reason to use force once on board the tanker. The crew offered no resistance. In

(continued)

[75] The *I'm Alone* (Canada v. United States), 3 *R.I.A.A.* 1609 (1935).
[76] International Tribunal for the Law of the Sea (ITLOS), 29 ILM 1323 (1999).

indiscriminately firing, the officers showed little or no regard for the safety of the ship and persons on board. The gunfire caused considerable damage in the radio and engine rooms and seriously injured two crew members.

Note

This was the first case heard on merits by the ITLOS. It defined what states could not do under the definition of "sovereign" rights.

A NOTE ON REGIMES AND THE IDEA OF THE GLOBAL COMMONS

As we noted earlier, the idea that areas outside the exclusive jurisdiction of any state formed part of the *global commons*—that is, spaces open to all states on an equal basis—had become part of the traditional law by the end of the eighteenth century. At that point, only the area of the high seas really mattered. Over the next 200 years or so, as scientific and technical advances generated new concerns (control of airspace, pollution of the atmosphere and sea, and conservation and management of fisheries) and expanded the ability of individuals to explore new vistas (deep sea and outer space) and tap into new sources of valuable mineral deposits, questions of what areas ought to be included in the definition of *commons* became hotly debated. In addition to the high seas (and deep seabed), Antarctica, outer space, and the atmosphere above the high seas can be included as parts of the global commons.

The first part of this chapter has addressed many of the political trends that permitted states to extend their claims for absolute control, or for an exclusive management role, over large portions of the seas once considered part of the global commons. In this respect, the events and negotiations that produced UNCLOS III created a series of new *regimes*[77] to govern specific areas: territorial sea, contiguous zone, EEZ, continental shelf, and high seas. A regime includes all of the legal principles, institutions, practices, and expectations relevant to a specific issue area. If we consider the regime of the high seas alone, we find that our discussion in this chapter, appropriate for an introductory undergraduate text, has barely scratched the surface of the complex of rules, institutions, regulations, and procedures relevant to everyday operations.

To give some idea of the importance of *regime* as a consideration and where it fits in our overall discussion of law, we will briefly describe the activities of the International Maritime Organization (IMO).[78] The IMO provides

> machinery for *cooperation* among Governments in the field of governmental *regulation* and *practices* relating to technical matters of all kinds affecting

---

[77]A *regime* entails "a set of implicit or explicit principles, norms, rules, and decision-making procedures around which actors' expectations converge in a given area of international relations." S. D. Krasner, "Structural Causes and Regime Consequences: Regimes as Intervening Variables," in *International Regimes*, edited by S. D. Krasner (1983), 1.

[78]Originally created as the Intergovernmental Maritime Consultative Organization (IMCO, 1958), the organization changed names in 1982 with the opening of UNCLOS III for signature. See www.imo.org/Pages/home.aspx.

shipping engaged in international trade; to encourage and facilitate the general adoption of the highest practicable standards in matters concerning maritime safety, efficiency of navigation and prevention and control of marine pollution from ships. (Emphasis added)

IMO activities include the development of new conventions to codify practice (Safety of Life at Sea, 1960) or deal with emerging issues such as air and sea pollution from ship operations (MARPOL). IMO has spearheaded efforts to simplify issues of liability and compensation for tanker spills and accidents, to improve ship communications (International Mobile Satellite Organization), or to develop the new safety measures such as the recent Global Maritime Distress and Safety System (GMDSS). UNCLOS III may provide an overarching set of principles to govern each regime (a "charter" or "constitution" of sorts), but practical operations demand a myriad of other administrative and technical regulations to give operational reality to the general principles of the treaty. This brief introduction should emphasize the dynamic nature of regimes. They change and evolve to meet new circumstances and challenges. Consider that within states, administrative law and regulations form a major part of the legal code. Ask any interstate trucker about the "regime" that governs his or her operations.

The Deep Seabed

The debate over access to the deep seabed (as well as Antarctica and outer space) has evolved within the context of the "North–South" divide among states, more so than for any other area of the sea. In this case, the states in the "South" have championed a new principle, the Common Heritage of Mankind (CHM), as governing access to, and distribution of, the resources of global common spaces. In 1970, the UN General Assembly adopted the Declaration of Principles Governing the Seabed and Ocean Floor and the Subsoil Thereof, Beyond the Limits of National Jurisdiction.[79] The declaration stated that this space, now designated as "the Area," and all its resources were to be considered as the common heritage of humankind. No state could claim any portion by asserting a sovereign or other right. The CHM principle mandated that the benefits from any exploitable resources found in the global commons should accrue to all states. The success of the "South" in structuring the deep seabed mining regime (Part XI, Annex III, Annex IV)[80] to reflect CHM principles resulted in the refusal of the United States, the United Kingdom, and a number of other major maritime states to sign UNCLOS III even though the balance of the treaty clearly favored their interests.

To move the process of ratification forward, states working under the auspices of the UN General Assembly developed a supplementary agreement that altered the provisions of Part XI, limiting the full implementation of the deep seabed regime to the contingency where such activities become economically viable

---

[79]Of December 17, 1970, A/RES/2749 (XXV).

[80]Part XI defined the deep seabed area beyond national jurisdiction (the Area); Annex III established the basic conditions of prospecting, exploration, and exploitation; and Annex IV created the Enterprise or operating (mining) arm of the Seabed Authority.

under free market principles.[81] The agreement paved the way for the states of the European Community (EC) that had not signed or acceded, as well as other maritime powers such as Japan, to ratify or submit a document of accession to the convention. The United States signed the agreement, but as of this writing (November 2011) the Senate still has not ratified UNCLOS III. Note that because the greatest part of the treaty was considered as a codification of customary law to which the United States has given its consent, the treaty, except for the seabed mining provisions, can be cited as evidence of customary practice in any litigation by a state party in litigation against the United States.

While the CHM principle formed the objection of states in the "North," other considerations came into play as well. For example, the possibility of extracting manganese and copper from the ocean floor set up a direct conflict with states in the "South" whose economic well-being relied upon the mining and export of these metals.[82] Access to metals may highlight the discussion, but other, more seemingly mundane, resources—such as sand, gravel, and shellfish remains—are also relevant. Some estimates have suggested that the resources from the ocean floor may far exceed the remaining deposits on land. In this instance, the important point is that analysts often treat the "South" as a unified entity. Yet many different issues cut across the announced common interests.

In the original plan, the International Seabed Authority (hereafter, the "Authority") would govern all activities in the Area to ensure compliance with CHM—that is, to ensure the equitable distribution of benefits. The Authority would carry out its task through the Enterprise, its operating arm. Certain states would gain "pioneer" investor status, which would permit exploration before the convention's entry into force and would then give them preferred status in the award of contracts for actual mining operations.

The United States (and other developed maritime states) argued that the original regime had several flaws. It presumed a centrally planned economic model that preempted free market private enterprise. It did not give states with major economic interests in seabed mining a decision-making role commensurate with their interests and potential investments. The membership of the council overseeing the Enterprise would be dominated by developing countries, while the United States could be excluded. Finally, the system of payments to the Authority and other requirements could severely reduce the commercial viability of seabed mining. The 1994 Agreement addressed these issues to the satisfaction of all, including the United States. Articles 1 and 2 of the Agreement stipulate that Part XI of the 1982 Convention and the Agreement stand as a single instrument. In the event of a conflict, the provisions of the Agreement control. States can accede to the Agreement only if they also consent to the 1982 Convention. Under the revised regime, if deep seabed mining does become an economic reality, it will be a market-based system.

---

[81]Agreement Relating to the Implementation of Part XI of the United Nations Convention on the Law of the Sea of 10 December 1982, adopted by General Assembly Resolution 48-263, on July 28, 1994 (48th session).

[82]For a very good discussion of the types of resources involved, see C. L. Antrim, "Mineral Resources of Stateless Space: Lessons from the Deep Seabed," 59 *Journal of International Affairs* 55 (2005).

SUGGESTED READINGS

JURISDICTION OVER VESSELS: GENERAL

Anderson, "Legal Implications of the Entry into Force of the UN Convention on the Law of the Sea," 44 *ICLQ* 313 (1995).

Byers, "Policing the High Seas: The Proliferation Security Initiative," 98 *AJIL* 526 (2004).

"International Law: Law of the Sea" (short summary and links), http://foreignaffairs. gov.ie/international-law/TheLawoftheSea. asp.

Whiteman, IX: 1.

CASES

Cunard Steamship Co. v. Mellon, U.S. Supreme Court, 1923, 262 U.S. 100. "Extraterritorial Application of U.S. Law to Crimes on Foreign Vessels," 97 *AJIL* 183 (2003).

Payne v. S.S. Tropic Breeze, U.S. Ct. of Appeals, 1st Cir., 1970, 423 F.2d 236, in 64 *AJIL* 953 (1970).

Sea Hunt, Inc. v. Unidentified Shipwrecked Vessel or Vessels, 221 F.3d 634 (4th Cir. 2000), *cert. denied,* 121 S. Ct. 1079 (2001).

United States v. Conroy, U.S. Ct. of Appeals, 5th Cir., 1979, 589 F.2d 1258, in 73 *AJIL* 696 (1979).

United States v. Cortes, U.S. Ct. of Appeals, 1979, 588 Fed. Reporter, 2nd Series 106, in 73 *AJIL* 514 (1979).

FLAGS OF CONVENIENCE

Walker, *The Tanker War, 1980–88: Law and Policy* (2000).

CASES

Hellenic Lines, Ltd. et al. v. Zacharias Rhoditis, U.S. Supreme Court (1970), in 9 *ILM* 769 (1970); decision of U.S. Ct. of Appeals (July 3, 1969) in 64 *AJIL* 703 (1970).

McCulloch, Chairman, National Labor Relations Board, et al. v. Sociedad Nacional de Marineros de Honduras; McLeod, Regional Director, National Labor Relations Board v. Empresa Hondurena de Vapores, S.A.; National Maritime Union of America, AFL-CIO v. Empresa Hondurena de Vapores, S.A., U.S. Supreme Court, 1963, 372 U.S. 10.

TERRITORIAL WATERS

Bederman, "United States v. Alaska. 117 S. Ct. 1888 (1997)," 92 *AJIL* 82 (1998).

Charney, "Central East Asian Maritime Boundaries and the Law of the Sea," 89 *AJIL* 724 (1995).

Charney and Alexander, eds, *International Maritime Boundaries* (3 vols. 1993); 1-vol. ed. (2002).

Hackworth, I: 642, 651.

Hollick, "The Origins of 200-Mile Offshore Zones," 71 *AJIL* 494 (1977).

Kim, "The 1992 Chinese Territorial Sea Law in the Light of the UN Convention," 43 *ICLQ* 894 (1994).

Lauterpacht, *Oppenheim,* I: 487.

Maritime Zones Act, East Timor, www. timorseaoffice.gov.tp/mza.htm.

Nelson, "The Role of Equity in the Delimitation of Maritime Boundaries," 84 *AJIL* 837 (1990).

Prescott, *The Maritime Political Boundaries of the World* (1986).

Strohl, *The International Law of Bays* (1963).

Territorial Sea of the United States of America, Presidential Proclamation No. 5928 (December 27, 1988), 54 F.R. 777, http:// chartmaker.ncd.noaa.gov/shalowitz/ App_g.pdf.

Weil, *The Law of Maritime Delimitations— Reflections* (1989).

Whiteman, IV: 1.

CASES

Alaska v. United States, 125 S. Ct. 2137; 162 L. Ed. 2d 57; 2005 U.S. LEXIS 4654; 73 U.S.L.W. 4441.

The International Court of Justice has a number of cases currently under litigation concerning maritime boundaries: see www.icj-cij.org/icjwww/idecisions. htm.

Treasure Salvors, Inc. v. Abandoned Sailing Vessel, U.S. Dist. Ct., S.D. Florida, 1976 (amended February 4, 1976), 408 F. Supp. 907, in 71 *AJIL* 151 (1977).

United States v. State of Maine et al., 516 U.S. 365; 116 S. Ct. 872; 134 L. Ed. 2d 4; 1996 U.S. LEXIS 1549.

STRAITS

Alexandersson, *The Baltic Straits* (1982).

Lapidoth-Eschebacher, *The Red Sea and the Gulf of Aden* (1982).

Leifer, *Malacca, Singapore and Indonesia* (1978).

Ramazani, *The Persian Gulf and the Strait of Hormuz* (1979).

Truver, *The Strait of Gibraltar and the Mediterranean* (1980).

CONTIGUOUS ZONES

CASES

Cook v. United States, U.S. Supreme Court, 1933, 288 U.S. 102.

The Grace and Ruby, U.S. Dist. Court, Mass., 1922, 283 F. 574.

THE CONTINENTAL SHELF

Chiu, "Some Problems Concerning the Application of the Delimitation of Maritime Boundary Provisions of the 1982 United Nations Convention on the Law of the Sea," 4 *Chinese Yearbook of International Law and Affairs* (CYILA) 66 (1984).

Iceland-Norway: Agreement on the Continental Shelf Between Iceland and Jan Mayen (Oslo, October 22, 1981), 21 *ILM* 1220 (1982); see also 20 *ILM* 797 (1981) for the report of the conciliation commission on the same subject.

Karl, "Islands and the Delimitation of the Continental Shelf: A Framework for Analysis," 71 *AJIL* 642 (1977).

Research Centre for International Law (Cambridge University), *International Boundary Cases: The Continental Shelf* (2 vols. 1991).

Richardson, "Jan Mayen in Perspective," 82 *AJIL* 443 (1988).

Whiteman, IV: 740.

CASES

Anglo-French Continental Shelf Arbitration (United Kingdom v. France), Permanent Court of Arbitration, 1977, in 72 *AJIL* 95 (1978), *id.,* 73, 60, and 112 (1979).

Bonser v. La Macchia, Australia, High Court, 1969 (43 *Austral, L. J. R.* 275), in 64 *AJIL* 435 (1970).

Continental Oil Company v. London Steam-Ship Owners' Mutual Insurance Association, Ltd., U.S. Ct. of Appeals, 5th Cir., 417 F.2d 1030, in 64 *AJIL* 695 (1970).

North Sea Continental Shelf Case (West Germany v. Denmark and the Netherlands), International Court of Justice, 1969 ICJ Rep. 3, in 63 *AJIL* 536 and 591 (1969).

Occidental of Umm al Qaywayn, Inc. v. A Certain Cargo of Petroleum Laden Aboard the Tanker Dauntless Colocotronis, U.S. Ct. of Appeals, 5th Cir., August 9, 1978, in 17 *ILM* 1190 (1978).

United States v. California, U.S. Supreme Court, 1965, 381 U.S. 139, in 59 *AJIL* 930 (1965), and its supplementary decree, January 31, 1966, 382 U.S. 448, excerpted in 60 *AJIL* 588 (1966). See also the *Note* by Moreau in 7 *Harvard Int'l Law Club J.* 339 (1966), on this case and its background.

United States v. Ray, U.S. Dist. Court, S.D. Florida, January 3, 1969, in 63 *AJIL* 642 (1969); and see also *Time* (January 24, 1969), 55, on this case.

United States v. States of Maine, New Hampshire, Massachusetts, Rhode Island, New York, New Jersey, Delaware, Maryland, Virginia, North Carolina, South Carolina, Georgia and Florida, U.S. Supreme Court, October Term, 1968, in 8 *ILM* 850 (1969).

EXCLUSIVE ECONOMIC ZONES

Attard, *The Exclusive Economic Zone in International Law* (1987).

Dahmani, *The Fisheries Regime of the Exclusive Economic Zone* (1987).

Davies, "The EC/Canadian Fisheries Dispute in the Northwest Atlantic," 44 *ICLQ* 927 (1995).

The "Hoshinmaru" Case (Japan v. Russian Federation), International Tribunal for the Law of the Sea, Case No. 14, Judgment of 6 August 2007 (EEZ).

The 53rd Tomimaru (Japan v. Russian Federation), International Tribunal for the Law of the Sea, Case No. 15, Judgment of 6 August 2007 (EEZ).

Lowe and Evans, "The M/V Saiga: The First Case in the International Tribunal for the Law of the Sea," 48 ICLQ 187 (1999).

Mahmoudi, "Capri Marine Ltd. v. Chief State Prosecutor. Case No. 2004:26," 99 AJIL 472 (2005).

Vicuña, The Exclusive Economic Zone (1989).

THE HIGH SEAS: GENERAL

Bowett, The Legal Regime of Islands in International Law (1979).

Churchill and Lowe, The Law of the Sea, 2nd rev. ed. (1988).

Hailbronner, "Freedom of the Air and the Convention on the Law of the Sea," 77 AJIL 490 (1983).

Kurabayashi, Tadao, and Miles, eds, The Law of the Sea in the 1990s (1992).

Marcopoulos, "Flags of Terror: An Argument for Rethinking Maritime Security Policy Regarding Flags of Convenience," 32 Tulane Maritime L.J. 277 (2007).

McDougal and Burke, The Public Order of the Oceans (1987).

O'Connell, The International Law of the Sea, edited by Shearer (2 vols. 1983, 1984).

Whiteman, IV: 631 (on landlocked states).

POLICE ACTIVITIES AT SEA

"International Convention Relating to the Arrest of Sea-Going Ships" (Brussels, May 10, 1952); text in 53 AJIL 539 (1959).

Murphy, ed., "Contemporary Practice of the United States Relating to International Law: Extraterritorial Application of U.S. Law to Crimes on Foreign Vessels," 97 AJIL 183 (2003).

CASES

United States v. Warren, U.S. Ct. of Appeals, 5th Cir., 1978, 578 F.2d 1058, in 73 AJIL 143 (1979).

Whiteman, IV: 683, 686.

HOT PURSUIT

Gilmore, "Hot Pursuit: The Case of R. v. Mills and Others," 44 ICLQ 949 (1995).

Maidment, "Historical Aspects of the Doctrine of Hot Pursuit," 46 British Yearbook of Int'l Law 365 (1972–1973).

CASES

Church v. Hubbart, U.S. Supreme Court, 1804, 2 Cranch (6 U.S.) 187 ["Hovering" Vessels].

The I'm Alone, U.S. Department of State, Arbitration Series, No. 2 (1–7), 1931–1935; The I'm Alone Arbitration (Canada v. United States), Claims Commission, 1933 and 1935, in 23 AJIL 351 (1929), id. 29 at 296, 326 (1935).

The Katina, Egypt, Mixed Court of Appeal of Alexandria, 1929, in 24 AJIL 175 (1930) [Hot Pursuit].

United States v. Conroy, U.S. Ct. of Appeals, 1979, 589 Fed. Reporter, 2nd Series 1258, in 73 AJIL 696 (1979).

UNITED NATIONS THIRD CONFERENCE ON THE LAW OF THE SEA

Allott, "Power Sharing in the Law of the Sea," 77 AJIL 1 (1983).

Former Legal Advisers' Letter on Accession to the Law of the Sea Convention (Herbert J. Hansell; Roberts B. Owen; Davis R. Robinson; Abraham D. Sofaer; Edwin D. Williamson; Conrad K. Harper; David R. Andrews; Michael J. Matheson) 98 AJIL 307 (2004).

Senate Testimony regarding U.S. Adherence to Law of the Sea Convention, 98 AJIL, 173 (2004).

DEEP SEABED RESOURCES AND MINING

Antrim, "Mineral Resources of Stateless Space: Lessons from the Deep Seabed," *59 Journal of International Affairs 55* (2005).

Consult also the documents in Deep Sea Ventures, Inc. [United States]; "Notice of Discovery and Claim of Exclusive Mining Rights, and Request for Diplomatic Protection and Protection of Investment," filed November 15, 1974, in 14 *ILM* 51 (1975).

Friedman, "*Selden Redivivus*—Towards a Partition of the Seas" 65 *AJIL* 757 (1971).

Hopson, "Miners Are Reaching for Metal Riches on the Ocean's Floor," *Smithsonian* (January 1981), 51.

Kronmiller, *The Lawfulness of Deep Seabed Mining* (2 vols. 1979).

Statement on "Deep Seabed Mining and the 1982 Convention on the Law of the Sea," 82 *AJIL* 363 (1988).

U.S. Department of State, "Statement on Claim of Exclusive Mining Rights by Deepsea Ventures, Inc.," *id.,* 66; Comments by Government of Canada (re Deepsea Ventures Claim), *id.,* 67–68; "Reply of the Australian Government," *id.,* 795; and "Reply of British Government," *id.,* 796.

Jurisdiction Over Air Space and Outer Space

NATIONAL AIRSPACE

The invention of the balloon and more especially the airplane made it necessary to clarify the rights of states in the air above their territory. As with any newly emerging area of concern, writers advanced a number of theories: (1) states had complete freedom in airspace, just as on the high seas; (2) states could claim territorial jurisdiction in airspace up to about 1,000 feet above the ground, with the upper air again free, as in the case of the high seas; (3) states could claim the entire airspace above a state with no upper limit, but only with a servitude of innocent passage granted to all aircraft registered in friendly foreign countries; and (4) states had absolute and unlimited sovereignty over national airspace, with no upper limit.[1]

The last proposition quickly received general approval when the outbreak of World War I led all belligerent states to assert full sovereignty over their national airspace. Neutrals, in turn, denied all right of passage to belligerent aircraft, thus aligning national airspace with the rules applying to the land surface rather than with those applicable to neutral territorial waters. In fact, both the Swiss and the Dutch armed forces, maintaining the integrity of their neutral airspaces, brought down a number of belligerent aircraft that had penetrated their national airspaces. By the end of the conflict, national sovereignty over airspace had gained almost universal acceptance. The 1919 Paris Convention for the Regulation of Aerial Navigation[2] embodied the idea of full sovereignty (Article I) but also contained a right of innocent passage for private aircraft subject to the rules of the convention.

No question exists today about the legal status of national airspace—states have complete and exclusive sovereignty over the air above their territories (including the

---

[1]"The United States Government has not recognized any top or upper limit to its sovereignty." From a speech by the legal adviser to the Department of State (May 14, 1958), reported in 38 *Department of State Bulletin* 962 (1958). Consult also H. B. Jacobini, "International Aviation Law: A Theoretical and Historical Survey," 2 *J Politics* 314 (1953), and the excellent legal and historical survey by A. M. Dula, "Frontier Law 1977," 97 *Analog* (August 1977), 60.

[2]October 13, 1919; text in 17 *American Journal of International Law* AJIL 195 (1923).

territorial sea but not the contiguous zone). The 1944 Chicago Convention on Civil Aviation,[3] which still provides the essential structure for modern commercial and private aviation operations, reaffirmed the rule from the Paris Convention. Furthermore, Articles 6 and 7 of the Chicago Convention specifically state that no scheduled international flights may come into the territory of a state party without explicit previous authorization. Still, a group of concepts emerged from the Chicago conference that became known as the "five freedoms of the air":

1. The privilege of flying over the territory of another state without landing
2. The privilege of landing in another state for technical reasons only (i.e., refueling)
3. The privilege of landing in another state to discharge passengers, cargo, or mail picked up in one's own state
4. The privilege of landing in another state to pick up passengers, cargo, or mail destined for one's own state
5. The privilege of landing in another state to pick up or discharge passengers, cargo, or mail from a third state.

Article 5 of the convention would seemingly give other flights—that is, those "not engaged in scheduled international air services"—the first two freedoms, but for the most part, state practice has ignored the difference between "scheduled" and "unscheduled."[4] States struggled with the multiplicity of issues raised by these ideals but failed to create a multilateral regime governing traffic rights (the last three freedoms) for scheduled air service.[5] As a result, permission for international commercial air operations is granted primarily only through an unwieldy set of bilateral treaties that deal with routes, capacities, and other matters of concern.

The doctrine of absolute sovereignty means that aircraft have no right of innocent passage through national airspace, though most states clearly have the right to assign entry and exit lanes, if only for purposes of control induced by considerations of national defense. This includes the right to delineate routes or lanes over its territory through which planes may traverse the national airspace. States may designate specified areas as closed to foreign aircraft in the interest of national security. In fact, most countries require that foreign commercial airlines in transit passage obtain prior permission to cross national territory and, in many cases, pay a standard overflight charge per flight. Specific permission is required if foreign *military* aircraft wish to enter the national airspace. For example, in the April 1986 raid on Libya, American planes had to fly a circuitous route from bases in Great Britain because France had refused overflight permission.[6]

The Chicago Convention also created the International Civil Aviation Organization (ICAO) as the operational arm that would promote technical and administrative

---

[3]T.I.A.S. 1591, 15 U.N.T.S. 295. The convention also set up the International Civil Aviation Organization. Text at www.icao.int/cgi/goto_m.pl?/icao/en/chicago_conf/convention.html.

[4]This stands as an instance where practice has actually modified a treaty provision. For further discussion, see Chapter 4.

[5]See O. J. Lissitzyn, "Bilateral Agreements on Air Transport," 30 *J. of Air L. & Commerce* 248 (1964).

[6]"France Barred Overflights," *The Washington Post* (April 16, 1986), A23.

cooperation among states parties to the convention. Another major component of the air law regime is the International Air Transport Association (IATA), a private organization that represents the industry regarding issues of mutual concern.[7] Until airline deregulation in the late 1970s, the IATA operated as a cartel through which (subject to government approval) airlines set ticket prices and other fees. Today the IATA provides a forum for discussion of common concerns besides acting a lobbyist in various other situations when the industry wishes to present a common front.

Jurisdiction

As we noted in Chapter 12, like ships, aircraft also have nationality (Article 17). Unlike the law of the sea, no "flags of convenience" exist for aircraft. Indeed, many states directly own and operate airline companies. In many respects, the rules of jurisdiction parallel those for ships. Within foreign national territorial airspace or airports, both the foreign state and the "flag" state have concurrent jurisdiction. Just as with ships, "territory" trumps "flag" if the foreign state chooses to exert its authority in a specific case. For aircraft, the concept of flag extends much further than it does for ships. Beyond the territorial sea, coastal states *do not* have jurisdiction over the airspace above their contiguous zones, the continental shelves, or their exclusive economic zones (EEZs). Once outside of the territorial sea, for aircraft the flag forms the basis of exclusive jurisdiction.

Occasionally, new circumstances may produce gaps in domestic laws because legislators have not thought ahead. By its very definition, law must have a basis for application. Consider the circumstances in the following case. The defendant clearly committed the acts charged to him, but the court, upon a search, found that no legislation existed to prescribe punishment. In this case, the court had to ask whether an airplane is a vessel, within the meaning of the statute, because Congress had not updated federal law to cover the circumstances of the case.

▌ UNITED STATES V. CORDOVA

U.S. Dist. Ct. E.D. N.Y. (1950) 89 F. Supp. 298

Facts

On August 2, 1948, while over the high seas en route from San Juan, Puerto Rico, to New York, Cordova assaulted the pilot of an airplane owned by Flying Tigers, Inc., an American corporation. At the same time and place, Cordova assaulted the stewardess (Ms. Santiago) of the air carrier and then assaulted the codefendant, Santano. Finally, at the same time and place, Santano assaulted Cordova. The defendant was charged with assault in a U.S. flag air carrier over the high seas.

(continued)

---

[7]See www.iata.org/index.htm. The IATA lists 265 airlines as members, representing 94 percent of all passenger traffic in the world.

Issues

1. Is an airplane a vessel within the meaning of the statute cited?
2. If so, do the acts of the defendant(s) come within the admiralty and maritime jurisdiction of the United States?

Decision

No to both questions, because an airplane cannot be considered a "vessel" within the meaning of the applicable statute.

Reasoning

The statute that speaks of crimes committed *upon* the high seas or *on* other waters cannot be extended to include a plane in flight *over* the high seas. As defined by statute, the question turns on whether an airplane is a vessel within the meaning of the statute, and obviously the answer should be in the negative. The judge said, "It is perhaps irrelevant, but I have little doubt that had it wished to do so, Congress could, under its police power, have extended federal criminal jurisdiction to acts committed on board an airplane owned by an American national, even though such acts had no effect upon national security."

So because an airplane cannot be considered a vessel within the meaning of the applicable statute, and because the statute that speaks of crimes committed *upon* the high seas or *on* other waters cannot be extended to include a plane in flight *over* the high seas, although the defendant was found guilty of the acts charged, the court arrested judgment of conviction because of lack of federal jurisdiction to punish such acts. The judge noted: "I, therefore, find Cordova guilty of the acts charged. But I must arrest judgment of conviction since there is no federal jurisdiction to punish those acts."

Needless to say, shortly after this decision, the Congress enacted appropriate legislation to address this situation.

On the other hand, states have asserted a right to enact measures for air defense that extend into areas of airspace outside of their territorial waters. The United States and Canada have established an air defense identification zone (ADIZ) that, among other regulations, requires the filing of detailed flight plans.[8] The United States also mandates a distant early warning identification system (DEWIZ) adjacent to Alaska's coastal waters. After September 11, 2001, a special ADIZ around Washington, DC (and Ronald Reagan National Airport), went into effect. Several instances of violations of the DC ADIZ have caused plans for evacuation and protection of government personnel to go into effect. In one instance, the senior commander at NORAD noted that he came close to giving an order to an F-16 chase plane to shoot down an errant aircraft that had on board the governor of Kentucky, who was on his way to former President Ronald Reagan's funeral.[9]

When we discussed the law of the sea, we noted the important relationship between private international law (conflict of laws) and the issues of public

---

[8]See 14 C.F.R. § 99; discussion at www.docstoc.com/docs/835226/Washington-D-C-ADIZ-FRZ (accessed May 10, 2009).

[9]A. Russell, "US Fighter 'Minutes Away' from Firing on VIP Plane" (London), *Daily Telegraph* (July 9, 2004), 16. See also C. Gordon and S. Adcock, "D.C. Told: 'Run!' as Plane Strays," *Newsday* (May 12, 2005), A16; and A. Lengel and S. Kehaulani, "Plane Sets Off Evacuation of Capitol," *The Washington Post* (June 30, 2005), A2.

international law. For air law, the greatest majority of the issues litigated (e.g., civil liability and compensation for various alleged losses) have revolved around the Warsaw Convention (1929). The *Convention for International Carriage by Air* (Montreal 1999) updated and modernized the Warsaw Convention.[10] While differing standards of liability and compensation among countries constitute important problems, these problems do not form part of the essential material for an undergraduate text in *public* international law because they require considerable background in the principles and application of civil law for an adequate understanding of the issues.[11] The following case illustrates the symbiotic relationship between the two spheres of law in terms of application.

CHUMNEY V. NIXON

U.S. Court of Appeals (6th Cir., 1980)
615 F.2d 389

Facts

Chumney and his wife,[12] both American nationals, were returning from Rio de Janeiro to Memphis, Tennessee, on a flight chartered by the Shrine Temple of Memphis. During the flight, Chumney alleged that Nixon, an American national and an official of Shelby County, Tennessee (and others, also American nationals), broke some of his teeth and inflicted some other injuries. At the time of the alleged assault, all parties agreed that the position of the plane was at 29,000 feet over Brazilian territory.

Issue

1. Did U.S. federal courts have jurisdiction over an offense that occurred on board an American aircraft within the territorial limits of Brazil?
2. Do the plaintiffs then have grounds for a civil action against the defendants?

Decision

First, U.S. courts, by statute and treaty, clearly have jurisdiction over any offense committed on board an aircraft registered in the United States.

Second, because of that jurisdiction, the plaintiffs may proceed with their civil case.

Reasoning

In deciding the first issue, the court noted that Congress clearly intended 18 U.S.C. § 113 to establish criminal jurisdiction over any criminal activity on board an aircraft of U.S. registry. Law-abiding citizens should be protected.

On the second issue, the court engaged in some interesting and innovative reasoning: "It seems to this court to be an appropriate step under the legal doctrines that we have outlined earlier to approve a civil cause of action for damages derived from criminal statutes that plaintiffs alleged were violated in this case."

---

[10]Convention for International Carriage by Air, May 28, 1999, S. Treaty Doc. No. 106-45, 2242 U.N.T.S. 350. Entered into effect in the United States on November 4, 2003.

[11]For a guide to recent issues, see O. Beiersdorf and J. Guidea, "Recent Developments in Aviation Law," 72 *J. Air L. & Com.* 207 (2007).

[12]Compare "Sailor's Snug Harbor" in Chapter 12. We encourage students to read the full transcript of the plaintiff's allegations in this case. In today's era, this case would have made the Jerry Springer show.

In this case, the questions of public international law clearly involved competence. Did any U.S. court, state or federal, have jurisdiction? Did the United States have a right to assert jurisdiction based upon the nationality of the aircraft, or would Chumney have to seek relief in a Brazilian court? The court found the issues of criminal jurisdiction had a straightforward answer. On the other hand, the civil aspects of the case raised interesting problems in relation to domestic law. Did the Congress intend that "criminal" jurisdiction in the circumstances also would permit a corresponding civil case?

Questions such as these (and those in *Cordova*) led to the ICAO taking the initiative to develop the 1963 Tokyo Convention on Offenses and Certain Other Acts Committed on Board Aircraft.[13] The convention addresses possible gaps in jurisdiction by making sure that at least one state (normally the "flag" state) will have a basis to assert jurisdiction no matter where the aircraft was flying at the time of the incident. Article 4 reflects a "peace of the port" doctrine for aircraft in flight. In normal circumstances, a territorial state may not interfere with an aircraft in flight unless the offense has some dimension that affects security or traffic rules.[14] Perhaps as important as the jurisdiction issues, the convention specifically establishes the authority of the aircraft commander to deal with offenses on board (Articles 5–10). This includes the authority to restrain passengers who have committed an offense and to land as soon as practicable to offload them to local authorities.

AIR HIJACKING

A peculiar and distressing accompaniment to the successful development of air transportation has been the forcible seizure of aircraft (hijacking). Incidents of this nature took place occasionally in connection with large-scale disturbances in various countries (Czechoslovakia in 1950, China, and Cuba) in the late 1940s and the 1950s, but modern hijacking on a large scale began on May 1, 1961. On that day, Antulio Ramirez Ortiz, a Cuban using the pseudonym of El Pirata Cofrisi (the name of an eighteenth-century Spanish pirate), diverted a National Airlines plane and forced the pilot to land in Havana.

After this event, dozens of passenger planes were diverted to Cuba, with such incidents sometimes occurring as often as twice a day. Planes, crews, and passengers were always permitted to return to their scheduled routing, with the hijackers remaining in Cuba. The resulting publicity surrounding hijackings with Cuba as their destination focused increased public and governmental attention on the problem. In 1961, President John F. Kennedy signed a bill declaring the hijacking of aircraft an act of piracy and authorizing penalties for the offense ranging up to death. The law also provided for a $1,000 fine for carrying concealed weapons aboard an aircraft and for sentences of up to five years in prison for giving false information

---

[13]20 U.S.T. 1641; entered into force for the United States on December 4, 1969. Text: www.iasl. mcgill.ca/airlaw/public/aviation_security/tokyo1963.pdf. As of this writing, the convention has 185 states parties.

[14]For the purposes of the convention, an aircraft is considered in flight "from the moment when all of its doors are closed" (Article 5.2).

on plane hijacking. Application of such legislation proved to be almost impossible; however, in almost all instances, the "pirates" remained in Cuba, beyond the jurisdiction of American courts. In a few instances, on the other hand, the hijackers were subdued before the aircraft left the United States or reached Cuba. In such cases, prosecution of the individuals in question took place. In February 1973, the United States and Cuba negotiated an understanding on hijacking (both of aircraft and of vessels) that provided for either prosecution or extradition.[15]

The motivation behind air hijackings varies from case to case. In some instances (the diversions to Cuba are the best examples), individuals either harbor some grudge against their own government or have other, quite personal reasons for wishing to leave their country of residence and to go to another place. In other instances, ransom for the plane and passengers plays a major role, either for the hijacker's personal enrichment or to finance some underground or rebel movement (many hijackings by Middle Eastern groups are examples of this variety of motivation). Again, aircraft have been hijacked as a lever for bringing about the release of certain political (or other types of) prisoners, or, quite frequently, for drawing attention to a political or social cause through the publicity created by the hijacking. In still other instances, hijackings have been caused by the desire of an individual or small groups to escape from a regime that is objectionable to them (most of the hijackings of Eastern European planes and one People's Republic of China plane were examples).

During the early period of modern air hijackings, those guilty of the acts in question pleaded for asylum on the grounds that they were political offenders. That defense of the seizure of aircraft held true in many cases, but increasingly, the courts and governments of many countries became cognizant of the danger to the safety of the aircraft, its crew, and its passengers—and realized that this danger was most clearly out of proportion to the claims of personal endangerment, persecution, and so on brought forward by hijackers. It has thus become gradually accepted that the dangers posed to property as well as to innocent people should not be overshadowed by real or alleged political aspects. Consequently, a large proportion of more recent air hijackings have been classified by such bodies as the Organization of American States as "common crimes," particularly when the seizure of hostages has been involved in the act.

International reaction to criminal acts connected with aircraft began in a rather modest way when the Convention of Offenses and Certain Other Acts Committed on Board Aircraft was signed in Tokyo on September 14, 1963, at the end of a conference called by the ICAO. Representatives of 16 countries, including the United States, signed the agreement.[16] The Tokyo Convention entered into force just as an epidemic of so-called skyjackings (aircraft hijackings) occurred. The

[15]U.S.-Cuba, "Memorandum of Understanding on Hijacking and Vessels and Other Offenses" (February 15, 1973): text in *New York Times* (February 16, 1973), 4; see also the memorandum's relation to the right of asylum, as analyzed by the U.S. Department of State, in 67 *AJIL* 535 (1973).

[16]Text in 2 *International Legal Materials* 1042 (1963); see also the detailed analysis of the convention in S. Shubber, *Jurisdiction Over Crime on Board Aircraft* (1973). The convention entered into force on December 4, 1969.

Tokyo Convention had dealt briefly with the possibility of skyjacking (Article 11), but the delegates who drafted it had clearly not anticipated the political climate of the late 1960s. In 1968–1969, there were *109* recorded seizures of aircraft—more than twice the number for all previous years of powered flight.[17] Most of the perpetrators claimed political motives.[18] Prodded by the United States, the ICAO undertook to draft another convention specifically aimed at skyjacking: the 1970 Hague Convention for the Suppression of Unlawful Seizure of Aircraft (December 16, 1970).[19]

One indication of how serious the problem had become was the speed with which states acted. The treaty was drafted and open for signature in less than two years. It entered into force less than a year (October 14, 1971) after it opened for signature. The convention represents a major innovation in that it gives state parties a grant of *universal jurisdiction* over the crimes defined in the treaty.[20] Perhaps more practically, the treaty specifically gives concurrent jurisdiction to the state of registration as well as to any state where the aircraft may land with the offender(s) still aboard. Moreover, if a state party apprehends a perpetrator, the treaty requires authorities to extradite or try the person. To this end, Articles 7 and 8 stipulate that aircraft hijacking will be added as an offense to all existing extradition treaties and is to be included as an offense under any future extradition treaties. Article 7 attempts to eliminate the political exception loophole by stipulating that states are obligated "without exception whatsoever" to try if they do not extradite. Authorities must "take their decision in the same manner as in the case of any ordinary offense of a serious nature under the laws of that state." If no extradition treaty exists between two states, Article 8 states that the convention itself may serve as the treaty agreement for the purposes of the convention.

Unlike the Tokyo Convention, the Hague instrument made air hijacking a distinct separate crime and gave the receiving state no real discretion on the issue of prosecution of a hijacker. The language of the convention excluded motivation from consideration.[21] Many commentators were somewhat critical of several provisions of the Hague agreement. They felt (correctly, in the view of the present writers) that Article 4 of the treaty could have based jurisdiction simply on the "universality principle," arguing that when certain crimes against international law have been committed, jurisdiction is vested in any state able to secure possession of the guilty

---

[17]By 1976, the total reached 385, http://encyclopedia.laborlawtalk.com/Aircraft_hijacking.

[18]Review Chapter 11 on the problems that claims of "political motivation" may cause. An exception is the 1971 incident where D. B. Cooper demanded and received a $200,000 ransom for the plane and passengers. Cooper parachuted from the rear door of the 727 (an action that caused a major retrofit for that jet) and was never seen again, although some parts of the ransom were later found, www.crimelibrary.com/criminal_mind/scams/DB_Cooper/.

[19]22 U.S.T. 164. Text: www.iasl.mcgill.ca/airlaw/public/aviation_security/hague1970.pdf; 10 *ILM* 133 (1971); and 65 *AJIL* 440 (1971 Supp.). The key articles of the agreement are nos. 4 and 7.

[20]See 49 U.S.C. § 1301(38) and 49 U.S.C. § 1472. The United States had to redefine its special aircraft jurisdiction and extend its own law to implement Article 4 of the convention.

[21]See also R. L. Brooks, "Skyjacking and Refugees: The Effect of the Hague Convention upon Asylum," 16 *Harvard Int'l Law J.* 93 (1975), referring to the wording and the U.S. government's understanding of the crucial Article 7 of the treaty.

party or parties, regardless of where the offense in question has taken place or of the nationality of the apprehended individual.[22]

In September 1971, the ICAO held its Diplomatic Conference on Air Law in Montreal, where still another agreement was concluded: The Montreal Convention to Discourage Acts of Violence Against Civil Aviation (1971),[23] unanimously accepted by the representatives of 30 countries, agreed that hijackers could be tried if found in the territory of a state other than the state in which the aircraft in question had been registered (Article 4, para. 3). Enforcement provisions in the new agreement again were weak, even in the view of the sponsoring ICAO. Consequently, a special subcommittee met in Washington, DC, in September 1972 to consider a convention providing for the cutting off of air service and for other boycott activity against states that failed to comply with the rules laid down in the Tokyo, Hague, and Montreal conventions. Afterward, the ICAO Council decided to convene an extraordinary session of its assembly and a diplomatic conference in Rome in August–September 1973. The 25-day meeting ended on September 21, 1973, after voting down all the proposals calling for tougher action against air hijackers.

On December 27, 1985, Palestinian terrorists attacked the Israeli airline (El Al) desks at both the international airports in Rome and Vienna. Eighteen persons, including four of the terrorists, were killed, and more than 100 were injured. Because of those episodes and others, particularly in the Mediterranean area, the ICAO moved to supplement the coverage of offenses against aircraft by the Montreal Convention of 1971. It drafted the Protocol for the Suppression of Unlawful Acts of Violence at Airports Serving International Civil Aviation. That instrument was signed at Montreal on February 23, 1988, by 46 countries.[24]

The record of the United Nations in dealing with the problem of air hijacking has been less than impressive over the years. Following General Assembly Resolution 2551 (XXIV) of December 12, 1969, in which the dangers of hijacking were recognized and prosecution of all guilty persons was recommended, the Security Council, called into urgent session by the United States and the United Kingdom, met briefly and passed its Resolution 286 (1970) on September 9, 1970. The resolution consisted of three sentences, the last of which called on states to take all possible legal steps to prevent further hijackings or any other interference with international civil air travel. This was followed by General Assembly Resolution 2645 (XXV) of November 25, 1970, in which the General Assembly, in essence, endorsed the declarations adopted at the 1970 Montreal meeting of the ICAO and subsequent instruments developed by that agency. After there had been several hijackings and after a 24-hour strike by airline pilots, the Security Council adopted by consensus on June 20, 1972, a "decision" in which it urged states to put an end

---

[22]For example, Y. Dinstein, "Criminal Jurisdiction Over Aircraft Hijacking," 7 *Israel Law Review* (1972), 195–197.

[23]Text in 10 *ILM* 1151 (1971); the Montreal Convention entered into force on January 26, 1973; the United States is a party.

[24]Background, content summary, and text in 27 *ILM* 627 (1988); entered into force August 6, 1989. The U.S. Senate gave advice and consent to ratification on November 22, 1989.

to hijacking by adopting cooperative international efforts. Needless to say, that decision had no measurable effects on the problem.

Following a renewed outbreak of hijacking, 42 countries (mostly Western nations) jointly asked the General Assembly, on October 22, 1977, to schedule a debate on safety of international civil aviation. The 149-member Special Political Committee approved by consensus a resolution that was then adopted by the General Assembly, without a vote, on November 3, 1979.[25] One of the interesting Arab- and African-sponsored amendments to the resolution stressed the importance of the concept of national sovereignty. This amendment implied, according to observers, that the 1977 West German rescue of crew and passengers of a hijacked Lufthansa craft in Somalia was acceptable, in view of Somalia's approval of the action to be taken, whereas Israel's 1976 rescue of hostages from Entebbe in Uganda was not acceptable, in view of Ugandan opposition.[26] (See "Unusual Hijackings with Special Legal Implications," later in this chapter.)

The failure of international agencies to develop effective measures aimed at air hijackers resulted in regional, bilateral, and unilateral plans of action. Thus, 13 countries—including the United States, Israel, and the Federal Republic of Germany—had created, by the middle of October 1977, commando units trained to rescue hijacked hostages.[27] In July 1978, representatives of the United States and six other major non-Communist industrial countries attended an economic summit in Bonn, West Germany, and resolved to act jointly in suspending air traffic to and from states that failed to quickly turn over hijacked aircraft and hijackers.[28]

On a bilateral basis, the United States and Cuba arrived at the Memorandum of Understanding on the Hijacking of Aircraft and Vessels (February 15, 1973).[29] That agreement provided for the return of hijackers to the country in which the aircraft or vessel in question had been registered or for their trial in the country whose territory the hijackers had reached. Both parties also agreed to provide severe punishment for the promoters of, and participants in, hostile expeditions of any kind from either state to the other state. In the fourth part of the memorandum, it was agreed that the receiving country

> may take into consideration any extenuating or mitigating circumstances in those cases in which the persons responsible for the acts were being sought for strictly political reasons and were in real and imminent danger of death without a viable alternative for leaving the country, provided there was no financial extortion or physical injury to the members of the crew, passengers, or other persons in connection with the hijacking.

On a unilateral basis, country after country has amended its domestic legislation to provide for the trial and punishment of air hijackers (to list a few examples

---

[25]Text in 16 *ILM* 1545 (1977).

[26]See *New York Times* (November 4, 1977), sec. A.1

[27]See *New York Times* (October 22, 1977), 7, for a survey of the types of units then in existence and of some of the actions in which several had been involved; consult also *Time* (October 31, 1977), 44.

[28]*New York Times* (July 18, 1978), A1, A6; and (August 2, 1978), A7.

[29]Text in *New York Times* (February 16, 1973), 4; and 12 *ILM* (1973), 370–376.

only: Cuba, the Soviet Union, the German Democratic Republic, and China). In the United States, Congress had passed an antihijacking law as early as October 14, 1970 (the Act to Implement the Convention on Offenses and Certain Acts Committed on Board Aircraft, Pub. L. No. 91–449, 84 Stat. 921).[30] Congress later passed Public Law 93–366 on August 5, 1974, which amended the Federal Aviation Act of 1958[31] in order to implement the Hague Convention of 1970. It is interesting to note that Public Law 93–366 refers to air piracy, a term used in the domestic legislation of several countries though not in international agreements. The 1974 law also provided for the death penalty (or life imprisonment) if the death of another person resulted from the commission or attempted commission of an air hijacking.

Politics and Practice

Agreeing to extradite or try may leave states with some interesting dilemmas in the real world. What should a government do in the case of individuals who are genuinely fleeing from an oppressive regime and in fear of their lives, and who "hijack" an airliner as the means of their escape? What happens when principles conflict? Consider the following incident because it illustrates the tension between events as characterized by the ideal of the law—hijackers ought to be punished—and the *political* (and moral) questions faced by the West German government.

▶ THE TIEDE–RUSKE CASE

In 1978, Hans Detlev Tiede (an East German national), accompanied by Ingrid Ruske (an East German national), hijacked a Polish airliner en route from Gdansk, Poland, to East Berlin and forced it to land at Tempelhof Air Base in the American sector of West Berlin.[32] From the standpoint of the West German public, the two hijackers merited a hero's welcome for their successful escape from "behind the wall" separating the two Germanies. On the other hand, as we have noted, the United

States had long taken a hard line against skyjacking. Both the United States and West Germany were states parties to the 1970 Hague Convention with its "extradite or try" provisions. In addition, approximately six weeks before this incident, the major industrial states of the West (OECD) had jointly signed and publicly proclaimed the Bonn Declaration, which stipulated that these states would initiate a civil aviation boycott against any country that failed in its duty to extradite or try aerial hijackers.

(continued)

---

[30]See O. J. Lissitzyn, "In-Flight Crime and United States Legislation," 67 *AJIL* 306 (1973), for an analysis of the law.

[31]Text in 13 *ILM* 1515 (1974). See also the *New York Times* (September 14, 1976), 1, 32, for an arraignment of "air pirates."

[32]*United States v. Tiede and Ruske*, Berlin, U.S. Court for Berlin, March 14, 1979 (Criminal Cases No. 78-001 and 78-001A), in 19 *ILM* 179; see also A. Lowenfeld, "Hijacking, Freedom, and the 'American Way,'" 83 *Mich. L. R.* 1000 (1985); and H. J. Stern, *Judgment in Berlin* (New York: Universe Books, 1984). Stern was the presiding judge at the trial.

At this time, diplomatic relations between the United States and West Germany were strained over President Jimmy Carter's decision to cancel deployment of the neutron bomb. This had placed West German Chancellor Helmut Schmidt in a difficult political position because of his vigorous campaign to have the West German public accept the weapon. The Tiede–Ruske incident was a political time bomb for Schmidt because West German public opinion would not support either a trial or an extradition back to Poland for the two. Finally, West Germany was in the midst of negotiating a refugee exchange with East Germany.

The case takes on an additional element of complexity because the plane landed in Berlin, "the city where World War II never quite ended and the Cold War never thawed."[33] Technically, Berlin was still under occupation and controlled by the Four Power Agreement. West Germany and the United States worked out an arrangement whereby Germany would bear the financial cost of the trial while the United States would bear the political costs. Trial would take place in the "United States Court for Berlin." An artifact of the occupation, the court had never heard a case and had no standing arrangements (i.e., no judges, bailiffs, clerks, or courtrooms). The U.S. ambassador to the Federal Republic (not the president of the United States) had the authority to appoint all officials and presumably would also then serve to hear any appeals of the court's decisions.[34]

The trial took place using *American procedure* (rules of evidence, etc.), but the jury would apply *German substantive law*. Judge, prosecution, and defense spoke only English. The six jurors were West German citizens who spoke only German. Authorities dropped charges against Ms. Ruske because of violations of her rights under American procedure (extended detention without charge, no Miranda warning, etc.). Tiede was convicted and sentenced to nine months' imprisonment. Since he had already spent that much time in jail awaiting trial, the sentence was commuted to time served.

The really interesting question here is unanswerable. What would have happened if Tiede had directed the plane to another city in the Federal Republic—Bonn or Frankfurt?

Unusual Hijackings with Special Legal Implications

Several cases of hijacking provided unusual and interesting problems, as well as unorthodox solutions, in the sphere of international law. On September 16, 1980, the Cuban government announced that it would either punish or return to the United States any person hijacking an aircraft to Cuba from the United States. That decision had been made after nine U.S. airplanes had been skyjacked to Havana since early August 1980. A number of similar arrangements were concluded between other countries, such as one between France and the United States (1970) and between Cuba and Mexico (1973).

---

[33]Lowenfeld, note 32, at 1001.

[34]The trial itself raises many issues that Judge Stern did not address in his book and that are beyond the scope of this text. The most interesting of these involves the extent to which the Constitution applies outside the territorial borders of the United States (and to extensions such as aircraft and ships of American registry).

In the famous episode referred to as the Entebbe Raid, the problems raised were debated, unsuccessfully, before the UN Security Council. The facts were fairly clear: On June 28, 1976, a group of Palestinian Liberation Organization (PLO) terrorists hijacked an Air France plane in a flight from Israel to France with a crew of 12 and 256 passengers aboard. The terrorists seized the aircraft just after it had left Athens. After a detour to Libya, the plane finally landed at Entebbe Airport in Uganda. The hijackers demanded the release of over 150 terrorists jailed in several European countries, in Israel, and in Kenya. The hijackers released 164 passengers and held the others as hostages. The Ugandan government appears to have done nothing to assist the crew in regaining control of the craft. On July 3, an Israeli military commando unit liberated the surviving hostages (three had died) and flew them to Israel. The crew remained with the plane. During the fighting involved in the rescue operation, one Israeli soldier, seven terrorists, and several Ugandan military personnel were killed; much of the Entebbe Airport was wrecked, as were a number of Ugandan military aircraft found on the ground.[35]

On July 12, 1976, two draft resolutions were introduced in the Security Council: One by Tanzania, Libya, and Benin condemned Israel for violating the territorial integrity and sovereignty of Uganda; the other by the United Kingdom and the United States condemned hijacking but affirmed the need to respect the territorial integrity and sovereignty of all states.[36] When the matter came up for a vote on July 14, 1976, the UK–U.S. resolution failed to obtain the nine affirmative votes needed, and the African resolution was not pressed for a vote. On July 22, 1976, President Idi Amin of Uganda informed the French government that he would release the hijacked aircraft. Its crew thereupon flew it back to France.

A series of events in many respects similar to the Entebbe Raid occurred in the Mogadishu Raid of October 1977.[37] On October 13 of that year, a Lufthansa aircraft was hijacked and eventually landed (after traveling over much of the Middle East). Two planeloads of West German specialist troops of the Border Protection Force (also trained to act against hijackers) had trailed the aircraft for some time before its landing. Some 110 hours after the hijackers had taken control of the aircraft, the German units attacked and captured the plane, killing three of the four hijackers in the process. In contrast with the Entebbe incident, the Mogadishu recapture was undertaken with the full knowledge and explicit approval of the Somalian government.

On other occasions, commandos brought in by permission of the country in which the hijacked aircraft was located attacked the airliner and liberated the hostages: In April 1981, Indonesian commandos stormed an Indonesian plane at the Bangkok (Thailand) Airport; in July 1984, Venezuelan commandos took a hijacked

---

[35]See the *Introductory Note* by McDowell, 15 *ILM* 1124 (1976), on which much of the above account has been based; *New York Times* (July 5, 1976), 1, 4, for French charges of Ugandan collusion with the hijackers; and also *Newsweek* (July 19, 1976), 42, for a detailed account of the rescue operation.

[36]Texts in 15 *ILM* 1226 (1976) see *id.*, 1228, excerpts from the most interesting presentations of various members of the Security Council; also *Time* (July 26, 1976), 39–40.

[37]A detailed account, with map, of the entire incident may be found in *Time* (October 31, 1977), 42.

Venezuelan aircraft at the airport in Willemstad, Curaçao; and in November 1985, Egyptian commandos captured Egyptian hijackers at the Valetta Airport in Malta.

The frequency of major hijackings of aircraft declined sharply in the 1990s. In March 1991, four Pakistanis were killed at the Singapore Airport by commandos after they had seized a Singapore Airlines jet during its flight from Malaysia; in August 1992, an Ethiopian jetliner was hijacked to Djibouti, where all passengers and crew members were released; in September 1993, three Russian hijackers forced a Russian aircraft to land in Norway, where they sought political asylum; and in October of the same year, four hijackers seized a Nigerian Airlines jet and diverted it to Niamey, capital of Niger, only to be captured by a commando raid after a four-day hostage drama. And in February 1994, three Algerian policemen hijacked a domestic flight and forced it to land in Spain. On December 25, 1994, four Muslim terrorists seized a Paris-bound French airliner with 239 passengers and crew aboard in Algiers. Three of the passengers were killed, and female passengers were released. Then, after a 40-hour standoff, the jet was flown to Marseille. There, the hijackers demanded that the craft be fully refueled. French police commandos, however, stormed the jet and killed all four hijackers—who, it was later discovered, apparently had planned to explode the aircraft over Paris. Also, in 1994 a disgruntled employee seized Federal Express Flight 705 as it left Memphis, Tennessee. He intended to use it as a cruise missile against FedEx headquarters. He was subdued by the flight crew before an emergency landing back at Memphis.

In 1996, Ethiopian Airlines Flight 961 crashed into the Indian Ocean near a beach in the Comoros Islands after hijackers refused to allow the pilot to land and refuel the plane. A total of 125 passengers died, and 50 survived. In 1999, a lone man hijacked All Nippon Airways Flight 61. He killed the pilot before being subdued. In 1999, Kashmiri militants hijacked Indian Airlines Flight 814 and diverted it to Kandahar. After a weeklong standoff, India agreed to release three jailed Kashmiri militants in exchange for the hostages. The militants killed a hostage before the agreement was reached.

The most devastating incidents occurred on September 11, 2001, when nineteen terrorists hijacked four planes: American Airlines Flight 11, American Airlines Flight 77, United Airlines Flight 93, and United Airlines Flight 175. The hijackers used two of the planes—United Airlines Flight 175 and American Airlines Flight 11—as missiles, deliberately crashing into each of New York City's Twin Towers. American Airlines Flight 77 was used in a similar fashion at the Pentagon in Washington, DC. These are by far the three most deadly of all aircraft hijackings. In the fourth case, the passengers, learning of the fate of the other three planes, attacked the cockpit, causing the hijackers to crash the plane in rural Pennsylvania, killing all on board. By official count, 2,752 people died at the World Trade Center; 189 died in Washington, DC; and 44 died in Pennsylvania. In the 10 years since 9/11, 10 other hijackings have occurred, but none resulted in casualties.

Aerial Intrusions

The penetration of national airspace by foreign aircraft has led to numerous disputes and claims between countries, to one case brought before the International Court of Justice, and, in at least one instance, to a serious international crisis and the cancelation of a proposed "summit" conference. Under the doctrine of exclusive sovereignty over the national airspace, authorities may adopt one of several actions when a foreign aircraft intrudes into that space without permission: they may ignore the intruder; they may attempt (in the event of a landing) to exercise administrative and possibly judicial authority over the craft and its occupants; they may attempt to destroy the craft after intrusion has become a fact; or they may attempt to force the craft to leave the sovereign's airspace, change course, or land in a designated area. That airspace, though currently varying from country to country, will probably correspond at some future time to the 12-mile border limit laid down in the UNCLOS III Convention.

The procedures just outlined do not make a distinction between military and civilian planes. There would be few recriminations if a bomber from an unfriendly country were to intrude, refuse to land or turn back, and be attacked. On the other hand, what if a civilian plane, especially one carrying passengers, were to follow similar tactics after intruding into another country's airspace? Or what if the ostensibly civilian plane were actually a spy aircraft, manned by government personnel and engaged in an electronic survey of the country whose airspace had been violated?

Driven by Cold War concerns, major disputes over aerial intrusion surfaced soon after the end of World War II. The following are some of the more spectacular intrusions and state reactions.

- In 1948, the Yugoslav government sent a note to the UN secretary-general for circulation among the members of the Security Council, in which it charged the United States with numerous violations of Yugoslav airspace.[38]
- In July 1955, a Bulgarian fighter shot down a commercial aircraft of El Al Israel Airline. Bulgaria finally agreed to pay a total of US $195,000, which excluded compensation for the loss of the aircraft.[39]
- In May 1960, the Soviet Union brought down an American U-2 engaged in aerial reconnaissance. The incident served as the Russian excuse for abandoning the planned Paris Summit Conference between President Dwight D. Eisenhower and Premier Nikita Khrushchev. Francis Gary Powers, the captured pilot, was later traded for a Russian spy, Rudolph Abel.[40]

---

[38]*New York Times* (September 4 and October 10, 1946); detailed documentation in 15 *Dept. of State Bulletin,* 415 and 502 (1946).

[39]*Case Concerning the Aerial Incident of July 27, 1955 (Israel v. Bulgaria)* [Preliminary Objections, Judgment of May 26, 1959], *ICJ Reports, 1959,* 127. Consult L. Gross, "The Jurisprudence of the World Court: Thirty-Eighth Year (1959)," 57 *AJIL* 751 at 753–771; and L. C. Caflisch, "The Recent Judgment of the International Court of Justice in the Case Concerning the Aerial Incident of July 27, 1955, and the Interpretation of Article 36(5) of the Statute of the Court," 54 *AJIL* 855 (1960).

[40]See Q. Wright, "Legal Aspects of the U-2 Incident," 54 *AJIL* 836 (1960); O. J. Lissitzyn, "Some Legal Implications of the U-2 and RB-47 Incidents," 56 *AJIL* 135 (1962); as well as the copious literature cited in those sources. For the aftermath of the incident, consult also T. B. Ross and D. Wise, *The U-2 Affair* (1962). See also "Legal Aspects of Reconnaissance in Airspace and Outer Space," 61 *Columbia L. R.* 1074 (1961); R. J. Stanger, ed., *Essays on Espionage and International Law* (1963); Francis Gary Powers with Curt Gentry, *Operation Overflight* (1970); as well as *New York Times* (August 2, 1977), 12.

- In July 1960, an American military patrol craft (RB-47) was shot down over Soviet territorial waters off the northern coast after it had "intruded deliberately" into Soviet airspace and had disobeyed an order to land. The Soviets interned two crew members for approximately six months.

- In April 1969, North Korean MIGs shot down a U.S. Navy EC-121M reconnaissance plane, some 90 miles off the North Korean coast, with a total loss of the 31-man crew.

- In February 1973, Israeli military aircraft shot down a Libyan airliner that had strayed into the Sinai airspace; 106 lives were lost. The assembly of the ICAO condemned the Israeli action, and the ICAO Council instructed the agency's secretary-general to institute a fact-finding investigation. The latter was then undertaken by ICAO secretariat experts.[41]

- In March 1973, Libyan jet fighters attacked a U.S. Air Force "transport plane" (really an electronic reconnaissance craft), claimed by the United States to have been, at the time in question, over 80 miles off the Mediterranean coast of Libya.[42]

- In August 1973, Israeli military aircraft intercepted a civil airliner of Middle East Airlines in Lebanese airspace outside Beirut and forced it to land on a military air base in Israel. The claimed purpose of the act was to capture four leaders of Arab terrorist organizations. After two hours, the craft and all aboard were permitted to depart.[43]

- In September 1981, Sudanese air defense forces shot down an intruding Libyan bomber, killing its two pilots.

- Between 1950 and 1983, Soviet military aircraft attacked at least 35 foreign aircraft, in the name of defending against aerial intruders: 16 military planes were attacked, another 16 were downed, and 76 lives were lost. Three civilian planes were attacked, resulting in a loss of three lives.[44] The scenes of these attacks varied greatly. Some took place over the Soviet Union itself, others were near the borders (the Baltic, Poland, Czechoslovakia, East Germany, the Siberian coast), and still others were over the Japanese islands or over clearly international waters (the Baltic, the Sea of Japan).

- In September 1983, the Soviet Union destroyed KAL Flight 007 causing a loss of 269 lives. The Korean aircraft strayed into Soviet airspace over the Kamchatka Peninsula, the Sea of Okhotsk, and Sakhalin Island. Eventually, after the alleged failure of attempts to communicate with the aircraft and after it had turned away from Soviet airspace, a Soviet fighter pilot

---

[41]*New York Times* (March 1, 1973), 7; text of the ICAO Council Resolution of June 4, 1973, in 12 *ILM* 1180 (1973).

[42]*New York Times* (March 22, 1973), 1, 9; (March 24, 1973), 5; (May 31, 1973), 2; see also "Letter Dated 18 June 1973 from the Permanent Representative of the United States of America to the United Nations to the President of the Security Council," in 12 *ILM* 1277 (1973).

[43]*New York Times* (August 11, 1973–August 16, 1974), passim; UN Security Council condemnation (15 to 0) of Israel in Resolution 337 (1973) on August 15, 1973, *New York Times* (August 16, 1973), 13; and a second condemnation of Israel by the Council, August 20, 1973, in 12 *ILM* 1280 (1973); see also 68 *AJIL* 111 (1974) concerning the episode.

[44]Special Report, "Secrets of the Cold War," *U.S. News and World Report* (March 15, 1993), 30.

destroyed the airliner with an air-to-air missile.[45] The Soviet Union subsequently claimed that the airliner at some time that night had been mistaken for a U.S. RC-135 spy plane and that the Soviet pilots had believed that the Korean plane had been collecting military intelligence.

- In May 1987, a 19-year-old West German pilot defied Soviet air defenses by landing a single-engine plane on the edge of Red Square.[46]
- On April 1, 2001, a U.S. reconnaissance aircraft flying over the ocean at least 50 miles southeast of China's Hainan Island collided with a Chinese jet fighter that had been tracking its movements. The U.S. aircraft made an emergency landing in China. The Chinese jet crashed. The pilot of the U.S. aircraft did not obtain verbal permission from China to land, and all crew members on board were interned. The Chinese pilot was presumed dead at sea.[47]

Right of Distress

The right to penetrate national airspace and to land on national territory in the event of distress or of unfavorable weather conditions has been generally accepted and is based on analogous rights of vessels in distress. National regulations govern the rights of aircraft in this category of intrusion into the national airspace.[48] In the last incident listed earlier, the U.S. aircraft was flying over the ocean beyond the recognized 12-mile limit of China's territorial sea. Although not within "territorial limits," it did come within an air defense identification zone (ADIZ) claimed by China. After the collision, the U.S. aircraft then landed on Chinese territory without verbal clearance. It did so in distress. Consider this analysis from the commentary posted by the American Society of International Law:[49]

> Customary international law recognizes that ships at sea have a right to enter another state's port in distress. By analogy a similar right probably extends to

---

[45]See 22 *ILM* 1109 (1983) for a collection of the documents covering the incident, including Security Council meetings, ICAO deliberations, diplomatic notes to the Soviet Union, national actions taken by the United States and other states as a result of the downing of the airliner, actions by the International Federation of Air Line Pilots, as well as the "Rules of the Air," signals to be used in plane-to-plane communications, and so forth. For general accounts of the Korean Airlines (KAL) incident, see *Time* (September 12, 1983), 10–18; and *Newsweek* (September 12, 1983), 16–30, passim. See also Union of Soviet Socialist Republics, "Law on the State Boundary of the U.S.S.R." (entered into force on March 1, 1983), in 22 *ILM* 1055, esp. 1058, 1063 (1983); "Japan–U.S.–USSR: Memorandum of Understanding Concerning Air Traffic Control" (Tokyo, July 29, 1985) in 25 *ILM* 74 (1986); A. Dallin, *Black Box, KAL 007 and the Superpowers* (1985); L. Goodrich in *Christian Science Monitor* (October 23, 1992), 6, and J. Barron, "KAL 007: The Hidden Story," *Reader's Digest* (November 1991), 71.

[46]C. Bohlen, "W. German Pilot, 19, Flies Unchallenged to Red Square; Aviation Buff Took Off From Helsinki," *The Washington Post* (May 30, 1987), A1.

[47]J. Dao, "U.S. and China Resume High-Level Military Talks After 20 Months," *New York Times* (December 10, 2002), 15.

[48]See, for example, the U.S. regulations, http://tfmlearning.faa.gov/Publications/atpubs/AIM/Chap6/aim0603.html.

[49]See F. L. Kirgis, "United States Reconnaissance Aircraft Collision with Chinese Jet," www.asil.org/insights/insigh66.htm, for a discussion.

aircraft in distress, including state aircraft, although the Chicago Convention does not contain an express exception to article 3(c) for state aircraft in distress. Article 25, which applies to civil aircraft rather than to noncommercial state aircraft, says that "Each contracting State undertakes to provide such measures of assistance to aircraft in distress as it may find practicable."[50]

The following case has some interesting elements concerning U.S. views of what regulations may apply to an aircraft that lands within U.S. territory in distress.

▶ LEISER V. UNITED STATES OF AMERICA

U.S. Court of Appeals First Circuit (1956); cert. denied 234 F.2d 648; 1956

Facts

The appellant, Samuel Leiser, with diamonds in his possession, was traveling by air from Frankfurt, Germany, to Gander, Newfoundland, by way of Paris. His ultimate destination was Bermuda. His tickets called for no stop in the United States, but owing to adverse weather conditions, his plane overflew Gander. Contrary to his original expectation and intent, the plane landed at Boston, Massachusetts, early on the morning of June 7, 1954. Before any customs officer approached him in Boston, he made arrangements to return to Canada by the next available plane (scheduled to leave at 7 A.M.). Appellant failed to declare the diamonds in his possession. Subsequent discovery by the customs officers led ultimately to a criminal indictment alleging that "appellant . . . did knowingly and willfully . . . smuggle and clandestinely introduce into the United States certain merchandise" and "did fraudulently and knowingly . . . bring into the United States certain merchandise . . . contrary to law, in that said merchandise was not included

in the declaration and entry as made, and was not declared either orally or in writing before examination of his baggage was begun as required by law." The diamonds were seized as contraband. In January 1955, appellant was tried and acquitted on both counts of the criminal indictment. Shortly thereafter, appellee instituted the present proceedings to recover the diamonds in question.

Issue

Do exemptions from customs regulations normally accorded ships in distress apply to individuals arriving involuntarily by air as well?

Decision

By law, the circumstances do not matter. Even if Leiser violated the law in good faith, the diamonds are still subject to forfeiture. A violation is a violation no matter the intent.

Reasoning

The court rejected the appellant's construction of the term *arrival,* noting that "the collector may cause an

(continued)

---

[50]*Ibid.,* note 32.

examination to be made of the baggage of any person arriving in the United States in order to ascertain what articles are contained therein and whether subject to duty, free of duty, or prohibited notwithstanding a declaration and entry therefore has been made."

"Moreover if it had been the intent of Congress to extend . . . exemptions to such individuals, we believe it would not have been done inferentially by relying upon some highly technical interpretation of an ordinary word such as 'arriving', but, on the contrary, would have been spelled out in some detail."

In March 1992, twenty-five states signed a Treaty on Open Skies. This unusual agreement permits surveillance flights over North America, Europe, and the former Soviet Union to ensure compliance with arms control agreements. It established an annual quota of overflights for each country.[51]

Satellites

The development of both reconnaissance satellites and digital photography has rendered long-range overflights by manned aircraft somewhat obsolete. These craft pass over states at such altitudes as to be practically invulnerable to normal defense measures. In fact, the Soviet Union and the United States came to a tacit agreement, and other countries soon joined them, that satellites have to be tolerated. In recent years the U.S. government has made available, for purely nominal sums and to any country desiring them, satellite photographs showing agricultural development, locations of mineral deposits, and so on.[52]

TELECOMMUNICATIONS

A different use of airspace involves wireless transmission into the state's airspace, and perhaps, through it. The invention of wireless telegraphy at the beginning of the twentieth century resulted in discussions similar to those posed by the advent of aircraft. In 1906, a number of states signed an International Wireless Telegraph Convention (Berlin); this was superseded by the International Wireless Convention of London (1912). Both instruments attempted to deal with the technical aspects of radio communications. In 1927, a conference in Washington, DC, resulted in the International Radio Convention, signed by representatives of 78 governments. That instrument expanded controls and required private radio stations to obtain government licenses. It also provided for the use and allocation of radio frequencies and types of transmitters permitted.

Many states sought to maintain strict controls over telecommunications through state monopolies. The problem of regulating telecommunications parallels

---

[51]See details in "Open Skies Treaty," 88 *AJIL* 96 (1994).

[52]See *U.S. News and World Report* (September 12, 1983), 24; and (September 8, 1986), 59. Consult also G. C. Staple, "The New World Order: A Report from Geneva," 80 *AJIL* 699 (1986). The first artificial satellite, Sputnik, went into orbit around the earth on October 4, 1957.

that of regulating aircraft in another respect. With the rapid changes occurring in technology during this period, telecommunications quickly expanded in scope and sophistication. Consequently, more modern methods of control became desirable. The Madrid Telecommunications Convention of 1932 created a new international agency, the International Telecommunications Union (ITU).[53] The convention creating the ITU established a central office in Berne, Switzerland (now moved to Geneva), and gave it control of all varieties of telecommunications, thus consolidating into a single regime areas previously governed by separate treaties. The ITU developed a separate set of regulations to govern each mode of communication. Subsequently, the union has convened a number of conferences to discuss common problems. In 1982, the ITU produced a new Telecommunications Convention, which entered into force on January 1, 1984. Regional telecommunications conventions have evolved in the Americas (Havana, 1937; Rio de Janeiro, 1945) and in Asia (Asian Broadcasting Union, 1964). The latest global convention (Malaga–Torremolinos, 1973) entered into force on January 1, 1975 (for the United States, April 7, 1976). In addition, global radio regulations (Geneva, December 6, 1979) entered into force on January 1, 1982 (except for certain provisions on February 1, 1983); for the United States, on October 27, 1983.

As the power of transmitters increased, states and others recognized the potential for propaganda, both in terms of supporting domestic regimes and as a relatively low cost foreign policy option. The British Broadcasting Company (BBC) began BBC Empire Service in December 1932, with broadcasts aimed toward Australia and New Zealand. Other early international broadcasters included Radio Moscow, the official service of the Soviet Union (1923), which began broadcasting on long-wave in 1923 (renamed the Voice of Russia, following the collapse of the Soviet Union); PCJJ (the Netherlands) targeting Indonesia; and Vatican Radio (February 1931). Germany, with the ascension to power of the Nazi Party (1933), quickly realized the potential of broadcast media as a tool of policy. Post World War II, not only international "information" broadcasts were a staple of Cold War politics, but many other states such as Egypt, Iran, and the two Koreas mounted sustained campaigns to promote their goals.[54]

Among the basic regulations adopted by the ITU was the requirement that all radio stations must be operated in such a manner that avoided interference with the communications services of all contracting governments or agencies authorized by them. Questions always arose about the exact content of this requirement. My co-author noted that this regulation was violated on a wholesale basis by the governments of Soviet Bloc states, which set up extensive systems of radio stations purposely designed to interfere with (jam) broadcasts from the BBC, the German Deutsche

---

[53]See www.itu.int/home/ (accessed April 22, 2009).

[54]See, J. Hale, *Radio Power: Propaganda and International Broadcasting* (1975); R. Johnson, *Radio Free Europe and Radio Liberty: The CIA Years and Beyond* (2010); P. C. Washburn, *Broadcasting Propaganda: International Radio Broadcasting and the Construction of Political Reality* (1992); C. M. Kim, "Research Presentation [North-South Korean Propaganda & International Law]," *Global Media and International Law* (April 21, 2011), http://blogs.nyu.edu/blogs/cmk396/globalmediainternationallaw/2011/04/research_presentation_northsou.html.

Welle, and the American Voice of America, Radio Free Europe, and Radio Liberty.[55] The real question, however, revolves around the right of a state to "invade" the "airwaves" of other states, deliberately or not. Jamming in this case could be considered a legitimate right of self-defense. Questions continue about the status of Radio Martí (1984, TV Marti, 1990), a U.S.-government-funded operation aimed at Cuba.

"Pirate" Broadcasting We noted that many governments sought to keep tight controls over telecommunications through state monopolies. For example, the BBC originated as a state monopoly. In 1958, a new phenomenon in the communications sphere made its appearance. Privately owned radio stations, located on vessels anchored or sailing outside the territorial sea or established on artificial islands beyond territorial jurisdictions, began broadcasting into the territory of states whose governments did not permit, or controlled rigorously, the transmission of commercial advertising. The ITU rules prohibited such commercial broadcasting from international waters, but the responsibility for enforcement rested on the country in which the vessel in question was registered.[56]

In 1962, the "Voice of Slough" began operations off the English coast. In 1964, it was joined by Radio Caroline—a large-scale operation on a former ferry, staffed by two disc jockeys and a crew. Soon after, other stations began operating off the coasts of Denmark and the Netherlands. When the British government protested to the ITU, the flag state of the *Caroline,* the ITU reminded Panama of its responsibilities. Previously, Panama had agreed to withdraw its registration from vessels housing illegal radio stations off the Dutch and Danish coasts. Meanwhile, the owners of the *Caroline* acquired a second vessel, which soon began to broadcast off the British coast near Liverpool.[57]

In January 1965, the Council of Europe opened the European Agreement for the Prevention of Broadcasts Transmitted from Stations Outside National Territories for signature.[59] In 1967, the United Kingdom enacted the Marine and Broadcasting Offenses Act, making it a criminal offense to assist a pirate station in any manner, after enacting an earlier (1964) Territorial Waters Order in Council that was aimed at the stations located on fixed tower sites.[58] UNCLOS III (Chapter 12) contained several provisions that gave states the right to close down stations.[59] The phenomenon disappeared as states liberalized domestic laws and began to license private stations.

---

[55]See G. von Glahn, "The Case for Legal Control of 'Liberation' Propaganda," 31 *Law and Contemporary Problems* (Duke University, Summer 1966), 554; *Christian Science Monitor* (March 24, 1993), 18 and 19; (June 17, 1993), 2; (October 20, 1993), 14; and (March 9, 1994), 17. On the concept of a "Free Radio" for China, see *Christian Science Monitor* (July 30, 1992), 18; and B. J. Wattenberg, "Time for a Radio Free Asia," *Reader's Digest* (September 1992), 179.

[56]See *United States v. McIntyre,* U.S. Dist. Ct., D. New Jersey, 1973, 365 F. Supp. 618, reported in 68 *AJIL* 339 (1974); *Newsweek* (September 24, 1973), 93, on McIntyre's activities; Whiteman, IX: 789; and Henkin, 384, on pirate stations.

[57]Consult *Time* (January 14, 1973), 34; and *The (Vancouver, B.C.) Province* (August 2, 1978), 13, on Radio Caroline.

[58]See *Regina v. Kent Justices, ex Parte Lye et al.,* Great Britain, Queen's Bench, 1966 (1966), 2 W.L.R., reported in 61 *AJIL* 1077 (1967) and noted, with elaborate documentation, by Watts in 9 *Harvard Int'l L. J.* 317 (1968).

[59]See, for example, UNCLOS III, Articles 33, 109(3) and 110(c).

OUTER SPACE

The problems of the law of the air have not ended with the questions posed by the increasingly common penetration of the upper layers of Earth's atmosphere. Outer space has become one of the next targets for voyages of discovery. Already the legal implications of space travel have begun to appear. The United Nations maintains an Office for Outer Space Affairs in Vienna.[60]

United Nations Action

Late in 1961, the General Assembly adopted the Resolution on Peaceful Uses of Outer Space, which asserted that international law, including the Charter of the United Nations, applied to outer space as well as to celestial bodies and that both such space and such bodies were to be regarded as free for exploration and use by all states.[61] These concepts were expanded in 1963 by the General Assembly's Declaration of Legal Principles Governing Activities in Outer Space. That declaration, though not a binding treaty, summarized neatly the consensus arrived at after serious debate in the General Assembly. It provided that (1) space exploration and the use of space were to be for the benefit of all humankind; (2) states conducting activities related to space would be responsible for their acts; (3) all activity in space was to be guided by the principles of cooperation and mutual assistance; (4) states launching objects and personnel were to retain jurisdiction over them in space and on their return to Earth, no matter where they might land; (5) states were to be liable for any damages on Earth, in the airspace, or in outer space caused by objects launched by them into outer space; and (6) astronauts were to be considered envoys of humankind and, in case of accident, all states were to be bound to render them all possible assistance and to return them promptly to the state in which their space vehicle was registered.

Outer Space Treaty

On May 7, 1966, President Lyndon Johnson announced that the United States would seek a UN agreement to prevent any state from claiming title to the moon and other celestial bodies. The Legal Committee (on Outer Space, now composed of 28 members) quickly began to draft such an agreement, adding sections on the prohibition of weapons of mass destruction in outer space or on celestial bodies. After reconciling the differences between the views of the United States and the Soviet Union, the draft was approved unanimously in the General Assembly on December 19, 1966.[62] On January 27, 1967, the treaty was signed at an unusual ceremony in the White House attended by representatives of 60 nations, and

---

[60]See www.oosa.unvienna.org/oosa/SpaceLaw/treaties.html (accessed May 10, 2009). All resolutions and treaties discussed in this section are available from this website.

[61]Res. 1721 (XVI), UN General Assembly, 16th Session, reprinted in 56 *AJIL* 946 (1962 Supp.); see also J. Simsarian, "Outer Space Co-operation in the United Nations," 57 *AJIL* 854 (1963).

[62]G.A. Res. 2222 (XXI), December 19, 1966.

thereafter, the treaty was open for ratification. The U.S. Senate gave its consent on April 25, and the United States then ratified the treaty, which entered into force on October 10, 1967.[63] An examination of this Treaty on Principles Governing the Activities of States in the Exploration and Use of Outer Space reveals that despite the exaggerated claims put forth in 1967, the instrument represents little more than a declaration of "principles." In essence (without enforcement provisions), it is only a set of "self-denying" statements.[64]

One major development in the sphere of outer space law was the drafting of a treaty by the UN Committee on Outer Space on the Rescue of Astronauts, the Return of Astronauts and the Return of Objects Launched into Outer Space.[65] As soon as the General Assembly had approved the draft, the agreement was opened to signature and ratification. It entered into effect on December 3, 1968. Of the six substantive articles in the treaty, one pertains to the recovery and the return of artificial space objects, one to the inclusion of international agencies as launching authorities affected by the agreement, and the other four to the rescue and return of astronauts on Earth as well as in space. In contrast with the relevant provisions in the Outer Space Treaty, the 1968 instrument contains detailed and well-thought-out provisions concerning the duties and rights of states respecting the rescue and return of astronauts who have crash-landed on Earth. On the other hand, the treaty's provisions dealing with the rescue of astronauts who have encountered difficulties in space are incomplete. The situation appears logical because some of the problems likely to be encountered in such a contingency have not yet appeared in fact, and solutions are problematic at best. Among the problems left unanswered is the important question of who would meet the staggering monetary costs of an Earth-to-space rescue effort. Next, the Convention on International Liability for Damage Caused by Space Objects was concluded in 1972.[66] In January 1979, this instrument was invoked for the first time by Canada as a result of damage claimed to have been caused by the *Soviet Cosmos 954*.[67]

By November 1974, the UN Committee on the Peaceful Uses of Outer Space had completed a draft treaty, the Convention on Registration of Objects Launched into Outer Space.[68] That draft was approved by the General Assembly on January

---

[63]Consult also the analysis of the agreement by Ambassador Goldberg, 56 *Department of State Bulletin* 78 (1967), or 61 *AJIL* 586 (1967) for his views; and T. R. Adams, "The Outer Space Treaty: An Interpretation in Light of the No-Sovereignty Provision," 9 *Harvard Int'l L. J.* 140 (1968). By the end of December 1984, a total of 92 states had ratified the treaty, but 30 signatories had failed to do so.

[64]See the comprehensive survey of S. H. Lay and H. J. Taubenfeld, *The Law Relating to Activities of Man in Space* (1970), 63, on this point.

[65]*New York Times* (December 17, 1968), 1 (for the text of the treaty, see *New York Times*, 66) and 63 *AJIL* 382 (1969). Consult also R. C. Hall, "Rescue and Return of Astronauts on Earth and in Outer Space," 63 *AJIL* 197 (1969).

[66]Text in 66 *AJIL* 702.

[67]See 18 *ILM* 899 (1979) for the relevant diplomatic correspondence; and 20 *ILM* 689 (1981) for the protocol (April 2, 1981) on settlement of Canada's claim for damages caused by *Soviet Cosmos 954*. See also C. Q. Christol, "International Liability for Damage Caused by Space Objects," 74 *AJIL* 346 (1980).

[68]Text in 14 *ILM* 44 (1975).

14, 1975, and the secretary-general opened it for adherence; the convention entered into force on September 15, 1976. A major reason for the enactment of that instrument was the ever-increasing number of artificial objects floating through space. According to a recent study by NASA, "space trash" by 1991 was composed of dust, tens of thousands of small bits, and some 7,000 larger objects, all of these orbiting at around 17,000 miles an hour.[69]

On October 30, 1980, the Convention for the Establishment of a European Space Agency, drawn up in Paris, entered into force; it was ratified by France, Belgium, Denmark, the Federal Republic of Germany, Italy, the Netherlands, Spain, Sweden, Switzerland, and the United Kingdom.[70] Finally, after seven years' work, the 47-member UN Committee on the Peaceful Uses of Outer Space approved (July 3, 1979) a modified version of the Agreement Governing the Activities of States on the Moon and Other Celestial Bodies (commonly called the Moon Treaty).[71] The concept was originally proposed by the Soviet Union in 1971. A major cause of the delay in arriving at a compromise solution had been the Soviet Union's unwillingness to express in treaty terms the idea that the moon's resources were "the common heritage of mankind." The version finally approved by the committee states that neither the surface nor the subsurface of the moon shall become the national property of any country. The draft agreement was to become a binding convention upon passage by the UN General Assembly during its regular session in 1979 and ratification by a minimum of five members. As of this writing, serious objections to U.S. ratification have been voiced in the United States, primarily by a number of business concerns as well as by the L-5 Society. On July 11, 1984, the Moon Treaty entered into force, following the fifth ratification of the agreement; 11 states have ratified or acceded to the treaty. France, the only major signatory, has not ratified it.[72]

The most recent international instruments related to outer space were the USSR–U.S. Agreement on Cooperation in the Exploration and Use of Outer Space for Peaceful Purposes, of April 15, 1987; and the United Nations' General Assembly Resolution and Principles Relevant to the Use of Nuclear Power Sources in Outer Space of December 14, 1992.[73]

---

[69]See *Christian Science Monitor* (March 21, 1989), 13; and (June 17, 1992), 15. See also H. A. Baker, *Space Debris: Legal and Policy Implications* (1989); G. C. M. Reijnen and W. De Graaff, *Pollution of Outer Space, in Particular of the Geostationary Orbit* (1989); and Q. He, "Environmental Impact of Space Activities and Measures for International Protection," 16 *J. of Space Law* 117 (1988).

[70]Final Act of the 1975 meeting and the text of the convention appear in 14 *ILM* 855 (1975).

[71]Text in 18 *ILM* 1434 (1979); see also *New York Times* (July 4, 1979), A4; and (July 8, 1979), E18.

[72]See *Christian Science Monitor* (February 20, 1980), 11; *Time* (March 24, 1980), 47; *Note* by Spitz in 21 *Harvard Int'l L. J.* 579 (Spring 1980); and especially C. Q. Christol, "The Moon Treaty Enters into Force," 79 *AJIL* 163 (1985).

[73]Text and agreed list of cooperative projects in 26 *ILM* 622 (1987); text of "Resolution" in 32 *ILM* 917 (1993).

SUGGESTED READINGS

Banner, *Who Owns the Sky?* (2008).

Grief, *Public International Law in the Airspace of the High Seas* (1994).

Lauterpacht, *Oppenheim*, I, 517.

Masson-Zwaan and de Leon, eds, *Air and Space Law: de Lege Ferenda* (1992).

McWhinney and Bradley, *The Freedom of the Air* (1969).

Post Cold War, the most interesting cases in these areas tend to involve questions of liability or other similar issues that require a level of knowledge and expertise in civil law far beyond the scope of an undergraduate introductory course. The following represents essential reading, but deals only with the issues of *public* international law.

Whiteman, IX: 312, 634.

Williams, "The Interception of Civil Aircraft Over the High Seas in the Global War on Terror," 59 *Air Force L. Rev.* 73 (2007).

CASES

American Institute of Aeronautics and Astronautics, *Proceedings of the Twenty-Third Colloquium on the Law of Outer Space,* New York (1981).

Appeal Relating to the Jurisdiction of the ICAO Council (India v. Pakistan), ICJ Reports, 1972, 46, reported in 67 *AJIL* 127 (1973).

Beiersdorf and Guidea, "Recent Developments in Aviation Law," 72 *J. Air L. & Com.* 207 (2007).

DeMay, "Recent Developments in Aviation Law," 73 *J. Air L. & Com.* 131 (2008).

TELECOMMUNICATIONS AND CYBERSPACE

Contemporary Practice of the United States Relating to International Law, "U.S. Policy Regarding Internet Governance," 99 *AJIL* 258 (2005).

"Developments in the Law: The Law of Cyberspace," 112 *Harvard Law Review* 1574 (1999).

Edwards and Waelde, eds, *Law & the Internet: Regulating Cyberspace* (1997).

European Agreement for the Prevention of Broadcasts Transmitted from Stations Outside National Territories (January 22, 1965), in 62 *AJIL* 814 (1968).

Notes, "Nothing but Internet," 110 *Harvard L. Rev.* 1143 (1997).

OUTER SPACE

Gangale, *The Development of Outer Space: Sovereignty and Property Rights in International Space Law* (2009).

Hurwitz, *State Liability for Outer Space Activities* (1992).

Jasentuliyana, United Nations Conference on the Exploration and Peaceful Uses of Outer Space (3rd ed., 1999), *International Space Law and the United Nations* (1999).

Moltz, *The Politics of Space Security: Strategic Restraint and the Pursuit of National Interests* (2008).

Sreejith, "Whither International Law, Thither Space Law: A Discipline in Transition," 38 *Cal. W. Int'l L.J.* 331 (2008).

United Nations Institute for Disarmament Research, *Safeguarding Space for All: Security and Peaceful Uses: Conference Report 25–26 March 2004* (2005).

Wassenbergh, *Principles of Outer Space Law* (1991).

Wolter, *Common Security in Outer Space and International Law* (2006).

Agents of International Intercourse Immunities

One of the most controversial and often misunderstood sections of international law deals with questions relating to the norms and practices associated with agents engaged in the diplomatic enterprise. Diplomacy constitutes an essential element in the conduct of modern foreign policy, but any basic international relations textbook will point out that it comprises only one set of techniques among many others available to statesmen.[1] Normally diplomacy, in its narrow sense, is associated with negotiation and other peaceful means of developing cooperation or resolving disputes.[2] This chapter will first briefly discuss the history of diplomatic practice and then will examine the legal regime within which modern diplomatic and consular relations take place.

DIPLOMATIC AGENTS

At the root of all diplomatic practice is the need for communication. From the beginning of recorded history, whenever they have come into contact, states, empires, or other entities—friendly or otherwise—have felt the need for special organs of communications. For millennia, however, these organs, called *ambassadors* (diplomatic agents),[3] did not possess the character of permanent representatives; instead, they were used only on occasion for the purpose of achieving certain tasks. An ambassador would be sent to a certain country to conclude an alliance, to make a trade agreement, to seek the hand of a princess for his king, to arrange

---

[1] R. P. Barston, *Modern Diplomacy*, 3rd ed. (2006), 1.

[2] T. C. Schelling, *Arms and Influence* (1966); A. L. George and W. E. Simons, eds, *The Limits of Coercive Diplomacy* (1994); and R. J. Art and P. M. Cronin, eds, *The United States and Coercive Diplomacy* (Washington, DC: United States Institute of Peace, 2003).

[3] In the following discussion, we emphasize the distinction between diplomatic agents and consular agents. Consular agents are primarily concerned with facilitating business and tourism ("low politics"), rather than with matters of foreign policy/diplomacy ("high politics"). Matters of foreign policy and diplomacy are the work of diplomatic agents.

for a marriage dowry, or to carry out whatever special purpose was at hand. Upon succeeding or failing in his mission, the ambassador returned home. Nevertheless, classical antiquity, particularly among the Greek city-states, witnessed the development of rules governing the sending of such agents. In ancient Greece at the time of Homer, the *herald* performed many tasks. One of the more important tasks was escorting diplomatic missions. For religious and other reasons, the heralds, not the diplomats, were considered inviolable.[4] The status of the herald presumably guaranteed safe conduct to those involved in the mission. By the time of Thucydides, the role of the herald had declined, and customary practice had evolved a complex set of rules and procedures associated with diplomatic missions. Another remarkable institution was that of the *proxenos*.[5] *Proxenoi* were those who in their own cities looked after the affairs of other city-states. While there are obvious parallels with modern consular practice, a *proxenos* also had some diplomatic responsibilities in addition to the consular functions.

Northern India, China, Rome, Byzantium, the Muslim states of the Middle East, and the Catholic Church all developed elaborate sets of rules and practices to govern diplomatic interaction.[6] In Western practice, the term *ambassador* appeared in Italy sometime near the end of the twelfth century. Expanding trade and political contacts with Constantinople and west Asia led Venice to develop a diplomatic model based on the Byzantine model. Venice, Mantua, and Milan exchanged resident ambassadors in the late fourteenth century, but permanent representatives did not appear at other foreign capitals until the middle of the fifteenth century. The first permanent legations outside of Italy came in 1463, when Milan and Venice both sent permanent representatives to the court of Louis XI at Paris. These first agents often combined the diplomatic and commercial consular functions.

Over time, the utility of having permanent agents abroad overcame the distrust with which courts viewed a foreign ambassador. All too many of them saw an ambassador as nothing more than an official spy—of noble birth, to be sure, but nonetheless a spy of the sending state. Thus Russia, until the reign of Peter the Great, resisted successfully all attempts to locate permanent foreign representatives in its capital. Other states in Western Europe, on the other hand, quickly realized the many advantages accruing from the permanent presence of representatives abroad, and the custom quickly spread. Some states persisted for quite a while in ensuring the right to send ambassadors by means of bilateral agreements, but the majority regarded such a right as an aspect of sovereign independence. After the Treaty of Westphalia (1648), the establishment of permanent diplomatic missions became the rule in Europe.[7]

Until the Reformation, Rome and the pope occupied a central place in European diplomatic life. Yet problems persisted. Questions of protocol involving rank,

---

[4]D. Bederman, *International Law in Antiquity* (2001), 96–99; see also J. T. Greene, *The Role of the Messenger and the Message in the Ancient Near East* (1989).

[5]I have used the consular analogy here, but as many have pointed out, there are differences between modern consuls and the role of *proxenoi*. See Bederman, note 4, at 130–131; C. Phillipson, *The International Law and Custom of Ancient Greece and Rome* (1911), 149.

[6]See H. Nicolson, *The Evolution of Diplomacy* (1966).

[7]See M. S. Anderson, *The Rise of Modern Diplomacy, 1450–1919* (1993); and W. J. Roosen, *The Age of Louis XIV: The Rise of Modern Diplomacy* (1976).

precedence, and prestige became matters of great importance. While several popes attempted to set an order of diplomatic precedence among states, matters of protocol continued to provoke "affairs of honor" (duels) until the Treaties of Vienna (1815) and Aix-la-Chapelle (1818) provided simple solutions. Indeed, even after the settlement at Westphalia (1648), France and Spain continued at war for another 11 years. Questions of protocol and prestige were among the important issues.

Right of Representation

The right of diplomatic intercourse is divided into an *active* and a *passive* right. The active right consists of the authority to send diplomatic agents abroad. This is an unquestioned right of every independent member of the family of nations. The problem of who will exercise this right in any given state is an internal constitutional question. As a rule, the monarch in a monarchy or the president (or prime minister) in a republic (alone or in conjunction with some legislative body) will exercise the right. Corresponding to the active right to send diplomatic agents is the passive right: to receive such agents. Normally an international person having the former right also has the latter. Generally, however, the right of representation, being a common attribute of sovereign states, has posed questions only in the relatively few instances when it had to be determined whether a given community was entitled to this right (see Chapter 7). On rare modern occasions, an entity that is neither a recognized member of the community of nations nor a legal person in the form of an international organization has been accorded by a few countries a right of diplomatic representation. Thus India, on January 9, 1975, granted full diplomatic status to the representative of the Palestine Liberation Organization (PLO), the first time this had been done by a non-Arab state (see Chapter 7).

Codification of Rules

Until 1815, the rules governing diplomatic intercourse were based primarily on customary international law, supplemented by practices founded on comity. The classification of diplomatic ranks and certain issues of protocol achieved at the Congress of Vienna and amended in the Protocol of Aix-la-Chapelle (1818) clarified and systematized existing practices without adding materially to the corpus of rules. Not until 1927 did states seriously consider a possible codification of those rules. In that year, the League of Nations Committee of Experts for the Progressive Codification of International Law reported to the Council of the League that it regarded the subject of diplomatic privileges and immunities as "sufficiently ripe for international regulation." The council, however, rejected the committee's conclusion. On the other hand, the Sixth Conference of American states (Havana, 1928) adopted the Convention on Diplomatic Officers.[8] This instrument, subsequently ratified by 12 American states, was signed but not ratified by the United States, which objected to the inclusion of provisions approving the granting of diplomatic asylum.

Post World War II, the International Law Commission of the United Nations selected the subject of diplomatic intercourse and immunities as one of 14 topics

---

[8]Text of the convention in 22 *American Journal of International Law* 142 (1928).

for codification but gave it a low priority when the original list was drawn up (1949). At its seventh session, in 1952, however, the General Assembly passed a resolution requesting the commission to codify the subject. In 1954, the commission initiated a study of diplomatic intercourse and immunities. Work on a proposed draft convention proceeded, and the commission succeeded in completing a final draft by 1959.

On December 7, 1959, the General Assembly, by Resolution 1450 (XIV), decided to convene an international conference to consider the question of diplomatic intercourse and immunities. This gathering, the United Nations Conference on Diplomatic Intercourse and Immunities, met in Vienna, from March 2 to April 14, 1961. It prepared three instruments: (1) Vienna Convention on Diplomatic Relations, (2) Optional Protocol Concerning Acquisition of Nationality, and (3) Optional Protocol Concerning the Compulsory Settlement of Disputes.[9] Of these, the Convention on Diplomatic Relations, of April 14, 1961, is the most important (hereinafter Vienna Convention). Although it largely followed the draft convention prepared by the International Law Commission, there were significant departures in several articles of the Vienna Convention. On April 18, 1961, the representatives of 75 states signed the convention, and the instrument entered into force on April 24, 1964 (for the United States, December 13, 1972). At this writing, the convention has 187 states parties—indicating that it has acquired almost universal acceptance among contemporary states. Despite the near-universal acceptance, we should note that the final paragraph of the preamble to the convention declares that the signatory states affirm "that the rules of customary international law should continue to govern questions not expressly regulated by the provisions of the present Convention."

Representation

From a legal point of view, each sovereign state has complete freedom to decide whether, and in which foreign states, it wishes to be represented by diplomatic agents. Should a state decide, for some reason, to deviate from what certainly has become a general custom and attempt to live in solitude, such deviation would be regarded by other states, at the very least, as an international incivility. And if the state in question resolved also to bar all foreign diplomatic agents from its jurisdiction, it would effectively remove itself from further membership in the community of nations.

On the other hand, no state maintains diplomatic representation at all capitals of the world and with all international organizations.[10] Most countries could

---

[9]The texts of the convention, the protocols, and resolutions in 55 *AJIL* 1062 (1961 Supp.); also at http://untreaty.un.org/ilc/index.html (accessed May 10, 2009).

[10]"The U.S. Government has diplomatic relations with about 180 countries. In most of these countries, the U.S. maintains an embassy, which usually is located in the capital. The U.S. also may have branches of the embassy, called consulates, in other locations within the country. When the U.S. does not have full diplomatic relations with a nation, the U.S. may be represented by only a Liaison Office or Interests Section. In addition, the U.S. has representation or missions at international organizations. There are more than 250 missions or posts throughout the world," www.usembassy.gov/ (accessed May 10, 2009).

not afford either the personnel or the enormous monies needed for such an enterprise. They might properly decide that little interaction—and hence few interests in maintaining relations with a given foreign state—would not warrant the expense of a diplomatic mission. Thus, some states content themselves with being represented in certain capitals through the diplomatic mission of a friendly third state or with maintaining an ambassador at one capital who acts as their accredited representative to a number of other states. Thus, Western Samoa, independent since 1962, has decided for economic reasons not to join the United Nations and not to establish diplomatic missions abroad. Its limited foreign relations were entrusted by special agreement to the embassies maintained by New Zealand in various parts of the world. Monaco has a similar agreement with France.

Just as states have a right to establish diplomatic relations, they also have a right to break off diplomatic relations with another state. For the state breaking off relations, this act involves recalling its diplomatic agents. Note that a decision to break relations **does not** mean the withdrawal of recognition from the government or the state (Chapter 7). It merely indicates a level of displeasure with current events. Such an occurrence usually does not dissolve all relations between the states in question. After the rupture of diplomatic relations with the Castro administration in Cuba, the U.S. government continued to accord to the Cuban government such rights as accrue to the government of a sovereign state under international law.

Occasionally, as a gesture of protest against some host government policy or act, only the top-level diplomats are withdrawn by governments: After Sweden criticized the U.S. bombing of Hanoi and Haiphong, the United States and Sweden were without ambassadors in their respective capitals from 1972 until ambassadors were finally exchanged again in March 1974. Great Britain conducted its diplomatic relations with the People's Republic of China through respective missions, each headed by a chargé d'affaires for 20 years until ambassadors were finally exchanged by both countries in 1971. In 1975, fifteen European countries temporarily recalled their ambassadors from Madrid to protest the Spanish execution of five terrorists. Mexico, then having no embassy in Spain, expressed its displeasure with the executions by cutting off postal communications with Spain. On May 11, 1992, the 12-member European Community recalled its ambassadors from the rump Yugoslavia (Serbia and Montenegro) in protest of Serbian involvement in the civil war under way in Bosnia–Herzegovina.

Special Interest Sections

Often the need for ongoing communication leads both states to arrange for representation by a third state, which then acts as an intermediary. As we noted, the official rupture of diplomatic relations may be mitigated by the establishment of special interest sections by the two states involved. This act may take one of two forms: sections created at the outset of a "limited exchange" of diplomats, preceding an eventual resumption of full diplomatic relations, or sections established on the rupture of such relations. An example of the first form occurred when, after a seven-year break, relations were resumed between the United States and Syria in 1974 on a "limited-exchange" basis. The former American Embassy building in Damascus (hitherto in the custody of Italy) was redesignated the Embassy of

Italy: Section for the Protection of the Interests of the United States of America, with the American flag flying above it. A similar name change took place at the former Syrian Embassy building in Washington. In 1972, the Swiss ambassador to Cuba represented his own state as well as nine others (including the United States) in Havana until the 16-year-old rupture of diplomatic relations ended in 1977. Switzerland had maintained custody of the U.S. Embassy building in Havana, and Czechoslovakia of the Washington Embassy building of Cuba. Special interest sections were established in the respective facilities, which were still designated as the "protecting power's" embassy.

The United States and Iran severed diplomatic relations in 1980. The United States established a special interest section at the Swiss Embassy in Tehran, and no U.S. citizens were employed there. Iran set up the Iranian Special Interests Section as a part of, but not physically in, the Algerian Embassy in Washington. It was staffed by ethnic Iranians who were either naturalized Americans or resident aliens. Algeria permitted the section to use its diplomatic bag or pouch. In 1987, Switzerland operated a British Special Interest Section in Buenos Aires, besides representing 14 other states around the world (Iran in Israel, etc.).

Initiation of a Diplomatic Mission

No state is required to accept every individual proposed as the principal agent of a foreign state. Consider that because of the very essence of the position, the agent must enjoy the confidence of the receiving state's government. Should the receiving state decide that a given nominee, for any reason, is not suitable as the representative of his or her government, it may reject the appointment. In late 2001, Iran indicated that it could not accept the appointment of David Reddaway as the new British ambassador to Teheran.[11] When Iran rejected (June 1979) the U.S. Ambassador-Designate Walter Cutler, it noted alleged American intervention in Zaire at a time when Cutler served as the American ambassador there. In February 1982, Afghanistan asked the United States to withdraw the visa application of Archer Blood, the current chargé d'affaires-designate, on the grounds that while posted in New Delhi, Blood had been in contact with Afghan citizens hostile to the regime. The United States unsuccessfully protested the request as being unacceptable and labeled the explanation as "irrelevant and immaterial."

As a matter of prudent statecraft, before a diplomatic agent is appointed, the sending state should inquire of the receiving state whether the nominee is acceptable—that is, if he or she is *persona grata*. If such advance notification does not occur, the receiving state can simply refuse to admit the nominee. Rejection of the nominee as *persona non grata* may or may not be accompanied by reasons for the decision. Traditionally, no reason is given or expected. Still, the United States and Great Britain have, on occasion, not only insisted on being given reasons for the rejection of one of their nominees, but indeed also asserted their right to approve or reject those reasons as valid. This attitude had to be abandoned by both states because in practice, any receiving state can simply refuse to accept an individual

---

[11]www.payvand.com/news/02/apr/1052.html (accessed April 22, 2009).

whom it has judged to be *persona non grata*. Here, common sense and pragmatism should rule. Given the nature of the diplomatic enterprise, the ability to communicate effectively with the foreign government obviously depends upon the willingness of the other government to deal with the agent.

The legal basis of each diplomatic office is the agreement of the receiving state to admit a foreign mission. The receiving state will maintain a *diplomatic list* that identifies those individuals officially accredited. The receiving state has the right to lay down the rules governing the legal position and activities of foreign diplomats, but in each instance, the state is bound by the valid and applicable principles of international law, both customary and conventional.[12] In effect, the receiving state concedes to the foreign diplomat certain rights, privileges, and spheres of activity that are subject to international law. Thus, each diplomatic activity carried out by agents of a state rests upon both the agreement (concession) of the receiving state and the instructions issued to them within the framework of that concession by the sending state.

The appointment of diplomatic agents is a constitutional act of the sending state. The rights and duties of agents begin formally with the handing over and acceptance of credentials *(lettre de créance)* in the receiving state. By its formal acceptance of these credentials, the receiving state recognizes the position of the individual concerned as the agent of his or her government. The credentials are accepted, depending on the rank of the agent by either the chief of state or the minister of foreign affairs (in the United States, the secretary of state) or through some specially designated protocol officer or functionary.

Note here one other important set of considerations. *Reciprocity* and self-interest play a great role. Vattel's Golden Rule of Sovereigns applies with special force here. As a decision maker, if you wish *your* diplomats to be treated with courtesy and respect, then you must treat diplomats stationed in *your* country with equal courtesy and respect. This simple observation goes a long way toward explaining why the diplomatic system works. States and governments have a fundamental interest in seeing that it does. Every diplomat abroad represents a potential hostage. This does not mean that all governments in every case value the system. Pariah states[13] such as Khomeini's Iran and al-Gaddafi's Libya, which care little for their own image and reputation (or people) abroad, have engaged in actions that violate the fundamental values of the regime. The seizure of the American Embassy in Teheran and its aftermath stand as an egregious example of violation, as do the actions of China during the Cultural Revolution. Finding a solution to such glaring disregard for the law is often difficult because reciprocity operates outside the narrow confines of diplomatic law as well. In writing about the British response to the 1984 Libyan People's Bureau in London, Rosalyn Higgins (now a judge on the International Court of Justice [ICJ]) noted:[14]

---

[12]See the U.S. Department of State Memorandum of December 12, 1974, setting forth the requirements for accreditation by the United States; relevant excerpts in 69 *AJIL* 394 (1975).

[13]See, e.g., T. Niblock, *Pariah States & Sanctions in the Middle East: Iraq, Libya, Sudan* (2001).

[14]R. Higgins, "The Abuse of Diplomatic Privileges and Immunities: Recent United Kingdom Experience," 79 *AJIL* 641 (1985), 645.

It became clear that balancing diplomatic law is not only about the balancing of legitimate interests between the sending state and the receiving state. There is another factor often at play: the presence abroad in the sending state, of an expatriate community of the receiving state.

Recall our discussion of the problems of enforcement and the interrelationship of interests in Chapter 1. International legal problems seldom exist in a context isolated from a multitude of other considerations. In this case, the British government had to consider how much its actions might place some 8,000 British citizens then in Libya at risk. Moreover, the British government (like the American government in the Iranian case) had to consider the implications of its actions from a multilateral standpoint. It had an interest in maintaining the general principle of absolute inviolability of chancellery premises and principal agents regardless of the provocation or perception of abuse owing to the extensive nature of its diplomatic presence overseas as well as that of its partners in the European Union.[15]

Termination of a Mission

The Vienna Treaty contains no provisions concerning the termination of diplomatic missions other than in time of war. Clearly, a mission may end by mutual consent or when the sending state decides that it no longer wishes to maintain a presence in the receiving state. In time of war, the receiving state has the duty to permit diplomatic personnel to exit in timely fashion and to facilitate their exit (Article 44). Obviously, a diplomatic mission ends with the disappearance of the sending or receiving state. An unusual exception to this normal and logical rule took place in the case of the diplomatic representatives of the Republic of Latvia following that country's absorption into the Soviet Union in 1940. Because most of the world's governments refused to recognize the annexation of Latvia, Estonia, and Lithuania by the Soviet Union, the diplomatic agents of the three Baltic republics continued to occupy their posts in all nonrecognizing states. The Latvian envoy in London, as the senior diplomatic agent of Latvia abroad, assumed the emergency powers of his government.[16] Thus, a diplomatic representative assumed the status of a government-in-exile and claimed sovereignty over all Latvian citizens living in Western countries. Such jurisdiction naturally was limited to states in which Latvian diplomatic agents were still accredited. This event has led to some interesting questions. Yet, as with many treaties, circumstances may arise that fall outside the explicit provisions of the instrument.

A constitutional change in either the sending or receiving government through election or agreed succession does not necessarily require renewal of credentials. This will depend upon the practice of the two states. Guillermo Sevilla-Sacasa served as Nicaraguan ambassador to the United States for over 30 years. Anatoly Dobrynin served 24 years as the Soviet ambassador to Washington. On the other hand, U.S. ambassadors tend to rotate with each presidential election.

---

[15]Higgins, note 14, at 650.

[16]See *Mrs. J. W v. Republic of Latvia*, Germany, Landgericht, Berlin, October 3, 1953, digested in 48 *AJIL* 161 (1954).

When a fundamental change occurs in the *governments* of the sending or receiving state (see Chapter 7 on recognition), the affected diplomats will have to go through the process of official accreditation again. For instance, the U.S. ambassador to Russia, David R. Francis, reported to the Department of State on March 17, 1917, that the imperial government of Russia had been overthrown by revolution. He requested authorization to recognize the new government, which he received two days later from Secretary of State Lansing. On March 22, Francis called on the new Council of Ministers and presented his new credentials as U.S. ambassador. When the provisional government was in turn ousted on November 7, 1917, Ambassador Francis did not receive new credentials, and presumably, his diplomatic mission terminated with the overthrow of the provisional government. The United States did not recognize the successor Bolshevik government until 1933. Ambassador Francis remained in Russia as a liaison, though unaccredited, until he was formally recalled in late July 1918. Presumably, he continued to enjoy the immunities granted to diplomatic agents.

The unanswered question in the example just given as well as in the Vienna Convention concerns the status of missions in interim situations. More recently, Iraq has provided two interesting cases concerning the status of missions. Following its invasion and occupation of Kuwait, the Iraqi government on August 20, 1990, ordered all foreign embassies in Kuwait to close by August 23. The United States and 20 other governments refused to comply with that order and kept their embassies open, albeit with reduced staffs. After three Canadian naval vessels sailed for the Persian Gulf, Iraq surrounded first the Canadian and then the rest of the foreign embassies with troops. Iraq also announced that Canadian and other diplomats in Iraq would be prohibited from leaving because their embassies in Kuwait remained open. The U.S. Department of State denounced this step as "an outrageous breach of international law."

On August 25, 1990, Iraq cut off water and electricity to several of the open embassies and maintained that beginning at midnight on August 24, the diplomats of the remaining embassies had lost their immunity and would be detained as hostages. By September 3, telephone communications had been severed to most of the embassy compounds. On September 15, 1990, Iraqi soldiers invaded the residence of the French ambassador in Kuwait City and seized four French citizens— including the military attaché, who was released later. Iraqi military personnel also entered the Belgian and Dutch Embassy compounds and the residence of the Canadian ambassador. Iraq denied the incidents, labeling the foreign compounds as "former diplomatic missions." At that time, 17 foreign embassies in Kuwait City had refused to obey the Iraqi order to close. The UN Security Council unanimously condemned the raids on diplomatic missions in occupied Kuwait (September 16, 1990).[17] As time went on, one country after another evacuated its embassy and consular staffs until only the British and American missions remained. These two embassies finally closed in December 1990.

Iraq's invasion and occupation raised the issue of the legitimacy of its authority within Kuwait. The refusal of the missions to close their doors rested upon the

---

[17]UNSC 667 (1990). For text of the resolution, see www.worldpress.org/specials/iraq/unscr667.htm (accessed April 22, 2009).

simple premise that, because Iraq clearly intended to incorporate Kuwait as a province (i.e., extinguish it as an independent state), the invasion and occupation were illegal (see Chapter 20). Because these other governments continued to recognize the authority of the Kuwaiti government (now in exile), Iraq had no legitimate authority to terminate missions accredited by that government (see Chapter 7).

The second case also involves Iraq and a set of parallel issues. In June 2003, after Operation Iraqi Freedom removed Saddam Hussein from power, a representative of the U.S. State Department announced:

> There are diplomats who were previously accredited to the Saddam regime, who have been residing in former mission residences, who are still there. We do not regard those as diplomatic missions. They're accredited to a regime that is no longer existent, and, therefore, their accreditation would have lapsed.[18]

Although the Vienna Convention does talk about war, it does not cover this situation. It raises an interesting question: Do the immunities of diplomatic agents and missions terminate if the government that extended accreditation ceases to exist? Clearly the occupying power (or powers) has no authority to accredit diplomatic agents. A tension exists here between the presumed need for formal accreditation and the practical aspect represented by the functions of diplomatic missions. Even though the Hussein government no longer exists, the interests of sending states may continue.[19] As we have seen in the first case discussed, in other situations where changes of governments have occurred through revolution, coup, or other irregular means, the presumption has been that immunities continue until a new regime comes to power. At that point, both the new government in the receiving state and governments of sending states have decisions to make concerning recognition and the continuation of diplomatic representation.

Diplomatic Ranks

When there were no permanent representatives abroad, distinctions between diplomatic agents depended almost entirely on the relative strength and importance of the sending state. But as soon as permanent representatives became a fixture, bitter quarreling ensued between the representatives of various powers stationed in the same capital. Generally, no one questioned that the representatives of monarchs *(ambaxatores)* occupied the highest category in rank. Besides "ambassadors," there emerged one other important class of representatives—the ministers, or residents, titled, since the middle of the seventeenth century, *envoyés (envoys)*. After some time, this second group became divided into two classes—ordinary and extraordinary envoys. The latter began to claim special privileges and higher rank than the former had. More and more states named *envoyés extraordinaires,* insisting that these constituted a class distinct from ambassadors and residents, even when their duties and powers corresponded in every detail to those of the residents.

---

[18]Cited in F. L. Kirgis, "Diplomatic Immunities in Iraq," *ASIL Insights* (June 2003), www.asil.org/insights/insigh109.htm (accessed April 22, 2009).
[19]*Ibid.*

At the beginning of the eighteenth century, practice had evolved three basic classes of diplomats: ambassadors, envoys extraordinary, and residents (soon called *ministers resident*). By the end of the century, a fourth category had made its appearance—the *chargés d'affaires,* occupying the bottom rank among diplomatic agents. The emergence of definite categories did not, however, end the disputes among diplomats—within each class, quarrels concerning precedence continued. The Congress of Vienna finally cleared up a totally confused state of affairs when it adopted, on March 19, 1815, the Règlément sur le Rang Entre les Agents Diplomatiques, a document supplemented later by the Protocol of Aix-la-Chapelle of November 21, 1818. The categories set up by these two instruments still exist today (even though one class of diplomats, added by the 1818 protocol, has disappeared from the world scene and is not listed anymore in the Vienna Diplomatic Convention of 1961). There are today four classes, or categories, of diplomatic representatives:

1. Ambassadors (ambassadors extraordinary, ambassadors plenipotentiary) and papal nuncios
2. Ministers (envoys extraordinary, ministers plenipotentiary, and papal internuncios)
3. Ministers resident
4. Chargés d'affaires and chargés d'affaires ad interim

Those diplomats granted *plenipotentiary status* (i.e., possessing the *plena potens*) have the capacity to bind their government by word or signature. The chargé d'affaires, once customarily sent only to small, backward, unimportant states, is today primarily an assistant, with specified administrative functions, to an ambassador or minister. Normally he or she assumes, on an acting basis (ad interim), the functions of his or her superior during the latter's absence from the diplomatic mission or until a replacement is sent to the mission.

States customarily exchange diplomatic agents of the same rank, even though there have been exceptions to this practice. In the past, ambassadors were exchanged only between the great powers, but in the past 60 years or so, this custom has been abandoned in most cases—notably by the United States. Sending an ambassador to a small country supposedly formally acknowledges the formal principal of legal equality. Thus the United States, in pursuance of the "good neighbor" policy adopted during the presidency of Franklin Roosevelt, elevated all heads of missions in Latin American states to the rank of ambassador.

The Vienna Conference also solved the problem of precedence within the diplomatic community by initiating a seniority system. Order of procession, for example, for any diplomatic function will be determined by the date of accreditation to a particular state. The diplomat with the longest continuous service will have the title of dean *(doyen)* of the diplomatic corps. In Washington, DC, this has meant that, at one time or another, the ambassador from the Soviet Union (Anatoly Dobrynin) and the ambassador from the Cape Verde Islands have served as dean. As of this writing, the ambassador from Djibouti has the honor.[20]

---

[20]U.S. State Department, "Order of Precedence and Date of Presentation of Credentials," www.state.gov/s/cpr/rls/dpl/29710.htm (accessed April 22, 2009).

Diplomats take the matter of precedence quite seriously. During President Truman's administration, Dr. Guillermo Sevilla-Sacasa (Nicaragua), then dean in Washington, lost his accreditation because of a coup in Managua. The new government did not last long, but when Dr. Sevilla received a new appointment after the coup had been reversed, the State Department refused to acknowledge his previous service. State insisted that the position of dean depended upon continuous service. During the interim between his appointments, Dr. Sevilla sent some roses to Mrs. Truman, who had undergone minor surgery. President Truman sent a thank-you note in return that began, "Dear Mr. Ambassador." Dr. Sevilla produced the note and argued that President Truman, their superior, had considered him ambassador, even if the people at the State Department had not. Dr. Sevilla noted that he would abide by the president's judgment, not theirs. State relented and reinstated the title.

Below the ambassador or minister, a diplomatic mission may contain hundreds of persons. On occasion, distinctions are drawn between the official and nonofficial personnel of such a mission. The official personnel include all persons employed by the sending state or the chief of mission, to whom they are subordinate. This group comprises all of the mission's various functionaries, including the affiliated military or technical *attachés* as well as the clerical staff (typists, secretaries, file clerks, interpreters, code clerks, and so forth). In a U.S. Embassy overseas, not all personnel are necessarily employees of the State Department. Many other Cabinet-level departments (e.g., Treasury and Commerce) may have agents attached to the mission as well.

Functions of Diplomatic Agents

The functions of the diplomat may be classified under six main headings:[21]

1. *Negotiation.* The original reason for having diplomats—the intention of having a representative in a foreign capital empowered to negotiate agreements with the receiving state—was to "deal" directly with the foreign government. This basic function has been downgraded considerably in the past half century or so, in part because of progress in communications, which makes the diplomat more of a spokesman than a true negotiator, and in part because of a tendency to substitute foreign ministers' meetings or summit meetings for negotiation at the ambassadorial level.
2. *Representation.* The diplomatic agent is the representative of the government of his state. He acts as such on ceremonial occasions but also files protests or inquiries with the receiving government. A diplomatic agent presents the policies of his government to the host state.
3. *Information.* A diplomat's basic duty is to report to his government on political events, policies, and other related matters. He is not a spy in the orthodox meaning of the term—even though a few heads of missions have been spies in the true sense of the word, and others have acted as paymasters to spies.
4. *Protection.* The diplomat has a duty to look after the interests, persons, and property of citizens of his own state in the receiving state. A diplomat must

---

[21]See B. Sen, *A Diplomat's Handbook of International Law and Practice* (1988).

be ready to assist such citizens when they get into trouble abroad, may have to take charge of their bodies and effects if they happen to die on a trip, and must in general act as "troubleshooter" for his fellow nationals in the receiving state (Chapter 11).

5. *Public relations.* The diplomat continually tries to create goodwill for his own state and its policies. This propaganda–public relations function means giving and attending parties and dinners; giving lectures and other speeches; attending dedications of monuments, buildings, and (lately) foreign assistance projects; and so on. The effectiveness of such public relations activities is questionable, however, because it is difficult to measure. Only one thing is certain: If the diplomat refrains from participating in such activities, it creates ill-will.

6. *Administration.* The chief of a diplomatic mission is the administrative head of the group, even though, in a large mission, he may have a subordinate personnel office and department heads. In the last resort, the ambassador or minister is responsible for the operation and administration of the embassy or legislation.

In the absence of consular relations (discussed later in this chapter) between two countries, diplomatic officers customarily perform various functions normally performed by consular officers, always provided that the host (receiving) state does not object to the practice.

DIPLOMATIC PRIVILEGES AND IMMUNITIES

A person with diplomatic status enjoys a considerable range of privileges and immunities[22] based on customary as well as conventional international law. The obvious intent behind this grant of privilege has been the desire to enable diplomatic agents to exercise their duties and functions without being impeded by the authorities of the receiving state. Diplomats, if in fear of their own lives or of the safety of their families and staff members, cannot effectively carry out their duties.

On the other hand, immunities can generate great controversy and public misunderstanding. Within areas that have great concentrations of individuals who enjoy diplomatic status, minor complaints involving shoplifting, parking, and speeding are common. But Rosalyn Higgins noted in a report in the wake of the incident at the Libyan People's Bureau in London that 546 "serious incidents" involving abuse of immunity had occurred in the United Kingdom between 1974 and 1984.[23] Perceptions of widespread abuse in the United States at about the same time led Senator Jesse Helms to sponsor legislation to redefine the bounds of diplomatic immunity.[24] While generating much publicity, the legislation did not

---

[22]To remove conflicts between existing U.S. law and the 1961 Vienna Convention on Diplomatic Relations, Congress enacted the Diplomatic Relations Act of 1978. Text in 17 *International Legal Materials* 149 (1979).

[23]Higgins, note 14, at 643. This goes beyond the "nuisance" crimes of shoplifting and parking and speeding violations.

[24]E. Pianin, "Bounds of Diplomatic Immunity: Victims to Testify in Support of Helm's Bill Limiting Exemptions," *The Washington Post* (August 5, 1987), B1. See, in particular, C. Ashman and P. Trescott, *Diplomatic Crime: Drugs, Killings, Thefts, Rapes, Slavery and Other Outrageous Crimes* (Washington, DC: Acropolis Books, 1987). This book formed the centerpiece of the case for limiting immunities.

pass. As the state with the largest number of diplomats abroad, the United States has an interest in maintaining the integrity of the regime.

Personal Inviolability

Personal inviolability forms perhaps the oldest diplomatic practice. Article 29 of the Vienna Convention states that the person of a diplomatic agent (defined in Article 1(e)) is inviolable. Diplomatic agents may not be detained, arrested, or otherwise harassed. The families, residence, papers, correspondence, and property of such agents held in conjunction with their official duties also have inviolable status. Diplomatic agents are also exempt from all taxes and customs duties. Practically this means, under normal circumstances, that diplomatic agents and their families enjoy almost *complete* immunity from the legal system of the receiving state.[25] As a condition of this immunity, they have an obligation to be law abiding. As a rhetorical question, can you imagine that any diplomatic agent could be an effective representative, if he or she were not respectful of the laws of the receiving state?

Common exceptions to the immunity from the civil and administrative jurisdiction of the receiving state include (1) a real action relating to private immovable property situated in the receiving state, unless the diplomatic agent holds it on behalf of the sending state for the purposes of the mission; (2) an action relating to succession in which the agent is involved as executor, administrator, heir, or legatee as a private person and not on behalf of the sending state; and (3) any action relating to any professional or commercial activity exercised by the diplomatic agent in the receiving state outside his official functions (Article 31(1)). In regard to the third of these exemptions, the Vienna Convention prohibits such outside professional or commercial activity for personal profit (Article 42).

Diplomatic agents are also exempt from certain fiscal obligations normally payable in or to the receiving state. They do not have to pay any direct national, regional, or municipal dues and taxes relating to the premises of the mission (Article 23(1)).[26] They are exempt from all dues and taxes, personal or real, in the receiving state, except for indirect taxes normally included in the cost of goods or services;[27] taxes on real estate in the receiving state owned privately by the agent; estate, succession, or inheritance duties on personal property (except in the event of the

---

[25]See Articles 29–37 of the Vienna Convention, note 9. Some limited civil liability and responsibility does exist. For example if a diplomat has a private business or owns property for his or her own private purposes, he or she cannot plead their immunity in matters that concern the business or property. The diplomat must pay relevant taxes and observe building codes, local property ordinances, etc. These are not of importance for the discussion here. See Article 31(1) of the Vienna Convention. For an extended discussion, see E. Denza, *Diplomatic Law* (1998), 226–233. Also, U.S.C. §4304b—Crimes Committed by Diplomats.

[26]See *United States v. City of Glen Cove*, U.S. Dist. Ct., E.D.N.Y., 1971, 322 F. Supp., 149, reported in 65 *AJIL* 832 (1971); see also *United States v. County of Arlington, Virginia*, U.S. Ct. of Appeals, 4th Cir., February 1, 1982, in 21 *ILM* 109 (1982).

[27]The U.S. Department of State introduced a new policy (February 1985) on sales tax for foreign diplomats living in the United States to reflect the treatment of American diplomats living abroad. The new system is one of "reciprocity" and reflects foreign collection of sales and value-added taxes from U.S. embassies and diplomatic staffs.

▶ UNITED STATES V. WILLIAM TAPIA

U.S. Dist. Ct, Eastern District of New York 1991
U.S. Dist. LEXIS 10462

Facts

Tapia served as the first secretary in charge of the Nicaraguan Consulate General in Tokyo during the Sandinista regime. His indictment alleged that he conspired to import heroin into the United States and distributed heroin in Thailand with the purpose of having it imported into the United States. Tapia moved for dismissal on the basis that at the time, as a Nicaraguan diplomatic officer, he possessed diplomatic immunity under the Vienna Convention.

The arrest came about as the result of information given by Jorges Rueda, the chargé d'affaires for the Guatemalan Embassy in Tokyo. Rueda claimed that he and Tapia jointly engaged in drug trafficking. The new (1990) Nicaraguan government did not assert a claim of diplomatic immunity on Tapia's behalf.

Issues

Did the United States, Japan, and Nicaragua err in failing to honor Tapia's diplomatic immunity?

Decision

The United States, Nicaragua, and Japan acted within the law.

Reasoning

Nicaragua has no obligation to assert the right of immunity on behalf of Tapia. This right belongs to Nicaragua—not to Tapia, who has no standing to claim this right as an individual. Treaty rights belong to sovereign states, not to individuals. If Nicaragua chooses not to assert the right, Tapia has no defense.

agent's death, when his or her movable property is treated as tax exempt); taxes on private income and on investments made in commercial enterprises in the receiving state; and certain fees and duties relating to real estate (Articles 34 and 39(4)).

Restraints on Diplomatic Agents

The primary duty international law places on all diplomatic agents is abstention from interference—by word or deed—in the internal affairs of the receiving state. This prohibition is all-inclusive: Diplomats may not discuss pending legislation, may not comment on political controversies, and may not endorse or criticize the host government, political parties, or party platforms.[28] They may not correspond with the press and other news media on any matter that is still a subject of communication between their own government and the host government. They may not make public a communication from their government to that of the receiving state before the latter has received it nor publish any correspondence from the latter without obtaining prior authorization. Equally prohibited but difficult to prove

---

[28]See *Time* (February 1, 1960), 28, for an amusing example; and *New York Times* (July 1, 1976), 4, for another illustration of the rule.

are the use of an embassy or a legation as a center for the dissemination of propaganda on a matter on which the two governments concerned may disagree and the conversion of any diplomatic mission into a center of subversive or spy activities in favor of the ideological or national interests of the sending state. And, of course, spying is prohibited to diplomats, as is the smuggling of goods.[29] A very modern and quite obvious prohibition in regard to diplomatic activities is assistance to or participation in terrorist activities in the host country.[30]

Dismissal of Agents

A minor violation of some of these restraints on the diplomat's activities may be overlooked or may lead to a protest by the appropriate authorities of the receiving state. But if the violation is repeated or is of a serious nature, the receiving state is fully within its rights if it requests the recall of the offender or, as quite often happens, expels him at once. Motor vehicle accidents and parking violations have been continuing problems. Since 1984, all diplomatic personnel in the United States must carry automobile liability insurance with a minimum limit of $1 million.[31] In the early 1990s, the State Department also began assisting authorities in the District of Columbia and New York City in an effort to crack down on parking violations.[32] The State Department undertook this action with some reluctance; as one diplomat noted in response, U.S. diplomats abroad would now need to read parking signs very carefully because *"Everything in diplomacy works on the basis of reciprocity"*[33] (Emphasis added). The reader must keep this statement in mind while working through the following discussion.

The personal immunity diplomats enjoy seems to many "a license to sin" as an article in Spiegel (Germany) graphically described it.[34] For some, at lower levels, this may hold true. It is hard to get a complete picture because the State Department does not publish statistics on crimes by the diplomatic community. If a serious

---

[29]See *New York Times* (October 16, 1976), 5; (October 21, 1976), 4; (October 23, 1976), 5; and (October 26, 1976), 5 (all dealing with Scandinavian investigations of smuggling by North Korean diplomats). See also *New York Times* (December 30, 1976), 5 (Peru); and (*Toronto*) *Globe & Mail* (July 29, 1983), 4.

[30]*New York Times* (August 15, 1973), 6 (Norway); (July 11, 1975), 1, 6 (France); (July 28, 1978), A2 (Great Britain).

[31]On all these details, consult Rieser's *Note* on diplomatic immunity in 19 *Harvard Int'l L. J.* 1019 (1978); 73 *AJIL* 125 (1979); *New York Times* (February 2, 1976), 25; (August 12, 1977), A4; (August 14, 1977), E4; and (April 4, 1979). See Department of State regulations concerning compulsory liability insurance for diplomats, 18 *ILM* 871 (1979).

[32]See R. E. Stassen-Berger, "Letter from the Tow-Away Zone: What's 'Petty Cash' to New York Is Big-Ticket Concern for Envoys," *The Washington Post* (December 13, 1993). For example, during 1990 in New York City, the Soviet Union had received more than 11,000 citations worth about $364,300. As a group, the diplomatic community in New York had amassed $6.3 million in outstanding citations.

[33]Quoted in Stassen-Berger, note 32.

[34]"Licensed to Sin: Diplomats in Berlin Use Immunity to Commit Crimes," Spiegel Online International (February 27, 2007), www.spiegel.de/international/spiegel/0,1518,468715,00.html; K. Donaldson, "Murder, Rape, Assault: The Secret Crimes of London's Diplomats," *The Independent* (London) (February 16, 2006).

indent occurs, the host state has two main options: ask for a waiver of immunity, or declare the alleged offender persona non grata if the waiver is not forthcoming. Agents cannot personally waive their immunities because the right belongs to the sending state, not the individual. In normal practice, for top officials, the right will rest with the appropriate constitutional authorities in the sending state. For others, including administrative and technical staff, the head of mission may have the authority. Individuals can, however, voluntarily yield their immunities by simply resigning their position and remaining in the country. This occurred most recently when Venezuela refused to waive the immunities of an agent charged with sexual assault by his former fiancée. The refusal by Venezuela would have resulted in U.S. authorities declaring the agent persona non grata. Venezuela had already indicated they would recall him. He decided instead to resign his position and have his day in court.[35] We should emphasize the rarity of this decision.

On the other hand, upon request, Georgia did waive the diplomatic immunity of Gueorgui Makharadze, the deputy chief of mission at the Georgian Embassy in Washington, DC, so that he could be prosecuted in the U.S. courts on the charge of manslaughter committed while driving under the influence of alcohol. Makharadze had a blood alcohol level considerably above the legal limit on the night of January 3, 1997, when he caused a five-car accident that resulted in the death of a 16-year-old teenager in downtown Washington. In October 1997, the diplomat pleaded guilty to criminal charges in connection with the accident.[36] If declared persona non grata, the agent *must* be withdrawn by the sending state. A third possibility does exist, but cost and circumstance make it a distant possibility. Immunities and privileges are role or function specific. They do not attach to the person, but to the office. They cease upon leaving the country at the end of a term—or, if no longer serving for other reasons (i.e., being declared persona non grata), after a reasonable period of time in which to leave. The immunities of a diplomat who is no longer accredited as such are governed by Article 39(2) of the Vienna Convention on Diplomatic Relations. When the functions of such a person have ended, a diplomat's privileges and immunities "normally cease when he leaves the country, or on expiry of a reasonable period in which to do so, but shall subsist until that time, even in the case of armed conflict."

U.S. Department of State (1987) has stated that, under the convention, the immunities of ex-diplomats do not continue to apply if acts performed during the performance of diplomatic functions were not done so in the exercise of functions as a member of the diplomatic mission. Hence, if the incident or crime *did not* involve official duties, immunity only suspends arrest and process *at the time*. Immunities and privileges do not last forever and *do not* remove culpability for any offense an individual agent may have committed outside his or her official

---

[35]B. A. Masters, "Former Diplomat Faces Sexual Assault Trial," *The Washington Post* (April 16, 1997), B6.

[36]"Georgian's Diplomatic Immunity Waived," www.lubbockonline.com/news/021697/georgian. htm (accessed April 22, 2009). In a case with similar circumstances, see "Canada Requests Immunity Waiver for Russian Diplomats," *Saint Petersburg Times* (January 30, 2001), 1; see also the discussion in J. Shaw, "Privilege of Diplomatic Immunity Facing Challenges from All Sides," *Washington Diplomat* (March 2002), www.washdiplomat.com/02-03/a5_02_03.html (accessed April 22, 2009).

duties.[37] The person who enjoyed the immunity could be prosecuted as a private person at a later time if the receiving state can find a way to exercise a valid in personam jurisdiction. If any question occurs about the status of a particular individual, in the United States the State Department has the final say.

A diplomat who is no longer persona grata is normally given a time limit within which to leave the receiving state's jurisdiction. Should the diplomat refuse to leave, he or she may be placed under detention and escorted to the frontier for expulsion. In July 1980, the United States recalled Ambassador Frederic L. Chap from Ethiopia at the request of the latter's revolutionary government. On many recent occasions during the Cold War, the dismissal of diplomatic agents represented merely a retaliatory action, caused by a similar dismissal (usually for purely political reasons) of agents by the sending state. The British government ordered (September 24, 1971) 105 Soviet Embassy and trade agency staff members to leave within two weeks, accusing them of espionage and attempting to infiltrate saboteurs. In turn, the Soviet Union expelled 13 British Embassy staff members on October 6, 1971. On December 18, 1979, the U.S. Department of State announced that at least 183 Iranian diplomatic staff members would be expelled within five days, leaving only 35 Iranian diplomatic personnel in the country. The United States justified this action as a reprisal for the seizure of the American Embassy and hostages in Teheran. Note that the United States refrained from seizing the Iranian Embassy. While the short-term circumstances might have justified such an act in reprisal, the broader context did not. Here, one must consider reciprocity and precedent. The United States has more embassies than any other country. The United States did not wish to establish a precedent that seemingly would permit the seizure of an embassy, no matter what the provocation.[38]

Contemporary practice records a number of expulsions for political reasons. Table 14.1 gives a representative sample, not a complete log:

Status of Administrative and Technical Staff

Members of the administrative and technical staff (and their households), provided they are not nationals or permanent residents of the receiving state, have immunity as well. If they are nationals or permanent residents, administrative and technical staff have immunity *only* for activities connected with their official duties. Article 38 stipulates that if any diplomatic agent is a national of the receiving state, he or she need only be granted immunity for activities connected with official duties. Members of the service staff also have immunity for acts performed in the course of their official duties.

---

[37]See the discussion of an accident involving the ambassador to the U.S. from Papua New Guinea in 81 *AJIL* (1987), 937 ff. See also G. V. McClanahan, *Diplomatic Immunity: Principles, Practices, Problems* (1989); "Diplomatic Immunity," *Gist* (U.S. Department of State), October 4, 1990; "Crimes by Foreign Mission Personnel: Corrective Measures," 82 *AJIL* 106 (1988); "U.S. Dept. of State: Guidance for Law Enforcement Officers with Regard to Personal Rights and Immunities of Foreign Diplomatic and Consular Personnel (February 1988)," 27 *AJIL* 1617 (1988); "Prosecution of Former Diplomats for Nonofficial Acts," 81 *AJIL* 937 (1987); M. Nash, "Diplomatic Privileges and Immunities: Motor Vehicles, Traffic Citations and Fines," 88 *AJIL* 312 (1994).

[38]R. Shaplen, "Eye of the Storm," *New Yorker* (June 9, 1980), 48, esp. 82.

> ### Table 14.1
>
> **Expulsion of Diplomats for Political Reasons 2007–2011**
>
> United Kingdom–Russia 2007[39]
> Belarus–United States 2008[40]
> Bolivia and Venezuela–United States 2008[41]
> Britain–Israel 2010[42]
> Canada–Libya 2011[43]
> Ecuador–United States 2011[44]

Inviolability extends to diplomatic communication. Diplomatic correspondence is immune from seizure, search, and censorship by the receiving state. A mission may employ codes and ciphers in its communications, but embassies may install and operate radio transmitters *only* with the consent of the receiving state. Diplomatic couriers, traveling on diplomatic passports, may not be arrested or impeded. The contents of their pouch or baggage cannot be inspected or confiscated.

Immunities and privileges begin from the moment the person enters the state, but they depend upon acknowledgment of the agent by the receiving state. More simply, merely entering a state with a diplomatic passport does not automatically confer immunities and privileges unless the person is in direct transit to a post or on some official business or duty recognized by the state.[45]

Immunity and Inviolability of Embassy Buildings

The embassy or legation quarters, as well as the residence of a diplomatic agent, are inviolable. The agents of the receiving state may not enter any official buildings except with the explicit consent of the head of the diplomatic mission. This restriction has led to some interesting problems. During the Cold War, a major fire broke out at the Soviet Embassy in Washington, DC. The firefighters had to follow the instructions of embassy personnel concerning where they could go and where they could not. Still, inviolability carries with it the following duty (Article 41(3)):

> The premises of the mission must *not* be used in any manner incompatible with the functions of the mission as laid down in the present Convention or

---

[39]"British Government Expels 4 Russian Diplomats," *International Herald Tribune* (July 16, 2007).

[40]"Diplomats Expulsion from Belarus Angers U.S.," *International Herald Tribune* (May 2, 2008).

[41]"Expulsion of US Ambassadors: Ecuador, Honduras Support Bolivia & Venezuela," Centre for Research on Globalization, www.globalresearch.ca/index.php?context=va&aid=10193.

[42]"Britain Expels Israeli Diplomat Over Dubai Passport Row," BBC News (March 23, 2010); http://news.bbc.co.uk/2/hi/uk_news/8582518.stm.

[43]B. Bouzane, "Diplomatic Expulsions Often Fly Under Radar, Says Intelligence Expert," *Montreal Gazette* (May 18, 2011).

[44]"Ecuador Expels U.S. Ambassador in WikiLeaks Flap," *USA Today* (April 5, 2011).

[45]Regina v. Governor of Pentonville Prison, ex parte Teja, 2 QB 274, 54 International Law Reports, 368.

UNITED STATES V. IBRAHIM AHMED AL-HAMDI

United States Court of Appeals, Fourth Circuit
356 F.3d 564; 2004 U.S. App. LEXIS 1034

Facts

U.S law prohibits possession of firearms by nonimmigrant aliens. Ibrahim Ahmed Al-Hamdi, a citizen of Yemen, had been prosecuted and convicted of possessing a firearm in contravention of this statute. Al-Hamdi argued that as a family member of a diplomat, he had diplomatic immunity at the time of his arrest. He further claimed that the U.S. State Department had tried to revoke that immunity retroactively. Such action would have been a violation of the Vienna Convention on Diplomatic Relations and the U.S. Constitution.

Al-Hamdi came to the United States in 1993, when his father was appointed as a Minister in the Republic of Yemen's embassy in Washington, DC. At that point, both Al-Hamdi and his father possessed diplomatic immunity. Al-Hamdi celebrated his twenty-first birthday in November 1998. His identity card, given to all persons with diplomatic immunity, expired in December 1998. The Yemeni Embassy applied for a new identity card for Al-Hamdi in December 1999. U.S. regulations specify that for adult children over 21 to continue to be regarded as members of a diplomat's household for purposes of extended immunity, they must be enrolled in school full-time. Because Al-Hamdi was not enrolled in school at the time, the State Department requested more information before it would grant the request. The embassy did not reply, and Al-Hamdi never received a new identity card. Al-Hamdi argued that the Vienna Convention does not allow for age restrictions and that

he remained a member of his father's household because his father continued to support him financially. Police arrested Al-Hamdi in February 2003. On March 31, 2003, the State Department sent a letter to the Yemeni embassy stating that Al-Hamdi's father also no longer qualified for diplomatic immunity because he was not employed full-time.

Issues

1. Did the State Department's action in placing an age limit on "members of the household" fall within permissible actions with respect to the Vienna Convention?
2. Did Al-Hamdi have diplomatic immunity at the time of his arrest and subsequent prosecution? Did the State Department revoke his immunity retroactively?

Decision

1. Yes. States have a right to formulate reasonable definitions of ambiguous treaty phrases.
2. No. The State Department had not renewed his certificate. He lost his diplomatic immunity upon turning 21 in 1998.

Reasoning

The determination of whether a person has diplomatic immunity turns on interesting questions of fact and law. In 1989, the State Department had established a policy that "members of the family" as

(*continued*)

set forth in the Vienna Convention did not include children over the age of 21 unless those children were legitimately enrolled in school. Children enrolled in school would enjoy diplomatic immunity until their twenty-third birthday. States have a right to formulate reasonable definitions elaborating the language in the Vienna Convention.

Under the Constitution, the executive branch has the power to send and receive ambassadors. Hence, the certificate of the secretary of state is the best evidence to prove the status of a person who claims to be a minister. Courts cannot "assume to sit in judgement upon the decision of the executive in reference to the public character of a person claiming to be a foreign minister."

by other rules of general international law or by any special agreements in force between the sending State and the receiving state. (Emphasis added)

An important question arises because, while receiving states have other remedies available for individuals who violate local laws, if a state violates the duty not to use the embassy or other protected buildings for purposes that violate the public policy of the receiving state, what recourse does the receiving state have?[46]

In dealing with this question, we should note that a staple plot in action movies or television dramas has an agent (or intrepid reporter) ready to penetrate a foreign embassy to gain information or perhaps locate someone imprisoned on its premises. In preparation, his handler will warn him, "Be careful. You know that if you are caught, you are on their territory; you are subject to their law and they can do what they want." Recent episodes of the franchise TV shows *CSI Miami* and *Law and Order* have revolved around crimes committed that involved this aspect of immunity. In each of these episodes, the writers have presumed that embassies and consulates have *extraterritorial status;* that is, the writers have assumed that the inviolable nature of the embassy translates into sovereign rights over the premises. This is a common misperception, but inviolability *does not mean* that embassies and other protected buildings have been granted extraterritoriality. Despite their inviolable status, embassies and consulates remain the territory of the receiving states.[47] As with personal inviolability, the law simply *suspends*

---

[46]For a discussion of the debate over this issue in the United Kingdom after the incident at the Libyan People's Bureau, see R. Higgins, "The Abuse of Diplomatic Privileges and Immunities: Recent United Kingdom Experience," 79 *AJIL* 641 (1984); and R. Higgins, "UK Foreign Affairs Committee Report on the Abuse of Diplomatic Immunities and Privileges: Government Response and Report," 80 *AJIL* 135 (1985).

[47]See *Fatemi v. United States,* U.S. Dist. Court, DC, 1963, At. 2d 525, in which the court stated

> (1) that a foreign embassy is not to be considered the territory of the sending state; and (2) that local police have the authority and responsibility to enter a foreign embassy if the privilege of diplomatic inviolability is not invoked when an offense is committed there in violation of local law.

In this case, the ambassador had invited the DC police into the embassy to arrest demonstrators who had occupied part of the building. The Court of Appeals for the District of Columbia Circuit (opinion on rehearing) reached the same result in holding that the embassy of the United States in Teheran was not U.S. territory under the terms of the Foreign Sovereign Immunities Act of 1976. *Persinger v. Islamic Republic of Iran,* 729 F.2d 835, *cert. denied,* 469 U.S. 881, 105 S. Ct. 247 (1984).

RADWAN V. RADWAN

England, Family Division 1972 (1972) 3 W.L.R. 735

Facts

Mrs. Mary Isobel Radwan filed a petition for divorce in November 1970. Her husband was a subject of the United Arab Republic (Egypt) but was then living in England. In April 1970, her husband, an adherent of Islam, had gone to the Egyptian Consulate in London and had before witnesses performed the prescribed ceremony for divorce in accordance with Egyptian law. After the prescribed 90 days, the divorce was finalized in accordance with Egyptian law. The consul stated that the Egyptian Consulate in London is regarded by Egypt as being Egyptian territory on Egyptian soil.

Issues

Does the Egyptian Consulate (or its embassy) have extraterritorial status because of its inviolable status? (Does Egyptian law or English law apply within the premises?)

Decision

Embassies and consulates do not have extraterritorial status. They stand squarely within the territory of the received state. The divorce is invalid because it did not conform to English law.

Reasoning

In examining both the Vienna Convention on Consular Relations and the Vienna Convention on Diplomatic Relations, the court noted:

> The premises of a mission are inviolable and the local authorities may enter them only with the consent of the head of the mission. But this does not make the premises foreign territory or take them out of the reach of the local law for many purposes: for example, a commercial transaction in an embassy may be governed by the local law, particularly the tax law; marriages may be celebrated there only if conditions laid down by the local law are met; and a child born in it will, unless his father has diplomatic status, acquire the local nationality.

certain rights normally associated with the control of territory.[48] Thus, if a crime is committed within an embassy, that crime occurs on the soil of the *receiving state*, not that of the sending state. If embassy personnel apprehend a burglar on the premises, they have no right to try and impose sentence. They must hand him or her over to the authorities of the sending state for prosecution.

The *sending* state does have the right to punish *its own* officers and nationals for crimes committed within diplomatic premises (active nationality principle). In *United States v. Erdos*,[49] the chargé d'affaires at the American Embassy in the Republic of Equatorial Guinea was convicted of killing another embassy employee within the American Embassy compound. The court found that the

---

[48]See *Time* (July 21, 1958), 20, for the lively tale of Sam Sary, Cambodian ambassador to Great Britain, who wrongly maintained that he had every right under Cambodian law to whip a concubine with the assistance of his number 1 wife; Sary justified his action by asserting that his embassy was "Cambodia in London." See also the *Asylum case (Columbia-Peru), ICJ Reports* (1950), 274.

[49]474 F.2d 157 (4th Cir. 1973).

special maritime and territorial jurisdiction of the United States applied to U.S. embassies in foreign countries.[50]

Security of Diplomatic Premises

Local authorities have the responsibility to provide adequate security for embassies. Because the embassy forms part of its territory, the receiving state—not the sending state—has primary responsibility for ensuring the security of legation premises from attack or damage (Article 22 (2)):

> The receiving State is under a special duty to take all appropriate steps to protect the premises of the mission against any intrusion or damage and to prevent any disturbance of the peace of the mission or impairment of its dignity.

Between 1998 and 2003, forty violent attacks were directed against embassies in various countries.[51] Not unexpectedly, many of these were directed at American legations, but attacks also occurred on embassies accredited to China, Jordan, France, Thailand, and Iraq. For example, upon anticipating trouble in the wake of the invasion of Iraq in March 2003, Spanish authorities deployed heavily armed police to guard the American and British embassies in Madrid.[52]

In the United States, during the 1960s, harassment of certain foreign diplomats and inconsequential attacks on foreign mission buildings—particularly those of the USSR—led to passage of the Protection of Diplomats Act (1972), Pub. L. No. 92–539.[53] Because that new law did not appear to meet fully the needs of the times, Congress enacted additional legislation in 1976: the Act for the Prevention and Punishment of Crimes Against Internationally Protected Persons, Pub. L. No. 94–467.[54] The purpose of that legislation was to bring Title 18 of the U.S. Code into conformity with two international conventions ratified by the United States: the 1971 OAS Convention to Prevent and Punish the Acts of Terrorism Taking the Form of Crimes Against Persons That Are of International Significance[55] and the 1973 UN Convention on the Prevention and Punishment of Crimes Against Internationally Protected Persons, Including Diplomatic Agents.[56]

The UN Convention, which entered into force on February 20, 1977, provides in Article 7 that "the State Party in whose territory the alleged offender is

---

[50]18 U.S.C. § 7(3).

[51]"In Depth: Embassy Attacks," www.cbc.ca/news/background/embassy/ (accessed April 22, 2009). See the following about security problems of diplomatic premises: "Can U.S. Buy Embassy Safety?" *U.S. News & World Report* (April 14, 1986), 22; G. D. Moffett, "US Embassies Under Siege of Terrorism," *Christian Science Monitor* (January 29, 1986), 14; and *Current Policy No. 788*, "Enhancing Diplomatic Security" (February 1986), and *No. 923*, "How Much Security Is Enough?" (March 1987).

[52]"Spain Steps Up Embassy Security," www.cnn.com/2003/WORLD/europe/03/19/sprj.irq.spain.security/ (accessed April 22, 2009).

[53]Text of the Act for the Protection of Foreign Officials and Official Guests of the United States in 67 *AJIL* 622 (1973).

[54]See 71 *AJIL* 134 (1977).

[55]Text in 10 *ILM* 255 (1971).

[56]Text in 67 *AJIL* 383 (1974); and in 13 *ILM* 41 (1974).

present shall, if it does not extradite him, submit, without exception whatsoever and without undue delay, the case to its competent authorities for the purpose of prosecution, through proceedings in accordance with the laws of that State." Note that this wording eliminates the possibility of giving asylum by declaring the act a political offense. This article caused prolonged and somewhat heated debate in the UN General Assembly. Nonetheless, the overwhelming majority of member governments agreed that the offenses in question represented crimes under international law rather than political activities that were in some manner excusable.[57]

Status of Diplomatic Persons in Transit

As we have noted, the rights and privileges of diplomatic personnel apply only in the receiving state because no legal relationship exists between a diplomat and a third state. Nonetheless, as a matter of courtesy and because it forms a question of interest and convenience to all states, third states usually have granted diplomats in direct transit to their posts the same privileges as they would have in the receiving state.

A classic case is *Bergman v. De Sieyes*.[58] The defendant had been served with process in a tort action in New York while on his way to Bolivia, where he had been accredited as the French minister. The District Court had dismissed the complaint, holding that although De Sieyes was not entitled to immunity under Title 22, Section 252, of the U.S. Code, that section was declaratory of existing international law, and hence, under that law, the French diplomat should be granted immunity. The Circuit Court upheld the dismissal on appeal. The latter reviewed previous New York State court decisions in point and concluded that due to changing concepts of diplomatic immunity and changing conditions of travel, "the courts of New York would today hold that a diplomat *in transitu* would be entitled to the same immunity as a diplomat *in situ*."

However, a diplomat *must be en route* on an official mission in order to enjoy immunity. The Guatemalan ambassador to Belgium and the Netherlands flew to New York from Europe on a personal visit and was arrested on a narcotics charge. His motion to dismiss because of diplomatic immunity was denied because of the nature of his trip. Similarly, in *Ludovicus v. Astenavondt,* the chancellor of the Belgian Embassy in New Delhi, India, was arrested with seven others in New York City (on May 26, 1985) after he delivered 22 pounds of heroin to an FBI agent. He apparently served as a courier for a smuggling ring.[59]

---

[57]See L. M. Bloomfield and G. F. Fitzgerald, *Crimes Against Internationally Protected Persons: Prevention and Punishment* (1975), for a detailed analysis of the provisions of the UN Convention; and R. D. Kearney, "The Twenty-Fourth Session of the International Law Commission," 67 *AJIL* 84, esp. 85–92 (1973). See also Bayles, "Hostage Crisis Still Haunts Nation," AP Dispatch (October 28, 1984); and Chapter 13.

[58]U.S. Court of Appeals, 2d Cir., 1948, 170 F.2d 360, digested in 43 *AJIL* 373 (1949).

[59]*United States v. Rosal*, U.S. Dist. Court, S.D.N.Y., 1960, 191 F. Supp. 663, reported briefly in 55 *AJIL* 986 (1961); AP Dispatch (June 6, 1985) re Vastenavondt. See also *Christian Science Monitor* (May 18, 1988), 2. "Britain Quits Zimbabwe After Diplomacy Gaff," *The Independent* (March 9, 2000). Britain recalled its ambassador from Zimbabwe to protest the opening of British diplomatic baggage by local customs authorities.

Immunity and Travel

Immunity does not automatically give diplomatic personnel freedom of movement in the receiving state. The receiving state may create, by its law or regulations, zones into which entry is prohibited or restricted for reasons of security. Occasionally, this action may be in response to what a government perceives as an unfriendly action by another government. In August 1967, Great Britain limited the embassy personnel of the People's Republic of China to an area 5 miles from the center of London. During the Cold War, both the United States and the Soviet Union imposed strict travel guidelines on diplomatic agents. One of the most extensive travel limitations on record was imposed in January 1952, when the Soviet government converted 80 percent of the area of the Soviet Union into a forbidden zone—including the capitals of the allegedly independent Ukrainian and Byelorussian republics, both members of the United Nations. The ban was reduced in extent in 1974.[60] The most drastic restrictions on the movement of diplomats were those imposed in Cambodia under the Pol Pot government: Members of the 11 foreign missions accredited to Cambodia lived under virtual house arrest, being forbidden to venture more than 200 yards from their compounds; missions were not permitted to operate automobiles; and meals had to be ordered daily through Khmer Rouge military personnel, who then delivered them to each mission.[61]

In 1985, the U.S. secretary of state, to reduce spying, ordered some 300 Soviet nationals employed by the United Nations to report almost all travel outside of a 25-mile radius of Columbus Circle in New York City. The Soviet contingent, along with 20 Afghans, 30 Cubans, 50 Iranians, 40 Libyans, and 15 Vietnamese employees, was ordered to make all future airline and hotel reservations through the Department of State's Office of Foreign Missions. In late 1985 and early 1986, the Department of State notified the UN missions of Bulgaria, Czechoslovakia, the German Democratic Republic, and Poland of the same report and reservation requirements for their nationals employed by the United Nations.

Special Categories of Agents

Several countries, notably the United States, have on occasion utilized the services of special officers of various types, in addition to the generally recognized categories of diplomatic personnel. Almost invariably the sending states have attempted to secure diplomatic status, with its attendant privileges and immunities, for such special officers. Conversely, the receiving states have generally opposed such efforts. In essence, whatever status is granted to such officers depends on the decision of the receiving state, because these categories fall outside the practice of both customary and conventional rules of law.

---

[60]Y. Liang, "Diplomatic Intercourse and Immunities as a Subject for Codification," 47 *AJIL* 439, at 443 (1953). See *New York Times* (February 20, 1974), 6 and (February 3, 1977), 2 (with maps showing 1977 restricted areas in both the United States and the Soviet Union); also (February 2, 1977), A2, on travel by UN diplomats from governments not recognized then by the United States.

[61]See *Time* (October 24, 1977), 58; and K. Müller, "Scenes from Hermetic Cambodia," 28 *Swiss Review of World Affairs* (May 1978), 6.

The U.S. Treasury Department has employed a group of officers attached to embassies and legations in Europe and styled, at different times, as special commissioner, customs attaché, customs representative, and treasury attaché. Despite repeated efforts to have these individuals accorded diplomatic status, only France has accepted the Treasury Department's agents as full-fledged diplomats. Other countries have been willing to grant to them only an exemption from income taxes on their salaries.

An innovation in diplomatic practice was recorded on February 22, 1973, when the United States and the People's Republic of China announced agreements to establish liaison offices in Peking and Washington in order to speed up the normalization of their relations. The announcement was remarkable because the United States had not then recognized the Chinese government. Staff members of both missions were to have diplomatic privileges, including the right to communicate in code with the respective home governments.[62]

Special envoys are usually granted temporary diplomatic status and, in recent decades, have been equipped with a diplomatic rank. Thus, heads of delegations to international conferences are commonly styled as ambassadors or envoys extraordinary. Similarly, members of arbitration tribunals and boundary commissions are on occasion granted diplomatic privileges and immunities.

Diplomatic Asylum

Because embassies do not have extraterritorial status, the question of granting asylum poses interesting questions of law, politics, and policy. To state the obvious, once someone enters legation premises, inviolability means that local authorities can demand return but cannot enter to detain or arrest.[63] Historically, those individuals guilty of political offenses or the object of political or religious persecution have, for political or religious reasons, often sought refuge (asylum) in embassies or consulates located within their own state. Receiving states have long asserted that an unlimited right to grant asylum represents an unwarranted intervention in the internal affairs of the host state. Outside of Latin America, where the practice has been employed so consistently that it may form a principle of "regional international law,"[64] other states have struggled with the issues. Most recently, the incidence of North Korean refugees seeking asylum at foreign embassies in Beijing and

---

[62]See 67 *AJIL* 536 (1973); full text of joint communiqué in 12 *ILM* 431 (1973).

[63]See "Seoul Protests Over Asylum Scuffle," BBC News, http://news.bbc.co.uk/1/hi/world/asia-pacific/2043212.stm (accessed April 22, 2009), for an incident where allegedly Chinese authorities entered a South Korean consulate to remove North Koreans who had entered demanding asylum.

[64]On Latin American instances, see A. E. Evans, "The Colombian-Peruvian Asylum Case: The Practice of Diplomatic Asylum," 46 *AJIL* 142, esp. 144 (1952); *Haya de la Torre* case (*Columbia v. Peru*), International Court of Justice (June 13, 1950), www.icj-cij.org/docket/index.php?p1=3&p2=3&code=haya&case=14&k=d4 (accessed May 11, 2009); and more recently, L. O. Monasterio, "Guatemalan Refugees in Mexico: A Happy Ending," Department of International Legal Affairs, Organization of American States, www.oas.org/juridico/english/ortize.html (accessed April 22, 2009).

other capitals has kept the issue on the front burner.[65] Tension arises here because many cases potentially involve issues of human rights (see Chapter 16).

One of the more bizarre episodes in the history of modern asylum practice, the "Mariel Cuban" exodus, began in March 1980, when six Cubans forced their way into the Peruvian Embassy compound in Havana and demanded asylum. The total inside the embassy soon grew to 30 Cubans. The Cuban government then withdrew all guards from the embassy. Over the next few days, over 10,000 more Cuban citizens crowded into the embassy. Peru offered to accept 1,000 of the crowd; Costa Rica indicated a willingness to take up to 10,000; and the United States, 3,500. The Cuban government lifted its opposition to transporting these individuals out of the country and designated the port of Mariel as an official departure point. A fleet of small boats, estimated at more than a thousand, chartered or manned by Cuban exiles in the United States began moving refugees to Key West. When the operation ended in June 1980, nearly 124,000 individuals had entered the United States.[66]

The official U.S. policy has been fairly consistent for the past 130 years or so. American diplomatic agents receive instructions not to grant such asylum except temporarily to persons whose lives are threatened by mob violence. The United States does not accept diplomatic asylum as a practice sanctioned by international law. The U.S. position is that, at most, it may represent a "permissive local custom," or a temporary measure. In ratifying the 1928 Havana Convention on Asylum,[67] the United States submitted a reservation to this effect and refused to sign another convention adopted by Latin American delegations to the 1933 Montevideo Conference.

On occasion, U.S. practice has departed from state policy. U.S. diplomats have granted asylum in embassies and legations on various occasions not involving mob violence. Perhaps the most notable recent departure occurred when, after the failed Hungarian uprising in 1956, the United States permitted József Cardinal Mindszenty political asylum in its embassy in Budapest until his death in 1971. In June 1978, seven Russian Pentecostal dissidents made their way into the U.S. Embassy in Moscow.[68] They were granted an unofficial and temporary asylum pending Soviet acceptance of a U.S. proposal for assurances of nonpunishment. Six members of the group remained in the embassy until April 1983, when they were finally persuaded to return home and then were permitted to emigrate with their families in June 1983. After the Chinese government crushed the pro-democracy movement at Tiananmen Square in June 1989, the United States also granted diplomatic asylum

---

[65]See, for example, "N. Koreans Beg Asylum from French in Vietnam," Agence France Press (December 17, 2004); "The Status of North Korean Asylum Seekers and the US Government Policy Towards Them," U.S. Department of State (February 28, 2005); D. Sconfield, "No Asylum in Canada for North Korean Diplomat," *Asia Times Online* (February 13, 2004), www.atimes.com/atimes/Korea/FB13Dg05.html (accessed May 11, 2009).

[66]For a concise summary, see www.globalsecurity.org/military/ops/mariel-boatlift.htm (accessed April 22, 2009).

[67]Text in 47 *AJIL* 446 (1953).

[68]For the Soviet Pentecostals, see *New York Times* (June 24, 1979), 3; (September 22, 1979), 2; and the (*Victoria, B.C.*) *Times-Colonist* (July 17, 1983).

in its Beijing Embassy to Fang Lizhi[69] and his wife. The Fangs were permitted to leave China for England a year later.

When the United States invaded Panama ("Operation Just Cause") in December 1989, U.S. troops sought to capture General Manuel Antonio Noriega and bring him to trial in the United States for drug trafficking.[70] Noriega hid from capture for four days and then found asylum in the Vatican Embassy in Panama City. If Noriega had been caught by agents of the new Panamanian government, his extradition to the United States would have been forbidden by the Panamanian Constitution. If he wanted to leave for a third country, he would have had to receive safe passage from Panama to a country willing to accept him.

When the papal nuncio refused a U.S. request for custody of Noriega, American troops surrounding the embassy set up loudspeakers and played rock and roll at top volume 24 hours a day.[71] The Vatican failed to find a state willing to take Noriega. The new Panamanian government announced that it would ask for Noriega's surrender on charges of murder. Finally, in early January 1990, Noriega surrendered to American troops.

When dissidents seized the U.S. Embassy in Teheran in 1979, the Canadian government quietly granted diplomatic asylum to five U.S. consular employees and one U.S. agricultural attaché. The six had escaped via a back door of the U.S. Embassy. The Canadians quietly arranged for transport out of Iran on forged Canadian passports when Canada closed its embassy. The Iranian foreign minister denounced the Canadian action as a "flagrant violation of international law."

AGENTS OF INTERNATIONAL ORGANIZATIONS: PRIVILEGES AND IMMUNITIES

The development of international organizations has been accompanied by a number of problems connected with the privileges and immunities of the officials and agents of the organizations in question. Article 7(4) of the Covenant of the League of Nations conferred on the representatives of the member states and the agents of the League full diplomatic privileges and immunities. In some respects, these paragraphs represent definite innovations when compared with earlier practices. In contrast with Article 7 of the Covenant, the corresponding Article 105(2)

---

[69]See A. P Rubin, "Diplomatic Asylum and Fang Lizhi," 1 *Diplomacy & Statecraft* (1990), 84–89.

[70]See V. P. Nanda, "The Validity of United States Intervention in Panama Under International Law," 84 *AJIL* 494 (1990); T. Farer, "Panama: Beyond the Charter Paradigm," *id.,* 503; see A. Lowenfeld's heavily documented study, "U.S. Law Enforcement Abroad: The Constitution and International Law, Continued," 84 *AJIL* 444 (1990); T. Farer, "Panama: Beyond the Charter Paradigm," *id.,* 503; A. D'Amato, "The Invasion of Panama Was a Lawful Response to Tyranny," *id.,* 516; and A. P. Rubin, "Is Noriega Worth Subverting US Law?" *Christian Science Monitor* (March 19, 1990), 18. Examine *United States v. Verdugo-Urquidez,* U.S. Supreme Court, February 28, 1990, in 29 *ILM* 441 (1990), in which the Court ruled that the Fourth Amendment did not apply to aliens in foreign territory or in international waters. Any restrictions on foreign searches or seizures had to be imposed by Congress, based on diplomatic negotiations, or found in the provisions of treaties.

[71]As a curious aside, during the "codfish war" (1973) between Iceland and the United Kingdom, the British ambassador attempted to disperse a protesting mob near his embassy by loudly playing selections from a bagpipe band.

of the UN Charter grants to the representatives of the member states "such privileges and immunities as are necessary for the independent exercise of their functions in connection with the Organization."[72]

As one of its very first acts, the General Assembly adopted the General Convention on the Privileges and Immunities of the United Nations.[73] Because the headquarters of the new organization would be located in the United States, arrangements had to be worked out with the prospective host government. The initial step was passage by Congress on December 29, 1945, of the Statute Extending Privileges, Exemptions, and Immunities to International Organizations and to the Officers and Employees Thereof (International Organizations Immunities Act).[74] Negotiations between the secretary-general and the United States resulted in the definitive Headquarters of the United Nations Agreement Between the United States of America and the United Nations of June 26, 1947 (in force November 21, 1947), and an interim agreement of December 18, 1947, applying relevant provisions of the June 26 agreement to the temporary headquarters of the United Nations at Lake Success, New York.[75]

Diplomatic Privileges and Immunities of Member States

These rights apply to delegates to the principal and subsidiary organs of the United Nations and to conferences convened by that organization, but only while these representatives exercise their functions and during their travel to and from the place of meeting. The privileges listed include immunity from arrest or detention and seizure of personal luggage; immunity from legal process of every kind for all acts (and words spoken or written) in their capacity as representatives; inviolability of all papers and documents; the right to use codes and receive correspondence and papers by courier or in sealed bags; exemption for representatives and their spouses from immigration restrictions or national service obligations en route or while visiting in the exercise of their functions; and equality of treatment as respects currency or exchange restrictions with representatives of foreign governments on temporary official missions. In acknowledgment of the theory of functional necessity, Section 14 of Article 4 states:

> [P]rivileges and immunities are accorded to representatives of Members not for the personal benefit of the individuals themselves, but in order to safeguard the independent exercise of their functions in connection with the United Nations. Consequently a Member not only has the right but is under a duty to waive the immunity of its representative in any case where in the opinion of the Member the immunity would impede the course of justice, and it can be waived without prejudice to the purpose for which the immunity is accorded.

---

[72]On the general subject of the immunity of UN officials, consult the excellent and heavily documented summary in Bishop, 614.

[73]Text in 43 *AJIL* 1 (1949 Supp.).

[74]Text in 40 *AJIL* 85 (April 1946 Supp.); see 68 *AJIL* 316 (1974), on 1973 amendments relative to the OAU and the OAS.

[75]Texts of agreements, together with notes and the required joint congressional resolution of August 4, 1947, in 43 *AJIL* 8 (1949 Supp.).

The secretary-general has the right to designate categories of officials of the United Nations who will enjoy substantially the same privileges and immunities as representatives of member states, under Article 5 of the convention. Experts performing missions for the United Nations are also to be accorded substantially the same privileges (Article 6, Section 22).

The Headquarters Agreement with the United States outlines the rules governing the Headquarters District in New York City. The federal, state, and local laws of the United States and the jurisdiction of the federal, state, and local courts of the United States apply within the district, except as specified in the General Convention or in the Headquarters Agreement. Normally, however, the United Nations makes regulations for the district, and no federal, state, or local law of the United States conflicting with such regulations can be applied within (Article 3, Section 8). The district is inviolable. Federal, state, or local officers or officials of the United States, whether administrative, judicial, military, or police, cannot enter the district without the consent of and under the conditions agreed to by the secretary-general. On the other hand, the district may not become a place of asylum (Article 3, Section 9-b).

The various levels of U.S. authorities may not impede travel *to or from* the district by the representatives of members, by the families of such persons, by experts performing missions for the United Nations, by representatives of media of mass communications who have been accredited by the United Nations or one of its agencies at its discretion after consultation with the United States, or by other persons summoned to or having official business with the United Nations and its Specialized Agencies (Article 4, Section 11). Otherwise, the United States can restrict (and has done so) travel of delegates accredited to the United Nations within the United States, just as it has the right to do with those agents accredited to embassies in Washington, DC.

The resident representatives to the United Nations, as specified in Article 5, Section 15, of the agreement, are entitled in the territory of the United States to the same privileges and immunities as are enjoyed by diplomatic agents accredited to the United States. In the case of member states whose governments are not recognized by the United States, such privileges and immunities need be extended to such representatives only within the Headquarters District, at their residences or offices outside the district, in transit between the district and their residences or offices, and in transit on official business to and from foreign countries.

As with agents accredited to the receiving state, agents accredited to the United Nations are subject to waiver of immunities. In the "oil for food" scandal, the secretary-general waived the immunities of two UN officials, Alexander Yakovlev and Benon Sevan.[76] Yakovlev pleaded guilty to conspiracy, wire fraud, and money laundering. Investigations continue into Sevan's activities, which include accusations of kickbacks for contracts.

The United Nations and Immunities

Almost as soon as the United Nations began its operations in the United States, cases pertaining to the immunities of representatives, officials, and servants of both

[76]"Oil-for-Food Report Hits 2 Ex-U.N Officials," www.foxnews.com/story/0,2933,165028,00.html (accessed April 22, 2009).

categories began to occur.[77] In the most recent decisions dealing with such immunities, the functional necessity theory influenced the courts' decisions. This was particularly true in the *Advisory Opinion of April 11, 1949, on Reparations for Injuries Suffered in the Service of the United Nations,*[78] in which the ICJ clearly embraced the idea of functional necessity regarding the immunities of persons serving as employees of the United Nations.

Responding to the need to develop adequate guidelines, the International Law Commission drew up successive draft articles, culminating in a treaty—the Vienna Convention on the Representation of States in Their Relations with International Organizations of a Universal Character.[79] To discuss in detail the various immunities exceeds the needs of a general text. Suffice it to note that *representatives* to international organizations as defined in the convention enjoy the same privileges as granted to their colleagues under the Vienna Convention on Diplomatic Relations. An unusual feature of the convention is the high level of privileges and immunities granted to agents, as well as the fact that the service staff and the private staff of mission members are exempted from taxes on their salaries.

Observer Missions

Several governments maintain observer missions at the United Nations. Like consular officials, staff members of these missions possess only "functional immunity"—that is, immunity with tasks or events directly related to their work. Thus, O Nam Chol, a third secretary in North Korea's observer mission who had avoided arrest for almost 11 months by hiding in the mission premises (inviolable), surrendered on July 26, 1983, and pleaded guilty to a reduced charge of third-degree sexual abuse (a misdemeanor; the original charge had been a felony).

The important questions here concern the right of a host state to control agents accredited to the organization. The attempt of the United States to close the Palestine Liberation Organization (PLO) Observer Mission to the United Nations in 1987 resulted not only in interesting diplomatic maneuvering but also in decisions by a U.S. district court and by the ICJ. In 1987, several bills were introduced in Congress to require, among other things, the closing of the PLO Permanent Observer Mission to the United Nations. Although the U.S. Department of State opposed those measures on the grounds that they violated provisions of the 1947 U.S.–UN Headquarters Agreement,[80] the proposed ban on the PLO UN Mission became a part of the Foreign Relations Appropriation Act for 1988 and 1989, as

---

[77]See *Westchester County on Complaint of Donnelly v. Ranollo,* 187 Misc. 777, 67 N.Y.S.2d 31 (City Ct. New Rochelle 1946); see also the analysis of early instances in L. Preuss, "Immunity of Officers and Employees of the United Nations for Official Acts: The Ranallo [*sic*] Case," 41 *AJIL* 555 (1947); *People v. Von Otter,* 114 N.Y.S. (2d) 195 (City Ct. New Rochelle, July 30, 1952), reported in 47 *AJIL* 151, n. 1 (1953); *Tsiang v. Tsiang* (1949), 194 Misc. 259, 86 N.Y.S. (2d) 556; and Q. Wright, "Responsibility for Injuries to United Nations Officials," 43 *AJIL* 95 (1949).

[78]*ICJ Reports* (1949), 174.

[79]Text in 69 *AJIL* 730 (1975); see also Fennessy's analysis of the convention, 70 *AJIL* 62 (1976).

[80]Text of relevant portions in *Time* (December 12, 1988), 36.

the Anti-terrorist Appropriation Act of 1987 (ATA).[81] The UN concerns about the ATA were discussed in the UN General Assembly Committee on Relations with the Host Country. The U.S. representatives admitted that closing the mission would be a violation of the Headquarters Agreement. Eventually, the General Assembly voted (December 17, 1987, Res. 42/210 B) 145–1 (with Israel dissenting and the United States abstaining), requesting the United States to observe the obligations assumed under the Headquarters Agreement.

True to a promise made by the attorney general, the Department of Justice on March 22, 1988, filed a complaint against the PLO, its UN Mission, and all members of the same in the U.S. District Court (S.D.N.Y): *United States of America v. Palestine Liberation Organization, et al.* (88 Div. 1962).[82] In response, on March 23, 1988, a group of 65 U.S. citizens and organizations filed a countercomplaint against the attorney general (*Mendelsohn v. Meese*, 88 Civ. 2005), asking that the ATA not be enforced.

The UN secretary-general requested that the law not be applied in such a manner as to interfere with the operations of the PLO Mission. The United States rejected the request. The secretary-general then invoked the settlement-of-disputes provisions of the Headquarters Agreement. The General Assembly passed two more resolutions. The first called upon the United States to honor its treaty obligations. The second requested an Advisory Opinion from the ICJ. The United States informed the secretary-general that the attorney general had decided that under the ATA, he had to close the PLO Mission and that submission to arbitration "would not serve a useful purpose." The attorney general then notified the PLO Mission that operation of the mission after March 21, 1988, would be unlawful.

In its Advisory Opinion (April 26, 1988), the ICJ unanimously held that the United States was obligated to submit the dispute to arbitration.[83] The decision of the district court in *United States v. Palestine Liberation Organization* came on June 29, 1988.[84] The decision illustrates the approach of U.S. judges discussed in Chapter 4 when potential conflicts arise between international law and legislation. The court held that, while the final decision on the manner in which the United States would honor its treaty obligations had to be left to the U.S. executive branch, the closing of the PLO Mission would be contrary to the manner in which the United States dealt with other Observer Missions. Under the provisions of the Headquarters Agreement, the United States should not interfere with the PLO Mission. The court then concluded after an analysis of the ATA that it could not find any expression of a congressional intent to violate U.S. obligations under the Headquarters Agreement, and hence did not require a closing of the PLO Mission. The court decided that the ATA applied to PLO activities except for those

[81]Text in 27 *ILM* 756 (1988). See the informative collection of "Documents Concerning the Controversy Surrounding the Closing of the Palestine Liberation Organization Observer Mission to the United Nations," 27 *ILM* 712 (1988).

[82]Text in 27 *ILM* 789 (1988).

[83]Applicability of the Obligation to Arbitrate under Section 21 of the United Nations Headquarters Agreement of 26 June 1947, Advisory Opinion of 26 April 1988, http://domino.un.org/UNISPAL. NSF/0/ccaf886d4630dd8185256df800581849?OpenDocument (accessed April 22, 2009).

[84]Text in 27 *ILM* 1055 (1988).

connected with the UN Mission. The latter existed by invitation of the United Nations (since 1974) and was therefore protected by the Headquarters Agreement. In effect, the district court's decision also represented a decision in the *Mendelsohn v. Meese* litigation. On August 29, 1988, the Department of Justice announced that it would not appeal the decision of the district court, asserting that "on balance, the interests of the United States are best served by not appealing."

CONSULAR AGENTS

Practice in classical antiquity developed certain institutions resembling the modern consul in a number of details. In the Greek city-states could be found officials *(proxenoi)* responsible for the welfare of resident aliens in a given state. Rome developed the office of the *praetor peregrinus*. All of these officials, however, were citizens of the territorial sovereign and not of the states whose nationals were in their charge. The end of Greek independence, followed eventually by the collapse of the Roman Empire, meant the disappearance of these predecessors of the modern consul.

The modern consulate had its true beginning during the medieval period, in the Mediterranean area. Alien merchants settling in a port received the permission of the host state to establish a sort of corporation with a limited right of self-government and jurisdiction over its members. This function soon ended up in the hands of judges who, beginning in the eleventh century, were chosen by the merchants from among their own number. The competence of these judges extended primarily into the sphere of commercial disputes. Their titles varied—*consules mercatorium, consuls de commerce, juges consuls*—but *consules mercatorium* was most commonly used. In the twelfth century, these officials were increasingly regarded not only as the heads of the foreign merchants' guild but also as officials (frequently appointed) of the territorial sovereign.

The usefulness of specialized agents to deal with commercial matters became so apparent after a short time that the consular institution began to spread from Italy into other parts of the Mediterranean world, particularly to the Near East and North Africa. As increasing numbers of merchants established branches there, the home government sent out agents *(consules missi)* to take charge of the settlers' interests and to exercise both criminal and civil jurisdiction over them. Most historians of consular institutions point out that a number of these consuls, now stationed abroad, were elected by the emigrant merchants *(consules electi)* but that such personages had, in general, less authority than did those sent abroad by governments.

In the Western states themselves, expansion of the practice of stationing permanent diplomatic representatives in foreign capitals tended to minimize the institution of the consul until the growth of international commerce around the early part of the eighteenth century. It then became apparent to many governments that the presence of commercial representatives in other countries might indeed be advantageous. Soon scores of consuls appeared and began to fulfill important nonpolitical functions abroad. Since then, the institution has proliferated; until today, several thousand consuls of various ranks are scattered all over the world.

Consular Relations

Codification of Rules

For many years, the greater part of a consul's functions—and rights—have been based on special bipartite agreements (consular treaties) between the state whose agent he is and the state within which he performs his functions.[85] The UN International Law Commission, at its seventh session in 1955, began the study of consular relations. The United Nations Conference on Consular Relations met in Vienna from March 4 to April 22, 1963, and prepared (1) the Vienna Convention on Consular Relations (VCCR), (2) the Optional Protocol Concerning Acquisition of Nationality, and (3) the Optional Protocol Concerning the Compulsory Settlement of Disputes.[86] Of these, the VCCR obviously was the most important. On April 24, 1963, the treaty opened for signature; it entered into force on March 19, 1967 (for the United States, on December 24, 1969). The Optional Protocol entered into force on the same dates.

We should emphasize that *consuls are not diplomatic representatives of their state,* because generally the consul's duties are more commercial than political (diplomatic) in their nature. The establishment of consular relations between states takes place by mutual consent. Normally the consent required for the establishment of diplomatic relations also implies consent to the establishment of consular relations. On the other hand, a severance of diplomatic relations does not, ipso facto, mean a breaking off of consular relations. It is also possible to establish consular relations between states that do not have diplomatic relations with each other. In this situation, the consular relations represent the only permanent official relations between the states in question. In most instances of this sort, the consular relations constitute a preliminary to diplomatic relations.

Consular relations are normally exercised through consular posts (Vienna Consular Convention, Article 3), but it is possible for them to be carried out through diplomatic missions. If members of such a mission are assigned to consular functions, they may continue to enjoy diplomatic privileges and immunities (Article 15; see also Article 3(2) of the 1961 Vienna Convention on Diplomatic Relations). Under certain rare circumstances, consular relations may be carried on through the creation of "liaison offices." Thus, the United States and Vietnam, in the absence of normal diplomatic and consular relations, agreed on the opening of such offices, in Hanoi and Washington, in February 1994. The offices were to operate, initially, at the level of consulate general. Staff members and their families were to enjoy all privileges and immunities provided for in the VCCR. The location of consulates or branches thereof and the boundaries of the districts assigned to each of them are

---

[85]See, for example, the Consular Convention (France–United States), signed on July 18, 1966 (in force January 7, 1968), in 62 *AJIL* 551 (1968 Supp.); the Consular Convention of U.S.-USSR, 1964, in force since 1968; text in 50 *Department of State Bulletin* 979 (1964); see also S. Lay, "The United States–Soviet Consular Convention," 59 *AJIL* 876 (1965), and the "Consular Convention Between the United States of America and the People's Republic of China" (September 17, 1980) and related letters, in 19 *ILM* 1119 (1980).

[86]The texts of the convention and of the protocols are reprinted in 57 *AJIL* 993 (1963); and see L. T. Lee, *The Vienna Convention on Consular Relations* (1966), and his useful "Vienna Convention on Consular Relations," *International Conciliation* (January 1969), 41. The convention will be cited hereafter as *Vienna Consular Convention*.

determined by mutual agreement between the sending state and the receiving state; subsequent changes in either sphere must receive the consent of the receiving state (VCCR, Article 4). It is possible for a sending state to entrust a consulate located in a particular state with the exercise of consular functions in a third state. However, this may be done only with the consent of both other states (VCCR, Article 7).

Functions of Consular Agents The major functions exercised by consuls may be summarized as follows:

1. Protecting in the receiving state the interests of the sending state and its nationals within the limits set by international law
2. Promoting trade and the development of economic, cultural, and scientific relations between the two states in question
3. Reporting to the government of the sending state on conditions and developments in the economic, cultural, and scientific life of the receiving state as well as giving such information to interested persons and firms
4. Issuing passports and travel documents to nationals of the sending state and visas or similar documents to persons desiring to go to that state
5. Assisting in all legitimate ways the nationals of the sending state
6. Acting as notary and civil registrar and performing certain administrative functions, particularly in the safeguarding of the interests of nationals of the sending state in cases of succession (caused by death) in the territory of the receiving state
7. Representing nationals of the sending state before the courts and other authorities of the receiving state when, for some reason or other, those nationals are unable to assume the defense of their rights, so as to preserve, on a provisional basis, those rights in accordance with the law of the receiving state
8. Serving judicial documents or executing commissions to take evidence for the courts of the sending state in accordance with existing treaties or, in their absence, in accordance with the laws of the receiving state
9. Exercising rights of supervision and inspection, under the laws and regulations of the receiving state, in respect of vessels having the nationality of the sending state and of aircraft registered in that state, and in respect of their crews; examining the stamping ships' papers, conducting investigations into any incidents that have occurred during the voyage, and settling disputes between the master, the officers, and the seamen to the extent that such settlement is authorized by the laws of the sending state (VCCR, Article 5)

The nationals of the sending state are to be free to communicate with the consulates of their state, and, in turn, the consular officials of that state are to be free to communicate with the nationals of their state located in the receiving state (VCCR, Article 36, para 1-a). The competent authorities of the receiving state have an obligation to notify the consulate of a sending state without undue delay if in the relevant district a national of the sending state is committed to prison or to custody pending trial or is detained in any other manner. Equally, any communication from such nationals is to be forwarded to the relevant consulate without undue delay (VCCR, Article 36, para 1-b). Consular officials have the right to visit any national of the sending state who is in prison, custody, or detention for the purpose of gaining information about the case and of arranging for his legal representation (VCCR, Article 36, para 1-c). Obviously these rights would have to be exercised in accordance with the laws and regulations of the receiving state, provided that the laws or regulations do not nullify the rights of consular officials.

The question of consular access has had a high profile over the past ten years. Several cases in which foreign nationals had been tried, convicted, and given the death penalty gained prominence because of appeals that claimed local officials had not informed the defendants of their right to consult with consular officials.[87] Honduras, Paraguay, Germany, and Mexico had all filed formal complaints with the State Department alleging that the United States had breached its obligations under international law. Both the Inter-American Court of Human Rights (2000)[88] and the ICJ (2004)[89] issued opinions highly critical of the United States for failure to observe the treaty obligation. The ICJ ruled that the United States had violated the rights of 51 Mexican nationals awaiting execution because they had been denied the opportunity to avail themselves of consular aid and advice. President Bush responded to the ICJ decision by requesting that Texas grant the 51 individuals new hearings. On the other hand, the United States also formally withdrew from the Optional Protocol to the VCCR in March 2005 even though the United States had originally proposed the measure and was the first to use it before the ICJ during the Iranian Embassy hostage crisis in 1979.[90] The Optional Protocol requires signatories of the VCCR to use the ICJ as the forum for adjudicating allegations of nonperformance of obligations.[91]

The decision to withdraw from the Optional Protocol illustrates an ongoing dilemma with respect to U.S. policy concerning human rights that we will explore more thoroughly in Chapter 15. The president, by his actions in requesting new trials, indicated that the United States does take the issues raised seriously. On the

---

[87]See "Agora: Breard," 92 *AJIL* (1998), 666–712. This includes articles by J. I. Charney, W. M. Reisman, C. A. Bradley, J. L. Goldsmith, L. Henkin, C. M. Vázquez, J. J. Paust, L. F. Damrosch, F. L. Kirgis, and A-M. Slaughter; this collection addresses the issues connected with the Paraguayan case.

[88]E. Hegstrom, "OAS Court Says Foreign Inmates Denied Rights," *Houston Chronicle* (February 18, 2000), 30.

[89]*Avena and Other Mexican Nationals (Mexico v. United States of America)*, International Court of Justice (March 31, 2004), www.icj-cij.org/docket/index.php?p1=3&p2=3&k=11&case=128} (accessed May 11, 2009). The court considered 52 cases, but found that the United States had carried out its obligations in one instance. See also, the second application of Mexico, in 2008, requesting an interpretation of the original verdict, Request for Interpretation of the Judgment of 31 March 2004 in the Case Concerning Avena and Other Mexican Nationals (Mexico *v.* United States of America), www.icj-cij.org/docket/index.php?p1=3&p2=3&code=musa&case=139&k=11.

[90]C. Lane, "U.S. Quits Pact Used in Capital Cases," *The Washington Post* (March 10, 2005), A1. *Optional Protocol Governing the Compulsory Settlement of Disputes* (April 18, 1963), http://untreaty.un.org/ilc/texts/instruments/english/conventions/9_2_1963_disputes.pdf (accessed May 11, 2009).

[91]In May 2005, the U.S. Supreme Court in a 5–4 decision dismissed a writ of certiorari in the case of Jose Ernesto Medellin, a Mexican national on death row in Texas who claimed he had been denied access to Mexican consular authorities. The majority felt Medellin had not exhausted his options in Texas courts. *Medellin v. Dretke*, 125 S. Ct. 2088; 161 L. Ed. 2d 982; 2005 U.S. LEXIS 4344; 73 U.S.L.W. 4381.

one hand, a clear intrusion into matters of domestic jurisdiction (a sovereignty issue) and focusing upon a highly contentious issue (the death penalty) engendered very deep resentment. The United States is both proud and protective of its justice system. The decision to opt out of the Optional Protocol will limit the future possibility of another such intrusion. On the other hand, this choice comes at some risk. The United States had championed the Optional Protocol as a high-profile forum where it could take allegations of abuse against its citizens. The question now becomes, how much has this decision undermined the position of American nationals overseas? As we have pointed out, reciprocal obligation plays a large role in this area.

Honorary Consuls   Many portions (notably Articles 58–68) of the Vienna Consular Convention refer in whole or in part to honorary consuls. In contrast with career consuls, who are always nationals of the sending state, honorary consuls are recruited from among the nationals of the receiving state. Most honorary consuls carry on a private gainful activity in addition to their consular functions, and indeed some states classify as an honorary consul any consular official, regardless of nationality, who engages in such private activity. Consular officials, as a rule, possess the nationality of the sending state. However, such officials may be appointed from among the nationals of the receiving state or of a third state—subject to the consent of the receiving state, which may be withdrawn at any time (Article 22). It is still fairly common for smaller or new states to follow these practices.

Consular Privileges and Immunities

Inviolability of Consular Premises   Consular premises are inviolable, and the agents of the receiving state may not enter them except with the consent of the head of the consular post. The receiving state is under a special duty to take appropriate measures to protect the consular premises, which are immune from any search, requisition, attachment, or execution (VCCR, Article 31). These premises are also exempt, under international law, from state and local real estate taxes.[92] A few consular treaties and the municipal law of some states also recognize inviolability of a consul's residence, but this innovation has not gained widespread acceptance. Consular archives and documents, wherever they may happen to be, are inviolable (VCCR, Article 33).

Inviolability of Means of Communication   The receiving state permits a consulate free communication for all *official* purposes. The consulate may employ diplomatic or consular couriers and the diplomatic or consular bag, and it may send and receive messages in code or cipher. It may install and use a wireless transmitter only with the express consent of the receiving state. The official correspondence of a consulate is inviolable from all interference, including inspection and censorship (VCCR, Article 35).

---

[92]See letter from Legal Adviser, U.S. Department of State, dated January 27, 1969, excerpted in 63 *AJIL* 559 (1969).

KASHIN V. KENT

U.S. District Court for the Southern District of California 333 F. Supp. 2d 926; 2004 U.S. Dist. LEXIS 17381

Facts

Douglas Barry Kent served as consul general of the United States to the Republic of Russia. In October 1998, he was involved in a late-night automobile accident in Vladivostok while driving from a gymnasium to his home. The accident left Aleksandr Kashin, a passenger in another car, severely injured. The Department of Internal Affairs in Vladivostok brought an action against Kent on behalf of Kashin. Kent claimed diplomatic immunity. Actions in Russia terminated upon Kent's departure in July 2000. Kashin then filed suit in the United States. Kent again raised the defense of consular immunity and asked the attorney general of the United States to certify that he was acting within the official scope of his office or employment at the time of the accident. The attorney general denied the request.

Issues

1. Did Kent possess full diplomatic immunity?

2. Did the activities surrounding the accident qualify as "conduct within the scope of employment," thus sustaining Kent's claim to consular immunity?

Decision

Immunity of any kind did not attach to the activities surrounding the accident.

Reasoning

While his job may have required working at odd hours, Kent was not engaged in any diplomatic or consular activity at the time of the accident. His contention that the workouts at the gym formed part of his duties because he had to pass regular medical checkups has no merit. No essential connection existed between his official duties and the physical workout. Moreover, the attorney general's "scope of employment" determination was made on the basis of information submitted by Kent. He has no basis for complaint.

Personal and Family Immunity *If* a consular official appears on the *diplomatic list* (the official roster of accredited diplomats in a state), he or she will have full diplomatic immunity. Otherwise, the VCCR (Article 43) states that personal immunity applies to consular officials *only* for actions performed as part of their official duties. Under this standard, a consular officer does not have immunity from all legal process, but must respond to any process and plead and prove immunity on the ground that the act or omission underlying the process was in the performance of his or her official function.

Waiver of Immunity The sending state alone may, of course, waive its consular official's immunity, but such a waiver must in all cases be express. If the sending state waives the immunity of its officials, for the purpose of civil or administrative proceedings, the waiver does not constitute a waiver of immunity from measures of execution resulting from a judicial decision. A separate waiver, again express in nature, would be required for such measures (Article 45). A consular official who initiates proceedings in a matter in which he might normally enjoy immunity is precluded from invoking such immunity from local jurisdictions in respect of any counterclaim directly connected with the principal claim (reciprocity).

SUGGESTED READINGS

Documentation of the *Case Concerning United States Diplomatic and Consular Staff in Tehran* (*United States v. Iran*).

Government of the Democratic and Popular Republic of Algeria, *Declaration on the Settlement of the Iran Hostage Crisis* (January 20, 1981), in 20 *ILM* 224 (1981), in 75 *AJIL* 418 (1981), and in *Department of State Bulletin*, No. 2047 (February 1981), 1; Algeria, Text of the *United States Government–Iran Government Settlement of Claims Agreement* and *Escrow Agreement* (January 19, 1981), in 20 *ILM* 229 (1981), and in 75 *AJIL* 431 (1981); United States, *Executive Order 12283* (Nonprosecution of Claims of Hostages and for Actions at the United States Embassy and Elsewhere), January 19, 1981, in 75 *AJIL* 430 (1981).

Gross, "The Case Concerning United States Diplomatic and Consular Staff in Tehran: Phase of Provisional Measures," 74 *AJIL* 395 (1980).

International Court of Justice, *Case Concerning United States Diplomatic and Consular Staff in Tehran: Judgment* (May 24, 1980), in 19 *ILM* 553 (1980) (including one separate and two dissenting opinions), and in 74 *AJIL* 746 (1980) (judgment only).

International Court of Justice, *Case Concerning United States Diplomatic and Consular Staff in Tehran, Order on Discontinuance* (May 12, 1981), in 20 *ILM* 889 (1981).

International Court of Justice, *United States Application and Request for Interim Measures of Protection in Proceeding Against Iran* (November 29, 1979). Text in 74 *AJIL* 258 (1980) and in 18 *ILM* 1464 (1979).

The oral argument presented before the court, as well as the order below, are reproduced in U.S. Department of State, "Selected Documents No. 15: World Court Rules on Hostage Case" (1979), as well as in 18 *ILM* 1464 (1979), and in 19 *ILM* 248 (1980).

United Nations Security Council, *Resolution 457 (1979) of December 4, 1979* (Calling for the Immediate Release of the Hostages), reproduced in 18 *ILM* 1644 (1979).

United States, *Executive Orders 12276–12281*, January 19, 1981, in 20 *ILM* 286 (1981).

United States, *Executive Order 12284* (Restrictions on the Transfer of Property of the Former Shah of Iran), January 19, 1981, in 75 *AJIL* 431 (1981), and in 20 *ILM* 292 (1981).

DIPLOMATIC AGENTS: GENERAL

Bassiouni, "Protection of Diplomats Under Islamic Law," 74 *AJIL* 609 (1980).

Brierly, 254.

Charnovitz, "Nongovernmental Organizations and International Law," 100 *AJIL* (2006).

Dembinski, *The Modern Law of Diplomacy* (1988).

E. Denza, *Diplomatic Law*, 3rd ed. (Oxford: Oxford University Press, 2008).

E. Denza, "Diplomatic Privileges and Immunities", *Harvard Research in International Law, Contemporary Analysis and Appraisal*, edited by J. P. Grant and J. C. Barker (Buffalo, New York: William S. Hein & Co, 2007).

Dickinson, "Status of Forces Under the UN Convention on State Immunity," *55 ICLQ* 427 (2006).

Frey and Frey, *The History of Diplomatic Immunity* (1999).

Lauterpacht, *Oppenheim*, I: 769.

E. Satow (ed. Ivor Roberts), *Guide to Diplomatic Practice*, 6th ed. (2009).

Stewart, "The UN Convention on Jurisdictional Immunities of States and Their Property," 99 *AJIL* 194 (2005).

CASES

Dickinson v. Del Solar, Great Britain, King's Bench Division, 1920, [1930] 1 K.B. 376.

Hellenic Lines, Ltd. v. Moore, U.S. Ct. of Appeals, D.C. Cir., 1965, 345 F.2d 978, in *59 AJIL* 927 (1965).

Holbrook, Nelson & Co. v. Henderson, United States, Supreme Court of the City of New York, 1839, 6 N.Y. Super. Court (4 Sandford 619).

Mrs. J. W. v. Republic of Latvia, Germany, Berlin Landesgericht, 1953, in 48 *AJIL* 161 (1954).

Shaffer v. Singh, U.S. Ct. of Appeals, D.C. Cir., 1965, 343 F.2d 324; see also the extensive *Note* on this case by Levit, *Harvard Int'l L. J.* 153 (Winter 1965).

United States v. Erdos, U.S. Ct. of Appeals, 1973, 474 F.2d 157, in 67 *AJIL* 785 (1973).

United States v. Egorov, U.S. Dist. Ct., E.D.N.Y, 1963, 222 F. Supp. 106, in 58 *AJIL* 513 (1964).

CONSULAR AGENTS: GENERAL

Lee, *Consular Law and Practice,* 2nd ed. (1991).

Roosaare, "Consular Relations Between the United States and the Baltic States," *Baltic Review* (January 1964).

CASES

Bliss v. Nicolaeff, United States, New York, Appellate Division, 1948, 79 N.Y.S. (2d) 63, in 42 *AJIL* 944 (1948).

Radwan v. Radwan, United Kingdom, Probate, Divorce, and Admiralty Division, May 11, 1972, in 66 *AJIL* 875 (1972).

Santovincenzo v. Egan, U.S. Supreme Court, 1931, 223 U.S. 317.

International Law and the Individual

The Individual and International Law

Human Rights

THE INDIVIDUAL: FROM OBJECT TO SUBJECT

Before the twentieth century, the belief prevailed that the treatment of its citizenry by a state fell outside the province of international law, inasmuch as the individual, alone or collectively, was merely an object and not a subject of the law of nations. Since World War I, the community of nations has become increasingly aware of the need to safeguard the minimal rights of the individual. Consequently, human rights have become a matter of vital and sometimes acrimonious concern to the traditional subjects of international law. The individual has begun to emerge, to some extent at least, as a direct subject of that law. In this chapter, we discuss the development and content of those instruments that guarantee fundamental human rights. In Chapter 16, we will cover offenses, such as genocide and participation in the slave trade, that give rise to *individual criminal liability* rather than *collective responsibility*. Finally, in Chapter 20, we will examine war crimes. In each of these areas, international law has progressively evolved norms that either grant rights directly to the individual or impose a duty or an obligation on the individual.

Before proceeding, we need to issue two caveats. First, in dealing with human rights, always keep in mind the distinction between substantive law, statements of aspirational goals, and the rules of morality as we perceive and understand them. This is not to say that these three categories are unrelated, but in the midst of a situation that involves questions of human rights, sorting out legal obligation from moral outrage can yield painful conclusions. Second, we need to keep in mind that others, in other societies, may have very different conceptions. While few would dispute that some fundamental (universal) human rights exist, we do not need to look far to find instances of grave disagreement over what constitutes a fundamental human right. One should look no farther than the 1948 Universal Declaration of Human Rights (UDHR)[1] to see some contentious propositions about rights that

---

[1]General Assembly Resolution 217 A (III) of December 10, 1948; text at www.un.org/Overview/rights.html (accessed April 22, 2009); text also in *Yearbook of the United Nations, 1948–1949*, 535, and in many other readily available sources. The communist states later accepted the declaration in the Final Act of the Helsinki Conference of 1975.

every human being should possess. In this respect, consider only Article 25(1) of the UDHR and the debate it still generates within the United States:

> Everyone has the *right* to a standard of living adequate for the health and well-being of himself and of his family, including food, clothing, housing and *medical care and necessary social services,* and the right to security in the event of unemployment, sickness, disability, widowhood, old age or other lack of livelihood in circumstances beyond his control. (Emphasis added)

As a General Assembly Resolution, the UDHR stands as a statement of desired goals rather than black letter, substantive, law. Nonetheless, as we shall see, as a powerful and clear statement, it has played an important role in the evolution of human rights law over the past 60-plus years.

International law and international organization in their various incarnations both flow from a productive interaction of idealism and pragmatism. Without idealism to set goals that transcend the demands of the immediate as defined by the narrow self-interest of particular states, the essential exchanges in political interaction would remain on the most basic level. Without a leavening dialectic with the "art of the possible"—the traditions gleaned from conservative statesmanship and experience—ideals would remain undeveloped, ethereal, and isolated from political life. The tension between the ideals and narrow self-interest reflected in the ebb and flow of decisions ensures that the mix at any specific time will never fully satisfy advocates of either position. Yet any idea of progress must take both into account. Progress depends upon the development and application of new ideas and approaches. The practical statesman will attempt to adapt these to changing circumstances by grafting them to rootstock gleaned from those practices deemed useful and successful in the past. The story of the development of human rights law in the twentieth century gives us a vivid illustration of the process. In this chapter (and the next), we will examine both the evolution of the substantive law and the development of the international institutions and procedures associated with promoting and protecting those rights.

RESTRICTIONS ON THE JURISDICTION OF STATES OVER THEIR NATIONALS

Before World War I, international law said little about the individual and left the question of rights to municipal law. Early concern about human rights was limited to a guarantee of certain religious rights to minority groups within the populations of given states. The broader concerns with the rights of human beings to life, liberty, and equality before the law were mostly unformulated politically and legally until the last decades of the nineteenth century. The spread of democratic forms of government, particularly post World War II, brought these ideas into the international arena as desirable goals.

The numerous changes in territorial ownership occurring after World War I pointed up the need for an expansion of the rights guaranteed to minorities, particularly due to the growth of nationalistic sentiments and the very real danger of suppression and oppression faced by racial, ethnic, linguistic, and religious minorities. In consequence, the Principal Allied and Associated Powers concluded a number of treaties with such countries as Czechoslovakia, Austria, Greece, Bulgaria, Hungary, Poland, Turkey, Rumania, and Yugoslavia in which those states promised just and equal treatment of their minority groups.

Sometime later, Albania, Estonia, Iraq, Latvia, and Lithuania gave similar guarantees as conditions of their admission to the League of Nations. Unlike the earlier guarantees, however, these subsequent grants of rights to minorities took the form of unilateral declarations by the countries in question. In turn, various resolutions adopted by the Council of the League of Nations created legal obligations for those declarations.

THEORY AND PRACTICE

To ensure practical observance of the various rights guaranteed to minorities, the affected sovereign states had to acknowledge that the "minorities clauses" constituted "fundamental laws." They further agreed that the clauses were "placed under the guarantee of the League of Nations" and would not be altered without the consent of a majority of the League's Council. The League, in turn, worked out a definitive procedure to deal with any questions arising under the clauses in question.

All this looked fine on paper, but trouble appeared as soon as implementation became the issue. Regardless of the motives that had inspired acquiescence in the guarantees extended to minorities, the governments in question all too soon shared a growing conviction that the guarantees represented *intolerable intrusions into the domestic jurisdictions of sovereign states.* This points up the inherent tension between the Westphalian idea of the "hard-shell" sovereign state and the idea that governments do not have an unlimited right to mistreat their own citizens or subjects. Human rights law aims to protect individuals from the excesses of states and governments. In the interwar period, the Permanent Court of International Justice had to point out again and again that mere laws were not enough; the prohibitions laid down in the minorities clauses had to operate in fact. A law supposedly general in its effects but actually discriminating against members of minority groups constituted a violation of obligations.[2]

During World War II, the necessity of promoting and preserving human freedoms and rights was affirmed in such statements as the Atlantic Charter (August 14, 1941), the Declaration by the (wartime) United Nations (January 1, 1942), and the Tehran Declaration (December 1, 1943). The Nuremberg War Crimes Trials implicitly assumed that certain laws applied directly to individuals.[3] However, after the war, none of the various peace treaties included provisions for the protection of minorities, except on a very selective basis.

[2]See Advisory Opinion relating to *German Settlers in Poland*, Ser. B, No. 6; Advisory Opinion on the *Treatment of Polish Nationals in Danzig*, Ser. A/B, No. 44; and Advisory Opinion on *Minority Schools in Albania*, Ser. A/B, No. 64.

[3]P. Jessup, *A Modern Law of Nations* (1946), 161; and Q. Wright, *Contemporary International Law: A Balance Sheet* (1945), 19.

THE UNITED NATIONS AND HUMAN RIGHTS

In the United Nations, interest in the subject of human rights has arisen sporadically. Beginning with the founding conference at San Francisco in 1945, the organization has been at the center of a modern disposition to enlarge the sphere of legitimate international interest or concern.[4] The Charter of the United Nations asserts in the sweeping terms of its Preamble that the members are "determined to reaffirm faith in fundamental human rights, in the dignity and worth of the human person, in the equal rights of men and women." Article 1 of the Charter lists, among the purposes of the organization, the "promoting and encouraging [of] respect for human rights and for fundamental freedoms for all without distinction as to race, sex, language, or religion." Article 13 assigns to the General Assembly the task of initiating and making recommendations directed to the accomplishment of these purposes. Article 55(c) commits the United Nations to promote "universal respect for, and observance of, human rights and fundamental freedoms." Article 62 directs the Economic and Social Council to make recommendations in pursuance of Article 55(c), and Article 68 sets up a commission for the "promotion of human rights." This multitude of provisions, however, did not spell out any bill of human rights, beyond mentioning discrimination, nor did it command the members to enact and enforce appropriate domestic legislation. Presumably the Security Council could find that abuses of human rights within a state constituted a "threat to international peace" under Article 39, but the Charter contains no sanctions or enforcement machinery specifically related to human rights. Only Article 56 represented a pledge by all member states to take joint and separate action to achieve the purposes outlined in Article 55.

The tension we noted earlier between traditional conceptions of sovereignty and evolving standards of human rights is built into the Charter. While the Preamble and several articles commit states to promote human rights, Article 2(7) of the UN Charter denies authority to the United Nations "to intervene in matters which are essentially within the domestic jurisdiction of any state." This *explicit* prohibition appeared to limit the rights of the organization to deal with alleged violations of human rights beyond discussion in the General Assembly and passage of recommendations regarding such violations. Furthermore, it appeared that if any member state heeded such recommendations and acted on them against a state accused of violating human rights, a charge of illegal intervention in the internal affairs of a sovereign state could be lodged.

To achieve positive protection of human rights, the Economic and Social Council (ECOSOC) began in early 1946 to produce multilateral conventions through the Commission on Human Rights as a drafting body. The obvious by-product of such an endeavor, if successful, would be the shift of the individual into the position of a partial subject of international law. On December 10, 1948, the General Assembly approved the UDHR, with no opposition but with eight abstentions (the Soviet Bloc, Yugoslavia, Saudi Arabia, and South Africa).[5] To emphasize an earlier point, the Universal Declaration is *not* a treaty. It was intended to lay

---

[4]See E. Luard, ed., *The International Protection of Human Rights* (1967).

[5]See note 1.

down "a common standard of achievement for all peoples and all nations." Being merely a declaration, it possesses no legal binding force, being comparable in this respect to the hortatory clauses found in some of the older state constitutions in the United States. Legal obligations can be created only through the ratification by member states of some convention on human rights, not by a voting consensus of the General Assembly. Furthermore, Article 22 of the declaration recognized that the realization of the rights in question had to be in accordance with the organization and resources of each state.

Still, though not a binding obligation upon members, the UDHR has to be considered an expository interpretation of the Charter's very general human rights provisions.[6] The Charter provisions represent, at least in theory, binding obligations on all member states. The UDHR has also served as a convenient standard by which many jurists and even national courts have evaluated compliance with the broad human rights provisions of the UN Charter. The UDHR should, therefore, be viewed as marking a definite advance toward the realization of human rights, on a global basis, and as somewhat distinct from other declarations adopted by the General Assembly.[7] In this respect, some publicists have argued that the UDHR (or at least certain of its provisions) has become part of customary international law.[8] Remember our discussion of the impact of law in Chapter 1. Many different factors affect the response of states and governments to events and circumstances. The Vienna Declaration and Programme of Action,[9] adopted in June 1993 at the United Nations Conference on Human Rights, characterized the UDHR as the "source of inspiration" and the "basis for the United Nations in making advances in standard setting as contained in existing international human rights instruments." In this respect, the UDHR has generated a "developmental push" perhaps unexpected by its sponsors at the time.

At first, the UN Commission on Human Rights proposed a single instrument, covering all aspects of the rights identified in the UDHR. The omnibus covenant encountered fierce opposition in the General Assembly. As a result, the General Assembly produced several different instruments: the International Covenant on Civil and Political Rights (ICCPR); the International Covenant on Economic, Social, and Cultural Rights (ICESCR); and the Optional Protocol to the Covenant on Civil and Political Rights. Although initial drafts of the treaties were completed by 1954,

---

[6]To summarize quickly, the UDHR constitutes one (of many possible) expository interpretation. Critics would deny that it is the expository interpretation.

[7]Advocates have made claims that the declaration has acquired the status of customary international law. The present writers disagree with that view. There is a wide differential between hortatory support and state practice in many areas. Nonetheless, a good case exists for arguing that some of the rights listed in the declaration (such as freedom from torture, slavery, murder, etc.) do form norms of customary international law. For example, see *American Law Institute, Restatement of the Law, Third, the Foreign Relations Law of the United States* 2 at 161 (para. 702); also T. Meron, *Human Rights and Humanitarian Norms as Customary International Law* (1989).

[8]See the discussion in R. Jennings and A. Watts, eds, *Oppenheim's International Law*, 9th ed. (1992), 1001, 1002; see also J. O'Manique, "Universal and Inalienable Rights: A Search for Foundations," 12 *Human Rights Quarterly* 465 (1990).

[9]Text 32 *ILM* at 1661, 1663; www.unhchr.ch/huridocda/huridoca.nsf/(Symbol)/A.CONF.157.23. En?OpenDocument (accessed April 22, 2009).

bitter disagreements about the contents and enforcement provisions in both the General Assembly and its Third Committee (Social, Humanitarian, and Cultural Affairs) resulted in delay and in considerable redrafting. Finally, the General Assembly adopted the instruments in December 1966 (the covenants, 106–0, and the protocol, 66–2). The two covenants represented the achievement of the "international bill of rights" contemplated by the assembly when it adopted the Universal Declaration in 1948.[10] The UDHR, ICCPR, and ICESCR form the "International Bill of Rights."

THE INTERNATIONAL BILL OF HUMAN RIGHTS

Universal Declaration of Human Rights (1948)

International Covenant on Economic, Social and Cultural Rights (1966)

International Covenant on Civil and Political Rights (1966)

Optional Protocol to the International Covenant on Civil and Political Rights

Second Optional Protocol to the International Covenant on Civil and Political Rights (aiming at abolition of the death penalty)

Three other important human rights treaties were drafted in the period immediately following World War II: the Convention on the Prevention and Punishment of the Crime of Genocide (1948), the Convention Relating to the Status of Refugees (1951), and the European Convention for the Protection of Human Rights and Fundamental Freedoms (1950). We will analyze the genocide treaty in Chapter 16. The other two treaties are covered later in this chapter. Human rights treaties differ in one important respect from other treaties. Human rights treaties do not create a system of rights, duties, and obligations between states. They seek to protect the rights of individuals; hence, some have argued that they form a category of obligations *erga omnes*.[11] Obligations *erga omnes* are those protecting and promoting basic values and common interests of all states.

INTERNATIONAL COVENANT ON CIVIL AND POLITICAL RIGHTS

The ICCPR guarantees, among other rights, equality of treatment by laws and courts, freedom of religious expression, peaceful assembly, and freedom of movement within states and between states. It prohibits inhuman treatment as well as

---

[10]Texts of the three instruments reprinted in 61 *American Journal of International Law* 861 (1967); see also L. Henkin, ed., *The International Bill of Rights: The Covenant on Civil and Political Rights* (1981). See also ICCPR at www.unhchr.ch/html/menu3/b/a_ccpr.htm, ICESCR at www.unhchr.ch/html/menu3/b/a_cescr.htm, and Optional Protocol at www.unhchr.ch/html/menu3/b/a_opt.htm (all accessed April 22, 2009).

[11]Literally, "towards all." In the Barcelona Traction case (1970), the International Court of Justice identified a separate category of international obligations that, rather than being owed to a specific state on a bilateral basis, are owed to the international community as a whole, with all states having an interest in their protection. See further the discussions of genocide and slavery in Chapter 17.

arbitrary arrest or detention, asserts a right to life and to a fair trial, and provides for the protection of all varieties of minorities. Under the provisions of the First Optional Protocol, individuals and groups are granted the right to appeal to the 32-member UN Commission on Human Rights. Both the covenant and the Optional Protocol entered into force on March 23, 1976. As of July 2011, a total of 167 states had ratified or acceded to the covenant. The United States finally ratified this treaty in June 1992.[12] South Africa became a state party in 1998. China signed the treaty in 1998 but has not yet ratified it. Saudi Arabia has neither signed nor ratified. The Covenant on Civil and Political Rights also has generated an optional protocol on abolition of the death penalty (December 15, 1989). The United States has not signed the Second Optional Protocol (abolition of the death penalty). Similar protocols were adopted for the European Convention on Human Rights and the American Convention on Human Rights.[13]

INTERNATIONAL COVENANT ON ECONOMIC, SOCIAL, AND CULTURAL RIGHTS

The ICESCR embraces the right to work, education, medical care, and related economic and social benefits. It entered into force in January 1976. In January 2005, it had 151 states parties. President Jimmy Carter signed the treaty on behalf of the United States in October 1977, but the U.S. Senate has not yet ratified it.[14] Both the ICCPR and the ICESCR became objects of bitter criticism. Several presidents failed to transmit the two instruments to the U.S. Senate. A considerable body of public opinion in the United States arguably agreed with the following view concerning the ICESCR:

> We believe that under present conditions "economic and social rights" are really more in the nature of aspirations and goals than "rights." This semantic distinction is highly important. It does not make sense to proclaim that a particular level of economic and social entitlements are rights if most governments are not able to provide them. *In contrast, any government can guarantee political and civil rights to its citizens*[15]. (Emphasis added)

OTHER HUMAN RIGHTS INSTRUMENTS

Nine multilateral treaties (including the ICCPR and the ICESCR) form the core of the international human rights regime. Each of these conventions establishes a legal obligation for states parties to abide by the specific rights defined therein.

---

[12]See H. Hannum and D. D. Fischer, eds, *U.S. Ratification of the International Covenants on Human Rights* (1993). Consult also U.S. Senate Committee on Foreign Relations, "Report on the International Covenant on Civil and Political Rights," 31 *International Legal Materials* 645 (1992).

[13]Covenant, 29 ILM 1464 (1990); European Convention, 22 ILM 538 (1983); and OAS American Convention, 29 ILM 1447 (1990). See also W. Schabas, *The Abolition of the Death Penalty in International Law* (1993). The United States has signed but not ratified the American Convention on Human Rights.

[14]See P. Alston, "U.S. Ratification of the Covenant on Economic, Social and Cultural Rights: The Need for an Entirely New Strategy," 84 *AJIL* 365 (1990).

[15]P. Dobriansky, "U.S. Human Rights Policy: An Overview," *Current Policy* (September 1988), 2.

We should note that some of the treaties are supplemented by optional protocols dealing with specific concerns. Note also that because the duties contained in the Optional Protocols constitute obligations not included in the original treaty, the protocols *apply only* to those states that have chosen to sign and ratify them separately from the original treaty (Chapter 4).

As a fundamental principle, *nondiscrimination* forms a major theme of these treaties with respect to individuals as well as groups. For example, slightly predating the ICCPR, the International Convention on the Elimination of All Forms of Racial Discrimination (ICERD) was opened for signature in 1965 and entered into force in 1969. It defined racial discrimination as

> any distinction, exclusion, restriction or preference based on race, colour, descent or national or ethnic origin which has the purpose or effect of nullifying or impairing the recognition, enjoyment or exercise, on an equal footing of human rights and fundamental freedoms in the political, economic, social cultural or any other field of public life.[16]

Article 26 of the ICCPR prohibits "any discrimination . . . on any ground such as race, colour, sex, language, religion, political or other opinion, national or social origin, property, birth or other status."[17]

MAJOR HUMAN RIGHTS INSTRUMENTS

Charter of the United Nations
The Core International Human Rights Instruments
(and their monitoring bodies)

Treaty	Monitoring Body[18]
International Convention on the Elimination of All Forms of Racial Discrimination, December 21, 1965	CERD
International Covenant on Civil and Political Rights, December 16, 1966	HRC
International Covenant on Economic, Social, and Cultural Rights, December 16, 1966	CESCR

(continued)

---

[16]Article 1(1), www.unhchr.ch/html/menu3/b/d_icerd.htm (accessed April 22, 2009).

[17]Compare with Article 1 of the Convention on the Elimination of All Forms of Discrimination Against Women:

> For the purposes of the present Convention, the term "'discrimination against women'" shall mean any distinction, exclusion or restriction made on the basis of sex which has the effect or purpose of impairing or nullifying the recognition, enjoyment or exercise by women, irrespective of their marital status, on a basis of equality of men and women, of human rights and fundamental freedoms in the political, economic, social, cultural, civil or any other field.

See www.unhchr.ch/html/menu3/b/e1cedaw.htm (accessed April 22, 2009).

[18]See www.ohchr.org/EN/HRbodies/Pages/HumanRightsBodies.aspx (accessed July 1, 2011).

Treaty	Monitoring Body
Convention on the Elimination of All Forms of Discrimination Against Women, December 18, 1979	CEDAW
Convention Against Torture and Other Cruel, Inhuman or Degrading Treatment or Punishment, December 10, 1984	CAT
Convention on the Rights of the Child, November 20, 1989	CRC
International Convention on the Protection of the Rights of All Migrant Workers and Members of Their Families, December 18, 1990	CMW
First Optional Protocol to the International Covenant on Civil and Political Rights, December 16, 1966	HRC
Second Optional Protocol to the International Covenant on Civil and Political Rights (abolition of the death penalty), December 15, 1989	HRC
Optional Protocol to the Convention on the Elimination of Discrimination Against Women, December 10, 1999	CEDAW
Optional Protocol to the Convention on the Rights of the Child on the Involvement of Children in Armed Conflict, May 25, 2000	CRC
Optional Protocol to the Convention on the Rights of the Child on the Sale of Children, Child Prostitution and Child Pornography, May 25, 2000	CRC
Optional Protocol to the Convention against Torture and Other Cruel, Inhuman or Degrading Treatment or Punishment, December 18, 2002	CAT
Convention on the Rights of Persons with Disabilities (December 13, 2006)	CRPD
International Convention for the Protection of All Persons from Enforced Disappearance (December 20, 2006)	CED

HRC	Human Rights Committee—International Covenant on Civil and Political Rights (1966) and its optional protocols
CESCR	The Committee on Economic, Social, and Cultural Rights—the International Covenant on Economic, Social, and Cultural Rights (1966)
CERD	The Committee on the Elimination of Racial Discrimination—International Convention on the Elimination of All Forms of Racial Discrimination (1965)
CEDAW	The Committee on the Elimination of Discrimination Against Women—Convention on the Elimination of All Forms of Discrimination against Women (1979)

(*continued*)

CAT	The Committee Against Torture—Convention Against Torture and Other Cruel, Inhuman or Degrading Treatment
CRC	The Committee on the Rights of the Child—Convention on the Rights of the Child (1989) and its optional protocols
CMW	The Committee on Migrant Workers—International Convention on the Protection of the Rights of All Migrant Workers and Members of Their Families (1990)
CRPD	The Committee on the Rights of Persons with Disabilities—Convention on the Rights of Persons with Disabilities (2006)
CED	Committee on Enforced Disappearances

Each treaty body receives secretariat support from the Treaties and Commission Branch of OHCHR in Geneva except CEDAW, which is supported by the Division for the Advancement of Women (DAW). CEDAW meets at UN headquarters in New York; the other treaty bodies generally meet at the UN Office in Geneva, although the Human Rights Committee usually holds its March session in New York.

Of the nine instruments listed, the Convention on the Rights of the Child has gained the most support from members of the international community (193 states parties); the Convention for the Protection of All Persons from Enforced Disappearance the least (27 states parties). The Convention on the Elimination of All Forms of Discrimination Against Women (CEDAW) illustrates another problem. The treaty currently has 186 states parties, but many states have joined with reservations aimed at minimizing the impact of certain provisions (particularly Articles 2 and 16). Article 28.2 of CEDAW, drawing on the principle from the Vienna Convention on the Law of Treaties (Chapter 4), prohibits impermissible reservations. Though its intent is clear, the provision has not deterred states from attempting to add reservations.[19] This in turn raises important questions concerning the permissibility of reservations to human rights treaties in general.

The ICCPR (Article 20.2) also explicitly prohibits reservations incompatible with its object and purpose. The Human Rights Commission, in examining the problem, noted:[20]

---

[19]"The Special Rapporteur considers that control of the permissibility of reservations is the primary responsibility of the States parties. However, the Committee again wishes to draw to the attention of States parties its grave concern at the number and extent of impermissible reservations. It also expresses concern that, even when States object to such reservations there appears to be a reluctance on the part of the States concerned to remove and modify them and thereby comply with general principles of international law," www.un.org/womenwatch/daw/cedaw/reservations.htm (accessed April 22, 2009).

[20]U.N. Doc. CCPR/c/21/Rev.1/Add.6 (1994). See also O. Schachter, "The Obligation of the Parties to Give Effect to the Covenant on Civil and Political Rights," 73 *AJIL* 462 (1979); and Report of the Committee on the Elimination of Discrimination Against Women, GAOR 53rd Sess., Supp. no. 38, A/53/38/Rev. 1 (1998) at 47 (paras. 1–25), www.un.org/womenwatch/daw/cedaw/reports/18report.pdf (accessed April 22, 2009).

Because of the special character of a human rights treaty, the compatibility of a reservation with the object and purpose of the Covenant must be established objectively by reference to legal principles, and the Committee is particularly well placed to perform this task. The normal consequence of an unacceptable reservation is not that the Covenant will not be in effect at all for a reserving party. *Rather, such a reservation will generally be severable, in the sense that the Covenant will be operative for the reserving party without benefit of the reservation.* (Emphasis added)

The point, simply stated, is that reservations should not engender a situation where states, by weakening the obligations, produce a state of affairs that would preclude the attainment of international human rights standards.

IMPLEMENTATION

Beyond the question of reservations, the difficulty comes in ensuring effective implementation. In effect, states have promised to take effective domestic measures. The question then becomes, what remedies do individuals have if states fail to honor their promises? The CERD became the first UN-sponsored treaty to set up a monitoring system.[21] Nonetheless, while ostensibly set up to safeguard individual rights, individuals often have no right to seek redress directly from the monitoring bodies. Only five of the monitoring bodies listed earlier (HRC, CAT, CDAW, CERD, and CRPD)[22] permit individual petitions under severely restricted circumstances. For example, to generate any action by the HRC, a petition must satisfy three preliminary conditions. First, the state involved must have ratified the First Optional Protocol to the ICCPR. Second, the individual must have exhausted local remedies (see Chapter 11). Third, the individual must not have submitted the petition to any other international body.[23]

None of the monitoring bodies serve an adjudicative function.[24] They are not courts that can issue binding decisions on cases received. They have no powers to institute sanctions in instances of a finding that a state has violated the convention.[25] When a monitoring body does find a violation, often the only sanction is public disapproval and calls for action by the state party to take appropriate action. The statement concerning reservations by CEDAW serves as an example: "The Committee in two of the general recommendations and its statement on reser-

---

[21]See E. Schwelb, "The International Convention on the Elimination of All Forms of Racial Discrimination," 15 *International and Comparative Law Quarterly* 996 (1966).

[22]The CMW will be added to this list when ten state parties have made the necessary declaration under Article 77.

[23]See Commission on Human Rights, Complaint Procedures, www.ohchr.org/english/bodies/chr/complaints.htm (accessed April 22, 2009).

[24]For an examination of the practice of treaty bodies, see M. K. Addo, "Practice of United Nations Human Rights Treaty Bodies in the Reconciliation of Cultural Diversity with Universal Respect for Human Rights," 32 *Human Rights Quarterly* (2010), 601–664.

[25]For cases that have come before the Human Rights Committee, see www.worldlii.org/int/cases/UNHRC/ or www1.umn.edu/humanrts/undocs/undocs.htm (both accessed April 22, 2009).

vations has called on the States to re-examine their self-imposed limitations to full compliance with all the principles in the Convention by the entry of reservations."

Several of the treaties contain provisions to allow states parties (on the basis of consent and reciprocity) to complain to the relevant treaty body about alleged violations of the treaty by another state party, but this has never occurred. In consequence, the various monitoring bodies depend primarily upon periodic reports generated by the states parties themselves (ICCPR mandates every five years).[26] Common sense should suggest that because governments themselves submit the reports, none will contain an open admission of a treaty violation. Some states parties are habitually lax or late in submission. This does not necessarily mean the reports are totally without value. The exercise of having to compose a document for *public* consumption explaining in detail the actions taken toward fulfilling a set of treaty obligations does place a state on the record for all to see.

While not a formal part of the treaty regime, nongovernmental organizations (NGOs) play an active role as well.[27] Amnesty International, Human Rights Watch, Freedom House, the International Commission of Jurists, and Derechos Human Rights are high-profile transnational organizations that constantly monitor the status of human rights in various countries. For example, Amnesty International claims to have a membership of 1.8 million from 150 countries.[28] Many human rights NGOs have consultative status with the Human Rights Commission under the Economic and Social Council (ECOSOC) and actively participate and observe in various conferences and other activities.

Perhaps the greatest hindrance comes from a lack of resources and funding. Funding for the Office of the High Commissioner for Human Rights (OHCHR) comes from both the United Nations' regular budget and voluntary contributions. The Charter obligates all member states to pay a portion of the budget. Each state's contribution is calculated on the basis of its share of the world economy. Many states fail to pay even the minimum dues (currently around $13,000), and others have refused to pay for specific operations or have deliberately withheld funds as a means of forcing reforms or signaling discontent with decisions.[29] The organization itself faces a continuing budget crisis. Funding from the regular budget covers only 33 percent of the OHCHR's activities.[30] Fundraising takes time and effort that might otherwise be devoted to other tasks.

OHCHR also receives voluntary contributions from governments, NGOs, foundations, and other private sources. The good news is that voluntary contributions have increased fourfold in the past ten years.[31] The bad news comes from the

---

[26]Latest reports available at www.unhchr.ch/tbs/doc.nsf/newhvdocsbytype?OpenView&Start=1&Count=750&Expand=20#20 (accessed April 22, 2009).

[27]For a list, see http://billie.lib.duke.edu/pubdocs/ngo/rights.asp (accessed April 22, 2009); see also R. Thakur, "Human Rights: Amnesty International and the United Nations," 31 *Journal of Peace Research* 143 (1994).

[28]See http://web.amnesty.org/pages/aboutai-index-eng (accessed April 22, 2009).

[29]See T. Deen, "U.N. Threatened with Budgetary Shutdown," Inter Press Service News Agency (December 21, 2005), www.ipsnews.net/news.asp?idnews=31533 (accessed April 22, 2009).

[30]See OHCHR, "Funding and Budget," www.ohchr.org/EN/AboutUs/Pages/FundingBudget.aspx.

[31]Idem.

very constricted nature of the donor base. *Ten* donors provided 79.4 percent of voluntary contributions. The second problem is that relying upon yearly voluntary contributions makes it difficult to plan a consistent long-term program of action because contributions may vary greatly from year to year. Finally, donors sometimes earmark or tie funds to specific projects or activities.

The funding crisis points to another set of related issues. The continuing proliferation of monitoring bodies and activities clearly makes the funding crisis more acute. Beyond the resource question, the multiplicity of bodies and programs also raises issues of consistency in interpretation and application. In recognition of the problem, since 1994, chairpersons of treaty bodies have had annual meetings to discuss areas of common concern. For the moment, and the foreseeable future, resources form a real constraint on efforts to do more.

COMMISSION ON HUMAN RIGHTS/ HUMAN RIGHTS COUNCIL

In 1948, the United Nations established the Human Rights Commission under the Economic and Social Council (ECOSOC) as the mechanism to develop human rights programs, as laid down in the Charter and in the UDHR. Composed of 53 members, elected from as many member states, the commission meets annually for five weeks. Each member serves a three-year term.[32] In its endeavor to promote the further development of the human rights concept, the UN General Assembly created (on December 20, 1993) the post of high commissioner for Human Rights, with the rank of under-secretary-general.[33]

Because of its composition and elective status, the commission was a highly political body. Before the end of the Cold War and the transition in South Africa, the commission was criticized severely for confining its investigations to South Africa, Chile, and the Israel-occupied Arab territories at a time when wholesale violations of human rights were taking place in dozens of other countries—Uganda, North Korea, Cambodia, Bolivia, Argentina, and Uruguay, to mention a few of the most egregious cases. For example, Uganda served as a member when gross violations of human rights occurred during the regime of Idi Amin. Commission subgroups, to be sure, have reviewed complaints about countries that showed a consistent pattern of gross violations. Although the subgroups reported to the commission, no action in the form of an inquiry was taken, except for the perennial three cases just mentioned.

A September 2005 report by former Secretary-General Kofi Annan called for reform, saying the commission had been undermined by "declining credibility and professionalism" because states with questionable human rights records had

---

[32]The fifty-three seats of the Commission were distributed as follows: African states, 15; Asian states, 12; Eastern European States, 5, Latin American and Caribbean states, 11; and Western Europe and other states, 10.

[33]UN General Assembly, "Resolution on the High Commissioner for the Promotion and Protection of All Human Rights," 33 *ILM* 303 (1994). See also Hartzman's analysis in *ASIL Newsletter* (January–February 1994); 13.

banded together to block scrutiny of their actions.[34] In April 2006, the General Assembly passed resolution 60/251 replacing the commission with a new Human Rights Council (HRC).[35] The council consists of 47 member states, who serve three-year terms, elected by a majority vote of the General Assembly. Approximately one-third of the membership is elected each year. States may serve two consecutive terms. The resolution mandated an "equitable geographical distribution" among five regional groups: Africa (13), Asia (13), Eastern Europe (6), Latin American and Caribbean (8), and Western European/others (7).[36]

The change has not measurably improved performance. The "equitable geographical distribution" provision ensures, for the moment, that membership contains a high proportion of autocratic governments. These states have been buoyed up by the decay in the moral high ground enjoyed previously by leading pro-human rights countries as a result of what many see as excesses associated with the "war on terrorism" after September 11, 2001.[37] Council members tend to vote in Blocs rather than as measured responses to individual issues. The bulk of resolutions still single out Israel while ignoring or downplaying other situations. During the seventh session in 2008, debate over the renewal of the mandate of the special rapporteur on freedom of expression sparked controversy. Citing inflammatory caricatures and documentaries about Islam, the Organization of the Islamic Conference sponsored an amendment in which religious discrimination would not be protected by freedom of expression.[38] Although Western states opposed the move as an attack on free speech, the mandate passed with the amendment. In 2010, the General Assembly elected Libya to the HRC. Surprisingly, the General Assembly then reversed itself in March 2011 by voting (for the first time ever) to remove Libya from the council in the wake of the violent uprising and response of the Gaddafi government.[39] The HRC then approved a Western proposal to appoint a special rapporteur to investigate actions against dissenters by the Iranian government.[40]

The use of special rapporteurs (or investigators) has been one of the main methods used by the HRC as well as its processor.[41] Depending upon their mandate from the council, special rapporteurs can perform consultative, advisory, and/or monitoring services. Some have thematic mandates (freedom of speech, use of mercenaries), while others have country-specific assignments (Iran). They may make specific recommendations to the council, but these have no legal significance. This feature

---

[34]See Report of the Secretary-General, "In Larger Freedom," UNGA Doc. A/59/2005 (March 21, 2005), para. 182.

[35]UN General Assembly, A/RES/60/251 (April 3, 2006).

[36]UNGA RES 60/251, note 34, para. 7.

[37]S. Subedi, "Protection of Human Rights through the Mechanism of UN Special Rapporteurs," 33 *Human Rights Quarterly* (2011), 204.

[38]L. Vriens, "Troubles Plague UN Human Rights Council," Council on Foreign Relations (May 13, 2009), www.cfr.org/un/troubles-plague-un-human-rights-council/p9991.

[39]"U.N. Suspends Libya from Rights Council," *USA Today* (March 1, 2011).

[40]We should note the vote on Iran: 22–7 with 14 abstentions and 4 not casting a vote. N. Cumming-Bruce, "U.N. Rights Council Backs Investigator on Iran," *NY Times* (March 24, 2011).

[41]S. Subedi, "Protection of Human Rights through the Mechanism of UN Special Rapporteurs," 33 *Human Rights Quarterly* (2011), 203.

survived the transition from commission to council in 2006, but until recently, had been under attack. Some have feared that the country-specific monitors might disappear after the 2011 review of the council by the General Assembly.[42] This would deprive the council of at least some semi-independent eyes and ears.

Currently, the council lists a wide variety of issue area concerns as exemplified by various working groups. We have noted several of those in the discussion of the major covenants. The breadth and diversity of the other issues may come as a surprise. Bioethics, the environment, physical and mental health, globalization, AIDS, internal displacement, and mercenaries form a short list.[43] To note how politics may define priorities, because of an ongoing concern from African states about the role of mercenaries in various African conflicts (going back to 1960), since 1987 the commission has approved a special rapporteur to monitor the purported use of mercenaries in contemporary conflicts.[44] Because of the contemporary activities of private military companies and private security companies (PMCs and PSCs), the issue remains a hot-button topic.

REGIONAL HUMAN RIGHTS INITIATIVES

Europe

Europe[45] has developed one of the strongest records in the contemporary world in terms of advancing human rights. In 1950, under the auspices of the newly formed Council of Europe (COE),[46] the European Convention for the Protection of Human Rights and Fundamental Freedoms (ECPHR)[47] emerged as one of the first efforts to build on the UDHR.[48] The convention has had an important impact in a number of different ways: (1) it set up the European Court of Human Rights (ECHR);[49] (2) it has become a living document in the sense that, unlike most treaties, it has evolved over time; and (3) the COE has used accession to the convention as a basic requirement for new applicants for membership.

These three elements form part of a synergistic process that has transformed the rhetoric of the UDHR into the reality of legal obligation. Of most interest is the continuing evolution of the regime. As of this writing, 14 amendments (pro-

---

[42]Subedi, note 41, at 204.

[43]See www.ohchr.org/english/issues/ (accessed April 22, 2009).

[44]For the genesis and practice, see J. L. Taulbee, "Mercenaries, Private Armies and Contemporary Policy Options," 37 *International Politics* 433 (2000).

[45]See D. Gomien, *Short Guide to the European Convention on Human Rights* (2005); C. Ovey and R. Wright, *Jacobs and White: The European Convention on Human Rights* (4th ed., 2006); Council of Europe, *Human Rights Today: European Legal Texts* (2nd ed., 1999); and P. Alston et al., eds., *The EU and Human Rights* (1999). For a complete listing of COE treaties and conventions, see http://conventions.coe.int/Treaty/EN/CadreListeTraites.htm (accessed April 22, 2009).

[46]For background and information on current activities, see http://www.coe.int (accessed April 22, 2009). The Council of Europe currently has 46 members. The Council of Europe *is often mistaken* for the Council of the European Union. These are quite different and distinct bodies. The Council of the European Union has no role.

[47]Of November 4, 1950; entered into force, September 1953. Text at http://conventions.coe.int/treaty/en/Treaties/Html/005.htm.

[48]In turn, we might note the ICCPR drew on the ECHR.

[49]See www.echr.coe.int/echr (accessed April 22, 2009).

tocols) have entered into force—an impressive record, considering that adoption requires unanimous consent. The amending protocols fall into two categories: those that streamline the institutional procedures to accommodate changing circumstances and those that have added substantive rights. Of the former, Protocol 11 codified or superseded all prior protocols dealing with institutional issues. It also radically changed the procedures for submitting petitions. Protocol 11 (1998) abolished the commission, which had served a prescreening role for the ECHR, and eliminated any role for the Council of Ministers. The protocol permitted individuals to have direct access to the ECHR in that it abolished the requirement that any petition would require the consent of the state against which the complaint had been made. Petitioners still have to exhaust local remedies. It also established the ECHR as full-time and authorized it to give advisory opinions to the Council of Ministers. Making the ECHR a full-time occupation of the judges forms the most important change. This reflects the increasing caseload. Protocol 13 abolished the death penalty in all cases. Protocol 14, approved in 2010, updated and streamlined ECHR procedures to reflect the expanded membership of the COE. The ECHR has ruled that each state in its domestic law must ensure that the safeguards are effective and practical.[50]

The court has an unusual composition in two respects. First it has a number of judges equal to the number of states parties to the European Convention (47 as of August 2011). Second, while judges are elected by the Parliamentary Assembly of the COE on behalf of member states, the nationality of judges so elected does not have to be that of the sponsoring country. This means that a judge of German nationality could be elected on behalf of Luxemburg for example. Judges are presumed to serve as impartial arbiters, not as national representatives.[51] Judges serve nine-year terms and cannot be reelected. Its rulings are binding on governments.

The court has had a heavy caseload. Between 1959 and 2010, it handed down 13,697 decisions.[52] After the reform of the convention system in 1998, the caseload of the court has increased considerably. Ten years after the reform, the court delivered its 10,000th judgment. More than 90 percent of the court's judgments since its creation in 1959 were delivered between 1998 and 2009. At the end of May 2011, it had 151,150 applications under review. Currently, almost one quarter of the complaints involve four states: Russia, Turkey, Romania, and Ukraine.[53]

The Americas

The American Declaration of the Rights and Duties of Man (Bogotá, 1948)[54] was the world's first international human rights instrument of a general nature. It preceded the UDHR by more than six months. Nonetheless, the Americas lagged

---

[50]*Soering v United Kingdom* 11 Eur. Ct. H.R. (ser. A) (1989) at 34.

[51]Note, however, the Russian Federation refused to ratify Protocol 14 until given assurances that a Russian judge would always be involved on panels involving complaints against Russia. E. Barry, "Russia Ends Opposition to Rights Court, *NY Times* (January 14, 2010).

[52]Table, Violation by Article and by Country: 1959-2010, ECHR, www.echr.coe.int/ECHR/EN/ Header/Reports+and+Statistics/Statistics/Statistical+information+by+year/.

[53]European Court of Human Rights, *50 Years of Activity: The European Court of Human Rights Some Facts and Figures*, www.echr.coe.int.

[54]www.cidh.org/Basicos/basic2.htm (accessed April 22, 2009).

somewhat behind Europe in moving to establish a regional regime that had the capacity to monitor implementation. As with the UDHR, the American Declaration is technically an aspirational statement, not a legally binding treaty. Still the Inter-American Commission on Human Rights and the Inter-American Court of Human Rights have treated the declaration as a source of binding obligation for all Organization of American States (OAS) member states. In complaint proceedings, if a member state has not ratified the American Convention on Human Rights,[55] the commission relies upon the American Declaration (Statute, Article 64).

The OAS approved the Statute of the Inter-American Commission on Human Rights (IACHR) in 1959 and incorporated it as a principal organ in 1971.[56] As with the European system, the important factor is the evolution and development of the commitment to human rights. This corresponds to the evolution and development of democratic regimes in South and Central America.[57] Twenty-five years ago, a great many Latin American states had authoritarian governments that became notorious for torture, murder, and arbitrary imprisonment of political opponents. Today, Cuba stands alone in the hemisphere in having a nonelected government.

The IACHR consists of seven members who serve in their personal capacities. Each member serves a four-year term and may be reelected one time. In theory, as noted earlier, the commission has powers over all member states of the OAS whether they have ratified the American Convention or not. The commission has authority to receive and investigate complaints from individuals. It also has the authority to observe the general human rights situation in member states and publish special reports when appropriate. Petitioners must have exhausted local remedies or show that such an exercise would be futile. In terms of action, the commission will try to broker a friendly settlement. In cases that fail, it may both publish its findings and refer the matter to the Inter-American Court.[58] The state concerned (but not the individual) may also choose to have the court hear the case.

The Inter-American Court has seven judges elected for six-year terms by the OAS General Assembly. No state may have two judges on the court at the same time. Judges may be reelected for a second six-year term. Unlike IAHCR commissioners, judges may hear cases involving their home states. If a state involved in a case does not have a judge of its own nationality on the court, it may appoint an ad hoc judge (Article 55). Under Article 64, the court also has an advisory jurisdiction with regard to the interpretation of the American Convention as well as other conventions concerning the protection of human rights in American states.

The case of *Caesar v. Trinidad and Tobago* illustrates the working relationship between the Inter-American Commission and the court. It also involves a number of important procedural and substantive principles. The interesting aspect

---

[55]San Jose, Costa Rica (November 22, 1969); entered into force July 18, 1978. Text at www.oas.org/juridico/english/Treaties/b–32.htm (accessed April 22, 2009). The United States has signed but not ratified the treaty.

[56]See www.cidh.org (accessed April 22, 2009).

[57]See E. L. Lutz and K. Sikkink, "International Human Rights Law and Practice in Latin America," 54 *International Organization* 633 (2000).

[58]In 2008, the Commission received 1,323 complaints. For *Annual Reports of the IACHR,* see www.cidh.oas.org/annualrep/2008eng/TOC.htm (accessed May 14, 2009).

of the Inter-American Court is the extent to which it has been willing to look at the practice and jurisprudence associated with the universal regional instruments as well as that of the European Court. The court has taken the view that a fundamental purpose of the American Convention was to blend together the various systems of human rights.[59] In particular, in the *Caesar* case the court referenced its earlier advisory opinion on the "Effects of Reservations"[60] to make the point that a reservation incompatible with the purpose of the convention can have no effect with respect to obligations in the treaty.

CAESAR V. TRINIDAD AND TOBAGO

Inter-American Court of Human Rights Series C No. 123 Judgment of March 11, 2005

Facts

The Inter-American Commission referred the case to the Court in February 2003. The Commission had received the original petition in May 1999. The alleged victim in this case, Winston Caesar, was convicted before the High Court of Trinidad and Tobago of the offense of attempted rape. He received a sentence of 20 years in prison and additionally was to receive 15 strokes of the "cat-o-nine-tails." The Court of Appeal of Trinidad and Tobago confirmed his conviction and sentence. Twenty-three months after the final confirmation of his sentence, Mr. Caesar's punishment of flogging was carried out. He has been in jail since September 1991.

The Commission found that, given the nature of the violations for which the State should be held responsible, Trinidad and Tobago must provide Mr. Caesar with an effective remedy, which includes compensation for the moral damage suffered by him. In addition, the Commission sought an order requiring the State to adopt legislative and other measures as necessary to give effect to the right to a trial within a reasonable time, to abrogate the punishment of flogging as provided under its Corporal Punishment Act, and to ensure that conditions of detention in the State's prisons satisfy the minimum standards of humane treatment provided for under the Convention.

Trinidad and Tobago had accepted the compulsory jurisdiction of the Court in May 1999. Subsequently in May 1998 (effective a year later), Trinidad and Tobago denounced and withdrew from the Convention regime. According to Article 78 of the Convention, a denunciation will not release the denouncing state from its obligations under the Convention with respect to acts of that state occurring prior to the effective date of the denunciation that may constitute a violation of the Convention. Trinidad and Tobago did not respond to the Commission's report on the petition; nor, after referral to the Court, did they select an ad hoc judge. They did not participate in any fashion in the hearing. Article 27 of the

(continued)

---

[59]See Advisory Opinion Oc–1/82 of September 24, 1982, "Other Treaties" Subject to the Consultative Jurisdiction of the Court (Article 64 *American Convention on Human Rights*).

[60]Advisory Opinion Oc–2/82 of September 24, 1982, *The Effect of Reservations on the Entry into Force of The American Convention on Human Rights* (Articles 74 and 75).

Court's rules of procedure provide, "When a party fails to appear in or continue with a case, the Court shall, on its own motion, take such measures as may be necessary to complete the consideration of the case."

Issues

1. Did Trinidad and Tobago fail to provide humane treatment in prison?
2. Did Trinidad and Tobago violate Mr. Caesar's right to a fair trial?
3. Did the sentence of corporal punishment violate the "cruel and unusual" standard?

Decision

The Court had held in previous cases that when a state does not specifically contest the application, the facts on which it remains silent are presumed to be true, provided that the evidence before the Court is found to be consistent with those facts.

Reasoning

Many international and national tribunals and authorities have considered that corporal punishment is incompatible with national and international guarantees against torture and other inhuman treatment. By imposing upon Mr. Caesar a sentence of 15 strokes with the cat-o-nine-tails, the state violated his right to physical, mental, and moral integrity under Article 5.1 of the Convention, and his right not to be subjected to torture or other cruel, inhuman, or degrading treatment or punishment under Article 5.2 of the Convention. The lapse of time in which Mr. Caesar waited for the punishment caused him great anguish, stress, and fear. He was forced to view the suffering of other inmates subjected to corporal punishment on four separate occasions. The fact that the treatment given to Mr. Caesar was imposed as a form of criminal sanction does not affect the state's obligation to comply with the requirements of Articles 5.1 and 5.2 of the Convention. The prohibition of torture and other cruel, inhuman, or degrading punishment or treatment is absolute. In the present case, the state failed to meet domestic and international standards on conditions of detention. Between January 1991 and November 1999, Mr. Caesar was subjected to an overcrowded cell with poor sanitation, and little light and ventilation, as well as inadequate medical treatment. These all violated his right to have his physical, mental, and moral integrity respected and constituted a cruel, inhuman, or degrading punishment or treatment.

"It is well settled in international jurisprudence that a judgment constitutes, *per se,* a form of reparation. However, considering the circumstances of the present case and its nonpecuniary consequences, the Court deems it appropriate that the moral damages must also be repaired, on grounds of equity, through the payment of compensation. . . . Taking all of the elements of the present case into account, the Court sees fit, on grounds of equity, to direct Trinidad and Tobago to grant an indemnity of US $50.000,00 (fifty thousand United States of America dollars) to Mr. Winston Caesar for moral damages."

"Having found that the Corporal Punishment Act is incompatible with the terms of Article 5(1) and 5(2) of the Convention the Court directs the State to adopt, within a reasonable time, such legislative or other measures as may be necessary to abrogate the Corporal Punishment Act. *Trinidad and Tobago, as a Party to the Convention at the time that the acts took place, cannot invoke provisions of its domestic law as justification for failure to comply with its international obligations.* The state must pay the compensation ordered within one year of the notification of this judgment and to adopt the other measures of reparation ordered in accordance with the provisions of paragraphs 131 to 134 of this judgment (emphasis added)."

HUMAN RIGHTS AND TERRITORIAL ASYLUM

In Chapter 10, we dealt with the issues raised by claims for asylum based upon the justification that certain crimes characterized as political offenses would exempt individuals from the possibility of extradition. This section deals with a slightly different set of questions relating to individuals who have fled from an oppressive regime or who have been displaced by war or state policy. Giving political asylum to any individual or group constitutes a *permissive* action by the granting state.[61] International law neither designates the conditions for granting asylum nor prescribes a positive duty to do so. It merely sanctions the practice, leaving the details to each domestic legal and political system. In the case of asylees, as with the admission of aliens in general, the issues come not from any presumed right of entry, but from the duties of the state with respect to their status and treatment *after entry*.[62] Interestingly, *illegal* entry does not change the nature of the duty.[63]

Convention Relating to the Status of Refugees

As a practice, territorial asylum does flow directly from human rights concerns—the right to live free from discrimination and persecution.[64] The events before, during, and after World War II led to millions of displaced people. The problem prompted the UN General Assembly to establish the Office of the High Commissioner for Refugees[65] in 1950 and to develop the Convention Relating to the Status of Refugees. Article 14(1) of the UDHR underpins the principal rationale of the Refugee Convention: "Everyone has the right to *seek* and to enjoy in other countries asylum from persecution" (Emphasis added). Article 1 of the Refugee Convention defines a refugee as one who has a "well-founded fear of being persecuted for reasons of race, religion, nationality, membership of a particular social group or political opinion"; is "outside the country of his nationality"; and is "unable or unwilling to return or take advantage of the protection of that country" because

---

[61]For interesting treatments of this issue from a philosophical and moral perspective, see M. Gibney, "Liberal Democratic States and Responsibilities to Refugees," 93 *American Political Science Review* 169 (1999); and C. Boswell, "European Values and the Asylum Crisis," 76 *International Affairs (Royal Institute of International Affairs 1944–)* 537 (2000).

[62]In *Kleindienst v. Mandel*, 408 U.S. 763 (1972) at 765, the court noted that the legal power to exclude aliens is "inherent in sovereignty, [as it is] necessary for maintaining normal international relations and defending the country against foreign encroachments and dangers." See also *Sale v. Haitian Ctrs. Council*, 113 S. Ct. 2549, 113 S. Ct. 2549, 125 L. (92–344), 509 U.S. 155 (1993). For U.S. practice, see P. Schuck, "The Transformation of Immigration Law," 84 *Colum. L. Rev.* 1 (1984); and VerKuil, "A Study of Immigration Procedure," 31 *UCLA L. Rev.* 1141 (1984).

[63]*Convention Relating to the Status of Refugees*, Geneva, July 28, 1951 (entry into force April 22, 1954), currently 140 states parties, www.unhchr.ch/html/menu3/b/o_c_ref.htm; and Protocol Relating to the Status of Refugees, December 16, 1966, www.unhchr.ch/html/menu3/b/o_p_ref.htm, currently 138 states parties. The United States did not sign the convention but did adhere to the protocol in 1968.

[64]For example, see Articles 31(1) and 33(1) of the Convention Relating to the Status of Refugees, note 57.

[65]See G. Goodwin-Gill, *The Refugee in International Law*, 2nd ed. (1996); and Steiner, Gibney, and Loescher, eds, *Problems of Protection: The UNCHR, Refugees, and Human Rights* (2003).

of the fear. The intent of the original convention was clear from the qualifying phrase in the definition: "as a result of events occurring in Europe before 1 January 1951." At the time of signature, ratification, or accession, each state party had to declare if it would apply the definition only to Europe or to "events occurring in Europe or *elsewhere* before 1 January 1951." A protocol removing the time and geographic restrictions entered into force in October 1967.

Nonetheless, *along with other immigration concerns* as the number of displaced persons has risen exponentially because of internal wars, failed states, natural disasters, and various other events, the issues surrounding refugees and grants of asylum rank among the most highly charged political issues in contemporary politics. By the beginning of 2010, the UN Office of the High Commissioner of Refugees estimated the world total of forcibly displaced persons at 43.2 million people.[66] Those who qualify as refugees under the mandate of UNHCR had actually fallen to 15.2 million. Interestingly, the number of asylum requests for asylum in industrialized countries had dropped significantly over the past 10 years. The cause for the drop is uncertain. The UN High Commissioner for Refugees António Guterres has noted: "We need to study the root causes to see if the decline is because of fewer push factors in areas of origin, or tighter migration control in countries of asylum."[67]

For 30 years after World War II, the questions relating to asylum remained quite distinct from those pertaining to immigration.[68] Refugees fled political oppression; immigrants sought economic opportunity. For the United States and its allies, the Cold War set the parameters for grants of asylum. They welcomed those fleeing Communism as individuals who were making important political statements by "voting with their feet." Viktor Korchnoi, a Soviet chess grand master and at the time the second-ranked player in the world, defected to the Netherlands. Arkady N. Shevchenko, UN under-secretary-general for political and security affairs, chose to stay in the United States rather than return to Moscow. Asylum also formed an avenue of protest against American policy: Sweden, emphasizing its policy of neutrality, granted asylum to some 500 American citizens who actively resisted the Vietnam War.

Immigration not only had a different meaning, but also signified different perceptions for countries depending upon perceptions of the motives of those seeking to immigrate. For states such as the United States and Canada, whose origins lay in large-scale immigration, immigrants were people who wished to settle permanently. In contrast, many states in Western Europe saw immigrants as temporary workers who probably would return home after reaping the benefits of the rapidly redeveloping European economy.

---

[66]www.unhcr.org/4c176c969.html.

[67]"Asylum-seeker numbers nearly halved in last decade, says UNHCR," UNHCR (March 28 2011), www.unhcr.org/4d8cc18a530.html.

[68]See L. Lucassen, *The Immigrant Threat: The Integration of Old and New Migrants in Western Europe since 1850* (2005); M. Gibney, *The Ethics and Politics of Asylum: Liberal Democracy and the Response to Refugees* (2004); R. Hansen and P. Weil, eds., *Towards a European Nationality: Citizenship, Immigration, and Nationality Law in the EU* (2001); and R. Karapin, "The Politics of Immigration Control in Britain and Germany," 31 *Comparative Politics* 423 (1999).

Since the early 1970s, when large numbers of refugees began to emerge in the developing world, the ideas of asylum and immigration have become almost synonymous in Western Europe. By the early 1970s, France, Germany, Switzerland, and Scandinavia had all ended or severely modified policies that encouraged labor migration from Southern Europe and from former colonies or the Third World. Nonetheless, asylum requests dramatically increased after the end of the Cold War and the outbreak of civil war as the former Yugoslavia disintegrated. Between 1985 and 1995, Western European states received over *5 million* requests for asylum.[69]

Here we need to make a clear distinction between the *domestic issues* created by the presence of refugees (welfare, work status, etc.) and the obligations states may have with respect to international law. The principal difficulty in international law comes from the obligation of *nonrefoulement*. *Refoulement* means "the expulsion of persons who have the right to be recognized as refugees," according to the definition in Article 1 of the Convention. Article 33(1) states:

> No Contracting State shall expel or return (*refouler*) a refugee in any manner whatsoever to the frontiers of territories where his life or freedom would be threatened on account of his race, religion, nationality, membership of a particular social group or political opinion.

This article applies not only to the country of origin or citizenship but also to *any* state where the individual might suffer persecution. The dilemma arises because even if a particular state denies asylum (and hence permanent residence) to a refugee, authorities may not be able to find another country that fulfills the nonthreatening stipulation and has the willingness to accept the individual in question.[70] In consequence, several countries have a large number of individuals who lack the qualifications for permanent residence through asylum but literally have no other place to go.

The difficulties, both legal and political, explain why many states enacted measures to keep potential refugees from entering the territory. These involve measures such as enhanced visa regimes targeting states likely to produce refugees; carrier sanctions that level fines on ships, planes, or land vehicles that bring foreign nationals without documentation into a country; inspection regimes; definitions and redefinitions of territory for immigration purposes; and other measures of "proactive" interdiction. The events in the *Maersk Dubai* case (Chapter 12) resulted from the Captain's desire to avoid the considerable fine Canada would have imposed for bringing in undocumented aliens. The incident involving M/V *Tampa* gives us a concise snapshot of a recent government reaction to the issues.

---

[69]M. Gibney and R. Hansen, *Deportation and the Liberal State: the Forcible Return of Asylum Seekers and Unlawful Migrants in Canada, Germany and the United Kingdom,* New Issues in Refugee Research Working Paper Series, no. 77, UNHCR, Geneva (February 2003), 4. See also P. Barkham, "No Waltzing in Woomera: As Britain Offers an Increasingly Sour Welcome to Asylum Seekers," *The Guardian* (London) (May 25, 2002), 24.

[70]Many other questions arise here as well. Consider in this respect both time and cost. See Gibney and Hansen, note 69, at 11–12 for a concise discussion.

THE M/V TAMPA[71]

On August 24, 2002, an Indonesian ferry, the *Palapa,* sent a distress call indicating that it was stranded and sinking. The ship had sailed from a port in Indonesia with 460 (primarily Afghani) asylum seekers intending to land at Christmas Island. A Norwegian freighter, the M/V *Tampa,* answered the distress call and took the individuals on board (August 26). The captain of the *Tampa* then faced an interesting problem. The refugees insisted that he take them to Christmas Island (Australian territory), but Australian authorities denied him permission to dock at Christmas Island. The government of Indonesia also refused permission to dock. For the next five days the *Tampa* remained at sea—until the captain, citing the conditions on board, moved the ship into Australian territorial waters just off Christmas Island. The Australian government did send medical supplies but also responded by sending its Special Air Services (SAS) unit to board the ship. Norway and the United Nations pressured the Australian government to permit the ship to dock. Negotiation finally produced an agreement where New Zealand would accept 150 passengers, while Nauru would temporarily take in the rest to permit Australia time to process their applications for asylum.

The *Tampa* was the latest incident involving asylum seekers. In the two weeks preceding the arrival of the *Tampa,* over 1,000 individuals had sought entry through Christmas Island. On August 16, a vessel carrying 350 Iraqis had arrived; on August 22, another vessel carrying 360 Afghanis had docked. The influx had put a severe strain on facilities and resources. Australia charged four members of the *Palapa* with people smuggling. The government then instituted policies that removed Christmas Island along with other sovereign territories in the Indian Ocean from Australia's "migration zone."[72] Australia also began a vigorous program of naval patrol in the seas toward Indonesia with the goal of intercepting other ships before they could enter territorial waters.

Australia's hard line caused a storm of criticism from around the world. Australia did enlist the aid of the UN high commissioner for refugees (UNHCR) in deciding the eventual disposition of the detainees.[73] As of August 2005, all but 32 of those originally detained in Nauru had been resettled in another country or had returned to their country of origin.

The United States formerly utilized the naval facility at Guantánamo Bay to process the requests of Haitians seeking asylum because U.S. courts had ruled that while the base is subject to U.S. jurisdiction, it does not constitute U.S. territory in terms of the rights accorded to individuals under the Constitution.[74] As a matter of observation in passing, U.S. policy toward the Haitian boat people seeking entry has alternated between prescreening and indiscriminately returning them to their point of origin. One problem with aggressive interdiction of this nature is that it does increase the possibility of *refoulement.*

---

[71]"Australia: Refugees on Freighter Refused Entry," Facts on File, August 27, 2001, Lexis-Nexis.

[72]Martin, "Australia Targets Illegal Immigrants: New Law Will Mean No Seeking Asylum from Island Outposts," *The Daily Telegraph* (Sydney) (September 24, 2001), C15, Lexis-Nexis.

[73]Australia granted asylum to only seven of the Afghanis rescued by the *Tampa.* Madigan, "UN Search for Refugee Homes," *The Courier Mail* (Queensland) (April 11, 2002), 3, Lexis-Nexis; and Fickling, "Refugees on Nauru to be Sent Home," *The Guardian* (London) (September 11, 2002), 14, Lexis-Nexis.

[74]*Sale v. Haitian Ctrs. Council,* 113 S. Ct. 2549, 113 S. Ct. 2549, 125 L. (92–344), 509 U.S. 155 (1993).

U.S. Practice

The United States still maintains a clear distinction between refugees and immigrants.[75] The revised immigration law of 1990 created a flexible cap of 675,000 immigrants each year. It exempted certain categories of people from that limit. Apart from ordinary immigration, the attorney general has *discretion* to grant *asylum* to a person who qualifies as a "refugee" within the meaning of section 101(a)(42)(A) of the Immigration and Nationality Act.[76] The Act, drawing on the 1951 Refugee Convention, defines a refugee as

> any person who is outside any country of such person's nationality or, in the case of a person having no nationality, is outside any country in which such person last habitually resided, and who is unable or unwilling to return to, and is unable or unwilling to avail himself or herself of the protection of, that country because of persecution or a well-founded fear of persecution on account of race, religion, nationality, membership in a particular social group, or political opinion.

The statute definition is broader than that of the convention because it includes stateless individuals. The Congress, however, has set numerical limits here as well. Each year, the State Department prepares a report to Congress on proposed *refugee* admissions. The president then consults with Congress and establishes the proposed ceilings for refugee admissions for the fiscal year.[77]

Aliens already present in the United States may follow two paths. They may apply for asylum directly with the U.S. Citizenship and Immigration Services (USCIS) bureau,[78] or they may seek asylum before a Department of Justice Executive Office for Immigration Review (EOIR) judge during removal proceedings. Aliens who arrive at an entry point into the United States without appropriate documents have one avenue to avoid expedited removal. A claim that they have a "fear of persecution" will generate a "credible fear" hearing with an USCIS asylum officer. If the fear is found "credible," the officer will refer them to an EOIR judge for a hearing.[79] The Illegal Immigrant Reform and Immigrant Responsibility Act of 1996[80] instituted a number of procedural changes aimed at streamlining the process and severely limiting judicial review for those summarily excluded. This includes those found not to have a "credible fear" of persecution.[81]

---

[75]See R. E. Wasem, "U.S. Immigration Policy for Asylum Seekers," Congressional Research Service (May 5, 2005), www.fas.org/sgp/crs/misc/RL32621.pdf (accessed April 22, 2009).

[76]See 8 U.S.C. § 1158(b)(1).

[77]For the 2005 fiscal year (i.e., October 1, 2004–September 30, 2005), the total ceiling was set at 70,000 admissions and allocated to six geographic regions: Africa (20,000 admissions), East Asia (13,000 admissions), Europe and Central Asia (9,500 admissions), Latin America/Caribbean (5,000 admissions), and Near East/South Asia (2,500 admissions), with a 20,000 reserve.

[78]This bureau is now in the Department of Homeland Security.

[79]Wasem, note 75. The USCIS received 42,114 claims for asylum in fiscal year 2003. At the close of the fiscal year, there were 262,102 cases pending. *Id.*

[80]Pub. Law No. 104–208 (1996).

[81]Wasem, note 75, at CRS–5.

The pivotal case governing asylum claims in the United States is *INS v. Cardoza-Fonseca*.[82] Ms. Cardoza-Fonseca, a Nicaraguan national then living in Nevada, claimed that the Sandinista government would persecute her if she returned to her homeland. On first hearing, the immigration judge (IJ) decided that Ms. Cardoza-Fonseca had not established a "clear probability" of persecution as required under U.S. law. He rejected her petition for withholding deportation and asylum. The Board of Immigration Appeal agreed with the IJ. On appeal, the U.S. Court of Appeals (Ninth Circuit) ruled that the previous decision had erroneously narrowed the "clear probability of persecution" standard. The Supreme Court agreed. The Supreme Court held that the law required only a "well-founded fear" of persecution if returned. Consider the following case in defining the parameters of "credible" or "well-founded fear."

▌ RRESHPJA V. GONZALES

United States Court of Appeals, Sixth Circuit 420 F.3d 551; 2005 U.S. App. LEXIS 17127; 2005 FED App. 0341P (6th Cir.)

Facts

Vitore Rreshpja is a citizen of Albania. She arrived in the United States in November 2001 with a fraudulently obtained nonimmigrant visa after an unknown man attempted to abduct her in her home country. The Immigration and Naturalization Service (INS) initiated removal proceedings against her several months later. Rreshpja requested a grant of asylum or, in the alternative, the withholding of removal and protection under the Convention against Torture (CAT). She claimed that she would be at risk of being forced to work as a prostitute if returned to Albania. The immigration judge (IJ) denied her application. Rreshpja appealed the denial to the Board of Immigration Appeals (BIA), which affirmed the IJ's decision without issuing its own opinion on the matter.

Issue

Does Ms. Rreshpja have a valid request for asylum or withholding based upon a fear of torture and persecution if returned to Albania?

Decision

No.

Reasoning

An applicant claiming to be a refugee must present specific facts demonstrating that she suffered past persecution or that she has a well-founded fear of future persecution. An applicant's fear of persecution must be both "*subjectively genuine and objectively reasonable*"[83] (Emphasis added). She must demonstrate "an 'objective situation' under which her fear can be deemed reasonable. First, the "social group" in which Ms. Rreshpja claims membership

(*continued*)

---

[82]480 U.S. 421, 423, 438, 440, 107 S. Ct. 1207, 94 L. Ed. 2d 434 (1987).
[83]*Perkovic v. INS,* 33 F.3d 615, 620–21 (6th Cir. 1994).

(young attractive Albanian females) does not fall within the parameters of the relevant definition in the Immigration and Nationality Act. Actually, if accepted, then any young, attractive Albanian woman, subjectively determined, would qualify for asylum in the United States.[84] Second, Rreshpja failed to demonstrate that her attempted kidnapping or her fear of being forced into prostitution if she is returned to Albania is the result of her membership in that social group or due to the unfortunate consequences of widespread crime in Albania. "Although Rreshpja has established her subjective fear of future persecution, she has not demonstrated an objectively reasonable possibility that she will be persecuted if she is forced to return to Albania. The isolated and apparently random attempt to abduct Rreshpja in 2001 by an unknown assailant is simply not sufficient to establish persecution by the government of Albania. A humanitarian grant of asylum is therefore unwarranted."

Cuba and Haiti

Most discussions of U.S. asylum policy focus on the differential treatment of asylum seekers from Cuba and Haiti because both have a history of repressive governments and human rights violations. Both have generated large numbers of asylum seekers. Post Cuban Revolution, the two groups have been treated very differently. In July 1991, a group of 161 Haitians left the island in a small fishing boat in an attempt to reach the United States. During the journey, they picked up two Cubans from a sinking raft. Before the boat reached U.S. territorial waters, the U.S. Coast Guard intercepted it. After processing through USCIS, the two Cubans received asylum, but almost all of the Haitians were returned.[85] Cubans do receive more favorable treatment than nationals from any other country because of the Cuban Adjustment Act (CAA) of 1966.[86]

Outside of south Florida, individuals may recall the 1980 Mariel boatlift, in which 125,000 Cubans came to the United States. The CAA was passed in response to an earlier influx. The Camarioca boatlift in September–November of 1965 generated approximately 200,000 Cuban refugees. The earlier exodus came after Fidel Castro made a public announcement that any Cuban citizens who had relatives in the United States could leave if their relatives came for them by boat.[87] Looking for a way to regularize the process, the Johnson administration negotiated an airlift ("freedom flights"). Over the next year, these initiatives brought another 45,000 Cubans to the United States. In response to the boatlift and subsequent airlift, Congress passed the CAA in 1966.

---

[84]The court cited *Gomez v. INS*, 947 F.2d 660, 663–64 (2d Cir. 1991), which held that a Salvadoran woman who had been beaten and raped by Salvadoran guerillas during her youth was not for that reason a member of a particular social group for asylum purposes.

[85]"The Cuban Adjustment Act of 1966: Mirando por los Ojos de Don Quixote o Sancho Panza," 114 *Harvard Int'l L. R.* 902 (2001) at 902; C. Miranda, "Haiti and the United States during the 1980s and 1990s: Refugees, Immigration and Foreign Policy," 32 *San Diego L. Rev.* 673 (1995).

[86]Pub. Law No. 89–732; 80 Stat. 1161 (1966); codified as amended at 8. U.S.C. § 1255 (1994 & Supp. II 1996).

[87]"Cuban Adjustment Act," note 85, at 904.

The CAA put Cuban refugees on a fast track to permanent residence. They did not have to satisfy the "well-founded fear" test, and officials seldom questioned them closely about their reasons for leaving Cuba.[88] The act has been considered by refugees and politicians as an open-ended entitlement to permanent residence in the United States. A new policy established in May 1995 created some important exceptions. Before 1995, any Cuban immigrant, including those intercepted at sea before entry into the United States, was virtually guaranteed admission. The new policy mandates that those refugees intercepted at sea are immediately returned to Cuba unless they can meet the "credible fear of persecution" threshold. For those who make it to U.S. soil, preferential treatment continues.[89] In November 2004, forty-nine members of a Cuban dance troupe that had been touring and performing in the United States defected. The United States granted their applications for asylum in July 2005.

U.S. PRACTICE AND HUMAN RIGHTS CONVENTIONS

When dealing with the ideas underlying the rise to prominence of the international human rights movement, one cannot ignore the central role played by the United States in placing and keeping human rights as items of consequence on the contemporary agenda of concerns among states.[90] Within the American justice system, questions of individual rights dominate constitutional jurisprudence. Since the Carter administration, presidents have routinely declared that a dedication to human rights constitutes a fundamental tenet of American foreign policy. Yet in comparison with many other democracies, the United States has only a modest record when it comes to formal adoption of international human rights conventions.[91]

The American record on international human rights displays two complementary attitudes: A deep pride in the accomplishments reflected in the Constitution and Bill of Rights, and an unwillingness to subject American practice to any type of examination and criticism by non-Americans.[92] A third attitude surfaced dur-

---

[88]"Cuban Adjustment Act," note 85, at 906.

[89]Wasem, note 75, at CRS–20, 21.

[90]L. Henkin, *The Age of Rights* (1990), 65 et seq.

[91]See N. H. Kaufman, *Human Rights Treaties and the Senate: A History of Opposition* (1990), 1–36; D. P. Forsythe, *Human Rights and U.S. Foreign Policy: Congress Reconsidered* (1988), 1–23. Since the publication of Kaufman's book, the Senate has ratified the International Covenant on Civil and Political Rights (ICCPR), December 16, 1966, 999 U.N.T.S. 171, in 1992. In 1994, it ratified both the International Convention on the Elimination of All Forms of Racial Discrimination, March 7, 1966, 660 UNTS 195 (hereinafter the Racial Discrimination Convention) and the Convention Against Torture and Other Cruel, Inhuman or Degrading Treatment or Punishment, June 26, 1987 1465 UNTS 85 (hereinafter the Torture Convention). In 1996 the Senate Committee on Foreign Relations recommended that the Senate consent to ratification of the Convention on the Elimination of All Forms of Discrimination Against Women, December 18, 1979, 1249 UNTS 13, but as of the end of the 2005 session, the Senate had not acted on the recommendation.

[92]Professor Louis Sohn cut to the heart of American attitudes and fears:

> I think on the one hand we always say to everybody else that our standards are higher than those of anyone else; but we will discover if we are subject to international supervision, that there are some skeletons in our closet and they will be paraded in public, and we do not like that idea.

International Human Rights Treaties: Hearings Before the Comm. on Foreign Relations, 96th Cong. 103 (1979) (statement of Louis B. Sohn) (hereinafter, Testimony 1979).

ing the post–World War II debates over the Genocide Convention and the Bricker Amendment—the fear that the call for international standards masked an effort to dilute the essential essence of "Americanism."[93] The perceived discrepancy between cautious practice and hortatory statements, juxtaposed with the determination to exercise an active and often interventionist leadership role, has occasioned great debate. For example, a century and a half ago, in a remarkably prescient statement directed at the avidness with which certain congressmen advocated overt support for Louis Kossuth (a leader of the 1848 Hungarian Revolution), Henry Clay eloquently pointed out the dilemmas involved in an active interventionist human rights policy. He noted that in undertaking such ventures, the United States would expose itself "to the reaction of foreign Powers, who, when they see us assuming to judge of their conduct, will undertake in their turn to judge of our conduct."[94] That possibility was no more appealing then than it is now.

Focus from abroad on the United States with respect to issues concerning the death penalty and prison conditions graphically illustrates the continued American sensitivity to criticism. Senator Jesse Helms, chairman of the Senate Foreign Relations Committee, sent a letter of complaint to UN Ambassador Bill Richardson concerning visits to a number of U.S. prisons by a UN investigative team, led by Senegalese jurist Bacre Waly Ndiaye. Ndiaye's team focused on "extrajudicial, summary and arbitrary executions." Helms's indignant letter reflected the essence of American concern by questioning the legitimacy of such activity. Why should the United States be subject to other people's judgment, particularly by individuals from countries where their own government's commitment to human rights in its own internal affairs is dubious?[95] The announcement in October 1998 by Amnesty International of its plans to conduct a yearlong

---

[93]This viewpoint often translates into an assertion that, by embracing international standards, Americans would actually find their rights curtailed in important ways. Frank E. Holman, a former president of the American Bar Association, provides a concise statement of these fears:

> Most of those who support a program like UNESCO, designed to influence our educational curriculum along international lines—inculcating into the youth the desirability of "world citizenship" over American citizenship—are also opposed to the Bricker Amendment, for programs like UNESCO can be more easily achieved through the treaty process—and without the American people knowing much about them. (Holman, *The Story of the Bricker Amendment* (1954), 21)

[94]Cong. Globe, 31st Cong., 1st Sess. 116 (1850). Conventional diplomatic wisdom holds that failure to embrace international standards wholeheartedly has consistently undermined U.S. credibility on human rights issues because others interpret American reluctance as simple hypocrisy and evidence of a questionable commitment. Former ambassador to the United Nations, Charles Yost, noted 25 years ago, "Many are . . . inclined to believe that our whole human rights policy is merely a cold war exercise or a display of self-righteousness directed against governments we dislike." Testimony 1979, note 92, at 4.

[95]Senator Helms stated,

> Bill, is this man confusing the United States with some other country, or is this an intentional insult to the US and our nation's legal system?. . . It is clear that Mr. Ndiaye's strange "investigation" is intended to be merely a platform for more outrageous accusations from U.S. critics at the United Nations. ("Helms Protests UN Human Rights Probe in US," AP Wire, October 7, 1997)

As a result of Ndiaye's report, the United States had to defend the use of the death penalty before the UN Human Rights Commission.

probe to highlight abuses in the United States further confirmed the worst fears of those who see the U.S. Constitution, laws, and judicial practice as the archetype for all others.[96]

In the recent past, the United States has reacted to adverse decisions concerning policy by withdrawing from agreements. In the wake of the Nicaragua decision by the International Court of Justice (ICJ), the United States terminated its consent to compulsory jurisdiction. Reacting to another adverse decision by the ICJ, in March 2005, the United States gave notice that it "hereby withdraws" from the Optional Protocol to the Vienna Convention on Consular Relations.[97] The United States had originally proposed the protocol in 1963 and ratified it along with the rest of the Vienna Convention in 1969 (see Chapter 15).

The last action occurred as the Supreme Court took up *Medellin v. Dretke,* which involves an April 2004 ruling by the ICJ that the United States had violated the Vienna Convention on Consular Relations (right of diplomatic protection) by failing to tell 51 Mexican nationals charged with capital murder that they had a right under the convention to meet with diplomats from their home country. Jose Ernesto Medellin, one of the 51, had argued that the ICJ ruling is binding in U.S. courts. The State of Texas, citing Supreme Court rulings, countered that the ICJ could not override state procedural rules under which Medellin had forfeited his right to invoke the Vienna Convention by not asserting it until 1998, rather than originally at his trial in 1994.[98] The ICJ ruling raised not only the question of the relationship between international and domestic law but also very contentious issues concerning the balance of rights between individual states in the United States and the federal government. It also raised an interesting question concerning the relationship between the judiciary and the executive because President George W. Bush argued that he alone had the power to decide how the country should react to the ICJ decision. He declared that the various state courts involved should give those party to the suit a new hearing, and he requested the Supreme Court to bow out.[99]

This event illustrates an interesting pattern. Apart from the recent actions, over the years the arguments against U.S. ratification of various human rights

---

[96]G. Gedda, "Alleged US Abuses to Be Highlighted," AP Wire, October 5, 1998. "The country that so often sits in judgment of others is being judged itself. Amnesty International, the London-based human rights group, plans a yearlong campaign to expose perceived rights shortcomings in the United States." Human Rights Watch: World Report 1999, United States: Human Rights Development (www.hrw.org/legacy/worldreport99/ (accessed May 14, 2009) (discussing police abuse, prison and jail conditions, asylum and immigration practices, the death penalty, continued racial and gender discrimination, and resistance to international requirements for reporting and observation as areas in which the United States falls short of international standards).

[97]C. Lane, "U.S. Quits Pact Used in Capital Cases: Foes of Death Penalty Cite Access to Envoys," *Washington Post* (March 10, 2005): A1; and T. Jackman, "Supreme Court to Review Fairfax Case; Convicted of Murder, Honduran Says Police Denied Him Access to Embassy," The *Washington Post* (November 8, 2005), A4.

[98]C. Lane, "Justices Consider Rights of Foreigners; Power of International Court at Issue," The *Washington Post* (March 29, 2005), A4.

[99]Ibid.

treaties have involved a mix of technical considerations, emotional appeals, and special pleadings based upon perceptions of internal political imperatives. The arguments reflect five major themes or concerns,[100] which first appeared in the Senate debates surrounding the initial discussions of the Genocide Convention and the introduction of the Bricker Amendment in the early 1950s.[101] Though modified in committee and by Bricker himself over time, the amendment, in its various forms, sets the initial tone for the debate of human rights in the Congress and has since cast a long shadow over subsequent efforts to seek ratification and implementation of international conventions by the U.S. Senate. Critics fear that under the guise of setting an international standard, the treaties may have the following effects:

1. The treaties could abridge or deny rights currently guaranteed to U.S. citizens under the Constitution, such as freedom of speech and press and trial by jury.
2. The treaties could radically alter the balance of rights between the states and the federal government by giving powers to the federal government that by law and usage belong to the states. Self-executing treaties, in particular, embody this risk (remember the issues in *Missouri v. Holland*).
3. The treaties would erode U.S. sovereignty and promote world government.
4. The treaties would create perennial opportunities for those inimical to the policies and practices of the United States to criticize and create embarrassing situations.
5. Some treaties contain provisions that both undermine values fundamental to the free enterprise system and promote socialism or Communism.

Beginning with the ratification of the Genocide Convention, the U.S. Senate, as a condition of its consent, has systematically appended a number of reservations, understandings, and declarations (RUDs) to each human rights treaty, the intent of which is to limit the impact of certain provisions on domestic

---

[100]See Kaufman, note 90, at 204–205; D. Tannenbaum, *The Bricker Amendment Controversy: A Test of Eisenhower's Political Leadership* (1988), 1–15. See L. J. LeBlanc, *The United States and the Genocide Convention* (1991), 151–174, 237–244 for a discussion of the original negotiations. Ironically, the concerns of the USSR (e.g., diminution of sovereign prerogatives) expressed during the negotiations mirrored many of the concerns expressed by members of the U.S. Senate during the first, and subsequent, debates over possible ratification.

[101]Between 1950 and 1955, Senator John W. Bricker of Ohio led a movement to amend the U.S. Constitution in ways designed to make it impossible for the United States to adhere to human rights treaties. The campaign for the Bricker Amendment apparently represented a move by anti–civil rights and pro–"states' rights" forces to prevent bringing an end to racial discrimination and segregation by international treaty. On January 7, 1953, Senator Bricker introduced a joint resolution calling for an amendment to the U.S. Constitution. The Bricker Amendment clearly intended to restrict the power of the president to commit the United States through treaty or executive agreement. Amendment of Constitution Relating to Treaties and Executive Agreements, S.J. Res. 1-A, 83d Cong. (1953) is the most often cited, but see also S.J. Res 102, 82d Cong. (1951); S.J. Res. 130, 82d Cong. (1952); and S.J. Res. 181, 83d Cong. (1954). See, generally, Tannenbaum, note 99; and C. J. Nolan, "The Last Hurrah of Conservative Isolationism: Eisenhower, Congress and the Bricker Amendment," 22 *Pres. Stud.* Q. (1992): 337, 337–344.

law and practice.[102] Each set of RUDs bears the imprint of the Bricker legacy. The five traditional themes have translated into five axioms of contemporary political wisdom:

1. The United States will not commit to any treaty obligation deemed inconsistent with the U.S. Constitution.[103]
2. The United States will not submit to the jurisdiction of the ICJ with regard to application or interpretation of any human rights convention.[104]
3. The United States will not regard any human rights treaty as self-executing; all treaties will require enabling legislation.[105]
4. Human rights treaties do not create a basis for litigation by individuals (note the nature of the enabling legislation).
5. The United States will not undertake any treaty obligation that might change the balance of rights between the federal government and the states.

The question as to the extent to which these RUDs may actually mute the potential international responsibility of the United States lies beyond the scope of this chapter. However, their general tenor and purpose form an important part of the context in any analysis of U.S. policy regarding international initiatives to expand human rights.

SUGGESTED READINGS

Addo, "Practice of United Nations Human Rights Treaty Bodies in the Reconciliation of Cultural Diversity with Universal Respect for Human Rights," 32 *Human Rights Quarterly* (2010), 601–664.

Alston, *The United Nations and Human Rights* (1992).

Anderson, "Human Rights and the Structure of International Law," N.Y. *Law School J. of Int. & Comp. Law* 1 (1991).

---

[102]L. Henkin, "U.S. Ratification of Human Rights Conventions: The Ghost of Senator Bricker," 89 *AJIL* 341 (1995); and see Genocide Convention, S. Rep. No. 99–2, at 26–27 (1985); International Covenant on Civil and Political Rights, S. Rep. No. 102–23, at 10–20 (1992); and International Convention on the Elimination of All Forms of Racial Discrimination, S. Rep. No. 103–29, at 9 (1994). See also David P. Stewart, "United States Ratification of the Covenant on Civil and Political Rights: The Significance of the Reservations, Understandings, and Declarations," 42 *DePaul L. Rev.* 1183 (1993). For a discussion of the reasoning behind the reservations to the Racial Discrimination Convention, see Marian Nash (Leich), "Contemporary Practice of the United States Relating to International Law," 88 *AJIL* 721 (1994).

[103]See the U.S. reservations to the Racial Discrimination and Torture Conventions.

[104]For example, see the statement and answers to questions of Conrad K. Harper, legal adviser, U.S. Department of State, during the ratification of the Racial Discrimination Convention. International Convention on the Elimination of All Forms of Racial Discrimination; Hearings before the Senate Comm. on Foreign Relations, 103d Cong. 13, 21 (1994) (statement of Conrad K. Harper, legal advisor, U.S. Department of State).

[105]At present, Congress has not enacted any implementing legislation for the ICCPR or Racial Discrimination Convention. For the legislation accompanying the Genocide Convention, see 18 U.S.C. §§ 1091–1093 (1998). For material relevant to the Torture Convention, see the Torture Victim Protection Act, 28 U.S.CA. § 1350 (1998).

Buergenthal, Shelton, and Stewart, *International Human Rights in a Nutshell,* 3rd ed. (2002).

Dinstein, *The Protection of Minorities and Human Rights* (1992).

Donnelly, *Universal Human Rights in Theory and Practice*, 2nd ed. (2002).

Forsythe, *Human Rights in International Relations,* 2nd ed. (2006).

Franck, *Human Rights in Third World Perspective* (1982).

Hannum, *Autonomy, Sovereignty, and Self-Determination: The Accommodation of Conflicting Rights* (1996).

Hannum and Fischer, eds, *United States Ratification of the International Covenants on Human Rights* (1993).

Henkin, *The Age of Rights* (1990).

Lauren, *The Evolution of International Human Rights: Visions Seen,* 2nd ed. (2003).

Meron, *Human Rights and Humanitarian Norms As Customary Law* (1989).

Merrills, *The Development of International Law by the European Court of Human Rights* (1993).

Mertus, *United Nations and Human Rights: A Guide for a New Era* (2005).

Murphy, "Objections to Western Conceptions of Human Rights," *Hofstra L. R.* 433 (1981).

Saulle, *International Code of the Rights of the Child* (1994).

Sikkink, "Transnational Politics, International Relations Theory, and Human Rights," 31 *PS: Political Science and Politics* 516 (1998).

Steiner and Alston, *International Human Rights in Context: Law, Politics, Morals,* 2nd ed. (2000).

Thornberry, *International Law and the Rights of Minorities* (1991).

Wilson, ed., *Human Rights in the "War on Terror"* (2005).

EUROPEAN CONVENTION ON HUMAN RIGHTS

Alston et al., eds, *The EU and Human Rights* (1999).

Council of Europe, *Human Rights Today: European Legal Texts,* 2nd ed. (1999).

Gomien, *Short Guide to the European Convention on Human Rights* (2005).

Ovey, *Jacobs and White: The European Convention on Human Rights,* 3rd ed. (2002).

THE AMERICAS

Buergenthal, "The Advisory Practice of the American Human Rights Court," 79 *AJIL* 1 (1985).

Buergenthal, Norris, and Shelton, *Protecting Human Rights in the Americas: Selected Problems* (1982).

Latin American Network Information Center (LANIC), "Human Rights," http://lanic.utexas.edu/la/region/hrights/.

Nydell, "The Inter-American Court of Human Rights," 76 *AJIL* 231 (1982).

TERRITORIAL ASYLUM

Gibney, *The Ethics and Politics of Asylum: Liberal Democracy and the Response to Refugees* (2004).

Goodwin-Gill, *The Refugee in International Law,* 2nd ed. (1996).

Hansen and Weil, eds, *Towards a European Nationality: Citizenship, Immigration, and Nationality Law in the EU* (2001).

Karapin, "The Politics of Immigration Control in Britain and Germany," 31 *Comparative Politics* 423 (1999).

Lucassen, *The Immigrant Threat: The Integration of Old and New Migrants in Western Europe since 1850* (2005).

Steiner, Gibney, and Loescher, eds, *Problems of Protection: The UNCHR, Refugees, and Human Rights* (2003).

International Criminal Law

As we discussed earlier (Chapter 10), one aspect of the universal principle of jurisdiction acknowledges that some activities, undertaken by both states and individuals, require an authority vested in all community members to punish these acts wherever or whenever they may occur, even absent a link between the state and the parties or the acts in question.[1] Throughout the earlier chapters, we have noted the evolution of international law with respect to these questions as well as the areas where they overlap with more traditional areas of the law. We pointed out earlier (Chapters 1 and 11) that individuals normally do not represent a subject of international law, although the scope of human rights law (Chapter 15) has expanded over the past 60 years. International criminal law (ICL) forms a subcategory of the human rights regime. Not every human rights norm falls into the category of ICL. Certain crimes, however, have such international significance that the community of nations has felt compelled to make those who commit them directly subject to international law.

Until the emergence of the ad hoc criminal tribunals and the International Criminal Court (ICC) in the 1990s, writers tended to define ICL as that part of a state's legal code that dealt with transnational crimes.[2] This reflected the simple fact that, as states moved to attach criminal liability to certain categories of acts, they left implementation in terms of prosecution and punishment to national courts rather than establishing new international institutions. With the appearance of international courts in the 1990s, many sought to define ICL as comprising only those crimes punishable by an international court. This distinction has produced an anomaly. Many crimes, such as piracy and engaging in the slave trade, that once defined ICL now fall into the transnational (transboundary) category.

Thus, from a narrow technical viewpoint, *international crime* (and hence ICL) now refers to violations that fall under the jurisdiction of an international

---

[1]S. Macedo, *Universal Jurisdiction: National Courts and the Prosecution of Serious Crimes Under International Law* (2004), 28.

[2]R. Cryer, H. Friman, D. Robinson, and E. Wilmshurst, *An Introduction to International Criminal Law* (2007), 3.

court. International crimes presumably reflect violation of values fundamental to all members of the international community. For example, the Rome Statute of the ICC uses the phrase "the most serious crimes of concern to the international community as a whole."[3] Confusion may occur because few of the conventions (treaties) that define international criminal offenses use the term *international crime*.[4] In contrast, transnational crimes generally fall solely under the jurisdiction of national courts. Rather than explore that distinction, we have elected to discuss both under the rubric of ICL.

Hence, for our purposes, ICL embraces two categories. The first includes the crimes included in the statutes of the international courts: genocide, war crimes, crimes against peace (aggression or waging aggressive war), and the group of somewhat ill-defined acts that comprise crimes against humanity.[5] The second category includes the slave trade, piracy, air hijacking, terrorism, peacetime taking of hostages, and torture. With regard to the second category, international law requires that each state pass appropriate laws and take appropriate action to suppress the practices. Though clearly both piracy and the slave trade have international dimensions, no current international court has jurisdiction to try individuals for alleged acts that violate the prohibitions. Alleged offenders will be tried before national courts. The same holds true for international acts of terrorism and drug trafficking. Hence, transnational criminal law includes a focus on domestic criminal law as well as on mechanisms for interstate cooperation such as extended jurisdiction and extradition.[6]

The term *international crime* does not appear in any current international treaty, though the phrase "crime under international law" does.[7] The question then becomes, how can we talk about ICL? This may appear as a nitpicking distinction, but the observation illustrates the evolutionary and fragmented nature of the discipline. Note the emphasis on *crimes* here. It marks an important distinction that the reader must keep in mind. Traditional international law engages the collective responsibility of the state (Chapter 11). ICL places responsibility directly on individuals. It does not depend upon an individual having a responsible position as part of a state's governing authority. At the moment, a comprehensive international criminal code does not exist. Hence, definitions of what should be included in the category of *ICL* vary. The International Law Commission's (ILC)

---

[3]Articles 1 and 5(1). *Rome Statute of the International Criminal Court, www2.icc-cpi.int/NR/rdonlyres/EA9AEFF7-5752-4F84-BE94-0A655EB30E16/0/Rome_Statute_English.pdf* (accessed May 12, 2009).

[4]M. C. Bassiouni, An *Introduction to International Criminal Law* (2003), 158–161.

[5]Most aspects of traditional categories of international crimes are covered comprehensively in M. Bassiouni, *An Introduction to International Criminal Law* (New York: Transnational Publishers, 2002); A. Cassese, *International Criminal Law* (2003); G. Mettraux, *International Crimes and the Ad Hoc Tribunals* (2005); W. Schabas, *The UN International Criminal Tribunals: The Former Yugoslavia, Rwanda and Sierra Leone* (2006). For an updated bibliography, see G. Raisch and M. Partin, "Features–International Criminal Law: A Selective Resource Guide," www.llrx.com/features/int_crim.htm (accessed April 22, 2009).

[6]N. Boister, "Transnational Criminal Law," 14 *European Journal of International Law* 953 (2003).

[7]Bassiouni, note 4, at 166–167. Indeed, Bassiouni notes that the term *crime under international law* appears in only 34 of 281 relevant international instruments.

long-standing effort to develop a comprehensive criminal code produced agreement on only five international crimes: aggression, genocide, war crimes, crimes against humanity, and crimes against UN personnel.[8] We will discuss aggression and war crimes in Chapters 20 through 22.

CRIMES AGAINST HUMANITY AND GENOCIDE

The Charter of the Nuremberg International Military Tribunal first defined crimes against humanity[9] and waging aggressive war as international crimes for which individuals could have personal (individual) criminal responsibility. The term *genocide* had not yet entered into general usage. The charges elicited many protests about "victor's justice" because of questions about whether these alleged "crimes" had been identified and specifically "criminalized" in the sense of making individuals personally responsible for their acts. Nonetheless, the precedent set by Nuremberg and its counterpart at Tokyo firmly established the principle that individuals could be held directly responsible for certain acts.

Presumably as categories of crime that permit an exercise of universal jurisdiction, all states may exercise their jurisdiction in prosecuting a perpetrator regardless of where these crimes occurred. All states have a duty to prosecute or extradite, so that no person charged with that crime may claim the "political offense exception" to extradition. States also have the duty to assist each other in securing evidence needed to prosecute. No perpetrator may claim the defense of "obedience to superior orders," and no statute of limitation contained in the laws of any state can apply. Last, no one is immune from prosecution for such crimes—not even former heads of state or other high officials.[10]

Crimes Against Humanity

Like many other terms, ordinary usage often misuses the idea of *crimes against humanity*. In popular parlance, it has come to mean anything atrocious committed on a large scale.[11] This does not reflect either the original meaning or the contemporary technical legal one. The term originated in the Preamble to the 1907 Hague Convention, which codified the customary law of armed conflict. The convention presumed to draw on existing state practice that derived from those values and principles deemed to constitute the "laws of humanity," as reflected throughout history in different cultures. After World War I, the Allies, in connection with the Treaty of Versailles, established a commission to investigate war crimes that relied

---

[8]*Draft Code of Crimes Against the Peace and Security of Crimes of Mankind,* May 6–July 26, 1996, *Report of the International Law Commission,* GAOR Supp. No. 10, U.N. doc. A/51/10.

[9]For an excellent guide to the materials associated with crimes against humanity, genocide, and other war crimes, see the New England School of Law Library, www.nesl.edu/research/warcrim.cfm (accessed April 22, 2009).

[10]Taulbee, *International Crime and Punishment* (2009), ch. 2.

[11]M. C. Bassiouni, "Crimes Against Humanity," www.crimesofwar.org/a-z-guide/crimes-against-humanity/.

on the 1907 Hague Convention as the applicable law. In addition to war crimes committed by the Germans, the commission also found that Turkish officials committed "crimes against the laws of humanity" for killing Armenian nationals and residents during the period of the war. The United States and Japan strongly opposed making such conduct criminal on the grounds that crimes against the "laws" of humanity were violations of moral and not positive law.[12]

At conferences in Moscow (1943), Teheran (1943), Yalta (1945), and Potsdam (1945), the Big Three powers (the United States, USSR, and Great Britain) had agreed to try as well as punish those responsible for war crimes. In 1945, the United States and other Allies negotiated the Agreement for the Prosecution and Punishment of the Major War Criminals of the European Axis and Charter of the International Military Tribunal (IMT).[13] From November 20, 1945, until October 1, 1946, the IMT convened in the principal courtroom for criminal cases (room No. 600) at the Nuremberg Palace of Justice. The agreement contained the following definition of crimes against humanity in Article 6(c):

> Crimes against humanity: murder, extermination, enslavement, deportation, and other inhumane acts committed against civilian populations, before or during the war; or persecutions on political, racial or religious grounds in execution of or in connection with any crime within the jurisdiction of the Tribunal, whether or not in violation of the domestic law of the country where perpetrated, could not be regarded any longer as domestic acts or whether they constituted crimes against humanity.

The Nuremberg Charter represented the first time that crimes against humanity were asserted as part of positive international law. The IMT for the Far East, at Tokyo, followed the Nuremberg Charter, as did Control Council Law No. 10 of Germany, under which the Allies prosecuted Germans in their respective zones of occupation.[14] Curiously, however, no specialized international convention on crimes against humanity has emerged, although the category has been included in the statutes of the International Criminal Tribunal for the Former Yugoslavia (ICTY) and the International Criminal Tribunal for Rwanda (ICTR), as well as in the statute of the ICC.

Still, a quick search of contemporary international documents reveals 11 texts that include definitions of crimes against humanity. All differ slightly in detail but share the idea that crimes of humanity are specific acts of violence associated with, and directed toward, the persecution of a group of persons. The list of the specific crimes contained within the meaning of crimes against humanity has been

---

[12]*Ibid.*; see also G. Bass, *Stay the Hand of Vengeance: The Politics of War Crimes Tribunals* (2000), 58–146.

[13]Text in 39 *American Journal of International Law* 257 (1945 Supp.); consult International Conference on Military Trials, London, 1945 (Department of State Publication 3080) for the texts of all proposals at the meeting. The principles contained in the 1945 Agreement were recognized as binding in international law by UN General Assembly Resolution 95(I) (December 11, 1946). See also www.justiz.bayern.de/olgn/imt/imte.htm (accessed April 22, 2009).

[14]On Tokyo, see R. J. Pritchard and S. M. Zaide, *The Tokyo War Crimes* Trial (5 vols, New York: Garland, 1981–1987); and R. R. Minear, *Victors' Justice: The Tokyo War Crimes Trial* (1971).

expanded since Article 6(c) of the IMT to include, in the ICTY and the ICTR, rape and torture. The statute of the ICC (Article 7) also expands the list of specific acts. In particular, the ICC statute adds the crimes of enforced disappearance of persons and apartheid.[15] Further, the ICC statute contains clarifying language that more precisely defines the specific crimes of extermination, enslavement, deportation or forcible transfer of population, torture, and forced pregnancy.

To some extent, crimes against humanity overlap with genocide and common war crimes. We can distinguish crimes against humanity from genocide in that they do not require an intent to destroy a group "in whole or in part," according to the definition of genocide in the 1948 Convention. Crimes against humanity require only that the target group is the victim of a policy that condones widespread or systematic violations. We can distinguish crimes against humanity from ordinary war crimes in that they apply in wartime as well as in peacetime.[16]

Increasingly, states have incorporated enabling statutes into their domestic legal codes.[17] Practically, the *time, money, and cooperation* needed to mount a successful prosecution may militate against any state undertaking to try a particular case. Canada's experience may prove instructive here. From 1987 to 1992, after extensive investigation (883 potential cases), charges were filed under the Criminal Code in four cases. None resulted in convictions (including that of the notorious Imre Finta).[18] Canada redrafted its legislation. The first case under the new law came in October 2005. After five years of investigation that included extensive interviews with numerous witnesses in Rwanda, Europe, and Canada, the Royal Canadian Mounted Police War Crimes Section arrested Désiré Munyaneza of Rwanda on seven charges under the Crimes Against Humanity and War Crimes Act (CAHWC), including two counts of genocide, two counts of crimes against humanity, and three counts of war crimes.[19] On May 22, 2009, Munyaneza, was convicted on seven counts related to genocide, war crimes, and crimes against humanity.[20] Despite some demands for additional trials, authorities have not moved to issue new indictments.

---

[15]Rome Statute of the International Criminal Court, http://untreaty.un.org/cod/icc/statute/romefra.htm.

[16]www.nesl.edu/research/warcrim.cfm; see also B. Goodman, "Crimes Against Humanity During the Gulf War: A Hyperlinked Pathfinder Research Tool" (June 22, 1998), http://web.archive.org/web/20010812004424/http://diana.law.yale.edu/diana/db/war10.html (accessed April 22, 2009).

[17]See, for example, Department of Justice, Canada, Crimes Against Humanity and War Crimes Act, http://laws.justice.gc.ca/en/C–45.9/; and Interpol, Genocide, War Crimes and Crimes Against Humanity, www.international.gc.ca/court-cour/war-crimes-guerres.aspx?view=d.

[18]During this period, revocation of citizenship and deportation proceedings under the Immigration Act was also initiated in the case of Jacob Luitjens. These proceedings resulted in the deportation of Luitjens to the Netherlands, where he was immediately incarcerated for an earlier conviction of collaboration.

[19]Judgment, Superior Court of Canada (Quebec), May 22, 2009, www.scribd.com/doc/15764096/Judgement-Desire-Munyaneza-Canada-22-May-2009.

[20]R. Boyagoda, "Désiré Munyaneza Tested Our Principles–and Lost," *Toronto Globe & Mail* (October 29, 2009).

Genocide

Genocide means "an act committed with the intent to destroy, in whole or in part, a national, ethnic, racial, or religious group." The word itself was coined by Dr. Raphael Lemkin in his *Axis Rule in Occupied Europe.*[21] The practices of the German government before and especially during World War II, pertaining to the attempt to eliminate entire groups of its own citizens and later citizens of occupied states, led to the question of whether such acts of destruction could be regarded as solely domestic acts or whether they constituted a class of crimes against humanity. Genocide in practice went beyond the killing of people. It includes other acts of depredation such as forced abortion, sterilization, artificial infection, the working of people to death in special labor camps, and the separation of families or sexes in order to depopulate specific areas.

Commentators have characterized genocide as the "international crime among crimes," the one considered most heinous above all others. In an Advisory Opinion, the International Court of Justice (ICJ) defined *genocide* as "a crime under international law involving a denial of the right of existence of entire human groups, a denial which shocks the conscience of mankind and results in great losses to humanity, and which is contrary to moral law and to the spirit and aims of the United Nations."[22] The Armenian genocide and the events of World War II led to the creation of the Genocide Convention (1948).[23] Yet the hope embodied in this document rapidly faded. The cry "never again" unfortunately gave way to the reality of "again and again." One analyst noted, "Five decades of non-enforcement have left the Genocide Convention's core terms shrouded in considerable ambiguity, making it that much easier for recalcitrant politicians to equivocate."[24] Antonio Cassese, who served as a judge on the ICTY, states, "at the *enforcement* level the Convention has long proved a failure"[25] (Emphasis in the original). Though visualized in the convention, no *international* court with jurisdiction to try *individuals* accused of genocide existed until the UN Security Council authorized the ad hoc tribunals for Yugoslavia and Rwanda. As the first permanent international court, the ICC Statute includes genocide as a crime within its jurisdictions. Still, not until a half-century after the original draft of the convention opened for signature and ratification did a trial and conviction of an individual for crimes comprising genocide occur. In 1998, the ICTR found Jean-Paul Akayesu guilty of genocide

---

[21](1944), 79. See also Lemkin's "Genocide as a Crime Under International Law," 41 *AJIL* 145 (1947); and International Conference Commemorating its 60th Anniversary, www.genocide-convention2008. de/Genocide-Conference-Reader.pdf.

[22]Advisory Opinion, Reservations to the Convention on the Preservation and Punishment of the Crime of Genocide, 28 May 1951, ICJ Reports 1951, 23. Text at www.icj-cij.org/docket/index.php?p1=3&p2 =4&k=90&case=12&code=ppcg&p3=4 (accessed April 22, 2009).

[23]Convention on the Prevention and Punishment of the Crime of Genocide, December 9, 1948; text at www.oas.org/dil/1948_Convention_on_the_Prevention_and_Punishment_of_the_Crime_of_Genocide. pdf.

[24]D. F. Orentlicher, "Genocide" in *Crimes of War: What the Public Should Know*, edited by R. Gutman and D. Reiff (New York: W.W. Norton, 1999), 153.

[25]Cassese, note 5, at 97.

and direct and public incitement to commit genocide.[26] Bosnia brought the first case alleging *collective responsibility* for genocide by Serbia to the ICJ in 1993.[27]

The Genocide Convention Immediately after World War II, the UN General Assembly moved quickly to address the issues raised by the Holocaust. On December 13, 1946, the General Assembly unanimously adopted Resolution 96(I), in which it condemned genocide as a crime under international law. The assembly also requested the Economic and Social Council (ECOSOC) to begin studies toward a draft convention on genocide. The council, in turn, asked the secretary-general to prepare a first draft and to circulate it among the members for comment. In 1948, the ECOSOC appointed an ad hoc committee consisting of seven members to revise the original draft. Upon completion of the draft, ECOSOC—after a general debate—decided on August 26, 1948, to send the draft to the General Assembly for study and action. After further study in Paris by the Legal Committee of the General Assembly, action followed in the parent body. On December 9, 1948, the General Assembly adopted the Convention on the Prevention and Punishment of the Crime of Genocide.[28]

The convention affirms the criminality of genocide in time of peace as well as in time of war (Article 1). Article 2 defines the offense:

> In the present Convention, genocide means any of the following acts committed with intent to destroy, in whole or in part, a national, ethnical, racial or religious group, as such:
>
> a. Killing members of the group;
> b. Causing serious bodily or mental harm to members of the group;
> c. Deliberately inflicting on the group conditions of life calculated to bring about its physical destruction in whole or in part;
> d. Imposing measures intended to prevent births within the group;
> e. Forcibly transferring children of the group to another group.

Persons committing any of the acts listed in Article 3 are punishable, whether they are constitutionally responsible rulers, public officials, or private individuals (Article 4). The parties to the convention undertook the obligation to enact the necessary domestic legislation to give effect to the convention and, in particular,

---

[26]Prosecutor v. Akayesu, ICTR, Trial Chamber, Judgment of 2 September 1998 (ICTR-96-4).

[27]Application of the Convention on the Prevention and Punishment of the Crime of Genocide (Bosnia and Herzegovina v. Serbia and Montenegro), 1993; Judgment of 11 July 1996. Application for Revision of the Judgment of 11 July 1996 in the Case Concerning Application of the Convention on the Prevention and Punishment of the Crime of Genocide (Bosnia and Herzegovina v. Yugoslavia), Judgment of 26 February 2007.

[28]Text in 45 *AJIL* 6 (1951 Supp.). For a discussion of the original negotiations, see L. LeBlanc, The United States and the Genocide Convention (1991), 151–174. Ironically, the concerns of the USSR (e.g., diminution of sovereign prerogatives) expressed during the negotiations mirrored many of the concerns expressed by members of the U.S. Senate during the first, and subsequent, debates over possible ratification. See also J. L. Kunz, "The United Nations Convention on Genocide," 43 *AJIL* 738 (1949); Whiteman, XI: 848; and M. Nash, "Genocide Convention," 80 *AJIL* 612 (1986); also note G. J. Andreapoulos, *Genocide: Conceptual and Historical Dimensions* (1994).

to provide effective penalties for persons guilty of the forbidden acts (Article 5). Persons charged with any of the enumerated acts are to be tried by a competent tribunal of the state in which the act was committed or by such international penal tribunal as may have jurisdiction over those contacting parties that have accepted its jurisdiction (Article 5). This would now include the ICC if conditions for exercise of its jurisdictional reach are met.

In passing, we should note what the definition in the convention does *not* cover. It does not cover "all groups" of people; however, one may define a group. Except for religious groups, where membership clearly may be voluntary, the convention definitions apply to groups constituted by *involuntary* membership through birth.[29] This means that, except for religious organizations, the groups that an individual may join by voluntary choice would not qualify. It does not provide an extended definition of the categories, nor does it provide criteria one might use to construct an operational definition. It does *not* encompass political, cultural, or economic genocide. Because of definitional difficulties, these three concepts were deliberate omissions. As Cassese notes, intending to kill all the communists in a country may constitute a horrific crime, but it would not qualify as genocide.[30] Hence, the definition covers "ethnic cleansing" in Bosnia but would not apply to Stalin's systematic elimination of dissidents or to his extermination of an economic class (the *kulaks*—independent farmers). On the other hand, given the widespread and systematic nature of the attacks, Stalin might have been charged with crimes against humanity.

The Genocide Convention, originally signed by 25 states, came into force on January 12, 1951. The United States refrained from ratification until 1986. The legislative history of the ratification is rather interesting.[31] By the end of 1985, the convention had been pending in the U.S. Senate for almost 36 years. Both President Carter and President Reagan had urged the Senate to give consent to ratification, but to no avail. The Senate finally gave its consent to the ratification of the convention in February 1986, by a vote of 83–11. Because the treaty was considered *non-self-executing* (Chapter 4), it took two more years to gain congressional passage of legislation needed to implement the treaty by making genocide punishable under federal laws and setting penalties for violators.[32] The House then passed the implementing legislation in April 1988, and the Senate did so on October 15, 1988.[33]

---

[29]Prosecutor v. Akayesu, para. 511. Note that the Trial Chamber in this case did hold that the convention applied to any stable and permanent group. The statement has had very limited impact because others have chosen to interpret the convention conservatively and literally.

[30]Cassese, note 5, at 96–97. See also B. van Schaack, "The Crime of Political Genocide: Repairing the Genocide Convention's Blind Spot," 106 *Yale Law Journal* 2259 (1996–1997).

[31]For a discussion of this in context of the ratification of other human rights treaties, see Chapter 15.

[32]Note the discussion in Chapter 15 concerning U.S. attitudes toward human rights treaties. All are regarded as non-self-executing, thus requiring explicit legislation for implementation.

[33]Text, with Joyner's introductory note and the "Lugar Report," 28 *International Legal Materials* 754 (1989). As of November 2005, the convention had 133 states parties. The Senate version of the bill was officially called the Proxmire Act in honor of Senator William Proxmire (WI), who with unmatched dedication had delivered over 3,300 speeches in favor of ratification. He had repeated his call for action on every day the Senate was in session since January 11, 1967.

Contemporary history has seen instances of genocide after the drafting of the instrument. These have graphically illustrated the need for universal acceptance and enforcement of its provisions. Recent examples of genocide not directly connected with international war are supplied by the intermittent (1959–1973 and 1988) massacres that took place in Burundi during intertribal fighting between the Tutsi and Hutu groups, the reported slaughter of large numbers of Ugandans during the rule of former President Idi Amin, the reported slaying of dissidents in Equatorial Africa in the decade after independence was secured from Spain in 1968, the wholesale killing of Cambodians at the hands of their own government during the reign of Pol Pot, and the reported mass killings of members of the Muslim minority in Chad in 1979.[34]

New impetus to the prevention of genocide was given by the internecine strife in parts of the former Yugoslavia. Starting with a UN General Assembly Resolution and Declaration on the Rights of Persons Belonging to National or Ethnic, Religious, and Linguistic Minorities (1992),[35] Bosnia–Herzegovina instituted proceedings (March 20, 1993) in the ICJ against the Federal Republic of Yugoslavia (Serbia and Montenegro).[36] The court ordered provisional measures concerning application of the Genocide Convention on two occasions.[37] Croatia brought suit against Serbia in June 2000.[38] As of August 2011, the court had not rendered a judgment, but had set a date of November 4, 2011, for receipt of final written pleadings.

A large-scale killing of a population occurred in the African state of Rwanda in April 1994, with casualties among the Tutsi element estimated at 800,000. The United Nations appointed a special investigator for human rights, who soon called for trials of those guilty of the massacres. He asserted that the crimes were "well-orchestrated" and blamed the then current Rwandan government.[39] On July 1, 1994, the UN Security Council ordered an investigation of "acts of genocide" and in November 1994 approved setting up a war crimes tribunal. The UN tribunal had authority to try only crimes committed in 1994. Rwandan courts could examine acts dating back to 1990. By December 1994, more than 15,000 people had been arrested by the new government.[40]

---

[34]See W. Shawcross, *Deliver Us from Evil: Peacekeepers, Warlords and a World of Endless Conflict* (2000); and S. Power, *A Problem from Hell: America and the Age of Genocide* (2002).

[35]Text in 32 *ILM* 911 (1993).

[36]Case Concerning Application of the Convention on the Prevention and Punishment of the Crime of Genocide (Bosnia and Herzegovina v. Yugoslavia [Serbia and Montenegro]).

[37]See 32 *ILM* 888 (1993) and 87 *AJIL* 505 (1993), as well as Order of September 12, 1993, in 32 *ILM* 1599 (1993). See also A. D'Amato, "Peace v. Accountability in Bosnia," 88 *AJIL* 500 (1994), Paust's criticism of same, in *id.*, 715 (1994); and the detailed analysis by C. Bassiouni, "The United Nations Commission of Experts Established Pursuant to Security Council Resolution 780" (1992), in *id.*, 784 (1994).

[38]Application of the Convention on the Prevention and Punishment of the Crime of Genocide (Croatia v. Serbia), June 27, 2000.

[39]See press release in *Christian Science Monitor* (July 1, 1994), 7; (October 21, 1994), 3; and US News & World Report, November 28, 1994.

[40]See P. J. Magnarella, "The Background and Causes of the Genocide in Rwanda," 3 *Journal of International Criminal Justice* 801 (2005); J. Mukimbiri, "The Seven Stages of the Rwandan Genocide," 3 *JICJ* 837 (2005); L. Melvern, "The Security Council in the Face of Genocide," 3 *JICJ* 847 (2005); E. Møse, "Main Achievements of the ICTR," 3 *JICJ* 920 (2005); P. Akhavan, "The Crime of Genocide in the ICTR Jurisprudence," 3 *JICJ* 989 (2005); G. Prunier, *The Rwanda Crisis* (1997).

The Stockholm Declaration on Genocide Prevention[41] Talk and declarations of intent are cheap. Effective intervention is not. The reluctance to engage in timely fashion remains the Achilles heel of effective prevention. Still, states easily support the principles of prevention. Fifty-five countries—including the United States, United Kingdom, Canada, France, Germany, Japan, and Russia—signed the Stockholm Declaration on Genocide Prevention in January 2004 just as the situation in Darfur came to world attention. The signatory states pledged to cooperate in developing early detection mechanisms, to *support research* into methods of prevention, and to *explore* "seriously and actively, the options presented at the Forum for action against genocidal threats, mass murders, deadly conflicts, ethnic cleansing as well as genocidal ideologies and incitement to genocide." As a declaration, the document has no legal force, even though many human rights advocates hailed it as the most significant step forward since the signing of the Genocide Convention in 1948. The issue, however, remains one of political will, not resources. One should not be totally cynical here, however. Over time, support of those commitments that many originally considered as "mouth honor"—that is, saying the appropriate words in public to indicate commitment without the concomitant political will to carry out the obligations—has come back to haunt governments.

Crimes Against Humanity and Genocide The defendants at Nuremberg, if prosecuted today, would be charged with genocide. As we noted earlier, the Genocide Convention explicitly states that genocide may occur in peacetime as well as in times of conflict, whether international or intrastate (Article 1). Genocide forms a special category within the broader ambit of crimes against humanity. While the requirements for genocide somewhat resemble those establishing "persecution" as a crime against humanity, acts related to genocide require a *specific intent* to produce a *specific result*. Persecution applies to civilian populations in general; genocide requires "an *intent* to destroy, in whole or in part, a national, ethnical, racial or religious group, as such" (Emphasis added).[42] Persecution depends upon objective circumstantial thresholds that do not require a specific intent to *destroy or eliminate* a group; genocide does. Moreover, genocide has no threshold requirements for scale or gravity. The victim in the crime of genocide is the group, not the individual members, but a great difficulty arises because persons accused of genocide must be found guilty on the basis of their own individual acts. However, consider the challenge faced in making that case without some assessment of a collective effort that gives context to the individual acts. The Rome Statute of the ICC addresses this question by adding a contextual requirement. Article 6 of the Elements of Crimes states: "The term 'in the context of' would include the initial acts in an *emerging pattern*" (Emphasis added). This would seem a reasonable addition, but note that only the ICC is bound to apply this requirement.

The crisis in Darfur illustrates the problems of determining a group in a manner that falls within the definitions of the convention. The media and others have used the word *genocide* to describe the ongoing situation. Again, few outside the

---

[41]The Stockholm Declaration on Genocide Prevention (January 28, 2004), www.preventgenocide.org/prevent/conferences/StockholmDeclaration28Jan2004.htm (accessed April 22, 2009).

[42]Article 1, Genocide Convention, note 21.

government of Sudan dispute the evidence of large-scale, indiscriminate killing. The problem with this characterization arises because the victims of the attacks do not make up ethnic, racial, or religious groups distinct from those mounting the attacks. Gerard Prunier accurately describes the Darfur crisis as "The Ambiguous Genocide."[43] The groups share religion and language, although increasingly the divide has been characterized as between "Arabs" who support the government and "Africans" who do not. The UN Commission established to investigate concluded: "The various tribes that have been the object of attacks and killings (chiefly the Fur, Masalit, and Zaghawa tribes) do not appear to make up ethnic groups distinct from the ethnic group to which persons or militias that attack them belong."[44] These comments do not mean that crimes have not been committed, only that the characterization of genocide may not necessarily provide the best *legal* characterization of the situation.

Courts and Cases   Almost all of the cases before the ICTR have involved charges of genocide. In contrast, very few trials before the ICTY and none before the SCSL (Sierra Leone) have done so. In large part, this discrepancy flows from the difference in the statutes, which reflected a difference in legislative concerns. While both ICTR and ICTY statutes include genocide as a listed crime, the SCSL statute does not. When the UN Security Council established the ICTR, the Preamble to the resolution authorizing the tribunal specifically voiced the concern that "genocide and other systematic, widespread and flagrant violations of international humanitarian law had been committed in Rwanda."[45] In the case of the SCSL, the secretary-general explicitly noted that genocide had been excluded from the draft presented to the Security Council because no evidence existed to show that the killings, while widespread and systematic, were directed against any of the protected groups in the convention.[46]

The Slave Trade

The movie *Amistad* (1997),[47] based upon a real incident, illustrated many of the political and legal issues of the time. Great Britain abolished slavery within its realm in 1807 and then ordered its navy to stop and search vessels suspected of being engaged in the slave trade. At the Congress of Vienna (1815), the British government proposed the creation of economic boycotts against any country refusing to

---

[43]G. Prunier, *Darfur: The Ambiguous Genocide*, 3rd ed. (Ithaca, NY: Cornell University Press, 2008); W. A. Schabas, "Darfur and the 'Odious Scourge': The Commission of Inquiry's Findings on Genocide," 18 *Leiden Journal of International Law* 4 (2005), 871–885.

[44]International Commission of Inquiry on Darfur, Report to the Secretary-General, U.N. Doc. S/2005/60 (January 25, 2005), para. 508.

[45]UN SCOR, S/RES/955 (1994), Preamble, para. 3.

[46]Schabas, note 5, at 162.

[47]For an exploration of the issues here, see www.law.umkc.edu/faculty/projects/ftrials/amistad/AMISTD.HTM (accessed April 22, 2009); see also H. Thomas, *The Slave Trade* (1997); and H. Jones, *Mutiny on the Amistad: The Saga of a Slave Revolt and Its Impact on American Abolition, Law, and Diplomacy* (1987).

abolish slavery (Sweden had done away with the institution in 1813, and the Netherlands did so in 1814). The assembled delegations received the suggestion with little enthusiasm. Only the British Navy would have been in a position to enforce such a prohibition. No one at Vienna harbored any desire to strengthen British rule of the oceans. Hence, only a solemn condemnation of "the trade in negroes" was passed, with no enforcement detailed. The British government then concluded a series of bilateral agreements with several countries, providing in each case for reciprocal rights of visit and search by public ships and private vessels flying the flag of the other party. The United States—because of Article I, Section 9, of the Constitution—did not forbid the importation of slaves into its territory until 1808. In that year, Congress did prohibit the further importation of slaves. In 1820, it made the international trade in slaves an act of piracy.[48]

After 1840, a number of multilateral conventions were developed, culminating in the *Convention of St. Germain* (1919). That instrument provided for the complete abolition of slavery and any trade in slaves on land or by sea. Bassiouni lists 28 relevant international instruments (1815–2000) directly related to the problem, and 47 others with provisions that relate in some way to this category.[49] Among those most relevant was the *Convention to Suppress the Slave Trade and Slavery* (Geneva, 1926; amended by a protocol in 1953), entered into force in 1927 (for the United States, in 1929).[50] That instrument reaffirmed much more emphatically, and for many more countries, the contents of the St. Germain agreement. It was updated and enlarged through the *Supplementary Convention on the Abolition of Slavery, the Slave Trade, and Institutions and Practices Similar to Slavery* (Geneva, 1956), in force April 30, 1957 (for the United States, since 1967). The latest is the *Protocol to Prevent, Suppress and Punish Trafficking in Persons, Especially Women and Children*.[51] The protocol adds "trafficking in persons" as an offense to the *United Nations Convention Against Transnational Organized Crime*.[52] While not all trafficking in persons is associated with the slave trade, and some practices do not involve trafficking, the instrument does extend the authority of states to deal with that aspect of slavery. None of the foregoing agreements have realistic enforcement provisions.

Moreover, not unexpectedly, the governments within whose territories indisputable evidence of slavery has been found deny that such an institution exists. They may, in some instances, point to solemn governmental prohibitions of the practice. But slavery in some form does appear to continue in a broad belt of states extending from northwestern Africa to the eastern borders of the Arabian Peninsula, and possibly in isolated pockets beyond into the Asian mainland.[53]

---

[48]A. Sheikh, *International Law and National Behavior* (1974), 18.

[49]C. Bassiouni, "List of Conventions," *Introduction to International Criminal Law* 145 (2003), 242–245.

[50]Lauterpacht, Oppenheim, I: 620.

[51]UN GAOR, Doc. A/Res/55/25 (November 15, 2000). Entered into force December 25, 2003; currently 124 states parties.

[52]UN GAOR, Doc. A/Res/55 (November 15, 2000).

[53]K. Bales, *Disposable People: New Slavery in the Global Economy* (rev. ed. 2004); E. B. Skinner, *A Crime So Monstrous: Face-to-Face with Modern-Day Slavery* (2008); D. Batstone, *Not for Sale* (2008).

Despite all efforts, traditional forms of slavery still persist in some parts of the world. A recent case before the Community Court of the Economic Community of West Africa (ECOWAS) involved the status of a 24-year-old woman, Hadijatou Mani, born into slavery in Niger. The court found Niger in breach of its own laws and international obligations in protecting its citizens from slavery. Nonetheless, *The Economist* has stated that there are still more than 40,000 "inheritance slaves" in Niger alone.[54] The problem here, as with piracy (see the following section), stems from the lack of political will across the board to enforce the prohibitions of existing instruments—and, as in Niger, of states to enforce their own internal laws.

The international agreements require states to pass appropriate domestic legislation guided by the language of the relevant instruments. Article 3 of the protocol on trafficking serves as an example: "Each State Party shall adopt such legislative and other measures as may be necessary to establish as criminal offences the conduct set forth in article 3 of this Protocol, when committed intentionally." In addition, the protocol specifies that participation as an accomplice and organizing or directing others should be included. The Convention Against Transnational Organized Crime states in Article 4:

1. States Parties shall carry out their obligations under this Convention in a manner consistent with the principles of sovereign equality and territorial integrity of States and that of non-intervention in the domestic affairs of other States.
2. Nothing in this Convention entitles a State Party to undertake in the territory of another State the exercise of jurisdiction and performance of functions that are reserved exclusively for the authorities of that other State by its domestic law.

Article 6.2(c) also contains a "double criminality" provision in that any activity included in the domestic legislation of one state must also constitute a criminal offense in the other. States have a duty to supply the Conference of Parties to the Convention their plans for implementation; the Conference of Parties has the authority only to review and suggest, based upon information supplied by the states parties themselves. In addition, the 1982 UN Convention on the Law of the Sea (UNCLOS III) provides in Article 99 that every state shall take effective measures to prevent and punish the transport of slaves in ships authorized to fly the flag of that state and to prevent the unlawful use of its flag for that purpose. Any slave taking refuge on board any ship, whatever its flag, shall ipso facto be free. Article 110(1-b) of the same convention reaffirms the right of all public vessels to stop, visit, and search any merchant vessel on the high seas when there is reasonable ground for suspecting that the ship in question is engaged in the slave trade.

The extent of current practice is highly debatable because no accurate statistics are available. Our assumptions about what constitutes slavery tend to flow from the practices associated with the plantation system in the American South. This scenario does not provide an accurate picture of contemporary practices.

---

[54]"Slavery in West Africa: A Continuing Abomination," *The Economist* (November 1, 2008), 57.

Moreover, the definitions used in the relevant conventions may not cover many contemporary practices. As Bales points out, the problem of precise definition constitutes a problem in two important ways.[55] First, without a definition that specifies types (forms), one can neither estimate the scope of the problem nor develop explicit prohibitions. Second, prosecuting a violation requires a clear statement of what has been forbidden. Needless to say, as with most of the crimes discussed in this section, developing a more comprehensive definition takes one into a political minefield.

Under the auspices of the Commission on Human Rights, the United Nations established a Working Commission on Slavery in 1975. After recognizing the changing nature of the issues, it became the Working Commission on Contemporary Forms of Slavery in 1988.[56] The commission has identified an extensive list of problems focusing mainly on the exploitation of children. Bales notes that the new slavery, with few exceptions, avoids ownership and the problems associated with it (cost of purchase, maintenance, etc.). The key factors are low cost, high profits, and often a short-term relationship. Because of a glut of potential workers, slaves can be added or discarded as circumstances dictate.[57] Bales divides the problem into three basic categories: chattel slavery, debt bondage, and contract slavery. Others would add forced labor and specifically single out sexual slavery, though it may result from the conditions defined within the three basic forms.[58]

In every case, the root is extreme poverty. Yet calls for complete abolition have to face some interesting moral and pragmatic problems. As Bales argues, liberation is a *process,* not a single event. It involves questions of determining how individuals may support themselves, assessing their capacity to adapt to a situation where they must make fundamental decisions about their daily lives, and ensuring that they have the skills to survive in the "free" environment.[59] At the very least, liberation involves raising awareness of the scope of the problem as the foundation for more focused efforts to deal with the problems.

PIRACY

Piracy, an age-old occupation of certain enterprising individuals, has not yet disappeared completely from the world's oceans. The status of pirates has an interesting history. Most of us have romantic notions about piracy. After all, the pirate serves as the ultimate icon of "in your face" resistance to any authority (on par with the "hit man" of organized crime lore). The reality of piracy clashes with the romanticism of piracy just as the reality of what a hit man does clashes with the romanticism associated with the deed in current popular culture. Many texts and other

---

[55]For a description of the problem, see Bales, note 52, at 8–9.

[56]"Fact Sheet 14: Contemporary Forms of Slavery," Office of the High Commissioner for Human Rights (June 1991), www.ohchr.org/Documents/Publications/FactSheet14en.pdf.

[57]Bales, note 52, at 15–16.

[58]Anti-slavery, "What Is Modern Slavery?," www.antislavery.org/english/slavery_today/what_is_modern_slavery.aspx.

[59]Bales, note 52, at 252–258.

sources will quote Cicero to support the idea that pirates have always stood outside the law.[60] Yet, in the ancient Greek world, pirates were both feared and admired. Consider that Ulysses (Odysseus) made his fortune as a "sea raider" or "pirate."[61] Eustathius asserts that raiding and robbing was an art or a craft, not at all "blameworthy or shameful."[62] Entities without navies regularly made alliances with pirates when they needed ships to counter those of a rival in a conflict. Herodotus reports that Psammetichus recruited Ionian and Carian raiders "who had left home in search of rich pickings" to aid him in his rebellion.[63] Herodotus also spends some time discussing the exploits of Polycrates of Samos (c. 532–522 B.C.), whose ships cruised the Aegean seizing Greek and foreigner ships alike, as well as extorting payment for safe passage. We should note that Cicero's quote stands almost alone and forms a minuscule part (indeed, almost an aside) of a moral, not a legal, discourse.[64]

In early modern Europe, *Sir* Frances Drake and *Sir* Henry Morgan received their honors in part because of their successful careers as pirates (against Spanish but not English ships, of course).[65] Nonetheless, in modern practice, by the mid-seventeenth century, states had agreed the pirate had become an outlaw. Note that the prohibition against piracy constitutes one of the few instances prior to the twentieth century concern with human rights, where international law directly proscribed the activities of *private* individuals.

Contemporary international law mandates that each state pass appropriate national legislation to control piracy. In that all states have a duty to suppress piracy (Article 100, UNCLOS III), we can speak of "universal jurisdiction" in this instance. Since the early 1970s, true acts of piracy have occurred with embarrassing

---

[60]Cicero, De Officiis 3.29, G. R. Crane, ed., The Perseus Project, www.perseus.tufts.edu (September 1999). One should not interpret Plutarch's reference to "the common enemies of the world" as any more than hyperbole, much as one should also discount Cicero's single use of communis hostis omnium in a discussion of moral duties, because neither forms any part of the justification for any Roman action against "pirates."

[61]When asked how he acquired his wealth, Odysseus replied:

> I had nine times led warriors and swift-faring ships against foreign folk, and great spoil had ever fallen to my hands. Of this I would choose what pleased my mind, and much I afterwards obtained by lot. Thus my house straightway grew rich, and thereafter I became one feared and honored among the Cretans. (*Odyssey* 14.230)

[62]Eustathius (archbishop of Thessalonica) used the word *technê*—an art, a craft, or a cunning—sometimes meant in a derogatory sense to characterize the function of raids in early Hellenic culture. Cited in W. K. Pritchett, *The Greek State at War*, vol. 5 (1991), 316. See also M. Finley, *The World of Odysseus* (2nd rev. ed. 1978), 48–49, 63–64.

[63]Herodotus, *The Histories*, trans. R. Waterfield (Oxford: Oxford University Press, 1998), 2.152.4.

[64]In 67 B.C., the Senate gave Pompey proconsular power over the Mediterranean and land to the extent of 50 miles from the coast for three years with authority to raise troops and money and to build ships as required. Pompey's rapid progress in eliminating the problem surprised his contemporaries. In 40 days, he cleared the west; in three months, he forced the surrender of the major strongholds in Cilicia itself. The end of the operation demonstrates that the Romans perceived the problem as a political one to be solved by war and treaties, not as an operation against criminals and outlaws. Pompey offered generous treaty terms that required resettlement, but not execution or slavery. Plutarch, Pompey, 28.

[65]See J. E. Thomson, *Mercenaries, Pirates, and Sovereigns: State-Building and Extraterritorial Violence in Early Modern Europe* (1996).

frequency off the western coast of Thailand and in the Gulf of Thailand, the Sulu Sea, the Java Sea, and the Celebes Sea.[66] In the aftermath of the Vietnam War, news reports highlighted pirate attacks on the so-called boat people or refugees in the South China Sea and in the Gulf of Thailand. According to representatives of the UN high commissioner of refugees, pirates killed more than 2,000 boat people and abducted hundreds of young women, who were then sold to brothels in Thailand and elsewhere on the mainland. In particular, South Asian seas remain notorious as an area where pirate ships still prey on merchant vessels that pass through busy choke points in large numbers. The Strait of Malacca between Indonesia, Malaysia, and Singapore—the shortest sea route connecting the Indian and Pacific oceans—is the location of many such raids. Over 50,000 vessels a year pass through the strait.[67]

Over the past few years, many high-profile incidents have occurred off the coast of Somalia.[68] In early November 2005, pirates attacked the cruise ship *Seabourn Spirit* as it sailed in the Indian Ocean off the coast of Somalia. Two ships carrying aid for the UN World Food Program were among the vessels attacked.[69] The largest vessel taken was a 74,000-ton bulk carrier, fully laden with coal.[70] In late September 2008, Somali pirates hijacked the Ukrainian cargo ship *Faina*, with a crew of 20, carrying a cargo that included 33 battle tanks and assorted heavy weaponry.[71] In early November, a gang of Somali pirates captured a Saudi Arabian oil tanker off the coast of Kenya.[72] The vessel carried 2 million barrels—more than a fourth of Saudi Arabia's daily production. During the first two quarters of 2011, the International Maritime Bureau (IMB) listed 243 incidents (154 off the coast of Somalia).[73]

The Problem of Definition   *Piracy* is a word often used indiscriminately to describe various actions. As with many terms, common usage does not necessarily correspond

---

[66]See, e.g., *New York Times* (November 23, 1977), A-6; *Time* (July 31, 1978), 35; *The Washington Post* (September 2, 1980), A-14; Time (November 9, 1981), 56; *Christian Science Monitor* (January 7, 1982), 8; (February 9, 1984), 13; (February 28, 1984), 3; (June 9, 1986), 18; and especially Armstrong in *id.* (April 30, 1985), at 3–4; AP Dispatches of April 24, 1985; December 25, 1985; November 8, 1986; May 5, 1989; August 8, 1989; and April 6, 1990; the detailed account in the Duluth (MN) News Tribune (May 9, 1993), 5, from the Boston Globe; and "Today's Pirates Pose Double Trouble," *Parade Magazine* (April 3, 1994), 16.

[67]"South Asian Pirates Back on the Rampage," . www.voanews.com/english/news/a-13-2005-03-15-voa48-66378827.html.

[68]A. de Nesnera, "Pirates Step Up Attacks on Vessels in Gulf of Aden, Off Somalia Coast," newsVOA.com (November 4, 2008), http://newsvoa.com (accessed April 22, 2009).

[69]"Cruise Ship Repels Somali Pirates," BBC News (November 5, 2006), http://news.bbc.co.uk/2/hi/africa/4409662.stm; and "Cruise Ship Britons Attacked by Pirates," *The Sunday Times* (November 6, 2005), www.timesonline.co.uk/article/0,2087–1859626,00.html (websites accessed April 22, 2009).

[70]de Nesnera, note 67.

[71]J. S. Burnett, "Pirates of the 21st Century: Today's Swashbucklers Wield High-Powered Weapons and Demand Millions in Ransom," *LA Times* (October 4, 2008), A21.

[72]"Pirates Capture Saudi Oil Tanker," BBC News (November 18, 2008).

[73]ICC Commercial Crime Service, "Piracy News & Figures," www.icc-ccs.org/piracy-reporting-centre/piracynewsafigures.

to the legal definition. For example, we speak of "piracy" with regard to the unauthorized copying and sale of videos, tapes, and discs. We do need, however, to focus on the rather narrow specific definition of piracy in international law; moreover, we need also to be aware of an important change in the definition of piracy in contemporary international law. The *traditional* definition of piracy is found in Oppenheim:

> Piracy, in its original and strict meaning, is every unauthorized act of violence committed by a private vessel on the open sea against another vessel with intent to plunder (*animo furandi*).
>
> If a definition is desired which really covers all such acts as are in practice treated as piratical, piracy must be defined as *every unauthorized act of violence against persons or goods committed on the open sea either by a private vessel against another vessel or by the mutinous crew or passengers against their own vessel.*[74] (Emphasis in original)

A shorter definition is found in the classic case of *In re Piracy Jure Gentium,* when the court endorsed as "nearest to accuracy" the definition of "piracy is any armed violence at sea which is not a lawful act of war."[75]

Piracy in the 1982 UNCLOS III Convention   The 1982 UN Convention (UNCLOS III) deals with piracy in Articles 101 through 107 and 110(a). The most important of these is the definition in Article 101:

> Piracy consists of any of the following acts: (a) any illegal act of violence, detention or any act of depredation, *committed for private ends* by the crew or the passengers of a private ship or a private aircraft, and directed: (i) on the high seas, against another ship or aircraft, or against persons or property on board such ship or aircraft; (ii) against a ship, aircraft, persons or property in a place outside the jurisdiction of any State; (b) any act of voluntary participation in the operation of a ship or of an aircraft with knowledge of facts making it a pirate ship or aircraft; (c) any act of inciting or of intentionally facilitating an act described in subparagraph (a) or subparagraph (b) of this article. (Emphasis added)

ARTICLE 105

On the high seas, or in any other place outside the jurisdiction of any State, *every State* may seize a pirate ship or aircraft, or a ship taken by piracy and under the control of pirates, and arrest the persons and seize the property on

---

[74]Lauterpacht, Oppenheim, I: 608. See A. P. Rubin, *Piracy, Paramountcy and Protectorates* (1974) and his *The Law of Piracy* (1988), the most comprehensive study available; Whiteman, IV: 648; and for historical background, J. de Montmorency, "The Barbary States in International Law," *Transactions of the Grotius Society* 87 (1919).

[75]In re Piracy Jure Gentium, Great Britain, Judicial Committee of the Privy Council, 1934 [1934] A.C. 586, in 29 AJIL 140 and 508 (1935). We should point out that certain "authorized" acts of a nature that today would be called piracy (then known as privateering) were abolished and declared illegal by Article 1 of the Declaration of Paris in 1856.

board. The courts of the State which carried out the seizure may decide upon the penalties to be imposed, and may also determine the action to be taken with regard to the ships, aircraft or property, subject to the rights of third parties acting in good faith. (Emphasis added)

ARTICLE 107

A seizure on account of piracy may be carried out only by warships or military aircraft, or other ships or aircraft clearly marked and identifiable as being on government service and authorized to that effect.

UNCLOS III made *two* important changes to the traditional law governing piracy. First, it added the phrase "for private ends" in Article 101. Second, it specifically excluded private individuals from undertaking actions against suspected pirates (Article 107). The phrase "for private ends" has proven troublesome. No official definition exists in either the Geneva instruments or their predecessors. In considering the phrase, perhaps a clue may come if we recall the era that produced the draft treaty. The *travaux préparatoires* ("preparatory work") of a number of meetings indicate that "for private ends" was meant to exclude acts of unrecognized rebels who restricted their attacks to the state from which they sought independence.[76] We address this problem later when discussing the *Santa Maria* and *Achille Lauro* cases.

But UNCLOS III created another problem as well. As defined, the characterization of piracy applies only to acts "on the high seas." The question of what types of jurisdiction states have the exclusive right to exercise within the exclusive economic zone (EEZ), which can extend 200 nautical miles from the coast, remains a subject of debate. The EEZ embraces about *a third* of the marine environment. *All* of the world's important seas and gulfs are composed entirely, or mainly, of waters within 200 miles of some coastal state. While clearly the test of "open" or "high" seas does not apply to the EEZ, questions remain concerning the scope of the jurisdiction a coastal state may exercise. Presumptions here tend to fall on the conservative side—though Bernard Oxman, a distinguished scholar and activist, recently noted: "The International Tribunal for the Law of the Sea has been careful in its decisions to keep the competence of the coastal state in the 24-mile contiguous zone confined to that area, and to resist open-ended assertions of similar competence beyond that limit."[77] Logically, this would mean that except for the specific activities listed in UNCLOS III, the regime of the high seas would apply within the EEZ to the extent that it does not impinge upon the right of the coastal state to enact measures for conservation and management of the living resources (primarily fish) in the zone.[78] Such a definition would permit states to actively pursue and arrest pirates in the EEZ without violating the rights of the coastal state. In practice, other EEZ issues such as fishing rights have taken precedence. Clearly,

---

[76]M. Halberstam, "Terrorism on the High Seas: The Achille Lauro, Piracy and the IMO Convention on Maritime Safety," 82 *AJIL* 269 (1988), 277.

[77]B. H. Oxman, "The Territorial Temptation: A Siren Song at Sea," 100 *AJIL* 837 (2006).

[78]*Ibid.*, 837.

the issue of whether other states may exercise a right of apprehension involves an interesting tension between the desire of states to extend jurisdiction on the basis of security concerns, the touchiness of many of these states concerning their sovereign rights, and the desire to create a regime of effective enforcement.

The problems in enforcement stem largely from the lack of will or capacity on the part of coastal states. Many lack the resources to control areas on land from which the pirates operate, let alone mount effective patrols at sea. Actually, controlling the land area is the most important. Without bases or outlets from which to operate and from which to dispose of goods, exchange monies, or transact other business, pirates could not exist except on a very diminished basis. Somalia stands as a case in point. In March 2008, the UN Security Council finally persuaded the Transitional Federal Government (TFG) in Somalia to accept a resolution that would permit states, with the express prior agreement of the TFG, to enter the country's territorial waters for a period of six months to use "all necessary means" to repress acts of piracy and armed robbery at sea.[79] The product of two years of international mediation, the TFG is the *fourteenth* attempt to create a functioning government in Somalia since the end of Muhammad Siad Barre's rule in 1991. The Secretary General of the UN announced a new UN initiative in February 2011.[80] The difficulty is that at the moment the initiative is little more than a hortatory call for more attention and cooperation.

Some countries have arrested and convicted Somali pirates under their own national legal systems. As of August 2011, there were a total of 1,011 pirates in detention in 20 countries. Kenya is holding 119 pirates and has convicted 50; the Netherlands is holding 29 and convicted 5. The United States detains 28 and has convicted 8. Yemen arrested 120 and convicted all of them. But the largest number of detained pirates remain in Somalia: Puntland has 290 and convicted 240; Somaliland has 94 and convicted 68. Proposals have been made to set up an international court in Somalia, but the cost of such a tribunal (estimated US $24 million) may prove an insurmountable barrier.[81]

Burnett notes that "defining the crime [piracy] has become somewhat of a political football."[82] The International Maritime Organization (IMO) has advocated dividing acts of piracy into the geographical and legal categories of maritime zones: Piracy on the high seas would be defined as "piracy" in accordance with UNCLOS III; piracy in ports or national waters (internal waters and territorial seas) would be defined as "armed robbery against ships." This division has an obvious shortcoming. Piracy and armed robbery are not equivalents. Pirate attacks have become increasingly violent, particularly when the pirates wish to take the ship and cargo. Two incidents, the M/V *Cheung Son* and the *Ten-yu*, sparked international outrage. The pirates systematically murdered the 23-member crew of the *Cheung*

---

[79]UN SCOR, S/RES/1806 (March 20, 2008).

[80]"Somalia: UN Launches New Anti-piracy Plan Calling for Greater Global Naval Support," UN News Centre (February 3, 2011), www.un.org/apps/news/story.asp?NewsID=37457&Cr=somalia &Cr1.

[81]"UN: Somali Pirate Trials Would Cost More Than 24 Million Dollars," M&C News (June 16, 2011).

[82]J. S. Burnett, *Dangerous Waters* (2002), 158.

Son; the crew of the *Ten-yu* was never found. The *Ten-yu* later turned up in an eastern Chinese port bearing a new name, a paint job in appropriate places, and an Indonesian crew. The Chinese government did prosecute those responsible for the massacre aboard the *Cheung Son,* but pleading lack of jurisdiction and evidence, the Chinese returned those suspected in the *Ten-yu* to Indonesia.[83]

Today the *warships* of any state may seize, on the high seas or in any other place outside the territorial waters of another state, a pirate ship or aircraft—or a ship taken in piracy and under the control of pirates—and arrest the persons and seize the property on board. The craft and prisoners are supposed to be taken to the nearest appropriate court of the arresting state. That court will decide upon the penalties to be imposed and on the disposition of the craft and its contents. Although private crafts are banned from hunting down pirates today, should a merchant vessel overpower its attacker, the "arrest" of the pirate craft and crew by the merchant vessel would be lawful. Normally, the merchant vessel would then summon a warship to its assistance and turn the captured craft and crew over to the custody of that warship. Essentially, the capture of pirate craft today may be undertaken only by warships or military aircraft, unless other ships or aircraft on government service have been authorized to undertake such capture.

If an individual is found guilty of piracy, the state of which he is a national or citizen has, under customary international law, no right to defend or represent him in any further proceedings. If, on the other hand, a ship, an aircraft, or individuals on suspicion of piracy have been seized without adequate grounds, the state making the seizure is liable to the state whose nationality is possessed by the craft or individuals in question for any loss or damage caused by the seizure.[84]

Because the words *pirate* and *piracy* are often used indiscriminately (and have been a source of controversy because definitions in municipal statutes may differ), we must urge caution in automatically assuming that a particular incident on the high seas constitutes "piracy." The following incident illustrates many of the ambiguities and complexities associated with characterizing a particular event in terms of legal categories.

THE SANTA MARIA

In January 1961, an armed group seized the Portuguese cruise ship *Santa Maria*[85] off the coast of St. Lucia. The raid resulted in the death of one crewman and the wounding of several others. Led by Captain Henrique Galvao, a retired member of the Portuguese army, the group claimed to be acting in support of General Humberto Delgado and

(continued)

---

[83]*Ibid.,* 225.

[84]See the celebrated case of the Virginius, in Moore, II: 895; and, for comparison, the well-known case of the Marianna Flora, U.S. Supreme Court, 1826, 11 Wheaton 1.

[85]See *New York Times* (January 24–31, 1961); see also *Time* (February 3, 1961), 19, for a detailed account of the events, including a useful map. B. Day, *Perilous Passage* (1962); and H. Zeiger, *The Seizing of the Santa Maria* (1961) also have extended accounts of the incident.

against the dictatorial regime of Portuguese dictator Antonio Salazar. Other than trying to create publicity and international support for Delgado, the questions all related to how seizing the cruise ship fit with the announced goal of fomenting a political insurrection against Salazar. Portuguese authorities labeled the group "pirates," but subsequently, upon communication with Galvao, both British and U.S. authorities resisted this characterization. After 12 days, Galvao negotiated an agreement with U.S. and Brazilian authorities for release of the passengers and crew. Brazil eventually granted members of Galvao's group political asylum.[86]

Note that while the incident does not fit the contemporary definitions of piracy, it also does not meet the "objective" test for political crimes found in *Castioni*.[87] Certainly Brazil was within its rights to award asylum as a political act within its sovereign prerogatives, but the question of how one might characterize Galvao's actions from a legal standpoint formed an interesting and troublesome question.

The *Achille Lauro*

From our previous discussion, in response to a crime that occurs outside its territorial jurisdiction but over which it may assert jurisdiction, a state has three options in attempting to bring the guilty parties to justice: (1) it may rely on an extradition treaty with the asylum state to have the offenders returned for trial; (2) it may persuade the asylum state to try the offenders under its own laws in its own courts; or (3) all else failing, it may try to capture the offenders and abduct them to its own jurisdiction for trial. The seizure of the Italian cruise ship *Achille Lauro* and its sequel illustrated both procedures and problems encountered in practice.[88] It also represents the first time the United States officially employed the third option listed.

On October 7, 1985, five Palestinian hijackers seized control of the Italian cruise ship *Achille Lauro,* en route from Alexandria to Port Said, Egypt. The hijackers demanded the release of 50 prisoners held by Israel and threatened to destroy the vessel if attacked. While under the control of the hijackers, one of the ship's passengers, an American citizen named Leon Klinghoffer, was shot and thrown overboard with his wheelchair. On October 9 the ship, its crew, and all passengers aboard were released when the *Achille Lauro* reached Egypt. The hijackers surrendered to a PLO representative, were taken to Cairo, and the next day were placed aboard a chartered Egyptian airliner with a plan to fly to Tunis. When the airliner had left Egyptian air space, four U.S. Navy fighter-interceptor jets met the plane

[86]C. Fenwick, "'Piracy' in the Caribbean," 55 *AJIL* 426 (1961); B. Forman, "The International Law of Piracy and the Santa Maria Incident," 15 *JAG Journal* (October–November 1961), 143, 166; F. Váli, "The Santa Maria Case," 56 *NW University L. R.* 168 (March–April 1961); T. Franck, "'To Define and Punish Pirates'—The Lessons of the Santa Maria: A Comment," 36 *NYU L. R.* 839 (1961).

[87]Nor do the actions fit any of the legal tests to identify "political crimes" used by other countries. See J. L. Taulbee, "Terrorism, the Right to Rebel and Political Crimes," in *Terrorism and Political Violence*, edited by H. L. Han (1993).

[88]The incident was made into a television movie in 1990, *Voyage of Terror: The* Achille Lauro *Affair.* An opera, *The Death of Klinghoffer*, opened to great controversy in 1991. In 2003, a movie version of the opera appeared.

over international waters; the jets forced the aircraft to land at an Italian NATO airbase in Sicily. There, Italian forces took the hijackers into custody. A dispute quickly developed between Italy and the United States concerning the exercise of criminal jurisdiction over the hijackers and the leader Muhammad Abbas (aka Abu el-Abbas and Muhammad Zaydan).[89]

On October 11, a judge of the U.S. District Court in the District of Columbia had issued an arrest warrant for Abbas, charging him with hostage taking, piracy on the high seas, and conspiracy. The Italian judicial authorities, faced with an American request to arrest Abbas and eventually extradite him (and the hijackers) to the United States, demurred on the grounds that there was insufficient evidence to arrest Abbas. The Italian authorities permitted him to leave for Yugoslavia, where he traveled under the protection of an Iraqi diplomatic passport.

On July 11, 1986, an Italian court in Genoa convicted Abbas (in absentia) and the five perpetrators in custody of the hijacking and of the killing of the American passenger. Abbas and two others were sentenced to life in prison; the others received 15- to 30-year terms in prison.[90] This action meant, moreover, that under a "double jeopardy" provision in the 1963 U.S.–Italy extradition treaty, the six could not be tried again in the United States for the offenses. As an aside, that treaty is a modern instrument devoid of the traditional list of offenses but calling for extradition for any crime punishable under the laws of both parties. A more interesting feature is that the treaty (Article 3) does not limit extraditable offenses to those committed on the territory of the requesting state, but it permits extradition for *extraterritorial crimes,* so long as the offense meets the criterion of double criminality. Article 7 of the treaty provides that extradition could be refused if the authorities of the requested (asylum) state were proceeding against the wanted persons for the same offense for which extradition had been requested.

The seizure of the *Achille Lauro* raised an interesting question. Certainly the actions fell under the traditional definition of piracy, but given the avowed purpose, did they meet the modern definition?[91] If they could be considered pirates, they could be brought to justice by the military authorities of *any* country. Under this interpretation, the American diversion of the airliner could be viewed as legally correct. Clearly, U.S. authorities asserted the position that the actions did constitute piracy.

---

[89]See the extensive collection of documents and treaty texts on the whole affair in 24 *ILM* 1509 (1985) and the heavily documented study by Halberstam, note 75; and M. K. Bohn, *The Achille Lauro Hijacking: Lessons in the Politics and Prejudice of Terrorism* (2004).

[90]The fate of those convicted of the hijacking varied: Bassam al-Asker was granted parole in 1991. He died on February 21, 2004. Ahmad Marrouf al-Assadi disappeared in 1991 while on parole. Youssef al Molqi was sentenced to 30 years; left the Rebibbia prison in Rome on February 16, 1996, on a 12-day furlough; and fled to Spain, where he was recaptured and extradited to Italy. Abu Abbas left the jurisdiction of Italy and was convicted in absentia. In 1996, he made an apology for the hijacking and murder, and then advocated peace talks between Palestine and Israel; the apology was rejected by the U.S. government and Klinghoffer's family, who insisted Abbas be brought to justice. Abbas was captured in Iraq in 2003 by the U.S. military during its 2003 invasion of Iraq. He died in custody on March 8, 2004.

[91]J. Paust, "Extradition of the Achille Lauro Hostage-Takers: Navigating the Hazards," 20 *Vanderbilt J. Transnat'l L.* 235 (1987); "Getting Even," *Newsweek* (October 21, 1985), 20; *Time* (October 21, 1985), 22; G. V. Gooding, "Fighting Terrorism in the Late 1980s: The Interception of the Achille Lauro Hijackers," 2 *Yale J. Int'l L.* 158 (1987); M. Cassese, *Terrorism, Politics and Law: The Achille Lauro Affair* (1989).

The legal adviser of the Department of State[92] secured arrest warrants charging the hijackers with hostage taking, conspiracy, and "piracy on the high seas."

As a direct result of the seizure of the *Achille Lauro,* the IMO developed the 1988 Convention for the Suppression of Unlawful Acts Against the Safety of Maritime Navigation (SUA).[93] The SUA currently has 156 states parties, representing 98.5 percent of the world's registered tonnage. Due to the evolution of new threats and concerns, amendments to the 1988 SUA Convention and its related protocol were adopted by the Diplomatic Conference on the Revision of the SUA Treaties held from October 10 to 14, 2005. The amendments were adopted in the form of protocols to the SUA treaties (the 2005 Protocols).[94]

Among the unlawful acts covered by the SUA Convention in Article 3 are the seizure of ships by force, acts of violence against persons on board ships, and the placing of devices on board a ship that are likely to destroy or damage it. The 2005 Protocol to the SUA Convention adds a new Article 3b, which states that a person commits an offense within the meaning of the convention if that person unlawfully and intentionally tries to "intimidate a population, or to compel a Government or an international organization to do or to abstain from any act." The protocol also addresses questions of transporting substances, including radioactive and other hazardous materials (including biological, chemical, and nuclear [BCN] weapons) intended to be used to cause death, serious injury, or damage. It expressly prohibits the use of any ship in any manner that might cause death, serious injury, or damage. Finally, it provides that none of the offenses in the protocol should be considered a political offense for the purposes of extradition.[95]

---

[92]*New York Times* (December 30, 1985), A-1.

[93]Text at http://cns.miis.edu/inventory/pdfs/aptmaritime.pdf. . The convention entered into force March 1, 1992. See also Halberstam, note 75, at 291–309.

[94]There are nine current SUA treaties. The protocol would amend all of them:

1. Convention for the Suppression of Unlawful Seizure of Aircraft, done at The Hague on December 16, 1970
2. Convention for the Suppression of Unlawful Acts Against the Safety of Civil Aviation, done at Montreal on September 23, 1971
3. Convention on the Prevention and Punishment of Crimes Against Internationally Protected Persons, including Diplomatic Agents, adopted by the General Assembly of the United Nations on December 14, 1973
4. International Convention Against the Taking of Hostages, adopted by the General Assembly of the United Nations on December 17, 1979
5. Convention on the Physical Protection of Nuclear Material, done at Vienna on October 26, 1979
6. Protocol for the Suppression of Unlawful Acts of Violence at Airports Serving International Civil Aviation, supplementary to the Convention for the Suppression of Unlawful Acts Against the Safety of Civil Aviation, done at Montreal on February 24, 1988
7. Protocol for the Suppression of Unlawful Acts Against the Safety of Fixed Platforms Located on the Continental Shelf, done at Rome on March 10, 1988
8. International Convention for the Suppression of Terrorist Bombings, adopted by the General Assembly of the United Nations on December 15, 1997
9. International Convention for the Suppression of the Financing of Terrorism, adopted by the General Assembly of the United Nations on December 9, 1999

[95]This provision offers a major exception in that it contains what now has become a standard "loophole": "if the requested state has substantial ground for believing that, among other things, the request for extradition has been made for the purpose of prosecuting or punishing a person on account of his race, religion, nationality, ethnic origin or political opinion."

PEACETIME HOSTAGE TAKING

The peacetime taking of hostages is not a mere by-product of aircraft or ship hijacking or of other types of terrorist activities: It has been recognized, at least since 1979, as a separate international crime.[96] The intention of hostage takers has been either to enable them to bring pressure to bear on those against whom their activity is aimed or to protect themselves against attack or reprisal. In the latter case, the hostage taking either by itself or coupled with another terrorist act would be the reason for any antiterrorist action.

The most widely publicized modern instance of hostage taking followed the takeover of the U.S. Embassy complex in Teheran, Iran, on November 4, 1979, by a group alleged to consist of students (but subsequently referred to as "militants"). Some 100 hostages were seized initially, including 63 American citizens, mostly members of the embassy staff. While these events were taking place, the UN General Assembly drafted and then approved a convention (December 17, 1979) that for the first time prohibited the taking of hostages in time of peace: the *International Convention Against the Taking of Hostages*.[97] The convention, as with the other eight SUA treaties, contains the "extradite or try" requirement as well as the "political exception" clause (Article 9). Article 12 of the treaty contains another artifact of the era. It states:

> [T]he convention shall not apply to any act of hostage-taking committed in the course of armed conflicts as defined in the Geneva Conventions of 1949 in which people are fighting against *colonial domination and alien occupation and against racist regimes in the exercise of their right of self-determination.* (Emphasis added)

Between 1984 and 1990 in Lebanon, at least 92 foreign citizens were abducted and held as hostages by Middle Eastern terrorists. Eight of the captives died or were executed in captivity, and three others remained missing. The taking of foreign hostages by Iraq in 1990 was the largest in modern history. On August 15, twelve days after the invasion of Kuwait, Iraq announced that it would hold all (male) foreigners from "aggressive nations" until the threat of war against Iraq had ended. Some 600 foreigners in Kuwait and Iraq were transported to key installations, mostly of a military or weapons-manufacturing nature, to serve as deterrence ("human shields") against a potential U.S. attack.[98] On August 18, the UN Security Council demanded unanimously that Iraq allow the immediate departure of the thousands of foreigners trapped there. It also insisted that consular officials

---

[96]See also J. J. Lambert, *Terrorism and Hostages in International Law* (1990).

[97]Text in 18 *ILM* 1456 (1979) and in 74 *AJIL* 277 (1980). The convention went into force after ratification by 22 states; for the United States on January 6, 1985. See also W. D. Verwey, "The International Hostages Convention and National Liberation Movements," 75 *AJIL* 69 (1981), and esp. Lambert, note 95.

[98]BBC, "1990: Outrage at Iraqi IV Hostage Show," August 23, 1990, http://news.bbc.co.uk/onthis-day/hi/dates/stories/august/23/newsid_2512000/2512289.stm (accessed April 22, 2009). For a timeline, see History Commons, "Context of 'December 6, 1990: Hussein Releases American Hostages'," www.historycommons.org/context.jsp?item=a120690hostagesreleased (accessed April 22, 2009).

be permitted to see the hostages (called "guests" by Iraq's leaders) and that nothing be done to jeopardize the safety and health of the hostages.[99] The relevant resolution of the Security Council invoked the mandatory provisions of Chapter VI of the UN Charter. On November 18, Iraq announced that all remaining foreign hostages could leave over a period of time starting at Christmas, unless something marred "the atmosphere of peace." However, on December 6, President Hussein told the Iraq National Assembly that all foreign hostages in both Iraq and Kuwait were to be freed immediately.[100]

Torture

In the era after World War II, government-sanctioned torture of prisoners became "a way of life" in several dozen countries. In 1974, Amnesty International listed 61 states in which barbarous tortures regularly occurred.[101] In response to this ever-spreading phenomenon, the UN-sponsored Congress on Crime Prevention and Treatment of Offenders (Geneva, 1975) drafted a declaration banning torture. Approved by the General Assembly in November 1975 as the Declaration on the Protection of All Persons from Being Subjected to Torture and Other Cruel, Inhuman or Degrading Treatment or Punishment,[102] the instrument—as a mere declaration—imposed no obligations on UN members. The event produced no noticeable immediate policy effects in those countries then suspected of using torture as a matter of policy. In 1984, the UN General Assembly adopted the *Convention Against Torture and Other Cruel, Inhuman or Degrading Treatment or Punishment*.[103] The United States has ratified the convention, but with several reservations.

Definition Unlike the terrorism conventions, the UN Torture Convention does have an explicit definition of torture. Article 1.1 defines torture as

> Any act by which severe pain or suffering, whether physical or mental, is intentionally inflicted on a person for such purposes as obtaining from him or a third person information or a confession, punishing him for an act he or a third person has committed or is suspected of having committed, or intimidating or coercing him or a third person, or for any reason based on discrimination of any kind, when such pain or suffering is inflicted by or at the

---

[99]UN SCOR, S/RES/664 (1990) of August 18, 1990.

[100]BBC, "1990: Iraq Frees British Hostages," December 10, 1990, http://news.bbc.co.uk/onthisday/hi/dates/stories/december/10/newsid_2544000/2544281.stm (accessed April 22, 2009).

[101]See *New York Times* (August 4, 1974), E-5; and Amnesty International, *Report on Torture* (1975), as well as its *Torture in the Eighties* (1984), listing abuses in 98 countries.

[102]G. A. Res. 3452. 30 GAOR, Supp. [No. 34] 91, UN Doc. A/10034–1975. Text in 19 *ILM* 972 (1980); see also UN "Draft Convention Against Torture and Other Cruel, Inhuman or Degrading Treatment or Punishment" [1984], 23 *ILM* 1027 (1984). See also *Time* (August 16, 1976), 31, for an illuminating account of the modern use of torture.

[103]Text in 23 *ILM* 1027 (1984), with changes in 24 *ILM* 535 (1985); see also 85 *AJIL* 335 (1991) on the delayed ratification on the part of the United States, as well as H. Burgers and H. Danelius, eds, The United Nations Convention Against Torture (1988).

instigation of or with the consent or acquiescence of a public official or other person acting in an official capacity. It does not include pain or suffering arising only from, inherent in or incidental to lawful sanctions.

Article 1.2 also provides that states may enact a broader prohibition if they choose to do so. In addition, states have obligations to enact appropriate domestic criminal legislation; to prevent, punish, or extradite individuals accused of such activities in territories under their control; and to provide effective remedies for victims of torture.

From the beginning, the definition proved divisive. Some states argued that the concept of torture should be legally distinct from that of "cruel, inhuman or degrading treatment or punishment." They argued that punishment forms part of all criminal justice regimes and that a distinction needed to be made between justifiable forms and those that would fall outside the standard.[104] Additional questions revolved around standards for terms such as *severe* and *mental*, the extent to which omissions might engage liability, or whether the convention should specifically list "purposes."[105] The title of the convention speaks for itself vis-à-vis the outcome of the first of these controversies. Obviously, the broader characterization carried the day. Parameters of the others were left to courts to work out in practice. Similarly, in the debate over the detainees at Guantánamo Bay, administration lawyers have argued that while the Torture Convention bans both torture and "cruel, inhuman, or degrading treatment," the enabling legislation criminalizes only torture.[106]

On the other hand, the European Human Rights Convention (which also condemned torture) served as a vehicle to produce an important and interesting decision by the European Court of Human Rights. In *Ireland v. United Kingdom* (January 18, 1978),[107] the complaint centered on the (successful) Irish contention of mistreatment of arrested persons by British forces in Northern Ireland. The court relied heavily on the UN Declaration on Torture in interpreting the European Convention of Human Rights. The issues revolved around interrogation methods used by the British in Northern Ireland commonly known as the five techniques: wall-standing, hooding, subjection to noise, deprivation of sleep, and deprivation of food and drink. The court decided:

> Although the five techniques, as applied in combination, undoubtedly amounted to inhuman and degrading treatment, although their object was the

---

[104]A. Boulesbaa, *The UN Convention on Torture and the Prospects for Enforcement* (1999), 6.

[105]For a thorough discussion of the drafting process, see Boulesbaa, note 103, at ch. 1, particularly 16–23.

[106]The argument also involves the reach of the Constitution. The Attorney General of the United States, Alberto Gonzalez, argued that the prohibitions applied only to actions on sovereign U.S. Territory. Guantánamo as leased territory did not qualify as "U.S. territory." D. Luban, "Liberalism, Torture and the Ticking Bomb," 91 *Virginia L. Rev.* 1458 (2005).

[107]Ireland v. United Kingdom. European Court of Human Rights (ECHR), Judgment of 18 January 1978 (No. 91), www.humanrights.is/the-human-rights-project/humanrightscasesandmaterials/cases/regionalcases/europeancourtofhumanrights/nr/2607, para. 167, ext. of judgment in 17 *ILM* 680 (1978). See also the following related materials: *New York Times* (February 9, 1977), 3; R. J. Spjut, "Torture Under the European Convention on Human Rights," 73 *AJIL* 267 (1979); and the earlier but most valuable and heavily documented study by M. O'Boyle, "Torture and Emergency Powers Under the European Convention on Human Rights: Ireland v. The United Kingdom," 71 *AJIL* 674 (1977); and see the interesting case of Pratt & Morgan v. Attorney General for Jamaica [1993], 4 All E.R. 769, Judicial Committee of the Privy Council, November 2, 1993, in 88 *AJIL* 775 (1994).

extraction of confessions, the naming of others and/or information and although they were used systematically, they did not occasion suffering of the particular intensity and cruelty implied by the word torture as so understood.

Not torture perhaps, but still the court concluded "that recourse to the five techniques amounted to a practice of inhuman and degrading treatment."[108]

In 1987, the Council of Europe approved the European Convention for the Prevention of Torture and Inhuman or Degrading Treatment or Punishment.[109] Within less than a year, the 15 countries of the EEC (then the European Economic Community) ratified the treaty. Apart from the constitutional and legislative provisions in these countries, Article 5 of this instrument furnishes a powerful incentive to observe its provisions. The Committee of Ministers elects 15 members of the Special Committee, which is empowered under the treaty to visit any place of detention operated by a public authority (in the ratifying states) and to make recommendations for greater protection of detainees from torture or inhuman and degrading treatment or punishment.

The Organization of American States (OAS) adopted (on December 9, 1985) the Inter-American Convention to Prevent and Punish Torture.[110] Under this instrument, a public servant or employee who orders, instigates, or induces the use of torture—as well as any person who does so at the instigation of his or her superior—is culpable. Acting under the orders of a superior does not exempt an individual from criminal liability under the convention. At this writing, only 16 of the 34 states of the OAS had ratified the convention. Uruguay and Paraguay have joined, but the United States, Canada, and Colombia have not.

The Alien Tort Claims Act (Alien Tort Statute) The U.S. Congress adopted the Alien Tort Claims Act (ATCA) in 1789 as part of the original Judiciary Act. In its original form, the act made no assertion about legal rights; it simply provided that "[t]he district courts shall have original jurisdiction of *any civil action by an alien for a tort* only, committed in violation of the law of nations or a treaty of the United States"[111] (Emphasis added). For almost two centuries, the statute remained unnoticed, supporting jurisdiction in only two cases during that time.[112] Then in 1978, Joel Filartiga, a Paraguayan dissident living in New York City, filed suit against Américo Peña-Irala (the inspector general of police in Asunción) alleging that Peña-Irala had abducted and tortured to death Filartiga's son. Filartiga had attempted to commence

---

[108]*Ireland v. United Kingdom*, para. 168.

[109]Text in 27 *ILM* 1152 (1988); see also 82 *AJIL* 806 (1988).

[110]Text in 25 *ILM* 519 (1986); also at www.oas.org/juridico/english/treaties/a-51.html.

[111]28 U.S.C. § 1350. Since *Filartiga*, proponents of the so-called modern position who seek to use Section 1350 to incorporate international human rights norms have employed the name "Alien Tort Claims Act (ATCA)," referring to the 1789 version as included in the Judiciary Act. Opponents have referred to the Alien Tort Statute (ATS), the modified version, emphasizing that the statute merely grants jurisdiction and does not establish a cause of action—that is, the right to make a claim for damages. In *Sosa v. Alvarez-Machain,* 124 S. Ct. 2739 (2004), the Supreme Court chose to use ATS. See N. Norberg, "The US Supreme Court Affirms the *Filartiga* Paradigm," 3 *J. of Int'l Criminal Justice* (2005).

[112]See Filartiga v. Peña-Irala, 630 F.2d 876, 887 & n.21 (2d Cir. 1980).

a criminal action against Peña-Irala in Paraguay, but had in turn been arrested. He and his daughter (Dolly) then immigrated to the United States. Peña-Irala entered the United States on a visitor's visa in 1978. When Dolly Filartiga learned of his presence, she informed the Immigration and Naturalization Service. INS agents arrested Peña-Irala and a female companion. During his detention, the Filartigas had Peña-Irala served with a civil complaint alleging his participation in the torture and death. They asked for $10 million in compensatory and punitive damages.

Peña-Irala moved to dismiss the complaint on the ground that the courts lacked subject matter jurisdiction. Peña's lawyer also asked for dismissal on the ground of *forum non conveniens,*[113] in particular that Paraguayan law provided adequate remedies for the wrong alleged. The Filartigas submitted affidavits by noted legal scholars, who unanimously agreed that international law absolutely prohibited the use of torture. On May 15, 1979, the U.S. District Court (E.D.N.Y.) dismissed the complaint on jurisdictional grounds. Shortly afterward, Peña and his companion returned to Paraguay.

The plaintiffs appealed, and on June 30, 1980, the Circuit Court of Appeals decided in their favor, reversed the decision of the district court, and remanded the case. The court of appeals relied heavily on a most interesting and heavily documented memorandum, filed at the court's request by the U.S. Department of Justice jointly with the Department of State.[114] The memorandum, asserting that official torture violated international law, centered on the interpretation of the ATCA. The memorandum pointed out that the view that a state's treatment of its own citizens was beyond the purview of international law was once widely held. However, due to changing standards of behavior in the community of nations, an international law of human rights had begun to develop. This did not mean that all such rights could be judicially enforced. But one thing became clear: The assumption that a state had no obligation to respect the human rights of its citizens was incorrect. Through both treaties and the continuing development of customary law, states had accepted as law a duty to observe basic human rights, and that customary law had been upheld in decisions of the ICJ (e.g., *Nuclear Tests* (*Australia v. France*), 1974; and Advisory Opinion on *Legal Consequences of Continued Presence of South Africa in Namibia,* 1970).

The court argued that among the fundamental human rights protected by every relevant multilateral treaty was freedom from torture and that customary international law condemned torture as well. Every state accused of torture has denied the accusation, and none has tried to justify torture. Hence, it could be asserted correctly that official torture was a tort "in violation of the law of nations." In January 1984, the same district court (E.D.N.Y.) awarded the plaintiffs $10 million in compensatory and

---

[113]Forum non conveniens, literally translated, simply means "inconvenient forum." In some instances a court may have appropriate jurisdiction, but the location would result in great inconvenience for the witnesses or parties. If a party makes an adequate showing of inconvenience, the principle of forum non conveniens permits a judge to decline to hear, or perhaps to transfer, a case even though the court is an appropriate court for the case.

[114]See Memorandum filed by the United States, 19 *ILM* 585 (1980); and J. M. Blum and R. G. Steinhardt, "Federal Jurisdiction Over International Human Rights Claims: The Alien Tort Claim Act after Filartiga v. Peña-Irala," 22 *Harvard Int'l L. J.* 53 (Winter 1981).

punitive damages for further proceedings.[115] We should note that the court in *Filartiga* had slightly modified the Act of State Doctrine enunciated in the 1964 *Sabbatino* case (see Chapter 7). The dicta in *Sabbatino* prohibited U.S. courts from examining the actions of foreign governments upon their own soil. In *Filartiga*, the court had held that the Act of State Doctrine does not extend to justify torture under the color of law.

The success of the suit resulted in a number of other cases. Because of increasing international concern with human rights issues, litigants have begun to seek redress more frequently under the ATCA.[116] *Filartiga v. Peña-Irala* held that deliberate torture perpetrated under the color of official authority violates universally accepted norms of international human rights law *and* that such a violation of international law constituted a violation of the domestic law of the United States. In *Kadic v. Karadzic*,[117] the court held that the ATCA reaches to the conduct of private parties provided that their conduct is undertaken under the aegis of state authority or violates a norm of international law that is recognized as governing the conduct of private parties. Passage of the Torture Victim Protection Act (TVPA) in 1991 specifically permitted suit in U.S. courts against individuals who, acting in an official capacity for any foreign nation, committed torture and/or extrajudicial killing.[118]

Needless to say, the expansion in litigation has caused a great deal of controversy. An interesting recent development has been the effort to use the ATCA to sue transnational corporations for violations of international law in countries outside the United States.[119] Human rights advocates argue that the ATCA could be a valuable and potent tool to increase corporate accountability.[120] Critics maintain that judges have intruded into issues and subject matter that interfere with the management of

---

[115]*Filartiga v. Peña-Irala*, 630 F.2d 876 (2d Cir. 1980), June 30, 1980, on remand, 577 F. Supp. 860 (E.D.N.Y. 1984). See B. Stephens, "Translating *Filartiga*: A Comparative and International Law Analysis of Domestic Remedies for International Human Rights Violations," 27 *Yale J. Int'l L.* 1 (2002).

[116]See, e.g., Abebe-Jira v. Negewo, 72 F.3d 844 (11th Cir. 1996) (alleging torture of Ethiopian prisoners); Kadic v. Karadzic, 70 F.3d 232 (2d Cir. 1995) (alleging torture, rape, and other abuses orchestrated by Serbian military leader); In re Estate of Ferdinand Marcos, 25 F.3d 1467 (9th Cir. 1994) (alleging torture and other abuses by former President of Philippines); Tel-Oren v. Libyan Arab Republic, 726 F.2d 774 (D.C. Cir. 1984) (alleging claims against Libya based on an armed attack upon a civilian bus in Israel); and Xuncax v. Gramajo, 886 F. Supp. 162 (D. Mass.1995) (alleging abuses by Guatemalan military forces).

[117]70 F.3d 232 (2d Cir.).

[118]Pub. L. No. 102–256, March 12, 1992, 106 Stat. 73.

[119]Wiwa v. Royal Dutch Petroleum Co., 226 F.3d 88 (2d Cir. Sept. 14, 2000), cert. denied, 2001 U.S. LEXIS 2488 (26 March 2001); Wiwa v. Royal Dutch Petroleum Co., 2002 U.S. Dist. LEXIS 3293 (S.D.N.Y. Dist. Ct. 2002); "Wiwa v. Royal Dutch Petroleum/Wiwa v. Anderson: Description and Status,"www.ccrjustice.org/ourcases/current-cases/wiwa-v.-royal-dutch-petroleum.com. See also Doe v. UNOCAL (and Roe v. UNOCAL). These cases were settled in April 2005. "The US oil company Unocal has agreed to compensate Burmese villagers who sued the firm for complicity in forced labor, rape and murder. The abuses were committed in the mid–1990's by soldiers providing security for Unocal's natural gas pipeline in southern Burma." See "Historic Advance for Universal Human Rights: Unocal to Compensate Burmese Villagers," www.earthrights.org/news/press_unocal_settle.shtml.

[120]See L. Gettler, "Liability Forges a New Morality" (August 3, 2005), www.globalpolicy.org/intljustice/atca/2005/0803morality.htm (accessed April 22, 2009); and D. Weissbrodt and M. Kruger, "Norms on the Responsibilities of Transnational Corporations and Other Business Enterprises with Regard to Human Rights," 97 *AJIL* 901 (2003).

foreign affairs by the executive and the legislative authority of the Congress. The argument is interesting in that almost no information exists concerning legislative intent. Why did Congress find it necessary to pass the Alien Tort Statute of 1789? We have no extant legislative findings to illuminate the problems that lawmakers sought to address. The Supreme Court stepped into this controversy in 2004, when it heard *Sosa v. Alvarez-Machain.*[121]

SOSA V. ALVAREZ-MACHAIN

United States Supreme Court 124 S. Ct. 2739 (2004)

Facts

For the original case, see the discussion in Chapter 9. After his acquittal in the original case, Alvarez-Machain sued the United States for false arrest under the Federal Tort Claims Act (FTCA) and Sosa under the ATCA (ATS) for violation of international law. The district court dismissed the FTCA claim but granted summary judgment with damages ($25,000) on the ATCA (ATS) suit. Both the government and Sosa appealed. Both argued that the ATCA is a simple grant of subject matter jurisdiction that provides no substantive basis on which to create a cause of action. The government also argued that allowing suits for damages could inhibit the war on terrorism. Sitting en banc, the Ninth Circuit Court ruled in favor of Alvarez-Machain. Upon the request of the Bush administration, the Supreme Court granted certiorari. All ATCA (ATS) litigation in progress was suspended pending the decision.

Issues

1. Does the ATCA (ATS) offer a substantive basis on which to create a cause for action?
2. If so, what are the limits?

Decision

Yes. The ATCA (ATS) does constitute a grant of subject matter jurisdiction. The common law provides the substantive cause of action for the relatively limited number of violations thought to carry personal liability under international law.

Reasoning

The court clearly cited the need for judicial caution concerning the application of the statute, but noted that modern international law "is very much concerned with just questions and apt to stimulate calls for vindicating private interests in [these] cases."[122] Equally, "courts have not sought out and defined new and debatable violations of the law of nations." In fact, in the 24 years of litigation since the *Filartiga* decision, Congress has taken no action against ATCA (ATS) litigation. The court noted that norms that have the same definite content and acceptance among civilized nations as the historic examples (piracy, safe conduct, and crimes against ambassadors) define the substantive reach. This effectively limits application to those crimes widely accepted as subject to universal jurisdiction.[123]

---

[121]*Sosa v. Alvarez-Machain*, 124 S. Ct. 2739 (2004).

[122]*Ibid.*, at 2763.

[123]See, for example, International Law Association, *Final Report on the Exercise of Universal Jurisdiction in Respect of Gross Human Rights Offences* (2000), 3.

The Pinochet Case The case of General Augusto Pinochet Ugarte,[124] former president of Chile, illustrates the evolution of human rights law and the controversies surrounding efforts to ensure compliance. It also gives us one of the best contemporary examples of the intricate interplay between international law and politics. The case demonstrates the continuing tension between the fundamental principle of sovereign immunity and the demands for punishment for gross violations of fundamental human rights. Do violations of international human rights law override the traditional protection afforded by the idea of sovereign immunity? Byers concisely summarizes this perspective:[125]

> [T]he proceedings posed, in the most direct terms, a choice between two competing visions of the international legal order. On the one hand, there was the international law of the past whereby a head of state could do what he wished and rely, for the rest of his life, on the fact that he was immune before the courts. On the other hand, there was the international law of the present and future, in which a former head of state was not immune from claims brought by, or in relation to, egregious wrongs perpetrated on innocent victims.

Second, the case raises important questions of procedure and venue associated with universal jurisdiction: Should states undertake unilateral action to rectify perceived violations, or should the task be left to multilateral or international tribunals? Third, the case exemplifies the role that nongovernmental organizations (NGOs) increasingly play in human rights issues. Fourth, it involves a request for extradition that raised some complex questions of double criminality.

Finally, the Pinochet case highlights a controversy that we cannot address within the limits of an introductory text: Should any tribunal, national or international, have authority to seize these issues for consideration if Chilean authorities have settled them domestically as part of an important step in the peaceful transition to democracy? This, of course, again highlights the tension between sovereign rights and the pressures generated by international judgment from human rights advocates, but over an entirely different set of issues. It forms an important philosophical debate among human rights advocates.[126]

---

[124]For a summary discussion of the legal issues, see M. Carrasco, M. del Carmen, and J. Alcaide-Fernandez, "In re Pinochet. Spanish National Court, Criminal Division (Plenary Session) Case 19/97, November 4, 1998; Case 1/98, November 5, 1998." 93 *AJIL* 690 (1999); B. Stern, "In re Pinochet. French Tribunal de Grande Instance (Paris)," 93 *AJIL* 696 (1999); C. Chinkin, "In re Pinochet. United Kingdom House of Lords. Regina v. Bow Street Stipendiary Magistrate Ex Parte Pinochet Ugarte (no. 3) [1999] 2 WLR 827," 93 *AJIL* 703 (1999); L. Reydems, "In re Pinochet. Belgian Tribunal of First Instance of Brussels (Investigating Magistrate), November 8, 1998" 93 *AJIL* 700 (1999); C. Bradley and J. Goldsmith, "Pinochet and International Human Rights Litigation," 97 *Mich. L. Rev.* 2129 (1999); G. Fox, C. Warbrick, and D. McGoldrick, "The First Pinochet Case: Immunity of a Former Head of State," 48 *International Criminal Law Quarterly* 207 (1999); and M. Byers, "The Law and Politics of the Pinochet Case," 10 *Duke J. of Comp. & Int'l L.* 415 (2000).

[125]Byers, note 123, at 421–422.

[126]See G. Bass, *Stay the Hand of Vengeance* (2000), 3–36; and M. Amstutz, *The Healing of Nations: The Promise and Limits of Political Forgiveness* (2005), chs. 1–4, 6.

The government headed by General Pinochet came to power in 1973 through a military coup d'état that removed the elected government headed by Dr. Salvador Allende.[127] The new regime immediately began to pursue a systematic policy of terror and repression aimed at those it perceived as political opponents. The tactics included arbitrary arrests, long detention under appalling conditions, torture, execution, and murder. An estimated 3,000 persons simply disappeared without any explanation.[128] Outside of Chile, agents tracked down and assassinated many dissidents who had fled into exile. As part of the transition back to civilian rule in 1990, Pinochet negotiated an amnesty with the new government that provided constitutional and legal protection for all actions during his years as president. He continued to serve as head of the Chilean armed forces until 1997 and to occupy a seat in the Chilean Senate until 2002. Despite the grant of amnesty, a number of local and transnational NGOs—Amnesty International being the most prominent—had continued to press for the prosecution of Pinochet for crimes against humanity.

In September 1998, General Pinochet went to the United Kingdom for medical treatment.[129] On October 16, British authorities arrested him on a warrant from a British magistrate based in turn upon a request for extradition issued by a Spanish judge alleging that Pinochet had been responsible for the murder of Spanish citizens in Chile between 1973 and 1983. On October 22, 1998, the British court issued a second warrant based upon additional charges being received from Spain alleging that General Pinochet had also been responsible for acts of torture and murder.

Before proceeding, we need to review the genesis of the Spanish request.[130] The allegations in the warrant had to clear many hurdles imposed by Spanish domestic law (Chapter 6) before Spanish authorities issued the request for extradition. The Progressive Union of Prosecutors of Spain filed complaints in 1996 with Spanish Investigating Court #5 against the militaries of both Argentina and Chile in a Spanish investigative court. Article 26(4) of the Judicial Branch Act of 1985 (LOPJ) stated that the Spanish courts have jurisdiction over crimes committed abroad by Spanish or foreign citizens when such crimes can be considered crimes of *genocide* or terrorism, as well as "any other [crime] which according to international treaties or conventions must be prosecuted by Spain." This provision raised the issues of retroactive application (ex post facto) because most of the alleged acts occurred between 1973 and 1983. Subsequently, the complaint focused only upon

---

[127]For details of the coup, see B. Loveman, *Chile: The Legacy of Hispanic Capitalism* (1979, 2001); A. Valenzuela, "Chile," in *Democracy in Developing Countries: Latin America*, edited by L. Diamond, J. Hartlyn, J. Linz, and S. Lipset (1999).

[128]The official report of the Chilean National Commission on Truth and Reconciliation concluded that 2,279 known deaths had occurred during the Pinochet years and that 2,115 of these were executions carried out by agents of the secret police. Comisión Nacional de Verdad y Reconciliación, Report of the Chilean National Commission on Truth and Reconciliation, trans. by P. Berryman (1993); and P. Kornbluh, *The Pinochet File: A Declassified Dossier on Atrocity and Accountability* (2004).

[129]For a timeline of events connected with the case, see www.globalpolicy.org/intljustice/wanted/2001/pino2.htm (accessed April 22, 2009).

[130]For a summary of the domestic issues in Spain, see Carrasco et al., note 123.

those acts alleged to have occurred after passage of the LOPJ. The Investigating Court also adopted a social definition of genocide influenced by the 1971 definition (destruction of a "national ethnic, social or religious group"). The court found that although the individuals the Argentine and Chilean governments sought to exterminate formed a heterogeneous set, they still formed a distinctive group because they were characterized as not fitting into the new order of the state. This potentially could have been a stumbling block if British courts found the definition did not fit any crime under British law or did not fit the treaty definition.

The Spanish court decided in February 1997 that Spain could assert jurisdiction over a limited set of alleged events in Chile (but not Argentina). Upon learning of Pinochet's presence in the United Kingdom, the court—citing the Spanish Criminal Procedure Act and the 1957 European Convention on Extradition—ordered the Spanish government to use diplomatic channels to request that the British government detain Pinochet for extradition to Spain. The Spanish requests accused Pinochet of torture and conspiracy to torture between January 1, 1988, and December 1992; detention of hostages and conspiracy to detain hostages between January 1, 1982, and December 31, 1982; and conspiracy to commit murder between January 1976 and December 1992. After his arrest, Pinochet sought a writ of habeas corpus and moved for review by the Divisional Court of the Queen's Bench Division. The Divisional Court quashed the warrants on two grounds: (1) the original request failed because the offenses did not meet the test of double criminality and (2) as head of state, Pinochet enjoyed immunity from prosecution of the acts he may have committed.

On appeal, the House of Lords, concerned that the Divisional Court did not fully appreciate the significance of the international legal issues involved, invited an amicus curiae brief from Amnesty International.[131] This first panel (Pinochet 1) ruled 3–2 in favor of extradition. The involvement of the NGO became an issue when allegations surfaced that one of the judges and his wife had close ties to Amnesty International and its activities. The appearance of possible bias resulted in authorities constituting a new panel of seven judges to rehear the appeal (Pinochet 2). In the second set of proceedings, the panel solicited briefs from Amnesty International as well as a number of other parties (including the government of Chile). Spanish authorities then presented an extended list of charges in support of extradition (Pinochet 3).[132]

After long deliberation, the panel voted 6–1 for extradition, but on a reduced set of charges: The allegation of torture committed in pursuance of a conspiracy to

---

[131]See Chinkin, note 123; Bradley and Goldsmith, note 123; Fox et al., note 123, and Byers, note 123, for discussions of the issues. In this instance, we have not dealt with the internal issues of British process. For these see Byers, note 123, at 427–428. The Law Lords knew that the executive (the Home Secretary Jack Straw) had already gone on record as not opposing the extradition—that is, as essentially permitting the process to go forward in the courts without intervention.

[132]Regina v. Bow Street Metropolitan Stipendiary Magistrate, ex parte Pinochet Ugarte (No. 3) 1 A.C. 147; International Law Review 119, 135 (2000). As Byers notes, the judge worked within an extremely constrained environment. Precedent matters. To reject the earlier decision would send a message that "justice" depends upon the luck of the draw with respect to appeal. Byers, note 123, at 434.

commit torture and the single act of torture allegedly committed after December 8, 1988, when Pinochet was deemed to have lost immunity. Chile then requested that Britain free Pinochet on humanitarian grounds, citing his deteriorating health. Following independent medical tests carried out on the general, British Home Office Secretary Jack Straw (March 2, 2000) announced the government would release Pinochet because of health reasons. The medical report, leaked to the media, concluded that Pinochet suffered from a deteriorating brain condition and would be unable to understand and answer questions at a trial. On March 2, 2000, Straw ordered the release of Pinochet after 503 days in detention.[133]

Issues   The various panels of courts in Britain had to deal directly with the issues of immunity, universal jurisdiction, and requirement for extradition (double criminality). Based upon their interpretation of the State Immunity Act of 1978, the panel noted that while the immunity of a current head of state is absolute, the immunity of a former head of state persists only with respect to acts performed in the exercise of the functions as head of state *(acta jure imperii)*, whether at home or abroad. The determination of an official act must be placed in the context of international law. The question then becomes whether torture and other international high crimes can be official acts of a head of state. The majority of the Law Lords found that torture can never constitute an official act of state, although murder and conspiracy to commit murder may be protected by sovereign immunity.[134]

As we noted earlier, any claim to exercise of universal jurisdiction has to overcome the presumptive sovereign territorial rights that form the fundamental premise of traditional international law. In the case of the Pinochet 3 panel, the crucial question for the judges became whether British courts could have lawfully exercised jurisdiction over the alleged crimes at the time of their commission (as opposed to the date of the extradition request).[135] This question somewhat conflated the issue of universal jurisdiction and double criminality. In this instance, the Law Lords assumed that universal jurisdiction could issue only from a treaty, not from customary international law.[136] By this reasoning, even though British law may have outlawed torture within the United Kingdom for many years, British courts could claim *extraterritorial* jurisdiction only from the time the United Kingdom had formally ratified the Torture Convention.[137] Further, British courts could then claim extraterritorial jurisdiction only with respect to other states parties to

---

[133]Upon his return to Chile, the recently elected government moved to strip Pinochet of his immunity and instituted charges based upon his involvement with the "Caravan of Death" in 1973. Defense attorneys continue to raise the issue of Pinochet's health as a barrier to prosecution. The Santiago Appeals Court ruled that Pinochet was unfit to stand trial as an accessory to 75 cases of politically motivated kidnapping and murder in 1973. The tribunal suspended the charges indefinitely.

[134]This statement summarizes the conclusion, but ignores the rather convoluted (and muddled) reasoning employed by various members of the panel.

[135]We should note that the divisional court had found that jurisdiction need exist only at the time of the extradition request, not at the time of commission of the alleged offenses. The Pinochet 1 panel did not address the issue of double criminality.

[136]Among others, Byers has characterized this reasoning as severely flawed. See Byers, note 123, at 436.

[137]The treaty entered into force for the United Kingdom on September 29, 1988.

the Torture Convention. In this case, Chile was a state party to the Torture Convention (ironically, ratified in 1984 during Pinochet's tenure in office). This set of circumstances limited the offenses considered to the single instance that occurred after the date of Chilean accession to the convention. For many reasons, we should not be surprised at the approach because, as we noted in Chapter 6, the mode of search and decision for judges in domestic courts generally begins with the familiar ground of statute and treaty.

TERRORISM

The events of September 11, 2001, caught attention worldwide. Nonetheless, before 9/11, few terrorist incidents had occurred within the territory of the United States. In contrast, the governments of the United Kingdom, Germany, Italy, Canada, and Spain had faced the problem of dealing with well-organized terrorist movements that carried out numerous attacks on national territory. Given the diverse nature and extent of the American presence outside the country, overseas targets always formed more attractive options for reasons of pragmatism and effect. Indeed, according to State Department statistics during 1984, a total of 652 terrorist attacks occurred worldwide. About half of these (300) were against American targets. The *Achille Lauro* and TWA incidents captured the attention of the American public for a while, but the concern over terrorism faded as these events receded from collective memory and other even more spectacular events occurred. During the 1990s, the number of attacks worldwide as well as the number against U.S. installations had actually declined over time. Up to 9/11, the most devastating attack on U.S. soil, on the Alfred P. Murrah Federal Building in Oklahoma City, had come from within. Until the rise of groups driven by apocalyptic religious beliefs or ethnic fervor, terrorists tended to choose targets that produced a lot of publicity, not a lot of people dead. The September 11 attacks reflect the evidence of a disturbing trend confirmed by the bombings in Madrid in March 2004 and London in July 2005.

Drawing attention to their cause and manipulating target governments toward some goal formed the essence of what we might term "traditional" strategy. Whether of the political right or the political left, these groups had some appreciation of the idea—no matter how perverse the calculus may seem to us—that violence in service to political aims must be calculated and controlled for effect. A leader of the Irish Republican Army once said, "You just don't bloody well kill people just for the sake of killing them."

Groups motivated primarily by ethnic or religious zeal have no such reservations. While publicity remains an important by-product of their terrorism, they have as much interest in punishment as publicity. The new breed of terrorists see themselves as representatives of a particular constituency. The appeals and the effects of any action are directed to this narrow constituency rather than to society at large. Justification comes from the reactions of approval from this constituency. The terrorists may or may not have given any systematic thought to how a specific act may influence target governments on particular issues. Any political calculus clearly forms a secondary motive to retribution for transgressions, real or imagined. As a result, those who see themselves as acting on behalf of these constituencies see little need for restraint.[138] Concerns are well founded that if a group such as al-Qaeda came into possession of working chemical, bacteriological, or nuclear weapons (weapons of mass destruction, or WMDs), they would not hesitate to use them.[139]

Our focus and concern here are on the international linkages between groups and the international legal means available to help states combat the threats. These linkages are not new. Terrorist groups have collaborated on intelligence, training, finances, and operation many times in the past. The case of the Japanese Red Army group in 1972 (Rengo Sekigun-ha) illustrates the transnational connection among various terrorist groups. The unit, composed of Japanese citizens, was allegedly trained in North Korea, picked up funds in West Germany, had further training in both Syria and Lebanon, acquired its arms and ammunition in Italy, and then attacked the Lod Airport in Israel on behalf of the Popular Front for the Liberation of Palestine.

More recently, in December 2002, Spanish Marines acting upon a request from the United States intercepted a North Korean freighter (the *So San*) in the Arabian Sea.[140] The marines found 15 Scud missiles hidden under the bags of cement listed as the official cargo on the manifest. Subsequently, Yemeni officials declared they had purchased the missiles. Reluctantly, the Spanish and American governments permitted the ship to continue on its way.[141] Nothing in international law prevented North Korea from selling missiles to Yemen.[142] No law permitted seizure of the goods on the high seas (see Chapter 12), no matter what the suspicions about their eventual end use.

---

[138]See B. Hoffman, *Inside Terrorism* (1999), for the best brief introduction to issues and groups; for the list of groups currently considered terrorist by the United States, see U.S. State Department, www. state.gov/s/ct/list/.A separate list also includes states identified as supporting terrorism and www.state. gov/s/ct/c14151.htm.

[139]See C. D. Ferguson and W. C. Potter, *The Four Faces of Nuclear Terrorism* (2004); G. Allison, *Nuclear Terrorism: The Ultimate Preventable Catastrophe* (2004); and for links and short discussions of chemical and biological weapons, see the website of the Federation of American Scientists, www. fas.org/programs/bio/chemweapons/index.html.

[140]T. Shanker, "Threats and Responses: Arms Smuggling; Scud Missiles Found on Ship of North Korea," *New York Times* (December 11, 2002), A1.

[141]D. E. Sanger and T. Shanker, "Threats and Responses: War Materiel; Reluctant U.S. Gives Assent for Missiles to Go to Yemen," *New York Times* (December 12, 2002), A1.

[142]Neither state was bound by the voluntary guidelines of the Missile Technology Control Regime. For an extended analysis of the issues here, see M. Byers, "Policing the High Seas: The Proliferation Security Initiative," 98 *AJIL* 526 (2004).

[143]Note that during the negotiations on the Statute of the International Criminal Court, many states supported adding terrorism to the list of crimes over which the court would have jurisdiction. This proposal was not adopted. However, the statute provides for a review conference to be held seven years after the entry into force of the statute. The proposed review will consider (among other things) an extension of the court's jurisdiction to include terrorism.

Definitions

A major problem connected with legal control of "terrorism" is developing an agreed-on definition[143] of the term and of the acts to be included as part of the definition. Part of the problem is that changes in meaning and usage have evolved to reflect the political climate of different eras.[144] In the present era, people use many euphemisms designed to deflect attention from the central reality of terrorist acts. Terrorist groups look to "convoluted semantic obfuscations" to deflect the pejorative connotation associated with *terrorism*.[145] Observers often resort to the sentiment that one person's criminal is another person's freedom fighter or hero. Within the context of many conflicts, that statement certainly describes the view of participants and supporters. Nonetheless, this view only makes the development of a definition difficult—but not impossible. It may mean that many are reluctant to apply the definition because of political calculations and considerations of the moment, not that it cannot be done. The same problem exists with respect to political asylum (see Chapter 10). In thinking about issues of definition, consider these two incidents:[146]

- In Russia, a prosecutor has recently accused human rights defender Stanislav Dmitrievsky of "inciting hatred" because his human rights advocacy has a "tendency to reflect negatively on the policy of the Russian president and soldiers of the Russian forces."
- President Mugabe of Zimbabwe told his critics in 2001 that they would be treated like terrorists. He threatened journalists who had reported on human rights violations that "we too will not make any difference between terrorists and their friends and supporters."

The United Nations and Terrorism

In fact, over the past ten years, the international community has made some progress in this area by focusing upon specific activities rather than attempting to construct a comprehensive definition.[147] In 1996, the General Assembly established the Ad Hoc Committee on Terrorism charging it with the task of drafting an international convention for the suppression of terrorist bombings—and, subsequently, with drafting an international convention for the suppression of acts of nuclear terrorism—to supplement related existing international instruments.[148] To date, the committee has successfully produced texts resulting in the adoption (and entry into force) of two treaties: the International Convention for

---

[144]Hoffman, note 137, at 28.

[145]*Ibid.*, at 29.

[146]www.un.org/en/sc/ctc/rights.html.

[147]The earliest international effort to create treaty law to combat terrorism was the abortive League of Nations' Convention for the Prevention and Punishment of Terrorism (1937), drafted in consequence of the assassination of King Alexander of Yugoslavia. That instrument, to date, has received only one ratification. Obviously, it never entered into force.

[148]See the 2005 report of the Chair at www.unis.unvienna.org/unis/pressrels/2005/13084.html (accessed April 22, 2009).

the Suppression of Terrorist Bombings (December 15, 1997)[149] and the International Convention for the Suppression of the Financing of Terrorism (December 9, 1999).[150] While the avowed goal of the committee is to develop a comprehensive definition of terrorism, each instrument has rather specific definitions of prohibited activities. For example, Article 2(1) of the Convention for the Suppression of Terrorist Bombings provides the following:

1. Any person commits an offence within the meaning of this Convention if that person unlawfully and intentionally delivers, places, discharges or detonates an explosive or other lethal device in, into or against a place of public use, a State or government facility, a public transportation system or an infrastructure facility:
   a. With the intent to cause death or serious bodily injury; or
   b. With the intent to cause extensive destruction of such a place, facility or system, where such destruction results in or is likely to result in major economic loss.

Sections 2 and 3 deal with accomplices and other contingencies. As with the associated treaties (see the previous discussion of SUA treaties), these treaties contain an extradite-or-try provision as well as a prohibition on granting political asylum (Article 11).[151]

In the wake of the September 11, 2001, attack on the World Trade Center, the UN Security Council condemned global terror as a tactic. The Security Council also recognized a right of self-defense under Article 51 as a response to these attacks.[152] Perhaps the most important initiative came with the adoption of SC Resolution 1373 (September 28, 2001), which established the Counter-Terrorism Committee (CTC). The resolution declares international terrorism a threat to "international peace and security" and imposes a binding obligation on all member states to support efforts to suppress it.[153] The willingness of the Security Council to take action marks a new direction because prior discussion had been almost entirely within the

---

[149]Entered into force on May 2001; U.S. ratified September 1999. Text at www.unodc.org/unodc/en/terrorism_convention_terrorist_bombing.html. As we noted in our discussion in Chapter 16, the Senate ratified with a series of Reservations, Understandings and Conditions. First it opted out of Article 20(1), which would refer disputes over the Convention to the ICJ. Second, it narrowed the definition of Armed Conflict in Article 19(2) to exclude internal disturbances such as riots or other sporadic acts of violence. Third, it equated the phrase "international humanitarian law" with the phrase "law of war." Fourth, it defined coverage to exclude the activities of military forces of the state, those who direct or organize them, and civilians acting in support of, and under the command of, these forces. Fifth, it prohibited extradition to the International Criminal Court. Sixth, it affirmed the supremacy of the U.S. Constitution; www.amicc.org/docs/Terrorbombings98.pdf (accessed April 22, 2009).

[150]Entered into force on April 2002. Text at http://untreaty.un.org/English/Terrorism/Conv12.pdf (accessed April 22, 2009).

[151]See note 91 and accompanying text.

[152]See N. Rostow, "Before and After: The Changed U.N. Response to Terrorism Since September 11th," 35 *Cornell Int'l L.J.* 475 (2002).

[153]For an analysis, see E. Rosand, "Security Council Resolution 1373: The Counter-Terrorism Committee and the Fight Against Terrorism," 97 *AJIL* 333 (2003). See also "UN Action against Terrorism," www.un.org/terrorism/sc.htm (accessed April 22, 2009).

General Assembly. Resolution 1373 references Security Council duties and powers under Chapter VII (threats to the peace, breaches of the peace), but does not seek to define terrorism. Rather, it creates a set of uniform obligations for all members, thus pulling within its reach those states that have not signed or ratified the existing conventions and instruments.

The CTC does not operate as a sanctions committee and has specifically rejected that role. It seeks to work with states to upgrade their legislation and capacities to implement the resolution.[154] It also has engaged in dialogue with other international, regional, and subregional organizations as appropriate mechanisms to discuss and identify appropriate regional policies as well as potentially providing monitoring capacity.[155] The lack of an agreed-on definition still inhibits more vigorous action. In part, the success of the CTC has come because it has avoided dealing with questions of precise definition. In the long term, the CTC cannot avoid dealing with the issues. When or if the committee moves beyond its current role of encouraging states to build technical capability to the issues of implementation and monitoring, the definitional questions will become of central rather than peripheral importance for its work.

Two further actions deserve mention. In 2004, the Security Council unanimously approved Resolution 1566 (October 8, 2004) in response to the deaths of 338 individuals in September 2004 from an attack on a school in Beslan, Russian Federation, and the suicide bombings that destroyed two Russian airliners.[156] After some debate, the final text eliminated all attempts at definition, relying instead on the restatement of actions considered offenses under current international conventions. More important, the Security Council decided to establish a working group, apart from the CTC, to consider and submit recommendations to the council on "practical measures" that could be taken against "individuals, groups or entities involved in or associated with terrorist activities." More recently, Security Council Resolution 1624 (September 14, 2005) targets the *incitement* of terrorist acts. After restating the duties to cooperate in denying safe havens, it condemned all acts of terrorism regardless of their motivation and called on all states to prohibit by law incitement to commit terrorist acts and to take necessary and appropriate measures to prevent such conduct.

A further complicating factor potentially arises from the proviso in Resolution 1624 that "*Stresses* that States must ensure that any measures taken to implement . . . this resolution comply with all of their obligations under international law, in particular international human rights law, refugee law, and humanitarian law." The UN high commissioner for human rights has voiced

---

[154]Rosand, note 152, at 335.

[155]See H.E. Permanent Representative of Denmark to the United Nations Ambassador Ellen Margrethe Løj, "Briefing by the Chairman of the Counter-terrorism Committee to the Security Council" (October 26, 2005), www.sikkerhedsraadet.um.dk/en/menu/DanishStatements/UNSCBriefingByChairmanOfCTC.htm (accessed April 22, 2009).

[156]See W. Hoge, "UN Council Initiates Effort Against Terror," *New York Times* (October 9, 2004), A6.

concern over the possibility that actions to suppress terrorism (however defined) may be used as a justification for abridging or infringing upon human rights. The CTC has resisted the effort to make this a concern, citing the limitations of its mandate, but publicity from interested advocates will certainly keep the questions in the spotlight.

INTER-AMERICAN CONVENTION AGAINST TERRORISM

On October 7, 2005, the U.S. Senate voted its approval of the Inter-American Convention Against Terrorism.[157] On November 2, 2005, President Bush signed the instrument of ratification. The United States became a state party 30 days after the deposit of the instrument of ratification with the Organization of American States (November 15, 2005). The convention does not contain a definition of terrorism. As with other recent instruments, it draws upon offenses defined in the existing SUA treaties[158] and requires that states take appropriate domestic action in strengthening their laws relating to financial transactions. States also pledge cooperation and mutual assistance in dealing with the offenses defined. Articles 11–13 preclude a state granting political asylum or refugee status to a person charged with any of the listed offenses.

CONCLUSION

Virtually all commentators on the phenomenon of international terrorism have agreed that no real progress in combating hijacking, hostage taking, and other terrorist activities can be expected until three basic concepts have been incorporated in global conventions and are then implemented without exception: (1) the states of the world must agree not to permit their territories to be used as places of asylum by terrorists, regardless of their nationality; (2) extradition of individuals charged with terrorist offenses must be granted on submission of evidence of presumed guilt; and (3) if no extradition is granted, the receiving (or host) state must vigorously prosecute the alleged terrorists. These provisions depend upon a clearly defined characterization of terrorists as criminals. While some progress has occurred, the international community still has far to go in turning these conditions into effective principles.

---

[157]Text at www.oas.org/juridico/english/treaties/a–66.htm (accessed April 22, 2009); the convention was adopted by the OAS General Assembly June 3, 2002 (AG/Resolution 1840 [XXXII–0/02]). The convention entered into force internationally on July 10, 2003, after six countries became party. As of November 30, 2005, there were 34 signatories and 13 parties to the convention (Antigua and Barbuda, Brazil, Canada, Chile, Dominica, El Salvador, Honduras, Mexico, Nicaragua, Panama, Paraguay, Peru, and Venezuela).

[158]See note 94 and accompanying text.

SUGGESTED READINGS

Raisch and Partin, "International Criminal Law: A Selective Resource Guide," http://www.llrx.com/features/int_crim.htm.

GENERAL

Bassiouni, *An Introduction to International Criminal Law* (2002).

Bassiouni and Manikas, *The Law of the International Criminal Tribunal for the Former Yugoslavia* (1996).

Boister, "Transnational Criminal Law," 14 *European Journal of International Law* 953 (2003).

Cassesse, *International Criminal Law* (2005).

Cryer, *Prosecuting International Crimes: Selectivity and the International Criminal Law Regime* (2005).

Cryer, Friman, Robinson, and Wilmshurst, *An Introduction to International Criminal Law* (2007).

Drumbl, *Atrocity, Punishment and International Law* (2007).

Kissinger, "The Pitfalls of Universal Jurisdiction" 80 *Foreign Affairs* 86 (2001).

Macedo, *Universal Jurisdiction: National Courts and the Prosecution of Serious Crimes Under International Law* (2004).

Roth, "The Case for Universal Jurisdiction," 80 *Foreign Affairs* 150 (2001).

Zahar and Sluiter, *International Criminal Law: A Critical Introduction* (2008).

SLAVERY

Bales, *Disposable People: New Slavery in the Global Economy* (rev. ed., 2004).

Jones, *Mutiny on the Amistad: The Saga of a Slave Revolt and Its Impact on American Abolition, Law, and Diplomacy* (1987).

Kapstein, "The New Global Slave Trade," 85 *Foreign Affairs* 103 (2006).

Thomas, *The Slave Trade* (1997).

PIRACY

Bohn, *The Achille Lauro Hijacking: Lessons in the Politics and Prejudice of Terrorism* (2004).

Cassese, *Terrorism, Politics and the Law: The Achille Lauro Affair* (1989).

Halberstam, "Terrorism on the High Seas: The *Achille Lauro,* Piracy and the IMO Convention on Maritime Safety," 82 *AJIL* 269 (1988).

Johnson and Valencia, eds, *Piracy in Southeast Asia: Status, Issues and Responses* (2005).

Rubin, *The Law of Piracy,* 2nd ed. (1998).

HOSTAGE TAKING

Griffiths, *Hostage: The History, Facts, and Reasoning Behind Political Hostage Taking* (2003).

Lambert, *Terrorism and Hostages in International Law* (1990).

Poland and McCrystle, *Practical, Tactical and Legal Perspectives of Terrorism and Hostage-Taking* (2000).

CRIMES AGAINST HUMANITY

The New England School of Law Library, www.nesl.edu/research/warcrim.cfm.

Bassiouni, *Crimes Against Humanity in International Criminal Law* (1999).

May, *Crimes Against Humanity: A Normative Account* (2004).

Robertson, *Crimes Against Humanity: The Struggle for Global Justice,* 3rd ed. (2006).

GENOCIDE

Chalk and Jonassohn, *The History and Sociology of Genocide: Analyses and Case Studies* (1990).

Dadrian, "Genocide As a Problem of National and International Law: The World War I Armenian Case and Its Contemporary Legal Ramifications," 14 *Yale Journal of International Law* 221 (1989).

Kiernan, *Blood and Soil: A World History of Genocide and Extermination from Sparta to Darfur* (2007).

LeBlanc, *The United States and the Genocide Convention* (1991).

Magnarella, "The Background and Causes of the Genocide in Rwanda," 3 *Journal of International Criminal Justice* 801 (2005).

Power, *A Problem from Hell: America and the Age of Genocide* (2002).

TORTURE

Jessberger, "Bad Torture—Good Torture? What International Criminal Lawyers May Learn from the Recent Trial of Police Officers in Germany," 3 *Journal of International Criminal Justice* 1059 (2005).

Luban, "Liberalism, Torture and the Ticking Bomb," 91 *Virginia Law Review* 1458 (2005).

O'Boyle, "Torture and Emergency Powers Under the European Convention on Human Rights: *Ireland v. The United Kingdom*," 71 AJIL 674 (1977).

ALIEN TORT CLAIMS STATUTE

Abebe-Jira v. Negewo, 72 F.3d 844 (11th Cir. 1996) (alleging torture of Ethiopian prisoners).

In re Estate of Ferdinand Marcos, 25 F.3d 1467 (9th Cir. 1994) (alleging torture and other abuses by former President of Philippines).

Kadic v. Karadzic, 70 F.3d 232 (2d Cir. 1995) (alleging torture, rape, and other abuses orchestrated by Serbian military leader).

Norberg, "The US Supreme Court Affirms the Filartiga Paradigm," 3 *J. of Int'l Criminal Justice* (2005).

Stephens, "Translating Filartiga: A Comparative and International Law Analysis of Domestic Remedies for International Human Rights Violations," 27 *Yale Journal of International Law* 1 (2002).

Tel-Oren v. Libyan Arab Republic, 726 F.2d 774 (D.C. Cir.1984) (alleging claims against Libya based on an armed attack upon a civilian bus in Israel).

Xuncax v. Gramajo, 886 F. Supp. 162 (D. Mass. 1995) (alleging abuses by Guatemalan military forces).

PINOCHET

Bradley and Goldsmith, "Pinochet and International Human Rights Litigation," 97 *Mich. L. Rev.* 2129 (1999).

Byers, "The Law and Politics of the Pinochet Case," 10 *Duke J. of Comp. & Int'l L.* 415 (2000).

Kornbluh, *The Pinochet File: A Declassified Dossier on Atrocity and Accountability* (2004).

TERRORISM

Bianchi, ed., *Enforcing International Law Norms Against Terrorism* (2004).

Ferguson and Potter, *The Four Faces of Nuclear Terrorism* (2004).

Rosand, "Security Council Resolution 1373: The Counter-terrorism Committee and the Fight Against Terrorism," 97 AJIL 333 (2003).

Rostow, "Before and After: The Changed U.N. Response to Terrorism Since September 11th," 35 *Cornell Int'l L. J.* 475 (2002).

Saul, *Defining Terrorism in International Law* (2006).

Process and Issues

Adjudication

Dealing with disputes, either to prevent them altogether or to settle them, constitutes one of the major purposes of law at any level. Dispute settlement at the international level has many different facets. Dispute settlement at the international level has many different facets. Chapter 5 dealt with methods other than adjudication. Chapter 6 addressed how national courts deal with disputes that fall within their jurisdiction. This chapter focuses on adjudication by *international* arbitral tribunals and *international* courts. International adjudication as a method involves the use of an *impartial third-party* tribunal that will result in a *binding decision* based upon law. For reasons discussed later in this chapter, formal legal proceedings form a minor method of dispute resolution in international relations. While negotiation, mediation, and conciliation as methods do not necessarily produce legally binding decisions (unless the agreement results in a treaty), and the outcomes do not necessarily reflect principles of law, states may still prefer them. This chapter focuses on the role(s), advantages, and disadvantages of adjudication in relationship to other methods of dispute resolution.[1]

Expectations about what an effective "rule of law" at the international level would require inevitably reflect the vision of the perceived central role of courts in the domestic legal order where adjudication by permanent courts with standard rules of procedure forms the ideal method of dispute settlement. Needless to say, if this is the true measure, given the relatively limited scope accorded to adjudication in contemporary practice, the current system falls far short of the ideal. Simply put, states have seldom submitted disputes involving important interests to arbitral tribunals or courts. Yet one needs to remember the discussion in Chapter 11 about reparations and redress—and that adjudication, as mentioned, forms but

---

[1]See R. Bilder, "Adjudication: International Arbitral Tribunals and Courts," in *Peacemaking in International Conflict: Methods and Techniques,* edited by I. W. Zartman and J. L. Rasmussen (1997), 155. For a concise discussion, see also B. Spangler, "Adjudication," in *Beyond Intractability*, edited by G. Burgess and H. Burgess, www.beyondintractability.org/essay/adjudication/ (accessed April 22, 2009); and J. G. Merrills, *International Dispute Settlement,* 3rd ed. (1998).

one method of dispute settlement, even in domestic societies. Remember as well that techniques of dispute resolution are not mutually exclusive exercises. For a starter, negotiation will almost always play a role in any dispute resolution effort no matter what method(s) states eventually choose for final resolution.[2] To build on the earlier discussion in Chapter 11, states will weigh the advantages and disadvantages of various techniques against the advantages and disadvantages of other means available.

Indeed, at least in the United States, mediation and other forms of alternative dispute resolution have become the preferred techniques for many varieties of disputes involving civil law.[3] Note as well the following advice from the U.S. Department of Commerce about settling commercial disputes in China: "Simple negotiation with your partner is usually the best method of dispute resolution. It is the least expensive and it can preserve the working relationship of the parties involved"[4] (Emphasis added). Add to this the following advice from another source: "The best approach in dealing with individual disputes varies from case to case."[5]

ADVANTAGES AND DISADVANTAGES OF ADJUDICATION

Earlier in Chapter 1, we noted that "law" may not provide an adequate solution to every dispute. Here, even if law has relevance, adjudication may not be the best method of dealing with the issues. As with every technique of dispute resolution, adjudication has advantages and disadvantages. State decision makers will weigh these factors in electing a course of action.

States resort to adjudication because they see it as impartial, impersonal, principled, and authoritative.[6] As a strategy, it may buy time and defuse the situation. It can help develop international law. At least in theory, the ideas of impartiality and neutral principle underlie all adjudication by third parties. Arbitrators or judges presumably apply the rules of relevant law or other agreed-on principles rather than relying upon personal preference or political factors associated with the dispute. Adjudication also embodies the idea of an impersonal process in that neither

---

[2]Bilder, note 1, at 157. Bilder also suggests that the unique characteristics of international politics—a relatively small group in continuous interaction—may require institutions and techniques very different from those designed to deal with domestic problems, *id*.

[3]See "ADR," Cornell Law School, www.law.cornell.edu/wex/index.php/ADR (accessed April 22, 2009). Note that at the domestic level, most lists of *alternative dispute resolution* (ADR) methods will include *arbitration* as distinguished from *litigation* in any list of alternative methods. The reason flows from the broad definition given ADR on this website: "any means of settling a dispute outside the courtroom." Note also the following advice from the International Trade Forum: "Competition means conflict, but the courts are rarely the best way to settle disputes in business. Trials can be expensive, lengthy and sometimes embarrassingly public." "Dispute Resolution: Bridge Building in a New World," *International Trade Forum* (April 2004), www.intracen.org/Dispute-Resolution-Bridge-building-in-a-New-World/.

[4]"Dispute Avoidance and Dispute Resolution in China," *FindLaw*, http://library.findlaw.com/2002/Nov/1/132533.html (accessed April 22, 2009).

[5]"Dispute Avoidance and Dispute Resolution," www.mac.doc.gov/china/dispute.pdf.

party presumably can influence the decision except through persuasive argument based upon facts and appropriate substantive law and principles. The process of having to structure opposing claims within a legal framework may clarify the facts and issues in dispute. Decisions of impartial tribunals convey strong claims for legitimacy to other states. Each use of legal principles to assert a claim, however cynical or self-interested it may be, still bolsters legal development in reinforcing the authority of the principles and the process.

To understand why judicial settlement may not be appropriate to all cases, one must address several problems: expense, lack of control, possible delay, limitation on relevant issues, limitation on possible solutions, the winner–loser context, and possible effects on the parties. These issues are interrelated. Litigation is expensive and time consuming. Moreover, to a great extent, control moves from the parties to the lawyers and judges actively involved in the case (the experts). The costs of preparing and hearing the case flow from the necessity of framing all the issues in terms of the law perceived to be relevant law *even if doing so does not adequately capture the underlying issues in the case or address longer-term considerations* (see the discussion of litigation over environmental issues in Chapter 19). Issues in litigation often become couched in terms of money when the real questions involve trust, respect, or other emotional issues.[7] Having to frame any solution in terms of relevant law *limits* the possibility of the parties finding common ground for solution other than that dictated by application of the law. The winner–loser framework adds to the possible psychological costs and impact over time. Add to this the nature of the adversarial process, which requires each side to present its case in strongest possible terms while critiquing the case and conduct of its opponent. One need look no further than the process and outcomes of high-profile divorce cases (or perhaps divorce litigation, high profile or not) to understand the potential problems. Adjudication may also limit solutions in that it tends to look for principles of existing law rather than for principles to develop the law if needed. States may in theory enable tribunals to decide on the basis of "reasonable and fair" (ex aequo et bono) but have seldom done so.[8] Finally, some have argued that a principal focus on adjudication reflects a Western bias toward adversarial methods and ignores the long practice of many non-Western societies for nonadversarial methods that emphasize mediation and accommodation.[9]

On balance, the argument cannot be resolved in the abstract. As Bilder points out, even if relatively few international disputes are resolved through judicial methods, this does not mean that adjudication can be relegated to a shadowy corner of the dispute resolution landscape. A number of situations lend themselves to resolution through adjudication. Among these are disputes that do not involve a significant interest, but for which governments may feel unable to make

---

[6]Based upon Bilder, note 1, at 174–175.

[7]Spangler, note 1.

[8]The ICJ has used a standard of "equitable result" in maritime boundary cases. See *Libya v. Tunisia*, Chapter 13.

[9]See, for example, the discussion in A. Alibekova and R. Carrow, eds, *International Arbitration and Mediation from the Professional's Perspective* (2007), 66–67.

concessions in direct negotiations because they do involve highly charged emotional issues such as borders or maritime boundaries, and disputes that involve difficult factual or technical questions.[10] A quick perusal of International Court of Justice (ICJ) cases quickly establishes that territorial and maritime questions have formed a great part of the workload of the court. Since 2000, a total of 6 out of 12 contentious cases heard by the court have involved territorial or maritime questions.

INTERNATIONAL ADJUDICATION

Generally, as we have noted, adjudication has played a relatively minor role in dispute settlement at the international level. The jurisdiction of all international courts relies upon *formal state consent*. Unless a treaty or other agreement—to which a state has assented (Chapter 4)—designates a specific court or arbitration as the process for dispute settlement, no rule of *customary law* mandates a compulsory rule for dispute settlement. Certainly, no rule of customary law mandates that states submit disputes to judicial determination. An international court or arbitration panel may render a binding decision *if, and only if,* the states involved have given their consent in some form to the proceedings.

Many treaties specify the ICJ as the method of resolving disputes over disputes (or interpretations), but obviously treaties require consent (Chapter 4). Some treaties, like the ones setting up the World Trade Organization or the regime of UNCLOS III (see M/V *Saiga,* Chapter 12), have their own dispute resolution mechanisms that may employ a form of adjudication. Others (see Chapter 18) require states to negotiate in good faith. The following sections focus on the two principal means of international adjudication: arbitration and settlement by an international court.

ARBITRATION

The procedure known as arbitration is one of the oldest methods used by Western countries to settle international disputes.[11] The Greek city-states not only evolved comprehensive procedural details for arbitration, used in the peaceful solution of many disagreements, but also concluded many treaties under which the parties agreed in advance to submit either all or specified categories of disputes to arbitration. In the medieval period, there was occasional recourse to the procedure, usually in the form of a papal arbitration. Almost every one of the classical writers on international law, from Vitoria and Suárez through Grotius to Vattel, endorsed arbitration. Some of these writers, notably Grotius, even advocated arbitration of disputes by assemblies or conferences of the Christian powers.

---

[10]Bilder, note 1, at 179.

[11]Consult the standard historical treatment of the subject in J. H. Ralston, *International Arbitration from Athens to Locarno* (1929), and see A. M. Stuyt, *Survey of International Arbitration, 1794–1989,* 3rd. ed. (1990), for a contemporary analysis.

Although arbitration began to be used increasingly as a civil procedure, particularly between merchants, it did not play a prominent part in modern international relations until 1794, when Jay's Treaty provided for the use of arbitration to settle disputes between the United States and Great Britain. One single arbitration under the provisions of the treaty resulted in more than 500 awards to private claimants. American interest in arbitration has continued ever since that agreement. Thus, the New York Society of Peace (founded in 1815) and the Massachusetts Peace Society carried on consistent propaganda campaigns to promote arbitration of disputes as a permanent aspect of American foreign policy. Their efforts bore some fruit. Article 21 of the Guadalupe-Hidalgo Treaty with Mexico (1848) provided for the arbitration of all future disputes before either country had recourse to war. Another Anglo-American arbitral tribunal, operating under the provisions of the Treaty of London in 1853, settled more than 100 claims. An American–Mexican commission established under a treaty concluded in 1868 handled more than 2,000 claims, dismissing about 1,700 of these.

The single event that suddenly called attention to the usefulness of the procedure was the successful Alabama Claims arbitration (Chapter 5) under the Washington Treaty of 1871 (Geneva, 1872). The United States received an award of $15.5 million in compensation for the direct losses caused by Confederate cruisers illegally supplied to the South by British interests (see the discussion in Chapter 5). As early as 1875, the private Institute of International Law drafted a body of arbitral procedure rules. At the First International Conference of American States (Washington, DC, 1889–1890), a comprehensive Plan of Arbitration was proposed but not ratified.

The acceptance of arbitration on a large scale came at the Hague Peace Conference of 1899. The Convention for the Pacific Settlement of International Disputes (revised in 1907) established the Permanent Court of Arbitration (PCA). Actually, this title is a misnomer because the treaty did not create a tribunal in the orthodox sense of the term. Instead, the "court" consisted of a panel, a list of four names of individuals submitted to a central office in The Hague by each signatory to the convention. When states agreed to refer a dispute to the court, each party selected two arbitrators from the panel. Only one of the two could be a national of the state in question. The four arbitrators then selected an umpire. Thus, while a permanent panel of arbitration existed, the court itself had to be constituted anew for each case. To make the matter more complex, bringing the Hague machinery into operation required a network of bipartite arbitration treaties to supplement the 1899 Convention (specific element of consent). Despite the relative simplicity and inexpensive nature of the Hague procedure, the court handled only a very small number of disputes (14 awards between 1902 and 1914). The organization remains in existence today.[12] Its caseload is relatively light. Currently, it has nine pending cases.

---

[12]www.pca-cpa.org/showpage.asp?pag_id=363 (accessed April 22, 2009).

Although the nations of the world have bypassed the institution of the Hague Court, they nevertheless used arbitration to an increasing extent during the twentieth century. Hundreds of bipartite compulsory arbitration treaties have come into existence. The largest accumulation of claims (over 70,000) were handled by the more than 40 mixed arbitral tribunals established after World War I to cover claims by nationals of the Allied and Associated Powers against the three Central Powers. In contemporary practice, arbitration has become the method of choice for settling many international business disputes.[13]

Arbitration: Form and Procedure

In modern form, arbitration[14] differs from formal settlements by a permanent court in that panels are ad hoc, constituted for each specific dispute through an agreement usually called a *compromis*. In arbitration, states have a choice in designating panel members; they can specify the issues deemed relevant (scope of jurisdiction), the procedures, and even the body of law or other rules applicable. Once the panel finishes its work, it is disbanded. On occasion, panels designated as "claims commissions" have been established to deal with a large number of disputes in the same issue area. Chapter 11 discussed the work of both the Mexican–American Mixed Claims Commission and the Iran–U.S. Claims Tribunal.

A typical panel would consist of three individuals—one chosen by each party and a neutral individual. The procedure for selecting the neutral individual will be specified in the *compromis*. Sometimes the two arbitrators from the parties will mutually select the third; sometimes the parties will mutually agree on a neutral third party (secretary-general of the United Nations or president of the ICJ) who will then select an individual. Other than efficiency or pragmatism, no rule of international law mandates a number. New Zealand and France chose a sole arbitrator, the UN secretary-general, for the *Rainbow Warrior* case. William Howard Taft served as the sole arbitrator in the Tinoco case. The Alabama Claims commission had five members. The Iran–U.S. Tribunal had nine members. The *compromis* for the Iran–U.S. Tribunal designated the Arbitration Rules of the UN Commission on International Trade Law as the procedural model to follow.[15]

The following case involves several different techniques of settlement—good offices, negotiation, and finally arbitration. In this case, the issue does not turn so much on legal principles as it does on determining the facts.[16]

---

[13]See the website of the International Chamber of Commerce, www.iccwbo.org/id93/index.html?cookies=no, and the International Court of Arbitration, www.iccwbo.org/court/.

[14]See Merrills, note 1, at 88ff. The following text does not discuss the rather extensive private law literature.

[15]www.jus.uio.no/lm/un.arbitration.rules.1976/ (accessed April 22, 2009).

[16]See also the Taba Arbitration (1988), which involved the border between Egypt and Israel. 27 *International Legal Materials* 1421, 1427 (1989); this involved a five-member commission.

THE RANN OF KUTCH ARBITRATION

India v. Pakistan (1968)

Facts

The Rann of Kutch[17] comprises about 5.19 million acres (21,000 km^2) lying largely in the state of Gujarat in western India. Some portion of the area extends into eastern Pakistan. Although the area can flood during monsoon season, it is largely treeless and barren, consisting of salt marshes and mudflats. The two states had disputed possession since partition, with open hostilities breaking out in 1965. In 1968, the two states agreed to arbitration by an international panel under the auspices of the United Nations.

India claimed title to the whole area as the legitimate successor state to the former princely state of Kutch. Pakistan, as the successor state to British rule in Sindh province, advanced the argument that the Rann was an inland sea in which the median line should be the border and that Sindh had traditionally exercised control over the northern half of the Rann. When conflict over the area threatened to escalate in 1965, British Prime Minister Harold Wilson stepped in with a series of proposals to defuse the crisis. The two countries agreed to first try bilateral negotiations at the ministerial level. If this effort failed to produce agreement in two months, the two governments agreed to settlement by an international tribunal. The negotiations did not result in a mutually agreed settlement.

In consequence, in 1967 a three-member panel was constituted with Geneva as the place of meeting. India nominated a diplomat from Yugoslavia (Ales Bebler); Pakistan nominated an Iranian diplomat (Nasrollah Entezam). The secretary-general of the United Nations nominated a Swedish judge (Gunnar Lagergren) as the chair.

Issues

Where should the border between India and Pakistan be drawn?

Decision

In February 1968, the tribunal decided that India would get 90 percent of the Rann; Pakistan would get 10 percent.

Reasoning and Evidence

In coming to its decision, the panel of commissioners had to study documents of the former British administration as well as the ex-princely states of Kutch and Sindh, going back nearly 200 years. Both India and Pakistan had produced evidence in the form of maps and other documents confirming exercises of jurisdiction that supported their claims. Pakistan produced considerable evidence to show that, during the British period, Sindh's jurisdiction also extended to the northern half of the Rann. Criminal cases in this region had always been handled by the police of Sindh on the premise that the northern half of the Rann belonged to Sindh Province. Pakistan also produced documented evidence that in 1885, the senior British officer in Nagarparkar, the Sindh district adjacent to the Rann of Kutch, had contended to higher officials that the northern half of the Rann

(continued)

---

[17]See J. G. Wetter, "The Rann of Kutch Arbitration," *65 AJIL* 346 (1971); see also S. Saeed, "The Rann of Kutch Arbitration," Karachi University International Relations Department, www.ribt.org/kuird/html/samiasaeed.htm (accessed April 22, 2009).

had always been considered to belong to Sindh. No one had argued at that time that the whole of the Rann belonged to Kutch.

The chair, Judge Lagergren, became the principal author of the compromise settlement. He drew a new borderline dividing the area with 90 percent to India, 10 percent to Pakistan. The Iranian commissioner (Pakistan) acceded to the agreement in order to produce a majority settlement. Despite fears that India would reject the settlement and throw up obstacles to the demarcation of the border, Indian Prime Minister Indira Gandhi affirmed India would honor the decision. She also said that India would never again use arbitration.

In May 2010, Pakistan, invoking treaty provisions in the 1960 Indus Waters Treaty, initiated arbitral proceedings against India utilizing the PCA. The Indus is a strategic and vital resource for Pakistan's economy. Pakistan has alleged that India has violated the terms of the 1960 Treaty by building dams on the river in violation of the 1960 agreement.[18] The panel had not reached a decision as of July 2011.

Revision, Appeal, and Rejection of Awards

An arbitral award may be binding but *not necessarily* final. This statement may seem somewhat counterintuitive because the obvious purpose of the arbitration is to end the dispute. However, "it may be open to the parties to take further proceedings to interpret, revise, rectify, appeal from or nullify the decision."[19] The possibilities here rely partly upon general international law but also, more importantly, upon the terms of the *compromis*. Normally, the power to interpret, appeal, or seek revision of any award must come from an express grant. Considering the purpose of arbitration, the right to appeal is rarely included. The right to seek clarification (which does not challenge the ruling, but often the scope of its application) is more commonly included.[20] For example, the case of the *Continental Shelf Arbitration (United Kingdom–France)* centered on the delimitation of the shelf in parts of the English Channel, in the area of the Scilly Islands, and in areas to the north and northwest of the Channel Islands. This arbitration required two decisions, the second one asked for by the United Kingdom under the terms of the *compromis* of July 10, 1975, concerning the scope and meaning of the decision.[21]

The *Rainbow Warrior* case (Chapter 11) offers an interesting insight into the possibilities and limitations here. The difficulties that arose between New Zealand and France over implementation of the initial settlement in *Rainbow Warrior* were explored in Chapter 12. Here, the unique structure of the settlement offers some insight into the rest of the story. The original *compromis* did not deal with the question of disputes over implementation of the agreement, but the settlement did. New Zealand, fearing that France might not honor the bargain, insisted that any dispute over implementation would be subject to compulsory arbitration. The sole arbitrator, the UN secretary-general, noted that France did not seem opposed to this and so included the procedures

---

[18]Indus Waters Kishanganga Arbitration (*Pakistan v. India*), Permanent Court of Arbitration, www.pca-cpa.org/showpage.asp?pag_id=1392.

[19]Merrills, note 1, at 105.

[20]*Id.* at 105–106. As noted in the text, this was the case with respect to the UK–France arbitration.

[21]Text of first decision (June 30, 1977) in 18 *ILM* 398 (1979); text of second decision (March 14, 1978), *id.*, 462 (including appended map).

in the settlement.[22] This eventually led to the second arbitration (1990), when New Zealand complained that France had not honored its bargain with the two agents.[23] A three-member panel decided the case. It did not award damages but made a finding of "illegality."[24] It also recommended the creation of a joint fund to promote friendly relations between the two states, to which France did make an initial contribution.

Only if the arbitrators disregard the instructions laid down in the *compromis* by not following specified rules, principles, or terms of settlement may a party rightfully claim not to be bound by the decision. A contemporary illustration comes from the 1991 ICJ Case concerning the Arbitral Award of 31 July 1989 (*Guinea-Bissau v. Senegal*),[25] which involved a dispute over the validity of an award delivered by an arbitration tribunal. In August 1989, Guinea-Bissau instituted proceedings in the ICJ against Senegal. Guinea-Bissau contended that, notwithstanding the negotiations pursued from 1977 onward, the two states had not reached a settlement of a dispute concerning the maritime delimitation between them. The two states consented, by an arbitration agreement dated March 12, 1985, to submit that dispute to an arbitration tribunal composed of three members. Guinea-Bissau indicated that, according to the terms of Article 2 of that agreement, the tribunal had been asked to rule on two questions:

1. Does the agreement on the maritime boundary concluded by an exchange of letters between France and Portugal in April 1960 have the force of law in the relations between the two states?
2. In the event of a negative answer to the first question, what should be the line delimiting the maritime territories of the Republic of Guinea-Bissau and the Republic of Senegal?

Guinea-Bissau asserted that the decision had no validity because the records of the deliberations did not support the decision and because the tribunal did not produce a map. The two states then *agreed* to submit this contention to the ICJ. Negotiations continued between the two parties resulting in an agreement in 1994 and the removal of the case from the ICJ's docket.

JUDICIAL SETTLEMENT

Judicial settlement utilizes permanent courts that make legally binding decisions in disputes. Unlike the ad hoc nature of arbitration, the jurisdiction, rules of procedure, selection of judges, and other pertinent machinery are already established and continue after the court renders any particular decision. The Central American Court of Justice (1907–1918) emerged as the first permanent international court, but the Permanent Court of International Justice (PCIJ), which was established

---

[22]The secretary-general also gave himself the power to designate *all* members of the commission (national and neutral alike) in case the states failed to do so.

[23]*Rainbow Warrior* (*New Zealand v. France,* 1986), Ruling by UN Secretary-General Javier Pérez de Cuéllar, New York, July 5, 1986; text in *International Legal Materials* 26 (1987), 1346, including statement of facts and legal briefs by New Zealand and France.

[24]*New Zealand v. France,* New York (April 30, 1990), based on the supplementary agreement (arbitration compromise) of February 14, 1989. See L. Guruswamy, G. Palmer, and B. Weston, *International Environmental Law and World Order* (1994), 163–168, for text and discussion.

[25]Arbitral Award of July 31, 1989 (*Guinea-Bissau v. Senegal*), 31 ILM 32 (1992); abstract in 86 *AJIL* 553 (1992), www.haguejusticeportal.net/eCache/DEF/6/231.html.

under the authority of the League of Nations and began deliberations in 1922 at The Hague, constituted the first international court with a potential global jurisdiction. The contemporary ICJ, the principal judicial organ of the United Nations, is generally considered to be the successor to the PCIJ.

The ICJ is certainly the most prominent international court, but other international courts that have more specialized jurisdictional mandates, regional and/or functional (war crimes, human rights), have also emerged in the post–World War II era (see sidebar). The European Court of Justice and the Caribbean Court of Justice have regional mandates, while the newly formed International Criminal Court (ICC) has a specific functional mandate in that it hears only cases of individuals charged with war crimes or genocide. The European Court of Human Rights and the Inter-American Court of Human Rights combine regional and specific functional mandates.

War Crime Tribunals

We will discuss war crime tribunals in Chapter 22. These courts constitute a special case. On the one hand, these courts have been set up by agreement when needed for a specific task and will disband after accomplishment of that task (and thus are ad hoc). On the other hand, they have the formal features of permanent courts in that they have permanent machinery (judges, prosecutors, and rules of procedure) for formal trials of individuals for the duration of the task. For Yugoslavia, Rwanda, and Sierra Leone, the task of hearing the cases may take many years. As a method of adjudication, these tribunals fall between mixed claims commissions and truly permanent international courts.

PERMANENT INTERNATIONAL COURTS

Central American Court of Justice (1907–1918)—heard ten cases

Permanent Court of International Justice (PCIJ) (1922–1940)[26]

International Court of Justice (ICJ)[27]

International Court of Arbitration[28]

Corte Centroamericana de Justicia (1962)[29]

Inter-American Court of Human Rights (1979)[30]

European Court of Justice (European Union)

European Court of Human Rights (Council of Europe)

International Tribunal on the Law of the Sea (November 16, 1994)[31]

Caribbean Court of Justice (2001)[32]

International Criminal Court (2002)[33]

---

[26]www.icj-cij.org/pcij/index.php?p1=9.

[27]www.icj-cij.org (accessed April 22, 2009).

[28]www.iccwbo.org/court/.

[29]www.portal.ccj.org.ni/ccj2/.

[30]www.corteidh.or.cr/index.cfm (accessed April 22, 2009).

[31]www.itlos.org/ (accessed April 22, 2009).

[32]www.caribbeancourtofjustice.org (accessed April 22, 2009).

[33]www.icc-cpi.int/Menus/ICC.

Permanent Court of International Justice

Article 14 of the Covenant of the League of Nations called on the council to "formulate and submit to the members of the League for adoption, plans for the establishment of a Permanent Court of International Justice."[34] This provision reflected a desire to have a true international court to settle legal disputes between states. As a result of this provision, the council appointed an advisory council of jurists. They met in The Hague in June 1920 to draft the basic instrument (statute) of such a tribunal. The result of the meeting, called a *draft scheme*, was submitted to the council and assembly. After debate and some changes, the two bodies approved the statute. Established by treaty, the statute would bind only those states that signed and ratified the Protocol of Signature dated December 16, 1920. Over its existence, certain amendments adopted in 1928–1929 were submitted to member states for ratification in the form of a second protocol in 1929.[35] By December 1940, the original protocol had been ratified by 51 states. States parties included all major powers except the United States.

The PCIJ did not convene during World War II. In January 1946, the remaining judges of the PCIJ formally resigned, and the former Assembly of the League of Nations formally dissolved the court. The Charter of the United Nations established the new ICJ as the successor to the PCIJ. In most details, the statute of the new court duplicated that of the old one, but there are certain significant differences. The most important of these is that all member states of the United Nations are automatically parties to the statute of the new court, whereas in the case of the 1920 statute, only those states that signed and ratified the PCIJ Statute were bound. States not members of the United Nations may ratify the Statute of the Court. This observation applied to Switzerland until it became a UN member in 2002.

The International Court of Justice

As the judicial arm of the United Nations, the ICJ is the *only* international court that exercises a truly global jurisdiction. The ICJ is often referred to as the "World Court," which reflects its position. This statement requires some elaboration. The ICJ does not have individual *criminal* jurisdiction. *Litigants must be states*, but the statute does not limit the range of issues that states may refer to the court. On the other hand, the ICC functions only among states parties and tries individuals accused of the delimited set of crimes described in the Rome Statute.

The ICJ has 15 judges, serving in their personal capacities (i.e., in principle, they do not serve as representatives of their national governments), elected for staggered nine-year terms (five judges elected every three years). Judges may be reelected (no term limits). The court may not have two judges of the same nationality. If a nominee has dual nationality, the statute provides that "a national of more

---

[34]www.worldcourts.com/pcij/eng/ (accessed April 22, 2009).

[35]The major documents relating to the court are found in "Instruments Relating to the Permanent Court of Justice" (with an introduction by Hudson), *International Conciliation*, 388 (March 1943), 137.

than one state shall be deemed to be a national of the one in which he ordinarily exercises civil and political rights" (Article 3(2)). When delegations vote, Article 9 adds another consideration for them:

> At every election, the electors shall bear in mind not only that the person to be elected should individually possess the qualifications required, but also that in the body as a whole the representation of the *main forms of civilization and of the principal legal systems of the world should be assured.* (Emphasis added)

Even though the presumption is that judges serve in their personal capacities, the statute addresses potential "political" problems. In contentious cases, judges of the nationality of each of the parties shall retain their right to sit in the case before the court. If a party does not have a judge sitting on the court, it has the right to appoint one (Article 31), preferably from the list of eligible candidates for election to the court (see next section). The ad hoc judge so chosen will not necessarily be of the same nationality. In its case against the United States,[36] Nicaragua chose a French national, Claude-Albert Colliard, to represent it on the ICJ.[37]

During their term, no member of the court may exercise any political or administrative function, or engage in any other occupation of a professional nature or act as "an agent, counsel in any case" (Articles 16 and 17), nor may a member participate in any case where he or she has acted as an agent, a counsel, or an advocate or in any other capacity, whether fact-finding or adjudicative, at any level. Judges enjoy diplomatic immunity while engaged in the business of the ICJ (Article 19). Finally, each judge takes an oath to exercise his or her powers "impartially and conscientiously" (Article 20).

Nomination of Candidates for the ICJ   Understanding how an individual might become a judge on the ICJ requires some historical background.[38] Both of the Hague Conferences (1899 and 1907) discussed the idea of a permanent international court. The stumbling block was disagreement over a system to elect judges. They did agree, however, on a convention establishing a PCA. That convention provides that each state party to the convention has the right to name four jurists as arbitrators who will be available to consider a concrete matter for international arbitration. When the PCIJ came into existence after World War I, a solution was found for the difficult problem of electing judges. The legal experts named as potential arbitrators under the Hague Convention became the nominating committee. The League of Nations then elected the judges from among the slate of proposed nominees.

---

[36]Military and Paramilitary Activities in and Against Nicaragua (*Nicaragua v. United States of America*), *ICJ Reports* (1984), www.icj-cij.org/icjwww/icases/inus/inusframe.htm (accessed April 22, 2009).

[37]For a list of judges ad hoc, see "World Court Digest," Max Planck Institute for International and Comparative Law, www.mpil.de/ww/en/pub/research/details/publications/institute/wcd.cfm?judges02.cfm (accessed April 22, 2009).

[38]R. R. Baxter, "The Procedures Employed in Connection with the United States Nominations for the International Court in 1960," *55 AJIL* 445 (1961). For a concise discussion of the mechanics and politics of election, see www.securitycouncilreport.org/site/c.glKWLeMTIsG/b.1140925/k.1FF5/November_2005brElection_of_Five_Judges_of_the_International_Court_of_Justice.htm (accessed April 22, 2009).

The selection system for the ICJ has in essence preserved this procedure. To ensure that candidates are not mere government nominees, nominees must be members either of the PCA or of similar groups specially constituted in countries that are not members of the PCA. No national group may nominate more than four persons, and only two of those may bear the nationality of the group. Article 2 of the ICJ Statute[39] establishes the minimum qualifications for a nominee:

> The Court shall be composed of a body of independent judges, elected regardless of their nationality from among persons of high moral character, who possess the qualifications required in their respective countries for appointment to the highest judicial offices, or are jurisconsults of recognized competence in international law.

The list of candidates then goes to the United Nations. To be elected, a candidate must obtain an absolute majority in the Security Council and the General Assembly, both bodies voting independently and simultaneously. If more than one candidate of the same nationality obtains the required votes, the eldest is elected.

ICJ Jurisdiction (Competence)   Articles 34 through 38 and Article 65 outline the competence of the court. The court may hear contentious cases and give advisory opinions. Article 36 defines its jurisdiction as all legal disputes concerning the interpretation of a treaty, any other question of international law, and/or fact-finding and determination of the extent of a breach of any international obligation. Many multilateral treaties specify the ICJ as the method to resolve any dispute relating to the treaty. For example, Article 22 of the International Convention on the Elimination of All Forms of Racial Discrimination states:

> Any dispute between two or more States Parties with respect to the interpretation or application of this Convention, which is not settled by negotiation or by the procedures expressly provided for in this Convention, shall, at the request of any of the parties to the dispute, be referred to the International Court of Justice for decision, unless the disputants agree to another mode of settlement.

In contentious cases, the court serves as a trial court. Only states may be litigants. This means that neither the United Nations nor any other IGO or NGO can bring a contentious case. Neither can individuals. If individuals desire to bring a case before the court, they must depend on the willingness of their own government to take up the case. The *Nottebohm* case (Chapter 9) came to the ICJ only because Liechtenstein filed a complaint against Guatemala concerning the mistreatment of an individual they claimed as a national. The ICJ heard the case of Jose Medellin and 51 other Mexican nationals (Chapter 15) because Mexico filed against the United States claiming a violation of a treaty with respect to their detention and trial.[40] Moreover, the court has no criminal jurisdiction and has no basis to try individuals for alleged violations of international criminal law.

---

[39]See www.icj-cij.org/documents/index.php?p1=4&p2=2&p3=0.

[40]*Avena and Other Mexican Nationals (Mexico v. United States of America)*, March 31, 2004; *ICJ Report* (2004), 128; 43 *ILM* 581 (2004), www.icj-cij.org/docket/files/128/8190.pdf.

The ICJ also may render advisory opinions "on any legal question at the request of whatever body may be authorized by or in accordance with the Charter of the United Nations to make such a request." Two of the last three requests came from resolutions of the General Assembly. In December 2003, the General Assembly requested an advisory opinion on the Legal Consequences of the Construction of a Wall in the Occupied Palestinian Territory.[41] In 2008, it requested an opinion on the unilateral declaration of independence by Kosovo. Prior to this case, the World Health Organization (WHO) jointly with the General Assembly had in 1994 requested an opinion on the question, "Is the threat or use of nuclear weapons in any circumstance permitted under international law?"[42] The General Assembly has granted this privilege to all specialized agencies, except the Universal Postal Union. The latest request (2010) came from the International Labor Organization.[43] In the case of the United States, a provision of the 1947 Headquarters Agreement, which calls for arbitration of differences between the United States and the United Nations, also calls for an advisory opinion by the ICJ, which is to be taken into consideration by the arbitral tribunal.

As a trial court, the ICJ is a court of *original* jurisdiction, meaning that the greatest majority of cases have not had a previous judicial determination. Unlike judges on the U.S. Supreme Court, the judges of the ICJ do not have the benefit of the pleadings and decision from lower courts. This is a significant limitation because the proceeding of lower courts can be extraordinarily helpful in that they often clarify the factual context, leaving courts of appeals to wrestle with the legal issues alone. In this respect, the *Guinea-Bissau v. Senegal* case discussed earlier stands as an anomaly—it did come as an appeal from an arbitration panel. Not only is the ICJ the original trial court, but it is also the court of final resort. It serves as the ultimate arbiter. States cannot appeal ICJ decisions (Article 60), although they may ask for clarification in terms of application.[44]

In theory, the court is not bound by its previous decisions. Article 59 states that the decisions of the court have "no binding force except between the parties and in respect of that particular case." In reality, the high-profile decisions made by 15 prominent jurists have an impact—whether formally acknowledged in the statute or not. Other than the voluntary acceptance and implementation of a decision, the ICJ has no direct means to ensure compliance with its verdicts and orders. Individual states may appeal to the Security Council if any party

---

[41]For the details of the request and the decision, see www.icj-cij.org/icjwww/idocket/imus/imusframe. htm (accessed April 22, 2009).

[42]Legality of the Threat or Use of Nuclear Weapons (1994–1996).

[43]www.icj-cij.org/docket/index.php?p1=3&p2=4&code=fida&case=146&k=ad.

[44]States also may not "reserve" a right to object at a later time:

The fact that a State purports to "reserve its rights" in respect of a future decision of the Court, after the Court has determined that it has jurisdiction, is clearly of no effect on the validity of that decision. Under Article 36, paragraph 6, of its Statute, the Court has jurisdiction to determine any dispute as to its own jurisdiction, and its judgment on that matter, as on the merits, is final and binding on the parties under Articles 59 and 60 of the Statute. (*Corfu Channel, Judgment of 15 December 1949, ICJ Rep.* (1949), 248, www.icj-cij.org/icjwww/icases/icc/iccframe.htm [accessed April 22, 2009]).

to a case fails to perform the obligations incumbent upon it under a judgment rendered by the ICJ (Charter, Article 94(2)). The Security Council may, if it deems necessary, make recommendations or decide upon measures to be taken to give effect to the judgment.

Of interest is that Article 94(2) refers to "awards or decisions," thus including arbitration in the enforcement text. Thus far, Article 94(2) has been invoked only once, in the "interim-measures-of-protection" decision in the Anglo-Iranian Oil Company case. Great Britain brought the case before the Security Council on a contention that the latter had the right to take action to deal with interim measures ordered by the court but not carried out by Iran. The Security Council, however, decided to postpone any action until the ICJ had decided whether it was itself competent to handle the case, and when the court decided that it lacked jurisdiction, the order for the measures of protection lapsed—and with it, all question of enforcement by the Security Council.

The Politics of ICJ Jurisdiction   Although the jurisdiction of the ICJ comprises all cases that the parties refer to it and all other matters especially provided for in the UN Charter or in treaties in force, the court has always found it necessary to justify its competence in great detail. The question of jurisdiction seldom forms a basis of contention in domestic law, but questions of jurisdiction always become a question of first magnitude in international cases. Records of ICJ proceedings will often appear in at least two different stages: *jurisdiction,* sometimes titled *preliminary objections* (see Chapter 11 on claims),[45] and *merits*. More than once, questions over the scope of the court's competence to decide an issue have generated almost as much discussion and justification as the final result.[46]

For any international court, the question is never as simple as the dichotomous choice between jurisdiction or no jurisdiction (sometimes expressed as jurisdiction *vel non*). In this respect, recall the rather extended reasoning of the British panels in the Pinochet case (Chapter 16). The statement of the majority in the case Nicaragua brought against the United States in the ICJ yields a good outline for discussion of the salient issues that follow:[47]

> The Court's jurisdiction, as it has frequently recalled, is based on the *consent of States*, expressed in a variety of ways including *declarations* made under Article 36, paragraph 2, of the Statute. It is the declaration made by the United States under that Article which defines the categories of dispute for which the United States consents to the Court's jurisdiction. If therefore that declaration, because of a *reservation* contained in it, excludes from the disputes for which it accepts the Court's jurisdiction certain disputes arising under multilateral treaties, the Court must take that fact into account. (Emphasis added)

---

[45]These can include questions concerning nationality, exhaustion of local remedies, and the like.

[46]See, for example, the very first case of the court, *The Corfu Channel Case* (*United Kingdom v. Albania, 1947–1949*), www.icj-cij.org/docket/index.php?p1=3&p2=3&k=cd&case=1.

[47]Judgment of 26 November 1984: Jurisdiction of the Court and Admissibility of the Application at 32, www.icj-cij.org/docket/index.php?sum=367&code=nus&p1=3&p2=3&case=70&k=66&p3=5.

In this case, one should note that while all judges agreed that consent formed the basis of jurisdiction, the judges divided the issues into three separable sets of questions:

1. Did the court have jurisdiction under Article 36 (paragraphs 2 and 5) of the Statute? (Vote, 11–5 yes)
2. Did the court have jurisdiction to interpret the 1956 Treaty of Friendship, Commerce and Navigation between the United States and Nicaragua? (Vote, 14–2 yes)
3. Did the court have jurisdiction to "entertain" the case? (Vote, 15–1 yes)

Article 36(2) stipulates that states may declare that they recognize the jurisdiction of the ICJ as "compulsory" in relation to any other state *accepting the same obligation* with respect to the subject matter detailed in the article. Commentaries often refer to Article 36(2) as the "optional clause."[48] The language reflects a compromise. Note that the article does not require that states submit all disputes to compulsory jurisdiction. States joining the UN automatically became members of the court with the *option* of accepting compulsory jurisdiction through a declaration (in essence, through expressing formal consent). The obligation to submit certain disputes to the ICJ would then be in effect only with respect to other states that had also formally consented (Chapter 4). If one state party to a dispute has made a declaration under the optional clause and the other has not, the ICJ cannot hear the dispute unless the other party expressly consents to using the court. The process has one other interesting twist. In submitting their declarations, states can further specify the circumstances (and thus further limit the possibilities) under which they would submit disputes to the ICJ.[49] As noted in the excerpt from the Nicaragua case earlier in text, the court must first establish the element of consent and *then consider the extent* of that consent.

States have used a number of methods to limit the authority of the ICJ. Many include either time limits or the idea of "reciprocity." In this context, reciprocity refers to the simple calculation that not all states making declarations under the optional clause will have accepted the court's jurisdiction on identical terms. Specifying reciprocity is an attempt to "level the playing field" in terms of applicable rules. In a dispute, a state declaring reciprocity as the basis for its declaration then would have the opportunity to take advantage of a declaration made by the other party to the dispute if that declaration mandated a narrower basis for accepting the ICJ as the method of resolution. In the case of Certain Norwegian Loans (France v. Norway), in its consideration of preliminary objections, the court[50]

> considered the second ground of this Objection and noted that the jurisdiction of the Court in the present case depended upon the Declarations made

---

[48]At present, of the five permanent members of the UN Security Council, only the United Kingdom remains a party to the optional clause. France and the United States have withdrawn; the People's Republic of China repudiated, by letter, in September 1972, the acceptance of compulsory jurisdiction by the Republic of China in 1946. Russia had never filed a declaration of any type.

[49]While the term *declaration* is used here, in form the statements actually constitute *reservations* to the statute.

[50]See *Case of Certain Norwegian Loans* (*France v. Norway*), Judgment of July 6, 1957, www.icj-cij. org/icjwww/idecisions/isummaries/ifnsummary570706.htm (accessed April 22, 2009).

by the Parties on condition of *reciprocity;* and that since two unilateral declarations were involved *such jurisdiction was conferred upon the Court only to the extent to which the Declarations coincided* in conferring it. Consequently, the common will of the Parties, which was the basis of the Court's jurisdiction, existed within the narrower limits indicated by the French reservation. (Emphasis added)

This finding effectively precluded the ICJ from hearing the case because of the restrictions in the French declaration.[51]

The U.S. declaration[52] contained the famous Connally Amendment, according to which the United States excluded from its acceptance of the compulsory jurisdiction of the court "disputes with regard to matters which are essentially within the domestic jurisdiction of the United States of America *as determined by the United States of America"* (Emphasis added). The italicized phrase represents the amendment.[53] The declaration also exempted the United States from any dispute where other tribunals may have jurisdiction (at the time of submission or in the future) and any dispute arising under a multilateral treaty unless all parties to the treaty affected by the decision are parties to the case or if the United States "specially agrees" to jurisdiction. The declaration also reserved to the United States the right to terminate the declaration with six months' written notice.

In April 1984, the United States announced that it rejected the authority of the ICJ over Central American questions for the next two years. The American action followed a number of well-known precedents, including denial of jurisdiction by the United Kingdom in a commercial disagreement with Saudi Arabia, by India in its dispute with Portugal over rights of passage in several of the latter's enclaves in India, by Australia in a fishing dispute with Japan, and by Canada in an effort to bar claims for marine pollution by Canada. Subsequently, the United States formally withdrew from the proceedings instituted by Nicaragua.[54] The ICJ then ruled that the U.S. decision was invalid, citing the requirement to first give the court six months' notice. The United States then refiled its intent (October 1985) to withdraw from the court's jurisdiction.[55]

---

[51]See also the discussion in "Land and Maritime Boundary Between Cameroon and Nigeria, Preliminary Objections, Judgment," *ICJ Report* (1998), 275, www.icj-cij.org/icjwww/idocket/inc/incjudgment/inc_ijudgment_19990325_frame.htm (accessed April 22, 2009).

[52]Text of U.S. Declaration of August 14, 1946, in 41 *AJIL* 11 (1947). The literature on the amendment is enormous; consult the valuable ideas in A. D'Amato, "Modifying U.S. Acceptance of the Compulsory Jurisdiction of the World Court," 79 *AJIL* 385 (1985); V. F. DeCain, "The Connally Amendment," 10 *National Review* (March 11, 1961), 143; and L. Preuss, "The International Court of Justice, the Senate, and Matters of Domestic Jurisdiction," 40 *AJIL* 720 (1946). See also the monographic study of the subject by H. W. Briggs, "Reservations to the Acceptance of the Compulsory Jurisdiction of the International Court of Justice," 93 *Hague Academy Recueil des Cours* (1958, I), 223–367.

[53]This neutralizes Article 36(6) of the statute, which gives the ICJ the authority to make this determination. Also note that many writers mistakenly refer to the entire declaration as the Connally Amendment.

[54]79 *AJIL* 439 (1985); see also K. Highet, "Litigation Implications of the U.S. Withdrawal from the *Nicaragua* Case," *id.,* 79, 992.

[55]See also G. Scott and C. Carr, "The ICJ and Compulsory Jurisdiction: The Case for Closing the Clause," 81 *AJIL* 57 (1987).

The following case demonstrates the approach of the ICJ to issues of jurisdiction. More than that, in its discussion the court addresses many issues of treaty interpretation and obligation covered earlier in the text. Due to the extensive nature of the submissions by the Democratic Republic of the Congo (DRC), the summary of the reasoning in this case does not address all of the contentions put forward to justify ICJ jurisdiction.

ARMED ACTIVITIES ON THE TERRITORY OF THE CONGO (NEW APPLICATION: 2002)

Democratic Republic of the Congo v. Rwanda Jurisdiction of the Court and Admissibility of the Application International Court of Justice Judgment of February 3, 2006

Facts

On May 28, 2002,[56] the government of the Democratic Republic of the Congo (hereinafter, "the DRC") filed an application with the court instituting proceedings against the Republic of Rwanda (hereinafter, "Rwanda"). The application alleged "massive, serious and flagrant violations of human rights and of international humanitarian law." In the application, the DRC stated, "[the] flagrant and serious violations [of human rights and of international humanitarian law]" in breach of the "International Bill of Rights (see Chapter 16), other relevant international instruments and mandatory resolutions of the United Nations Security Council." The DRC complained these resulted "from acts of armed aggression perpetrated by Rwanda on the territory of the Democratic Republic of the Congo in flagrant breach of the sovereignty and territorial integrity of [the latter], as guaranteed by the Charters of the United Nations and the Organization of African Unity."

To validate the jurisdiction of the court, the DRC, referring to Article 36(1) of the statute, invoked Article 22 of the International Convention on the Elimination of All Forms of Racial Discrimination; Article 29(1) of the Convention on the Elimination of All Forms of Discrimination Against Women; Article IX of the Convention on the Prevention and Punishment of the Crime of Genocide; Article 75 of the Constitution of the World Health Organization; Article XIV(2) of the Constitution of the United Nations Educational, Scientific, and Cultural Organization; Article 9 of the Convention on the Privileges and Immunities of the Specialized Agencies of November 21, 1947; Article 30(1) of the Convention Against Torture and Other Cruel, Inhuman, or Degrading Treatment or Punishment; and Article 14(1) of the Montreal Convention for the Suppression of Unlawful Acts Against the Safety of Civil Aviation. The DRC further contended in its application that Article 66 of the Vienna Convention on the Law of Treaties of May 23, 1969, established the

(*continued*)

---

[56]www.icj-cij.org/icjwww/idocket/icrw/icrwframe.htm. See also *Certain Criminal Proceedings in France* (*Republic of the Congo v. France*, 2003), www.icj-cij.org/icjwww/idocket/icof/icoff500frame.htm (accessed April 22, 2009).

jurisdiction of the court to settle disputes arising from the violation of peremptory norms (*jus cogens*) in the area of human rights, as those norms were reflected in a number of international instruments.

Judges

Since the court did not have a sitting judge of the nationality of the parties, each of them availed itself of the right (Article 31) to choose a judge ad hoc to sit in the case. The DRC chose Mr. Jean-Pierre Mavungu, and Rwanda chose Mr. Christopher John Robert Dugard.

Procedure

At a meeting held on September 4, 2002, by the president of the court with the agents of the parties, Rwanda proposed that the procedure provided for in Article 79, paragraphs 2 and 3, of the Rules of Court be followed, and that the questions of jurisdiction and admissibility in the case therefore be determined separately before any proceedings on the merits. Rwanda requested the court to declare that (1) it lacks jurisdiction over the claims brought against the Republic of Rwanda by the *authorities* within the *international* legal order" (Emphasis added). The Vienna Convention on the Law of Treaties applies here. No evidence exists that Rwanda took the appropriate international action to withdraw the reservations. Hence, the passage of the domestic law by Rwanda did not as a matter of international law effect a withdrawal of its reservation to the Genocide Treaty. Moreover, the ICJ noted as a matter of the law of treaties that when Rwanda acceded to the Genocide Convention and made the reservation, the DRC made no objection to it.

Democratic Republic of the Congo; and (2) in the alternative, that the claims brought against the Republic of Rwanda by the Democratic Republic of the Congo are inadmissible.

Issues

1. Has Rwanda given its formal consent to the proceeding brought by the DRC?
2. Is the application of the DRC admissible?

Decision

By a vote of 15–2, the ICJ found that it had no jurisdiction to entertain the application filed by the DRC on May 28, 2002.

Reasoning

In accordance with the decision taken in its Order of September 18, 2002, the court addressed only the questions of whether it is competent to hear the dispute and whether the DRC's application is admissible. The DRC had alleged 11 separate bases of jurisdiction. The court examined and rejected each one. The court's reasoning with respect to the Genocide Convention illustrates most of the principal points raised in the discussion of the other contentions.

The court noted that Rwanda "has expressly and repeatedly objected to its jurisdiction at every stage of the proceedings." Thus, its attitude cannot be regarded as "an unequivocal indication" of a desire to accept the jurisdiction of the court in a "voluntary and indisputable" manner. Rwanda's participation in the proceedings cannot be taken as acquiescence because the purpose of the participation was to contest any claim to jurisdiction.

Genocide Convention: Both Rwanda and the DRC are parties to the Genocide Convention. Rwanda's accession to the convention contained a reservation that exempted it from Article IX. Article IX stipulates the ICJ as the forum for dispute resolution. The issue turned on whether a Rwandan domestic law passed in 1995 that mandated the withdrawal of all

(*continued*)

reservations to international treaties had effect. The court noted that there is a clear distinction to be drawn "between a *decision to withdraw a reservation* to a treaty taken within a State's *domestic* legal order and the *implementation* of that decision by the competent *national authorities within the international legal order*" (Emphasis added). No evidence exists that Rwanda took the appropriate *international* action to withdraw the reservations.

Moreover, the ICJ noted as a matter of the law of nations that when Rwanda acceded to the Genocide Convention and made the reservations, the DRC made no objections.

The DRC also contended that the obligations under the Genocide Treaty constituted *jus cogens.* The court recognized that the "rights and obligations enshrined by the Convention are rights and obligations *erga omnes.* Nonetheless, the universal character of a norm and the rule of consent to jurisdiction are two different things. The mere fact that an obligation *erga omnes* or a peremptory norm is at issue in a dispute does not thereby establish the court's jurisdiction."

Ad Hoc Chambers of the Court The use of an ad hoc chamber of three or five judges by the ICJ is authorized by Articles 26–29 of the court's statute. This option was not utilized until the case of the *Delimitation of the Maritime Boundary in the Gulf of Maine Area* (see Chapter 12).[57] This use of a chamber followed an earlier agreement to that effect (1979) by the litigants.[58] The chamber procedure was used again in *Frontier Dispute (Burkina Faso v. Mali),*[59] in *Elettronica Sicula S.p.A. (ELSI) (U.S. v. Italy),*[60] and in *Land, Island and Maritime Frontier Dispute (El Salvador v. Honduras).*[61] A judgment given by a chamber is to be considered as a judgment by the court. The chambers may sit elsewhere than at The Hague with the consent of the parties. The Revised Rules adopted by the ICJ (Article 17) provide that either party may file a request for the formation of a chamber at any time until the closure of written proceedings. Both parties then would be consulted to determine their views regarding the composition of the chamber. If the other party then agrees, a chamber would be formed. The major advantage accruing from the use of a chamber is that it enables the court to handle a much greater caseload than would otherwise be possible. Also, if a chamber were to sit physically close to the litigants, the procedure may well be much less expensive than if everyone had to journey to The Hague. Finally, Article 17 of the rules permits input by the parties concerning the composition of the chamber perhaps making it an attractive option as opposed to a hearing by the full complement of judges.

---

[57]Constitution of Chamber, *ICJ Report* (1982), 3 (Order of January 20), www.icj-cij.org/icjwww/icases/icigm/icigm_ijudgment/icigm_ijudgment_19841012.pdf (accessed April 22, 2009).

[58]See the authoritative coverage by S. Schwebel, "*Ad Hoc* Chambers of the International Court of Justice," 81 *AJIL* 831 (1987).

[59]Constitution of Chamber, *ICJ Report* (1985), 6 (Order of April 3), www.icj-cij.org/icjwww/icases/iHVM/ihvm_iorders/ihvm_iorder_19870409.pdf (accessed April 22, 2009).

[60]Constitution of Chamber, *ICJ Report* (1987), 3 (Order of March 2), www.icj-cij.org/icjwww/icases/ielsi/ielsiframe.htm (accessed April 22, 2009).

[61]Constitution of Chamber, *ICJ Report* (1987), 10 (Order of May 8), www.icj-cij.org/icjwww/icases/ish/ishframe.htm (accessed April 22, 2009). See also S. Oda, "Further Thoughts on the Chambers of the International Court of Justice," 82 *AJIL* 556, at 557, n. 6 (1988).

Nonappearance Before the ICJ   The decision of the United States to withdraw from the Nicaragua case focused attention on the problem of nonappearance and nonresponse when the court has found it has jurisdiction.[62] In the very first case before the ICJ, Albania declined to participate. Only a short time before the Nicaragua case, Iran had refused to acknowledge the ICJ in the *Diplomatic and Consular Staff in Tehran* case. Because of the experience of the PCIJ, the Statute of the ICJ (Article 53) anticipated the problem. Whenever one of the parties does not appear before the court, or fails to defend its case, the other party may call upon the court to decide in favor of its claim. Before doing so, the ICJ must satisfy itself not only that it has jurisdiction in accordance with Articles 36 and 37 but also that the claim is well founded in fact and law.

The Avena Case   The *Avena* case raises a number of interesting issues concerning the relationship between the ICJ and national judicial practice. The Vienna Convention on Consular Relations (Chapter 14), to which the United States, Mexico, and 164 other states are parties, requires the authorities of each party to inform the consulate of the other party when one of the other party's nationals is arrested. The convention also requires the authorities to inform the person concerned without delay of his or her right to communicate with the consulate. Authorities must forward without delay any communication the arrested person addresses to the consulate. The consular authorities have the right to visit and correspond with that person and to arrange for appropriate legal representation.

These requirements seemingly were not widely known or followed by U.S. law enforcement and judicial agencies and officers. In a number of homicide cases resulting in the death penalty, defense attorneys had failed to raise the issue during the original trials. If they raised it later on appeal or in a habeas corpus proceeding after conviction, courts denied its relevance. They found either that, having not raised the issue at trial, it was now too late (the "procedural default rule") or that the Consular Convention does not create rights for individuals who seek to enforce its provisions in U.S. courts.[63]

Before the Avena case, Paraguay and Germany had filed applications in the ICJ contesting U.S. practice.[64] In the Paraguay case, in its preliminary hearings, the ICJ called on the U.S. government to take measures to ensure that the Paraguayan national Angel Francisco Breard would not be executed before a final decision by the ICJ. The U.S. secretary of state did request the governor of Virginia to suspend Breard's impending execution while Breard sought immediate relief in U.S. courts. The U.S. Supreme Court denied his petitions for habeas corpus and for certiorari,

[62]The nonappearance problem is covered well in Highet's review article of J. B. Elkind, *Nonappearance Before the International Court of Justice: Functional and Comparative Analysis* (1984); and H. W. Thirlway, *Non-appearance Before the International Court of Justice* (1985), in 81 *AJIL* 237 (1987).

[63]See F. L. Kirgis, "President Bush's Determination Regarding Mexican Nationals and Consular Convention Rights," *ASIL Insights* (March 2005), www.asil.org/insights/2005/03/insights050309.html (accessed April 22, 2009).

[64]*Case Concerning the Vienna Convention on Consular Relations (Paraguay v. United States)*, *ICJ Report* (1998), 248; 37 *ILM* 810 (1998); *LeGrand* case (*Germany v. United States*), *ICJ Report* (2001), 466; 40 *ILM* 1069 (2001).

relying on the procedural default rule.[65] The governor of Virginia rejected the secretary of state's request for a further stay. Virginia executed Breard before the ICJ could decide the merits of the case.

The ICJ decided the German case (LeGrand) on its merits, finding that the United States had violated the Consular Convention and was therefore obligated to review and reconsider the convictions and sentences by taking account of the rights set forth in that convention.[66] More interestingly, the ICJ also held that use of the procedural default rule to preclude review and reconsideration in these cases would violate the Consular Convention.[67] The United States had argued that the Vienna Convention must be implemented subject to the laws of each state party. In the case of the United States, this meant operation of the convention was subject to the doctrine of procedural default. The ICJ found that domestic laws could not limit the rights of the accused under the convention. Domestic laws could only specify the means through which individuals could exercise those rights. The United States had also argued that the Vienna Convention did not grant rights to individuals, only to states. The ICJ rejected this argument on the grounds that the U.S. interpretation contradicted the plain meaning of the convention (Chapter 4).

The LeGrand case marks one other important decision. Despite provisional orders by the ICJ, Arizona executed the two LeGrand brothers in 1999. The ICJ continued its consideration of the case including Germany's contention that provisional measures ordered by the court were legally binding (Article 41). The binding nature of provisional measures had been a subject of great dispute in international law. The English text of the Statute of the ICJ implies that such measures are not binding, while the French text implies that they are. Faced with a contradiction between two equally authentic texts of the statute, the ICJ considered which interpretation better served the objects and purposes of the statute. Choosing the French text, the court found that provisional measures are binding (see Chapter 11).[68] This was the first time in the history of the ICJ that it had ruled as such.

The Avena case raises many of the same issues, but also gave the ICJ a rare opportunity to assess an ongoing situation. We discussed some of the implications in Chapter 15 (*Medellin v. Dretke*) of U.S. action after the Avena decision. Looking at the nature of the charges in LeGrand and Avena should give a good idea of

---

[65]*Breard v. Greene,* 523 U.S. 371, 118 S. Ct. 1352 (1998). The Supreme Court said that the convention "arguably" confers on an individual the right to consular assistance following arrest, but it did not finally decide the point.

[66]See F. L. Kirgis, "World Court Rules Against the United States in LeGrand Case Arising from a Violation of the Vienna Convention on Consular Relations," *ASIL Insights* (July 2001), www.asil.org/insights/insigh75.htm (accessed April 22, 2009).

[67]Kirgis, note 66.

[68]Article 41(1):

   1. The Court *shall have the power* to indicate, if it considers that circumstances so require, any provisional measures which ought to be taken to preserve the respective rights of either party.
   -(*La Cour* a le pouvoir d'indiquer, *si elle estime que les circonstances l'exigent, quelles mesures conservatoires du droit de chacun doivent etre prises à titre provisoire.*)

The French text says directly in terms of its translation into English, "The Court has the power."

why states, and particularly powerful states, may avoid arenas where they cannot exercise at least some control over the outcome. As we noted in Chapter 16 and elsewhere, the United States is particularly proud of its criminal justice system and has never thought that "international standards" might improve the process. Keep that in mind as you read the following case.

▶ CASE CONCERNING AVENA AND OTHER MEXICAN NATIONALS

Mexico v. United States of America International Court of Justice Judgment of March 31, 2004

Facts

On January 9, 2003, the United Mexican States (Mexico) instituted proceedings against the United States of America for "violations of the Vienna Convention on Consular Relations" of April 24, 1963 (Vienna Convention), allegedly committed by the United States. In its application, Mexico based the jurisdiction of the ICJ on Article 36(1) of the Statute of the Court and on Article I of the Optional Protocol Concerning the Compulsory Settlement of Disputes, which accompanies the Vienna Convention (Optional Protocol).

Mexico alleged that the United States of America, in arresting, detaining, trying, convicting, and sentencing the 52 Mexican nationals on death row (described in Mexico's Memorial), violated its international legal obligations to Mexico. The United States had deprived Mexico of the exercise of its right to *diplomatic protection* of its nationals by failing to inform, without delay, the 52 Mexican nationals after their arrest of their right to consular notification and access under Article 36(1)(b) of the Vienna Convention on Consular Relations. By depriving Mexico of its right to provide consular protection, the 52 nationals were denied their right to receive such protection as Mexico would provide under Article 36(1) (a) and (c) of the convention.

Judges

Since the court did not include a judge of Mexican nationality, Mexico chose Mr. Bernardo Sepúlveda to sit as judge ad hoc in the case. Mr. Thomas Burgenthal of the United States sat on the court as an elected judge.

Jurisdiction

The United States advanced the following objections to jurisdiction:

1. Mexico's submissions invite the ICJ to rule on the operation of the U.S. criminal justice system. Enquiry into the conduct of criminal proceedings in U.S. courts is a matter belonging to the merits.
2. Mexico has failed to exhaust local remedies.
3. Certain of those individuals included in the petition have American nationality.
4. The ICJ lacks jurisdiction to determine whether consular notification is a human right.
5. Mexico's request for remedies goes beyond the court's jurisdiction.
6. Mexico had knowledge of a breach but failed to act in expeditious fashion.
7. Mexico has invoked standards that it does not follow in its own practice.

In sum, the United States contended that the ICJ lacked jurisdiction to decide many

(*continued*)

of Mexico's claims, because its submissions in the memorial asked the court to decide questions that do not arise out of the interpretation or application of the Vienna Convention and that the United States has never agreed to submit to the court.

Decision on Jurisdiction

The ICJ dismissed the U.S. objections to jurisdiction (no recorded vote) and moved to consider the merits.

Issues

1. Has the United States violated its obligations under Article 36(1)(b) of the Vienna Convention on Consular Relations?
2. Does the United States have adequate and appropriate procedures for undertaking the review and reconsideration of sentences mandated by the LeGrand case?

Decision

Voted 14–1 to uphold Mexico's allegations.

Reasoning

The court, although recognizing the efforts by the United States to raise awareness of consular assistance rights, noted with regret that "the United States program, whatever its components, has proven ineffective to prevent the regular and continuing violation by its competent authorities of consular notification and assistance rights guaranteed by Article 36." The court also noted, "While it is a matter of concern that, even in the wake of the LeGrand Judgment, there remain a substantial number of cases of failure to carry out the obligation to furnish consular information to Mexican nationals."

With regard to the "review and reconsideration" (clemency) procedure, the court pointed out that the issue in the present case is whether the clemency process as practiced within the criminal justice systems of different states in the United States can qualify as an appropriate means for undertaking the effective "review and reconsideration of the conviction and sentence by taking account of the violation of the rights set forth in the Convention," as the court prescribed in the LeGrand judgment. The court noted that the clemency process, as currently practiced within the United States criminal justice system, does not appear to meet the prescribed standards and that it therefore is not sufficient in itself to serve as an appropriate means of "review and reconsideration" as envisaged by the ICJ in the LeGrand decision.

The court also emphasized a point of importance. The findings of the court in the present judgment cannot be interpreted to imply that the conclusions apply only to Mexican nationals. They apply equally to other foreign nationals finding themselves in similar situations in the United States.

The following case illustrates another aspect of the changing nature of the international legal landscape. To understand the genesis of this case, consider the precedent set by the attempted prosecution of Augusto Pinochet Ugarte (Chapter 16). Consider the implications here of claims to universal jurisdiction over certain crimes. Note in particular the sensitivity of the ICJ to the question of the appropriate role of courts with respect to the possibility that they might "legislate" by their ruling. Consider in this respect the earlier discussion about the jurisdiction of the ICJ and what issues it chose to seize for decision. On the other hand, when thinking about issues of enforcement and compliance, consider the difficulties encountered by Mr. Ndombasi after issuance of the warrant.

ARREST WARRANT OF APRIL 11, 2000

Democratic Republic of the Congo v. Belgium International Court of Justice Judgment of February 14, 2002

Facts

In April 2000, an investigating judge of the Brussels *tribunal de première instance* ("court of original jurisdiction") issued an international arrest warrant in absentia against Mr. Abdulaye Yerodia Ndombasi, charging him, as perpetrator or co-perpetrator, with offences constituting grave breaches of the Geneva Conventions of 1949 and of the Additional Protocols thereto, and with crimes against humanity. The arrest warrant circulated internationally through Interpol. At the time when the arrestwarrant was issued, Mr. Yerodia served as the minister for foreign affairs of the Congo, thus covered by sovereign immunity. The crimes with which Mr. Yerodia was charged were punishable in Belgium under the Law of 16 June 1993 "concerning the Punishment of Grave Breaches of the International Geneva Conventions of 12 August 1949 and of Protocols I and II of 8 June 1977 Additional Thereto," as amended by the Law of 19 February 1999 "concerning the Punishment of Serious Violations of International Humanitarian Law" (Belgian law).

In its application to the ICJ, the DRC contended that Belgium had violated the "principle that a State may not exercise its authority on the territory of another State," the "principle of sovereign equality among all Members of the United Nations, as laid down in Article 2, paragraph 1, of the Charter of the United Nations," as well as "the diplomatic immunity of the Minister for Foreign Affairs of a sovereign State, as recognized by the jurisprudence of the Court and following from Article 41, paragraph 2, of the Vienna Convention of 18 April 1961 on Diplomatic Relations."

Judges

The ICJ did not include a judge of the nationality of either of the parties. Each party proceeded to exercise the right conferred by Article 31(3) of the Statute to choose a judge ad hoc to sit in the case. The Congo chose Mr. Sayeman Bula-Bula, and Belgium chose Ms. Christine Van den Wyngaert.

Jurisdiction

Belgium contested the DRC application on the following bases:

1. Mr. Yerodia Ndombasi is no longer either a minister for foreign affairs of the DRC or a minister occupying any other position in the DRC government.
2. The case as it now stands is materially different to that set out in the DRC's application instituting proceedings, and the court accordingly lacks jurisdiction in the case and/or the application is inadmissible.
3. Given new circumstances, the case has assumed the character of an action of diplomatic protection but one in which the individual being protected has failed to exhaust local remedies.

Decision on Jurisdiction

The abstract issues of law raised by this case go to the heart of the debate about individual responsibility for the commission

(*continued*)

of international crimes. The court noted, "Against this background, a judgment of the Court on the merits in this case would—no matter in what direction that judgment was to go—inevitably influence the course of this debate. Two related questions are thus relevant. First, would it be appropriate, in circumstances in which there is no longer a concrete dimension to the dispute before it, for the Court to render, in the context of bilateral adjudicatory proceedings, what would in effect be an advisory opinion on matters on which the wider international community has an interest? Second, in the absence of a subsisting concrete dispute or an appropriate request for an advisory opinion, would it in any event be appropriate for the court to address such matters given that this would place the court in a *quasi-legislative* role as opposed to an adjudicatory or declaratory role?" By a vote of 15–1, the court found it had jurisdiction.

Issues

Does Belgium have the right to issue an arrest warrant for the crimes alleged?

Decision

Belgium has no authority to do so (vote, 13–3).

Reasoning

The ICJ found that, in the case of the issue of the warrant, the international circulation from June 2000 by the Belgian authorities effectively infringed Mr. Yerodia's immunity as the DRC's incumbent minister for foreign affairs. The international circulation of the warrant affected the ability of the DRC to conduct its foreign affairs. Because Mr. Yerodia in his capacity as minister of foreign affairs needed to undertake travel in the performance of his duties, the international circulation of the warrant—even in the absence of "further steps" by Belgium—could have resulted, in particular, in his arrest while abroad. The court observes in this respect that Belgium itself cites information to the effect that Mr. Yerodia, on applying for a visa to go to two countries, (apparently) learned that he ran the risk of being arrested as a result of the arrest warrant issued against him by Belgium. Concerning the warrant, the court found, "The violations of international law underlying the issue and international circulation of the arrest warrant of 11 April 2000 preclude any State, including Belgium, from executing it."

International Politics and International Law In looking forward to Chapter 18, one recent ICJ case seems relevant to many themes in that chapter, as well as to many other areas discussed earlier. In its discussion of the Nuclear Weapons case, the ICJ noted:

> The fact that this question also has political aspects, as, in the nature of things, is the case with so many questions which arise in international life, does not suffice to deprive it of its character as a "legal question" and to "deprive the Court of a competence expressly conferred on it by its Statute."[69]

Earlier, in the Interpretation of the Agreement of 25 March 1951 between the WHO and Egypt, the ICJ said, "Indeed, in situations in which political considerations

---

[69]Advisory Opinion, "Legality of the Threat or Use of Nuclear Weapons," *ICJ Report* (1995), 234.

TABLE 17.1

New Cases Before the International Court of Justice, 2009–2012

Request for interpretation of the Judgment of 15 June 1962 in the case concerning the Temple of Preah Vihear (*Cambodia v. Thailand*, 2011)

Certain Activities carried out by Nicaragua in the border area (*Costa Rica v. Nicaragua*, 2010)

Frontier Dispute (*Burkina Faso/Niger*, 2010)

Whaling in the Antarctic (*Australia v. Japan*, 2010)

Request for Advisory Opinion, 2010, Judgment No. 2867 of the Administrative Tribunal of the International Labour Organization upon a complaint filed against the International Fund for Agricultural Development

Jurisdiction and Enforcement of Judgments in Civil and Commercial Matters (*Belgium v. Switzerland*, 2009)

Certain questions concerning diplomatic relations (*Honduras v. Brazil*, 2009)

Questions relating to the obligation to prosecute or extradite (*Belgium v. Senegal*, 2009)

---

are prominent it may be particularly necessary for an international organization to obtain an advisory opinion from the Court as to the legal principles applicable with respect to the matter under debate."[70]

Current Cases Before the ICJ   Between January 1, 2009, and July 31, 2012, the ICJ received applications to hear seven contentious cases and one request for an advisory opinion. This brought to fourteen the number of active cases before the court (Table 17.1).

With the end of the Cold War, the caseload of the court increased significantly. Still, note both the issue areas involved and the states that filed claims. Then, note the discussion that runs throughout this book about the place adjudication. None of the case discussed earlier involve "vital" issues? Japan might be considered a major player on the contemporary stage of international politics, but the issue involves a minor concern (though a major issue in terms of the issue area of conservation) in the hierarchy of Japanese foreign policy concerns. Note also, that border issues form the largest issue area for claims brought to the court.

These observations are gauged to place the court in the context of the international political process. Within its defined areas of competence, the ICJ has played an important role in defining *international* standards of conduct. As we have noted, "losers" are often not happy. While we have noted some of the reactions of the United States when ICJ decisions have found its conduct in violation of international standards, we should also point out that the United States does not stand alone here.

---

[70]Advisory Opinion, "Interpretation of the Agreement of 25 March 1951 Between the WHO and Egypt," *ICJ Rep*ort (1980), 87, para. 33.

SUGGESTED READINGS

GENERAL

Hamilton, Requena, van Scheltinga, and Shifman, *The Permanent Court of Arbitration: International Arbitration and Dispute Resolution* (1999).

International Bureau of the Permanent Court of Arbitration Staff, *International Alternative Dispute Resolution: Past, Present and Future—The Permanent Court of Arbitration Centennial Papers* (2003).

Merrills, *International Dispute Resolution*, 4th ed. (2009).

O'Connell, *International Dispute Resolution: Cases and Materials* (2006).

INTERNATIONAL COURT OF JUSTICE

Aljaghoub, *The Advisory Function of the International Court of Justice 1946–2005* (2007).

Bedi, *The Development of Human Rights Law by the Judges of the International Court of Justice* (2007).

Bowett, *International Court of Justice: Process, Practice and Procedure* (1997).

Franck, *Judging the World Court* (1986).

International Court of Justice, *The International Court of Justice: Questions and Answers About the Principal Judicial Organ of the United Nations* (2000).

Lowe and Fitzmaurice, *Fifty Years of the International Court of Justice: Essays in Honour of Sir Robert Jennings* (1996).

Schulte, *Compliance with Decisions of the International Court of Justice* (2005).

Van den Biesen and Burroughs, *The Legality of Threat or Use of Nuclear Weapons: A Guide to the Historic Opinion of the International Court of Justice* (1998).

Zimmermann, Oellers-Frahm, Tomuschat, and Tams, *The Statute of the International Court of Justice: A Commentary* (2006).

International Law and Protection of the Environment

In 1969, Thor Heyerdahl of *Kon-Tiki* fame undertook another perilous expedition. He had noted a design similarity between boats on Lake Titicaca (Peru and Bolivia) and those depicted on tomb walls in Egypt. Theorizing that ancient Egyptians might have had some contact with the Americas, Heyerdahl attempted to sail from North Africa to South America in a papyrus reed boat.[1] During the voyage of *Ra I*, the crew encountered areas of the ocean littered by lumps of "tar" large enough to pose a hazard to a small reed boat. The lumps had resulted from the then current practice of supertankers washing out their empty tanks in the open sea. The practice had seemed harmless because few believed that, given the breadth and depth of the oceans, such minor and sporadic episodes would cause permanent harm. This incident formed part of a global "wake-up call" that directed attention to the conservation of the global environment as an important issue. Almost forty-five years later, a simple list of concerns commands attention because of the breadth, interrelated nature, and complexity of the problems. Deforestation and desertification, biodiversity (extinction of species), global warming, air and ocean pollution, and disposal of hazardous wastes constitute areas of immediate and growing concern. The Millennium Ecosystem Assessment Synthesis Report, completed in March 2005, concluded that approximately 60 percent of the ecosystem services that support life on Earth—such as fresh water, capture fisheries, air and water regulation, and the regulation of regional climate, natural hazards, and pests—are being degraded or used unsustainably.[2]

---

[1] T. Heyerdahl, *The Ra Expeditions* (1970), 208.

[2] The study involved 1,300 environmental experts from 95 countries. See www.maweb.org/en/index. aspx for a quick summary, see J. Amos, "Study Highlights Global Decline," BBC News (March 30, 2005), news.bbc.co.uk/1/hi/sci/tech/4391835.stm (accessed April 22, 2009).

THE ENVIRONMENT AND TRADITIONAL INTERNATIONAL LAW

During the past 40 years, international environmental law has emerged as a distinct and separable concern from state responsibility. We emphasize "distinct and separable" because some environmental concerns have long formed part of general international law. For example, states have always had a duty to control activities that might have adverse effects within the territories of their neighbors.[3] The heightened interest and proliferation of effort has come from the realization that transboundary problems form only one aspect of environmental concerns. Atmospheric pollution, global warming, marine pollution, ozone depletion, disposal of radioactive and other hazardous wastes, and questions of conservation and management of wildlife and fish stocks are problems that states may have in common, but no one state, no matter how powerful, can solve these questions by itself. Over the past 40 years, a concern for *damage to the environment itself* apart from damage to the environment of a particular state has slowly become part of the international agenda. Modern concerns embody not only potential transboundary problems but also more general threats to the atmosphere and global commons.

We emphasize this important distinction because, as with human rights, the structure and assumptions of traditional international law militate against major innovation. Curiously, although we must rely upon expanding scientific knowledge about the planet as the basis for effective action, the structure and nature of modern scientific inquiry also pose a set of problems. This observation about the law may seem obvious; that about modern science less so, to the point of being counterintuitive. Regarding the law, the simple fact that states, and therefore evidence of state consent, are still the essential element in developing legal obligations means that regimes develop only as states recognize that protecting their individual interests requires a cooperative effort. As we know, recognition of necessity—that is, of a common problem—does not necessarily lead to effective cooperative action. Illustrations that run from Rousseau's parable of the Stag Hunt to the more modern "tragedy of the commons"[4] and discussions of the logic surrounding the politics of collective goods[5] and bargaining detail the incentives and pitfalls. At the center of the controversy stands an indisputable fact—many of the activities that form the basis for industrial society, and the idea of progress and economic development that produces a better standard of living for all, may also generate effects that have deleterious impacts on the environment. Because many of the issues here do have direct economic consequences, the incentives to

---

[3]Trail Smelter arbitration, *United States vs. Canada, Arbitral Tribunal,* Montreal, April 16, 1938, and March 11, 1941; UN Reports of International Arbitral Awards 3 (1947), 1905; 33 *American Journal of International Law* 182 (1939) and 35 *AJIL* (1941). See also J. W. Meyer, D.J. Frank, A. Hironaka, E. Schofer, and N. B. Tuma, "The Structuring of a World Environmental Regime, 1870–1990," 51 *International Organization* 623 (1997).

[4]G. Hardin, "Tragedy of the Commons," 162 *Science* 1243 (1968), http://dieoff.org/page95.htm (accessed April 22, 2009).

[5]M. Olson, *The Logic of Collective Action: Public Goods and the Theory of Groups* (1971); and R. Axelrod, *The Evolution of Cooperation* (1984).

maximize or preserve short-run benefits because of the perceived cost of long-run gains have real, not theoretical, impacts on government calculations. Hence, even though progress seems rapid over the past 40 years—as measured in numbers of multilateral conventions (and the starting point)—questions of scope, effectiveness, and compliance remain at the heart of the effort. We still have much to learn about the complex interplay between the natural and the social world. As one recent study noted:[6]

> Truly effective international environmental institutions would improve the quality of the global environment. Much of this activity, however, is relatively new, and . . . on none of the issues . . . do we yet have good data about changes in environmental quality as a result of international institutional action. So we must focus on observable political effects of institutions rather than directly on environmental impact.

In this respect, the nature of modern scientific inquiry—coupled with concerns for the extent and accuracy of current findings—can serve as an inhibiting factor as well. This observation points up an interesting problem and dilemma. Certainly, effective action requires accurate and reliable scientific knowledge, *but* how scientists conceptualize problems has an impact on the nature of the information generated. Modern science owes much of its success to patterns of investigation that "encourage the disaggregation of problems into their component parts and reward efforts to tackle individual issues piecemeal."[7] Extrapolating this approach to the sociopolitical world, the nature of the scientific enterprise explains in part the often piecemeal nature of environmental regulation.[8]

On the other hand, the development of environmental law absolutely depends upon science—the need to understand the "laws of nature." Biology, chemistry, physics, and the other "hard sciences" form the heart of effective steps to regulate those activities that produce deleterious effects. Few other areas of the law absolutely depend upon scientific knowledge. Most areas of law attempt to regulate variable and often unpredictable human relationships. *In contrast, environmental law uses science to predict and regulate the consequences of human behavior on natural phenomena.*[9]

This means that we have an ongoing fundamental question concerning the reliability of what we think we know and do not know about environmental processes. For example, a recent study has called into question the long-held belief that simply planting trees will significantly reduce the effects of the greenhouse gas CO_2 (carbon dioxide) closely associated with hypotheses about global warming. These researchers found that trees (and other plants) give off significant amounts

---

[6]P. Keohane, R. Haas, and M. Levy, "The Effectiveness of International Environmental Institutions," in *Institutions for the Earth: Sources of Effective International Environmental Protection*, edited by R. Haas, P. Keohane, and M. Levy (1993), 7.

[7]O. R. Young, *International Governance* (1994), 47.

[8]Note the debate here in that Nazli Choucri and others have argued for a "holistic" approach. See N. Choucri, ed., *Global Accord: Environmental Challenges and International Responses* (1993).

[9]A. Kiss and D. Shelton, *International Environmental Law*, 3rd ed. (2004), 21.

of methane, another greenhouse gas.[10] If this proves true, the questions of controlling the processes associated with global warming have become infinitely more complex and difficult.

The ideology associated with globalization also presents a problem, but so does that associated with ideas of local development. Accepting the logic of the market economy without considering the impact on resources can produce the "tragedy of the commons."[11] The following discussion notes the tension between market principles, resource conservation, and the desire for economic development. These are not necessarily incompatible principles, but in devising strategies to reconcile the three, we face the rather daunting obstacle of overcoming "default assumptions" (see Chapter 1) deeply held by decision makers. This applies to the "market economy" (globalization) rationales as well as the "entitlement" perspectives of the Group of 77.

THE LIMITS OF THE LIABILITY/TRADITIONAL LAW FRAMEWORK

The structure and processes of the traditional law, apart from the questions relating to accepted scientific knowledge, form additional barriers. Law is a technique to preserve cooperative agreements but is not necessarily the technique best suited to develop them. For example, the obvious limitations of the traditional law as a technique for dealing with new areas of concern are reflected in the application of the responsibility/liability framework to environmental problems. As we discussed in Chapter 11, the idea that legal responsibility for injury should be imposed upon the party that caused the damage has an old and honorable history ("Polluters should pay"). The principal difficulty arises because establishing a law of environmental protection in this manner requires that we proceed on a case-by-case basis. Apart from the time and cost involved in international adjudication (and the questions of evidence, scope of competence, etc.), the major long-term environmental issues do not necessarily present themselves as a discrete set of problems, each with a definite technical and/or legal solution. Focusing on liability makes us think in terms of oil spills, when the major potential long-term threats may flow from the interconnected effect of many different everyday activities—such as the use of pesticides such as DDT (for mosquitoes) or chlordane (for termites) or the generation of electric power through the burning of fossil fuels.

Beyond the episodic character of the liability framework lies the consideration that the results of any particular litigation using the liability framework provide only a standard for levels *not* permitted. Seldom does litigation in liability cases serve the dual function of imposing responsibility for past acts and allocating the costs of future ones. Closely associated is the question of what

---

[10]"Plants Revealed As Methane Source," BBC News (January 11, 2006), http://news.bbc.co.uk/2/hi/science/nature/4604332.stm (accessed April 22, 2009); and P. N. Spotts, "Do Trees Share Blame for Global Warming?" *Christian Science Monitor* (January 19, 2006), 1.

[11]Hardin, note 4.

action in redress would be appropriate for violators. Does the idea that "polluters should pay" go far enough? How do we assess the extent of the compensation? Is repair and restoration a sufficient standard, or should the idea of punishment and punitive damages be incorporated as a matter of course? Consider the large-scale destruction caused by the actions of Iraqi armed forces as they retreated from Kuwait. They set fire to over 700 oil wells, causing almost unimaginable damage:[12]

> Day vanished into night, black rain fell from the sky, and a vast network of lakes was born . . . lakes of oil as deep as six feet. . . . Saddam also poured 10 million barrels of oil into the sea. Thousands of birds perished, and the people of the Persian Gulf became familiar with new diseases.

Add to these observations the problem of adducing proof. Again, lawyers tend to think in terms of paradigm cases, like oil spills, where the problems of proof are relatively easy.[13] As we noted earlier, many environmental problems such as global warming do not occur as discrete, bounded events. Consider the problem of proof in the case of injury to fisheries at some distance from the coast caused by land- or ocean-based sources that discharge relatively small quantities of pollutants but do so relatively often. Even in the case of discrete, bounded events, proof may be hard to adduce. The Rhine fish kill of 1969 provides an example of the difficulties authorities may have in establishing the cause of an injury as well as the origin of the injurious substance.[14] Unknown offenders discharged highly toxic Thiodan into the river Rhine near Bingen. This resulted in the death of at least 40 million whitings and eels downstream in Germany and the Netherlands. Authorities never established the identity of those responsible.

REGIMES AND THE LAW

Because of the extraordinarily complex nature of the problems, much of the research in the area of international environmental protection has concentrated on the idea of *regimes*. Scholars still dispute the exact definition of a regime, but

---

[12]R. Chilcote, "Kuwait Still Recovering from Gulf War Fires," CNN (January 3, 2003), www.cnn.com/2003/WORLD/meast/01/03/sproject.irq.kuwait.oil.fires/ (accessed April 22, 2009). As a result of this incident, the UN Compensation Commission (UNCC) was created in 1991 as a subsidiary organ of the UN Security Council. Its mandate is to process claims and pay compensation for losses and damages suffered as a direct result of Iraq's unlawful invasion and occupation of Kuwait in August 1990. The funds are raised through a tax on Iraqi oil exports. The UNCC's approach to reparation is strictly limited to *compensation*. As of January 24, 2006, a little over half of the 2,686,108 claims filed with the commission had been processed. The compensation awarded against the claims processed so far amounts to US $52.5 billion. The problem now clearly comes from the lack of revenue to pay settled claims; www.uncc.ch/.

[13]For example, the classic cases of the *Torrey Canyon*, www.guardian.co.uk/environment/2010/jun/24/torrey-canyon-oil-spill-deepwater-bp; *Amoco Cadiz*, news.bbc.co.uk/onthisday/hi/dates/stories/march/24/newsid_2531000/2531211.stm; and *Exxon Valdez*, www.eoearth.org/article/Exxon_Valdez_oil_spill?topic=58075.

[14]For a list of environmental "events," see www.gein.de/html/calendar/en/calDisasters.html (accessed April 22, 2009).

for our purposes, the original put forth by Stephen Krasner will suffice. Krasner defined regimes as "implicit or explicit principles, norms, rules and decision-making procedures around which actors' expectations converge in a given area of international relations."[15] Hence, even though law has an important function, an emphasis on regimes focuses attention more broadly on the importance of institutions and nonbinding political arrangements (e.g., "soft law"; see Chapter 2)[16] as well as issues of compliance. Regimes may serve many purposes apart from norm generation and standard setting (hard and soft laws). For example, other functions include dispute resolution, implementation, monitoring, technical support, and communication.

From the beginning, many organizations other than states, operating at many different levels, have played significant roles in developing international environmental policy. Myriad transnational institutions and organizations established by domestic law exist alongside the formal intergovernmental organizations established by treaties among states. These include nongovernmental organizations (NGOs), corporations, "epistemic communities,"[17] and other interest groups. As with human rights, the United Nations and the United Nations Environmental Programme (UNEP) stand at the center of the effort. NGOs[18] at many different levels are engaged in many different activities, providing essential support. Apart from the UN system, very few organizations have broad global interests.

Environmental NGOs include professional societies (Caretakers of the Environment International), foundations (Ford, Rockefeller),[19] federations of national organizations (Friends of the Earth, International Chamber of Commerce, Climate Action Network), public interest research groups (PIRGs),[20] and those devoted to specific tasks (Clean Up the World, Comitè Arctique International) to promote environmental awareness. Some groups actively lobby for legislation and policy changes, others engage in scientific research, many focus on a particular environmental project such as protecting wetlands, and still others find their mission in training or disseminating information. We also find an interesting array of hybrid organizations such as the International Union for Conserva-

---

[15]S. Krasner, "Structural Causes and Regime Consequences: Regimes As Intervening Variables," in *International Regimes,* edited by S. Krasner (1983), 3.

[16]See, inter alia, Reykjavik Declaration on Responsible Fisheries in the Marine Ecosystem (2001), www.fao.org/docrep/meeting/004/Y2211e.htm; FAO, Code of Conduct for Responsible Fisheries (1995), Ministerial Declaration of the Fifth International Conference on the Protection of the North Sea, 2002, www.eurocbc.org/page149.html; and Ministerial Declaration on the Protection of the Black Sea, 1993, http://eelink.net/~asilwildlife/odessa.pdf (accessed April 22, 2009).

[17]An "epistemic community" is a network of knowledge-based experts (or groups) with an authoritative claim to policy-relevant knowledge within the domain of their expertise. Members hold a common set of causal beliefs and share notions of validity based on internally defined criteria for evaluation, common policy projects, and shared normative commitments. See P. Haas, "Introduction: Epistemic Communities and International Policy Coordination," 46 *International Organization* 1 (1992), 3.

[18]For a directory, see www.ourearth.org/activism/default.html?gclid=CJL9ndjUxawCFcqa7Qod33taqg.

[19]See www.environmentalgrants.com (accessed April 22, 2009).

[20]www.pirg.org (accessed April 22, 2009).

tion of Nature and Natural Resources (IUCN),[21] whose membership comprises representatives from both governments and NGOs. This short list serves as only a minimal representation of the range and variety of activity associated with environmental regimes.

In analyzing the impact and importance of the Stockholm Conference, two prominent political scientists concisely summarized many of the issues touched on in the preceding discussion:[22]

> "Environment" as an issue has no simple bounds. To be concerned with assessing the impact of scientific and technological developments on the environment requires being concerned with the full array of issues affecting civilization, from disposal of waste . . . to the calculation of the real costs of economic growth. . . . Inevitably, as international institutions develop their concern and capacity for analyzing environmental impact issues, they will find themselves involved in many questions touching on major political, economic and social problems.

As with human rights, the diversity of efforts means fragmentation (specialization) that has often resulted in a lack of coordination, let alone formal cooperation or collaboration, among organizations working on similar problems. Lack of coordination also may stem from competition for scarce resources and funds. At the national level, even in smaller countries, groups often do not know of each other's existence. At the international level, the growth in the number of specialized organizations means that individuals and organizations need to spend increasing amounts of energy and resources in simply keeping abreast of research and other activities in the same area of interest. Nonetheless, the growth in efforts to deal with environmental questions continues at a rapid pace.

Over the years, four guiding principles have emerged as common elements in declarations, treaties, and other instruments. At present, the debate continues over the extent to which these principles have become "hard law" through treaty, court decisions, and customary practice or whether they simply remain aspirational goals. The four principles are as follows:

1. Consultation and cooperation on issues that might affect others
2. Precaution or prudence—avoidance of policies that could adversely affect the environment
3. Good neighbors—the extension of precaution to avoidance of policies that may have adverse joint effects
4. Intergenerational equity—the duty to preserve the environment for the future

---

[21]The International Union for Conservation of Nature and Natural Resources (IUCN) was established according to the Civil Code of Switzerland in 1948. As an international, nongovernmental organization, IUCN provides the World Heritage Committee with technical evaluations of natural heritage sites. Through its worldwide network of specialists, it provides reports on the state of conservation of listed properties. See www.iucn.org (accessed April 22, 2009).

[22]D. Kay and E. Skolnikoff, "International Institutions and the Environmental Crisis: A Look Ahead," 26 *International Organization* 469 (1972), 472.

The first case decided by an international tribunal illustrates the first three of these principles. In particular, the last sentence of the award in the *Trail Smelter* case expresses "strong hope" that future investigations in conjunction with the issues would be conducted jointly.

THE TRAIL SMELTER CASE

United States vs. Canada Arbitral Tribunal, Montreal (April 16, 1938, and March 11, 1941) U.N. RIAA wards 3 (1947) 1905; 33 AJIL 182 (1939) 182, and 35 AJIL 716 (1941)

Facts

The arbitration arose from claims involving transboundary air pollution by a smelter factory located in Trail (Province of British Columbia, Canada) about 12 miles north of the U.S. border.[23] Owned by the private Consolidated Mining & Smelting Co. of Canada, the smelter roasted sulfur-bearing ores and emitted sulfur dioxide fumes (SO_2) into the air. Between 1926 and 1937, the emissions caused damage to privately owned agricultural and forest lands near the township of Northport (State of Washington, United States). On August 7, 1928, the issue was referred to the International Joint Commission (IJC) established by the 1909 U.S.–Canadian Boundary Waters Treaty. The IJC submitted a report on February 28, 1931, recommending compensation and remedial measures.

After further representations by the United States in 1933, the two countries concluded a *compromis* on April 15, 1935, whereby Canada agreed to pay $350,000 for damage caused up to 1932, while the question of subsequent liability and prevention was submitted to an arbitral tribunal (Jan Frans Hostie, Belgium; Robert A. E. Greenshields, Canada; and Charles Warren, United States). Article IV of the *compromis* provided that the tribunal was to apply the law and practice followed in the United States as well as international law and practice.

Issues

1. Had damage been done to Washington State by the smelter since January 1, 1932?
2. If the smelter was found to have done damage, should it be made to refrain from doing so in the future?
3. Should the smelter operate under any restrictions?
4. Should any compensation be paid in light of the answers to questions 2 and 3?

Decisions

In its first decision on April 16, 1938, the tribunal addressed question 1 in the

(*continued*)

---

[23]So much written about this case takes its authority for granted. For a good recent reassessment, see C. Romano, *The Peaceful Settlement of International Environmental Disputes: A Pragmatic Approach* (2000), 261–278.

affirmative and evaluated the further damage between 1932 and 1937 at $78,000. It prescribed provisional remedial measures.

The second decision mandated that the Trail Smelter should refrain from causing any future damage to the State of Washington from its sulfur dioxide emissions. It required that the smelter maintain equipment to measure the wind velocity and direction, turbulence, atmospheric pressure, barometric pressure, and sulfur dioxide concentrations at Trail in order to keep the SO_2 emissions at or below levels determined by the tribunal.

Reasoning

The tribunal knew of *no prior case* in which a government had sought or been allowed indemnity for expenses incurred in preparing the proof or presenting a national or private claim before an international tribunal. In the absence of international cases on the subject, the members turned to decisions of the Supreme Court of the United States dealing with disputes between U.S. states that dealt with both air pollution and water pollution (Article IV of the *compromis*). They noted that these cases may legitimately be taken as a guide in this field of international law *where*

no contrary rule prevails in international law and no reason for rejecting such precedents can be induced from the limitation of sovereignty inherent in the Constitution of the United States.[24] The tribunal held that under the principles of international law, as well as the law of the United States, no state has the right to use or permit the use of its territory in such a manner as to cause injury by fumes in or to the territory of another or the properties or persons therein, when the case is of serious consequence and the injury is established by clear and convincing evidence.[25]

Note

In November 1949, the U.S. secretary of state wrote a letter to the Canadian ambassador to the United States offering to refund to the Canadian government US $8,828 of the money that the Canadians had paid to the United States as compensation for damages caused by operation of the Trail Smelter. This money was the balance left over from the US $428,179 Canada had paid in damages after the U.S. government had satisfied the claims of individual property owners in Washington State against the Trail Smelter. The Canadian government accepted this refund in January 1950.

The *Lac Lanoux* **arbitration** between France and Spain shows how the process of prior consultation and negotiation has been interpreted by an international arbitral tribunal. The panel drew on a treaty stipulation (the Bayonne Treaty of 1866 between France and Spain), but more important, it treated the requirement as a principle of customary law.[26] The questions in the arbitration turned on the principle that equitable utilization is based on the *equality of rights, not* on equal division of the water resource. This means that the interests of each party must be balanced against the other so as to achieve an equitable distribution of rights.

---

[24]See *State of Georgia v. Tennessee Copper Company and Ducktown Sulphur Copper, and Iron Company, Ltd.,* 206 U.S. 230 (1907); *Missouri v. Illinois,* 200 U.S. 496 (1906); and *New York v. New Jersey,* 200 U.S. 496 (1906).

[25]Sometimes called the *sic utere* principle ("Do not use property such as to harm others").

[26]12 U.N. RIAA 281 (1957).

THE LAC LANOUX CASE

France v. Spain November 9, 1957, 12 U.N. RIAA 281 (1957)

Facts

The Lac Lanoux *negotiations* began in 1917. The two states agreed to arbitration in 1956. Lake Lanoux is located on the French side of the Pyrenees mountain chain. It is fed by many streams rising in France and running only in French territory. The water of the lake feeds the headwaters of the river Carol, which crosses the Spanish border about 15 miles from the lake. Approximately 4 miles into Spanish territory, the Carol joins the Segre, which ultimately flows into the Ebro. The Treaty of Bayonne (1866) fixed the frontier between France and Spain. An Additional Act to the treaty contained regulations for the joint use of the water resources.

Beginning in 1917, the French government had proposed various schemes to divert the Lake Lanoux waters for public utility. The French utility proposed to divert the river Carol water but return it in total at the point where it flowed into Spain. Spain maintained that France would need Spanish consent for interference with the water.

Issues

Does France have to consult Spain concerning a project that lies wholly within the borders of France?

Decision

While France is entitled to exercise her rights, it cannot ignore Spanish interests. Spain is entitled to demand that its rights be respected and its interests be taken into account.

Reasoning

In examining the agreement between the two countries (Treaty of Bayonne, 1866, and Additional Act), the tribunal found that the conflicting interests generated by the industrial use of international rivers must be reconciled through negotiations in good faith with respect to the relevant documents. By way of a dictum, the tribunal stated that there existed a customary rule prohibiting an upper riparian state from altering the waters of a river in circumstances calculated to do serious injury to the lower riparian state. In the present case, the tribunal was of the opinion that "the French scheme complied with the obligations of Article 11 of the treaty." Because Spain was not able to submit evidence showing any injury, there was no need for the tribunal to consider what would amount to so-called serious injury. Thus, that threshold was left undecided.

Consultations and negotiation in good faith are necessary not only as a mere formality but also as an attempt to conclude an agreement for the prevention of conflicts.

Gabĉikovo–Nagymaros Project 1997 (Hungary/Slovakia)

Under a special agreement, Hungary and Slovakia[27] submitted to the International Court of Justice (ICJ) certain issues arising out of differences regarding the implementation and the termination of the Budapest Treaty of September 16, 1977, on

---

[27]*Case Concerning the Gabĉikovo-Nagymaros* (Hungary/Slovakia), *1996 ICJ Reports*, www.icj-cij. org/docket/index.php?p1=3&p2=3&code=hs&case=92&k=8d.

the construction and operation of the Gabcíkovo-Nagymaros barrage system. In 1989, Hungary suspended and subsequently abandoned work on the locks project, alleging that it entailed grave risks to the environment and the water supply of Budapest. Slovakia denied these allegations and insisted that Hungary comply with its 1977 treaty obligations. When it did not, Slovakia then initiated a unilateral plan for an alternative project built only on Slovakia's territory. However, the project would affect Hungary's access to the water of the Danube.

The ICJ found that both Hungary and Slovakia had breached their legal obligations: Hungary was not entitled to suspend and abandon the project unilaterally. Slovakia was perfectly entitled to take countermeasures, but had also breached international law by unilaterally assuming control of a shared resource in a way that deprived Hungary of its right to an equitable and reasonable portion. Slovakia failed to respect the *proportionality* required by international law. The court called on both states to *negotiate in good faith* in order to ensure the achievement of the objectives of the 1977 Budapest Treaty, which it declared was still in force, while taking account of the situation that had developed since 1989. In September 1998, Slovakia requested the ICJ for an additional judgment (Chapter 17), claiming that Hungary had demonstrated an unwillingness to implement the measures in the original judgment (lack of good faith). In support of its request, Slovakia submitted that Hungary had "breached Article 5(3) of the Special Agreement signed at Brussels on 7 April 1993 by itself and Hungary with a view to the joint submission of their dispute to the Court."[28] As of August 1, 2011, Hungary had not responded.

ORGANIZATIONS AND REGIMES

The International Whaling Commission

As one of the first international organizations set up with a conservation mission (1946), the International Whaling Commission (IWC)[29] had the formal mission to provide "for the proper conservation of whale stocks and thus make possible the orderly development of the whaling industry."[30] The IWC is currently composed of 66 states parties,[31] and membership is open to any state that wishes to ratify the convention. The IWC has a small secretariat (in Cambridge, England). The politics surrounding the history of the IWC illustrates the dilemmas associated with developing "hard law" standards for many perceived environmental threats. The dual nature of the mission—conservation and orderly development of the industry—has

---

[28]Press Release ICJ, "Gabcíkovo-Nagymaros Project (Hungary/Slovakia) Slovakia Requests an additional Judgment" (September 3, 1998), www.icj-cij.org/docket/index.php?pr=268&p1=3&p2=1&case=92&p3=6 (accessed April 22, 2009).

[29]Set up by the International Convention for the Regulation of Whaling of December 2, 1946, www.iwcoffice.org/commission/convention.htm#convention (accessed April 22, 2009). For background, see G. P. Donovan, "The International Whaling Commission and the Revised Management Procedure" (1993), www.highnorth.no/Library/Management_Regimes/IWC/th-in-wh.htm (accessed April 22, 2009).

[30]www.iwcoffice.org/commission/iwcmain.htm (accessed April 22, 2009).

[31]For membership list, see www.iwcoffice.org/commission/iwcmain.htm#nations (accessed April 22, 2009).

often produced open rifts between member states committed to commercial whaling and those opposed.

While commercial whaling has been banned since 1986, Japan has continued the practice under a loophole that permits killing whales for scientific purposes.[32] Norway has a long-standing protest against the zero-catch policy and has refused to abide by it since 1992.[33] Iceland, a new member, has started a "scientific whaling" program.[34] Statements by African and Caribbean delegates to the annual conference of the IWC (June 2005) show the interconnection they perceive between the necessities of economic development and the economic opportunities they see in commercial whaling.[35]

The key to the convention is the Schedule, a document that mandates protection of certain species, designates certain areas as whale sanctuaries, sets limits on the numbers and size of catches, prescribes open and closed seasons and areas for whaling, and controls aboriginal subsistence whaling.[36] The convention specifies that any amendments to the Schedule "shall be based on scientific findings" (Article V.2.b). Hence, the findings of the Scientific Committee are the key to redefining the Schedule. In 1975, the IWC adopted a new management schedule designed to bring all stocks to the levels that would sustain the greatest long-term harvests. It did so by setting catch limits for individual stocks below their sustainable yields. Problems arose due to lack of confidence in the scientific analyses, largely because of the difficulty in obtaining the complex data required. The decision to declare a moratorium on commercial whaling beginning in 1986 followed.

The IWC Scientific Committee then undertook a mission to develop a Revised Management Program (RMP). After eight years, based on the report of the Scientific Committee, the IWC set up a Revised Management Scheme (RMS) Working Group in 1994. The record from the 2005 annual conference proves instructive. The official website notes:[37]

> In the Commission, different views remained regarding the elements that should be included in an RMS "package" and on whether adoption of an RMS should be linked in any way to the lifting of the commercial whaling moratorium. Japan put forward a proposed Schedule amendment for an RMS

---

[32]See the material of the Japanese Whaling Association at www.whaling.jp/english/ (accessed April 22, 2009). For the Japanese view, see also K. Nakai, "The Whaling Controversy Between Japan and the U.S." (1997), www.geocities.com/Athens/Styx/9189/whaligcon.html (accessed April 22, 2009).

[33]See Ministry of Foreign Affairs, "Norwegian Minke Whaling" (2001), http://odin.dep.no/odin/engelsk/norway/environment/032001-990108/ (accessed April 22, 2009).

[34]A. Kirby, "Iceland Bids to Resume Whaling," BBC (April 3, 2003), http://news.bbc.co.uk/1/hi/sci/tech/2910655.stm (accessed April 22, 2009).

[35]R. Black, "Caribbean Call to Resume Whaling," BBC (June 22, 2005), http://news.bbc.co.uk/2/hi/science/nature/4117888.stm (accessed April 22, 2009). One minister told BBC News, "The key point is that if commercial whaling is resumed, then countries in the Caribbean would be given a quota." He also noted, ". . . Even though we might not catch whales ourselves, we could then sell the quota, like we do our tuna quota under ICCAT" (the International Commission for the Conservation of Atlantic Tuna), *id.*

[36]www.iwcoffice.org/commission/schedule.htm (accessed April 22, 2009).

[37]www.iwcoffice.org/conservation/rms.htm (accessed April 22, 2009).

that *inter alia* would have lifted the moratorium. The proposal did not attract the required three-quarter majority to be adopted (23 votes in favour, 29 against and 5 abstentions).

In evaluating the history of the IWC, consider that no state has acted totally in "bad faith." The Caribbean states may make statements (to gain negotiating leverage), but they still work through the IWC. The protesters—Japan, Norway, and Iceland—have problems with the prohibition on commercial whaling. Each state has been conservative in its "scientific" harvest, but more important, all three states have had to justify their policies in terms of the convention. Most certainly, this requirement has had a positive effect.

The Stockholm Conference and Declaration

The emergence of the environment as a major concern for transnational consideration came with the 1972 Stockholm Conference. The conference produced the Declaration of the United Nations Conference on the Human Environment (Twenty-Six Principles)[38] and provided the impetus for creation of the UNEP by the UN General Assembly.[39] In this sense, the Stockholm Declaration occupies the same "founding" position in contemporary environmental law as the Universal Declaration of Human Rights (Chapter 16) has in the evolution and development of human rights law. From the standpoint of the evolution of future legal norms, while the declaration itself contains no standards, it mentions several specific forms of potential damage states have a duty to address (e.g., ocean dumping, toxic discharges, and nuclear weapons) and states three general legal principles as guides for future development:

1. All human beings have a "fundamental right to "freedom, equality and adequate conditions of life, in an environment of a quality that permits a life of dignity and well-being." Individuals bear a "solemn responsibility to protect and improve the environment for present and future generations. In this respect, policies promoting or perpetuating apartheid, racial segregation, discrimination, colonial and other forms of oppression and foreign domination stand condemned and must be eliminated." (Principle 1)
2. "States shall cooperate to develop further the international law regarding liability and compensation for the victims of pollution and other environmental damage caused by activities within the jurisdiction or control of such States to areas beyond their jurisdiction." (Principles 21–22)
3. States have a duty to cooperate through international agreements to "prevent, eliminate or reduce and effectively control adverse environmental effects resulting from activities conducted in all sphere in such a way that due account is taken of the sovereignty and interests of all States." (Principle 24)

---

[38]Text at www.unep.org/Documents.multilingual/Default.asp?DocumentID=97&ArticleID=1503 (accessed April 22, 2009).

[39]www.unep.org (accessed April 22, 2009).

Two of the general principles (Principles 21–22 and 24) merely reflect the traditional structure of international law and the liability framework with the environment as an explicit focus. The third (Principle 1) marks an interesting departure from traditional law in that it embodies the idea of an *individual right* to a clean and healthy environment *as well as* that of *intergenerational equity* reflected in an *individual duty* to "protect and improve" the environment for future generations.

Many of the other principles note particular problems such as the depletion of nonrenewable resources, rapid population growth, and the need for education, scientific research, and wildlife preservation, but these have significance only as a laundry list of potential future agenda items. Based on Indira Gandhi's impassioned presentation, the declaration also addressed the question of the relationship between environmental protection and the drive for economic development in lesser developed countries (LDCs).[40] This issue continues as a major concern because of the expense associated with more modern "clean" technologies. Maintaining a balance between development and the need for environmental protection once again illustrates the tensions between state sovereignty (potent individual interests) and the need for broad international cooperation. LDCs would choose smoking factories if they meant a better standard of living over no factories at all—if all that *no factories* meant was a clean "environment" with no improvement in the basic economic living conditions of their citizens.

The United Nations Environmental Programme

Established by the UN General Assembly in 1972, the UNEP stands at the center of environmental law and policymaking. As a subsidiary organ of the United Nations, UNEP has a Governing Council composed of 58 states, elected in staggered terms for four years. The rapid growth of the UNEP in terms of issue areas and regional reach illustrates both progress and problems. In the past 35 years, UNEP has become a remarkably complex operation. Besides the headquarters in Nairobi (which also houses the regional office for Africa), the organization has six regional offices (Africa, Asia-Pacific, West Asia, Latin America–Caribbean, Europe, and North America), eight divisions, and a multitude of linkages with NGOs and private organizations.[41] UNEP has been the catalyst for development of more than 40 formal international agreements—some global, some regional—and for promoting discussions that have produced a number of "ministerial declarations" and other soft-law pronouncements suggesting guidelines and principles for developing future standards in many issue areas.[42]

UNEP stands at the center of UN efforts on environmental matters. It has a principal role in identifying new problems and monitoring progress, coordination, and promotion. Yet this status should not draw attention from the fact that other UN agencies (e.g., the Food and Agricultural Organization [FAO] and the

---

[40]E. P. Morgan, "The Clean (but Impossible) Dream," *Foreign Policy* (1972).

[41]See, for example, the "UNEP Finance Incentive: Innovative Financing for Sustainability," described as a global partnership between UNEP and the financial sector, www.unepfi.org (accessed April 22, 2009).

[42]See note 14.

World Health Organization [WHO]), some even before UNEP was established, have been very much concerned with environmental issues. Indeed, as testament to our earlier observation concerning fragmentation of effort, UNEP has only the power of persuasion in promoting and coordinating environmental programs and initiatives. As with human rights programs, finance is a continuing concern. The costs of maintaining the Governing Council and the Secretariat come from the UN regular budget.[43] Funds for other activities come solely from voluntary contributions. While the base of donors has increased significantly over time, contributions have seldom been sufficient to fund all programs fully.

THE UN SYSTEM AND THE ENVIRONMENT: SELECTED INTERNET SITES

CSD	www.un.org/esa/dsd/csd/csd_aboucsd.shtml
FAO	www.fao.org
IAEA	www.aea.org/
IBRD (World Bank)	
Inspection Panel	www.worldbank.org/html/ins-panel
CGIAR	www.cgiar.org/
ICAO	www2.icao.int/en/home/default.aspx
ILO	www.ilo.org
IMO	www.imo.org
ITTO	www.lincmedia.co.jp/itto
UNCC	www.un.org/wcm/content/site/climatechange/gateway
UNCCD	www.unccd.ch
UNCLOS	www.un.org/Depts/los
UNDP	www.beta.undp.org/undp/en/home.html
UNECE	www.unece.org/env
UNEP	www.unep.org
Basel Secretariat	www.basel.int/
CBD Secretariat	www.biodiv.org
CITES Secretariat	www.cites.org/eng/disc/sec/index.php
CMS Secretariat	www.cms.int/secretariat/index.htm
Ozone Secretariat	www.ozone.unep.org/new_site/en/index.php
Regional Seas	www.unep.org/regionalseas/
UNESCO	
World Heritage	www.whc.unesco.org/en/list

(continued)

---

[43]For 2011–2012, the contribution from the UN regular budget represented 3.1 percent of funds needed for various activities, www.unep.orgVrms/en/Financing_of_UNEP/Regular_Budget/index.asp.

UNFCCC	www.unfccc.de
UNITAR	www.unitar.org
UNOLA (Treaties)	www.un.org/Depts/Treaty
WHO	
Ecosystem	www.who.int/topics/ecosystems/en/
Environmental health	www.who.int/topics/environmental_health/en/
Pollution	www.who.int/topics/environmental_pollution/en
WIPO	www.wipo.int
WMO	www.wmo.ch
WTO	
Trade and Environment	www.wto.org/english/tratop_e/envir_e/envir_e.htm

THE EARTH SUMMIT (RIO CONFERENCE)

The UN Conference on Environment and Development, better known as the Earth Summit, held at Rio de Janeiro in 1992, marked a second significant milestone. Attended by 172 governments and 2,400 representatives from NGOs, the conference generated two soft-law statements of general principles (the Rio Declaration, forest conservation) and a program for future action (Agenda 21). As planning for the meeting took place, two conventions were prepared for final action at the conference—the UN Framework Convention on Climate Change (UNFCCC)[44] and the Convention on Biodiversity (CBD).[45]

The Rio Declaration[46] dealt with the problems associated with development and environmental quality and protection. The themes that states have a duty to consult, cooperate, and take effective domestic action run throughout the document. Between Stockholm and Rio, several treaties had incorporated these principles. For example, Article 5 of the Long-Range Transboundary Air Pollution Convention (1979)[47] says that consultation shall be held upon request if an activity may have an effect in other states. Other treaties have stronger requirements, such as environmental impact assessments (e.g., Article 204 of UNCLOS III; the Antarctic Environmental Protocol, 1991[48]). The debate continues over the status of these principles as new *customary* rules of international law.

---

[44]http://unfccc.int/resource/docs/convkp/conveng.pdf (accessed April 22, 2009); entered into force on March 21, 1994. Currently, 189 states parties. The United States has ratified the convention.

[45]www.biodiv.org/convention/articles.asp (accessed April 22, 2009); 188 states parties. The United States has signed, but not ratified, the treaty.

[46]Text at www.unep.org/Documents.multilingual/Default.asp?DocumentID=78&ArticleID=1163 (accessed April 22, 2009).

[47]Text at www.unece.org/env/lrtap/full%20text/1979.CLRTAP.e.pdf (accessed April 22, 2009). Currently 49 states parties. The United States has signed and ratified the convention.

[48]Text at www.antarctica.ac.uk/About_Antarctica/Treaty/protocol.html (accessed April 22, 2009); entered into force on January 14, 1998. Currently 27 states parties. The United States has signed and ratified the protocol.

While the document reemphasized the principles of Stockholm (cooperation, consensus, and intergenerational equity), Principle 3 speaks of a "right" to development, and Principle 4 defines *environmental protection* as an "integral part of the development process." Perhaps the most interesting statement comes in Principle 7, which departs from the traditional equality assumption to talk about differential responsibility in terms of environmental and developmental issues:

> The developed countries acknowledge the responsibility that they bear in the international pursuit to sustainable development in view of the pressures their societies place on the global environment and of the technologies and financial resources they command.

Because it is characterized as soft law, the declaration does not bind states to specific *legal* obligations. Yet, as we have noted in these discussions, the importance and impact flowing from public expectations can turn political statements into future commitment. For example, Article 3(1) of the UNFCCC reflects the principle of *differential responsibility* (differential duties) in providing that the states parties should deal with the questions of climate change on the basis of "equity" and "in accordance with their common but differentiated responsibilities and respective capabilities." Article 3(2) emphasizes the "special needs and circumstances of developing countries."[49] Article 20(4) of the Biodiversity Convention states this differential clearly:

> The extent to which developing country Parties will effectively implement their commitments under this Convention will depend on the effective implementation by developed country Parties of their commitments under this Convention related to financial resources and transfer of technology and will take fully into account the fact that economic and social development and eradication of poverty are the first and overriding priorities of the developing country Parties.

Agenda 21 Often mentioned as the blueprint for developing future management plans for all sectors of the environment, this document has 40 chapters and runs to more than 800 pages.[50] Like the Rio Declaration, Agenda 21 does not generate binding obligations. Its importance lies in the restatement and elaboration of many general principals and perspectives regarding specific areas of concern. Again, as with certain areas of human rights law, understanding the delays involved with disputes over *definitions*, states made the decision that it was important to move ahead with *general statements of goals* with an understanding that the details would still require much negotiation. In international politics, the devil is always in the details, but this should not diminish the giant step involved in the production of Agenda 21.

Regarding Agenda 21, future steps in developing solutions to the extensive list of problems identified (let alone the prospect that new ones may emerge) may

---

[49]For an examination of this idea in relationships to other areas, see C. D. Stone, "Common but Differentiated Responsibilities in International Law," 98 *AJIL* 276 (2004).

[50]For a table of contents with hyperlinks to text, see www.unep.org/Documents.multilingual/Default.asp?DocumentID=52&ArticleID= (accessed April 22, 2009).

occur very slowly, for many reasons. While statements noting the need for cooperation and consultation run throughout the document, most of these goals depend on the actions of independent states in establishing appropriate domestic goals and mechanisms for their achievement. As a general comment, the document glosses over some continuing areas of deep division, such as the terms of technology transfer, trade barriers, adequacy and availability of development assistance, financial support for international programs in general, and questions of timetables for plans of action to achieve the goals.

The definition (and goals) of "sustainable development" continues as a problem. Sustainable development implies the necessity to reconcile the competing demands of global social equity, environmental protection, and economic efficiency.[51] Adding sustainable development as a requirement takes environmental planning far outside the normal frames of reference. Doing so also raises substantive issues about appropriate goals and measures of progress. Moreover, as a new and somewhat ambiguous goal, factoring in global equity concerns in future planning presents two additional challenges. First, because many goals demand action through domestic planning, those involved must proceed in ways not part of their prior experience. Second, domestic planning will always be responsive to local evaluations of where global equity concerns rank in terms of domestic priorities.

The Commission on Sustainable Development   As part of the machinery established to implement the goals of the Earth Summit, the General Assembly created the Commission on Sustainable Development (CSD; under the Economic and Social Council) to monitor progress toward achievement of the Rio Declaration and Agenda 21 objectives. The CSD meets every two years, at each meeting focusing on a specific set of thematic issues.[52] The Earth Summit mandated that every five years, an international conference should convene to examine and evaluate the progress toward the standards contained in Agenda 21. The World Summit on Sustainable Development (WSSD) in Johannesburg in the late summer of 2002 marked the second follow-up meeting. The 2002 Conference saw a shift in priorities from the UN perspective. The 1997 conference had identified the global threats as defined by the developed nations—climate change and loss of biodiversity, for example—as the top priorities. The 2002 Conference reflected Indira Gandhi's challenge of 30 years before—the idea that improvement at the "micro" level formed an essential component of sustainable development as important as the concerns at the "macro" level. Safe drinking water, sanitation, and basic health care moved ahead of global warming and extinction of species as priorities.[53] The WSSD produced another plan of implementation.[54] Yet progress over

---

[51]See J. Meadowcroft, "The Politics of Sustainable Development: Emerging Arenas and Challenges for Political Science," 20 *International Political Science Review* 219 (1999), 224 et seq.

[52]See www.un.org/esa/sustdev/csd/aboutCsd.htm (accessed April 22, 2009).

[53]Text at www.un.org/esa/sustdev/documents/WSSD_POI_PD/English/POIToc.htm (accessed April 22, 2009).

[54]Text at www.johannesburgsummit.org/html/documents/summit_docs/131302_wssd_report_reissued.pdf (accessed April 22, 2009).

the years after Rio seems modest. A considerable gap has seemed to exist between the pledges made with such idealism at Rio and performance in terms of implementation since.

TREATIES

Treaties have formed one of the main instruments for environmental regulation. Reports vary as to the number of global and regional agreements now in force. A recent estimate gave the number as "more than 500."[55] The greatest majority of these address regional issues; one environmental website identifies 225 treaties that have entered into force since 1972.[56] Many of these set up their own governance and monitoring structures. Rather than an extended and detailed tour through the various treaties, in this discussion we will address thematic areas and patterns.

Biodiversity and Land Management

The initiative for the Convention on Biodiversity (CBD)[57] dates from 1981. First proposed by the IUCN, it brought together in legal form a number of policies and proposals that had been part of many conference agendas as well as action programs of advocacy organizations at all levels. The primary goal of the CBD is to preserve and protect the variety of life on Earth. Article 2 offers the following definitions:

> "Biological diversity" means the variability among living organisms from all sources including, inter alia, terrestrial, marine and other aquatic ecosystems and the ecological complexes of which they are part; this includes diversity within species, between species and of ecosystems.
>
> "Biological resources" includes genetic resources, organisms or parts thereof, populations, or any other biotic component of ecosystems with actual or potential use or value for humanity.

Potentially, the treaty applies to the simplest organism as well as the complex ecosystems of rainforests.

The issues in this area clearly demonstrate the complexity and interdependence of environmental processes. Preservation of species has obvious links to

---

[55]C. Joyner, *International Law in the 21st Century* (2005), 210.

[56]Environmental Treaties and Resource Indicators, http://sedac.ciesin.columbia.edu/entri/treatySearch. jsp (accessed April 22, 2009).

[57]See note 37. President George H. W. Bush did not sign the CBD because of questions involving technology transfer, intellectual property rights, and financial commitments. President Bill Clinton subsequently signed the CBD in 1993 and submitted it to the Senate for ratification. When it became clear that the treaty did not have sufficient votes to pass, Senate Majority Leader George Mitchell requested that it be withdrawn from consideration. The United States is the only major power that has not ratified the CBD. For a brief description of events, see "How the Convention on Biodiversity Was Defeated," www.sovereignty.net/p/land/biotreatystop.htm (accessed April 22, 2009).

deforestation[58] and desertification[59] because these processes obviously produce loss of habitat. For example, deforestation, as well as desertification, can result from a number of activities associated with development: conversion of forests and woodlands to agricultural land for food production; development of cash crops and cattle ranching, both of which earn hard currency for tropical countries; commercial logging (e.g., teak, mahogany, and ebony), often in conjunction with development of land for agriculture; and cutting trees for firewood. The presence of livestock compacts the substrata, reducing the percolation rate of the soil and in erosion by wind and water. Grazing and the collection of firewood reduce or eliminate plants that help to bind the soil. These activities can produce extreme land degradation because, despite the often lush appearance of the rainforest, the soils of the tropics lack depth and coherence. Without amendment and conservation, they cannot support agriculture or ranching for long. A cycle begins—people then must move on and clear more forests in order to maintain production. Both the Statement of Forest Principles and the Convention on Biodiversity cite "sustainable" exploitation as a priority. Article 15(7) of the Biodiversity Convention states that lesser developed countries must develop conservation plans, while developed states must provide expertise and financial assistance in the expectation of a "far and equitable sharing" of any benefits.

Desertification has received a great deal of publicity from the news media, but scientific knowledge in many areas still remains sparse. Almost 20 years ago, Ridley Nelson pointed out in an important scientific paper written for the World Bank ("Dryland Management: The Desertification Problem") that desertification problems and processes are not clearly defined. This still remains the case. No consensus exists among researchers as to the specific causes, extent, or degree of desertification. Desertification occurs in many different areas of the world with very different ecosystems. It is not just a problem of lesser developed countries. The "Dust Bowl" saga of the American prairie lands in the 1930s stands as a reminder of what can happen in the absence of prudent land management plans—as do areas of Arizona and New Mexico currently. In Canada, portions of the three Prairie provinces—Alberta, Saskatchewan, and Manitoba—comprise vulnerable drylands. In these areas, ordinary activity without careful planning can have long-term effect.

Convention on International Trade in Endangered Species

Sponsored by IUCN, the Convention on International Trade in Endangered Species of Wild Fauna and Flora (CITES)[60] emerged as the first post-Stockholm environmental instrument. As with many other treaties in the environmental area, CITES does not substitute for national legislation. It has guidelines that provide a *framework* within

---

[58]See www.botany.uwc.ac.za/Envfacts/facts/deforestation.htm; J. Revington, "The Causes of Tropical Deforestation," www.ru.org/32defore.html; and "Forest Holocaust," *National Geographic*, www. nationalgeographic.com/eye/deforestation/effect.html (accessed April 22, 2009).

[59]For a pioneering study, see R. Nelson, *Dryland Management: The Desertification Problem* (World Bank Technical Paper, 1990). For a good summary of current problems, see www.fao.org/ desertification/default.asp?lang=en (accessed April 22, 2009).

[60]www.cites.org/eng/disc/parties/index.php; Currently 175 states parties.

which each state party must develop appropriate domestic legislation. Although we have adopted Stockholm (1972) as a significant transitional event, the preparatory work for this convention dates back to 1963—a reminder of the often lengthy process associated with developing important international norms.

CITES merits note not only because it has evolved as an effective regime but also because we need to distinguish between what the term *framework* means with regard to the obligations it mandates in contrast with what it means with regard to other treaty regimes such as the Vienna Convention[61] (1985) and the Montreal Protocol[62] (1987). In the broader sense, the Vienna Convention provides a "framework" in that it sets general guidelines with the expectation that future negotiations will deal with standard setting in specific areas through protocols or substantive amendments guided by the general principles in the "framework treaty." The protocols will contain explicit standards and targets. Confusion can result because the resulting protocols often have utilized the framework guideline approach of CITES in mandating the passage of appropriate legislation at the domestic level. The Montreal Protocol stands as a prime example. To summarize quickly, CITES is not a framework convention per se in the sense of guiding the future development of *international* law; rather, it sets guidelines for the development of *national* law.

To reinforce an earlier point about knowledge and international concern about the environment, note that when IUCN first proposed that certain species needed protection from extinction, few states had thought a problem existed. Today, CITES regulates international trade worth several billion dollars in over 30,000 species (more than 25,000 are plants).[63] The trade comprises live animals and plants as well as the products derived from them, including food products, exotic leather goods, wooden musical instruments, timber, tourist curios, and medicines (or exotic health treatments). Monitoring includes factors such as level of exploitation (demand) and loss of habitat. The treaty has three areas of concern: (1) endangered species or those threatened with extinction; (2) species not endangered, but needing monitoring to ensure *sustainability;* and (3) species designated by at least one country as protected, where the state has asked international cooperation in controlling the trade. The treaty has two administrative levels: international and domestic. At the *international* level, the Conference of the Parties (COP) meets biennially. The COP has responsibility for amendments to the three categories of protected species and for any new resolutions affecting the implementation of the treaty. The CITES standing committee, which meets once or twice a year depending upon demand, takes care of issues arising between meetings of the COP. The CITES secretariat, administered by UNEP, takes care of the everyday business associated with communications, dissemination of information, monitoring, and assistance to field operations. Financing of the core activities associated with COP, the standing committee, and the secretariat comes from the CITES trust fund. Replenishment of the trust fund comes from contributions from the parties to the convention, based on the UN scale of assessment and adjusted to account

---

[61]Text at www.unescap.org/drpad/vc/orientation/legal/3_vienna.htm.

[62]Text at www.unescap.org/drpad/vc/orientation/legal/3_vienna.htm.

[63]See "How CITES Works," www.cites.org/eng/disc/how.shtml (accessed April 22, 2009).

for the fact that not all members of the United Nations are parties to the convention.[64] Funds for other activities must be raised from private sources.

At the national level, CITES works by requiring that states parties enact certain controls with respect to international trade in specimens of selected species. All import, export, reexport, and introduction from the sea of species covered by the convention must be authorized through a licensing system. Each party to the convention must designate one or more management authorities in charge of administering that licensing system as well as at least one scientific authority to advise them on the effects of trade on the status of the species.[65]

Other Relevant International Conventions (Wildlife and Land Management)

Ramsar Convention on Wetlands Signed at Ramsar (Iran) in 1971, the Convention on Wetlands was the first international treaty aimed at the conservation of natural resources.[66] The convention provides guidelines for national action with regard to the preservation, restoration, and wise use of areas designated as wetlands. Its international administrative structure consists of the Conference of Contracting Parties (COCP), which meets every three years to discuss policy issues and to report on the activities of the previous three years through national reports; the standing committee, which meets annually; the secretariat; and the scientific and technical review committee. The secretariat of the Convention on Wetlands is housed by IUCN. The treaty secretariat is an independent body serving the contracting parties to the convention, and the standing committee. Ramsar staff receive the benefits and services as IUCN staff members and are legally considered IUCN personnel. The Convention on Wetlands is not part of the United Nations or UNEP system of environmental treaties.

At the national level, each state party designates an administrative authority as the focal point for implementation of the convention. The convention suggests that parties should establish national wetland committees to coordinate all government institutions, as well as interested NGOs, in dealing with water resources, development planning, protected areas, biodiversity, education, and development assistance. Ramsar sites facing problems in maintaining their ecological character can be placed by the country concerned on a special list, the *Montreux Record,* and receive technical assistance to help solve the problems.[67]

Bonn Convention on Migratory Species of Wildlife The Stockholm Conference produced the initiative for the Bonn Convention on Migratory Species of Wildlife (CMS).[68] In part, CMS mirrors the structure of CITES; it sets guidelines for

---

[64]"How Is CITES Financed," www.cites.org/eng/disc/fund.shtml (accessed April 22, 2009).

[65]See "U.S. Fish and Wildlife Service, International Affairs," www.fws.gov/international/DMA_DSA/CITES/CITES_home.html.

[66]Text at www.ramsar.org (accessed April 22, 2009). Presently the convention has 150 contracting parties. The United States became a party in 1987. The United States currently has 18 listed sites.

[67]www.ramsar.org/key_brochure_2004_e.htm (accessed April 22, 2009).

[68]Text at www.cms.int/documents/convtxt/cms_convtxt.htm (accessed April 22, 2009). Entered into force 1983.

national legislation, and its international administrative structure (conference of parties, standing committee, secretariat) has the same component institutions. In scope, the convention lists two categories of concern: (1) species threatened with extinction and (2) migratory species that would benefit from international cooperation. The treaty seeks to have states establish regulations that would protect and conserve habitats, eliminate obstacles to migration, and deal with other conditions that pose a threat. As with CITES, UNEP administers the secretariat. A scientific council, consisting of experts appointed by individual member states and by the COP, gives advice on technical and scientific matters.[69]

Unlike CITES, the Bonn Convention serves as a "framework treaty" with respect to both international and national laws. The convention consists of six agreements and eight memoranda of understandings (MoUs). Because states parties are not necessarily interested in all problems of all migratory wildlife, the international structure is quite complex; states may choose to ratify some agreements and MoUs and not others. States may elect not to join CMS (i.e., not to sign or ratify the treaty) and yet still participate in one or more of the MoUs. The United States has not joined CMS but participates in the Marine Turtle/Indian Ocean MoU. In passing, we should point out the overlap in issue area with the IWC (cetacean agreements).

CMS (BONN) CONVENTION: AGREEMENTS AND MoUs[70]

Populations of European Bats

Cetaceans of the Mediterranean Sea, Black Sea, and Contiguous Atlantic Area

Small Cetaceans of the Baltic and North Seas

Seals in the Wadden Sea

African–Eurasian Migratory Waterbirds

Albatrosses and Petrels

MEMORANDA OF UNDERSTANDING

Siberian Crane

Slender-Billed Curlew

Marine Turtles of the Atlantic Coast of Africa

Marine Turtles of the Indian Ocean and Southeast Asia

Middle European Population of the Great Bustard

Bukhara Deer

Aquatic Warbler

West African Populations of the African Elephant

---

[69]"Introduction to the Convention on Migratory Species," www.cms.int/about/intro.htm.

[70]See www.cms.int/pdf/en/party_list/Partylist_eng.pdf.

Climate, Atmosphere, and Other Transboundary Problems

Acid rain, air quality, ozone depletion, global warming/climate change and transport, control, and disposal of hazardous compounds and wastes comprise some of the core problems in this issue area.[71] As many have pointed out, questions of air quality are not new. We have reliable reports of significant air pollution from ancient smelting operations, from the burning of coal for heat in the Middle Ages, and later from factories as the industrial revolution took hold.[72] In 1908, Glasgow, Scotland, had a winter inversion that trapped smoke and killed 1,000 people. Sixty years ago, many cities in the United States, particularly those with large steel industries—like Pittsburgh, Birmingham (AL), East Chicago, and Gary—were infamous for the smoky fog ("smog") constantly hovering over them. In October 1948, twenty people were asphyxiated and another 7,000 hospitalized in Donora, Pennsylvania (population 14,000). Known as the Donora Smog, it was described as a killer fog that "dropped dogs and cats in their tracks."[73] Tokyo in the 1960s had oxygen stations strategically placed, so that for the equivalent of a quarter, you could get "fresh air" if needed. A cartoon published in the late 1960s shows two extraterrestrial beings landing in a flying saucer with one saying to the other: "The rules here are simple: in developing countries, don't drink the water; in developed countries, don't breathe the air."

The difficulties here, as with other issue areas, stem from the traditional structure of international law. Each state clearly has responsibility for the airspace (or other activities that occur within) above its territorial jurisdiction. The contemporary questions come from responsibility for areas outside the territorial domain of any state. For effective regimes to develop, a more effective sense of the atmosphere as a shared resource and common concern must evolve. Time becomes an important issue, both because responsible regulation necessitates a timetable for phasing out pollutants and converting to alternative substances and because of the long-term persistence of the pollutants already in the air. Some chlorofluorocarbons (CFCs) may take 50 years or more to become totally inert.[74] Table 18.1 highlights some important issues and themes.

Framework Convention on Long-Range Transboundary Air Pollution[75] Sponsored by the United Nations Economic Commission for Europe (UNECE),[76] the Framework Convention on Long-Range Transboundary Air Pollution (LRTAP) addresses the problem of acid rain. The convention now has 51 states parties. This includes the United States and Canada.[77] LRTAP is an international framework convention

---

[71]For a concise discussion of many of the problems in this issue area, see "Encyclopedia of the Atmospheric Environment," www.ace.mmu.ac.uk/eae/english.html (accessed April 22, 2009).

[72]In 1306, Edward I forbade coal burning while Parliament was in session. See "Green Crusades: Environmental Conflict in History," www.combusem.com/HIST.HTM (accessed April 22, 2009).

[73]See www.dep.state.pa.us/dep/Rachel_Carson/donora.htm (accessed April 22, 2009).

[74]For a short summary of the issues, see G. Handl, "International Efforts to Protect the Atmosphere: Too Little Too Late?" 1 *European Journal of International Law* 250 (1990), www.ejil.org/journal/Vol1/No1/art14.html (accessed April 22, 2009).

[75]www.unece.org/env/lrtap/lrtap_h1.htm.

[76]Text at www.unece.org/env/lrtap/full%20text/1979.CLRTAP.e.pdf.

[77]Summary table on accession and ratification at www.unece.org/env/lrtap/status/Status%20of%20the%20Convention.pdf (accessed April 22, 2009).

> **TABLE 18.1**

Treaty	Type	Settlement	Sponsor/Dispute Subject Matter	Governance
Long-Range Transboundary Air Pollution (LRTAP) (1979)	Regional framework	UNECE negotiation or other mutually agreed method	Acid rain	Executive Body EMEP (Scientific Programme) Working Group on Effects Working Group on Strategies Working Group on Strategies Secretariat (UNECE)
Vienna Convention for Protection of the Ozone Layer/Montreal Protocol (1985/1987)	International framework	UNEP negotiation	Regulates 96 chemicals that have ozone-depleting properties	Conference of Parties Technology/Economic Assistance Panel Secretariat (TEAP) (Ozone, UNEP)/ Implementation Committee
Framework Convention on Climate Change/ Kyoto Protocol (1994/1997)	International framework	United Nations/ Compliance Committee, Conference of Parties	Reduction of greenhouse gases	Conference of Parties Subsidiary Body for Scientific and Technical Advice Subsidiary Body for Implementation Partner Agencies Secretariat (Bonn)
Basel Convention (1989)[78]	Conventional-multilateral[79]/ requires domestic legislation	UNEP/Compliance Committee	Control transboundary movements of hazardous wastes and their disposal	Conference of Parties Compliance Committee Secretariat
Stockholm Convention on Persistent Organic Pollutants (2001)	International framework	UNEP/negotiation or other mutually agreed method	Twelve priority toxic organic compounds[80]	Conference of Parties POP Review Committee Secretariat

---

[78]See also the 1999 Protocol on Liability and Compensation: The Protocol on Liability and Compensation, adopted in December 1999, established rules on liability and compensation for damages caused by accidental spills of hazardous waste during export or import, or during disposal.

[79]Article 11 encourages bilateral, multilateral, and regional agreements to carry out the purposes of the treaty. For a list of these agreements, see www.basel.int/article11/index.html.

[80]These 12 priority POPs are aldrin, chlordane, dichlorodiphenyltrichloroethane (DDT), dieldrin, endrin, heptachlor, mirex, toxaphene, polychlorobiphenyls (PCBs), hexachlorobenzene, dioxins, and furans. The treaty contains a very restricted exemption for DDT use to combat mosquitoes that carry malaria because affordable substitutes are not readily available.

that to date has eight protocols addressing specific problems (see Table 18.1). The executive secretary of UNECE performs the secretariat function. The treaty has modest goals. States agree to limit and gradually reduce air pollution, particularly pollution that may have transboundary impact. The regime established does not deal with questions of potential liability from damage caused by transboundary pollution. While progress here remains slow, each of the protocols continues to gain acceptance as evidenced by new state ratification.

LRTAP PROTOCOLS

All protocols[81] have entered into force.

The 1999 Protocol to Abate Acidification, Eutrophication and Ground-Level Ozone; 26 parties

The 1998 Protocol on Persistent Organic Pollutants (POPs); 30 parties

The 1998 Protocol on Heavy Metals; 30 parties

The 1994 Protocol on Further Reduction of Sulphur Emissions; 29 parties

The 1991 Protocol Concerning the Control of Emissions of Volatile Organic Compounds or Their Transboundary Fluxes; 29 parties

The 1988 Protocol Concerning the Control of Nitrogen Oxides or Their Transboundary Fluxes; 34 parties. Entered into force February 14, 1991

The 1985 Protocol on the Reduction of Sulphur Emissions or Their Transboundary Fluxes by at Least 30 Percent; 25 parties

The 1984 Protocol on Long-Term Financing of the Cooperative Programme for Monitoring and Evaluation of the Long-Range Transmission of Air Pollutants in Europe (EMEP); 43 parties

---

Vienna Convention for the Protection of the Ozone Layer (1985) A widespread concern with the effects of CFCs on the ozone layer prompted action that produced the international framework treaty.[82] To understand the myriad factors involved in effective action here, one merely needs to note that Freon—at the time, a widely used gas in refrigeration and air conditioning units as well as aerosol spray cans—is a CFC. Phasing out the use of Freon, developed explicitly for refrigeration purposes, by itself had very real economic costs in terms of retooling and conversion. In 1987, states negotiated the Montreal Protocol on Substances That Deplete the Ozone Layer,[83] which set explicit goals for reduction of both CFCs and halons (widely used in fire extinguishers). By 1989, concern had arisen that the original goals in the protocol were too lenient. The parties then adopted the Helsinki Declaration on the Protection of the Ozone Layer, which specified a 2000 deadline for the total phaseout of CFCs and the phaseout of halons as soon as eco-

---

[81]www.unece.org/env/lrtap/status/lrtap_s.htm.

[82]Text at http://ozone.unep.org/pdfs/viennaconvention2002.pdf.

[83]Text at www.globelaw.com/Climate/montreal.htm.

nomically feasible.[84] Now ratified by 196 states, the Vienna/Montreal regime has been considered a success story.[85]

Framework Convention on Climate Change (1994) Aimed at reducing the emissions of carbon dioxide (CO_2) and other greenhouse gases,[86] the UNFCC achieved immediate and almost universal acceptance. The difficulties came with the follow-on Kyoto Protocol.[87] Negotiations to provide standards began at the first COP at Berlin in 1995 and resulted in the adoption of the Kyoto Protocol at the third COP in Kyoto, Japan, in 1997. Many countries signed the Kyoto Protocol (including the United States), but did not carry through with ratification and/or acceptance due to the treaty's lack of specificity in monitoring and compliance rules. A second round of negotiations finally produced the Marrakesh Accords, adopted at the seventh COP. The protocol entered into force in February 2005 after ratification by the Russian Federation.[88]

The treaty reflects the development debate by placing the main burden of reducing emissions on the developed countries.[89] The UNFCC website notes:

> Because economic development is vital for the world's poorer countries—and because such progress is difficult to achieve even without the complications added by climate change—the Convention accepts that the share of greenhouse gas emissions produced by developing nations will grow in the coming years. It nonetheless seeks to help such countries limit emissions in ways that will not hinder their economic progress.

The United States has refused to ratify the Kyoto Protocol. In rejecting the protocol, President George W. Bush questioned the underlying science and noted that the treaty requirements would harm the U.S. economy and would diminish U.S. sovereignty over its own economy. President Bush also objected to the exemption for India and China, which rank in the top five of current CO_2 producers.[90]

---

[84]The regime has undergone seven revisions in all: London 1990, Nairobi 1991, Copenhagen 1992, Bangkok 1993, Vienna 1995, Montreal 1997, and Beijing 1999.

[85]A. C. Kiss and D. Shelton, *Guide to International Environmental Law* (2007), ch. 6.

[86]Many chemical compounds found in Earth's atmosphere act as "greenhouse gases." These gases allow sunlight to enter the atmosphere freely. When sunlight strikes Earth's surface, some of it is reflected back toward space as infrared radiation (heat). Greenhouse gases absorb this infrared radiation and trap the heat in the atmosphere. Carbon dioxide (CO_2), methane, and nitrous oxide (NO2) represent the three most prevalent gases, with CO_2 comprising 82 percent of total U.S. human-made emission. In the United States, greenhouse gas emissions come mostly from energy use (petroleum and natural gas). The United States produces about 25 percent of *global* carbon dioxide emissions from burning fossil fuels for energy needs. For a quick overview and summary, see Energy Information Administration, www.eia.doe.gov/oiaf/1605/ggccebro/chapter1.html.

[87]Text at http://unfccc.int/resource/docs/convkp/kpeng.pdf.

[88]Entry into force required the ratification, acceptance, or accession of a minimum of 55 states. These states among them had to produce 55 percent of *developed* country CO_2 emissions. The 55-state marker was reached in 2002 with ratification by Iceland.

[89]Referred to as "Annex I states" because they are listed in Annex I of the treaty.

[90]See "Making an Excellent Case Against Kyoto Protocol," *Atlanta Journal-Constitution* (March 29, 2001), 22A; W. Drozdiak, "U.S. Left Out of Warming Treaty; EU-Japan Bargain Saves Kyoto Pact," *Washington Post* (July 24, 2001), A1.

The Kyoto Protocol expires in 2012. Negotiations for a successor instrument began in June 2009. This produced no agreement, neither did a follow-on in Mexico in 2010. While negotiations continue, we should note that changes in the Protocol will mean a new round of ratifications by governments. Even if agreement is reached in the two scheduled rounds of negotiation in 2011 and 2012, this would probably mean a gap in "obligation" between the date of expiration and the date when the new protocol enters into force.

One of the more interesting problems that has emerged in the negotiations centers on emissions from agricultural production. New Zealand, Australia, Canada, and Japan have resisted demands by developed countries for additional cuts to emissions in this sector.[91] *The arguments illustrate some important issues involved in reconciling the view that developing countries should receive some preference with the realities of projected impacts in the developed world of granting that preference.* The dissenters argue that these emissions constitute only a miniscule problem that can be resolved only by cutbacks in production. Such cutbacks run a twofold risk in the contemporary world. First, they would shift production to countries that have less efficient production methods, perhaps resulting in an overall net increase, not a decrease. Second, in an era where food has become increasingly scarce, such a shift to less efficient producers could result in a decrease in food security across the board. This would affect the lesser developed countries to a greater extent than the developed ones.

Nuclear Problems

The resumption of nuclear testing by the Soviet Union and the United States in 1962, together with the growing problem of how to dispose of dangerous radioactive waste materials, pointed up the relevance of including Article 25 in the 1958 Convention on the High Seas. The article provided that each state should take measures to prevent pollution of the seas from the dumping of radioactive waste, taking into account any standards and regulations that might be formulated by competent international organizations. The treaty also called for cooperation by all states with the relevant international agency in taking measures to prevent pollution of the seas—or the airspace above—resulting from any activities with radioactive materials or other harmful agents.

The question of *nuclear tests* was partially settled outside the framework of any international organization. After 425 announced test blasts, the United States, Great Britain, and the Soviet Union succeeded in producing the Partial Nuclear Test Ban Treaty (PTBT, Moscow Treaty) of 1963. The instrument, in force on October 10, 1963, represented an agreement among the three powers to "prohibit, to prevent, and not to carry out any nuclear weapons test explosions or any other nuclear explosion" in the atmosphere, in outer space, or under water. Underground testing was excluded deliberately because of Russian insistence that adequate inspection of such tests would open the way to espionage. The three par-

---

[91]See, New Zealand Ministry of Foreign Affair and Trade, "Treaties and International Law Kyoto Protocol to the UN Framework Convention on Climate Change, 13 February 2002," www.mfat.govt.nz/Treaties-and-International-Law/03-Treaty-making-process/2-National-Interest-Analyses/0-Kyoto-Protocol-Part-I.php.

ties also agreed in the treaty to refrain "from causing, encouraging or in any way participating in the carrying out of any nuclear weapons test whatever."

This provision was quite obviously aimed at France and the People's Republic of China, both of which continued open-air testing.[92] France halted all testing in 1996, but still has not acceded to the PTBT. China has traditionally been reluctant to participate in the international regimes restricting nuclear testing. It originally criticized the PTBT as a "fraud" designed to preserve the superpowers' nuclear monopoly. However, although China has not signed the PTBT, it has been in de facto compliance with the treaty since its last atmospheric nuclear test on October 16, 1980. On March 21, 1986, China stated that it had not conducted atmospheric testing for years and announced a permanent end to its aboveground testing. China also did not sign or state its adherence to the Threshold Test Ban Treaty (TTBT, which restricts underground test yields to below 150 kilotons), but has been in de facto compliance with the treaty since its 660-kiloton explosion on May 21, 1992.

The omission of underground testing in the 1963 agreement was rectified in part when the United States and the Soviet Union concluded a treaty on the Limitation of Underground Nuclear Weapon Tests, signed in Moscow on July 3, 1974, and entering into force on the day of exchange of ratifications.[93] This treaty, in turn, was followed by the American–Soviet Treaty on Underground Nuclear Explosions for Peaceful Purposes (Moscow and Washington, May 28, 1976).[94] These last two agreements were supplemented by an agreement, initially of five years' duration, on ceilings for underground nuclear tests.

Testing continued, and by 1989 the United States had recorded 932 test explosions as against 638 for the Soviet Union. The latter had resumed underground testing on February 28, 1987, after a 19-month moratorium, following repeated unsuccessful calls for the United States to follow suit. After conducting an underground nuclear test on July 29, 1996 (its 45th test), China began a self-imposed moratorium on testing, effective July 30, 1996. On September 24, 1996, China signed the Comprehensive Test Ban Treaty (CTBT), even though the treaty draft banned peaceful nuclear explosions (PNEs) while allowing national technical means (NTM) of verification. China insisted that the PNE ban be reviewed after 10 years, that NTM not be abused to infringe on Chinese sovereignty, and that the CTBT be considered only a first step toward more general disarmament.[95] The United States has signed but not ratified the CTBT.

Transboundary Problems Until the Soviet nuclear plant accident at Chernobyl caused widespread atmospheric and river pollution, the only relevant treaty was the 1963 *Vienna Convention on Civil Liability for Nuclear Damage*.[96] Following

---

[92]See also J. McBride, *The Test Ban Treaty* (1967). The text of the agreement is found in 57 *AJIL* 1026 (1963). At the time of this writing, France and the People's Republic of China are the only major countries that have not signed or ratified the agreement or adhered to it.

[93]Text, with protocol, in *New York Times* (July 4, 1964), 2; and in 68 *AJIL* 805 (1974).

[94]Text in 15 *ILM* 891 (1976).

[95]"China's Nuclear Testing," Center for Nonproliferation Studies, http://cns.miis.edu/research/china/coxrep/testpos.htm (accessed April 22, 2009).

[96]Text at www.iaea.org/Publications/Documents/Infcircs/1996/inf500.shtml; currently 38 states parties. The United States has not signed the convention.

the Chernobyl event, the International Atomic Energy Agency (IAEA), utilizing a conference of experts (1986), developed a comprehensive *Convention on Early Notification of a Nuclear Accident*[97] and a *Convention on Assistance in the Case of a Nuclear Accident or Radiological Emergency.* The Soviet Union has ratified both. Both have entered into force. The IAEA also developed a 1994 *Convention on Nuclear Safety* (78 states parties).[98] A 1997 Convention that would amend the 1963 Vienna Convention and a separate 1997 Convention on compensation for nuclear damage have been signed but are not yet in force.[99] Beyond these conventions, customary international law imposes an obligation on all states not to permit activities on their territories that might cause significant environmental injury to other nations. Finally, the *United Nations Convention on the Law of the Sea*, although not drafted with nuclear accidents in mind, is arguably relevant with regard to the release of contaminated cooling water into international waters.

The Fukushima nuclear plant, destroyed by a giant tsunami in March 2011, again raised fears of widespread contamination. In terms of severity of impact, officials raised the level of risk to a 7, the highest on the International Nuclear Events Scale, ranking it with Chernobyl.[100] Given the extended lives of many of the radioactive elements released, the area around plant may have to remain uninhabited for many decades. Still, despite the rating, the long-term impact is likely to be much less severe than Chernobyl. The major difference between Fukushima and Chernobyl flows from the sequence of events. The Chernobyl accident started with a huge explosion and a major release of radioactive material high into the atmosphere, with a radioactive cloud that deposited fallout over a large part of Europe. The releases at Fukushima have been over a longer period and a smaller area, but the scale of evacuation and other population protection measures necessitated by the accident has clearly surpassed everything except Chernobyl.[101]

Under both the existing nuclear conventions and the proposed protocols, TEPCO, as the "operator" of the Fukushima plant, is liable under international law to parties injured by the plant's radioactive releases. This presumes, however, that the injured parties have access to a court with jurisdiction over the operator. Moreover, the monetary amount of that liability could far exceed both TEPCO's assets (if any such assets remain after payments to Japanese victims) and any insurance or international compensation fund established for accident victims under the pending protocols to the Vienna Convention.[102]

---

[97]Texts and related documents in 25 *ILM* 1370 (1986). See also P. Cameron, L. Hancher, and W. Kuhn, eds, *Nuclear Energy After Chernobyl* (1988); A. Adede, *The IAEA Notification and Assistance Conventions in Case of a Nuclear Accident* (1987); and P. Sands, ed., *Chernobyl: Law and Communication: Transboundary Nuclear Air Pollution—The Legal Materials* (1988).

[98]Text at www.iaea.org/Publications/Documents/Infcircs/Others/inf449.shtml; United States has ratified.

[99]Texts at www-pub.iaea.org/MTCD/publications/PDF/Pub1279_web.pdf.

[100]The Three Mile Island disaster, which involved a partial reactor meltdown in Harrisburg, Pennsylvania in 1979, was rated as a 5.

[101]For updates, see All Things Nuclear, Union of Concerned Scientists, www.ucsusa.org/.

[102]For a concise analysis, see S. Kassi, "International Law Lessons from the Fukushima Nuclear Disaster," *New York Law Journal* (April 29, 2011), www.clm.com/publication.cfm/ID/324.

Marine Pollution and Dumping   Pollution through the dumping of nuclear wastes became a problem not yet solved. Although all "nuclear nations" had adhered to the International Convention on the Prevention of Marine Pollution by Dumping of Wastes and Other Matter (London, 1972), several countries ignored the prohibitions established through that instrument. The Soviet Union and later the Russian Federation admittedly dumped, over decades, nuclear reactors and nuclear wastes from warships and icebreakers into the Arctic Ocean and the Sea of Japan. As late as October 11, 1993, a Russian military tanker dumped 237,000 gallons of nuclear wastes into the ocean some 300 miles north of Japan. Norway and Japan have been particularly worried about long-term destruction of fishing waters. Despite international protests, the Russian government indicated that such dumping would continue. Under the 1992 Start II Treaty, Russia agreed to dismantle part of its nuclear submarine fleet. Decommissioning of nuclear submarines at naval facilities on the Kola Peninsula in the north and at Vladivostok in the Far East has evoked international concern. However, on October 21, 1993, the Russian government announced that such disposal of radioactive wastes in oceans would cease, provided other countries would help to build treatment facilities. In late 1993, Russia had 225 nuclear-powered submarines, 3 nuclear battleships, and 7 icebreakers, with a total of 407 reactors producing 26,000 cubic meters of liquid and solid reactor wastes each year. The Environmental Protection Agency (EPA) noted that fuels are being stored in vessels not designed for this purpose off Murmansk, the largest population center north of the Arctic Circle. Fears of mishap are growing in that area.[103]

The United States had dumped radioactive wastes some 19 miles offshore from Gloucester, Massachusetts, between 1946 and the 1970s. Dumping also occurred in the Farallon Islands area near San Francisco. There, some 47,500 barrels of wastes were dumped 30 miles from shore.[104]

In November 1993, a total of 42 of the 71 countries represented at the formulation of the 1972 Convention attended a meeting in London. At the meeting, 37 of those countries agreed on a permanent prohibition on the dumping of radioactive wastes at sea. The five states abstaining were Russia, England, France, China, and Belgium. Two previous opponents of the ban, the United States and Japan, supported it.

CONCLUSION

The negotiations surrounding the evolution of international environmental law clearly illustrate the "politics" and hence the problems of legal development because the issues involved the classic dilemma of immediate satisfaction versus

---

[103]See O. Funke, "Environmental Issues and Russian Security," in *Russian Forces at the Dawn of the Millennium,* edited by M. Curtcher (U.S. Army War College, 2000), 54–55.

[104]See also M. Waldichuk, "Control of Marine Pollution," 4 *Ocean Development and Int'l Law Journal* 269 (1977); A. Boyle, "Marine Pollution Under the Law of the Sea Convention," 79 *AJIL* 367 (1985); Brown in *Christian Science Monitor* (February 20, 1991), 8; Hajost and Pfirman, *id.* (February 8, 1993), 18; *id.* (November 15, 1993), 15; and Murkowski, "The Soviet Union's Deadly Legacy in the Arctic," *Christian Science Monitor* (April 21, 1992), 19.

long-term costs. Most environmental issues require that governments take conscious decisions to address issues that can have short-term, adverse economic effects on their states in return for promised long-term benefits for all states. Programs to deal with environmental issues clearly directly connect the issues of real short-term costs weighed against projected long-term benefits in tangible ways that many other areas do not. As a result, we have many treaties that do no more than impose a duty to consult and coordinate—many soft-law incentives and few hard-law imperatives. Finance and the "sustainable development" question continue as core problems in need of solutions.

SUGGESTED READINGS

GENERAL

American Society of International Law, "Guide to Environmental Law," www.asil.org/resource/env1.htm.

IUCN, "ECOLEX: A Gateway to Environmental Law," www.ecolex.org/index.php.

Axelrod, Downie, and Vig, eds, *The Global Environment: Institutions, Law, and Policy,* 2nd ed. (2005).

Bodansky, Brunnee, and Hey, *The Oxford Handbook of International Environmental Law* (2008).

Dupuy, *"Soft Law and the International Law of the Environment,"* 12 Mich. J. Int'l L. 420 (1991).

Freestone, *The Burden of Proof in Natural Resources Legislation: Some Critical Issues for Fisheries Law* (1996).

Freestone and Hey, *The Precautionary Principle in International Law: The Challenge of Implementation* (1996).

Holder and Lee, *Environmental Protection, Law and Policy: Text and Materials* (2007).

Kiss and Shelton, *Guide to International Environmental Law* (2007).

Kiss and Shelton, *International Environmental Law,* 3rd ed. (2004).

Rajamani, *Differential Treatment in International Environmental Law* (2006).

Young, *Creating Regimes: Arctic Accords and International Governance* (1998).

INSTITUTIONS AND CIVIL SOCIETY

Ba and Hoffman, eds, *Contending Perspectives on Global Governance: Coherence, Contestation and World Order* (2005).

Bodansky, "The Legitimacy of International Governance: A Coming Challenge for International Environment Law," 93 AJIL 614 (1999).

Mushkat, *International Environmental Law and Asian Values: Legal Norms and Cultural Influences* (2005).

Potter, *NGOs and Environmental Policies: Asia and Africa* (1996).

Scovazzi, *The Protection of the Environment in a Context of Regional Economic Integration* (2001).

Young, *The Effectiveness of International Environmental Regimes: Causal Connections and Behavioral Mechanisms* (1999).

EUROPEAN UNION

Kramer, *Casebook on EU Environmental Law* (2002).

Oberthur and Genring, eds, *Institutional Interaction in Global Environmental Governance: Synergy and Conflict Among International and EU Policies* (2006).

International Economic Law

ECONOMIC THEORY AND ECONOMIC LAW

Before World War II, in comparison with postwar development, we can speak only of rudimentary international economic law. No overarching international economic regime existed, although agreements like the Berlin Act of 1885 (Congo and colonial expansion in Africa) did govern some limited areas.[1] Even though many states had adopted economic policies based upon the ideas of liberal political economy that had developed over the past 150 years,[2] the Great Depression witnessed a return to neo-mercantilist policies based upon the narrow, self-interested "every state for itself" mentality. Understanding the genesis of post–World War II economic law requires that we first briefly explore the roots of many of the theories underlying the propositions that promote "globalism" and "globalization" as the central goals of state policy.[3]

Mercantilism

Mercantilism emerged as a dominant economic theory during the state-building era in Western Europe (A.D. 1500–1800). "National" kings began to centralize

---

[1]F. Botchway, ed., *Documents in International Economic Law* (2005), ch. 3.

[2]See, for example, E. Silberner, *The Problem of War in Nineteenth Century Economic Thought* (1946). Please note the use of the lowercase *l* here to differentiate the liberal philosophical tradition from the contemporary American use of the term, capital-L Liberalism. To confuse matters further, many of the ideas associated with social and economic American "Conservatives" stem from the small-*l* liberal strain of political thought.

[3]The two terms, though often used as synonyms, represent different concepts. Globalism describes the state of "interconnectedness," while globalization describes the process whereby globalism increases or decreases. For a brief discussion, see J. Nye, "Globalism Versus Globalization," *The Globalist* (April 15, 2002), www.theglobalist.com/StoryId.aspx?StoryId=2392 (accessed April 22, 2009).

governmental functions (authority) in an effort to diminish the power of regional and local magnates (earls, dukes, counts, viscounts, barons) over important matters such as justice and tax collecting. As a doctrine, mercantilism had a twofold purpose: (1) to make the interests of the "state" paramount in the economic realm and thus increase the power of the state and (2) to reduce the vulnerability of the state, particularly in times of war, by achieving self-sufficiency or *autarky*. Because of the prevalence of war as a method of resolving disputes, being able to generate the resources necessary to support war-making on a regular basis and reducing the ways in which an adversary might weaken you were both important goals. In this sense, mercantilism as a doctrine of *political economy* formed a complement to the ideas of political realism.[4]

Mercantile system theorists postulated that Earth had only a fixed quantity of resources. Economic competition thus was a zero-sum game. One state's gain represented an absolute loss to others. From this perspective, there can be no *mutual* net gain from trade with other countries. Protectionism rather than competition in the marketplace was the rule. The goal was to maximize exports while minimizing imports. States maintained high tariffs on imports and discouraged the import of luxury goods. This attitude also underlaid the drive for colonies. Colonies provided raw materials and food as well as a closed market for goods. This situation explains the benign attitude of English authorities toward the activities of men such as *Sir* Francis Drake and *Sir* Henry Morgan, who essentially made their reputations and fortunes in the sixteenth and early seventeenth centuries by robbing Spanish ships carrying gold from Spanish colonies in the New World. It also explains the drive by Spanish explorers to find sources of gold and silver in the New World because presumably the size of a state's treasury and accumulation of bullion were measures of its power.

Adam Smith (1723–1790) and Modern Economic Thought

Others, like the philosopher David Hume (1711–1776), had explored many of the themes developed by Adam Smith in *The Wealth of Nations* (1776), but Smith remains the pivotal figure in the development of modern political economy. Smith is perhaps best known for his "invisible hand" theory of how rational self-interest in a free market economy increases the well-being of all. He also pioneered the idea of division of labor, which underlies modern manufacturing methods. Though the concept is often portrayed as laissez-faire economics (i.e., governments should have no role in regulation), this is a misreading. As influenced by Locke (1632–1704), Smith argued that government should intervene only when absolutely necessary. He also argued that the American colonies were not worth

---

[4]The best explication of mercantilism remains that by E. F. Heckscher, *Mercantilism* (2 vols, 1934; 2nd ed., 1955). See also L. Magnusson, *Mercantilism: The Shaping of an Economic Language* (1994); D. Omrod, *The Rise of Commercial Empires: England and the Netherlands in the Age of Mercantilism, 1650–1770* (2003).

keeping,[5] thus presaging rationales for colonial independence that would come into vogue 170 years later. Regarding international economic policy, Smith clearly rejected what he named the "mercantile system." He argued that merely maintaining a favorable trade balance (and bullion in the treasury) did not necessarily increase wealth. The primary advantage of competitive trade ("free" trade) came from opening up new markets for goods and providing many commodities at a lower cost. Obviously, this view ran completely counter to the idea of protecting domestic industry from competition and keeping foreign goods out. Acceptance of these ideas by policymakers had to counter opposition from those who had benefited from the old policies. We still see "mercantilist" ideas emerge in domestic economic debates when industries demand "protection" from international competition.

Political economist David Ricardo (1772–1823) is credited with developing the theory of *comparative advantage* that forms the basis for modern theories of international exchange. Simply explained, comparative advantage holds that every country can produce certain items less expensively than others because of the relative values of inputs (land, labor, capital). This being so, every country should maximize its production of those items that it produces most efficiently in terms of inputs and trade for products that others can produce more efficiently in terms of inputs (lower cost). Ricardo's essay in retrospect has some obvious problems: It utilized agricultural products (wool and wine), and it used only a two-country exchange. However, the premises he developed have become the central assumption underlying the General Agreement on Tariffs and Trade, and the World Trade Organization (WTO) as its successor—namely, free trade benefits all.

Only with the advent of the Industrial Revolution did the new theory take hold. During the nineteenth century, John Stuart Mill elaborated the rationales and benefits of a free trade regime.[6] To note the difference between the older rationale and the new, liberal political economists, he argued that war was irrational because it disrupted the essential trading links between countries. Whatever the presumptive gains from war, they could never offset the losses from the interruptions of the normal trading relationships between countries.[7] While this argument

---

[5] "A great empire has been established for the sole purpose of raising up a nation of customers who should be obliged to buy from the shops of our different producers all the goods with which these could supply them. For the sake of that little enhancement of price which this monopoly might afford our producers, the home-consumers have been burdened with the whole expense of maintaining and defending that empire. For this purpose, and for this purpose only, in the two last wars, more than a hundred and seventy millions [in pounds] has been contracted over and above all that had been expended for the same purpose in former wars. The interest of this debt alone is not only greater than the whole extraordinary profit, which, it ever could be pretended, was made by the monopoly of the colony trade, but than the whole value of that trade, or than the whole value of the goods, which at an average have been annually exported to the colonies." Smith, *Wealth of Nations* (vol. 4, ch. VIII), http://oll.libertyfund.org/200/111936/2316261 (accessed April 22, 2009). Note that Marx (and Lenin) made this same argument: States undertake wars that benefit the privileged few, but "the many" bear the costs.

[6] See *Principles of Political Economy and Some of the Applications to Social Philosophy* (1848).

[7] Silberner, note 2.

presaged World War I by 60 years, it proved accurate in terms of the devastating economic consequences of the two wars that defined the twentieth century.

WORLD WAR I AND THE GREAT DEPRESSION

World War I proved as devastating as prewar liberal critics had forecast.[8] Though Great Britain's losses at first did not seem as extensive as those suffered by the continental countries—ships at the bottom of the sea and lost markets were far less tangible consequences than destroyed landscape in northern France—she had to draw down her overseas assets to finance the war.[9] No European country emerged from the war in healthy financial shape. While the United States and Japan seemed to benefit from European woes (the United States went from being a net debtor to being a net creditor during the war), the initial boom of the 1920s turned into a major economic crisis.

The Great Depression was a worldwide phenomenon. It spread because of neo-mercantilist assumptions still held by governments. Earlier we noted that political realism and mercantilism shared philosophical roots. Every country acted in its own self-interest, narrowly conceived, in an effort to achieve its goal. Each government saw the answer to its problems as increasing exports and limiting imports. Without a central international agency to regulate policies, each country could determine what it needed to do. To regenerate demand, they raised tariffs and devalued their currency to discourage imports and make their exports more attractive. Devaluing the currency would make their goods more desirable to consumers in other countries because the exchange rate made the goods less expensive in terms of other currencies. The high tariff wall discouraged imports, in addition to their already more expensive price due to cheapening one's own currency. For an individual country, this constitutes a rational strategy. Post Civil War, the United States had always had a "protectionist" attitude: "High tariffs were a means not only of protecting infant industries, but of generating revenue for the federal government."[10] This relaxed somewhat during the Wilson presidency (1913–1921). In the wake of the Wall Street collapse in 1929, the U.S. Congress enacted the Smoot–Hawley Tariff Act of June 1930. The legislation raised U.S. tariffs to historically high levels—the most protectionist tariffs in U.S. history.

Similarly, for about 40 years before World War I, many western European States (and the United States) had adhered to a gold standard. Briefly, this meant that for international transactions, these currencies had fixed value in terms of a certain weight of gold. If you presented a £100 note, or a $100 bill, at the British Bank of England or the U.S. Treasury, the person behind the counter would give you a specified, fixed, unchanging quantity of gold: about 4.5 (troy) ounces in the case of the $100 bill, and about 22 (troy) ounces in the case of the £100 note.[11] Note that this meant that 1 pound had about five times the value of 1 dollar in

---

[8]See, for example, the classic, I. Bloch, *Is War Now Impossible?: Being an Abridgement of the Future of War* (1899).

[9]P. Kennedy, *The Rise and Fall of British Naval Mastery* (1976, reprint 2004), 267–272.

[10]U.S. Department of State, "Protectionism in the Interwar Period," www.state.gov/r/pa/ho/time/id/17606.htm (accessed April 22, 2009). See also J. M. Jones, *Tariff Retaliation: Repercussions of the Hawley-Smoot Bill* (1934).

terms of international purchasing power. A central problem of the gold standard was that gold production was insufficient to support the increasing level of international transactions. Lacking gold, other countries valued their currencies with respect to these *key currencies* (American dollar, British pound, French franc, and German mark) and kept these currencies as reserves in their central banks because they were "as good as gold." In this case, the British pound emerged as the most important of the key currencies principally due to the extent of British holdings in overseas investments and colonies and the consequent volume of trade associated with both. The outbreak of World War I caused most gold standard countries to suspend convertibility to meet the costs of the war. Great Britain restored convertibility in 1925 but then had to suspend it again in 1931. Other European states followed. The United States held out until 1933, when newly elected President Franklin Roosevelt promoted and signed legislation to unhook the dollar from gold.

By unhooking its currency from a common standard of value, a government—as with tariffs—could attempt to manipulate the value of its own currency to promote exports and curb imports. A simple illustration will suffice here. Earlier we noted that 1 British pound (£) on the gold standard equaled 5 American dollars ($; see Table 19.1). At this exchange rate, if Americans used dollars to purchase an item priced at £2, they would pay $10. Conversely, £2 would buy an item priced at $10. Now consider if Great Britain devalued the pound in terms of the dollar by 10 percent—£2 will buy only $9 of American goods, but from the American side, it will take only $9 to buy a £2 item that used to cost $10. The American dollar has gained 10 percent more purchasing power in terms of international transactions with Great Britain, while the British pound has lost the same. Presumably, this would make British products more attractive to American consumers (lower prices) while discouraging Britons from buying American products (higher prices). In Table 19.1, note that after devaluation, the Cadillac will cost British customers 10 percent more while Americans can purchase the Jaguar for 10 percent less. The domestic prices of the two cars will remain the same for domestic consumers. Hence, the Jaguar will continue to cost £3,000 for domestic British customers, and the Cadillac will still cost American customers $15,000.

The logic here should not require elaboration. When every country (or individual) pursues the same self-interested policy directed at maximizing returns, regardless of consequences, everyone loses to the extent that no one buys. This attitude is often described as a "beggar-thy-neighbor" policy.[12] In the pursuit of economic recovery at home, no one is willing to sacrifice a short-term gain (self-interest narrowly calculated) for themselves in anticipation of a long-term gain for all. Consider the parallel here with the famous "tragedy of the commons" example by Garrett Hardin.[13] The point of the Hardin story is that individuals could not overcome

---

[11]J. B. DeLong, *Slouching Towards Utopia?: The Economic History of the Twentieth Century*, ch. VIII, www.j-bradford-delong.net/tceh/Slouch_Gold8.html (accessed April 22, 2009). A troy ounce is about 10 percent heavier than the standard (avoirdupois) ounce used in common measures.

[12]For a concise definition, see "Beggar-thy-neighbor," http://financial-dictionary.thefreedictionary.com/Beggar-thy-neighbor (accessed April 22, 2009).

[13]G. Hardin, "The Tragedy of the Commons," 162 *Science* 1243 (1968), www.dieoff.org/page95.htm (accessed April 22, 2009). Consider also the security dilemma paradigm.

Table 19.1		
Devaluation and Exchange Rates*		
	Pound British Consumer	Dollar American Consumer
Before devaluation	1	5
Jaguar	3,000	15,000
Cadillac	3,000	15,000
After devaluation	1	4.50
Jaguar	3,000	13,500
Cadillac	3,300	15,000

*Values are for illustration only.

their own narrow economic self-interest in order to preserve a common (*collective*) good. Consider also the solution. Hardin noted that the problem was solved only when a *third-party intervention* resulted in the fencing of the commons and the regulation of the number of sheep any one person could graze on common land. Note the parallel to the discussion of development of post–World War II international economic institutions. Note also that policies adopted during the Great Depression established a precedent for increased government intervention into the regulation of domestic economies. Issues such as employment levels, growth, and the security of financial transactions, once considered outside the public domain, became central elements of public policy.

PRELUDE: MODERN ECONOMIC THEORY AND POLITICAL ECONOMY

As we will see in the following discussion, a tension exists between international economic theory and the political and economic consequences that may result from strictly adhering to its precepts.[14] For example, the theory of comparative advantage postulates that as conditions shift in terms of "comparative" efficiencies, adjustments will occur in terms of falling wages and workers migrating to other jobs in a rational response to economic conditions. As Lowenfeld points out, this theory ignores qualitative factors such as types of skills (e.g., custodians, engineers, managers, pilots, bus drivers) involved as well as the quality of different areas of land (e.g., what crops could replace tobacco in North Carolina—should it all be converted to factories?).[15] The Ricardian model (and its elaboration by

---

[14]Note that an additional problem here arises because while we talk about states, governments, and countries, in fact the relevant data may involve the efficiencies of individual companies in utilizing these essential economic factors. Does not much of the debate surrounding the American automobile industry involve the differences in terms of principles and practices between Toyota, Honda, et al. and American companies, even for Japanese cars assembled in the United States?

[15]A. F. Lowenfeld, *International Economic Law*, 2nd ed. (2008), 7.

Heckscher and Ohlin) assumes a relatively easy and short-term mobility among the factors of production. Hence, farmers can become factory workers or factory workers can become farmers, as the relative costs and efficiencies among factors dictate. But not all factors in every country are equally mobile. Moreover, we need only look at the current debate over the status of the American automobile industry to realize that other factors, such as the centrality of an industry to a particular economy, also play a role.

In this respect, Lowenfeld notes two additional problems that underlie much of international trade law: (1) the extent to which government intervention may alter the balance between various factors (i.e., subsidies, training programs, etc.) and (2) the problem of how to construct a regime that allows time for adjustments that will enable a disadvantaged country, or disadvantaged sectors within countries, to develop policies for adjustment without creating permanent distortions of the overall regime.[16] Taken together, these issues often emerge in the debate as the proposition that, while trade must be *free*, it must also be *fair*. Clearly, this task involves a minefield even if we try to define what is fair only in a particular context. Despite their shortcomings, the general principles still form the basis for the development of contemporary trade law. We will discuss the political problems of domestic economic adjustment regarding international monetary arrangements—that is, the gap between theory and political reality—in the following section on the Bretton Woods Agreements.

Two other observations are necessary here. First, understanding the current international economic crisis requires that we expand our understanding of money in the contemporary world. It is not just a medium of exchange, a unit of account, and a store of value.[17] It is also an investment asset with markets, derivatives,[18] index trading, and other features that one would not expect to be present from the usual rather narrow definition. Second, with respect to the post–World War II international monetary regime, the line between "hard law" and "soft law" (Chapter 3) has become very blurred. Unlike discussions of international trade, many discussions of institutions, practices, and transactions associated with monetary policy proceed with no reference to law at all. This approach seems curious in that, *as sources of law,* the constitutive documents of the International Monetary Fund (IMF) and the International Bank for Reconstruction and Development (IBRD) established much stronger institutions and controls than those associated with the General Agreement on Tariffs and Trade (GATT). Ironically, the twenty-first century has witnessed the decline of the monetary regime and strengthening of the trade regime. Still, the full story requires that we examine the obligations that states have been willing to assume as well as those that states have abandoned or refused to take on at all.[19]

---

[16]Lowenfeld, note 15, at 8.

[17]M. Moffatt, "What Is Money?" www.economics.about.com/cs/studentresources/f/money.htm.

[18]The term *derivative* refers to securities whose prices are based on the price of another underlying investment.

[19]Lowenfeld, note 15, at 594.

THE BRETTON WOODS SYSTEM

The lessons of the interwar period generated the post–World War II effort to bring stability to international trade and financial transactions.[20] Curiously, though related, the negotiations proceeded on two different tracks. Stabilizing international monetary and financial arrangements took priority. The questions in both cases clearly involved how much authority to grant to a centralized agency to regulate transactions. The monetary regime emerged from a conference—delegates representing 44 countries attended—held in July 1944 at Bretton Woods, a resort in New Hampshire at the foot of Mount Washington. The agreements established two basic organizations: the IMF and the IBRD (often called the World Bank). They entered into force in December 1945.[21] Establishing *legal* obligations to prohibit the practices that all believed had contributed to the Great Depression constituted a central goal. Under Article XX(2)(a) of the original agreements, upon joining the fund, each state pledged that "it has accepted this Agreement in accordance with its law and has taken all steps necessary to enable it to carry out all of its obligations under this Agreement." The type of assistance offered defines the difference in function between the two organizations. The IMF was designed to provide short- and medium-term assistance (3–5 years) to countries with balance-of-payments problems.[22] The IBRD would make available longer-term loans (5–15 years) for specific reconstruction or development projects such as rural electrification, roads, airports, or similar "bankable" infrastructure improvements.[23] At the beginning, the two agencies carefully observed the distinction. Over the past 30 years, the clear separation became blurred as the World Bank has moved toward funding projects that focus on education, training, and health care—that is, the development of *human capital assets*—while the IMF has had to deal with the long-term problems created by the adjustment problems of the lesser developed world.[24]

THE INTERNATIONAL MONETARY FUND

The system set in place by the IMF consisted of rules governing both exchange rates and mechanisms for balance-of-payments adjustments. The agreements included several innovations. First, they established central institutional control over international financial transactions. Second, they instituted a system of fixed, but adjustable, exchange rates. Third, they created a central stabilization fund to help states that needed to address short-term balance-of-payments problems. Fourth, the system aimed at universal participation. Fifth, unlike most other intergovernmental

---

[20]See F. Cesarano, *Monetary Theory and Bretton Woods: The Construction of an International Monetary Order* (2006), chs 5–7.

[21]*Articles of Agreement of the International Monetary Fund*, July 22, 1944 (Bretton Woods, NH); entered into force December 27, 1945; text at www.imf.org/external/pubs/ft/aa/index.htm.

[22]Fund, Articles of Agreement, I and V(3).

[23]Bank, Articles of Agreement, I and III(I).

[24]See, in particular, N. Woods, *The Globalizers: The IMF, the World Bank, and Their Borrowers* (2007).

organizations, the IMF has a weighted voting scheme based upon the size of each country's contributions to the stabilization fund.[25] Sixth, the IMF permitted governments to enact *exchange controls* as a means of controlling capital flows (Article VI(3)). Many of these restrictions remained in place until the late 1970s.

The regime did not attempt to return to a strict gold standard, though gold formed the fundamental basis of value. Only the U.S. dollar had a formal tie to gold. The *par value* (base value) of other currencies was "pegged" to the U.S. dollar, valued at $35 per ounce of gold. Because the dollar defined the standard, these currencies also had a relative value in gold, but not all currencies necessarily could be exchanged for gold. Other countries, lacking gold, again kept U.S. dollars in their central banks as a key currency because the dollar was "as good as gold." The system afforded some short-term flexibility to states in that they could, under circumstances defined in the agreements, unilaterally adjust the "pegged rate" up or down once by 10 percent without obtaining approval from the IMF.[26] Otherwise, if a state wished to change the par value of its currency, it had to inform the IMF in advance and secure its approval. These requirements sought to ensure that the change in par value was necessary—neither too small to be effective nor too large to give an unfair competitive advantage. Presumably, if a state violated these provisions, its drawing rights could be suspended—or in an extreme case, it might face expulsion from the organization. The use of gold as the standard as well as the central role of the U.S. dollar became knotty political problems during the 25 or so years the initial system stayed in place.

Balance-of-payments accounting formed the core of the new regime. The regime was meant to help states manage situations that entailed a fundamental disequilibrium in their balance of payments. No official document precisely defines *fundamental disequilibrium,* although it is generally understood to refer to circumstances involving an extremely large imbalance. Under these limited circumstances, states could devalue or revalue their currencies as needed to mitigate the extent of domestic economic adjustments that otherwise would have to be made to bring its balance of payments into equilibrium[27] Table 19.2 gives a simplified version of the accounting scheme. All three of the categories—Current Account, Capital Account, and Gold/Reserves—involve a net balance between inflow and outflow (gains and losses). So, for example, a state could run a negative balance on Current Account but have a positive balance on Capital Account because the inflow to domestic opportunities exceeded the outflow to investment in various overseas ventures. This explains why, although running a significant deficit on Current Account, Great Britain was able to survive economically between the two wars by liquidating its overseas investments and repatriating the proceeds.[28] It also explains why the United States, for almost four decades, has been able to offset a glaring imbalance—particularly on trade and remittances—by attract-

---

[25]One should not overplay this scheme, because the fund seldom votes, and when it does, the issues often require supermajorities (70 percent, 85 percent) for approval.

[26]For a concise discussion of the issues here, see T. Oatley, *International Political Economy: Interests and Institutions in the Global Economy* (2004), 232–236.

[27]Oatley, note 26, at 232.

[28]This is a central theme of Kennedy, note 9.

> **Table 19.2**
>
> ### Elements of Balance-of-Payments Accounting: Bretton Woods
>
> **Current Account (Net +/−)**
>   Exports (+)
>   Imports (−)
>   Income from investments (interest and dividends) (+/−)
>   Travel/Tourism (+/−)
>   Remittances (+/−)
> **Capital Account (Net +/−)**
>   Short term in (demand deposits, Treasury Bills, etc.)
>   Short term out
>   Long term in (e.g., BMW, Toyota building plants in the United States)
>   Long term out
> **Gold and Reserves (Net +/−)**
>   Reserves on hand (gold and key currencies)
>   Reserves in (+)
>   Reserves out (−)

ing offsets in the form of foreign direct investment and sales of U.S. government securities.[29] In passing, we need to make a special note concerning *remittances* in Current Account. This category has played an important role in the history of U.S. balance-of-payments accounting post World War II due to the extent of U.S. military commitments overseas.[30] Items such as pay for U.S. military personnel stationed abroad, spent within the country of assignment, are continuing expenditures without a corresponding inflow (unilateral transfers) for the United States.

As suggested by its title IMF, creating a central pool of resources based upon mandatory member contributions (quotas) constituted an essential function of the IMF.[31] The pool would be available for states to draw upon for balance-of-payments purposes. When a government had insufficient foreign exchange reserves to cover a small deficit, it could draw from the fund. This alleviated the pressure for that state to make adjustments without devaluing its currency or imposing import restrictions through tariffs and/or quota.[32] Each state's contribution depended upon its rank in the world economy, adjusted for various political and economic

---

[29]See C. Conte and A. R. Karr, *An Outline of the U.S. Economy* (2009), ch. 10, http://usa.usembassy.de/etexts/oecon/chap10.htm (accessed April 22, 2009).

[30]Actually, also because of the number of U.S. citizens who are drawing pensions and Social Security payments in dollars, but have chosen to live outside the United States because the cost of living is lower.

[31]International Monetary Fund, "A Factsheet: IMF Quotas" (September 2008). At the end of August 2008, the Fund stood at approximately $341 billion, www.imf.org/external/np/exr/facts/quotas.htm (accessed April 22, 2009).

[32]For a detailed description, see J. K. Horsefield, *The International Monetary Fund, 1945–1965* (1969), 23–24.

A NOTE ON SPECIAL DRAWING RIGHTS

The IMF created the idea of Special Drawing Rights (SDR) in 1969 to support the Bretton Woods fixed exchange rate system.[34] The perception at the time was that the two key reserve assets, gold and the U.S. dollar, could not continue to support the volume of trade projected for the future. The international community decided to create a new international reserve asset under the auspices of the IMF. Two years later, the Bretton Woods system collapsed and the major currencies shifted to a floating exchange rate regime. Additionally, the growth in international capital markets facilitated borrowing by creditworthy governments. Both of these developments lessened the need for SDRs as reserved assets.

Today, the SDR has only limited use as a reserve asset. *Instead, it now serves as the unit of account for the IMF* as well as for some other international organizations and purposes. For example, the Montreal Convention (1999) uses SDRs to specify liability limits for international air carriers.[35] The value of the SDR is defined in terms of a basket of four major currencies—the euro (e), Japanese yen (¥), pound sterling (£), and U.S. dollar ($). The U.S. IMF posts the dollar value of the SDR daily on its website. The value is calculated as the sum of specific amounts of the four currencies valued in U.S. dollars, on the basis of exchange rates quoted at noon each day in the London market.

factors through negotiation at the time of entry. The agreements required that 25 percent of the quota would be paid in hard assets[33] (gold in the original) and 75 percent would be paid in the member's national currency. From the outset, the United States, as the world's largest economy, had the largest quota (as of August 2008, 17.09 percent). Table 19.3 gives a snapshot of some current obligations.

From the beginning of the IMF's operation, several problems emerged. The central legal issue became the conditions under which states might draw on IMF resources. The United Kingdom (John Maynard Keynes) and the United States (Harry Dexter White) had very different perspectives. The United Kingdom pushed for an automatic entitlement. The United States argued that withdrawal should occur only with an understanding that the borrowing government will follow conditions set by the IMF. The original agreements did not resolve the controversy. Subsequent interpretations of the agreements by the executive directors[36] did establish the idea of *conditionality*—that is, the idea that borrowing states would have to negotiate the loan terms, which would include explicitly identifying the measures the borrower would take to redress the problem.[37] IMF conditionally requires countries to rectify balance-of-payments problems using stringent fiscal

---

[33]"Hard assets" refers to currency such as the dollar, euro, yen, or pound sterling that does not fluctuate much in value and that can be freely and universally *converted* into other currencies.

[34]International Monetary Fund, "Special Drawing Rights (SDRs)" (September 2008), www.imf.org/external/np/exr/facts/sdr.htm (accessed April 22, 2009).

[35]*Convention for the Unification of Certain Rules for International Carriage by Air,* Montreal (May 28, 1999). Currently, the convention has 87 states parties. This includes the United States, European Union, Canada, China, and Japan.

[36]Executive directors are permanent country representatives to the Fund.

[37]Woods, note 24, at 40–41.

▶ **Table 19.3**

Selected IMF Quotas (December 1, 2008)[38]

Country	SDRs (in millions)*	Percentage
Canada	6,369.2	2.93
Germany	13,008.2	5.99
Japan	13,313.8	6.13
Palau	3.1	0.001
Russian Federation	5,945.4	2.74
Saudi Arabia	6,985.5	3.21
United States	37,149.3	1,709

*Special Drawing Rights; 1 SDR = $1.51.

and monetary policy measures. Actual practice has been more flexible. From the early 1950s, an understanding developed whereby states could draw up to the first 25 percent of its quota (the gold portion was later called the reserve *tranche*), provided that it was fully subscribed. Any drawing beyond that would require conditions. The greater the amount borrowed, the more stringent the IMF demands in terms of demonstrating commitment to policies of domestic adjustment or reform. Needless to say, this policy has proven very controversial because the "conditions" preferred by the IMF often resulted in states having to pursue deflationary policies that involved measures such as reducing public spending and employment in the public sector.

A second set of issues involved the nature of the assets deposited and withdrawn. In theory, all assets a state contributed would be available for withdrawal by member states. As a matter of practicality, only those assets the states contributed that were generally acceptable as either convertible or hard currencies were really useful. No state needed a currency that others would not accept for international payments. In the initial period of the IMF, given the devastation of Europe and Japan, few if any states had gold or dollars in the required amounts. None of the continental states had a convertible currency. The United Kingdom suspended the convertibility of the pound early in 1947. This meant the American dollar then served not only as the principal medium of exchange in international transactions but as the primary reserve asset as well. The United States also held more than 60 percent of the world's total gold supply.

Because of the discrepancy between the ideal system visualized in the agreements and the status of the world economy post World War II, the system never quite worked as drawn up.[39] Given that the dollar formed the only stable currency for international exchange, governments desperately needed dollars to fund postwar reconstruction projects that depended upon importing necessary materials. In

---

[38]International Monetary Fund, "IMF Members' Quotas and Voting Power" (December 1, 2008), www.imf.org/external/np/sec/memdir/members.htm (accessed April 22, 2009).

[39]See J. Gold, "Unauthorized Changes of Par Value and Fluctuating Exchange Rates in the Bretton Woods System," 65 *American Journal of International Law* (1971), 113–128.

the period immediately after World War II, analysts talked of the *dollar gap*—the difference between dollars needed and dollars in circulation. Under these circumstances, the U.S. Current Account deficit (along with aid programs) funded the system. Over the years, as Europe and Japan recovered and more currencies once again became convertible, the need for the dollar decreased, but the United States did not take steps to reduce its continuing Current Account deficits. By the late 1950s, analysts now talked of a *dollar glut*—an excess of dollars held by foreign banks and others. Concern grew as the number of dollars held overseas continued to increase while U.S. gold reserves continued to decrease during the 1960s. This situation gave rise to talk of a *dollar overhang*—the gap between the value of unrepatriated dollars versus the amount of gold held by the United States.[40]

In August 1971, President Richard Nixon suspended the convertibility of foreign-held dollars into gold. He also indicated that the United States would not intervene in exchange markets to maintain the par value of the dollar against other currencies. The issues illustrate the problems of treaty interpretation (Chapter 4). The immediate questions centered on whether the actions taken breached the IMF Agreement. Some question existed as to the obligation of the United States to maintain the gold window (Article IV(4)(b)). On the other hand, the fact that the United States had maintained the gold connection created the situation where many countries had held dollars based upon the expectations created by the system (a customary norm?).[41] Presumably, even if the United States did have the legal right to abandon the convertibility of the dollar to gold, it still would then have to honor its obligation to maintain the par value of the dollar within the prescribed parameters of the treaty (Article IV(3)). It did not, but then neither did any of the other major players.

Immediately, many proposals for reform floated. Before a new system could be put in place, several events occurred that placed more strain on the system. The most important effect flowed from the "oil shock" following the 1973 Yom Kippur War. The Organization of Petroleum Exporting Countries (OPEC) succeeded in raising oil prices to a level that created recession in many countries. This single event pushed the negotiations away from a return to fixed exchange rates. Consider also that by this time, the lesser developed countries (LDCs) had a voice. Further negotiations eventually produced a set of amended articles in March 1976. The Amended Articles of Agreement entered into effect on April 1, 1978, after 78 member states had notified the IMF of acceptance. Based on the weighted voting scheme, this represented three-fifths of the members (130) but four-fifths of the voting power.[42]

The amended articles had as their purpose the reestablishment of a legal regime over monetary transactions. While not explicitly putting in place a system of floating exchange rates, the agreement did the following:

---

[40]For a comprehensive discussion, see J. E. Spero and J. A. Hart, *The Politics of International Economic Relations,* 6th ed. (2009), ch. 2.

[41]Lowenfeld, note 15, at 625.

[42]Lowenfeld, note 15, at 633. Note that the amended articles changed the special majority necessary to implement change from 80 to 85 percent; see also K. W. Dam, *The Rules of the Game: Reform and Evolution in the International Monetary System* (1982).

- Eliminated references to gold and the "gold tranche"
- Established the SDR as the unit of accounting replacing dollars or gold
- Required states to maintain the international value of their currency, but permitted a choice of methods
- Reasserted the principle that the IMF "shall oversee the international monetary system" and "oversee the compliance of each member with its obligations" (Article IV(3)(a))

The agreement permitted governments to choose the ways they wish to establish the exchange rate of their currency. In effect, the amended agreements established the system of floating exchange rates.[43]

Perhaps the most important aspect of the amended articles was the Principles of Fund Surveillance. This instrument moved beyond the focus on exchange rate policies to authorize a comprehensive analysis of the general economic situation and economic policy strategy of member states when questions of compliance arise. Lowenfeld notes that the wording of the principles seemingly gave the managing director the authority to raise "almost any matter of the member's economic policy that has effect on the member's exchange rate or the international economy."[44] While there still may be a line between matters that lie solely within the domestic jurisdiction of a member, specifying exactly where that line might be drawn has proven difficult—except to note that while the basic outlines of monetary and fiscal policies may come under scrutiny by the IMF, detailed policy choices still remain the province of the member state.[45]

Enforcement of Obligations to the IMF

Interestingly, the IMF has not characterized the programs subject to conditionality as binding legal obligations.[46] If a member state does not follow through on the economic program agreed to in the letter of intent, or fails to meet established goals in a timely fashion, the IMF may suspend borrowing privileges, but it does not characterize such actions as sanctions or even "enforcement."[47] The IMF has worked out a process to prod states that have not met their obligations.[48] It begins with a cable reminding the member of its obligation as soon as a government misses a due date. The member has two weeks to respond. If it does not, this lapse triggers a set of procedures whereby successive levels of decision makers become involved each time a member fails to respond. If no answer to the various communications has been received within six weeks, the managing director informs the

---

[43]Actually, the agreement permitted states that wished to "peg" to do so—and those that preferred to float to do so.

[44]Lowenfeld, note 15, at 639.

[45]Lowenfeld, note 15, at 640.

[46]See para. 7 of the Guidelines on Conditionality, Sec. 19.5(c).

[47]Lowenfeld, note 15, at 663.

[48]See Overdue Obligations to the Fund, Selected Decisions, 715–743 (31st issue, 2006); Procedures for Dealing with Members with Overdue Financial Obligations to the General Department and the SDR Department Executive Board Meetings 89/100 and 89/101, July 27, 1989, www.imf.org/external/pubs/ft/sd/index.asp?decision=EBM/89/101 (accessed April 22, 2009).

state in default that a formal complaint will be issued to the IMF Executive Board in two weeks' time. The Executive Board, under Article XXVI(2)(a) of the Articles of Agreement, can suspend the member from use of IMF resources. This suspension would occur only in circumstances where the member has refused payment and has not cooperated with the IMF in working out a plan to repay. Potentially, a member could face compulsory withdrawal.[49]

The Third Amendment to the Articles of Agreement in 1992 provided for another measure between ineligibility for IMF resources and compulsory withdrawal. New Article XXVI(2)(b) specifies that, by a 70 percent majority of the total voting power, the IMF can suspend the voting rights of a member that persists in failing to honor its obligations to the fund. To date, this article has been used against the Sudan and the Democratic Republic of the Congo during the 1990s.

The IMF in Transition

Since the transition to floating exchange rates, the IMF has not played a major role as a source of funds for the advanced industrial states.[50] On the other hand, it became very important to LDCs whose currencies were not freely convertible and not held by other countries. For these countries, the IMF continues as a source of assistance. Since the 1990s, this has also been true for the countries of Eastern Europe and the former Soviet Union as they make the transition from central planning to market economies. Perhaps the IMF's most important new role, and one of its most controversial, was in imposing some discipline (conditionality) on states (and private institutions) involved in the various debt crises in the 1980s and 1990s. Though still an important forum for international financial issues, ironically the IMF probably does *not* completely "oversee the international monetary system in order to ensure its effective operation" (Article IV(3)(a)).

THE GENERAL AGREEMENT ON TARIFFS AND TRADE

The United States took the lead in trying to restore order to international trading relations.[51] Based upon extended conversations with the United Kingdom, the United States issued a set of proposals calling for a new charter that would seek to reduce restraints on free trade and create a new international organization—the International Trade Organization (ITO)—to oversee the process. The ITO would also provide a mechanism for dispute settlement, a forum for continued negotiation, and a system for collecting relevant statistics and other information. Unconditional acceptance of the *most favored nation* (MFN) principle would comprise the central

---

[49]No state has ever been required to withdraw; also, the executive directors for Sudan recommended the action for several years.

[50]See Woods, note 24, at 39–64.

[51]See C. Wilcox, *A Charter for World Trade* (1949); G. Curzon, *Multilateral Commercial Diplomacy: The General Agreement of Tariffs and Trade and Its Impact on National Commercial Policies and Techniques* (1965); R. N. Gardner, *Sterling Dollar Diplomacy: The Origins and the Prospects of Our International Economic Order,* (rev. ed. 1980); R. E. Hudec, *The GATT Legal System and World Trade Diplomacy,* 2nd ed. (1990).

legal obligation of the new regime.[52] The United States wasted little time in moving forward. The first meeting of the UN Economic and Social Council (ECOSOC) in February 1946 established a Preparatory Committee (19 countries) to draft a document.[53] The process resulted in a conference on trade and development that met in Havana in November 1947 to discuss the draft proposal for the ITO.

Over the same period, the United States pursued a second path as well. It invited the 19 countries on the ITO Preparatory Committee plus 8 others to Geneva to engage in a series of "round-robin" bilateral negotiations specifically aimed at cutting tariffs. Between April and October of 1947, a total of 123 sets of negotiations occurred that were aimed at achieving low rates or duty-free entry.[54] These initial negotiations had an impact still felt 60 years later in terms of procedures and policies. They set a precedent for all future negotiating sessions (eight total) and set a policy that all the provisions involving tariffs and other "concessions" would apply to all the participants. All of the negotiated agreements were embodied in a single document, the General Agreement on Tariffs and Trade (GATT), that contained the appropriate schedules and a code of conduct.[55]

At the time, participating states viewed the GATT as an interim measure that would be in place only long enough for the ITO to become a reality. The structure of the GATT also reflected a desire to circumvent the potentially lengthy process of ratification—especially in the U.S. Congress, which was still seen as parochial, protectionist, and isolationist. Because it was presented as a "trade agreement" negotiated under an existing—but soon expiring—grant of authority to the president by the Congress, the treaty could not include any elaborate organizational structures. To be fair, many European states would have faced some formidable obstacles in achieving ratification as well because of a view that reconstruction would require policies.

For many reasons associated with post–World War II political events, the ITO proposal went from being a top priority to an unwanted orphan.[56] Until replaced by the WTO in 1995, the GATT would form the backbone of the international trade regime. Even then, the principles and procedures of the GATT continued to form the core of WTO obligations. By the time of its transformation, the GATT had 125 signatories and governed 90 percent of world trade.[57] Currently, WTO membership has grown to 153 (December 2011).

---

[52]The most favored nation principle holds that a country should not discriminate between its trading partners (giving them equally "most-favored-nation" status), and it should not discriminate between its own and foreign products, services, or nationals (giving them "national treatment").

[53]Interestingly, although ECOSOC is a principal organ of the UN—and the one that receives 75 percent of the regular budget—after this initial flurry of activity, ECOSOC has not played a great role in economic relations, particularly among the developed states.

[54]Wilcox, note 51, at 46–47.

[55]*General Agreement on Tariffs and Trade,* October 30, 1947; entered into force January 1, 1948; text at www.wto.org/english/docs_e/legal_e/gatt47_e.pdf (accessed April 22, 2009). Note that the code of conduct largely reflected the draft Charter for the ITO.

[56]See Lowenfeld, *Trade Controls for Political Ends,* 2nd ed. (1983), ch. 1.

[57]"General Agreement on Tariffs and Trade," *Encyclopædia Britannica 2009,* Encyclopædia Britannica Online (January 23, 2009), http://search.eb.com/eb/article-9036358 (accessed April 22, 2009). Note that the end of the Uruguay Round of negotiations in 1994 finally produced a permanent organization (WTO), but the essential obligations of the GATT remained intact.

The interesting aspect of the GATT arises because, in expectation that the ITO Charter would eventually be ratified, the agreement did not create an ongoing organizational structure.[58] The GATT speaks of contracting parties (and contracting *parties* to refer to the collective whole), not members or member states. Yet, for the regime to survive over the long term, it would need to develop mechanisms for dispute settlement and would need to address other problems of implementation and compliance—such as requests for temporary exemptions and waivers—as well as other problems that would arise as circumstances changed. The response to the situation required some remarkable footwork in creating procedures and making adjustments as problems arose. As an example, we should consider the evolution of dispute resolution procedures. The GATT did foresee some necessity for ways to deal with disputes among signatories. Article XXII states that each contracting party "shall accord sympathetic consideration" to concerns about "any matter" that may be raised by another contracting party. In addition, if sufficiently serious in that a matter posed a basic challenge to any of the fundamental principles in the GATT, a matter could be referred to the "CONTRACTING PARTIES" (emphasis in the original document) or the entire, collective body of signatories (Article XXIII). It specified no procedures for submission or methods for arriving at a decision, although it did permit sanctions in the form of suspension of obligations.[59] Lowenfeld describes the process as somewhat akin to arbitration, but in many ways also similar to the methods an exclusive club may use to keep its members in line:

> The GATT as a dispute resolution forum had ebb and flow, as prevailing views moved back and forth between a desire to compose disputes and keep controversies from spreading, and a desire to arrive at clear rules with law-making effect. In fact more than 200 formal complaints were filed over the first 45 years of the GATT, alleging either violations of the General Agreement or one of the codes subsequently adopted.[60]

Because the contracting parties had to avoid any presumption that the GATT had created a permanent organization, in the early period, business had to be done during the periodic meetings of the signatories. These were called sessions. No neutral arbitral or judicial mechanisms existed. Thus, early legal complaints had to be dealt with in the few weeks that the contracting *parties* remained in session. As Hudec notes, an assembly of diplomats, each representing his or her own government's interest, hardly seemed an appropriate forum for rendering an impartial legal decision.[61] On the other hand, the early GATT decisions seemed attuned to

---

[58]The ITO idea died largely because, with the onset of the Cold War, the United States (and its Allies) preferred the relative flexibility of the GATT to what would have been a more demanding set of standards in the ITO.

[59]R. E. Hudec, *Enforcing International Trade Law* (1993), 274–276. Many of the delegates had been involved in the negotiation and implementation of the agreements; they shared a common history and understanding of the purposes.

[60]Lowenfeld, note 15, at 45.

[61]R. E. Hudec, "The Role of the GATT Secretariat in the Evolution of the WTO Dispute Settlement Procedure," in *The Uruguay Round and Beyond: Essays in Honour of Arthur Dunkel,* edited by J. Bhagwati and M. Hirsch (1998), 104.

context in that rather than the harsh language of law, they utilized the language of diplomacy. The art was to suggest the necessary conclusions without explicitly saying what everyone knew they meant.[62] Over time, other methods evolved. We shall deal with these later when we discuss the dispute resolution procedures in the WTO.

Avoiding the idea that the GATT had created an organizational structure led to one of the more curious arrangements in the history of international organization. The pretense meant that the GATT could not create its own secretariat to manage its business. To overcome the problem, GATT member governments simply *borrowed* a secretariat. The United Nations had created a secretariat to manage the Havana negotiations to finalize the ITO. At the end of the conference, that organization had continued on an ad hoc basis as the Interim Commission for the International Trade Organization (ICITO) that presumably would make the final preparations to give life to the ITO. After the ITO became a dead issue, the ICITO had no official function, but the GATT signatories had adopted the group as a convenient solution to the problem of organizing its business. ICITO continued to exist for the next 45 years with the sole purpose of giving a legal basis for the operation of a GATT secretariat.

General Principles

The GATT represented a work in progress.[63] While it had clear principles, because of the pragmatic qualifications and exceptions contained within the original, these served as goals to be achieved in many cases rather than hard law to be immediately applied and observed. In principle, each signatory pledged

- To conduct trade on a *nondiscriminatory* basis (MFN, Article I)
- Not to increase trade barriers; changes should occur in the form of reductions, not increases
- To utilize tariffs only; these should be computed on an *ad valorem* basis or similar fashion where charges apply per unit
- Not to impose measures such as discriminatory national taxation or other regulations
- To conduct regular, ongoing multilateral negotiations aimed at reducing trade barriers; the series of conferences convened to negotiate issues forms a distinguishing feature of international trade law

Exceptions and Exemptions

The difficulty with the GATT was that almost every principle was fraught with exemptions and exceptions.[64] These included the preservation of certain preferences. Other exemptions were based on national legislation, national security, or other political objections. One should not, however, draw the conclusion that the

---

[62]*Ibid.*, 106.

[63]Note that the original agreement concerned only *goods*. Concerns about services and other areas such as intellectual property did not arise until the Uruguay Round (1986–1994) of negotiations.

[64]See J. M. Finger, "Legalized Backsliding: Safeguard Proposals in GATT," in *The Uruguay Round and the Developing Economies*, edited by W. Martin and L. A. Winters (1995), 285–304.

exemptions and exceptions totally undermined the principles. Despite the exemptions and exceptions, the principles have survived and evolved.

Perhaps the most notable set of exceptions involved a concession by the United States that permitted Great Britain, France, Belgium, and other colonial powers to maintain the preferential arrangements they had because of their colonial holdings and policies. These clearly violated the MFN principle, but given the political and economic circumstances following the war, the dispensation seemed a necessary, if perhaps temporary, allowance. On the other hand, Article I clearly states that the margin of such preferences could not be increased over the level that existed at the start of the Geneva negotiating sessions. While a major factor at the time, because of the anticolonial revolution, these preferences have played a relatively minor and declining role over time.[65]

A second important exemption came from a calculation involving expediency. The GATT did not require that contracting parties repeal or revise any existing domestic legislation that might contravene obligations in the treaty regarding subsidies, dumping, or other discriminatory practices (Protocol of Provisional Application).[66] This exemption permitted the United States as well as others to avoid the formal ratification process (Chapter 4) because the GATT would not require any changes in legislation. The protocol obligated the signatories to implement Parts I and III of the agreement (fundamental principles, procedural provisions), but required states to comply with Part II—the code of conduct—only "to the fullest extent not inconsistent with existing legislation." In practice over time, GATT panels sought to limit the impact of the protocol:

> "Not inconsistent with existing legislation" was interpreted . . . to justify implementation of a measure contrary to a provision of the GATT only when such a measure was *required* under pre-existing law, as contrasted with merely being *authorized*. Also, a GATT panel held that when a pre-existing law expired and was re-enacted with a brief gap, the new law could not regain the benefit of the Protocol of Provisional Application.[67]

Note that here the United States, as well as others, took full advantage of the exemptions. A focus on U.S. law with respect to imposing countervailing duties on imports that benefited from subsidies formed a principal issue as late as the Tokyo Round (1973–1979) of negotiations.[68] The protocol proved more durable than provisional. It lasted in some form until the WTO replaced the GATT in 1995.

A third set of exemptions centered on national security. Article XXI provided that

> Nothing in this Agreement shall be construed (*a*) to require any contracting party to furnish any information the disclosure of which it considers contrary

---

[65]The one exception—the corresponding role that preferences played in the politics surrounding the European Economic Community. See "The EEC and the GATT," *European Navigator* (June 28, 2006), www.ena.lu/the-eec-and-the-gatt-020100229.html (accessed May 15, 2009).

[66]For a lengthy and detailed discussion, see Hudec, note 51, at 135–157.

[67]Lowenfeld, note 15, at 34.

[68]See WTO, "The GATT Years: From Havana to Marrakesh," www.wto.org/english/thewto_e/whatis_e/tif_e/fact4_e.htm (accessed May 15, 2009).

to its essential security interests; or (*b*) to prevent any contracting party from taking any action which it considers necessary for the protection of its essential security interests.

The language clearly makes Article XXI a self-judging or permissive measure. In fact, no procedural guidelines have ever been created to examine a claim based on Article XXI. Considering the level and scope of political tensions during the early years of the agreement, this seemingly offered a huge potential loophole for evading some of the more onerous obligations. Interestingly, disputes alleging abuse of Article XXI have seldom arisen. The question of whether a contracting party affected by a trade measure could bring a complaint has never been definitively settled.[69] When disputes have arisen, member states have sought to utilize international pressure and diplomacy rather than formal third-party panels.[70]

In one of the few cases brought to the GATT, Nicaragua challenged the imposition of an embargo by the United States. While a dispute panel was established, it concluded that it could not address the validity of the U.S. use of Article XXI because it was precluded from doing so by the terms of Article XXI as well as the terms of its mandate.[71] Other tribunals have also upheld the self-judging aspect of the article. As part of its decision in the case Nicaragua brought against the United States in the International Court of Justice, the court used the language of Article XXI as a comparative standard. It noted that the treaty in question contained an objective standard—national security measures must be *necessary*, rather than the subjective, self-judging standard of Article XXI—a country may take measures *it considers* necessary.[72]

Fourth, the question arose concerning states that had long-standing antagonistic relations with one another. During the Havana Conference to finalize the ITO Charter, India proposed a solution. When states first joined the GATT, they could declare that they would not enter into negotiations with another state and would not apply the GATT provisions with respect to that state. When a state acceded to the GATT on a bilateral basis, it could elect not to apply GATT provisions with regard to another state. On the other hand, states already "members" could also choose not to apply GATT provisions with regard to the new entrant. This provision was added to the GATT as Article XXXV. While one might understand the cases of Egypt and Israel, or India and Pakistan, the most egregious use of Article XXXV occurred in 1955, when many states invoked it to avoid giving MFN status to Japanese goods.[73] Many of these restrictions lasted until the late 1980s.

A fifth exemption involved restrictions that largely had to do with agricultural products, although it potentially could apply to other sectors. Most countries

---

[69]P. Lindsay, "The Ambiguity of GATT Article XXI: Subtle Success or Rampant Failure," 52 *Duke Law Journal* (2003), 1278.

[70]*Ibid.*, 1279.

[71]GATT, *Analytical Index: Guide to GATT Law and Practice*, 6th ed. (1995), 601.

[72]*Military and Paramilitary Activities in and Against Nicaragua (Nicaragua v. United States)*, *ICJ Reports* (1986), 116–117.

[73]For a thorough discussion, see A. Forsberg, "The Politics of GATT Expansion: Japanese Accession and the Domestic Political Context in Japan and the United States, 1948–1955," 27 *Business and Economic History* 185 (1998).

want to protect domestic agriculture. As with other sectors, if a competing product could be imported freely, then it might undermine domestic production. Article XI first prohibits any quantitative restrictions (quotas) but then permits them under a number of restrictive conditions (Article XXXV).[74] In fact, the practice here produced the reality that agriculture stood outside the primary rules. Sharma describes the situation:

> Agriculture has had a difficult history in the GATT. The GATT does not say much about agriculture specifically, which meant that in theory agricultural trade was to be treated essentially like trade in other goods. However, some GATT articles provided exceptional status for agricultural products, an indication that the drafters of the GATT were well aware of the unique political status that agriculture enjoyed in some major countries at that time. But agriculture was not forgotten altogether—the subject was brought in all successive rounds—but without much success. At the same time, it attracted a large number of trade disputes.[75]

Again, in evaluating this statement about practice, we should consider Article XIII—stating that any quota should be applied on a nondiscriminatory basis. Nonetheless, a common standard of discrimination still results in discrimination.

Other Issues and Problems

The question of regional arrangements such as *customs unions* also formed an issue from the beginning. Belgium, the Netherlands, and Luxembourg (Benelux), three founding members of the GATT, had entered into a regional arrangement to eliminate trade barriers among themselves. The dilemma flows from the nature of a customs union. On the one hand, the very definition of a customs union is inconsistent with MFN treatment because clearly those within the agreement will receive special treatment. On the other hand, the very idea of a customs union—in that it eliminates trade barriers—is consistent with the overall goals of the GATT.[76] The solution to the dilemma came in the drafting of Article XXIV of the GATT. A customs union had to meet three conditions. It must cover substantially all of the trade between the prospective members; the external tariff may not be greater than the average of tariffs utilized by constituent states before the agreement, and, if the agreement includes a "phase-in" arrangement, this must be accomplished within a reasonable time. The negotiators working on the European Economic Community (EEC) clearly kept Article XXIV in mind as they developed the regime. In addition to the EEC (now the European Union, EU), we have the North American Free

---

[74]R. Sharma, "Agriculture and the GATT: A Historical Account," *Multilateral Trade Negotiations on Agriculture*, Module 4, FAO Corporate Document Repository, www.fao.org/DOCREP/003/X7352E/X7352E04.htm (accessed April 22, 2009).

[75]*Ibid.*, Sec. 4.1; D. E. Hathaway, "Agriculture and the GATT: Rewriting the Rules. Policy Analysis in International Economics," *Institute for International Economics* (1997).

[76]H. Konishi, C. Kowalczyk, and T. Sjöström, "Free Trade, Customs Unions, and Transfers," *Boston College Working Papers in Economics*, No. 568 (2003), 3–4, http://fmwww.bc.edu/EC-P/WP568.pdf (accessed April 22, 2009).

Trade Agreement (NAFTA), the Association of Southeast Asian Nations (ASEAN), the South Asian Association for Regional Cooperation (SAARC), the Common Market of the South (MERCOSUR), and the Australia–New Zealand Closer Economic Relations Agreement, to name a few. The WTO website states:

> By July 2005, only one WTO member—Mongolia—was not party to a regional trade agreement. The surge in these agreements has continued unabated since the early 1990s. By July 2005, a total of 330 had been notified to the WTO (and its predecessor, GATT). Of these: 206 were notified after the WTO was created in January 1995; 180 are currently in force; several others are believed to be operational although not yet notified.[77]

A substantial body of practice has developed concerning the relationships between the various regional arrangements and the GATT (now WTO).

A second set of continuing issues has centered on questions of dumping, subsidies (Article XVI), and nontariff barriers. Dumping occurs when a country sells in overseas markets for prices less than those charged in its home market (often less than true production costs).[78] Governments have a right to impose an "antidumping duty" to offset the unfair pricing. Often, dumping may be linked with government subsidies that offset the actual cost to companies. The problem with subsidies is the fine line between using them as part of a domestic program to promote growth or development in certain sectors or areas and using them to improve the competitiveness of a product in international trade. States had a right to impose a "countervailing duty" to offset the subsidy.[79] Interestingly, in the original agreement, dumping was "condemned" but not prohibited; subsidies were neither condemned nor prohibited. The issues again revolved around the fear that states would abuse the right to take corrective action to enact protectionist measures.[80] Over time, as duties were reduced, the questions of dumping, subsidies, and nontariff barriers became the primary elements in ongoing discussions of "unfair" trade practices. In particular, potential distortions in the guise of health and safety standards, product quality standards, or environmental regulations have been continuing concerns. To give but one example here, the equipment necessary to bring an automobile into compliance with Environmental Protection Agency (EPA) clean air standards has meant that a large number of automobiles available in Europe are not sold in the United States. Foreign manufacturers do not believe the cost involved in altering designs and adding extra equipment to meet the emissions standards can be justified by sales volume. Hence, these models are effectively excluded from the U.S. domestic market.

Another ongoing problem involved waivers of obligation (Article XXV(5)). The collective body *(contracting parties)* could grant waivers by a two-thirds majority vote for "exceptional circumstances." Over 100 waivers were granted in

---

[77]"Understanding the WTO: Cross-Cutting and New Issues—Regionalism: Friends or Rivals?" www.wto.org/english/thewto_e/whatis_e/tif_e/bey1_e.htm#top (accessed April 22, 2009).

[78]See A. C. Sobel, *Political Economy and Global Affairs* (2006), 258.

[79]*Ibid.*, 258.

[80]Wilcox, note 51, at 55–56.

[81]Lowenfeld, note 15, at 44.

the first 40 years.[81] Again, this represented a pragmatic response to potential political problems. It permitted the GATT to navigate through situations that might have threatened its very existence. Perhaps the most interesting and illustrative of this is the waiver given to the United States in 1955 that covered restrictions on imports of almost all agricultural products. This waiver remained in force for 40 years. It was phased out only after the agricultural settlement reached in the Uruguay Round of negotiations.[82] The agreement establishing the WTO retained the waiver requirement but raised the necessary vote of approval to three-quarters. It also requires that waivers have a termination date and that, if extended beyond a year, they will be subject to annual review.[83]

Getting to the World Trade Organization

As noted earlier, a commitment to ongoing negotiation constituted one of the primary obligations of states entering the GATT regime. Between 1947 and 1961, states held five sets of negotiations. These resulted in some modest, but not significant, cuts in tariffs. Dissatisfaction with the progress after the fourth round in 1956 led to a meeting of the foreign ministers of the Benelux countries, France, Federal Republic of Germany, and Italy to discuss the Spaak (Brussels) Report that called for the establishment of a Common Market.[84] The discussion excluded both the United States and the United Kingdom. The Treaty of Rome, creating the EEC (or Common Market), entered into force in 1968.[85]

The EEC presented the United States and United Kingdom with an interesting set of problems. On the one hand, it clearly enmeshed Germany within a multilateral setting that would permit it to take a more active role in Cold War politics in Europe. Still, the EEC could also be seen as an active barrier to U.S. interests in promoting free trade. Great Britain attempted to offset the EEC by putting together the European Free Trade Association (EFTA).[86] The Kennedy Round (1964–1967) saw the development of an Anti-dumping Agreement and establishment, in general, that the principle of reciprocity should be part of future negotiations. The Tokyo Round embodied a largely unsuccessful attempt at fundamental reform. It did not result in modifying practices associated with agricultural trade but did succeed in producing a series of agreements on nontariff barriers. In many

---

[82]FAO, "Impact of the Uruguay Round Agreements of Relevance to the Agricultural Sector: Winners and Losers," www.fao.org/trade/docs/TradeBrief_en.htm (accessed April 22, 2009).

[83]WTO Agreement, Article IX(3), www.wto.org/english/docs_e/legal_e/04-wto_e.htm (accessed April 22, 2009).

[84]Archive of European Integration, University of Pittsburgh, Intergovernmental Committee on European Integration. The Brussels Report on the General Common Market (abridged, English translation of document commonly called the Spaak Report) (June 1956), http://aei.pitt.edu/995/ (accessed April 22, 2009).

[85]www.europa.eu/legislation_summaries/institutional_affairs/treaties/treaties_eec_en.htm.

[86]See E. Benoit, *Europe at Sixes and Sevens: The Common Market, the Free Trade Association and the United States* (1960), for a good discussion of the politics. Originally EFTA consisted of Austria, Denmark, Norway, Portugal, Sweden, Switzerland, and the United Kingdom. EFTA still is in existence. It now has four member states: Iceland, Liechtenstein, Norway, and Switzerland; www.efta.int/about-efta/the-efta-states.aspx.

cases, only a relatively small number of industrialized GATT members subscribed to these agreements and arrangements. Because they were not accepted by the full GATT membership, they were often informally called "codes."[87] Several of these codes were amended and turned into multilateral agreements during the Uruguay Round.[88]

The UN Conference on Trade and Development

As the anticolonial movement gained momentum, many lesser developed states felt that the principles of the GATT, particularly those of nondiscrimination with respect to market access, worked against their interest in economic development. Many saw the GATT principles as a continuing license to steal phrased in the language of fair trade.[89] A coalition of developing countries pushed for a separate organization that would be more attuned to their interests and concerns. The organization became a reality with the formation of the United Nations Conference on Trade and Development (UNCTAD) in 1964. Over the next two decades, a coalition known as the Group of 77 (G77) pushed for a fundamental reform of the international trading system.[90] When this effort produced limited results, the group escalated its demands in the form of a set of proposals collectively known as the New International Economic Order (NIEO). Adopted by the UN General Assembly in 1974, the proposals sought a radical restructuring of the international economic system to subordinate international economic processes to the development needs of the poorer states (the global South).[91]

Beset with their own economic problems caused by the two oil crises (1973–1974, 1979), the advanced industrial states paid little heed. The NIEO slowly faded as an issue as the divergent interests of "the South" undermined the coalition, aided by a selective concessions strategy by the GATT countries. Moreover, by the mid-1980s, many states in the global South faced serious balance-of-payments and financial problems. They had to turn to the World Bank and IMF for financial assistance.[92] This gave the industrialized states enormous leverage during talks

---

[87]"Understanding the WTO: Basics, The GATT Years: From Havana to Marrakesh," www.wto.org/english/thewto_e/whatis_e/tif_e/fact4_e.htm (accessed April 22, 2009).

[88]For a list of these codes, see "Understanding the WTO: Basics," note 87.

[89]Much of this view stems from a number of neo-Marxist hypotheses popular in the 1960s and 1970s. In particular, the work of Singer and Prebisch suggested that the terms of trade between manufacturing states and states producing primary products would always decline over time. In economic terms, this decline would occur because the income elasticity of demand for manufactured goods is greater than that for primary products—especially food. Thus, as incomes rise, the demand for manufactured goods increases more rapidly than the demand for primary products. Some recent work has suggested that the hypothesis does find some support during the post–World War II period. See, for example, H. Bloch and D. Sapsford, "Whither the Terms of Trade? An Elaboration of the Prebisch-Singer Hypothesis," 24 *Cambridge Journal of Economics* (2000), 461–481; J. Toye and R. Toye, "The Origins and Interpretation of the Prebisch-Singer Thesis," 35 *History of Political Economy* (2003), 437–457.

[90]Though the group has grown in membership, it retains the G77 designation to honor the original members. See S. D. Krasner, *Structural Conflict: The Third World Against Global Liberalism* (1985).

[91]R. Gilpin, *The Political Economy of International Economic Relations* (1987), 299–300.

[92]Oatley, note 26, at 144–149.

concerned with development issues. While UNCTAD still exists as a forum for development issues, the WTO functions as the most important organization with respect to policy issues, negotiations, and implementation.[93]

The Uruguay Round in GATT

The Uruguay Round marked a significant milestone for many reasons. Perhaps the most important factor stemmed from the simple observation that circumstances and issues had changed substantially since the establishment of the GATT. The trade environment is not static. The ability to compete well in particular products can shift from company to company or country to country when the market changes or new technologies make cheaper and better products possible. Again, one only needs to look at the ebb and flow of the automobile industry, or the change in the mix of American imports and exports over the past 60 years. The GATT had succeeded in achieving major reductions in the average tariff rate on goods, but by the early 1980s, tariffs on manufactured good ceased to be the major concern.[94] For the first time, issues other than tariffs on manufactured goods and nontariff barriers appeared on the negotiating agenda: intellectual property,[95] services (any economic activity that does not involve manufacturing, farming, or resource extraction), and measures relating to investment and the concerns generated by the operations of multinational corporations. As a result, the WTO includes the agreements on Trade-Related Aspects of Intellectual Property (TRIPs), Trade-Related Investment Measures (TRIMs), and the General Agreement on Trade in Services (GATS).[96]

The Uruguay Round produced a new organization, the WTO, that in many important ways marked a departure for international trade law. Still, Article XVI(1) of the Marrakesh Agreements clearly states that governments saw this as an evolutionary continuation, not a replacement:

> Except as otherwise provided under this Agreement or the Multilateral Trade Agreements, the WTO shall be guided by the decisions, procedures and customary practices follow by the CONTRACTING PARTIES to GATT 1947 and the bodies established in the framework of GATT 1947.[97]

The agreements extended the authority of the new organization into many new aspects of international economic activity, while not surprisingly leaving others such as the environment for future negotiations. All in all, the Uruguay Round

---

[93]See UNCTAD, www.unctad.org/Templates/Startpage.asp?intItemID=2068&lang=1 (accessed April 22, 2009).

[94]J. H. Jackson, *The World Trading System: Law and Policy of International Economic Relations* (1997).

[95]"Creations of the mind": inventions (patents), literary and artistic works (copyright), and items such as pictures, corporate logos, movies, brand names, computer software, etc.

[96]Texts available on the WTO website, "WTO Legal Texts," www.wto.org/english/docs_e/legal_e/legal_e.htm (accessed April 22, 2009).

[97]*Marrakesh Agreement Establishing the World Trade Organization* (1994). Text at www.wto.org/english/docs_e/legal_e/04-wto_e.htm (accessed April 22, 2009).

resulted in 60 agreements totaling over 550 pages. The agreements include five groups of general principles:

- Principles of nondiscrimination
- Rules on market access
- Rules on unfair trade
- Rules on conflicts between trade liberalization and other societal values
- Rules promoting coordination and congruence with national regulations in certain fields[98]

Additionally, the regime includes procedural rules that govern decision making and dispute settlement.

A unique aspect of the WTO agreement concerned Annex 4. This instrument contained four agreements termed *plurilateral*. Under the WTO structure, a multilateral agreement binds all members (unless exceptions and exemptions apply); a plurilateral agreement applies only to those countries that had originally signed and ratified it. Two of the four original plurilateral agreements were terminated in 1997.[99] At present, only the Agreement on Trade in Civil Aircraft and the Agreement on Government Procurement remain. For our purposes, the most important aspect of these plurilateral arrangements is that they are exempted from the dispute settlement procedures in the WTO.

The Doha Round

Needless to say, the WTO is a work in progress. Continuing the original commitment to negotiations among contracting parties (now called members), ministers met in Doha, Qatar, in November 2001. The delegates approved an extensive program of future work that comprised an agenda of 21 issues. The agenda included ongoing issues such as dumping, nontariff barriers, market access, and agriculture as well as new items that stressed environmental issues and the concerns of the developing nations. In particular, the conference dealt with issues of implementation of the *Marrakesh Agreement*. The WTO website notes that *implementation* is shorthand for problems raised by developing countries about the implementation of the current WTO agreements. The website also includes fleshing out agreements on some other issues, such as the GATS, that had been approved basically as "framework agreements" that structured the issues for further negotiation. The work continued at Cancun (2003), Geneva (2004), and Hong Kong (2006). As of this writing, drafts negotiating texts on agriculture, non-agricultural market access (NAMA), rules, and refinement of the GATS have been distributed to members.[100]

---

[98]P. Van den Bossche, *The Law and Policy of the World Trade Organization*, 2nd ed. (2008), 37.

[99]The *International Dairy Agreement* and the *International Bovine Meat Agreement*.

[100]For a current listing, see "Doha Development Agenda: Negotiations, Implementation and Development," www.wto.org/english/tratop_e/dda_e/dda_e.htm (accessed April 22, 2009). This site receives regular updates on developments.

Dispute Settlement in the WTO

We noted earlier that the GATT had only minimal provisions for dispute settlement.[101] Note that the evolution of the procedures forms one of the best illustrations of how customary law develops. The process over time illustrates how "what was initially a rudimentary, power-based system" became transformed into "an elaborate, rule-based system for settling disputes through adjudication."[102] Since its inception in 1995, the WTO dispute settlement system has perhaps been the most widely used of all methods of international third-party arrangements. As of February 1, 2009, a total of 390 disputes had been brought to the organization for resolution.[103] Among the most active filers of complaints have been the United States and the European Union. Some of the more high-profile disputes have involved the EU ban on meat from cattle treated with growth hormones, the EU preferential import regime for bananas, and the EU measures affecting poultry meat and poultry meat products from the United States. Van den Bossche notes that in about a quarter of the disputes, states have been able to reach an amicable resolution through consultations or other methods without resorting to the formal process of adjudication.[104]

Annex 2 of the WTO agreement is titled "Understanding on Rules and Procedures Governing the Settlement of Disputes (DSU)."[105] The principal purpose of the dispute settlement system is the *prompt* settlement of disputes among members involving obligations under the agreements through *multilateral* rather than unilateral means. Article 3.10 requires that all members must "engage in these procedures in good faith in an effort to resolve the dispute." Good faith means that a government must not use the system in a contentious way and must have a genuine intention to resolve the dispute. The DSU does not extend to all trade agreements between members. Trade agreements negotiated within the context of WTO requirements, but that are neither attached to the WTO nor within covered agreements listed in Appendix 1 of the DSU, are exempted.

Drawing on Chapter 5, we should note that dispute settlement mechanisms in the WTO involve many different choices, not a single process applicable to all. Within the WTO, we can identify four methods: (1) good offices, conciliation, and mediation; (2) consultation or negotiation; (3) arbitration; and (4) adjudication by special panels or the appellate body. Indeed, the DSU encourages consultation, negotiation, and mediation. Article 3.7 of the DSU states:

> The aim of the dispute settlement mechanism is to secure a positive solution to a dispute. A solution mutually acceptable to the parties to a dispute and consistent with the covered agreements is clearly to be preferred.

---

[101]For information on any dispute, see WTO, "Find Dispute Cases," www.wto.org/english/tratop_e/dispu_e/find_dispu_cases_e.htm (accessed April 22, 2009).

[102]Van den Bossche, note 98, at 170.

[103]See WTO, "Chronological List of Dispute Cases," www.wto.org/english/tratop_e/dispu_e/dispu_status_e.htm (accessed April 22, 2009).

[104]Van den Bossche, note 98, at 169.

[105]Text at www.wto.org/english/tratop_e/dispu_e/dsu_e.htm (accessed April 22, 2009).

The Dispute Settlement Body (DSB) administers the Dispute Settlement Understanding (DSU).[106] It meets as often as needed to carry out its functions. Article 2.1 specifies its duties:

> Accordingly, the DSB shall have the authority to establish panels, adopt panel and Appellate Body reports, maintain surveillance of implementation of rulings and recommendations and authorize suspension of concessions and other obligations under the covered agreement.

If the members involved cannot come to a settlement through direct negotiation or mediation, then they may request the DSB to appoint an ad hoc panel with the specific purpose of recommending measures to resolve the dispute. The panels are not continuing, standing bodies—they are constituted for each specific dispute and are dissolved after making their reports. Constituting a panel can be a contentious process. In keeping with the prompt settlement requirement, if the parties to the dispute cannot agree on the composition of the panel, the director general has the authority to appoint members (Annex 2, Article 8(7)).[107] The panels act as independent bodies, subject only to the requirement that they deal with the dispute as defined by the parties. While the DSB potentially has the power to reject a report, it has seldom done so.

Relevant Law

In addition to the constitutive treaties and supporting materials that define the obligations of member and the jurisdiction of the WTO, panels may consider a number of other "sources" in coming to their decisions. These include WTO settlement reports (including old GATT panels), acts of WTO bodies, customary international law, general principles of law, relevant international agreements, practice of WTO members, and the negotiating history of the various agreements. Though prior reports form the most important written source, particularly when the issues involve clarification or interpretation of various agreements, the reports constitute guides rather than binding precedents.

The Appellate Body

The Appellate Body is a standing, permanent international tribunal. It consists of seven persons, appointed by the DSB, who serve four-year terms. They may be reappointed for a second term. Like other tribunals, the Appellate Body requires members to have expertise that qualifies them to deal with the legal issues of international trade and be unaffiliated with any government. In addition, Article 17.3 requires that "The Appellate Body membership shall be broadly representative of membership in the WTO." The Appellate Body can uphold, modify, or reverse the *legal* findings and conclusions of a panel. Practice indicates that unless inconsistent with Article 11 of the DSU, the factual findings of a panel are not subject to

---

[106]The DSB is comprised of ambassador-level diplomats of all WTO members.

[107]See Van den Bossche, note 98, at 244–246, for a concise discussion of the "rules" that apply.

review.[108] Appellate Body Reports, once adopted by the DSB, must be accepted by the parties to the dispute.

Trade and the Environment

Neither the GATT nor the agenda for the Uruguay Round had environmental issues as a principal focus. By the time of its formation, however, it was clear that the WTO would have to deal with the concerns of environmentalists. Lowenfeld argues that while particular cases may call for inquiry into facts (or motives), it is not impossible to reconcile the rules of the GATT/WTO with widely accepted *multilateral* regulations designed to protect the environment.[109] Difficulties arise when individual states attempt to enact and implement measures not widely accepted in the international community.

The *Tuna/Dolphin* cases[110] and the *Shrimp/Turtle* cases[111] illustrate the problems. We have chosen these cases because—unlike many trade cases that involve complex, contentious facts—the basic factual situations were not at issue. Moreover, the situations are relatively straightforward and easy to grasp. The *Tuna/Dolphin* cases involved the use of purse seine nets by commercial tuna fishermen. Dolphins and tuna are often found together. The methods used by the fishermen to harvest the tuna resulted in large numbers of injuries and deaths among dolphins. The United States passed legislation setting strict limits on the number that could be killed. The issue came to a head in 1984, when Congress amended the legislation to provide that tuna caught in foreign vessels could be imported only if that state had a comparable set of regulations. The United States subsequently imposed an embargo on imports of tuna from Mexico and several other countries on the grounds that they had not met the comparability standard.

Mexico requested consultation in the GATT. When that failed to resolve the issue, Mexico initiated a dispute settlement proceeding. The panel found the legislation and actions of the United States violated XI(1) of the GATT. The panel report was discussed at several meetings of the GATT, but never formally adopted.[112] The environmentalist community rejected the decision in the case. It became the symbol of the clash between the trade and environmental constituencies. Perhaps because of the nondecision in the first case, the European Community and the Netherlands brought a second complaint *(Tuna/Dolphin II)*. This resulted in a second decision that paralleled the first. Again, although a majority of the GATT Council favored the decision, that report was not formally adopted either.

---

[108]Van den Bossche, note 98, at 262–265.

[109]Lowenfeld, note 15, at 388.

[110]*United States—Restrictions on Imports of Tuna (Mexico v. U.S.; Tuna/Dolphin I)*, GATT Doc. DS21/R (1991); *United States—Restrictions on Imports of Tuna (EEC &Netherlands v. U.S.; Tuna/Dolphin II)*, GATT Doc. DS29/R (1994).

[111]*United States—Import Prohibition of Certain Shrimp and Shrimp Products (India, Malaysia, Pakistan, Thailand v. U.S.; Shrimp/Turtle)*, WT/DS58/R (May 15, 1998); *(Shrimp/Turtle I)*, Report of the Appellate Body, WT/DS58/AB/R (October 12, 1998).

[112]Lowenfeld, note 15, at 391.

Three years later, another case *(Shrimp/Turtle)* focused on similar U.S. actions banning import of commercial seafood as a measure of protection against the incidental killing of another species. What had changed was the emergence of the strengthened dispute mechanisms of the WTO. The issue was the incidental killing of sea turtles, which were considered an endangered species and identified as such in an international treaty (CITES).[113] India, Pakistan, Malaysia, and Thailand brought a complaint to the WTO, alleging violation by the United States of Article XI of the GATT. The panel once again found the United States had violated Article XI; the Appellate Body concurred, noting that the United States had unilaterally developed a trade policy rather than following the multilateral path.[114] In its decision, the Appellate Body attempted to dampen the controversy. It noted:

> In reaching these conclusions, we wish to underscore what we have not decided. We have *not* decided that the protection and preservation of the environment is of no significance to the Members of the WTO. We have not decided that the sovereign nations that are Members of the WTO cannot adopt effective measures to protect endangered species such as sea turtles. Clearly they can and should.[115]

The story does not end here. After the decision in *Shrimp/Turtle I*, the United States opened negotiations with Malaysia and others with an eye toward producing an agreement on the protection and conservation of sea turtles. This produced a nonbinding memorandum of understanding (MoU; see Chapter 18) but no widespread consensus. In 2000, Malaysia requested a panel to be constituted under Article 21.5 of the DSU, asserting that in the absence of a multilateral agreement on sea turtle conservation, the United States could not impose any import prohibitions *(Shrimp/Turtle II)*.[116] The panel rejected Malaysia's position, noting that the United States was required only to show "serious good faith efforts to reach an agreement before resorting to the type of unilateral measure currently in place."[117]

Some Notes on Investment

Good trading regimes often produce incentives to undertake more extensive foreign operations such as licensing to foreign manufacturers or establishing their own manufacturing operations in another country.[118] We need only look at the extent to which Japanese auto companies (and others such as BMW and Mercedes) have built assembly plants in the United States to illustrate this point. Foreign

---

[113]*Convention on International Trade in Endangered Species;* see Chapter 19.

[114]*Shrimp/Turtle I*, Report of the Appellate Body, para. 35; for a full discussion of the reasoning here, see Lowenfeld, note 15, at 395–398.

[115]*Shrimp/Turtle I*, Appellate Body Report, para. 193.

[116]*United States—Import Prohibition of Certain Shrimp and Shrimp Products—Recourse to Article 21.5 of the DSU by Malaysia (Shrimp/Turtle II)*. Report of the Appellate Body on Compliance, WT/DS58/AB/RW (October 22, 2001), para. 54.

[117]*Shrimp/Turtle II*, para. 5.67.

[118]In this section, we deal only with foreign direct investment, although portfolio investment is another important tool in establishing a presence abroad.

direct investment (FDI) creates an interesting situation. For our purposes, the investor—usually a wholly owned corporation formed under the law of the host country—establishes a legal presence in the foreign country. The story does not stop there. Not only do the laws of the host state apply, but in many cases so do those of the investor's home state. Additionally, the entity may be subject to rules in bilateral investment treaties (BITs), in regional arrangements such as NAFTA or the EU, as well as in the WTO. Most of the applicable law here comes from treaties.[119] The main exception may lie in the law of expropriation. As with trade law, the major policy objective has been trying to move toward removing controls from FDI. The liberal doctrine, as with trade, is that the market should determine the direction of international investment flows.[120]

Bilateral Investment Treaties

Much of the relevant law is found in BITs. According to the Office of the U.S. Trade Representative, the U.S. BIT program helps protect private investment, develop market-oriented policies in partner countries, and promote U.S. exports. The BIT program's basic aims are to

- Protect investment abroad in countries where investor rights are not already protected through existing agreements (such as modern treaties of friendship, commerce, and navigation, or free trade agreements)
- Encourage the adoption of market-oriented domestic policies that treat private investment in an open, transparent, and nondiscriminatory way
- Support the development of international law standards consistent with these objectives[121]

U.S. BITs impose six main obligations: (1) treatment equal to that given other competitors; (2) limits on expropriation or full compensation if expropriation occurs (Chapter 12); (3) right to transfer funds without delay; (4) limits on regulations for trade-distorting practices; (5) right to submit any dispute to *international* arbitration (Chapter 11, the Calvo Clause); and (6) the right to use top personnel of a country's choice regardless of nationality.[122] Since the 1990s, the United States and a number of other advanced industrial countries have worked to develop a network of BITs. Potential partners are expected to make a commitment to implement all WTO Trade-Related Aspects of Intellectual Property Rights (TRIPs) as soon as possible.

Dispute Settlement and International Investment

At this point, we suggest a brief review of Chapter 5. The first step in dispute settlement normally would be a private action by the investor to obtain redress in the

---

[119]"Foreign Direct Investment," in *The International Legal System: Cases and Materials,* 5th ed., edited by C. L. Blakesley, E. B. Firmage, R. F. Scott, and S. A. Williams (2001), 1007.

[120]For a discussion, see K. J. Vandevelde, "The Political Economy of a Bilateral Investment Treaty," 92 *AJIL* (1998), 624.

[121]Office of the U.S. Trade Representative, Summary of U.S. Bilateral Investment Treaty (BIT) Program (February 24, 2006), www.ustr.gov/trade-agreements/bilateral-investment-treaties.

[122]*Ibid.*

courts of the host state. One should recall that under normal circumstances, apart from the nationality requirement, claimants must have exhausted local remedies before requesting their government to intervene. Other options exist as well for *commercial disputes.* Investors, under certain circumstances, may file suit in the courts of a third country or resort to private arbitration (see *Texaco v. Libya*). As discussed earlier, in doing so, claimants potentially face issues of sovereign immunity or "acts of state" because courts in third countries will not pass judgment on the acts of foreign sovereigns within their own territories.

The brief discussion of U.S. BIT requirements provides a reasonably concise insight into the principal concerns of governments and investors. The first wave of decolonization saw a number of high-profile expropriations by governments. In particular, governments sought to gain control of the extractive industries (mining and oil) that were operating under favorable concession agreements negotiated by the controlling colonial power or under regimes that did not care for development so long as officials benefited personally from the arrangement. As we noted in Chapter 12, the issues involved questions of compensation. States resorted to traditional methods to resolve these disputes: arbitration (Libyan Nationalization Cases), the International Court of Justice (*Anglo-Iranian Case, Barcelona Traction Case*), and litigation in national courts. Drawing upon our introductory comments, two observations seem appropriate here. First, not all disputes involve expropriation, but other policies can be just as harmful. Second, the disputes involve three parties—the private interest or investor, the home state of the investor, and the host state.

The World Bank took the lead in developing a convention—the *Convention on the Settlement of Investment Disputes Between States and Nationals of Other States.*[123] The convention set up the International Center for Settlement of Investment Disputes (ICSID) within the World Bank. The convention has an interesting requirement. It is not open to all parties. It is open to all members of the World Bank, and with approval of the administrative council by a two-thirds vote, to any other state party to the Statute of the International Court of Justice (Article 67). In any dispute over investment issues, both states must be a party to the convention, and both must consent to arbitration using the ICSID. Once given, consent may not be withdrawn (Article 2.5(1)).

At the beginning, the convention generated opposition from Latin American states. They viewed it as an intrusion on sovereignty even though it had no requirement for compulsory arbitration. As of December 1, 2011, a total of 153 states had signed and 143 had completed the ratification process. Two states (Bolivia and Ecuador) have withdrawn. In Latin America, Brazil and Mexico also remain outside. China has ratified, but India has not.

Article 42(1) notes:

> The Tribunal shall decide a dispute in accordance with such rules of law as may be agreed by the parties. In the absence of such agreement, the Tribunal shall apply the law of the Contracting State party to the dispute (including its rules on conflict of laws) and such rules of international law as may be applicable.

---

[123]17 U. S. T. 1270, 575 U.N.T.S. 159; entered into force October 16, 1966; text at http://icsid. worldbank.org/ICSID/StaticFiles/basicdoc_en-archive/ICSID_English.pdf (accessed April 22, 2009).

This means that, in practice, the tribunal will first look at the relevant law of the host state and apply it. Then it will test the result against relevant international law. To the extent that the result under national law falls short of international law, the panel will follow international law. It will not explicitly deny the relevance of the host state's law, but simply not apply it.[124]

The Iran–United States Claims Tribunal[125]

Space precludes a detailed analysis of the practice of this tribunal, but it stands as one of the most important in terms of developing the idea of international arbitration of disputes. The dispute arose out of events preceding and surrounding the seizure of the American Embassy in Teheran. In 1979, the shah was deposed and exiled. The new regime targeted American businesses in Iran with threats, discriminatory legislations and action, and outright expropriation. The crisis came to a head with the taking of 52 hostages by the embassy invaders. They were held for 14 months.

Iranian banks had large deposits in U.S. banks and their European branches. The United States immediately moved to place a "freeze" on all Iranian assets within U.S. jurisdiction. U.S. claimants, alleging damages, also began filing suits in U.S. courts. Note here that claimants under private international law have choices regarding where they may file suits. For our purposes, the rather complex rules of jurisdiction under private international law are not relevant, though courts will always consider the jurisdictional issues. With the help of Algeria as a mediator, Iran and the United States signed the *Algiers Accords* (January 19, 1981).[126] The terms of the two agreements provided for the release of the hostages, the release and return of a large portion of the frozen assets to Iran, the termination of all litigation against Iran in U.S. courts,[127] and the establishment of a claims tribunal to hear all claims arising out of the incident. These included claims of Iranian nationals and companies against the United States as well as those of U.S. nationals and companies against Iran.

The tribunal consisted of nine members: three chosen by the United States, three chosen by Iran, and three neutrals chosen through negotiation of the two parties. Generally, the tribunal sat in chambers of three, composed of one member from each party and a neutral. On some occasions, the tribunal sat as a panel of nine. *The Claims Settlement Declaration* stipulated that the UNCITRAL (UN Commission on International Trade Law) Authoritative Rules would apply except when the parties agreed to modification. The tribunal, in interpreting the Algiers Accords, decided very early that two normal requirements would not apply—its jurisdiction did not depend upon exhaustion of local remedies, and the availability

---

[124]For an extended discussion, see A. Broches, "The Convention on the Settlement of Investment Disputes," 136 *Hague Recueil de Cours* (1972-II). Note that this requirement implies the *hierarchical* superiority of international law.

[125]Official website, www.iusct.org/index-english.html (accessed April 22, 2009).

[126]C. N. Brower and J. D. Brueschke, *The Iran-United States Claims Tribunal* (1998), 3–10. There are two basic documents: *The General Declaration* and *The Claims Settlement Declaration*.

[127]See *Dames & Moore v. Reagan*, 453 U.S. 654 (1981).

of local remedies was irrelevant.[128] The tribunal used the definitions in the ICSID Convention, the BITs, and the Multilateral Investment Guarantee Agency to define the nationality of individuals and corporations.[129]

The large number of cases, the large sums of money at stake, the high profile of the arbitrators, and the nature and scope of the issues have given the tribunal a central place in the development of international investment law. Lowenfeld lists several important principles confirmed by the decision of the tribunal:

- Affirmed that international law applies directly between states and foreign parties, not merely just between states
- Confirmed that states must respect the property rights of foreign investors and must pay appropriate compensation when an owner is deprived of those rights by an action imputable to the state
- Determined that a revolution or social upheaval does not automatically create liability, but does not excuse the state from its obligations to act in accordance with international law
- Confirmed that appropriate compensation for expropriation does not depend upon the perceived ability to pay (it requires full value)[130]

THE MULTILATERAL INVESTMENT GUARANTEE AGENCY[131]

As we noted earlier, the decolonization of the 1960s and 1970s brought development issues to the forefront of the international agenda. Several trends came together in the early 1980s that undermined the willingness of investors to seek opportunities in the LDCs. First, the debt crisis in Latin America had curtailed the pace of commercial bank lending to the LDCs. Second, a series of expropriations had further undermined the willingness of investors to take the risks.[132] The World Bank took the lead in developing the Multilateral Investment Guarantee Agency (MIGA) as a means of improving the climate for direct investment. To quote from its statement of purpose:

> Concerns about investment environments and perceptions of political risk often inhibit foreign direct investment, with the majority of flows going to just a handful of countries and leaving the world's poorest economies largely ignored. MIGA addresses these concerns by providing three key services: political risk insurance, foreign investments in developing countries, technical assistance to improve investment climates and promote investment opportunities in developing countries, and dispute mediations services, to remove possible obstacles to future investment.[133]

---

[128]Brower and Brueschke, note 126, at 20–22.

[129]*The Claims Settlement Declaration*, Article VII(2). Brower and Brueschke, note 126, at 26–56.

[130]Lowenfeld, note 15, at 553–554.

[131]www.miga.org/ (accessed April 22, 2009). See also M. D. Rowat, "Multilateral Approaches to Improving the Investment Climate of Developing Countries: The Cases of ICSID and MIGA," 33 *Harvard Int'l L.J.* (1992), 103.

[132]See Oatley, note 26, at 144–149.

[133]www.miga.org/about/index_sv.cfm?stid=1588 (accessed April 22, 2009).

MIGA came into existence with the ratifications of its convention by the United States and the United Kingdom on April 12, 1988. It currently has 173 member states.

Article 11 of the MIGA Convention[134] lists the covered risks: limits on currency transfers, expropriation, breaches of contract, and acts of war and civil disturbance. These include politically motivated acts of sabotage or terrorism. Article 12 provides that "Eligible investments shall include equity interest, including medium- or long-term loans made or guaranteed by holders of equity in the enterprise concerned, and such forms of direct investment as may be determined by the Board." The agency has an activist mission. Article 23 requires MIGA to "promote and facilitate the conclusion of agreements, among its members, on the promotion and protection of investments." Hence, it encourages developing countries to join the ICSID Convention or negotiate BITs or take other action that indicates an investor-friendly environment.

The final question may be the impact of the web of obligations just described. Lowenfeld raises the question of whether these agreements have contributed to an international law of international investment. Do states sign these treaties as a matter of a particular calculation of advantage rather than from a sense of obligation?[135] Are these merely temporary concessions? What do current events in Bolivia and Venezuela (and perhaps other countries) mean for the future? On the other hand, in the two decades since MIGA entered into force, we find very few major breaches when compared to the decades previous.

SUGGESTED READINGS

GENERAL

Guzman and Sykes, *Research Handbook in International Economic Law* (2007).

Jackson, *The World Trading System: Law and Policy of International Economic Relations* (1997).

Lowenfeld, *International Economic Law*, 2nd ed. (2008).

INTERNATIONAL POLITICAL ECONOMY

Oatley, *International Political Economy: Interests and Institutions in the Global Economy* (2008).

Sobel, *Political Economy and Global Affairs* (2006).

Spero and Hart, *The Politics of International Economic Relations* (2009).

Hudec, *The GATT Legal System and World Trade*, 2nd ed. (1990).

Van Den Bossche, *The Law and Political of the World Trade Organization* (2008).

Wilcox, *A Charter for World Trade* (1949).

IRAN–U.S CLAIMS TRIBUNAL

Brower and Brueschke, *The Iran-United States Claims Tribunal* (1998).

Lillich and Magraw, eds, *The Iran-United States Claims Tribunal: Its Contribution to the Law of State Responsibility* (1998).

Mouri, *The International Law of Expropriation As Reflected in the Work of the Iran-U.S. Claims Tribunal* (1994).

---

[134]www.miga.org/quickref/index_sv.cfm?stid=1583 (accessed April 22, 2009).

[135]Lowenfeld, note 15, at 591. He cites A. T. Guzman, "Why LDCs Sign Treaties That Hurt Them," 38 *Virginia J. of Int'l L.* (1998), 686–687, who advances this proposition.

Law and the Use of Force

The Use of Force

T he questions relating to law and the use of force clearly constitute the most contentious and frustrating areas of international law. Two thousand years ago, Cicero simply stated that "in war the laws are silent."[1] More recently, a prominent law professor expressed the frustration felt by many over what she perceived as the limitations of law in dealing with a modern tragedy: "How can an effort so broadly supported in its objectives—to stem Belgrade's expulsion of ethnic Albanians from Kosovo and block a gross violation of international law—be so uncertain in its legal basis?"[2] This chapter takes a broad view of the basic problems. The range of conflicts where states have resorted to force extends from responses to terrorism and/or transboundary guerrilla raids, to "cod wars" over fishing rights (Iceland and the United Kingdom) to classic invasions (Iraq and Iran, Vietnam and Cambodia). In this respect, we need to emphasize that the Charter of the United Nations (Article 2(4)) prohibits *the unilateral use of force* by member states (states parties), not just the resort to war.[3]

Historically, the law on the use of force has divided into two distinct categories: the *jus ad bellum* that presumably governed the resort to *war* and the *jus in bello* or the law governing individual conduct within war. This chapter primarily addresses questions relating to the *jus ad bellum,* slightly redefined to mean the right to resort

---

[1] *"Silent enim leges inter arma,"* Cicero, *Pro T. Annio Milone Oratio,* IV.11, *The Latin Library,* www. thelatinlibrary.com/cicero/milo.shtml (accessed April 22, 2009). English translation at the Perseus Digital Library, Crane, ed., www.perseus.tufts.edu/cgi-in/ptext?doc=Perseus:text:1999.02.0020&query=text%3 DMil.%3Atext%3DMil.%3Achapter%3D4%3Asection%3D11 (accessed April 22, 2009).

[2] R. Wedgwood, "Editorial Comments: NATO's Kosovo Intervention: NATO's Campaign in Yugoslavia," 93 *American Journal of International Law* 828 (1999).

[3] See M. O'Connell, *International Law and the Use of Force: Cases and Materials* (2005); C. Gray, *International Law and the Use of Force,* 2nd ed. (2004); Y. Dinstein, *War, Aggression and Self-Defense,* 3rd ed. (2001); A. Cassese, ed., *The Current Regulation of the Use of Force* (1986); and the classics, I. Brownlie, *International Law and the Use of Force by States* (1963); and J. Stone, *Legal Controls of International Conflict* (1954).

to *force.*[4] Chapter 21 will cover the basics of the *jus in bello* and Chapter 22 will examine modern war crime trials. In particular, the discussion will emphasize the importance of defining contexts. From the discussion earlier, one should quickly understand that the phrase "use of force" contains a legal minefield. Consider how many different descriptions of conflicts appear in the contemporary literature discussing various situations in which force has been used. In addition to war, one finds civil war, internal armed conflict, international armed conflict, humanitarian intervention, hostilities, and police actions, to name just a few.

THE CLASSIC DEFINITION OF WAR

War in the traditional sense may be defined as a contention, through the use of armed force and between states, undertaken for the purpose of overpowering another.[5] True, such a definition does not cover the modern development of what some have called a *status mixtus,* or intermediacy concept. The latter describes a condition between peace and war that, as the introduction notes, has increasingly become part of the modern political landscape. Still, the concept has not yet become a part of accepted international law despite its advocacy by several well-known jurists.[6] Because a large number of modern armed conflicts have taken place without an official declaration of a state of war, the term *armed conflict* has been used, when deemed to be desirable, in the discussion to follow.

---

[4]Even though the secular just war tradition, based upon natural law rather than transcendental sanction, that emerged during the latter part of the sixteenth century marked an important transition in the evolution of modern international law, it produced no meaningful restraints on the resort to war, the *jus ad bellum.* The sixteenth- and early seventeenth-century writers considered to be the precursors to Grotius focused on clarifying the circumstances covered by the *jus ad bellum* with an eye toward strengthening and expanding the *jus in bello.* Legal theory had not yet shed the a priori principle that the right of princes to resort to arms, and in consequence that of combatants to be protected by the provisions of the *jus in bello,* still turned on the determination of just cause based upon fault. In the absence of vindicative grounds for the resort to violence, the vast majority of writers continued to argue that neither the combatants nor the results had any standing in law. As always, these writers struggled with the nexus between idealism and practice, often bowing to the idea that a conclusive determination of justice may fall beyond the power of men to ascertain objectively. If so, then in consequence princes have a duty to minimize damage to the innocent. The *twin principles of proportionality,* that of effect and that of value, should limit claims to military necessity. That is, did the end justify the means in terms of tangible costs (practical calculation in terms of economy of force, etc.), and did the end justify the means in terms of moral costs (idealism, justice, etc.)? In discussions of military necessity, the two principles are often conflated because it is extremely difficult to discuss one without the other. Often writers simply presume that proportionality of means will result in a proportionality of value.

[5]See Lauterpacht's *Oppenheim,* II: 201. There appear to be as many definitions as there are writers on the subject: see, inter alia, Hyde, vol. 3, 1686; Moore, VII: 154; H. Kelsen, *Principles of International Law* (1952), 26; and the collection of many different definitions in C. Eagleton, "The Attempt to Define War," 291 *International Conciliation* (June 1933), 237.

[6]G. Schwarzenberger, "Jus Pacis ac Belli?" 37 *AJIL* 460 (1943); and P. Jessup, "Should International Law Recognize an Intermediate Status Between Peace and War?" 48 *AJIL* 98 (1954). See also M. McDougal and F. Feliciano, "International Coercion and World Public Order: The General Principles of the Law of War," 67 *Yale Law J* 774 (1958); the position of the two authors is clarified at length in their heavily documented basic study, "The Initiation of Coercion: A Multi-temporal Analysis," 52 *AJIL* 241 (1958).

Before the twentieth century, the world of the international lawyer was much simpler. The resort to *war* was not illegal. Self-help and self-preservation formed the cornerstone, the essential underpinnings, of state sovereignty. Until the twentieth century, states had few ties that produced transactions or links of sufficient importance and magnitude to constitute an opportunity for exploitation. Apart from persuasion, subsidy, and bribery, forms of armed coercion were often the only means available. Force short of war and conduct within war (*jus in bello*) were ostensibly roughly governed by the twin principles of necessity and proportionality, but the resort to force remained deeply enshrouded within the umbra of an open-ended perception of necessity. States could and did use force to gain political advantage.[7] The real question concerning the customary law involved the scope of the right of self-defense.

In examining textbooks written before the UN Charter, one always finds two distinct sections (sometimes two distinct volumes): the law of peace and the law of war.[8] One set of laws governed states during peaceful relations; another set of laws governed states during war. International law said nothing about the transition from peace to war. The law did not prohibit war; rather, it viewed the institution as a normal function of sovereign states. The rights claimed did not have to have legal or moral merit. Failing to gain its objective by peaceful means, a state was free to pursue its aims by recourse to force. Doing so required only a formal declaration of war. A declaration of war set up a "state of war" in which the formal laws of war applied. Legally, a state of war did not have to mean overt clashes between armed forces. It only meant that relations between the two states, and between the two states and third-party states, were now controlled by the laws of war.

Curiously, while war was not governed by law, presumably the law did regulate the resort to force short of war (reprisal, retaliation).[9] As Brownlie points out, during the nineteenth century as mass armies, increasing interdependence, and public opinion made war more expensive and difficult to justify both politically and pragmatically, states increasingly resorted to more limited uses of force rather than war.[10] In the customary law, reprisal and retaliation were forms of self-help ostensibly governed by the twin principles of necessity and proportionality.

---

[7]See E. de Vattel, *Le droit de gens ou principes de la loi naturelle: appliqués à la conduite et aux affaires des nations and des souverains* 531–41 (1916) (reproduction of books I and II of the 1758 edition); and J. Verzijl, *International Law in Historical Perspective* 39–40 (1968). L. Oppenheim, *International Law: A Treatise,* 5th ed., vol. 2, edited by H. Lauterpacht (London, New York: Longmans, Green, 1935–1937); and J. L. Brierly, *The Law of Nations: An Introduction to the International Law of Peace* (Oxford: Clarendon Press, 1928).

[8]For example, see the first edition of Oppenheim (1905).

[9]See D. Bowett, "Reprisals Involving the Recourse to Armed Force," 66 *AJIL* 1 (1972); and R. W. Tucker (Comment), "Reprisals and Self Defense: The Customary Law," 66 *AJIL* 586 (1972); and J. L. Taulbee and J. Anderson, "Reprisal *Redux*," 16 *Case Western Reserve Journal of International Law* 309 (1984). In the customary law, self-defense and reprisal were forms of self-help governed by time frame (necessity), purpose (principle of proportionality), and appropriate targets. Before the 1920s, the literature on the customary law differentiated between retaliation and reprisal.

[10]Brownlie, note 3, at 27–28.

PRE-CHARTER ATTEMPTS TO REGULATE THE USE OF FORCE

Hague Conferences of 1899 and 1907

The arrival of the mass army and the continuing discoveries of more efficient weapons led in the late nineteenth century to the first serious attempts to limit war as a legally accepted method of enforcing legal rights and changing the rules of law. The two Hague Conferences of 1899 and 1907 represented early efforts to mitigate the impact of war.[11] Neither of these conferences seriously addressed the idea of limiting the right of states to resort to war. Rather, they concentrated upon the idea of making war more humane. The Preamble to the 1907 Hague Convention (IV) states:[12]

> Seeing that, while seeking means to preserve peace and prevent armed conflicts between nations, it is likewise necessary to bear in mind the case where the appeal to arms has been brought about by events which their care was unable to avert;
>
> Animated by the desire to serve, even in this extreme case, the interests of humanity and the ever progressive needs of civilization;
>
> Thinking it important, with this object, to revise the general laws and customs of war, either with a view to defining them with greater precision or to confining them within such limits as would mitigate their severity as far as possible.

The conferees had planned another meeting in 1914. Ironically, it was canceled because of war.

The Interwar Period

The Covenant of the League of Nations provided in its preamble an acceptance by the contracting parties of an obligation not to resort to war. On the other hand, the covenant did not totally outlaw war. Member states could still go to war under certain conditions (Article 12; Article 13; Article 15[7]; Article 17). Primarily, the assumption that debate and time could defuse situations that might otherwise erupt into overt conflict underlaid the procedures and obligations states had under the covenant. Article 16 of the covenant did provide for the imposition of sanctions against a member of the League of Nations that had resorted to war in violation of its obligations under the covenant. The article was applied in only one of the five major instances in which such a violation did take place. When Japan invaded Manchuria in 1931, the Assembly concluded that "without any declaration of war, part of the Chinese territory has been forcibly seized and occupied by the Japanese troops."[13] Nevertheless, the assembly finally decided, Japan had not resorted to war in violation of the covenant, and therefore Article 16 did not apply.

---

[11]See A. Eyffinger, *The 1899 Hague Peace Conference: "The Parliament of Man, the Federation of the World"* (1999).

[12]Laws and Customs of War on Land (Hague IV), October 18, 1907, www.yale.edu/lawweb/avalon/lawofwar/hague04.htm#iart1 (accessed April 22, 2009).

[13]League of Nations Assembly, "Report on the Sino-Japanese Dispute," 27 *AJIL* 146 (1933 Supp.).

In 1934, in connection with the Chaco War between Bolivia and Paraguay (1932–1935), many members of the League, all deciding that Paraguay had violated the covenant, began an arms embargo—originally imposed on both belligerents—to Paraguay alone. The Japanese invasion of China proper, in 1937, led to a decision by the assembly that Japan had violated the Nine-Power Treaty of 1922 as well as the Pact of Paris and that consequently Article 16 of the covenant now applied to the dispute. Each member state, however, was judged to be free to apply such individual enforcement action against Japan as it saw fit. None of them took any action. When the Soviet Union attacked Finland in late 1939, the assembly did act under Article 16(4) and expelled the Soviet Union from the organization. Expulsion was not implemented by any follow-on collective enforcement action.

Only in the case of the Italian invasion of Ethiopia, in 1935, did the assembly conclude that the invasion represented resort to war in violation of the covenant and that Article 16(1) was applicable. Collective economic sanctions were therefore authorized against Italy. These were not enough, however, and the failure to adopt the obviously effective measures of an embargo on oil shipments and a closing of the Suez Canal to Italian shipping led to Italy's successful defiance of the League and to the conquest of Ethiopia.

Kellogg–Briand Pact (Pact of Paris, 1928)[14]

Much has been written about the Kellogg–Briand Pact, deriding its idealism and lack of impact. Still, the agreement does stand at the center of the efforts to "outlaw" *aggressive* war. Note the adjective *aggressive* because none of these proposals really prohibited every kind of war. The General Treaty for the Renunciation of War (Kellogg–Briand Pact, or Pact of Paris) was signed in Paris on August 27, 1928, by representatives of 15 states and was ratified or adhered to by 65 nations. The key parts of the text of this famous instrument read as follows:[15]

> Art. 1. The High Contracting Parties solemnly declare in the names of their respective peoples that they condemn recourse to war for the solution of international controversies, and renounce it as an instrument of national policy in their relations with one another.
>
> Art. 2. The High Contracting Parties agree that the settlement or solution of all disputes or conflicts of whatever nature or of whatever origin they may be, which may arise among them, shall never be sought except by pacific means.

---

[14]More important, in some respects, were the efforts made to establish aggressive war as an illegal enterprise. As early as 1923, the Treaty of Mutual Assistance—which never came into force—attempted to identify wars of aggression as an international crime. The equally abortive Geneva Protocol of 1924 similarly labeled aggressive war a crime (preamble) and in its Article 2 imposed an obligation on all parties to the agreement to refrain from war except in the specific circumstances listed in the treaty. In 1927, the Assembly of the League passed a resolution under which all wars of aggression were said to be prohibited and only pacific means were to be employed to settle international disputes of every kind; this approach reflected the provisions of the Treaty of Mutual Guarantee (Locarno Treaty) of 1925. In 1928, the Sixth Pan-American Conference adopted a resolution asserting that a "war of aggression constitutes a crime against the human species—all aggression is illicit and as such is declared prohibited."

[15]Text at www.yale.edu/lawweb/avalon/imt/kbpact.htm. These two articles comprise the sum of the obligations in the treaty. Article 3 deals with the question of entry into force.

Interestingly enough, the pact contained no provision for denunciation and did not state a date of termination. It thus is an extremely rare modern instance of a perpetual agreement. This latter fact alone may be taken as an indication of the instrument's optimistic and unrealistic aspects.[16] The agreement did not abolish the institution of war as such. Under its terms, resort to war was still allowed in legally permissible self-defense and as an instrument of collective action to restrain an aggressor. As with the covenant, the treaty also did not abolish resort to war between a party to the treaty and a country not party to the treaty. The pact, furthermore, did not prohibit the resort to war against a country that had violated the treaty's provisions. The Pact of Paris failed to provide a means of enforcing compliance and, even more important, did not define the measures and methods through which relations between states might be changed without resorting to force.[17]

Both Kellogg–Briand and the covenant continue to raise important questions about how far and fast the law can evolve. Clearly, any rule, to be effective, must correspond to the needs of states and must equally correspond to the practice of states. Charles De Visscher expressed this concept well when he wrote, "A normative (lawmaking) treaty the content of which is too far in advance of development in international relations is stillborn, just as a treaty that ceases to be exactly observed in the practice of governments, is no longer valid in its formal expression."[18] Or, as the eminent lawyer who translated De Visscher's book observed, "Law cannot be built upon a heedless sacrifice of reality."[19] Yet progress depends upon a judicious blend of idealism and pragmatism; otherwise, the lowest common denominator will always define the norm. Carr notes:

> The ideal, once it is embodied in an institution, ceases to be an ideal and becomes the expression of a selfish interest, which must be destroyed in the name of a new ideal. This constant interaction of irreconcilable forces is the stuff of politics. Every political situation contains mutually incompatible elements of utopia and reality, of morality and power.[20]

The reason to spend some time in examination here has to do with the debate in Chapter 22 over the validity of several charges made at the Nuremberg War Crimes Trials.[21] Arguably, aggressive war had become a crime, but statesmen and

---

[16]For an interesting treatment of the politics of this era, see E. H. Carr, *The Twenty Years' Crisis 1919—1939,* 2nd ed. (1945). If readers can obtain a copy of the first edition, they might better understand Professor Carr's cryptic remarks in his introduction to the second edition about certain alterations and deletions.

[17]See R. S. Morris, "The Pact of Paris for the Renunciation of War: Its Meaning and Effect in International Law," *Proceedings* 88 (1929), and discussion of that paper, *id.,* 91; consult also Q. Wright, "The Meaning of the Pact of Paris," 27 *AJIL* 39 (1933); and especially E. Borchard, "The Multilateral Treaty for the Renunciation of War," 23 *AJIL* 116 (1929).

[18]C. De Visscher, *Theory and Reality in Public International Law,* trans. P. E. Corbett (1957), 133.

[19]Corbett, *id.,* viii.

[20]Carr, note 16, at 94.

[21]"War for the solution of international controversies includes a war of aggression, and such a war is therefore outlawed by the Pact." *Trial of the Major War Criminals Before the International Tribunal, Nuremberg, 14 November 1945–1 October 1946,* 1 (1947), 220.

lawyers alike still postulated an essential connection between the availability of force as a sanction and the preservation of state interests. Despite the trappings of a treaty, the instrument had little effect on state practice. Many of the states that had signed it denied validity through their own practice. Armed conflicts in the ensuing decade were both more numerous and more serious than they had been between 1919 and 1928.[22] As another prominent contemporary international lawyer has recently noted, "A process of decision making constitutes a normative system only when those affected believe that in general they have an obligation to obey its results."[23]

THE UNITED NATIONS

The experience of World War II and the approaching abolition of the League of Nations combined to bring out a renewed attempt to circumscribe resort to force by the provisions incorporated in the Charter of the United Nations. Article 2 of that document contains the key obligations:

> 2(3). All Members shall settle their international disputes by peaceful means in such a manner that international peace and security, and justice, are not endangered.
>
> 2(4). All Members shall refrain in their international relations from the *threat or use of force* against the territorial integrity or political independence of any state, or in any other manner inconsistent with the Purposes of the United Nations. (Emphasis added)

The Charter went beyond the provisions of the Pact of Paris in that the members of the United Nations renounced not only their right to go to war—except in instances of individual or collective self-defense (Articles 51 and 52)—but also their right unilaterally to resort to the threat or the use of force. One should note that the only reference to war in the Charter occurs in its preamble ("determined to save succeeding generations from the scourge of war"). Elsewhere, "threat or use of force" and "threat to the peace, breach of the peace, or act of aggression" are used in reference to situations in which the new organization, through the Security Council, could take action under specified conditions.

The divisive nature of the postwar world affected the organization's ability to respond as ideally planned, but so did the unexpected nature of the issues. The unanimity required for productive Security Council deliberation and action quickly fell prey to the imperatives of the Cold War. But, equally important, the Charter was constructed to deal with a particular kind of challenge. The Charter (as well as the customary law) rests upon a specific conception of military conflict and its

---

[22]See Brownlie, note 3, at 249–550; and A. C. Arend and R. J. Beck, *International Law and the Use of Force* (1993), 23–25. The authors do not share this view of the status of the customary law, Kellogg–Briand and Nuremberg pronouncements notwithstanding. We would argue the vague language in Kellogg–Briand and the retrospective judgment at Nuremberg placed no meaningful restraints on states in terms of developments in the customary law. We fail to see the basis for certainty that Browlie accords to practice in the 1930s.

[23]T. J. Farer, "Editorial Comment: Beyond the Charter Frame: Unilateralism or Condominium," 96 *AJIL* 359 (2002) at 361.

conduct. Charter operations presupposed that armed conflicts would be between two territorial states conducted by regular army forces that would be clearly identified through distinctive uniforms and insignia.[24] It presumed that states would have the capacity to control their own territories. Over the past 50 years, incidents that fit this characterization have been the exception rather than the rule. Nuclear weapons changed the prudential calculus associated with large-scale conventional war. The political dynamics of self-determination and economic justice displaced interstate war as a principal concern. Nonstate actors began to play major roles, sometimes as initiators of low-intensity transborder military activity against states. Weak states fell prey to internal wars fueled by societal cleavages of various types. The United Nations, so fundamentally tied to a statist foundation, had to face demands that it support and promote policies that transcended state claims to absolute primacy—such as human rights and, preeminently, self-determination.

Collective Security and the Security Council

In structure, the UN Charter plan sets up a centralized collective security system. Domestic legal orders are centralized collective security systems. In both, members have the right to use force in self-defense only in instances of "necessity," and then only until the centralized authority provides the requisite protection or assistance. The difference between the United Nations and the domestic context is obvious. In the domestic context, designated agents (law enforcement officers of various kinds) perform the enforcement function for the larger community. In the international context, the members of the society must themselves undertake the action necessary to redress violations.[25] Theoretically, all members of the United Nations take on an open-ended obligation to take appropriate action against those who transgress Charter norms through unauthorized uses of force if and when the Security Council has made an appropriate determination. The heart of the process is the willingness of the Security Council to make a determination that a threat to the peace, a breach of the peace, or an act of aggression has occurred (Chapter VII, Article 39).

The inclusion of the Security Council in the Charter follows the pattern of settlements since Westphalia that have assumed that great powers have special duties and responsibilities for the maintenance of the order produced by the settlement. The Security Council currently has five permanent members (United States, Russian Federation, People's Republic of China, France, and the United Kingdom) and ten nonpermanent members elected for two-year

---

[24]For the attempt to update the jus in bello to reflect the varieties of post–World War II conflict, see Protocol Additional to the Geneva Conventions of 12 August 1949, and Relating to the Protection of Victims of International Armed Conflicts (Protocol I) and Protocol Additional to the Geneva Conventions of 12 August 1949, and Relating to the Protection of Victims of Non-International Armed Conflicts (Protocol II); International Legal Materials 16 (1977), 1391–1449.

[25]The international obligation is somewhat akin to that in medieval English common law that required villagers, in the absence of "police" in the modern sense, to raise a "hue and cry" when a crime occurred. There was a collective duty to pursue the perpetrator. Failure to do so could result in a fine or other penalty imposed upon the village.

terms. The permanent members possess a "veto" power in that a negative vote by any one of the five will result in the defeat of a resolution or decision.[26] From the beginning, writers asserted that the principal chore of the Security Council centered on maintaining or restoring the peace. The means selected by the council may not coincide with strict maintenance of what lawyers see as "black letter" law in specific circumstances.[27] Security Council procedures do not in any way generate parallels with judicial proceedings.[28] In cases of conflict, a perception of urgency focuses debate on the requisites of taking immediate action to contain and pacify, omitting any extensive discussion of the legal basis for the action authorized. Article 24 confers the responsibility for maintenance of the peace on the Security Council. Chapter VII, Article 39, grants authority to the Security Council to intervene when a situation constitutes a threat to the peace, a breach of the peace, or an act of aggression. The language of Article 39 and of subsequent provisions in Chapter VII is vague and permissive. While the General Assembly has developed a definition of aggression,[29] the circumstances that may constitute a "threat to the peace" or a "breach of the peace" remain open ended.[30] The process of decision with regard to cases considered and actions adopted is both selective and arbitrary. Nothing in the Charter requires the acts that the Security Council deems as threats to the peace or breaches of the peace to be illegal, nor does the Charter explicitly require that responses be proportionate to the intensity of the breach or threat.

---

[26]To use an example, the vote on a resolution could be 14–1 for, but if the 1 is a permanent member, the resolution has not passed.

[27]H. Kelsen, *Law of the United Nations* (New York: Praeger, 1950), 294. Kelsen's alternative argument, that forcible interference in the sphere of interests of a state (Articles 41 and 42) required a prior violation of the law to square the grant with the requirements of general international law, raised still another interesting issue. See also R. Higgins, *The Development of International Law Through the Political Organs of the United Nations* (1963), 168ff.

[28]To be very strict constructionist, Article 1(1) associates justice with the peaceful resolution of disputes, not with peace maintenance:

> To maintain international peace and security, and to that end: to take effective collective measures for the prevention and removal of threats to the peace, and for the suppression of acts of aggression or other breaches of the peace, and *to bring about by peaceful means, and in conformity with the principles of justice* and international law, adjustment or settlement of international disputes or situations which might lead to a breach of the peace. (Emphasis added)

Council proceedings under Chapter VII could be seen as part of a process that promotes the return to a situation where peaceful means become relevant to settlement.

[29]GA Res. 3314 (XXIX), December 14, 1974; text with commentary in 69 *AJIL* 224 (1975).

[30]For example, the Security Council's Summit Declaration of January 31, 1991, which states that threats to the peace can come from the "economic, social, humanitarian and ecological field." UN Doc. S/2411 (1992). Deviating from well-established practice, in SC Res/1160 (March 31, 1998) concerning Kosovo, the Council condemned "the use of excessive force by Serbian police forces against civilians and peaceful demonstrators in Kosovo, as well as all acts of terrorism by the Kosovo Liberation Army," without first making a finding that a threat to international peace and security exists. The Council backtracked, however, in SC Res/1199 (September 23, 1998) "by affirming that the deterioration of the situation in Kosovo, Federal Republic of Yugoslavia, constitutes a threat to peace and security in the region."

Defining the Scope of Self-Defense: Early Problems

As we noted earlier, from the beginning the system did not work as designed. This situation engendered a number of interesting debates. The first raged over the scope of self-defense. Given that the machinery of collective security did not work as envisioned, states sought to define the situations that might give rise to the right of "self-defense" as broadly as possible. For example, one of the first cases to come to the Security Council, involved a claim for self determination in the form of a demand to end to the colonial rule of the Dutch in Indonesia. The government of the Netherlands sought unsuccessfully to claim a right of self-defense in justification of its attempts to suppress the uprising. This pointed to the problem of defining what exactly constituted an "armed attack." States could agree on the abstract principles that governed the exercise of self-defense. The twin principles of *necessity* and *proportionality* presumably govern all uses of force, even in wartime.[31] The questions concerned defining the scope of circumstances, the *necessity,* that would permit a valid exercise of the right.

The initial debate actually had two separable themes. One theme focused on the language of Article 51, which begins with the phrase "If an *armed attack* occurs". (Emphasis added). The second focused on the ineffectiveness of the Charter regime. In the first theme, did the opening phrase represent *the* single contingency that absolutely defined self-defense, or did it represent only a suggestion of one contingency under which states might exercise self-defense?[32] Did the right of self-defense include a right of preemptive action?[33] If it included a right of preemptive action, did that right extend to a preemptive nuclear strike? Does support for revolutionary groups constitute an armed attack? Do other forms of so-called indirect aggression constitute an armed attack? The camps were divided—some feared expansion of the right to the point where the norm provided no restraint and thus sought to define *necessity* as narrowly as possible; others argued that given the paralysis (and slow procedures) of the Security Council, states needed a relatively broad grant to ensure their security.[34]

---

[31]See the heavily documented analysis by J. G. Gardam, "Proportionality and Force in International Law," 87 *AJIL* 391 (1993).

[32]Consider here the argument made by Judge Steven Schwebel in his dissent in the Nicaragua case. Judge Schwebel argued that Article 51 does not say "*if, and only if,* an armed attack occurs" (emphasis added). Thus, it does not explicitly limit the *inherent* exercise of self-defense only to the circumstance in which an armed attack has occurred. Case Concerning Military and Paramilitary Activities in and against Nicaragua (*Nicaragua v. U.S.*), Merits, International Court of Justice (judgment of June 27, 1986), dissent of Judge Schwebel.

[33]Note that the case often cited to define the circumstances of self-defense, the *Caroline,* involved a preemptive strike by British forces across the Niagara River.

[34]Arend and Beck argue, "[The] restrictionist theory most accurately reflects both the intentions of the Charter's framers and the common sense meaning of the Charter's texts," note 21, at 136. See also Brownlie, note 3 at 278ff.; D. W. Bowett, *Self-defense in International Law* (1958); O. Schachter, "Self-defense and the Rule of Law," 83 *AJIL* 259 (1989); and M. B. Baker, "Terrorism and the Inherent Right of Self-Defense (A Call to Amend Article 51 of the United Nations Charter)," 10 *Houston J. Int'l L.* 25 (1987). Note here that the ICJ has held in the *Nicaragua* case that the United States could not justify its aid to the Nicaragua Contras on the claim that it was acting in collective self-defense since there was insufficient evidence of a Nicaraguan "armed attack" on the United States (*Nicaragua v. United States, Merits,* paras. 210–211, 246–249).

The second theme did not necessarily preclude the first. It focused on the phrase in Article 51 that states, "Nothing in the present Charter shall impair the inherent right of individual or collective self-defense if an armed attack occurs against a Member of the United Nations, until the Security Council has taken the measures necessary to maintain international peace and security." It held very simply that if the Charter provisions were ineffective; that is, if the Security Council did not act, the customary law governing the use of force remained intact. The difficulty with this argument is its presumption that pre-Charter customary law specified a well-defined, normative set of principles. As discussed earlier in the section on the interwar period, this presumption itself is debatable. At the very least, however, pre-Charter customary law would have permitted states to justify their action in terms of reprisal and retaliation. Interestingly, their actions notwithstanding, states have chosen to justify their actions in the language of the Charter, not in that of the customary law. This approach can lead to some interesting formulations. For example, in justifying its invasion of East Pakistan in 1971, India claimed self-defense on the basis of "refugee aggression" by Pakistan.[35] Despite their perception that the United Nations would provide no relief, the Israelis continued to rely upon an "accumulation of events" rationale (several "provocations add up to a major retaliation in self defense) to justify a contention of self-defense in response to Palestinian attacks rather than resorting to the older reprisal or retaliation framework.[36] The gap between justification and practice led a number of scholars to question the continuing relevance of the Charter prohibition on the use of force narrowly defined.[37]

The debates here constitute a graphic example of the ongoing tension with respect to law and order at the international level (see Chapter 1). Events such as those associated with 9/11 will always raise calls for immediate retaliatory action, couched in terms of redress and justice. The questions will often center on the question of whether those actions that states feel are "necessary" to vindicate their rights will undermine or promote the rule of law. States acting on the basis of immediacy may set precedents of unilateral self-help that serve perceived short-term needs without regard to the longer-term implications for a stable order. Responses to terrorism are not the only area where these questions arise. The long-standing debate over "humanitarian intervention" reflected in the question at the beginning of this chapter raises similar issues.

---

[35] N. J. Wheeler, Saving Strangers: Humanitarian Intervention in International Society (2000): 16.

[36] See Bowett, note 9, 5ff.

[37] While Franck does not make exactly the argument stated in the text in this article, his position is interesting in that it foreshadows the evolution of the debate. T. M. Franck, "Who Killed Article 2(4)? or: Changing Norms Governing the Use of Force by States," 64 *AJIL* 809 (1970); and L. Henkin, "The Reports of the Death of Article 2(4) Are Greatly Exaggerated," 65 *AJIL* 544 (1971). See also A. M. Weisburd, Use of Force: The Practice of States since World War II (1997). For a summary of Security Council practice with regard to these issues, see J. L. Taulbee, "Governing the Use of Force: Does the Charter Matter Anymore?" 4 Civil Wars 1 (2001).

THE *CAROLINE* CASE

R. Y. Jennings (Jennings later served as a judge on the ICJ) asserts that "it was in the *Caroline* case that self-defense was changed from a political excuse to a legal doctrine."[38] Certainly, modern texts and casebooks agree. Few bother to analyze other cases, taking *Caroline* as the paradigm that defines the elements necessary to establish a claim to self-defense. On close examination, however, *Caroline* raises as many questions as it answers concerning its relevance to modern practice. In his article, Professor Jennings provides extensive quotes from the reports associated with the immediate events and their aftermath as well as a wonderfully detailed analysis of the diplomatic exchanges between the United States and Great Britain; but he offers no systematic analysis of events after settlement of the 1837 incident to validate this claim. Jennings himself does note that the textbook writers—including Wheaton, Hall, Phillimore, Halleck, and Oppenheim—still viewed self-preservation as the controlling principle.[39] This makes less convincing Jennings's assertion that once the phrase had been introduced, "it was possible for lawyers of a later day to give it a legal content."[40] He cites no twentieth-century practice, although the article appeared in 1938.

Reducing the situation in the *Caroline* to its essential elements produces the following summary:

- A challenge to the legitimacy of British authority in the form of a provisional government formed with the specific goal of replacing British rule in Canada.

- A series of minor raids from Navy Island and other parts of U.S. territory, which inflicted little damage in Canada. There are no reports of any Canadian casualties, civilian or military, resulting from the raids.

- A perception that the rebels operated with impunity from adjacent territory. Authorities in Canada believed that local authorities in New York State lacked effective capacity to control the activities of the rebels. They did not believe that anyone in authority supported the rebellion even through a policy of benign blindness.

- A *preemptive* strike to *remove* an essential element of the threat posed by the rebels.

In context, the rebel force on Navy Island represented little more than a dangerous nuisance. The question becomes why the British chose to utilize self-defense, a term not found in the legal texts of the day, rather than simply relying upon self-preservation or, indeed, reprisal (the United States had indicated it lacked capacity to inhibit the raids).

In fact, specific references to a right of self-defense as opposed to the more general right of self-preservation are notably lacking in nineteenth- and early twentieth-century texts. The most conspicuous aspect of the case may be the definition of *self-defense* put forward by Secretary of State Daniel Webster. Webster demanded that the British government prove a "*necessity* of self-defense, instant, overwhelming, leaving no choice of means, and no moment for deliberation" (Emphasis added).[41] In relation to legal development, the insistence that necessity formed a definable limiting factor on the exer-

(continued)

---

[38]R. Y. Jennings, "The *Caroline* and *McLeod* Cases," *32 AJIL* 82 (1938).

[39]Ibid., 91.

[40]Ibid., 92.

[41]Ibid., 89.

cise of the right of self-preservation and/or self-defense marks an important departure from previous practice, even if "the diplomatists were almost certainly not consciously attempting to introduce a new concept into the law."[42] Nonetheless, a superlative definition does not by itself establish new legal doctrine without subsequent practice to validate the principle as a new norm of international law. As we have noted many times already, the law evolves as circumstances change and new situations evolve. Still no text, until post World War I, including the first *three* editions of Oppenheim, mentioned "self defense" as a rationale. They analyze the broader idea of "self preservation."

Keep these points in mind because they have special relevance to the evolution of the ideas associated with self-defense. [41]

Aggression: Another Controversy Over Definitions

An interesting feature of the evolution of law in the twentieth century stems from the massive amount of effort spent in trying to define *aggression*. For many, defining aggression became important. As developed through the 1920s and 1930s, self-defense, the legitimate use of force, was in response to aggression, or the illegitimate and/or illegal use of force. Curiously, in the period between the two world wars, a divergence of opinion emerged among jurists and statesmen over whether it was desirable to advance a legal definition of aggression. The League of Nations had spent much time in trying to develop a definition of aggression. The efforts of the League and others reflect a "legislative" perspective in that those engaged sought to develop definitions and standards to guide future practice through consultation, debate, and parliamentary diplomacy. On the other hand, others felt that a definition should evolve through state responses on a case-by-case basis. They believed that the complexity of circumstances dictated that a definition emerge from actions in actual situations and the resulting judgments of the collective organs of the international community. This scenario would permit a full appreciation of the facts in any particular situation that might arise. Those holding this view argued that a rigid definition might be abused by an unscrupulous state to fit in with its aggressive design. An opinion widely held in Britain rejected the attempts to define *aggression* because it would be "a trap for the innocent and a signpost for the guilty."[43] Frank B. Kellogg (of Kellogg–Briand) noted:[44]

> It seems to me that any attempt to define the word "aggression," and by exceptions and qualifications to stipulate when nations are justified in going to war with one another, would greatly weaken the effect of any treaty such as that under consideration and virtually destroy its positive value as a "guaranty of peace."

---

[42]Idem.

[43]E. Borchard. "The Renunciation of War" (1928), http://avalon.law.yale.edu/20th_century/kbbor.asp (accessed May 15, 2009).

[44]Quoted in Borchard, note 42. For a modern critique of the efforts to define aggression, see J. Stone, Aggression and World Order (1958). Kellogg was U.S. secretary of state at the time.

The United Nations spent a great deal of time on the issue as well.[45] Unlike the League, the General Assembly did approve a definition Resolution 3314 (XXIX) by "consensus" (without vote).[46] Keep in mind that General Assembly resolutions do *not* create obligatory rules of international law. Of more interest here is the change in styles of justification over the past 35 years. As a legal term, *aggression* has somewhat fallen out of use. Recent texts in international law have spent little or no time in examining this debate.[47]

Post World War II, the legal significance of the term *war* has all but disappeared. Those who write about conflicts may still use the term to describe serious conflicts; and statesmen may use the term to describe a seriousness of effort. At present, the United States has asserted that it is engaged in a war on terrorism; but this has little *international legal* significance. States no longer declare war in the legal sense. The Geneva Conventions and the two Protocols Additional apply to "armed conflicts" (see Chapter 22).[48] The commentaries on Common Article 2 of the four conventions note, "There is no need for a formal declaration of war, or for recognition of the existence of a state of war, as preliminaries to the application of the convention. The occurrence of *de facto* hostilities is sufficient." The commentary then notes that the insertion of the phrase *"armed conflict"* was deliberate because[49]

> [a] State which uses arms to commit a hostile act against another State can always maintain that it is not making war, but merely engaging in a police action, or acting in legitimate self-defence. The expression "armed conflict" makes such arguments less easy. Any difference arising between two States and leading to the intervention of members of the armed forces is an armed conflict within the meaning of Article 2, even if one of the Parties denies the existence of a state of war. It makes no difference how long the conflict lasts, or how much slaughter takes place.

---

[45]For a sample of the debate here, see "Question of Defining Aggression," Summary of the Record of the 93rd Meeting (May 31, 1951), Yearbook of the ILC, 89. UN Doc. A/CN.4/SR93, http://untreaty.un.org/ilc/documentation/english/a_cn4_sr93.pdf (accessed April 22, 2009).

[46]Text, with explanatory comments by the Special Committee, in 69 *AJIL* 480 (1975). See J. Stone, "Hopes and Loopholes in the 1974 Definition of Aggression," 71 *AJIL* 224 (1977); and B. Ferencz, "The United Nations Definition of Aggression: Sieve or Substance?" 2 World Issues (April–May 1977): 26–28. See also Time (November 14, 1983): 32, quoting a number of legal scholars on "What Is Aggression?" As with self-defense, the restrictionists sought a very broad, inclusive definition; thus, such ideas as "ideological aggression" and "economic aggression" often were included in discussions.

[47]See, for example, O'Connell, note 3, which discusses "armed conflict" but not aggression.

[48]Common Article 2 of the four original conventions mentions "all cases of declared war or of any other armed conflict." Note also Protocol Additional to the Geneva Conventions of 12 August 1949, and Relating to the Protection of Victims of International Armed Conflicts (Protocol I) and Protocol Additional to the Geneva Conventions of 12 August 1949, and Relating to the Protection of Victims of Non-international Armed Conflicts (Protocol II); ILM 16 (1977): 1391–1449.

[49]International Committee of the Red Cross, Commentary, International Humanitarian Law: Treaties and Documents, Chapter 1, para. 1, www.helpicrc.org/ihl.nsf/COM/370-580005?OpenDocument (accessed April 22, 2009).

This statement still leaves open a number of questions. Sporadic border raids or other occasional "hostilities" involving the armed forces of two states would appear to fall short of an armed conflict because, intuitively, an armed conflict would seem to imply a level of intensity and some duration beyond an occasional raid or clash.[50] Other issues arise concerning the scope of application of the Geneva Conventions, but we will defer these until Chapter 22. Still other questions arise regarding how *domestic* courts may define the issues here.[51]

For the moment, the question becomes the standards for determining the threshold of armed attack. The International Court of Justice (ICJ) explored these questions in the *Nicaragua* case (see Chapter 17). The United States had submitted in the preliminary stages of the proceedings that El Salvador, Costa Rica, and Honduras had suffered armed attacks from Nicaragua of a nature to permit action in collective self-defense. The court first noted that states must refrain from many "less grave forms of the use of force." Citing the Declaration on Principles of International Law concerning Friendly Relations and Co-operation Among States in Accordance with the Charter of the United Nations,[52] the court then specifically listed reprisals involving the use of force; any forcible action that might deprive persons of the right to self-determination, freedom, and independence; organizing or encouraging any kind of transborder raid or terrorist act; and any act that might aid in the violent overthrow of or cause civil strife in another country.[53] The ICJ then observed that, in and of themselves, while prima facie not permissible, these activities do not necessarily constitute "armed attack" *unless* they pose significant problems. Hence, the court noted that sending armed bands across a border in significant numbers would constitute an armed attack. Merely providing assistance in the forms of weapons, logistics, or finance would not.[54] Thus, in defining *armed attack,* the ICJ used a test that might be labeled *intensity in context.* Given the evidence at its disposal, the court found that Nicaragua had assisted in supplying arms to the opposition in El Salvador, but that "[e]ven at a time when the arms flow was at its peak . . . that would not constitute such armed attack." Lacking a situation that rose to a level constituting armed attack, the ICJ found the U.S. claim of collective self-defense to have no merit.

---

[50]For a discussion of these issues with respect to differentiating between self-defense and reprisal, see Taulbee and Anderson, note 9, 316ff.

[51]See Hamdi v. Rumsfeld, 542 U.S. 507, 124 S. Ct. 2633 (2004).

[52]General Assembly Resolution 2625 (XXV) (October 24, 1970), www.hku.edu/law/conlawhk/conlaw/outline/Outline4/2625.htm (accessed April 22, 2009).

[53]Nicaragua v. United States, paras. 191, 192.

[54]One must also consider the limited nature of ICJ jurisdiction in this case. Because of the U.S. reservation in its declaration (Chapter 18) excluding interpretation of multilateral treaties from the compulsory jurisdiction of the Court, the ICJ could discuss the customary law only on the use of force as they perceived it had developed post World War II.

TERRORISM AND SELF-DEFENSE

Here we build on some points made earlier.[55] The framers of the Charter clearly did not foresee the rise of non-state actors capable of carrying out activities that would pose major threats to international peace and security.[56] States have an inherent right to use force to defend themselves. Yet, as discussed in Chapter 16, no generally accepted definition of terrorism exists in terms of international criminal law.[57] Note that the discussion to this point has proceeded on the basis of some important underlying assumptions—an armed attack involves a significant *ongoing* set of actions by a *state* or *states* that could seriously affect the security and stability of another state (or set of states). The events of September 11, 2001, raise an interesting set of contingencies characterized by the simple question of trying to assimilate the sporadic actions of terrorist groups to the idea of armed attack in order to justify a *legal* response in terms of self-defense. The reader must keep in mind that, at present, the fundamental structure of international law depends upon the state as principal actor even when discussing human rights and international criminal law. First and foremost, the events of 9/11 and those earlier directed against U.S. targets (the *USS Cole,* and the Kenyan and Tanzanian embassies) represent armed attacks by *nonstate* actors. The difficulty in dealing with all of these attacks lies first in finding an appropriate characterization of the act in terms of *international* law and, second, in determining what that characterization might mean in light of permissible responses with respect to *international* law. Third, it has to deal with a third issue of state responsibility with respect to the states that might provide "terrorists" a safe haven from which to operate.

To frame the question simply: the events of 9/11 certainly involve individual criminal acts, *but* to what extent do they generate *state* responsibility (Chapter 11) under international law? State responsibility requires an act of sufficient significance *imputable* to the state. Under international law, can a nonstate actor carry out an "armed attack" within the meaning of the current law? *If* the group responsible does not meet the test of being either a state or an agent of a state, the

---

[55]The *AJIL* has provided a forum for a vigorous exchange of opinions. Given our earlier characterization of the debate over self-defense, the following two cites represent the case for a "restrictive" multilateral approach (Farer) and the case for an expanded unilateral (and preemptive) right (Reisman). T. J. Farer, "Editorial Comment: Beyond the Charter Frame: Unilateralism or Condominium?" 96 *AJIL* 359 (2002); and W. M. Reisman, "Editorial Comment: Assessing Claims to Revise the Laws of War," 97 *AJIL* 82 (2003).

[56]A. Cassese, "Terrorism Is Also Disrupting Some Crucial Legal Categories of International Law, 12 European Journal of International Law 993 (2001). Between 1993 and 2000, Professor Cassese served as a judge on the International Criminal Tribunal for the Former Yugoslavia. See also M. J. Glennon, "The Fog of Law: Self Defense, Inherence and Incoherence in Article 51 of the United Nations Charter," 25 *Harvard J. L. and Pub. Policy* 539 (2002).

[57]When some states proposed that terrorism be considered as one of the international crimes to be subjected to the jurisdiction of the International Criminal Court (ICC), several states (including the United States) opposed this proposal. See Cassese, "Terrorism" note 63, at 994, and Chapter 22. Interestingly enough, the definition of "crimes against humanity" in the ICC Statute (Article 7(2)) may give the court jurisdiction over activities of individuals apart from any state connection. Moreover, crimes against humanity may occur outside of the existence of an "armed conflict."

acts have the quality of *ordinary criminal acts*. Equally, *if* the states most closely identified with the nonstate group lack the capacity to control the group's activities, then the acts have the quality of ordinary criminal acts.[58] The Security Council could find the attack to be a "breach of the peace" or "act of aggression" under its authority in Article 39, but that still leaves open the question of the appropriate target(s) of any action to redress the situation.

All of these contingencies raise the same problem—appropriate responses. Given the diffuse nature of al-Qaeda, even if the Security Council has determined that a breach of the peace or act of aggression has occurred, what does that mean? Does the magnitude of the destruction (or persistence of the problem) necessitate a broadening of the right of inherent self-defense to use force against any state perceived to be involved? Does it mean a state has a right to take action in efforts to gain custody of those responsible if governments prove unwilling or unable to assist? Even more controversial, does the right of self-defense extend to the possibility of using force to effect a regime change in states that continue to support certain activities deemed as unlawful and as threats to international peace and security? These questions remain the focus of intense debate.

Terrorism and Preemptive Self-Defense Much of the renewed debate centers on the claim that states have a right to *anticipatory* action in self-defense. Indeed, the *Caroline* involved just such an action. Although a point of discussion early in the self-defense debate post World War II, the possibility of nuclear war tended to promote a consensus around a narrower set of parameters that excluded anticipatory action. Critics also pointed out that anticipatory self-defense as a rationale is open to potential abuse and self-serving claims in ways that narrower interpretations are not.[59] On the other hand, the change in circumstances even before 9/11 had regenerated the debate over the permissibility of anticipatory action. This time, the debate had a new wrinkle. The questions revolved around the possibility of *preemptive* action in self-defense. The difference between anticipatory (preventive) and preemptive rests upon the nature of the contingencies addressed. Anticipatory self-defense depends upon a "palpable and imminent threat" in the sense of Webster's definition in the exchange over the *Caroline*.[60] Preemptive self-defense moves the nature of the contingency back from imminent and threatening to "an incipient development that is not yet operational . . . but permitted to mature could then be neutralized only at a higher and possibly unacceptable cost."[61] Consider the difference in definition in evaluating the response to the following incident.

---

[58]Due to the magnitude of destruction, describing the events as ordinary criminal acts tends to generate a feeling that something is terribly wrong; this characterization does not in any way capture the nature of the acts. On this point, see M. A. Drumbl, "Judging the 11 September Terrorist Attack," 24 *Human Rights Quarterly* 323 (2002): 341.

[59]Reisman, note 55, at 84.

[60]Reisman, note 55, at 87

[61]Ibid.

THE OSIRAK REACTOR

On June 7, 1981, Israeli planes attacked and destroyed a French-built nuclear reactor located approximately 18 miles south of Baghdad. Although the Iraqis denied intentions to produce nuclear weapons, Israeli intelligence had developed information to the contrary. The type of reactor and the fact that Iraq had little reason to develop nuclear power to produce electricity reinforced suspicions. The raid took place before the reactor had become "hot"—that is, stocked with nuclear fuel. In addition to the reactor, construction, and technical assistance, the French had sold approximately 12.5 kg of highly enriched uranium fuel (HEU) to the Iraqi government. The Israelis justified the action by noting, "Under no circumstances will we allow an enemy to develop weapons of mass destruction against our people."[62] Israel's ambassador to the United Nations noted, "Israel was exercising its inherent and natural right of self-defense as understood in general international law and well within the meaning of Article 51 of the Charter."[63] Even though the Security Council condemned the raid, the curiosity of the debate over this incident arises because many states addressed directly the issues of anticipatory self-defense. Many of these states took a counter-restrictionist position based upon the *Caroline* case. Most denied that the circumstances warranted the attack because the potential threat lacked an "imminent" character.[64]

The United States has claimed the right to engage in preemptive action in self-defense for some time. President Bill Clinton and British Prime Minister Tony Blair used it implicitly in their justification of the continued action to keep Iraqi military capabilities at relatively low levels.[65] President Clinton disclosed that his administration had plans to attack North Korean nuclear facilities if they resumed activity.[66] President George W. Bush echoed these themes in more explicit terms in asserting, "We must take the battle to the enemy, disrupt his plans and confront the worst threats before they emerge."[67]

Have weapons of mass destruction (WMD) and the ongoing threat of terrorism changed operational reality to the extent that states need a less restrictive set of conditions under which they may *unilaterally* use force to protect their security? The debate centers on questions that can only be answered in time. While the broad question of the continued relevance of the Charter underlies this discussion, the issues here focus on process. Presently, the *Caroline* offers a standard for judging

---

[62]"On This Day," BBC, http://news.bbc.co.uk/onthisday/hi/dates/stories/june/7/newsid_3014000/3014623.stm (accessed April 22, 2009).

[63]U.N. Doc. No. S/PV. 1024-51, June 12, 1981, at 16.

[64]For an analysis, see A. C. Arend, "International Law and the Preemptive Use of Military Force," 26 *The Washington Quarterly* 89 (2003): 95.

[65]P. Shenon, "Attack on Iraq: The Strategy; U.S. Declares It Might Need More Strikes on Iraq Soon," New York Times (December 21, 1998): A12; "We May Strike Again; Blair Promises to Keep Saddam 'in His Cage' as Doubts Grow over Iraq Attacks," The Guardian (London) (December 21, 1998): 1.

[66]D. E. Sanger, "Threats and Responses: Nuclear Anxiety; U.S. Eases Threat on Nuclear Arms for North Korea," New York Times (December 30, 2002): A1.

[67]George W. Bush, Commencement Address at the U.S. Military Academy in West Point (June 1, 2002), www.whitehouse.gov/news/releases/2002/06/20020601-3.html (accessed April 22, 2009).

anticipatory acts based on "necessity" (and, by implication, proportionality). The demand that preemption should form a new standard under changed circumstances raises the question of what standards should apply in evaluating claims that seemingly extend the *Caroline* paradigm.

At the very least, the fundamental principle that states must observe stems from a simple obligation that applies to *any* claim in law—*the party demanding redress must furnish sufficient evidence to permit judgment.* In the cases that follow, this obligation means the connection between the original events and the targets must be explicit. To the extent that states have found the norms governing self-defense irrelevant or constraining, is there an alternative set of standards that will find the extensive consent and support among the members of the community of nations to be considered law? Some tentative answers may be gleaned from a brief examination of some cases: the U.S. response to the embassy bombings in Kenya and Tanzania, and the U.S. and allied invasion of Afghanistan. Because of its special context, the action against Iraq will be considered as part of the discussion of the events (and expectations) flowing from the aftermath of the Iraqi invasion of Kuwait.

Kenya and Tanzania

In August 1998, bombs destroyed U.S. embassies in Kenya and Tanzania. Two weeks later, the United States launched military strikes against targets in Afghanistan and the Sudan, justifying the strikes as "retribution" and "a measure of self-defense against the imminent threat of terrorism."[68] Russia condemned the strikes as "aggression," but agreed one day later to issue a statement condemning terrorism.[69] The government of the Sudan protested the missile strike on Sudan as did the Taliban Islamic movement, along with Iran, Iraq, Libya, Pakistan, Russia, Yemen, Palestinian officials, and certain Islamic militant groups. The Secretariat of the League of Arab States condemned the attack on Sudan as a violation of international law but was silent as to the attack on Afghanistan. Saudi Arabia expressed qualified support. Australia, France, Germany, Japan, Spain, and the United Kingdom expressed varying degrees of support for the U.S. action.[70] Instead of a resolution condemning the United States, the General Assembly expressed "its grave concern at persistent violations of human rights and breaches of international humanitarian law in Afghanistan, as exemplified by reports of mass killings and atrocities committed by combatants against civilians and prisoners of war."[71]

---

[68]Foreign news in brief, ITAR-TASS News Agency, August 21, 1998 (Lexis-Nexis).

[69]"Russia Favours Joint Struggle against Terrorism," ITAR-TASS News Agency, August 21, 1998 (Lexis-Nexis).

[70]ITAR-TASS, note 75.

[71]GA Res. 53/203A, February 12, 1999. To continue:

> Strongly condemning the armed attacks against United Nations personnel in territories controlled by the Taliban, in which United Nations staff members were murdered or injured; Also strongly condemning the capture by Taliban militia of the Consulate-General of the Islamic Republic of Iran in Mazar-e Sharif and the killing of diplomatic and consular personnel of the Consulate-General and the correspondent of the Islamic Republic News Agency, and stressing that these unacceptable acts constitute violations of the Vienna Convention on Diplomatic Relations and the Vienna Convention on Consular Relations.

Justifying either of the events just described as an exercise in self-defense clearly stretches the essential parameters defining *necessity*. In looking at the response to the Sudan–Afghanistan bombing, it appears that the criticism was much more intense regarding the chosen targets in the Sudan than those in Afghanistan because, upon close examination, the Sudanese installation was perceived as being less directly connected to Osama bin Laden. The target was seen as a civilian installation that had little to do with support of terrorist activity.[72] The criticism from small states and Muslim fundamentalists must be analyzed in light of subsequent General Assembly action in approving the resolution critical of Afghanistan.

Afghanistan

The Security Council had previously passed Resolution 1267 on October 15, 1999.[73] Resolution 1267 demanded that the Taliban cease its activities in support of international terrorism. It also demanded the extradition of Osama bin Laden to the appropriate authorities to bring him to trial for the bombings of two U.S. embassies in Africa in August 1998. To enforce these demands, the Council imposed a flight ban on any aircraft "owned, leased or operated by or on behalf of the Taliban," and put a freeze on all financial resources controlled by the organization. The Resolution also announced the establishment of a Sanctions Monitoring Committee. In Resolution 1333 (2000), it further refined and strengthened the sanctions imposed in Resolution1267.[74]

Promptly after the events of 9/11, the Security Council passed Resolution 1368 unanimously.[75] The resolution

1. *Unequivocally condemns* in the strongest terms the horrifying terrorist attacks which took place on 11 September 2001 in New York, Washington, DC, and Pennsylvania and *regards* such acts, like any act of international terrorism, as a threat to international peace and security. . . .
2. *Expresses* its readiness to take all necessary steps to respond to the terrorist attacks of 11 September 2001, and to combat all forms of terrorism, in accordance with its responsibilities under the Charter of the United Nations.

The Security Council subsequently passed Resolution 1373 on September 28, 2001. In light of the previous discussion, and subsequent action by the United States citing this resolution as justification, the language and comprehensive nature of the resolution become important.

---

[72]ITAR-TASS, note 75.

[73]S/RES/1267 (October 15, 1999), www.apgml.org/conventions/documents/UNSCR1267pdf.pdf (accessed April 22, 2009).

[74]S/RES/1333 (December 19, 2000), www.ustreas.gov/offices/enforcement/pdf/unscr1333.pdf (accessed April 22, 2009). S/RES/1373 (2001) of September 28, 2001.

[75]S/RES/1368 (2001), United Nations A/RES/56/1 (2001).

S/RES/1373 (2001) OF SEPTEMBER 28, 2001

Adopted by the Security Council at its 4,385th meeting,
on September 28, 2001

The Security Council,

Acting under Chapter VII of the Charter of the United Nations,

1. Decides that all States shall:
   a. Prevent and suppress the financing of terrorist acts;
   b. Criminalize the wilful provision or collection, by any means, directly or indirectly, of funds by their nationals or in their territories with the intention that the funds should be used, or in the knowledge that they are to be used, in order to carry out terrorist acts;
   c. Freeze without delay funds and other financial assets or economic resources of persons who commit, or attempt to commit, terrorist acts or participate in or facilitate the commission of terrorist acts; of entities owned or controlled directly or indirectly by such persons; and of persons and entities acting on behalf of, or at the direction of such persons and entities, including funds derived or generated from property owned or controlled directly or indirectly by such persons and associated persons and entities;
   d. Prohibit their nationals or any persons and entities within their territories from making any funds, financial assets or economic resources or financial or other related services available, directly or indirectly, for the benefit of persons who commit or attempt to commit or facilitate or participate in the commission of terrorist acts, of entities owned or controlled, directly or indirectly, by such persons and of persons and entities acting on behalf of or at the direction of such persons;

2. Decides also that all States shall:
   a. Refrain from providing any form of support, active or passive, to entities or persons involved in terrorist acts, including by suppressing recruitment of members of terrorist groups and eliminating the supply of weapons to terrorists;
   b. Take the necessary steps to prevent the commission of terrorist acts, including by provision of early warning to other States by exchange of information;
   c. Deny safe haven to those who finance, plan, support, or commit terrorist acts, or provide safe havens;
   d. Prevent those who finance, plan, facilitate or commit terrorist acts from using their respective territories for those purposes against other States or their citizens;
   e. Ensure that any person who participates in the financing, planning, preparation or perpetration of terrorist acts or in supporting terrorist acts is brought to justice and ensure that, in addition to any other measures against them, such terrorist acts are established as serious criminal offences in domestic laws and regulations and that the punishment duly reflects the seriousness of such terrorist acts;
   f. Afford one another the greatest measure of assistance in connection with criminal investigations or criminal proceedings relating to the financing or support of terrorist acts, including assistance in obtaining evidence in their possession necessary for the proceedings;

(continued)

g. Prevent the movement of terrorists or terrorist groups by effective border controls and controls on issuance of identity papers and travel documents, and through measures for preventing counterfeiting, forgery or fraudulent use of identity papers and travel documents;

3. Calls upon all States to:

   1. Cooperate, particularly through bilateral and multilateral arrangements and agreements, to prevent and suppress terrori st attacks and take action against perpetrators of such acts;

4. Notes with concern the close connection between international terrorism and transnational organized crime, illicit drugs, money-laundering, illegal arms-trafficking, and illegal movement of nuclear, chemical, biological and other potentially deadly materials, and in this regard emphasizes the need to enhance coordination of efforts on national, subregional, regional and international levels in order to strengthen a global response to this serious challenge and threat to international security;

5. Declares that acts, methods, and practices of terrorism are contrary to the purposes and principles of the United Nations and that knowingly financing, planning and inciting terrorist acts are also contrary to the purposes and principles of the United Nations;

6. *Expresses its determination to take all necessary steps in order to ensure the full implementation of this resolution, in accordance with its responsibilities under the Charter;* (Emphasis added)

On October 7, 2001, the United States, Australia, and the United Kingdom initiated military action against Afghanistan.[76] This action generated a heated debate, more among lawyers than among states.[77] Many doubted that the two resolutions authorized unilateral action in retaliation. Much of the commentary revolved around technical questions of interpretation—can one interpret the language of the two Security Council resolutions to justify the unilateral use of force in self-defense? Kofi Annan, the secretary-general of the United Nations, affirmed that the states that launched the strikes did so within the parameters of the two resolutions.[78] Resolution 1378 (November 14, 2001)[79] did not mention the invasion, but did support "international efforts to root out terrorism." Pakistan, despite its links with the Taliban, characterized the invasion as "an action against terrorists . . . and their sanctuaries and their supporters."[80] The editorial pages of major

[76]Note that France provided logistical support. See also BBC (September 16, 2001), http://news.bbc.co.uk/1/hi/world/americas/1546289.stm (accessed April 22, 2009).

[77]For example, see Discussion Forum on the Attack on the World Trade Center, "Security Council Resolutions 1368 (2001) and 1373 (2001): What They Say and What They Do Not Say," *EJIL*, www.ejil.org/forum_WTC/messages/15.html (accessed April 22, 2009).

[78]Statement of UN Secretary-General Kofi Annan, "Secretary-General's Statement on the Situation in Afghanistan" (October 8, 2001).

[79]S/RES/1378 (November 14, 2001), http://yale.edu/lawweb/avalon/sept_11/unsecres_1378.htm (accessed April 22, 2009).

[80]BBC (October 8, 2001), http://news.bbc.co.uk/1/hi/world/south_asia/1586353.stm (accessed April 22, 2009).

European papers clearly supported the invasion.[81] Japan, Turkey, Egypt, Jordan, Nigeria, and South Africa supported the strikes. Russia offered use of bases within its territory.[82] China, while relatively noncommittal, did not overtly oppose. Iran, Sudan, Indonesia, and Malaysia were openly in opposition. Saudi Arabia refused permission to use bases in their territory as a staging area. The balance of state opinion seemed to accept the *evidence* of connection between the Taliban government and the activities of al-Qaeda (state responsibility) sufficient to support the coalition's justification for the invasion.[83]

UN Forces

Article 42 of the UN Charter authorizes a UN military command. It has never been implemented. Nonetheless, multinational forces operating under the aegis of UN approval have taken several different forms. In two cases, the invasion of South Korea by North Korea in 1950 and the invasion of Kuwait by Iraq in 1991, the United Nations has authorized the use of force to redress the situation; but the most interesting development here involves the evolution of innovative and alternative means to promote or preserve peace in specific situations. The United Nations has posted military observer groups to supervise truces, cease-fires, and borders. To note a current debate over the role of the United Nations, should the United Nations authorize "peacekeepers" or "peacemakers"?

The question of the legal basis for the United Nations to use armed forces posed immense and practical problems for the future work of the organization in keeping the peace.[84] The authority of the United Nations to create armed forces comes from Articles 1(1), 39, 41, and 42. Should the Security Council consider that measures provided for in Article 41 would be inadequate or have proved to be inadequate, it may authorize such action by air, sea, or land forces as may be necessary to maintain or restore international peace and security. Such action may include demonstrations, blockade, and other operations by air, sea, or land forces of members of the United Nations.

Note that the Security Council, not the General Assembly, is the agency mentioned in Article 42. In December 1946, the Security Council authorized the first "peacekeeping" experience of the United Nations to investigate the post–World War II boundary disputes between Greece, Bulgaria, Albania, and Yugoslavia. The Council created a Commission of Investigation. However, in September 1947, the Council shifted the disputes to the General Assembly. A month later the Assembly established in fact the first nonmilitary peacekeeping unit, a Special Committee (UNSCOB) that

---

[81]BBC (October 8, 2001), http://news.bbc.co.uk/1/hi/world/europe/1585826.stm (accessed April 22, 2009). See also "EU Wants New Afghan Government," BBC (October 8, 2001), http://news.bbc.co.uk/1/hi/world/europe/1586366.stm (accessed April 22, 2009).

[82]"Powell Welcomes Russian Support," BBC (September 25, 2001), http://news.bbc.co.uk/1/hi/world/americas/1562329.stm (accessed April 22, 2009).

[83]For analyses that question this conclusion, see Drumbl, note 65, at 328ff. and Farer, note 22, at 361ff.

[84]See especially J. W. Halderman, "Legal Basis for United Nations Armed Forces," *56 AJIL 971* (1962).

lasted from 1947 to 1954.[85] The General Assembly acted later to establish the first of the UN Emergency Forces (UNEF I) during the Suez crisis (1956) and the West Irian Security Force, but outside those particular occasions, the organization of peacekeeping activities by the United Nations has remained in the hands of the Security Council.

United Nations Command: South Korea

The Korean conflict marked the first direct test of the collective security system. The situation began in June 1950 with the movement of troops trained in North Korea across the 38th parallel into territory occupied by the Republic of Korea.[86] Both Korean entities claimed the right to govern the entire peninsula. In the absence of the USSR, the Security Council determined that the attack constituted a breach of the peace, fixed responsibility on North Korea for an armed attack, and called for an immediate cessation of hostilities followed by withdrawal of North Korean troops to behind the 38th parallel.[87]

Two factors facilitated the decision: strong U.S. support and the presence in Korea of a United Nations Temporary Commission, charged with assisting in unification, that provided an independent confirmation of the circumstances surrounding the attack.[88] While the decision in form appeared as a collective response, the United States engineered the decision.[89] Fifteen other states contributed nominal amounts of troops and other logistical support, but the United States bore the brunt of the cost of field operations in terms of material and manpower.[90] When the Soviet Union returned to block further action by the Security Council, the United States moved, through the Uniting for Peace Resolution,[91] to empower the General Assembly to carry on supervision of the war effort. An expansion of the original mandate to restore the status quo ante led to intervention by the People's Republic of China (PRC) and a two-year stalemate before a negotiated armistice. The General

---

[85]See R. Higgins, United Nations Peacekeeping, Documents and Commentary, IV: Europe 1946–1979 (1981). The series of Higgins's coverage of UN peacekeeping activities is the accepted early standard reference work on the subject.

[86]The Republic of Korea (ROK) was established after an election supervised by the United Nations. Koreans in the area north of the 38th parallel were prevented from participating. The General Assembly Nations recognized the ROK but without specifying whether the grant applied to the whole peninsula. The Soviet Union vetoed its application for membership. The Democratic People's Republic of Korea (DPRK) in the north was proclaimed with Soviet assistance at about the same time. This represents another case of an armistice line serving as a de facto border, a factor that somewhat complicates the issues of characterizing conflicts (e.g., the extended legal debate over aspects of the Vietnam War).

[87]S/1501 (Res. 82), June 25, 1950, 473rd mtg.; S/1511 (Res. 83), June 27, 1950, 474th mtg.; and S/1588 (Res.84) June 27, 1950, 474th mtg.

[88]See L. Gordenker, The United Nations and the Peaceful Unification of Korea (The Hague: Martinus Nijhoff, 1959), on the work of the commission. The commission had been in South Korea since its inception in 1948. When the North frustrated attempts at unification, the commission stayed as observers in the expectation of a confrontation between the two.

[89]See Dean Acheson, Present at the Creation (New York: W. W. Norton, 1969), 402–413, for a detailed account of American concerns.

[90]Five other states contributed medical supplies and miscellaneous equipment.

[91]GA. Res. 377 (V) GAOR, 5th sess., supp. no. 20, 10.

Assembly found that "by giving direct aid and assistance to those who were already committing aggression in Korea," the Chinese had "engaged in aggression."[92]

If the United States had not taken the lead and pushed, one can speculate that the organization would have ignored the conflict and that other major states, occupied with their own troubles at home (major domestic economic reconstruction), would have acquiesced in whatever result ensued because Korea did truly stand on the extreme periphery of their interest.[93] The action in Korea still highlighted what the United States and its supporters perceived to be an important principle, though tainted somewhat by ideological overtones, the lack of a truly collective character in prosecution of the war, and the failure to exercise prudential restraint at critical moments. Despite these shortcomings, rhetorical support by Communist bloc members for the DPRK (North Korea), and the Chinese intervention (but, presumably, based on its own security interest), the weight of opinion falls on the restrictive rather than the permissive side.

The United Nations: Traditional Invasion

As violent as the post–World War II era has been, the remarkable fact is that invasion in the classic sense has occurred so few times. When an invasion has occurred, international reaction has on the whole condemned the initiator, and sanctions have been forthcoming.[94] Considering the exceptions—Tanzania–Uganda, Iran–Iraq, and Vietnam–Cambodia (Kampuchea)—the rule may well be that pariah states should expect no protection from the good citizens of the community. Of equal relevance is that, whether from prudence or other motives, *states have exhibited a strong reluctance to authorize or initiate armed coercion as a sanction except as an absolute last resort.*[95]

Suez: UNEF I

The force (UNEF I) was established in connection with the Suez crisis of 1956 through action by the General Assembly rather than by the Security Council. In contrast to

---

[92]GA Res. 498 (V), February 1, 1951. The reader should note that in this instance, the United Nations created only a "unified command." The term United Nations Command was widely used but did not correspond to the technical fact that only a unified command under the United States could be attributed juridically to the United Nations. The forces operating in Korea were not, legally speaking, a UN expeditionary force. The command has been replaced by a mutual defense agreement between the United States and South Korea (1976).

[93]Considering this, the role of Secretary of State Dean Acheson's statements before the conflict that indicated Korea lay outside the perimeter of U.S. security interest still remains an open question. One can argue that the United States had an interest in opposing aggressors (the Truman Doctrine), but the question has always revolved around which aggressors and where.

[94]See Weisburd, note 37, at 58, for speculation and analysis of why the states in these instances were not the object of sanctions. Weisburd concludes that of the three, Iran–Iraq actually stands alone with no possible redeeming factor other than fear of Iran's sponsorship of subversion.

[95]The Iraqi–Kuwaiti situation and the tussle with Iraq over observance of the terms of the peace agreement illustrate this principle wonderfully well.

Korea, the organizational response to Suez stands as an inventive mechanism put in place to skirt the recent memories and perceived lessons of Korea.[96] Indeed, in justifying the force, delegates took great pains to emphasize that the operation was not an enforcement action and had no military objectives in the usual sense.[97] The initial concern was, with the Security Council hamstrung by the certainty of vetoes by Britain and France, whether the organization could in fact do anything at all to effect a resolution. The Suez incident consisted of a twofold invasion of Egypt—a joint venture by Britain and France, and a separate action by Israel—involving three different motives. Of the three principals, only Israel justified its actions as self-defense. The justification of Britain and France drew more straightforwardly on the traditional doctrine of *self-help* (vital national interests, and protection of lives and/or property of nationals).

The actual force was created by a variety of devices: General Assembly Resolution of November 5, 1956, established the command; the commanding officer and the initial group of officers were taken from the United Nations Truce Supervision Organization in Palestine; and the remainder—some 5,000 men—were supplied by states *other than* the permanent members of the Security Council. As to the legal basis for these methods and for the establishment of UNEF itself, the General Assembly relied entirely on the provisions of the Charter as developed by the 1950 Uniting for Peace Resolution.[98]

Response from third-party states to the invasions (apart from New Zealand and Australia) was uniformly negative. The parties received threats from the Soviet Union, open and continued criticism from the United States, and a string of resolutions from the General Assembly urging a cease-fire, withdrawal of troops, and an embargo on shipment of military goods into the area.[99] The public outcry forced a British and, more reluctantly, a French withdrawal.[100] The Israelis proved more resistant, ignoring a number of General Assembly resolutions and initially resisting any deployment of UNEF on its side of the armistice line. A combination of international supervision of key areas and American threats and

---

[96]S. Hoffmann, "Sisyphus and the Avalanche: The United Nations, Egypt and Hungary," 11 International Organization 446–469 (1957). H. Thomas, Suez (New York: Harper, 1967), is still the standard treatment. A. Eden, Full Circle (Cambridge, MA: Houghton-Mifflin, 1960), contains a full discussion of the positions of the principals. R. Neustadt, Alliance Politics (New York: Columbia University Press, 1970), and P. Calvocoressi, Suez Ten Years After (New York: Pantheon Books, 1967), examine the tensions and rifts the action caused within the Atlantic alliance. A. James, The Politics of Peacekeeping (New York: Praeger, 1969), and O. Young, The Intermediaries: Third Parties in International Conflicts (Princeton, NJ: Princeton University Press, 1967), contain insightful discussions of UN operations.

[97]L. M. Goodrich and G. L. Rosner, "The UN Emergency Force," 11 International Organization 413 (1957); and L. Sohn, "Authority of the UN to Establish and Maintain a Permanent UN Force," 52 AJIL 229 (1958).

[98]See Goodrich and Rosner, note 104, for materials relating to the Suez crisis of 1956 and UNEF. The text of the "Uniting for Peace" Resolution has been reprinted in 45 AJIL 1 (1951 Supp.), and in Bishop, 770–771. See also the important study by J. I. Garvey, "United Nations Peacekeeping and Host State Consent," 64 AJIL 241 (1970).

[99]E.g., GA Res. 997 (ES-1), Nov. 2, 1956.

[100]Actually, once the British decided to withdraw, the French had little choice due to the joint composition of the invasion force.

guarantees finally secured Israeli withdrawal in March 1957. The evidence shows virtually no positive support from third parties for the justifications advanced by the principals (Britain and France). The overwhelming majority of states clearly and strenuously rejected the claims.

The Iraqi Invasion of Kuwait (1991)

On August 2, 1991, Iraq invaded Kuwait.[101] This occurred after a yearlong crisis in which Iraq had put pressure on Kuwait in a bid to gain aid, economic concessions, and debt relief.[102] At first Iraq claimed that the government of Kuwait had been overthrown in a coup d'état and that the new government had asked for aid.[103] Saddam Hussein then attempted to justify the annexation of Kuwait through radical Islamic rhetoric by claiming that the annexation had constituted a religious duty because the al-Sabah family (Kuwait's ruling family) had presided over an artificial state set up by the British. Hussein contended that the invasion was a jihad that had liberated Kuwait from dominance by Western infidels.[104]

On August 6, the Security Council—by a 13–0 vote—put in place a trade and financial boycott of Iraq and of occupied Kuwait (Resolution 661).[105] The European Union, Japan, and the greatest majority of countries in the region had quickly denounced the invasion.[106] By a unanimous vote, on August 10, the Council (in Resolution 662) declared the seizure and occupation "null and void under international law."[107] The United States almost immediately acted to position troops in the Gulf. Both the United Kingdom and France sent troops, while Germany and Japan pledged financial support. When Iraq failed to withdraw, the Council

---

[101]"On This Day: 1990: Iraq Invades Kuwait," BBC (August 2, 1990), http://news.bbc.co.uk/onthis-day/hi/dates/stories/august/2/newsid_2526000/2526937.stm (accessed April 22, 2009).

[102]M. Curtius, "Iraq Presses Designs on Gulf; US Navy and Emirates Reply with 'Short-Notice' Exercises in Region," Boston Globe (July 25, 1990): 2; S. Nasrawi, "Iraq Accuses Kuwait of Plot with U.S., American Forces on Exercise," Associated Press (June 24, 1990), Lexis-Nexis.

[103]See T. L. Friedman, "The Iraqi Invasion," New York Times (August 5, 1990): 12; and Murphy, "Iraq Creates New 'Army,' Government in Kuwait," Toronto Star (August 5, 1990): A1.

[104]P. Lewis, "Confrontation in the Gulf; UN Council Declares Void Iraqi Annexation of Kuwait," New York Times (August 10, 1990): A11. See also L. Freedman and E. Karsh, The Gulf Conflict 1990–91 (1993), 28–62; and G. Kepel, Jihad: The Trail of Political Islam (2002), 208ff.

[105]Cuba and Yemen abstained. S/Res/0661 (August 6, 1990), www.fas.org/news/un/iraq/sres/sres0661.htm (accessed April 22, 2009). See also Gertz, "Cuba, Libya Ignore Sanction," Washington Times (August 30, 1990): A1, Lexis-Nexis.

[106]Williams, "European Community Slaps Iraq with Sanctions," Toronto Star (August 5, 1990): A2; C. J. Hanley, "Saddam Urges Ouster of Emirs; Arabs Counter with Military Plan," Associated Press (August 10, 1990), Lexis-Nexis. At the meeting of the Arab League in Cairo on August 10, 1990, only Iraq, Libya, and the PLO voted against the resolution. Algeria and Yemen abstained. Twelve Arab nations voted for the resolution. However, Mauritania, Jordan, and the Sudan petitioned to be listed in a separate category as having "expressed reservations."

[107]S/Res/0662 (August 10, 1990), www.fas.org/news/un/iraq/sres/sres0662.htm (accessed April 22, 2009); E. Sciolino, "Confrontation in the Gulf; Peacekeeping in a New Era: The Superpowers Act in Harmony," New York Times (August 28, 1990): A13.

passed Resolution 665 on August 25 that authorized states to use military means to enforce a blockade.[108] Twenty-three states eventually sent ships in support of the action. With Iraq standing firm in its refusal to withdraw, on November 29, 1990, the UN Security Council (Resolution 678) voted to authorize the United States and its allies to expel Iraq from Kuwait by force if Iraq refused to withdraw by January 15, 1991.[109] Further attempts to resolve the situation through negotiation produced no results. The United States, France, the United Kingdom, and Saudi Arabia initiated air strikes against Iraq on January 16, 1991.[110] When this action and continued negotiation again failed to secure an Iraqi withdrawal, the coalition mounted a concerted ground attack on February 24. That attack resulted in the total expulsion of the Iraqi Army from Kuwait by February 28.[111] On April 7, 1991, the coalition proclaimed the northern "no-fly zone" over Iraq (north of 36 degrees latitude) to protect the Kurds. In August 1992, the coalition announced a similar southern no-fly zone to protect Iraq's Shi'a majority. On April 11, Iraq consented to UN Resolution 687 (passed on April 3). Under its terms, Iraq agreed to destroy or remove all long-range ballistic missiles and all nuclear, biological, and chemical weapons (WMD).[112]

We need to note the nature of the dissent here. While the greatest majority of Arab states supported the action, few lesser developed states did so. In the Americas, only Argentina provided active support. Even in what seems the paradigm case, many states were reluctant to authorize the use of force when other sanctions failed to provide redress. While the European Union openly condemned Iraq's invasion as a violation of law, and many members contributed military forces or financial support, others seemed less willing to move beyond economic sanctions.[113]

The United States, the United Nations, and Iraq (2003)

After the first Gulf War,[114] the community of nations struggled with the questions dealing with the ongoing resistance of Iraqi authorities to the application of Security Council Resolution 683. Even before 9/11, the United States had pushed hard on questions concerning Iraqi compliance. As we have noted, debate over proper use of force had been a continuing point of contention. Bosnia, Somalia, Rwanda,

---

[108]S/Res/0665 (August 25, 1990), www.fas.org/news/un/iraq/sres/sres0665.htm (accessed April 22, 2009).

[109]S/Res/0678 (November 29, 1990), www.fas.org/news/un/iraq/sres/sres0678.htm (accessed April 22, 2009); Graham, "Five Permanent Members in U.N. Agree on Use-of-Force Resolution," Associated Press (November 26), 1990, Lexis-Nexis. Yemen and Cuba opposed the resolution; China abstained.

[110]In response, on January 18 and 19, Iraq fired Scud missiles into Israel, killing 3 people and injuring 70. P. Constable, S. Kurkjian, et al., "Israel Decides against a Strike," Boston Globe (January 20, 1991): 1.

[111]R. W. Stevenson, "In the Age of the 'Black Box' War," New York Times (January 20, 1991), sect. 3, p. 1.

[112]S/Res/0687 (April 3, 1991), www.fas.org/news/un/iraq/sres/sres0687.htm (accessed April 22, 2009).

[113]See Weisburd, note 36, at 58 ff.

[114]For a guide to the debate, see "Iraq War Debate 2002/2006," University of Michigan Library, www.lib.umich.edu/govdocs/iraqwar.html (accessed April 22, 2009).

and Kosovo, each representing a different set of contextual issues, generated sharp debates over the efficacy of, and the costs associated with, the use of military force. Opinions differed widely over the efficacy of the use of armed force as a method of obtaining or maintaining peace. The Security Council approved a series of resolution termed *oil for food* to permit Iraq to meet its domestic economic needs. Resolution 1194[115] illustrates the ongoing problem. It states:

> Recalling all its previous relevant resolutions, and in particular its resolutions 687 (1991) of 3 April 1991, 707 (1991) of 15 August 1991, 715 (1991) of 11 October 1991, 1060 (1996) of 12 June 1996, 1115 (1997) of 21 June 1997 and 1154 (1998) of 2 March 1998,
>
> Noting the announcement by Iraq on 5 August 1998 that *it had decided to suspend cooperation with the United Nations Special Commission and the International Atomic Energy Agency (IAEA)* on all disarmament activities and restrict ongoing monitoring and verification activities at declared sites, and/or actions implementing the above decision, . . .
>
> Demands that Iraq rescind its above-mentioned decision and cooperate fully with the Special Commission and the IAEA in accordance with its obligations under the relevant resolutions and the Memorandum of Understanding as well as resume dialogue with the Special Commission and the IAEA immediately; . . .
>
> *Decides not to conduct the review scheduled for October 1998* provided for in paragraphs 21 and 28 of resolution 687 (1991), *and not to conduct any further such reviews until Iraq rescinds its above-mentioned decision of 5 August 1998* and the Special Commission and the IAEA report to the Council that they are satisfied that they have been able to exercise the full range of activities provided for in their mandates, including inspections. (Emphasis added)

Over a dozen years, the UN framework aimed at "containment" seemed to work, if only at a minimal level. The events of 9/11 changed the U.S. perspective.

On September 12, 2002, President George W. Bush detailed U.S. complaints before the General Assembly. He specifically noted repeated Iraqi resistance to the full implementation of the 16 Security Council resolutions directed toward Iraq since the first Gulf War. In particular, President Bush charged that Iraq continued to shelter terrorist organizations, buy weapons, and develop WMD.[116] Over the next two months, the United States continued to press the argument that continued Iraqi resistance to full compliance with Council mandates posed a potential threat to international peace and security. In October 2002, the U.S. Congress passed the Joint Resolution to Authorize the Use of United States Armed Forces Against Iraq, which gave President Bush the power to use military force with or without Security Council approval.[117]

---

[115]S/Res/1194 (September 9, 1998), www.casi.org.uk/info/undocs/scres/1998/sres1194.htm (accessed April 22, 2009).

[116]See the White House, "President's Remarks at the United Nations General Assembly," www.white-house.gov/news/releases/2002/09/20020912-1.html (accessed April 22, 2009).

[117]www.whitehouse.gov/news/releases/2002/10/20021002-2.html (accessed April 22, 2009).

Intense diplomatic activity at the United Nations produced Security Council Resolution 1441,[118] which passed unanimously early in November 2002. In Resolution 1441, the Council required that inspections, which had been suspended, would begin again within 45 days. It also decided that it would convene immediately upon the receipt of any reports from inspection authorities that Iraq was interfering with their activities. France had misgivings about the phrase "serious consequences." It repeatedly noted that any "material breach" found by the inspectors should not automatically lead to war. The use of force would require an explicit authorization.

After the inspections began, the United States and United Kingdom again voiced doubts about Iraqi compliance. On February 5, 2003, U.S. Secretary of State Colin Powell presented a case for military intervention in Iraq to the UN Security Council. On the other side, in mid-February 2003, French Foreign Minister Dominique de Villepin stated, "Such intervention could have incalculable consequences for the stability of this scarred and fragile region. It would compound the sense of injustice, increase tensions and risk paving the way to other conflicts."[119] Even if Iraq did have an ongoing chemical and nuclear weapons program, Villepin went on to say that he believed the presence of UN weapons inspectors had produced positive results. Villepin also suggested that France would veto any resolution allowing military intervention offered by the United States or Britain, even if a majority of the UN Security Council members voted for it. The PRC was aligned with France. Opinion seemed heavily against the use of force.[120]

On March 17, 2003, President George W. Bush delivered an ultimatum to Saddam Hussein. Two days later, the president announced the beginning of military operations ("a coalition of the willing" that comprised 48 states, including the United Kingdom, Italy, Poland, and Spain) aimed at unseating the Iraqi government.[121] The debate over the legality of the action continues.[122] Unlike the first Gulf War (the Iran operation in 1991), UN Secretary General Kofi Annan characterized the invasion of Iraq as "illegal."[123] A number of states—including Spain, the Ukraine, and Bulgaria—have withdrawn their troops, citing changes in policy and increasing opposition at home.

---

[118]S/Res/1441 (November 8, 2002), www.un.org/News/Press/docs/2002/SC7564.doc.htm (accessed April 22, 2009).

[119]"Dominique de Villepin's Statement to the UN Security Council," http://www.globalpolicy.org/security/issues/iraq/unmovic/2003/0214dominiquestate.htm (accessed April 22, 2009).

[120]See "Security Council Hears over 60 Speakers in Two-Day Debate on Iraq's Disarmament; Many Say Use of Force Should Be Last Resort, Others Urge Swift Action," February 19, 2003, www.un.org/News/Press/docs/2003/sc7666.doc.htm (accessed April 22, 2009).

[121]See "Operation Iraqi Freedom," the White House, www.whitehouse.gov/news/releases/2003/03/20030319-17.html (accessed April 22, 2009). For a list of states and their contributions, see http://en.wikipedia.org/wiki/Multinational_force_in_Iraq#List_of_nations_in_the_Coalition (accessed April 22, 2009).

[122]See, for example, M. J. Glennon, "Why the Security Council Failed," 82 Foreign Affairs (2003); and E. C. Luck et al., "Stayin' Alive: The Rumors of the UN's Death Have Been Greatly Exaggerated," 82 Foreign Affairs (2003).

[123]"Iraq War Is Illegal Says Annan," BBC (September 16, 2004); http://news.bbc.co.uk/1/hi/world/middle_east/3661134.stm (accessed April 22, 2009).

The United Nations: Postimperial, Continuation, and/or Border Wars

The UN Charter regime presupposes stable governments operating within well-defined and accepted territorial borders with an identifiable and integrated population. None of these conditions have obtained over the past 60 years. It is in these issue areas that the failure of the United Nations to evolve as a center of authoritative procedures for resolving disputes by peaceful means has most importance. Is it reasonable to expect that a design for a stable world that never existed should totally govern the rather chaotic one that does? Based on the preceding discussion, between Cold War strictures and anticolonial imperatives, no forum apart from state-to-state negotiation existed for resolution of outstanding or newly generated issues. Using *disrespect* as a term to describe a situation implies that the law has some relevance to the issue. The availability of authoritative and legitimate procedures for settlement has to be an important factor.

In this environment, the UN approach of fostering negotiation seemed appropriate. In surveying the cases, the decisions (or "no calls") reflect an important attitude—*the unwillingness to impose any one version of the status quo as defined by past practice.* In many cases of border conflicts, the question of who decided the original border—or disputes over historical claims to areas left unresolved for other reasons—has no clear resolution on the basis of preexisting understandings.

Similarly, with wars of continuation, wars of postimperial succession, and postimperial wars, the lack of a widely accepted, preexisting, stable status quo as a benchmark against which to make judgments constitutes the best explanation of state reactions to these cases. As Weisburd notes, "[I]t would have made no sense for the international community to insist that the parties keep the peace when there was no peace to keep."[124] To reiterate a previous point, law is a conservative technique that depends upon a broad underlying agreement of the values to be conserved for its effectiveness. If the participants in Cyprus, Kashmir, and the Arab–Israeli conflicts all see themselves as victims of a continuing wrong at one another's hands that produces an unacceptable future risk with no effective redress available through third-party intervention, the value of restraint on other than short-term prudential calculation has little payoff. *The violence here did not breach a long-standing, peaceful status quo.* Rather, the wars mark short-term phases where violent contexts become *relatively more violent.* Accordingly, the costs of coercively restraining the parties would be enormous, requiring major commitments of military and political resources.[125] Third-party states have threatened sanctions in some cases, but their efforts have focused largely on creating the conditions that might eventually produce an acceptable status quo.

124Weisburd, note 36, at 68.

125Consider as well the political limitations of the Cold War throughout most of the period under discussion.

Humanitarian Intervention

The doctrine of humanitarian intervention[126] furnishes another instance of the tension between state sovereignty and the active international protection of human rights. In retrospect, scholars have made more of this rationale than states have.[127] In 1986, Bowett noted, "we have no true example of a clear reliance on this right of intervention by any State since 1945." On the other hand, we do have at least one example—Vietnam's invasion of Cambodia (Kampuchea), which unseated one of the most criminal governments of the twentieth century (the Khmer Rouge). At the time the action received widespread condemnation.

Fernando Tesón has produced a thoughtful and compelling examination of the topic.[128] He argues that the "promotion of human rights is as important a purpose in the Charter as is the control of international conflict."[129] The difficulty with the argument is that it only makes the case for a more focused collective effort, not for the right of individual states to act on behalf of their perceptions.[130] Indeed, Tesón's sentiment had found little resonance among statesmen until the end of the Cold War.[131] The view from 2006, which includes almost two decades of inconsistent Security Council decisions, seems a little different. Somalia and Rwanda marked the beginnings of a new willingness to act under Chapter VII even though no armed attack had occurred.

Both Kosovo and Haiti mark significant precedents in terms of departures from previous practice. The precedent of having to deal with the turmoil created

---

[126]We have excluded missions to protect and/or rescue a state's own nationals from this category, limiting this discussion to the use of force to "promote/preserve" human rights. While we have not presented systematic evidence here, except in passing, states have generally tolerated limited uses of force to rescue nationals. The missions have generated the usual negative response from small states and, depending upon circumstances and time, from Cold War adversaries and their allies. Yet in no case did the actions result in more than the simple formulaic denunciation, sometimes in a single General Assembly Resolution.

[127]Indeed, the literature here is extensive. See, inter alia, M. Akehurst, "Humanitarian Intervention," in *Intervention in World Politics*, edited by H. Bull (1984), 112ff.; D. W. Bowett, "The Use of Force for the Protection of Nationals Abroad," in *The Current Legal Regulation of the Use of Force*, edited by A. Cassese (1986), 49; L. Brilmayer, *Justifying International Acts* (1989) at 139–141; N. Ronzitti, Rescuing Nationals Abroad through Military Coercion and Intervention on the Grounds of Humanity (1985); and F. R. Tesón, *Humanitarian Intervention* (3rd rev. ed., 1988).

[128]Tesón, note 127.

[129]Tesón, note 127, at 131, 134.

[130]For a summary of these arguments, see Arend and Beck, note 23 at 132–134, and accompanying footnotes. In answer to the argument that Article 56 authorizes joint and separate action in cooperation with the organization for the achievement of purposes set out in Article 55, it does so regarding the use of force only when the Security Council has made an appropriate finding under Article 39. Accordingly, the argument that absent a decision under Chapter VII, the collective impact of Articles 1, 55, and 56 establishes the permissibility of unilateral *self-help* borders on sheer silliness, unless one wishes to argue that human rights obligations have acquired the status not only of *jus cogens* but also of vital interests that generate the same imperatives as defending one's own territory. Additionally, the argument as stated totally distorts the primary purposes and procedural requirements because the authors fervently *believe* that armed force *ought* to be available in service of these goals. Finally, as noted earlier, the parallel assertion (as with the issue of self-defense) that paralysis of the collective security machinery leaves open the customary right of humanitarian intervention raises the question: *what* was the substantive content of the relevant "law"?

[131]For a detailed critique of the alleged customary right, see S. Chesterman, Just War or Just Peace? Humanitarian Intervention and International Law (2001).

by failed states would lead eventually to peacekeeping forces for Sierra Leone and the Democratic Republic of the Congo. The hostilities stemmed solely from civil strife generated by domestic divisions that posed no manifest threat to the vital interests of other states. In Haiti, the Security Council clearly went beyond the traditional Charter interpretation. In 1994, with Resolution 940, the Security Council found that the situation in Haiti threatened peace in the region— even though no armed threat existed—and authorized a detachment of primarily American troops to use armed force to restore democracy.[132] The authorization of military intervention to restore democracy in a place where a government held effective control represented the zenith of the Council's expansion of the heretofore conservative definitions of what situations legitimately fell under Chapter VII.[133] The implication of the Security Council finding is that a particular form of government and the manner in which it came to power could constitute a threat to international peace.

As the first large-scale military action in NATO's history, Kosovo raises questions of a different sort, both substantively and procedurally.[134] Procedurally, the operation was undertaken by a powerful and responsible multilateral organization with only the tacit acceptance of the Security Council. Operationally, it has raised many issues of appropriateness.[135] The issues center on those often cited as providing the rationale for the invasions of Uganda, the Central African Empire, and Cambodia (Kampuchea). The problem here is simple—in none of these cases does the diplomatic record indicate that the states involved used arguments based upon

---

[132]SC Res/940 (July 31, 1994). In this case the United States used the Security Council rather than the OAS to "multilateralize" the operation. See D. L. Donoho, "Evolution or Expediency: The United Nations Response to the Disruption of Democracy," 29 Cornell Int'l L. J. 329 (1996).

[133]See M. J. Glennon, "Sovereignty and Community After Haiti: Rethinking the Collective Use of Force," 89 *AJIL* 70 (1995).

[134]The United States asserted that it and its allies have the authority to use force based upon claimed implicit Security Council authorization. Did Resolution 1199 (September 23, 1998), while it condemned Yugoslavia's actions in Kosovo, explicitly authorize the use of force? The resolution does not mention the use of force. After the vote, Russia explicitly stated that it had voted for it because no measures of force and no sanctions were introduced by the Security Council. Moreover, Resolution 1199, in paragraph 16, states that the Security Council "decides, should the concrete measures demanded in this resolution and Resolution 1160 (March 31, 1998) not be taken, to consider further action and additional measures to maintain or restore peace and stability in the region." See SC Res/1203 (October 24, 1998); SC Res/1244 (June 10, 1999).

[135]From the standpoint of formal analysis of "the law," the operation would seem to violate the fundamental purpose of the NATO treaty, which specifies that the use of force should be in collective self-defense. North Atlantic Treaty, April 4, 1949, Art. 5, TIAS No. 1964, 34 UNTS 243. Chinkin alleges, "The NATO bombing was disproportionate for being both excessive in its impact on the human rights of one civilian population and inadequate by dint of the absence of ground forces to protect the other population." C. Chinkin, "Editorial Comments: NATO's Kosovo Intervention: Kosovo: A 'Good' or 'Bad' War" 93 *AJIL* 841 at 846 (1999). Chinkin argues that the "'reinvention' of NATO in the post–Cold War era is at the expense of the agreed normative order." Id. at 844.

humanitarian concerns as a primary justification. In her commentary on Kosovo, Wedgwood argues the following:[136]

> The lack of any single source of rules or ultimate arbiter of disputes in international affairs means that *state practice* remains key to the shaping of legal norms. When action is deemed morally urgent by a majority of states—even an action involving the use of force—it is likely to shape a legal justification to match. (Emphasis added)

She might have added that when the action is undertaken by, is supported by, or receives acquiescence from the largest and most powerful, the incident becomes a compelling example for future reference.

How much of a precedent these cases set remains an open question. That the Russians and Chinese were isolated in the Security Council when they tried to condemn NATO suggests that there were reserves of outrage toward Belgrade that might have been tapped by convening the General Assembly. India and some smaller states also opposed. Of more consequence will be the costs, both in human and material terms; and the complexity and nature of the problems *created* by this course of action may preclude future ventures except in the direst of circumstances. Yet one must also consider the expectations created. What does this mean in light of the perceived future responsibilities of regional or multilateral organizations with regard to stepping in to prevent wholesale slaughter?[137] At this point, the answer is far from self-evident.

The Responsibility to Protect   The International Commission on Intervention and State Sovereignty used this concept as the central theme of its 2001 report, *The Responsibility to Protect*. The report built on "the idea that sovereign states have a responsibility to protect their own citizens from avoidable catastrophe—from mass murder and rape, from starvation—but that when they are unwilling or unable to do so, that responsibility must be borne by the broader community of states."[138] The idea became an important part of the 2004, debate on United Nations reform.

---

[136]R. Wedgwood, "Editorial Comments: NATO's Kosovo Intervention: NATO's Campaign in Yugoslavia," 93 *AJIL* 828 (1999).

[137]That is, will the commitment to human rights that humanitarian intervention supposedly entails mean equality of rights worldwide? Clearly, the willingness of states and organizations to engage in meaningful fashion suggests that the human rights of some people are more worth protecting than those of others. Military intervention on behalf of the victims of human rights abuses has not occurred in, inter alia, Sudan, Afghanistan, or Ethiopia. It was wretchedly inadequate and delayed in Rwanda. The Security Council did nothing to stop the slaughter in Rwanda in the spring of 1994, although the conflict involved the crossing of many borders in the region. Moreover, the UN had already consented to be there. Nevertheless, showing its then new reticence at becoming involved in such complicated conflicts, the Security Council shied from authorizing intervention. Rather, it withdrew the peacekeeping force it had sent earlier. For a devastating critique, see W. Shawcross, *Deliver Us from Evil: Peacekeepers, Warlords and a World of Endless Conflict* (2000), 124–145.

[138]International Commission On Intervention And State Sovereignty: *The Responsibility To Protect*, at VIII (2001), www.iciss.ca/report-en.asp.

Given the lack of international response to the successive humanitarian disasters in Somalia, Bosnia–Herzegovina, Rwanda, Kosovo, and Darfur (Sudan) the High-Level Panel on Threats, Challenges and Change stated in its report that they found a growing acceptance of a new interpretation of sovereign rights: that sovereign governments have the primary responsibility to protect their own citizens from such catastrophes, when they are unable or unwilling to do so that responsibility should be taken up by the wider international community.[139] The Security Council made its first express reference to the concept in Resolution 1674 (2006) on the protection of civilians in armed conflict.[140] Interestingly, this initiative draws from a long tradition in political thought based upon Thomas Hobbes' account of why individuals seek to form a government as a way to escape the conditions of the state of nature. It involves reconceptualizing sovereignty from an emphasis on the right to control to the idea of sovereignty as entailing responsibilities.

The responsibility to protect principle means that matters pertaining to the life of the citizens and subjects of a state are no longer considered solely subject to the discretion of the domestic ruler. Violation of minimum standards of treatment would be come issues of concern to the broader international community (e.g., third states, multilateral institutions, and nonstate actors). This development is part of a growing trend in international law, fueled by concerns for human rights, to redefine the parameters of sovereignty in terms of placing limits on the right of governing elites to do what they please with regard to their subjects/citizens; and, on the other side, defining a minimum standard of performance from governments in terms of protecting basic rights.[141] Presumably the trigger for invoking the doctrine would be situations that comprise genocide, crimes against humanity or widespread war crimes.

Prior to its elaboration in the 2001 UN Report, variants of this rationale, sovereignty as responsibility, were used to justify certain military interventions in failed states (e.g., Somalia) where the government lacked the capacity to protect, in situations where the government was unwilling to act (e.g., Kosovo), and where the government deliberately undertook policies that put citizens/subjects at risk (e.g., Bosnia). Advocates argued that interventions based upon this principle would not run counter to the principles of sovereignty and territorial integrity of the host state.[142] The rationale upon which the obligation of nonintervention is based does not apply when the domestic sovereign violates the rights of its own population. Tesòn argues:

Force used in defense of fundamental human rights is not therefore a use of force in consistent with the purposes of the United Nations. States sovereignty makes sense only as a shield for persons to organize themselves freely in political communities. A. condition for respecting state sovereignty is, therefore that

---

[139]*A More Secure World: Our Shared Responsibility,* Report of the High-Level Panel on Threats, Challenges and Change, U N Doc. A/59/565, at 56–57, para. 2.01 (2004), www.un.org/secureworld/report.pdf.

[140]S C Res. 1674, para. 4 (April 8, 2006) ("reaffirming the provisions of paragraph 138 and 139 of the 2005 World Summit Outcome Document regarding the responsibility to protect populations from genocide, war crimes, ethnic cleansing and crimes against humanity").

[141]C. Stahn, "Responsibility to Protect: Political Rhetoric or Emerging Legal Norm?" 101 *AJIL* 99 (2007).

[142]Charter Articles 2(4) and 2(7)

sovereign governments (minimally) respect human rights. Delinquent government forfeit the protection afforded by Article4 (2).[143]

Needless to say this has produced a heated debate between the defenders of the hard shell traditional idea of sovereign rights and prerogatives, and those who wish to move toward the idea that as a definition of their position, sovereign authorities have certain duties to ensure certain fundamental rights that international law mandates for their subjects/citizens. India, China, Russia and many small states resist any rationale that would permit outside intervention under any circumstances. The legacy of colonialism has not disappeared. Lesser developed states, despite the record of breakdowns and abuses, see the idea as just the latest excuse to justify intervention by the strong against the weak.

As you should understand at this point, the position raises a number of issues with respect to implementation. Who would decide and on what criteria? Would it be limited to a collective decision by the Security Council or could other regional bodies take actions. Would a unilateral initiative ever be permissible? Scholars and others have attempted to produce a set of guidelines to flesh out circumstances under which "responsibility to protect" would apply, and develop corresponding criteria to guide response.[144] Nonetheless, at this juncture, the uncertainty surrounding the consequences of noncompliance and the conditions under which intervention might be justifiable still raises broad question of principle as well as practical problems of implementation. The rather amorphous formulations and uses in justification shed doubt on the notion that responsibility to protect has evolved into a hard norm of international law. It perhaps remains in the realm "soft law" as a desirable option in some circumstances.[145]

SUGGESTED READINGS

CLASSICS

Brownlie, *International Law and the Use of Force by States* (1963).

Hyde, vol. 3.

Lauterpacht's *Oppenheim*, II.

McDougal and Feliciano, *Law and Minimum World Public Order: Legal Regulation and International Coercion* (1961).

Moore, VII.

Stone, *Legal Controls of International Conflict* (1954).

GENERAL

Arend and Beck, *International Law and the Use of Force* (1993).

Byers, *War Law* (2005).

Bzsostek, *Why Not Pre-empt? Security, Law Norms, and Anticipatory Military Activity* (2008).

Corr and Sloan, *Low-Intensity Conflict: Old Threats in a New World* (1992).

Dinstein, *War, Aggression and Self-Defense,* 3rd ed. (2001).

Gazzini, *The Changing Rules on the Use of Force in International Law* (2005).

Gray, *International Law and the Use of Force,* 2nd ed. (2004).

O'Connell, *International Law and the Use of Force: Cases and Materials* (2005).

Weisburd, *Use of Force: The Practice of States since World War II* (1997).

---

[143]F. Tesòn, *Humanitarian Intervention: An Inquiry into Law and Morality* (3d rev. ed. 2005), 217.

[144]See for example, A. L. Bannon, "The Responsibility to Protect: The U.N. World Summit and the Question of Unilateralism," 115 *Yale Law Journal* (2006), 1157-1165

[145]Stahn, n. 148, 118.

KELLOGG-BRIAND PACT

Barnhard, "The Multilateral Treaty for the Renunciation of War," 23 *AJIL* 116 (1929).

Wright, "The Meaning of the Pact of Paris," 27 *AJIL* 39 (1933).

May, *Aggression and Crimes Against Peace* (2008)

SELF-DEFENSE

Bowett, *Self-Defense in International Law* (1958).

Gardam, "Proportionality and Force in International Law," 87 *AJIL* 391 (1993).

Jennings, "The *Caroline* and *McLeod* Cases," 32 *AJIL* 82 (1938).

Taulbee and Anderson, "Reprisal *Redux*," 16 *Case Western Reserve Journal of International Law* 309 (1984).

Tucker (Comment), "Reprisals and Self-Defense: The Customary Law," 66 *AJIL* 586 (1972).

TERRORISM AND SELF-DEFENSE

Arend, "International Law and the Preemptive Use of Military Force," 26 *Washington Quarterly* 89 (2003).

Farer, "Editorial Comment: Beyond the Charter Frame: Unilateralism or Condominium?" 96 *AJIL* 359 (2002).

Glennon, "The Fog of Law: Self Defense, Inherence and Incoherence in Article 51 of the United Nations Charter," 25 *Harvard J. L. and Pub. Policy* 539 (2002).

Reisman, "Editorial Comment: Assessing Claims to Revise the Laws of War," 97 *AJIL* 82 (2003).

THE UNITED NATIONS AND IRAQ

Glennon, "Why the Security Council Failed," 82 *Foreign Affairs* (2003).

Luck et al., "Stayin' Alive: The Rumors of the UN's Death Have Been Greatly Exaggerated," 82 *Foreign Affairs* (2003).

HUMANITARIAN INTERVENTION

Bellamy, *Global Politics and the Responsibility to Protect: From Words to Deeds* (2011).

Chesterman, *Just War or Just Peace? Humanitarian Intervention and International Law* (2001).

Nardin and Williams, eds., *Humanitarian Intervention* (2006).

Orford, *International Authority and the Responsibility to* Protect (2011).

Tesón, *Humanitarian Intervention* (1988).

Wheeler, *Saving Strangers: Humanitarian Intervention in International Society* (2000).

International Humanitarian Law

War Crimes

THE LAWS OF WAR (*JUS IN BELLO*): INTERNATIONAL HUMANITARIAN LAW

International law has always been concerned as much with the conduct of states engaged in war as with their relations in time of peace. Indeed, the authors of the classics in the law gave priority in space and attention to hostile relations among nations, a practice justified by the "normality" of such relations, compared with the relative abnormality of peace among the states of Europe. The gradual development of a stable international order favored the growth of rules governing the rights and duties of states in time of peace, and in modern times, the "law of peace" occupies the bulk of any treatise on international law. In contemporary form, the *jus in bello* is often termed *international humanitarian law*. The International Committee of the Red Cross (ICRC) provides a concise summary:[1]

> International humanitarian law is a set of rules which seek, for humanitarian reasons, *to limit the effects of armed conflict*. It protects persons who are not or are no longer participating in the hostilities and restricts the means and methods of warfare. International humanitarian law is also known as the law of war or the law of armed conflict.

The devastation caused by the Thirty Years' War (1618–1648) impressed upon both governments and military leaders that a regularization of the conduct of hostilities was highly desirable in order to avoid needless suffering and unnecessary loss of property.[2] Grotius wrote his famous *De jure belli ac pacis* ("On the law of war and peace") as a response to many of the atrocities committed during these hostilities. A relatively elaborate set of customary rules concerning the behavior of states during war evolved between the end of the Thirty Years' War

---

[1]ICRC, www.icrc.org/web/eng/siteeng0.nsf/html/humanitarian-law-factsheet (accessed April 22, 2009).

and the middle of the nineteenth century. Toward the end of the Thirty Years' War, isolated instances of humane practice in the conduct of hostilities acquired in the course of time the status of usages and came to be regarded as customs, as binding legal obligations to be observed by states at war with one another. The laws of war apply to armed conflicts, whether or not they are called wars: Article 2, common to all four Geneva Conventions of 1949, applies "to all cases of declared war or of any other armed conflict that may arise between two or more of the High Contracting Parties, even if the state of war is not recognized by one of them."

International humanitarian law covers two areas: (1) the protection of those who do not take part, or who are no longer taking part, in fighting; and (2) restrictions on the *means* of warfare (in particular, weapons) and the *methods* of warfare, such as military tactics.[3] Lauterpacht pointed out that three principles have determined the growth of the "laws of war": the principle that a belligerent is justified in applying any amount and any kind of force considered necessary to achieve the goal of a conflict—the defeat of the enemy; the principle that because of humanitarian considerations, any violence not necessary for the achievement of that goal should be prohibited; and the principle that a certain amount of chivalry, the spirit of fairness, should prevail in the conduct of hostilities—that certain practices smacking of fraud and deceit should be avoided.[4] The laws of war took the initial form of rules of customary law, beginning even before the sixteenth century. Their modern development, however, has taken place through the application of conventional law, through the conclusion of a number of multilateral treaties.[5]

EARLY DEVELOPMENT OF THE LAW OF WAR

The middle of the nineteenth century witnessed the birth of modern attempts to develop a *jus in bello*. The Declaration of Paris (1856) abolished privateering and formulated regulations for blockades and contraband goods. The true beginning of present-day rules applicable to land warfare came in 1863, when Dr. Francis Lieber's *Instructions for the Government of Armies of the United States in the Field* was issued to the Union Army during the American Civil War on April 24, 1863, as General Orders No. 100. The thoroughness of Lieber's work impressed military men elsewhere. The *Instructions* became the model for numerous national manuals (Italy, 1896 and 1900; Russia, 1904; and France, 1901 and 1912).

---

[2]Grotius, *The Law of War and Peace* = *De jure belli ac pacis*, trans. L. R. Loomis (1949); and Grotius, *Hugonis Grotii de jure belli ac pacis libri tres: in quibus jus naturae & gentium, item juris publici præ cipua explicantur: cum annotatis auctoris, ex postrema ejus ante obitum cura multo nunc auctior; accesserunt & annotata in Epistolam Pauli ad Philemonem*, trans. F. W. Kelsey (1995, reissue of 1922 ed.).

[3]ICRC, note 1.

[4]Lauterpacht's *Oppenheim*, II: 227.

[5]The ICRC has identified 99 relevant instruments. For a list, see ICRC, www.icrc.org/ihl.

Two private attempts at codification merit brief mention. In 1880, the Institute of International Law prepared the so-called *Oxford Manual* (*Manuel de Lois de la Guerre sur Terre*).[6] In 1894, the German writer Geffcken prepared a private code, anticipating several important aspects of the 1899 and 1907 Hague Conventions. The *Oxford Manual* was such an excellent effort, considering the type of warfare then current, that it is still cited with approval by European writers. Far more important than those early attempts were the conventions and regulations produced at the two Hague Peace Conferences in 1899 and 1907.

The Hague Conferences

In 1899, the First Peace Conference at The Hague resulted in the signing of the Convention with Respect to the Laws and Customs of War on Land, derived from the *Instructions*. The Second Peace Conference, which met in 1907 in The Hague, revised the earlier convention, and the new version is known as Convention IV (Convention Respecting the Laws and Customs of War on Land, The Hague, October 18, 1907). The drafters of the document realized full well that many aspects of the conduct of hostilities had not been covered fully or had been omitted from the document altogether. Hence, the preamble of the convention included toward its end the significant statement "It has not, however, been found possible at present to concert Regulations covering all the circumstances that arise in practice." It should be noted that both Hague conventions were considered declaratory of the existing rules of customary international law. Annexed to the Fourth Convention of 1907 (Convention Respecting the Laws and Customs of War on Land) were regulations detailing the conduct of hostilities. Those regulations remain of key importance even today. Both world wars showed the inadequacy of many of the 1907 rules as well as the great gaps in the body of law presumably governing war on land.

World War I and World War II

Few anticipated the nature of World War I. The last major conflict between two European adversaries, the Franco-Prussian War, had occurred in 1870–1871. Military planners and statesmen had believed that technology would make war short, thus limiting casualties on the battlefield and the impact on noncombatants. World War I proved both assumptions tragically wrong. The advent of the submarine, the machine gun, and longer-range, more powerful cannon coupled with the evolution of the airplane produced circumstances that the delegates to the 1907 Hague Conference did not foresee.[7] The devastation and human carnage did spark additional attempts to write new rules. States made repeated attempts to revise the rules (in

---

[6]The complete text of the *Manual* may be found in J. B. Scott, ed., *Resolutions of the Institute of International Law Dealing with the Law of Nations* (1916), 26. Geffcken's code may be found in his "Règlement des Lois et Coutumes de la Guerre," 26 *Revue de Droit International* 586 (1894).

[7]See, for example, the rules concerning the lawful use of submarines. The advent of armed escorts for merchant convoys made this rule a "nonstarter" given the vulnerability of submarines on the surface.

Madrid, Monaco, and Liège, various years), but the effort only produced the ban on chemical and bacteriological weapons.[8]

The aftermath of World War II produced a concerted effort to update the rules. The United Nations and the ICRC spearheaded the drive to develop international humanitarian law. The Geneva Diplomatic Conference of 1949 drafted four conventions: Amelioration of the Condition of the Wounded and Sick in Armed Forces in the Field (Geneva I); Amelioration of the Condition of Wounded, Sick and Shipwrecked Members of Armed Forces at Sea (Geneva II); Treatment of Prisoners of War (Geneva III); and Protection of Civilian Persons in Time of War (Geneva IV). The ICRC organized two sessions of a Conference of Government Experts (1971 and 1972) in Geneva to draft additional concrete rules applicable to armed conflicts (primarily in the form of additional protocols to the 1949 Geneva Conventions), followed by the Diplomatic Conference on Reaffirmation and Development of International Humanitarian Law Applicable in Armed Conflicts (1974–1977). On June 8, 1977, the conference adopted by consensus two conventions: Additional Protocol to the Geneva Conventions of 12 August 1949, and Relating to the Protection of Victims of International Armed Conflicts (AP-I) and Additional Protocol to the Geneva Conventions of 12 August 1949, and Relating to the Protection of Victims of Non-international Conflicts (AP-II). Both treaties amplify many of the rules developed in the 1949 Geneva Conventions and also add some new regulations. Both entered into force on December 7, 1978.[9]

LAW OF NONINTERNATIONAL WARS

At the 1974–1977 Diplomatic Conference, the West German delegate stated that 80 percent of the victims of armed conflicts after World War II were the victims of noninternational conflicts, and the Soviet delegate asserted that the figure should be raised to 90 percent.[10] Moreover, until December 1978, when AP-II of 1977 came into force, the only conventional (treaty-based) international law rule applicable to internal war was common Article 3 of the four Geneva Conventions of 1949, which in Farer's felicitous phrase, was not more than a statement of "affectionate

---

[8]*Protocol for the Prohibition of the Use in War of Asphyxiating, Poisonous or Other Gases, and of Bacteriological Methods of Warfare* (June 17, 1925); text at www.nti.org/e_research/official_docs/inventory/pdfs/geneva.pdf.

[9]Texts of the 1907 Hague Conventions (and annexes) are in 2 *American Journal of International Law* 90, 117, 153, 167 (1908); the text of most important treaties dealing with war (up to 1982) are in Roberts and Guelff, *Documents on the Laws of War*, 2nd ed. (1989); on air war, see U.S. Air Force, *International Law—the Conduct of Armed Conflict and Air Operations* (1976); on naval war, see U.S. Navy, *Law of Naval Warfare* in R. W. Tucker, *The Law of War and Neutrality* (1957) or U.S. Department of the Navy, NWIP 10–20, *Law of Naval Warfare* (1955, as amended in July 1959); and on Protocols I and II, texts in 16 *International Legal Materials* 1391 and 1442 (1977). On specialized treaties restricting the use of certain weapons and/or methods of warfare, see 7 *ILM* 809 (1968), on nuclear proliferation; 19 *ILM* 1523 (1980) and 20 *ILM*, at 567, 795, 1287 (1981), on certain weapons; 11 *ILM* 309 (1972), on bacteriological and toxin weapons; and 16 *ILM* 90 (1977), on environmental modification.

[10]In D. P. Forsythe's heavily documented "Legal Management Internal War: The 1977 Protocol on Noninternational Armed Conflicts," 72 *AJIL* 272 (1978).

generalities."[11] Nevertheless, Article 3 was the first example of a worldwide rule of international law requiring a state to treat its own citizens, rebels though they might be, in accordance with the minimum standards laid down by the "family of nations."

AP-II of 1977 itself is a rather interesting document. It reaffirms common Article 3 of the 1949 Conventions (Preamble), disavows the legitimacy of any form of discrimination in its application (Article 2(1)), and supplies a list of fundamental guarantees for those not taking a direct part or who have ceased to take part in hostilities, including a categorical prohibition of taking hostages and committing acts of "terrorism" (Article 4). It provides additional minimum safeguards for those whose liberty has been restricted (Article 5); offers detailed guidelines for the prosecution and punishment of criminal offenses related to the armed conflict, including a prohibition of punishment except after trial before an independent and impartial court (Article 6); outlines procedures to be applied concerning the wounded, the sick, and the shipwrecked (Articles 7–12); and supplies minimum protection directives for the civilian population, relative to the latter's being bombed or shelled. Its survival requirements prohibit attacks on installations containing "dangerous forces," for example, dams, dikes, and nuclear electric-generating stations—even if such should be genuine military objectives—if such attacks would cause severe civilian losses (Articles 13–18).[12]

Because almost all countries participating in the formulation of AP-II were opposed to incorporating any sort of enforcement mechanism in the instrument, the determination of its applicability still rests, in essence, with the governments and other agencies (including rebel movements) involved in any given noninternational armed conflict. But the fact that such an admittedly "weak" treaty dealing with such an explosive and emotionally upsetting topic as internal wars could come into being and achieve ratification by enough countries to enter into force gives hope for the future of the international regulation of internal wars. This is especially true in view of the evidence so carefully marshaled by Forsythe; namely, that in a very considerable proportion of the post–World War II civil wars, either or both parties involved accepted the obligations imposed by the common Article 3 of the Geneva Conventions of 1949.[13]

What Is a War Crime?

Generally, a war crime is any act for which soldiers or other individuals may be punished by the enemy on capture of the offender. The category includes acts committed in violation of international law and the laws of the combatant's own country as well as acts in violation of the laws of war undertaken *by order* and in the interest of the combatant's state of nationality. Current ideas about the nature of war crimes clearly depart from traditional legal attitudes toward the subject. For many years, offenses against the laws of war constituted crimes against the

---

[11]T. J. Farer, *The Laws of War 25 Years After Nuremberg* (International Conciliation no. 538 1971), 31. See also E. Luard, ed., *The International Regulation of Civil Wars* (1972); and J. N. Moore, ed., *Law and Civil War in the Modern World* (1974).

[12]See also G. Aldrich, "Human Rights and Armed Conflict," *Proceedings* (1973), 67 *AJIL* 141 (1973).

[13]See Forsythe, note 10, at 294.

municipal law of belligerents.[14] The defenses of act-of-state and superior orders conditioned prosecution for war crimes. The asserted *municipal* character of penal offenses against the laws of war was based also on the orthodox belief that individuals were not subjects of international law. Again, none of the pre-1914 conventions dealing with war crimes designated sanctions to be applied to states or to individuals for violations of the rules governing warfare. Article 3 of the Fourth Hague Convention of 1907 forms an exception. It called for payment of compensation by the belligerent state found guilty of violating the treaty.

Major Types of War Crimes

Most authorities agree on four types of war crimes:

1. Violations of the rules governing warfare
2. Hostile armed acts committed by persons who are not members of recognized armed forces
3. Espionage, sabotage, and war treason
4. All marauding acts

The first two headings raise the question of the definition of a *lawful combatant*. First developed in Article 1 of the Fourth Hague Convention of 1907, the definition has not varied a great deal since:

> The laws, rights and duties of war apply not only to armies, but also to militia and volunteer corps fulfilling the following conditions:
>
> 1. To be commanded by a person responsible for his subordinates
> 2. To have a fixed distinctive emblem recognizable at a distance
> 3. To carry arms openly
> 4. To conduct their operations in accordance with the laws and customs of war

Under the laws of warfare, lawful combatants should be permitted certain "privileges" if captured.[15] A lawful combatant possessing this privilege must be given "prisoner of war" (POW) status upon capture and immunity from criminal prosecution under the domestic law of his captor for his hostile acts that do not violate the laws and customs of war.[16]

The Geneva Conventions provide different schemes of protection depending upon the status of a particular individual under the conventions. Special rights in judicial proceedings are expressly provided for those having the status of POWs under the Third Convention and, in certain circumstances, for "protected persons" under the Fourth Convention. Protected or privileged combatants can be tried only for specific violations of the laws of war; that is, they cannot be tried for hostile acts that fall within the law. Unlike privileged combatants, captured unlawful

---

[14]G. Manner, "The Legal Nature and Punishment of Criminal Acts of Violence Contrary to the Laws of War," 37 *AJIL* 407, esp. 407, 414–415 (1943).

[15]The so-called privileged or lawful combatant is a person authorized by a party to an armed conflict to engage in hostilities and, as such, is entitled to the protections encompassed in the "combatant's privilege."

[16]R. K. Goldman and B. D. Tittemore, "Unprivileged Combatants and the Hostilities in Afghanistan: Their Status and Rights Under International Humanitarian and Human Rights Law," American Society of International Law (ASIL) Task Force on Terrorism (December 2002), www.asil.org/taskforce/goldman.pdf.

combatants can be tried and punished under municipal law for their unprivileged belligerency, even if their hostile acts complied with the laws of war. The status of "unprivileged" combatants and the means for determining that status have become controversial topics in the wake of the U.S. operations in Afghanistan and Iraq. We examine this issue briefly in the context of the contemporary law relating to POWs.

PRISONERS OF WAR

Prisoners taken in war have always posed a special problem. In antiquity, they were either killed or sold into slavery. After the coming of Christianity and until the sixteenth century, enslavement continued. St. Thomas Aquinas, for example, justified it by treating the reduction of prisoners to slaves as punishment for cowardice in combat and as a judgment of God under the concept of the ordeal by battle, in which only the just side would win and then was entitled to enslave its surviving opponents. Noble prisoners, on the other hand, normally were released on payment of a ransom, the amount depending on their rank and resources. Still later, special cartel arrangements for the treatment and return of prisoners were concluded, either at the outbreak of hostilities or soon thereafter. The end of the Thirty Years' War saw also the end of enslavement, and gradually humane considerations began to govern the treatment of captive enemies. An American–Russian Treaty of Friendship, concluded in 1785, is now generally regarded as containing the first stipulations of the decent treatment of POWs: it prohibited confinement in convict prisons (Article 24) and the employment of irons, and it required facilities for exercise.

Hague Conferences of 1899 and 1907

By the nineteenth century, the customary rules of law dictated the treatment of POWs at a standard comparable to that of the captor's own troops. There were no conventional rules on the subject until the Hague Conferences of 1899 and 1907. The 1907 Hague Regulations (Articles 4–20) provided in detail for the humane treatment of prisoners. Unfortunately, the actual practices of belligerents during World War I illustrated the inadequacy of the rules and the many gaps that needed to be filled. In July 1929, the representatives of 47 states met in Geneva at the invitation of the Swiss government in order to improve the earlier conventional law. The conference succeeded in drawing up two instruments—the Convention for the Amelioration of the Condition of the Wounded and Sick in Armies in the Field and the Convention relative to the Treatment of Prisoners of War. Following widespread ratification, both conventions were in effect when World War II began.[17] Only relations between Germany and the Soviet Union were not governed by those two instruments during the conflict. But, again, belligerent practices indicated the need for further conventional safeguards for POWs.

The Soviet Union committed one of the most serious violations of customary rules through its failure to repatriate its POWs at the end of World War II. A report published at the beginning of July 1952 by the Information Section of the North Atlantic Treaty Organization (NATO) indicated that of the more than 7 million prisoners taken by the Soviet Union, fewer than half had been repatriated by the middle of 1952.

---

[17]Convention Between the United States of America and Other Powers, Relating to Prisoners of War, July 27, 1929, The Avalon Project at Yale Law School, www.yale.edu/lawweb/avalon/lawofwar/geneva02.htm (accessed April 22, 2009).

About 1 million were reported dead or still held in the Soviet Union, and some 2.5 million were completely unaccounted for, including about 370,000 members of the Japanese forces in Manchuria who were captured at the very end of the war.[18]

The 1949 Geneva Conventions

The Geneva Conference of 1949 produced the new Convention Relative to the Treatment of Prisoners of War. This convention incorporated many new provisions based on the experiences of the last war. States ratified this new instrument quickly. It entered into effect on October 21, 1950. Owing to the extreme length of the 1949 Convention (143 articles) and the details incorporated in its provisions, an exhaustive analysis of the instrument would exceed the proper limits of a general text.[19] Hence, only a few significant features are mentioned here, together with some illustrative case materials.[20]

Comments on the 1949 Geneva Convention

As discussed in Chapter 21, under Article 2 of the convention, the instrument applies not only to all cases of declared war but also to all other armed conflicts that may arise between two or more of the contracting parties, even if the existence of a state of war is not recognized by one of them. The convention also applies to all cases of partial or total occupation of the territory of a contracting party, even if the occupation has not met with any armed resistance. Again, the convention applies in a war with a state that is not a party to the agreement, provided the latter accepts and applies the instrument's provisions. POWs *are to be regarded as in the custody of the capturing state* and not of particular armies or military units. They are entitled to humane treatment. They are entitled to the same maintenance as are troops of the same rank of the captor state. They are to be confined only to the extent that their detention is guaranteed and must not be punished except for acts committed by them after their capture.[21]

Under Article 17 of the convention, a POW, when questioned, "is bound to give only his surname, first names and rank, date of birth, and army regimental, personal or serial number, or failing this, equivalent information." Article 17(4) provides, "No physical or mental torture, nor any other form of coercion, may be inflicted on prisoners of war to secure from them information of any kind whatsoever."

[18]For further details from the report, see *Time* (July 7, 1952), 33. See also excerpts from *Kamibayashi et al. v. Japan*, Japan, Tokyo District Court (April 18, 1989), with introductory note by Adachi, in 29 *ILM* 391 (1990).

[19]See H. Fiisher, "Protection of Prisoners of War," in *The Handbook of Humanitarian Law in Armed Conflicts*, edited by D. Fleck (1995), 321–367, ch. 7; and Lauterpacht's *Oppenheim*, II: 369, for two exhaustive analyses of the provisions of the 1949 Convention. Consult also J. S. Pictet, "The New Geneva Conventions for the Protection of War Victims," 45 *AJIL* 462 (1951); R. T. Yingling and R. W. Ginnane, "The Geneva Conventions," 46 *AJIL* 393 (1952); and the thorough study by S. Levie, "Prisoners of War and the Protecting Power," 55 *AJIL* 374 (1961).

[20]One of the worst recorded crimes committed against prisoners of war was the execution by Soviet forces of more than 4,000 captured Polish officers in the Katyn Forest in 1940. The Soviet government admitted and apologized for the mass killing on April 13, 1990. Before then, it had denied responsibility and blamed the massacre on Nazi German forces. The Iraqi government violated several provisions of the Geneva Convention on January 21, 1991, when it telecast "interviews" with captured Allied personnel and announced that prisoners of war would be used as "human shields" against Allied air attacks.

[21]See D. P. Forsythe, "Who Guards the Guardians? Third Parties and the Law of Armed Conflict," 70 *AJIL* 41 (1976).

Insofar as the use of POWs as human shields is concerned, the 1949 Convention provides in Article 19(1), "Prisoners of war shall be evacuated, as soon as possible after their capture, to camps situated in an area far enough from the combat zone for them to be out of danger." In particular, Article 23(1) asserts, "No prisoner of war may at any time be sent to, or detained in, areas where he may be exposed to the fire of the combat zone, *nor may his presence be used to render certain points or areas immune from military operations*" (Emphasis added).

REX v. BROSIG

Ontario Court of Appeal, March 1, 1945, 2 D.L.R. 232

Facts

Brosig[22] was a German prisoner of war who was moved to Canada for detention. On December 21, 1943, he hid in a prisoner-of-war mailbag that was placed in the mail car of a Canadian train, next to a radiator in the car. The prisoner cut open the bag from the inside and then opened another mailbag containing parcels. From these he took some cigarettes, some chewing gum, and a bottle of perfume. He smoked some of the cigarettes and used some of the gum and also some of the perfume. He was later captured and charged with theft from the mails. The magistrate's court trying the initial case dismissed the charge, and the Crown appealed to the Court of Appeal.

Issue

Could an escaping prisoner of war be charged with the theft of goods stolen in the course of his escape and used by him?

Decision

The appeal was allowed, and a conviction of theft from the mails was recorded. A jail sentence of two months' duration was imposed, after which Brosig was to be returned to his prisoner-of-war camp.

Reasoning

The looting of the mailbag was not an act necessary to Brosig's escape. It served no military purpose and represented an offense against civil authority for the personal advantage of the prisoner of war. The court cited with approval the finding of the Magistrate's Court: "With regard to the perfume, I have given him the benefit of the doubt and say that he used it in order to assist his escape by concealing the extreme odour of perspiration. With regard to the cigarettes and gum I am unable to see that they would assist his escape materially and I feel that he took them for his own comfort."

Enlisted personnel may be put to work not directly assisting the war effort of the captor state and are to be paid for such work. Officers cannot lawfully be forced to perform such work but may do so on a purely voluntary basis (Articles 50–68). All prisoners are to be paid at the rate applicable to their rank at the time of capture, the actual terms of payment being outlined in the convention (Article 69).

---

[22]On the acceptance of the Potsdam Declaration by the Japanese government, some 600,000 Japanese soldiers surrendered to Soviet forces in Manchuria, Sakhalin, and the Kurile Islands. Most of the captives were deported to northern Soviet regions to perform reconstruction work. Some 68,000 of the prisoners died before repatriation. See the interesting case of war claims by former prisoners in *Kamibayashi et al. v. Japan*, Tokyo District Court, April 18, 1989, in 29 *ILM* 391 (1990).

Article 85 of the convention specifies, "Prisoners of war prosecuted under the laws of the Detaining Power for acts committed prior to capture shall retain, even if convicted, the benefits of the present convention." Until the United States ratified the convention in 1956, the American official attitude had been that POWs tried for war crimes were not entitled to the judicial safeguards of the 1929 Geneva Convention.[23]

An unsuccessful attempt to escape may result only in disciplinary punishment; on the other hand, force may be used against prisoners to prevent an escape, and it is considered lawful to shoot at, and kill, an escaping prisoner. If, on the other hand, an escaping prisoner commits criminal offenses not directly connected with his escape, he may be punished for those acts. This rule was illustrated clearly in the following case.

Allegations of mistreatment of Iraqi POWs by British and American troops surfaced in May 2003.[24] In late July, the U.S. Army filed charges against four members of the military police accused of hitting Iraqi prisoners and breaking their bones at Camp Bucca in southern Iraq. Eight marines, including the commanding officer, were charged in the death of Nagam Sadoon Hatab at Camp Whitehorse. An investigation into alleged abuses at Abu Ghraib prison outside Baghdad began in January 2004. A full-scale scandal flared in April 2004, when damning photographs of American personnel abusing prisoners were published. Seventeen soldiers, including officers, were removed from duty. The army charged ten with "maltreatment, aggravated assault, battery, and dereliction of duty." Four were convicted by court-martial. Six others reached plea deals, and all except one received prison sentences. All received dishonorable discharges. The army demoted the commanding officer at the prison from brigadier general to colonel.[25]

A Note on Determining "Unlawful Combatants": The United States, al-Qaeda, and Afghanistan

The Geneva Conventions contain references to combatants, POWs, and civilians. A recent commentary notes:[26]

> Whereas the terms "combatant," "prisoner of war," and "civilian" are general[ly] used and defined in the treaties of international humanitarian law, the terms "unlawful combatant," [and] "unprivileged combatant/belligerent" do not appear in them. They have, however, been frequently used at least

---

[23]See In re Yamashita, 327, U.S. 1 (1946). See also Chapter 22.

[24]M. Lacey, "Aftereffects: Human Rights; Iraqi Detainees Claim Abuse by British and U.S. Troops," *New York Times* (May 17, 2003), 11. Three of the four detainees accepted nonjudicial punishment in lieu of a court-martial. Punishment included an administrative discharge and forfeiture of two months' pay. Two detainees accepted a reduction in rank. Charges were dropped against the fourth.

[25]D. S. Cloud, "Private Gets 3 Years for Iraq Prison Abuse," *New York Times* (September 28, 2005), 20.

[26]K. Dormann, "The Legal Situation of 'Unlawful/Unprivileged Combatants,'" 85 *Int'l Rev. Red Cross* 849 (2003), 46.

since the beginning of the last century in legal literature, military manuals and case law. The connotations given to these terms and their consequences for the applicable protection regime are not always very clear.

The important question here is, what status does an unprivileged belligerent have? One long-standing opinion is that designation as an unlawful combatant leaves individuals with few or none of the protections they would have as POWs.[27] This reflects the traditional idea of war as state against state. Acting on behalf of a state has historically formed the rationale for most obligations and rights provided by international law. Hence, a soldier deserving POW status legitimately acts on behalf of a state. An unlawful combatant unlike a POW would be liable for all activities, including "killing the enemy." The difficulties caused by this assumption in the original four Geneva Conventions are reflected in the efforts to develop AP-I and AP-II.[28] Still, the uncertain status of those characterized as illegitimate participants "is evidenced by the variety of terms used to describe them such as unlawful combatants, unprivileged belligerents, enemy combatants, terrorists or insurgents."[29] More recent commentary has supported the idea that while unprivileged status may deprive combatants of the benefits of POW status, it cannot deprive them of a right to humane treatment.[30]

After 9/11, the United States has held a number of suspected terrorists without charges and without access to attorneys or courts.[31] Much of the controversy involves the legal status of individuals captured in Afghanistan who fought for the Taliban and/or were associated with al-Qaeda. Secretary of Defense Donald Rumsfeld stated that the United States would treat the detainees humanely as a matter of policy, but denied any *legal* obligation to do so.[32] The U.S. attorney in the *Hamdi v. Rumsfeld* case, Paul J. McNulty, stated, "[I]t is well-settled that the

---

[27]R. R. Baxter argues, "Privileged [belligerents] have a protected status upon capture, whilst other belligerents not so identified do not benefit from any comprehensive scheme of protection." Baxter, "So-Called 'Unprivileged Belligerency': Spies, Guerrillas and Saboteurs," *British Yearbook of International Law* 328 (1951), 343. For other evidence supporting this position, see D. Jinks, "The Declining Significance of POW Status," 45 *Harvard Int'l L. J.* 367 (2004), 368–370.

[28]The possibility of extending combatant status to "terrorists" formed one reason given by the United States for refusing to ratify AP-I. President Ronald Reagan stated that the perceived legitimization of "wars of national liberation" and the granting of combatant status to irregular forces that do not satisfy the traditional criteria for legitimate participation "would endanger civilians among whom terrorists and other irregulars attempt to conceal themselves." See "Letter of Transmittal, Agora: The U.S. Decision Not to Ratify Protocol I to the Geneva Conventions on the Protection of War Victims," 81 *AJIL* 81, 911 (1987).

[29]K. Watkin, "Warriors Without Rights? Combatants, Unprivileged Belligerents, and the Struggle over Legitimacy," Program on Humanitarian Policy and Conflict Research, Harvard University Occasional Paper Series, no. 2 (2005), 5–6.6, www.hpcr.org/pdfs/OccasionalPaper2.pdf (accessed April 22, 2009).

[30]See Dorman, note 26; and Jinks, note 27.

[31]P. Shenon, "Appeals Court Keeps an American Detainee and His Lawyer Apart," *New York Times* (July 13, 2002), 8.

[32]Fact Sheet, White House Press Office, "Status of Detainees at Guantanamo," February 7, 2002, www.whitehouse.gov/news/releases/2002/02/20020207-13.html (accessed April 22, 2009).

military has the authority to capture and detain individuals whom it has determined are enemy combatants" and that such combatants "have no right of access to counsel to challenge their detention."[33] The *Hamdi* case involved Yaser Esam Hamdi, a 21-year-old detainee captured on the battlefield in Afghanistan. The government had characterized Hamdi, who was born in Louisiana but reared in Saudi Arabia, as an "enemy combatant" rather than a POW. The government claimed that the designation as an enemy (or unlawful) combatant presumably deprived Hamdi of the protection of the Geneva Conventions and U.S. courts of any claim to jurisdiction.[34]

In sifting through the problems here, we must first distinguish between applicable international law and the procedural complexities of American domestic law. Until the U.S. Supreme Court decisions in *Rasul v. Bush*[35] and *Hamdi v. Rumsfeld*[36] in June 2004, while lawyers debated the international legal ramifications of the Bush administration's position, U.S. courts focused on the scope of their competence to deal with many of the relevant issues. The areas of concern involved (1) the effective territorial reach of the U.S. Constitution—do federal courts have jurisdiction with respect to Guantánamo Bay (particularly the capacity to hear habeas corpus petitions);[37] (2) an interesting (but ongoing) separation of powers issue—whether the president has the *sole* authority (without judicial review) to define the status of detainees taken in various operations against the Taliban and al-Qaeda; and (3) questions relating to the status, non-self-executing or self-executing (Chapter 4), of the Geneva Conventions. The courts have yet to rule on the substantive questions of how to determine "enemy combatant" status. As a result of the two Supreme Court decisions, the Department of Defense established Combatant Status Review Tribunals (CSRTs).[38]

The Supreme Court decision in *Hamdan v. Rumsfeld* (November 2006) decided a number of these issues.[39] Salim Ahmed Hamdan had served as a driver and bodyguard for Osama Bin Laden and other high-ranking al-Qaeda members. Hamdan had challenged the constitutional basis of the Military Commissions. The court held that President Bush had exceeded his authority in unilaterally establishing the military commissions, that the commissions violated the Geneva Convention,

---

[33]K. Seelye, "Traces of Terror: The Courts; U.S. Defends Limits on American in Custody," *New York Times* (June 20, 2002), 20; and see T. Franck, "Criminals, Combatants or What? An Examination of the Role of Law in Responding to the Threat of Terror," 98 *AJIL* 686 (2004).

[34]See, in contrast, the case of John Walker Lindh, captured at the same time as Hamdi. After considerable debate, the government decided to try him in a civilian court. W. Washington, "Fighting Terror/American Taliban; Lindh Makes Deal, Enters Guilty Pleas Agrees to Aid Government, Faces 20-Year Sentence," *Boston Globe* (July 16, 2002), A1.

[35]124 S. Ct. 2686 (2004); decision of June 28, 2004.

[36]124 S. Ct. 2633 (2004), decision of June 28, 2004.

[37]The founders thought this important enough to include in the U.S. Constitution. For the definitive treatment, see R. Hertz and J. Liebman, *Federal Habeas Corpus Practice and Procedure*, 5th ed. (2 vols, 2005).

[38]See www.defenselink.mil/news/Mar2006/d20060315arb2.pdf (accessed April 22, 2009). This site is updated on a regular basis.

[39]Hamdan v. Rumsfeld, 548 U.S. 557 (2006).

and that the commissions violated U.S. military law.[40] The Congress almost immediately passed the Military Commissions Act of 2006.[41] Authorities again charged Hamdan with conspiracy to commit war crimes and material support for terrorism in February 2007. In April 2007, the Supreme Court dismissed a lawsuit by Hamdan and another detainee, Omar Khadr, challenging the legality of the trials.[42] In June 2007, a U.S. military judge dismissed all charges on the basis that Hamdan's status was that of an "enemy combatant," not that of an "unlawful enemy combatant"; thus the commission lacked jurisdiction to try them.[43]

In September, a newly constituted Court of Military Commission Review, established by the 2006 Military Commissions Act, reinstated the charges against Khadr. The panel held that a military judge presiding over a military commission may determine both the factual issue of an accused's "unlawful enemy combatant status" and the corresponding legal issue of the commission's jurisdiction to hear the case.[44] After an unsuccessful appeal to the Supreme Court, in December, a review panel found that Hamdan did not have POW status.[45] This permitted the trial before a Military Commission to go forward. The trial, held in late August July, resulted in Hamdan's conviction for providing material support for terrorism. He received a sentence of five-and-a-half years with credit for time served.[46]

A second trial before a Military Commission in late October 2008 found a second defendant, Ali Hamza al-Bahlul, guilty on 35 counts of solicitation for committing murder, providing material support for terrorism, and conspiracy.[47] He received a life sentence. In October 2010, Khadr pled guilty to murder in violation of the laws of war, attempted murder in violation of the laws of war, conspiracy, and two counts of providing material support for terrorism and spying. Under the plea deal, Khadr would serve one more year in Guantánamo Bay, and then be returned to Canada.[48] One other event merits mention here. In a July 2008 ruling, the Supreme Court declared some key parts of the Military Commissions Act unconstitutional.[49] Shortly afterward, another detainee—Mohamed Sulaymon Barre—filed a suit challenging his designation as an enemy combatant.[50] He was released and repatriated to Somalia in December 2009.

---

[40]Hamdan v. Rumsfeld, Summary of Judgment, paras. 3, 4.

[41]*Military Commissions Act of 2006*, S.3930, 10 U.S.C.S. §§ 948a et seq. (2006).

[42]A. Goldstein, "Justices Again Refuse Guantanamo Bay Cases," *Washington Post* (May 1, 2007), A04. When captured, Khadr was only 15 years old.

[43]W. Glaberson, "Military Judges Dismisses Charges for Two Detainees," *New York Times* (June 5, 2007), 1.

[44]J. White, "Court Reverses Ruling on Detainees," *Washington Post* (September 25, 2007), A04.

[45]B. Fox, "Guantanamo Judge: Bin Laden Driver No POW, Must Face Military Trial," AP Wire (December 20, 2007).

[46]W. Glaberson, "Panel Convicts Bin Laden Driver in Split Verdict," *New York Times* (August 7, 2008), 1.

[47]P. Finn, "Guantanamo Jury Sentences Bin Laden Aide to Life Term," *Washington Post* (November 4, 2008), A10.

[48]P. Koring, "Deal or No Deal No Justice for Khadr," *Toronto Globe and Mail* (October 25, 2010).

[49]Boumediene v. Bush, 128 S. Ct. 2229 (2008). In particular, the court found that the guarantee of habeas corpus was one of the core rights embedded in the Constitution even before the Bill of Rights.

[50]Barre v. Gates. See also Zalita v. Gates and Zalita v. Bush. See J. White and D. Weber, "Guantanamo Detainee to File Habeas Petition," *Washington Post* (July 26, 2008), A14.

In March 2009, the Obama Administration announced a new definitional standard for the government's authority to detain terrorist suspects, which does not use the phrase "enemy combatant" to refer to persons who may be properly detained. The new standard is similar in scope to the "enemy combatant" standard used by the Bush Administration to detain terrorist suspects. The standard would permit the detention of members of the Taliban, Al Qaeda, and associated forces, along with persons who provide "substantial support" to such groups, regardless of whether such persons were captured away from the battlefield in Afghanistan. Courts that have considered the executive's authority to detain under the AUMF[51] and law of war have reached differing conclusions as to the scope of this detention authority. In January 2010, a DC Circuit panel held that support for or membership in an AUMF-targeted organization may constitute a sufficient ground to justify military detention.[52]

Termination of Captivity

Other questions arise regarding length of detention. As noted earlier, the conventions visualize a situation of traditional war of state against state, not an open-ended conflict. Article 118 states:

> Prisoners of war shall be released and repatriated without delay after the cessation of active hostilities. In the absence of stipulations to the above effect in any agreement concluded between the Parties to the conflict with a view to the cessation of hostilities, or failing any such agreement, each of the Detaining Powers shall itself establish and execute without delay a plan of repatriation in conformity with the principle laid down in the foregoing paragraph.

Given the indeterminate nature of many conflicts, this raises some interesting questions with respect to the Guantánamo detainees as well as those Afghans and Iraqis who may have POW status. In the past, problems have occurred with repatriation because detainees did not wish to return or because of other continuing political differences between the former belligerents.[53] The 1929 Geneva Convention had stipulated merely that the repatriation of healthy prisoners should be effected as soon as possible after the conclusion of peace. The importance of the 1949 rule regarding the immediate release when *hostilities* have ended stemmed from problems encountered at the end of World War II. The experts at Geneva in 1949 had assumed that every POW would want to go home as soon as possible. This somewhat erroneous impression should not have prevailed in view of certain events that occurred at the end of World War II. Then, the Western Allies captured thousands of Russian citizens who had joined General Andrei Vlasov's anti-Communist army

---

[51]Authorization for Use of Military Force (September 18, 2001), Public Law 107-40 [S. J. RES. 23].

[52]J. K. Elsea and M. J. Garcia, *Enemy Combatant Detainees: Habeas Corpus Challenges in Federal Courts*, Congressional Research Service (February 3, 2010), www.fas.org/sgp/crs/natsec/RL33180.pdf.

[53]See P. B. Potter, "Repatriation of Korean Prisoners of War," 47 *AJIL* 661 (1953); J. P. Charmatz and H. M. Wit, "The Repatriation of Prisoners of War and the 1949 Geneva Convention," 62 *Yale L. J.* 391 (1953); and H. Levie, "Legal Aspects of the Continued Detention of the Pakistani Prisoners of War by India," 67 *AJIL* 512 (1973).

on the side of Germany and had fled westward as the Soviet armies advanced into Germany. Despite pleas not to be repatriated because of their well-founded fears of being tried for treason, these Russians were forcibly repatriated by the Western forces. Many, including General Vlasov, were executed as traitors.

The Korean conflict posed a different problem. Thousands of North Koreans as well as Chinese "volunteers" refused to be returned to their countries for ideological reasons. Concurrence in this request by the UN Command created a dilemma that proved to be a key reason for the delay until 1956 of U.S. ratification of the four Geneva Conventions of 1949. By then, those prisoners who were unwilling to return to North Korea or China had been screened and dispersed after release; by early 1954, slightly over 14,000 Chinese soldiers had already been transferred to Taiwan.[54]

After the Vietnam conflict, all U.S. POWs were repatriated within weeks after the conclusion of the Paris Peace Agreements of January 27, 1973. The exchange of captured personnel between the two Vietnams, on the other hand, was not completed until March 8, 1974. In the India–Pakistan conflict of 1971, repatriation was delayed for several years until a series of complicated solutions had been worked out in the India–Pakistan Agreement on Repatriation of Prisoners of War (August 28, 1973) and an instrument on Repatriation of Prisoners of War and Civilian Internees (April 9, 1974).[55] Treatment of POWs in these conflicts led to a reiteration and an expansion of the 1949 Geneva Convention provisions governing these individuals in the new AP-I of 1977 (Articles 44–45, 72–75). The major additions to the already existing regulations consisted of a much more carefully detailed description of the role and rights of an outside protecting power and a more detailed list of prohibited acts against POWs.

LIMITING THE MEANS OF WAR

The following list, although not complete, includes many of the major acts falling under the concept of violations of the laws of war, whether committed by lawful combatants or others:

1. Using poisoned or otherwise forbidden arms or munitions
2. Treachery in asking for quarter or simulating sickness or wounds
3. Maltreating corpses
4. Firing on localities that are undefended and without military significance
5. Abusing or firing on a flag of truce
6. Misusing the Red Cross or similar emblems
7. Troops wearing civilian clothes to conceal their identity during the commission of combat acts
8. Improperly using privileged (exempt, immune) buildings for military purposes
9. Poisoning streams or wells

---

[54]See J. Mayda, "The Korean Repatriation Problem," 47 AJIL 414 (1953); Potter's Note on "Repatriation of Prisoners," 46 *AJIL* 508 (1952).

[55]Texts in 12 *ILM* 1080 (1973) and 13 *ILM* 501 (1974); see also H. Levie, "The Indo-Pakistani Agreement of August 28, 1973," 68 *AJIL* 95 (1974); and India-Pakistan, "Agreement on the Release and Repatriation of Detained Persons" (New Delhi, April 9, 1974), in 13 *ILM* 603 (1974).

10. Pillaging or committing purposeless destruction
11. Compelling prisoners of war or civilians to engage in prohibited types of labor
12. Violating surrender terms
13. Killing or wounding military personnel who have laid down arms, have surrendered, or are disabled by wounds or sickness[56]
14. Ill-treating prisoners of war or the wounded and sick—including despoiling them of possessions not classifiable as public property[57]
15. Killing or attacking harmless civilians[58]
16. Willful killing, torture, or inhuman treatment, including biological experiments
17. Collective punishments
18. Taking of hostages
19. Acts of terrorism
20. Outrages upon personal dignity, in particular humiliating and degrading treatment, rape, enforced prostitution, and any form of indecent assault
21. Slavery and the slave trade in all their forms

A quick look at the list should convey an underlying principle—the right of belligerents to adopt means of injuring the enemy is not unlimited. The difficulty comes from the rather vague language of the articles in question. For example, do these cover starvation as a deliberate tactic? Does this practice, common in several modern wars, represent a violation because it may disregard another fundamental distinction between combatants and noncombatants?[59]

In this regard, consider that the idea that needless suffering should be avoided extends to weapons. Article 36 of Geneva AP-I represents an innovative addition to the law of war:[60]

> In the study, development, acquisition or adoption of a new weapon, means or method of warfare, a High Contracting Party is under an obligation to determine whether its employment would, in some or all circumstances, be prohibited by this Protocol or by any other rule of international law applicable to the High Contracting Party.

AP-I, Article 35(2), forbids the employment of arms, projectiles, and other material calculated to cause unnecessary suffering. The prohibition again is somewhat vague. It essentially leaves each state free to decide whether to utilize a certain weapon because in its judgment the weapon possesses or lacks the prohibited

---

[56]Such as the massacre of more than 4,000 captive Polish Army officers by the Russian secret police (NKVD) in the Katyn Forest in the spring of 1940 (see note 21).

[57]Geneva IV of 1949, Article 34; AP-I of 1977, Article 75(2c); and AP-II, Article 4(2c).

[58]Such as the German massacre of 33,771 Jews at Babi Yar (Soviet Union) on September 29–30, 1941, and, in 1944, of all but one of the 644 inhabitants of the French village of Oradour-sur-Glane: see W. Korey, "What Monument to Babi Yar?" *Saturday Review* (February 3, 1968), 18, 40; and "The Lammerding Affair," *Time* (January 11, 1971), 22.

[59]See AP-I, Article 54(1): "starvation of civilians is forbidden."

[60]Consult, inter alia, letters from the General Counsel, Department of Defense, to Chairman, Senate Foreign Relations Committee, in 66 AJIL 382 (1972); and the panel discussion by Matheson, Blix, Delessert, and Paust on "Should Weapons of Dubious Legality Be Developed?" Proceedings 26 (1978), as well as 69 AJIL 397 (1975).

effect. State practice has sanctioned the use of explosives in artillery shells, mines, and hand grenades. On the other hand, such weapons as lances with barbed heads, irregularly shaped bullets, shells filled with glass, and the application of some substance to bullets, intended to inflame a wound, have been accepted as forbidden. During World War I, both sides accused the other of using dum-dum bullets[61]—bullets designed to expand or fragment upon impact—but at most, only individual instances were substantiated.

The drafters of the 1977 Protocols had decided at the time that the prohibition of certain specific weapons should be left to a future meeting, to be called by the United Nations and to be restricted to that particular subject. The General Assembly thereupon convened the UN Conference on Prohibitions or Restrictions of Use of Certain Conventional Weapons Which May Be Deemed to Be Excessively Injurious or to Have Indiscriminate Effects. On October 10, 1980, the conference adopted the Convention on Prohibitions or Restrictions of Use of Certain Conventional Weapons Which May Be Deemed to Be Excessively Injurious or to Have Indiscriminate Effects (Geneva 1980 Convention); the Protocol on Non-detectable Fragments (1980 PA-1); the Protocol on Prohibitions or Restrictions on the Use of Mines, Booby-Traps and Other Devices (1980 PA-2); and the Protocol on Prohibitions or Restrictions on the Use of Incendiary Weapons (1980 PA-3).[62] The 1980 Geneva Convention and its protocols apply in the situations referred to in Article 2 common to the four Geneva Conventions of 1949, including any situation described in paragraph 4 of Article 1 of PA-1 (wars against colonial domination, alien occupation, and racist regimes).

The 1980 PA-2 relates to the use on land of mines, booby traps, and other devices—including mines laid to interdict beaches, waterways, or river crossings—but does not apply to the use of anti-ship mines at sea or in inland waterways. The protocol prohibits, in essence, the use of the instruments listed against the civilian population as such or against individual civilians, even by way of reprisals, and the indiscriminate use of devices that could be expected to cause loss of life or injury to civilians that is excessive in relation to the concrete and direct military advantage anticipated. The use of the weapons listed is also forbidden in any area primarily inhabited by civilians where no combat between ground forces is taking place, unless the device is planted on or next to a military objective.

Interest in banning land mines as a weapon culminated in the Ottawa Treaty of 1997 (currently 150 states parties).[63] A continuing major problem with land

---

[61]The dum-dum was a British military bullet developed in the late 1890s (at the Dum-Dum arsenal) for use in India. The dum-dum was a .303-caliber bullet with the jacket nose open to expose its lead core. The purpose was to improve the bullet's effective striking power by increasing its expansion upon impact. The term dum-dum later came to include any soft-nosed or hollow-point bullet. The Hague Convention of 1899 outlawed the use of dum-dum bullets during warfare. See FirstWorldWar. com, www.firstworldwar.com/atoz/dumdum.htm.

[62]Final act and texts of all instruments in 19 *ILM* 1523 (1980), 1536; see also 20 ILM 567, 795, 1287 (1981). The convention and its annexed protocols entered into force on December 2, 1983, but not for the United States. See, however, 88 *AJIL* 748 (1994).

[63]1997 Convention on the Prohibition of the Use, Stockpiling, Production and Transfer of Anti-Personnel Mines and on their Destruction (1997 Mine Ban Treaty, done at Ottawa on December 3, 1997), www.icbl.org/treaty/text/english (accessed April 22, 2009). The United States is not a state party.

mines is that 60–100 million uncleared antipersonnel mines still lie scattered in scores of countries. The countries with the highest concentration are Afghanistan (10–15 million), Angola (9 million), Cambodia (4–7 million), Iraqi Kurdistan (4 million), the former Yugoslavia (almost 3 million), and Mozambique (2 million).[64]

Incendiary Weapons

In accordance with the Declaration of St. Petersburg of December 11, 1868, seventeen states had agreed to prohibit, for themselves and such other states as would adhere to the declaration, the use of any projectile weighing less than 14 ounces (400 grams) that is charged with some inflammable substance or is explosive in nature. By contrast, the use of weapons employing fire (tracer ammunition, flamethrowers, napalm bombs, or sprayers) is not prohibited by any rule or treaty. Napalm, used extensively in World War II, the Korean War, the Vietnamese conflict, and the first Gulf War, has frequently been characterized as an illegal weapon and singled out for regulation. Hence the 1980 PA-2, dealing with incendiary weapons, proved to be the most controversial of the protocols. During negotiations, some of the nonaligned countries (Mexico, Syria, and others) insisted that restrictions against aerial bombardment with napalm or other firebombs should be included. The United States, the Soviet Union, and the other major military powers refused to consider an absolute ban on incendiary weapons but did reach a compromise. The 1980 PA-3 prohibits the use of incendiary weapons against civilian populations and the use of air-delivered incendiary weapons against a military objective located in a concentration of civilians (Article 2(2)).

Poison Gas and Related Weapons

The First Hague Conference (1899) adopted a declaration, signed by 16 states, that prohibited the parties from using shells to distribute asphyxiating gases. This prohibition was, obviously, fully in accord with outlawing the use of poison and with the humane endeavor to avoid causing unnecessary suffering. The U.S. delegation refused to sign this prohibition as inconsistent with already accepted methods of warfare.

When Germany used poison gas—chlorine, then mustard gas—in World War I (1917), the Allies retaliated in kind, justifying their action as a reprisal. Both sides stopped gas warfare upon discovering that they could not control the drift of clouds of poison gas. The peace treaties ending the conflict reiterated the prohibition on asphyxiating gases. On June 17, 1925, the Geneva Gas Protocol prohibiting the use in war of asphyxiating, poisonous, or other gases, as well as of bacteriological methods of warfare, was signed by the U.S. delegate as well as the representatives of 28 states (in force April 3, 1929).[65] The U.S. Senate, however, did not give its

---

[64]For up-to-date information on the status of activities connected with the treaty, see International Campaign to Ban Landmines, www.icbl.org/lm/2004/developments (accessed April 22, 2009).

[65]Text in 64 *AJIL* 387 (1970). Consult also W. O'Brien, "Biological/Chemical Warfare and the International Law of War," 51 *Georgetown L. J.* 1 (Fall 1962); and the valuable, thoroughly documented study by R. R. Baxter and T. Buergenthal, "Legal Aspects of the Geneva Protocol of 1925,"

consent to ratification until December 16, 1974. Because 128 countries are now bound by the protocol, most writers today agree that the Geneva instrument is binding on all states through the development of a general rule of customary international law springing from the provisions of the protocol. The United States was not bound prior to Senate ratification because, since 1925, the U.S. government had consistently objected to the rules involved. Interestingly, the Geneva Protocol does not prohibit the production, acquisition, stockpiling, or use for nonwar purposes of the forbidden substances of warfare—only their use in conflict.

Post World War I, despite the Geneva Protocol, there have been many alleged uses of chemical weapons: Italy in Ethiopia (1935–1936), Japan in China (1939–1944), United States in Vietnam (Agent Orange, 1962–1968), Egypt in Yemen (1967), USSR in Afghanistan (1980–1984), Ethiopia against Eritrean rebel forces (1980), Iraq against Iran (1984–1985), and Iraq against the Kurds (Halabja, 1988). Chemical and bacteriological weapons were not used to any extent during World War II, even though both sides were prepared for such an eventuality. The major reason for abstaining from use of such weapons probably may be found in an inability to protect military and civilians alike against the retaliatory use of similar weapons by an enemy and the practical logistical difficulties of using them effectively. On April 2, 1990, Iraqi President Saddam Hussein declared that his country possessed nerve gas weapons and would use them against Israel if attacked—apparently a reference to a possible second Israeli attack on Iraq's nuclear reactor complex.[66]

In November 1969, U.S. President Richard Nixon renounced a first use of lethal chemical weapons and extended that renunciation to the first use of incapacitating chemicals. He also renounced any use of any method of biological warfare (restricting research in related subject matter to purely defensive measures) and ordered the disposal of existing stocks of bacteriological weapons. The president also urged the Senate to approve ratification of the Geneva Protocol.[67] In February 1970, the president extended the ban on the production and use of biological weapons to cover military toxins—that is, poisons biologically produced but used as chemical warfare agents. Subsequently, in December 1974, the U.S. Senate gave its consent to the ratification of the 1925 Protocol. The instrument entered into force for the United States on February 10, 1975.[68]

After more than 20 years of negotiation, the 39-nation UN Conference on Disarmament at Geneva completed a new comprehensive treaty banning the production, possession, and use of chemical weapons in November 1992: the UN Convention on the Prohibition of the Development, Production, Stockpiling and Use of Chemical Weapons and on Their Destruction.[69] The long instrument (192

---

[66]*AJIL* 853 (1970). Federation of American Scientists (FAS), "Weapons of Mass Destruction, Chemical Weapons Programs: History," www.fas.org/nuke/guide/iraq/cw/program.htm.

[67]Text in 64 *AJIL* 386 (1970). On the subject of chemical, bacteriological, and biological warfare, see the excellent analyses by Thatcher, "Poison in the Wind" [A Special Christian Science Monitor Report], Christian Science Monitor (December 13, 1988), B1–16; (December 14, 1988), B1–12; (December 15, 1988), B1–12; and (December 16, 1988), B1–12.

[68]See 14 *ILM,* 299, 794 (1975), for relevant documents.

[69]Text in *ILM* 800 (1993); see also "Chemical Weapons Convention," 88 *AJIL* 323 (1994), for a summary.

pages; two-thirds of the text relates to verification) currently has 185 states parties (including the United States).[70] Almost all countries in the world have joined
the Chemical Weapons Convention (CWC). As of June 2011, a total of 188 states
are party to the CWC. Of the states remaining outside the regime, two—Burma
and Israel—have signed but not yet ratified the treaty; five—Angola, North Korea,
Egypt, Somalia, and Syria—have not signed.[71]

Following the development of numerous drafts, the UN General Assembly
adopted—on February 20, 1972—the Convention on the Prohibition of the Development, Production and Stockpiling of Bacteriological (Biological) and Toxin
Weapons and on Their Destruction. The convention was signed by representatives
of 61 governments on April 10, 1972, in ceremonies in Washington, London, and
Moscow. It entered into force on March 26, 1975.[72] In this instance, alleged violations are to be reported to the Security Council for investigation and report. The
virtually unanimous support for the 1972 Convention resulted from two factors:
the splitting off of biological weapons from the general category of chemical weapons and the realization by the major powers that no defensible rationale existed for
the use of biological weapons.

Nuclear Weapons

Most controversial—although not a problem before World War II—has been
the use of nuclear weapons, whether delivered by land, sea, or air forces. As yet,
there is no *specific* conventional rule outlawing or limiting the use of atomic or
nuclear weapons.[73] Responsible authorities, notably the late Sir Hersch Lauterpacht, believe that the use of any such weapons ought to be prohibited if it
could be demonstrated that the aftereffects of their use would place them in the
sphere of "biological" warfare, while at the same time not objecting to their use
against strictly military objectives.[74] Lauterpacht expressed deep concern over the
abandonment—insofar as bombing was concerned—of the traditional distinction
between combatants and noncombatants, writing that to admit the impossibility
of preserving that distinction was "to admit that in modern conditions there is
no longer room for one of the most fundamental aspects of the traditional law of
war."[75] He then went on to state that even with the use of atomic weapons, the
distinction would invariably be obliterated.

---

[70]See www.cwc.gov/cwc_about.html.

[71]The treaty is monitored by an independent organization, the Organization for the Prohibition of
Chemical Weapons (OPCW), www.opcw.org/chemical-weapons-convention/.

[72]Text on the convention (and related documents) in 11 *ILM* 309 (1972). The U.S. Senate gave its
consent to ratification on December 16, 1974. See also S. Wright, ed., *Preventing a Biological Arms
Race* (1990), review by Weston in 86 *AJIL* 849 (1992).

[73]Thus, the United States Law of Naval Warfare (current edition) states in para. 613, "there is at
present no rule of international law expressly prohibiting states from the use of nuclear weapons in
warfare. In the absence of express prohibition, the use of such weapons against enemy combatants
and other military objectives is permitted."

[74]Lauterpacht's *Oppenheim*, II: 348.

[75]Ibid., 350. This would be true in an all-out nuclear war, as distinct from the use of tactical nuclear
weapons in battlefield situations (present writer's comment).

There can be little doubt that the destruction of existing nuclear weapons, together with the creation of a working system of inspection to make certain that no more such weapons were being manufactured on the sly, would represent a great advance. Unfortunately, all attempts to reach such an agreement have failed thus far. In 1963, the United States, the United Kingdom, and the Soviet Union signed the Partial Test Ban Treaty (PTBT) banning nuclear tests in the atmosphere, outer space, and under water, but not underground. Underground testing was continued by the United States, the Soviet Union, France, Great Britain, and China. Testing in the Pacific areas was ended by the Western countries (except for France) some 30 years ago. However, after years of negotiations, the Nuclear Non-proliferation Treaty was signed by more than 60 states on July 1, 1968, at parallel ceremonies in Washington, London, and Moscow.[76] By 2009, a total of 191 states had ratified the treaty.

The agreement specified that the sponsoring powers would not give nuclear weapons—or control over them—to other states, nor would they help others make such weapons. Parties to the treaty not possessing nuclear weapons waived their right (for 25 years) to acquire or manufacture such weapons for their own defense. One of the key articles (Article 3) recognized the International Atomic Energy Agency as the authority exercising overall control over safeguards in all peaceful nuclear activities in any state party to the treaty. Inspections were to be carried out by the agency. The nuclear powers also pledged to provide immediate assistance to any nonnuclear state facing nuclear aggression or threats of such aggression.

In 1991, states parties to the PTBT held an amendment conference that year to discuss a proposal to convert the treaty into an instrument banning all nuclear weapon tests. With strong support from the UN General Assembly, negotiations for a comprehensive test-ban treaty began in 1993. Very quickly, different priorities emerged. The nonaligned movement countries focused upon so-called *vertical* proliferation (increasing numbers and new bomb technology), while the nuclear powers focused on *horizontal* proliferation (nuclear weapons produced by states other than themselves). The Comprehensive Test Ban Treaty opened for signature in September 1996. As of June, 2011, the treaty had been ratified by 154 states and signed by another 28, but it had not entered into force because of the peculiar requirement that all 44 states named in Annex 2 must ratify. As of this writing, only 35 of the 44 states named in Annex 2 had ratified the convention.[77] Three had not signed. The U.S. Senate rejected the treaty (48–51) in October 1999. While advocates have urged reconsideration, this does not seem a possibility in the near future.

Nuclear-Free Zones   In 1983, the UN General Assembly appointed the UN Study Group on the Question of Nuclear-Weapon-Free Zones. That 21-member panel, including all five nuclear weapon powers, attempted to plan nonnuclear zones in the Middle East, the Balkans, Northern Europe, Africa, South Pacific, and South Asia. After two years of fruitless discussion, the study group disbanded in February

---

[76]Text in 7 *ILM* 809 (1968).

[77]For text, see www.ctbto.org. For ratification requirements, see Article XIV and Annex 2. For a summary of the history and debates, see J. Medalia, "CRS Issue Brief for Congress: Nuclear Weapons: Comprehensive Test Ban Treaty" (March 22, 2006), www.fas.org/sgp/crs/nuke/IB92099.pdf.

1985.[78] Despite the failure of this effort, regional nonnuclear zones have emerged. These include Antarctica (1959), outer space (1967), the deep seabed (1971), Latin America (Treaty of Tlatelolco, 1968), the South Pacific (Treaty of Rarotonga, 1986), and Mongolia (by unilateral declaration, 1992). The Treaty of Pelindaba that would establish an African nuclear-free zone entered into force in July 2009.

BELLIGERENT OCCUPATION

On May 1, 2003, President George W. Bush announced that major combat operations in Iraq had ended.[79] At that point, the status of the United States and its Allies changed from "belligerent" to "occupying power." *Belligerent occupation* means military occupation begun *before* the formal end of hostilities in a given conflict. The present rules governing the occupation of enemy territory in wartime (belligerent occupation, hostile occupation, and/or military occupation) were drawn up after centuries during which no distinction was made between mere occupation and conquest. The general assumption guiding heads of states was that conquest of enemy territory created annexation to the conqueror's own realm. Hence, no restrictions on the invader's actions in the annexed territory were laid down. Conquest created title. Today, the accepted view is that the annexation of occupied territory is a violation of international law (Chapter 20); thus, belligerent occupation is assumed to be a temporary condition. The question then becomes, what *rights and obligations* ought to govern the actions of an occupying power?[80]

The basic rules of the relevant modern law were developed at the Hague Peace Conferences of 1899 and 1907. The 1899 Convention laid the basis for most of today's rules governing military occupation in wartime. The later (1907) Fourth Convention Respecting the Laws and Customs of War on Land, and its appended Regulations (especially Articles 23g, 23h, and 42–56), detailed the rules adopted officially by most of the states of the world in their military manuals.[81] (The appended regulations are hereafter cited as "HR.") As mentioned earlier, it is accepted today that the *regulations are part of customary international law* and thus *binding on all states,* unless they had objected to a particular rule from its very beginning.[82] The provisions of Geneva IV (and the customary law) now apply in Iraq.[83]

---

[78]For current progress, see "Nuclear Weapons Free Zones Around the World," www.opanal.org/nwfz/nwfz.htm.

[79]The White House, "Operation Iraqi Freedom" (May 1, 2003), www.whitehouse.gov/news/releases/2003/05/20030501-15.html (accessed April 22, 2009).

[80]Note that Geneva Additional Protocol I has the most up-to-date codification of the law. AP-I does not apply because neither the United States nor Iraq has ratified it.

[81]The Avalon Project at Yale Law School, Laws of War: Laws and Customs of War on Land (Hague IV), October 18, 1907.

[82]See Judgment of the International Military Tribunal (Nuremberg), Cmd. 6963, 64, 125; Judgment of the International Military Tribunal for the Far East (1948), as shown in Lauterpacht's *Oppenheim*, II: 234; Supreme Court of Israel, The Beit-El Case, P.D. 33(2) 113, H.C. 606/78, 610/78 1979 33; and Supreme Court of Israel, Dwikat v. the Government of Israel. H.C.J. 390–79, P.D. 34(1)1, October 22, 1979.

[83]Note 10; see Pictet, note 20; J. Gutteridge, "The Geneva Conventions of 1949," 26 *BYIL* 294 (1949); and Yingling and Ginnane, note 19. The complete text of the Fourth Convention was reprinted in 50 *AJIL* 724 (1956 Supp.)

Territory is considered occupied when it is actually placed under the authority of the hostile army, according to Article 42 of the 1907 Hague Regulations. Invasion precedes but does not correspond to occupation, which occurs when the enemy government has been rendered incapable of exercising its authority in a given area. The invader (occupant) then substitutes its own authority for that of the legitimate sovereign. As a result, under belligerent occupation, three distinct systems of law potentially apply: the indigenous law of the sovereign, to the extent that it has not been suspended; the laws (legislation, orders, decrees, proclamations, and regulations) of the occupant; and the applicable rules of customary and conventional international law. Belligerent occupation does not transfer sovereignty. Instead, it transfers to the occupant the authority to exercise some of the rights of sovereignty. The occupant, therefore, exercises a temporary right of administration, on a trusteeship basis until the occupation ceases in one way or another.[84] "The exercise of these rights results from the established power of the occupant and from the necessity of maintaining law and order indispensable both to the inhabitants and to the occupying force."[85]

FOURTH GENEVA CONVENTION AND AP-I

The major provisions of Geneva IV are discussed in the remainder of this chapter. Article 2 of Geneva IV merits brief comment because it states that the convention applies in declared wars as well as in all other armed conflicts between two or more of the contracting parties, even if a state of war was not recognized by one of them. The convention applies, furthermore, even if partial or total occupation of a party's territory met with no armed resistance. If, in a future conflict, one of the parties concerned was not a contracting party to the convention, it still would apply to all other parties in their mutual relations. If the noncontracting party to a war accepted and applied the convention's provisions, all contracting parties were bound to apply the instrument to the noncontracting party.

Article 2 of Geneva IV is particularly relevant to the refusal of Israel (which had ratified the convention) to apply that instrument in its treatment of the inhabitants of the areas occupied since the 1967 Six-Day War. According to the Israeli view, the Fourth Convention does not apply to all cases of armed conflict, despite the wording of its second article. Israel has consistently relied on the wording of the *second* paragraph of Article 2 (Geneva IV): "The Convention shall also apply to all cases of partial or total occupation of the territory of a High Contracting Party, even if the said occupation meets with no armed resistance." Israel has asserted that the entire theory of the convention rested on an ouster of the legitimate sovereign and occupation of portions of the latter's territory. Israel has never recognized the legal rights

---

[84]On this point, see Law of Land Warfare, paras. 281–282 and 358, as well as United States v. Rice, U.S. Supreme Court, 1819, 4 Wheaton 246. Consult also Whiteman, I: 947–51; G. Schwarzenberger, "The Law of Belligerent Occupation: Basic Issues," 30 *Nordisk Tidsskrift for International Recht* 10 (1960); and the Case of Solazzi and Pace, Italy, Court of Cassation (Penal), 1953, 37 *Riv. di Dir. Int.* 387, noted in 49 *AJIL* 423 (1955).

[85]Law of Land Warfare, 138, 140.

of Syria, Jordan, and Egypt to the territories they occupied since 1948 in the former Palestine Mandate. Furthermore, Israel has emphasized that no Arab government ever acknowledged the annexation of the West Bank to Jordan in 1950.

Denying that its opponents had legal titles to Israeli-captured territories (including East Jerusalem), Israel maintains that its conquests in 1967 equaled, in validity, the rights of the Arab states in question.[86] On the other hand, Israeli spokesmen have also maintained consistently since 1971 (and possibly earlier) that, in practice, the occupant has applied the humanitarian aspects of Geneva IV; they always, however, refer officially and privately to the "administered territories" and not to the "occupied territories." In other words, Israel insists that it has applied and is applying the Hague Regulations and Geneva IV de facto but has not been obliged to do so de jure. Israeli legal experts have also long asserted that the extended occupation of the West Bank and the Gaza Strip since the 1967 war rendered it unique and that, in consequence, not all legal restraints concerning a "normal" occupation should or could apply to Israel.[87]

In contrast, the UN Security Council in Resolution 465 (March 1, 1980), non-Israeli government officials, and almost all legal writers have held that the applicability of Geneva IV to any occupation rests primarily on the wording of paragraph 1 of Article 2:

> In addition to the provisions which shall be implemented in peacetime, the present Convention shall apply to all cases of declared war or of any other armed conflict which may arise between two or more of the High Contracting Parties, even if the state of war is not recognized by one of them.

By that standard, Geneva IV applied in full to the Israeli "administered territories" during the hostilities and for a year after the general close of hostilities. Afterward, Articles 1–12, 27, 29–34, 47, 49, 51–53, 59, 61–77, and 143 still applied to the administered territories, in accordance with Article 6 of Geneva IV. Overall coverage of occupation by the regulations, on the other hand, is explained in beautifully simple language in paragraph 1 of Article 42: "Territory is considered occupied when it is actually placed under the authority of the hostile army." That simple sentence avoids all reference to legitimate sovereigns, to the previous legal status of the territory occupied, and so on. And as long as the word *legitimate* appears here, it should be noted that experts all agree today: The Regulations and all other instruments pertaining to occupations apply to both legitimate (lawful) and unlawful occupants. A better choice of words would be "displaced de facto government" or, simply, "displaced government."

---

[86]The literature on this topic has grown to considerable proportions. Among the best brief analyses are W. T. Mallison and S. V. Mallison, *The Palestine Problem* (1986), 243, 252; A. Gerson, "Trustee-Occupant: The Legal Status of Israel's Presence in the West Bank," 14 *Harvard Int'l L. J.* 1 (1973); A. Gerson, "War, Conquered Territory, and Military Occupation in the Contemporary International Legal System," 18 Harvard Int'l L. J. 525 (1977); and T. Meron, "Applicability of Multilateral Conventions to Occupied Territories," 72 *AJIL* 542 (1978). All four sources cited have impressive documentation; see also Letter from U.S. Legal Adviser Hansell (April 21, 1978) in 17 *ILM* 777 (1978).

[87]See Israel National Section of the International Commission of Jurists, *The Rule of Law in the Areas Administered by Israel* (1981), 95.

Rights and Obligations of the Occupant

International law does not require the issuance of a formal proclamation of belligerent occupation, but recent practice has favored such an announcement to the indigenous population. Territory is considered occupied when it is actually placed under the authority of the hostile army, according to Article 42 of the 1907 Hague Regulations. Invasion, therefore, precedes but does not correspond to occupation. Occupation begins when the enemy government has been rendered incapable of exercising its authority in a given area. The invader (occupant) then substitutes its own authority for that of the legitimate sovereign. So-called fictitious occupations, created by the dispatch of flying columns into enemy territory, are not lawful occupations. The result of belligerent occupation is that three distinct systems of law apply in territory under an enemy occupant: the indigenous law of the sovereign, to the extent that it has not been necessary to suspend it; the laws (legislation, orders, decrees, proclamations, and regulations) of the occupant, which are gradually introduced; and the applicable rules of customary and conventional international law.

The sovereignty of the legitimate government is suspended in the area for the duration of the belligerent occupation. The occupant, therefore, exercises a temporary right of administration—that is, the authority to exercise some of the rights of sovereignty—on a sort of trusteeship basis until the occupation ceases in one way or another.[88] Although the local law should be retained in force to the greatest possible extent, the occupant is of course free to legislate in the occupied territory, as long as its ordinances are in accordance with conventional or customary international law. The suspension of laws injurious to the interests of the occupant or to its war aims is legitimate. Conscription laws, travel regulations, the right to bear arms, suffrage legislation, and local rights of free speech and assembly are categories of legislation subject to immediate suspension, for obvious reasons. "The exercise of these rights results from the established power of the occupant and from the necessity of maintaining law and order [*l'ordre et la vie publics*] indispensable both to the inhabitants and to the occupying force."[89] On the other hand, occupied territory is generally considered a part of the occupant's realm in regard to belligerent purposes (bombardment, contraband of war, and so on).

Modern belligerent occupants, even if they have permitted some or all of the native courts to function, have tended to establish their own tribunals in occupied enemy territory. This practice is based on customary law and the practice of states, and has now been made a part of conventional law through the provisions of Articles 66–76 of Geneva IV. Space does not permit a detailed examination of the new rules.[90] It should be pointed out, however, that an occupant may create its own tribunals when the local judicial system has disintegrated or has had to be suspended for good reasons. The occupant may also establish its own courts to try offenses committed by local inhabitants against occupation personnel. And it may set up its courts to deal with all native violations of its orders, regulations, and

---

[88]Note 82.

[89]Law of Land Warfare, 138, 140.

[90]The literature on military occupation courts is very extensive: see Von Glahn, 111, and the sources cited in the relevant footnotes.

occupation statutes. Naturally, the occupant may also create its own tribunals to try offenses committed by its own armed forces or civil occupation administration. Such a court would not be called an *occupation court,* however, for its basis would be found in the occupant's own domestic law and not in international law.

It is unlawful under Article 47 of Geneva IV for a belligerent occupant to annex occupied territory or to create a new state therein.[91] Any attempt to supplant the legitimate sovereign (displaced government) by absorption of occupied territory during the course of a war must be considered an unlawful annexation. A number of decisions arising out of events during World War II led to the conclusion that legislation by the lawful sovereign intended to interfere with the occupant's legitimate rule has no effective force in occupied territory. But if such legislation does not conflict with the legitimate rule of the occupying power, it may apply in the territory.

Rights and Obligations of the Indigenous Population

Article 43 of the 1907 Hague Regulations provides that an occupant "shall take all measures in his power to restore and insure, as far as possible, public order and safety, while respecting, unless absolutely prevented, the laws in force in the [occupied] country." Likewise, Article 64 of Geneva IV requires (subject to certain exceptions) that the penal laws of the occupied territory remain in force. Normally an occupant would honor this rule because the administration of enemy territory would be greatly facilitated by using existing and known local laws and regulations.

Most of the older texts in international law asserted the existence of a "duty of obedience" by the local inhabitants toward a belligerent occupant and thus favored the latter at the expense of the civilian population. Numerous justifications have been advanced for this duty, some of them highly ingenious.[92] More recently, that viewpoint has changed; it can be said that, at the most, the inhabitants should give an obedience equal to that previously given to the laws of their legitimate sovereign. At the very least, they should obey the occupant to the extent that such a result can be enforced through the latter's military supremacy.

Unarmed but Violent Resistance

Resistance by the indigenous population to a belligerent occupant has given rise to a great body of literature as well as to acts of great brutality and many diplomatic protests. A *levée en masse*—armed resistance by civilians—is lawful under Article 2 of the Hague Regulations, provided this resistance is offered to an invader *from as-yet-unoccupied territory.* Unfortunately for those supporting such a view, few, if any, cases of genuine *levée en masse* in occupied territory are on record after the 1911 Italo-Turkish War. The *intifada* was, by definition, not a *levée en masse.*

---

[91]See International Military Tribunal, Trial of the Major War Criminals, vol. 22, 411, 497–98. On Israel's early changes in the status of Jerusalem, see UN General Assembly Res. 2253 (ES-V) of July 4, 1967, asserting that "these measures are invalid" and were to be rescinded. The General Assembly repeated this demand in Res. A/2254 (ES-V) of July 14, 1967.

[92]See R. R. Baxter, "The Duty of Obedience to the Belligerent Occupant," 27 *BYIL* 235 (1950).

An armed uprising inside the occupied territory is not forbidden by international law, but persons engaging in such an activity would be in a state of unprivileged belligerency: They would not enjoy the protection (privileges) extended to other inhabitants by the various instruments concerned with belligerent occupation. Presumably, however, those regulations applicable to guerrillas would also be applicable to participants in an armed uprising against an occupant. During the German invasion of the Soviet Union (World War II), several fairly large areas behind the German lines were not under the control of the German armed forces and instead became the homes of guerrilla groups of varying sizes. The areas in question were unoccupied Soviet territory, and in many instances the guerrilla groups were supplied by air from behind the Soviet lines.

The occupant is entitled to detain or otherwise punish inhabitants who resist, by one means or another, its lawful orders. However, penalties must be in accordance with specified procedures and within specified limits, such as when Article 68 of Geneva IV states that imprisonment is to be proportionate to the offense committed. It must always be kept in mind that since the end of the nineteenth century, resistance to an occupant has not been forbidden, or supported, by rules of international law. Such resistance therefore cannot be viewed as an ipso facto violation of that law.

On the other hand, the civilian inhabitants of an occupied territory have a right to protection, especially in regard to their personal rights. After being initially and sketchily detailed in Article 46 of the Hague Regulations, these personal rights were outlined in considerably expanded form in Geneva IV, Article 27, and have now been outlined in detail in PR-1, Articles 72–77, representing a long list of guarantees to the indigenous population. Briefly, civilian inhabitants are guaranteed respect for their persons, honor, family rights, religious convictions and practices, and manners and customs. Women are protected especially against any attack on their honor, in particular against rape, enforced prostitution, or any form of indecent assault. Article 32 of the same treaty prohibits certain practices associated with the Axis treatment of civilians, such as extermination, murder, torture, corporal punishment, mutilation, medical or scientific experiments not required by the medical treatment of an individual, and any other measures of brutality.

Article 70 of Geneva IV prohibits the arrest, prosecution, or conviction of members of the indigenous population for acts committed or opinions expressed before the occupation or during a temporary suspension thereof, except for breaches of the laws and customs of war. Article 50 of Geneva IV provides that the occupant should facilitate the proper operation of educational institutions, with the cooperation of the native authorities in the territory, but several authors have recently contended that the article does not apply to institutions of higher learning.

The deportation (expulsion) by the occupant of inhabitants from an occupied territory is strictly forbidden by Article 49(1) of Geneva IV. The International Military Tribunal (at Nuremberg) had judged deportation of civilians from occupied territories to be illegal, a war crime, and a crime against humanity.[93] Again, Article 9 of the Universal Declaration of Human Rights as well as Article 12(4) of the International Covenant on Civil and Political Rights of 1966 prohibit deportation

---

[93]International Military Tribunal, Trial of Major War Criminals, I, at 227, 293, 296.

in the one case and denial of the right to enter one's own country in the other. A frequent Israeli claim that Article 44(1) of Geneva IV reflected and referred only to World War II German practices is invalid in view of the clear wording of Article 44(1). It is lawful, however, under Article 44(2) for an occupant to undertake partial or total evacuation of a given area if the security of the population or imperative military reasons so demand.

Termination of Belligerent Occupation

The belligerent occupation of enemy territory may terminate in a number of different ways. The area may be set free by the forces of the sovereign or of his allies, liberated by a successful uprising of the indigenous population, and returned to the control of its legitimate sovereign under the terms of a peace treaty. It may also be annexed by the occupant under the provisions of such a treaty. Most modern occupations have ended with the return of the occupied territory to its legitimate sovereign, but even this normal situation has been complicated by many problems. For example, what laws and ordinances issued by the occupant will lose their validity after occupation ceases? No clear-cut answer can be given. If any of the occupant's decrees or laws violate customary or conventional international law, they will be null and void in the eyes of the returning legitimate sovereign; if they correspond to what the occupant could do legally in the occupied territory, then the returning sovereign will decide whether to keep the occupant's legislation in force as his or her own.

RULES OF CONFLICT IN THE AIR

The use of balloons to transport mail and newspapers from besieged Paris during the Franco-Prussian War had led to considerable speculation toward the end of the nineteenth century as to the possibilities of aerial warfare. At the Hague Conference of 1899, a declaration, renewed at the Second Conference in 1907, prohibited until the end of a Third Peace Conference "the discharge of projectiles and explosives from balloons and by other new methods of a similar nature." Very few states signed the instrument in 1899. In 1907, France, Germany, Italy, Japan, and Russia refused to sign it primarily because these countries, impressed by the advance in aviation, desired to wait and see what promising and possibly legal use could be made of the newfound ability to fly. Italy then became a pioneer, using balloons in the Italo-Turkish War of 1911–1912 both for spotting enemy troops and for dropping explosives (bombs) on them. The first "dogfight" actually took place between two mercenary pilots using pistols during the Mexican Civil War in 1912.[94]

Air Warfare in World War I

The outbreak of war in 1914 brought the airplane, and later the dirigible, into immediate prominence. Both sides fought each other in the air and proceeded to

---

[94]For a speculative piece on the law of war in space, see R. A. Ramey, "Armed Conflict on the Final Frontier: The Law of War in Space," 48 *Air Force L. Rev.* 1 (2000).

bomb enemy targets. The bombing, all too soon, expanded to "undefended" cities. Both sides piously insisted that their aviators received strict orders to attack only points of military importance and, in the case of cities, to bomb only genuine military targets. The usefulness of such instructions—even if the willingness to carry them out could have been proved—was nil, for the speed of an airplane and the absence of bombsights or other aiming devices left the ultimate destination of a dropped bomb to chance and the aviator's skill. One did not have to be a cynic to say before the end of the war that every inhabited enemy community had become a legitimate target, an attitude reinforced by the concept of the nation-in-arms. The distinction between undefended and defended communities had become meaningless, except in the rare cases of genuine "hospital towns," declared as such and subject to neutral inspection.

Regulation Post World War I

The application of the rules of land warfare to the new weapon failed to prevent indiscriminate bombing. After World War I, therefore, the possibility of developing a separate code of air warfare was considered. Here, however, military considerations of the greatest magnitude intruded. The airplanes, as perfected by 1918, had become the weapon of the future to many military staffs, and they successfully opposed any code promising to cripple this new item in the military hardware closet. The Spanish Civil War and the Japanese invasion of China showed that new rules governing aerial bombardment were needed most urgently. In 1938, British Prime Minister Neville Chamberlain, in addressing the House of Commons, asserted that three principles ought to be observed by all participants in future wars: (1) a deliberate attack on civilian populations was a clear violation of international law; (2) "targets which are aimed at from the air must be legitimate military objectives and must be capable of identification"; and (3) "reasonable care must be taken in attacking these military objectives so that by carelessness a civilian population in the neighborhood is not bombed."[95] Later that year, the Assembly of the League of Nations unanimously adopted a resolution embodying the three principles.

World War II saw the manned plane in its heyday; pilots carried out even greater bombing of enemy locations, beginning with the German attack on Poland. Without going into great detail, it can be said that by 1945, strategic bombing from the air, without warning, was a generally accepted method of warfare and that those who attempted to punish the captured perpetrators of those air raids by execution would end up as war criminals themselves. Since then the manned bomber, at least, seems to be on the way out, and its replacement, the unmanned intermediate or intercontinental ballistic missile, together with its relatives aboard nuclear-powered submarines, has appeared on the scene.

Moreover, May 11, 1940, may be regarded as the very day on which virtually unrestricted air bombardment was "legitimized." On that date, the British Cabinet decided on strategic air attacks on the enemy's interior—a decision that resulted,

---

[95]Cited in Lauterpacht's *Oppenheim*, II: 523.

on August 8, 1940, in the German "reprisal" raids against English nonmilitary targets, including the city of Coventry. At present, there is no global treaty governing war in the air. Only by analogy with the rules laid down for hostilities on the ground can rules be detected that apply to air warfare, and they are relatively limited in number and scope. In 1976, the U.S. Department of the Air Force, after some 20 years of research and planning, issued its regulations for the conduct of air operations—a welcome product in view of the scarcity of accepted international rules.[96]

Some of the more interesting "rules" include the assertion that urban areas containing military targets remain subject to attack (Chapters 5–8 of the manual). Dikes, dams, and nuclear generating stations may also be attacked if "under the circumstances ruling at the time, they are lawful military objectives." Area bombing is judged to be in accordance with existing international law rules (Chapters 1–15). In agreement with what has been stated before, the employment of nuclear weapons does not violate currently existing international law but should be used only at the direction of the president (Chapter 6). Interestingly enough, the Air Force manual justifies aerial overflights if they are based on the right of self-defense (Chapters 02–6), but admits the undoubted right of every state to prevent (i.e., attack and destroy, if possible) foreign military aircraft from unauthorized aerial intrusions (Chapters 2–6). Medical aircraft and their protection are covered in the U.S. Air Force manual in Chapters 2, 4, 13, and 14—and now also in AP-I, Articles 24 to 31—in great detail. The American manual represents the first comprehensive official effort to describe, backed with impressive documentation, the subject of modern air war from both a legal and a practical point of view. Despite some gaps and certain vague statements, the manual could well serve as the basis for the negotiation of a global convention on the subject, perhaps through another Geneva diplomatic conference.

NAVAL WARFARE

The rules governing warfare at sea appear to have survived the passage of two global wars to a far greater extent than have the rules applicable to land warfare. Apart from the abolition of privateering by the Declaration of Paris (1856), nothing of significance has changed in the past 150 years.[97] This situation has a simple explanation—the character of naval warfare did not undergo the profound changes that took place in land warfare. In World War I and World War II, naval warfare per se was governed primarily by the actual practices of the major bel-

---

[96]U.S. Air Force, *International Law—the Conduct of Armed Conflict and Air Operations*, Pamphlet 110 (1976). See also M. W. Lewis, "The Law of Aerial Bombardment in the 1991 Gulf War," 97 *AJIL* 481 (2003).

[97]Given the move toward "privatization" in contemporary times, the practice of privateering has a certain modern ring. Privateering gave individual (and intrepid) entrepreneurs the right to apply for a letter of marque from the government. A letter of marque granted the right to outfit a private ship to act as a commerce raider against enemy shipping during wartime. As noted in Chapter 13, the taking of enemy shipping as prizes could be very profitable. The French effort against the United States during the "undeclared war" of 1797–1801 consisted primarily of approving privateers to harass American shipping.

ligerents rather than by any code of naval warfare adopted by international agreement. In fact, after the end of World War I, the only phase of actual hostilities at sea "regulated" by treaty was the use of submarines against merchant vessels by the Treaty of Washington of 1922.[98] To be sure, the battleship became obsolete, submarines emerged as a potent weapon, and the air forces of belligerents began to play an ever more important part in hostilities, but the factors that conditioned the war at sea in 1914 did not significantly differ from those that governed the war at sea during World War II. The conferees decided to postpone modernization of the rules when the 1977 Protocols to the Geneva Convention of 1949 were drafted.

SUGGESTED READINGS

GENERAL

Byers, *War Law: Understanding International Law and Armed Conflict* (2005).

Delissen, ed., *Humanitarian Law of Armed Conflict* (1991).

Dinstein, *The Conduct of Hostilities Under the Law of International Armed Conflict* (2004).

Farer, *The Laws of War 25 Years After Nuremberg* (*International Conciliation no. 528*) (1971).

Greenwood, "The Concept of War in Modern International Law," *ICLQ* 283 (1987).

Jinks, "The Declining Status of POW Status," 45 *Harvard Int'l L. J.* 367 (2004).

Kalshoven and Sondoz, eds, *Implementation of International Humanitarian Law* (1989).

Levie, *The Code of International Armed Conflicts* (2 vols, 1986).

McCoubrey, *International Humanitarian Law* (1990).

McDougal and Feliciano, *The International Law of War* (1994).

Meron, *Henry's Wars and Shakespeare's Laws: Perspectives on the Law of War in the Later Middle Ages* (1993).

Schindler and Toman, eds, *The Laws of Armed Conflict,* 3rd ed. (1988).

Watkin, "Warriors Without Rights? Combatants, Unprivileged Belligerents, and the Struggle Over Legitimacy," Program on Humanitarian Policy and Conflict Research, Harvard University Occasional Paper Series, no. 2 (2005), 5–6.6, www.hpcr.org/pdfs/OccasionalPaper2.pdf (accessed April 22, 2009).

ADDITIONAL PROTOCOLS I AND II

Fleck, ed., *The Handbook of Humanitarian Law in Armed* Conflicts (1995).

Forsythe, "Legal Management of International Wars: The 1977 Protocol on Non-international Armed Conflict," 72 *AJIL* 272 (1978).

Levie, *Protection of War Victims: Protocol I to the 1949 Geneva Conventions* (1979–1981).

Meron, "The Time Has Come for the United States to Ratify Geneva Protocol I," 88 *AJIL* 678 (1994).

Meyer, ed., *Armed Conflict and the New Law: Aspects of the 1977 Geneva Protocols and the 1981 Weapons Convention* (1989).

Sofaer, "The US Decision Not to Ratify Protocol I to the Geneva Conventions on the Protection of War Victims," 82 *AJIL* 784 (1988).

---

[98]For an extended treatment of the subject (and still the standard), consult R. W. Tucker, *The Law of War and Neutrality at Sea* (1957). Tucker's volume also contains, in an appendix, the official U.S. Navy Manual, *Law of Naval Warfare.* See Whiteman, X: 614, 644, and XI: 1, 115; G. P. Politakis, *Modern Aspects of the Laws of Naval Warfare and Maritime Neutrality* (1998); and J. J. Busuttil, *Naval Weapons Systems and the Contemporary Law of War* (1998).

ILLEGAL WEAPONS

CHEMICAL-BACTERIOLOGICAL WARFARE

Lundin, ed., *Non-production by Industry of Chemical-Warfare Agents* (Technical Verification Under a Chemical Warfare Convention) (1989).

Sims, *International Organization for Chemical Disarmament* (1987).

HERBICIDES

Johnstone, "Ecocide and the Geneva Protocol," 49 *Foreign Affairs* 711 (1971).

Verwey, *Riot Control Agents and Herbicides in War* (1977).

"U.S. Department of Defense Position with Regard to Destruction of Crops Through Chemical Agents (April 1971)," 10 *ILM* 1300 (1971).

NUCLEAR WEAPONS

Alley, *Nuclear-Weapon-Free Zones: The South Pacific Proposal* (Stanley Foundation, 1977).

Singh and McWhinney, *Nuclear Weapons and Contemporary International Law,* 2nd ed. (1988).

Weston, "Nuclear Weapons Versus International Law: A Contextual Reassessment," 28 *McGill L. J.* 542 (1983).

Weston, "The 'Sources' of International Law Revisited: The Case of Nuclear Weapons," 4 *Chinese Yearbook of Int. Law* 7 (CYILA–1985).

INTERNAL WAR

Bethlehem and Weller, eds, *The "Yugoslav" Crisis in International Law* (1994).

Cassese, "The Status of Rebels Under the 1977 Geneva Protocol on Non-international Armed Conflicts," 30 *ICLQ* 416 (1981).

Levie, ed., *The Law of Non-international Armed Conflict: Protocol II to the 1949 Geneva Conventions* (1987).

Meron, *Human Rights in Internal Strife: Their International Protection* (1988).

Wilson, *International Law and the Use of Force by National Liberation Movements* (1988).

PRISONERS OF WAR

Falk, "International Law Aspects of Repatriation of Prisoners during Hostilities," 67 *AJIL* 465 (1973); Levie, "A Reply," *id.,* 693; Falk, "Reply," 68 *AJIL* 104 (1974).

Hingorani, *Prisoners of War,* 2nd ed. (1982).

Levie, *Prisoners of War in International Armed Conflicts* (1978).

Otterman, "IRAQ: International Law and POWs," Council on Foreign Relations (March 31, 2003).

Rodley, *The Treatment of Prisoners Under International Law* (1987).

AIR WAR

Lewis, "The Law of Aerial Bombardment in the 1991 Gulf War," 97 *AJIL* 481 (2003).

U.S. Air Force, *International Law—the Conduct of Armed Conflict and Air Operations,* Pamphlet 110 (1976).

MODERN NAVAL WARFARE

Busuttil, *Naval Weapons Systems and the Contemporary Law of War* (1998).

Mallison and Mallison, "A Survey of the International Law of Naval Blockades," 102 *U.S. Naval Institute Proceedings* 44 (February 1976).

Politakis, *Modern Aspects of the Laws of Naval Warfare and Maritime Neutrality* (1998).

Tucker, *The Law of War and Neutrality at Sea* (1957).

War Crime Tribunals

The movement to construct institutions and regimes that would allow the international prosecution of those individuals who have committed genocide, war crimes, and other crimes against humanity has become a salient force in contemporary international politics. Presumably, the modern laws of war would preclude Alexander the Great's punishment of the citizens of Tyre for their resistance (he crucified 2,000 young men, positioning them along the main road along the Lebanese coast) or the Roman "final solution" to Cato's perception of threat presented by Carthage (*Carthago delenda est,* or "Carthage must be destroyed"). Perhaps the first modern trials were those of individuals (Bonapartists charged with treason) who helped Napoleon escape from exile in Elba and then joined in the Hundred Days in which he attempted to regain power. As a recent commentator noted, in contrast, in the twentieth century, international war crime tribunals have become "a recurring modern phenomenon with discernible patterns."[1] Nuremberg stands as the model, but Leipzig and Constantinople after World War I; the less well known Tokyo trials after World War II; the ad hoc tribunals for Rwanda, Sierra Leone, and the former Yugoslavia; and the permanent International Criminal Court (ICC) also need examination.

Many have questioned the need for war crime tribunals. The short and simple reply flows from notions of justice and accountability for heinous deeds done. Before the twentieth century, world leaders as well as soldiers in the field could act with virtual impunity because international law did not hold them accountable. The twentieth century witnessed both a change in attitude (see Chapters 16 and 20) and some of the worst incidents of mass murder in recorded history: Germany (6 million during the Nazi regime), China (5 million during the Cultural Revolution), Cambodia (2 million during the Khmer Rouge regime), East Timor (200,000), Uganda (750,000 during the Idi Amin regime), Rwanda (800,000 Hutu in ethnic fighting with the Tutsi), and Bosnia (250,000). Add to these numbers the incidences of rape, torture, and other abuses that push individuals to become

---

[1]G. J. Bass, *Stay the Hand of Vengeance: The Politics of War Crimes Trials* (2000), 5.

refugees in search of a safe haven. As one strong advocate has succinctly stated the issue, "[T]he pledge of 'never again' quickly became the reality of 'again and again.'"[2] UN Secretary General Kofi Annan, during a visit to the International Criminal Tribunal for Yugoslavia (ICTY) in 1997, declared, "Impunity cannot be tolerated, and will not be. In an interdependent world, the Rule of the Law must prevail."[3] On the other hand, if interested states had acted earlier to stop the slaughter, these courts would not have found a reason for existence. The dilemmas of humanitarian intervention persist (see Chapter 20).

The UN tribunals for Sierra Leone (SCSL), Rwanda (ICTR), and the former Yugoslavia (ICTY) do address the legal responsibilities of individuals who have committed crimes of war and crimes against humanity. The international demand to punish these crimes seems to have tapped a resonant chord. The ICC presumably will take this process further. In addition, advocates argue that prosecution of the individuals responsible for specific acts will avoid the attribution of collective guilt to an entire nation, provide victims with a sense that their grievances have been addressed, and establish an impartial historical record of the crimes and events. Ideally, successful apprehension and prosecution would also serve as a deterrent.[4]

Yet trials by their nature seem an extraordinarily awkward and unwieldy way to deal with the types of problems presented by certain types of war crimes. Courts require "proof" adduced through application of a strict set of rules. Such proof may not always be readily available considering the circumstances.[5] The ICTY initially acquitted Dusko (Dusan) Tadic on seven murder charges. The judges then dismissed 11 of 31 charges against him on the grounds that he could not have violated the Geneva Conventions because the war in Bosnia was not an international one (see Chapter 20).[6] Are processes such as the Truth and Reconciliation Commission in South Africa more appropriate in some cases?[7] Given the nature of the atrocities in Rwanda and Bosnia, in what sense may we speak of appropriate punishment as fulfilling justice? The sheer scale of genocidal crimes—involving thousands upon thousands of killers—can overwhelm almost any judicial system. The Pol Pots, Idi Amins, and Slobodan Milosevics did not act alone. But what tribunal could hope to punish all of the guilty?

Many believe that war crime trials, no matter how carefully conducted, still represent nothing more than "victor's justice."[8] The Soviet Union participated in

---

[2]M. P. Scharf, *Balkan Justice* (1997), xiii.

[3]www.un.org/icty/glance-e/index.htm (accessed April 22, 2009).

[4]See *Making Justice Work*, Report of the Century Foundation/Twentieth Century Fund Task Force on Apprehending Indicted War Criminals (1998), 27–29. See also Bass, note 1, at 28–33. Bass argues that liberal states "commonly see their enemies not as mere foes, but as war criminals deserving punishment" (p. 35).

[5]For example, in the aftermath of what happened in Rwanda, what are the probabilities of finding credible testimony from both witnesses and relevant documents to support specific cases?

[6]Bass, note 1, at 13ff; and Scharf, note 2, at 213–214, 271–288.

[7]See Truth and Reconciliation Commission, www.doj.gov.za/trc/; and for the report, see www.info.gov.za/otherdocs/2003/trc/ (accessed April 22, 2009).

[8]Bass, note 1, at 15ff., argues that the phrase *victor's justice* has little meaning. The question should always be which victor and what justice?

the Nuremberg trials even though Josef Stalin was responsible for an estimated 4 million deaths of Soviet citizens, and some interesting questions do arise concerning the possible culpability of Allied air commanders and other senior political officials for the decisions that resulted in the massive destruction of civilian life at Hamburg and Dresden. From another view, the spectacle produced by Slobodan Milosevic before the ICTY (as well as the length of the trial) before his death as well as the seeming unwillingness of the NATO powers to seek out and arrest Ratko Mladic and Radovan Karadzic even though the ICTY had issued indictments represent ongoing practical problems of political will and calculation. Milosevic (as Hermann Goering did at Nuremberg) used the trials as a forum to challenge the authority of those conducting the proceedings.

Yet the Nuremberg trials, by focusing on the alleged crimes of individuals rather than on "holding Germany guilty" (collective responsibility), did provide an important impetus for the development of the post–World War II human rights regime as well as the rehabilitation of Germany into an ally. In a partial answer to skeptics, the Special Court for Sierra Leone, the ICTY, and the ICTR, once established, have persisted despite all obstacles. They may not have functioned as well in the short run as idealist advocates had hoped, but they have had an impact.[9] Although they evaded capture for several years, Mladic and Karadzic, internationally indicted war criminals, were eventually found and arrested. Milosevic did eventually surrender to international authority for trial. Despite a woeful lack of funding (and often local cooperation) for their task, the ICTY and the ICTR continue. The ICC, despite U.S. opposition, quickly became a reality.

THE TREATY OF VERSAILLES AND THE COMMISSION OF FIFTEEN

The first major attempt to punish offenders guilty of committing war crimes as defined in Chapter 20 took place at the end of World War I. On January 25, 1919, the Preliminary Peace Conference created the Commission of Fifteen to investigate and report on violations of international law that could be charged against Germany and its allies.[10] The commission, in its report, specifically denied immunity from responsibility to high officials of the Central Powers, including even chiefs of states. It recommended the establishment of the International High Tribunal to apply "the principles of the law of nations as they result from the usages established among civilized peoples, from the laws of humanity, and from the dictates of public conscience"—words taken from the preamble to the Hague Conventions of 1899 and 1907. The American representatives on the commission differed with their Allied colleagues and wanted the law to be limited to the laws

---

[9]See www.un.org/icty/cases-e/index-e.htm (accessed April 22, 2009) for relevant documents and decisions.

[10]The report of the "Commission on the Responsibility of the Authors of the War and on the Enforcement of Penalties" is in 14 *American Journal of International Law* 95 (1920 Supp.). For a lengthy discussion of the debates, see Bass, note 1, at 58–105.

and customs of war only. The American delegation advanced three main reasons to oppose the charges as drawn:[11]

> The first of these is the uncertainty of the law to be administered, in that liability is made to depend not only upon violations of the laws and customs of war, but also upon violations "of the laws of humanity." The second of these reasons is that heads of states are included within the civil and military authorities of the enemy countries to be tried and punished. . . . They also believe that the Commission erred in seeking to subject heads of state to trial and punishment by a tribunal to whose jurisdiction they were not subject when the alleged offences were committed.
>
> The American representatives believe that the Commission has exceeded its mandate in extending liability to violations of the laws of humanity. . . . The American representatives know of no international statute or convention making a violation of the laws and customs of war—not to speak of the laws or principles of humanity—an international crime, affixing a punishment to it, and declaring the court which has jurisdiction over the offence.

The Japanese delegation, while noting that "many crimes have been committed by the enemy in the course of the present war," using parallel arguments, also argued against trials.[12]

The deliberations here became increasingly bitter. Over the dissenting views of the United States and Japanese members, the view of the majority was adopted, and Article 227 of the Treaty of Versailles provided for the creation of a tribunal of five judges to be appointed to try the ex-emperor of Germany—not for war crimes, but for "a supreme offense against international morality and the sanctity of treaties." Because the Kaiser had found asylum in the Netherlands and the government refused to surrender him to the Allied and Associated Powers, the scheme came to naught.

LEIPZIG

The Allies after 1919 faced an interesting difficulty. Although they had defeated Germany, they did not occupy the territory. Early in February 1920, the Allied powers submitted a list of 854 names of persons accused of war crimes to the German government.[13] These included some of Germany's most prominent military leaders: Helmuth von Moltke, Erich Ludendorff, Paul von Hindenburg, and Alfred von Tirpitz. Following strong German resistance to the surrender of those persons, a compromise was reached on German suggestions. On May 7, 1920, a sample "abridged" list of 45 names was sent to the German government. These individuals were to be tried before the German Supreme Court at Leipzig.

---

[11]Memorandum of Reservations Presented by the Representatives of the United States to the Report of the Commission on Responsibilities, 14 *AJIL* 127 (1920), 144ff.

[12]*Ibid.*

[13]P. H. Maguire, *Law and War: An American Story* (2000), 80. Maguire notes that, depending upon the source used, the numbers cited for this original list may vary.

The trial began on May 23, 1921. Only 12 of the 45 persons named on the "test list" were actually tried. Only six of them were found guilty. Of the three generals tried (all for mistreatment of POWs), all were found not guilty, although Major Benno Cruscius received a two-year sentence for allegedly passing on an illegal order (to kill POWs) issued by one of the generals (Karl Stenger).[14] In the case of Commander Karl Neumann, accused of deliberately sinking a hospital ship the *Dover Castle*, the court explicitly accepted a defense of superior orders, noting, "The accused accordingly sank the *Dover Castle* in obedience to a service order of his highest superiors, an order which he considered to be binding. He cannot, therefore, be punished for his conduct."[15] The sentences imposed on those convicted were nominal, ranging from 6 months to a maximum of 4 years in prison. The final bizarre touch of these regrettable proceedings was added by the escape from detention of Lieutenants John Boldt and Ludwig Dithmar, submarine officers who had received four-year sentences for firing on the lifeboats of the hospital ship *Llandovery Castle*.[16] The Allies then ceased all further attempts to continue the war crimes trials.[17]

CONSTANTINOPLE

At the end of World War I, Germany also refused to hand over to the Allies Mehmed Tâlat Pasha,[18] the acting head of the Turkish government. In this case, the British formed the driving force behind the desire to punish those accused of forcibly deporting and killing Greeks and Armenians resident in the Ottoman state during the war. The Turks had previously been implicated in the Hamidian massacres (1894–1897)[19] in Armenia and Turkey. Great Britain, France, and

---

[14]The charge was reduced to "killing through negligence." Maguire, note 13, at 82. Major Cruscius had testified against General Stenger, who was considered a war hero, having lost a leg in 1914 after being wounded by a French artillery barrage.

[15]*Judgment in the Case of Comander Karl Neumann* (June 4, 1921), Supreme Court at Leipzig; text in 16 *AJIL* 704 (1922), at 708.

[16]For a firsthand account of this trial, see "The War Crime Trial—Llandovery Castle," www.gwpda.org/naval/lcastl12.htm (accessed April 22, 2009).

[17]For a more detailed account, told more in sorrow than in anger, consult S. Glueck, *War Criminals, Their Prosecution and Punishment* (1944), 19; see also J. W. Garner, *Recent Developments in International Law* (1925), 455–463; G. A. Finch, "Retribution for War Crimes," 37 *AJIL* 81 (1943); A. Levy, "The Law and Procedure of War Crimes Trials," 37 *American Political Science Review* 1052, esp. 1056–1063 (1943); and G. Schwarzenberger, *International Law and Totalitarian Lawlessness* (1943), 68, 113–147, for copious excerpts from the decisions at the Leipzig trials. The most complete account of the early trials is by J. F. Willis, *Prologue to Nuremberg: The Politics and Diplomacy of Punishing War Criminals of the First World War* (1982).

[18]The three "pashas" ("young turks") who emerged after the 1909 "revolution" were Mehmed Tâlat, Ismail Enver, and Ahmed Djemal. The following draws upon V. N. Dadrian, "Genocide As a Problem of National and International Law: The World War I Armenian Case and Its Contemporary Legal Ramifications," 14 *Yale J. Int'l Law* 221 (1989); and Bass, note 1, at 106–146. Little has been written about the trials, though much has been written about the events leading up to them.

[19]Named for Abdul-Hamid II (Abd al-Hamid II), sultan of Turkey (deposed 1909).

Russia (the Triple Entente) had issued a warning to the Turkish government in May 1915. Turkey ignored the warning. Until the end of the war, evidence indicates a systematic campaign of slaughter waged against Armenians and other ethnic groups (an estimated 1,500,000 deaths).[20] At the end of the war, Britain demanded the surrender for trial of those Turks accused of criminal acts. Mustafa Kemal,[21] head of the newly formed Ankara government, refused, indicating that he could not recognize "a kind of right of jurisdiction on the part of a foreign government over [an] act of a Turkish subject in the interior of Turkey herself."[22] Under continued British pressure (Britain still had 320,000 troops in Turkey), the Turkish government eventually agreed that Turkey would agree to the same conditions for trial of those accused that Germany had accepted (June 1921). Under continued British diplomatic pressure, the Turkish minister of the interior drew up a list of 60 people purportedly responsible for the campaign against the Armenians for detention for potential trial. The Turkish government systematically pursued a program of arrest. These included many prominent and popular political figures.

The first trial resulted in a death sentence (actually carried out against Kemal Bay) for acts that were "against *humanity and civilization*. They are never compatible in any manner to human considerations"[23] (Emphasis added). For future reference, this verdict stands as important because it addressed two questions critical to the future development of the law: command responsibility and the idea of crimes against *humanity*. The decision and execution sparked a severe backlash in Turkey against the verdicts and further trials, but the Turkish government still proceeded. A court sentenced Mehmed Tâlat, Ismail Enver, and other "young Turk" leaders to death, but did so with the defendants in absentia. Others were released "after investigation."

The rest of the story revolves around circumstance and *political* decisions. Britain had a large number of troops in Turkey at the end of the war. Political considerations demanded their steady withdrawal. Those remaining would suddenly pose a problem.[24] Ostensibly, the British had some leverage in that they still held a number of Turkish prisoners at Malta. When fighting broke out within Turkey in 1921, Kemal seized a number of British soldiers. He then offered a prisoner swap. The subsequent negotiations, resulting in the exchange of prisoners (November 1921), essentially precluded any future trials. They also effectively ended any further prosecutions or attempts to enforce sentences already meted out by the government in Turkey. The final treaty, signed in July 1923 with Turkey, made no mention of war crimes.

---

[20]For a concise, relatively non-polemic, account (a rarity!), see www.historyplace.com/worldhistory/genocide/armenians.htm (accessed April 22, 2009).

[21]Later, Mustafa Kemal Atatürk.

[22]Cited in Dadrian, note 18, at 221.

[23]Bass, note 1, at 125.

[24]Bass, note 1, at 107.

THE INTERNATIONAL MILITARY TRIBUNAL: NUREMBERG

The deliberate violations of the laws of war at the hands of the Axis powers and their minor allies led early in World War II to demands for an effective postwar punishment of the guilty individuals.[25] Two prefatory comments seem important here. First, statesmen and lawyers had labored to place some restrictions on the unilateral resort to force in the period after World War I. Nonetheless, as noted in the American and Japanese dissents, many questions still remained open. Second, contemporary writers often treat Nuremberg as if the establishment of the tribunal was a clear, predetermined choice. It was not. Feelings ran high. Britain at first opposed trials because the "guilt was so black" that it was "beyond the scope of judicial process."[26] U.S. Secretary of the Treasury Henry Morgenthau Jr. and U.S. Secretary of State Cordell Hull supported summary executions. Secretary of War Henry L. Stimson at first embraced summary executions and then became a strong advocate for trials.

Stimson believed that trials were necessary to establish beyond doubt the idea of *organizational* responsibility as well as the guilt of individuals responsible for the worst atrocities. Organizational responsibility did *not* mean collective responsibility, but rather that the leaders of the mainstays of the Nazi apparatus, the Gestapo and SS, would be held responsible for the atrocities committed because of their policies and orders. Needless to say, Stalin had no problem with summary executions. In a widely reported incident, at a banquet with President Franklin D. Roosevelt and Prime Minister Winston Churchill, Stalin proposed a toast: "I drink to the quickest possible justice for all German war criminals. I drink to the justice of a firing squad. . . . Fifty thousand must be shot."[27] Eventually, Stimson's advocacy would form the basis for postwar action. These discussions remained private because of fear that the German leadership would lose all restraint with regard to POWs if any details of the discussions became public knowledge. Public statements did warn of retribution for atrocities, but almost always in very general terms.

The London Agreement

In August 1945, the United States, the United Kingdom, France, and the Soviet Union concluded the London Agreement for the Prosecution and Punishment of the Major War Criminals of the European Axis (August 8).[28] This instrument (also known as the London Charter) provided the details for the establishment of the

---

[25]Consult Whiteman, XI: 874.

[26]T. Taylor, *The Anatomy of the Nuremberg Trials* (1992), 29.

[27]Quoted in Scharf, note 2, at 5.

[28]Text in 39 *AJIL* 257 (1945 Supp.); consult *International Conference on Military Trials, London, 1945* (Department of State Publication 3080), for the texts of all proposals at the meeting. The principles contained in the 1945 Agreement were recognized as binding in international law by UN General Assembly Resolution 95 (I) (December 11, 1946).

International Military Tribunal (IMT). The tribunal would consist of four judges, each appointed by a party to the agreement, together with four alternates similarly chosen. The conferees chose Nuremberg as the site for symbolic reasons. It was the location for an annual mass demonstration orchestrated by the Nazi Party and the location where the anti-Semitic "Nuremberg Laws" had been proclaimed in 1935.[29]

In assessing the negotiations that led to the adoption of the agreement, one should consider the enormous difficulties involved in reconciling the different legal traditions and conceptions represented by the United States and Britain, on the one hand (common law), and France and the Soviet Union, on the other (civil law). For example, in civil law procedure, officers of the court system assemble the evidence for both sides, the court conducts the questioning of witnesses, and cross-examination by a defending counsel rarely occurs. Hearsay evidence is permitted, as are trials in absentia. Defendants do not have a right to testify on their own behalf. In contrast, American and British procedures rely upon examination and cross-examination in open court as a method of establishing the facts, defendants have a right to confront their accusers and offer testimony on their own behalf, and the use of hearsay evidence is limited. The compromise involved a blend of elements from both systems. The Anglo-American method of examination, cross-examination, would be used. Defendants not only could testify on their own behalf, but also, contrary to Anglo-American practice, could be compelled to testify by the court. Because the trials would not involve juries, the Anglo-American technical rules of evidence would not apply. The court could consider any evidence it found to have probative value.[30] The defendants were permitted counsel of their own choice or could have counsel appointed by the IMT. The Charter provided no right of appeal.

The Soviet Union demanded that the charges for crimes be confined to acts committed by the European Axis powers. This represented a basic problem. If the secret protocol of the 1939 Soviet nonaggression pact with Germany became public, the Soviet Union could also be charged with the crime of aggression against Poland.[31] The final language in the Charter simply stated that the purpose of the IMT was prosecution of *Axis* crimes. Another controversy erupted over the definition of "crimes against humanity" (Article 6(c) of the London Charter). This involved a seemingly minor grammatical change, insertion of a semicolon rather than a comma, but the change resulted in limiting IMT jurisdiction with respect to crimes against humanity committed before the German invasion of Poland on September 1, 1939 (the accepted date for the beginning of the war). Scharf notes, "While the public perception is that the Nuremberg trial provided a comprehensive account of the Holocaust, in fact that was the one thing the Nuremberg Tribunal was legally precluded from doing."[32]

---

[29]Taylor, note 26, at 61.

[30]Taylor, note 26, at 61–64.

[31]J. C. Watkins and J. P. Weber, *War Crimes and War Crime Trials: From Leipzig to the ICC and Beyond* (2005), 81.

[32]Scharf, note 2, at 9.

Article 6 of the London Charter defined the following acts as within its jurisdiction.[33] All generated individual responsibility. Unlike Leipzig, the Charter specifically rejected any defense based upon superior orders.

a. Crimes against Peace: Namely, planning, preparation, initiation or waging of a war of aggression, or a war in violation of international treaties, agreements or assurances, or participation in a common plan or conspiracy for the accomplishment of any of the foregoing [Emphasis added]

b. War Crimes: Namely, violations of the laws or customs of war. Such violations shall include, but not be limited to, murder, ill-treatment or deportation to slave labor or from any other purpose of civilian population of or in occupied territory, murder or ill-treatment of prisoners of war or persons on the seas, killing of hostages, plunder of public or private property, wanton destruction of cities, towns or villages, or devastation not justified by military necessity;

c. Crimes against Humanity: Namely, murder, extermination, enslavement, deportation, and other inhumane acts committed against any civilian population, before or during the war[;] or persecutions on political, racial or religious grounds in execution of or in connection with any crime within the jurisdiction of the Tribunal, whether or not in violation of the domestic law of the country where perpetrated.

The IMT conducted 22 trials. Twenty-one defendants (Martin Bormann, deputy for Nazi Party affairs, was tried *in absentia*) were present when the trials began on November 20, 1945. The trial lasted for 284 days. Each prosecuting team had a specific charge to present: the United States had the duty of presenting the conspiracy charges, the British detailed the "aggressive warfare" charges, and the French and the Soviets were to deal with war crimes and crimes against humanity, the French for Western Europe and the Soviets for Eastern Europe.[34] The defense raised four major issues: (1) international law applies to the acts of sovereign states only, thus no basis exists for punishing individuals; (2) individuals cannot be held responsible for "acts of state"; (3) the law applied was ex post facto; and (4) obedience to superior orders, either political or military, is a valid defense. The tribunal regarded none of these issues as sufficient. The tribunal gave its judgment on September 30, 1946,[35] and sentences were pronounced on October 1, 1946. Nineteen of the 22 defendants were found guilty; 12 were sentenced to death by hanging. Those sentences were carried out almost immediately, on October 16, 1946.

---

[33]See note 42.

[34]Watkins and Weber, note 31, at 82–83.

[35]Text of judgment and the sentences reprinted in 41 *AJIL* 172–332 (1947); see also Whiteman, XI: 880; G. Ginsburg and V. N. Kudriavtsev, eds, *The Nuremberg Trial and International Law* (1990); and J. E. Persico, *Nuremberg: Infamy on Trial* (1994).

Evaluation

The trials stand open to critique from many different perspectives. Certainly, from the standpoint of American legal standards, they violated many rules of due process associated with domestic trials. Second, the Allies were not without guilt with respect to certain activities (the *tu quoque* defense—you did it too), but this does not lessen the culpability of those accused and tried. Third, for all of the purported shortcomings, the trials set the tone for other trials of lesser figures. The Tokyo trials drew upon the London Charter as a model, as did other venues. Fourth, the trials put the idea that, under certain circumstances, international law does place duties directly upon the individual center stage. Presumably sovereignty could not serve as a blanket explanation to excuse atrocities.

INTERNATIONAL MILITARY TRIBUNAL FOR THE FAR EAST

Closely related to the Nuremberg trials was the establishment of the International Military Tribunal for the Far East (IMTFE, Tokyo). In this instance, the charter in question specified the categories of war crimes, crimes against peace, and crimes against humanity, together with a separate grouping of a crime of conspiracy to commit the foregoing crimes. Even though the course of the war in the Pacific produced instances of behavior comparable to that in Europe, the IMTFE has received far less attention than its European counterpart. Though influenced by the London Charter, the IMTFE resulted from the Proclamation of the Supreme Commander for the Allied Powers (January 19, 1946) signed by General Douglas MacArthur.[36] Although the 11 belligerents who had fought against Japan had the right to nominate judges, General MacArthur had sole authority of appointment. Judges who served came from Australia, Canada, China, Great Britain, France, India, the Netherlands, New Zealand, the Philippines, the Soviet Union, and the United States. The accused faced three charges: (1) murder, (2) crimes against peace, and (3) other conventional war crimes and crimes against humanity.[37] In all, 28 individuals were indicted and tried.[38]

Even before the beginning of the trials, controversy erupted over the decision to exempt the Japanese Emperor Hirohito from trial as a war criminal.[39] The trials

---

[36]Text of Charter in 14 *Department of State Bulletin* 361 (1946).

[37]Watkins and Weber, note 31, at 286.

[38]During the trials, two defendants died and one was unable to stand trial because of mental incompetence. For a critical treatment, see R. H. Minear, *Victor's Justice: The Tokyo War Crimes Trial* (1971). For an interesting dissent attacking the basis for the charges against the defendants, see the opinion of Judge R. M. Pal (India) in *The United States of America, et al. Against Sadeo Araki, et al.* reprinted in Watkins and Weber, note 31, at 337–343. Judge Pal argues, "The acts alleged are, in my opinion, all acts of state and whatever these accused are alleged to have done, they did that in working the machinery of the government, the duty and responsibility of working the same having fallen on them in due course of events." Pal, 338.

[39]For a discussion, see K. C. O'Neill, "A New Customary Law of Head of State Immunity: Hirohito and Pinochet," 38 *Stan. J. Int'l L.* 289 (2002).

began on June 4, 1946, and the judgment was given on November 4, 1948. The IMTFE found all of the defendants guilty. Seven were sentenced to death, and 16 to life imprisonment. No defendant who received a prison sentence actually served more than ten years.[40] In 1948, in a significant decision, the Supreme Court of the United States ruled that the tribunal was not a court of the United States and that consequently the Supreme Court had no jurisdiction to review or to set aside the tribunal's judgments.[41]

TRIALS BY NATIONAL TRIBUNALS

The publicity given to the proceedings of the two international military tribunals overshadowed the fact that most of the accused war criminals of World War II were tried by military courts of individual occupants, or they were returned to the scenes of their offenses and were tried by local courts and under local laws.[42] In some countries, where domestic legislation required, the accused offenders were tried in ordinary criminal courts for violating the local criminal laws. Most offenders, however, were brought before military courts of particular states for violating the laws and customs of war.

By late November 1948, a total of 7,109 defendants had been arrested for war crimes, including the "major cases" at Nuremberg and Tokyo. The trials that took place resulted in 3,686 convictions and 924 acquittals. Of those convicted, 1,019 received death sentences and 33 defendants committed suicide. Prison sentences were received by 2,667, and 2,499 cases were still pending. By the end of 1948, the Western Allies had convicted 5,025 Germans of war crimes, with 806 receiving the death penalty (486 were actually executed); the Soviet Union had convicted around 10,000, many of whom were sentenced to 25 years in jail and others to death. In the years since 1948, many other culprits have been discovered by their own governments (mostly in France and West Germany) and have been tried for war crimes. Unfortunately, the space available in a general text does not permit a detailed account of the thousands of national trials conducted and all of the hearings for deportation proceedings and/or for denaturalization purposes lately held in the United States (see Chapter 9).[43]

---

[40]Watkins and Weber, note 31, at 287.

[41]*Koki Hirota et al. v. Douglas MacArthur*, U.S. Supreme Court, 1948, 338 U.S. 197, digested in 43 *AJIL* 170 (1949); consult also Whiteman, XI: 965–1009, 1017–19; and especially P. R. Piccigallo, *The Japanese on Trial: Allied War Crimes Operations in the East, 1945–1951* (1979), which covers the Tokyo trials as well as the thousands of national trials in the Pacific area.

[42]See M. Koessler, "American War Crimes Trials in Europe," 39 *Georgetown L.J.* 18 (1950); W. B. Cowles, "Trials of War Criminals (Non-Nuremberg)," 42 *AJIL* 299 (1948); and Whiteman XI: 934.

[43]See, for illustrative purposes, H. Blum, *Wanted: The Search for Nazis in America* (1977); *New York Times* (January 20, 1975), 17; (August 29, 1975), 1, 4; (October 3, 1976), 1, 22; (October 18, 1976), 16; (November 28, 1976), E-5; and (November 10, 1978), A-3; *Time* (July 13, 1981), 43; and *Newsweek* (November 26, 1979), 93; and (February 25, 1980), 56.

AFTER NUREMBERG

The end of the Cold War promised an era of peace, cooperation, and development. Instead, it engendered wars that unleashed pent-up hostilities. The massacres and widespread hostilities in Yugoslavia, Rwanda, and Sierra Leone prompted the UN Security Council to set up several ad hoc courts to try the worst offenders. The events also spurred the development of a permanent ICC.

Yugoslavia

Yugoslavia began disintegrating in 1991. The drive by Serbia to assert dominance and resist secession produced a number of ugly incidents that included the shelling of Dubrovnik and the devastation of Vukovar.[44] The international community was extremely slow in its reaction. In October, the UN Security Council voted to establish a five-member commission of experts to investigate war crimes in the former Yugoslavia. The commission faced both financial and political problems in carrying out its task. Certainly, none of the permanent members of the Security Council seemed to have an interest of sufficient salience to bring the issue to discussion until media reports detailing the carnage began to appear and influence public opinion. Moreover, many believed that a press toward international prosecution would stymie peace negotiations.[45] Subsequently, in February 1993, the Security Council by Resolution 827 established the International Tribunal for the Prosecution of Persons Responsible for Serious Violations of International Humanitarian Law Committed in the Territory of the Former Yugoslavia since 1991 (ITFY).[46] In November, a special (chief) prosecutor was named.[47] Even at that point, establishment of the court seemed a token gesture. Bass concludes, "NATO had the troops. In all of the Hague's early difficulties, the fundamental hurdle was the West's refusal to take military action against war criminals in ex-Yugoslavia."[48] While prosecutions began, not until 1998 did the political climate really support the tribunal.

Rwanda[49]

The movie *Hotel Rwanda* focused on events during the genocide in Rwanda.[50] The movie fails to capture the true horror of what happened. In fact, the events

---

[44]See Bass, note 1, at 210–219; and Scharf, note 2, at 25–36; for short accounts of the events leading up to the establishment of the tribunal.

[45]See Bass, note 1, at 274ff.

[46]"United Nations: Secretary-General's Report on Aspects of Establishing an IT," 32 *International Legal Materials* 1163, 1192 (1993); International Tribunal, "Rules of Procedure and Evidence," 33 *ILM* 484 (1994); see also O'Brien's detailed analysis in 87 *AJIL* 639 (1993); and D. Orentlicher, "Yugoslavia War Crimes Tribunal," *ASIL Newsletter* (June–August 1993), *ASIL Focus* no. 1.

[47]T. Meron, "War Crimes in Yugoslavia and the Development of International Law," 88 *AJIL* 78 (1994).

[48]Bass, note 1, at 224.

[49]G. Prunier, *The Rwanda Crisis* (1997); S. Straus, *The Order of Genocide: Race, Power, and War in Rwanda* (2008); D. Temple-Raston, *Justice on the Grass: Three Rwandan Journalists, Their Trial for War Crimes, and a Nation's Quest for Redemption* (2005), 1–46; United Human Rights Council, "Genocide in Rwanda," www.unitedhumanrights.org/genocide/genocide_in_rwanda.htm.

[50]www.imdb.com/title/tt0395169/.

of 1994 simply represented the latest in a long line of massacres. The first Tutsi refugees had fled to Uganda to escape ethnic purges that occurred in 1959. These resulted from the "social revolution" of 1959 that overthrew the Tutsi-led monarchy. Initially, 50,000–70,000 Tutsi fled, but the refugee population had swelled to about 200,000 by 1990. The Rwandan Patriotic Front (RPF) had its origin in 1987, when Tutsi refugees in Uganda banded together. The stated purpose of the RPF was to facilitate repatriation of Tutsi to Rwanda. President Juvenal Habyarimana had taken a hard line against the return. On October 1, 1990, the Rwandan Patriotic Army (RPA), the armed wing of the RPF, invaded northern Rwanda. At first, Habyarimana did not see the rebels as a serious threat, but that changed when the RPA rapidly advanced and threatened the capital, Kigali. After that initial success, troops from France and Zaire, called in to aid the Habyarimana regime, forced the RPA to retreat in some disarray. The RPA then—in classic Mao fashion—retreated to the "hills," regrouped under Paul Kagame, and began a guerilla campaign to unseat the government. The war reached a stalemate. In July 1992, the two sides entered into peace negotiations that lasted a year and resulted in the signing of the *Arusha Accords* in early August 1993. The agreement would have created a government in which Hutu and Tutsi would share power. A UN peacekeeping force (UNAMIR) was to oversee the implementation.

On April 6, 1994, a plane carrying President Juvénal Habyarimana of Rwanda and President Cyprien Ntaryamira of Burundi crashed at Kigali Airport, killing all on board. Following the deaths of the two presidents, widespread killings—having both political and ethnic dimensions—began in Kigali and spread to other parts of Rwanda. Radical elements in Rwanda used the death to promote a wholesale slaughter of the Tutsi minority. Estimates range from 600,000 to 800,000 casualties. The slaughter stopped only with the invasion and ultimate success of an expatriate rebel force that succeeded in unseating the successor government. On July 1, 1994, the UN Security Council asked the secretary-general to appoint a commission to accumulate evidence of war crimes in Rwanda. After copious supporting material on massacres had been secured, on November 8, 1994, the Security Council, acting on its authority under Chapter VII of the Charter, adopted the Statute of the International Tribunal for Rwanda.[51]

Sierra Leone

The events that led to the establishment of the Special Court for Sierra Leone (SCSL) began in the late 1980s. The roots of the violence stemmed primarily from attempts to control the diamond industry.[52] The civil war in neighboring Liberia contributed as well. Charles Taylor, leader of the National Patriotic Front of Liberia (NPFL), provided money and support to Foday Sankoh to form the Revolutionary United Front (RUF). In return, Taylor received diamonds from Sierra

---

[51]Security Council Resolution 955 of November 8, 1994; text in 33 *ILM* 1598 (1994), and at http://69.94.11.53/ENGLISH/basicdocs/statute.html (accessed April 22, 2009).

[52]The 2006 film *Blood Diamonds* (Leonard DiCaprio) took its plot line from the events in Sierra Leone.

Leone.[53] The RUF launched its first campaign into eastern Sierra Leone from Liberia in late March 1991. In the months following, over 100,000 refugees fled the conflict into Guinea. The government was unable to mount an effective counterattack.

The RUF's signature tactic was terror through physical mutilation. An estimated 20,000 civilians suffered amputation of arms, legs, ears, and other body parts from machetes and axes. Fighting continued in the ensuing months, with the RUF gaining control of the diamond mines. The Sierra Leone Army seemed totally ineffective. A military coup in April 1992 unseated the government, but those who staged the coup seemed no more equipped than their predecessors to deal with the challenge presented by the RUF. In desperation the new government contracted the private military firm, Executive Outcomes (South Africa).[54] In approximately six weeks, the situation changed dramatically—the RUF was reduced to existence in border enclaves.

Under the auspices of the United Nations, President Kabbah and RUF leader Foday Sankoh negotiated a Peace Accord. The agreement made Sankoh vice-president and gave other RUF members positions in the government. It called for an international peacekeeping force (UNAMSIL) under the auspices of the United Nations. Almost immediately, however, the RUF began to violate the agreement, most notably by holding hundreds of UNAMSIL personnel hostage and capturing their arms and ammunition in the first half of 2000. In May 2000, the situation deteriorated to the point that British troops intervened to evacuate foreign nationals and establish order. They stabilized the situation and were the catalyst for a cease-fire and ending of the civil war.

Not until January 2002 did the fighting end. In June 2000, President Kabbah wrote to UN Secretary-General Kofi Annan requesting the United Nations to authorize a court to deal with crimes during the conflict. In August 2000, the UN Security Council adopted Resolution 1315 requesting the secretary-general to start negotiations with the Sierra Leonean government to create a Special Court. On January 16, 2002, the United Nations and the government of Sierra Leone signed an agreement establishing the court.[55] The Special Court for Sierra Leone has authority to try those who bear the greatest responsibility for serious violations of international humanitarian law and Sierra Leonean law committed in the territory of Sierra Leone since November 30, 1996.

THE COURTS: STRUCTURE AND ORGANIZATION

The events just described spurred the development of international courts. The disintegration of the former Yugoslavia and the internal strife in Rwanda and Sierra Leone prodded the international community to take action to deal with those who

---

[53]In December 2000, the UN General Assembly unanimously adopted a resolution on the role of diamonds used to fund conflicts, particularly in Africa. UN GAOR A/RES/55/56 (December 1, 2000). The General Assembly recognized that "conflict" (blood) diamonds formed a crucial element in the ongoing wars in parts of Africa.

[54]For concise discussions of the role of Executive Outcomes, see J. L. Taulbee, "Mercenaries, Private Armies and Contemporary Policy Options" 37 *International Politics* 433; and Taulbee, "The Privatization of Security: Modern Conflict, Globalization and Weak States," 5 *Civil Wars* 1 (2002).

[55]UN SCOR S/RES/1315 (January 16, 2002).

TABLE 22.1

International Criminal Courts[56]

Court	Number of Judges	Selection	Term of Office	Seat
ICTY	16 permanent, 12 ad litem (temporary increased to 16 in 2008)	Elected by the UN General Assembly	Permanent—4 years (can be reelected), ad litem—4 years (no reelection)	The Hague (Netherlands)
ICTR	16 permanent, 9 ad litem (maximum)	Elected by the UN General Assembly	Permanent—4 years (can be reelected), ad litem—4 years (no reelection)	Arusha (Tanzania)
SCSL	11 permanent	Trial: 4 appointed by UN secretary-general; 2 by the government of Sierra Leone Appeals: 3 appointed by UN secretary-general, 2 by government of Sierra Leone	3-year terms	The Hague (Netherlands)
ICC	18 permanent	Elected by the Assembly of States Parties	9-year terms (can be reelected); 1/3 elected every 3 years	The Hague (Netherlands)

had ordered, instigated, or otherwise taken part in the large-scale atrocities that defined these conflicts. In response to specific conflicts, the UN Security Council authorized three ad hoc courts: the International Criminal Tribunal for Yugoslavia (ICTY), the International Criminal Tribunal for Rwanda (ICTR), and the Special Court for Sierra Leon (SCSL).[57] In addition to the temporary courts, work proceeded on establishing a permanent ICC. The treaty establishing the ICC (Rome Statute) was opened for signature on July 17, 1998. The ICC became a reality when the Statute entered into force in July 1, 2002, with deposit of the 60th instrument of ratification. Table 22.1 summarizes the structure of the ICTY, ICTR, SCSL, and the ICC. The SCSL differs from the ICTY and ICTR in that it was created under the joint authority of the government of Sierra Leone and of the United Nations to try those accused of violations of international humanitarian law (and the law of Sierra Leone) within the territory of Sierra Leone since November 30, 1996.[58]

Each court has three main organs: chambers (judges), office of the prosecutor, and registry (administrative division). In the three ad hoc courts, the chambers are divided into trial chambers and an appeals chamber. The ICC differs somewhat in

---

[56]J. L. Taulbee, International Crime and Punishment (2009), ch. 3.

[57]The Security Council has authorized a fourth ad hoc court—the Special Tribunal for Cambodia. We have chosen to limit our discussion to the functioning international courts.

[58]"About the Special Court," www.sc-sl.org/ABOUT/tabid/70/Default.aspx.

that it has a pretrial chamber that passes on indictments brought by the prosecutor as well as trial chambers and an appeals chamber. The ICTY and ICTR began with two trial chambers, but the Security Council authorized a third in 1998 as the volume of prosecutions increased. Each trial chamber has three judges; the appeals chamber has five.[59] The SCSL began with only one trial chamber; a second was established in 2005.

None of the courts have a separate investigative or police branch. The prosecutors operate as independent agents and are responsible for overseeing investigations. The tribunals have no independent means of enforcement beyond the active cooperation of national authorities. Until February 2003, the ICTY and ICTR shared an appeals chamber and prosecutor. In the interest of speeding up the process, the Security Council increased the number of judges on the ICTR and authorized additional judges *ad litem* for both tribunals, as well as a separate prosecutor and appeals chamber for the ICTR. The ICTY, ICTR, and SCSL have a mandate to finish all original trials by 2010 and all appeals by 2011.[60] The ICC, as a permanent court, will continue as the "court of last resort" with respect to prosecutions for violations of international criminal law.

The ICTY and ICTR have authority to prosecute four clusters of offenses: grave breaches of the 1949 Geneva Conventions, violations of the laws or customs of war, genocide, and crimes against humanity committed on the territory of—and within the time frame specified—in their charters. The SCSL Statute does not include genocide as a crime. Unlike the Nuremberg court, the courts have jurisdiction only over natural persons, not over organizations, political parties, administrative entities, or other legal subjects. The ad hoc courts have concurrent jurisdiction with national courts, but in any case in an ad hoc court, the jurisdiction of the international court overrides that of any national court.[61]

As with the tribunal at Nuremberg, the ICTY and ICTR had to deal with the difficulties inherent in trying to draw from both the civil and common law traditions as well as international human rights law.[62] The tribunal's first trial was held in the case of *Prosecutor v. Tadic,* from May 7 to November 28, 1996.[63] The judges had three main issues:[64] (1) Was the war in Bosnia an international armed conflict? (2) Did widespread and systematic abuse against Serbs occur? and (3) Did Tadic personally engage (and to what extent) in criminal acts against non-Serbs? The first issue divided the court (2–1, Judge McDonald dissenting), resulting in not-guilty verdicts on several counts on the basis that individuals within the sector

---

[59]"ICTY at a Glance," www.un.org/icty/glance-e/index.htm (accessed April 22, 2009).

[60]Security Council Resolution 955 of November 8, 1994; text in 33 *ILM* 1598 (1994) and at www.un.org/ictr/english/Resolutions/955e.htm.

[61]"ICTY at a Glance," note 100. On April 7, 2006, the Appeals Chamber upheld the decision to refer the Mejakic et al. case, involving four accused, to Bosnia and Herzegovina for trial. The Appeals Chamber dismissed eight of the grounds in the Joint Defence Appeal, and allowed one in part; www.un.org/icty/latest-e/index.htm (accessed April 22, 2009).

[62]See F. King and A. LaRosa, "The Jurisprudence of the Yugoslavia Tribunal: 1994–1996," 8 *EJIL* (1997), 123–179, www.ejil.org/pdfs/8/1/1403.pdf.

[63]ICTY Case No. IT-94-1-T, www.un.org/icty/tadic/trialc2/judgement/tad-sj970714e.pdf (accessed April 22, 2009).

[64]Scharf, note 2, at 208.

did not have "protected status."[65] The defendant did not really contest the second, and sufficient testimony from witnesses confirmed a number of charges related to the third. The sentencing judgment was rendered on July 14, 1997.[66]

Despite the Security Council mandate, at the beginning the ICTY had problems in rounding up the principal planners and instigators of the events for trial. The lack of political will on the part of all involved continually undermined efforts to arrest the individuals most responsible for the atrocities in the Balkans. A decision by Prime Minister Tony Blair in 1998 resulted in British troops acting as peacekeepers in the Balkans, actively pursuing those wanted. Even with the very slow start, with the July 2008 arrest of Radovan Karadzic and the May 2011 arrest of Ratko Mladic, of those formally indicted, only Goran Hadzic remains at large. As of July 2011, the ICTY had issued 161 indictments. Of these, there have been 80 convictions, 13 acquittals, and 13 referrals to national courts. The tribunal had 14 additional trials then in progress.

The former president of the Federal Republic of Yugoslavia, Slobodan Milosevic, became the highest-profile defendant to stand trial since Nuremberg.[67] As one of the principal players in the breakup of Yugoslavia, Milosevic was accused of complicity in persecution based upon political, racial, or religious grounds; genocide; willful killing and torture; willful and wanton destruction of property unconnected to military necessity; unlawful attacks on civilians; and other crimes against humanity. After Milosevic's defeat in a September 2000 election, his successor, Zoran Djindjic, arranged for his arrest and extradition to The Hague in April 2001.[68] As Hermann Goering had at Nuremberg, Milosevic pleaded not guilty to all of the charges, but he vehemently rejected the idea that the tribunal had any authority to pass judgment on him. He died in March 2006, before the defense phase of the trial had begun. At that point, the prosecution had called 294 witnesses.

ICTR As of July 2011, the ICTR had issued 92 indictments. Nine of those indicted still remain at large. The tribunal has finished 54 trials with 18 cases still on appeal. It has acquitted 8. Ten trials were in progress. Four indictments were withdrawn (two died in custody). Two cases had been referred to national authorities.

For the ICTR, the first case, that of Jean-Paul Akayesu, began with his indictment in May 1996. In August 2003, the Security Council adopted Resolution 1503, which urged both the ICTR and the ICTY to complete all investigations by 2004, all trials by 2008, and all appeals by 2010.[69] As of December 2011, the court had completed 32 cases—19 in the appeal stage, 10 more in progress, and 1 individual awaiting trial. Ten indictees remain at large.[70]

---

[65]See Article 2 of the statute creating the court: www.un.org/icty/legaldoc-e/index.htm (accessed April 22, 2009).

[66]www.un.org/icty/tadic/trialc2/judgement/tad-sj970714e.pdf (accessed April 22, 2009).

[67]ITCY case IT-02-54, "Bosnia and Herzegovina," summary at www.un.org/icty/cases-e/index-e.htm (accessed April 22, 2009).

[68]See D. Williams and R. Smith, "Crusader for Serb Honor Was Defiant Until the End," *Washington Post* (March 12, 2006), A16. Subsequently, a gunman assassinated Djindjic in March 2003.

[69]International Criminal Tribunal for Rwanda (ICTR), www.unictr.org/AboutICTR/GeneralInformation/tabid/101/Default.aspx.

[70]*Ibid.*

The *Akayesu* case, which follows, is the first in which an international tribunal had to apply the definition of genocide as defined in the Convention for the Prevention and Punishment of the Crime of Genocide (1948). The trial chamber recalled that *genocide* means, as described in the convention, "the act of committing certain crimes, including the killing of members of the group or causing serious physical or mental harm to members of the group with the intent to destroy, in whole or in part, a national, racial or religious group, as such."

THE PROSECUTOR OF THE TRIBUNAL AGAINST JEAN PAUL AKAYESU

Allegations of Fact

Between January 1, 1994, and December 31, 1994, in the commune of Taba, prefecture of Gitarama, territory of Rwanda, Jean-Paul Akayesu[71] as the mayor had the duty to perform executive functions and maintain public order within his commune, subject to the authority of the prefect. He had exclusive control over the communal police as well as any gendarmes put at the disposition of the commune. He was responsible for the execution of laws and regulations and the administration of justice, also subject only to the prefect's authority.

Between April 7 and the end of June 1994, hundreds of civilians (hereinafter "displaced civilians") sought refuge at the bureau communal. The majority of these displaced civilians were Tutsi. During this time, female displaced civilians were regularly taken by armed local militia and/or communal police and subjected to sexual violence, and/or beaten on or near the bureau communal premises. Displaced civilians were also murdered frequently on or near the bureau communal premises. These acts of sexual violence were generally accompanied by explicit threats of death or bodily harm. The female displaced civilians lived in constant fear, and their physical and psychological health deteriorated as a result of the sexual violence and beatings and killings.

Akayesu "knew that the acts of sexual violence, beatings and murders were being committed and was at times present during their commission. He facilitated the commission of the sexual violence, beatings and murders by allowing the sexual violence and beatings and murders to occur on or near the bureau communal premises. By virtue of his presence during the commission of the sexual violence, beatings and murders and by failing to prevent the sexual violence, beatings and murders, he encouraged these activities." In addition to these general charges, the indictment details a number of specific incidents.

Charges

Akayesu was charged with 15 offenses that included genocide, complicity in genocide, direct incitement to commit genocide, and various crimes against humanity (as defined in the statute of the court).

Defense

During the trial, the defense argued that Akayesu was a "scapegoat" who found himself accused only because he was a Hutu and a mayor at the time of the massacres. In his closing argument, the defense attorney claimed that witnesses were

(continued)

---

[71]*Ibid.*

colluding in a "syndicate of informers" that would denounce a particular individual for political reasons or in order to take over his property. In this connection, he quoted Rene Degni-Segui, the special rapporteur of the Commission on Human Rights on Rwanda, who recounted a story of a demonstrably innocent Rwandan who had been denounced by 15 witnesses as a participant in the genocide.

Verdict

"The Chamber holds that, as a blanket allegation to undermine the credibility of prosecution witnesses, this allegation can carry no weight, for two reasons. First, an attack on credibility which is not particularised with respect to individual witnesses is no attack at all on those witnesses' credibility; it is merely a generalised and unsubstantiated suspicion. Doubt can only arise where the criteria for

doubt are fulfilled. . . . It is to be noted that during the trial the Defence did not put, nor even suggest, to a single prosecution witness that he or she was lying because he or she had been drawn into a syndicate of informers and instructed as to how to testify against the accused, or that the witness was lying because he or she wished to take the accused's property."

The chamber found him guilty on 9 of the 15 counts named in the indictment. These included genocide (murder) and crimes against humanity (rape, torture, and extermination). He received a sentence of life in prison. In addition, for the first time, the chamber also determined that rape and sexual violence may constitute genocide in the same way as any other act of serious bodily or mental harm, if such acts were committed with the intent to destroy a particular group targeted as such.

The following case, dubbed "the Media trial," gained a great deal of attention because it raises interesting issues of freedom of speech.[72] Many countries have decided that there is a point at which hate speech should be stopped. Article 19 of the ICCPR (Chapter 15) states, "Everyone shall have the right to hold opinions without interference," but it also states that the exercise of the rights "carries with it special duties and responsibilities." Restrictions may be lawfully placed on speech to protect "the rights or reputations of others," and for "the protection of national security of public order or of public health or morals."[73]

The three men named in the indictment were charged as being responsible for the venomous broadcasts of RTLM, which Rwandans called "Radio Hate."[74] Ferdinand Nahimana and Jean-Bosco Barayagwiza were the founders of RTLM; Hassan Ngeze was the editor of *Kangura* magazine, which ran vicious anti-Tutsi propaganda pieces that were often read or discussed on the air.[75] One witness in

---

[72]Also called the "Radio Machete" trial.

[73]See also Article 10(2) of the European Convention on Human Rights. For an interesting exchange on these issues, see Human Rights Brief, "Point/Counterpoint," www.wcl.american.edu/hrbrief/03/2point.cfm (accessed April 22, 2009). See also Radio Free Europe, "Europe: Case of Swedish Pastor Convicted of Hate Speech Tests Limits of Freedom," www.rferl.org/featuresarticle/2005/01/d0e0334d-17b74d39-82c7-a012302d48f6.html (accessed April 22, 2009).

[74]D. Temple-Raston, "Radio Hate," *Legal Affairs* (September–October 2002), www.legalaffairs.org/issues/September-October-2002/feature_raston_sepoct2002.msp (accessed April 22, 2009).

[75]For brief profiles of the three, see ICTR, "The Media Trial," http://69.94.11.53/default.htm (accessed April 22, 2009).

the trial said that RTLM "spread petrol throughout the country little by little, so that one day it would be able to set fire to the whole country."[76] In the 80-page indictment, the three were charged before the ICTR with inciting fellow Hutus to commit genocide. These men were the first journalists accused of such serious crimes since 1946, when the Nazi editor Julius Streicher was sentenced to hang at Nuremberg for calling for the murder of Jews.[77]

In Rwanda, people get most of their information from radio broadcasts. Until 1993, Rwanda had only one national station, the government-owned Radio Rwanda. Then the government gave a license to Nahimana and Barayagwiza to start RTLM. It denied licenses to other applicants who might have offered competing viewpoints.[78] RTLM introduced talk radio to Rwanda. The station was the country's first and only privately owned alternative to government programming. The following case excerpt focuses on the role of RTLM in the events of 1994.

THE PROSECUTOR V. FERDINAND NAHIMANA, JEAN-BOSCO BARAYAGWIZA, AND HASSAN NGEZE

International Criminal Tribunal for Rwanda Trial Chamber I Case No. ICTR-99-52-T (2003)

Allegations of Fact

The indictment alleged that the programming on RTLM promoted ethnic stereotyping in a manner that promoted contempt and hatred for the Tutsi population. RTLM broadcasts called on listeners to seek out and take up arms against the enemy. The enemy was identified as the RPF, the Inkotanyi, the Inyenzi, and their accomplices, all of whom were effectively equated with the Tutsi ethnic group by the broadcasts. After April 6, 1994, the virulence and the intensity of RTLM broadcasts propagating ethnic hatred and calling for violence increased. These broadcasts called explicitly for the extermination of the Tutsi ethnic group.

Nahimana was seen as the founder and director of the company. Barayagwiza was seen as his second in command. They represented RTLM externally in an official capacity. Internally, they controlled the financial operations of the company and held supervisory responsibility for all activities of RTLM, taking remedial action when they considered it necessary to do so. Nahimana also played an active role in determining the content of RTLM broadcasts, writing editorials and giving journalists texts to read.

On several RTLM broadcasts, Ngeze called for the extermination of the Tutsi and of Hutu political opponents. He defended the extremist Hutu ideology that called for extermination of the Tutsi.

Charges

The three accused were charged in separate indictments, but tried jointly. All were charged on counts of genocide, conspiracy

(continued)

---

[76]ICTR, "Judgment and Sentence," http://69.94.11.53/default.htm (accessed April 22, 2009), 23.

[77]"Tribunal at a Glance," note 111.

[78]Temple-Raston, note 74.

to commit genocide, direct and public incitement to commit genocide, complicity in genocide, and crimes against humanity (persecution and extermination). In addition, Ngeze was charged with crimes against humanity (murder). All were charged with individual criminal responsibility under Article 6(1) of the statute for these crimes. Nahimana was additionally charged with superior responsibility under Article 6(3) in respect of direct and public incitement to commit genocide and the crime against humanity of persecution. Barayagwiza and Ngeze were additionally charged with superior responsibility under Article 6(3) in respect of all the counts except conspiracy to commit genocide.

Defense

Jean-Bosco Barayagwiza elected not to attend his trial. He stated that he did not have confidence that he would be afforded a fair trial in light of the Appeal Chamber's reversal of its decision ordering his release before the trial.

The defense raised the free speech standards of the United States. It also argues the need to promote vigilance with respect to an armed and dangerous enemy.

Verdict

All were convicted of genocide and conspiracy to commit genocide. Nahimana and Ngeze were convicted on 5 of 7 charges; Barayagwiza, on 5 of 9 charges. Nahimana and Ngeze received life sentences. Because of what it considered violations of his rights, Barayagwiza received a sentence of 35 years less time already served (8 years).

Special Court for Sierra Leone

At this writing, the court has 11 individuals, associated with all three of the former warring factions, in custody.[79] The court has completed trials of three former leaders of the Armed Forces Revolutionary Council (AFRC), and of two members of the Civil Defence Forces (CDF), including appeals. Testimony has ended in the trial of three former Revolutionary United Front (RUF) leaders, and a trial judgment was expected early in 2009. The highest-profile trial conducted by the SCSL is that of former Liberian President Charles Taylor. The court initially indicted him on 650 counts of war crimes and crimes against humanity. The case at trial involves only 11 counts. Allegedly, Taylor had provided active support for the rebel forces (RUF) during the civil war in Sierra Leone. The trial finally concluded in March 2011.

A Note on Costs

International justice does not come at bargain basement prices. Consider the fixed costs of salary for judges and support personnel as well as the costs associated with maintaining necessary facilities. For example, the ICTY has 1,200 staff. To the ongoing fixed costs, add those of actual trial costs.[80] Trials may last two years. Some defense costs may be reduced because since 2003, defense lawyers are paid

---

[79]"About the Special Court," www.sc-sl.org/about.html (accessed April 22, 2009).

[80]S. de Bertodano, "What Price Defence? Resourcing the Defence at the ICTY," 2 *Journal of International Criminal Justice* 503 (2004).

on a lump-sum basis. The savings here, however, may be offset by the increased number of high-level defendants, who have produced more complex trials.[81] In addition to fees for defense attorneys, one must consider other administrative costs related to operating in an international environment. For example, fairness demands that all have easy access to the relevant documents. This may require several copies in several different languages. Consider as well the costs of transport and maintenance for witnesses. The biannual budget for the ICTY for 2008 and 2009 was US $347,566,900.[82] The Taylor trial by the SCSL received $36 million for 2008.[83] The Tadic trial cost $20 million to convict a low-level foot soldier.

THE INTERNATIONAL CRIMINAL COURT

History

Tracing the history of efforts to construct the ICC involves following two separate tracks: the effort to draft an international criminal code and initiatives for an independent international court. In November 1947, the General Assembly charged the International Law Commission (ILC) with two tasks: first, to formulate the principles of international law recognized in the Charter and Judgment of the Nuremberg Tribunal; and second, with careful attention to these principles, to prepare a draft code of offenses against the peace and security of humankind.[84] The creation of the court was tied to other negotiations then in progress. During the preparatory work that produced the Genocide Convention, representatives from the United States pushed hard for inclusion of language authorizing the creation of an international tribunal.

Delegates from the Soviet Union, among others, expressed major reservations.[85] Unlike the International Court of Justice, where jurisdiction was limited to disputes between countries, the ICC was envisioned as a court that would assert jurisdiction directly over individuals for certain crimes not otherwise punished in national courts.[86] Article VI of the convention emerged as a compromise, providing for trial "by a competent tribunal of the State in the territory of which the act was committed, or by such international penal tribunal as may have jurisdiction with respect to those Contracting Parties which shall have accepted its jurisdiction."[87]

---

[81]*Ibid.,* 504–505.

[82]ICTY Weekly Press Briefing, January 16, 2008.

[83]BBC, "Sierra Leone UN court has enough funds to complete Taylor trial—registrar" (November 27, 2008).

[84]G.A. Res. 177(II), UN Doc. A/519 (1947).

[85]For a discussion of the original negotiations, see L. LeBlanc, *The United States and the Genocide Convention* (1991), 151–174. Ironically, the concerns of the USSR (e.g., diminution of sovereign prerogatives) expressed during the negotiations mirrored many of the concerns expressed by members of the U.S. Senate during the first, and subsequent, debates over possible ratification.

[86]A permanent court that would hear cases of international criminal law has been widely discussed by scholars for over a century and seriously debated since the conclusion of World War I. See H. H. Jescheck, "International Criminal Law: Its Object and Recent Developments," in 1 *International Criminal Law,* edited by M. C. Bassiouni and V. P. Nanda (1973), 49, 72.

[87]Convention on the Prevention and Punishment of the Crime of Genocide, December 9, 1948, 78 U.N.T.S. 277 (hereinafter Genocide Convention).

The Sixth Committee (UN General Assembly) recommended the creation of an ad hoc committee to produce a draft statute to take the debate out of the realm of conjecture and hypothetical argument.[88] The Committee on International Criminal Jurisdiction produced a report late in 1953. Reacting to the charge that the proposed court would have little positive law to utilize, the General Assembly subsequently linked consideration of that report to the development of the draft code of offenses against the peace and security of humankind, which was still part of the working agenda of the ILC. In 1954 the ILC submitted the draft of a convention, with extensive commentaries, to the General Assembly.[89]

At this juncture, another issue arose. The General Assembly noted that while the ILC's draft code listed aggression as the first offense, the General Assembly had already entrusted a Special Committee with the task of preparing a report on a draft definition of *aggression*.[90] The assembly decided to postpone consideration of the draft code until the Special Committee had submitted its report.[91] That decision effectively ended active consideration of the issues for the next 25 years. Not until 1981 did the General Assembly invite the ILC to resume its work on the draft code.[92] Another 15 years passed before the commission finally produced a second draft code.[93]

In 1989, Trinidad and Tobago raised the possibility of a court to deal with international drug trafficking, but it took the events in the former Yugoslavia and Rwanda to move the issue forward.[94] While the ILC again debated the questions concerning the definition of *offenses against peace and security,* in the early 1990s, events in the Balkans and Rwanda gave renewed impetus to the idea of an international court. In late 1992, the General Assembly requested that the ILC undertake

[88]1950 U.N.Y.B. 857, 861 (1951); and V. Pella, "Towards an International Criminal Court," 44 *AJIL* 37 (1950).

[89]1957 U.N.Y.B. 376 (1958). See also J. W. Bridges, "The Case for an International Court of Criminal Justice and the Formulation of International Criminal Law," 13 *International Criminal Law Quarterly* 1255, 1255–1281 (1964); and C. Bassiouni, "The Proscribing Function of International Criminal Law in the Process of International Protection of Human Rights," 9 *Yale J. World Pub. Ord.* 193, 195–196 (1982).

[90]On the basis of the recommendations of the Special Committee, the General Assembly finally adopted the Definition of Aggression by consensus in 1974. G.A. Res. 3314, UN GAOR, 29th Sess., Supp. 31, UN Doc. A/9631 (1974).

[91]G.A. Res. 897(IX), UN GAOR, 9th Sess., Supp. No. 21, UN Doc A/2890 (1954).

[92]UN GAOR, 36th Sess., UN Doc. A/Res/36/106 (1981). From 1982 to 1991, the special rapporteur, Doudou Thiam (Senegal), produced nine yearly reports for the Commission. See [1983] 2 *Y.B. Int'l L. Comm'n,* UN Doc. A/CN.4/364; [1984] 2 *Y.B. Int'l L. Comm'n* 89, UN Doc. A/CN.4/377; [1985] 2 *Y.B. Int'l L. Comm'n* 63, UN Doc. A/CN.4/387; [1986] 2 *Y.B. Int'l L. Comm'n* 53, UN Doc. A/CN.4/398; [1987] 2 *Y.B. Int'l L. Comm'n* 1, UN Doc. A/CN.4/404; [1988] 2 *Y.B. Int'l L. Comm'n* 197, UN Doc. A/CN.4/411; [1989] 2 *Y.B. Int'l L. Comm'n* 81, UN Doc. A/CN.4/419; [1990] 2 *Y.B. Int'l L. Comm'n* 27, UN Doc. A/CN.4/430; and [1991] 2 *Y.B. Int'l L. Comm'n* 37, UN Doc. A/CN.4/435.

[93]Report of the International Law Commission on the Work of Its Forty-eighth Session, UN GAOR, 51st Sess., Supp. No. 10, at 14, UN Doc. A/51/10 (1996) (hereinafter, 1996 Draft Code).

[94]See International Criminal Responsibility of Individual and Entities Engaged in Illicit Trafficking in Narcotic Drugs Across National Frontiers and Other Transnational Criminal Activities: Establishment of an International Criminal Court with Jurisdiction over Such Crimes, G.A. Res. 44/39, UN GAOR, 44th Sess., Supp. No. 49 at 311, UN Doc. A/444/49 (1989).

the "elaboration of a draft statute for an international criminal court."[95] Subsequently, in 1993 and 1994, the Security Council authorized ad hoc tribunals for the former Yugoslavia and for Rwanda. The ILC moved expeditiously on the ICC assignment, issuing its report in 1994.[96] Because of continuing division over the desirability of establishing a permanent court, the assembly first established an Ad Hoc Committee to study the issue further, and then two years later authorized a Preparatory Committee to prepare a statute for consideration by a conference of plenipotentiaries.[97] Early in 1998, the Preparatory Commission produced a consolidated text of a statute regarding the establishment of a permanent ICC for adoption at a diplomatic conference held in Rome on June 15–17, 1998.[98] Even though post Nuremberg, the paucity of prosecutions at any level for war crimes and other gross violations of humanitarian law, combined with the checkered success of the more recent ad hoc tribunals, strongly suggested a continuing lack of political will to exert pressure for full compliance on reluctant parties by both the Security Council and the broader international community, nevertheless, states voted to establish a permanent court by an overwhelming majority (120–7, with 21 abstentions). The Rome Statute entered into force on July 1, 2002 (60 ratifications). Of the five permanent members of the UN Security Council, Britain and France have ratified the statute, the Russian Federation has signed it (September 2000), China has not signed, and the United States has "withdrawn" its signature (see Chapter 4). Of others, Germany and Italy have ratified, Japan did not sign, Iran signed (December 2000), and Iraq did not. Neither India nor Pakistan signed. In 2011, Tunisia became the 116th state to ratify the statute.

---

[95]UN GAOR, 47th Sess., UN Doc. A/Res/50/46 (1992).

[96]The ILC draft statute and commentaries are found in Report of the International Law Commission on the Work of Its Forty-sixth Session, UN GAOR, 49th Sess., Supp. No. 10, at 43, UN Doc. A/49/10 (1994) (hereinafter, Draft Statute).

[97]There is no formal written record of the deliberations of the Preparatory Committee. For summaries, see C. K. Hall, "The First Two Sessions of the UN Preparatory Committee on the Establishment of an International Criminal Court," 91 *AJIL* 177, 177–187 (1997) (hereinafter, Hall 1); Hall, "The Third and Fourth Sessions of the UN Preparatory Committee on the Establishment of an International Criminal Court," 92 *AJIL* 124 (1998) (hereinafter, Hall 2); Hall, "The Fifth Session of the UN Preparatory Committee on the Establishment of an International Criminal Court," 92 *AJIL* 331 (1998) (hereinafter, Hall 3); and Hall, "The Sixth Session of the UN Preparatory Committee on the Establishment of an International Criminal Court," 92 *AJIL* 548 (1998) (hereinafter, Hall 4). See also Summary of the Proceedings of the Preparatory Committee During the Period 25 March–12 April 1996, UN Doc. A/AC.249/1 (1996); Draft Set of Rules of Procedure and Evidence for the International Criminal Court, UN Doc. A/AC.249/L.2 (1997); Report of the Working Group on Definition of Crimes, UN Doc. A/AC.249/1997/L.2 (1997); Report of the Working Group on General Principles of Criminal Law and Penalties, UN Doc. A/AC.249/1997/L.3 (1997); Decision Taken by the Preparatory Committee at Its Session Held from 11 to 21 February 1997, UN Doc. A/AC.249/1997/L.5 (1997); UN Doc. A/AC.249/1997/L.6 (1997); Report of the Working Group on Procedural Matters, UN Doc. A/AC.249/1997/L.7 (1997); Decision Taken by the Preparatory Committee at Its Session Held from 4 to 15 August 1997, UN Doc. A/AC.249/1997/L.8 (1997); Decision Taken by the Preparatory Committee at Its Session Held From 4 to 15 August 1997, UN Doc. A/AC.249/1997/L.8/Rev.1 (1997); and UN Doc. A/AC.249/1997/L.9 (1997).

[98]Rome Statute of the International Criminal Court, July 17, 1998, 37 *ILM* 999 (hereinafter, Rome Statute). The vote was 120–7, with 21 abstentions; www.icc-cpi.int/home.html.

Structure and Jurisdiction

The ICC sits at The Hague and operates as an independent international organization.[99] In accordance with Article 2 of the Rome Statute, the Negotiated Relationship Agreement Between the International Criminal Court and the United Nations governs the relationship.[100] The Assembly of States Parties forms the management oversight and legislative body for the court. The assembly has established a permanent secretariat and a bureau (interim oversight) to manage the everyday operations of the court. Article 5 establishes the grant of subject matter jurisdiction as being "limited to the most serious crimes of concern to the international community as a whole"—genocide, crimes against humanity, war crimes, and aggression.[101] The Rome Statute, rather than referencing the relevant treaties, contains definitions of the crimes within its substantive jurisdiction listed in Article 5 within the body of the treaty.[102] More importantly, the *in personam* jurisdiction of the court was designed to be *complementary* to that of national courts, meaning that it may try cases only where "a state is *unwilling or unable* to carry out the investigation or prosecution (Article 17(1)(a))" (Emphasis added). Two further limitations on jurisdiction exist as well. The court may seize only cases where the events (or portions of the events) have occurred after July 1, 2002, when the Rome Statute entered into effect. Second, double jeopardy applies as well. The court may not try individuals if they have already been tried in another court unless the trial was a sham designed to absolve the person of any guilt (Article 20). On the other hand, no accused may claim immunity of any kind (head of state, diplomatic, or special grant).

Getting Started

In February 2003, the Assembly of States Parties elected the 18 judges of the ICC. In the future, judges will have nine-year terms—the Rome Statute provides that six will be elected every three years—however, for the first election (as with the ICJ), judges were elected for terms of three, six, and nine years. The judges constitute a forum of international experts who represent the world's principal legal systems.[103] Judges must be nationals of states parties to the statute. The election process itself contains an interesting requirement because the Rome Statute specifies

---

[99]Article 4 states, "The Court shall have international legal personality."

[100]Text at www.icc-cpi.int/library/asp/ICC-ASP-3-Res1_English.pdf (accessed April 22, 2009).

[101]Article 5(2) has a caveat, 2:

> The Court shall exercise jurisdiction over the crime of aggression once a provision is adopted in accordance with articles 121 and 123 defining the crime and setting out the conditions under which the Court shall exercise jurisdiction with respect to this crime. Such a provision shall be consistent with the relevant provisions of the Charter of the United Nations.

Considering the history of international efforts to define aggression (Chapter 20), the provisions for amending the statute (seven-eighths of the Assembly of States Parties) raise serious doubts about future incorporation of this crime into the court's mandate.

[102]Note that attempts to include drug trafficking and "terrorism" in the list failed.

[103]Seven are from the Western European Group (and others), four from the Latin American Caribbean Group, three from the Asian Group, three from the African Group, and two from the Group of Eastern Europe. Seven are female and 11 are male judges.

two different sets of qualifications that define eligible candidates. One list consists of candidates with established competence in criminal law and procedures as well as the necessary relevant experience, whether as judge, as prosecutor, as advocate, or in other similar capacity in criminal proceedings. The second list consists of candidates with established competence in relevant areas of international law, such as international humanitarian law and the law of human rights, and extensive experience in a professional legal capacity that is of relevance to the judicial work of the court (Article 36(5)).

Operations

Cases may come to the court through several different avenues. States parties may refer cases, as may the UN Security Council. The prosecutor may initiate investigative proceedings (*proprio motu,* on his or her own initiative) with the consent of a majority vote (two of three) of judges sitting in a pretrial chamber. At this writing (July 2011), three states parties to the Rome Statute—Uganda, the Democratic Republic of the Congo, and the Central African Republic—have referred situations occurring on their territories to the court. The prosecutor has opened investigations into all three situations. In March 2010, Pre-Trial Chamber II granted the prosecution authorization to open an investigation proprio motu in the situation of Kenya. The UN Security Council has referred two cases: the Darfur (Sudan, March 2005) and Libya (February 2011).[104] These referrals are interesting because three of the five permanent members of the Security Council (China, Russia, and the United States) are not states parties to the court.

SUMMARY OF CASES BEFORE THE ICC JULY 2011

Uganda:	Four warrants of arrest have been issued against four top leaders of the Lord's Resistance Army (LRA).
Democratic Republic of the Congo:	Four cases are being heard by the relevant chambers with two others at the pre-trial stage.
Sudan:	Four cases are before Pre-Trial Chamber I:
Central African Republic:	The case *The Prosecutor v. Jean-Pierre Bemba Gombo* is at the trial stage.
Kenya:	On March 7–8, 2011, six people voluntarily appeared before Pre-Trial Chamber II. Confirmation of charges hearing in the case of *The Prosecutor v. William Samoei Ruto, Henry Kiprono Kosgey, and Joshua Arap Sang* were scheduled to start on September 1, 2011.[105]

---

[104]www.icc-cpi.int/Menus/ICC/Situations+and+Cases/.

[105]ICC, Weekly Update, April 11, 2011.

Perhaps the most controversial indictment to date came in July 2008, when the prosecutor requested that the ICC issue an arrest warrant for Omar Hassan Ahmad al-Bashir, president of Sudan, on the charge of genocide and crimes against humanity.[106] The request raised a storm of protest from many who feared this would impede a diplomatic settlement in Darfur. These arguments were raised as well with respect to the ICTY.[107] Prior to his capture and death in October 2011, the court had issued an arrest warrant for Muammar Gaddafi (June 2011), the leader of Libya. Critics again argued that this would impede a solution to the crisis because fear of extradition to the court would prevent his going into exile.[108] More to the point, the seeming focus of the court on Africa (and perhaps now the Middle East) has also led to a charge of an inherent Western (and Great Power) bias. They see the court as intent on holding the weak to strict accountability while letting the rich and powerful do as they please.[109] The court has a number of African members, but of the Arab states, only Jordan has joined.

Finance continues as a major concern as does the ponderous nature of its process.[110] The ICC is not cheap. It has an annual budget of nearly $150 million. Many complain that it offers little value for money spent, having so far yielded only a dozen arrest warrants and indictments, all relating to Africa.[111] The idea that human rights abuses and war crimes should be punished gained ground in the 1990s, as democratic regimes replaced authoritarian ones in many parts of the world, and the horrors of Bosnia and Rwanda surfaced. But it is hard to apply consistently. Conflict zones abound where the only credible participants in a peace process happen to be rebel leaders or warlords.

U.S. Objections to the International Criminal Court

In his brief testimony before the Senate Committee on Foreign Relations, Ambassador David Scheffer advanced nine specific objections to the statute as

---

[106]ICC, Press Release, "ICC Prosecutor presents case against Sudanese President, Hassan Ahmad Al-Bashir for genocide, crimes against humanity and war crimes in Darfur," July 14, 2008, www.icc-cpi.int/press/pressreleases/406.html.

[107]See H. Kissinger, "The Pitfalls of Universal Jurisdiction," 80 *Foreign Affairs* (2001); and the response by K. Roth, "The Case for Universal Jurisdiction," 80 *Foreign Affairs* (2001).

[108]M. Steinglass and M. Peel, "ICC Issues Arrest Warrant for Gaddafi," *Financial Times* (June 28, 2011); "In the past countries such as France and Belgium argued that offering tyrants an escape route prevented bloodshed and eased transitions in their homelands. Today most countries that ex-dictators would regard as livable are bound by extradition treaties and human-rights conventions to bundle the big and bad back home or off to a trial in The Hague." "Exile for Autocrats: You Can Run. But Can You Hide?" *The Economist* (May 19, 2011).

[109]"The International Criminal Court Bares Its Teeth," *The Economist* (May 14, 2011), 57–58.

[110]"ICC budget 'under pressure" to fund Libya probe," Reuters (April 14, 2011).

[111]"Courting Disaster?" *The Economist* (May 27, 2010).

adopted.[112] There were no surprises in his presentation. Each objection relates to a position articulated in some detail by the United States during the preparatory work and more generally to the attitudes outlined in Chapters 16 and 17. What runs through the ambassador's testimony and that of others who oppose the court is the constant idea that the statute, as adopted, provides unlimited "potential for mischief" by those unfriendly to the United States. In the first warning shots fired across the bow in anticipation of Senate debate or perhaps to head off reconsideration by the administration, on the same day Ambassador Sheffer testified, the committee also heard additional statements that characterized the statute as unconstitutional and unwise. The critics raised the old shibboleths of surrender of sovereignty, national security, and the perils of foreign jealousy.[113] In the eyes of the critics, the ICC "would represent an unprecedented cession of our right to self government."[114]

Evaluating American Objections

Many critics have easily dismissed American concerns over the potential reach of the ICC, citing the complementarity provisions as sufficient protection. After all,

---

[112]Prepared Statement of David J. Scheffer, ambassador-at-large for war crimes issues and head of the U.S. delegation to the UN diplomatic conference before the Senate Committee on Foreign Relations, Federal News Service, July 23, 1998, available in Lexis-Nexis Library (hereinafter, Scheffer Statement): (1) The United States objected to the method of defining the jurisdiction of the ICC. By the formula adopted, the ICC would not be able to seize directly offenses flowing from the most common circumstances of contemporary conflict—those arising from internal war. (2) The statute would permit the court to assert jurisdiction over the nationals of non-signatories, a novelty that seemingly contradicts both customary practice and black letter treaty law. (3) The United States rejected the right of the court to decide for itself questions of jurisdiction because the ambiguous definition of some offenses ("crimes against humanity") included in the statute afford considerable latitude for a "potential for mischief" by those unfriendly to the United States. (4) The methods by which cases may be referred to the court would give too much latitude to individual states and prosecutors, yielding another "potential for mischief." (5) The provisions that permit states to opt out of the statute after ratification if they find the regime "unfair" are too restrictive. (6) The statute provides for new or added crimes to become part of the court's jurisdiction without adequate review by the states parties. (7) The statute lacks sufficient mechanisms to hold prosecutors and judges accountable for their decisions and actions. (8) Inclusion of terrorism and drugs extends the court's competence to areas better left to national investigation and effort, and risks diluting the focus and impact on more serious crimes. (9) The treaty permits no reservations as a condition of accession, which leaves no wiggle room. States are either in or out; if ratifying, they accept the package "as is."

[113]B. Crossette, "Helms Vows to Make War on UN Court," *New York Times* (March 27, 1998), A9. Senator Helms is quoted as saying the treaty would be "dead on arrival" if the United States did not have veto power. Senator Helms refers to the Rome treaty as "an irreparably flawed and dangerous document," and further asserts that "rejecting the Rome treaty is not enough. The US must fight the treaty. . . . We must be aggressively opposed because, even if the US never joins the court, the Rome treaty will have serious implications for US foreign policy." J. Helms, "We Must Slay This Monster," *Financial Times* (July 31, 1998), 18.

[114]Prepared Statement of Lee A. Casey and David B. Rivkin before the Senate Foreign Relations Committee, Federal News Service (July 23, 1998), available in Lexis-Nexis; Prepared Statement of John Bolton Before the Senate Foreign Relations Committee, International Operations Subcommittee, Federal News Service (July 23, 1998), available in Lexis-Nexis Library. See also F. Hiatt, "The Trouble with the War-Crimes Court," *Washington Post* (July 26, 1998), C7; and M. Vo, "Why US Won't Back a World Criminal Court," *Christian Science Monitor International* (July 24, 1998), 6.

Canada, the United Kingdom, and France have had little problem in ratifying the treaty. This misses the real fear. The United States has focused upon the ordinary soldier in its public campaign against the ICC. Yet it is not the Lt. Calley case that fuels the real resistance, but the Slobodan Milosevic example. True, the United States has always been very protective of its soldiers. The Scott O'Grady incident, involving a pilot shot down over Bosnia in 1995, clearly demonstrates this stance. If captured, Captain O'Grady could have faced a grim future (possibly trial as a war criminal) given Serbian views of the legality of the air raids. No one should dismiss the official statements of concern here as other than genuine. Certainly, U.S. Senator John McCain can testify to the realities of being captured. Yet the real concerns lie in the incidents in Canada, where protesters tried to have President George W. Bush arrested or expelled, and in France, where antiwar groups sought to have the French government arrest former Secretary of Defense Donald Rumsfeld on war crimes charges.

The justifications for the ICC do not rest upon prosecuting individual soldiers case by case for war crimes. The underlying model is Nuremberg. Prosecuting the Idi Amins (Uganda), Pol Pots (Cambodia), Charles Taylors (Liberia), and Slobodan Milosovics (Serbia) of the world spurred the effort, not the case of Lt. Calley or concern for Scott O'Grady. As we have noted all through our previous discussion, politics "happens." Considering the bitter division in world opinion over aspects of the U.S. "war" on terrorism and the invasion of Iraq, one might understand the U.S. reluctance to join the court. On the other hand, critics still argue that if the United States is conducting its policies within accepted international standards, why should it fear international judgment?

SUGGESTED READINGS

WAR CRIMES: GENERAL

Baird, ed., *From Nuremberg to My Lai* (1972).

Bass, *Stay the Hand of Vengeance: The Politics of War Crimes Trials* (2003).

Cowles, "Trial of War Criminals (Non-Nuremberg)," 41 *AJIL* 299 (1948).

Freeman, "War Crimes by Enemy Nationals Administering Justice in Occupied Territory," 41 *AJIL* 579 (1947).

Friedman, ed., *The Law of War: A Documentary History* (2 vols, 1972), contains relevant rules as well as a number of post–World War II decisions.

Hart, "Yamashita, Nuremberg and Vietnam: Command Responsibility Reappraised," 25 *Naval War College Review* 19 (1972).

Maguire, *Law and War: An American Story* (2000).

Parks, "Command Responsibility for War Crimes," 62 *Military Law Review* 1 (1973).

Robertson, *Crimes Against Humanity*, 3rd ed. (2006).

Rogat, *The Eichmann Trial and the Rule of Law* (1961).

Schabas, *An Introduction to the International Criminal Court,* 3rd ed. (2007).

Schabas, *The UN International Criminal Tribunals* (2006).

Scharf, *Balkan Justice* (1997).

Taulbee, *International Crime and Punishment* (2009).

Tutorow, *War Crimes, War Criminals, and War Crimes Trials: An Annotated Bibliography and Source Book* (1986; 4,500 references).

Watkins and Weber, *War Crimes and War Crime Trials: From Leipzig to the ICC and Beyond* (2005).

NUREMBERG WAR CRIMES TRIALS

The American Road to Nuremberg: The Documentary Record, 1944–1945 (1982).

Borkin, *The Crime and Punishment of I. G. Farben* (1978).

Davidson, *The Trial of the Germans* (1967), and his *The Nuremberg Fallacy: Wars and War Crimes since World War II* (1973).

The documentary material covering the trial is forbidding in scope: International Military Tribunal, Nuremberg, *Trial of the Major War Criminals Before the International Military Tribunal, Nuremberg, 14 November 1945–1 October 1946* (42 vols, 1947–1949). Consult, *inter alia*, the following sources:

Glueck, *The Nuremberg Trial and Aggressive War* (1946).

Jackson, *The Case Against the Nazi War Criminals* (1946).

Levy, "The Law and Procedure of War Crime Trials," 37 *APSR* 1052 (1943).

Smith, *Reaching Judgment at Nuremberg* (1979).

von Knieriem, *The Nuremberg Trials* (1959).

Woetzel, *The Nuremberg Trials in International Law* (1950).

Wright, "The Law of the Nuremberg Trial," 41 *AJIL* 38 (1947).

SUBJECT AND NAME INDEX

Page numbers followed by "b" indicates box material, "n" indicates notes material, and "t" indicates table material.

INDEX OF CASES

Page numbers followed by "b" indicates box material, "n" indicates notes material, and "t" indicates table material.